Substance Abuse:
Therapist Jean Obert
"Being addicted to heroin is one of the most difficult things to kick."

Substance Abuse:
Therapist Louise Roberts
"You try to make sense out of an addiction that doesn't make sense."

Anorexia Nervosa—Binge-Eating/ Purging Type:
The Case of Jessica
"The diet started being my only way of getting control."

Bulimia:
The Case of Ann
"I was just afraid to go home and be around food."

Anorexia Nervosa:
The Case of Tamora
"If someone had told me how ugly I looked, being that thin, I wouldn't have done it. I mean, it was...part beauty and...part power."

Attention-Deficit/Hyperactivity Disorder (ADHD):
The Case of Jimmy
"Sometimes I just drift off."

Eating Disorders:
Nutritionist Alise Thresh
"Some people are normal eaters...some people are concerned about their eating...and to an extreme, there is an eating disorder."

Gender Identity Disorder:
The Case of Denise
"My earliest memories, back when I was about 4 years old...I remember cross-dressing back then, all the way until really around my puberty."

Childhood Sexual Abuse:
The Case of Karen
"He started when I was six years old...He would always get one bed in motel rooms because he said he needed to save money."

Schizophrenia:
The Case of Larry
"I have all kinds of voices."

Autism:
Dr. Kathy Pratt

Attention-Deficit/Hyperactivity Disorder (ADHD):
Dr. Raun Melmed

Schizophrenia:
The Case of Georgiana
"Then it got out of hand, where I couldn't control coming and going, back and forth, and in my body, out of my body, it was no longer under my control."

Schizoaffective Disorder:
The Case of Josh
"I looked out the window and saw this guy with a machete chasing one of the psychiatrists."

Antisocial Personality Disorder:
The Case of Paul
"I went to prison for kicking down my wife's door."

Borderline Personality Disorder:
The Case of Liz
"I have problems with anger management."

Autism:
The Case of Xavier
"He'll watch a DVD, same scene over and over and over again."

Alzheimer's Disease:
The Case of Wilburn "John"
"You kinda have hope whenever you have cancer...but then, [with] Alzheimer's...you die, just a little each day."

Abnormal Psychology in a Changing World

SIXTH EDITION

JEFFREY S. NEVID
St. John's University

SPENCER A. RATHUS
New York University

BEVERLY GREENE
St. John's University

PEARSON

Prentice
Hall

Upper Saddle River, New Jersey 07458

Library of Congress Cataloging-in-Publication Data

Nevid, Jeffrey S.
   Abnormal psychology in a changing world / Jeffrey S. Nevid, Spencer A. Rathus, Beverly Greene.— 6th ed.
    p. cm.
   Includes bibliographical references and index.
   ISBN 0-13-191678-5
   1. Psychology, Pathological.   2. Psychiatry.   I. Rathus, Spencer A.   II. Greene, Beverly.   III. Title.
   RC454.N468 2005
   616.89—dc22

                   2004024788

Senior Editor: Jeff Marshall
Editorial Director: Leah Jewell
Sponsoring Editor: Stephanie Johnson
Editorial Assistant: Patricia Callahan
Senior Media Editor: David Nusspickel
Director of Marketing: Heather Shelstad
Marketing Assistant: Julie Kestenbaum
Development Editor: Elaine Silverstein
Assistant Managing Editor: Maureen Richardson
Production Liaison: Fran Russello
Manufacturing Buyer: Ben Smith
Art Director: Kathy Mrozek
Interior & CoverDesign: Jon Boylan
Cover Illustration/Photo: White Packert / Image Bank / Getty Images, Inc.
Illustrator (Interior):
Photo Researcher: Mary Ann Price
Image Permission Coordinator: Debbie Latronica
Composition/Full-Service Project Management: Pine Tree Composition, Inc.
Printer/Binder: Courier Companies, Inc.

Credits and acknowledgments borrowed from other sources and reproduced, with permission, in this textbook appear on the appropriate pages.

Pearson Education LTD. London
Pearson Education Singapore, Pte. Ltd
Pearson Education, Canada, Ltd
Pearson Education—Japan
Pearson Education Australia PTY, Limited
Pearson Education North Asia Ltd
Pearson Educación de Mexico, S.A. de C.V.
Pearson Education Malaysia, Pte. Ltd
Pearson Education, Upper Saddle River, New Jersey

10 9 8 7 6 5 4 3 2 1

ISBN 0-13-191678-5

BRIEF CONTENTS

Contents

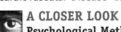

CHAPTER 7

Dissociative and Somatoform Disorders   208

CHAPTER 8

Mood Disorders and Suicide   240

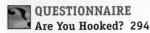

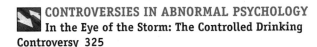

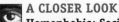

CHAPTER 15
Cognitive Disorders and Disorders Related to Aging 508

CHAPTER 16
Abnormal Psychology and the Law 532

We are pleased to offer the 6th edition of *Abnormal Psychology in a Changing World*. The text has been thoroughly updated with more than 1,000 references to scientific findings published since the year 2000. We hope that students will take away from this course a richer understanding of contemporary theory and research into the causes and treatments of these perplexing disorders. But we also hope that students gain a better appreciation of the human side of abnormal psychology.

A textbook on abnormal psychology is not a diagnostic or treatment manual. We seek to put a human face on the study of abnormal psychology by including many illustrative case examples in the narrative text and in the accompanying video CD-ROM. With this edition, we also introduce a new feature that takes this approach an important step further—the "I" feature.

PUTTING A HUMAN FACE ON THE STUDY OF ABNORMAL PSYCHOLOGY

The New "I" Feature

The "I" feature takes us directly into the world of people affected by psychological disorders. This feature presents first-person accounts of people struggling with various psychological disorders we discuss in the text.

Each chapter begins with one or more of these first-hand accounts. These personal accounts help students learn what it is like to experience depression, schizophrenia, eating disorders, autism, panic disorder, and other mental health problems. The people sharing their experiences would like us to better understand their personal struggles and the efforts they have made to cope with the many challenges they face.

Susanna—"A Girl, Interrupted"

Suicide is a form of murder—premeditated murder. It isn't something you do the first time you think of doing it. It takes getting used to. And you need the means, the opportunity, the motive. . . .

My motives were weak: an American-history paper I didn't want to write and the question I'd asked months earlier, Why not kill myself? Dead, I wouldn't have to write the paper. Nor would I have to keep debating the question. . . .

Anything I thought or did was immediately drawn into the debate. Made a stupid remark—why not kill myself? Missed the bus—better put an end to it all. Even the good got in there. I liked that movie—maybe I shouldn't kill myself.

Actually, it was only part of myself I wanted to kill: the part that wanted to kill herself, that dragged me into the suicide debate and made every window, kitchen implement, and subway station a rehearsal for tragedy.

I didn't figure this out, though, until after I'd swallowed the fifty aspirin.

I had a boyfriend named Johnny who wrote me love poems—good ones. I called him up, said I was going to kill myself, left the phone off the hook, took my fifty aspirin, and realized it was a mistake. Then I went out to get some milk, which my mother had asked me to do before I took the aspirin.

New Video Case Examples

An exciting development with this edition of the text is the inclusion of a broader base of video case vignettes on the accompanying student CD-ROM, and on the VHS and DVD segments available to instructors. Video case examples provide students with opportunities to see and hear individuals who are diagnosed with different types of psychological disorders. Students can read about the clinical features of specific disorders and with a few clicks of a computer mouse, see a video case example that illustrates the concepts discussed in the text. The video case examples are highlighted in the margins of the text with a CD-ROM icon. The CD-ROM now offers fifteen new segments from the *Speaking Out* series, which includes interviews with persons who have been diagnosed with major depressive disorder, obsessive compulsive disorder, anorexia, bulimia, PTSD, alcoholism, schizophrenia, autism, ADHD, bipolar disorder, social phobia, hypochondriasis, and personality disorders. These fifteen segments are available free to instructors in longer, presentational format on VHS or DVD (see description under the Ancillaries section of the preface).

The video case examples supplement the many case examples we include in the text itself. Putting a human face on the subject matter helps make complex material more accessible. Many of these case examples are drawn from our own clinical files and those of leading mental health professionals.

Major Depression:
The Case of Everett
"You feel absolute worthlessness."

INTEGRATION OF DIVERSITY

We thank the many reviewers and users over the years who have commented favorably on our integration of material relating to diversity in the field of abnormal psychology. Throughout the text, we examine relationships between abnormal behavior patterns and ethnicity, cultural factors, gender, sexual orientation, and socioeconomic status. We believe that students need to understand how issues of diversity affect the conceptualization of abnormal behavior as well as the diagnosis and treatment of psychological disorders. We also believe that coverage of diversity is inseparable from the broader discussion of disorders and their treatments, and as a result, we integrate multicultural and other diversity material directly within the body of the text, rather than setting it off in boxed features.

Since this material is embedded within the text, we have prepared the following tabbing guide to help instructors identify the passages of text in which material relating to diversity appears:

Acculturative stress (Chapter 5)

Cross-cultural differences in symptoms of schizophrenia (Chapter 12)

Cultural bases of abnormal behavior (Chapter 1)

BUILDING UPON AN EFFECTIVE LEARNING SYSTEM

We continually examine our pedagogical approach to find better ways of helping students succeed in this course. As with previous editions of this book, we believe that a textbook should do more than offer a portrait of a field of knowledge. It should primarily be a teaching device—a means of presenting information that excites student interest and encourages understanding and critical thinking. We have provided a number of features to achieve these goals—some new to this edition, like the chapter-opening "I" feature, and some that have been popular for several editions.

NEW: The First-Person "I" Feature

As described above, the new "I" feature opens each chapter with first-person accounts of people struggling with various psychological disorders we discuss in that chapter. These personal accounts span a wide range of disorders, including depression, schizophrenia, eating disorders, autism, panic disorder, and other mental health problems.

NEW: Video Case Examples on CD-ROM

A revised and expanded CD-ROM accompanies every new copy of the 6th edition, and offers video case examples that are highlighted in the margins of the text with a CD-ROM icon. The video case examples reinforce and expand the student's understanding of the clinical features of the disorder and expose them to first-hand experiences of people suffering from specific disorders. As noted above, the CD-ROM now offers sixteen new segments from the *Speaking Out* series, including interviews with persons who have been diagnosed with major depressive disorder, obsessive compulsive disorder, anorexia, bulimia, PTSD, alcoholism, schizophrenia, autism, ADHD, bipolar disorder, social phobia, hypochondriasis, and personality disorders. (These sixteen segments are also available free to instructors in longer, presentational format on VHS or DVD—see description under the Ancillaries section of the preface).

NEW: Streamlined Organization

We streamlined the text by reducing the number of chapters from 17 to 16. We accomplished this reorganization by moving material from the previous chapter on violence and abuse directly into chapters covering related material. Previous users may also notice a change in the order of the chapter on personality disorders. We surveyed user opinion and found that many instructors prefer teaching the major types of Axis I disorders before Axis II personality disorders. Consequently, we moved the chapter on personality disorders to follow the chapter on schizophrenia and directly precede the chapter on developmental disorders. Instructors who prefer to cover personality disorders earlier in the semester may continue to do so, as the chapter is written to stand on its own.

NEW: Controversies in Abnormal Psychology

With this edition, we introduce a new feature called **Controversies in Abnormal Psychology.** Some controversies in the field are long simmering, such as Szasz's charge that mental illness is a myth and the heated disputes over controlled drinking and recovered memories. Other controversies reflect contemporary issues in our changing world that affect the field, such as cybersex addiction, use of the Internet to deliver psychological services, and psychological first-aid in response to trauma survivors.

In each chapter we focus on a particular controversy in the field. These boxed features raise the student's awareness that many issues in abnormal psychology remain unsettled. These controversy boxes also encourage the development of critical thinking skills by posing a set of critical thinking questions following the discussion of the issues. Here is a listing of the controversy features we include:

- What is Abnormal Behavior? (Chapter 1)
- Is It All in the Genes? (Chapter 2)
- Should Interviewers Be Replaced by Computers? (Chapter 3)
- Online Therapy: A New Therapeutic Tool or Pandora's Box? (Chapter 4)
- Psychological First-Aid Following Trauma: Does it Help? (Chapter 5)
- EMDR: Fad or Find? (Chapter 6)
- Are Recovered Memories Credible? (Chapter 7)
- Why Are More Women Depressed? (Chapter 8)
- In the Eye of the Storm: The Controlled Drinking Controversy (Chapter 9) special guest feature by Mark and Linda Sobell
- Should Barbie Be Banned? (Chapter 10)
- Cybersex Addiction—New Psychological Disorder? (Chapter 11)
- Is Mental Illness A Myth? (Chapter 12)
- Are Personality Disorders Sexist? (Chapter 13)
- Are We Overmedicating Our Kids? (Chapter 14)
- Genetic Testing: Should People at Risk Be Tested? (Chapter 15)
- What Should We Do About the Wild Man of West 96th Street? (Chapter 16)

Tying it Together Helps Students Integrate Theoretical Perspectives

We approach our writing with the belief that a better understanding of abnormal psychology is gained by adopting an orientation that takes into account the roles of psychological, biological, and sociocultural factors and their interactions in the development of abnormal behavior patterns. Students often feel as though one theoretical perspective must ultimately be right and all the others wrong. The *Tying it Together* features help students integrate the theoretical discussions and examine possible causal pathways involving interactions of multiple factors in explaining many forms of abnormal behavior, including anxiety disorders, dissociative disorders, mood disorders, substance abuse and dependence, and schizophrenia. In this edition, we have added a visual dimension to each *Tying it Together* section to help students see the interactions of causal factors even more clearly. We hope to impress upon students the importance of taking a broader view of the complex problems we address by considering the influences of multiple factors and their interactions.

Overview Charts

Overview charts are capsulized summaries of the features, causes, and treatments of various disorders. Students can see at a glance how the information presented in the chapter fits together. We are gratified by the many comments from adopters who have cited the value of the overview charts in helping students review and organize their knowledge about the major types of disorders. In this edition, we expanded the information in the charts to include a summary of prevalence rates for particular disorders gleaned from sources presented in the narrative text.

Overview of Mood Disorders

TYPES OF MOOD DISORDERS/PREVALENCE RATES (approx., in parentheses)		
	Description	Features
Major Depressive Disorder 10%–25% in women; 5%–12% in men)	Episodes of severe depression	• A range of features may be present, from downcast mood to appetite and sleep disturbance, to lack of interest and motivation • Seasonal affective disorder and postpartum depression are subtypes of major depression
Dysthymic Disorder 8% in women, 4%–5% in men)	Long-standing mild depression	• Feeling "down in the dumps" most of the time, but not as severely depressed as people with major depressive disorder • Double depression is characterized by major depressive episodes occurring during the course of dysthymia
Bipolar Disorder (0.4%–1.6%; or 4 to 16 people in 1,000)	Mood swings between elation and depression	• The two general subtypes are bipolar I disorder and bipolar II disorder • In rapid cycling, mania and major depression alternate without intervening periods of normal mood
Cyclothymia (0.4%–1%, or 4 to 10 people in 1,000)	Milder mood swings than bipolar disorder	• Chronic, cyclical pattern of shifting mood states from hypomanic episodes to states of mild depression • Frequent periods of depressed mood or loss of interest or pleasure in activities, but not at the level of severity of a major depressive episode

Closer Look Boxes Explore Key Issues in Our Changing World

Closer Look boxed features provide opportunities for further exploration of selected topics that reflect contemporary issues or areas of study in the field as well as concerns that directly touch the lives of many students, including sleep problems, binge drinking, and threats of suicide made by friends or acquaintances.

Several *Closer Look* features provide information and resources that enable students to apply information in the text to their own lives. Examples include:

- Thinking Critically About Abnormal Psychology (Chapter 1)
- How Do I Find Help? (Chapter 4)
- Warning Signs of Trauma-Related Stress (Chapter 5)
- Psychological Methods for Lowering Arousal (Chapter 5)
- Coping with a Panic Attack (Chapter 6)
- Suicide Prevention (Chapter 8)
- To Sleep, Perchance to Dream (Chapter 10)

Other *Closer Look* features focus on intriguing research findings or emerging developments in the field.

- Something Fishy About This (Chapter 8)
- Magnetic Therapy for Depression (Chapter 8)
- Did Samson Have Antisocial Personality Disorder? (Chapter 13)
- In Cold Blood: Peering into the Minds of Psychopathic Murderers (Chapter 13)

Still others focus on specific topical issues, providing opportunities for more in-depth exploration of these topics:

- Emotions and the Heart (Chapter 5)
- Münchausen Syndrome (Chapter 7)

- Binge Drinking, a Dangerous College Pastime (Chapter 9)
- Homophobia: Social Prejudice or Personal Psychopathology? (Chapter 11)
- The Love Delusion (Chapter 12)
- The Savant Syndrome (Chapter 14)

Truth-or-Fiction? Chapter Openers

To foster deeper understanding, we must first engage student interest. Each chapter begins with a set of *Truth-or-Fiction?* questions that whet students' appetites for the subject matter within the chapter. Some items challenge preconceived ideas and common folklore, and debunk myths and misconceptions, while others highlight new research in the field. The new design format encourages students to answer the questions at the start of the chapter, and then compare their answers to the *Truth or Fiction Revisited* features found in the margins of the chapter. This gives students immediate feedback on the accuracy (or inaccuracy) of their preconceptions regarding the disorders discussed. Instructors and students have repeatedly reported that these items stimulate and challenge students.

Truth or Fiction?

T☐ F☐ Some men in India develop a psychological disorder involving excessive concerns or anxiety over losing semen. (p. 75)

T☐ F☐ People are more likely to report more personal problems when they are questioned by a live interviewer, rather than by a computer. (p. 80)

T☐ F☐ The most widely used personality inventory includes a number of questions that bear no obvious relationship to the traits the instrument purports to measure. (p. 84)

T☐ F☐ One of the most widely used tests of personality asks people to interpret what they see in a series of inkblots. (p. 87)

T☐ F☐ People in weight-loss programs who carefully monitor what they eat tend to lose less weight than people who are less-reliable monitors. (p. 92)

T☐ F☐ Despite advances in technology, physicians today must perform surgery to study the workings of the brain. (p. 96)

T☐ F☐ Cocaine cravings in people addicted to cocaine have been linked to parts of the brain that are normally activated during pleasant emotions. (p. 96)

Self-Scoring Questionnaires

Questionnaires involve students in the discussion at hand and permit them to evaluate their own attitudes and behavior patterns. In some cases, students may become more aware of troubling concerns, such as states of depression or problems with drug or alcohol use, which they may wish to bring to the attention of a professional. We have screened the questionnaires to ensure that they will provide students with useful information to reflect upon as well as serve as a springboard for class discussion. Examples include the following:

- The Life Orientation Test (Optimism Scale) (Chapter 5)
- Are You Type A? (Chapter 5)
- The Dissociative Experiences Scale (Chapter 7)
- Are You Depressed? (Chapter 8)
- The Fear of Fat Scale (Chapter 10)
- Examining Your Attitudes Toward Aging (Chapter 15)

Running Glossary

We include a running glossary within the text itself so that students will not need to thumb to the back of the book to find definitions of key terms. Key terms are boldfaced in the text and defined in both the glossary in the back of the book and in the margins of the text where the terms appear. The origins of key terms are often discussed. By learning to attend to commonly found Greek and Latin word origins, students can acquire skills that will help them decipher the meanings of new words. These decoding skills are a valuable objective for general education as well as a specific asset for the study of abnormal psychology. **New** to this edition is a full glossary at the end of the book that contains general vocabulary terms found in the text as well as key terms from the running glossary.

Summing-Up Chapter Summaries

The *Summing-Up* chapter summaries are organized in a question-and-answer format, rather than a traditional narrative summary. We believe that students learn better when material is framed in terms of questions to answer rather than just narrative text. This format encourages recitation of knowledge, not simply recognition skills.

ANCILLARIES

No matter how comprehensive a textbook is, today's instructors and students require a complete teaching package to advance teaching and comprehension. *Abnormal Psychology in a Changing World* is accompanied by the following ancillaries.

NEW for 2005: Current Directions in Abnormal Psychology

Prentice Hall is pleased to announce the **American Psychological Society (APS)** reader series, *Current Directions in Psychological Science.* For classes starting in 2005, you can package the Current Directions in Abnormal Psychology reader for *free* with this text.

This Reader contains selected articles from APS's journal *Current Directions in Psychological Science. Current Directions* was created as a means by which scientists could quickly and easily learn about new and significant research developments outside their major field of study. The journal's concise reviews span all of scientific psychology, and because of the journal's accessibility to audiences outside specialty areas, it is a natural fit for use in college courses. These Readers offer a rich resource that connects students and scholars directly to leading scientists working in psychology today.

The American Psychological Society is the only association dedicated solely to advancing psychology as a science-based discipline. APS members include the field's most respected researchers and educators representing the full range of topics within psychological science. The Society is widely recognized as a leading voice for the science of psychology in Washington, and is focused on increasing public understanding and use of the knowledge generated by psychological research.

Print Supplements for Instructors
Instructor's Resource Manual (0-13-191682-3)

Nicole T. Buchanan of Michigan State University has prepared an instructor's resource manual with *Lecture and Discussion* suggestions, *Student Activities, Classroom Demonstration* ideas, and suggestions on how to integrate the new *Abnormal Psychology* CD-ROM into your course. The *Instructor's Resource Manual* now includes notes and suggestions on how to integrate the new *Speaking Out* video segments into your course.

Test Item File (0-13-191680-7)

Developed by Malcolm Kahn of University of Miami, this comprehensive test bank has been updated to include new questions on revised text material. It contains over 4,000 multiple choice, true/false, short answer, and essay questions.

PH Color Transparencies for *Abnormal Psychology Series II* (0-13-080451-7)

This set of full-color transparencies includes illustrations, figures, and graphs from the text, as well as images from a variety of other sources. It has been designed with lecture hall visibility and convenience in mind.

Media and On-line Resources for Instructors
NEW Video—*Speaking Out: Interviews with People who Struggle with Psychological Disorders*

This new set of sixteen video segments allows students to see first-hand accounts of patients with various disorders. The interviews were conducted by licensed clinicians and range in length from 8–25 minutes. Disorders include major depressive disorder, obsessive compulsive disorder, anorexia nervosa, PTSD, alcoholism, schizophrenia, autism, ADHD, bipolar disorder, social phobia, hypochondriasis, borderline personality disorder, and adjustment to physical illness. These video segments are available on VHS cassettes or on DVD, and the *Instructor's Resource Guide* provides background notes and suggested discussion questions.

New Instructor's Resource Center on CD-ROM

This valuable, time-saving supplement provides you with an electronic version of a variety of teaching resources all on one disk so that you may customize your lecture notes and media presentations. This CD-ROM includes PowerPoint slides, electronic versions of the artwork, electronic versions of the overhead transparencies, the electronic Instructor's Resource Manual, and the Test Item File.

Patients as Educators: Video Cases in Abnormal Psychology

Created by James H. Scully, Jr., M.D., and Alan M. Dahms, Ph.D., Colorado State University, this VHS tape includes a series of ten patient interviews illustrating a range of disorders. Each interview is preceded by a brief history of the patient and a synopsis of some major symptoms of the disorder, and ends with a summary and brief analysis.

TestGen Testing Software

Prentice Hall TestGen Software (0-13-191681-5). Available on one dual-platform CD-ROM, this test generating software provides instructors *Best in Class* features in an easy to use program. Create tests using the TestGen Wizard and easily select questions with drag-and-drop or point-and-click functionality. Add or modify test questions using the built-in Question Editor and print tests in a variety of formats. The program comes with full technical support.

Nevid On-line Instructor Resources
(www.prenhall.com/psychology)

This site is password-protected for instructors' use only, and allows you online access to all Prentice Hall Psychology supplements at any time. You'll find a multitude of resources—both text-specific and non-text-specific—for teaching abnormal psychology. From this site, you can download any of the key supplements for *Nevid 6e: Instructor's Resource Manual*, Test Item File, and PowerPoint presentations. Contact your local sales representative for the User ID and Password to access this site.

PowerPoint Presentations
(on the Companion Website)

This PPT set includes two sets of PowerPoint presentations, one with graphics and one without, to give you even greater flexibility in using PowerPoint in your lectures. Both presentations highlight all of the key points in *Nevid 6e*.

Student Supplements

Revised! *Videos in Abnormal Psychology* CD-ROM 2.0

With every new copy of *Nevid 6e*, students will receive a *free* CD-ROM containing video clips showing skilled clinicians inter-

viewing real patients who have been diagnosed with various disorders. Sixteen new segments have been added to the CD-ROM, which now covers disorders such as panic disorder, schizophrenia, anorexia nervosa, bipolar disorder, PTSD, major depression, autism, ADHD, borderline personality disorder, hypochondriasis, alcoholism, and others. Icons in the text margins indicate when students should go to the CD-ROM to find video interviews.

Companion Website *(www.prenhall.com/nevid)*

All of the online resources on the Companion Website have been carefully created and selected to reinforce students' understanding of the concepts in the text. Students can take online quizzes and get immediate scoring and feedback, use interactive flashcards to test themselves on key terms, access PowerPoint presentations for each chapter, and link to related websites for more information on each chapter's topics.

Research Navigator

Research Navigator is an online resource that features three exclusive databases full of source material, including:

- EBSCO's *ContentSelect Academic Journal Database,* organized by subject. Each subject contains 50 to 100 of the leading academic journals by keyword, topic, or multiple topics. Articles include abstract and citation information and can be cut, pasted, e-mailed, or saved for later use.
- *The New York Times Search-by-Subject One Year Archive,* organized by subject and searchable by keyword or multiple keywords. Instructors and students can view the full text of the article.
- *Link Library,* organized by subject, offers editorially selected best of the Web sites. Link Libraries are continually scanned and kept up to date, providing the most relevant and accurate links for research assignments.

To see how this resource works, take a tour at www.researchnavigator.com, or ask your local Prentice Hall representative for more details.

Study Guide (0-13-191683-1)

Ruth Hallongren of Triton College has created a study guide that includes numerous review and study questions, crossword puzzles, and other learning aids to help reinforce students' understanding of the concepts covered in the text.

ACKNOWLEDGMENTS

With each new edition, we try to capture a moving target, as the literature base that informs our understanding continues to expand. We are deeply indebted to the thousands of talented scholars and investigators whose work has enriched our understanding of abnormal psychology. We are also greatly indebted to our many professional colleagues who have reviewed our manuscript through earlier editions and continue to help us refine and strengthen our presentation of this material.

Reviewers of the Sixth Edition

Sally Bing, *University of Maryland Eastern Shore*
Barbara L. Brown, *Georgia Perimeter College*
Lorry Cology, *Owens Community College*
Nancy T. Dassoff, *University of Illinois-Chicago*
David Dooley, *University of California at Irvine*
Karla J. Gingerich, *Colorado State University*
Bernard Gorman, *Nassau Community College*
Robert Kapche, *California State University at Los Angeles*
Cynthia Diane Kreutzer, *Georgia Perimeter College*
Tom Marsh, *Pitt Community College*
Martin M. Oper, *Erie Community College*
Ramona Parish, *Guilford Technical Community College*
Robert Sommer, *University of California-Davis*
Linda Sonna, *University of New Mexico, Taos*
Stephanie Stein, *Central Washington University*
Joanne Hoven Stohs, *California State University-Fullerton*

Reviewers of Previous Editions

Christiane Brems, *University of Alaska Anchorage*
Heinz Fischer, *Long Beach City College*
John H. Forthman, *Vermillin Community College*
Pam Gibson, *James Madison University*
Bernard Gorman, *Nassau Community College*
Gary Greenberg, *Connecticut College*
John K. Hall, *University of Pittsburgh*
Bob Hill, *Appalachian State University*
Stuart Keeley, *Bowling Green State University*
Shay McCordick, *San Diego State University*
Linda L. Morrison, *University of New England*
Joseph J. Palladino, *University of Southern Indiana*

Carol Pandey, *L.A. Pierce College*
J. Langhinrichsen-Rohling, *University of Nebraska-Lincoln*
Esther D. Rosenblum, *University of Vermont*
Harold Siegel, *Nassau Community College*
Ari Solomon, *Williams College*
Larry Stout, *Nicholls State University*
Theresa Wadkins, *University of Nebraska-Kearny*
Max Zwanziger, *Central Washington University*

We also wish to recognize the exemplary contributions of the publishing professionals at Prentice Hall who helped guide the development of this edition, especially Stephanie Johnson, Sponsoring Editor; Jeff Marshall, Senior Editor; and Elaine Silverstein, Developmental Editor. For the fresh new look of the sixth edition, our thanks go to the production and design team, including Leslie Osher, Creative Director; Jon Boylan, who designed the interior and the cover; Maureen Richardson, Associate Managing Editor for Production; and Fran Russello, who provided expert guidance throughout the production process. Thanks also to Dawn Stapleton, Associate Editor, for managing the complex array of print supplements that accompany the sixth edition, and David Nusspickel, Media Editor, for shepherding the production of all the media supplements, including the new and improved CD-ROM.

Finally, we especially wish to thank the two people without whose inspiration and support this effort would never have materialized or been completed, Judith Wolf-Nevid and Lois Fichner-Rathus.

J.S.N
New York, New York

S.A.R.
Short Hills, New Jersey

B.A.G
Brooklyn, New York

Jeffrey S. Nevid is Professor of Psychology at St. John's University in New York, where he directs the Doctoral Program in Clinical Psychology, teaches graduate courses in research methods, psychological assessment, and behavior therapy, and supervises doctoral students in clinical practicum work. He completed his doctoral degree in clinical psychology at the University at Albany of the State University of New York and served as a staff psychologist at Samaritan Hospital in Troy, New York. He later completed a National Institute of Mental Health Post-Doctoral Fellowship in Mental Health Evaluation Research at Northwestern University. He has numerous research publications in the areas of clinical and community psychology, health psychology, training models in clinical psychology, methodological issues in clinical research, and pedagogical research. He holds a Diplomate in Clinical Psychology from the American Board of Professional Psychology and is a Fellow of the American Academy of Clinical Psychology. Dr. Nevid has served as a consulting editor for several professional journals, including *Health Psychology,* and most recently served as an Associate Editor of the *Journal of Consulting and Clinical Psychology.* He is also author of several books, including *Choices: Sex in the Age of STDs* and the introductory psychology text, *Psychology: Concepts and Applications.* Dr. Nevid coauthored several other books with Spencer A. Rathus and has been an invited speaker at a number of conferences on the teaching of psychology, including the National Institute on the Teaching of Psychology, the Annual Conference on Undergraduate Teaching of Psychology, and the Midwest Institute for Students and Teachers of Psychology.

Spencer A. Rathus received his Ph.D. from the University at Albany of the State University of New York and teaches at New York University. He has engaged in clinical practice in hospital and private settings. His interests include deviant behavior, human sexuality, developmental disorders, and cognitive-behavior therapy. He has published numerous arti-cles and authored several textbooks, including *Psychology: Concepts and Connections* and *Children and Adolescents: Voyages in Development.* Together with Jeffrey Nevid, he coauthored the textbooks *Human Sexuality in a World of Diversity* and *Psychology and the Challenges of Life* and the popular book, *Behavior Therapy.* His professional activities include service on the American Psychological Association Task Force on Diversity Issues at the Precollege and Undergraduate Levels of Education in Psychology, and on the Advisory Panel, American Psychological Association, Board of Educational Affairs (BEA) Task Force on Undergraduate Psychology Major Competencies.

Beverly A. Greene is Professor of Psychology at St. John's University and is a Fellow of the American Psychological Association, the American Orthopsychiatric Association, and the American Academy of Clinical Psychology. She holds a Diplomate in Clinical Psychology and serves on the editorial boards of numerous scholarly journals. She received her Ph.D. in Clinical Psychology from Adelphi University and worked in public mental health for more than a decade. She was founding co-editor of the APA Society for the Study of Lesbian, Gay and Bisexual Issues series, *Psychological Perspectives on Lesbian, Gay and Bisexual Issues.* The author of over 70 professional publications, Dr. Greene was the recipient of the APA 2003 Committee on Women in Psychology Distinguished Leadership Award, the 1996 Outstanding Achievement Award from the APA Committee on Lesbian, Gay and Bisexual Concerns, the 2004 Distinguished Career Contributions to Ethnic Minority Research Award from the APA Society for the Study of Ethnic Minority Issues, the 2000 Heritage Award from the APA Society for the Psychology of Women, and the 1995, 1996, and 2000 (co-winner) Psychotherapy with Women Research Award from The Society for the Psychology of Women. One of her papers was honored with the 2000 Women of Color Psychologies Publication Award; an award she previously received in 1991 and 1995. Her co-edited book, *Psychotherapy with African American Women: Innovations in Psychodynamic Perspectives and Practice,* also was honored with the Association for Women in Psychology's 2001 Distinguished Publication Award.

Abnormal Psychology
in a Changing World

Introduction and Methods of Research

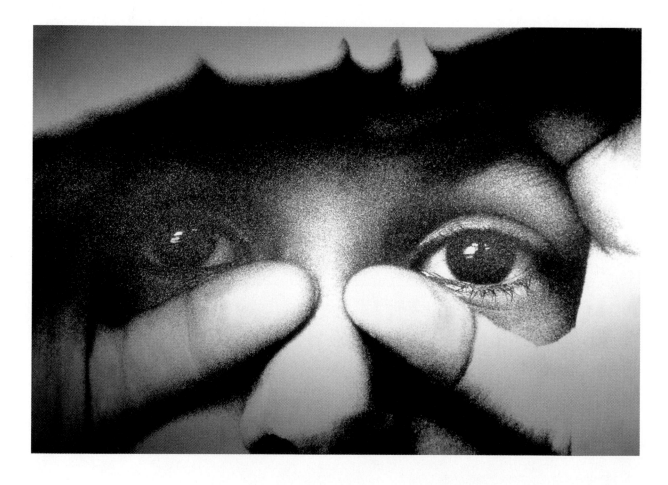

"I"

"Pretty Grisly Stuff"

I never thought I'd ever see a psychologist or someone like that, you know. I'm a police photographer and I've shot some pretty grisly stuff, corpses and all. Crime scenes are not like what you see on TV. They're more grisly. I guess you kind of get used to it. It never bothered me, just maybe at first. Before I did this job, I worked on a TV news chopper. We would take shots of fires and rescues, you know. Now I get uptight sitting in the back seat of car or riding an elevator. I'll avoid taking an elevator unless I really have no other choice. Forget flying anymore. It's not just helicopters. I just won't go in a plane, any kind of plane.

I guess I was younger then and more daring when I was younger. Sometimes I would hang out of the helicopter to shoot pictures with no fear at all. Now, just thinking about flying makes my heart race. It's not that I'm afraid the plane will crash. That's the funny thing. Not ha-ha funny, but peculiar, you know. I just start trembling when I think of them closing that door, trapping us inside. I can't tell you why.

—Phil, 42, a police photographer

Source: The Author's Files

"I"

Cowering Under the Covers

When I start going into a high, I no longer feel like an ordinary housewife. Instead I feel organized and accomplished and I begin to feel I am my most creative self. I can write poetry easily. I can compose melodies without effort. I can paint. My mind feels facile and absorbs everything. I have countless ideas about improving the conditions of mentally retarded children, of how a hospital for these children should be run, what they should have around them to keep them happy and calm and unafraid. I see myself as being able to accomplish a great deal for the good of people. I have countless ideas about how the environment problem could inspire a crusade for the health and betterment of everyone. I feel able to accomplish a great deal for the good of my family and others. I feel pleasure, a sense of euphoria or elation. I want it to last forever. I don't seem to need much sleep. I've lost weight and feel healthy and I like myself. I've just bought six new dresses, in fact, and they look quite good on me. I feel sexy and men stare at me. Maybe I'll have an affair, or perhaps several. I feel capable of speaking and doing good in politics. I would like to help people with problems similar to mine so they won't feel hopeless.

It's wonderful when you feel like this. . . . The feeling of exhilaration—the high mood— makes me feel light and full of the joy of living. However, when I go beyond this stage, I become manic, and the creativeness becomes so magnified I begin to see things in my mind that aren't real. For instance, one night I created an entire movie, complete with cast, that I still think would be terrific. I saw the people as clearly as if watching them in real life. I also experienced complete terror, as if it were actually happening, when I knew that an assassination scene was about to take place. I cowered under the covers and became a complete shaking wreck. . . . My screams awakened my husband, who tried to reassure me that we were in our bedroom and everything was the same. There was nothing to be afraid of. Nevertheless, I was admitted to the hospital the next day.

—A firsthand account of a 45-year-old woman with bipolar disorder

Source: Fieve, 1975, pp. 27–28

Truth or Fiction?

T☐ F☐ Psychological disorders affect only a few of us. (p. 6)

T☐ F☐ Behavior deemed abnormal in one society may be perceived as normal in another. (p. 11)

T☐ F☐ A night's entertainment in London a few hundred years ago might have included gaping at the inmates at the local asylum. (p. 14)

T☐ F☐ Despite changing attitudes in society toward homosexuality, the psychiatric profession still continues to classify homosexuality as a mental disorder. (p. 17)

T☐ F☐ You always learn more about the American population by surveying one million people than 1,500 people. (p. 27)

T☐ F☐ Case studies are only conducted on living people who can participate in the study. (p. 30)

"I"

Thomas Hears Voices

I've been diagnosed as having paranoid schizophrenia. I also suffer from clinical depression. Before I found the correct medications, I was sleeping on the floor, afraid to sleep in my own bed. I was hearing voices that, lately, had turned from being sometimes helpful to being terrorizing. The depression had been responsible for my being irritable and full of dread, especially in the mornings, becoming angry over frustrations at work, and seemingly internalizing other people's problems. . . .

The voices, human sounding, and sounding from a short distance outside my apartment, were slowly turning nearly all bad. I could hear them jeering me, plotting against me, singing songs sometimes that would only make sense later in the day when I would do something wrong at work or at home. I began sleeping on the floor of my living room because I was afraid a presence in the bedroom was torturing good forces around me. If I slept in the bedroom, the nightly torture would cause me to make mistakes during the day. A voice, calling himself Fatty Acid, stopped me from drinking soda. Another voice allowed me only one piece of bread with my meals.

—*Thomas, a young man diagnosed with schizophrenia and major depression*

Source: Campbell, 2000, reprinted with permission of the National Institute of Mental Health

---

psychological disorders Abnormal behavior pattern that involves a disturbance of psychological functioning or behavior.

abnormal psychology The branch of psychology that deals with the description, causes, and treatment of abnormal behavior patterns.

psychologist A professional who has completed advanced graduate training in psychology and obtained a license to practice psychology.

psychiatrist A medical doctor who specializes in the diagnosis and treatment of emotional disorders.

medical model A biological perspective in which abnormal behavior is viewed as symptomatic of underlying illness.

THESE THREE PEOPLE—LIKE MANY OF THE PEOPLE YOU WILL MEET IN THIS TEXT—struggle with problems that mental health professionals classify as psychological or mental disorders. A **psychological disorder** is a pattern of abnormal behavior that is associated with states of emotional distress, such as anxiety or depression, or with impaired behavior or ability to function, such as difficulty holding a job or even distinguishing reality from fantasy. **Abnormal psychology** is the branch of psychology that studies abnormal behavior and ways of helping people who are affected by psychological disorders.

The problem of abnormal behavior might seem the concern of only a few of us. After all, relatively few people are ever admitted to a psychiatric hospital. Most people never seek the help of a **psychologist** or **psychiatrist.** Fewer still ever plead not guilty to crimes on grounds of insanity. Most of us probably have at least one relative we consider "eccentric," but how many of us have relatives we consider "crazy"? And yet, the truth is that abnormal behavior affects all of us in one way or another. If we limit ourselves to diagnosable mental disorders, about one in two of us are directly affected at some point in our lives (see Figure 1.1). From about one fifth to about one third of us suffer from a diagnosable psychological disorder in any given year (Narrow et al., 2002 USDHHS, 1999a; WHO World Mental Health Survey Consortium, 2004). If we also include the mental health problems of our family members, friends, and coworkers and take into account those who foot the bill for treatment in the form of taxes and health insurance premiums and lost productivity due to sick days, disability leaves, and impaired job performance inflating product costs, then clearly all of us are affected to one degree or another.

The study of abnormal psychology is illuminated not only by the extensive research on the causes and treatments of psychological disorders reported in scientific journals, but also by the personal stories of people affected by these problems. In this text, we will learn from these people as they tell their stories in their own words. Through first-person narratives, case examples, and video interviews, we enter the world of people struggling with various types of psychological disorders that affect their moods, thinking, and behavior. Some of these stories may remind you of the experiences of people close to you, or perhaps even yourself. We invite you to explore with us the nature and origins of these disorders and ways of helping people who face the many challenges they pose.

Let us pause for a moment to raise an important distinction. Though the terms *psychological disorder* and *mental disorder* are often used interchangeably, we prefer using the term *psychological disorder*. The major reason is that the term *psychological disorder* puts the study of abnormal behavior squarely within the purview of the field of psychology. Moreover, the term *mental disorder* is associated with the **medical model** perspective that considers abnormal behavior patterns to be symptoms of underlying illness. *Mental illness is*

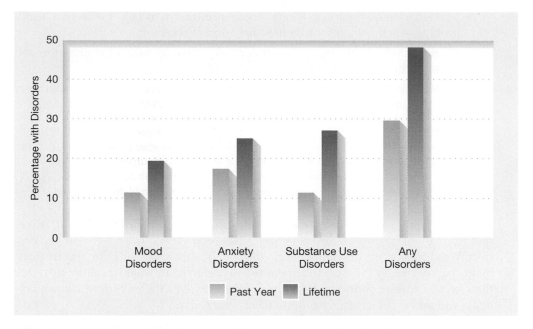

FIGURE 1.1 Lifetime and past-year prevalences of psychological disorders.
This graph is based on a nationally representative sample of U.S. residents in the 15- to 49-year-old age range. Here we see percentages of individuals with diagnosable psychological disorders either during the past year or at some point in their lives for several major diagnostic categories. The mood disorders category includes major depressive episode, manic episode, and dysthymia (discussed in chapter 8). Anxiety disorders includes panic disorder, agoraphobia without panic disorder, social phobia, specific phobia, and generalized anxiety disorder (discussed in chapter 6). Substance use disorders include abuse or dependence disorders involving alcohol or other drugs (discussed in chapter 10).

Source: National Comorbidity Survey (Kessler et al., 1994)

another term derived from the medical model to describe psychological or mental disorder. Although the medical model is a prominent perspective for understanding abnormal behavior, we believe that other perspectives, especially psychological and sociocultural perspectives, need to be considered to provide a more complete view of abnormal behavior.

We also adopt a more neutral language in this text in describing abnormal behavior patterns. For example, we often refer to "features" or "characteristics" of psychological disorders rather than to "symptoms"—the term that reflects the medical model. But our adoption of nonmedical jargon is not an absolute rule. In some cases, there may be no handy substitutes for terms that derive from the medical model, such as the term *remission* or the reference to patients in mental hospitals as "mental patients." In other cases we may use terms such as *disorder, therapy,* and *treatment* because they are commonly used by psychologists who "treat" "mental disorders" with psychological "therapies."

Recently, the U.S. Surgeon General issued a report on the nation's mental health. Here are some key conclusions from the report (Satcher, 2000; USDHHS, 1999b):

- Mental health reflects the complex interaction of brain functioning and environmental influences.

- Effective treatments exist for most mental disorders, including psychological interventions such as psychotherapy and counseling and psychopharmacologic or drug therapies. Treatment is often more effective when psychological and pharmacological treatments are combined.

- Progress in developing effective prevention programs in the mental health field has been slow because we do not know the causes of mental disorders or ways of altering known influences, such as genetic predispositions. Nonetheless, some effective prevention programs have been developed.

- Though 15% of American adults receive some form of help for mental health problems each year, many who need help do not receive it.
- Mental health problems are best understood when we take a broader view and consider the social and cultural contexts in which they occur.
- Mental health services need to be designed and delivered in a manner that takes into account the viewpoints and needs of racial and ethnic minorities.

The Surgeon General's report forms a backdrop for our study of abnormal psychology. As we shall see throughout the text, we believe that understandings of abnormal behavior are best revealed through a lens that takes into account interactions of biological and environmental factors. We also believe that social and cultural (or *sociocultural*) factors need to be considered in the attempt to both understand abnormal behavior and develop effective treatment services.

In this chapter we first address the difficulties of defining abnormal behavior. We see that throughout history, abnormal behavior has been viewed from different perspectives. We chronicle the development of concepts of abnormal behavior and its treatment. We see that in the past, treatment usually referred to what was done *to,* rather than *for,* people with abnormal behavior. We then describe the ways in which psychologists and other scholars study abnormal behavior today.

HOW DO WE DEFINE ABNORMAL BEHAVIOR?

We all become anxious or depressed from time to time, but is this abnormal? Becoming anxious in anticipation of an important job interview or a final examination is perfectly normal. It is appropriate to feel depressed when you have lost someone close to you or when you have failed at a test or on the job. So, where is the line between normal and abnormal behavior?

One answer is that emotional states such as anxiety and depression may be considered abnormal when they are not appropriate to the situation. It is normal to feel down when you fail a test, but not when your grades are good or excellent. It is normal to feel anxious before a college admissions interview, but not to panic before entering a department store or boarding a crowded elevator.

Abnormality may also be suggested by the magnitude of the problem. Although some anxiety is normal enough before a job interview, feeling that your heart might leap from your chest—and consequently canceling the interview—is not. Nor is it normal to feel so anxious in this situation that your clothing becomes soaked with perspiration.

Criteria for Determining Abnormality

Mental health professionals apply various criteria in making judgments about whether behavior is abnormal. The most commonly used criteria include the following:

1. *Unusualness.* Behavior that is unusual is often considered abnormal. Only a few of us report seeing or hearing things that are not really there; "seeing things" and "hearing things" are almost always considered abnormal in our culture, except, perhaps, in the case of certain types of religious experiences (USDHHS, 1999a). Moreover, "hearing voices" and other forms of hallucinations under some circumstances are not considered unusual in some preliterate societies.

   Becoming overcome with feelings of panic when entering a department store or when standing in a crowded elevator is uncommon and considered abnormal in our culture. Uncommon behavior is not in itself abnormal. Only one person can hold the record for swimming the fastest 100 meters. The record-holding athlete differs from the rest of us but, again, is not considered abnormal. Thus rarity or statistical deviance is not a sufficient basis for labeling behavior abnormal; nevertheless, it is one yardstick often used to judge abnormality.

2. *Social deviance.* All societies have norms (standards) that define the kinds of behaviors acceptable in given contexts. Behavior deemed normal in one culture may

When is anxiety abnormal? Negative emotions such as anxiety are considered abnormal when they are judged to be excessive or inappropriate to the situation. Anxiety is generally regarded as normal when it is experienced during a job interview (left), so long as it is not so severe that it prevents the interviewee from performing adequately. Anxiety is deemed to be abnormal if it is experienced whenever one boards an elevator (right).

be viewed as abnormal in another. For example, people in our culture who assume that all male strangers are devious are usually regarded as unduly suspicous or distrustful. But such suspicions were justified among the Mundugumor, a tribe of cannibals studied by anthropologist Margaret Mead (1935). Within that culture, male strangers *were* typically malevolent toward others, and it was normal to feel distrustful of them. Norms, which arise from on the practices and beliefs of specific cultures, are relative standards, not universal truths.

Is this abnormal? One of the criteria used to determine whether or not behavior is abnormal is whether it deviates from acceptable standards of conduct or social norms. The behavior and attire of these men is abnormal in a classroom or workplace, but not at a football game.

Thus, clinicians need to weigh cultural differences while determining what is normal and abnormal. Moreover, what strikes one generation as abnormal may be considered normal by the next. For example, until the mid-1970s homosexuality was classified as a mental disorder by the psychiatric profession (see *Controversies in Abnormal Psychology* box on page 18). Today, however, the psychiatric profession no longer considers homosexuality a mental disorder, and many people argue that contemporary societal norms should include homosexuality as a normal variation in behavior.

Another result of basing normality on compliance with social norms is the tendency to label nonconformists as mentally disturbed. We may come to brand behavior that we do not approve as "sick" rather than accept that the behavior may be normal, even as it offends or puzzles us.

3. *Faulty perceptions or interpretations of reality.* Normally, our sensory systems and cognitive processes permit us to form accurate mental representations of the environment. Seeing things and hearing voices that are not present are considered hallucinations, which in our culture are generally taken as signs of an underlying mental disorder. Similarly, holding unfounded ideas or *delusions,* such as *ideas of persecution* that the CIA or the Mafia are out to get you, may be regarded as signs of mental disturbance—unless, of course, they *are.* (As former Secretary of State Henry Kissinger is said to have remarked, "Even paranoid people have enemies.")

   It is normal in the United States to say that one "talks" to God through prayer. If, however, a person insists to have literally seen God or heard the voice of God—as opposed to, say, being divinely inspired—we may come to regard her or him as mentally disturbed.

4. *Significant personal distress.* States of personal distress caused by troublesome emotions, such as anxiety, fear, or depression, may be abnormal. As we noted earlier, however, anxiety and depression are sometimes appropriate responses to the situation. Real threats and losses do occur in life, and *lack* of an emotional response to them would be regarded as abnormal. Appropriate feelings of distress are not considered abnormal unless they persist long after the source of anguish has been removed (after most people would have adjusted) or if they are so intense that they impair the individual's ability to function.

5. *Maladaptive or self-defeating behavior.* Behavior that leads to unhappiness rather than self-fulfillment can be regarded as abnormal. Behavior that limits our ability to function in expected roles, or to adapt to our environments, may also be considered abnormal. According to these criteria, heavy alcohol consumption that impairs health or social and occupational functioning may be viewed as abnormal. Agoraphobic behavior, characterized by intense fear of venturing into public places, may be considered abnormal in that it is both uncommon and maladaptive because it impairs the individual's ability to fulfill work and family responsibilities.

6. *Dangerousness.* Behavior that is dangerous to oneself or other people may be considered abnormal. Here, too, the social context is crucial. In wartime, people who sacrifice themselves or charge the enemy with little apparent concern for their own safety may be characterized as courageous, heroic, and patriotic. But people who threaten or attempt suicide because of the pressures of civilian life are usually considered abnormal.

   Football and hockey players who occasionally get into fistfights altercations with opposing players may be normal enough. Given the nature of the sports, unaggressive football and hockey players would not last long in college or professional ranks. But individuals involved in frequent altercations may be regarded as abnormal. Physically aggressive behavior is most often maladaptive in modern life. Moreover, physical aggression is ineffective as a way of resolving conflicts—although it is by no means uncommon.

Abnormal behavior thus has multiple definitions. Depending on the case, some criteria may be weighted more heavily than others. But in most cases, a combination of these criteria is used to define abnormality.

Let's now return to the three cases we introduced at the beginning of the chapter. Consider the criteria we can apply in determining that the behaviors reported in these case vignettes are abnormal. For one thing, the abnormal behavior patterns in these three cases are unusual in the statistical sense. Most people do not encounter these kinds of problems, although we should add that these problems are far from rare. The problem behaviors also meet other criteria of abnormality, as we shall see.

Phil suffered from *claustrophobia,* an excessive fear of enclosed spaces. (This is an example of an anxiety disorder and is discussed more fully in Chapter 6). His behavior was unusual (relatively few people are so fearful of confinement that they avoid flying in airplanes or riding on elevators) and was associated with significant personal distress. His fear also impaired his ability to carry out his occupational and family responsibilities. But he was not hampered by faulty perceptions of reality. He recognized that his fears exceeded a realistic appraisal of danger in these situations.

What criteria of abnormality applies in the case of the woman who cowered under the blankets? She was diagnosed with *bipolar disorder* (formerly, manic-depression), a type of mood disorder in which a person experiences extreme mood swings from the heights of elation and seemingly boundless energy to the depths of depression and despair. (The vignette described the manic phase of the disorder.) Bipolar disorder, which is discussed in Chapter 8, is associated with extreme personal distress and difficulty functioning effectively in normal life. It is also linked to self-defeating and dangerous behavior, such as reckless driving or exorbitant spending during manic phases and suicide during depressive phases. In some cases, like the one presented here, people in manic phases sometimes have faulty perceptions or interpretations of reality, such as hallucinations and delusions.

Thomas, whose story was featured in the third vignette, suffered from both schizophrenia and depression. It is not unusual for people to have more than one disorder at a time. In the parlance of the psychiatric profession, these clients present with *comorbid* (co-occurring) diagnoses. Comorbidity complicates treatment, because clinicians need to design a treatment approach that focuses on treating two or more disorders. Schizophrenia meets a number of criteria of abnormality in addition to statistical infrequency (it affects about 1% of the general population). The clinical features of schizophrenia include socially deviant or bizarre behavior, disturbed perceptions or interpretations of reality (delusions and hallucinations), maladaptive behavior (difficulty meeting responsibilities of daily life), and personal distress. (See Chapter 13 for more detail on schizophrenia.) Thomas, for example, was plagued by auditory hallucinations (terrorizing voices), which were certainly a source of significant distress. His thinking was also delusional, as he believed that "a presence" in his bedroom was "torturing good forces" that surrounded him and causing him to make mistakes during the day. In Thomas's case, schizophrenia was complicated by depression that involved feelings of personal distress (irritability and feelings of dread). Depression is also associated with dampened or downcast mood, maladaptive behavior (difficulty getting to work or school or even getting out of bed in the morning), and potential dangerousness (possible suicidal behavior).

It is one thing to recognize and label behavior as abnormal; it is another to understand and explain it. Philosophers, physicians, natural scientists, and psychologists have used various approaches, or *models,* in the effort to explain abnormal behavior. Some approaches have been based on superstition; others have invoked religious explanations. Some current views are predominantly biological; others are psychological. In considering various historical and contemporary approaches to understanding abnormal behavior, let's first look further at the importance of cultural beliefs in determining which behavior patterns are deemed abnormal.

A traditional Native American healer. Many traditional Native Americans distinguish between illnesses believed to arise from influences external to their own culture ("white man's sicknesses") and those that emanate from a lack of harmony with traditional tribal life and thought ("Indian sicknesses"). Traditional healers such as the one shown here may be called on to treat "Indian sickness," whereas "white man's medicine" may be sought to help people deal with problems whose causes are seen as lying outside the community, such as alcoholism and drug addiction.

Cultural Bases of Abnormal Behavior

As noted, behavior that is normal in one culture may be deemed abnormal in another. Australian aborigines believe they can communicate with the spirits of their ancestors and that people, especially close relatives, share their dreams. These beliefs are considered normal within Aboriginal culture. But were such beliefs to be expressed in our culture, they would likely be deemed delusions, which professionals regard as a common feature of schizophrenia. Thus, the standards we use in making judgments of abnormal behavior must take into account cultural norms.

Kleinman (1987) offers an example of "hearing voices" among Native Americans to underscore the ways in which judgments about abnormality are embedded within a cultural context:

> Ten psychiatrists trained in the same assessment technique and diagnostic criteria who are asked to examine 100 American Indians shortly after the latter have experienced the death of a spouse, a parent or a child may determine with close to 100% consistency that those individuals report hearing, in the first month of grieving, the voice of the dead person calling to them as the spirit ascends to the afterworld. [While such judgments may be consistent across observers] the determination of whether such reports are a sign of an abnormal mental state is an interpretation based on knowledge of this group's behavioural norms and range of normal experiences of bereavement. (p. 453)

To these Native Americans, bereaved people who report hearing the spirits of the deceased calling to them as they ascend to the afterlife are normal. Behavior that is normative within the cultural setting in which it occurs should not be considered abnormal.

Concepts of health and illness have different meanings in different cultures. Traditional Native American cultures distinguish between illnesses that are believed to arise from influences outside the culture, called "White man's sicknesses," such as alcoholism and drug addiction, from those that emanate from a lack of harmony with traditional tribal life and thought, which are called "Indian sicknesses" (Trimble, 1991). Traditional healers, shamans, and medicine men and women are called on to treat "Indian sickness." When the problem is thought to have its cause outside the community, help is sought from "White man's medicine."

Abnormal behavior patterns take different forms in different cultures (USDHHS, 1999a). Westerners experience anxiety, for example, in the form of worrying about paying the mortgage, losing a job, and so on. Yet "[I]n a number of African cultures, anxiety is expressed as fears of failure in procreation, in dreams and complaints about witchcraft" (Kleinman, 1987). Australian aborigines can develop intense fears of sorcery, accompanied by the belief that one is in mortal danger from evil spirits (D. J. Spencer, 1983). Trancelike states in which young aboriginal women are mute, immobile, and unresponsive are also quite common. If these women do not recover from the trance within hours or, at most, a few days, they may be brought to a sacred site for healing.

The very words that we use to describe psychological disorders—words such as *depression* or *mental health*—have different meanings in other cultures or no equivalent meaning at all. This doesn't mean that depression doesn't exist in other cultures. Rather, it suggests we need to learn how people in different cultures experience emotional distress, including states of depression and anxiety, rather than imposing our perspectives on their experiences. Among people in China and other countries in the Far East, depression is often expressed through the development of physical symptoms, such as headaches, fatigue, or weakness, rather than by the feelings of guilt or sadness that are more common in the West (American Psychiatric Association, 2000; Draguns & Tanaka-Matsumi, 2003; Parker, Gladstone, & Chee, 2001).

These differences demonstrate how important it is that we determine whether our concepts of abnormal behavior are valid before we apply them to other cultures (Dana, 2000). Research efforts along these lines have shown that the abnormal behavior pattern associated with our concept of schizophrenia exists in countries as far flung as Colombia, India, China, Denmark, Nigeria, and the former Soviet Union, among others (Jablensky et al., 1992). Furthermore, rates of schizophrenia appear similar among the countries studied. However, differences have been observed in some of the features of schizophrenia across cultures (Thakker & Ward, 1998).

Views about abnormal behavior vary from society to society. In our culture, models based on medical disease and psychological factors are prominent in explaining abnormal behavior. But in traditional native cultures, models of abnormal behavior often invoke supernatural causes, such as possession by demons or the devil (Lefley, 1990). In Filipino folk society, for example, psychological problems are often attributed to the influence of "spirits" or the possession of a "weak soul" (Edman & Johnson, 1999).

HISTORICAL PERSPECTIVES ON ABNORMAL BEHAVIOR

Throughout the history of Western culture, concepts of abnormal behavior have been shaped, to some degree, by the prevailing worldview of the time. For hundreds of years, beliefs in supernatural forces, demons, and evil spirits held sway. (And, as we've just seen, these beliefs still hold true in some societies.) Abnormal behavior was often taken as a sign of possession. In modern times, the predominant—but by no means universal—worldview has shifted toward beliefs in science and reason. In our culture, abnormal behavior has come to be viewed as the product of physical and psychosocial factors, not demonic possession.

The Demonological Model

Why would anyone need a hole in the head? Archaeologists have unearthed human skeletons from the Stone Age with egg-sized cavities in the skull. One interpretation of these holes is that our prehistoric ancestors believed abnormal behavior was caused by the inhabitation of evil spirits. These holes might be the result of **trephination**—the drilling of the skull to provide an outlet for those irascible spirits. Fresh bone growth indicates that some people did survive this "medical procedure."

Just the threat of *trephining* may have persuaded some people to comply with tribal norms. Because no written accounts of the purposes of trephination exist, other explanations are possible. For instance, perhaps trephination was simply a form of surgery to remove shattered pieces of bone or blood clots that resulted from head injuries (Maher & Maher, 1985).

The notion of supernatural causes of abnormal behavior, or demonology, was prominent in Western society until the Age of Enlightenment. The ancients explained nature in terms of the actions of the gods: The Babylonians believed the movements of the stars and the planets expressed the adventures and conflicts of the gods. The Greeks believed the gods toyed with humans, unleashed havoc on disrespectful or arrogant humans, and clouded their minds with madness.

In ancient Greece, people who behaved abnormally were sent to temples dedicated to Aesculapius, the god of healing. The Greeks believed that Aesculapius would visit the afflicted while they slept in the temple and offer them restorative advice through dreams. Rest, a nutritious diet, and exercise were also part of the treatment. Incurables were driven from the temple by stoning.

Origins of the Medical Model: In "Ill Humor"

Not all ancient Greeks believed in the demonological model. The seeds of naturalistic explanations of abnormal behavior were sown by Hippocrates and developed by other physicians in the ancient world, especially Galen.

trephination A harsh, prehistoric practice of cutting a hole in a person's skull, possibly in an attempt to release demons.

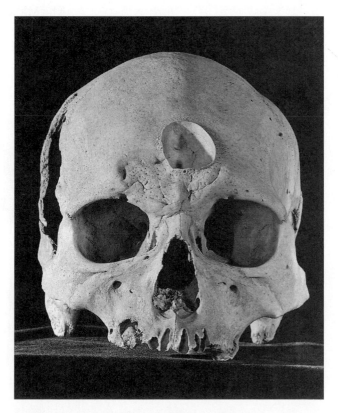

Trephination. Trephination refers to a procedure by which a hole is chipped into a person's skull. Some investigators speculate that the practice represented an ancient form of surgery. Perhaps trephination was intended to release the demons responsible for abnormal behavior.

humors According to the ancient Hippocratic belief system, the vital bodily fluids (phlegm, black bile, blood, yellow bile).

Hippocrates (ca. 460–377 B.C.E.), the celebrated physician of the Golden Age of Greece, challenged the prevailing beliefs of his time by arguing that illnesses of the body and mind were the result of natural causes, not possession by supernatural spirits. He believed the health of the body and mind depended on the balance of **humors,** or vital fluids, in the body: phlegm, black bile, blood, and yellow bile. An imbalance of humors, he thought, accounted for abnormal behavior. A lethargic or sluggish person was believed to have an excess of phlegm, from which we derive the word *phlegmatic.* An overabundance of black bile was believed to cause depression, or *melancholia.* An excess of blood created a *sanguine* disposition: cheerful, confident, and optimistic. An excess of yellow bile made people "bilious" and *choleric*—quick-tempered, that is.

Though we no longer subscribe to Hippocrates's theory of bodily humors, his theory is important because of its break from demonology. It foreshadowed the modern medical model, the view that abnormal behavior results from underlying biological processes. Hippocrates made other contributions to modern thought and, indeed, to modern medical practice. He classified abnormal behavior patterns, using three main categories that still find equivalents today: *melancholia* to characterize excessive depression, *mania* to refer to exceptional excitement, and *phrenitis* (from the Greek "inflammation of the brain") to characterize the bizarre behavior that might today typify schizophrenia. To this day, medical schools honor Hippocrates by having students swear an oath of medical ethics that he originated, the Hippocratic oath.

Galen (ca. 130–200 C.E.), a Greek physician who attended Roman emperor–philosopher Marcus Aurelius, adopted and expanded on the teachings of Hippocrates. Among Galen's contributions was the discovery that arteries carry blood, not air, as had been formerly believed.

Medieval Times

The Middle Ages, or medieval times, cover the millennium of European history from about 476 C.E. through 1450 C.E. After the passing of Galen, belief in supernatural causes, especially the doctrine of possession, increased in influence and eventually dominated medieval thought. This doctrine held that abnormal behaviors were a sign of possession by evil spirits or the devil. This belief was part of the teachings of the Roman Catholic Church, the central institution in western Europe after the decline of the Roman Empire. Although belief in possession preceded the Church and is found in ancient Egyptian and Greek writings, the Church revitalized it. The Church's treatment of choice for possession was exorcism. Exorcists were employed to persuade evil spirits that the bodies of the "possessed" were no longer habitable. Methods of persuasion included prayer, incantations, waving a cross at the victim, beating and flogging, even starving the victim. If the victim continued to display unseemly behavior, there were yet more persuasive remedies, such as the rack, a device of torture. No doubt, recipients of these "remedies" fondly wished the devil would vacate the premises immediately.

The Renaissance—a great revival of classical learning, art, and literature—began in Italy in the 1400s and spread throughout Europe. Ironically, although the Renaissance is considered the transition from the medieval to the modern world, the fear of witches also reached its height during this period.

Witchcraft

The late 15th through the late 17th centuries were especially bad times to annoy your neighbors. These were times of massive persecutions, particularly of women, who were accused of witchcraft. Church officials believed that witches made pacts with the devil,

Exorcism. This medieval woodcut illustrates the practice of exorcism, which was used to expel the evil spirits that were believed to have possessed people.

practiced satanic rituals, ate babies, and poisoned crops. In 1484, Pope Innocent VIII decreed that witches be executed. Two Dominican priests compiled a notorious manual for witch-hunting, called the *Malleus Maleficarum* (The Witches' Hammer), to help inquisitors identify suspected witches. Over 100,000 accused witches were killed in the next two centuries.

Witch-hunting required innovative "diagnostic" tests. In the case of the water-float test, suspects were dunked in a pool to certify they were not possessed by the devil. The test was based on the principle that pure metals settle to the bottom during smelting, whereas impurities bob up to the surface. Suspects who sank and drowned were ruled pure. Suspects who kept their heads above water were judged to be in league with the devil. As the saying went, you were "Damned if you do and damned if you don't."

Modern scholars once believed these so-called witches were actually people with psychological disorders who were persecuted because of their abnormal behavior. Many suspected witches did confess to bizarre behaviors, such as flying or engaging in sexual intercourse with the devil, which suggests the types of disturbed behavior associated with modern conceptions of schizophrenia. Yet these confessions must be discounted because they were extracted under torture by inquisitors who were bent on finding evidence to support accusations of witchcraft (Spanos, 1978). We know today that the threat of torture and other forms of intimidation are sufficient to extract false confessions. Although some of those who were persecuted as witches probably did show abnormal behavior patterns, most did not (Schoenman, 1984). Rather, accusations of witchcraft appeared to be a convenient means of disposing of social nuisances and political rivals, of seizing property, and of suppressing heresy (Spanos, 1978). In English villages, many of the accused were poor, unmarried elderly women who were forced to beg their neighbors for food. If misfortune befell the people who declined to give help, the beggar might be accused of having cast a curse on the household. If the woman was generally unpopular, the accusation of witchcraft was likely to follow.

Demons were believed to play roles in both abnormal behavior and witchcraft. However, although some victims of demonic possession were perceived to be afflicted as retribution for their own wrongdoing, others were considered to be innocent victims—possessed by demons through no fault of their own. Witches, on the other hand, were believed to have renounced God and voluntarily entered into a pact with the devil. Witches were generally seen as more deserving of torture and execution (Spanos, 1978).

Historical trends do not follow straight lines. Although the demonological model held sway during the Middle Ages and much of the Renaissance, it did not completely supplant belief in naturalistic causes (Schoenman, 1984). In medieval England, for example, demonic possession was only rarely invoked in cases in which a person was held to be insane by legal authorities (Neugebauer, 1979). Most explanations for unusual behavior involved natural causes, such as physical illness or trauma to the brain. In England, in fact, some disturbed people were kept in hospitals until they were restored to sanity (Alldridge, 1979). The Renaissance Belgian physician Johann Weyer (1515–1588) also took up the cause of Hippocrates and Galen by arguing that abnormal behavior and thought patterns were caused by physical problems.

Asylums

By the late 15th and early 16th centuries, asylums, or madhouses, began to crop up throughout Europe. Many were former leprosariums, which were no longer needed because of the decline in leprosy after the late Middle Ages. Asylums often gave refuge to beggars as well as the mentally disturbed, and conditions were appalling. Residents were chained to their beds and left to lie in their own waste or to wander about unassisted. Some asylums became public spectacles. In one asylum in London, St. Mary's of Bethlehem Hospital—from which the word *bedlam* is derived—the public could buy tickets

The water-float test. This so-called test was one way in which medieval authorities sought to detect possession and witchcraft. Managing to float above the water line was deemed a sign of impurity. In the lower right-hand corner, you can see the bound hands and feet of one poor unfortunate who failed to remain afloat, but whose drowning would have cleared away any suspicions of possession.

"Bedlam." The bizarre antics of the patients at St. Mary's of Bethelem Hospital in London in the 18th century were a source of entertainment for the well-heeled gentry of the town, such as the two well-dressed women in the middle of the painting.

TRUTH or FICTION? *REVISITED*

A night's entertainment in London a few hundred years ago might have included gaping at the inmates at the local asylum.

☑ **TRUE.** A night on the town for the gentry of London sometimes included a visit to a local asylum, St. Mary's of Bethlehem Hospital, to gawk at the patients. We derive the word *bedlam* from Bethlehem Hospital.

to observe the antics of the inmates, much as we would pay to see a circus sideshow or animals at the zoo.

The Reform Movement and Moral Therapy

The modern era of treatment begins with the efforts of the Frenchmen Jean-Baptiste Pussin and Philippe Pinel in the late 18th and early 19th centuries. They argued that people who behave abnormally suffer from diseases and should be treated humanely. This view was not popular at the time; mentally disturbed people were regarded as threats to society, not as sick people in need of treatment.

From 1784 to 1802, Pussin, a layman, was placed in charge of a ward for people considered "incurably insane" at La Bicêtre, a large mental hospital in Paris. Although Pinel is often credited with freeing the inmates of La Bicêtre from their chains, Pussin was actually the first official to unchain a group of the "incurably insane." These unfortunates had been considered too dangerous and unpredictable to be left unchained. But Pussin believed that if they were treated with kindness, there would be no need for chains. As he predicted, most of the shut-ins were manageable and calm after their chains were removed. They could walk the hospital grounds and take in fresh air. Pussin also forbade the staff from treating the residents harshly, and he fired employees who ignored his directives.

Pinel (1745–1826) became medical director for the incurables' ward at La Bicêtre in 1793 and continued the humane treatment Pussin had begun. He stopped harsh practices, such as bleeding and purging, and moved patients from darkened dungeons to well-ventilated, sunny rooms. Pinel also spent hours talking to inmates, in the belief that showing understanding and concern would help restore them to normal functioning.

The philosophy of treatment that emerged from these efforts was labeled *moral therapy.* It was based on the belief that providing humane treatment in a relaxed and decent environment could restore functioning. Similar reforms were instituted at about this

The unchaining of inmates at La Bicêtre by 18th-century French reformer Philippe Pinel. Continuing the work of Jean-Baptiste Pussin, Pinel stopped harsh practices, such as bleeding and purging, and moved inmates from darkened dungeons to sunny, airy rooms. Pinel also took the time to converse with inmates, in the belief that understanding and concern would help restore them to normal functioning.

time in England by William Tuke and later in the United States by Dorothea Dix. Another influential figure was the American physician Benjamin Rush (1745–1813)—also a signatory to the Declaration of Independence and an early leader of the antislavery movement (Farr, 1994). Rush, considered the father of American psychiatry, penned the first American textbook on psychiatry in 1812: *Medical Inquiries and Observations Upon the Diseases of the Mind.* He believed that madness is caused by engorgement of the blood vessels of the brain. To relieve pressure, he recommended bloodletting, purging, and ice-cold baths. But he did advance humane treatment by encouraging the staff of his Philadelphia Hospital to treat patients with kindness, respect, and understanding. He also favored the therapeutic use of occupational therapy, music, and travel (Farr, 1994). His hospital became the first in the United States to admit patients for psychological disorders.

Dorothea Dix (1802–1887), a Boston schoolteacher, traveled about the country decrying the deplorable conditions in the jails and almshouses where mentally disturbed people were placed. As a result of her efforts, 32 mental hospitals devoted to treating people with psychological disorders were established throughout the United States.

A Step Backward

In the latter half of the 19th century, the belief that abnormal behaviors could be successfully treated or cured by moral therapy fell into disfavor (USDHHS, 1999a). A period of apathy ensued in which patterns of abnormal behavior were deemed incurable (Grob, 1994). Mental institutions in the United States grew in size but provided little more than custodial care. Conditions deteriorated. Mental hospitals became frightening places. It was not uncommon to find residents "wallowing in their own excrements," in the words of a New York State official of the time (Grob, 1983). Straitjackets, handcuffs, cribs, straps, and other devices were used to restrain excitable or violent patients.

Deplorable hospital conditions remained commonplace through the middle of the 20th century. By the mid-1950s, the population in mental hospitals had risen to half a million patients. Although some state hospitals provided decent and humane care, many were described as little more than human snakepits. Residents were crowded into wards that lacked even rudimentary sanitation. Mental patients in back wards were essentially *warehoused;* that is, they were left to live out their lives with little hope or expectation of recovery or return to the community. Many received little professional care and were abused by poorly trained and supervised staffs. Finally, these appalling conditions led to calls for reforms of the mental health system.

The Community Mental Health Movement: The Exodus from State Hospitals

In response to the growing call for reform, Congress in 1963 established a nationwide system of community mental health centers (CMHCs) that was intended to offer an alternative to long-term custodial care in bleak institutions. CMHCs were charged with providing continuing support and care to former hospital residents who were released from state mental hospitals under a policy of deinstitutionalization. Another factor that laid the groundwork for the mass exodus from mental hospitals was the development of a new class of drugs—the *phenothiazines.* This group of antipsychotic drugs, which helped quell the most flagrant behavior patterns associated with schizophrenia, was introduced in the 1950s. *Phenothiazines* reduced the need for indefinite hospital stays and permitted many people with schizophrenia to be discharged to halfway houses, group homes, and independent living. The mental hospital population across the United States plummeted from more than 550,000 in 1955 to fewer than 130,000 by the late 1980s (D. Braddock, 1992; Kiesler & Sibulkin, 1987). Some mental hospitals were closed entirely.

The community mental health movement and the policy of deinstitutionalization were developed with the hope that mental patients could return to their communities and assume more independent and fulfilling lives (Lamb, 2001; Lamb & Weinberger, 2001). Yet critics contend that the exodus from state hospitals abandoned tens of thousands of marginally functioning people to communities that lack adequate housing and other forms of support. Even today, many of the homeless we see wandering city streets and sleeping in bus terminals and train stations are discharged mental patients. (In Chapter 4, we take a closer look at the policy of deinstitutionalization and the problems faced by the psychiatric homeless population.)

Contemporary Perspectives on Abnormal Behavior

Beliefs in possession or demonology, as we have seen, persisted until the 18th century, when society began to turn toward reason and science to explain natural phenomena and human behavior. The nascent sciences of biology, chemistry, physics, and astronomy promised knowledge derived from scientific methods of observation and experimentation. Scientific observation in turn uncovered the microbial causes of some kinds of diseases and gave rise to preventive measures. Scientific models of abnormal behavior also began to emerge, including models representing biological, psychological, sociocultural, and biopsychosocial perspectives. We briefly discuss each of these models here, particularly in terms of their historical background, which will lead to a fuller discussion in Chapter 2.

The Biological Perspective Against the backdrop of advances in medical science, the German physician Wilhelm Griesinger (1817–1868) argued that abnormal behavior was rooted in diseases of the brain. Griesinger's views influenced another German physician, Emil Kraepelin (1856–1926), who wrote an influential textbook on psychiatry in 1883 in which he likened mental disorders to physical diseases. Griesinger and Kraepelin paved the way for the modern medical model, which attempts to explain abnormal behavior on the basis of underlying biological defects or abnormalities, not evil spirits. According to the medical model, people behaving abnormally suffer from mental illnesses or disorders that can be classified, like physical illnesses, according to their distinctive causes and symptoms. Adopters of the medical model don't necessarily believe that every mental disorder is a product of defective biology, but they maintain that it is useful to classify patterns of abnormal behavior as disorders that can be identified on the basis of their distinctive features or symptoms.

Kraepelin specified two main groups of mental disorders or diseases: **dementia praecox** (from roots meaning "precocious [premature] insanity"), which we now call schizophrenia, and manic–depressive psychosis, which is now labeled *bipolar disorder*. Kraepelin believed that dementia praecox was caused by a biochemical imbalance and manic–depressive psychosis by an abnormality in body metabolism. His major contribution was the development of a classification system that forms the cornerstone for current diagnostic systems.

The medical model gained support in the late 19th century with the discovery that an advanced stage of *syphilis*—in which the bacterium that causes the disease directly invades the brain itself—led to a form of disturbed behavior called **general paresis** (from the Greek *parienai,* meaning "to relax"). General paresis is associated with physical symptoms and psychological impairment, including personality and mood changes, and with progressive deterioration of memory functioning and judgment. With the advent of antibiotics for treating syphilis, general paresis has become extremely uncommon.

General paresis is of interest to us mostly for historical reasons. With the discovery of the connection between general paresis and syphilis, scientists became optimistic that other biological causes would soon be discovered for many other types of disturbed behavior. Though advances have been made in understanding the biological underpinnings of psychological disorders, that early optimism has not been fulfilled. Today we realize that psychological disorders are complex phenomena that involve the interplay of factors we are still struggling to understand.

Much of the terminology used in abnormal psychology has been "medicalized." Because of the medical model, we commonly speak of people whose behavior is abnormal as being mentally ill. Because of the medical model we commonly refer to the symptoms of abnormal behavior, rather than the features or characteristics of abnormal behavior.

dementia praecox The term given by Kraepelin to the disorder now called schizophrenia.

general paresis A degenerative brain disease occurring when the bacterium that causes syphilis directly invades brain tissue.

Other terminological offspring of the medical model include *mental health, syndrome, diagnosis, patient, mental patient, mental hospital, prognosis, treatment, therapy, cure, relapse,* and *remission.*

The medical model is a major advance over demonology. It inspired the idea that abnormal behavior should be treated by learned professionals, not punished. Compassion supplanted hatred, fear, and persecution. But the medical model has also led to controversy over the extent to which certain behavior patterns should be considered forms of mental illness. We address this controversy in the accompanying feature, *"What is Abnormal Behavior?"*

The Psychological Perspective Although the medical model gained influence in the 19th century, some scientists argued that organic factors alone could not explain the many forms of abnormal behavior. In Paris, a respected neurologist, Jean-Martin Charcot (1825–1893), experimented with the use of hypnosis in treating *hysteria,* a condition characterized by paralysis or numbness that cannot be explained by any underlying physical cause. [Interestingly, cases of hysteria were common in the Victorian period, but are rare today (Spitzer et al., 1989).] The thinking at the time was that people with hysteria must have an affliction of the nervous system, which caused their symptoms. Yet Charcot and his associates demonstrated that these symptoms could be removed in hysterical patients or, conversely, induced in normal patients, by means of hypnotic suggestion.

Among those who attended Charcot's demonstrations was a young Austrian physician named Sigmund Freud (1856–1939). Freud reasoned that if hysterical symptoms could be made to disappear or appear through hypnosis—the mere "suggestion of ideas"—they must be psychological, not biological, in origin (E. Jones, 1953). He concluded that whatever psychological factors give rise to hysteria, they must lie outside the range of conscious awareness. This insight underlies the first psychological perspective on abnormal behavior—the **psychodynamic model.** "I received the proudest impression," Freud wrote of his experience with Charcot, "of the possibility that there could be powerful mental processes which nevertheless remained hidden from the consciousness of men" (as cited in Sulloway, 1983, p. 32).

Freud was also influenced by the Viennese physician Joseph Breuer (1842–1925), 14 years his senior. Breuer too had used hypnosis to treat a 21-year-old woman, Anna O., with hysterical complaints for which there was no apparent medical basis, such as paralysis in her limbs, numbness, and disturbances of vision and hearing (E. Jones, 1953). A "paralyzed" muscle in her neck prevented her from turning her head. Immobilization of the fingers of her left hand made it all but impossible for her to feed herself. Breuer believed there was a strong psychological component to her symptoms. He encouraged her to talk about her symptoms, sometimes under hypnosis. Recalling and talking about events connected with the appearance of the symptoms—especially events that evoked feelings of fear, anxiety, or guilt—provided symptom relief, at least for a time. Anna referred to the treatment as the "talking cure" or, when joking, as "chimney sweeping."

The hysterical symptoms were taken to represent the transformation of these blocked-up emotions, forgotten but not lost, into physical complaints. In Anna's case, the symptoms disappeared once the emotions were brought to the surface and "discharged." Breuer labeled the therapeutic effect *catharsis,* or emotional discharge of feelings (from the Greek word *kathairein,* meaning to clean or to purify).

Freud's theoretical model was the first major psychological model of abnormal behavior. As we'll see in Chapter 2, other psychological perspectives on abnormal behavior soon

psychodynamic model The theoretical model of Freud and his followers, in which abnormal behavior is viewed as the product of clashing forces within the personality.

Charcot's teaching clinic. Parisian neurologist Jean-Martin Charcot presents a woman patient who exhibits the highly dramatic behavior associated with hysteria, such as falling faint at a moment's notice. Charcot was an important influence on the young Sigmund Freud.

CONTROVERSIES IN ABNORMAL PSYCHOLOGY
What Is Abnormal Behavior?

The question of where to draw the line between "normal" and "abnormal" behavior continues to be a subject of debate within the mental health field and the broader society. Unlike medical illness, a psychological or mental disorder cannot be identified by a spot on an X-ray or from a blood sample. Classifying these disorders involves clinical judgments, not findings of fact; and as we have noted, these judgments can change over time and can vary from culture to culture. For example, medical professionals once considered masturbation a form of mental illness. Although some people today may object to masturbation on moral grounds, professionals no longer regard it as a mental disturbance.

Consider other behaviors that may blur the boundaries between normal and abnormal: Is body-piercing abnormal, or is it simply a fashion statement? (How much piercing do you consider "normal"?) Might excessive shopping behavior or overuse of the Internet be forms of mental illness? Is bullying a symptom of an underlying disorder, or is it just "bad behavior"? The judgments that mental health professionals make are informed by the kinds of criteria we have outlined in this text. But even in professional circles, debate continues about whether some forms of behavior should be classified as abnormal or, in the parlance of the psychiatric profession, as mental disorders or mental illnesses.

One of the longest of these debates concerns homosexuality. Until 1973, the American Psychiatric Association classified homosexuality as a mental disorder. In that year, however, the organization voted to drop homosexuality from its listing of classified mental disorders in its diagnostic manual, the *Diagnostic and Statistical Manual of Mental Disorders,* or DSM (discussed in Chapter 3). The DSM retained, however, a diagnostic classification that could be applied to individuals who are distressed or confused about their sexual orientation.

The decision to declassify homosexuality as a mental disorder was not unanimous among the nation's psychiatrists. Many argued that the decision was motivated more by political reasons than by good science. Some objected to basing such a decision on a vote. After all, would it be reasonable to drop cancer as a recognized medical illness based on a vote? Shouldn't scientific criteria determine these kinds of judgments, rather than a popular vote?

What do you think? Is homosexuality a variation in the normal spectrum of sexual orientation, or is it a form of abnormal behavior? What is the basis of your judgment? What criteria did you apply in forming a judgment? What evidence do you have to support your beliefs?

Within the DSM system, mental disorders are recognized on the basis of behavior patterns associated with either emotional distress and/or significant impairment in psychological functioning. Researchers have found that people with a gay male or lesbian sexual orientation tend to have a greater frequency of suicide and of states of emotional distress, especially anxiety and depression, than people with a heterosexual orientation (Bagley & D'Augelli, 2000; Cochran, Sullivan, & Mays, 2003; Skegg et al., 2003). We also have learned that gay males are more likely than heterosexual males to develop eating disorders, including anorexia nervosa and bulimia nervosa (Fergusson et al., 1999).

Even if gay males and lesbians are more prone to develop psychological problems, it doesn't necessarily follow that these problems are the result of their sexual orientation. Gay adolescents in our society come to terms with their sexuality against a backdrop of deep-seated prejudices and resentment toward gays. The process of achieving a sense of self-acceptance against this backdrop of societal intolerance can be so difficult that many gay adolescents seriously consider or attempt suicide (Bagley & D'Augelli, 2000; Simonsen et al., 2000). As adults, gay men and lesbians continue to bear the brunt of prejudice and negative attitudes toward them, including negative reactions from family members that often follow the disclosure of their sexual orientation. The social stress associated with stigma, prejudice, and discrimination that gay people encounter may directly cause mental health problems (Meyer, 2003).

Understood in this context, it is little wonder that many gay males and lesbians develop psychological problems. As a leading authority in the field, psychologist J. Michael Bailey (1999) wrote, "Surely, it must be difficult for young people to come to grips with their homosexuality in a world where homosexual people are often scorned, mocked, mourned, and feared."

Should we then accept the claim that societal intolerance is the root cause of psychological problems in people with a homosexual orientation? As critical thinkers, we should recognize that other factors may be involved. We need more evidence before we can arrive at any judgments concerning why gay males and lesbians are more prone to psychological problems, especially suicide.

One of these other factors may be lifestyle choice. A classic study of gay couples showed that those living in committed, close relationships were as well adjusted as married heterosexual couples (Bell & Weinberg, 1978). Differences in psychological adjustment or mental health may be more of a reflection of lifestyle factors than sexual orientation.

Imagine a society in which homosexuality was the norm and heterosexual people were shunned, scorned, or ridiculed. Would we find that heterosexual people are more likely to have psychological problems? Would this evidence lead us to assume that heterosexuality is a mental disorder? What do you think?

Critical Thinking

- How do you decide when any behavior, such as social drinking or even shopping or Internet use, crosses the line from "normal" to "abnormal"?
- Is there a set of criteria you use in all cases? How does your criteria differ from the criteria specified in the text?
- Do you believe that homosexuality is abnormal? Why or why not? ∎

Is homosexuality a mental disorder? Do you consider homosexuality abnormal? Until 1973, homosexuality was classified as a mental disorder by the American Psychiatric Association. What criteria should be used to form judgments about determining whether particular patterns of behavior comprise a mental or psychological disorder?

followed based on behavioral, humanistic, and cognitive models. Each of these perspectives, as well as the contemporary medical model, spawned particular forms of therapy to treat psychological disorders.

Sigmund Freud and Bertha Pappenheim. Freud is shown here at around age 30. Pappenheim (1859–1936) is known more widely in the psychological literature as "Anna O." Freud believed that her hysterical symptoms represented the transformation of blocked-up emotions into physical complaints.

The Sociocultural Perspective Mustn't we also consider the broader social context in which behavior occurs to understand the roots of abnormal behavior? Sociocultural theorists believe the causes of abnormal behavior may be found in the failures of society rather than in the person. Accordingly, psychological problems may be rooted in the ills of society, such as unemployment, poverty, family breakdown, injustice, ignorance, and the lack of opportunity. Sociocultural factors also focus on relationships between mental health and social factors such as gender, social class, ethnicity, and lifestyle.

Sociocultural theorists also observe that once a person is called "mentally ill," the label is hard to remove. It also distorts other people's responses to the "patient." Mental patients are stigmatized and marginalized. Job opportunities may disappear, friendships may dissolve, and the "patient" may feel increasingly alienated from society. Sociocultural theorists focus our attention on the social consequences of becoming labeled as a "mental patient." They argue that we need to provide access to meaningful societal roles, as workers, students, and colleagues to people with long-term mental health problems, rather than shunt them aside.

The Biopsychosocial Perspective Aren't patterns of abnormal behavior too complex to be understood from any one model or perspective? Many leading scholars today endorse the view that abnormal behavior is best understood by taking into account multiple causes representing the biological, psychological, and sociocultural domains. The **biopsychosocial perspective,** or interactionist model, informs this text's approach toward understanding the origins of abnormal behavior. We believe it's essential to consider the interplay of biological, psychological, and sociocultural factors in the development of psychological disorders. Although our understanding of these factors may be incomplete, we must consider all possible pathways and account for multiple factors, influences, and interactions.

biopsychosocial model An integrative model for explaining abnormal in terms of the interactions of biological, psychological, and sociocultural factors.

scientific method A systematic method of conducting scientific research in which theories or assumptions are examined in the light of evidence.

Perspectives on psychological disorders provide a framework not only for explanation but also for treatment (see Chapter 4) The perspectives we use also lead to the predictions, or *hypotheses,* that guide our research or inquiries into the causes and treatments of abnormal behavior. The medical model, for example, fosters inquiry into genetic and biochemical treatment methods. In the next section, we consider the ways in which psychologists and other mental health professionals study abnormal behavior.

RESEARCH METHODS IN ABNORMAL PSYCHOLOGY

Abnormal psychology is a branch of the scientific discipline of psychology. Research in the field is based on the application of the **scientific method.** How are we to apply the scientific method in investigating abnormal behavior?

Imagine you are a brand-new graduate student in psychology and are sitting in your research methods class on the first day of the term. The professor, a distinguished woman of about 50, enters the class. She is carrying a small wire-mesh cage containing a white rat. The professor removes the rat from the cage and places it on the desk. She asks the class to observe its behavior. As a serious student, you attend closely. The animal moves to the edge of the desk, pauses, peers over the edge, and seems to jiggle its whiskers at the floor below. It maneuvers along the edge of the desk, tracking the perimeter. Now and then the rat pauses and vibrates its whiskers downward in the direction of the floor.

The professor picks up the rat and returns it to the cage. She asks the class to describe the animal's *behavior.*

A student responds, "The rat seems to be looking for a way to escape."

Another student says, "It is reconnoitering its environment, examining it." "Reconnoitering?" you think. That student has seen too many war movies.

The professor writes each response on the blackboard. Another student raises her hand. "The rat is making a visual search of the environment," she says. "Maybe it's looking for food."

The professor prompts other students for their descriptions.

"It's looking around," says one.

"Trying to escape," says another.

Your turn arrives. Trying to be scientific, you say, "We can't say what its motivation might be. All we know is that it's scanning its environment."

"How so?" the professor asks.

"Visually," you reply, confidently.

The professor writes the response and then turns to the class, shaking her head. "Each of you observed the rat," she said, "but none of you described its *behavior.* Instead, you made *inferences* that the rat was 'looking for a way down' or 'scanning its environment' or 'looking for food,' and the like. These are not unreasonable inferences, but they are inferences, not descriptions. They also happen to be wrong. You see, the rat is blind. It's been blind since birth. It couldn't possibly be looking around, at least not in a visual sense."

Description, Explanation, Prediction, and Control: The Objectives of Science

Description is one of the primary objectives of science. To understand abnormal behavior, we must first learn to describe it. Description allows us to recognize abnormal behavior and provides the basis for explaining it.

Descriptions should be clear, unbiased, and based on careful observation. Our anecdote about the blind rat illustrates that our observations and our attempts to describe our observations are influenced by our expectations. Our expectations reflect our models, and they may incline us to perceive events—such as the rat's movements and other people's behavior—in certain ways. Describing the rat in the classroom as "scanning" and "looking" for something is an inference, or conclusion, we draw from our observations based on our model of how animals explore their environments. In contrast, description would involve a precise accounting of the animal's movements around the desk, measuring how far in each direction it moves, how long it pauses, how it bobs its head from side to side, and so on.

Nevertheless, inference is important in science. Inference allows us to jump from the particular to the general—to suggest laws and principles of behavior that can be woven into a model or **theory** of behavior. Without a way of organizing our descriptions of phenomena in terms of models and theories, we would be left with a buzzing confusion of unconnected observations.

Theories help scientists explain puzzling data and predict future data. Prediction entails the discovery of factors that anticipate the occurrence of events. Geology, for example, seeks clues in the forces affecting the earth that can forecast natural events such as earthquakes and volcanic eruptions. Scientists who study abnormal behavior seek clues in overt behavior, biological processes, family interactions, and so forth, to predict the development of abnormal behaviors as well as factors that might predict response to various treatments. It is not sufficient for theoretical models to help us explain or make sense of events or behaviors that have already occurred. Useful theories must allow us to predict the occurrence of particular behaviors.

The idea of controlling human behavior—especially the behavior of people with serious problems—is controversial. The history of societal response to abnormal behaviors, including abuses such as exorcism and cruel forms of physical restraint, render the idea particularly distressing. Within science, however, the word *control* does not imply that people are coerced into doing the bidding of others, like puppets dangling on strings. Psychologists, for example, are committed to the dignity of the individual, and the concept of human dignity requires that people be free to make decisions and exercise choices. Within this context, *controlling behavior* means using scientific knowledge to help people shape their own goals and more efficiently use their resources to accomplish them. Today, in the United States, even when helping professionals restrain people who are violently disturbed, their goal is to assist them to overcome their agitation and regain the ability to exercise meaningful choices in their lives. Ethical standards prohibit the use of injurious techniques in research or practice.

Psychologists and other scientists use the *scientific method* to advance the description, explanation, prediction, and control of abnormal behavior.

The Scientific Method

The scientific method tests assumptions and theories about the world through gathering objective evidence. Gathering evidence that is objective requires thoughtful observational and experimental methods. Here let us focus on the basic steps involved in using the scientific method in experimentation.

1. *Formulating a research question.* Scientists derive research questions from previous observations and current theories. For instance, based on their clinical observations and theoretical understanding of the underlying mechanisms in depression, psychologists may formulate questions about whether certain experimental drugs or particular types of psychotherapy help people overcome depression.

2. *Framing the research question in the form of a hypothesis.* A **hypothesis** is an "educated guess" that is to be tested in an experiment. For example, scientists might hypothesize that people who are clinically depressed will show greater improvement on measures of depression if they are given an experimental drug than if they receive an inert placebo ("sugar pill").

3. *Testing the hypothesis.* Scientists test hypotheses through experiments in which variables are controlled and the differences observed. For instance, they can test the hypothesis about the experimental drug by giving the drug to one group of people with depression and giving another group the placebo. They can then test to see if the people who received the active drug showed greater improvement over a period of time than those who received the placebo.

theory A formulation of the relationships underlying observed events.

hypothesis An assumption that is tested through experimentation.

4. *Drawing conclusions about the hypothesis.* In the final step, scientists draw conclusions from their findings about the accuracy of their hypotheses. Psychologists use statistical methods to determine the likelihood that differences between groups are significant, as opposed to chance fluctuations. Psychologists can be reasonably confident that group differences are significant—that is, not due to chance—when the probability that chance alone can explain the difference is less than 5%. When well-designed research findings fail to bear out hypotheses, scientists rethink the theories from which the hypotheses are derived. Research findings often lead to modifications in theory, new hypotheses, and in turn, subsequent research.

Let us consider the major research methods used by psychologists and others in studying abnormal behavior. Before we do so, however, let us consider some of the principles that guide ethical conduct in research.

Ethics in Research

Ethical principles are designed to promote the dignity of the individual, protect human welfare, and preserve scientific integrity (APA, 2002). Psychologists are prohibited by the ethical standards of their profession from using methods that cause psychological or physical harm to subjects or clients. Psychologists also must follow ethical guidelines that protect animal subjects in research (APA, 2002).

Institutions such as universities and hospitals have review committees, called *institutional review boards* (IRBs), that review proposed research studies in the light of ethical guidelines. Investigators must receive IRB approval before they are permitted to begin their studies. Two of the major principles on which ethical guidelines are based are (a) *informed consent* and (b) *confidentiality.*

informed consent The principle that subjects should receive enough information about an experiment beforehand to decide freely whether to participate.

The principle of **informed consent** requires that people be free to choose whether they wish to participate in research studies. They must be given sufficient information in advance about the study's purposes and methods, and its risks and benefits, in order to make an informed decision about their participation. Subjects must also be free to withdraw from a study at any time without penalty. In some cases, researchers may withhold certain information until all the data are collected. For instance, subjects in placebo control studies of experimental drugs are told that they may receive an inert placebo rather than the active drug. In studies in which information was withheld or deception was used, subjects must be debriefed afterward. That is, they must receive an explanation of the true methods and purposes of the study and why it was necessary to keep them in the dark. After the study is concluded, participants who received the placebo would be given the option of receiving the active treatment, if warranted.

confidentiality Protection of the identity of participants by keeping records secure and not disclosing their identities.

Subjects also have a right to expect that their identities will not be revealed. Investigators are required to protect their **confidentiality** by keeping the records of their participation secure and by not disclosing their identities to others.

We turn now to discussion of the research methods used to investigate abnormal behavior.

Naturalistic Observation

naturalistic observation A form of research in which behavior is observed and measured in its natural environment.

In **naturalistic observation,** the investigator observes behavior in the field, where it happens. Anthropologists have observed behavior patterns in preliterate societies to study human diversity. Sociologists have followed the activities of adolescent gangs in inner cities. Psychologists have spent weeks observing the behavior of homeless people in train stations and bus terminals. They have even observed the eating habits of slender and overweight people in fast-food restaurants, searching for clues to obesity.

Scientists try to ensure that their naturalistic observations are unobtrusive, so as to minimize interference with the behavior they observe. Nevertheless, the presence of the observer may distort the behavior that is observed, and this must be taken into consideration.

Naturalistic observation provides information on how subjects behave, but it does not reveal why they do so. Men who frequent bars and drink, for example, are more likely to get into fights than men who do not. But such observations do not show that alcohol *causes* aggression. As we see in the following pages, questions of cause and effect are best approached by means of controlled experiments.

The Correlational Method

A **correlation** is a statistical measure of the relationships between two factors, or **variables.** In using the correlational method, the investigator does not manipulate or control the variables of interest. Rather, the investigator uses statistical techniques to determine the degree to which different variables are related to each other. For example, in Chapter 8 we will see that there is a statistical relationship, or correlation, between negative thinking and depressive symptoms. When higher values in one variable (negative thinking) are associated with higher values in the other variable (depressive symptoms), there is a *positive correlation* between the variables. If higher levels of one variable are associated with lower values of another variable, there is a *negative correlation* between the variables. Correlation coefficients can vary between −1.00 and +1.00. Positive correlations carry positive signs; negative correlations carry negative signs. The closer the correlation coefficient is to either −1.00 or +1.00, the stronger the correlation or statistical relationship is between the variables.

A correlation between variables does not prove that the variables are causally related to each other. Sometimes there is no causal connection between variables that are merely correlated. For example, children's foot size is correlated with their vocabulary, but growth in foot size does not cause the growth of vocabulary. Depressive symptoms and negative thoughts are correlated, as we shall see in Chapter 8. Though negative thinking may be a causative factor in depression, it is also possible that the direction of causality works the other way—that depression gives rise to negative thinking. Or perhaps the direction of causality works both ways, with negative thinking contributing to depression and depression in turn influencing negative thinking. Then again, depression and negative thinking may both reflect a common causative factor, such as stress, and not be causally related to each other at all. In sum, we cannot tell from a correlation alone whether or not variables are causally linked.

Although the correlational method cannot determine cause-and-effect relationships, it does serve the scientific objective of prediction. When two variables are correlated, we can use one to predict the other. Knowledge of correlations among alcoholism, family history, and attitudes toward drinking helps us predict which adolescents are at great risk of developing problems with alcohol, although causal connections are complex and somewhat nebulous. Knowing which factors predict future problems helps direct preventive efforts toward high-risk groups.

The Longitudinal Study   One type of correlational study is the **longitudinal study,** in which subjects are studied at periodic intervals over lengthy periods, perhaps for decades. By studying people over time, researchers can investigate the events associated with the onset of abnormal behavior and, perhaps, learn to identify factors that predict the development of such behavior. However, this type of research is time consuming and costly. It requires a commitment that may literally outlive the original investigators. Therefore, long-term longitudinal studies are relatively uncommon. In Chapter 13 we examine one of the best-known longitudinal studies, the Danish high-risk study that has tracked, since 1962, a group of children whose mothers had schizophrenia and who were themselves at increased risk of developing the disorder (Mednick, Parnas, & Schulsinger, 1987; Parnas et al., 1993).

Naturalistic observation. Psychologists take their research into the streets when they conduct naturalistic observation studies—and into the homes, restaurants, schools, and other settings where behavior can be directly observed. For example, psychologists have unobtrusively positioned themselves in school playgrounds to observe how aggressive or socially anxious children interact with peers.

correlation   A relationship or association between variables.

variables   Factors that are measured (dependent variables) or manipulated (independent variables) in experiments.

longitudinal study   A research study in which subjects are followed over time.

The Experimental Method

Prediction is based on the *correlation* between events or factors that are separated in time. As in other forms of correlational research, we must be careful not to infer *causation* from *correlation*. A *causal relationship* between two events involves a time-ordered relationship in which the second event is the direct result of the first. We need to meet two strict conditions to posit a causal relationship between two factors:

1. The effect must follow the cause in a time-ordered sequence of events.

2. Other plausible causes of the observed effects (rival hypotheses) must be eliminated.

The **experimental method** allows scientists to demonstrate causal relationships by first manipulating the causal factor and then measuring its effects under controlled conditions that minimize the risk of other factors explaining these effects.

The term *experiment* can cause some confusion. Broadly speaking, an experiment is a trial or test of a hypothesis. From this vantage point, any method that seeks to test a hypothesis could be considered experimental—including naturalistic observation and correlational studies. But investigators usually limit the use of the term *experimental method* to refer to studies in which researchers seek to uncover cause-and-effect relationships by manipulating possible causal factors directly.

The factors or variables hypothesized to play a causal role are manipulated or controlled by the investigator in experimental research. These are called the **independent variables.** The observed effects are labeled **dependent variables** because changes in them are believed to depend on the independent or manipulated variable. Dependent variables are observed and measured, not manipulated, by the experimenter. Examples of independent and dependent variables of interest to investigators of abnormal behavior are shown in Table 1.1.

In an experiment, subjects are exposed to an *independent variable,* for example, the type of beverage (alcoholic vs. nonalcoholic) they consume in a laboratory setting. They are then observed or examined to determine whether the independent variable makes a difference in their behavior, or more precisely, whether the independent variable affects the dependent variable—for example, whether they behave more aggressively if they consume alcohol. Studies need to have a sufficient number of participants (subjects) to be able to detect statistically meaningful differences between experimental groups.

Experimental and Control Groups Well-controlled experiments assign subjects to experimental and control groups at random. The **experimental group** is given the experimental treatment, whereas the **control group** is not. Care is taken to hold other conditions constant for each group. By using **random assignment** and holding other conditions constant, experimenters can be reasonably confident that the experimental treatment, and not uncontrolled factors, such as room temperature or differences between the types of sub-

experimental method A scientific method that aims to discover cause-and-effect relationships by manipulating independent variables and observing the effects on the dependent variables.

independent variables Factors that are manipulated in experiments.

dependent variables Outcomes of an experiment believed to be dependent on the effects of an independent variable.

experimental group In an experiment, a group that receives the experimental treatment.

control group In an experiment, a group that does not receive the experimental treatment.

random assignment A method of assigning research subjects at random to experimental or control groups to balance these groups on the characteristics of people that comprise them.

TABLE 1.1

Examples of Independent and Dependent Variables in Experimental Research

Independent Variables	Dependent Variables
Type of treatment: for example, different types of drug treatments or psychological treatments	Behavioral variables: for example, measures of adjustment, activity levels, eating behavior, smoking behavior
Treatment factors: for example, brief vs. long-term treatment, inpatient vs. outpatient treatment	Physiological variables: for example, measures of physiological responses such as heart rate, blood pressure, and brain wave activity
Experimental manipulations: for example, types of beverage consumed (alcoholic vs. nonalcoholic)	Self-report variables: for example, measures of anxiety, mood, or marital or life satisfaction

jects in the experimental and control groups, brought about the differences in outcome between the experimental and control groups (Ioannidis & Karassa, 2001).

Why should experimenters assign subjects to experimental and control groups at random? Consider a study intended to investigate the effects of alcohol on behavior. Let's suppose we allowed subjects themselves to decide whether or not they wanted to be in an experimental group that drank alcohol or a control group that drank a nonalcoholic beverage. If this were the case, then differences between the groups might be due to an underlying **selection factor** rather than the experimental manipulation.

For example, subjects who *chose* the alcoholic beverage might differ in their personalities from those who chose the control beverage. They might be more willing to explore or to take risks, for example. Therefore, we would not know whether the independent variable (type of beverage) or a selection factor (difference in the kinds of subjects making up the groups) was ultimately responsible for observed differences in behavior. Random assignment controls for selection factors by ensuring that subject characteristics are randomly distributed across groups. Thus it is reasonable to assume that differences between groups result from the treatments they receive rather than from differences between the subjects making up the groups. Still, it is possible that apparent treatment effects stem from subjects' expectancies about the treatments they receive rather than from the active components in the treatments themselves. In other words, knowing you are being given an alcoholic beverage to drink might affect your behavior, quite apart from the alcoholic content of the beverage itself.

selection factor A type of bias in which differences between experimental and control groups result from differences in the subjects placed in the groups, not from the independent variable.

Controlling for Subject Expectancies   To control for subject expectancies, experimenters rely on procedures that render subjects **blind,** or uninformed about the treatments they are receiving. For example, the taste of an alcoholic beverage such as vodka may be masked by mixing it with tonic water in certain amounts, so as to keep subjects unaware of whether the drinks they receive contain alcohol or tonic water only. In this way, subjects who truly receive alcohol should have no different expectations than those receiving the nonalcoholic control beverage. Similarly, drug treatment studies are often designed to control for subjects' expectations by keeping subjects in the dark as to whether they are receiving the experimental drug or an *inert* placebo control.

blind A state of being unaware of whether one has received an experimental treatment.

The term **placebo** derives from the Latin meaning "I shall please," referring to the fact that belief in the effectiveness of a treatment (its pleasing qualities) may inspire hopeful expectations that help people mobilize themselves to overcome their problems—regardless of whether the substance they receive is chemically active or inert. In medical research on drug therapy, a placebo—also referred to as a "sugar pill"—is an inert substance that physically resembles an active drug. By comparing the effects of the active drug with those of the placebo, the experimenter can determine whether the drug has specific effects beyond those accounted for by expectations (Charney et al., 2002; Kaptchuk et al., 2002).

placebo An inert medication or bogus treatment that is intended to control for expectancy effects.

In a *single-blind placebo-control study,* subjects are randomly assigned to treatment conditions in which they receive an active drug (experimental condition) or a placebo (placebo-control condition), but they are kept blind, or uninformed, about which drug they are receiving. It is also helpful to keep the dispensing researchers blind as to which substances the subjects are receiving, lest the researchers' own expectations affect the results. So in the case of a *double-blind placebo design,* neither the researcher nor the subject is told whether an active drug or a placebo is being administered.

Double-blind studies are used to control for both subject and experimenter expectancies. But a major limitation of single-blind and double-blind studies is that subjects and experimenters can sometimes "see through" the blind (Mooney, White, & Hatsukami, 2004). Telltale side effects or obvious drug effects can break the blind, making it seem more like a Venetian blind with the slats slightly open. Still, the double-blind placebo control is among the strongest and most popular experimental designs, especially in drug treatment research (Leber, 2000; Leon, 2000).

Though placebos are routinely used in clinical research, evidence suggests that the effects of placebos are generally weak (Bailar, 2001; Hrobjartsson & Gotzsche, 2001). Evidence

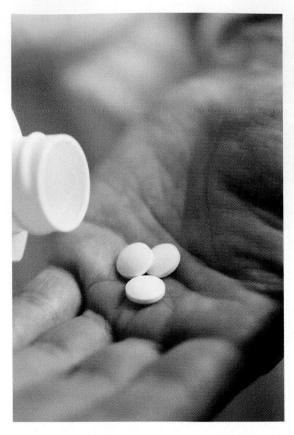

The real thing or a placebo? Placebos are inert pills that physically resemble active drugs. What are the two major types of placebo-control studies? What are they intended to control? What is the major limitation of these designs?

internal validity The degree to which manipulation of the independent variables can be causally related to changes in the dependent variables.

external validity The degree to which experimental results can be generalized to other settings and conditions.

of placebo effects is strongest in pain studies, presumably because pain is a subjective experience that may be influenced more by the power of suggestion than other medical conditions that rely on objective measures, such as blood pressure.

Placebo-control groups are also used in psychotherapy research to control for subject expectancies. Assume you were to study the effects of therapy method A on mood. We could assign the experimental group to therapy A randomly and the control group to a no-treatment waiting list. But in that case, the experimental group might show improvement because of group participation, not because of therapy method A. Participation might raise expectations of success, and these expectations might be sufficient to engender improvement. Changes in control subjects placed on the "waiting list" would help to account for effects due to the passage of time, but they would not account for placebo effects, such as the benefits of therapy that result from instilling a sense of hope.

An *attention-placebo* control group design can be used to separate the effects of a particular form of psychotherapy from placebo effects. In an attention-placebo group, subjects are exposed to a believable or credible treatment that contains the nonspecific factors that all therapies share—such as the attention and emotional support of a therapist—but not the specific ingredients of therapy represented in the active treatment. Attention-placebo treatments commonly substitute general discussions of participants' problems for the specific ingredients of therapy contained in the experimental treatment. Unfortunately, although attention-placebo subjects may be kept blind as to whether or not they are receiving the experimental treatment, the therapists themselves are generally aware of which treatment is being administered. Therefore, the attention-placebo method may not control for therapists' expectations.

Experimental Validity Experimental studies are judged on whether they are valid, or sound. There are many aspects of validity, including *internal validity, external validity,* and *construct validity.* We will see in Chapter 3 that the term *validity* is also applied in the context of tests and measures to refer to the degree to which these instruments measure what they purport to measure.

Experiments have **internal validity** when the observed changes in the dependent variable(s) can be causally related to the independent or treatment variable. Assume a group of depressed subjects is treated with a new antidepressant medication (the independent variable), and changes in their mood and behavior (the dependent variables) are tracked over time. After several weeks of treatment, the researcher finds most subjects have improved and claims the new drug is an effective treatment for depression. Not so fast! How does the experimenter know that the independent variable and not some other factor was causally responsible for the improvement? Perhaps the subjects improved naturally as time passed, or perhaps they were exposed to other events responsible for their improvement. Experiments lack internal validity to the extent they fail to control for other factors (called *confounds,* or threats to validity) that might pose rival hypotheses for the results.

Experimenters *randomly assign* subjects to treatment and control groups to help control for such rival hypotheses. Random assignment helps ensure that subjects' attributes—intelligence, motivation, age, race, and so on—are randomly distributed across the groups and are not likely to favor one group over the other. Through the random assignment to groups, researchers can be reasonably confident that significant differences between the treatment and control groups reflect the effects of independent (treatment) variables and not confounding selection factors. Studies need to include large enough samples of subjects to be able to randomize sufficient numbers of participants to experimental conditions and to be able to discern significant statistical differences between groups.

External validity refers to the generalizability of results of an experimental study to other subjects, settings, and times. In most cases, researchers are interested in generalizing the results of a specific study (for example, effects of a new antidepressant medication on a sample of people who are depressed) to a larger population (people in general who are depressed). The external validity of a study is strengthened to the degree that the *sample* is representative of the target population. In studying the problems of the urban homeless, it is essential to recruit a representative sample of the homeless population, for example, rather than focusing on a few homeless people who happen to be available. One way of obtaining a representative sample is by means of random sampling. In a *random sample,* every member of the target population has an equal chance of being selected.

Researchers may seek to extend the results of a particular study by replication, which refers to the process of repeating the experiment in other settings, with samples drawn from other populations, or at other times. A treatment for hyperactivity may be helpful with economically deprived children in an inner-city classroom but not with children in affluent suburbs or rural areas. The external validity of the treatment may be limited if its effects do not generalize to other samples or settings. That does not mean the treatment is less effective, but rather that its range of effectiveness may be limited to certain populations or situations.

Construct validity is a conceptually higher level of validity. It is the degree to which treatment effects can be accounted for by the theoretical mechanisms or constructs represented in the independent variables. A drug, for example, may have predictable effects but not for the theoretical reasons claimed by the researchers.

Consider a hypothetical experimental study of a new antidepressant medication. The research may have internal validity in the form of solid controls and external validity in the form of generalizability across samples of seriously depressed people. However, it may lack construct validity if the drug does not work for the reasons proposed by the researchers. Perhaps the researchers assumed that the drug would work by raising the levels of certain chemicals in the nervous system, whereas the drug actually works by increasing the sensitivity of receptors for those chemicals. "So what?" we may ask. After all, the drug still works. True enough—in terms of immediate clinical applications. However, a better understanding of why the drug works can advance theoretical knowledge of depression and give rise to the development of yet more effective treatments.

We can never be certain about the construct validity of research. Scientists recognize that their current theories about why their results occurred may eventually be toppled by other theories that better account for the findings.

Epidemiological Studies

Epidemiological studies examine the rates of occurrence of abnormal behavior in various settings or population groups. One type of epidemiological study is the **survey method,** which relies on interviews or questionnaires. Surveys are used to ascertain the rates of occurrence of various disorders in the population as a whole and in various subgroups classified according to such factors as race, ethnicity, gender, or social class. Rates of occurrence of a given disorder are expressed in terms of **incidence,** the number of new cases occurring during a specific period of time, and **prevalence,** the overall number of cases of a disorder existing in the population during a given period of time. Prevalence rates, then, include both new and continuing cases.

Epidemiological studies may point to potential causal factors in illnesses and disorders, even though they lack the power of experiments. By finding that illnesses or disorders "cluster" in certain groups or locations, researchers can identify distinguishing characteristics that place these groups or regions at higher risk. Yet such epidemiological studies cannot control for selection factors—that is, they cannot rule out the possibility that other unrecognized factors might play a causal role in putting a certain group at greater risk. Therefore they must be considered suggestive of possible causal influences that must be tested further in experimental studies.

Samples and Populations   In the best of possible worlds, we would conduct surveys in which every member of the population of interest would participate. In that way, we could be sure the survey results accurately represent the population we wish to study. In reality, unless the population of interest is rather narrowly defined (say, for example, designating the population of interest as the students living on your dormitory floor), surveying every

---

construct validity The degree to which treatment effects can be accounted for by the theoretical mechanisms (constructs) represented in the independent variables.

epidemiological studies Research studies that track rates of occurrence of particular disorders among different population groups.

survey method A research method in which large samples of people are questioned by means of a survey instrument.

incidence The number of new cases of a disorder that occurs within a specific period of time.

prevalence The overall number of cases of a disorder in a population within a specific period of time.

member of a given population is extremely difficult if not impossible. Even census takers can't count every head in the general population. Consequently, most surveys are based on a sample, or subset, of the population. Researchers must take steps when constructing a sample to ensure that it *represents* the target population. For example, a researcher who sets out to study smoking rates in a local community by interviewing people drinking coffee in late-night cafés will probably overestimate its true prevalence.

One method of obtaining a representative sample is random sampling. A **random sample** is drawn in such a way that each member of the population of interest has an equal probability of selection. Epidemiologists sometimes construct random samples by surveying at random a given number of households within a target community. By repeating this process in a random sample of U.S. communities, the overall sample can approximate the general U.S. population, based on even a tiny percentage of the overall population.

Random sampling is often confused with random assignment. *Random sampling* refers to the process of randomly choosing individuals within a target population to participate in a survey or research study. By contrast, *random assignment* refers to the process by which members of a research sample are assigned at random to different experimental conditions or treatments.

Kinship Studies

Kinship studies attempt to disentangle the roles of heredity and environment in determining behavior. Heredity plays a critical role in determining a wide range of traits. The structures we inherit make our behavior possible (humans can walk and run) and at the same time place limits on us (humans cannot fly without artificial equipment). Heredity plays a role in determining not only our physical characteristics (hair color, eye color, height, and the like) but also many of our psychological characteristics. The science of heredity is called *genetics.*

Genes are the basic building blocks of heredity. They regulate the development of traits. *Chromosomes,* rod-shaped structures that house our genes, are found in the nuclei of the body's cells. A normal human cell contains 46 chromosomes, organized into 23 pairs. Chromosomes consist of large complex molecules of deoxyribonucleic acid (DNA). Genes occupy various segments along the length of chromosomes. Scientists suspect there may be about 30,000 genes in the nucleus of a human body cell, but they admit that the actual number may turn out to be higher or lower (Wade, 2003).

The set of traits specified by our genetic code is referred to as our **genotype.** Our appearance and behavior are not determined by our genotype alone. We are also influenced by environmental factors such as nutrition, learning, exercise, accident and illness, and culture. The constellation of our actual or expressed traits is called our **phenotype.** Our phenotype represents the interaction of genetic and environmental influences. People who possess genotypes for particular psychological disorders are said to have a *genetic predisposition* that makes them more likely to develop the disorder in response to stress or other factors, such as physical or psychological trauma.

The more closely people are related, the more genes they have in common. Children receive half their genes from each parent. Thus there is a 50% overlap in genetic heritage between each parent and his or her offspring. Siblings (brothers and sisters) similarly share half their genetic heritage. Aunts and uncles related by blood to their nephews and nieces have a 25% overlap; first cousins, a 12.5% overlap (see Figure 1.2).

To determine whether abnormal behavior runs in a family, as we would expect if genetics plays a role, researchers locate a person with the disorder and then study how the disorder is distributed among the person's family members (Nestadt et al., 2000; Tillfors et al., 2001). The case first diagnosed is referred to as the index case, or **proband.** If the distribution of the disorder among family members of the proband approximates their degree of kinship, there may be a genetic involvement in the disorder. However, the closer their kinship, the more likely people also are to share environmental backgrounds. For this reason, twin and adoptee studies are of particular value.

---

random sample A sample that is drawn in such a way that every member of a population has an equal chance of being included.

TRUTH or FICTION? *REVISITED*

You always learn more about the American population by surveying one million people than 1,500 people.

☑ **FALSE.** A representative nationwide sample of about 1,500 people may be more accurate than a haphazard sample of millions.

genotype The set of traits specified by an individual's genetic code.

phenotype An individual's actual or expressed traits.

proband The case first diagnosed of a given disorder.

Twin Studies Sometimes a fertilized egg cell (or *zygote*) divides into two cells that separate, so each develops into a separate person. In such cases, there is a 100% overlap in genetic makeup, and the off-spring are known as identical twins, or monozygotic (MZ) twins. Sometimes a woman releases two egg cells, or ova, in the same month, and they are both fertilized. In such cases, the *zygotes* develop into fraternal twins, or dizygotic (DZ) twins. DZ twins overlap 50% in their genetic heritage, just as other siblings do.

Identical, or MZ, twins are important in the study of the relative influences of heredity and environment because differences between MZ twins are the result of environmental rather than genetic influences. MZ twins look more alike and are closer in height than DZ twins. In twin studies, researchers identify individuals with a specific disorder who are members of MZ or DZ twin pairs and then study the other twins in the pairs. A role for genetic factors is suggested when MZ twins are more likely than DZ twins to share a disorder. Differences in the rates of *concordance* (agreement for the given trait or disorder) for MZ versus DZ twins are found for some forms of abnormal behavior, such as schizophrenia and bipolar disorder, suggesting a strong genetic component.

Even among MZ twins, though, environmental influences cannot be ruled out. Parents and teachers, for example, often encourage MZ twins to behave in similar ways. Put in another way: If one twin does X, everyone expects the other to do X also. Expectations have a way of influencing behavior and making for self-fulfilling prophecies. We should also note that twins might not be typical of the general population, so we need to be cautious when generalizing the results of twin studies to the larger population. Twins tend to have had shorter gestational periods, lower birth weights, and a greater frequency of con-

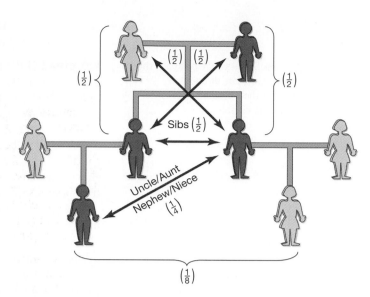

FIGURE 1.2 A family tree showing the proportion of shared inheritance among relatives.
This figure shows the proportion of shared genes among blood relatives. The more closely people are related, the more genes they have in common. For example, each parent shares half of his or her genes with each offspring; uncles and aunts share one-fourth of their genes in common with their nephews and nieces. How do researchers use this information in determining whether psychological disorders age genetically based? What are the limitations of this approach?

Twin studies. Identical twins have 100% of their genes in common, as compared to 50% overlap among fraternal twins or any two other siblings. Establishing that identical twins are more likely to share a given disorder than are fraternal twins provides strong evidence for a genetic contribution to the disorder.

genital malformations than nontwins (Kendler, 1994). Perhaps differences in prenatal experiences influence their later development in ways that set them apart from nontwins.

adoptee studies Studies that compare the traits and behavior patterns of adopted children to those of their biological parents and their adoptive parents.

Adoptee Studies **Adoptee studies** can provide powerful arguments for or against a role for genetic factors in the appearance of psychological traits and disorders. Assume that children are reared by adoptive parents from a very early age—perhaps from birth. The children share environmental backgrounds with their adoptive parents but not their genetic heritages. Then assume we compare the traits and behavior patterns of these children to those of their biological parents and their adoptive parents. If the children show a greater similarity to their biological parents than their adoptive parents on certain traits or disorders, we have strong evidence for genetic factors in these traits and disorders.

The study of monozygotic twins reared apart can provide even more dramatic testimony to the relative roles of genetics and environment in shaping abnormal behavior. However, this situation is so uncommon that few examples exist in the literature. Although adoptee studies may represent the strongest source of evidence for genetic factors in explaining abnormal behavior patterns, we should recognize that adoptees, like twins, may not be typical of the general population. In later chapters we explore the role that adoptee and other kinship studies play in ferreting out genetic and environmental influences in many psychological disorders.

Case Studies

Case studies have been important influences in the development of theories and treatment of abnormal behavior. Freud developed his theoretical model primarily on the basis of case studies, such as that of Anna O. Therapists representing other theoretical viewpoints have also reported cases studies.

case study A carefully drawn biography based on clinical interviews, observations, and psychological tests.

Types of Case Studies **Case studies** are intensive studies of individuals. Some case studies are based on historical material, involving subjects who have been dead for hundreds of years. Freud, for example, conducted a case study of the Renaissance artist and inventor Leonardo da Vinci. More commonly, case studies reflect an in-depth analysis of an individual's course of treatment. They typically include detailed histories of the subject's background and response to treatment. The therapist attempts to glean information from a particular client's experience in therapy that may be of help to other therapists treating similar clients.

Despite the richness of material that case studies can provide, they are much less rigorous as research designs than experiments. Distortions or gaps in memory are bound to occur when people discuss historical events, especially those of their childhoods. Some people may intentionally color events to make a favorable impression on the interviewer; others aim to shock the interviewer with exaggerated or fabricated recollections. Interviewers themselves may unintentionally guide subjects into reporting histories that mirror their theoretical preconceptions.

TRUTH or FICTION? *REVISITED*

Case studies are only conducted on living people who can participate in the study.

☑ **FALSE.** Case studies have been conducted on people who have been dead for hundreds of years, such as Freud's study of Leonardo. Such studies rely on historical records rather than interviews.

single-case experimental design A type of case study in which the subject is used as his or her own control.

Single-Case Experimental Designs The lack of control available in the traditional case-study method led researchers to develop more sophisticated methods, called **single-case experimental designs** (sometimes called *single-participant research designs*), in which subjects are used as their own controls (Morgan & Morgan, 2001). One of the most common forms of the single-case experimental design is the A-B-A-B, or **reversal design** (see Figure 1.3). The reversal design consists of the repeated measurement of clients' behavior across four successive phases:

reversal design An experimental design that consists of repeated measurement of a subject's behavior through a sequence of alternating baseline and treatment phases.

1. A baseline phase (A). The baseline phase occurs prior to the inception of treatment and is characterized by repeated measurement of the target problem behaviors at periodic intervals. This measurement allows the experimenter to establish a baseline rate for the behavior before treatment begins.

2. A treatment phase (B). Now the target behaviors are measured as the client undergoes treatment.

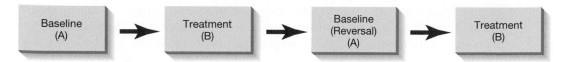

FIGURE 1.3 Diagram of an A-B-A-B reversal design.

3. A second baseline phase (A, again). Treatment is now temporarily withdrawn or suspended. This is the reversal in the reversal design, and it is expected that the positive effects of treatment should now be reversed because the treatment has been withdrawn.

4. A second treatment phase (B, again). Treatment is reinstated, and the target behaviors are assessed yet again.

Clients' target behaviors or response patterns are compared from one phase to the next to determine the effects of treatment. The experimenter looks for evidence of a correspondence between a subject's behavior and the particular phase of the design to determine whether the independent variable (that is, the treatment) has produced the intended effects. If the behavior improves whenever treatment is introduced (during the first and second treatment phases) but returns (or is reversed) to baseline levels during the reversal phase, the experimenter can be reasonably confident the treatment had the intended effect.

A reversal design is illustrated by a case in which Azrin and Peterson (1989) used a controlled blinking treatment to eliminate a severe eye tic—a form of squinting the eyes shut tightly for a fraction of a second—in a 9-year-old girl. The tic occurred about 20 times a minute when the girl was at home. In the clinic, the rate of eye tics or squinting was measured for 5 minutes during a baseline period (A). Then the girl was prompted to blink her eyes softly every 5 seconds (B). The experimenters reasoned that voluntary "soft" blinking would activate motor (muscle) responses incompatible with those producing the tic, thereby suppressing the tic. As you can see in Figure 1.4, the tic was virtually eliminated in but a few minutes of practicing the incompatible, or com-

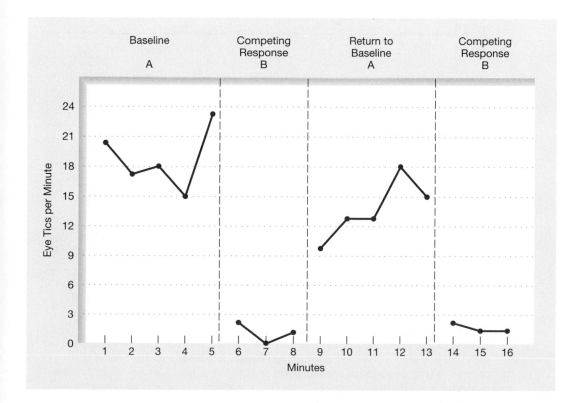

FIGURE 1.4 Use of an A-B-A-B reversal design in the Azrin and Peterson study.
Notice how the target response, eye tics per minute, decreased when the competing response was introduced in the first "B" phase. The rate then increased to near baseline levels when the competing response was withdrawn during the second "A" phase. It decreased again when the competing response was reinstated in the second "B" phase.

peting, response ("soft" blinking) but returned to near baseline levels during the reversal phase (A), when the competing response was withdrawn. The positive effects were quickly reinstated during the second treatment period (B). The child was also taught to practice the blinking response at home during scheduled 3-minute practice periods and whenever the tic occurred or she felt an urge to squint. The tic was eliminated during the first 6 weeks of the treatment program and remained absent at a follow-up evaluation 2 years later.

Although reversal designs offer better controls than traditional treatment case studies, it is not always possible or ethical to reverse certain behaviors or treatment effects. For instance, participants in a stop-smoking program who reduce or quit smoking during treatment cannot be allowed to revert to their baseline smoking rates while treatment is temporarily withdrawn during a reversal phase.

The *multiple-baseline design* is a type of single-case experimental design that does not require a reversal phase. In a multiple-baseline design *across behaviors,* treatment is applied, in turn, to two or more behaviors following a baseline period. A treatment effect is inferred if changes in each of these behaviors corresponded to the time at which each was subjected to treatment. Because no reversal phase is required, problems associated with reversal designs are avoided.

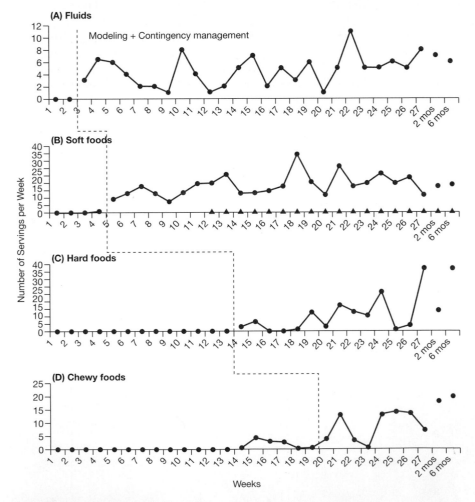

FIGURE 1.5 A multiple-baseline design.
The dotted line shows the point at which the behavioral treatment program was applied to each category of food. The immediacy of the changes, combined with the finding that changes in food consumption occurred when and only when treatment was applied to the particular food category, provides evidence that the effects were due to treatment.

Source: Adapted from Nock, 2002. Reprinted with permission.

A multiple-baseline design was used to evaluate the effectiveness of a behavioral treatment program for food phobia in a 4-year-old Latino boy (Nock, 2002). Food phobia is an uncommon childhood disorder in which children show a fear or avoidance of chewing or swallowing food or fluids. The phobia appears to be connected with a fear of choking rather than a fear of food per se. It occurs most often in cases of children who had suffered incidents of choking or vomiting and consequently developed a fear of eating or swallowing. The child in this study had refused to eat solid foods since choking on partially solid baby food when he was 7 months old. Since that time he had consumed only soft baby food, oatmeal, and liquids.

The treatment followed a behavioral program in which the clinician and parents participated as trainers. During the course of 21, one-hour-long treatment sessions, the clinician and parents modeled (demonstrated) proper eating behaviors and rewarded the child in the form of attention, praise, and small toys for performing the desired eating behaviors. The treatment program was phased in sequentially across four different categories of food: fluids, soft foods, hard foods, and then chewy foods. Treatment was first applied to consuming fluids, then eating soft foods, then hard foods and finally chewy foods. You can see in Figure 1.5 how food consumption increased

A CLOSER LOOK
Thinking Critically About Abnormal Psychology

We are exposed to a flood of information about mental health streaming through the popular media—television, radio, and print media, including books, magazines, and newspapers, and increasingly, the Internet. We may hear a news report touting a new drug as a "breakthrough" in the treatment of anxiety, depression, or obesity, only to later learn that the so-called breakthrough doesn't live up to expectations or carries serious side effects. Some reports in the media are accurate and reliable, whereas others are misleading, biased, or contain half-truths, exaggerated claims, or unsupported conclusions.

To sort through the welter of confusion, we need to ready ourselves with the skills of critical thinking, to adopt a questioning attitude toward the information we hear and read. Critical thinkers weigh evidence to see if claims stand up to scrutiny. Becoming a critical thinker means never taking claims at face value. It means looking at both sides of the argument. Most of us take certain "truths" for granted. Critical thinkers, however, evaluate assertions and claims for themselves.

We encourage you to apply critical thinking skills as you study this book. Adopt a skeptical attitude toward information you receive. Carefully examine the definitions of terms. Evaluate the logical bases of arguments. Evaluate claims in the light of available evidence. Here are some key features of critical thinking:

1. *Maintain a skeptical attitude.* Don't take anything at face value, not even claims made by respected scientists or textbook authors. Consider the evidence yourself. Seek additional information. Investigate the credibility of your sources.
2. *Consider the definitions of terms.* Statements may be true or false depending on how the terms they use are defined. Consider the statement, "Stress is bad for you." If we define *stress* in terms of hassles and work or family pressures that stretch to the max our ability to cope, then there is substance to the statement. However, if we define stress (see Chapter 5) as conditions that require us to adjust, which may include such positive life events as a new marriage or the birth of a child, then certain types of stress can be positive, even if they are stressful. Perhaps, as we'll see, we all need some amount of stress to be energized and alert.
3. *Weigh the assumptions or premises on which arguments are based.* Consider a case in which we are comparing differences in the rates of psychological disorders across racial or ethnic groups in our society. Assuming we find differences, should we conclude that ethnicity or racial identity accounts for these differences? This conclusion might be valid if we can assume that all other factors that distinguish one racial or ethnic group from another are held constant. However, ethnic or racial minori-

ties in the United States and Canada are disproportionately poor, and the poor are more apt to develop more severe psychological disorders. Thus, the differences we find among racial or ethnic groups may be a function of poverty, not race or ethnicity. These differences may also be due to stereotyping of minorities by clinicians in making diagnostic judgments, rather than to differences in underlying rates of the disorder.

4. *Bear in mind that correlation is not causation.* Consider the relationship between depression and stress. Evidence shows a positive correlation between these variables, which means depressed people tend to have higher levels of stress in their lives (Hammen & de Mayo, 1982; Pianta & Egeland, 1994). But does stress cause depression? Perhaps it does. Or perhaps depression leads to greater stress. After all, depressive symptoms are stressful in themselves and may lead to additional stress as the person finds it increasingly difficult to meet life responsibilities, such as keeping up with work at school or on the job. Perhaps the two variables are not causally linked at all but are linked through a third variable, such as an underlying genetic factor. Is it possible that people inherit clusters of genes that make them more prone to both depression and stress?
5. *Consider the kinds of evidence on which conclusions are based.* Some conclusions, even seemingly "scientific" conclusions, are based on anecdotes and personal endorsements, not sound research. There is much controversy today about so-called recovered memories that are said to suddenly arise in adulthood, usually during psychotherapy or hypnosis, and usually involving incidents of sexual abuse committed during childhood by the person's parents or family members. Are recovered memories accurate? (See Chapter 7.)
6. *Do not oversimplify.* Consider the statement, "Alcoholism is inherited." In Chapter 10, we review evidence suggesting that genetic factors may create a predisposition to alcoholism, at least in males. But the origins of alcoholism, as well as of schizophrenia, depression, and physical health problems such as cancer and heart disease, are complex and reflect the interplay of biological and environmental factors. For instance, people may inherit a predisposition to develop a particular disorder but may be able to avoid developing it if they live in a healthy environment or learn to manage stress effectively.
7. *Do not overgeneralize.* In Chapter 7, we consider evidence showing that a history of severe abuse in childhood figures prominently in the great majority of cases of people who later develop multiple personalities. Does this mean that most abused children go on to develop multiple personalities? Actually, very few do. ■

markedly when, and only when, the treatment was applied to consuming each particular category of food.

To show a clear-cut treatment effect, changes in target behaviors should occur only when they are subjected to treatment. In some cases, changes in the treated target behaviors may lead to changes in the yet-untreated target behaviors, apparently because of generalization of the effect. However, generalization effects tend to be the exception rather than the rule in experimental research (Kazdin, 1992).

No matter how tightly controlled the design, or how impressive the results, single-case designs suffer from weak external validity because they cannot show whether a treatment effective for one person is effective for others. Replication with other individuals can help strengthen external validity. But results from controlled experiments on groups of indivdiuals are needed to provide more convincing evidence of treatment effectiveness and generalizability.

Scientists use different methods to study phenomena of interest to them. But all scientists share a skeptical, hard-nosed way of thinking called **critical thinking.** When thinking critically, we adopt a willingness to challenge the conventional wisdom that many of us take for granted. We find *reasons* to support beliefs rather than relying on feelings or gut impressions. We maintain an open mind and seek evidence to support or refute beliefs or claims. In the *"A Closer Look"* feature on page 34, we examine the features of critical thinking and how they can be applied to our study of abnormal psychology.

critical thinking Adoption of a questioning attitude and careful scrutiny of claims and arguments in the light of evidence.

SUMMING UP

How Do We Define Abnormal Behavior?

What criteria do mental health professionals use to determine that behavior is abnormal? Psychologists consider behavior abnormal when it meets some combination of the following criteria: when behavior is (a) unusual or statistically infrequent, (b) socially unacceptable or in violation of social norms, (c) fraught with misperceptions or misinterpretations of reality, (d) associated with states of severe personal distress, (e) maladaptive or self-defeating, or (f) dangerous. Psychological disorders are patterns of abnormal behavior associated with disturbances in states of emotional distress or impaired functioning.

How do views about abnormal behavior vary across cultures? Behaviors deemed normal in one culture may be considered abnormal in another. Concepts of health and illness are different in different cultures. Abnormal behavior patterns also take different forms in different cultures, and societal views or models explaining abnormal behavior also vary across cultures

Historical Perspectives on Abnormal Behavior

How have views about abnormal behavior changed over time? Ancient societies attributed abnormal behavior to divine or supernatural forces. In medieval times, abnormal behavior was a sign of possession by the devil, and exorcism was intended to rid the possessed of the evil spirits that afflicted them. The 19th-century German physician Wilhelm Grie-

singer argued that abnormal behavior was caused by diseases of the brain. He and another German physician who followed him, Emil Kraepelin, were influential in the development of the modern medical model, which likens abnormal behavior patterns to physical illnesses.

How has the treatment of people with mental disorders changed over time? Asylums, or madhouses, arose throughout Europe in the late 15th and early 16th centuries. Conditions in these asylums were dreadful. With the rise of moral therapy in the 19th century, conditions in mental hospitals improved. Proponents of moral therapy believed that mental patients could be restored to functioning if they were treated with dignity and understanding. The decline of moral therapy in the latter part of the 19th century led to the belief that the "insane" could not be treated successfully. During this period of apathy, mental hospitals deteriorated, offering little more than custodial care. Not until the middle of the 20th century did public concern about the plight of mental patients lead to the development of community mental health centers as alternatives to long-term hospitalization.

What are the major contemporary models of abnormal behavior? The medical model conceptualizes abnormal behavior patterns, like physical diseases, in terms of clusters of symptoms, called syndromes, which have distinctive causes that are presumed to be biological in nature. Psychological models focus on the psychological roots of abnormal behavior and derive from psychoanalytic, behavioral, humanistic, and cognitive perspectives. The sociocultural model emphasizes a broader perspective that takes into account the social contexts in which abnormal behavior occurs. Today, many theorists subscribe to a biopsychosocial model that posits that multiple causes—representing biological, psychological, and sociocultural domains—interact in the development of abnormal behavior patterns.

Research Methods in Abnormal Psychology

What are the basic objectives of the scientific method, and what steps are involved in applying it? The scientific approach focuses on four general objectives: description, explanation, prediction, and control. There are four steps to the scientific method: formulating a research question, framing the research question in the form of a hypothesis, testing the hypothesis, and drawing conclusions about the correctness of the hypothesis. Psychologists follow the ethical principles of the profession that govern research.

What are the methods psychologists use to study abnormal behavior? In naturalistic observation, the investigator carefully observes behavior under naturally occurring conditions. The correlational method of research explores relationships between variables, which may help predict future behavior and suggest possible underlying causes of behavior. However, correlational research cannot directly demonstrate cause-and-effect relationships. Longitudinal research is a correlational method in which a sample of subjects is repeatedly studied at periodic intervals over long periods of time, sometimes spanning decades.

In the experimental method, the investigator manipulates or controls the independent variable under controlled conditions to reveal cause-and-effect relationships. Experiments use random assignment as the basis for determining which subjects (called experimental subjects) receive an experimental treatment and which others (called control subjects) do not. Experiments are evaluated in terms of internal, external, and construct validity.

Epidemiological studies examine the rates of occurrence of abnormal behavior in various population groups or settings. Kinship studies, such as twin studies and adoptee studies, attempt to differentiate the contributions of environment and heredity.

Case studies provide rich material, but are limited by difficulties obtaining accurate and unbiased client histories, by possible therapist biases, and by the lack of control groups. Single-case experimental designs are intended to help researchers overcome some of the limitations of the case-study method.

KEY TERMS

psychological disorder *(p. 4)*
abnormal psychology *(p. 4)*
psychologist *(p. 4)*
psychiatrist *(p. 4)*
medical model *(p. 4)*
trephination *(p. 11)*
humors *(p. 12)*
dementia praecox *(p. 16)*
general paresis *(p. 16)*
psychodynamic model *(p. 17)*
biopsychosocial model *(p. 19)*
scientific method *(p. 20)*
theory *(p. 21)*
hypothesis *(p. 21)*
informed consent *(p. 22)*

confidentiality *(p. 22)*
naturalistic observation *(p. 22)*
correlation *(p. 23)*
variables *(p. 23)*
longitudinal study *(p. 23)*
experimental method *(p. 24)*
independent variables *(p. 24)*
dependent variables *(p. 24)*
experimental group *(p. 24)*
control group *(p. 24)*
random assignment *(p. 24)*
selection factor *(p. 25)*
blind *(p. 25)*
placebo *(p. 25)*
internal validity *(p. 26)*

external validity *(p. 26)*
construct validity *(p. 27)*
epidemiological studies *(p. 27)*
survey method *(p. 27)*
incidence *(p. 27)*
prevalence *(p. 27)*
random sample *(p. 28)*
genotype *(p. 28)*
phenotype *(p. 28)*
proband *(p. 28)*
adoptee studies *(p. 30)*
case studies *(p. 30)*
single-case experimental designs *(p. 30)*
reversal design *(p. 30)*
critical thinking *(p. 34)*

WEB TOOLS

The companion website offers tools to enrich your learning experience and help you succeed in class. Go to www.prenhall.com/nevid for the gateway to the following resources:

- **VIDEO** links to connect to the video case files on the companion CD-ROM. VIDEO icons in the margins of the chapter highlight the case examples included in the CD-ROM. You can also access the CD-ROM directly if you do not have a Web connection.

- **QUIZ** links to self-scoring quizzes corresponding to each section of the chapter. The quizzes help you review your knowledge of the content in each chapter.

- **WEB** links to direct you to related sites that enhance your learning of abnormal psychology.

CHAPTER TWO

Contemporary Perspectives on Abnormal Behavior

"I"

Jessica's "Little Secret"

I don't want Ken (her fiancé) to find out. I don't want to bring this into the marriage. I probably should have told him, but I just couldn't do it. Every time I wanted to I just froze up. I guess I figured I'd get over this before the wedding. I have to stop bingeing and throwing up. I just can't stop myself. You know, I want to stop, but I get to thinking about the food I've eaten and it sickens me. I picture myself getting all fat and bloated and I just have to rush to the bathroom and throw it up. I would go on binges, and then throw it all up. It made me feel like I was in control, but really I wasn't.

I have this little ritual when I throw up. I go to the bathroom and run the water in the sink. Nobody ever hears me puking. It's my little secret. I make sure to clean up really well and spray some Lysol before leaving the bathroom. No one suspects I have a problem. Well, that's not quite true. The only one who suspects is my dentist. He said my teeth were beginning to decay from stomach acid. I'm only 20 and I've got rotting teeth. Isn't that awful?

. . . Now I've started throwing up even when I don't binge. Sometimes just eating dinner makes me want to puke. I've just got to get the food out of my body—fast, you know. Right after dinner, I make some excuse about needing to go to the bathroom. It's not every time but at least several times a week. After lunch sometimes too. I know I need help. It's taken me a long time to come here, but you know I'm getting married in three months and I've got to stop.

—*Jessica, a 20-year-old communications major.*

Source: From the Author's Files

JESSICA EXCUSES HERSELF FROM THE DINNER TABLE, GOES TO THE BATHROOM, STICKS a finger down her throat to gag, and throws up her dinner. Sometimes she binges first and then forces herself to throw up. You'll recall that in Chapter 1 we described the criteria that mental health professionals generally use to classify behavior patterns as abnormal. Jessica's behavior clearly meets several of these criteria. Bingeing and throwing up is a source of personal distress and is maladaptive in the sense that it can lead to serious health consequences, such as decaying teeth (see Chapter 10), and social consequences (which is why she kept it a secret and feared it would damage her forthcoming marriage). It is also statistically infrequent, though perhaps not as infrequent as you might think. Jessica was diagnosed with *bulimia,* a type of eating disorder that we discuss in Chapter 10.

How can we understand such unusual and maladaptive behavior? In this chapter we examine contemporary approaches to understanding abnormal behavior from the vantage points offered by the biological, psychological, and sociocultural perspectives. Each perspective provides a window for examining abnormal behavior, but none captures a complete view of the subject. Many scholars today believe that abnormal behavior patterns are complex phenomena that are best understood by taking into account the contributions of multiple factors representing these different perspectives, rather than from any one causal factor.

Since earliest times, humans have sought explanations for strange or deviant behavior. As we saw in Chapter 1, through the Middle Ages, most people believed that abnormal behavior was caused by demons and other supernatural forces. But even in ancient times, some scholars, such as Hippocrates and Galen, looked for natural explanations of abnormal behavior. Today, of course, superstition and demonology have given way to theoretical models from the natural and social sciences. These approaches pave the way not only for a scientifically based understanding of abnormal behavior but also for ways of treating people with psychological disorders.

In this chapter we examine the biological, psychological, and sociocultural perspectives on abnormal behavior. Each perspective provides a window for examining abnormal behavior, but none captures a complete view of the subject. Many scholars today believe that abnormal behavior patterns are complex phenomena that are best understood by taking into account these multiple perspectives.

THE BIOLOGICAL PERSPECTIVE

The *medical model*, inspired by physicians from Hippocrates through Kraepelin, remains a powerful force in contemporary understandings of abnormal behavior. We prefer the term *biological perspective*, which we use to refer to attempts to understand the biological bases of abnormal behavior and the use of biologically based approaches, such as drug therapy, to treat psychological disorders. We can speak of biological perspectives without adopting the tenets of the medical model, which treats abnormal behavior patterns as *disorders* and their features as *symptoms*. For example, a behavior pattern such as shyness may have a strong genetic (biological) component but not be considered a "symptom" of an underlying "disorder" or illness.

Our understanding of the biological underpinnings of abnormal behavior has grown in recent years. In Chapter 1 we focused on the methods of studying the role of heredity or genetics. Genetics plays a role in many forms of abnormal behavior, as we shall see throughout the text.

We also know that other biological factors, especially the functioning of the nervous system, are involved in the development of abnormal behavior (Cravchik & Goldman, 2000). To better understand the role of the nervous system in abnormal behavior patterns, we first need to learn how the nervous system is organized and how nerve cells communicate with each other. In Chapter 5 we examine another body system, the *endocrine system*, and the important roles that it plays in the body's response to stress.

The Nervous System

Perhaps if you did not have a nervous system, you would never feel nervous—but neither would you see, hear, or move. However, even calm people have nervous systems. The nervous system is made up of **neurons,** nerve cells that transmit signals or "messages" throughout the body. These messages allow us to sense an itch from a bug bite, coordinate our vision and muscles to ice skate, write a research paper, solve a math problem, and in the case of hallucinations, hear or see things that are not really there.

Every neuron has a cell body that contains the nucleus of the cell and metabolizes oxygen to carry out the work of the cell (see Figure 2.1). Short fibers called **dendrites** project from the cell body to receive messages from adjoining neurons. Each neuron has a single **axon** that projects, trunklike, from the cell body. Axons may branch and project in various directions; they can extend as long as several feet, if they are conveying messages between the toes and the spinal cord. Axons terminate in small branching structures that are aptly called **terminals.** Neurons convey messages in one direction, from the dendrites or cell body along the axon to the axon terminals. The messages are then conveyed from the terminals to other neurons, muscles, or glands.

Neurons transmit messages to other neurons by means of chemical substances called **neurotransmitters.** Neurotransmitters induce chemical changes in receiving neurons. These changes cause axons to conduct the messages in electrical form.

The junction or small gap between a transmitting neuron and a receiving neuron is termed a **synapse.** The message does not jump across the synapse like a spark. Instead, axon terminals release neurotransmitters into the cleft like myriad ships casting off into the seas (Figure 2.2).

Each kind of neurotransmitter has a distinctive chemical structure. It will fit only into one kind of harbor, or **receptor site,** on the receiving neuron. Consider the analogy of a lock and key. Only the right key (neurotransmitter) operates the lock, causing the *postsynaptic* (receiving) neuron to forward the message.

Once released, some molecules of a neurotransmitter reach port at receptor sites of other neurons. "Loose" neurotransmitters may be broken down in the synapse by enzymes or be reabsorbed by the axon terminal (a process termed *reuptake*), so as to prevent the receiving cell from continuing to fire.

neurons Nerve cells.

dendrites The rootlike structures at the ends of neurons that receive nerve impulses from other neurons.

axon The long, thin part of a neuron along which nerve impulses travel.

terminals The small branching structures at the tips of axons.

neurotransmitters Chemical substances that transmit messages from one neuron to another.

synapse The junction between the terminal knob of one neuron and the dendrite or soma of another through which nerve impulses pass.

receptor site A part of a dendrite on a receiving neuron that is structured to receive a neurotransmitter.

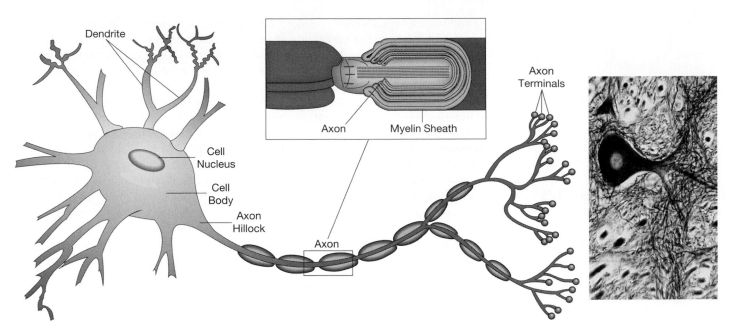

FIGURE 2.1 Anatomy of a neuron.
Neurons typically consist of cells bodies (or somas), dendrites, and one or more axons. The axon of this neuron is wrapped in a myelin sheath, which insulates it from the bodily fluids surrounding the neuron and facilitates transmission of neural impulses (messages that travel within the neuron).

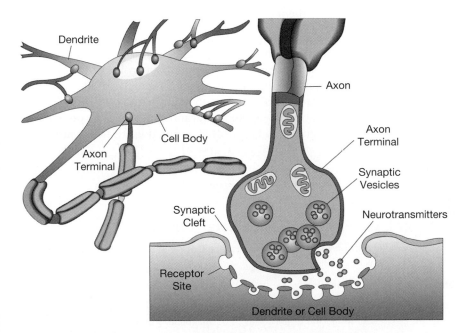

FIGURE 2.2 Transmission of neural impulses across the synapse.
The diagram here shows the structure of the neuron and the mode of transmission of neural impulses between neurons. Neurons transmit messages, or neural impulses, across synapses, which consist of the axon terminal of the transmitting neuron, the gap or synapse between the neurons, and the dendrite of the receiving neuron. The "message" consists of neurotransmitters that are released into the synapse and taken up by receptor sites on the receiving neuron. Somehow the patterns of firing of many thousands of neurons give rise to psychological events such as thoughts and mental images. Many patterns of abnormal behavior have been associated with irregularities in the transmission or reception of neural messages.

Psychiatric drugs, including drugs used to treat anxiety, depression, and schizophrenia, work by affecting the availability of neurotransmitters in the brain (Snyder, 2002). Consequently, many scientists suspect that irregularities in the workings of neurotransmitter systems in the brain play important roles in the development of these abnormal behavior patterns (see Table 2.1).

Depression is linked to chemical imbalances in the brain involving irregularities in the functioning of several neurotransmitters, especially serotonin (Bremner et al., 2003; Harmer et al, 2003; Meyer et al., 2003) (see Chapter 8). Serotonin is a key brain chemical involved in regulating moods, so it is not surprising that it would play a role in depression (Gupta, 2003). The most widely used antidepressant drugs—Prozac and Zoloft—belong to a class of drugs that increase the availability of serotonin in the brain. Serotonin is also linked to anxiety disorders, sleep disorders, and eating disorders.

Alzheimer's disease, a brain disease in which there is a progressive loss of memory and cognitive functioning, is associated with reductions in the levels of the neurotransmitter *acetylcholine* in the brain (see Chapter 15). Irregularities involving the neurotransmitter *dopamine* are implicated in the development of schizophrenia (see Chapter 12). Antipsychotic drugs used to treat schizophrenia apparently work by blocking dopamine receptors in the brain.

Although neurotransmitter systems are implicated in many psychological disorders, the precise causal mechanisms remain to be determined.

Parts of the Nervous System The nervous system consists of two major parts, the **central nervous system** and the **peripheral nervous system.** The two parts are also divided. The central nervous system consists of the brain and spinal cord. The peripheral nervous system is made up of nerves that (a) receive and transmit sensory messages (messages from sense organs such as the eyes and ears) to the brain and spinal cord, and (b) transmit messages from the brain or spinal cord to the muscles, causing them to contract, and to glands, causing them to secrete hormones.

Central Nervous System We begin our overview of the parts of the central nervous system with the back of the head, where the spinal cord meets the brain, and work forward (see Figure 2.3). The lower part of the brain, or *hindbrain,* consists of the medulla, pons, and cerebellum. Many nerves that link the spinal cord to higher brain levels pass through the **medulla.** The medulla plays roles in such vital functions as heart rate, respiration, and blood pressure, and also in sleep, sneezing, and coughing. The **pons** transmits information about body movement and is involved in functions related to attention, sleep, and respiration.

central nervous system The brain and spinal cord.

peripheral nervous system The somatic and autonomic nervous systems.

medulla An area of the hindbrain involved in regulation of heartbeat and respiration.

pons A structure in the hindbrain involved in respiration.

TABLE 2.1		
Neurotransmitter Functions and Relationships with Abnormal Behavior Patterns		
Neurotransmitter	**Functions**	**Associations with Abnormal Behavior**
Acetylcholine (ACh)	Control of muscle contractions and formation of memories	Reduced levels found in patients with Alzheimer's disease
Dopamine	Regulation of muscle contractions and mental processes involving learning, memory, and emotions	Overutilization of dopamine in the brain may be involved in the development of schizophrenia
Norepinephrine	Mental processes involved in learning and memory	Imbalances linked with mood disorders such as depression
Serotonin	Regulation of mood states, satiety, and sleep	Irregularities may be involved in depression and eating disorders

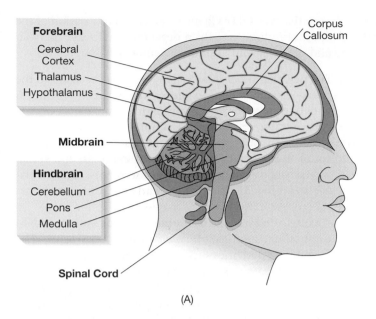

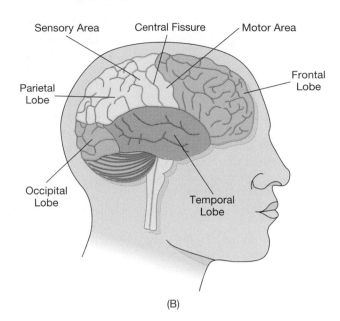

FIGURE 2.3 The geography of the brain.
Part A shows parts of the hindbrain, midbrain, and forebrain. Part B shows the four lobes of the cerebral cortex: frontal, parietal, temporal, and occipital. In B, the sensory (tactile) and motor areas lie across the central fissure from one another. Researchers are investigating the potential relationships between various patterns of abnormal behavior and irregularities in the formation or functioning of the structures of the brain.

Behind the pons is the **cerebellum** (Latin for "little brain"). The cerebellum is involved in balance and motor (muscle) behavior. Injury to the cerebellum may impair motor coordination and cause stumbling and loss of muscle tone.

The midbrain lies above the hindbrain and contains nerve pathways that link the hindbrain with the forebrain. The **reticular activating system** (RAS) starts in the hindbrain and rises through the midbrain into the lower forebrain. The RAS, which consists of a weblike network of neurons, plays vital roles in sleep, attention, and arousal. RAS stimulation triggers messages that heighten alertness. *Depressant drugs,* such as alcohol, which dampen central nervous system activity, lower RAS activity.

Important areas in the frontal part of the brain, or *forebrain,* are the thalamus, hypothalamus, limbic system, basal ganglia, and cerebrum. The **thalamus** relays sensory information (such as touch and vision) to higher brain regions. The thalamus is also involved in sleep and attention, in coordination with other structures, such as the RAS.

The **hypothalamus** is a tiny structure located between the thalamus and the pituitary gland. The hypothalamus is vital in regulating body temperature, concentration of fluids, storage of nutrients, and motivation and emotion. By implanting electrodes in parts of the hypothalamus of animals and observing the effects when a current is switched on, researchers have found that the hypothalamus is involved in a range of motivational drives and behaviors, including hunger, thirst, sex, parenting behaviors, and aggression.

The hypothalamus, together with parts of the thalamus and other structures, make up the **limbic system.** The limbic system plays a role in memory and in regulating the more basic drives involving hunger, thirst, and aggression. The **basal ganglia** lie in front of the thalamus and help to regulate postural movements and coordination.

The **cerebrum** is your "crowning glory" and is responsible for the round shape of the human head. The surface of the cerebrum is convoluted with ridges and valleys. This surface is the **cerebral cortex,** the thinking, planning, and executive center of the brain.

Abnormalities in specific brain structures are implicated in different forms of abnormal behavior. For example, investigators find abnormalities in parts of the cerebral cortex and limbic system in schizophrenia patients (Chapter 12). The hypothalamus is

cerebellum A structure in the hindbrain involved in coordination and balance.

reticular activating system Brain structure involved in processes of attention, sleep, and arousal.

thalamus A structure in the forebrain involved in relaying sensory information to the cortex and in processes related to sleep and attention.

hypothalamus A structure in the forebrain involved in regulating body temperature, emotion, and motivation.

limbic system A group of forebrain structures involved in learning, memory, and basic drives.

basal ganglia An assemblage of neurons located between the thalamus and cerebrum, involved in coordinating motor (movement) processes.

cerebrum The large mass of the forebrain, consisting of the two cerebral hemispheres.

cerebral cortex The wrinkled surface area of the cerebrum, it is responsible for processing sensory stimuli and controlling higher mental functions, such as thinking and use of language.

implicated in certain types of sleep disorders (see Chapter 10), and deterioration of the basal ganglia is associated with Huntington's disease, a degenerative disease that can lead to disturbances of mood and paranoia and even to dementia (see Chapter 15).

Peripheral Nervous System   The peripheral nervous system connects the brain to the outer world. Without the peripheral nervous system, people could not perceive the world or act on it. The two main divisions of the peripheral nervous system are the *somatic nervous system* and the *autonomic nervous system*.

The **somatic nervous system** transmits messages about sights, sounds, smells, temperature, body position, and so on to the brain. Messages from the brain and spinal cord to the somatic nervous system regulate intentional body movements, such as raising an arm, winking, or walking; breathing; and subtle movements that maintain posture and balance.

Psychologists are particularly interested in the **autonomic nervous system** (ANS) because its activities are linked to emotional response. *Autonomic* means "automatic." The ANS regulates the glands and involuntary activities such as heart rate, breathing, digestion, and dilation of the pupils of the eyes, even when we are sleeping.

The ANS has two branches or subdivisions, the **sympathetic** and the **parasympathetic.** These branches have mostly opposing effects. Many organs and glands are served by both branches of the ANS. The sympathetic division is most involved in processes that mobilize the body's resources in times of stress, such as drawing energy from stored reserves to prepare the person to deal with imposing threats or dangers (see Chapter 5). When we face a threat or dangerous situation, the sympathetic branch of the ANS accelerates the heart rate and breathing rate, which helps prepare our bodies to either fight or flee. Sympathetic activation in the face of a threatening stimulus is associated with emotional responses such as fear or anxiety. When we relax, the parasympathetic branch decelerates the heart rate. The parasympathetic division is most active during processes that replenish energy reserves, such as digestion. Because the sympathetic branch dominates when we are fearful or anxious, fear or anxiety can lead to indigestion because activation of the sympathetic nervous system curbs digestive activity.

The Cerebral Cortex   The human activities of thought and language involve the two hemispheres of the cerebrum. Each hemisphere is divided into four parts, or lobes, as shown in Figure 2.3. The *occipital lobe* is primarily involved in vision; the *temporal lobe* is involved in processing sounds or auditory stimuli. The *parietal lobe* is involved in determining sensations of touch, temperature, and pain. The *sensory area* of the parietal lobe receives messages from skin sensors all over the body. Neurons in the motor area (or *motor cortex*) of the *frontal lobe* are involved in controlling muscular responses, which enables us to move our limbs. The *prefrontal cortex* (the part of the frontal lobe that lies in front of the motor cortex) is involved in higher mental functions such as thinking, problem solving, and use of language.

Evaluating Biological Perspectives on Abnormal Behavior

Biological structures and processes are involved in many patterns of abnormal behavior, as we will see in later chapters. Disturbances in neurotransmitter functioning and underlying brain abnormalities or defects are implicated in many psychological disorders. For some disorders, such as Alzheimer's disease, biological processes play the direct causative role. (Even then, however, the precise causes remain unknown.) But for most disorders, we need to examine the interaction of biological and environmental factors.

We each possess a unique genetic code, and scientists suspect that buried in that code are sequences of DNA that play important roles in determining our risk of developing many physical and mental disorders. Evidence suggests that genes play a role in many psychological disorders, including schizophrenia, bipolar (manic–depressive) disorder, major depression, alcoholism, autism, dementia due to Alzheimer's disease, anxiety disorders, dyslexia, and antisocial personality disorder (Merikangas & Risch, 2003; NIMH, 2003; Plomin & McGuffin, 2003; Waterworth et al. 2002). Scientists are actively attempting to identify the specific genes involved in particular psychological disorders

somatic nervous system   The division of the peripheral nervous system that relays information from the sense organs to the brain and transmits messages from the brain to the skeletal muscles.

autonomic nervous system   The division of the peripheral nervous system that regulates the activities of the glands and involuntary functions.

sympathetic   Pertaining to the division of the autonomic nervous system whose activity leads to heightened states of arousal.

parasympathetic   Pertaining to the division of the autonomic nervous system whose activity reduces states of arousal and regulates bodily processes that replenish energy reserves.

(Gottesman & Gould, 2003; Tecott, 2003). They are even hopeful that gene therapy techniques, once the province of science fiction, will be developed to manipulate genetic material to prevent or treat psychological disorders (Sapolsky, 2003). Yet genetic factors alone do not account for any psychological disorder (Carey & DiLalla, 1994). In other words, environmental factors are also key contributors to the development of psycho-

CONTROVERSIES IN ABNORMAL PSYCHOLOGY
Is It All in the Genes?

It's not stretching a point to say that progress in genetic research in recent years has been nothing less than remarkable. The highlight of these achievements was the cracking of the human genome, the complete genetic blueprint of a human being. The genome consists of the precise chemical sequence in human DNA—a recipe for determining the features or traits of human beings (International Human Genome, 2001; Wade, 2003b). We are now able to read the coded instructions that comprise the genetic script of a human being. The genome has even been published on the Internet for scientists to use in their studies (Baltimore, 2000).

We've long known that genetics plays a determining role in many physical traits, including eye color and hair color. But we are learning that genetics also plays important roles in many behavioral traits, including shyness, intelligence, novelty seeking, aggressiveness, and sociability, to name but a few (Ellis & Bonin, 2003; Garlick, 2003; Plomin & Crabbe, 2001; Schwartz et al., 2003). Genetics also plays important roles in many psychological disorders, as we shall see through the course of this text—disorders such as schizophrenia, mood disorders, substance abuse and dependence, and autism (Merikangas & Risch, 2003; Plomin & McGuffin, 2003; Waterworth et al., 2002; Yu et al., 2002).

Now that the genome has been cracked, scientists are turning their attention to discover the particular genes involved in a host of physical illnesses and psychological disorders such as schizophrenia, depression, and autism (Bunney et al., 2003; Plomin, 2003; Plomin et al., 2003; Tecott, 2003). Scientists hope that one day in the not-too-distant future, it will be possible to repair defective or harmful genes, perhaps by blocking their actions (Phillips et al., 2002; Plomin & McGuffin, 2003; Sapolsky, 2003).

Against the backdrop of increasing evidence of genetic contributions across a wide swath of behavior, the question remains, "Is it all in the genes?" More specifically, is the development of psychological disorders a matter of luck in the genetic draw?

These questions touch on a long-standing debate in psychology, arguably the longest debate—the nature versus nurture debate. The debate is framed today in terms of the question of how much of our behavior is a product of nature (genes) and how much is a product of nurture (environment). As the long debate continues, let us offer a few key points to consider.

1. *Genes do not dictate behavioral outcomes.* The evidence of a genetic contribution in psychological disorders is arguably strongest in the case of schizophrenia. But as discussed in Chapter 12, even for monozygotic twins who share 100% genetic overlap, when scientists find one schizophrenic MZ twin, the chance of the other twin having schizophrenia is slightly less than 50%. In other words, genetics alone does not account for schizophrenia.
2. *Genetic factors create a predisposition or likelihood—not a certainty—that certain behaviors or disorders will develop.* Factors such as life experiences, family background, and levels of stress interact with genetic fac-

tors in determining these outcomes (Frank & Kupfer, 2000; Sapolsky, 2000). Recent evidence shows that even factors of ethnicity and gender influence how genes operate in the body (Williams et al., 2003).
3. *Multigenic determinism.* Where genetic factors play a role in psychological disorders, multiple genes are involved, not individual genes alone (Plomin, 2003; Uhl & Grow, 2004). We have yet to find any psychological disorder that can be explained by defects or variations on a single gene (USDHHS, 1999a).
4. *Genetic factors and environmental influence interact with each other in shaping our personalities and determining our vulnerability to a range of psychological disorders* (Andreasen, 2003; Johnston & Edwards, 2002; Plomin et al., 2003; Ridley, 2003). The contemporary view of the nature–nurture debate is best expressed in terms of nature *and* nurture acting together, not nature *versus* nurture (Angier, 2003).

Critical Thinking

- How might investigators determine the role of genetic factors in the development of psychological disorders? (Consider the research methods discussed in Chapter 1).
- What would you say to someone who believes that genetics is destiny when it comes to determining one's risk of developing psychological disorders such as depression or schizophrenia?

A human being, decoded. Here we see a portion of the human genome, the genetic code of a human being. Scientists recognize that genes play an important role in determining predispositions for many psychological traits and disorders. But whether these predispositions are expressed depends on the interactions of genetic and environmental influences.

logical disorders (see *Controversies in Abnormal Psychology* feature). Scientists recognize that we need to go beyond the old "nature–nurture" (gene vs. environment) debate to study the complex interactions between genes and other factors, including environmental influences, to better understand the development of psychological disorders (Andreasen, 2003; Angier, 2003; Plomin et al., 2003).

Although we continue to learn more about the biological foundations of abnormal behavior patterns, the interface between biology and behavior is a two-way street. Researchers have uncovered links between psychological factors and many physical disorders and conditions (see Chapter 5). Researchers are also investigating whether the combination of psychological and drug treatments for such problems as depression, anxiety disorders, and substance abuse disorders, among others, may increase the therapeutic benefits of either of the two approaches alone.

THE PSYCHOLOGICAL PERSPECTIVE

At about the time that biological models of abnormal behavior were becoming prominent in the late 19th century with the contributions of Kraepelin, Griesinger, and others, another approach to understanding abnormal behavior began to emerge. This approach emphasized the psychological roots of abnormal behavior and was most closely identified with the work of the Austrian physician Sigmund Freud. Over time other psychological models would emerge from the behaviorist, humanistic, and cognitivist traditions. Let us begin our study of psychological perspectives with Freud's contribution and the development of psychodynamic models.

Psychodynamic Models

Psychodynamic theory is based on the contributions of Sigmund Freud and his followers. Freud's **psychoanalytic theory** is based on the belief that psychological problems such as *hysteria* are driven by unconscious motives and conflicts that can be traced to childhood. These underlying conflicts revolve around our primitive sexual and aggressive instincts and the need to keep these primitive impulses out of conscious awareness. Why must we keep these impulses hidden? Because if we were aware of our most basic urges—which, according to Freud, include the wish to murder one parent and marry the other—our conscious selves would be flooded with crippling anxiety. In the Freudian view, abnormal behavior patterns represent "symptoms" of the dynamic struggles taking place within the mind. In the case of hysteria, the "symptom" represents the *conversion* of an unconscious psychological conflict into a physical problem. We are aware of the symptom, but not the unconscious conflict at its root.

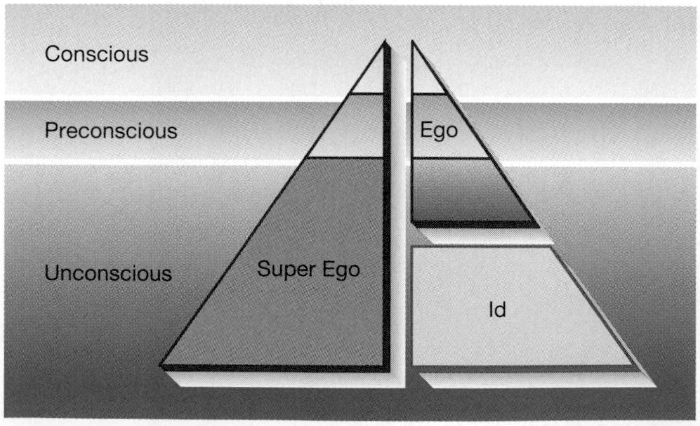

psychoanalytic theory The theoretical model of personality developed by Sigmund Freud; also called psychoanalysis.

conscious To Freud, the part of the mind that corresponds to our present awareness.

TRUTH or FICTION? *REVISITED*

Freud likened the mind to a giant iceberg, with only the tip rising into conscious awareness.

☑ **TRUE.** Freud believed that the larger part of the mind remains below the surface of consciousness.

preconscious To Freud, the part of the mind whose contents lie outside present awareness but can be brought into awareness by focusing attention.

unconscious To Freud, the part of the mind that lies outside the range of ordinary awareness and that contains instinctual urges.

id The unconscious psychic structure, present at birth, that contains primitive instincts and is regulated by the pleasure principle.

The Structure of the Mind Freud's clinical experiences led him to conclude that the mind is like an iceberg: only the tip is visible (Figure 2.4). Freud called this region "above the surface" the **conscious** part of the mind. It is the part of the mind that corresponds to our present awareness. The larger part of the mind remains below the surface of consciousness. The regions that lie beneath the surface of awareness were labeled the *preconscious* and the *unconscious*.

In the **preconscious** are memories that are not in awareness, but that can be brought into awareness by focusing on them. Your telephone number, for example, remains in the preconscious until you focus on it. The **unconscious,** the largest part of the mind, remains shrouded in mystery. Its contents can only be brought to awareness with great difficulty, if at all. Freud believed the unconscious is the repository of our basic biological impulses or drives, which he called instincts—primarily sexual and aggressive instincts.

The Structure of Personality According to Freud's structural hypothesis, the personality is divided into three mental entities, or psychic structures: the *id, ego,* and *superego*.

The **id** is the original psychic structure, present at birth. It is the repository of our baser drives and instinctual impulses, including

FIGURE 2.4 The parts of the mind, according to Freud.
In psychodynamic theory, the mind is akin to an iceberg; only a small part of it rises to conscious awareness at any moment in time. Although material in the preconscious mind may be brought into consciousness by focusing our attention on it, the impulses and ideas in the unconscious tend to remain veiled in mystery.

hunger, thirst, sex, and aggression. The id, which operates completely in the unconscious, follows the **pleasure principle:** It demands instant gratification of instincts without consideration of social rules or customs or the needs of others.

During the first year of life, the child discovers that every demand is not instantly gratified. He or she must learn to cope with the delay of gratification. The **ego** develops during this first year to organize reasonable ways of coping with frustration. Standing for "reason and good sense" (Freud, 1933/1964, p. 76), the ego seeks to curb the demands of the id and to direct behavior in keeping with social customs and expectations. Gratification can thus be achieved, but not at the expense of social disapproval. Let's say the id floods your consciousness with hunger pangs. Were it to have its way, the id might prompt you to wolf down whatever food is at hand or even to swipe someone else's plate. But the ego creates the idea of walking to the refrigerator, making a sandwich, and pouring a glass of milk.

The ego is governed by the **reality principle.** It considers what is practical and possible, as well as the urgings of the id. The ego lays the groundwork for developing a conscious sense of ourselves as distinct individuals.

During middle childhood, the **superego** develops from the internalization of the moral standards and values of our parents and other key people in our lives. The superego serves as a conscience, or internal moral guardian, that monitors the ego and passes judgment on right and wrong. It metes out punishment in the form of guilt and shame when it finds that the ego has failed to adhere to the superego's moral standards. Ego stands between the id and the superego. It endeavors to satisfy the cravings of the id without offending the moral standards of the superego.

Defense Mechanisms Although part of the ego rises to consciousness, some of its activity is carried out unconsciously. In the unconscious, the ego serves as a kind of watchdog, or censor, that screens impulses from the id. It uses **defense mechanisms** (psychological defenses) to prevent socially unacceptable impulses from rising into consciousness. If not for these defense mechanisms, the darkest sins of our childhoods, the primitive demands of our ids, and the censures of our superegos might disable us psychologically. *Repression,* or motivated forgetting (the banishment of unacceptable ideas

pleasure principle The governing principle of the id, involving demands for immediate gratification of needs.

ego The psychic structure that corresponds to the concept of the self, governed by the reality principle and characterized by the ability to tolerate frustration.

reality principle The governing principle of the ego, which involves considerations of social acceptability and practicality.

superego The psychic structure that incorporates the values of the parents and important others and functions as a moral conscience.

defense mechanisms The reality-distorting strategies used by the ego to shield the self from awareness of anxiety-provoking materials.

Ego and Id. Psychodynamic theorists believe the ego curbs the instinctual demands of the id. The ego seeks socially acceptable ways of channeling these demands. When you share a meal with other people, you do not grab their food or snatch away the serving dish.

or motives to the unconscious), is the most basic of the defense mechanisms. Others are described in Table 2.2.

A dynamic unconscious struggle thus takes place between the id and the ego. Biological drives that are striving for expression (the id) are pitted against the ego, which seeks to restrain them or channel them into socially acceptable outlets. When these conflicts are not resolved smoothly, they can lead to the development of features associated with psychological disorders, such as hysterical symptoms, phobias, and behavioral problems. Because we cannot view the unconscious mind directly, Freud developed a method of mental detective work called *psychoanalysis,* which is described in Chapter 4.

The use of defense mechanisms to cope with feelings such as anxiety, guilt, and shame is considered normal. These mechanisms enable us to constrain impulses from the id as we go about our daily business. Freud believed that slips of the tongue and ordinary forgetfulness could represent hidden motives that are kept out of consciousness by repression. If a friend means to say, "I hear what you're saying," but it comes out, "I hate what you're saying," perhaps the friend is expressing a repressed emotion. If a lover storms out in anger but forgets his umbrella, perhaps he is unconsciously creating an excuse for returning. Defense mechanisms may also give rise to abnormal behavior, however. The person who regresses to an infantile state under pressures of enormous stress is clearly not acting adaptively to the situation.

Stages of Psychosexual Development   Freud argued that sexual drives are the dominant factors in the development of personality, even in childhood. Freud believed that the child's basic relationship to the world in its first several years of life is organized around the pursuit of sensual or sexual pleasure. In Freud's view, all activities that are

TABLE 2.2

Some Defense Mechanisms of the Ego, According to Psychodynamic Theory

Defense Mechanism	Definition	Examples
Repression	The ejection of anxiety-evoking ideas from awareness.	A student forgets a difficult term paper is due. A patient in therapy forgets an appointment when anxiety-evoking material is to be discussed.
Regression	The return, under stress, to a form of behavior characteristic of an earlier stage of development.	An adolescent cries when forbidden to use the family car. An adult becomes highly dependent on his parents following the breakup of his marriage.
Rationalization	The use of self-deceiving justifications for unacceptable behavior.	A student blames her cheating on her teacher's leaving the room during a test. A man explains his cheating on his income tax by saying, "Everyone does it."
Displacement	The transfer of ideas and impulses from threatening or unsuitable objects onto less-threatening objects.	A worker picks a fight with her spouse after being criticized sharply by her supervisor.
Projection	The thrusting of one's own unacceptable impulses onto others so that others are assumed to harbor them.	A hostile person perceives the world as being a dangerous place. A sexually frustrated person interprets innocent gestures of others as sexual advances.
Reaction formation	Assumption of behavior in opposition to one's genuine impulses in order to keep impulses repressed	A person who is angry with a relative behaves in a "sickly sweet" manner toward that relative. A sadistic individual becomes a physician.
Denial	Refusal to accept the true nature of a threat.	Belief that one will not contract cancer or heart disease although one smokes heavily ("It can't happen to me").
Sublimation	The channeling of primitive impulses into positive, constructive efforts.	A person paints nudes for the sake of "beauty" and "art." A hostile person directs aggressive energies into competitive sports.

physically pleasurable, such as eating or moving one's bowels, are in essence "sexual." (The word *sensuality* is probably closer in present-day meaning to what Freud meant by *sexuality*.)

The drive for sexual pleasure represents, in Freud's view, the expression of a major life instinct, which he called Eros—the basic drive to preserve and perpetuate life. He called the energy contained in Eros that allows it to fulfill its function *libido*, or sexual energy. Freud believed libidinal energy is expressed through sexual pleasure in different body parts, called *erogenous zones*, as the child matures. In Freud's view, the stages of human development are psychosexual in nature, because they correspond to the transfer of libidinal energy from one erogenous zone to another. Freud proposed the existence of five psychosexual stages of development: oral (first year of life), anal (second year of life), phallic (beginning during the third year of life), latency (from around age 6 to age 12), and genital (beginning in puberty).

In the first year of life, the *oral stage*, infants achieve sexual pleasure by sucking their mothers' breasts and by mouthing anything that happens to be nearby. Oral stimulation, in the form of sucking and biting, is a source of both sexual gratification and nourishment. During the *anal stage* of psychosexual development, the child experiences sexual gratification through contraction and relaxation of the sphincter muscles that control elimination of bodily waste.

The next stage of psychosexual development, the *phallic stage*, generally begins during the third year of life. The major erogenous zone during the stage is the phallic region (the penis in boys, the clitoris in girls). Perhaps the most controversial of Freud's beliefs was his suggestion that phallic-stage children develop unconscious incestuous wishes for the parent of the opposite gender and begin to view the parent of the same sex as a rival. Freud dubbed this conflict the *Oedipus complex*, after the legendary Greek king Oedipus, who unwittingly slew his father and married his mother. The female version of the Oedipus complex has been named by some followers (although not by Freud himself) the *Electra complex*, after the character of Electra, who, according to Greek legend, avenged the death of her father, King Agamemnon, by slaying her father's murderers—her own mother and her mother's lover. Freud believed the Oedipus conflict represents a central psychological conflict of early childhood and that failure to successfully resolve the conflict can set the stage for the development of psychological problems in later life.

Successful resolution of the Oedipus complex involves the boy repressing his incestuous wishes for his mother and identifying with his father. This identification leads to development of the aggressive, independent characteristics associated with the traditional masculine gender role. Successful resolution of the complex for the girl involves repression of the incestuous wishes for her father and identification with her mother, leading to the acquisition of the

Denial? Denial is a defense mechanism in which the ego fends off anxiety by preventing recognition of the true nature of a threat. Failing to take seriously warnings of health risks from cigarette smoking can be considered a form of denial.

The oral stage of psychosexual development? According to Freud, the child's early encounters with the world are largely experienced through the mouth.

Are young children interested in sex? According to Freud, even young children have sexual impulses. Freud's view of childhood sexuality shocked the scientific establishment of his day, and many of Freud's own followers believe that Freud placed too much emphasis on sexual motivation.

Fixation In Freudian theory, a constellation of personality traits associated with a particular stage of psychosexual development, resulting from either too much or too little gratification at the stage.

archetypes Primitive images or concepts that reside in the collective unconscious.

more passive, dependent characteristics traditionally associated with the feminine sex role.

The Oedipus complex comes to a point of resolution, whether fully resolved or not, by about the age of 5 or 6. From the identification with the parent of the same gender comes the internalization of parental values in the form of the superego. Children then enter the *latency stage* of psychosexual development, a period of late childhood during which sexual impulses remain in a latent state. Interests become directed toward school and play activities.

Sexual drives are once again aroused with the *genital stage,* beginning with puberty, which reaches fruition in mature sexuality, marriage, and the bearing of children. The sexual feelings toward the parent of the opposite gender that had remained repressed during the latency period emerge during adolescence but are displaced, or transferred, onto socially appropriate members of the opposite gender. In Freud's view, successful adjustment during the genital stage involves attaining sexual gratification through sexual intercourse with someone of the opposite gender, presumably within the context of marriage.

One of Freud's central beliefs is that the child may encounter conflict during each of the psychosexual stages of development. Conflict during the oral stage, for example, centers around whether or not the infant receives adequate oral gratification. Too much gratification could lead the infant to expect that everything in life is given with little or no effort on his or her part. In contrast, early weaning might lead to frustration. Too little or too much gratification at any stage could lead to **fixation** in that stage, which leads to the development of personality traits characteristic of that stage. Oral fixations could include an exaggerated desire for "oral activities," which could become expressed in later life in smoking, alcohol abuse, overeating, and nail biting. Like the infant who depends on the mother's breast for survival and gratification of oral pleasure, orally fixated adults may also become clinging and dependent in their interpersonal relationships. In Freud's view, failure to successfully resolve the conflicts of the phallic stage (i.e., the Oedipus complex) can lead to the rejection of the traditional masculine or feminine roles and to homosexuality.

Other Psychodynamic Theorists Psychodynamic theory has been shaped over the years by the contributions of psychodynamic theorists who shared certain central tenets in common with Freud, such as that behavior reflects unconscious motivation, inner conflict, and the operation of defensive responses to anxiety. However, many psychodynamic theorists deviated sharply from Freud's positions on many issues. For example, they tended to place less emphasis than Freud on basic instincts such as sex and aggression and greater emphasis on conscious choice, self-direction, and creativity.

Swiss psychiatrist Carl Jung (1875–1961) was a member of Freud's inner circle. His break with Freud came when he developed his own psychodynamic theory, which he called *analytical psychology.* Jung believed that an understanding of human behavior must incorporate the facts of self-awareness and self-direction as well as the impulses of the id and the mechanisms of defense. He believed that not only do we have a *personal* unconscious, a repository of repressed memories and impulses, but we also inherit a collective unconscious. The collective unconscious contains primitive images, or **archetypes,** which reflect on the history of our species, including vague, mysterious mythical images like the all-powerful God, the fertile and nurturing mother, the young hero, the wise old man, and themes of rebirth or resurrection. Although archetypes remain unconscious, in Jung's view, they influence our thoughts, dreams, and emotions and render us responsive to cultural themes in stories and films.

Alfred Adler (1870–1937), like Jung, had held a place in Freud's inner circle, but he broke away as he developed his own beliefs that people are basically driven by an inferiority complex, not by the sexual instinct, as Freud had maintained. For some people, feelings of inferiority are based on physical deficits and the resulting need to compensate for them. But all of us, because of our small size during childhood, encounter feelings of inferiority to some degree. These feelings lead to a powerful drive for superiority, which motivates us to achieve prominence and social dominance. In the healthy personality, however, strivings for dominance are tempered by devotion to helping other people.

Adler, like Jung, believed self-awareness plays a major role in the formation of personality. Adler spoke of a *creative self,* a self-aware aspect of personality that strives to overcome obstacles and develop the individual's potential. With the hypothesis of the creative self, Adler shifted the emphasis of psychodynamic theory from the id to the ego. Because our potentials are uniquely individual, Adler's views have been termed *individual psychology.*

Some psychodynamic theorists, such as Karen Horney (1885–1952) (pronounced HORN-eye) and Harry Stack Sullivan (1892–1949), focused on the social context of psychological problems and stressed the importance of child–parent relationships in determining the nature of later interpersonal relationships. Sullivan, for example, maintained that children of rejecting parents tend to become self-doubting and anxious. These personality features persist and impede the development of close relationships in adult life.

More recent psychodynamic models also place a greater emphasis on the self or the ego and less emphasis on the sexual instinct than Freud. Today, most psychoanalysts see people as motivated on two tiers: by the growth-oriented, conscious pursuits of the ego as well as by the more primitive, conflict-ridden drives of the id. Heinz Hartmann (1894–1970) was one of the originators of **ego psychology,** which posits that the ego has energy and motives of its own. The choices to seek an education, dedicate oneself to art and poetry, and further humanity are not merely defensive forms of sublimation, as Freud had seen them. Erik Erikson (1902–1994) attributed more importance to children's social relationships than to unconscious processes. Whereas Freud's developmental theory ends with the genital stage, beginning in early adolescence, Erikson focused on developmental processes that he believed continue throughout adulthood. The goal of adolescence, in Erikson's view, is to achieve *ego identity,* a clearly defined and firm sense of who we are and what we believe in.

The power of archetypes. One reason adventure stories such as *Lord of the Rings* and the *Star Wars* saga are so compelling is that it features archetypes such as the struggle between good and evil characters.

One popular contemporary psychodynamic approach, **object-relations theory,** focuses on how children come to develop symbolic representations of important others in their lives, especially their parents. The object-relations theorist Margaret Mahler (1897–1985) saw the process of separating from the mother during the first 3 years of life as crucial to personality development (discussed further in Chapter 13).

According to psychodynamic theory, we introject, or incorporate, into our own personalities parts of parental figures in our lives. For example, you might introject your father's strong sense of responsibility or your mother's eagerness to please others. Introjection is more powerful when we fear losing others because of death or rejection. Thus we might be particularly apt to incorporate elements of people who *disapprove* of us or who see things differently.

In Mahler's view, these symbolic representations, which are formed from images and memories of others, come to influence our perceptions and behavior. We experience internal conflict as the attitudes of introjected people battle with our own. Some of our perceptions may be distorted or seem unreal to us. Some of our impulses and behavior may seem unlike us, as if they come out of the blue. With such conflict, we may not be able to tell where the influences of other people end and our "real selves" begin. The aim of Mahler's therapeutic approach was to help clients separate their own ideas and feelings from those of the introjected objects so they could develop as individuals—as their own persons.

Psychodynamic Views on Normality and Abnormality In the Freudian model, mental health is a function of the dynamic balance among the psychic structures of id, ego, and superego (USDHHS, 1999a). In mentally healthy people, the ego is strong enough to control the instincts of the id and to withstand the condemnation of the

ego psychology Modern psychodynamic approach that focuses more on the conscious strivings of the ego than on the hypothesized unconscious functions of the id.

object-relations theory The psychodynamic viewpoint that focuses on the influences of internalized representations of the personalities of parents and other strong attachment figures (called "objects").

Karen Horney

Erik Erikson

Margaret Mahler

superego. The presence of acceptable outlets for the expression of some primitive impulses, such as the expression of mature sexuality in marriage, decreases the pressures within the id and, at the same time, lessens the burdens of the ego in repressing the remaining impulses. Being reared by reasonably tolerant parents might prevent the superego from becoming overly harsh and condemnatory.

In people with psychological disorders, the balance among the psychic structures is lopsided. Some unconscious impulses may "leak," producing anxiety or leading to psychological disorders, such as hysteria and phobias. The symptom expresses the conflict among the parts of the personality while it protects the self from recognizing the inner turmoil. A person with a fear of knives, for example, is shielded from becoming aware of her own unconscious aggressive impulses to use a knife to murder someone or attack herself. So long as the symptom is maintained (and the person avoids knives), the murderous or suicidal impulses are kept at bay. If the superego becomes overly powerful, it may create excessive feelings of guilt and lead to depression. People who intentionally hurt others without feeling guilty about it are believed to have an underdeveloped superego.

Freud believed that the underlying conflicts that give rise to psychological disorders originate in childhood and are buried in the depths of the unconscious. Through psychoanalysis, he sought to help people uncover and learn to deal with these underlying conflicts. This way, they can free themselves of the need to maintain the overt symptom.

Perpetual vigilance and defense take their toll. The ego can weaken and, in extreme cases, lose the ability to keep a lid on the id. When the urges of the id spill forth, untempered by an ego that is either weakened or underdeveloped, the result is **psychosis.** Psychosis is characterized, in general, by bizarre behavior and thoughts and by faulty perceptions of reality, such as hallucinations ("hearing voices" or seeing things that are not present). Speech may become incoherent; there may be bizarre posturing and gestures. Schizophrenia is the major form of psychosis (see Chapter 12).

Freud equated psychological health with the *abilities to love and to work*. The normal person can care deeply for other people, find sexual gratification in an intimate relationship, and engage in productive work. To accomplish these ends, sexual impulses must be expressed in a relationship with a partner of the opposite gender. Other impulses must

psychosis A severe form of disturbed behavior characterized by impaired ability to interpret reality and difficulty meeting the demands of daily life.

be channeled (sublimated) into socially productive pursuits, such as work, enjoyment of art or music, or creative expression. Other psychodynamic theorists, such as Jung and Adler, emphasized the need to develop a differentiated self—the unifying force that provides direction to behavior and helps develop a person's potential. Adler also believed that psychological health involves efforts to compensate for feelings of inferiority by striving to excel in one or more of the arenas of human endeavor. For Mahler, similarly, abnormal behavior derives from failure to develop our distinctive and individual identity.

Evaluating Psychodynamic Models Psychodynamic theory has pervaded the general culture. Even people who have never read Freud look for symbolic meanings in slips of the tongue and assume that abnormalities can be traced to early childhood. Terms like *ego* and *repression* have become commonplace, although their everyday meanings do not fully overlap with those intended by Freud.

The psychodynamic model led us to recognize that we are not transparent to ourselves (Panek, 2002)—that our behavior may be driven by hidden drives and impulses of which we are unaware or only dimly aware. Moreover, Freud's beliefs about childhood sexuality were both illuminating and controversial. Before Freud, children were perceived as pure innocents, free of sexual desire. Freud recognized, however, that young children, even infants, seek pleasure through stimulation of the oral and anal cavities and the phallic region. Yet his beliefs that primitive drives give rise to incestuous desires, intrafamily rivalries, and conflicts remain sources of controversy, even within psychodynamic circles.

Many critics, including some of Freud's followers, believe he placed too much emphasis on sexual and aggressive impulses and underemphasized social relationships. Critics have also argued that the psychic structures—the id, ego, and superego—may be little more than useful fictions, poetic ways to represent inner conflict. Many critics argue that Freud's hypothetical mental processes are not scientific concepts because they cannot be directly observed or tested. Therapists can speculate, for example, that a client "forgot" about an appointment because "unconsciously" she or he did not want to attend the session. Such unconscious motivation may not be subject to scientific verification, however. On the other hand, psychodynamically oriented researchers have developed scientific approaches to test many of Freud's concepts. They believe that a growing body of evidence supports the existence of unconscious processes that lie outside ordinary awareness, including defense mechanisms such as represssion (Cramer, 2000; Westen & Gabbard, 2002).

Learning Models

The psychodynamic models of Freud and his followers were the first major psychological theories of abnormal behavior. Other relevant psychologies also took shape early in the 20th century. The behavioral perspective is identified with the Russian physiologist Ivan Pavlov (1849–1936), the discoverer of the conditioned reflex, and the American psychologist John B. Watson (1878–1958), the father of **behaviorism.** The behavioral perspective focuses on the role of learning in explaining both normal and abnormal behavior. From a learning perspective, abnormal behavior represents the acquisition, or learning, of inappropriate, maladaptive behaviors.

From the medical and psychodynamic perspectives, abnormal behavior is *symptomatic,* respectively, of underlying biological or psychological problems. From the learning perspective, however, the abnormal behavior itself is the problem. In this perspective, abnormal behavior is learned in much the same way as normal behavior. Why do some people behave abnormally? It may be that their learning histories differ from most people's. For example, a person who was harshly punished as a child for masturbating might become anxious, as an adult, about sexuality. Poor child-rearing practices, such as capricious punishment for misconduct and failure to praise or reward good behavior, might lead to antisocial behavior. Children with abusive or neglectful parents might learn to pay more attention to inner fantasies than to the world outside and have difficulty distinguishing reality from fantasy.

behaviorism The school of psychology that defines psychology as the study of observable behavior.

Ivan Pavlov. Russian physiologist Ivan Pavlov (center, with white beard) demonstrates his apparatus for classical conditioning to students. How might the principles of classical conditioning explain the acquisition of excessive irrational fears that we refer to as phobias?

Watson and other behaviorists, such as Harvard University psychologist B. F. Skinner (1904–1990), believed that human behavior is the product of our genetic inheritance and environmental or situational influences. Like Freud, Watson and Skinner discarded concepts of personal freedom, choice, and self-direction. But whereas Freud saw us as driven by irrational forces, behaviorists see us as products of environmental influences that shape and manipulate our behavior. Behaviorists also believed that we should limit the study of psychology to behavior itself rather than focus on underlying motivations. Therapy, in this view, consists of shaping behavior rather than seeking insight into the workings of the mind. Behaviorists focus on the roles of two forms of learning in shaping both normal and abnormal behavior, classical conditioning and operant conditioning.

Role of Classical Conditioning The Russian physiologist Ivan Pavlov discovered the conditioned reflex (now called a *conditioned response*) quite by accident. In his laboratory, he harnessed dogs to an apparatus like that in Figure 2.5 to study their salivary response to food. Along the way he observed that the animals would salivate and secrete gastric juices even before they started to eat. These responses appeared to be elicited by the sound of the food cart as it was wheeled into the room. So Pavlov undertook an experiment that showed that animals could learn to salivate in response to other stimuli, such as the sound of a bell, if these stimuli were *associated* with feeding.

Because dogs don't normally salivate to the sound of bells, Pavlov reasoned that they had acquired this response. He called it a **conditioned response** (CR), or conditioned reflex, because it had been paired with what he called an **unconditioned stimulus** (US)—in this case, food—which naturally elicited salivation (see Figure 2.6). The salivation to food, an unlearned response, Pavlov called the **unconditioned response** (UR), and the bell, a previously neutral stimulus, he called the **conditioned stimulus** (CS).

Can you recognize **classical conditioning** in your everyday life? Do you flinch in the waiting room at the sound of the dentist's drill? The sound of the drill may be a conditioned stimulus that elicits conditioned responses of fear and muscle tension.

Phobias or excessive fears may be acquired by classical conditioning. For instance, a person may develop a phobia for riding on elevators following a

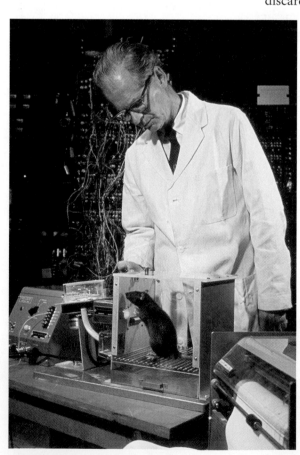

B. F. Skinner

FIGURE 2.5 The apparatus used in Ivan Pavlov's experiments on conditioning.
Pavlov used an apparatus such as this to demonstrate the process of conditioning. To the left is a two-way mirror, behind which a researcher rings a bell. After ringing the bell, meat is placed on the dog's tongue. Following several pairings of the bell and the meat, the dog learns to salivate in response to the bell. The animal's saliva passes through the tube to a vial, where its quantity may be taken as a measure of the strength of the conditioned response.

traumatic experience on an elevator. In this example, a previously neutral stimulus (elevator) becomes paired or associated with an aversive stimulus (trauma), which leads to the conditioned response (phobia).

From the learning perspective, normal behavior involves responding adaptively to stimuli, including conditioned stimuli. After all, if we do not learn to be afraid of putting our hand too close to a hot stove after one or two experiences of being burned or nearly burned, we might repeatedly suffer unnecessary burns. On the other hand, acquiring inappropriate and maladaptive fears on the basis of conditioning may cripple our efforts to function in the world. Chapter 6 explains how conditioning may help explain anxiety disorders such as phobias and posttraumatic stress disorder. In Chapter 10 we consider how the principles of classical conditioning can help explain the development of a common sleep disorder, insomnia.

Role of Operant Conditioning Classical conditioning can explain the development of simple, reflexive responses, such as salivating to cues associated with food, as well as

conditioned response In classical conditioning, a learned response to a previously neutral stimulus.

unconditioned stimulus A stimulus that elicits an unlearned response.

unconditioned response An unlearned response.

conditioned stimulus A previously neutral stimulus that evokes a conditioned response after repeated pairings with an unconditioned stimulus that had previously evoked that response.

classical conditioning A form of learning in which a response to one stimulus can be made to occur to another stimulus by pairing or associating the two stimuli.

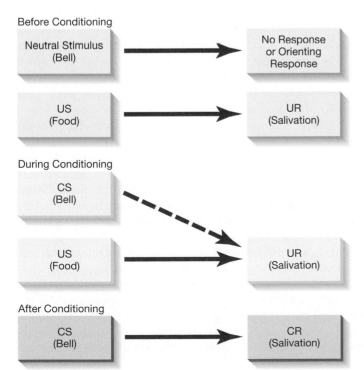

FIGURE 2.6 Schematic diagram of the process of classical conditioning.
Before conditioning, food (an unconditioned stimulus, or US) placed on a dog's tongue will naturally elicit salivation (an unconditioned response, or UR). The bell, however, is a neutral stimulus that may elicit an orienting response but not salivation. During conditioning, the bell (the conditioned stimulus, or CS) is rung while food (the US) is placed on the dog's tongue. After several conditioning trials have occurred, the bell (the CS) will elicit salivation (the conditioned response, or CR) when it is rung, even though it is not accompanied by food (the US). The dog is said to have been conditioned, or to have learned to display the conditioned response (CR) in response to the conditioned stimulus (CS). Learning theorists have suggested that irrational excessive fears of harmless stimuli may be acquired through principles of classical conditioning.

operant conditioning A form of learning in which behavior is acquired and strengthened when it is reinforced.

reinforcement A stimulus or event that increases the frequency of the response that it follows.

reward A pleasant stimulus or event that increases the frequency of the response that it follows.

positive reinforcers Reinforcers that, when introduced, increase the frequency of the preceding behavior.

negative reinforcers Reinforcers that on removal increase the frequency of the preceding behavior.

punishment Application of aversive or painful stimuli that reduces the frequency of the behavior it follows.

TRUTH or FICTION? *REVISITED*

Punishment does not eliminate undesirable behavior.

☑ **TRUE.** Punishment does not eliminate an undesirable behavior, but only suppresses it. The behavior may return when it is no longer punished.

the emotional response of fear to stimuli that have been paired with painful or aversive stimuli. But classical conditioning does not account for more complex behaviors, such as studying, working, socializing, or preparing meals. The behavioral psychologist B. F. Skinner (1938) called these types of complex behaviors *operant responses* because they operate on the environment to produce effects or consequences. In **operant conditioning,** responses are acquired and strengthened by their consequences.

We acquire responses or skills, such as raising our hand in class, that lead to **reinforcement.** Reinforcers are changes in the environment (stimuli) that increase the frequency of the preceding behavior.

A **reward** is a *pleasant* stimulus that increases the frequency of behavior, and so it is a type of reinforcer. Skinner found the concept of reinforcement to be preferable to that of reward because it is defined in terms of relationships between observed behaviors and environmental effects. In contrast to *reward,* the meaning of reinforcement does not depend on conjectures about what is "pleasant" to another person or lower animal. Many psychologists use the words *reinforcement* and *reward* interchangeably, however.

Behaviors that lead to rewarding consequences are strengthened—that is, they are more likely to occur again. Over time, such behaviors become habits (Staddon & Cerutti, 2003). For example, you likely acquired the habit of raising your hand in class on the basis of experiences early in grade school when your teachers responded to you only if you first raised your hand.

Skinner identified two types of reinforcers. **Positive reinforcers** boost the frequency of a behavior when they are introduced or presented. Most of Skinner's work focused on studying operant conditioning in animals, such as pigeons. If a pigeon gets food when it pecks a button, it will contine to peck a button until it has eaten its fill. If we get a friendly response from people when we hold the door open for them, we're more likely to develop the habit of opening the door for others. **Negative reinforcers** increase the frequency of behavior when they are *removed*. If picking up a crying child stops the crying, the behavior (picking up the child) is negatively reinforced (made stronger) by the removal of the negative reinforcer (the crying, an aversive stimulus).

Adaptive, normal behavior involves learning responses or skills that lead to reinforcement. We learn behaviors that allow us to obtain positive reinforcers, such as food, money, and approval, and that help us remove or avoid negative reinforcers, such as pain and disapproval. But if our early learning environments do not provide opportunities for learning new skills, we might be hampered in our efforts to develop the skills needed to obtain reinforcers. A lack of social skills, for example, may reduce our opportunities for social reinforcement (approval or praise from others), which may lead in turn to depression and social isolation. In Chapter 8, we examine links between changes in reinforcement levels and the development of depression. In Chapter 12, we examine how principles of reinforcement are incorporated in learning-based treatment programs to help people with schizophrenia develop more adapative social behaviors.

Punishment can be considered the flip side of reinforcement. Punishments are aversive stimuli that *decrease* the frequency of the behavior they follow. Punishment may take many forms, including physical punishment (spanking or use of other painful stimuli), removal of a reinforcing stimulus (turning off the TV), assessment of monetary penalties (parking tickets, etc.), taking away privileges ("You're grounded!"), or removal from a reinforcing environment ("time-out").

Before going further, let us distinguish between two terms that are often confused: *negative reinforcement* and *punishment.* The confusion arises from the fact that an aversive or painful stimulus can serve as either a negative reinforcer or a punishment, depending on the situation. With punishment, the *introduction* or application of the aversive or painful stimulus weakens the preceding behavior. With negative reinforcement, the removal of the aversive or painful stimulus strengthens the preceding behavior. A baby's crying can serve as a punishment (if it weakens the preceding behavior, such as turning your attention away from the baby) or a negative reinforcer (if it strengthens the behavior that leads to its removal, such as picking the baby up).

Punishment, especially physical punishment, may not eliminate undesirable behavior, though it may suppress it for the moment. The behavior may return when the punishment is withdrawn. Another limitation of punishment is that it does not lead to the development of more desirable alternative behaviors. It may also encourage people to withdraw from such learning situations. Punished children may cut classes, drop out of school, or run away. Moreover, punishment may generate anger and hostility rather than constructive learning and may cross the boundary into abuse, especially when it is repetitive and severe. Child abuse figures prominently in many abnormal behavior patterns, including some types of personality disorders (Chapter 13) and dissociative disorders (Chapter 7).

Psychologists recognize that reinforcement is more desirable than punishment. But rewarding good behavior requires paying attention to it, not just to misbehavior. Some children who develop conduct problems gain attention from others only when they misbehave. Consequently, other people may be inadvertently reinforcing these children for undesirable behavior. Learning theorists point out that adults need to teach children desirable behavior and regularly reinforce them for displaying it.

Let us now consider a contemporary model of learning, called *social-cognitive theory* (formerly called *social-learning theory*), which considers the role of cognitive factors in learning and behavior.

Social-Cognitive Theory **Social-cognitive theory** represents the contributions of theorists such as Albert Bandura (1925–), Julian B. Rotter (1916–), and Walter Mischel (1930–). Social-cognitive theorists emphasize the roles of thinking, or cognition, and of learning by observation, or **modeling,** in human behavior (Bandura, 2004). A phobia for spiders, for example, may be learned by observing the fearful reactions of others in real life, on television, or in the movies.

Social-cognitive theorists believe that people have an impact on their environment, just as their environment has an impact on them (Bandura, 2001, 2004). Social-cognitive theorists agree with traditional behaviorists like Watson and Skinner that theories of human nature should be tied to observable behavior. However, they argue that factors *within* the person, such as **expectancies** and the values placed on particular goals, also need to be considered in explaining human behavior. For example, we will see in Chapter 9 that people who hold more positive expectancies about the effects of a drug are more likely to use the drug and to use larger quantities of the drug than are people with less positive expectancies.

Evaluating Learning Models Learning perspectives have spawned a model of therapy, called *behavior therapy* (also called *behavior modification*), that involves systematically applying learning principles to help people change their behavior (see Chapter 4). Behavior therapy techniques have helped people overcome a wide range of psychological problems, including phobias and other anxiety disorders, sexual dysfunctions, and depression. Moreover, reinforcement-based programs are now widely used in helping parents learn better parenting skills and helping children learn in the classroom.

Critics contend that behaviorism alone cannot explain the richness of human behavior and that human experience cannot be reduced to observable responses. Many learning theorists, too—especially social-cognitive theorists—have been dissatisfied with the strict behavioristic view that environmental influences—rewards and punishments—mechanically control our behavior. Humans experience thoughts and dreams and formulate goals and aspirations; behaviorism does not seem to address much of what it means to be human. Social-cognitive theorists have broadened the scope of traditional behaviorism, but critics claim that social-cognitive theory places too little emphasis on genetic contributions to behavior and doesn't provide a

social-cognitive theory A learning-based theory that emphasizes observational learning and incorporates roles for both situational and cognitive variables in determining behavior.

modeling Learning by observing and imitating the behavior of others.

expectancies Beliefs about expected outcomes.

full enough account of subjective experience, such as self-awareness and the flow of consciousness. As we'll see next, subjective experience takes center stage in humanistic models.

Humanistic Models

A "third force" in modern psychology emerged during the mid-20th century—humanistic psychology. American psychologists Carl Rogers (1902–1987) and Abraham Maslow (1908–1970) believed that people have an inborn tendency toward **self-actualization**—to strive to become all they are capable of being. Each of us possesses a singular cluster of traits and talents that gives us our own set of feelings and needs and our own perspective on life. By recognizing and accepting our genuine needs and feelings, by being true to ourselves, we live *authentically*, with meaning and purpose. We may not decide to act out every wish and fancy, but awareness of our authentic feelings and subjective experiences can help us make more meaningful choices.

To understand abnormal behavior, in the humanist's view, we need to understand the roadblocks that people encounter in striving for self-actualization and authenticity. To accomplish this, psychologists must learn to view the world from clients' own perspectives, because clients' subjective views of their world lead them to interpret and evaluate their experiences in either self-enhancing or self-defeating ways. The humanistic viewpoint involves the attempt to understand the subjective experience of others, the stream of conscious experiences people have of "being in the world."

Humanistic Concepts of Abnormal Behavior Rogers held that abnormal behavior results from a distorted concept of the self. Parents can help children develop a positive self-concept by showing them **unconditional positive regard;** that is, by prizing them and showing them that they are worthy of love irrespective of their be-

Observational learning. According to social-cognitive theory, much human behavior is acquired through modeling, or observational learning.

self-actualization In humanistic psychology, the tendency to strive to become all that one is capable of being. The motive that drives one to reach one's full potential and express one's unique capabilities.

Carl Rogers and Abraham Maslow. Two of the principal forces in humanistic psychology.

havior at any given time. Parents may disapprove of a certain behavior but need to convey to their children that the behavior is undesirable, not the child. However, when parents show children **conditional positive regard**—accept them only when they behave in the way the parents want them to behave—the children may learn to disown all the thoughts, feelings, and behaviors their parents have rejected. Children will learn to develop *conditions of worth,* that is, they will think of themselves as worthwhile only if they behave in certain approved ways. For example, children whose parents seem to value them only when they are compliant may deny to themselves that they ever feel angry. Children in some families learn that it is unacceptable to hold their own ideas, lest they depart from their parents' views. Parental disapproval causes them to see themselves as "bad" and their feelings as wrong, selfish, or even evil. In order to retain their self-esteem, they may have to deny their genuine feelings or disown parts of themselves. The result can be a distorted *self-concept:* the children become strangers to their true selves.

Rogers believed we become anxious when we sense that our feelings and ideas are inconsistent with a distorted self-concept that mirrors what others expect us to be—for example, if our parents expected us to be docile and obedient but we sense ourselves becoming angry or defiant. Because anxiety is unpleasant, we may deny to ourselves that these feelings and ideas even exist. And so the actualization of our authentic self is bridled. We channel our psychological energy not toward growth but toward continued denial and self-defense. Under such conditions, we cannot hope to perceive our genuine values or personal talents. The result is frustration and dissatisfaction, which set the stage for abnormal behavior.

According to the humanists, we cannot fulfill all the wishes of others and remain true to ourselves. This does not mean that self-actualization invariably leads to conflict. Rogers believed that people hurt one another or become antisocial in their behavior only when they are frustrated in their endeavors to reach their unique potentials. When parents and others treat children with love and tolerance for their differences, children, too, grow up to be loving—even if some of their values and preferences differ from their parents' choices.

In Rogers's view, the pathway to self-actualization involves a process of self-discovery and self-acceptance, of getting in touch with our true feelings, accepting them as our own, and acting in ways that genuinely reflect them. These are the goals of Rogers's method of psychotherapy, called *client-centered therapy* or *person-centered therapy.*

Evaluating Humanistic Models The strength of humanistic models in understanding abnormal behavior lies largely in their focus on conscious experience and their therapy methods that guide people toward self-discovery and self-acceptance. The humanistic movement brought concepts of free choice, inherent goodness, personal responsibility, and authenticity into modern psychology. Ironically, the primary strength of the humanistic approach—its focus on conscious experience—may also be its primary weakness. Conscious experience is private and subjective, which makes it difficult to quantify and study objectively. How can psychologists be certain they accurately perceive the world through the eyes of their clients? Humanists may counter that we should not shrink from the challenge of studying consciousness because to do so would deny an essential aspect of what it means to be human.

Critics also claim that the concept of self-actualization—which is so basic to Maslow and Rogers—cannot be proved or disproved. Like a psychic structure, a self-actualizing force is not directly measurable or observable. It is inferred from its supposed effects. Self-actualization also yields circular explanations for behavior. When someone is observed engaging in striving, what do we learn by attributing striving to a self-actualizing tendency? The source of the tendency remains a mystery. Similarly, when someone is observed *not* to be striving, what do we gain by attributing the lack of endeavor to a blocked or frustrated self-actualizing tendency? We must still determine the source of frustration.

unconditional positive regard Valuing other people as having basic worth regardless of their behavior at a particular time.

conditional positive regard Valuing other people on the basis of whether their behavior meets one's approval.

Self-actualization. Humanistic theorists believe that there exists in each of us a drive toward self-actualization—to become all that we are capable of being. In the humanistic view, each of us, like artist Geraldine Pitts, shown here with one of her paintings, is unique. No two people follow quite the same pathway toward self-actualization.

TRUTH or FICTION? *REVISITED*

Children may acquire a distorted self-concept that mirrors what others expect them to be but which does not reflect who they truly are.

☑ **TRUE.** According to Rogers, children can develop a distorted self-concept that mirrors what others expect them to be but which is not true to themselves.

The makings of unconditional positive regard. Rogers believed that parents can help their children develop self-esteem and set them on the road toward self-actualization by showing them unconditional positive regard—prizing them on the basis of their inner worth, regardless of their behavior of the moment.

Cognitive Models

The word *cognitive* derives from the Latin *cognitio*, meaning "knowledge." Cognitive theorists study the cognitions—the thoughts, beliefs, expectations, and attitudes—that accompany and may underlie abnormal behavior. They focus on how reality is colored by our expectations, attitudes, and so forth, and how inaccurate or biased processing of information about the world—and our places within it—can give rise to abnormal behavior. Cognitive theorists believe that our interpretations of the events in our lives, and not the events themselves, determine our emotional states.

Information-Processing Models Many cognitive psychologists apply concepts of computer science to human cognition. Computers process information to solve problems. Information is fed into the computer (encoded so that it can be accepted by the computer as input) and placed in *memory* while it is manipulated. You can also place the information permanently in *storage*, on a floppy disk, a hard disk, or another device. Information-processing theorists discuss human cognition in terms such as *input* (based on perception), *manipulation* (interpreting or transforming information), *storage* (placing information in memory), *retrieval* (accessing information from memory), and *output* (acting on the information). Psychological disorders are seen as disturbances in these processes. The blocking or distortion of input or the faulty storage, retrieval, or manipulation of information can lead to distorted output (e.g., bizarre behavior). People with schizophrenia, for example, frequently jump from topic to topic in a disorganized fashion, which may reflect problems in retrieving and manipulating information. They also seem to have difficulty focusing their attention and filtering out extraneous stimuli, such as distracting noises, which may represent problems in the initial processing of input from their senses.

Manipulation of information may also be distorted by what cognitive therapists call *cognitive distortions,* or errors in thinking. For example, people who are depressed tend to develop an unduly negative view of their personal situation by exaggerating the importance of unfortunate events they experience, such as receiving a poor evaluation at work or being rejected by a dating partner (Meichenbaum, 1993). Cognitive theorists such as Albert Ellis (1913–) and Aaron Beck (1921–) have postulated that distorted or irrational thinking patterns can lead to emotional problems and maladaptive behavior.

Social-cognitive theorists, who share many basic ideas with the cognitive theorists, focus on the ways in which social information is encoded. For example, aggressive boys and adolescents are likely to incorrectly encode other people's behavior as threatening (see Chapter 14). They assume other people intend them ill when they do not. Aggressive children and adults may behave in ways that elicit coercive or hostile behavior from others, which serves to confirm their aggressive expectations (Meichenbaum, 1993). Rapists, especially date rapists, may misread a woman's expressed wishes. They may wrongly assume, for example, that the woman who says "no" really means yes and is merely playing "hard to get."

Albert Ellis Psychologist Albert Ellis (1977b, 1993), a prominent cognitive theorist, believes that troubling events in themselves do not lead to anxiety, depression, or disturbed behavior. Rather, it is the irrational beliefs we hold about unfortunate experiences that foster negative emotions and maladaptive behavior. Consider someone who loses a job and becomes anxious and despondent about it. It may seem that being fired is the direct cause of the person's misery, but the misery actually stems from the person's beliefs about the loss, not directly from the loss itself.

Ellis uses an "ABC approach" to explain the causes of the misery. Being fired is an *activating event* (A). The ultimate outcome, or *consequence* (C), is emotional distress. But the activating event (A) and the consequences (C) are mediated by various *beliefs* (B). Some of these beliefs might include "That job was the major thing in my life," "What a useless washout I am," "My family will go hungry," "I'll never be able to find another job as good," "I can't do a thing about it." These exaggerated and irrational beliefs compound depression, nurture helplessness, and distract us from evaluating what to do.

The situation can be diagrammed like this:

ACTIVATING EVENT → BELIEF → CONSEQUENCES

Ellis points out that apprehension about the future and feelings of disappointment are perfectly normal when people face losses. However, the adoption of irrational beliefs leads people to catastrophize their disappointments, leading to profound distress and states of depression. Irrational beliefs—"I must have the love and approval of nearly everyone who is important to me or else I'm a worthless and unlovable person"—impair coping ability. In his later writings, Ellis emphasized the demanding nature of irrational or self-defeating beliefs—tendencies to impose "musts" and "shoulds" on ourselves (Ellis, 1993, 1997). Ellis notes that the desire for others' approval is understandable, but it is irrational to assume that one must have it to survive or to feel worthwhile. It would be marvelous to excel in everything we do, but it's absurd to demand it of ourselves or believe that we couldn't stand it if we failed to measure up. Ellis developed a model of therapy, called *rational-emotive behavior therapy* (REBT), to help people dispute these irrational beliefs and substitute more rational ones. Ellis admits that childhood experiences are involved in the origins of irrational beliefs, but he maintains that it is repetition of these beliefs in the "here and now" that continues to make us miserable. For most people who are anxious and depressed, the key to greater happiness does not lie in discovering and liberating deep-seated conflicts, but in recognizing and modifying irrational self-demands.

Aaron Beck   Another prominent cognitive theorist, psychiatrist Aaron Beck, proposes that depression may result from errors in thinking or "cognitive distortions," such as judging oneself entirely on the basis of one's flaws or failures and interpreting events in a negative light (through blue-colored glasses, as it were) (A. T. Beck et al., 1979). Beck stresses the four basic types of cognitive distortions that contribute to emotional distress:

1. *Selective abstraction.* People may *selectively abstract* (focus exclusively on) the parts of their experiences that reflect on their flaws and ignore evidence of their competencies. For example, a student may focus entirely on the one mediocre grade received on a math test and ignore all the higher grades.

2. *Overgeneralization.* People may *overgeneralize* from a few isolated experiences. For example, a person may believe he will never marry because he was rejected by a date.

3. *Magnification.* People may blow out of proportion, or *magnify,* the importance of unfortunate events. For example, a student may catastrophize a bad test grade by jumping to the conclusion that she will flunk out of college and her life will be ruined.

4. *Absolutist thinking.* Absolutist thinking is seeing the world in black-and-white terms, rather than in shades of gray. Absolutist thinkers may assume that a work evaluation less than a total rave is a total failure.

Like Ellis, Beck has developed a major model of therapy, called *cognitive therapy,* that focuses on helping individuals with psychological disorders identify and correct faulty ways of thinking.

Evaluating Cognitive Models   As we'll see in later chapters, cognitive theorists have had an enormous impact on our understanding of abnormal behavior patterns and development of therapeutic approaches. The overlap between the learning-based and cognitive approaches is best represented by the emergence of *cognitive-behavioral therapy* (CBT), a form of therapy that focuses on modifying self-defeating beliefs in addition to overt behaviors.

Albert Ellis. Cognitive theorist Albert Ellis believes that negative emotions arise from the judgments we make about the events we experience, not from the events themselves.

TRUTH or FICTION? *REVISITED*

According to a leading cognitive theorist, emotional distress is caused by the beliefs people hold about their life experiences, not by the experiences themselves.

☑ **TRUE.** Ellis believed that emotional distress is determined by the beliefs we hold about events we experience, not by the events themselves.

Aaron Beck. Aaron Beck, a leading cognitive theorist, focuses on how errors in thinking, or cognitive distortions, set the stage for negative emotional reactions in the face of unfortunate events.

A major issue concerning cognitive perspectives is their range of applicability. Cognitive therapists have largely focused on emotional disorders relating to anxiety and depression. They have had less impact on the development of treatment approaches, or conceptual models, of more severe forms of disturbed behavior, such as schizophrenia. Moreover, in the case of depression, it remains unclear, as we see in Chapter 8, whether distorted thinking patterns are causes of depression or are themselves effects of depression.

THE SOCIOCULTURAL PERSPECTIVE

Does abnormal behavior arise from forces within the person, as the psychodynamic theorists propose, or from learned maladaptive behaviors, as the learning theorists suggest? Or, as the *sociocultural perspective* proposes, does a fuller accounting of abnormal behavior require that we consider the roles of social and cultural factors, including factors relating to ethnicity, gender, and social class? As we noted in Chapter 1, sociocultural theorists seek causes of abnormal behavior in the failures of society rather than in the person. Some of the more radical psychosocial theorists, like Thomas Szasz, even deny the existence of psychological disorders or mental illness. Szasz (1961, 2000) argues that "abnormal" is merely a label society attaches to people whose behavior deviates from accepted social norms. According to Szasz, this label is used to stigmatize social deviants.

Throughout the text we examine relationships between abnormal behavior patterns and sociocultural factors such as gender, ethnicity, and socioeconomic status. Here let us examine recent research on relationships between ethnicity and mental health.

Ethnicity and Mental Health

When Europeans first arrived on America's shores, the land was populated solely by Native Americans. By the time the United States achieved nationhood, the numbers of people of European descent were approaching those of Native Americans. During the 19th century, the nation became predominantly populated by White people. Although Euro-Americans (also called European Americans or non-Hispanic White Americans) remain in the majority today, the nation is becoming increasingly ethnically diverse, as a result of both an excess of births over deaths among U.S. ethnic groups and contemporary trends in immigration.

Figure 2.7 shows estimates of the ethnic composition of the U.S. population in 2005 and in the year 2050. Presently, African Americans, whose ancestors were forcibly brought to this country and enslaved, represent about 12% of the population. Latinos (Hispanic Americans) account for about 13% of the population, whereas Asian Americans/Pacific Islanders account for about 4% and Native Americans for nearly 1%. The terms *Hispanic American* or *Latino(a)* refer to persons of Mexican, Puerto Rican, Cuban, or other Central and South American or Spanish origin (USDHHS, 1999a).

The term *minority* is quickly becoming something of a misnomer, as traditionally identified minority groups now comprise the majority in many U.S. cities and in the nation's most populous state, California (Purdum, 2001, Schmitt, 2001a). Euro-Americans will constitute but the barest majority of the population by the year 2050 (see Figure 2.8). The largest anticipated increase will be among Latinos (Hispanic Americans), as their population ranks are expected to jump to about 24% by the year 2050. Latinos (Hispanics) now represent the nation's largest minority group, having surpassed African Americans for the first time in the nation's history (Clemetson, 2003; El Nasser, 2003; Navarro, 2004).

Ethnic designations are general categories that encompass many different subgroups. For example, Latinos include Spanish-speaking

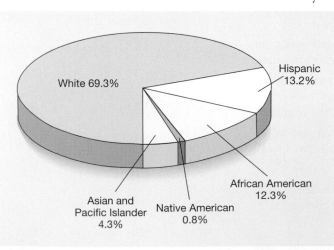

FIGURE 2.7 Ethnic/racial breakdown of the U.S. population in the year 2005 (est.).

Source: U.S. Census Bureau, Population Division, Population Projections Branch

people who may trace their heritage to Mexico, Puerto Rico, or Colombia. The population of Asian Americans/ Pacific Islanders includes people whose backgrounds and ancestries represent areas as diverse as China, Japan, Korea, Indochina, Thailand, the Philippines, India, and Pakistan. Asian Americans may perceive themselves as Filipino Americans or Chinese Americans rather than Asian Americans per se. When considering racial or ethnic distinctions, we must take into account differences among cultural and ethnic subgroups within our own culture.

We also need to recognize that traditional racial or ethnic distinctions are becoming increasingly blurry as increasing numbers of people in the United States and Canada identify themselves as biracial, multiracial, or multiethnic (Kristof, 2002; Meacham, 2000). Individuals of multiracial background, such as golfer Tiger Woods, baseball player Derek Jeter, and singer Mariah Carey, cannot easily be classified according to traditional racial groupings (See, 1999). Nearly seven million U.S. residents described themselves as multiracial in the most recent population census (Schmitt, 2001a, 2001b). Young people today are twice as likely as their parents to consider themselves multiracial (Takahashi, 2001).

Given the increasing ethnic diversity of the population, researchers have begun to study ethnic group differences in the prevalence of psychological disorders. Knowing that a disorder disproportionately affects one group or another can help planners direct prevention and treatment programs to the groups that are most in need. Researchers recognize that income level or socioeconomic status must be considered when comparing rates of a given diagnosis across ethnic groups. We also need to account for differences among ethnic subgroups, such as differences among the various subgroups that comprise the Hispanic American and Asian American populations. We find, for example, higher levels of depression among Hispanic immigrants to the United States from Central America than from Mexico, even when considering differences in educational backgrounds (Salgado de Snyder, Cervantes, & Padilla, 1990).

We should be cautious—and think critically—when interpreting ethnic group differences in rates of diagnoses of psychological disorders. Might these differences reflect ethnic or racial differences, or differences in other factors on which groups may vary, such as socioeconomic level, living conditions, or cultural backgrounds?

Prevalence rates of mental disorders are found to be higher among African Americans than among Euro-Americans (USDHHS, 1999a). However, these differences disappear when we control for socioeconomic status. In other words, the higher rates of mental disorder among African Americans are a function of their generally lower socioeconomic status, not their race or ethnicity. Evidence also shows few differences in rates of mental disorders between Hispanic Americans and Euro-Americans (USDHHS, 1999a).

Native Americans, on the whole, are among the most impoverished ethnic groups in the United States and Canada. Like other socially and economically disadvantaged groups, Native Americans also suffer from a much greater prevalence of mental health problems, including alcoholism, depression, suicide, drug abuse, and delinquency (T. J. Young & French, 1996). Native Americans, for example, have alcohol-related disorders at a rate six times that of other Americans (Rabasca, 2000a). The death rate due to suicide among adolescents in the 10- to 14-year-old age range is about four times higher among Native Americans than among other ethnic groups. Male Native American adolescents and young adults have the highest suicide rates in the nation (USDHHS, 1999a).

Asian Americans typically show lower rates of psychological disorders than the general U.S. population (Chang, 2002). But there are exceptions. When you envision stereotypes such as hula dancing, luaus, and wide tropical beaches, you may assume that Native Hawaiians are a carefree people. Reality paints a different picture, however. One reason for studying the relationship between ethnicity and abnormal behavior is to debunk er-

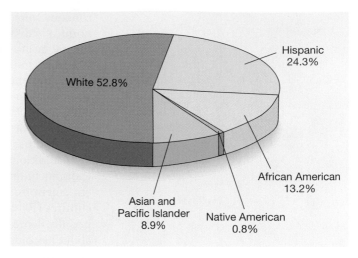

FIGURE 2.8 Projected ethnic/racial breakdown of the U.S. population in the year 2050.

Source: U.S. Census Bureau, Population Division, Population Projections Branch

TRUTH or FICTION? *REVISITED*

Rates of mental disorders are generally higher among African Americans than Euro-Americans, even when we account for income differences between these groups.

☑ **FALSE.** Rates of mental disorders overall are no higher among African Americans than those of Euro-Americans when differences in socioeconomic levels are taken into account.

roneous stereotypes. Native Hawaiians, like other Native American groups, are economically disadvantaged and suffer a disproportionate share of physical diseases and mental health problems. The death rate for Native Hawaiians is 34% higher than that of the general U.S. population, largely because of an increased rate of serious diseases, including cancer and heart disease (Mokuau, 1990). Native Hawaiians also have a 5- to 10-year lower life expectancy than other groups in Hawaii. Compared to other Hawaiians, Native Hawaiians experience higher rates of mental health problems, including higher suicide rates among males, higher rates of alcoholism and drug abuse, and higher rates of antisocial behavior.

In addition to economic disadvantage, the mental health problems of Native Americans, including Native Hawaiians, may at least partly reflect alienation and disenfranchisement from the land and a way of life that resulted from colonization by European cultures (Rabasca, 2000a). Native peoples often attribute mental health problems, especially depression and alcoholism, to the collapse of their traditional culture brought about by colonization (Timpson et al., 1988). Researchers recount how a Native Canadian elder in northwestern Ontario explained depression in his people (Timpson et al., 1988, p. 6):

> Before the White Man came into our world we had our own way of worshipping the Creator. We had our own church and rituals. When hunting was good, people would gather together to give gratitude. This gave us close contact with the Creator. There were many different rituals depending on the tribe. People would dance in the hills and play drums to give recognition to the Great Spirit. It was like talking to the Creator and living daily with its spirit. Now people have lost this. They can't use these methods and have lost conscious contact with this high power. The more distant we are from the Creator the more complex things are because we have no sense of direction. We don't recognize where life is from.

The depression so common among indigenous or native peoples apparently reflects the loss of a relationship with the world that was based on maintaining harmony with nature (Timpson et al., 1988). The description of the loss of this special relationship reminds us of the Western concept of alienation.

Whatever the underlying differences in psychopathology among ethnic groups, members of ethnic minority groups tend to underutilize mental health services compared to European (non-Hispanic White) Americans (USDHHS, 1999a). Those who do seek services are more likely to drop out prematurely from treatment. In Chapter 4 we consider barriers that limit the utilization of mental health services by various ethnic minority groups in our society.

Evaluating the Sociocultural Perspective

Lending support to the link between social class and psychological disturbance, a classic research study in New Haven, Connecticut, showed that people from the lower socioeconomic groups were more likely to be institutionalized for psychiatric problems (Hollingshead & Redlich, 1958). One reason may be that the poor have less access to private outpatient care.

An alternative view, the **social causation model,** holds that people from lower socioeconomic groups are at greater risk of severe behavior problems because living in poverty subjects them to a greater level of social stress than that faced by more well-to-do people (Costello et al., 2003). Yet another view, the **downward drift hypothesis,** suggests that problem behaviors, such as alcoholism, lead people to drift downward in social status, thereby explaining the linkage between low socioeconomic status and severe behavior problems.

Investigators recently had an opportunity to put the social causation model to the test. They focused on mental health problems among children on an American Indian reservation both before and after the introduction of a casino. The casino brought consid-

social causation model The belief that social stressors, such as poverty, account for the greater risk of severe psychological disorders among people of lower socioeconomic status.

downward drift hypothesis The theory that explains the linkage between low socioeconomic status and behavior problems by suggesting that problem behaviors lead people to drift downward in social status.

Roots of abnormal behavior? Sociocultural theorists believe that the roots of abnormal behavior are found not in the individual but in the social ills of society, such as poverty, social decay, discrimination based on race and gender, and lack of economic opportunity.

erable wealth to the previously impoverished Indian community, helping many families to rise out of poverty. Prior to the casino, Indian children showed a high rate of problem behaviors and psychiatric symptoms of depression and anxiety. But four years after the money from the casino began to flow to the community, Indian children whose families were no longer below the poverty line showed a significant reduction in problem behaviors. Levels of anxiety and depression were not reduced, however. This research lacked the experimental controls needed to firm up evidence of cause and effect, but it lends support to social causation model for at least some forms of problem behavior (Costello et al., 2003; Rutter, 2003).

Sociocultural theorists have focused much needed attention on the social stressors that can lead to abnormal behavior. Throughout the text we consider how sociocultural factors relating to gender, race, ethnicity, and lifestyle inform our understanding of abnormal behavior and our response to people deemed mentally ill. In Chapter 4, we consider how issues relating to race, culture, and ethnicity impact the therapeutic process.

THE BIOPSYCHOSOCIAL PERSPECTIVE

We have seen that there are several models or perspectives for understanding and treating psychological disorders. The fact that there are different ways of looking at the same phenomenon doesn't mean that one model must be right and the others wrong. No one theoretical perspective can account for the many complex forms of abnormal behavior we encounter in this text. Each perspective contributes something to our understanding, but none offers a complete view. Table 2.3 presents an overview of these perspectives.

The *biopsychosocial perspective* invites us to consider how multiple factors—biological, psychological, and social—are linked in the development of abnormal behavior patterns (Kiesler, 1999). For some disorders, the causes may be primarily or even ex-

TABLE 2.3

Perspectives on Abnormal Behavior

	Model	Focus	Key Questions
Biological Perspective	Medical model	Biological underpinnings of abnormal behavior	What role is played by neurotransmitters in abnormal behavior? By genetics? By brain abnormalities?
Psychological Perspective	Psychodynamic models	Unconscious conflicts and motives underlying abnormal behavior	How do particular symptoms represent or symbolize unconscious conflicts? What are the childhood roots of a person's problem?
	Learning models	Learning experiences that shape the development of abnormal behavior	How are abnormal patterns of behavior learned? What role does the environment play in explaining abnormal behavior?
	Humanistic models	Roadblocks that block self-awareness and self-acceptance	How do a person's emotional problems reflect a distorted self-image? What roadblocks did the person encounter in the path toward self-acceptance and self-realization?
	Cognitive models	Faulty thinking underlying abnormal behavior	What styles of thinking characterize people with particular types of psychological disorders? What role do personal beliefs, thoughts, and ways of interpreting events play in the development of abnormal behavior patterns?
Sociocultural Perspective		Social ills contributing to the development of abnormal behavior, such as poverty, racism, and prolonged unemployment; relationships between abnormal behavior and ethnicity, gender, culture, and socioeconomic level	What relationships exist between social-class status and risks of psychological disorders? Are there gender or ethnic group differences in various disorders? How are these explained? What are the effects of stigmatization of people who are labeled mentally ill?
Biopsychosocial Perspective		Interactions of biological, psychological, and sociocultural factors in the development of abnormal behavior	How might genetic or other factors predispose individuals to psychological disorders in the face of life stress? How do biological, psychological, and sociocultural factors interact in the development of complex patterns of abnormal behavior?

Source. Adapted from Nevid, J. S. (2003). *Psychology: Concepts and applications.* Boston: Houghton Mifflin. Reprinted with permission.

clusively biological in nature. For instance, certain forms of mental retardation have clear-cut biological causes, such as chromosomal abnormalities (see Chapter 14) or maternal alcohol consumption during pregnancy (see Chapter 9). Other disorders may arise directly from learning experiences. For example, phobias may be acquired based on associations of particular objects with traumatic or painful experiences (see Chapter 6). But in most psychological disorders, multiple causes are involved. We must consider not only the contributions of the multiple causes, but also the interactions among them. We are only beginning to unravel the complex web of factors that underlie many types of disorders. Here, let us consider a leading contemporary model that examines how the multiple causes interact in the development of psychological disorders.

The Diathesis–Stress Model

diathesis–stress model A model that posits that abnormal behavior problems involve the interaction of a vulnerability or predisposition and stressful life events or experiences.

diathesis A vulnerability or predisposition to a particular disorder.

The **diathesis–stress model** holds that psychological disorders arise from a combination or interaction of a **diathesis** (vulnerability or predisposition, usually genetic in nature) with stress (see Figure 2.9). Whether the disorder actually develops depends on the type and severity of stressors the person experiences in life. The life stressors that may contribute to the development of disorders include include birth complications, trauma or

FIGURE 2.9 The diathesis–stress model

serious illness in childhood, childhood sexual or physical abuse, prolonged unemployment, loss of loved ones, or other negative life events.

In some cases, people with a diathesis for a particular disorder, say schizophrenia, will remain free of the disorder or will develop a milder form of the disorder if the level of stress in their lives remains low or if they develop effective coping responses for handling the stress they encounter. However, the stronger the diathesis, the less stress is generally needed to trigger the disorder. In some cases the diathesis may be so strong that the disorder develops even under the most benign life circumstances.

The diathesis–stress hypothesis was originally developed as a framework for understanding schizophrenia (see Chapter 12). It has since been applied to other psychological disorders, including depression (Lewinsohn, Joiner, & Rohde, 2001; Ormel et al., 2001). The diathesis–stress model is not the only biopsychosocial account of how abnormal behavior patterns develop. Other models posit roles for biological and psychosocial influences, such as the cognitive model of panic disorder (see Chapter 6).

Not all forms of the diathesis–stress model are based on an interaction of a biological vulnerability and life stress. Psychological diatheses may also be involved, such as maladaptive personality traits and dysfunctional thinking patterns that increase the risk of developing a particular disorder in the face of stress (Harris & Curtin, 2002; Lewinsohn, Joiner, & Rohde, 2001). For example, the tendency to blame oneself for negative life events, such as a divorce or job loss, may put a person at greater risk of developing depression after these things happen (see Chapter 8) (Just, Abramson, & Alloy, 2001).

Evaluating the Biopsychosocial Perspective

The strength of the biopsychosocial model—its very complexity—may also be its greatest weakness. The model holds the view that with few exceptions, psychological disorders or other patterns of abnormal behavior are complex phenomena that arise from multiple causes. We cannot pinpoint any one cause that leads to the development of schizophrenia or panic disorder, for example. In addition, different people may develop the same disorder based on different sets of causal influences. Yet the complexity of understanding the interplay of underlying causes of abnormal behavior patterns should not deter us from the effort. The accumulation of a body of knowledge is a continuing process. We know a great deal more today than we did a few short years ago. We will surely know more in the years ahead.

The Case of Jessica—A Final Word

Let us briefly return to the case of Jessica, the young woman with bulimia whom we introduced at the beginning of the chapter. The biopsychosocial model leads us to consider the biological, psychological, and sociocultural factors that might account for bulimic behavior. As we shall consider further in chapter 10, evidence points to biological influences, such as genetic factors and irregularities in neurotransmitter activity in the brain. Evidence also points to contributions of sociocultural factors, such as the social pressures imposed on young women in our society to adhere to unrealistic standards of thinness, as well as psychological influences such as body dissatisfaction, cognitive factors such as thinking in perfectionistic and dichotomous ("black or white") terms, and underlying emotional and interpersonal problems. In all likelihood, multiple factors interact in leading to bulimia and other eating disorders. For example, we might apply the diathesis–stress model to frame a potential causal model of bulimia. From this perspective, we can propose that a genetic predisposition (diathesis) affecting the regulation of neurotransmitters in the brain interacts with stress in the form of social and family pressures, leading to the development of eating disorders.

We will return to consider these causal influences in Chapter 10. For now, let us simply note that psychological disorders like bulimia are complex phenomena that are best approached by considering the contributions and interactions of multiple factors.

SUMMING UP

The Biological Perspective

How is the nervous system organized? The nervous system consists of two major parts, the central nervous system and the peripheral nervous system. The central nervous system consists of the brain and spinal cord. The peripheral nervous system consists of two major divisions, the somatic nervous system, which transmits messages between the central nervous system and the sense organs and muscles, and the autonomic nervous system, which controls involuntary bodily processes. The autonomic nervous system has two branches or subdivisions, the sympathetic and the parasympathetic. The nervous system is composed of neurons, nerve cells that communicate with one another through chemical messengers, called neurotransmitters, that transmit nerve impulses across the tiny gaps, or synapses, between neurons.

What are the biological underpinnings of abnormal behavior? Biological factors such as disturbances in neurotransmitter functioning in the brain, heredity, and underlying brain abnormalities are implicated in the development of abnormal behavior.

The Psychological Perspective

What are the major psychological models of abnormal behavior? Psychodynamic perspectives reflect the views of Freud and his followers, who believed that abnormal behavior stemmed from psychological causes based on underlying psychic forces within the personality. Learning theorists posit that the principles of learning can be used to explain both abnormal and normal behavior. Humanistic theorists believe it is important to understand the obstacles that people encounter as they strive toward self-actualization and authenticity. Cognitive theorists focus on the role of distorted and self-defeating thinking in explaining abnormal behavior.

The Sociocultural Perspective

What is the basic idea underlying the sociocultural perspective on abnormal behavior? Sociocultural theorists believe we need to broaden our outlook on abnormal behavior by taking into account the role of social ills, including poverty, racism, and lack of opportunity, in the development of abnormal behavior patterns.

The Biopsychosocial Perspective

What is the distinguishing feature of the biopsychosocial perspective? The biopsychosocial perspective seeks an understanding of abnormal behavior based on the interplay of biological, psychological, and sociocultural factors.

What is the diathesis–stress model? The diathesis–stress model holds that a person may have a predisposition, or diathesis, for a particular disorder, but whether the disorder actually develops depends on the interaction of the diathesis with stress-inducing life experiences.

KEY TERMS

neurons (*p. 38*)
dendrites (*p. 38*)
axon (*p. 38*)

terminals (*p. 38*)
neurotransmitters (*p. 38*)
synapse (*p. 38*)

receptor site (*p. 38*)
central nervous system (*p. 40*)
peripheral nervous system (*p. 40*)

medulla *(p. 40)*
pons *(p. 40)*
cerebellum *(p. 41)*
reticular activating system *(p. 41)*
thalamus *(p. 41)*
hypothalamus *(p. 41)*
limbic system *(p. 41)*
basal ganglia *(p. 41)*
cerebrum *(p. 41)*
cerebral cortex *(p. 41)*
somatic nervous system *(p. 42)*
autonomic nervous system *(p. 42)*
sympathetic *(p. 42)*
parasympathetic *(p. 42)*
psychoanalytic theory *(p. 44)*
conscious *(p. 44)*
preconscious *(p. 44)*

unconscious *(p. 44)*
id *(p. 44)*
pleasure principle *(p. 45)*
ego *(p. 45)*
reality principle *(p. 45)*
superego *(p. 45)*
defense mechanisms *(p. 45)*
fixation *(p. 48)*
archetypes *(p. 48)*
ego psychology *(p. 49)*
object-relations theory *(p. 49)*
psychosis *(p. 50)*
behaviorism *(p. 51)*
conditioned response *(p. 53)*
unconditioned stimulus *(p. 53)*
unconditioned response *(p. 53)*
conditioned stimulus *(p. 53)*

classical conditioning *(p. 53)*
operant conditioning *(p. 54)*
reinforcement *(p. 54)*
reward *(p. 54)*
positive reinforcers *(p. 54)*
negative reinforcers *(p. 54)*
punishment *(p. 54)*
social-cognitive theory *(p. 55)*
modeling *(p. 55)*
expectancies *(p. 55)*
self-actualization *(p. 56)*
unconditional positive regard *(p. 57)*
conditional positive regard *(p. 57)*
social causation model *(p. 62)*
downward drift hypothesis *(p. 62)*
diathesis–stress model *(p. 64)*
diathesis *(p. 64)*

WEB TOOLS

The companion website offers tools to enrich your learning experience and help you succeed in class. Go to www.prenhall.com/nevid for the gateway to the following resources:

- **VIDEO** links to connect to the video case files on the companion CD-ROM. VIDEO icons in the margins of the chapter highlight the case examples included in the CD-ROM. You can also access the CD-ROM directly if you do not have a Web connection.

- **QUIZ** links to self-scoring quizzes corresponding to each section of the chapter. The quizzes help you review your knowledge of the content in each chapter.

- **WEB** links to direct you to related sites that enhance your learning of abnormal psychology.

CHAPTER THREE

Classification and Assessment of Abnormal Behavior

"I"

Jerry Has a Panic Attack on the Interstate

Interviewer: Can you tell me a bit about what it was that brought you to the clinic?

Jerry: Well, . . . after the first of the year, I started getting these panic attacks. I didn't know what the panic attack was.

Interviewer: Well, what was it that you experienced?

Jerry: Uhm, the heart beating, racing . . .

Interviewer: Your heart started to race on you.

Jerry: And then uh, I couldn't be in one place, maybe a movie, or a church . . . things would be closing in on me and I'd have to get up and leave.

Interviewer: The first time that it happened to you, can you remember that?

Jerry: Uhm, yeah I was . . .

Interviewer: Take me through that, what you experienced.

Jerry: I was driving on an interstate and, oh I might've been on maybe 10 or 15 minutes.

Interviewer: Uh huh.

Jerry: All of a sudden I got this fear. I started to . . . uh race.

Interviewer: So you noticed you were frightened?

Jerry: Yes.

Interviewer: Your heart was racing and you were perspiring. What else?

Jerry: Perspiring and uh, I was afraid of driving anymore on that interstate for the fear that I would either pull into a car head on, so uhm, I just, I just couldn't function. I just couldn't drive.

Interviewer: What did you do?

Jerry: I pulled, uh well at the nearest exit. I just got off . . . uh stopped and, I had never experienced anything like that before.

Interviewer: That was just a . . .

Jerry: Out of the clear blue . . .

Interviewer: Out of the clear blue? And what'd you think was going on?

Jerry: I had no idea.

Interviewer: You just knew you were . . .

Jerry: I thought maybe I was having a heart attack.

Interviewer: Okay.

—Exerpted from "Panic Disorder: The Case of Jerry," found on the "Videos in Abnormal Psychology" CD-ROM that accompanies this textbook.

Truth or Fiction?

T❏ F❏ Some men in India develop a psychological disorder involving excessive concerns or anxiety over losing semen. (p. 75)

T❏ F❏ People are more likely to report more personal problems when they are questioned by a live interviewer, rather than by a computer. (p. 80)

T❏ F❏ The most widely used personality inventory includes a number of questions that bear no obvious relationship to the traits the instrument purports to measure. (p. 84)

T❏ F❏ One of the most widely used tests of personality asks people to interpret what they see in a series of inkblots. (p. 87)

T❏ F❏ People in weight-loss programs who carefully monitor what they eat tend to lose less weight than people who are less-reliable monitors. (p. 92)

T❏ F❏ Despite advances in technology, physicians today must perform surgery to study the workings of the brain. (p. 96)

T❏ F❏ Cocaine cravings in people addicted to cocaine have been linked to parts of the brain that are normally activated during pleasant emotions. (p. 96)

JERRY BEGINS TO TELL HIS STORY, GUIDED BY THE INTERVIEWER. PSYCHOLOGISTS and other mental health professionals use clinical interviews and a variety of other means to assess abnormal behavior, including psychological testing, behavioral assessment, and physiological monitoring. The clinical interview is an important way of assessing abnormal behavior and arriving at a diagnostic impression—in this case, panic disorder. The clinician matches the presenting problems and associated features with a set of diagnostic criteria in forming a diagnostic impression.

The diagnosis of psychological or mental disorders represents a way of classifying patterns of abnormal behavior on the basis of their common features or symptoms. Abnormal behavior has been classified since ancient times. Hippocrates classified abnormal behaviors according to his theory of *humors* (vital bodily fluids). Although his theory proved to be flawed, Hippocrates' classification of some types of mental health problems generally correspond to diagnostic categories we use today. His description of melancholia, for example, is similar to our current conception of depression. During the Middle Ages some "authorities" classified abnormal behaviors into two groups, those that resulted from demonic possession and those due to natural causes.

The 19th-century German psychiatrist Emil Kraepelin was the first modern theorist to develop a comprehensive model of classification based on the distinctive features, or symptoms, associated with abnormal behavior patterns. The most commonly used classification system today is largely an outgrowth and extension of Kraepelin's work: the *Diagnostic and Statistical Manual of Mental Disorders (DSM)*, published by the American Psychiatric Association.

Why is it important to classify abnormal behavior? For one thing, classification is the core of science. Without labeling and organizing patterns of abnormal behavior, researchers could not communicate their findings to one another, and progress toward understanding these disorders would come to a halt. Moreover, important decisions are made on the basis of classification. Certain psychological disorders respond better to one therapy than another or to one drug than another. Classification also helps clinicians predict behavior: schizophrenia, for example, follows a more or less predictable course. Finally, classification helps researchers identify populations with similar patterns of abnormal behavior. By classifying groups of people as depressed, for example, researchers might be able to identify common factors that help explain the origins of depression.

This chapter reviews the classification and assessment of abnormal behavior, beginning with the *DSM*.

HOW ARE ABNORMAL BEHAVIOR PATTERNS CLASSIFIED?

The *DSM* was introduced in 1952. The latest version, published in 2000, is the *DSM-IV-TR*, the Text Revision (TR) of the Fourth Edition (*DSM-IV*) (APA, 2000). Another common system of classification, published by the World Health Organization, is used mainly for compiling statistics on the worldwide occurrence of disorders: the *International Statistical Classification of Diseases and Related Health Problems (ICD)*, which is now in its tenth revision (the *ICD*-10). The *DSM-IV* is compatible with the ICD, so that *DSM* diagnoses could be coded in the ICD system as well. Thus the two systems can be used to share information about the prevalences and characteristics of particular disorders. The *DSM* has been widely adopted by mental health professionals. However, many psychologists and other professionals criticize the *DSM* on several grounds, such as relying too strongly on the medical model. Our focus on the *DSM* reflects recognition of its widespread use, not an endorsement.

In the *DSM*, abnormal behavior patterns are classified as "mental disorders." *Mental disorders* involve either emotional distress (typically depression or anxiety), significantly impaired functioning (difficulty meeting responsibilities at work, in the family, or in society at large), or behavior that places people at risk for personal suffering, pain, disability, or death (e.g., suicide attempts, repeated use of harmful drugs).

Let us also note that a behavior pattern that represents an expected or culturally appropriate response to a stressful event, such as signs of bereavement or grief following the death of a loved one, is not considered disordered within the *DSM*, even if behavior is significantly impaired. If a person's behavior remains significantly impaired over an extended period of time, however, a diagnosis of a mental disorder might become appropriate.

The *DSM* and Models of Abnormal Behavior

The *DSM* system, like the medical model, treats abnormal behaviors as signs or symptoms of underlying disorders or pathologies. However, the *DSM* does not assume that abnormal behaviors necessarily reflect biological causes or defects. It recognizes that the causes of most mental disorders remain uncertain: Some disorders may have purely biological causes, whereas others may have psychological causes. Still others, probably most, are best explained within a multifactorial model that takes into account the interaction of biological, psychological, social (socioeconomic, sociocultural, and ethnic), and physical environmental factors.

The authors of the *DSM* recognize that their use of the term *mental disorder* is problematic because it perpetuates a long-standing but dubious distinction between mental and physical disorders (American Psychiatric Association, 1994, 2000). They point out that there is much that is "physical" in "mental" disorders and much that is "mental" in "physical" disorders. The diagnostic manual continues to use the term *mental disorder* because its developers have not been able to agree on an appropriate substitute. In this text we use the term *psychological disorder* in place of *mental disorder* because we feel it is more appropriate to place the study of abnormal behavior more squarely within a psychological context. Moreover, the term *psychological* has the advantage of encompassing behavioral patterns as well as strictly "mental" experiences, such as emotions, thoughts, beliefs, and attitudes.

Psychologist Jerome Wakefield (1992a, 1992b, 1997, 2001) proposed that the term *disorder* be conceptualized as "harmful dysfunction." A harmful dysfunction represents a failure of a mental or physical system to perform its natural function, resulting in negative consequences or harm to the individual. By this definition, dysfunction alone is not enough to constitute a disorder. For example, even though the body was naturally designed to have two kidneys, and it would be dysfunctional to have but one, a failure of one kidney to function properly (or even the loss of a kidney) may not be harmful to the individual's well-being. By contrast, a dysfunction in the brain's ability to store or retrieve memories would constitute a disorder if it leads to harmful consequences, such as memory deficits that make it difficult for the person to function effectively. We find Wakefield's concept instructive, although we recognize that not all psychologists share his viewpoint (see Lilienfeld & Marino, 1995). One problem is that we may not agree on what constitutes the "natural function" of mental systems (Bergner, 1997).

Finally, we should recognize that the *DSM* is used to classify disorders, not people. Rather than classify someone as a *schizophrenic* or a *depressive,* we refer to *an individual with schizophrenia* or *a person with major depression.* This difference in terminology is not simply a matter of semantics. To label someone a schizophrenic carries an unfortunate and stigmatizing implication that a person's identity is defined by the disorder he or she has.

Features of the *DSM* The *DSM* is descriptive, not explanatory. It describes the diagnostic features—or, in medical terms, symptoms—of abnormal behaviors; it does not attempt to explain their origins or adopt any particular theoretical framework, such as psychodynamic or learning theory. Using the *DSM* classification system, the clinician arrives at a diagnosis by matching a client's behaviors with the criteria that define particular patterns of abnormal behavior ("mental disorders"). Table 3.1 shows the diagnostic criteria for generalized anxiety disorder.

Abnormal behavior patterns are categorized according to the features they share. For example, abnormal behavior patterns chiefly characterized by anxiety, such as panic disorder or generalized anxiety disorder (see Table 3.1), are classified as anxiety disorders. Behaviors chiefly characterized by disruptions in mood are categorized as mood disorders. The *DSM* recommends that clinicians assess an individual's mental state according to five factors, or axes. Together the five axes provide a broad range of information about the individual's functioning, not just a diagnosis (see Table 3.2). The system contains the following axes.

1. *Axis I: Clinical Syndromes and Other Conditions That May Be a Focus of Clinical Attention.* This axis incorporates a wide range of clinical syndromes, including anxiety disorders, mood disorders, schizophrenia and other psychotic disorders, adjustment disorders, and disorders usually first diagnosed during infancy, childhood, or adolescence (except for mental retardation, which is coded on Axis II). Axis I also includes relationship problems, academic or occupational problems, and bereavement, conditions that may be the focus of diagnosis and treatment but that do not in themselves constitute definable psychological disorders. Also coded on Axis I are psychological factors that affect medical conditions, such as anxiety that exacerbates an asthmatic condition or depressive symptoms that delay recovery from surgery.

2. *Axis II: Personality Disorders and Mental Retardation.* Personality disorders are enduring and rigid patterns of maladaptive behavior that typically impair relationships with others and social functioning. These include antisocial, paranoid,

---

TABLE 3.1

Sample Diagnostic Criteria for Generalized Anxiety Disorder

1. Occurrence of excessive anxiety and worry on most days during a period of 6 months or longer.

2. Anxiety and worry are not limited to one or a few concerns or events.

3. Difficulty controlling feelings of worry.

4. The presence of a number of features associated with anxiety and worry, such as the following:

   a. experiencing restlessness or feelings of edginess

   b. becoming easily fatigued

   c. having difficulty concentrating or finding one's mind going blank

   d. feeling irritable

   e. having states of muscle tension

   f. having difficulty falling asleep or remaining asleep or having restless, unsatisfying sleep

5. Experiencing emotional distress or impairment in social, occupational, or other areas of functioning as the result of anxiety, worry, or related physical symptoms.

6. Worry or anxiety is not accounted for by the features of another disorder.

7. The disturbance does not result from the use of a drug of abuse or medication or a general medical condition and does not occur only in the context of another disorder.

Source. Adapted from *DSM-IV-TR* (APA, 2000).

TABLE 3.2

The Multiaxial Classification System of the *DSM-IV-TR*

Axis	Type of Information	Brief Description
Axis I	Clinical syndromes	The patterns of abnormal behavior ("mental disorders") that impair functioning and are stressful to the individual
	Other conditions that may be a focus of clinical attention	Other problems that may be the focus of diagnosis or treatment but do not constitute mental disorders, such as academic, vocational, or social problems, and psychological factors that affect medical conditions (such as delayed recovery from surgery due to depressive symptoms)
Axis II	Personality disorders	Personality disorders involve excessively rigid, enduring, and maladaptive ways of relating to others and adjusting to external demands.
	Mental retardation	Mental retardation involves a delay or impairment in the development of intellectual and adaptive abilities.
Axis III	General medical conditions	Chronic and acute illnesses and medical conditions that are important to the understanding or treatment of the psychological disorder or that play a direct role in causing the psychological disorder
Axis IV	Psychosocial and environmental problems	Problems in the social or physical environment that affect the diagnosis, treatment, and outcome of psychological disorders
Axis V	Global assessment of functioning	Overall judgment of current functioning with respect to psychological, social, and occupational functioning; the clinician may also rate the highest level of functioning occurring for at least a few months during the past year

Source: Adapted from the *DSM-IV-TR* (APA, 2000).

Assessment of level of functioning. The assessment of functioning takes into account the individual's ability to manage the responsibilities of daily living. Here we see a group home for people with mental retardation. The residents assume responsibility for household functions.

narcissistic, and borderline personality disorders (see Chapter 13). Mental retardation, which is also coded on Axis II, involves pervasive intellectual impairment (see Chapter 14)

People may be given either Axis I or Axis II diagnoses or a combination of the two when both apply. For example, a person may receive a diagnosis of an anxiety disorder (Axis I) *and* a second diagnosis of a personality disorder (Axis II).

3. *Axis III: General Medical Conditions.* All medical conditions and diseases that may be important to the understanding or treatment of an individual's mental disorders are coded on Axis III. For example, if *hypothyroidism* were a direct cause of an individual's mood disorder (such as major depression), it would be coded under Axis III. Medical conditions that affect the understanding or treatment of a mental disorder (but that are not direct causes of the disorder) are also listed on Axis III. For instance, the presence of a heart condition may determine whether a particular course of drug therapy should be used with a depressed person.

4. *Axis IV: Psychosocial and Environmental Problems.* The psychosocial and environmental problems that affect the diagnosis, treatment, or outcome of a mental disorder are placed on Axis IV. These include job loss, marital separation or divorce, homelessness or inadequate housing, lack of social support, the death or loss of a friend, or exposure to war or other disasters. Some positive life events, such as a job promotion, may also be listed on Axis IV, but only when they create problems for the individual, such as difficulties adapting to a new job. Table 3.3 lists other examples from this axis.

TABLE 3.3

Psychosocial and Environmental Problems

Problem Categories	Examples
Problems with primary support group	Death of family members; health problems of family members; marital disruption in the form of separation, divorce, or estrangement; sexual or physical abuse within the family; child neglect; birth of a sibling
Problems related to the social environment	Death or loss of a friend; social isolation or living alone; difficulties adjusting to a new culture (acculturation); discrimination; adjustment to transitions occurring during the life cycle, such as retirement
Educational problems	Illiteracy; academic difficulties; problems with teachers or classmates; inadequate or impoverished school environment
Occupational problems	Work-related problems including stressful workloads and problems with bosses or coworkers; changes in employment; job dissatisfaction; threat of loss of job; unemployment
Housing problems	Inadequate housing or homelessness; living in an unsafe neighborhood; problems with neighbors or landlord
Economic problems	Financial hardships or extreme poverty; inadequate welfare support
Problems with access to health care services	Inadequate health care services or availability of health insurance; difficulties with transportation to health care facilities
Problems related to interaction with the legal system/crime	Arrest or imprisonment; becoming involved in a lawsuit or trial; being a victim of crime
Other psychosocial problems	Natural or human-made disasters; war or other hostilities; problems with caregivers outside the family, such as counselors, social workers, and physicians; lack of availability of social service agencies

Source: Adapted from the *DSM-IV-TR* (APA, 2000).

5. *Axis V: Global Assessment of Functioning.* The clinician rates the client's current level of psychological, social, and occupational functioning using a scale similar to that shown in Table 3.4. The clinician may also indicate the highest level of functioning achieved for at least a few months during the preceding year. The level of current functioning indicates the current need for treatment or intensity of care. The level of highest functioning is suggestive of the level of functioning that might be restored.

Table 3.5 shows an example of a diagnosis in the *DSM* multiaxial system for a hypothetical case. The person receives two diagnoses, an Axis I diagnosis of generalized anxiety disorder (discussed in Chapter 6) and an Axis II diagnosis of dependent personality disorder (discussed in Chapter 13). The person also has a medical disorder (hypertension) and several psychosocial/environmental problems, as noted by the listing on Axis IV of marital separation and unemployment. The clinician also gives the person an overall rating of 62 on the level of functioning scale (GAF) on Axis V, which indicates that although the person is presenting with a mild level of symptoms or impaired functioning, he or she is functioning fairly well.

Culture-Bound Syndromes Some patterns of abnormal behavior, called **culture-bound syndromes,** occur in some cultures but are rare or unknown in others (Osborne, 2001).

Culture-bound syndromes may reflect exaggerated forms of common folk superstitions and belief patterns within a particular culture. For example, the psychiatric disorder *taijin-kyofu-sho*

culture-bound syndromes Patterns of abnormal behavior found within only one or a few cultures.

Cultural underpinnings of abnormal behavior patterns. Culture-bound syndromes often represent exaggerated forms of cultural beliefs and values. TKS is characterized by excessive fear that one may embarrass or offend other people. The syndrome primarily affects young Japanese men and appears to be connected with the emphasis in Japanese culture on politeness and avoiding embarrassing other people.

TABLE 3.4

Global Assessment of Functioning (GAF) Scale

Code	Severity of Symptoms	Examples
91–100	Superior functioning across a wide variety of activities of daily life	Lacks symptoms Handles life problems without them "getting out of hand"
81–90	Absent or minimal symptoms, no more than everyday problems or concerns	Mild anxiety before exams Occasional argument with family members
71–80	Transient and predictable reactions to stressful events, OR no more than slight impairment in functioning	Difficulty concentrating after argument with family Temporarily falls behind in schoolwork
61–70	Some mild symptoms, OR some difficulty in social, occupational, or school functioning, but functioning pretty well	Feels down, mild insomnia Occasional truancy or theft within household
51–60	Moderate symptoms, OR moderate difficulties in social, occupational, or school functioning	Occasional panic attacks Few friends, conflicts with coworkers
41–50	Serious symptoms, OR any serious impairment in social, occupational, or school functioning	Suicidal thoughts, frequent shoplifting Unable to hold job, has no friends
31–40	Some impairment in reality testing or communication, OR major impairment in several areas	Speech illogical Depressed man or woman unable to work, neglects family, and avoids friends
21–30	Strong influence on behavior of delusions or hallucinations, OR serious impairment in communication or judgment, OR inability to function in almost all areas	Grossly inappropriate behavior, speech sometimes incoherent Stays in bed all day, no job, home, or friends
11–20	Some danger of hurting self or others, OR occasionally fails to maintain personal hygiene, OR gross impairment in communication	Suicidal gestures, frequently violent Smears feces
1–10	Persistent danger of severely hurting self or others, OR persistent inability to maintain minimal personal hygiene, OR seriously suicidal act	Largely incoherent or mute Serious suicidal attempt, recurrent violence

Source: Adapted from the *DSM-IV-TR* (APA, 2000).

TABLE 3.5

Example of a Diagnosis in the Multiaxial *DSM* System

Axis I	Generalized Anxiety Disorder
Axis II	Dependent Personality Disorder
Axis III	Hypertension
Axis IV	Problem with Primary Support Group (marital separation); Occupational Problem (unemployment)
Axis V	GAF = 62

reliability In psychological assessment, the consistency of a measure or diagnostic instrument or system.

validity The degree to which a test or diagnostic system measures the traits or constructs it purports to measure.

(TKS) is common among young men in Japan but rare elsewhere. The disorder is characterized by excessive fear of embarrassing or offending other people (McNally, Cassiday, & Calamari, 1990). People with TKS may dread blushing in front of others not because they are afraid of embarrassing themselves, but for fear of embarrassing others. People with TKS may also fear mumbling their thoughts aloud, lest they inadvertently offend others. The syndrome primarily affects young Japanese men and is believed to be related to an emphasis in Japanese culture on not embarrassing others as well as deep concerns over issues of shame (McNally et al., 1990; Spitzer et al., 1994). Chang (1984) reports that TKS is diagnosed in 7% to 36% of the people treated by psychiatrists in Japan.

Culture-bound syndromes in the United States include anorexia nervosa (discussed in Chapter 10) and dissociative identity disorder (formerly called *multiple personality disorder*; discussed in Chapter 7). These abnormal behavior patterns are essentially unknown in less-developed cultures. Table 3.6 lists some other culture-bound syndromes identified in the *DSM-IV-TR*.

Evaluating the *DSM* System To be useful, a diagnostic system such as the *DSM* must demonstrate **reliability** and **validity.** The *DSM* may be considered reliable, or consistent, if different evaluators using the system are likely to arrive at the same diagnoses when they evaluate the same cases.

The most appropriate test of the validity of the *DSM* is its correspondence with observed behavior. If people diagnosed with social phobia show abnormal levels of anxiety in social situations, this evidence would help support claims of the validity of the diagnosis. We do have evidence supporting the reliability and validity of most *DSM* anxiety disorder and mood disorder categories (T. A. Brown et al., 2001; Turner et al., 1986). Yet questions about validity persist for some diagnostic classes, such as Axis II personality disorders, as well as Axis V, Global Assessment of Functioning (Moos, McCoy, & Moos, 2000). Overall, it is fair to say that the validity of the *DSM* remains a subject of ongoing debate and study (Kendell & Jablensky, 2003).

Many diagnostic categories also show *predictive validity,* or ability to predict the course the disorder is likely to follow or its response to treatment. For example, people diagnosed with bipolar disorder typically respond to the drug lithium (see Chapter 8). Likewise, persons diagnosed with specific phobias (such as fear of heights) tend to be highly responsive to behavioral techniques for reducing fears (see Chapter 6).

Many observers (e.g., Eisenbruch, 1992; Fabrega, 1992) have argued that the *DSM* should become more sensitive to cultural and ethnic diversity. The behaviors included as diagnostic criteria in the *DSM* are determined by consensus of mostly U.S.-trained psychiatrists, psychologists, and social workers. Had the American Psychiatric Association asked Asian-trained or Latin American–trained professionals to develop their diagnostic manual, for example, there might have been some different diagnostic criteria or even different diagnostic categories.

In fairness to the *DSM,* however, the latest edition does place greater emphasis than did earlier editions on weighing cultural factors when assessing abnormal behavior. It recognizes that clinicians unfamiliar with an individual's cultural background may incorrectly classify that individual's behavior as abnormal when it in fact falls within the normal spectrum in his or her culture. In Chapter 1 we noted that the same behavior might be deemed normal in one culture but abnormal in another. The *DSM-IV-TR* specifies that in order to make a diagnosis of a mental disorder, the behavior in question must not merely represent a culturally expectable and sanctioned response to a particular event, even though it may seem odd in the light of the examiner's own cultural standards. The *DSM-IV-TR* also recognizes that abnormal behaviors may take different forms in different cultures and that some abnormal behavior patterns are culturally specific (see Table 3.6). All told, the current edition of the *DSM,* the *DSM-IV-TR,* is widely recognized as an improvement over previous editions, even though questions still remain about the reliability and validity of certain diagnostic categories (Langenbucher et al., 2000; Thakker & Ward, 1998; Widiger & Clark, 2000).

Advantages and Disadvantages of the *DSM* System   The major advantage of the *DSM* may be its designation of specific diagnostic criteria. The *DSM* permits the clinician to readily match a client's complaints and associated features with specific standards to see which diagnosis best fits the case. For example, auditory hallucinations ("hearing voices") and delusions (fixed, but false beliefs, such as thinking that other people are devils) are characteristic symptoms of schizophrenia.

The multiaxial system paints a comprehensive picture of clients by integrating information concerning abnormal behaviors, medical conditions that affect abnormal behaviors, psychosocial and environmental problems that may be stressful to the individual, and level of functioning. The possibility of multiple diagnoses prompts clinicians to consider presenting current problems (Axis I) along with the relatively long-standing personality problems (Axis II) that may contribute to them.

Criticisms have also been leveled against the *DSM* system. Some critics challenge specific diagnostic criteria, such as the requirement that major depression be present for 2 weeks before diagnosis (Kendler & Gardner, 1998). Others challenge the reliance on the medical model. In the *DSM* system, problem behaviors are viewed as symptoms of underlying mental disorders in much the same way that physical symptoms are signs of underlying physical disorders. The very use of the term *diagnosis* presumes the medical model is an appropriate basis for classifying abnormal behaviors. But some clinicians feel that behavior, abnormal or otherwise, is too complex and meaningful to be treated as merely symptomatic. They assert that the medical model focuses too much on what

TRUTH or FICTION? *REVISITED*

Some men in India develop a psychological disorder involving excessive concerns or anxiety over losing semen.

☑ **TRUE.** Dhat syndrome is a culture-bound syndrome found in India in which men develop intense fears over loss of semen.

TABLE 3.6

Examples of Culture-Bound Syndromes from Other Cultures

Culture-Bound Syndrome	Description
Amok	A disorder principally occurring in men in Southeastern Asian and Pacific Island cultures, as well as in traditional Puerto Rican and Navajo cultures in the West, it describes a type of dissociative episode (a sudden change in consciousness or self-identity) in which an otherwise normal person suddenly goes berserk and strikes out at others, sometimes killing them. During these episodes, the person may have a sense of acting automatically or robotically. Violence may be directed at people or objects and is often accompanied by perceptions of persecution. A return to the person's usual state of functioning follows the episode. In the West, we use the expression "running amuck" to refer to an episode of losing oneself and running around in a violent frenzy. The word *amuck* is derived from the Malaysian word *amoq,* meaning "engaging furiously in battle." The word passed into the English language during colonial times when British colonial rulers in Malaysia observed this behavior among the native people.
Ataque de nervios ("attack of nerves")	A way of describing states of emotional distress among Latin American and Latin Mediterranean groups, it most commonly involves features such as shouting uncontrollably, fits of crying, trembling, feelings of warmth or heat rising from the chest to the head, and aggressive verbal or physical behavior. These episodes are usually precipitated by a stressful event affecting the family (e.g., receiving news of the death of a family member) and are accompanied by feelings of being out of control. After the attack, the person returns quickly to his or her usual level of functioning, although there may be amnesia for events that occurred during the episode.
Dhat syndrome	A disorder (described further in Chapter 7) affecting males found principally in India that involves intense fear or anxiety over the loss of semen through nocturnal emissions, ejaculations, or excretion with urine (despite the folk belief, semen doesn't actually mix with urine). In Indian culture, there is a popular belief that loss of semen depletes the man of his vital natural energy.
Falling out or blacking out	Occurring principally among southern U.S. and Caribbean groups, the disorder involves an episode of sudden collapsing or fainting. The attack may occur without warning or be preceded by dizziness or feelings of "swimming" in the head. Although the eyes remain open, the individual reports an inability to see. The person can hear what others are saying and understand what is occurring but feels powerless to move.
Ghost sickness	A disorder occurring among American Indian groups, it involves a preoccupation with death and with the "spirits" of the deceased. Symptoms associated with the condition include bad dreams, feelings of weakness, loss of appetite, fear, anxiety, and a sense of foreboding. Hallucinations, loss of consciousness, and states of confusion may also be present, among other symptoms.
Koro	Found primarily in China and some other South and East Asian countries, the syndrome (also discussed further in Chapter 7) refers to an episode of acute anxiety involving the fear that one's genitals (the penis in men and the vulva and nipples in women) are shrinking and retracting into the body and that death may result.
Zar	A term used in a number of countries in North Africa and the Middle East to describe the experience of spirit possession. Possession by spirits is often used in these cultures to explain dissociative episodes (sudden changes in consciousness or identity) that may be characterized by periods of shouting, banging of the head against the wall, laughing, singing, or crying. Affected people may seem apathetic or withdrawn or refuse to eat or carry out their usual responsibilities.

Source: Adapted from the *DSM-IV-TR* (APA, 2000); Osborne, 2001; and other sources.

may happen within the individual and not enough on external influences on behavior, such as social factors (socioeconomic, sociocultural, and ethnic) and physical environmental factors.

Another concern is that the medical model focuses on categorizing psychological (or mental) disorders rather than describing people's behavioral strengths and weaknesses. Nor does the *DSM* attempt to place behavior within a framework that examines the settings, situations, and cultural contexts in which behavior occurs. To behaviorally oriented psychologists, the understanding of behavior, abnormal or otherwise, is best approached by examining the interaction between the person and the environment. The *DSM* aims to determine what "disorders" people "have"—not how well they can function in particular situations. The behavioral model, alternatively, focuses more on behaviors than on underlying processes—more on what people "do" than on what they "are" or "have." Behaviorists and behavior therapists also use the *DSM,* of course, in part because mental health centers and health insurance carriers require the use of a diagnostic code and in part because they want to communicate in a common language with other practitioners. Many behavior therapists view the *DSM* diagnostic code as a convenient means of labeling patterns of abnormal behavior, a shorthand for a more extensive behavioral analysis of the problem.

Critics also complain that the *DSM* system might stigmatize people by labeling them with psychiatric diagnoses. Our society is strongly biased against people who are labeled as mentally ill. They are often shunned by others, including even family members, and subjected to discrimination—or **sanism** (Perlin, 1994), the counterpart to other forms of prejudice, such as racism, sexism, and ageism—in housing and employment.

The *DSM* system, despite its critics, has become part and parcel of the everyday practice of most U.S. mental health professionals. It may be the one reference manual found on the bookshelves of nearly all professionals and dog-eared from repeated use. Perhaps the *DSM* is best considered a work in progress, not a final product.

Now let us consider various ways of assessing abnormal behavior. We begin by considering the basic requirements for methods of assessment—that they be reliable and valid.

sanism The negative stereotyping of people who are identified as mentally ill.

STANDARDS OF ASSESSMENT

Important decisions are made on the basis of classification and assessment. For example, recommendations for specific treatment techniques vary according to our assessment of the problems clients exhibit. Therefore, methods of assessment, like diagnostic categories, must be *reliable* and *valid*.

Reliability

The reliability of a method of assessment, like that of a diagnostic system, refers to its consistency. A gauge of height would be unreliable if people looked taller or shorter at every measurement. A reliable measure of abnormal behavior must also yield the same results on different occasions. Also, different people should be able to check the yardstick and agree on the measured height of the subject. A yardstick that shrinks and expands with the slightest change in temperature will be unreliable. So will one that is difficult to read.

An assessment technique has *internal consistency* if the different parts of the test yield consistent results. For example, if responses to the different items on a depression scale are not highly correlated with each other, the items may not be measuring the same characteristic or trait—in this case, depression. On the other hand, some tests are designed to measure a set of different traits or characteristics. For example, the widely used personality test, the Minnesota Multiphasic Personality Inventory (MMPI), contains subscales measuring various traits related to abnormal behavior

An assessment method has *test–retest reliability* if it yields similar results on separate occasions. We would not trust a bathroom scale that yielded different results each time we weighed ourselves—unless we had stuffed or starved ourselves between weighings. The same principle applies to methods of psychological assessment.

Finally, an assessment method that relies on judgments from observers or raters must show *interrater reliability.* That is, raters must show a high level of agreement in their ratings. For example, two teachers may be asked to use a behavioral rating scale to evaluate a child's aggressiveness, hyperactivity, and sociability. The scale would have good interrater reliability if both teachers rated the same children in similar ways.

Validity

Assessment techniques must also be valid; that is, instruments used in assessment must measure what they intend to measure. Suppose a measure of depression actually turned out to be measuring anxiety. Using such a measure may lead an examiner to a wrong diagnosis. There are different ways of measuring validity, including *content, criterion,* and *construct validity.*

content validity The degree to which the content of a test or measure represents the content domain of the construct it purports to measure.

criterion validity The degree to which a test correlates with an independent, external criterion or standard.

construct validity The degree to which a test measures the hypothetical construct that it purports to measure.

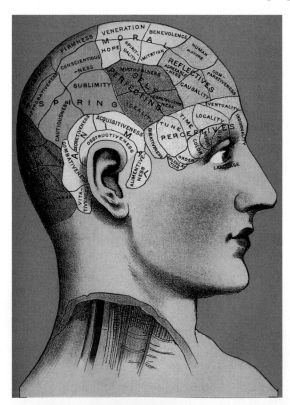

Phrenology. In the 19th century, some people believed that mental faculties and abilities were based in certain parts of the brain and that people's acumen in such faculties could be assessed by gauging the protrusions and indentations of the skull.

The **content validity** of an assessment technique is the degree to which its content represents the behaviors associated with the trait in question. For example, depression includes features such as sadness and refusal to participate in activities the person once enjoyed. In order to have content validity, then, techniques that assess depression should include items that address these areas.

Criterion validity represents the degree to which the assessment technique correlates with an independent, external criterion (standard) of what the technique is intended to assess. *Predictive validity* is a form of criterion validity. A test or assessment technique shows good predictive validity if it can be used to predict future performance or behavior. For example, a test measuring antisocial behavior would show predictive validity if people scoring high on the measure later showed more evidence of delinquent or criminal behavior than did low scorers.

Another way of measuring criterion validity of a diagnostic test for a particular disorder is to see if it is able to identify people who meet diagnostic criteria for the disorder. Two related concepts are important here: sensitivity and specificity. *Sensitivity* refers to the degree to which a test correctly identifies people who have the disorder the test is intended to detect. Tests that lack sensitivity produce a high number of *false negatives*—individuals identified as not having the disorder who truly have the disorder. *Specificity* refers to the degree to which the test avoids classifying people as having a particular disorder who truly do not have the disorder. Tests that lack specificity produce a high number of *false positives*—people identified as having the disorder who truly do not have the disorder. By taking into account sensitivity and specificity of a given test, we can determine the ability of a test to classify individuals correctly.

Construct validity is the degree to which a test corresponds to the theoretical model of the underlying construct or trait it purports to measure. Let's say we have a test that purports to measure anxiety. Anxiety is not a concrete object or phenomenon. It can't be measured directly, counted, weighed, or touched. Anxiety is a theoretical construct that helps explain phenomena like a pounding heart or the sudden inability to speak when you are asking someone out on a date. Anxiety may be indirectly measured by such means as self-report (the client rates the personal level of anxiety) and physiological techniques (measuring the level of sweat on the palms of the client's hands).

The construct validity of a test of anxiety requires the results of the test to predict other behaviors that would be expected, given your theoretical model of anxiety. Let's say your theoretical model predicts that socially anxious college students will have greater difficulties than calmer students in speaking coherently when asking someone for a date, but not when they are merely rehearsing the invitation in private. If the results of an experimental test of these predictions fit these predicted patterns, we could say the evidence supports the test's construct validity.

A test may be reliable (give you consistent responses) but still not measure what it purports to measure (be invalid). For example, 19th-century phrenologists believed they could gauge people's personalities by measuring the bumps on their heads. Their calipers provided reliable measures of their subjects' bumps and protrusions; the measurements, however, did not provide valid estimates of subjects' psychological traits. The phrenologists were bumping in the dark, so to speak.

METHODS OF ASSESSMENT

Clinicians use different methods of assessment to arrive at diagnoses, including interviews, psychological testing, self-report questionnaires, behavioral measures, and physiological measures. The role of assessment, however, goes further than classification. A careful assessment provides a wealth of information about clients' personalities and cognitive functioning. This information helps clinicians acquire a broader understanding of their clients' problems and recommend appropriate forms of treatment. In most cases, the formal assessment involves one or more clinical interviews with the client, leading to a diagnostic impression and a treatment plan. In some cases, more formal psychological testing probes the client's psychological problems and intellectual, personality, and neuropsychological functioning.

The Clinical Interview

The *clinical interview* is the most widely used means of assessment. It is employed by all helping professionals and paraprofessionals. The interview is usually the client's first face-to-face contact with a clinician. Clinicians often begin by asking clients to describe the presenting complaint in their own words, saying something like, "Can you describe to me the problems you've been having lately?" (Therapists learn not to ask, "What brings you here?" to avoid receiving such answers as, "A car," "A bus," or "My social worker.") The clinician will then usually probe aspects of the presenting complaint, such as behavioral abnormalities and feelings of discomfort, the circumstances regarding the onset of the problem, history of past episodes, and how the problem affects the client's daily functioning. The clinician may explore possible precipitating events, such as changes in life circumstances, social relationships, employment, or schooling. The interviewer encourages the client to describe the problem in her or his own words in order to understand it from the client's viewpoint. For example, the interviewer in the case vignette that opened the chapter asked Jerry to discuss the concerns that prompted him to seek help.

Although the format may vary, most interviews cover these topics:

Building rapport. By developing rapport and feelings of trust with a client, the skillful interviewer helps put the client at ease and encourages candid communication.

1. *Identifying data.* Information regarding the client's sociodemographic characteristics: address and telephone number, marital status, age, gender, racial/ethnic characteristics, religion, employment, family composition, and so on.

2. *Description of the presenting problem(s).* How does the client perceive the problem? What troubling behaviors, thoughts, or feelings are reported? How do they affect the client's functioning? When did they begin?

3. *Psychosocial history.* Information describing the client's developmental history: educational, social, and occupational history; early family relationships.

4. *Medical/psychiatric history.* History of medical and psychiatric treatment and hospitalizations: Is the present problem a recurrent episode of a previous problem? How was the problem handled in the past? Was treatment successful? Why or why not?

5. *Medical problems/medication.* Description of present medical problems and present treatment, including medication. The clinician is alert to ways in which medical problems may affect the presenting psychological problem. For example, drugs for certain medical conditions can affect people's moods and general levels of arousal.

Interview Formats There are three general types of clinical interviews. In an **unstructured interview,** the clinician adopts his or her own style of questioning rather than following a standard format. In a **semistructured interview,** the clinician follows a general outline of questions designed to gather essential information but is free to ask the questions in any particular order and to branch off into other directions to follow up on important information. In a **structured interview,** the interview follows a preset series of questions in a particular order.

The major advantage of the unstructured interview is its spontaneity and conversational style. Because the interviewer is not bound to follow any specific set of questions, there is an active give-and-take with the client The major disadvantage is the lack of standardization. Different interviewers may ask questions in different ways. For example, one interviewer might ask, "How have your moods been lately?" whereas another might pose the question, "Have you had any periods of crying or tearfulness during the

unstructured interview Interview in which the clinician adopts his or her own style of questioning rather than following any standard format.

semistructured interview Interview in which the clinician follows a general outline of questions designed to gather essential information but is free to ask them in any order and to branch off in other directions.

structured interview Interview that follows a preset series of questions in a particular order.

past week or two?" The clients' responses may depend to a certain extent on how the questions are asked. Also, the conversational flow of the interview may fail to touch on important clinical information needed to form diagnostic information, such as suicidal tendencies. A semistructured interview provides more structure and uniformity, but at the expense of some spontaneity. Some clinicians prefer to conduct a semistructured interview in which they follow a general outline of questions but allow themselves the flexibility to depart from the interview protocol when they want to pursue issues that seem important.

Structured interviews (also called *standardized interviews*) provide the highest level of reliability and consistency in reaching diagnostic judgments, which is why they are used frequently in research settings. The Structured Clinical Interview for the *DSM* (SCID) includes closed-ended questions to determine the presence of behavior patterns that suggest specific diagnostic categories and open-ended questions that allow clients to elaborate their problems and feelings. The SCID guides the clinician in testing diagnostic hypotheses as the interview progresses. Evidence supports the reliability of the SCID across various clinical settings (J. B. Williams et al., 1992).

In the course of the interview, the clinician may also assess the client's cognitive functioning with a **mental status examination.** The specifics of the examination vary, but they typically include features such as the following.

- *Appearance:* appropriateness of the client's attire and grooming
- *Mood:* prevailing emotions displayed during the interview
- *Level of attention:* ability to maintain focus and attend to the interviewer's questions
- *Perceptual and thinking processes:* ability to think clearly and discern reality from fantasy
- *Orientation:* knowing who they are, where they are, and the present date
- *Judgment:* ability to make sound life decisions in daily life

The interviewer arrives at a diagnostic impression by compiling all the information available: from the interview, from review of the client's background, and from the presenting problems.

Do clinical interviews need to be conducted by a trained, live interviewer? Today, many of us do our banking by computer, order airline tickets over the Internet, and organize our schedules electronically. Might the human interviewer be replaced by a computer? The *Controversies in Abnormal Psychology* feature focuses on the current debate over computerized assessment.

Psychological Tests

A psychological test is a structured method of assessment used to evaluate reasonably stable traits, such as intelligence and personality. Tests are usually standardized on large numbers of subjects and provide norms that compare clients' scores with the average. By comparing test results from samples of people who are free of psychological disorders with those of people who have diagnosable psychological disorders, we may gain some insights into the types of response patterns that are indicative of abnormal behavior. Though we tend to think of medical tests as a "gold standard" of testing, a recent analysis showed that many psychological tests were on par with many medical tests in their ability to predict criterion variables, such as underlying conditions or future outcomes (Daw, 2001; Meyer et al., 2001).

Here we examine two major types of psychological tests: intelligence tests and personality tests.

Intelligence Tests The assessment of abnormal behavior often includes an evaluation of intelligence. Formal intelligence tests are used to help diagnose mental retardation (discussed in Chapter 14). They evaluate the intellectual impairment that may be caused by other disorders, such as organic mental disorders caused by damage to the brain. They also provide a profile of the client's intellectual strengths and weaknesses to help develop a treatment plan suited to the client's competencies.

mental status examination A structured clinical assessment to determine various aspects of the client's mental functioning.

CONTROVERSIES IN ABNORMAL PSYCHOLOGY
Should Interviewers Be Replaced by Computers?

Clinicians obtain information about a client's presenting complaints and symptoms primarily by conducting a clinical interview. But what if instead of a clinician asking the questions, the client was "interviewed" by a set of questions on a computer screen? Would the computer be as effective at culling relevant information as the human interviewer?

Put yourself in the scene. You are seated before a computer screen. The message on the screen asks you to type in your name and press the return key. Not wanting to offend, you comply. This message then pops up: "Hello, my name is Sigmund. I'm programmed to ask you a set of questions to learn more about you. May I begin?" You nod your head yes, momentarily forgetting the computer can only "perceive" key strokes. You type "yes," and the interview begins.

The future, as the saying goes, is now. Clinicians have been using computerized clinical interviews for more than 25 years. A computerized interview system named CASPER, for example, presents the following interview questions and response options:

> *About how many days in the past month did you have difficulty falling asleep, staying asleep, or waking too early (include sleep disturbed by bad dreams)?*
>
> *During the past month, how have you been getting along with your spouse/partner? (1) Very satisfactory; (2) Mostly satisfactory; (3) Sometimes satisfactory, sometimes unsatisfactory; (4) Mostly unsatisfactory; (5) Very unsatisfactory. (Farrell et al., 1987, p. 692)*

The client responds to each item by pressing a numeric key. CASPER is programmed to follow up on problems suggested by the clients' responses. For example, if the client indicates difficulty in falling or remaining asleep, CASPER will ask whether sleep has become a major problem—"something causing you great personal distress or interfering with your daily functioning" (p. 693). If the client answers yes, the computer is programmed to ask the client to rate the duration and intensity of the problem. Clients may also add or drop complaints—change their minds, that is. Computers offer some potential advantages over traditional human interviewers (Farrell, Camplair, & McCullough, 1987). They can be programmed to ask a specific set of questions in a predetermined order. Human beings may omit critical items or steer the interview toward-less important topics. In addition, clients may be less embarrassed about relating personal matters to computers because computers will not respond emotionally to what the clients tell them. Finally, computerized interviews can free clinicians to spend more time providing direct clinical services.

Not everyone appreciates the use of computerized interviews. Some say that computers are just too mechanical. They lack the human touch needed to delve into sensitive concerns such as a person's deepest fears, relationship problems, sexual matters, and the like. A computer lacks the means of judging the nuances in people's facial expressions that may reveal more about their innermost concerns than their typed or verbal responses.

Though there is merit to both sides of the argument, evidence is accumulating to support the use of computerized interviews. For one thing, people tend to reveal as much if not more personal information to a computer than they do to a human interviewer (Kobak et al., 1997). The computer interview may actually be more helpful in identifying problems that clients are embarrassed or unwilling to report to a live interviewer (Taylor & Luce, 2003). Perhaps people feel less self-conscious if someone isn't looking at them when they are interviewed. Or perhaps the computer seems more willing to take the time to note all complaints.

Evidence also shows that computer programs are as capable as skilled clinicians at obtaining information from clients and reaching an accurate diagnosis (Kobak et al., 1996; Taylor & Luce, 2003). Computer programs are also less expensive and more time efficient than personal interviews.

The future of computerized assessment remains undetermined. Though most clients and clinicians respond favorably to computerized assessment, some do not (Richard & Bobicz, 2003). Most of the resistance to using computer interviews seems to come from clinicians rather than clients. Some clin-

icians believe that personal, eye-to-eye contact is necessary to tease out a client's underlying concerns. Though the computer may never completely replace the human interviewer, a combination of computerized and interviewer-based assessment may strike the best balance of efficiency and sensitivity.

Another change in the offing is the development of online assessments. Some psychologists are conducting psychological assessments via e-mail and the Internet (Buchanan, 2002; Naglieri et al., 2004; VandenBos & Williams 2000). Traditional paper-and-pencil psychological tests can now be reproduced as a page on the Internet. The respondent can enter the data by keyboard and have the answers automatically transmitted to the test administrator for scoring and interpretation.

Online therapy is also now available and is the focus of yet another controversy in the field (see Chapter 4). With the rapid pace of technological developments today, there may well come a day when computerized programs with interactive voice technology will be used as stand-alone "therapists."

Critical Thinking

- How can the reliability of computerized assessment be measured? the validity of this assessment technique?
- Would computerized assessment be more appropriate for people with people with certain disorders, such as social phobia, than for others, such as schizophrenia? Explain.

Computerized interview. Would you be more likely or less likely to tell your problems to a computer than to a person? Computerized clinical interviews have been used for more than 25 years, and some research suggests that the computer may be more sensitive than its human counterpart in teasing out problems.

Attempts to define intelligence continue to stir debate in the field. David Wechsler (1975), the originator of the most widely used intelligence tests, the Wechsler scales, defined intelligence as "capacity . . . to understand the world . . . and . . . resourcefulness to cope with its challenges." From his perspective, intelligence has to do with the ways in which we (a) mentally represent the world and (b) adapt to its demands.

Intelligence tests are designed to measure intelligence, which is usually expressed in the form of an intelligence quotient, or IQ. An IQ score is based on the relative difference (deviation) of a person's score on an intelligence test from the norms of the person's age group. A score of 100 is defined as the mean. People who answer more items correctly than the average obtain IQ scores above 100; those who answer fewer items correctly obtain scores of less than 100.

Different Wechsler scales of intelligence are used with different age groups. The Wechsler scales group questions into subtests or subscales, with each subscale measuring a different intellectual ability. (Table 3.7 shows examples from the adult version of the test.) The Wechsler scales are thus designed to offer insight into a person's relative strengths and weaknesses, and not simply yield an overall score. Another widely used intelligence test, the Stanford-Binet Intelligence Scale also measures intelligence in children and young adults.

Wechsler's scales include both *verbal* and *performance* subtests to compute verbal and performance IQs. Verbal subtests generally require knowledge of verbal concepts; performance subtests rely more on spatial relations skills. (Figure 3.1 shows items similar to those on the performance subscales of the Wechsler scales.)

Students from various backgrounds yield different profiles. College students, generally speaking, perform better on verbal subtests than on performance subtests. Australian Aboriginal children outperform White Australian children on performance-type tasks that involve visual–spatial skills (Kearins, 1981). It could be that such skills foster survival in the harsh Australian outback. Intellectual attainments, like psychological adjustment, are connected with the demands of particular sociocultural and physical environmental settings.

Wechsler IQ scores are based on how respondents' answers deviate from those attained by their age-mates. The mean whole test score at any age is defined as 100. Wechsler distributed IQ scores so that 50% of the scores of the population would lie within a "broad average" range of 90 to 110.

TABLE 3.7

Examples of Subtests from the Wechsler Adult Intelligence Scale (WAIS-III)

Verbal Subtests	Performance Subtests
Information Who wrote *Paradise Lost?*	**Digit Symbol** Given a key showing a set of symbols that correspond to particular numbers, fill in the correct symbols for a series of numbers.
Comprehension What do people need to obey traffic laws? What does the saying, "The early bird catches the worm," mean?	**Picture Completion** Identify the missing part from a picture, such as the picture of the watch in Figure 3.1.
Arithmetic John wanted to buy a shirt that cost $31.50, but only had 17 dollars. How much more money would he need to buy the shirt?	**Block Design** Using blocks such as those in Figure 3.1, match the design shown.
Similarities How are a stapler and a paper clip alike?	**Picture Arrangement** Arrange the pictures in the correct order to tell a story.
Digit Span (Forward order) Listen to this series of numbers and repeat them back to me in the same order: 6 4 5 2 7 3 (Backward order) Listen to this series of numbers and then repeat them backward: 9 4 2 5 8 7	**Object Assembly** Arrange the pieces of the puzzle so that they form a meaningful object.
Vocabulary What does *capricious* mean?	

Source: Adapted from "Examples of Items Similar to Those on the WAIS-III" from J. S. Nevid, *Psychology: Concepts and Applications*, p. 282. © 2003. Reprinted with permission of Houghton Mifflin Company.

Picture Arrangement
These pictures tell a story but they are in the wrong order. Put them in the right order so that they tell a story.

Picture Completion
What part is missing from this picture?

 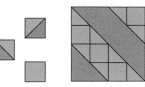

Block Design
Put the blocks together to make this picture.

Object Assembly
Put the pieces together as quickly as you can.

FIGURE 3.1 Items similar to those found on the performance subtests of the Wechsler Intelligence Scale (WAIS).
The Wechsler scales yield verbal and performance IQs that are based on the extent to which an individual's test scores deviate from the norm for her or his age group.

Source: Copyright (c) 1981 by the Psychological Corporation. Reproduced by permission. All rights reserved.

Most IQ scores cluster around the mean (see Figure 3.2). Just 5% of them are above 130 or below 70. Wechsler labeled people who attained scores of 130 or above as "very superior" and those with scores below 70 as "intellectually deficient."

Clinicians use IQ scales to evaluate a client's intellectual resources and to help diagnose mental retardation. IQ scores below 70 are one of the criteria used in diagnosing mental retardation. Next we consider two major types of tests used to assess personality: *self-report personality tests* and *projective tests*. Clinicians use personality tests to learn more about the client's underlying traits, needs, interests, and concerns.

Self-Report Personality Tests Do you like automobile magazines? Are you easily startled by noises in the night? Are you bothered by periods of anxiety or shakiness? **Self-report personality tests** use structured items, similar to these, to measure personality traits such as emotional instability, masculinity-femininity, and introversion. People are asked to respond to specific questions or statements about their feelings, thoughts, concerns, attitudes, interests, beliefs, and the like.

Self-report personality inventories are also called *objective tests* because the range of possible responses is limited. Tests might ask respondents to check adjectives that apply to them, to mark statements as true or false, to select preferred activities from lists, or

self-report personality test A structured personality test in which individuals give information about themselves by responding to items that require a limited type of response, such as "yes-no" or "agree-disagree."

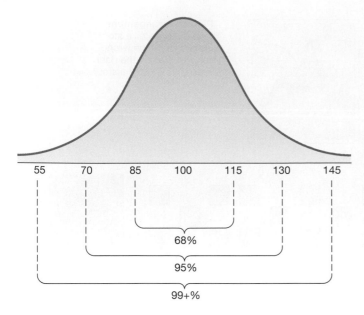

FIGURE 3.2 Normal distribution of IQ scores.
The distribution of IQ scores is based on a bell-shaped curve, which is referred to by psychologists as a normal curve. Wechsler defined the deviation IQ so that the average (mean) score was 100 and the standard deviation of scores was 15. A standard deviation is a statistical measure of the variability or dispersion of scores around the mean. Here we see the distribution of scores at one, two, and three standard deviations from the mean. Note also that 50% of the scores fall within the broad average range of 90 to 110.

TRUTH or FICTION? *REVISITED*

The most widely used personality inventory includes a number of questions that bear no obvious relationship to the traits the instrument purports to measure.

☑ **TRUE.** A leading personality inventory, the MMPI, contains items that bear no apparent relationship to the traits being measured. However, these items did differentiate between the response patterns of clinical diagnostic groups and normal reference groups.

to indicate whether items apply to them "always," "sometimes," or "never." For example, a test item may ask you to check either "true" or "false" to a statement like, "I feel uncomfortable in crowds." Here we focus on two of the more widely used personality tests in clinical settings, the Minnesota Multiphasic Personality Inventory (MMPI; now the MMPI-2) and the Millon Clinical Multiaxial Inventory (MCMI).

Minnesota Multiphasic Personality Inventory (MMPI-2) The MMPI-2 contains more than 500 true-false statements that assess interests habits, family relationships, physical (somatic) complaints, attitudes, beliefs, and behaviors characteristic of psychological disorders. It is widely used as a test of personality as well as to assist clinicians in diagnosing abnormal behavior patterns. The MMPI-2 consists of a number of individual scales composed of items that tended to be answered differently by members of carefully selected diagnostic groups, such as patients diagnosed with schizophrenia or depression, than by members of normal comparison groups.

Consider a hypothetical item: "I often read detective novels." If, for example, groups of depressed people tended to answer the item in a direction different from normal groups, the item would be placed on the depression scale. Many items that discriminate normal people from clinical groups are transparent in meaning, such as "I feel down much of the time." However, some items are more subtle in meaning or bear no obvious relationship to the measured trait. For example, a hypothetical item such as "I think people would be better off if they spent more time taking trains to flying whenever possible."

The items on the MMPI are divided into various clinical scales (see Table 3.8). A score of 65 or higher on a particular scale is considered clinically significant. The MMPI-2 also includes validity scales that assess tendencies to distort test responses in a favorable ("faking good") or unfavorable ("faking bad") direction. Other scales on the tests, called *content scales,* measure an individual's specific complaints and concerns, such as anxiety, anger, family problems, and problems of low self-esteem.

The MMPI-2 is interpreted according to individual scale elevations and interrelationships among scales. For example, a "2–7 profile," commonly found among people seeking therapy, refers to a test pattern in which scores for scales 2 ("Depression") and 7 ("Psychasthenia") are clinically significant. Clinicians may refer to "atlases," or descriptions, of people who usually attain various profiles.

MMPI-2 scales are regarded as reflecting continua of personality traits associated with the diagnostic categories represented by the test. For example, a high score on Scale 4, psychopathic deviation, suggests that the respondent holds a higher-than-average number of nonconformist beliefs and may be rebellious, which are characteristics often found in people with antisocial personality disorder. However, because it is not tied specifically to *DSM* criteria, this score cannot be used to establish a diagnosis. The MMPI, which was originally developed in the 1930s and 1940s, cannot provide diagnostic judgments consistent with the current version of the *DSM* system. Even so, MMPI profiles may suggest possible diagnoses that can be considered in the light of other evidence. Moreover, many clinicians use the MMPI to gain general information about respondents' personality traits and attributes that may underlie their psychological problems, rather than a diagnosis per se.

The validity of the MMPI-2 is supported by a large body of research findings (Garb, 2003; Kubisyzn et al., 2000). The test successfully discriminates between psychiatric patients and controls and between groups of people with different psychological disorders, such as anxiety versus depressive disorders (Ganellen, 1996; Graham, 2000). Moreover, the content scales of the MMPI-2 provide additional information to that provided by the clinical scales, which can help clinicians learn more about the client's specific problems (Graham, 2000; McGrath, Pogge, & Stokes, 2002).

TABLE 3.8

Clinical Scales of the MMPI-2

Scale Number	Scale Label	Items Similar to Those Found on MMPI Scale	Sample Traits of High Scorers
1	Hypochondriasis	My stomach frequently bothers me. At times, my body seems to ache all over.	Many physical complaints, cynical defeatist attitudes, often perceived as whiny, demanding
2	Depression	Nothing seems to interest me anymore. My sleep is often disturbed by worrisome thoughts.	Depressed mood; pessimistic, worrisome, despondent, lethargic
3	Hysteria	I sometimes become flushed for no apparent reason. I tend to take people at their word when they're trying to be nice to me.	Naive, egocentric, little insight into problems, immature; develops physical complaints in response to stress
4	Psychopathic deviate	My parents often disliked my friends. My behavior sometimes got me into trouble at school.	Difficulties incorporating values of society, rebellious, impulsive, antisocial tendencies; strained family relationships; poor work and school history
5	Masculinity-Femininity	I like reading about electronics. (M) I would like to work in the theater. (F)	Males endorsing feminine attributes: have cultural and artistic interests, effeminate, sensitive, passive Females endorsing male interests: Aggressive, masculine, self-confident, active, assertive, vigorous
6	Paranoia	I would have been more successful in life but people didn't give me a fair break. It's not safe to trust anyone these days.	Suspicious, guarded, blames others, resentful, aloof, may have paranoid delusions
7	Psychasthenia	I'm one of those people who have to have some thing to worry about. I seem to have more fears than most people I know.	Anxious, fearful, tense, worried, insecure, difficulties concentrating, obsessional, self-doubting
8	Schizophrenia	Things seem unreal to me at times. I sometimes hear things that other people can't hear.	Confused and illogical thinking, feels alienated and misunderstood, socially isolated or withdrawn, may have blatant psychotic symptoms such as hallucinations or delusional beliefs, or may lead detached, schizoid lifestyle
9	Hypomania	I sometimes take on more tasks than I can possibly get done. People have noticed that my speech is sometimes pressured or rushed.	Energetic, possibly manic, impulsive, optimistic, sociable, active, flighty, irritable, may have overly inflated or grandiose self-image or unrealistic plans
10	Social introversion	I don't like loud parties. I was not very active in school activities.	Shy, inhibited, withdrawn, introverted, lacks self-confidence, reserved, anxious in social situations

The Millon Clinical Multiaxial Inventory (MCMI) The MCMI was developed to help the clinician make diagnostic judgments within the multiaxial *DSM* system, especially in the personality disorders found on Axis II (Millon, 1982, 2003). The MCMI is the only objective personality test that focuses on personality style and disorders. The MMPI-2, in contrast, focuses on personality patterns associated with Axis I diagnoses, such as mood disorders, anxiety disorders, and schizophrenic disorders. Using the MCMI and MMPI-2 in combination may help the clinician make more subtle diagnostic distinctions than are possible with either test alone, because they assess different patterns of psychopathology (Antoni et al., 1986). However, relationships between the MCMI and the underlying personality disorders it is meant to assess remain under study. Though the MCMI may help clinicians discriminate among various Axis I and Axis II disorders and detect underlying personality characteristics (Kubiszyn et al., 2000; Salekin et al., 2003), some researchers voice concern that it may overdiagnose personality disorders (Guthrie & Mobley, 1994; Wetzler & Marlowe, 1993).

Evaluation of Self-Report Inventories Self-report tests are relatively easy to administer. Once the examiner has read the instructions to clients and made sure they can read and comprehend the items, clients can complete the tests unattended. Because the tests permit limited response options, such as marking items either true or false, they can be scored with high interrater reliability. Moreover, the accumulation of research findings on respondents provides a quantified basis for interpreting test responses. Such tests often reveal information that might not be revealed during a clinical interview or by observing the person's behavior. For example we might learn that a person harbors negative views of himself or herself—self-perceptions that may not be directly expressed in behavior or revealed during an interview. A disadvantage of self-rating tests is that they rely on clients as the source of data. Test responses may therefore reflect underlying response biases, such as a tendency to answer items in socially acceptable ways that may not reflect the person's true feelings. For this reason, self-report inventories, like the MMPI, contain validity scales to help ferret out response biases. Yet even these validity scales may not detect all sources of bias (Bagby, Nicholson, & Buis, 1998; Nicholson et al., 1997). Examiners may also look for corroborating information, such as interviewing others who are familiar with the client's behavior.

Tests are also only as valid as the criteria that were used to validate them. The original MMPI was limited in its role as a diagnostic instrument by virtue of the obsolete diagnostic categories that were used to classify the original clinical groups. Moreover, if a test does nothing more than identify people who are likely to belong to a particular diagnostic category, its utility is usurped by more economical means of arriving at diagnoses, such as the structured clinical interview. We expect more from personality tests than diagnostic classification, and the MMPI has shown its value in showing personality characteristics associated with people with certain response patterns. Psychodynamically oriented critics suggest that self-report instruments tell us little about possible unconscious processes. The use of such tests may also be limited to relatively high functioning individuals who can read well, respond to verbal material, and focus on a potentially tedious task. Clients who are disorganized, unstable, or confused may not be able to complete the tests.

projective tests Psychological tests that present ambiguous stimuli onto which the examinee is thought to project his or her personality and unconscious motives.

Projective Tests A **projective test,** unlike an objective test, offers no clear, specified response options. Clients are presented with ambiguous stimuli, such as inkblots, and asked to respond to them. The tests are called *projective* because they derive from the psychodynamic belief that people impose, or "project," their own psychological needs, drives, and motives, much of which lie in the unconscious, onto their interpretations of ambiguous stimuli.

The psychodynamic model holds that potentially disturbing impulses and wishes, often of a sexual or aggressive nature, are often hidden from consciousness by our defense mechanisms. Indirect methods of assessment, however, such as projective tests, may offer clues to unconscious processes. More behaviorally oriented critics contend, however, that the results of projective tests are based more on clinicians' subjective interpretations of test responses than on empirical evidence.

Many projective tests have been developed, including tests based on how people fill in missing words to complete sentence fragments or how they draw human figures and other objects. The two most prominent projective techniques are the Rorschach Inkblot Test and the Thematic Apperception Test (TAT).

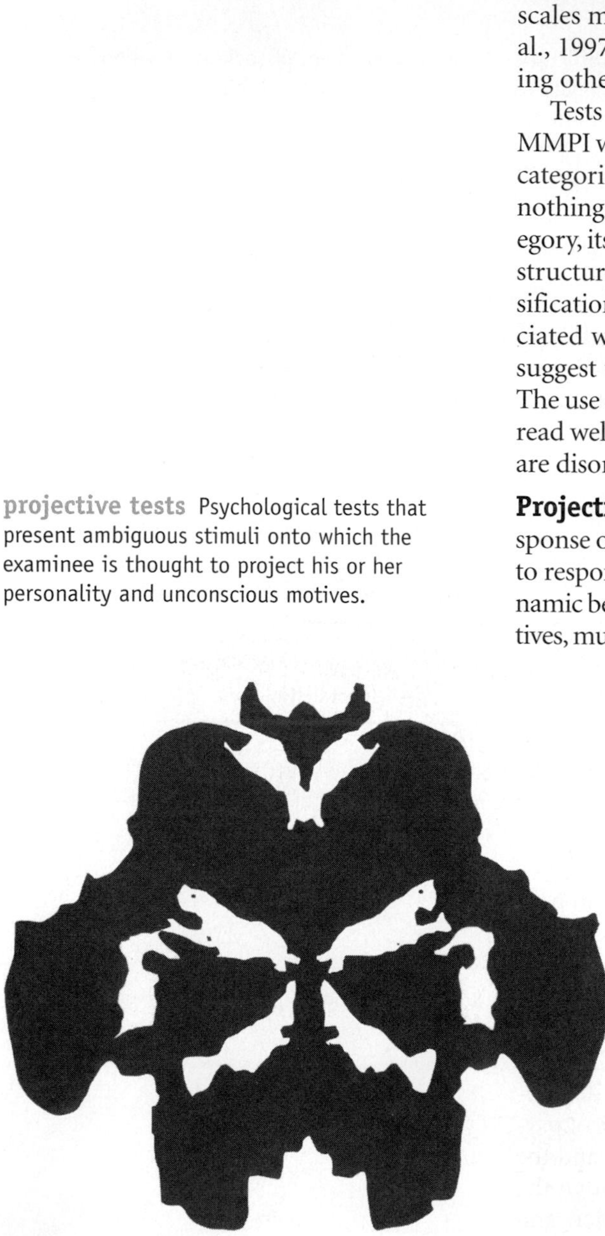

The Rorschach Test The Rorschach test was developed by a Swiss psychiatrist, Hermann Rorschach (1884–1922). As a child, Rorschach was intrigued by the game of dripping ink on paper and folding the paper to make symmetrical figures. He noted that people saw different things in the same blot, and he believed their "percepts" reflected their personalities as well as the stimulus cues provided by the blot. Rorschach's fraternity nickname was *Klex,* which means "inkblot" in German ("Time Capsule," 2000). As a psychiatrist, Rorschach experimented with hundreds of blots to identify those that could help in the diagnosis of psychological problems. He finally found a group of 15 blots that seemed to do the job and could be administered in a single session. Ten blots are used today because Rorschach's publisher did

FIGURE 3.3 An inkblot similar to those found on the Rorschach Inkblot Test.
What does the blot look like to you? What could it be? Rorschach assumed that people project their personalities into their responses to ambiguous inkblots.

not have the funds to reproduce all 15 blots in the first edition of the text on the subject. Rorschach never had the opportunity to learn how popular and influential his inkblot test would become. Sadly, seven months after the publication of the test that bears his name, Rorschach died at age 37 of complications from a ruptured appendix (Exner, 2002).

Five of the inkblots are black and white, and the other five have color (see Figure 3.3). Each inkblot is printed on a separate card, which is handed to subjects in sequence. Subjects are asked to tell the examiner what the blot might be or what it reminds them of. Then, they are asked to explain what features of the blot (its color, form, or texture) they used to form their perceptions.

Clinicians who use the Rorschach tend to interpret both the content and the form of the responses. For example, they may infer that people who use the entire blot in their responses show an ability to integrate events in meaningful ways. Those who focus on minor details of the blots may have obsessive–compulsive tendencies, whereas clients who respond to the negative (white) spaces may see things in their own idiosyncratic ways, suggesting underlying negativism or stubbornness.

A response consistent with the form or contours of the blot is suggestive of adequate **reality testing.** People who see movement in the blots may be revealing intelligence and creativity. Content analysis may shed light on underlying conflicts. For example, adult clients who see animals but no people may have problems relating to people. Clients who appear confused about whether or not percepts of people are male or female may, according to psychodynamic theory, be in conflict over their own gender identity.

The Thematic Apperception Test (TAT) The Thematic Apperception Test (TAT) was developed by psychologist Henry Murray (1943) at Harvard University in the 1930s. *Apperception* is a French word that can be translated as "interpreting (new ideas or impressions) on the basis of existing ideas (cognitive structures) and past experience." The TAT consists of a series of cards, each depicting an ambiguous scene (see Figure 3.4). It is assumed that clients' responses to the cards will reflect their experiences and outlooks on life—and, perhaps, shed light on their deep-seated needs and conflicts.

Respondents are asked to describe what is happening in each scene, what led up to it, what the characters are thinking and feeling, and what will happen next. Psychodynamic theorists believe that people will identify with the protagonists in their stories and project underlying psychological needs and conflicts into their responses. More superficially, the stories suggest how respondents might interpret or behave in similar situations in their own lives. TAT results may also be suggestive of clients' attitudes toward others, particularly family members and lovers.

Evaluation of Projective Techniques The reliability and validity of projective techniques have been the subject of extensive research and debate. One problem is the lack of a standard scoring procedure. Interpretation of a person's responses depends to some degree on the subjective judgment of the examiner. For example, two examiners may interpret the same Rorschach or TAT response differently.

Recent attempts to develop a comprehensive scoring approach for the Rorschach, such as the Exner system (Exner, 1991, 1993), have advanced the effort to standardize scoring of responses (Meyer et al., 2002). But debate over the reliability of the Rorschach, including the Exner system, continues (see Acklin et al., 2000; G. J. Meyer, 1997). Even if a Rorschach response can be scored reliably, the interpretation of the response—what it means—remains an open question.

The Rorschach continues to spark heated controversy in the field. Some reviewers find the overall validity of the Rorschach to

TRUTH or FICTION? *REVISITED*

One of the most widely used tests of personality asks people to interpret what they see in a series of inkblots.

☑ **TRUE.** The Rorschach is a widely used personality test in which a person's responses to inkblots are interpreted to reveal aspects of his or her personality

Reality testing. The ability to perceive the world accurately and to distinguish reality from fantasy.

FIGURE 3.4 Thematic Apperception Test (TAT). Psychologists ask test takers to provide their impressions of what is happening in the scene depicted in the drawing. They ask test takers what led up to the scene and how it will turn out. How might your responses reveal aspects of your own personality?

be generally on par with that of other psychological tests, such as the MMPI (e.g., Meyer et al., 2001; Meyer & Archer, 2001; Weiner, Spielberger, & Abeles, 2002, 2003). Evidence supports the validity of at least some specific Rorschach responses (e.g., Blais et al., 2001; Kubiszyn et al., 2000; G. J. Meyer, 2001; Viglione, 1999). For example, investigators find that Rorschach indicators can distinguish between different types of psychological disorders (Kubiszyn et al., 2000) and are helpful in detecting aggressive behavior (Baity & Hilsenroth, 2002), dependency behaviors, and forms of disturbed thinking (Lilienfeld, Fowler, & Lohr, 2003), as well as predicting psychotherapy outcomes (G. J. Meyer, 2000).

On the other hand, critics claim that the Rorschach can lead to overpredictions of psychopathology and has failed to meet overall tests of scientific utility or validity (Garb et al., 2002; Hamel et al., 2003; Hunsley & Bailey, 2001; Lilienfeld, Wood, & Garb, 2000). The debate over the validity and clinical utility of the Rorschach continues to rage between supporters and detractors with no resolution in sight (Garb, 2003; Meyer, 2001; Perry, 2003; Weiner, 2001). Recently, psychologist George Stricker (2003) appraised the present standoff in the field as follows: "The field remains divided between believers and nonbelievers, and each is able to marshal considerable evidence and discount the evidence of their opponents to support their point of view" (p. 728).

One criticism of the TAT is that the stimulus properties of some of the cards, such as cues depicting sadness or anger, may exert too strong a "stimulus pull" on the subject. If so, clients' responses may represent reactions to the stimulus cues rather than projections of their personalities (Murstein & Mathes, 1996). The validity of the TAT in eliciting deep-seated material or tapping underlying psychopathology also remains to be demonstrated. However, evidence does indicate that it can discriminate between different types of Axis I and Axis II disorders (Kubiszyn et al., 2000).

Proponents of projective testing argue that in skilled hands, tests like the TAT and the Rorschach can yield meaningful material that might not be revealed in interviews or by self-rating inventories (Stricker & Gold, 1999). Moreover, allowing subjects freedom of expression through projective testing reduces the tendency of individuals to offer socially desirable responses.

Neuropsychological Assessment

Neuropsychological assessment involves the use of tests to help determine whether psychological problems reflect underlying neurological impairment or brain damage. When neurological impairment is suspected, a neurological evaluation may be requested from a *neurologist*—a medical doctor who specializes in disorders of the nervous system. A clinical *neuropsychologist* may also be consulted to administer neuropsychological assessment techniques, such as behavioral observation and psychological testing, to reveal signs of possible brain damage. Neuropsychological testing may be used together with brain-imaging techniques such as the MRI and CT to shed light on relationships between brain function and underlying abnormalities (Fiez, 2001). The results of neuropsychological testing may not only suggest whether patients suffer from brain damage but also point to the parts of the brain that may be affected.

The Bender Visual Motor Gestalt Test   One of the first neuropsychological tests to be developed and still one of the most widely used neuropsychological tests is the Bender Visual Motor Gestalt Test (Raphael, Golden, & Cassidy-Feltgen, 2002). "The Bender" consists of geometric figures that illustrate various Gestalt principles of perception (Bender, 1938). The client is asked to copy nine geometric designs (see Figure 3.5). Signs of possible brain damage include rotation of the figures, distortions in shape, and incorrect sizing of the figures in relation to one another. The examiner then asks the client to reproduce the designs from memory, because neurological damage can impair memory functioning.

Although the Bender remains a convenient and economical means of uncovering possible organic impairment, it has been criticized for producing too many false negatives—that is, persons with neurological impairment who make satisfactory drawings (Bigler & Ehrhenfurth, 1981). In recent years, more sophisticated tests have been

neuropsychological assessment
Measurement of behavior or performance that may be indicative of underlying brain damage or defects.

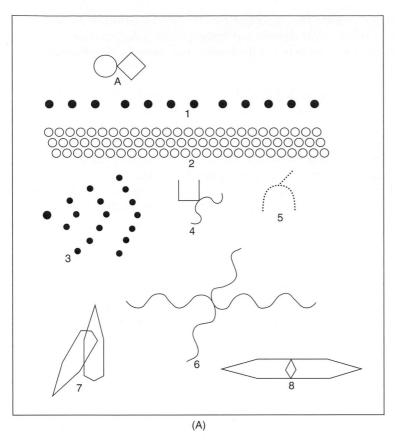
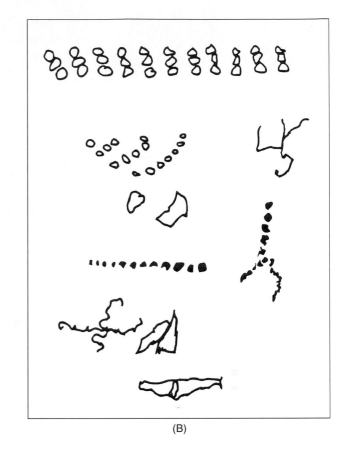

FIGURE 3.5 The Bender Visual Motor Gestalt Test.
The "Bender" is intended to assess organic impairment. Part A shows the series of figures respondents are asked to copy. Part B shows the drawings of a person who is known to be brain damaged.

developed. Two of the more widely used neuropsychological inventories today are the Halstead-Reitan Neuropsychological Battery and the Luria-Nebraska Neuropsychological Battery.

The Halstead-Reitan Neuropsychological Battery Psychologist Ralph Reitan developed the battery by adapting tests used by his mentor, Ward Halstead, an experimental psychologist, to study brain–behavior relationships among organically impaired individuals. The battery contains tests that measure perceptual, intellectual, and motor skills and performance. A battery of tests permits the psychologist to observe patterns of results, and various patterns of performance deficits are suggestive of certain kinds of organic defects, such as those that often occur following head trauma (Reitan & Wolfson, 2000). The tests in the battery include the following:

1. *The Category Test.* This test measures abstract thinking ability, as indicated by the individual's proficiency at forming principles or categories that relate different stimuli to one another. A series of groups of stimuli that vary in shape, size, location, color, and other characteristics are flashed on a screen. The subject's task is to discern the principle that links them, such as shape or size, and to indicate which stimuli in each grouping represent the correct category by pressing a key. By analyzing the patterns of correct and incorrect choices, the subject normally learns to identify the principles that determine the correct choice. Performance on the test is believed to reflect functioning in the frontal lobe of the cerebral cortex.

2. *The Rhythm Test.* This is a test of concentration and attention. The subject listens to 30 pairs of tape-recorded rhythmic beats and indicates whether the beats in each pair are the same or different. Performance deficits are associated with damage to the right temporal lobe of the cerebral cortex.

3. *The Tactual Performance Test.* This test requires the blindfolded subject to fit wooden blocks of different shapes into corresponding depressions on a form board. Afterward, the subject draws the board from memory as a measure of visual memory.

The Luria-Nebraska Neuropsychological Battery (LNNB). The Luria-Nebraska is based on the work of the Russian neuropsychologist Alexandr Luria and was developed by psychologists at the University of Nebraska (Purisch, 2001). Like the Halstead-Reitan, the Luria-Nebraska reveals patterns of skill deficits that are suggestive of particular sites of brain damage. The Luria-Nebraska is more efficiently administered than the Halstead-Reitan, requiring about one third the time to complete.

A wide range of skills is assessed. Tests measure tactile, kinesthetic, and spatial skills; complex motor skills; auditory skills; receptive and expressive speech skills; reading, writing, and arithmetic skills; and general intelligence and memory functioning.

Neuropsychological tests attempt to reveal underlying brain abnormalities without the need to resort to surgical procedures. Researchers find that when clinicians use batteries of neuropsychological tests, they can form reliable and accurate judgments about impaired cognitive functioning resulting from underlying brain damage (Garb, 2000; Kubiszyn et al., 2000). Moreover, these judgments cannot be derived simply on the basis of interviews or casual observations of patients' behaviors. We later consider other contemporary techniques that allow us to probe the workings of the brain without surgery.

Behavioral Assessment

Traditional personality tests such as the MMPI, Rorschach, and TAT were designed to measure underlying psychological traits and dispositions. Test responses are interpeted as *signs* of traits and dispositions believed to play important roles in determining people's behavior. For example, certain Rorschach responses are interpreted as revealing underlying traits, such as psychological dependency, that are believed to influence how people relate to others. In contrast, **behavioral assessment** treats test results as *samples* of behavior that occur in specific situations rather than as *signs* of underlying personality traits. According to the behavioral approach, behavior is primarily determined by environmental or situational factors, such as stimulus cues and reinforcement, not by underlying traits

Behavioral assessment aims to sample an individual's behavior in settings as similar as possible to the real-life situation, thus maximizing the relationship between the testing situation and the criterion. Behavior may be observed and measured in such settings as the home, school, or work environment. The examiner may also try to simulate situations in the clinic or laboratory that serve as analogues of the problems the individual confronts in daily life.

The examiner may conduct a *functional analysis* of the problem behavior—an analysis of the problem behavior in relation to antecedents, or stimulus cues that trigger it, and consequences, or reinforcements that maintain it. Knowledge of the environmental conditions in which a problem behavior occurs may help the therapist work with the client and the family to change the conditions that trigger and maintain it. The examiner may conduct a *behavioral interview* by posing questions to learn more about the history and situational aspects of problem behavior. For example, if a client seeks help because of panic attacks, the behavioral interviewer might ask how the client experiences these attacks—when, where, how often, under what circumstances. The interviewer looks for precipitating cues, such as thought patterns (e.g., thoughts of dying or losing control) or situational factors (e.g., entering a department store) that may provoke an attack. The interviewer also seeks information about reinforcers that may maintain the panic. Does the client flee the situation when an attack occurs? Is escape reinforced by relief from anxiety? Has the client learned to lessen anticipatory anxiety by avoiding exposure to situations in which attacks have occurred?

The examiner may also use observational methods to connect the problem behavior to the stimuli and reinforcements that help maintain it. Consider the case of Kerry.

behavioral assessment The approach to clinical assessment that focuses on the objective recording and description of problem behavior.

Kerry, the "Royal Terror"

A 7-year-old boy, Kerry, is brought by his parents for evaluation. His mother describes him as a "royal terror." His father complains he won't listen to anyone. Kerry throws temper tantrums in the supermarket, screaming and stomping his feet if his parents refuse to buy him what he wants. At home, he breaks his toys by throwing them against the wall and demands new ones. Sometimes, though, he appears sullen and won't talk to anyone for hours. At school he appears inhibited and has difficulty concentrating. His progress at school is slow, and he has difficulty reading. His teachers complain he has a limited attention span and doesn't seem motivated.

—The Authors' Files

The psychologist may use direct home observation to assess the interactions between Kerry and his parents. Alternatively, the psychologist may observe Kerry and his parents through a one-way mirror in the clinic. Such observations may suggest interactions that explain the child's noncompliance. For example, Kerry's noncompliance may follow parental requests that are vague (e.g., a parent says, "Play nicely now," and Kerry responds by throwing toys) or inconsistent (e.g., a parent says, "Go play with your toys but don't make a mess," to which Kerry responds by scattering the toys). Observation may suggest ways in which Kerry's parents can improve communication and cue and reinforce desirable behaviors.

Direct observation, or behavioral observation, is the hallmark of behavioral assessment. Through direct observation, clinicians can observe and quantify problem behavior. Observations may be videotaped to permit subsequent analysis of behavioral patterns. Observers are trained to identify and record targeted patterns of behavior. Behavior coding systems have been developed that enhance the reliability of recording.

There are both advantages and disadvantages to direct observation. One advantage is that direct observation does not rely on the client's self-reports, which may be distorted by efforts to make a favorable or unfavorable impression. In addition to providing accurate measurements of problem behavior, behavioral observation can suggest strategies for intervention. A mother might report that her son is so hyperactive he cannot sit still long enough to complete homework assignments. By using a one-way mirror, the clinician may discover that the boy becomes restless only when he encounters a problem he cannot solve right away. The child may then be helped by being taught ways of coping with frustration and of solving certain kinds of academic problems.

Direct observation also has its drawbacks. One issue is the possible lack of consensus in defining problems in behavioral terms. In coding the child's behavior for hyperactivity, clinicians must agree on which aspects of the child's behavior represent hyperactivity. Another potential problem is a lack of reliability, or inconsistency, of measurement across time or between observers. Reliability is reduced when an observer is inconsistent in the coding of specific behaviors or when two or more observers code behavior inconsistently.

Observers may also show response biases. An observer who has been sensitized to expect that a child is hyperactive may perceive normal variations in behavior as subtle cues of hyperactivity and erroneously record them as instances of hyperactive behavior. We can help minimize these biases by keeping observers uninformed or "blind" about the target subject they are observing.

Reactivity is another potential problem. Reactivity refers to the tendency for the behavior being observed to be influenced by the way in which it is measured. For example, people may put their best feet forward when they know they are being observed. Using covert observation techniques, such as hidden cameras or one-way mirrors, may reduce reactivity. Covert observation may not be feasible, however, because of ethical concerns or practical constraints. Another approach is to accustom subjects to observation by watching them a number of times before collecting data. Another potential problem is *observer drift*—the tendency of observers, or groups of raters, to deviate from the coding system in which they were trained as time elapses. One suggestion to help control this problem is to regularly retrain observers to ensure continued compliance with the coding system (Kazdin, 1992). As time elapses, observers may also become fatigued or distracted. It may be helpful to limit the duration of observations and to provide frequent breaks.

Behavioral observation is limited to measuring overt behaviors. Many clinicians also wish to assess subjective or private experiences—for example, feelings of depression and anxiety or distorted thought patterns. Such clinicians may combine direct observation with forms of assessment that permit clients to reveal internal experiences. Staunch behavioral clinicians tend to consider self-reports unreliable and to limit their data to direct observation.

In addition to behavioral interviews and direct observation, behavioral assessment may involve the use of other techniques, such as self-monitoring, contrived or analogue measures, and behavioral rating scales.

Self-Monitoring Training clients to record or monitor the problem behavior in their daily lives is another method of relating problem behavior to the settings in which it occurs. In **self-monitoring,** clients assume the responsibility for assessing the problem behavior in the settings in which it naturally occurs.

Behaviors that can be easily counted, such as food intake, cigarette smoking, nail biting, hair pulling, study periods, or social activities, are well suited for self-monitoring. Self-monitoring can produce highly accurate measurement, because the behavior is recorded as it occurs, not reconstructed from memory.

There are various devices for keeping track of the targeted behavior. A behavioral diary or log is a handy way to record calories ingested or cigarettes smoked. Such logs can be organized in columns and rows to track the frequency of occurrence of the problem behavior and the situations in which it occurs (time, setting, feeling state, etc.). A record of eating may include entries for the type of food eaten, the number of calories, the location in which the eating occurred, the feeling states associated with eating, and the consequences of eating (e.g., how the client felt afterward). In reviewing an eating diary with the clinician, a client can identify problematic eating patterns, such as eating when feeling bored or in response to TV food commercials, and devise better ways of handling these cues.

Today, clinicians are turning to the use of palmtop electronic devices, such as electronic diaries or personal digital assistants (PDAs) to help clients track specific behaviors. In one recent study, teenagers used palmtop devices to keep track of their smoking behavior and aggressive and depressive symptoms (Whalen et al., 2001).

Behavioral diaries can also help clients increase desirable but low-frequency behaviors, such as assertive behavior and dating behavior. Unassertive clients might track occasions that seem to warrant an assertive response and jot down their actual responses to each occasion. Clients and clinicians then review the log to highlight problematic situations and rehearse assertive responses. A client who is anxious about dating might record social contacts with the opposite gender. To measure the effects of treatment, clinicians may encourage clients to engage in a baseline period of self-monitoring before treatment is begun.

Self-monitoring, though, is not without its disadvantages. Some clients are unreliable and do not keep accurate records. They become forgetful or sloppy, or they underreport undesirable behaviors, such as overeating or smoking, because of embarrassment or fear of criticism. To offset these biases, clinicians may, with clients' consent, corroborate the accuracy of self-monitoring by gathering information from other parties, such as clients' spouses. Private behaviors such as eating or smoking alone cannot be corroborated in this way, however. Sometimes other means of corroboration, such as physiological measures, are available. For example, blood alcohol levels can be used to verify self-reports of alcohol use, or analysis of carbon monoxide levels in clients' breath samples can be used to corroborate reports of abstinence from smoking.

Recording undesirable behaviors may make people more aware of the need to change them. Thus, self-monitoring can be put to therapeutic use if it leads to adaptive behavioral changes. In one weight-loss study, for example, the more consistently participants monitored what they ate, the more weight they lost (Baker & Kirschenbaum, 1993). This is not to imply that self-monitoring alone is sufficient to produce a desired behavior change. Motivation to change and skills needed to make behavior changes are also important.

---

self-monitoring The process of observing or recording one's own behaviors, thoughts, or emotions.

TRUTH or FICTION? *REVISITED*

People in weight-loss programs who carefully monitor what they eat tend to lose less weight than people who are less-reliable monitors.

☑ **FALSE.** Investigators found that the more consistently weight-loss program participants monitored what they ate, the more weight they lost.

Analogue Measures   *Analogue measures* are intended to simulate the setting in which the behavior naturally takes place but are carried out in laboratory or controlled settings. Role-playing exercises are common analogue measures. For example, suppose a client has difficulty challenging authority figures, such as professors. The clinician might describe a scene to the client as follows: "You've worked very hard on a term paper and received a very poor grade, say a D or an F. You approach the professor, who asks, 'Is there some problem?' What do you do now?" The client's enactment of the scene may reveal deficits in self-expression that can be addressed in therapy or assertiveness training.

The Behavioral Approach Task, or BAT, is a widely used analogue measure of a phobic person's approach to a feared object, such as a snake. Approach behavior is broken down into levels of response, such as looking in the direction of the snake from about 20 feet, touching the box holding the snake, and touching the snake. The BAT provides direct measurement of a response to a stimulus in a controlled situation. The subject's approach behavior can be quantified by assigning a score to each level of approach. In a recent treatment study of phobic children, the effectiveness of treatment was gauged in part by comparing the children's ability to approach the phobic stimulus (e.g., live animal, insect) after treatment with their performance before treatment (Öst et al., 2001).

Behavioral Rating Scales   A *behavioral rating scale* is a checklist that provides information about the frequency, intensity, and range of problem behaviors. Behavioral rating scales differ from self-report personality inventories, in that items assess specific behaviors rather than personality characteristics, interests, or attitudes.

Behavioral rating scales are often used by parents to assess children's problem behaviors. The Child Behavior Checklist (CBCL) (Achenbach & Dumenci, 2001; Achenbach & Edelbrock, 1979), for example, asks parents to rate their children on more than 100 specific problem behaviors, including the following:

- ❏ refuses to eat
- ❏ is disobedient
- ❏ hits
- ❏ is uncooperative
- ❏ destroys own things

The scale yields an overall problem behavior score and subscale scores on dimensions such as delinquency, aggressiveness, and physical problems. The clinician can compare the child's score on these dimensions with norms based on samples of age-mates.

Cognitive Assessment

Cognitive assessment involves measurement of *cognitions*—thoughts, beliefs, and attitudes. Cognitive therapists believe that people who hold self-defeating or dysfunctional cognitions are at greater risk of developing emotional problems, such as depression, in the face of stressful or disappointing life experiences. They help clients replace dysfunctional thinking patterns with self-enhancing, rational thought patterns.

Several methods of cognitive assessment have been developed. One of the most straightforward is the thought record or diary. Depressed clients may carry such diaries to record dysfunctional thoughts as they arise. Aaron Beck (A. T. Beck et al., 1979) designed a thought diary or "Daily Record of Dysfunctional Thoughts" to help clients identify thought patterns connected with troubling emotional states. Each time the client experiences a negative emotion such as anger or sadness, entries are made to identify

1. The situation in which the emotional state occurred
2. The automatic or disruptive thoughts that passed through the client's mind

cognitive assessment   Measurement of thoughts, beliefs, and attitudes that may be associated with emotional problems.

Behavioral approach task.   One form of behavioral assessment of phobia involves measurement of the degree to which the person can approach or interact with the phobic stimulus. Here we see a woman with a snake phobia tentatively reaching out to touch the phobic object. Other people with snake phobias would not be able to touch the snake or even remain in its presence unless it was securely caged.

3. The type or category of disordered thinking that the automatic thought(s) represented (e.g., selective abstraction, overgeneralization, magnification, or absolutist thinking—see Chapter 2)

4. A rational response to the troublesome thought

5. The emotional outcome or final emotional response

A thought diary can become part of a treatment program in which the client learns to replace dysfunctional thoughts with rational alternative thoughts.

The *Automatic Thoughts Questionnaire* (ATQ-30; Hollon & Kendall, 1980) has clients rate the weekly frequency and degree of conviction associated with 30 automatic negative thoughts. (Automatic thoughts are thoughts that seem to just pop into our minds.) Sample items include the following:

- I don't think I can go on.
- I hate myself.
- I've let people down.

A total score is obtained by summing the frequencies of occurrence of each item. Higher scores are considered typical of depressive thought patterns. The scale discriminates between depressed and nondepressed subjects, and higher scores are indicative of more severe depressive symptoms (Blankstein & Segal, 2001). The scale is also used to measure cognitive changes occurring during cognitve-behavioral therapy (Furlong & Oei, 2002). The 30-item ATQ has been statistically sorted into four categories or factors of related thoughts (see Table 3.9).

Another cognitive measure, the *Dysfunctional Attitudes Scale* (DAS; A. N. Weissman & Beck, 1978), consists of an inventory of a relatively stable set of underlying attitudes or assumptions associated with depression (Blankstein & Segal, 2001). Examples include, "I feel like I'm nothing if someone I love doesn't love me back." Subjects use a 7-point scale to rate the degree to which they endorse each belief. The DAS taps underlying assumptions believed to predispose individuals to depression, so it may be sensitive to detecting vulnerability to depression (DeRubeis, Tang, & Beck, 2001; Weich, Churchill, & Lewis, 2003). However, some evidence indicates that the DAS may actually

TABLE 3.9

Items Defining Factors on the Automatic Thoughts Questionnaire

Factor 1: Personal maladjustment and desire for change	Something has to change. What's the matter with me? I wish I were a better person. What's wrong with me? I'm so disappointed in myself.
Factor 2: Negative self-concept and negative expectations	My future is bleak. I'm a failure. I'll never make it. My life's not going the way I wanted it to. I'm a loser. Why can't I ever succeed? I'm no good.
Factor 3: Low self-esteem	I'm worthless. I hate myself.
Factor 4: Giving up/helplessness	I can't finish anything. It's just not worth it.

Source: Adapted from Hollon & Kendall (1980).

measure depression itself, rather than vulnerability to depression (Calhoon, 1996). Whatever the case, it clearly taps into a style of thinking associated with depression.

Cognitive assessment opens a new domain to the psychologist in understanding how disruptive thoughts are related to abnormal behavior. Only in the past two decades or so have cognitive and cognitive-behavioral therapists begun to explore what B. F. Skinner labeled the "black box"—people's internal states—to learn how thoughts and attitudes influence emotional states and behavior.

The behavioral objection to cognitive techniques is that clinicians have no direct means of verifying clients' subjective experiences, their thoughts and beliefs. These are private experiences that can be reported but not observed and measured directly. However, even though thoughts remain private experiences, reports of cognitions in the form of rating scales or checklists can be quantified and validated by reference to external criteria.

Physiological Measurement

Physiological assessment is the study of people's physiological responses. Anxiety, for example, is associated with arousal of the sympathetic division of the autonomic nervous system (see Chapter 2). Anxious people therefore show elevated heart rates and blood pressure, which can be measured directly by means of the pulse and a blood pressure cuff. People also sweat more heavily when they are anxious. When we sweat, our skin becomes wet, increasing its ability to conduct electricity. Sweating can be measured by means of the *electrodermal response* or galvanic skin response (GSR). (*Galvanic* is named after the Italian physicist and physician Luigi Galvani, who was a pioneer in research in electricity.) Measures of the GSR assess the amount of electricity that passes through two points on the skin, usually of the hand. We assume the person's anxiety level correlates with the amount of electricity conducted across the skin.

The GSR is just one example of a physiological response measured through probes or sensors connected to the body. Another example is the *electroencephalograph (EEG)*, which measures brain waves by attaching electrodes to the scalp (Figure 3.6).

Changes in muscle tension are also often associated with states of anxiety or tension. They can be detected through the *electromyograph (EMG)*, which monitors muscle tension through sensors attached to targeted muscle groups. Placement of EMG probes on the forehead can indicate muscle tension associated with tension headaches.

Brain-Imaging and Recording Techniques Advances in medical technology have made it possible to study the workings of the brain without the need for surgery. One of the most common is the *electroencephalograph* (EEG), which is a record of the electrical activity of the brain. The EEG detects minute amounts of electrical activity in the brain, or brain waves, that are conducted between electrodes. Certain brain wave patterns are associated with mental states such as relaxation and with the different stages of sleep. The EEG is used to examine brain wave patterns associated with psychological disorders, such as schizophrenia, and with brain damage. It is also used to study various abnormal behavior patterns. The EEG is also used by medical personnel to reveal brain abnormalities such as tumors.

Brain-imaging techniques generate images that reflect the structure and functioning of the brain. In a *computed tomography (CT)* scan, a narrow X-ray beam is aimed at the head (Figure 3.7). The radiation that passes through is measured from multiple angles. The CT scan (also called CAT scan for *computerized axial tomography*) reveals abnormalities in shape and structure that may be suggestive of lesions, blood clots, or tumors. The computer enables scientists to integrate the measurements into a three-dimensional picture of the brain. Evidence of brain damage that was once detectable only by surgery may now be displayed on a monitor.

Another imaging method, *positron emission tomography (PET scan)*, is used to study the functioning of various parts of the brain (Figure 3.8). In this method, a small amount of a radioactive compound or tracer is mixed with glucose and injected into the bloodstream. When it reaches the brain, patterns of neural ac-

physiological assessment Measurement of physiological responses that may be associated with abnormal behavior.

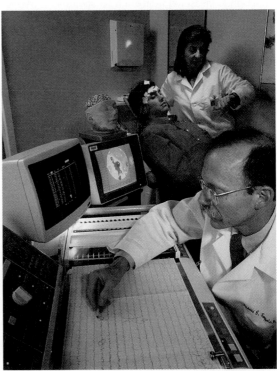

FIGURE 3.6 The electroencephalograph (EEG). The EEG can be used to study differences in brain waves between groups of normal people and people with problems such as schizophrenia or organic brain damage.

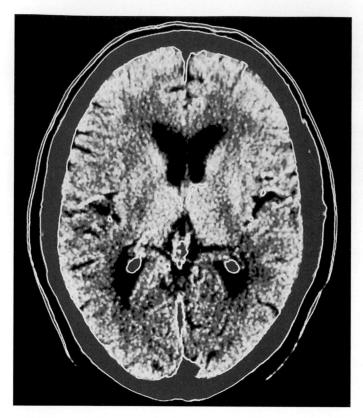

FIGURE 3.7 The computed tomography (CT) scan.
The CT scan aims a narrow X-ray beam at the head, and the resultant radiation is measured from multiple angles as it passes through. The computer enables researchers to consolidate the measurements into a three-dimensional image of the brain. The CT scan reveals structural abnormalities in the brain that may be implicated in various patterns of abnormal behavior.

TRUTH or FICTION? *REVISITED*

Despite advances in technology, physicians today must perform surgery to study the workings of the brain.

☑ **FALSE.** Advances in brain-imaging techniques make it possible to observe the workings of the brain without invasive surgery.

TRUTH or FICTION? *REVISITED*

Cocaine cravings in people addicted to cocaine have been linked to parts of the brain that are normally activated during pleasant emotions.

☑ **FALSE.** Just the opposite was the case. Cravings were associated with activation of parts of the brain that normally become active when watching depressing videotapes.

tivity are revealed by measurement of the positrons—positively charged particles—emitted by the tracer. The glucose metabolized by parts of the brain generates a computer image of neural activity. Areas of greater activity metabolize more glucose. The PET scan has been used to learn which parts of the brain are most active (metabolize more glucose) when we are listening to music, solving a math problem, or using language. It can also be used to reveal abnormalities in brain activity in people with schizophrenia (see Chapter 12).

A third imaging technique is *magnetic resonance imaging (MRI)*. In MRI, the person is placed in a donut-shaped tunnel that generates a strong magnetic field. The basic idea of the MRI, in the words of its inventor, is to stuff a human being into a large magnet (Weed, 2003). Radio waves of certain frequencies are then directed at the head. As a result, the brain emit signals that can be measured from several angles. As with the CT scan, the signals are integrated into a computer-generated image of the brain, which can reveal brain abnormalities associated with psychological disorders, such as schizophrenia and obsessive-compulsive disorder.

A new type of MRI, called *functional magnetic resonance imaging (fMRI)*, is used to identify parts of the brain that become active when people engage in particular tasks, such as vision, memory, or use of speech (Carpenter, 2000; Ingram & Siegle, 2001; Stern & Silbersweig, 2001) (see Figure 3.9). A recent fMRI study showed that when cocaine-addicted subjects experienced cocaine cravings, they showed increased activity in parts of the brain that were engaged when healthy subjects watched depressing videotapes (Wexler et al., 2001). This suggests there may be a physiological link between depressive feelings and drug cravings.

Brain electrical activity mapping (BEAM), a sophisticated type of EEG, uses the computer to analyze brain wave patterns and reveal areas of relative activity and inactivity from moment to moment (Figure 3.10) (F. H. Duffy, 1994; Silberstein et al., 1998). Twenty or more electrodes are

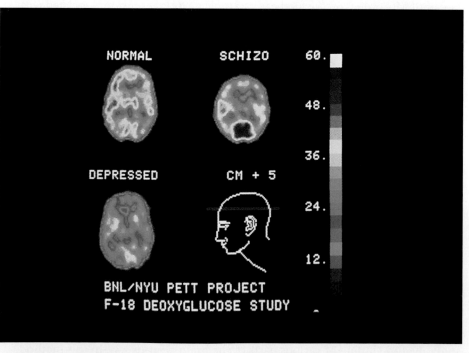

FIGURE 3.8 Positron emission tomography (PET) scan.
These PET scan images suggest differences in the metabolic processes of the brains of people with depression, schizophrenia, and controls who are free of psychological disorders

attached to the scalp and simultaneously feed information about brain activity to a computer. The computer analyzes the signals and displays the pattern of brain activity on a color monitor, providing a vivid image of the electrical activity of the brain at work. BEAM and other similar techniques have been helpful in studying the brain activity of people with schizophrenia and children with attention-deficit hyperactivity disorder, among other physical and psychological disorders. In later chapters we see how modern imaging techniques are furthering our understanding of various patterns of abnormal behavior.

SOCIOCULTURAL AND ETHNIC FACTORS IN ASSESSMENT

Researchers and clinicians must keep sociocultural and ethnic factors in mind when assessing personality traits and psychological disorders. When testing people from other cultures, careful translations are essential to capture the meanings of the original items (Butcher et al., 2002, 2003). However, assessment techniques that are reliable and valid within one culture may not be so in another, even when they are translated accurately (Bolton, 2001; Cheung et al., 2003).

For example, the Chinese version of the Beck Depression Inventory (BDI), a widely used inventory of depression in the United States, has shown good validity in distin-

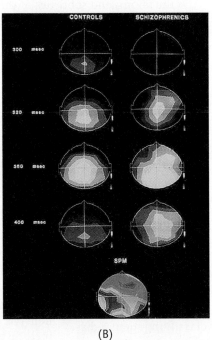

FIGURE 3.9 Functional magnetic resonance imaging (fMRI).
A fMRI is a specialized type of MRI that allows investigators to determine the parts of the brain that are activated during particular tasks. The areas depicted in red become activated when a person thinks about performing certain gestures (top), such as using a hammer or writing with a pen, and when the person actually performs these gestures (bottom). The right hemisphere is shown on the left side of the photographs, and the left hemisphere is shown on the right side.

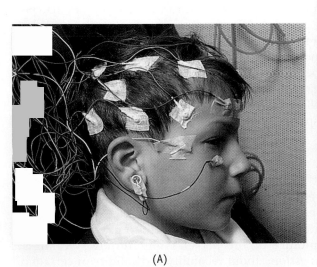

(A) (B)

FIGURE 3.10 Brain electrical activity mapping (BEAM).
BEAM is a type of EEG in which electrodes are attached to the scalp (Part A) to measure electrical activity in various regions of the brain. The left column of Part B shows the average level of electrical activity in the brains of 10 normal people ("controls") at 4 time intervals. The column to the right shows the average level of activity of subjects with schizophrenia during the same intervals. Higher activity levels are represented in increasing order by yellows, reds, and whites. The computer-generated image in the bottom center summarizes differences in activity levels between the brains of normal subjects and those with schizophrenia. Areas of the brain depicted in blue show small differences between the groups. White areas represent larger differences.

guishing people with depression from people without depression (Chan, 1991; Yeung et al., 2002). However, other investigators found that Chinese people in both Hong Kong and the People's Republic of China showed high levels of disturbed behavior when tested with a Chinese version of the MMPI (Cheung, Song, & Butcher, 1991). However, more careful analysis suggests that their test responses reflected cultural differences rather than greater psychopathology (Cheung, 1991; Cheung & Ho, 1997). In other words, researchers need to disentangle psychopathology from sociocultural factors. Translations of assessment instruments should not only translate words, but also provide instructions that encourage examiners to address the importance of cultural beliefs, norms, and values, so diagnosticians and interviewers will consider the client's background when making assessments of abnormal behavior patterns.

Studies in our own culture have put the MMPI-2 under a cultural microscope. Researchers have shown that the test is as accurate in predicting psychological adjustment of African Americans as non-Hispanic White Americans (Timbrook & Graham, 1994). Moreover, these researchers found only small differences in average test scores of African Americans and non-Hispanic White Americans when factors such as age, education, and income were taken into account. Overall, investigators find no evidence of clinically significant cultural bias on the MMPI-2 in comparing groups of African American and non-Hispanic White patients in either outpatient or inpatient settings (Arbisi, Ben-Porath, & McNulty, 2002; McNulty et al., 1997). In yet other research, investigators found that the MMPI-2 was sensitive to detecting problem behaviors and symptoms in American Indian tribal members (Greene et al., 2003; Robin et al., 2003).

Interviewers must also recognize that problems can arise when interviews are conducted in a language other than the client's mother tongue. Hispanics, for example, often are judged more disturbed when interviewed in English than in Spanish (Fabrega, 1990). Interviewers, too, who are using a second language sometimes fail to appreciate the idioms and subtleties of the language. One interviewer in a U.S. mental hospital, a foreign-born and -trained psychiatrist, reported that a patient exhibited the delusional belief that he was outside his body. The interviewer based this assessment on the patient's response when asked if he was feeling anxious. "Yes, Doc," the patient replied, "I feel like I'm jumping out of my skin at times."

In conclusion, people's psychological problems, which are no less complex than people themselves, are assessed in many ways. Clients are asked to explain their problems as best they can; sometimes a computer does the asking. Psychologists can draw on batteries of tests that assess intelligence, personality, and neuropsychological integrity. Many psychologists prefer to observe people's behavior directly. Modern technology has provided several means of studying the structure and function of the brain. The methods of assessment clinicians select reflect the problems of their clients, their theoretical orientations, and their mastery of specialized technologies.

SUMMING UP

Classification of Abnormal Behavior Patterns

What is the DSM and what are its major features? The *Diagnostic and Statistical Manual of Mental Disorders (DSM)* is the most widely accepted system for classifying mental disorders. The *DSM* uses specific diagnostic criteria to group patterns of abnormal behaviors that share common clinical features and a multiaxial system of evaluation.

Why is the DSM considered a multiaxial system? The *DSM* system consists of five axes of classification: Axis I (Clinical Syndromes), Axis II (Personality Disorders and Mental Retardation), Axis III (General Medical Conditions), Axis IV (Psychosocial and Environmental Problems), and Axis V (Global Assessment of Functioning).

What are the major strengths and weaknesses of the DSM? Strengths of the *DSM* include its use of specified diagnostic criteria and a multiaxial system to provide a comprehensive picture of the person's functioning. Weaknesses include questions about reliability and validity of certain diagnostic categories and, to some, the adoption of a medical model framework for classifying abnormal behavior patterns.

Standards of Assessment

What are the standards by which methods of assessment are judged? Methods of assessment must be reliable and valid. Reliability of assessment techniques is shown in various ways, including internal consistency, test–retest reliability, and interrater reliability. Validity is measured by means of content validity, criterion validity, and construct validity.

Methods of Assessment

What is a clinical interview? A clinical interview involves the use of a set of questions designed to elicit relevant information from people seeking treatment.

What are the three major types of clinical interviews? The three major types of clinical interviews are unstructured interviews (clinicians use their own style of questioning rather than follow a particular script), semistructured interviews (clinicians follow a general outline in directing their questioning but are free to branch off in other directions), and structured interviews (clinicians strictly follow a preset order of questions).

What are psychological tests? Psychological tests are structured methods of assessment used to evaluate reasonably stable traits such as intelligence and personality.

What are the major types of psychological tests? Tests of intelligence, such as the Wechsler scales, are used for various purposes in clinical assessment, including determining evidence of mental retardation or cognitive impairment, and assessing strengths and weaknesses. Self-report personality inventories, such as the MMPI, use structured items to measure psychological characteristics or traits, such as anxiety, depression, and masculinity-femininity. These tests are considered objective in the sense that they make use of a limited range of possible responses to items and are based on an empirical, or objective, method of test construction. Projective personality tests, such as the Rorschach and TAT, require subjects to interpret ambiguous stimuli in the belief their answers may shed light on their unconscious processes.

What is neuropsychological assessment? Neuropsychological assessment involves the use of psychological tests to indicate possible neurological impairment or brain defects. The Halstead-Reitan Neuropsychological Battery and Luria Nebraska Test Battery measure perceptual skills, cognitive skills, and motor skills and performance that relate to specific areas of brain function.

What are some of the methods used in behavioral assessment? In behavioral assessment, test responses are taken as samples of behavior rather than as signs of underlying traits or dispositions. The behavioral examiner may conduct a functional assessment, which relates the problem behavior to its antecedents and consequents. Methods of behavioral assessment include behavioral interviewing, self-monitoring, use of analogue or contrived measures, direct observation, and behavioral rating scales.

What is cognitive assessment? Cognitive assessment focuses on the measurement of thoughts, beliefs, and attitudes in order to help identify distorted thinking patterns. Specific methods of assessment include the use of a thought record or diary and the use of rating scales such as the Automatic Thoughts Questionnaire (ATQ) and the Dysfunctional Attitudes Scale (DAS).

How do clinicians and researchers study physiological functioning? Measures of physiological functioning include heart rate, blood pressure, galvanic skin response (GSR), muscle tension, and brain wave activity. Brain-imaging and recording techniques such as EEG, CT scans, PET scans, MRI, and BEAM probe the inner workings and structures of the brain.

Sociocultural and Ethnic Factors in Assessment

Why is it important to take cultural or ethnic factors into account in psychological assessment? We need to ensure that tests that are validated in one culture are reliable and valid when used with members of another culture.

KEY TERMS

WEB TOOLS

The companion website offers tools to enrich your learning experience and help you succeed in class. Go to www.prenhall.com/nevid for the gateway to the following resources:

- **VIDEO** links to connect to the video case files on the companion CD-ROM. VIDEO icons in the margins of the chapter highlight the case examples included in the CD-ROM. You can also access the CD-ROM directly if you do not have a Web connection.

- **QUIZ** links to self-scoring quizzes corresponding to each section of the chapter. The quizzes help you review your knowledge of the content in each chapter.

- **WEB** links to direct you to related sites that enhance your learning of abnormal psychology.

Methods of Treatment

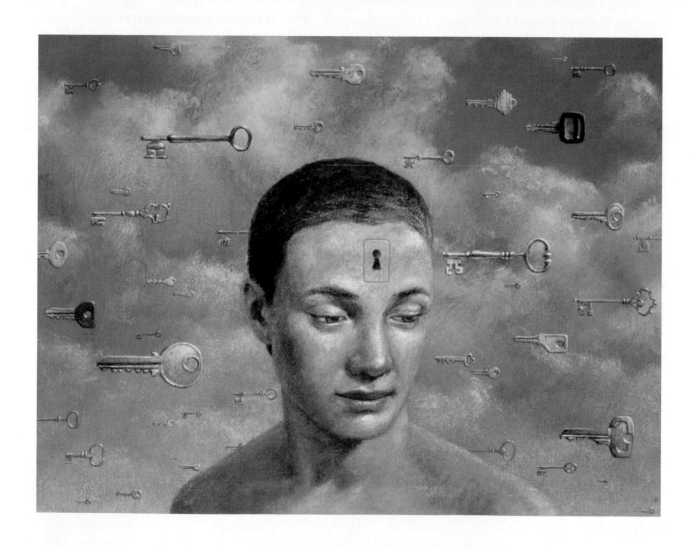

"I"

Susanna—"A Girl, Interrupted"

Suicide is a form of murder—premeditated murder. It isn't something you do the first time you think of doing it. It takes getting used to. And you need the means, the opportunity, the motive. . . .

My motives were weak: an American-history paper I didn't want to write and the question I'd asked months earlier, Why not kill myself? Dead, I wouldn't have to write the paper. Nor would I have to keep debating the question. . . .

Anything I thought or did was immediately drawn into the debate. Made a stupid remark—why not kill myself? Missed the bus—better put an end to it all. Even the good got in there. I liked that movie—maybe I shouldn't kill myself.

Actually, it was only part of myself I wanted to kill: the part that wanted to kill herself, that dragged me into the suicide debate and made every window, kitchen implement, and subway station a rehearsal for tragedy.

I didn't figure this out, though, until after I'd swallowed the fifty aspirin.

I had a boyfriend named Johnny who wrote me love poems—good ones. I called him up, said I was going to kill myself, left the phone off the hook, took my fifty aspirin, and realized it was a mistake. Then I went out to get some milk, which my mother had asked me to do before I took the aspirin.

Johnny called the police. They went to my house and told my mother what I'd done. She turned up in the A&P on Mass. Ave. just as I was to pass out over the meat counter.

As I walked the five blocks to the A&P I was gripped by humiliation and regret. I'd made a mistake and I was going to die because of it. I began to cry about my death. For a moment, I felt compassion for myself and all the unhappiness I contained. Then things started to blur and whiz. By the time I reached the store, the world had been reduced to a narrow, throbbing tunnel. I'd lost my peripheral vision, my ears were ringing, my pulse was pounding. The bloody chops and steaks straining against the plastic wrapping were the last things I saw clearly.

Having my stomach pumped brought me around. They took a long tube and put it slowly up my nose and down the back of my throat. That was like being choked to death. Then they began to pump. That was like having blood drawn on a massive scale—the suction, the sense of tissue collapsing and touching itself in a way it shouldn't, the nausea as all that was inside was pulled out. It was a good deterrent. Next time, I decided, I certainly wouldn't take aspirin.

But when they were done, I wondered if there would be a next time. I felt good. I wasn't dead, yet something was dead. Perhaps I'd managed my peculiar objective of partial suicide. I was lighter, airier than I'd been in years. . . .

The only odd thing was that suddenly I was a vegetarian. I associated meat with suicide, because of passing out at the meat counter. But I know there was more to it.

The meat was bruised, bleeding, and imprisoned in a tight wrapping. And, though I had a six-month respite from thinking about it, so was I.

—From Kaysen, 1994. Reprinted with permission of Random House

Truth or Fiction?

T☐ F☐ Some psychologists have been trained to prescribe drugs. (p. 102)

T☐ F☐ In many states people can set up shop as a psychotherapist without any kind of license or credentials. (p. 103).

T☐ F☐ In classical psychoanalysis, clients are asked to express whatever thought happens to come to mind, no matter how seemingly trivial or silly. (p. 104)

T☐ F☐ More psychotherapists identify with an eclectic approach than with any specific school of therapy. (p. 114)

T☐ F☐ The average client who receives psychotherapy is no better off than control clients who go without it. (p. 118)

T☐ F☐ Despite beliefs that it is a wonder drug, the antidepressant Prozac has not been shown to be any more effective than earlier antidepressants. (p. 124)

T☐ F☐ Severely depressed people who fail to respond to other treatments often show rapid improvement from electroconvulsive therapy. (p. 125)

EIGHTEEN-YEAR-OLD SUSANNA KAYSEN SPENT TWO YEARS ON A PSYCHIATRIC WARD after this halfhearted suicide attempt. Twenty-five years later she chronicled her experience as a psychiatric patient in her autobiographical book, *Girl, Interrupted*. Like Kaysen, many people who attempt or commit suicide have ambivalent feelings about taking their own lives. Kaysen called her boyfriend, giving him the opportunity to intervene. She survived, was able to get on with her life, and eventually wrote two novels and her memoir, which later became the subject of a motion picture of the same name. Unfortunately, many people who attempt suicide fail to get a second chance on life.

This chapter focuses on ways of helping people like Susanna who are struggling with psychological problems. Some forms of helping involve outpatient treatment, such as psychotherapy or drug therapy. In more severe cases, such as people who make suicide attempts or are suffering acute episodes of schizophrenia, treatment typically involves a period of inpatient care.

Girl, Interrupted. The memoir and movie of the same name chronicles the experiences of a young woman (played in the movie by actress Winona Ryder) who is hospitalized in a mental hospital after a halfhearted suicide attempt.

The treatment an individual receives depends not only the particular problem but also on the therapeutic orientation and training of the helping professional. Consider someone suffering from depression. A psychiatrist might recommend a course of antidepressant medication, perhaps in combination with psychotherapy. A cognitively oriented psychologist might suggest cognitive therapy to help identify faulty thinking patterns that underlie depression, whereas a psychodynamic therapist might probe for unconscious conflicts believed to lie at the root of the person's problems.

In this chapter we focus on these and other ways of treating psychological disorders. About one out of every seven people in the United States receives some form of mental health treatment in a given year (USDHHS, 1999a). In later chapters we examine the kinds of treatment approaches applied to particular disorders, but here we focus on the treatments themselves. We will see that the biological and psychological perspectives have spawned corresponding approaches to treatment. First, however, we consider the major types of mental health professionals who treat psychological or mental disorders and the different roles they play.

TYPES OF HELPING PROFESSIONALS

Many people are confused about the differences in qualifications and training of the various types of professionals who provide mental health care. It is little wonder people are confused, as there are many different types of professionals who represent a wide range of training backgrounds and areas of practice. For instance, psychologists are professionals who have completed advanced graduate training in psychology and obtained a license to practice psychology. Psychiatrists are medical doctors who specialize in the diagnosis and treatment of emotional disorders. There are also subgroupings within fields, such as between clinical psychologists and counseling psychologists. The major professional groupings of helping professionals, including clinical and counseling psychologists, psychiatrists, social workers, nurses, and counselors, are described in Table 4.1. Unfortunately, many states do not limit the use of the titles *therapist* or *psychotherapist* to trained professionals. In such states, anyone can set up shop as a psychotherapist and practice "therapy" without a license. Thus, people seeking help are advised to inquire about the training and licensure of helping professionals. If you or someone you know should seek the services of a psychologist, how would you find one? The "A Closer Look" feature, "How Do I Find Help?" offers some suggestions.

We now consider the major types of psychotherapy and their relationships to the theoretical models from which they derive.

psychotherapy A structured form of treatment derived from a psychological framework that consists of one or more verbal interactions or treatment sessions between a client and a therapist.

PSYCHOTHERAPY

Psychotherapy is a systematic interaction between a client and a therapist that draws on psychological principles to help bring about changes in the client's behaviors, thoughts, and feelings. Psychotherapy is used to help clients overcome abnormal behavior, solve problems in living, or develop as individuals. Let us take a closer look at these features of psychotherapy:

1. *Systematic interaction.* "Systematic" means that therapists structure their interactions with clients in ways that reflect their theoretical points of view.

2. *Psychological principles.* Psychotherapists draw on psychological principles, research, and theory in their practice.

TABLE 4.1	
Major Types of Helping Professionals	
Type	**Description**
Clinical psychologists	Have earned a doctoral degree in psychology (either a Ph.D., or Doctor of Philosophy, a Psy.D., or Doctor of Psychology, or an Ed.D., Doctor of Education) from an accredited college or university. Training in clinical psychology typically involves 4 years of graduate coursework, followed by a year-long internship and completion of a doctoral dissertation. Clinical psychologists specialize in administering psychological tests, diagnosing psychological disorders, and practicing psychotherapy. Psychologists cannot prescribe psychiatric drugs, except for a handful of specially trained psychologists within a special government program (Sammons & Brown, 1997; Seppa, 1997). Though the results of this pilot program showed that specially trained psychologists could prescribe psychiatric drugs safely and effectively (Dittman, 2003), the granting of prescription privileges to psychologists remains a hotly contested issue between psychologists and psychiatrists and within the field of psychology itself (McGrath et al., 2004; Welsh, 2003; Willis, 2003). By 2004, two states (New Mexico and Louisiana) had enacted laws granting prescription privileges to psychologists who meet specific training requirements (Holloway, 2004; Murray, 2003). Whether other states will follow suit remains to be seen.
Counseling psychologists	Also hold doctoral degrees in psychology and have completed graduate training preparing them for careers in college counseling centers and mental health facilities. They typically provide counseling to people with psychological problems falling in a milder range of severity than those treated by clinical psychologists, such as difficulties adjusting to college or uncertainties regarding career choices.
Psychiatrists	Have earned a medical degree (M.D.) and completed a residency program in psychiatry. Psychiatrists are physicians who specialize in the diagnosis and treatment of psychological disorders. As licensed physicians, they can prescribe psychiatric drugs and may employ other medical interventions, such as electroconvulsive therapy (ECT). Many also practice psychotherapy based on training they receive during their residency programs or in specialized training institutes.
Clinical or psychiatric social workers	Have earned a master's degree in social work (M.S.W.) and use their knowledge of community agencies and organizations to help people with severe mental disorders receive the services they need. For example, they may help people with schizophrenia make a more successful adjustment to the community once they leave the hospital. Many clinical social workers practice psychotherapy or specific forms of therapy, such as marital or family therapy.
Psychoanalysts	Typically are either psychiatrists or psychologists who have completed extensive additional training in psychoanalysis. They are required to undergo psychoanalysis themselves as part of their training.
Counselors	Have typically earned a master's degree by completing a graduate program in a counseling field. Counselors work in many settings, including public schools, college testing and counseling centers, and hospitals and health clinics. Many specialize in vocational evaluation, marital or family therapy, rehabilitation counseling, or substance abuse counseling. Counselors may focus on providing psychological assistance to people with milder forms of disturbed behavior or those struggling with a chronic or debilitating illness or recovering from a traumatic experience. Some are clergy members who are trained in pastoral counseling programs to help parishioners cope with personal problems.
Psychiatric nurses	Typically are R.N.s who have completed a master's program in psychiatric nursing. They may work in a psychiatric facility or in a group medical practice where they treat people suffering from severe psychological disorders.

Source: Adapted from Nevid, J. S. (2003). *Psychology: Concepts & applications.* Boston: Houghton Mifflin.

3. *Behavior, thoughts, and feelings.* Psychotherapy may be directed at behavioral, cognitive, and emotional domains to help clients overcome psychological problems and lead more satisfying lives.

4. *Abnormal behavior, problem solving, and personal growth.* At least three groups of people are assisted by psychotherapy. First are people with abnormal behavior problems such as mood disorders, anxiety disorders, or schizophrenia. Second are people who seek help for personal problems that are not regarded as abnormal, such as social shyness or confusion about career choices. Third are people who seek personal growth. For them, psychotherapy is a means of self-discovery that may help them reach their potentials as, for example, parents, creative artists, performers, or athletes.

Psychotherapies share other features as well. For one, they are all "talking therapies"—psychologically based treatment involving verbal interchanges between

TRUTH or FICTION? *REVISITED*

In many states people can set up shop as a psychotherapist without any kind of license or credentials.

☑ **TRUE.** It is legal in many states to use the title "psychotherapist" or to practice psychotherapy without a license or credentials.

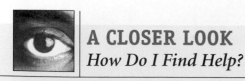

A CLOSER LOOK
How Do I Find Help?

In most areas in the United States and Canada, there are pages upon pages of psychologists and other mental health professionals in the telephone directory. Many people have no idea whom to call for help. If you don't know where to go or whom to see, there are a number of steps you can take to ensure that you receive appropriate care:

1. *Seek recommendations from respected sources, such as your family physician, course instructor, clergyperson, or college health service.*

2. *Seek a consultation with your college counseling center or health services center.* Most colleges and universities offer psychological assistance to students, generally without charge.

3. *Seek a referral from a local medical center or local community mental health center.* When making inquiries, ask about the services that are available or about opportunities for referral to qualified treatment providers in the area.

4. *Contact professional organizations for recommendations.* Many local or national organizations maintain a referral list of qualified treatment providers in your area. If you would like to consult a psychologist, contact the American Psychological Association in Washington, DC (by telephone at 202-336-5650, on the Web at www.apa.org), and ask for local referrals in your area. Alternatively, you can call your local or state psychology association in the United States or your provincial or territorial psychological association in Canada.

5. *Let your fingers do the walking—but be careful!* Look under "Psychologists," "Physicians," "Social Workers," or "Social and Human Services" in your local Yellow Pages. However, be wary of professionals who take out large ads and claim to be experts in treating many different kinds of problems.

6. *Make sure the treatment provider is a licensed member of a recognized mental health profession, such as psychology, medicine, counseling, or social work.* In many states, anyone can set up practice as a "therapist," even as a "psychotherapist." These titles may not be limited by law to licensed practitioners. Licensed professionals clearly display their licenses and other credentials in their offices, usually in plain view. If you have any questions about the licensure status of a treatment provider, contact the licensing board in your state, province, or territory.

7. *Inquire about the type of therapy being provided (e.g., psychoanalysis, family therapy, behavior therapy).* Ask the treatment provider to explain how his or her particular type of therapy is appropriate to treating the problems you are having.

8. *Inquire about the treatment provider's professional background.* Ask about the person's educational background, supervised experience, and credentials. An ethical practitioner will not hesitate to provide this information.

9. *Inquire whether the treatment provider has had experience treating other people with similar problems.* Ask about their results and how they were measured.

10. *Once the treatment provider has had the opportunity to conduct a formal evaluation of your problem, discuss the diagnosis and treatment plan before making any commitments to undertake treatment.*

11. *Ask about costs and insurance coverage.* Ask what types of insurance the provider accepts and whether copayments are required on your part. Ask whether the provider will adjust his or her fees on a sliding scale that takes your income and family situation into account. If you are eligible for Medicaid or Medicare, inquire whether the treatment provider accepts these types of coverage. College students may also be covered by their parents' health insurance plans or by student plans offered by their colleges. Find out if the treatment provider participates in any health maintenance organization to which you may belong.

12. *Find out about the treatment provider's policies regarding charges for missed or canceled sessions.*

13. *If medication is to be prescribed, find out how long a delay is expected before it starts working.* Also inquire about possible side effects, and about which side effects should prompt you to call with questions. Don't be afraid to seek a second opinion before undergoing any course of medication.

14. *If the treatment recommendations don't sound quite right to you, discuss your concerns openly.* An ethical professional will be willing to address your concerns rather than feeling insulted.

15. *If you still have any doubts, request a second opinion.* An ethical professional will support your efforts to seek a second opinion. Ask the treatment provider to recommend other professionals—or select your own.

Source: Adapted from Nevid, J. S. (2003). Psychology: Concepts and applications. Boston: Houghton Mifflin. Reprinted with permission

---

TRUTH or FICTION? *REVISITED*

In classical psychoanalysis, clients are asked to express whatever thought happens to come to mind, no matter how seemingly trivial or silly.

☑ **TRUE.** In classical psychoanalysis, clients are asked to report any thoughts that come to mind. The technique is called free association.

clients and therapists. In some cases, there is a continuous back-and-forth dialogue between the client and therapist. In others, such as traditional psychoanalysis, the client does virtually all the talking. Skillful therapists are also active listeners: they listen intently to what clients are saying to understand as clearly as possible what they are experiencing and attempting to convey. Therapists also express interest in what the client is saying through words as well as nonverbal gestures, such as establishing eye contact and leaning forward when the client is speaking. Skillful therapists are also sensitive to clients' nonverbal cues, such as gestures that may indicate underlying feelings or conflicts. Therapists also seek to convey empathy, or accurate understanding of the client's feelings and experiences. Therapist empathy is a consistent predictor of therapy outcome. Clients of therapists who are perceived as warmer and more empathic show greater improvement than clients of other therapists, whether the therapists are psychodynamic (Luborsky et al., 1988) or cognitive–behavioral (Burns & Nolen–Hoeksema, 1992) in their therapeutic approach.

Another common feature among different psychotherapies is the instilling in clients of a sense of hope of improvement. Clients generally enter therapy with expectations of receiving help to overcome their problems. Responsible therapists do not promise results or guarantee cures. They do instill hope, however, that they can help clients deal with their problems. Positive expectancies can become a type of self-fulfilling prophecy by leading clients to mobilize their efforts toward overcoming their problems. Responses to positive expectancies are termed *placebo effects* or *expectancy effects*.

These common features of psychotherapy that are not specific to any one form of therapy, such as the encouragement of hope and the display of empathy and attentiveness on the part of the therapist, are often referred to as **nonspecific treatment factors.** Nonspecific factors may have therapeutic benefits in addition to the specific benefits of particular forms of therapy. We will discuss these factors in greater detail in the section on evaluating psychotherapy.

Psychodynamic Therapy

Sigmund Freud was the first theorist to develop a psychological model—the *psychodynamic model*—of abnormal behavior (see Chapter 2). He was also the first to develop a model of psychotherapy, which he called **psychoanalysis,** to help people who suffered from psychological disorders. Psychoanalysis was the first **psychodynamic therapy.** Psychodynamic therapy helps individuals gain insight into, and resolve, the unconscious conflicts believed to lie at the root of abnormal behavior. Working through these conflicts, the ego would be freed of the need to maintain defensive behaviors—such as phobias, obsessive–compulsive behaviors, hysterical complaints, and the like—that shield it from recognition of inner turmoil.

Freud summed up the goal of psychoanalysis by saying, "Where id was, there shall ego be." This meant, in part, that psychoanalysis could help shed the light of awareness, represented by the conscious ego, on the inner workings of the id. Through this process a man might come to realize that unresolved anger toward his dominating or rejecting mother has sabotaged his intimate relationships with women during his adulthood. A woman with a loss of sensation in her hand that could not be explained medically might come to see that she harbored guilt over urges to masturbate. The loss of sensation might have prevented her from acting on these urges. Through confronting hidden impulses and the conflicts they produce, clients learn to sort out their feelings and find more constructive and socially acceptable ways of handling their impulses and wishes. The ego is then freed to focus on more constructive interests.

The major methods that Freud used to accomplish these goals were free association, dream analysis, and analysis of the transference relationship.

Free Association **Free association** is the process of uttering uncensored thoughts as they come to mind. Free association is believed to gradually break down the defenses that block awareness of unconscious processes. Clients are told not to censor or screen out thoughts, but to let their minds wander "freely" from thought to thought. Psychoanalysts do not believe that the process of free association is truly free. Repressed impulses press for expression or release, leading to a *compulsion to utter.* Although free association may begin with small talk, the compulsion to utter eventually leads the client to disclose more meaningful material.

The ego, however, continues to try to avert the disclosure of threatening impulses and conflicts. Consequently, clients may show *resistance,* an unwillingness or inability to recall or discuss disturbing or threatening material. Clients may report that their minds suddenly go blank when they venture into sensitive areas, such as hateful feelings toward family members or sexual yearnings. They may switch topics abruptly or accuse the analyst of trying to pry into material that is too personal or embarrassing to talk

The therapeutic relationship. In the course of successful psychotherapy, a therapeutic relationship is forged between the therapist and patient. Therapists use attentive listening to understand as clearly as possible what the client is experiencing and attempting to convey. Skillful therapists are also sensitive to clients' nonverbal cues, such as gestures and posture, that may indicate underlying feelings or conflicts.

nonspecific treatment factors Factors not specific to any one form of psychotherapy, such as therapist attention and support, and creating positive expectancies of change.

psychoanalysis The method of psychotherapy developed by Sigmund Freud.

psychodynamic therapy Therapy that helps individuals gain insight into, and resolve, unconscious conflicts.

free association The method of verbalizing thoughts as they occur without a conscious attempt to edit or censure them.

Dream analysis. Freud believed that dreams represent the "royal road to the unconscious." Dream interpretation was one of the principal techniques that Freud used to uncover unconscious material.

transference relationship In psychoanalysis, the client's transfer or generalization to the analyst of feelings and attitudes the client holds toward important figures in his or her life.

about. Or they may conveniently "forget" the next appointment after a session in which sensitive material is touched upon. The analyst monitors the dynamic conflict between the compulsion to utter and resistance. Signs of resistance are often suggestive of meaningful material. Now and then, the analyst brings interpretations of this material to the attention of the client to help the client gain better insight into deep-seated feelings and conflicts.

Dream Analysis To Freud, dreams represented the "royal road to the unconscious." During sleep, the ego's defenses are lowered and unacceptable impulses find expression in dreams. Because the defenses are not completely eliminated, the impulses take a disguised or symbolized form. In psychoanalytic theory, dreams have two levels of content:

1. *Manifest content:* the material of the dream the dreamer experiences and reports

2. *Latent content:* the unconscious material the dream symbolizes or represents

A man might dream of flying in an airplane. Flying is the apparent or manifest content of the dream. Freud believed that flying may symbolize erection, so perhaps the latent content of the dream reflects unconscious issues related to fears of impotence. Such symbols may vary from person to person. Analysts therefore ask clients to free-associate to the manifest content of the dream to provide clues to the latent content. Though dreams may have a psychological meaning, as Freud believed, there remains no independent way of determining what dreams mean (Squier & Domhoff, 1998).

Transference Freud found that clients responded to him not only as an individual but also in ways that reflected their feelings and attitudes toward other important people in their lives. A young female client might respond to him as a father figure, displacing, or transferring, onto Freud her feelings toward her own father. A man might also view him as a father figure, responding to him as a rival in a manner that Freud believed might reflect the man's unresolved Oedipus complex.

The process of analyzing and working through the **transference relationship** is considered an essential component of psychoanalysis. Freud believed that the transference relationship provides a vehicle for the reenactment of childhood conflicts with parents. Clients may react to the analyst with the same feelings of anger, love, or jealousy they felt toward their own parents. Freud termed the enactment of these childhood conflicts the *transference neurosis.* This "neurosis" had to be successfully analyzed and worked through for clients to succeed in psychoanalysis.

Childhood conflicts usually involve unresolved feelings of anger, rejection, or need for love. For example, a client may interpret any slight criticism by the therapist as a devastating blow, transferring feelings of self-loathing that the client had repressed from childhood experiences of parental rejection. Transference may also distort or color the client's relationships with others, such as a spouse or employer. A client might relate to a spouse as to a parent, perhaps demanding too much or unjustly accusing the spouse of being insensitive or uncaring. Or a client who had been mistreated by a past lover might not give new friends or lovers the benefit of a fair chance. The analyst helps the client recognize transference relationships, especially the therapy transference, and work through the residues of childhood feelings and conflicts that lead to self-defeating behavior in the present.

According to Freud, transference is a two-way street. Freud felt he transferred his underlying feelings onto his clients, perhaps viewing a young man as a competitor or a woman as a rejecting love interest. Freud referred to the feelings that he projected onto clients as **countertransference.** Psychoanalysts in training are expected to undergo psychoanalysis themselves to help them uncover motives that might lead to countertransferences in their therapeutic relationships. In their training, psychoanalysts learn to monitor their own reactions in therapy, so as to become better aware of when and how countertransferences intrude on the therapy process.

countertransference In psychoanalysis, the transfer of feelings or attitudes that the analyst holds towards other persons in her or his life onto the client.

Although the analysis of transference is a crucial element of psychoanalytic therapy, it generally takes months or years for a transference relationship to develop and be resolved. This is one reason why psychoanalysis is typically a lengthy process.

Modern Psychodynamic Approaches Although some psychoanalysts continue to practice traditional psychoanalysis in much the same manner as Freud, briefer and less-intensive forms of psychodynamic treatment have emerged. They are able to reach clients who are seeking briefer and less costly forms of treatment, perhaps once or twice a week (Grossman, 2003).

Like Freudian psychoanalysis, the newer psychodynamic approaches aim to uncover unconscious motives and break down resistances and psychological defenses. Yet they focus more on the client's present relationships and encourage the client to make adaptive behavior changes. Many contemporary psychodynamic therapists draw more heavily on the ideas of Erik Erikson, Harry Stack Sullivan, and other theorists than on Freud's

Modern psychodynamic psychotherapy. Modern psychodynamic therapists engage in more direct, face-to-face interactions with clients than do traditional Freudian psychoanalysts. Modern psychodynamic approaches are also generally briefer and focus more on the direct exploration of clients' defenses and transference relationships.

ideas. Treatment entails a more open dialogue and direct exploration of the client's defenses and transference relationships than was traditionally the case (Messer, 2001b). The client and therapist generally sit facing each other, and the therapist engages in more frequent verbal give-and-take with the client, as in the following vignette. Note how the therapist uses interpretation to help the client, Mr. Arianes, achieve insight into how his relationship with his wife involves a transference of his childhood relationship with his mother:

Offering an Interpretation

MR. ARIANES: I think you've got it there, Doc. We weren't communicating. I wouldn't tell her [his wife] what was wrong or what I wanted from her. Maybe I expected her to understand me without saying anything.

THERAPIST: Like the expectations a child has of its mother.

MR. ARIANES: Not my mother!

THERAPIST: Oh?

MR. ARIANES: No, I always thought she had too many troubles of her own to pay attention to mine. I remember once I got hurt on my bike and came to her all bloodied up. When she saw me she got mad and yelled at me for making more trouble for her when she already had her hands full with my father.

THERAPIST: Do you remember how you felt then?

MR. ARIANES: I can't remember, but I know that after that I never brought my troubles to her again.

THERAPIST: How old were you?

MR. ARIANES: Nine, I know that because I got that bike for my ninth birthday. It was a little too big for me still, that's why I got hurt on it.

THERAPIST: Perhaps you carried this attitude into your marriage.

MR. ARIANES: What attitude?

THERAPIST: The feeling that your wife, like your mother, would be unsympathetic to your difficulties. That there was no point in telling her about your experiences because she was too preoccupied or too busy to care.

MR. ARIANES: But she's so different from my mother. I come first with her.

THERAPIST: On one level you know that. On another, deeper level there may well be the fear that people—or maybe only women, or maybe only women you're close to—are all the same, and you can't take a chance at being rejected again in your need.

MR. ARIANES: Maybe you're right, Doc, but all that was so long ago, and I should be over that by now.

THERAPIST: That's not the way the mind works. If a shock or a disappointment is strong enough, it can permanently freeze our picture of ourselves and our expectations of the world. The rest of us grows up—that is, we let ourselves learn about life from experience and from what we see, hear, or read of the experiences of others, but that one area where we really got hurt stays unchanged. So what I mean when I say you might be carrying that attitude into your relationship with your wife is that when it comes to your hopes of being understood and catered to when you feel hurt or abused by life, you still feel very much like that nine-year-old boy who was rebuffed in his need and gave up hope that anyone would or could respond to him.

—From *Doing Psychotherapy* by M. F. Basch. Copyright © 1980 by Basic Books, pp. 29–30. Reprinted with permssion of Basic Books, a member of Perseus Books L. L. C.

Some modern psychodynamic therapies focus more on the role of the ego and less on the role of the id. These therapists, such as Heinz Hartmann, are generally described as *ego analysts*. Other modern psychoanalysts, such as Melanie Klein and Margaret Mahler, are identified with *object-relations* approaches to psychodynamic therapy. They focus on helping people separate their own ideas and feelings from the elements of others they have incorporated or *introjected* within themselves. Clients can then develop more as individuals—as their own persons, rather than trying to meet the expectations they believe others have of them.

Though psychodynamic therapy is no longer the dominant force in the field that it once was, it is still practiced widely. A recent survey of 177 practicing psychologists found that nearly half (45%) reported using psychodynamic techniques along with cognitive–behavioral techniques in their practice (Holloway, 2003; PracticeNet, 2003). Let's now turn to other forms of therapy, beginning with behavior therapy.

Behavior Therapy

behavior therapy The therapeutic application of learning-based techniques.

Behavior therapy is the systematic application of the principles of learning to the treatment of psychological disorders. Because the focus is on changing behavior—not on personality change or deep probing into the past—behavior therapy is relatively brief, lasting typically from a few weeks to a few months. Behavior therapists, like other therapists, seek to develop warm therapeutic relationships with clients, but they believe the special efficacy of behavior therapy derives from the learning-based techniques rather than from the nature of the therapeutic relationship.

Behavior therapy first gained widespread attention as a means of helping people overcome fears and phobias, problems that had proved resistant to insight-oriented therapies. Among the methods used are systematic desensitization, gradual exposure, and modeling. **Systematic desensitization** involves a therapeutic program of exposure (in imagination or by means of pictures or slides) to progressively more fearful stimuli while one remains deeply relaxed. First the person uses a relaxation technique, such as progressive relaxation (discussed in Chapter 5), to become deeply relaxed. The client is then instructed to imagine (or perhaps view, as through a series of slides) progressively more anxiety-arousing scenes. If fear is evoked, the client focuses on restoring relaxation. The process is repeated until the client can tolerate the scene without anxiety. The client then progresses to the next scene in the *fear-stimulus hierarchy*. The procedure is continued until the person can remain relaxed while imagining the most distressing scene in the hierarchy.

systematic desensitization A behavior therapy technique for overcoming phobias by means of exposure to progressively more fearful stimuli while one remains deeply relaxed.

gradual exposure A behavior therapy technique for overcoming fears through direct exposure to increasingly fearful stimuli.

In **gradual exposure** (also called in vivo, meaning "in life," exposure), people troubled by phobias purposely expose themselves to the stimuli that evoke their fear. Like systematic desensitization, the person progresses at his or her own pace through a hierar-chy of progressively more anxiety-evoking stimuli. The person with a fear of snakes, for example, might first look at a harmless, caged snake from across the room and then gradually approach and interact with the snake in a step-by-step process, progressing to each new step only when feeling completely calm at the prior step. Gradual exposure is often combined with cognitive techniques that focus on replacing anxiety-arousing ir-rational thoughts with calming rational thoughts.

In **modeling,** individuals learn desired behaviors by observing others perform them (Braswell & Kendall, 2001). For example, the client may observe and then imitate oth-ers who interact with fear-evoking situations or objects. After observing the model, the client may be assisted or guided by the therapist or the model in performing the target behavior. The client receives ample reinforcement from the therapist for each attempt. Modeling approaches were pioneered by Albert Bandura and his colleagues, who had re-markable success using modeling techniques with children to treat various phobias, es-pecially fears of animals, such as snakes and dogs (Bandura, Jeffery, & Wright, 1974; Braswell & Kendall, 2001).

Behavior therapists also use reinforcement techniques based on operant condition-ing to shape desired behavior. For example, parents and teachers may be trained to sys-tematically reinforce children for appropriate behavior by showing appreciation and to extinguish inappropriate behavior by ignoring it. In institutional settings, **token econ-omy** systems seek to increase adaptive behavior by rewarding patients with tokens for performing appropriate behaviors, such as self-grooming and making their beds. The to-kens can eventually be exchanged for desired rewards. Token systems have also been used to treat children with conduct disorders.

Other techniques of behavior therapy discussed in later chapters include *aversive con-ditioning* (used in the treatment of substance abuse problems like smoking and alco-holism), *social skills training* (used in the treatment of social anxieties and skills deficits associated with schizophrenia), and *self-control techniques* (used in helping people reduce excess weight and quit smoking).

Humanistic Therapy

Psychodynamic therapists tend to focus on unconscious processes, such as internal conflicts. By contrast, humanistic therapists focus on clients' subjective, conscious experiences. Like behavior therapists, humanistic therapists also focus more on what clients are experiencing in the present—the here and now—than on the past. But there are also similarities between the psycho-dynamic and humanistic therapies. Both assume that the past affects present behavior and feelings and both seek to expand clients' self-insight. The major form of humanistic therapy is **person-centered therapy** (also called *client-cen-tered therapy*), which was developed by the psychologist Carl Rogers.

Person-Centered Therapy Rogers (1951) believed that people have natural motivational tendencies toward growth, fulfillment, and health. In Rogers's view, psychological dis-orders develop largely from the roadblocks that other people place in the path toward self-actualization. When others are selective in their approval of our childhood feelings and be-havior, we may disown the criticized parts of ourselves. To earn social approval, we may don social masks or facades. We learn "to be seen and not heard" and may become deaf even to our own inner voices. Over time, we may develop distorted self-concepts that are consistent with others' views of us but

modeling A behavior therapy technique for helping an individual acquire a new behavior by means of having a therapist or another individual demonstrate a target behavior that is then imitated by the client.

token economy Behavioral treatment program in which a controlled environment is constructed such that people are reinforced for desired behaviors by receiving tokens that may be exchanged for desired rewards.

person-centered therapy The establishment of a warm, accepting therapeutic relationship that frees clients to engage in self-exploration and achieve self-acceptance.

Modeling. Modeling techniques are often used to help people overcome phobias. Here a therapist works with a man who has a canine phobia. As the client observes the therapist harmlessly petting a dog, he becomes more likely to imitate the behavior.

are not of our own making and design. As a result, we may become poorly adjusted, unhappy, and confused as to who and what we are.

Well-adjusted people make choices and take actions consistent with their personal values and needs. Person-centered therapy creates conditions of warmth and acceptance in the therapeutic relationship that help clients become more aware and accepting of their true selves. Rogers did not believe therapists should impose their own goals or values on their clients. His focus of therapy, as the name implies, is the person.

Person-centered therapy is *nondirective.* The client, not the therapist, takes the lead and directs the course of therapy. The therapist uses *reflection*—the restating or paraphrasing of the client's expressed feelings without interpreting them or passing judgment on them. This encourages the client to further explore his or her feelings and get in touch with deeper feelings and parts of the self that had become disowned because of social condemnation.

Rogers stressed the importance of creating a warm therapeutic relationship that would encourage the client to engage in self-exploration and self-expression. The effective therapist should possess four basic qualities or attributes: *unconditional positive regard, empathy, genuineness,* and *congruence.* First, the therapist must be able to express **unconditional positive regard** for clients. In contrast to the conditional approval the client may have received from parents and others in the past, the therapist must be unconditionally accepting of the client as a person, even if the therapist sometimes objects to the client's choices or behaviors. Unconditional positive regard provides clients with a sense of security that encourages them to explore their feelings without fear of disapproval. As clients feel accepted or prized for themselves, they are encouraged to accept themselves in turn. To Rogers, every human being has intrinsic worth and value. Rogers believed that people are basically good and are motivated to pursue *pro*social goals.

Therapists who display **empathy** are able to reflect or mirror accurately their clients' experiences and feelings. Therapists try to see the world through their clients' eyes or frames of reference. They listen carefully to clients and set aside their own judgments and interpretations of events. Showing empathy encourages clients to get in touch with feelings of which they may be only dimly aware.

Genuineness is the ability to be open about one's feelings. Rogers admitted he had negative feelings at times during therapy sessions, typically boredom, but he attempted to express these feelings openly rather than hide them (Bennett, 1985).

Congruence refers to the fit between one's thoughts, feelings, and behavior. The congruent person is one whose behavior, thoughts, and feelings are integrated and consistent. Congruent therapists serve as models of psychological integrity to their clients.

Here Rogers (C. R.) uses reflection to help a client focus more deeply on her inner feelings:

unconditional positive regard The expression of unconditional acceptance of another person's basic worth as a person.

empathy The ability to understand someone's experiences and feelings from that person's point of view.

genuineness The ability to recognize and express one's true feelings.

congruence The fit between one's thoughts, behaviors, and feelings.

Rogers Demonstrates Reflection

JILL: I'm having a lot of problems dealing with my daughter. She's 20 years old; she's in college; I'm having a lot of trouble letting her go. And I have a lot of guilt feelings about her; I have a real need to hang on to her.

C.R.:   A need to hang on so you can kind of make up for the things you feel guilty about. Is that part of it?

JILL: There's a lot of that. Also, she's been a real friend to me, and filled my life. And it's very hard . . . a lot of empty places now that she's not with me.

C.R.:   The old vacuum, sort of, when she's not there.

JILL: Yes. Yes. I also would like to be the kind of mother that could be strong and say, you know, "Go and have a good life," and this is really hard for me, to do that.

C.R.:   It's very hard to give up something that's been so precious in your life, but also something that I guess has caused you pain when you mentioned guilt.

JILL: Yeah. And I'm aware that I have some anger toward her that I don't always get what I want. I have needs that are not met. And, uh, I don't feel I have a right to those needs. You know . . . she's a daughter; she's not my mother. Though sometimes I feel as if I'd like her to mother me . . . it's very difficult for me to ask for that and have a right to it.

C.R.: So, it may be unreasonable, but still, when she doesn't meet your needs, it makes you mad.

JILL: Yeah I get very angry, very angry with her.

C.R.: (*Pause*) You're also feeling a little tension at this point, I guess.

JILL: Yeah. Yeah. A lot of conflict . . . (C.R.: M-hm.). A lot of pain.

C.R.: A lot of pain. Can you say anything more about what that's about?
 —From Farber, Brink, & Raskin, 1996, *The psychotherapy of Carl Rogers: Cases and commentary*, pp. 74–75. Reprinted with permission of The Guilford Press.

Cognitive Therapy

. . . there is nothing either good or bad, but thinking makes it so.

—*Shakespeare, Hamlet*

In these words, Shakespeare did not mean to imply that misfortunes or ailments are painless or easy to manage. His point, rather, was that the ways in which we evaluate upsetting events can heighten or diminish our discomfort and affect our ability to cope. Several hundred years later, cognitive therapists adopted this simple but elegant expression as a kind of motto for their approach to therapy.

Cognitive therapists focus on helping clients identify and correct maladaptive beliefs, automatic types of thinking, and self-defeating attitudes that create or compound emotional problems. They believe that negative emotions such as anxiety and depression are caused by the interpretations we place on troubling events, not on the events themselves. Here we focus on the contributions of two prominent types of **cognitive therapy:** Albert Ellis's rational emotive behavior therapy and Aaron Beck's cognitive therapy.

cognitive therapy A form of therapy that helps clients identify and correct maladaptive cognitions (thoughts, beliefs, and attitudes) believed to underlie their emotional problems and self-defeating behavior.

Rational Emotive Behavior Therapy Albert Ellis (1977b, 1993, 2001; Dryden & Ellis, 2001) believes that the adoption of irrational, self-defeating beliefs gives rise to psychological problems and negative feelings. Consider the irrational belief that one must have the approval almost all the time of the people who are important to you. Ellis finds it understandable to want other people's approval and love, but he argues that it is irrational to believe we cannot survive without it. Another irrational belief is that we must be thoroughly competent and achieving in virtually everything we seek to accomplish. We are doomed to eventually fall short of these irrational expectations, and when we do, we may experience negative emotional consequences, such as depression and lowered self-esteem. Emotional difficulties such as anxiety and depression are not directly caused by negative events, but rather by how we distort their meaning by viewing them through the dark-colored glasses of self-defeating beliefs. In Ellis's **rational emotive behavior therapy (REBT),** therapists actively *dispute* clients' irrational beliefs and the premises on which they are based and help clients to develop alternative, adaptive beliefs in their place.

rational emotive behavior therapy (REBT) A therapeutic approach that focuses on helping clients replace irrational, maladaptive beliefs with alternative, more adaptive beliefs.

Ellis and Dryden (1987) describe the case of a 27-year-old woman, Jane, who was socially inhibited and shy, particularly with attractive men. Through REBT, Jane identified some of her underlying irrational beliefs, such as "I must speak well to people I find attractive" and "When I don't speak well and impress people as I should, I'm a stupid, inadequate person!" (p. 68). REBT helped Jane discriminate between these irrational beliefs and rational alternatives, such as "If people do reject me for showing them how anxious I am, that will be most unfortunate, but I can stand it" (p. 68). REBT encouraged Jane to debate or dispute irrational beliefs by posing challenging questions to herself: (1) "*Why* must I speak well to people I find attractive?" and (2) "When I don't speak well and impress people, how does that make me a *stupid and inadequate person?*" (p. 69). Jane learned to form rational responses to her self-questioning, for example, (1) "There is no reason I must speak well to people I find attractive, but it would be desirable if I do so, so I shall make an effort—but not kill myself—to do so," and (2) "When I speak poorly and fail to impress people, that only makes me a *person who spoke unimpressively this time*—not a *totally stupid or inadequate person*" (p. 69). After 9 months of REBT, Jane was able to talk comfortably to men she found attractive and was preparing to take a job as a teacher, a position she had previously avoided due to fear of facing a class.

Rational emotive behavior therapists help clients substitute more effective interpersonal behavior for self-defeating or maladaptive behavior. Ellis often gives clients specific tasks or homework assignments, such as disagreeing with an overbearing relative or asking someone for a date. He assists them in practicing or rehearsing adaptive behaviors.

Beck's Cognitive Therapy As formulated by psychiatrist Aaron Beck and his colleagues (Beck, 1976; Beck et al., 1979; DeRubeis, Tang, & Beck, 2001), cognitive therapy, like REBT, focuses on clients' maladaptive cognitions. Cognitive therapists encourage clients to recognize and change errors in their thinking, called *cognitive distortions,* which affect their moods and impair their behavior, such as tendencies to magnify negative events and minimize personal accomplishments.

Cognitive therapists have clients record the thoughts that are prompted by upsetting events and note the connections between their thoughts and their emotional responses. They then help clients to dispute distorted thoughts and replace them with rational alternatives. Therapists also use behavioral homework assignments, such as encouraging depressed clients to fill their free time with structured activities, such as gardening or completing work around the house. Carrying out such tasks counteracts the apathy and loss of motivation that tend to characterize depression and may also provide concrete evidence of competence, which helps combat self-perceptions of helplessness and inadequacy.

Another type of homework assignment involves *reality testing.* Clients are asked to test their negative beliefs in the light of reality. For example, a depressed client who feels unwanted by everyone might be asked to call two or three friends on the phone to gather data about the friends' reactions to the calls. The therapist might then ask the client to report on the assignment: "Did they immediately hang up the phone? Or did they seem pleased you called? Did they express any interest at all in talking to you again or getting together sometime? Does the evidence support the conclusion that *no one* has any interest in you?" Such exercises help clients replace distorted beliefs with rational alternatives.

Consider this case in which a depressed man was encouraged to test his belief that he was about to be fired from his job. The case also illustrates several cognitive distortions or errors in thinking, such as selectively perceiving only one's flaws (in this case, self-perceptions of laziness) and expecting the worst (expectations of being fired).

Kyle Tests His Beliefs

Kyle, a 35-year-old frozen foods distributor, had suffered from chronic depression since his divorce six years earlier. During the past year the depression had worsened, and he found it increasingly difficult to call upon customers or go to the office. Each day that he avoided working made it more difficult for him to go to the office and face his boss. He was convinced that he was in imminent danger of being fired since he had not made any sales calls for more than a month. Since he had not earned any commissions in a while, he felt he was not adequately supporting his two daughters and was concerned that he wouldn't have the money to send them to college. He was convinced that his basic problem was laziness, not depression. His therapist pointed out the illogic in his thinking. First of all, there was no real evidence that his boss was about to fire him. His boss had actually encouraged him to get help and was paying for part of the treatment. His therapist also pointed out that judging himself as lazy was unfair because it overlooked the fact that he had been an industrious, successful salesman before he became depressed. While not fully persuaded, the client agreed to a homework assignment in which he was to call his boss and also make a sales call to one of his former customers. His boss expressed support and reassured him that his job was secure. The customer ribbed him about "being on vacation" during the preceding six weeks but placed a small order. The client discovered that the small unpleasantness he expe-

rienced in facing the customer and being teased paled in comparison to the intense depression he felt at home while he was avoiding work. Within the next several weeks he gradually worked himself back to a normal routine, calling upon customers and making future plans. This process of viewing himself and the world from a fresh perspective led to a general improvement in his mood and behavior.

—*Adapted from Burns & Beck, 1978, pp. 124–126*

REBT and Beck's cognitive therapy have much in common, especially the focus on helping clients replace self-defeating thoughts and beliefs with more rational ones. Perhaps the major difference between the two approaches is therapeutic style. REBT therapists tend to be more confrontational and forceful in their approach to disputing clients' irrational beliefs. Cognitive therapists tend to adopt a more gentle, collaborative approach in helping clients discover and correct the distortions in their thinking.

Cognitive–Behavioral Therapy

Today, most behavior therapists identify with a broader model of behavior therapy called **cognitive-behavioral therapy (CBT)** (also called *cognitive behavior therapy*). Cognitive-behavioral therapy attempts to integrate therapeutic techniques that help individuals make changes not only in their overt behavior but also in their underlying thoughts, beliefs, and attitudes. Cognitive-behavioral therapy draws on the assumption that thinking patterns and beliefs affect behavior and that changes in these cognitions can lead to desirable behavioral changes (Dobson & Dozois, 2001; McGinn & Sanderson, 2001).

Cognitive-behavioral therapists use an assortment of behavioral and cognitive techniques. The following case illustration shows how behavioral techniques (exposure to fearful situations) and cognitive techniques (changing maladaptive thoughts) were used in the treatment of *agoraphobia,* a type of anxiety disorder characterized by excessive fears of venturing out in public.

cognitive-behavioral therapy (CBT) A learning-based approach to therapy incorporating cognitive and behavioral techniques.

Mrs. X Uses CBT to Overcome Agoraphobia

Mrs. X was a 41-year-old woman with a 12-year history of agoraphobia. She feared venturing into public places alone and required her husband or children to accompany her from place to place. In vivo (actual) exposure sessions were arranged in a series of progressively more fearful encounters (a fear-stimulus hierarchy). The first step in the hierarchy, for example, involved taking a shopping trip while accompanied by the therapist. After accomplishing this task, Mrs. X gradually moved upwards in the hierarchy. By the third week of treatment, she was able to complete the last step in her hierarchy— shopping by herself in a crowded supermarket.

Cognitive restructuring was conducted along with the exposure training. Mrs. X was asked to imagine herself in various fearful situations and to report the self-statements she experienced. The therapist helped her identify disruptive self-statements, such as, "I am going to make a fool of myself." The therapist questioned this particular self-statement by asking whether it was realistic to believe that she would actually lose control and, secondly, by disputing the belief that the consequences of losing control, were it to happen, would truly be disastrous. Mrs. X progressed rapidly with treatment and became capable of functioning more independently, but she still worried about future relapses. The therapist focused at this point on deeper cognitive structures involving her fears of abandonment by the people she loved if she were to relapse and be unable to attend to their needs. In challenging these beliefs, the therapist helped Mrs. X realize that she was not as helpless as she perceived herself to be and that she was loved for other reasons than her ability to serve others. She also explored the question, "Who am I improving for?" She realized that she needed to find reasons to overcome her phobia that were related to meeting her own personal needs, not simply the needs of her loved ones.

At a follow-up interview nine months after treatment, she was functioning independently, which allowed her to pursue her own interests, such as taking night courses and seeking a job.

—Adapted from Biran, 1988, pp. 173–176

It could be argued that any behavioral method involving imagination or mental imagery, such as systematic desensitization, bridges behavioral and cognitive domains. Cognitive therapies such as Ellis's rational emotive behavior therapy and Beck's cognitive therapy also incorporate cognitive and behavioral treatment methods. The dividing lines between the psychotherapies may not be as clearly drawn as authors of textbooks—who are given the task of classifying them—might desire. Not only are traditional boundaries between therapies blurring, but many therapists today endorse an eclectic orientation in which they incorporate principles and techniques derived from different schools of therapy.

Before going forward, you may wish to review Table 4.2, which summarizes the major therapeutic approaches to psychotherapy.

Eclectic Therapy

Each of the major psychological models of abnormal behavior—the psychodynamic, behaviorist, humanistic and cognitive approaches—has spawned its own approaches to psychotherapy. Although many therapists identify with one or another of these schools of therapy, an increasing number of therapists practice **eclectic therapy,** in which they draw on techniques and teachings of multiple therapeutic approaches. Eclectic therapists seek to enhance their therapeutic effectiveness by incorporating principles and techniques from different therapeutic orientations. An eclectic therapist might use behavior therapy techniques to help a client change specific maladaptive behaviors, for example, along with psychodynamic techniques to help the client gain insight into the childhood roots of the problem.

A greater percentage of clinical and counseling psychologists identify with an eclectic or integrative orientation than any other therapeutic orientation (Bechtoldt et al., 2001; see Figure 4.1). Therapists who adopt an eclectic approach tend to be older and more experienced (Beitman, Goldfried, & Norcross, 1989). Perhaps they have learned through experience of the value of drawing on diverse contributions to the practice of therapy.

Eclecticism has different meanings for different therapists. Some therapists are *technical eclectics.* They draw on techniques from different schools of therapy without necessarily adopting the theoretical positions that spawned the techniques (Beutler, Harwood, & Caldwell, 2001; Lazarus, 1992). They assume a pragmatic approach in using techniques from different therapeutic approaches that they believe are most likely to work with a given client.

Other eclectic therapists are *integrative eclectics.* They attempt to synthesize and integrate diverse theoretical approaches—to bring together different theoretical concepts and therapeutic approaches under the roof of one integrated model of therapy (Beutler, Harwood, & Caldwell, 2001; Stricker & Gold, 2001). Though various approaches to integrative psychotherapy have been proposed, there is as yet no clear agreement as to the principles and practices that constitute therapeutic integration (Garfield, 1994). Perhaps multiple approaches are needed (Safran & Messer, 1997).

Not all therapists subscribe to the view that therapeutic integration is a desirable or achievable goal. They believe that combining elements of different therapeutic approaches will lead to a hodgepodge of techniques that lack a cohesive conceptual framework. Still, interest in the professional community in therapeutic integration is growing, and we expect to see new models emerging that aim to tie together the contributions of different approaches.

Group, Family, and Couple Therapy

Some approaches to therapy expand the focus of treatment to include groups of people, families, and couples.

---

eclectic therapy An approach to psychotherapy that incorporates principles or techniques from various systems or theories.

TRUTH or FICTION? *REVISITED*

More psychotherapists identify with an eclectic approach than with any specific school of therapy.

☑ **TRUE.** Surveys of therapists show that more endorse an eclectic approach than any other therapeutic orientation.

TABLE 4.2

Overview of Major Types of Psychotherapy

Type of Therapy	Major Figure(s)	Goal	Length of Treatment	Therapist's Approach	Major Techniques
Classical psychoanalysis	Sigmund Freud	Gaining insight and resolving unconscious psychological conflicts	Lengthy, typically lasting several years	Passive, interpretive	Free association, dream analysis, interpretation
Modern psychodynamic approaches	Erik Erikson Harry Stack Sullivan Heinz Hartmann Melanie Klein Margaret Mahler	Focus on developing insight, but with greater emphasis on ego functioning, current interpersonal relationships, and adaptive behavior than traditional psychoanalysis	Briefer than traditional psychoanalysis	More direct probing of client defenses; more back-and-forth discussion	Direct analysis of client's defenses and transference relationships
Behavior therapy	Various	Directly changing problem behavior through use of learning-based techniques	Relatively brief, typically lasting 10 to 20 sessions	Directive, active problem solving	Systematic desensitization, gradual exposure, modeling, reinforcement techniques
Humanistic, client-centered therapy	Carl Rogers	Self-acceptance and personal growth	Varies, but briefer than traditional psychoanalysis	Nondirective, allowing client to take the lead, with therapist serving as an empathic listener	Use of reflection, creation of a warm, accepting therapeutic relationship
Ellis's rational emotive behavior therapy	Albert Ellis	Replacing irrational beliefs with rational alternative beliefs; making adaptive behavioral changes	Relatively brief, typically lasting 10 to 20 sessions	Direct, sometimes confrontational challenging of client's irrational beliefs	Identifying and challenging irrational beliefs, behavioral homework assignments
Beck's cognitive therapy	Aaron Beck	Identify and correcting distorted or self-defeating thoughts and beliefs; making adaptive behavioral changes	Relatively brief, typically lasting 10 to 20 sessions	Collaboratively engaging client in process of logically examining thoughts and beliefs and testing them out	Identifying and correcting distorted thoughts; behavioral homework including reality testing
Cognitive-behavioral therapy	Various	Use of cognitive and behavioral techniques to change maladaptive behaviors and cognitions	Relatively brief, typically lasting 10 to 20 sessions	Direct, active problem solving	Combination of cognitive and behavioral techniques

Group Therapy In **group therapy,** a group of clients meets together with a therapist or a pair of therapists. Group therapy has several advantages over individual treatment. For one, group therapy is less costly to individual clients, because several clients are treated at the same time. Many clinicians also believe that group therapy is more effective in treating groups of clients who have similar problems, such as complaints relating to anxiety, depression, lack of social skills, or adjustment to divorce or other life stresses. Clients learn how people with similar problems cope and receive social support from the group as well as the therapist. Group therapy also provides members with opportunities to work through their problems in relating to others. For example, the therapist or other members may point out to a particular member patterns of behavior that mirror the client's behavior outside the group. Group members may also rehearse social skills with one another in a supportive atmosphere.

Despite these advantages, clients may prefer individual therapy for various reasons. For one, clients might not wish to disclose their problems in a group. Some clients pre-

group therapy A form of therapy in which a group of clients meets together with a therapist.

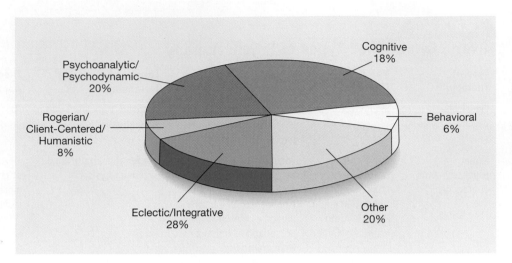

FIGURE 4.1 Therapeutic orientations of clinical and counseling psychologists.
An eclectic/integrative orientation is the most widely endorsed therapeutic orientation among clinical and counseling psychologists today.

Source: Adapted from Bechtoldt, H., Norcross, J. C., Wyckoff, L. A., Pokrywa, M. L., & Campbell, L. F., 2001.

fer the individual attention of the therapist. Others are too socially inhibited to feel comfortable in a group setting. Because of such concerns, group therapists require that group disclosures be kept confidential, that group members relate to each other supportively and nondestructively, and that group members receive the attention they need.

Family Therapy In **family therapy,** the family, not the individual, is the unit of treatment. Family therapy aims to help troubled families resolve their conflicts and problems so the family functions better as a unit and individual family members are subjected to less stress from family conflicts. In family therapy, family members learn to communicate more effectively and to air their disagreements constructively. Family conflicts often emerge at transitional points in the life cycle, when family patterns are altered by changes in one or more members. Conflicts between parents and children, for example, often emerge when adolescent children seek greater independence or autonomy. Family members with low self-esteem may be unable to tolerate different attitudes or behaviors from other members of the family and may resist their efforts to change or become more independent. Family therapists work with families to resolve these conflicts and help them adjust to life changes.

family therapy A form of therapy in which the family, not the individual, is the unit of treatment.

couple therapy A form of therapy that focuses on resolving conflicts in distressed couples.

Family therapists are sensitive to tendencies of families to scapegoat one family member as the source of the problem, or the "identified client." Disturbed families seem to adopt a sort of myth: Change the identified client, the "bad apple," and the "barrel," or family, will once again become functional. Family therapists encourage families to work together to resolve their disputes and conflicts, instead of scapegoating one member.

Many family therapists adopt a *systems approach* to understanding the workings of the family and problems that may arise within the family. They see problem behaviors of individual family members as representing a breakdown in the system of communications and role relationships within the family. For example, a child may feel in competition with other siblings for a parent's attention and develop enuresis, or bed-wetting, as a means of securing attention. Operating from a systems perspective, the family therapist may focus on helping family members understand the hidden messages in the child's behavior and make

Group therapy. What are some of the advantages of group therapy over individual therapy? What are some of its disadvantages?

CONTROVERSIES IN ABNORMAL PSYCHOLOGY
Online Therapy: A New Therapeutic Tool or Pandora's Box?

You can do almost anything on the Internet these days, from ordering concert tickets to downloading music (legally of course) or whole books. You can also receive counseling or therapy services from an online therapist. By the early years of the new millennium, more than 250 Web sites were offering counseling services (Kalb, 2001b). But as the numbers of online counseling services mushroomed, so did the controversy concerning their use.

Many professionals voice serious concerns about the clinical, ethical, and legal issues regarding Internet-based psychological services (Jacobs et al., 2001; Jerome et al., 2000; Reed, McLaughlin, & Milholland, 2000; Taylor & Luce, 2003). One problem they identify is that although psychologists are licensed in particular states, Internet communications easily cross state and international borders. It remains unclear whether psychologists or other mental health professionals can legally provide online services to residents of states in which they are not licensed. Ethical problems and liability issues arise when psychologists and other helping professionals offer services to clients they never meet in person. Many therapists also express concerns that interacting with a client only by computer would prevent them from evaluating nonverbal cues and gestures that might signal deeper levels of distress than are verbally reported or typed on a keyboard.

Yet another problem is that online therapists living at great distances from their clients may not be able to provide the more intensive services clients need during times of emotional crisis. Professionals also express concern about the potential for unsuspecting clients to be victimized by unqualified practitioners or "quacks." We presently lack a system for ensuring that online therapists are licensed and otherwise qualified practitioners (Lauerman, 2000; Stamm & Perednia, 2000).

Despite these drawbacks, many professionals believe that online consultation and counseling services have potential value (e.g, Chang & Yeh, 2003; Glueckauf et al., 2003; Houston et al., 2002; Palmiter & Renjilian, 2003;

Taylor & Luce, 2003;). For one thing, people who have hesitated to seek help because of shyness or embarrassment may prefer online consultation (Rabasca, 2000a). Online consultation may also make people feel more comfortable about receiving help and become a first step toward meeting a therapist in person. Online therapy may also provide people living in remote areas where finding a therapist is difficult, or those lacking mobility, with services they might not otherwise receive.

Recently, investigators found that participants in Internet-delivered behavioral programs for weight loss achieved better results than a comparison group who were simply given a list of weight loss education sites on the Web (Tate, Wing, & Winett, 2001). Online support groups may also be helpful to people who are depressed and have few social outlets (Houston et al., 2002). Internet-based treatment programs have also shown positive results in treating such varied problems as posttraumatic stress disorder (Lange et al., 2003), childhood encopresis (soiling) (Ritterband et al., 2003), and insomnia (Ström, Pettersson, & Andersson, 2004).

The bottom line about Internet counseling, says Russ Newman, executive director for professional practice of the American Psychological Association, is the need for monitoring and evaluation of this emerging technology (cited in Lauerman, 2000). Psychologists are not writing off so-called e-therapy, but they remain cautious in endorsing its widespread use. Let's turn the discussion around to you. Would you be willing to seek psychological assistance via the Internet? Why or why not?

Critical Thinking

- What ethical and practical problems do therapists who offer online therapy face?
- What are the potential benefits of online therapy? What are the potential risks?

---

changes in their relationships to meet the child's needs more adequately.

Couple Therapy **Couple therapy** focuses on resolving conflicts in distressed couples, including married and unmarried couples (Christensen et al., 2004). Like family therapy, couple therapy focuses on improving communication and analyzing role relationships. For example, one partner may play a dominant role and resist any request to share power. The couple therapist helps bring these role relationships into the open, so that partners can explore alternative ways of relating to one another that would lead to a more satisfying relationship.

Evaluating Methods of Psychotherapy

What, then, of the effectiveness of psychotherapy? Does psychotherapy work? Are some forms of therapy more effective than others? Are some forms of therapy more effective for some types of clients or for some types of problems than for others?

The effectiveness of psychotherapy receives strong support from the research literature. Reviews of the scientific literature often utilize a statistical technique called *meta-analysis*, which averages the results of a large number of studies to determine an overall level of effectiveness.

In the most frequently cited meta-analysis of psychotherapy research, M. L. Smith and Glass (1977) analyzed the results of

Family therapy. In family therapy, the family, not the individual, is the unit of treatment. Family therapists help family members communicate more effectively with one another, for example, to air their disagreements in ways that are not hurtful to individual members. Family therapists also try to prevent one member of the family from becoming the scapegoat for the family's problems.

some 375 controlled studies comparing various types of therapies (psychodynamic, behavioral, humanistic, etc.) against control groups. The results of their analyses showed that the average psychotherapy client in these studies was better off than 75% of the clients who remained untreated. A larger analysis based on 475 controlled outcome studies showed the average person who received therapy was better off at the end of treatment than 80% of those who did not (M. L. Smith, Glass, & Miller, 1980).

Other meta-analyses also show positive outcomes for psychotherapy, including analyses of behavior therapy (Bowers & Clum, 1988; Lipsey & Wilson, 1993, 1995), brief psychodynamic therapy (E. M. Anderson & Lambert, 1995; Crits-Christoph, 1992), child and adolescent psychotherapy (McLeod & Weisz, 2004), and group psychotherapy (McDermut, Miller, & Brown, 2001). Evidence indicates that psychotherapy is effective not only in the confines of clinical research centers, but also in settings that are more typical of ordinary clinical practice (Shadish et al., 2000).

Evidence also shows that the greatest gains in psychotherapy are typically achieved in the first several months of treatment (Barkham et al., 1996; Howard et al., 1986). About 50% of patients show clinically significant change in about 3 or 4 months of treatment; by about 6 months, this figure rises to about 75% (E. M. Anderson & Lambert, 2001; Messer, 2001a). However, many clients drop out prematurely, before therapeutic benefits can be achieved (Hansen, Lambert, & Forman, 2002).

Meta-analysis shows negligible differences among different forms of therapy in the magnitude of the outcomes they achieve relative to control groups (Crits-Christoph, 1992; M. L. Smith, Glass, & Miller, 1980; Wampold et al., 1997a, 1997b). This suggests that the effectiveness of psychotherapies may have more to do with nonspecific factors they have in common than with the specific techniques that set them apart (M. J. Lambert & Bergin, 1994). Nonspecific or common factors include expectations of improvement and features of the therapist–client relationship, including the following: (1) empathy, support, and attention shown by the therapist; (2) *therapeutic alliance,* or the attachment the client develops toward the therapist and the therapy process; and (3) the *working alliance,* or the development of an effective working relationship in which the therapist and client work together to identify and confront the important issues and problems the client faces (Busseri & Tyler; 2003; Klein et al., 2003; Perlman, 2001; Wampold, 2001).

Should we conclude that different therapies are about equally effective? One possibility is that different therapies are about equal in their effects overall but may not be equal in their effects with every patient (Wampold et al., 1997a). That is, a given therapy may be more effective for a particular patient or for a particular type of problem. Another possibilty is that the effectiveness of therapy may have more to do with effectiveness of the therapist than with the particular form of therapy (Wampold, 2001).

All in all, the question of whether some forms of therapy are more effective than others remains unresolved (Nathan, Stuart, & Dolan, 2000). But perhaps the time has come for investigators to turn more of their attention to examining the active ingredients that make some therapists more effective than others, such as skills of empathy and ability to develop a good therapeutic relationship (Hanna, 2003; Wampold, 2001). For example, evidence shows that personal qualities of the therapist, such as flexibilty, honesty, warmth, and trustworthiness, relate to the ability to form an effective therapeutic alliance (Ackerman & Hilsenroth, 2003).

Another approach to determining which therapies are effective for which types of problems is the effort of a task force of clinical psychologists to identify *empirically supported treatments* or ESTs (Addis, 2002; Chorpita et al., 2002; Deegear & Lawson, 2003). The task force concluded that sufficient evidence exists to support the therapeutic efficacy of a number of psychological treatments for specific problem behaviors or disorders (listed in Table 4.3) (Chambless & Ollendick, 2001; Weisz et al., 2000). Other treatment interventions may be added to the list as scientific evidence becomes available. We should caution you not to infer that the inclusion of a particular treatment guarantees that it is effective in every case.

It is thus insufficient to ask which therapy works best. We must ask, Which therapy works best for which type of problem? Which clients are best suited for which type of

TABLE 4.3	
Examples of Empirically Supported Treatments (ESTs)	
Treatment	**Conditions for Which Treatment Is Effective** (Chapter in text where treatment is discussed is shown in parentheses.)
Cognitive therapy	Headache (Chapter 5) Depression (Chapter 8)
Behavior therapy or Behavior modification	Depression (Chapter 8) Persons with developmental disabilities (Chapter 14) Enuresis (Chapter 14)
Cognitive-behavior therapy	Panic disorder with and without agoraphobia (Chapter 6) Generalized anxiety disorder (Chapter 6) Smoking cessation (Chapter 9) Bulimia (Chapter 10)
Exposure treatment	Agoraphobia and specific phobia (Chapter 6)
Exposure and response prevention	Obsessive–compulsive disorder (Chapter 6)
Interpersonal psychotherapy	Depression (Chapter 8)
Parent training programs	Children with oppositional behavior (Chapter 14)

therapy? What are the advantages and limitations of particular therapies? Behavior therapy, for example, has shown impressive results in treating various types of anxiety disorders, sleep disorders, and sexual dysfunctions and in improving the adaptive functioning of people with schizophrenia and mental retardation. Psychodynamic and humanistic approaches may be most effective in fostering self-insight and personality growth. Cognitive therapy has demonstrated impressive results in treating depression and anxiety disorders. By and large, however, the process of determining which treatment, practiced by whom, and under what conditions is most effective for a given client remains a challenge.

All in all, psychotherapy is a complex process that incorporates common features along with specific techniques that foster adaptive change. A strong therapeutic alliance between client and therapist is associated with better therapy outcomes (Barber et al., 2000; Klein et al., 2003; Martin, Garske, & Davis, 2000; Meyer et al., 2002). But therapeutic gains are not accounted for entirely by nonspecific factors (Grissom, 1996; Oei & Shuttlewood, 1996). In fact, investigators believe that specific techniques may account for about twice the magnitude of therapeutic change as nonspecific factors that different therapies have in common (Stevens, Hynan, & Allen, 2000). In the final analysis, therapeutic change most likely depends on the influence of specific and nonspecific factors, as well as their interactions (Ilardi & Craighead, 1994).

Managed Care or Managed Costs?   This is an appropriate juncture to note that the practice of psychotherapy has been influenced by changes in the general health care environment in recent years, especially the increasing role of **managed care systems,** such as health maintenance organizations (HMOs). Managed care systems typically impose limits on the number of treatment sessions they will approve for payment and the fees they will allow for reimbursement. Consequently, there is greater emphasis today on briefer, more direct forms of treatment, including cognitive-behavioral therapy and shorter-term psychodynamic therapies. Moreover, managed care has curbed costly inpatient mental health treatment, primarily through limiting the lengths of stay of patients in psychiatric hospitals (USDHHS, 1999a; Wickizer, Lessler, & Travis, 1996).

Though managed care may help trim costs, many people express concerns about the risks of sacrificing quality of care in the interests of cutting costs. A recent study found that quality of mental health care is lacking in many HMOs (Druss et al., 2002). Con-

managed care systems Health care delivery systems that impose limits on the number of treatment sessions they will approve for payment and the fees they will allow for reimbursement.

" IT'S YOUR INSURANCE COMPANY,
THEY SAY YOU'RE CURED. "

Managed care or managed costs?

sumers rank autonomy in treatment decisions (not having a particular treatment turned down for reimbursement by a managed care company), choice of therapists, copayments amounts, limits to confidentiality, and ease of access to care as the most important elements of psychotherapy service plans offered by managed care companies (Kremer & Gesten, 2003).

Though health care providers understand the need to curtail the spiraling costs of care, they are understandably concerned that the cost-cutting emphasis of managed care plans may discourage people with identifiable psychological disorders from seeking help or receiving adequate care (Landerman et al., 1994). According to a Surgeon General's report, "Excessively restrictive cost-containment strategies and financial incentives to providers and facilities to reduce specialty referrals, hospital admissions, or length or amount of treatment may ultimately contribute to lowered access and quality of care" (cited in USDDHS, 1999a, Chapter 6).

Overzealous cost-cutting policies may also be financially shortsighted because the failure to provide adequate mental health care when problems arise may lead to a need for more expensive care later. Evidence shows that for people with severe psychological disorders, such as schizophrenia, bipolar disorder, and borderline personality disorder, psychotherapy actually reduces health care costs by reducing the need for hospitalization and reducing work impairment (Fraser, 1996; Gabbard et al., 1997).

Multicultural Issues in Psychotherapy

We live in an increasingly diverse, multicultural society in which people bring to therapy not only their personal backgrounds and individual experiences but also their cultural learning, norms, and values (James & Prilleltensky, 2002; La Roche & Maxie, 2003). Therapists need to be culturally competent to provide appropriate services to people of varied backgrounds (Iwamasa, Soroccco, & Koonce, 2002; Stuart, 2004; Wong et al., 2003).

Therapists need to be sensitive to cultural differences and how they affect the therapeutic process. Cultural sensitivity involves more than good intentions (Rice & O'-Donohue, 2002). Therapists must also have accurate knowledge of cultural factors, ability to use that knowledge effectively in developing culturally sensitive interventions, and awareness of how one's own culture and values may bias one's interactions with members of other cultural groups. Therapists also need to avoid ethnic stereotyping and to demonstrate sensitivity to the values, languages, and cultural beliefs of members of racial or ethnic groups that are different than their own (Comas-Diaz & Griffith, 1988; Lee & Richardson, 1991). They also need to be able to engage clients in an open discussion about issues of race and ethnicity (Cardemil & Battle, 2003). Perhaps it shouldn't surprise us that clients who rate their therapists high on multicultural competence also tend to perceive them as having skills of empathy and general competence (Fuertes & Brobst, 2002).

Just because a given therapy works with one population does not mean that it will necessarily work with another population (Hall, 2003; Sue, 2003). We need to gather evidence that speaks directly to whether particular therapies are effective with different populations. Let us touch on some of the issues involved in treating members of the major ethnic minority groups in our society: African Americans, Asian Americans, Hispanic Americans, and Native Americans.

African Americans The cultural history of African Americans must be understood in the context of extreme racial discrimination (Boyd-Franklin, 1989; Greene, 1990). African Americans have needed to develop coping mechanisms for managing the pervasive racism they encounter in such areas as employment, housing, education, and access to health care (Greene, 1993a, 1993b). For example, the sensitivity of many African Americans to the potential for maltreatment and exploitation is a survival tool and may take the form of a heightened level of suspiciousness or reserve (Greene, 1986). Therapists need to be aware of the tendency of African American clients to minimize their vulnerability by being less self-disclosing, especially in early stages of therapy (Ridley, 1984).

Therapists should not confuse such suspiciousness with paranoia (Boyd-Franklin, 1989; Greene, 1986).

In addition to whatever psychological problems an African American client may present, the therapist often needs to help the client develop coping mechanisms to deal with societal racial barriers. Therapists also need to be attuned to tendencies of some African Americans to internalize the negative stereotypes about Blacks that are perpetuated in the dominant culture (Greene, 1985, 1992a, 1992b; Nickerson, Helms, & Terrell, 1994; Pinderhughes, 1989).

To be culturally competent, therapists not only must understand the cultural traditions and languages of the groups with which they work, but also must recognize their own racial and ethnic attitudes and how these underlying attitudes affect their clinical practice (Greene, 1985, 1992a, 1992b; Nickerson, Helms, & Terrell, 1994; Pinderhughes, 1989). Therapists are exposed to the same negative stereotypes about African Americans as other people in society and must recognize how these stereotypes, if left unexamined, can become destructive to the therapeutic relationships they form with African American clients. In effect, therapists must be willing to confront their own racism and prejudices and replace these attitudes with more realistic appraisals of African Americans (Mays, 1985).

Therapists must also be aware of the cultural characteristics of African American families, such as strong kinship bonds, often including people who are not biologically related (for example, a close friend of a parent may have some parenting role and may be addressed as "aunt"), strong religious and spiritual orientation, multigenerational households, adaptability and flexibility of gender roles (African American women have a long history of working outside the home), and distribution of child-care responsibilities among different family members (Boyd-Franklin, 1989; Collins, 1990; Ferguson-Peters, 1985; Greene, 1990; USDHHS, 1999a).

Asian Americans Culturally sensitive therapists not only understand the beliefs and values of other cultures but also integrate this knowledge within the therapy process. Generally speaking, Asian cultures, including Japanese culture, value restraint in talking about oneself and one's feelings. Therapists thus need to be patient and not expect instant self-disclosures from Asian clients (Henkin, 1985). Public expression of emotions is also discouraged in Asian cultures. Suppression of emotions, especially negative emotions, is valued, and failure to keep one's feelings to oneself is believed to reflect poorly on one's upbringing (Huang, 1994). Asian clients who appear emotionally restrained when judged by Western standards may be responding in ways that are culturally appropriate.

Clinicians also note that Asian clients often express psychological complaints in terms of physical symptoms. However, this tendency to *somaticize* emotional problems may be attributed in part to differences in communication styles (Zane & Sue, 1991). That is, Asians may use somatic terms to convey emotional distress.

In some cases, the goals of therapy may conflict with the values of a particular culture. The individualism of American society, which is expressed in therapeutic interventions that focus on development of the self, contrasts sharply with the group- and family-centered values of Asian cultures (Huang, 1994). Therapeutic approaches that emphasize individuality and self-determination may be inappropriate for Asian clients who adhere to traditional Asian cultural values, which emphasize the importance of the group over the individual (Ching et al., 1995; Henkin, 1985).

Hispanic Americans Although Hispanic American subcultures differ in various respects, many share certain cultural values and beliefs, such as adherence to a strong patriarchal (male-dominated) family structure and strong kinship ties. De la Cancela and Guzman (1991) identify some other values shared by many Hispanic Americans:

> One's identity is in part determined by one's role in the family. The male, or *macho*, is the head of the family, the provider, the protector of the family honor, and the final decision maker. The woman's role (*marianismo*) is to care for the family and the children. Obviously, these roles are changing, with women entering the work force and achieving greater

Cultural sensitivity. Therapists need to be sensitive to cultural differences and how they may affect the therapeutic process. They also need to avoid ethnic stereotyping and to demonstrate sensitivity to the values, languages, and cultural beliefs of members of racial or ethnic groups that are different than their own. Clients who are not fluent in English profit from having therapists who can conduct therapy in their own languages.

educational opportunities. Cultural values of *respeto* (respect), *confianza* (trust), *dignidad* (dignity), and *personalismo* (personalism) are highly esteemed and are important factors in working with many [Hispanic Americans]. (p. 60)

Therapists need to recognize that the traditional Hispanic American value of interdependency within the family may conflict with the values of independence and self-reliance that are stressed in the mainstream U.S. culture (De la Cancela & Guzman, 1991). Psychotherapeutic interventions should respect differences in values rather than attempt to impose values of majority cultures. Therapists should also be trained to reach beyond the confines of their offices to work within the Hispanic American community itself, in settings that have an impact on the daily lives of Hispanic Americans, such as social clubs, *bodegas* (neighborhood groceries), and neighborhood beauty and barber shops. We can further break down barriers that may impede utilization of mental health services by Hispanic Americans by recruiting bicultural/bilingual staff and creating a welcoming therapeutic atmosphere that is accepting of Hispanic American cultural values (Guarnaccia & Rodriguez, 1996).

Native Americans Among all the ethnic minority groups in the United States, Native Americans may be most in need of effective mental health treatment. Lifetime prevalence of psychological disorders may exceed 50% of the population of some Native American tribes. Despite the need, Native Americans remain severely underserved by mental health professionals, in part because of the cultural gap that exists between providers and recipients.

Kahn (1982) argues that if mental health professionals are to be successful in helping Native Americans, they must do so within a context that is relevant and sensitive to Native Americans' customs, culture, and values. For example, many Native Americans expect the therapist will do most of the talking and they will play a passive role in treatment. These expectations are in keeping with the traditional healer role but conflict with the client-focused approach of many forms of conventional therapy. There may yet be other differences in gestures, eye contact, facial expression, and other modes of nonverbal expression that can impede effective communication between therapist and client (Renfrey, 1992).

Psychologists recognize the importance of bringing elements of tribal culture into mental health programs for Native Americans (Rabasca, 2000a). For example, therapists can use indigenous ceremonies that are part of the client's cultural or religious traditions. Purification and cleansing rites are therapeutic for many Native American peoples in the United States and elsewhere, as among the African Cuban *Santeria,* the Brazilian *umbanda,* and the Haitian *vodoun* (Lefley, 1990). Cleansing rites are often sought by people who believe their problems are caused by failure to placate malevolent spirits or to perform mandatory rituals (Lefley, 1990).

Respect for cultural differences is a key feature of culturally sensitive therapies. Training in multicultural therapy is becoming more widely integrated into training programs for therapists (e.g., Neville et al., 1996). Culturally sensitive therapies adopt a respectful attitude that encourages people to tell their own personal story as well as the story of their culture (Coronado & Peake, 1992).

BIOMEDICAL THERAPIES

There is a growing emphasis in American psychiatry on biomedical therapies, especially the use of psychotherapeutic drugs (also called *psychotropic drugs*). Biomedical therapies are generally administered by medical doctors, many of whom have specialized training in psychiatry or **psychopharmacology.** Many family physicians or general practitioners also prescribe psychotherapeutic drugs for their patients.

Biomedical approaches have had dramatic success in treating some forms of abnormal behavior, though they also have their limitations. For one, drugs may have unwelcome or dangerous side effects. There is also the potential for abuse. One of the most commonly prescribed minor tranquilizers, Valium, has become a major drug of abuse among people who become psychologically and physiologically dependent on it. Psychosurgery has been all but eliminated as a form of treatment because of serious harmful effects of earlier procedures.

Drug Therapy

Different classes of psychotropic drugs are used in treating many types of psychological disorders. But all the drugs in these classes act on neurotransmitter systems in the brain, affecting the delicate balance of chemicals that ferry nerve impulses from neuron to neuron (Snyder, 2002). The major classes of psychiatric drugs are antianxiety drugs, antipsychotic drugs, antidepressants, and lithium, which is used to treat mood swings in people with bipolar disorder. The use of other psychotropic drugs, such as stimulants, will be discussed in later chapters.

Antianxiety Drugs Antianxiety drugs (also called *anxiolytics*, from the Greek *anxietas*, meaning "anxiety," and *lysis*, meaning "bringing to an end") combat anxiety and reduce states of muscle tension. They include mild tranquilizers, such as those of the *benzodiazepines* class of drugs, including *diazepam* (Valium) and *alprazolam* (Xanax), as well as hypnotic-sedatives, such as *triazolam* (Halcion) and *flurazepam* (Dalmane).

Antianxiety drugs depress the level of activity in certain parts of the central nervous system (CNS). In turn, the CNS decreases the level of sympathetic nervous system activity, reducing the respiration rate and heart rate and lessening states of anxiety and tension. Mild tranquilizers such as Valium grew in popularity when physicians became concerned about the use of more potent depressants, such as barbiturates, which are highly addictive and extremely dangerous when taken in overdoses or mixed with alcohol. Unfortunately, it has become clear that these tranquilizers also can, and often do, lead to physiological dependence (addiction). People who are dependent on Valium may go into convulsions when they abruptly stop taking it. Deaths have been reported among people who mix mild tranquilizers with alcohol or who are unusually sensitive to them.

Side effects of using antianxiety drugs include fatigue, drowsiness, and impaired motor coordination that can impair the ability to function or to operate an automobile. Regular usage of these drugs can also produce **tolerance,** a physiological sign of dependence, which refers to the need over time for increasing dosages of a drug to achieve the same effect. When used on a short-term basis, antianxiety drugs can be safe and effective in treating anxiety and insomnia. Yet drugs by themselves do not teach people more adaptive ways of solving their problems and may encourage them to rely on a chemical agent to cope with stress rather than to develop active means of coping. Drug therapy is thus often combined with psychotherapy to help people with anxiety complaints. However, combining drug therapy and psychotherapy may present special problems and challenges. For one, drug-induced relief from anxiety may reduce clients' motivation to try to solve their problems. For another, medicated clients who develop skills for coping with stress in psychotherapy may fail to retain what they have learned once the tranquilizers are discontinued or find themselves too tense to employ their newly acquired skills.

Rebound anxiety is another problem associated with regular use of tranquilizers. Many people who regularly use antianxiety drugs report that anxiety or insomnia returns in a more severe form once they discontinue them. For some, this may represent a fear of not having the drugs to depend on. For others, rebound anxiety might reflect changes in biochemical processes that are not well understood at present.

Antipsychotic Drugs Antipsychotic drugs, also called *neuroleptics* (sometimes called *major tranquilizers*) are commonly used to treat the more flagrant features of schizo-

psychopharmacology The field of study that examines the effects of therapeutic or psychiatric drugs.

antianxiety drugs Drugs that combat anxiety and reduce states of muscle tension.

tolerance Physical habituation to use of a drug.

rebound anxiety The experiencing of strong anxiety following withdrawal from a tranquilizer.

antipsychotic drugs Drugs used to treat schizophrenia or other psychotic disorders.

phrenia and other psychotic disorders, such as hallucinations, delusions, and states of confusion. Introduced during the 1950s, many of these drugs, including *chlorpromazine* (Thorazine), *thioridazine* (Mellaril), and *fluphenazine* (Prolixin), belong to the *phenothiazine* class of chemicals. Phenothiazines appear to control psychotic features by blocking the action of the neurotransmitter dopamine at receptor sites in the brain. Although the underlying causes of schizophrenia remain unknown, researchers suspect an irregularity in the dopamine system in the brain may be involved (see Chapter 12). *Clozapine* (Clozaril), a neuroleptic of a different chemical class than the phenothiazines, is effective in treating many people with schizophrenia whose symptoms were unresponsive to other neuroleptics (see Chapter 12). The use of clozapine must be carefully monitored, however, because of potentially dangerous side effects.

The use of neuroleptics has greatly reduced the need for more restrictive forms of treatment for severely disturbed patients, such as physical restraints and confinement in padded cells, and has lessened the need for long-term hospitalization. The introduction of the first generation of antipsychotic drugs in the mid-1950s was one of the major factors that led to a massive exodus of chronic mental patients from state institutions. Many formerly hospitalized patients have been able to resume family life and hold jobs while continuing to take their medications.

Neuroleptics are not without their problems, including potential side effects such as muscular rigidity and tremors. Although these side effects are generally controllable by use of other drugs, long-term use of antipsychotic drugs (possibly excepting clozapine) can produce a potentially irreversible and disabling motor disorder called *tardive dyskinesia* (see Chapter 12), which is characterized by uncontrollable eye blinking, facial grimaces, lip smacking, and other involuntary movements of the mouth, eyes, and limbs. Researchers are experimenting with lowered dosages, intermittent drug regimens, and new medications to reduce the risk of such complications.

Antidepressants Three major classes of **antidepressants** are used in treating depression: *tricyclics, monoamine oxidase (MAO) inhibitors,* and *selective serotonin-reuptake inhibitors (SSRIs).* Tricyclics and MAO inhibitors increase the availability of the neurotransmitters norepinephrine and serotonin in the brain. Some of the more common tricyclics are *imipramine* (Tofranil), *amitriptyline* (Elavil), and *doxepin* (Sinequan). The MAO inhibitors include such drugs as *phenelzine* (Nardil) and *tranylcypromine* (Parnate). Tricyclic antidepressants (TCAs) are favored over MAO inhibitors because they cause fewer potentially serious side effects.

The third class of antidepressants, selective serotonin-reuptake inhibitors, or SSRIs, have more specific effects on serotonin function in the brain. Drugs in this class include *fluoxetine* (Prozac) and *sertraline* (Zoloft). They increase the availability of serotonin in the brain by interfering with its reuptake by the transmitting neuron.

Evidence indicates that slightly more than half of the people with clinically significant depression who are treated with antidepressants of the tricyclic class will respond favorably (Depression Guideline Panel, 1993b). A favorable response to treatment does not mean depression is relieved, however. Overall, the effects of antidepressants appear to be modest at best (Kirsch et al., 2002). Nor does any particular antidepressant appear to be clearly more effective than any other (Depression Guideline Panel, 1993b). Even Prozac, which was hailed by some as a "wonder drug," produces about the same level of therapeutic benefit as the older generation of antidepressants, the TCAs (Greenberg et al., 1994). Prozac and other SSRIs may be preferred, however, because they are associated with fewer side effects, such as weight gain, and have a lower risk of lethal overdoses than the older tricyclics (Depression Guideline Panel, 1993b).

Antidepressants also have beneficial effects in treating a wide range of psychological disorders, including panic disorder, social phobia, obsessive–compulsive disorder (see Chapter 6), and eating disorders (see Chapter 10) (Barlow et al., 2000; Hudson et al., 2003; Liebowitz et al., 2002; McElroy et al., 2000). As research into the underlying causes of these disorders continues, we may find that irregularities of neurotransmitter functioning in the brain plays a key role in their development.

antidepressants Drugs used to treat depression that affect the availability of neurotransmitters in the brain.

Lithium Lithium carbonate, a salt of the metal lithium in tablet form, helps stabilize the dramatic mood swings in many cases of people with bipolar disorder (formerly *manic depression*) (Baldessarini & Tondo, 2000; Bowden et al., 2003; Grof & Alda, 2000). People with bipolar disorder may have to continue using lithium indefinitely to control the disorder. Because of potential toxicity associated with lithium, the blood levels of patients maintained on the drug must be carefully monitored.

Table 4.4 lists psychotropic drugs according to their drug class and category.

Ethnic Differences in Response to Psychotropic Medication

Cultural or ethnic factors may contribute to differences in responsiveness to psychotropic medications (Lefley, 1990; Lesser, 1992). African Americans, for example, tend to show a better response to antidepressants and phenothiazines than other groups. Hispanic Americans tend to show lower effective dosage levels (Lawson, 1986). However, some research suggests that African Americans are at greater risk of experiencing potentially serious side effects from psychiatric drugs, especially phenothiazines (Jeste et al., 1996). Differences in response patterns and risks of side effects among ethnic groups brings into perspective the need to conduct psychopharmacological research on diverse groups. Unfortunately, people of color, including African Americans, have been underrepresented in drug trials (Lawson, 1996).

Electroconvulsive Therapy

In 1939, the Italian psychiatrist Ugo Cerletti introduced the technique of **electroconvulsive therapy (ECT)** in psychiatric treatment. Cerletti had observed the practice in some slaughterhouses of using electric shock to render animals unconscious. He observed that the shocks also produced convulsions. Cerletti incorrectly believed, as did other researchers in Europe at the time, that convulsions of the type found in epilepsy were incompatible with schizophrenia and that a treatment method that induced convulsions might be used to cure schizophrenia.

After the introduction of the phenothiazines in the 1950s, the use of ECT became generally limited to the treatment of severe depression. The introduction of antidepressants has limited the use of ECT even further today. However, evidence indicates that about 50% of people with major depression who fail to respond to antidepressants show significant improvement following ECT (Prudic et al., 1996).

ECT remains a source of controversy for several reasons. First, many people, including many professionals, are uncomfortable about the idea of passing an electric shock through a person's head, even if the level of shock is closely regulated and the convulsions are controlled by drugs. Second, ECT carries potential side effects, including some memory loss. Permanent loss of memory may occur for events that happen during the months that precede ECT and for several weeks afterwards (Glass, 2001). Third, the relative effectiveness of ECT, as compared to antidepressant drugs and to alternative treatments, such as cognitive-behavioral therapy, remains under study. Fourth, no one yet knows why ECT works, although it is suspected that it might help correct neurotransmitter imbalances in the brain. Finally, ECT is associated with a high rate of relapse following treatment (Sackeim et al., 2001).

Although controversies concerning the use of ECT persist, increasing evidence supports its effectiveness in helping people with severe depression, including cases in which depressed people fail to respond to psychotherapy or antidepressant medication (Sackeim et al., 2001). ECT is generally considered a treatment of last resort, after less-intrusive methods have been tried and failed.

electroconvulsive therapy (ECT) A method of treating severe depression by administering electrical shock to the head.

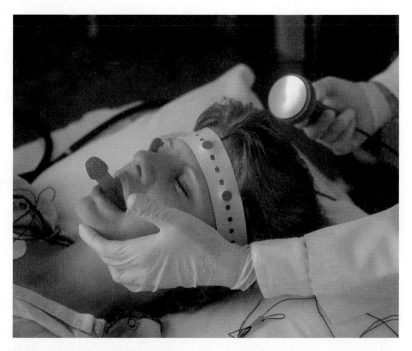

Electroconvulsive therapy (ECT). ECT is helpful in many cases of severe or prolonged depression that do not respond to other forms of treatment. Still, its use remains controversial.

TABLE 4.4

Major Psychotropic Drugs

Category	Drug Class	Generic Name	Trade Name
Antianxiety agents (also called anxiolytics)	Benzodiazepines	Diazepam	Valium
		Chlordiazepoxide	Librium
		Clorazepate	Tranxene
		Oxazepam	Serax
		Lorazepam	Ativan
		Alprazolam	Xanax
	Barbiturates	Meprobamate	Miltown
			Equanil
	Hypnotics	Flurazepam	Dalmane
		Triazolam	Halcion
		Zolpidem	Ambien
	Other anxiolytics	Busipirone	BuSpar
Antipsychotic drugs (also called neuroleptics or major tranquilizers)	Phenothiazines	Chlorpromazine	Thorazine
		Thioridazine	Mellaril
		Mesoridazine	Serentil
		Perphenazine	Trilafon
		Trifluoperazine	Stelazine
		Fluphenazine	Prolixin
	Thioxanthenes	Thiothixene	Navane
	Butyrophenones	Haloperidol	Haldol
	Dibenzoxazepines	Loxapine	Loxitane
	Dibenzodiazepines	Clozapine	Clozaril
Antidepressants	Tricyclic antidepressants (TCAs)	Imipramine	Tofranil
		Desipramine	Norpramin
		Amitriptyline	Elavil
		Doxepin	Sinequan
		Clomipramine	Anafranil
	MAO inhibitors (MAOIs)	Phenelzine	Nardil
		Tranylcypromine	Parnate
	Selective serotonin-reuptake inhibitors (SSRIs)	Fluoxetine	Prozac
		Sertraline	Zoloft
		Paroxetine	Paxil
		Fluvoxamine	Luvox
		Citalopram	Celexa
	Other antidepressants	Bupropion	Wellbutrin
		Nefazodone	Serzone
		Venlafaxine	Effexor
Antimanic agents		Lithium carbonate	Eskalith
		Carbamazepine	Tegretol
		Divalproex	Depakote
		Valproate	Depakene
Stimulants		Methylphenidate	Ritalin
		Pemoline	Cylert

Psychosurgery

Psychosurgery is yet more controversial than ECT and is rarely practiced today. Although it is no longer performed, the most widely used form of psychosurgery was the *prefrontal lobotomy,* in which the nerve pathways linking the thalamus to the prefrontal lobes of the brain are surgically severed. The operation was based on the theory that extremely disturbed patients suffer from overexcitation of emotional impulses that emanate from the lower brain centers, such as the thalamus and hypothalamus. It was believed that by severing the connections between the thalamus and the higher brain centers in the frontal lobe of the cerebral cortex, the patient's violent or aggressive tendencies could be controlled. The prefrontal lobotomy was developed by the Portuguese neurologist António Egas Moniz and was introduced to the United States in the 1930s. More than 1,000 mental patients received the operation by 1950. Although the operation did reduce violent and agitated behavior in many cases, it was not always successful. In a cruel ironic twist, a patient whom Moniz had treated later shot him, leaving him paralyzed from a bullet that lodged in his spine.

Many distressing side effects are associated with the prefrontal lobotomy, including hyperactivity, impaired learning ability and reduced creativity, distractibility, apathy, overeating, withdrawal, epileptic-type seizures, and even death. The occurrence of these side effects, combined with the introduction of the phenothiazines, led to the elimination of the operation.

More sophisticated psychosurgery techniques have been introduced in recent years. Generally speaking, they are limited to smaller parts of the brain and produce less damage than the prefrontal lobotomy. These operations have been performed to treat such problems as intractable aggression, depression, and psychotic behavior; chronic pain; some forms of epilepsy; and persistent obsessive–compulsive disorder (Baer et al., 1995; Irle et al., 1998; Sachdev & Hay, 1996). Follow-up studies of such procedures have shown marked improvement in about one quarter to one half of cases. But concerns about possible complications, including impaired intellectual functioning, have greatly reduced their use (Irle et al., 1998). Before leaving this topic, let us understand that psychosurgery should only be considered as a treatment of last resort.

Evaluation of Biological Approaches

There is little doubt that biological treatments have helped many people with severe psychological problems. Many thousands of people with schizophrenia who were formerly hospitalized are able to function in the community because of antipsychotic drugs. Antidepressant drugs have helped relieve depression in many cases and have shown therapeutic benefits in treating other disorders, such as panic disorder, obsessive–compulsive disorder, and eating disorders. ECT is helpful in relieving depression in many people who have been unresponsive to other treatments.

On the other hand, some forms of psychotherapy may be as effective as drug therapy in treating anxiety disorders and depression (see Chapters 6 and 8). Moreover, problems such as side effects persist. In addition, antianxiety agents, such as Valium, have often become drugs of abuse among people who become dependent on them for relieving the effects of stress. Medical practitioners have often been too quick to use their prescription pads to help people with anxiety complaints, rather than to help them examine their lives or refer for psychological treatment. Physicians often feel pressured, of course, by patients who seek a chemical solution to their life problems.

Although we continue to learn more about the biological foundations of abnormal behavior patterns, the interface between biology and behavior can be construed as a two-way street. Researchers have uncovered links between psychological factors and many physical disorders and conditions (see Chapter 5). Researchers are also investigating whether the combination of psychological and drug treatments for such problems as depression, anxiety disorders, and substance abuse disorders, among others, may increase the therapeutic benefits of either of the two approaches alone.

HOSPITALIZATION AND COMMUNITY-BASED CARE

People receive mental health services within various settings, including hospitals, outpatient clinics, community mental health centers, and private practices. In this section we explore the purposes of hospitalization and the movement toward community-based care. Due to **deinstitutionalization**—the policy of shifting the burden of care from state hospitals to community-based treatment settings—an exodus has taken place from state

deinstitutionalization The policy of shifting care for patients with severe or chronic mental health problems from inpatient facilities to community-based facilities.

mental hospitals. We will see that deinstitutionalization has had a profound impact on the delivery of mental health services as well as on the larger community.

Roles for Hospitalization

Different types of hospitals provide different types of mental health treatment. State mental hospitals provide care to people with severe psychological problems. Municipal and community-based hospitals tend to focus on short-term care for people with serious psychological problems who need a structured hospital environment to help them through a crisis. In these kinds of cases, psychotropic drugs and other biological treatments, such as ECT for severe cases of depression, are often used in combination with short-term psychotherapy. Hospitalization may be followed by outpatient treatment. Many private psychiatric hospitals provide longer-term care or are specialized to help people withdraw safely from alcohol or drugs. Susanna, whose case opened this chapter, was treated in such a hospital for nearly two years.

Most state hospitals today are better managed and provide more humane care than those of the 19th and early 20th centuries, but here and there deplorable conditions persist. Today's state hospital is generally more treatment oriented and focuses on preparing residents to return to community living. State hospitals today often function as part of an integrated, comprehensive approach to treatment. They provide a structured environment for people who are unable to function in a less-restrictive community setting. When hospitalization restores patients to a higher level of functioning, the patients are reintegrated in the community and given follow-up care and transitional residences, if needed, to help them adjust to community living. Patients may be rehospitalized as needed in a state hospital if a community-based hospital is not available or if they require more extensive care. For younger and less intensely disturbed people, the state hospital stay is typically briefer than it was in the past, lasting only until their condition allows them to reenter society. Older chronic patients may be unprepared to handle the most rudimentary tasks (shopping, cooking, cleaning, and so on) of independent life, however—in part because the state hospital may be the only home such patients have known as adults.

The Community Mental Health Center

Community mental health centers (CMHCs) perform many functions in the effort to reduce the need for hospitalization of new patients and rehospitalization of formerly hospitalized patients. A primary function of the CMHC is to help discharged mental patients adjust to the community by providing continuing care and closely monitoring their progress. Unfortunately, not enough CMHCs have been established to serve the needs of the hundreds of thousands of formerly hospitalized patients and to prevent the need to hospitalize new patients by providing intervention services and day hospital programs. Patients in *day hospitals* attend structured therapy and vocational rehabilitation programs in a hospital setting during the day but are returned to their families or homes at night. Many CMHCs also administer transitional treatment facilities in the community, such as *halfway houses.* Halfway houses provide a sheltered living environment to help discharged mental patients gradually adjust to the community as well as to offer people in crisis an alternative to hospitalization. CMHCs also provide consultative services to other professionals, such as training police officers to handle disturbed people.

One of the major functions of the community mental health center is prevention. "An ounce of prevention is worth a pound of cure," so goes the saying. In medical science, vaccines prevent people from contracting such diseases as smallpox and polio. In the mental health system, however, resources are generally directed toward treating mental health problems rather than attempting to prevent them from developing. A report by the prestigious Institute of Medicine (IOM) called for increased support for research on prevention and for programs to promote psychological well-being and reduce the risks of mental health disorders (Muñoz, Mrazek, & Haggerty, 1996).

Halfway house. The halfway house provides a sheltered living environment that can help mental patients make the transition from the psychiatric hospital to the community. These facilities also offer an alternative to hospitalization for people in crisis.

The Spectrum of Prevention Traditionally, the term *prevention* has been applied to interventions that run the gamut from programs designed to prevent the onset of mental disorders to those that attempt to reduce the impact of disorders once they develop (Kaplan, 2000). The IOM report, initiated by the U.S. Congress, limits the term *prevention* to interventions that occur before the onset of a diagnosable disorder (Muñoz et al., 1996). Interventions focusing on lessening the impact of already developed disorders are classified as *treatment interventions* rather than prevention.

The IOM report conceptualizes a mental health spectrum of interventions ranging from prevention efforts through treatment and maintenance interventions (see Figure 4.2). Three categories of prevention programs are identified: universal, selective, and indicated.

Universal preventive interventions are targeted toward the whole population or general public, such as programs designed to enhance prenatal health or childhood nutrition. *Selective preventive interventions* are targeted toward individuals or groups known to be at higher than average risk of developing mental disorders, such as children of schizophrenic parents. **Primary prevention** efforts—programs designed to prevent problems from arising—can be either universal or selective, depending on whether they are focused on the general population or "at-risk" groups.

Indicated preventive interventions are directed toward individuals with early signs or symptoms that foreshadow the development of a mental disorder but don't yet meet diagnostic criteria for the particular disorder. This form of prevention, commonly called **secondary prevention,** attempts to nip in the bud developing problems. For example, secondary preventive programs aimed at changing the drinking habits of high-risk drinkers or early problem drinkers may forestall the onset of more severe alcohol-related problems or alcohol dependence (Botelho & Richmond, 1996; Marlatt et al., 1998).

We have had some success in the health arena in developing effective prevention programs for teenage pregnancies, sexually transmitted diseases, and some forms of drug abuse (e.g., Blackman, 1996; Stover et al., 1996). Psychologist Martin Seligman and his colleagues have shown that teaching cognitive skills involved in disputing catastrophic, negative thoughts reduced the risk of depression in both college students and school-age children (Jaycox et al., 1994; Seligman, 1998). Still, we have much to learn about developing effective prevention programs to prevent psychological disorders. To develop effective preventive programs we must expand our knowledge of the underlying causes

primary prevention Efforts designed to prevent problems from arising.

secondary prevention Efforts to ameliorate existing problems at an early stage.

An ounce of prevention. Obtaining good prenatal care can help prevent health problems in both the mother and the fetus. Mental health professionals face the challenge of developing programs to reduce the risks of psychological disorders.

of these disorders as well as mount controlled investigations to examine ways of preventing them.

The challenge of preventing psychological disorders is before us. The question is whether the nation can muster the political will and financial resolve to meet the challenge.

Ethnic Group Differences in Use of Mental Health Services

A 2001 report by the U.S. Surgeon General concluded that members of racial and ethnic minority groups typically have less access to mental health care and receive lower-quality care than do other Americans (US-DHHS, 2001; see Table 4.5). A major reason for this disparity is that a disproportionate number of minority group members remain uninsured or underinsured, leaving them unable to afford mental health care. Consequently, minorities shoulder a greater burden of mental health problems that go undiagnosed and untreated (Stenson, 2001a).

Cultural factors are yet another reason for underutilization of mental health services by minority groups (Sanders Thompson et al., 2004). Mental health clinics are not typically the first places where African Americans go for help for emotional problems. They are more likely to turn first to the church and second to the emergency room of the local general hospital (Lewis-Hall, 1992). The National Survey of African Americans found that slightly more than half (54%) of those who reported experiencing feelings of a "nervous breakdown" failed to consult any type of professional for help with their problems (Neighbors, 1992). Another study found that only about 1 in 10 African Americans in a community-based sample who experienced major depression consulted a mental health professional (D. R. Brown, Ahmed, Gary, & Milburn, 1995).

Latinos who encounter emotional problems are more likely to seek assistance from friends and relatives or from spiritualists than to reach out to mental health facilities, which they perceive as cold and impersonal (De La Cancela & Guzman, 1991). Latinos are also more likely to seek assistance for emotional problems from primary-care physicians than from

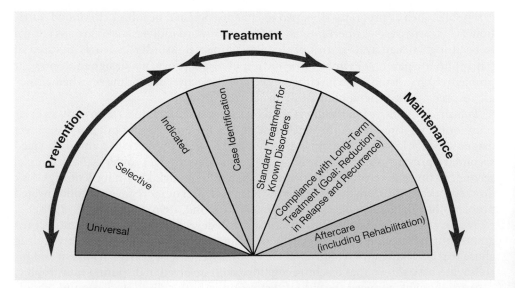

FIGURE 4.2 The mental health intervention spectrum for mental disorders.

Source: Mazrek, P. J., & Haggerty, R. J., *Reducing risks for mental disorders: Frontiers for preventive intervention research.* Copyright © 1994 by the National Academy of Sciences. Courtesy of the National Academy Press, Washington, D.C. Reprinted with permission.

TABLE 4.5

Culture, Race, Ethnicity, and Mental Health: **Major Findings of the Surgeon General's Report**

- The percentage of African Americans receiving needed care for mental health problems is only half that of non-Hispanic Whites. African Americans have less access to mental health care than Whites, partly because a greater percentage of African Americans lack health insurance.

- Of all American ethnic groups, Hispanic Americans are the least likely to have health insurance. Moreover, the limited availability of Spanish-speaking mental health professionals means that many Hispanic Americans who speak little or no English lack the opportunity to receive care from linguistically similar treatment providers.

- Largely because of lingering stigma and shame associated with mental illness, Asian Americans/Pacific Islanders often fail to seek care until their problems are more advanced than is the case with other groups. Moreover, accessibility is limited by scarcity of treatment providers with appropriate language skills.

- American Indians/Alaska Natives have a suicide rate that is 50% higher than the national average, but little is known about how many people within these groups receive needed care. In addition, the rural, isolated locations in which many Native Americans live places a severe constraint on the availability of mental health services.

Source: Adapted from Stenson, 2001a; USDHHS, 2001.

psychologists or psychiatrists, in part to avoid the perceived stigma of consulting a mental health provider (Kouyoumdjian, Zamboanga, & Hansen, 2003). Asian Americans/Pacific Islanders are also less likely than Euro Americans to seek help from mental health providers (Breaux, Matsuoka, & Ryujin, 1995).

We may better understand low rates of utilization of outpatient mental health services by ethnic minorities by examining the barriers that exist to receiving treatment, which include the following (adapted from Cheung, 1991; USDHHS, 1999a; Woodward, Dwinell, & Arons, 1992).

1. *Cultural mistrust.* People from minority groups often fail to use mental health services because of a lack of trust (Sanders Thompson et al., 2004). Mistrust may stem from a cultural or personal history of oppression, discrimination, or experiences in which service providers were unresponsive to their needs. When ethnic minority clients perceive majority therapists and the institutions in which they work to be cold or impersonal, they are less likely to place their trust in them.

2. *Institutional barriers.* Facilities may be inaccessible to minority group members because they are located at a considerable distance from their homes or because of lack of public transportation. Most facilities operate only during daytime work hours, which means they are inaccessible to working people. Moreover, minority group members feel staff members often make them feel stupid for not being familiar with clinic procedures, and their requests for assistance often become tangled in red tape.

3. *Cultural barriers.* Many recent immigrants, especially those from Southeast Asian countries, have had little, if any, previous contact with mental health professionals. They may hold different conceptions of mental health problems or view mental health problems as less severe than physical problems. In some ethnic minority subcultures, the family is expected to take care of members who have psychological problems and may resist seeking outside assistance. Other cultural barriers include cultural differences between typically lower socioeconomic strata minority group members and mostly White, middle-class staff members and incongruence between the cultural practices of minority group members and techniques used by mental health professionals. For example, Asian immigrants may find little value in talking about their problems or may be uncomfortable expressing their feelings to strangers. In many ethnic minority groups, personal and inter-

personal problems are brought to trusted elders in the family or religious leaders, not to outside professionals. In light of these factors, it is not surprising to find evidence that East Asian immigrants who are willing to seek psychological treatment tend to be older, more assimilated, and have better proficiency in English than their peers (Barry & Grilo, 2002).

4. *Language barriers.* Differences in language make it difficult for minority group members to describe their problems or obtain needed services. Many mental health facilities lack staff members who can communicate in the languages used by ethnic minority residents in their communities (Biever et al., 2002).

5. *Economic and accessibility barriers.* As mentioned earlier, financial burdens are often a major barrier to utilization of mental health services by ethnic minorities, many of whom live in economically distressed areas (Sanders Thompson et al., 2004). Moreover, many minority group members live in rural or isolated areas where mental health services may be lacking or inaccessible (USDHHS, 2001).

Cheung (1991) concludes that greater utilization of mental health services will depend to a great extent on the ability of the mental health system to develop programs that take cultural factors into account and build staffs that consist of culturally sensitive providers, including minority mental health professionals and paraprofessionals. Cultural mistrust of the mental health system among minority group members may be grounded in the perception that many mental health professionals are racially biased in how they evaluate and treat members of minority groups. Let's take a closer look at whether the evidence bears out this perception.

Racial Stereotyping and the Mental Health System

If you are African American, you are more likely to be admitted to a mental hospital and more likely to be involuntarily committed than if you are White (Lindsey & Paul, 1989). You are also more likely to be diagnosed with schizophrenia (Coleman & Baker, 1994; USDHHS, 1999a). The question is, why?

Relationships between ethnicity and diagnostic and admission practices are complex. They depend in part on differences in rates of mental disorders among different ethnic groups. If the rate of a given disorder is higher in a particular group, then it stands to reason that more members of the group will be diagnosed with the disorder. We know that African Americans as a group are no more likely to develop schizophrenia, a severe psychological disorder that often leads to hospitalization, than are Euro Americans of the same socioeconomic level (USDHHS, 1999a). However, we also know that African Americans are overrepresented among lower socioeconomic groups in our society, and people in the lower strata on the socioeconomic ladder are more likely to have severe psychological disorders, such as schizophrenia. Thus, differences in socioeconomic backgrounds offer at least a partial explanation of ethnic/racial differences in diagnostic practices and rates of psychiatric hospitalization.

Ethnic stereotyping by mental health professionals may also contribute to an overdiagnosis of severe psychological problems requiring hospitalization. For example, although African Americans and Hispanic Americans are more likely than Euro Americans to be diagnosed with schizophrenia, independent assessment of patients does not justify such differences in rates of diagnosis (Garb, 1997; Lawson et al., 1994). This evidence strongly suggests that bias comes into play in diagnosing members of ethnic minority groups. African Americans are also more likely than Euro Americans to receive psychiatric medication, including antipsychotic medication (Segal, Bola, & Watson, 1996). Investigators believe that clinician biases rather than clinical criteria may account for differences in prescription patterns (Frackiewicz et al., 1999).

How might bias affect a clinician's clinical judgments? As the recent Surgeon General's report on mental health points out, diagnostic and treatment decisions in mental health settings are based more on behavioral signs and patient reporting of symptoms than on more objective laboratory tests (USDHHS, 1999a). Consequently, clinician judgment plays an important role in determining whether someone receives a schizophrenia diagnosis and is deemed to be in need of hospitalization or antipsychotic medication.

Evaluation of Deinstitutionalization

Let us return to the issue of deinstitutionalization. Has this policy achieved its goal of successfully reintegrating mental patients into society, or does it remain a promise that is largely unfulfilled? Deinstitutionalization has often been criticized for failing to live up to its expectations. The criticism seems to be well founded. Among the most frequent criticisms is the charge that many hospital patients were merely dumped into the community and not provided with the community-based services they needed to adjust to demands of community living. A 1998 national study found that fewer than half of patients with schizophrenia were receiving adequate care (Winerip, 1999).

Though the community mental health movement has had some successes, a great many patients with severe and persistent mental health problems fail to receive the range of mental health and social services they need to adjust to life in the community (Jacobs, Newman, & Burns, 2001). One of the major challenges facing the community mental system is the problem of psychiatric homelessness.

Deinstitutionalization and the Psychiatric Homeless Population
The federal government estimates that about one third of homeless adults in the United States suffer from severe psychological disorders (NIH, 2003). Many formerly hospitalized mental patients were essentially dumped into local communities after discharge and left with little if any support. Lacking adequate support, they often face more dehumanizing conditions on the street, under deinstitutionalization, than they did in the hospital. Many compound their problems by turning to illegal street drugs such as crack. Also, some of the younger psychiatric homeless population might have been hospitalized in earlier times but are now, in the wake of deinstitutionalization, directed toward community support programs, when they are available.

The lack of available housing and transitional care facilities and effective case management plays an important role in homelessness among people with psychiatric problems. Some homeless people with severe psychiatric problems are repeatedly hospitalized for brief stays in community-based hospitals during acute episodes. They move back and forth between the hospital and the community as though caught in a revolving door. Frequently, they are released from the hospital with inadequate arrangements for housing and community care. Some are left essentially to fend for themselves. While many state hospitals closed their doors and others slashed the number of beds, the states never funded the support services in the community that were supposed to replace the need for long-term hospitalization (Winerip, 1999).

Problems of homelessness are especially severe for children. Not surprisingly, homeless children tend to have more behavior problems than housed children (Schteingart et al., 1995). The problem of psychiatric homelessness is not limited to urban areas, although it is on our city streets that the problem is most visible. The pattern in rural areas tends to be one of inconsistent housing and unstable living arrangements, rather than outright homelessness (Drake et al., 1991).

The mental health system alone does not have the resources to resolve the multifaceted problems faced by the psychiatric homeless population. Helping the psychiatric homeless escape from homelessness requires an integrated effort involving mental health and alcohol and drug abuse programs; access to decent, affordable housing; and provision of other social services (Dixon et al., 1997; Rosenheck, Kasprow et al., 2003). It also requires effective means of evaluating the mental health needs of homeless people and matching services to their specific needs (Jacobs, Newman, & Burns, 2001; Tolomiczenko, Sota, & Goering, 2000).

Another difficulty in meeting the challenge of psychiatric homelessness is that homeless people with severe psychological problems typically do not seek out mental health services. More intensive outreach and intervention efforts that focus on helping home-

The problem of psychiatric homelessness. Many homeless people have severe psychological problems but fall through the cracks of the mental health and social service systems.

less people connect with the services they need are likely to produce the best outcomes (Rosenheck, 2000). All in all, the problems of the psychiatric homeless population remain complex, vexing problems for the mental health system and society at large.

Deinstitutionalization: A Promise as Yet Unfulfilled Although the net results of deinstitutionalization may not have yet lived up to expectations, a number of successful community-oriented programs are available. However, they remain underfunded and unable to reach many people needing ongoing community support. Deinstitutionalization has worked best for those who experience acute episodes of disturbed behavior, who are hospitalized briefly and then returned to their homes, families, and jobs (Shadish et al., 1989). If deinstitutionalization is to succeed, patients need continuing care and opportunities for decent housing, gainful employment, and training in social and vocational skills.

New, promising services exist to improve community-based care for people with chronic psychological disorders—for example, psychosocial rehabilitation centers, family psychoeducational groups, supported housing and work programs, and social skills training. Unfortunately, too few of these services exist to meet the needs of many patients who might benefit from them. The community mental health movement continues to need expanded community support and adequate financial resources if it is to succeed in fulfilling its original promise.

SUMMING UP

Types of Helping Professionals

How do the three major groups of mental health professionals—clinical psychologists, psychiatrists, and psychiatric social workers—differ in their training backgrounds? Clinical psychologists complete graduate training in clinical psychology, typically at the doctoral level. Psychiatrists are medical doctors who specialize in psychiatry. Psychiatric social workers are trained in graduate schools of social work or social welfare, generally at the master's level.

Psychotherapy

What is psychotherapy? Psychotherapy involves a systematic interaction between a therapist and clients that incorporates psychological principles to help clients overcome abnormal behavior, solve problems in living, or develop as individuals.

What is psychodynamic therapy? Psychodynamic therapy originated with psychoanalysis, the approach to treatment developed by Freud. Psychoanalysts use techniques such as free association and dream analysis to help people gain insight into their unconscious conflicts and work through them in the light of their adult personalities. Contemporary psychodynamic therapy is typically briefer and more direct in its approach to exploring the patient's defenses and transference relationships.

What is behavior therapy? Behavior therapy applies the principles of learning to help people make adaptive behavioral changes. Behavior therapy techniques include systematic desensitization, gradual exposure, modeling, operant conditioning approaches, and social skills training. Cognitive-behavioral therapy integrates behavioral and cognitive approaches in treatment.

What is humanistic therapy? Humanistic therapy focuses on the client's subjective, conscious experience in the here and now. Rogers's person-centered therapy helps people increase their awareness and acceptance of inner feelings that had met with social condemnation and been disowned. The effective person-centered therapist possesses the qualities of unconditional positive regard, empathy, genuineness, and congruence.

What are two major approaches to cognitive therapy? Cognitive therapy focuses on modifying the maladaptive cognitions that are believed to underlie emotional problems and self-defeating behavior. Ellis's rational emotive behavior therapy focuses on disputing the irrational beliefs that occasion emotional distress and substituting adaptive beliefs and behavior. Beck's cognitive therapy focuses on helping clients identify, challenge, and replace distorted cognitions, such as tendencies to magnify negative events and minimize personal accomplishments.

What is cognitive-behavioral therapy? Cognitive-behavioral therapy is a broader form of behavior therapy that integrates cognitive and behavioral techniques in treatment.

What are the two major forms of eclectic therapy? These are technical eclecticism, a pragmatic approach that draws on techniques from different schools of therapy without necessarily subscribing to the theoretical positions represented by these schools, and integrative eclecticism, an approach that attempts to synthesize and integrate diverse theoretical approaches in an integrative model of therapy.

What are the general aims of group therapy, family therapy, and couple therapy? Group therapy provides opportunities for mutual support and shared learning experiences within a group setting to help individuals overcome psychological difficulties and develop more adaptive behaviors. Family therapists work with conflicted families to help them resolve their differences. Family therapists focus on clarifying family communications, resolving role conflicts, guarding against scapegoating individual members, and helping members develop greater autonomy. Couple therapists focus on helping couples improve their communications and resolve their differences.

Does psychotherapy work? Evidence from meta-analyses of psychotherapy outcome studies that compare psychotherapy with control groups supports the value of various approaches to psychotherapy. The question of whether there are differences in the effectiveness of different types of psychotherapy remains under study.

Biomedical Therapies

What are the major biomedical approaches to treating psychological disorders and how effective are they? The major biomedical therapies are drug therapy and electroconvulsive therapy (ECT). Antianxiety drugs, such as Valium, may relieve short-term anxiety but do not directly help people solve their problems or cope with stress. Antipsychotics help control flagrant psychotic symptoms, but regular use of these drugs is associated with the risk of serious side effects. Antidepressants can help relieve depression, and lithium is helpful in many cases in stabilizing mood swings in people with bipolar disorder. ECT often leads to dramatic relief from severe depression. Psychosurgery has all but disappeared as a form of treatment because of adverse consequences.

Hospitalization and Community-Based Care

What roles do mental hospitals and community mental health centers play in the mental health system? Mental hospitals provide structured treatment environments for people in acute crisis and for those who are unable to adapt to community living. Community mental health centers seek to prevent the need for psychiatric hospitalization by providing intervention services and alternatives to full hospitalization.

What factors account for underutilization of mental health services by racial or ethnic minorities in the United States? These include cultural factors regarding preferences for other forms of help, cultural mistrust of the mental health system, cultural barriers, linguistic barriers, and economic and accessibility barriers.

How successful is the policy of deinstitutionalization? Deinstitutionalization has greatly reduced the population of state mental hospitals, but it has not yet fulfilled its promise of providing the quality of care needed to restore discharged patients to a reasonable quality of life in the community. One example of the challenges yet to be met are the many homeless people with severe psychological problems who are not receiving adequate care in the community.

KEY TERMS

psychotherapy (p. 102)
nonspecific treatment factors (p. 105)
psychoanalysis (p. 105)
psychodynamic therapy (p. 105)
free association (p. 105)
transference relationship (p. 106)
countertransference (p. 106)
behavior therapy (p. 108)
systematic desensitization (p. 108)
gradual exposure (p. 108)
modeling (p. 109)
token economy (p. 109)
person-centered therapy (p. 109)
unconditional positive regard (p. 110)
empathy (p. 110)
genuineness (p. 110)
congruence (p. 110)
cognitive therapy (p. 111)
rational emotive behavior therapy (REBT) (p. 111)
cognitive-behavioral therapy (CBT) (p. 113)
eclectic therapy (p. 114)
group therapy (p. 115)
family therapy (p. 116)
couple therapy (p. 116)
managed care systems (p. 119)
psychopharmacology (p. 123)
antianxiety drugs (p. 123)
tolerance (p. 123)
rebound anxiety (p. 123)
antipsychotic drugs (p. 123)
antidepressants (p. 124)
electroconvulsive therapy (ECT) (p. 125)
deinstitutionalization (p. 127)
primary prevention (p. 129)
secondary prevention (p. 129)

WEB TOOLS

The companion website offers tools to enrich your learning experience and help you succeed in class. Go to www.prenhall.com/nevid for the gateway to the following resources:

- **VIDEO** links to connect to the video case files on the companion CD-ROM. VIDEO icons in the margins of the chapter highlight the case examples included in the CD-ROM. You can also access the CD-ROM directly if you do not have a Web connection.

- **QUIZ** links to self-scoring quizzes corresponding to each section of the chapter. The quizzes help you review your knowledge of the content in each chapter.

- **WEB** links to direct you to related sites that enhance your learning of abnormal psychology.

Stress, Psychological Factors, and Health

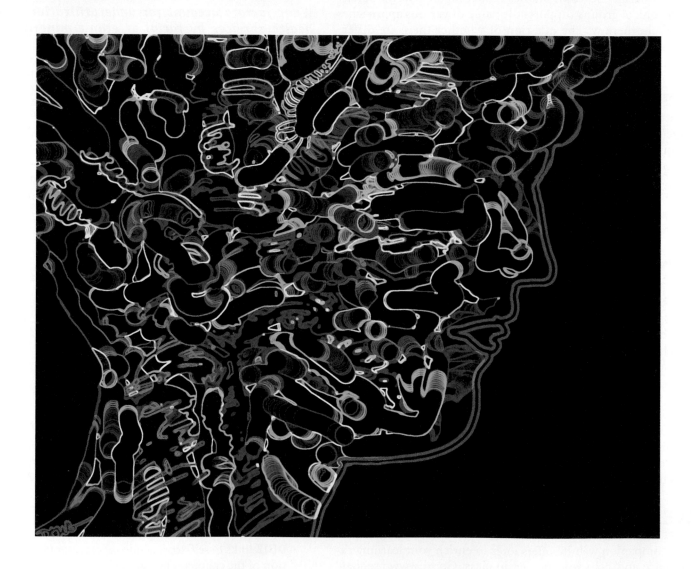

"Is there a problem?" I (J.S.N.) asked as I entered my classroom at St. John's University in Queens, New York, on the morning of September 11, 2001. The students were gathered around the window. None replied, but one pointed out the window with a pained expression on her face that I'll never forget. Moments later, I saw for myself the smoke billowing out of one of the towers of the World Trade Center, clearly visible some 15 miles to the west. Then the second tower suddenly burst into flames. We watched in stunned silence. Then the unthinkable occurred. Suddenly one tower was gone and then the other. A student who had come into the room asked, "Where are they?" Another answered that they were gone. The first replied, "What do you mean, gone?"

We watched from a distance the horror that we knew was unfolding. But many other New Yorkers experienced the World Trade Center disaster firsthand, including thousands like New York City police officer Terri Tobin, who risked their lives to save others. Here, Officer Tobin tells of her experience:

"Go! Go! It's Coming Down!"

Then I saw people running toward me, and they were screaming. "Go! Go! It's coming down!" Just for a second, I looked up and saw it. I thought, I'm not going to outrun this. *But then I thought,* Maybe I can make it back to my car and jump in the back seat. *Before I could make a move, the force of the explosion literally blew me out of my shoes. It lifted me up and propelled me out, over a concrete barrier, all the way to the other side of the street. I landed face-first on a grassy area outside the Financial Center, and after I landed there, I just got pelted with debris coming out of this big black cloud.*

And then I felt it, but what sticks with me is hearing it: The whomp of my helmet when I got hit in the head. The helmet literally went crack, split in half, and fell off my head. I realized then that I'd just taken a real big whack in the head. I felt blood going down the back of my neck, and when I was able to reach around, I felt this chunk of cement sticking out three or four inches from the back of my head. It was completely embedded in my skull.

Then it got pitch black, and I thought, I must have been knocked unconscious, because it's totally black. *But then I thought,* I wouldn't be thinking about how black it is if I'm unconscious. *And it was really hard to breathe. All I heard were people screaming. Screaming bloody murder. All sorts of cries. At that moment, I thought,* This is it. We're all going to die on the street.

—From Hagen & Carouba, 2002, Women at Ground Zero: Stories of Courage and Compassion

Truth or Fiction?

T❏ F❏ If concentrating on your schoolwork has become difficult because of the breakup of a recent romance, you could be experiencing a psychological disorder. (p. 139)

T❏ F❏ Stress actually makes you more resistant to developing the common cold. (p. 141)

T❏ F❏ Writing about traumatic experiences may be good for your health. (p. 142)

T❏ F❏ Immigrants show better psychological adjustment when they forsake their cultural heritage and adopt the values of the host culture. (p. 149)

T❏ F❏ Optimistic people recover more rapidly than pessimistic people from coronary artery bypass surgery. (p. 151)

T❏ F❏ People can relieve the pain of migraine headaches by raising the temperature in a finger. (p. 155)

T❏ F❏ Compelling evidence now exists that psychological treatment increases survival rates in cancer patients. (p. 163)

EXPOSURE TO STRESS, ESPECIALLY TRAUMATIC STRESS LIKE THAT EXPERIENCED BY many thousands of people on 9/11, can have profound and enduring effects on our mental and physical health. This chapter focuses on the psychological and physical effects of stress. In the next chapter, we discuss the types of psychological disorders that can arise from exposure to traumatic stress.

The effects of psychological forms of stress bring into context the age-old debate about the relationship between the mind and the body. The 17th-century French philosopher René Descartes (1596–1650) influenced modern thinking with his belief in *dualism*, or separateness, between the mind and body. Today, scientists and clinicians recognize that mind and body are closely intertwined—that psychological factors both influence and are influenced by physical functioning. In other words, mental health and physical health are inseparable (Kendler, 2001; Lemonick, 2003b). Psychologists who study the interrelationships between psychological factors and physical health are called **health psychologists** (Schneiderman et al., 2001).

We begin focusing on relationships between mind and body by examining the role of stress in both mental and physical functioning. The term *stress* refers to pressure or force placed on a body. In the physical world, tons of rocks that crash to the ground in

health psychologist A psychologist who studies the role of psychological factors in physical illness.

137

stress A demand made on an organism to adapt or adjust.

stressor A source of stress.

a landslide cause stress on impact, forming indentations or craters when they land. In psychology, we use the term **stress** to refer to a pressure or demand that is placed on an organism to adapt or adjust. A **stressor** is a source of stress. Stressors (or stresses) include psychological factors, such as examinations in school and problems in social relationships, and life changes, such as the death of a loved one, divorce, or a job termination. They also include daily hassles, such as traffic jams, and physical environmental factors, such as exposure to extreme temperatures or noise levels. The term *stress* should be distinguished from "distress," which refers to a state of physical or mental pain or suffering. Some degree of stress is probably healthy for us; it helps keep us active and alert. But stress that is prolonged or intense can overtax our coping ability and lead to emotional distress, such as states of anxiety or depression, and physical complaints, such as fatigue and headaches.

Stress is implicated in a wide range of physical and psychological problems. We begin our study of the effects of stress by discussing a category of psychological disorders called *adjustment disorders,* which involve maladaptive reactions to stress. We then consider the role of stress and other psychological and sociocultural factors in physical disorders.

adjustment disorder A maladaptive reaction to an identified stressor, characterized by impaired functioning or emotional distress that exceeds what would normally be expected.

ADJUSTMENT DISORDERS

Adjustment disorders are the first psychological disorders we discuss in this book, and they are among the mildest. An **adjustment disorder** is a maladaptive reaction to an identified stressor that develops within a few months of the onset of the stressor. According to the *DSM,* the maladaptive reaction is characterized by significant impairment in social, occupational, or academic functioning or by states of emotional distress that exceed those normally induced by the stressor. Prevalence estimates of the rates of the disorder in the population vary widely. However, the disorder is common among people seeking outpatient mental health care, with estimates indicating that between 5% and 20% of people receiving outpatient mental health services present with a diagnosis of adjustment disorder (APA, 2000).

Difficulty in concentrating or adjustment disorder? An adjustment disorder is a maladaptive reaction to a stressor that may take the form of impaired functioning at school or at work, such as having difficulties keeping one's mind on one's studies.

TABLE 5.1
Subtypes of Adjustment Disorders

Disorder	Chief Features
Adjustment Disorder with Depressed Mood	Sadness, crying, and feelings of hopelessness.
Adjustment Disorder with Anxiety	Worrying, nervousness, and jitters (or in children, separation fears from primary attachment figures).
Adjustment Disorder with Mixed Anxiety and Depressed Mood	A combination of anxiety and depression.
Adjustment Disorder with Disturbance of Conduct	Violation of the rights of others or violation of social norms appropriate for one's age. Sample behaviors include vandalism, truancy, fighting, reckless driving, and defaulting on legal obligations (e.g., stopping alimony payments).
Adjustment Disorder with Mixed Disturbance	Both emotional disturbance, such as depression or anxiety, and conduct disturbance of Emotions and Conduct (as described above).
Adjustment Disorder Unspecified	A residual category that applies to cases not classifiable in one of the other subtypes.

Source: Adapted from the *DSM-IV-TR* (APA, 2000).

For the diagnosis to apply, the stress-related reaction must not be sufficient to meet the diagnostic criteria for other clinical syndromes, such as anxiety disorders or mood disorders (see Chapters 6 and 8). The maladaptive reaction may be resolved if the stressor is removed or the individual learns to cope with it. If the maladaptive reaction lasts for more than 6 months after the stressor (or its consequences) have been removed, the diagnosis may be changed.

If your relationship with someone comes to an end (an identified stressor) and your grades are falling off because you are unable to keep your mind on schoolwork, you may fit the bill for an adjustment disorder. If Uncle Harry has been feeling down and pessimistic since his divorce from Aunt Jane, he too may be diagnosed with an adjustment disorder. So too might Cousin Billy if he has been cutting classes and spraying obscene words on the school walls or showing other signs of disturbed conduct. There are several subtypes of adjustment disorders that vary in terms of the type of maladaptive reaction (see Table 5.1).

The concept of "adjustment disorder" as a *mental disorder* highlights some of the difficulties in attempting to define what is normal and what is not. When something important goes wrong in life, we should feel bad about it. If there is a crisis in business, if we are victimized by a crime, or if there is a flood or a devastating hurricane, it is understandable that we might become anxious or depressed. There might, in fact, be something more seriously wrong with us if we did not react in a "maladaptive" way, at least temporarily. However, if our emotional reaction exceeds an expected response, or our ability to function is impaired (e.g., avoidance of social interactions, difficulty getting out of bed, or falling behind in schoolwork), then a diagnosis of adjustment disorder may be indicated. Thus, if you are having trouble concentrating on your schoolwork following the breakup of a romantic relationship and your grades are slipping, you may have an adjustment disorder.

STRESS AND ILLNESS

Psychological sources of stress not only diminish our capacity for adjustment, but also may adversely affect our health. Many visits to physicians, perhaps even most, can be traced to stress-related illness. Stress increases the risk of various types of physical illness, ranging from digestive disorders to heart disease (e.g., Cohen et al., 1993).

The field of *psychoneuroimmunology* studies relationships between psychological factors, especially stress, and the workings of the endocrine system, the immune system, and

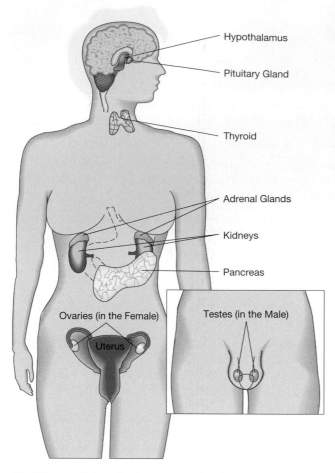

FIGURE 5.1 Major glands of the endocrine system.
The glands of the endocrine pour their secretions—called
hormones—directly into the bloodstream. Although hormones
may travel throughout the body, they act only on specific
receptor sites. Many hormones are implicated in stress reactions
and various patterns of abnormal behavior.

endocrine system The system of ductless
glands that secrete hormones directly into
the bloodstream.

hormones Substances secreted by
endocrine glands that regulate body
functions and promote growth and
development.

steroids A group of hormones that includes
testosterone, estrogen, progesterone, and
corticosteroids.

immune system The body's system of
defense against disease.

the nervous system (Ader, Felten, & Cohen, 2001). Here we examine what
we've learned about these relationships.

Stress and the Endocrine System

Stress has a domino effect on the **endocrine system,** the body's system of
glands that release their secretions, called **hormones,** directly into the
bloodstream. (Other glands, such as the salivary glands that produce saliva,
release their secretions into a system of ducts.) The endocrine system consists of glands distributed throughout the body. Figure 5.1 shows the major
endocrine glands in the body.

Several endocrine glands are involved in the body's response to stress.
First, the hypothalamus, a small structure in the brain, releases a hormone
that stimulates the nearby pituitary gland to secrete *adrenocorticotrophic
hormone* (ACTH). ACTH, in turn, stimulates the adrenal glands, which are
located above the kidneys. Under the influence of ACTH, the outer layer
of the adrenal glands, called the *adrenal cortex,* releases a group of hormones called **steroids** (cortisol and cortisone are examples). These cortical steroids (also called *corticosteroids*) have a number of different functions
in the body. They boost resistance to stress, foster muscle development, and
induce the liver to release sugar, which provides needed bursts of energy
for responding to a threatening stressor (for example, a lurking predator
or assailant) or an emergency situation. They also help the body defend
against allergic reactions and inflammation.

The sympathetic branch of the autonomic nervous system, or ANS,
stimulates the inner layer of the adrenal glands, called the *adrenal medulla,*
to release a mixture of epinephrine (adrenaline) and norepinephrine (noradrenaline). These chemicals function as hormones when released into
the bloodstream. Norepinephrine is also produced in the nervous system, where it functions as a neurotransmitter. Together epinephrine and
norepinephrine mobilize the body to deal with a threatening stressor by
accelerating the heart rate and by also stimulating the liver to release
stored glucose (sugar), making energy available where it can be of use in
protecting ourselves in a threatening situation.

The stress hormones produced by the adrenal glands help the body
prepare to cope with an impending threat or stressor. Once the stressor has
passed, the body returns to a normal state. This is perfectly normal and adaptive. However, when stress is enduring or recurring, the body regularly pumps out stress hormones and mobilizes other systems, which over time can tax the body's resources and
impair health (Kemeny, 2003). Chronic or repetitive stress can damage many bodily systems, including the cardiovascular system (heart and arteries) and the immune system.

Stress and the Immune System

Given the intricacies of the human body and the rapid advance of scientific knowledge,
we might consider ourselves dependent on highly trained medical specialists to contend with illness. Actually our bodies cope with most diseases on their own, through
the functioning of the immune system.

The **immune system** is the body's system of defense against disease. It combats disease in a number of ways. Your body is constantly engaged in search-and-destroy missions against invading microbes, even as you're reading this page. Millions of white blood
cells, or *leukocytes,* are the immune system's foot soldiers in this microscopic warfare.
Leukocytes systematically envelop and kill pathogens like bacteria, viruses, and fungi;
worn-out body cells; and cells that have become cancerous.

Leukocytes recognize invading pathogens by their surface fragments, called *antigens,*
literally *anti*body *gen*erators. Some leukocytes produce *antibodies,* specialized proteins
that attach to these foreign bodies, inactivate them, and mark them for destruction.

Special "memory lymphocytes" (lymphocytes are a type of leukocyte) are held in reserve rather than marking foreign bodies for destruction or going to war against them. They can remain in the bloodstream for years and form the basis for a quick immune response to an invader the second time around.

Though occasional stress may not impair our health, chronic or repetitive stress can weaken the body's immune system over time (Ader et al., 2001; Dougall & Baum, 2001; Epstein, 2003; Kemeny, 2003). A weakened immune system increases our susceptibility to common illnesses, such as colds and the flu, and possibly increases risk of developing chronic diseases, including cancer.

Exposure to physical sources of stress such as cold or loud noise, especially when intense or prolonged, can dampen immunological functioning. So too can various psychological stressors, ranging from sleep deprivation to final examinations (Maier, Watkins, & Fleshner, 1994). Medical students, for example, show poorer immune functioning during exam time than they do a month before exams, when their lives are less stressful (Glaser et al., 1987). Traumatic stress, such as exposure to earthquakes, hurricanes, or other natural or technological disasters, or to terrorist attacks or other forms of violence, can also dampen immunological functioning (Ironson et al., 1997; Solomon et al., 1997).

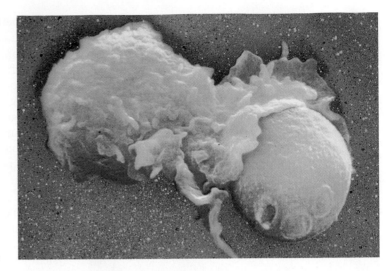

The War Within. White blood cells, shown here (colored purple) attacking and engulfing a pathogen, form the major part of the body's system of defense against bacteria, viruses, and other invading organisms.

Scientists recently discovered that one way chronic stress damages the body's immune system is by increasing levels of a chemical in the body called *interleukin-6* (Kiecolt-Glaser et al., 2003; "Scientists Learn," 2003). Sustained high levels of this chemical are linked to inflammation, which in turn can contribute to the development of many disorders, including cardiovascular disease, cancer, and arthritis.

Life stressors such as marital conflict, divorce, and chronic unemployment can also take a toll on the immune system (Kiecolt-Glaser et al., 2002; O'Leary, 1990). Chronic stress also makes it take longer for wounds to heal (Kiecolt-Glaser et al., 1995). Negative emotional states such as anxiety and depression are sources of emotional stress that also contribute to longer wound healing (Kiecolt-Glaser et al., 2002).

Social support appears to moderate the harmful effects of stress on the immune system. For example, investigators find that medical and dental students with large numbers of friends show better immune functioning than students with fewer friends (Jemmott et al., 1983; Kiecolt-Glaser et al., 1984). Consider too that lonely students show a greater suppression of the immune response than do students with greater social support (Glaser et al., 1985). Newly separated and divorced people also show evidence of a suppressed immune response, especially those who remain attached to their ex-partners (Kiecolt-Glaser et al., 1987, 1988).

Exposure to stress is linked to an increased risk of developing a common cold. In one study, people who reported high levels of daily stress, such as pressures at work, showed low levels in their bloodstreams of antibodies that fend off cold viruses (Stone et al., 1994). In another study, exposure to severe chronic stress lasting a month or longer (for example, unemployment or problems with family members or friends) was associated with a greater risk of developing a common cold after exposure to cold viruses (Cohen et al., 1998). Yet social support is linked to greater resistance to the common cold. Researchers found that people who have more varied social relationships—with spouses, children, other relatives, friends, colleagues, members of organizations and religious groups, and so on—were less likely than others with limited social networks to come down with a cold after exposure to cold viruses (Cohen & Mannarino, 1997; Gilbert, 1997b). And when they did get sick, they tended to develop milder symptoms.

We should caution that much of the research in the field of psychoneuroimmunology is correlational. Researchers examine immunological functioning in relation to different indices of stress, but do not (nor would they!) directly manipulate stress to observe its effect on subjects' immune systems or general health. Correlational research

TRUTH or FICTION? *REVISITED*

Stress actually makes you more resistant to developing the common cold.

☑ **FALSE.** Stress increases the risk of developing a cold.

Stress and the common cold. Are you more likely to develop a cold during stressful times in your life? Investigators find that people under severe stress are more likely to become sick after exposure to cold viruses.

helps us better understand relationships between variables and may point to possible underlying causal factors, but does not in itself demonstrate causal connections.

In addition to social support, expressing emotions through writing about stressful or traumatic events may enhance both psychological and physical well-being and perhaps even boost immune system responses (Esterling et al., 1999; Largo-Marsh & Spates, 2002; Sloan & Marx, 2004; Smyth & Pennebaker, 2001). This form of expressive writing even reduces symptoms in asthma and arthritis patients (Smyth et al., 1999; Stone et al., 2000). In addition, terminally ill cancer patients asked to write about their cancer had less sleep disturbance than control patients who wrote about neutral topics (de Moor et al., 2003).

Why might expressive writing be effective therapy? Perhaps keeping thoughts and feelings about traumatic events tightly under wraps places a stressful burden on the autonomic nervous system, which in turn may weaken the immune system and thereby increase susceptibility to stress-related disorders (Petrie, Booth, & Pennebaker, 1998). We should caution, however, that more research is needed before we can reach any definite conclusions about the effects of writing or other psychological interventions on the workings of the immune system (Miller & Cohen, 2001).

Terrorism-Related Trauma

The terrorist attacks on America of September 11, 2001, changed everything. Before 9/11 we may have felt secure in our homes, offices, and other public places from the threat of terrorism. But now, terrorism looms as an ever-present threat to our safety and sense of security. Still, we endeavor to maintain a sense of normalcy in our lives. We travel and attend public gatherings, though the ever-present security regulations are a constant reminder of the heightened concern about terrorism. Many of us who were directly affected by 9/11 or lost friends or loved ones may still be trying to cope with the emotional consequences of that awful day. Many survivors, like survivors of other forms of trauma such as floods and tornadoes, may experience prolonged, maladaptive stressful reactions, such as posttraumatic stress disorder (discussed in Chapter 6). But even if we are free of diagnosable psychological disorders, the events of 9/11 may affect us emotionally in one way or another (Galea et al., 2002).

Most Americans reported feeling depressed in the immediate aftermath of 9/11, and a substantial proportion reported difficulty concentrating or suffered from insomnia (see Table 5.2). Not surprisingly, factors such as direct exposure to the attacks in New York City and Washington, D.C., and time spent viewing TV coverage of the attacks were linked to higher levels of posttraumatic stress disorder (PTSD) symptoms (Schlenger et al., 2002). Though most people exposed to traumatic events do not develop PTSD, many do experience symptoms associated with the disorder, such as difficulties

TABLE 5.2

Stress-Related Symptoms Reported by Americans in the Week Following the Terrorists Attacks of September 11, 2001

	Depression	Lack of Focus (difficulty concentrating)	Insomnia
Men	62	44	26
Women	79	53	40
Genders combined	71	49	33

Source: Pew Research Center. (2002, September 20). *American psyche reeling from terror attacks.* www.people-press.org/terroist01rpt.htm

concentrating and high levels of arousal. In more than 60% of households in New York City, parents reported that their children were upset by the attacks. Since 9/11, many of us have become sensitized to the emotional consequences of traumatic stress. The accompanying *A Closer Look* feature focuses on the warning signs of trauma-related stress. The *Controversies in Abnormal Psychology* feature examines the debate over providing "psychological first-aid" to trauma survivors.

People vary in their reactions to traumatic stress. Investigators trying to pinpoint factors that account for resiliency in the face of stress suggest that positive emotions can play an important role. Evidence gathered since 9/11 shows that experiencing positive emotions such as gratitude and love, helped buffer the effects of stress (Frederickson et al., 2003).

The General Adaptation Syndrome

Stress researcher Hans Selye (1976) coined the term **general adaptation syndrome (GAS)** to describe a common biological response pattern to prolonged or excessive stress. Selye pointed out that our bodies respond similarly to many kinds of unpleasant stressors, whether the source of stress is an invasion of microscopic disease organisms, a divorce, or the aftermath of a flood. The GAS model suggests that our bodies, under stress, are like clocks with alarm systems that do not shut off until their energy is perilously depleted.

The GAS consists of three stages: the alarm reaction, the resistance stage, and the exhaustion stage. Perception of an immediate stressor (for example, a car that swerves in front of your own on the highway) triggers the **alarm reaction.** The alarm reaction mobilizes the body for defense. It is initiated by the brain and regulated by the endocrine system and the sympathetic branch of the autonomic nervous system (ANS). In 1929, Harvard University physiologist Walter Cannon termed this response pattern the **fight-or-flight reaction.** We noted earlier how the endocrine system responds to stress. During the alarm reaction, the adrenal glands, under control by the pituitary gland in the brain, pump out cortical steroids and stress hormones that help mobilize the body's defenses (see Table 5.3).

The fight-or-flight reaction most probably helped our early ancestors cope with the many perils they faced. The reaction may have been provoked by the sight of a predator or by a rustling sound in the undergrowth. But our ancestors usually did not experience prolonged activation of the alarm reaction. Once a threat was eliminated, the body reinstated a lower level of arousal. Our ancestors fought off predators or fled

general adaptation syndrome (GAS) The body's three-stage response to states of prolonged or intense stress.

alarm reaction The first stage of the GAS, characterized by heightened sympathetic activity.

fight-or-flight reaction The inborn tendency to respond to a threat by either fighting or fleeing.

TABLE 5.3

Stress-Related Changes in the Body Associated with the Alarm Reaction

Corticosteroids are released.

Epinephrine and norepinephrine are released.

Heart rate, respiration rate, and blood pressure increase.

Muscles tense.

Blood shifts from the internal organs to the skeletal muscles.

Digestion is inhibited.

Sugar is released by the liver.

Blood-clotting ability is increased.

Stress triggers the alarm reaction. The reaction is defined by secretion of corticosteroids, catecholamines, and activity of the sympathetic branch of the ANS. The reaction is defined by secretion of stress hormones and increased activity of the sympathetic branch of the ANS.

A CLOSER LOOK
Warning Signs of Trauma-Related Stress

People normally experience psychological distress in the face of trauma. If anything it would be abnormal to remain blasé at a time of crisis or disaster. But stress reactions that linger beyond a month and affect an individual's ability to function in everyday life can be a cause for concern. The American Psychological Association lists the following symptoms as warning signs of traumatic stress reactions.

- Recurring thoughts or nightmares about the event
- Having trouble sleeping or changes in appetite
- Experiencing anxiety and fear, especially when exposed to events or situations reminiscent of the trauma
- Being on edge, being easily startled, or becoming overly alert
- Feeling depressed, sad, and having low energy
- Experiencing memory problems including difficulty in remembering aspects of the trauma
- Feeling "scattered" and unable to focus on work or daily activities
- Having difficulty making decisions
- Feeling irritable, easily agitated, or angry and resentful

- Feeling emotionally "numb," withdrawn, disconnected or different from others
- Spontaneously crying, feeling a sense of despair and hopelessness
- Feeling extremely protective of, or fearful for, the safety of loved ones
- Not being able to face certain aspects of the trauma, and avoiding activities, places, or even people that remind you of the event

If you or a loved one has experienced these symptoms for more than a month, it would be worthwhile to seek professional mental health assistance. Assistance is available through your college health services (for registered students) or through networks of trained professionals. For more information or a referral, you may contact your local American Red Cross chapter or the American Psychological Association at 202/336-5800. See also the *Closer Look* in Chapter 4 for guidelines to follow in choosing a mental health professional.

Reprinted from Nevid & Rathus, 2005, with permission of Wiley & Sons, Inc. Source: American Psychological Association. Warning Signs of Trauma Related Stress. Web Posting, http://www.apa.org/practice/ptsd.html. Copyright 2002 by American Psychological Association. Reprinted by permission. ■

---

quickly; then their bodies returned to the normal, nonaroused state. Sensitive alarm reactions increased their chances of survival. Yet our ancestors did not remain for long in a state of heightened arousal after the immediate danger was past. In contrast, people today are continually bombarded with stressors—everything from battling traffic in the morning to balancing school and work, or rushing from job to job. Consequently, our alarm system is turned on much of the time, which may eventually increase the likelihood of developing stress-related disorders.

When a stressor is persistent, we progress to the **resistance stage,** or adaptation stage, of the GAS. Endocrine and sympathetic system responses (release of stress hormones, for example) remain at high levels, but not quite as high as during the alarm reaction. During this stage the body tries to renew spent energy and repair damage. But when stressors continue or new ones enter the picture, we may advance to the final or **exhaustion stage** of the GAS. Although there are individual differences in capacity to resist stress, all of us will eventually exhaust our bodily resources. The exhaustion stage is characterized by dominance of the parasympathetic branch of the ANS. Consequently, our heart and respiration rates decelerate. Do we benefit from the respite? Not necessarily. If the source of stress persists, we may develop what Selye termed "diseases of adaptation." These range from allergic reactions to heart disease—and, at times, even death. The lesson is clear: Chronic stress can damage our health, leaving us more vulnerable to a range of diseases and other physical health problems.

Cortical steroids are perhaps one reason that persistent stress may eventually lead to health problems. Although cortical steroids help the body cope with stress, they also suppress the activity of the immune system. Cortical steroids have negligible effects when they are only released periodically. Continuous secretion, however, weakens the immune system by disrupting the production of antibodies. As a result, we may become more vulnerable to various diseases, even the common cold (Cohen, Tyrrell, & Smith, 1991).

Although Selye's model speaks to the general response pattern of the body under stress, different biological processes may respond to particular kinds of stressors. For example, persistent exposure to excessive noise may invoke different bodily processes than other sources of stress, such as overcrowding, or psychological sources of stress, such as divorce or separation.

Stress and Life Changes

Researchers have investigated the stress–illness connection by quantifying life stress in terms of *life changes* (also called *life events*). Life changes are sources of stress because they force us to adjust. They include both positive events, such as getting married, and neg-

resistance stage The second stage of the GAS, involving the body's attempt to withstand prolonged stress and preserve resources.

exhaustion stage The third stage of the GAS, characterized by lowered resistance, increased parasympathetic activity, and eventual physical deterioration.

CONTROVERSIES IN ABNORMAL PSYCHOLOGY
Psychological First-Aid Following Trauma: Does It Help?

Following the terrorist attacks of September 11, 2001, thousands of counselors traveled to New York City to provide psychological assistance to rescue workers, people directly exposed to the violence, and family members of people who perished in the attack. More than 9,000 counselors offered immediate psychological assistance to anyone who was even remotely connected with the tragedy (Gist & Devilly, 2002). Most forms of psychological first-aid, or *early intervention,* encourage trauma survivors to discuss the trauma and reexperience their emotional reactions with a counselor or therapist (Litz et al., 2002; van Emmerik et al., 2002).

No one questions the good intentions of the helping professionals who sought to assist people coping with this horrific disaster. Nor does anyone deny that people who receive psychological first-aid following exposure to trauma believe it is helpful. No one is claiming that help should not be offered to trauma survivors. But controversy has arisen about whether such assistance is effective and whether it should be provided to all trauma survivors. The controversy has been framed around the question of whether immediate psychological assistance actually prevents the development of posttraumatic stress disorder in trauma survivors. On this point, investigators fail to find any convincing evidence that early intervention reduces the risk of PTSD (McNally, Bryant, & Ehlers, 2003; van Emmerik et al., 2002). In fact, some investigators argue that many people may be better off by not receiving any immediate emotional assistance and allowing the process of recovery to unfold naturally (Gist & Devilly, 2002; McNally, Bryant, & Ehlers, 2003).

Many people are naturally resilient in the face of traumatic stress or are able to bounce back without professional assistance. Many survivors seek support from other sources, such as family, friends, and religious groups. Perhaps these factors explain why, despite evidence of high levels of early PTSD symptoms shortly after the attacks, the number of cases of PTSD following 9/11 was far lower than anticipated (Galea et al., 2002; Gist & Devilly, 2002; North & Pfefferbaum, 2002; Simeon et al., 2003). Early intervention may be most helpful when no alternative forms of support are available. Early intervention may also be helpful for people who develop signs of PTSD and are unlikely to recover in the absence of treatment. Presently, however, we lack the ability to identify people who fall in this category (Ehlers et al., 2003).

Let's frame the controversy in a more personal way. If you or a loved one suffered a traumatic experience, would you want psychological assistance? What sort of help do you think would be most desirable—crisis intervention services, individual therapy, group therapy, antianxiety medication? To whom

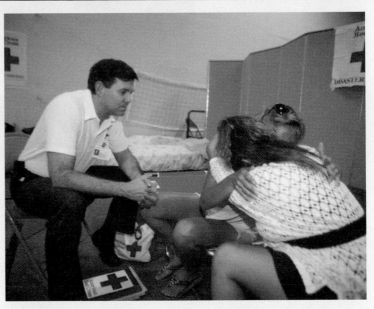

Psychological first aid. Controversy exists over whether it is a good idea to provide emergency psychological help to all trauma survivors. Does evidence support the view that psychological first-aid prevents PTSD in trauma survivors?

would you turn for help if you suffered a traumatic experience? To family and friends? Your church or religious group? To a helping professional?

Critical Thinking

- Should we assume that everyone experiencing trauma is better off if they receive immediate psychological assistance? Why or why not?
- What factors might determine whether trauma survivors would fare better if they received immediate psychological assistance?   ■

ative events, such as the death of a loved one. You can gain insight into the level of stressful life changes you may have experienced during the past year by completing the College Life Stress Inventory on page 147.

Exposure to life stressors, including life changes and daily hassles, is linked to increased risk of physical health problems and even increased risk of suffering sports injuries (Kanner et al., 1981; Smith, Smoll, & Ptacek, 1990; Stewart et al., 1994). Again, we need to be cautious in interpreting these findings. The reported links are correlational and not experimental. In other words, researchers did not (and would not!) assign subjects to conditions in which they were exposed to either a high or low level of life changes to see what effects these conditions might have on their health over time. Rather, existing data are based on observations of relationships, say, between life changes on the one hand and physical health problems on the other. Such relationships are open to other interpretations. It could be that physical symptoms are sources of stress in themselves and lead to more life changes. Physical illness may cause disruptions of sleep or financial burdens, and so forth. Hence, in some cases at least, the causal direction may be reversed: Health problems may lead to life changes. Existing research does not allow us to tease out the possible cause-and-effect relationships (Suls, Wan, & Blanchard, 1994).

Although both positive and negative life changes can be stressful, positive life changes seem to be less disruptive than negative life changes (Thoits, 1983). In other words, marriage tends to be less stressful than divorce or separation. Or to put it another way, a

For better or for worse. Life changes such as marriage and the death of loved ones are sources of stress that require adjustment. The death of a spouse may be one of the most stressful life changes that people ever face.

change for the better may be a change, but it is less of a hassle. Let us also note that "eventlessness" (i.e., the absence of life changes) can also be stressful and may be as strongly linked to the risk of physical health problems as negative life events (Theorell, 1992).

Acculturative Stress: Making It in America

Should Hindu women who immigrate to the United States give up the sari in favor of California casuals? Should Soviet immigrants continue to teach their children Russian in the home? Should African American children be acquainted with the music and art of African peoples? Should women from traditional Islamic societies remove the veil and enter the competitive workplace? How do the stresses of acculturation affect the psychological well-being of immigrants and their families?

Sociocultural theorists have alerted us to the importance of accounting for social stressors in explaining abnormal behavior. One of the primary sources of stress imposed on immigrant groups, or on native groups living in the larger mainstream culture, is the need to adapt to a new culture. *Acculturation* is the process of adaptation by which immigrants and native groups adjust to the new culture or majority culture through making behavioral and attitudinal changes (Rogler, Cortes, & Malgady, 1991). **Acculturative stress** is pressure that results from the demands placed on immigrant and ethnic minority groups to adjust to life in the mainstream culture.

Consider the challenges faced by Hispanic Americans. There are two general theories of the relationships between acculturation and adjustment (Griffith, 1983). One theory, dubbed the *melting pot theory,* holds that acculturation helps people adjust to living in the host culture. From this perspective, Hispanic Americans might adjust better by replacing Spanish with English and adopting the values and customs associated with mainstream American culture. A competing theory, the *bicultural theory,* holds that psychosocial adjustment is fostered by identification with both traditional and host cultures. That is, the ability to adapt to the ways of the new society, combined with a supportive cultural tradition and a sense of ethnic identity, may predict good adjustment. From a bicultural perspective, immigrants maintain their ethnic identity and traditional values while learning to adapt to the language and customs of the host culture.

We first must be able to measure acculturation if we are to investigate its relationship to mental health among immigrant and native groups. Measures of acculturation vary. In assessing acculturation among Hispanic Americans, for example, researchers assess variables such as the degree to which people favor English or Spanish in social situations,

acculturative stress Pressure to adjust to a host or mainstream culture.

QUESTIONNAIRE
Going Through Changes

How stressful has your life been lately? The College Life Stress Inventory contains a listing of stressful events that college students may face. Circle each of the events that you have experienced in the past year. Then compute your total, and look at the guide at the end of the chapter to interpret your score.

Event	Stress Rating
Being raped	100
Finding out that you are HIV-positive	100
Depression or crisis in your best friend	73
Difficulties with parents	73
Talking in front of a class	72
Lack of sleep	69
Change in housing situation (hassles, moves)	69
Competing or performing in public	69
Getting in a physical fight	66
Difficulties with a roommate	66
Job changes (applying, new job, work hassles)	65
Being accused of rape	98
Death of a close friend	97
Death of a close family member	96
Contracting a sexually transmitted disease (other than AIDS)	94
Concerns about being pregnant	91
Finals week	90
Concerns about your partner being pregnant	90
Oversleeping for an exam	89
Flunking a class	89
Having a boyfriend or girlfriend cheat on you	85
Ending a steady dating relationship	85
Serious illness in a close friend or family member	85
Financial difficulties	84
Writing a major term paper	83

Event	Stress Rating
Being caught cheating on a test	83
Drunk driving	82
Sense of overload in school or work	82
Two exams in one day	80
Cheating on your boyfriend or girlfriend	77
Getting married	76
Negative consequences of drinking or drug use	75
Declaring a major or concerns about future plans	65
A class you hate	62
Drinking or use of drugs	61
Confrontations with professors	60
Starting a new semester	58
Going on a first date	57
Registration	55
Maintaining a steady dating relationship	55
Commuting to campus or work, or both	54
Peer pressures	53
Being away from home for the first time	53
Getting sick	52
Concerns about your appearance	52
Getting straight As	51
A difficult class that you love	48
Making new friends; getting along with friends	47
Fraternity or sorority rush	47
Falling asleep in class	40
Attending an athletic event (e.g., football game)	20

Source. Renner, M. J., & Mackin, R. S. (1998). A life stress instrument for classroom use. Teaching of Psychology, 25, 46–48. Reprinted with permission.

when reading, or while watching media such as TV; preferences for types of food and styles of clothing; and self-perceptions of ethnic identity.

Researchers find that relationships between acculturation and psychological adjustment are quite complex. Findings from research with Latino (Hispanic) Americans highlight some psychological risks associated with acculturation.

- *Increased risk of heavy drinking among women.* Evidence shows that highly acculturated Hispanic American women are more likely than relatively unacculturated Hispanic women to develop heavy drinking (Caetano, 1987). In Latin American cultures, men tend to drink much more alcohol than women, largely because gender-based cultural prohibitions against drinking constrain alcohol use among women. These constraints appear to have loosened among Hispanic American women who adopt "mainstream" U.S. attitudes and values.

- *Increased risk of delinquency and smoking among adolescents.* Third-generation Mexican American male adolescents—who are more likely to be acculturated than first- or second-generation Mexican Americans—were at higher risk of delinquency (Buriel, Calzada, & Vasquez, 1982). Acculturation was also associated with an increased risk of smoking among Hispanic adolescents (Ribisl et al., 2000; Unger, Cruz, & Rohrbach, 2000).

- *Increased risk of disturbed eating behaviors.* Highly acculturated Hispanic American high school girls were more likely than their less-acculturated counterparts to show test scores associated with anorexia (an eating disorder characterized by excessive weight loss and fears of becoming fat—see Chapter 10) on an eating attitudes questionnaire (Pumariega, 1986). Acculturation apparently made these girls

Adapting to a new culture. The relationship between acculturation and mental health is complex and depends on such factors as financial status, economic opportunities, linguistic differences, and availability of strong family ties.

more vulnerable to the demands of striving toward the contemporary American ideal of the (very!) slender woman.

From this evidence, we might gather that acculturation has a negative influence on psychological adjustment. Yet other evidence points to some benefits of bicultural identification, in which the individual makes efforts to adjust to the host culture while also maintaining an identity with the traditional culture. Consider a study of Mexican American elders (Zamanian et al., 1992). Those who were minimally acculturated showed higher levels of depression than did those who were either acculturated or bicultural. The bicultural and highly acculturated groups were similar in levels of depression, whereas those who were minimally acculturated had a greater risk of depression. However, people who held a bicultural identity, in which they maintained an identification with their original culture while adapting to the new culture, experienced no greater vulnerability to depression.

Why might low acculturation status be linked to increased risk of depression? Low acculturation status is often a marker for low socioeconomic status (SES). People who are minimally acculturated often face economic hardship. Social stress resulting from financial difficulties, linguistic differences, and limited economic opportunities adds to the stress of adapting to the host culture, which can increase the risk of depression and other psychological problems (e.g., Ryder, Alden, & Paulhus, 2000; Yeh, 2003). Not surprisingly, evidence shows that Mexican Americans who are more proficient in English show fewer signs of depression and anxiety than those who are less proficient (Salgado de Snyder, 1987; Warheit et al., 1985). Yet SES isn't the only, or necessarily the most important, determinant of mental health in members of immigrant groups. In a northern California sample, researchers found better mental health profiles among Mexican immigrants than among people of Mexican descent born in the United States, despite the socioeconomic disadvantages faced by the immigrant group (Vega et al., 1998). Acculturation and "Americanization" may

Maintaining ethnic identity. Some studies point to psychological benefits in immigrant groups that adapt to the host culture while maintaining ethnic identity.

have damaging effects on the mental health of Mexican Americans, and the retention of cultural traditions may have a protective or "buffer" effect (Escobar, 1998).

In sum, the erosion of traditional family networks and traditional values in Hispanic immigrants that may accompany acculturation might increase the risk of some kinds of psychological problems in more acculturated groups (Ortega et al., 2000). Studies with other ethnic groups also point to the benefits of adapting to the host culture while maintaining ties to the traditional culture. Among Asian Americans, establishing contacts with the majority culture while maintaining one's ethnic identity appears to generate less stress than withdrawal and separation from the host culture (Huang, 1994; Phinney, Lochner, & Murphy, 1990). Maintaining one's ethnic identity also seems to hold a psychological benefit. Studies with Asian American adolescents show that those who have achieved an ethnic identity are better adjusted psychologically and have higher self-esteem (Huang, 1994; Phinney, 1989; Phinney & Alipuria, 1990). But a recent study of Asian immigrant adolescents in the United States showed that feelings of being alienated from both cultures or caught between the two—the United States and the traditional culture—can lead to mental health problems (Yeh, 2003).

Moreover, some outcomes need careful interpretation. For example, does the finding that highly acculturated Hispanic American women are more likely to drink heavily argue in favor of placing greater social constraints on women? Perhaps a loosening of restraints is a double-edged sword, and all people—male and female, Hispanic and non-Hispanic—encounter adjustment problems when they gain new freedoms.

Finally, we need to consider gender differences in acculturation. In one study, female immigrants showed higher levels of depression than male immigrants (Salgado de Snyder, Cervantes, & Padilla, 1990). Their depression may be linked to the greater level of stress women encountered in adjusting to changes in family and personal issues, such as the greater freedom of gender roles for men and women in U.S. society. Because they were reared in cultures in which men are expected to be breadwinners and women homemakers, immigrant women may encounter more family and internal conflict when they enter the workforce, regardless of whether they work because of economic necessity or personal choice. Given these factors, we shouldn't be surprised by findings that wives in more acculturated Mexican American couples report greater marital distress than those in less-acculturated couples (Negy & Snyder, 1997).

Psychological Factors That Moderate Stress

Stress may be a fact of life, but the ways in which we handle stress help determine our ability to cope with it. Individuals react differently to stress depending on psychological factors such as the meaning they ascribe to stressful events. For example, whether a major life event, such as pregnancy, is a positive or negative stressor depends on a couple's desire for a child and their readiness to care for one. We can say the stress of pregnancy is moderated by the perceived value of children in a couple's eyes and their self-efficacy—their confidence in their ability to raise a child. As we see next, psychological factors such as coping styles, self-efficacy expectancies, psychological hardiness, optimism, social support, and ethnic identity may moderate or buffer the effects of stress.

Styles of Coping   What do you do when faced with a serious problem? Do you pretend it does not exist? Like Scarlett O'Hara in the classic film *Gone With the Wind,* do you say to yourself, "I'll think about it tomorrow," and then banish it from your mind? Or do you take charge and confront it squarely?

Pretending that problems do not exist is a form of denial. Denial is an example of **emotion-focused coping** (Lazarus & Folkman, 1984). In emotion-focused coping, people take measures that immediately reduce the impact of the stressor, such as denying its existence or withdrawing from the situation. Emotion-focused coping, however, does not eliminate the stressor (a serious illness, for example) or help the individual develop better ways of managing it. In **problem-focused coping,** by contrast, people examine the stressors they face and do what they can to change them or modify their own reactions

emotion-focused coping A coping style that attempts to minimize emotional responsiveness rather than deal with the stressor directly.

problem-focused coping A coping style that attempts to confront the stressor directly.

to render stressors less harmful. These basic styles of coping—emotion-focused and problem-focused—have been applied to ways in which people respond to illness.

Denial of illness can take various forms, including the following.

1. Failing to recognize the seriousness of the illness
2. Minimizing the emotional distress the illness causes
3. Misattributing symptoms to other causes (for example, assuming the appearance of blood in the stool represents nothing more than a local abrasion)
4. Ignoring threatening information about the illness

Denial can be dangerous to your health, especially if it leads to avoidance of, or noncompliance with, needed medical treatment. Avoidance is another form of emotion-based coping. In one study, people who had an avoidant style of coping with cancer (for example, by trying not to think or talk about it) showed greater disease progression when evaluated a year later than did people who more directly confronted the illness (Epping-Jordan, Compas, & Howell, 1994). Like denial, avoidance may deter people from complying with medical treatments, which can lead to a worsening of their medical conditions. Avoidance may also contribute to heightened emotional distress and arousal, which may impair immunological functioning.

Another form of emotion-focused coping, the use of wish-fulfillment fantasies, is also linked to poor adjustment in coping with serious illness. Examples of wish-fulfillment fantasies include ruminating about what might have been had the illness not occurred and longing for better times. Wish-fulfillment fantasy offers the patient no means of coping with life's difficulties other than an imaginary escape.

Does this mean that people are invariably better off when they know all the facts concerning their illnesses? Not necessarily. Whether you will be better off knowing all the facts may depend on your preferred style of coping. A mismatch between the individual's style of coping and the amount of information provided may hamper recovery. In one study, cardiac patients with a repressive style of coping (relying on denial) who received information about their conditions showed a higher incidence of medical complications than repressors who were largely kept in the dark (Shaw et al., 1985). Sometimes ignorance helps people manage stress—at least temporarily.

Problem-focused coping involves strategies that address the source of stress, like seeking information about the illness through self-study and medical consultation. Information seeking may help the individual maintain a more optimistic frame of mind by creating an expectancy that the information will prove to be useful.

Self-Efficacy Expectancies **Self-efficacy expectancies** refer to our expectations regarding our abilities to cope with the challenges we face, to perform certain behaviors skillfully, and to produce positive changes in our lives (Bandura, 1982, 1986). We may be better able to manage stress, including the stress of coping with illness, if we feel confident (have higher self-efficacy expectancies) in our ability to cope effectively. A forthcoming exam may be more or less stressful depending on your confidence in your ability to achieve a good grade. In a classic study, Albert Bandura and colleagues found that spider-phobic women showed high levels of the stress hormones epinephrine and norepinephrine when they interacted with the phobic object, such as by allowing a spider to crawl on their laps (Bandura et al., 1985). As their confidence or self-efficacy expectancies for coping with these tasks increased, the levels of these stress hormones declined. Epinephrine and norepinephrine arouse the body by way of the sympathetic branch of the ANS. They make us feel shaky, have "butterflies in the stomach," and generally feel nervous. Because high self-efficacy expectancies appear to be associated with lower secretion of these stress hormones, people who believe they can cope with their problems may be less likely to feel nervous.

Psychological Hardiness **Psychological hardiness** refers to a cluster of traits that may help people manage stress. Suzanne Kobasa (1979) and her colleagues investigated business executives who resisted illness despite heavy burdens of stress. Three key

self-efficacy expectations Beliefs in one's ability to accomplish particular tasks.

psychological hardiness A cluster of stress-buffering traits characterized by commitment, challenge, and control.

traits distinguished the psychologically hardy executives (Kobasa, Maddi, & Kahn, 1982, pp. 169–170):

1. *Commitment.* Rather than feeling alienated from their tasks and situations, hardy executives involved themselves fully. That is, they believed in what they were doing.

2. *Challenge.* Hardy executives believed change was the normal state of things, not sterile sameness or stability for the sake of stability.

3. *Control over their lives* (Maddi & Kobasa, 1984). Hardy executives believed and acted as though they were effectual rather than powerless in controlling the rewards and punishments of life. In terms suggested by social-cognitive theorist Julian Rotter (1966), psychologically hardy individuals have an *internal locus of control.*

Coping with stress. Psychologically hardy people appear to cope more effectively with stress by adopting active, problem-solving approaches and by perceiving themselves as choosing high-stress situations.

Psychologically hardy people appear to cope more effectively with stress by using more active, problem-solving approaches (Williams, Wiebe, & Smith, 1992). They are also likely to report fewer physical symptoms and less depression in the face of stress than nonhardy people (Ouellette & DiPlacido, 2001; Pengilly & Dowd, 2000). Kobasa suggests that hardy people are better able to handle stress because they perceive themselves as *choosing* their stress-creating situations. They perceive the stressors they face as making life more interesting and challenging, not as simply burdening them with additional pressures. A sense of control is a key factor in psychological hardiness.

Optimism Research suggests that seeing the glass as half full is healthier than seeing it as half empty (Scheier & Carver, 1992). In one study on the relationships between optimism and health, Scheier and Carver (1985) administered a measure of optimism, the Life Orientation Test (LOT), to college students. The students also tracked their physical symptoms for 1 month. It turned out that those students who received higher optimism scores reported fewer symptoms such as fatigue, dizziness, muscle soreness, and blurry vision. (Subjects' symptoms at the beginning of the study were statistically taken into account, so it could not be argued that the study simply shows that healthier people are more optimistic.)

Other research also reveals links between optimism and better health outcomes. For example, pain patients who expressed more pessimistic thoughts during flare-ups of pain reported more severe pain and distress (Gil et al., 1990). The pessimistic thoughts included, "I can no longer do anything," "No one cares about my pain," and "It isn't fair I have to live this way." Optimism is associated with less emotional distress among breast cancer patients (Trunzo & Pinto, 2003). Among pregnant women, optimism is linked to a lower likelihood of postpartum depression (depression following childbirth) and higher infant birth weights (Carver & Gaines, 1987; Lobel et al., 2000). Heart disease patients with more optimistic attitudes showed less depression when evaluated a year later (Shnek et al., 2001). In a separate study, patients undergoing coronary artery bypass procedure who had more optimistic attitudes about the procedure showed better outcomes (fewer complications requiring additional hospitalization or surgery) than did more pessimistic patients (Scheier et al., 1999).

Research to date shows only correlational links between optimism and health. Perhaps we shall soon learn whether learning to alter attitudes—to learn to see the glass as half filled—plays a causal role in maintaining or restoring health. You can evaluate your own level of optimism by completing the Life Orientation Test in this section.

Social Support The role of social support as a buffer against stress is well documented (e.g., Wills & Filer Fegan, 2001). In one study, having a broad network of

TRUTH or FICTION? *REVISITED*

Optimistic people recover more rapidly than pessimistic people from coronary artery bypass surgery.

☑ **TRUE.** Investigators find that optimistic patients tend to recover more rapidly than pessimistic patients following coronary artery bypass surgery.

social contacts was associated with greater resistance to developing an infection following exposure to a common cold virus (Cohen & Mannarino, 1997). The investigators believe that having a wide range of social contacts may help protect the body's immune system by serving as a buffer against stress. Researchers in Sweden, as well as in the United States, find that people with a high level of social support are likely to live longer (Goleman, 1993). In the Swedish study, researchers followed middle-aged men who experienced a high level of emotional stress due to such factors as financial trouble or serious problems with a family member. Men who were highly stressed but lacked social support were three times more likely to die within a period of 7 years as were those whose lives were low in stress (Goleman, 1993). Yet men with highly stressed lives who had ample amounts of emotional support in their lives showed no higher death rates. Having other people available may help people find alternative ways of coping with stressors or simply provide them with the emotional support they need during difficult times.

Ethnic Identity   African Americans, on the average, stand a greater risk than Euro Americans of suffering chronic health problems, such as obesity, hypertension, heart disease, diabetes, and certain types of cancer (Anderson, 1991; Angier, 2000b). The particular stressors that African Americans often face, such as racism, poverty, violence, and overcrowded living conditions, may contribute to their heightened risks of serious health-related problems. Yet African Americans often demonstrate a high degree of resilience in coping with stress (Cutrona et al., 2000). Among the factors that help buffer stress among African Americans are strong social networks of family and friends, beliefs in one's ability to handle stress (self-efficacy), coping skills, and ethnic identity.

Ethnic identity is associated with perceptions of a better quality of life among African Americans (Utsey et al., 2002) and appears to be more strongly related to psychological well-being among African Americans than among White Americans (Gray-Little & Hafdahl, 2000). Acquiring and maintaining pride in one's racial identity and cultural heritage may help African Americans and other ethnic minorities withstand stresses imposed by racism. Although more research is needed to elucidate the links among racial identity, self-esteem, and tolerance of stress, the available evidence suggests that African Americans who become alienated from their culture develop more negative self-images and stand a greater risk of developing not only physical and psychological disorders, but also academic underachievement and marital conflicts (Anderson, 1991).

QUESTIONNAIRE
The Life Orientation Test

Do you see the glass as half full or half empty? Do you expect bad things to happen or do you find the silver lining in every cloud? The Life Orientation Test can afford you insight as to how optimistic or pessimistic you are.

Directions: Indicate whether or not each of the items represents your feelings by writing a number in the blank space according to the following code. Then turn to the scoring key at the end of the chapter.

4 = strongly agree
3 = agree
2 = neutral
1 = disagree
0 = strongly disagree

1. _____ In uncertain times, I usually expect the best.
2. _____ It's easy for me to relax.
3. _____ If something can go wrong for me, it will.
4. _____ I always look on the bright side of things.
5. _____ I'm always optimistic about my future.
6. _____ I enjoy my friends a lot.
7. _____ It's important for me to keep busy.
8. _____ I hardly ever expect things to go my way.
9. _____ Things never work out the way I want them to.
10. _____ I don't get upset too easily.
11. _____ I'm a believer in the idea that "every cloud has a silver lining."
12. _____ I rarely count on good things happening to me.

Source. Scheier, M. F., & Carver, C. S. (1985). Optimism, coping, and health: Assessment and implication of generalized outcome expectancies. Health Psychology, 4, 219–247. Reprinted by permission. ■

Ethnic pride as a moderator of the effects of stress. Pride in one's racial or ethnic identity may help the individual withstand the stress imposed by racism and intolerance.

PSYCHOLOGICAL FACTORS AND PHYSICAL DISORDERS

We noted at the start of the chapter that psychological factors can influence physical functioning; physical factors can also influence mental functioning. In these next sections we take a look at the role of psychological factors in various physical disorders. Physical disorders in which psychological factors are believed to play a causal or contributing role have traditionally been termed **psychosomatic** or *psychophysiological*. The term *psychosomatic* is derived from the Greek roots *psyche*, meaning "soul" or "intellect," and *soma*, which means "body." Disorders that involve psychological components range from asthma and headaches to heart disease.

psychosomatic Pertaining to a physical disorder in which psychological factors play a causal or contributing role.

Ulcers are another ailment traditionally identified as psychosomatic disorders. Ulcers affect about 1 in 10 people in the United States. However, their status as a psychosomatic disorder has been reevaluated in the light of recent landmark research that showed that a bacterium, *H. pylori*, not stress or diet, is the cause of the great majority of peptic ulcers (Boren et al., 1993; Mason, 1994). Researchers suspect that ulcers arise when the bacterium damages the protective lining of the stomach or intestines. Treatment with a regimen of antibiotics can help cure ulcers by attacking the bacterium directly (Altman, 1994). We don't yet know why some people with the bacterium develop ulcers and others don't. The virulence of the particular strain of *H. pylori* may be involved in determining whether infected people develop peptic ulcers (Spechler, Fischbach, & Feldman, 2000). It is possible that psychological stress is involved as well (Levenstein et al., 1999).

The field of psychosomatic medicine explores the possible health-related connections between the mind and the body. Today, evidence points to the importance of psychological factors in a much wider range of physical disorders than those traditionally identified as psychosomatic. In this section we discuss several of the traditionally identified psychosomatic disorders as well as two other diseases in which psychological factors may play a role in the course or treatment of the disease—cancer and AIDS.

Headaches

Headaches are symptoms of many medical disorders. When they occur in the absence of other symptoms, however, they may be classified as stress related. By far the most frequent kind of headache is the tension headache (Mark, 1998). Stress can lead to persistent contractions of the muscles of the scalp, face, neck, and shoulders, giving rise to periodic or chronic tension headaches. Such headaches develop gradually and are generally characterized by dull, steady pain on both sides of the head and feelings of pressure or tightness. A survey in the Baltimore area showed that 38% of respondents complained of occasional tension headaches, with women reporting a 16% higher rate than men (B. S. Schwartz et al., 1998).

Most other headaches, including the severe migraine headache, are believed to involve changes in the blood flow to the brain. Migraine headaches affect more than 28 million Americans ("Headache Coping," 2000). Typical migraines last for hours or days. They may occur as often as daily or as seldom as every other month. They are characterized by piercing or throbbing sensations on one side of the head only or centered behind an eye. They can be so intense that they seem intolerable. Coping with the misery of brutal migraine attacks can take its toll, impairing the quality of life and leading to disturbances of sleep, mood, and thinking processes (Lipton, Hamelsky et al., 2000).

Migraine attacks typically last from 4 to 72 hours. There are two major types of migraines: migraine without aura (formerly called *common migraine*) and migraine with aura (formerly called *classic migraine*) (Olesen, 1994). An *aura* is a cluster of warning sensations that precedes the attack. Auras are typified by perceptual distortions, such as flashing lights, bizarre images, or blind spots. About 1 in 5 migraine sufferers experiences auras. Other than the presence or absence of the aura, the two types of migraine are the same.

Theoretical Perspectives The underlying causes of headaches remain unclear and subject to continued study. One factor contributing to tension headaches may be increased sensitivity of the neural pathways that send pain signals to the brain from the face and head (Holroyd, 2002). With migraines, investigators suspect an underlying central nervous system disorder involving nerves and blood vessels in the brain ("What Causes Migraine Headaches?," 2001). The neurotransmitter serotonin is also implicated (Edelson, 1998). Falling levels of serotonin may cause blood vessels in the brain to contract (narrow) and then dilate (expand). This stretching stimulates sensitized nerve endings that give rise to the throbbing, piercing sensations associated with migraines. Evidence also points to a strong genetic contribution to migraine ("Scientists Discover," 2003).

Many factors may trigger a migraine attack. These include stress; stimuli such as bright lights; changes in barometric pressure; pollen; certain drugs; the chemical monosodium glutamate (MSG), which is often used to enhance the flavor of food; red wine; and even hunger (Martin & Seneviratne, 1997). Hormonal changes of the sort that affect women prior to and during menstruation can also trigger attacks, and the incidence of migraines among women is about twice that among men.

Treatment Commonly available pain relievers, such as aspirin, ibuprofen, and acetaminophen, may reduce or eliminate pain associated with tension headaches. A recent study reported that a combination of acetaminophen, aspirin, and caffeine (the ingredients in the over-the-counter pain reliever Excedrin) produced greater relief from the pain of migraine headaches than a placebo control (Lipton et al., 1998). Drugs that constrict dilated blood vessels in the brain or help regulate serotonin activity are used to treat the pain from migraine headache (Lipton, Stewart et al., 2000; Lohman, 2001; Silberstein et al., 2000).

Psychological treatment can also help relieve tension or migraine headache pain in many cases. These treatments include training in biofeedback, relaxation, coping skills training, and some forms of cognitive therapy (Blanchard & Diamond, 1996; Gatchel, 2001; Holroyd, 2002; Holroyd et al., 2001). **Biofeedback training (BFT)** helps people gain control over various bodily functions, such as muscle tension and brain waves, by giv-

biofeedback training (BFT) A method of feeding back to the individual information about bodily functions so that the person can gain some degree of control over these functions.

ing them information (feedback) about these functions in the form of auditory signals (e.g., "bleeps") or visual displays. People learn to make the signal change in the desired direction. Training people to use relaxation skills combined with biofeedback has also been shown to be effective. *Electromyographic* (EMG) biofeedback is a form of BFT that involves relaying information about muscle tension in the forehead. EMG biofeedback thus heightens awareness of muscle tension in this region and provides cues that people can use to learn to reduce it.

Some people have relieved the pain of migraine headaches by raising the temperature in a finger. This biofeedback technique, called thermal BFT, modifies patterns of blood flow throughout the body, including blood flow to the brain, which helps to control migraine headaches (Blanchard et al., 1990; Gauthier, Ivers, & Carrier, 1996). One way of providing thermal feedback is by attaching a *thermistor* to a finger. A console "bleeps" more slowly or rapidly as the temperature rises. The temperature rises because more blood is flowing into the limb—away from the head. The client can imagine the finger growing warmer to bring about changes in the body's distribution of blood.

Cardiovascular Disease

Cardiovascular disease (heart and artery disease) is the leading cause of death in the United States, claiming about 1 million lives annually and accounting for about 4 in 10 deaths, most often as the result of heart attacks or strokes (Hu & Willett, 2002; Nabel, 2003). *Coronary heart disease* (CHD) is the major form of cardiovascular disease, accounting for about 700,000 deaths annually, mostly from heart attacks. It may surprise you to learn that more women die from CHD than from breast cancer (Ansell, 2001).

About 10% of the population, some 22 million Americans, have CHD. In coronary heart disease, the flow of blood to the heart is insufficient to meet its needs. The underlying disease process in CHD is *arteriosclerosis*, or "hardening of the arteries," a condition in which artery walls become thicker, harder, and less elastic, which makes it more difficult for blood to flow freely. The major underlying cause of arteriosclerosis is *atherosclerosis*, a process involving the buildup of fatty deposits along artery walls that leads to the formation of artery-clogging plaque (Stoney, 2003). If a blood clot should form in an artery narrowed by plaque, it may nearly or completely block the flow of blood to the heart. The result is a heart attack (also called *myocardial infarction*), a life-threatening event in which heart tissue dies due to a lack of oxygen-rich blood. If a blood clot chokes off the supply of blood in an artery serving the brain, a *stroke* may occur, leading to death of brain tissue that can result in loss of function controlled by that part of the brain, coma, or even death.

The good news is that CHD is largely preventable (Nabel, 2003). How? By reducing the risk factors we can control. Some risk factors we can't control, such as age and family history. But a number of risk factors can be controlled through medical treatment or lifestyle changes—factors such as high cholesterol, hypertension (high blood pressure), smoking, overeating, heavy drinking, consuming a high-fat diet, and leading a sedentary lifestyle (e.g., Chobanian et al., 2003; Pickering, 2003; Tanasescu et al., 2002; Writing Group, 2003). Unfortunately, many of these factors remain uncontrolled. For example, only about one in four adults with hypertension take medications to control their blood pressures (Chobanian, 2001; Hyman & Pavlik, 2001). Rates of uncontrolled hypertension were highest among older adults.

Psychological factors, such as negative emotional states like anger, anxiety, and even depression are also risk factors for cardiovascular disorders. For example, depressed postmenopausal women are 50% more likely to die of cardiovascular disease than are nondepressed women (Wassertheil-Smoller et al., 2004). The nature of the link between depression and heart disease is unclear; that is, either condition may lead to the other. A personality pattern called the *Type A behavior pattern* poses yet another psychological risk factor in CHD.

Type A Behavior Pattern The **Type A behavior pattern (TABP)** is a style of behavior that characterizes people who are hard driving, ambitious, impatient, and highly

cardiovascular disease A disease or disorder of the cardiovascular system, such as coronary heart disease or hypertension.

Type A behavior pattern (TABP) A behavior pattern characterized by a sense of time urgency, competitiveness, and hostility.

A CLOSER LOOK
Psychological Methods for Lowering Arousal

Stress induces bodily responses such as excessive levels of sympathetic nervous system arousal, which if persistent may impair our ability to function optimally and possibly increase the risk of stress-related illnesses. Psychological treatments have been shown to lower states of bodily arousal that may be prompted by stress. In this feature, we consider two widely used psychological methods of lowering arousal: meditation and progressive relaxation.

Meditation

Meditation comprises several ways of narrowing consciousness to moderate the stressors of the outer world. Yogis (adherents to Yoga philosophy) study the design on a vase or a mandala. The ancient Egyptians riveted their attention on an oil-burning lamp, which is the inspiration for the tale of Aladdin's lamp. In Turkey, Islamic mystics called whirling dervishes fix on their motion and the cadences of their breathing.

There are many meditation methods, but they share the common thread of narrowing one's attention by focusing on repetitive stimuli. Through passive observation, the regular person–environment connection is transformed. Problem solving, worry, planning, and routine concerns are suspended, and consequently, levels of sympathetic arousal are reduced.

Many thousands of Americans regularly practice *transcendental meditation (TM),* a simplified kind of Indian meditation brought to the United States in 1959 by Maharishi Mahesh Yogi. Practitioners of TM repeat *mantras*—relaxing sounds like *ieng* and *om.*

Benson (1975) studied TM practitioners ages 17 to 41—students, businesspeople, artists. His subjects included relative novices and veterans of 9 years of practice. Benson found that TM yields a *relaxation response* in many people. The relaxation response is typically characterized by a reduced heart rate and metabolic rate and by reduced blood pressure in people with hypertension (Benson, Manzetta, & Rosner, 1973; Gatchel, 2001). Meditators also produced more alpha waves, brain waves connected with relaxation. Critics of meditation do not hold that meditation is without value; they suggest, instead, that meditation may have no distinct effects when compared to a restful break from a stressful routine.

Meditation can also produce measurable health benefits. Evidence shows that it can lower blood pressure and actually reduce the amount of fatty deposits on artery walls, both of which are major risk factors for heart attacks and strokes (Ready, 2000).

In *mindfulness meditation,* a form of meditation practiced by Tibetan Buddhists, the person focuses on conscious experience (thoughts, feelings, and sensations) on a moment-to-moment basis, without judging or evaluating the experience (Baer, 2003; Hayes & Wilson, 2003; Kabat-Zinn, 2003). This practice has been likened to observing the flow of a river. Mindfulness medi-

Going with the flow. Meditation is a popular method of managing the stresses of the outside world by reducing states of bodily arousal. This young woman practices yoga, a form of meditation. She "goes with the flow," allowing the distractions of her environment to in a sense "pass through." Contrast her meditative state with the apparently stressful features of the young man sitting behind her.

tation shows promise in treating various physical and mental health problems, including chronic pain and stress, as well as improving psychological well-being and reducing relapse rates in depressed patients (Baer, 2003; Brown & Ryan, 2003; Logsdon-Conradsen, 2002; Ma & Teasdale, 2004; Roemer & Orsillo, 2003).

Although there are differences among meditative techniques, the following suggestions illustrate some general guidelines.

1. Try meditation once or twice a day for 10 to 20 minutes at a time.
2. When you meditate, what you *don't* do is more important than what you do. So embrace a passive attitude: Tell yourself, "What happens, hap-

competitive. The Type A pattern is associated with a modestly higher risk of CHD (T. Q. Miller et al., 1991). Psychological interventions designed to reduce Type A behavior can significantly lower their risk of subsequent heart attacks in people who have already suffered a heart attack (Brody, 1996; Friedman et al., 1986). Perhaps there is a lesson in this for us all.

Hostility—quickness to anger—is the element of the Type A behavior pattern most closely linked to cardiovascular risk (Donker, 2000 Niaura et al., 2002) (see A Closer Look: Emotions and the Heart feature, p. 161). People with TABP tend to have "short fuses" and are prone to get angry easily.

The questionnaire on page 162 "Are You Type A?" helps you assess whether or not you fit the Type A profile. If you would like to begin modifying Type A behavior, a good place to start is with lessening your sense of time urgency. Here are some suggestions (Friedman & Ulmer, 1984):

pens." In meditation, you take what you get. You don't *strive* for more. Striving of any kind hinders meditation.

3. Place yourself in a hushed, calming environment. For example, don't face a light directly.

4. Avoid eating for an hour before you meditate. Avoid caffeine (found in coffee, tea, many soft drinks, and chocolate) for at least 2 hours.

5. Get into a relaxed position. Modify it as needed. You can scratch or yawn if you feel the urge.

6. For a focusing device, you can concentrate on your breathing or sit in front of a serene object like a plant or incense. Benson suggests "perceiving" (not "mentally saying") the word *one* each time you breathe out. That is, think the word, but "less actively" than you normally would. Other researchers suggest thinking the word *in* as you breathe in and *out*, or *ah-h-h*, as you breathe out. They also suggest mantras like *ah-nam*, *rah-mah*, and *shi-rim*.

7. When preparing for meditation, repeat your mantra aloud many times—if you're using a mantra. Enjoy it. Then say it progressively more softly. Close your eyes. Focus on the mantra. Allow thinking the mantra to become more and more "passive" so you "perceive" rather than think it. Again, embrace your "what happens, happens" attitude. Keep on focusing on the mantra. It may become softer or louder, or fade and then reappear.

8. If unsettling thoughts drift in while you're meditating, allow them to "pass through." Don't worry about squelching them, or you may become tense.

9. Remember to take what comes. Meditation and relaxation cannot be forced. You cannot force the relaxing effects of meditation. Like sleep, you can only set the stage for it and then permit it to happen.

10. Let yourself drift. (You won't get lost.) What happens, happens.

Progressive Relaxation

Progressive relaxation was originated by University of Chicago physician Edmund Jacobson in 1938. Jacobson noticed that people tense their muscles under stress, intensifying their uneasiness. They tend to be unaware of these contractions, however. Jacobson reasoned that if muscle contractions contributed to tension, muscle relaxation might reduce tension. But clients who were asked to focus on relaxing muscles often had no idea what to do.

Jacobson's method of progressive relaxation teaches people how to monitor muscle tension and relaxation. With this method, people first tense, then relax, selected muscle groups in the arms; facial area; the chest, stomach, and lower back muscles; the hips, thighs, and calves; and so on. The sequence heightens awareness of muscle tension and helps people differentiate feelings of tension from relaxation. The method is progressive in that people progress from one group of muscles to another in practicing the technique. Since the 1930s, progressive relaxation has been used by a number of behavior therapists, including Joseph Wolpe and Arnold Lazarus (1966).

The following instructions from Wolpe and Lazarus (1966, pp. 177–178) illustrate how the technique is applied to relaxing the arms. Relaxation should be practiced in a favorable setting. Settle back on a recliner, a couch, or a bed with a pillow. Select a place and time when you're unlikely to be disturbed. Make the room warm and comfortable. Dim sources of light. Loosen tight clothing. Tighten muscles about two thirds as hard as you could if you were trying your hardest. If you sense that a muscle could have a spasm, you are tightening too much. After tensing, let go of tensions completely.

Relaxation of Arms (time: 4–5 minutes)

Settle back as comfortably as you can. Let yourself relax to the best of your ability. . . . Now, as you relax like that, clench your right fist, just clench your fist tighter and tighter, and study the tension as you do so. Keep it clenched and feel the tension in your right fist, hand, forearm . . . and now relax. Let the fingers of your right hand become loose, and observe the contrast in your feelings. . . . Now, let yourself go and try to become more relaxed all over. . . . Once more, clench your right fist really tight . . . hold it, and notice the tension again. . . . Now let go, relax; your fingers straighten out, and you notice the difference once more. . . . Now repeat that with your left fist. Clench your left fist while the rest of your body relaxes; clench that fist tighter and feel the tension . . . and now relax. Again enjoy the contrast. . . . Repeat that once more, clench the left fist, tight and tense. . . . Now do the opposite of tension—relax and feel the difference. Continue relaxing like that for a while. . . . Clench both fists tighter and together, both fists tense, forearms tense, study the sensations . . . and relax; straighten out your fingers and feel that relaxation. Continue relaxing your hands and forearms more and more. . . . Now bend your elbows and tense your biceps, tense them harder and study the tension feelings . . . all right, straighten out your arms, let them relax and feel that difference again. Let the relaxation develop. . . . Once more, tense your biceps; hold the tension and observe it carefully. . . . Straighten the arms and relax; relax to the best of your ability. . . . Each time, pay close attention to your feelings when you tense up and when you relax. Now straighten your arms, straighten them so that you feel most tension in the triceps muscles along the back of your arms; stretch your arms and feel that tension. . . . And now relax. Get your arms back into a comfortable position. Let the relaxation proceed on its own. The arms should feel comfortably heavy as you allow them to relax. . . . Straighten the arms once more so that you feel the tension in the triceps muscles; straighten them. Feel that tension . . . and relax. Now let's concentrate on pure relaxation in the arms without any tension. Get your arms comfortable and let them relax further and further. Continue relaxing your arms even further. Even when your arms seem fully relaxed, try to go that extra bit further; try to achieve deeper and deeper levels of relaxation.

---

1. Increase social activity with family and friends.

2. Each day, spend a few minutes recalling distant events. Peruse photos of family and old friends.

3. Read books—biographies, literature, drama, politics, nature, science, science fiction. (Books on business and on climbing the corporate ladder are not recommended!)

4. Visit art galleries and museums. Consider works for their aesthetic value, not their prices.

5. Go to the movies, theater, concerts, ballet.

6. Write letters to family and old friends.

7. Take an art course; start violin or piano lessons.

Reducing Type A behavior. Slowing down the pace of your daily life and making time for loved ones are among the ways of reducing Type A behavior. Can you think of other ways that can help you decrease Type A behavior?

8. Keep in mind that life is by nature unfinished. You needn't have all your projects finished by a certain date.

9. Ask family members what they did during the day. *Listen* to the answer.

Here are some additional suggestions for reducing anger and hostility, the elements believed to be the most toxic components of the Type A profile (Brody, 1996; Friedman & Ulmer, 1984):

1. Don't get involved in discussions that you know lead to pointless arguments.

2. When others do things that disappoint you, consider situational factors that might explain their behavior. Don't jump to the conclusion that others intend to get you upset.

3. Focus on the beauty and pleasure in things.

4. Don't curse.

5. Express appreciation to people for their support and assistance.

6. Play for the fun of it, not to beat your opponent.

7. Check out your face in the mirror from time to time. Look for signs of anger and aggravation; ask yourself if you really need to look like that.

8. Don't sweat the small stuff. Let it go. Avoid grudges, and let bygones be bygones.

Social Environmental Stress *Social environmental stress* also appears to heighten the risk of CHD (Krantz et al., 1988). Such factors as overtime work, assembly-line labor, and exposure to conflicting demands are linked to increased risk of CHD (C. D. Jenkins, 1988). The stress–CHD connection is not straightforward, however. For example, the effects of demanding occupations may be moderated by factors such as psychological hardiness and whether or not people find their work meaningful (Krantz et al., 1988).

Other forms of stress are also linked to increased cardiovascular risk. Researchers in Sweden, for example, find that among women, marital stress triples the risk of recurrent cardiac events, including heart attacks and cardiac death (Foxhall, 2001; Orth-Gomér et al., 2000).

Ethnicity and CHD Coronary heart disease is not an equal opportunity destroyer. White men and Black (non-Hispanic) men and women have the highest rates of death due to coronary heart disease (see Figure 5.2). Factors such as obesity, smoking, dia-

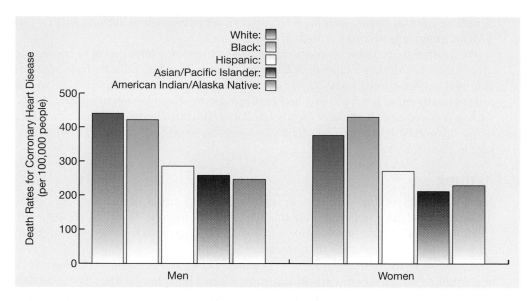

FIGURE 5.2 Coronary heart disease death rates in relation to race and ethnicity.
Deaths due to CHD in our society fall disproportionately on White men and on Black (non-Hispanic) men and women.

Source: Morbidity and Mortality Weekly Report, Centers for Disease Control, February 16, 2001, *50*(006), 90–93.

betes, and hypertension play important roles in determining relative risks of CHD and the rate of CHD-related deaths. For example, Black men and women have high rates of hypertension (see Figure 5.3) as well as obesity and diabetes. Moreover, a dual standard of care limits access to quality health care for minority group members. Black Americans with CHD who suffer heart attacks typically receive less-aggressive and potentially lifesaving treatments than do their White counterparts, leading to higher death rates (Chen et al., 2001; Stolberg, 2001). This dual standard of care may reflect discrimination

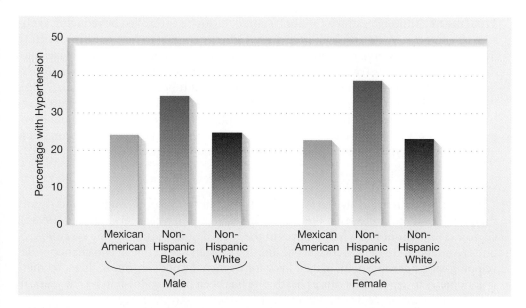

FIGURE 5.3 Hypertension among people ages 20 to 74, according to race/ethnicity.
Non-Hispanic Black Americans have disproportionately high rates of hypertension, a major risk factor for cardiovascular disease.

Source: USDHHS, Public Health Service (1991), *Health, United States 1990.* DHHS Pub. No. (PHS) 91-1232.

as well as cultural factors limiting utilization of services, such as cultural mistrust of African Americans toward the medical establishment.

We finish this section with encouraging news. Americans have begun to take better care of their health. The incidence of CHD and deaths from heart disease have been declining steadily during the past 50 years, thanks largely to reductions in smoking, to improved treatment of heart patients, and perhaps also to other changes in lifestyle habits, such as reduced overall intake of dietary fat. Better-educated people are also more likely to modify unhealthful behavior patterns and reap the benefits of change. Is there a message in there for you?

Asthma

Asthma is a respiratory disorder in which the main tubes of the windpipe—the bronchi—constrict and become inflamed, and large amounts of mucus are secreted. During asthma attacks, people wheeze, cough, and struggle to breathe in enough air. They may feel as though they are suffocating.

According to the Centers for Disease Control (CDC), an estimated 14 million adults and 5 million children in the United States are affected by asthma (CDC, 2001b, 2004a). Rates of asthma are on the rise, having doubled since 1980. Attacks can last from just a few minutes to several hours and vary notably in intensity. Series of attacks can harm the bronchial system, causing mucus to collect and muscles to lose their elasticity. Sometimes the bronchial system is weakened to the point where a subsequent attack is lethal.

Theoretical Perspectives Many causes are implicated in asthma, including allergic reactions; exposure to environmental pollutants, including cigarette smoke and smog; and genetic and immunological factors (Giembycz & O'Connor, 2000; Van Eerdewegh et al., 2002). Asthmatic reactions in susceptible people can be triggered by exposure to allergens such as pollen, mold spores, and animal dander; by cold, dry air; and by emotional responses such as anger or even laughing too hard. Psychological factors such as stress, anxiety, and depression can increase susceptibility to asthmatic attacks (Greengrass, 2002; Lehrer et al., 2002). Asthma, moreover, has psychological consequences. Some sufferers avoid strenuous activity, including exercise, for fear of increasing their demand for oxygen and tripping attacks.

Treatment Although asthma cannot be cured, it can be controlled by reducing exposure to allergens, by desensitization therapy ("allergy shots") to help the body acquire more resistance to allergens, by use of inhalers, and by drugs that open bronchial passages during asthma attacks (called *bronchodilators*) and others (called *anti-inflammatories*) that reduce future attacks by helping to keep bronchial tubes open (Sears et al., 2003). Psychological treatment may also help asthma sufferers apply the skills of muscle relaxation to improve their breathing (Lehrer et al., 1994), and for asthmatic children, family therapy that helps reduce family conflict (Lehrer et al., 1992). Family conflict is linked to increased rates of hospitalization for asthmatic children (Chen et al., 2003).

Cancer

The word *cancer* is arguably the most feared word in the English language and rightly so: One of every four deaths in the United States is caused by cancer (Stolberg, 1998a). Cancer claims about half a million lives in the United States annually, one every 90 seconds (Andersen, Golden-Kreutz, & DiLillo, 2001). Men have a one in two chance of developing cancer at some point in their lives; for women the odds are one in three. Yet there is good news to report: The cancer death rate has been inching down in recent years, in part due to better screening and treatment ("Mixed Progress," 2003).

Cancer is characterized by development of aberrant, or mutant, cells that form growths (tumors) that spread to healthy tissue. Cancerous cells can take root anywhere—the blood, the bones, lungs, digestive tract, and genital organs. When it is not contained early, cancer may *metastasize,* or establish colonies throughout the body, leading to death.

A CLOSER LOOK
Emotions and the Heart

Might your emotions be putting you at risk of developing coronary heart disease? It appears so. Evidence shows that both anxiety and anger are hazardous to a person's cardiovascular health (Suinn, 2001).

The Anxious Heart

Investigators have linked phobic anxiety, the type of anxiety characterized by unfounded fears and panicky feelings, to a greater risk of death in men as the result of irregular heart rhythms. A study of some 34,000 men, none of whom were diagnosed at the outset of the study with coronary heart disease, showed those scoring at the high end of an index of phobic anxiety were six times more likely to suffer sudden coronary death over a 2-year period than were less-anxious men (Hilchey, 1994; Kawachi et al., 1994). The researchers suspect that persistent, high levels of anxiety may produce "electrical storms" in the heart, resulting in irregular heart rhythms that may lead to sudden coronary death. Fortunately, the number of cardiac-related deaths during the 2-year study period was relatively small (only 16 among 34,000). Other investigators have also linked states of anxiety and tension with an increased risk of coronary symptoms and death in people with established CHD (Denollet et al., 1996; Gullette et al., 1997).

Researchers also find a connection between anxiety in middle-aged men and the later risk of developing hypertension, a major risk factor for CHD (Markovitz et al., 1993). Highly anxious men were about twice as likely as their more relaxed counterparts to develop hypertension. We don't yet know whether this relationship also applies to women.

Anger and Hostility

Occasional feelings of anger may not damage the heart in healthy people, but chronic anger—the type you see in people who seem angry all of the time—is linked to an increased risk of CHD and may even be as dangerous a risk factor as smoking, obesity, family history, or a high-fat diet (Rutledge & Hogan, 2002; Smith & Ruiz, 2002; J. E. Williams et al., 2000). Anger is closely associated with hostility—an attitude characterized by tendencies to blame others and to perceive the world in negative terms. Hostile people are quick to anger and become angry more often and more intensely when they feel they have been mistreated than do nonhostile people. Young people with high levels of hostility stand an increased risk of developing early signs of coronary heart disease (Clay, 2001b; Matthews et al., 2000).

Although anger and hostility are not direct causes of heart disease, they are associated with increased risks of death from cardiovascular disease (Kiecolt-Glaser et al., 2002; Suinn, 2001). Moreover, episodes of acute anger can actually trigger heart attacks and sudden cardiac death in people with established heart disease (Clay, 2001a).

Linking Emotions and the Heart

More research is needed to better understand the underlying mechanism linking negative emotions to heart disease, but investigators suspect that the stress hormones epinephrine and norepinephrine play significant roles (Januzzi & DeSanctis, 1999; Melani, 2001). Anxiety or anger triggers the adrenal glands to release these stress hormones, which then mobilize the body's resources to deal with threatening situations. They increase the heart rate, breathing rate, and blood pressure, which increases the flow of oxygen-rich blood to the muscles to prepare for defensive action—to fight or to flee—in the face of a threatening stressor. When people are persistently or repeatedly anxious or angry, the body

may remain overaroused for long periods of time, continuing to pump out these stress hormones, which eventually may have damaging effects on the heart and blood vessels. Stress hormones also appear to increase the stickiness of the clotting factors in blood, which might increase the chances that potentially dangerous blood clots will form (Januzzi & DeSanctis, 1999).

Anxiety and anger may also compromise the cardiovascular system by increasing blood levels of cholesterol, the fatty substance that clogs arteries and increases the risk of heart attacks (Suinn, 2001). People with higher levels of hostility tend to show markers of increased risks for heart attacks and strokes, including high blood pressure (Räikkönen et al., 1999; Smith, 2003a).

Cognitive-behavioral therapists help chronically angry people learn to control their emotional responses in anxiety-provoking or angering situations (e.g., Deffenbacher et al., 2000). Helping angry people learn to remain calm in provocative situations may have beneficial effects on the heart as well as the mind (Gidron & Davidson, 1996). Along these lines, men with CHD who received a hostility-reduction program showed less hostility and lower blood pressures after treatment than did controls (Gidron, Davidson, & Bata, 1999).

Investigators are finding additional links between coronary heart disease and other forms of emotional stress, including depression (Carney, Freedland, & Jaffe, 2001; Ferketich et al., 2000; Orth-Gomér et al., 2000). In one recent study, people without cardiac disease who were suffering from major depression were nearly four times more likely than nondepressed people to die from heart-related causes over a 4-year study period (Penninx et al., 2001). ■

Emotions and the heart. Emotional stress in the form of persistent negative emotions, such as anxiety and anger, is a risk factor in heart-related problems.

QUESTIONNAIRE
Are You Type A?

People with the Type A behavior pattern are impatient, competitive, and aggressive. They feel rushed, under pressure; they keep one eye glued to the clock. They are prompt and often arrive early for appointments. They walk, talk, and eat rapidly. They grow restless when others work slowly.

Type A people don't just stroll out on the tennis court to bat the ball around. They scrutinize their form, polish their strokes, and demand consistent self-improvement.

Are you Type A? Check the appropriate column on the following scale to indicate whether or not the item is generally true of you. Then consult the scoring key at the end of the chapter to determine whether you fit the Type A profile.

YES NO Do you . . .

☐ ☐ 1. Walk briskly from place to place or from meeting to meeting?
☐ ☐ 2. Strongly emphasize important words in your ordinary speech?
☐ ☐ 3. Think that life is by nature dog-eat-dog?
☐ ☐ 4. Get fidgety when you see someone complete a job slowly?
☐ ☐ 5. Urge others to complete what they're trying to express?
☐ ☐ 6. Find it exceptionally annoying to get stuck in line?
☐ ☐ 7. Envision all the things you have to do, even when someone is talking to you?
☐ ☐ 8. Eat while you're getting dressed, or jot down notes while you're driving?
☐ ☐ 9. Catch up on work during vacations?

YES NO Do you . . .

☐ ☐ 10. Direct the conversation to things that interest you?
☐ ☐ 11. Feel as if things are going to pot because you're relaxing for a few minutes?
☐ ☐ 12. Get so wrapped up in your work that you fail to notice beautiful scenery passing by?
☐ ☐ 13. Get so wrapped up in money, promotions, and awards that you neglect expressing your creativity?
☐ ☐ 14. Schedule appointments and meetings back to back?
☐ ☐ 15. Arrive early for appointments and meetings?
☐ ☐ 16. Make fists or clench your jaws to drive home your views?
☐ ☐ 17. Think that you've achieved what you have because of your ability to work fast?
☐ ☐ 18. Have the feeling that uncompleted work must be done *now* and fast?
☐ ☐ 19. Try to find more efficient ways to get things done?
☐ ☐ 20. Struggle always to win games instead of having fun?
☐ ☐ 21. Interrupt people who are talking?
☐ ☐ 22. Lose patience with people who are late for appointments and meetings?
☐ ☐ 23. Get back to work right after lunch?
☐ ☐ 24. Find that there's never enough time?
☐ ☐ 25. Believe that you're getting too little done, even when other people tell you that you're doing fine? ■

There are many causes of cancer, including regular exposure to cancer-causing chemicals in the environment and genetic factors, such as defective or mutant genes. Some cancers are caused by viruses. But many behavior patterns also contribute to the development of cancer, including dietary practices (high fat intake), heavy alcohol consumption, smoking, and sunbathing (ultraviolet light causes skin cancer). On the other hand, daily intake of fruits and vegetables may lower the risk of some forms of cancer. Death rates from cancer are lower in Japan than in the United States, where people ingest more fat, especially animal fat. The difference is not genetic or racial, however, because Japanese Americans whose fat intake approximates that of other Americans show similar death rates from cancer.

Stress and Cancer A weakened or compromised immune system may increase susceptibility to cancer. We've seen that psychological factors, such as exposure to stress, may affect the immune system. Research with animals has shown that exposure to stress can hasten the onset of a virus-induced cancer (Riley, 1981). Might exposure to stress in humans increase the risk of cancer? Some studies show an increased incidence of stressful life events, such as the loss of loved ones, preceding the development of some forms of cancer (e.g., Levenson & Bemis, 1991). However, other studies show no linkage between stress and cancer (e.g., McKenna et al., 1999). Clearly, the links between stress and cancer require further study (Delahanty & Baum, 2001; Dougall & Baum, 2001).

Psychological Factors in Treatment and Recovery Cancer is a physical disease treated medically by means surgery, radiation, and chemotherapy. Yet psychologists and mental health professionals can play key roles in helping cancer patients cope with the disease (Andersen, 2002). Feelings of hopelessness and helplessness are common reactions to receiving a cancer diagnosis, but such feelings may hinder recovery (Andersen, 1992), perhaps by depressing the patient's immune system.

In one study, breast cancer patients who maintained a "fighting spirit" experienced higher survival rates than those who resigned themselves to their illness (Pettingale, 1985). But more recent research casts doubt on whether a fighting spirit increases survival (Petticrew, Bell, & Hunter, 2002; Verghese, 2004). On the other hand, it is clear that group therapy contributes to emotional well-being in cancer patients, perhaps by providing a source of emotional support (K. L. Taylor et al., 2003). Though cancer patients who participate in group therapy tend to fare better emotionally, we lack evidence that psychological treatment increases survival rates (DeAngelis, 2002; Goodwin et al., 2001).

Investigators have examined the value of training cancer patients to use coping skills, such as relaxation, stress management, and coping thoughts, to relieve the stress and pain of coping with cancer. These interventions may also help cancer patients cope with the anticipatory side effects of chemotherapy. Cues associated with chemotherapy, such as the hospital environment itself, may become conditioned stimuli that elicit nausea and vomiting even before the drugs are administered. By pairing relaxation, pleasant imagery, and attentional distraction with these cues, investigators find that nausea and vomiting can be lessened (Redd, 1995; Redd & Jacobsen, 2001). Playing video games as a form of distraction has also helped lessen the discomfort of chemotherapy in children with cancer (Kolko & Rickard-Figueroa, 1985).

Learning to modify expectations is also important. Cancer patients who are able to maintain or restore their psychological well-being appear to be able to do so by readjusting their expectations of themselves in line with their present capabilities (Heidrich, Forsthoff, & Ward, 1994).

Acquired Immunodeficiency Syndrome (AIDS)

Acquired immunodeficiency syndrome (AIDS) is a disease caused by the human immunodeficiency virus (HIV). HIV attacks the person's immune system, leaving it helpless to fend off diseases it normally would hold in check. AIDS is one of history's worst epidemics. By the early years of the new millennium, more than 40 million people worldwide were living with HIV/AIDS, and the disease was responsible for taking some three million lives annually (U.N., 2003).

There are two primary reasons for including HIV/AIDS in our discussion of psychological factors in physical illness. First, people living with HIV/AIDS often develop significant psychological problems in adjusting to living with the disease. Secondly, behavioral patterns such as unsafe sexual and injection practices play the dominant role in determining risks of contracting and transmitting the virus.

HIV can be transmitted by sexual contact (vaginal and anal intercourse; oral–genital contact); direct infusion of contaminated blood, as from transfusions of contaminated blood, accidental pricks from needles used previously on an infected person, or needle sharing among injecting drug users; and from an infected mother to a child during pregnancy or childbirth or through breast-feeding. AIDS is not contracted by donating blood; by airborne germs; by insects; or by casual contact, such as using public toilets, holding or hugging infected people, sharing eating utensils with them, or living or going to school with them. Routine screening of the blood supply for HIV has reduced the risk of infection from blood transfusions to virtually nil. The majority of cases of HIV transmission worldwide involve heterosexual intercourse; in the United States, heterosexual intercourse accounts for 35% of new cases of HIV infections (CDC, 2004b).

There is no cure or vaccine for HIV infection, but the introduction of highly effective antiretroviral drugs has revolutionized treatment of the disease, raising hopes that it can become a chronic but manageable disease (Gallant, 2000; Sherbourne et al., 2000; Yeni et al., 2002). However, hopes are tempered by the fact that many patients fail to benefit fully from the newer antiviral drug combinations (Catz & Kelly, 2001; Cole et al., 2002) and that new drug-resistant strains of the virus have appeared (Lawrence et al., 2003; Little et al., 2002). The lack of a cure or effective vaccine means that prevention

Adjustment to Physical Illness/ HIV Positive:
The Case of Julia
"You're born into society to groups or classes that are marginalized."

AIDS support group. AIDS support groups offer emotional support and assistance to people with HIV/AIDS, their families, and their friends.

programs focusing on reducing or eliminating risky sexual and injection practices represent our best hope for controlling the epidemic.

Adjustment of People with HIV and AIDS Given the nature of the disease and the stigma suffered by people with HIV and AIDS, it is not surprising that many people with HIV, although certainly not all, develop psychological problems, most commonly anxiety and depression (Catz & Kelly, 2001; Heckman et al., 2004; Morrison et al., 2002). Investigators have reported that greater levels of depressive symptoms were associated with more rapid disease progression in women with HIV (Ickovics et al., 2001).

Psychologists and other mental health professionals are involved in providing treatment services to people affected by HIV/AIDS. Coping skills training and cognitive-behavioral therapy have been shown to help improve psychological functioning, ability to handle stress, and quality of life and to reduce feelings of depression and anxiety (Lechner et al, 2003; Lutgendorf et al., 1997). Treatment may incorporate training in active coping skills, such as stress management techniques like self-relaxation and positive mental imagery, and cognitive strategies to control intrusive negative thoughts and preoccupations. The importance of stress management skills is highlighted by recent findings that stressful life events and passive coping (use of denial) were associated with faster progression to AIDS in HIV-infected men (Leserman et al., 2000).

Antidepressant medication has also been found to be helpful in treating depression in people with HIV (Elliott et al., 1998). Whether treatment of depression or coping skills training for handling stress can improve immunological functioning or prolong life in people with HIV and AIDS remains an open question.

Psychological Interventions to Reduce Risky Behaviors Providing information about risk reduction alone is not sufficient to induce widespread changes in sexual behavior. Despite awareness of the dangers, many people continue to practice unsafe sexual and injection behaviors (Kalichman, 2000). Fortunately, psychological interventions are effective in helping people alter risky behaviors (e.g., Carey et al., 2004; Fisher et al., 2002; Kelly & Kalichman, 2002). These programs help raise people's awareness about risky behaviors and help them develop more adaptive behaviors, such as learning how to refuse invitations to engage in unsafe sex and how to communicate effectively with one's partner(s) about safer sex. The likelihood of engaging in safer sex practices is also linked to the avoidance of alcohol and drugs before sex and to the perception that safer sex practices represent the social norm (expected behavior) within one's peer group.

The advent of AIDS presents the mental health community with unparalleled opportunity to help prevent the spread of HIV and to treat people with HIV and AIDS. As frightening as AIDS may be, it is preventable.

Preventing AIDS For the first time, a generation of young people has come of age at a time when the threat of AIDS hangs over every sexual encounter. People may decrease the risk of being infected by HIV and other sexually transmitted diseases (STDs) by taking the following measures. Only the first two are sure paths to avoiding the sexual transmission of HIV. The others reduce the risk of infection, but cannot be certified as perfectly safe. If we are going to be sexually active without knowing (not guessing) whether we or our partners are infected with HIV or some other STD, we can speak only of safe(r) sex—not of perfectly safe sex.

1. *Maintaining lifelong celibacy.*

2. *Remaining in a lifelong monogamous relationship with an uninfected person who is doing the same thing.* Although these first two sexual career paths guarantee safety, they are not followed by the majority of students or other Americans.

3. *Being discerning in one's choice of sex partners.* Get to know another person before engaging in sexual activity. Still, getting to know a person is no guarantee the person is uninfected with HIV. Avoid contact with multiple partners or with people who are likely to have multiple partners.

4. *Being assertive with sex partners.* It is important to communicate concerns about AIDS clearly and assertively with sex partners.

5. *Inspecting one's partner's sex organs.* There are no obvious signs of HIV infection, but people who are infected with HIV are often infected by other sexually transmitted diseases as well. It may be feasible to visually inspect your partner's sex organs for rashes, chancres, blisters, discharges, warts, and lice during foreplay. Consider any disagreeable odor a warning sign.

6. *Using latex condoms.* Condoms protect men from infected vaginal fluids and stop infected semen from entering women. All condoms (including so-called natural condoms made of animal intestines or "skins") act as barriers to sperm, but only latex condoms can prevent transmission of HIV.

7. *Using spermicides.* Spermicides containing the ingredient nonoyxnol-9 kill HIV as well as sperm. Spermicides should be used along with latex condoms, not as a substitute for condoms.

8. *Consulting a physician following suspected exposure to a sexually transmitted disease (STD).* Antibiotics following unprotected sex may guard against bacterial STDs, but they are of no use against viral STDs such as genital herpes and HIV/AIDS. Consult with a physician before using any medications, including medications you may have stored away in your medicine cabinet.

9. *Seeking regular medical checkups.* Checkups and appropriate laboratory tests enable you to learn about and treat disorders that might have gone unnoticed.

10. *Avoiding sexual activity if there are doubts about safety.* None of the safer sex practices listed guarantees protection. Why not avoid sexual activity when doubts of safety exist?

In this chapter we focused on relationships between stress and health and on the psychological factors involved in health. Psychology has much to offer in the understanding and treatment of physical disorders. Psychological approaches may help in the treatment of such physical disorders as headaches and coronary heart disease. Psychologists also help people reduce the risks of contracting health problems such as cardiovascular disorders, cancer, and AIDS. Emerging fields like psychoneuroimmunology promise to further enhance our knowledge of the intricate relationships between mind and body.

SUMMING UP

Adjustment Disorders

What are adjustment disorders? Adjustment disorders are maladaptive reactions to identified stressors.

What are their features? Adjustment disorders are characterized by emotional reactions that are greater than normally expected given the circumstances or by evidence of significant impairment in functioning. Impairment usually takes the form of problems at work or school, or in social relationships or activities.

Stress and Illness

How is stress linked to physical illness? Evidence links exposure to stress to weakened immune system functioning, which in turn can increase vulnerability to physical illness. However, because this evidence is correlational, questions of cause and effect remain.

What is the general adaptation syndrome? This is the name given by Hans Selye to the generalized pattern of response of the body to persistent or enduring stress, as characterized by three stages: the alarm reaction, the resistance stage, and the exhaustion stage.

How are life changes related to physical health problems? Again, links are correlational, but evidence shows that people who experience more life stress in the form of life changes and daily hassles are at an increased risk of developing physical health problems.

What psychological factors buffer the effects of stress? These factors include coping styles, self-efficacy expectancies, psychological hardiness, optimism, and social support.

Psychological Factors and Physical Disorders

What roles do psychological factors play in the onset of headaches and their treatment? The most common headache is the muscle-tension headache, which is often stress related. Behavioral methods of relaxation training and biofeedback are of help in treating various types of headaches.

What behavioral or lifestyle factors increase the risk of coronary heart disease? Psychological factors that increase the risk of coronary heart disease include patterns of consumption, leading a sedentary lifestyle, Type A behavior pattern, and persistent negative emotions.

What role do psychological factors play in asthma? Psychological factors such as emotional stress, loss of loved ones, and sudden or intense disappointment may trigger asthma attacks in susceptible individuals.

What role do psychological factors play in the development of cancer and its treatment? Although relationships between stress and risk of cancer remain under study, behavioral risk factors for cancer include dietary practices (especially high fat intake), heavy alcohol use, smoking, and excessive sun exposure. Psychological interventions help cancer patients cope better with the symptoms of the disease and its treatment.

What roles do psychologists play in the prevention of HIV/AIDS and treatment of people with HIV? Our behavior patterns influence our risk for contracting HIV. Psychologists have become involved in the prevention and treatment of AIDS because AIDS, like cancer, has devastating psychological effects on victims, their families and friends, and society at large, and because AIDS can be prevented through reducing risky behavior.

Scoring Key for "The College Life Stress Inventory." Though we have no national norms by which to compare your score, the test developers obtained an average (mean) score of 1,247 based on a sample of 257 introductory psychology students. About two of three students obtained scores in the range of 806 to 1,688.

Computing your total score helps you gauge how you compare to the students in the original study sample in terms of your overall stress level. Bear in mind, however, that the same level of stress may affect different people differently. Your ability to cope with stress depends on many factors, including your coping skills and the level of social support you have available. If you are experiencing a high level of stress, you may wish to examine the sources of stress in your life. Perhaps you can reduce the level of stress you experience or learn more effective ways of handling the sources of stress you can't avoid.

Scoring Key for "The Life Orientation Test." To arrive at your total score for the test, first *reverse* your score on items 3, 8, 9, and 12. That is,

4 is changed to 0
3 is changed to 1
2 remains the same
1 is changed to 3
0 is changed to 4

Now add the numbers of items 1, 3, 4, 5, 8, 9, 11, and 12. (Items 2, 6, 7, and 10 are "fillers"; that is, your responses are not scored as part of the test.) Your total score can vary from 0 to 32.

Scheier and Carver (1985) provide the following norms for the test, based on administration to 357 undergraduate men and 267 undergraduate women. The average (mean) score for men was 21.03 (standard deviation = 4.56), and the mean score for women was 21.41 (standard deviation = 5.22). All in all, approximately 2 out of 3 undergraduates obtained scores between 16 and 26. Scores above 26 may be considered quite optimistic, and scores below 16 quite pessimistic. Scores between 16 and 26 are within a broad average range, and higher scores within this range are relatively more optimistic.

Scoring Key for "Are You Type A?" "Yes" answers suggest a Type A behavior pattern—and the more items to which you answered "yes," the stronger your TABP. You should have little difficulty determining whether you are strongly or moderately inclined toward this behavior pattern—that is, if you are honest with yourself.

KEY TERMS

health psychologist *(p. 137)*
stress *(p. 138)*
stressor *(p. 138)*
adjustment disorder *(p. 138)*
endocrine system *(p. 140)*
hormones *(p. 140)*
steroids *(p. 140)*
immune system *(p. 140)*

general adaptation syndrome (GAS) *(p. 143)*
alarm reaction *(p. 143)*
fight-or-flight reaction *(p. 143)*
resistance stage *(p. 144)*
exhaustion stage *(p. 144)*
acculturative stress *(p. 146)*
emotion-focused coping *(p. 149)*
problem-focused coping *(p. 149)*

self-efficacy expectations *(p. 150)*
psychological hardiness *(p. 150)*
psychosomatic *(p. 153)*
biofeedback training (BFT) *(p. 154)*
cardiovascular disease *(p. 155)*
Type A behavior pattern (TABP) *(p. 155)*

WEB TOOLS

The companion website offers tools to enrich your learning experience and help you succeed in class. Go to www.prenhall.com/nevid for the gateway to the following resources:

- **VIDEO** links to connect to the video case files on the companion CD-ROM. VIDEO icons in the margins of the chapter highlight the case examples included in the CD-ROM. You can also access the CD-ROM directly if you do not have a Web connection.

- **QUIZ** links to self-scoring quizzes corresponding to each section of the chapter. The quizzes help you review your knowledge of the content in each chapter.

- **WEB** links to direct you to related sites that enhance your learning of abnormal psychology.

Anxiety Disorders

"I" "I Felt Like I Was Going To Die Right Then And There"

I never experienced anything like this before. It happened while I was sitting in the car at a traffic light. I felt my heart beating furiously fast, like it was just going to explode. It just happened, for no reason. I started breathing really fast but couldn't get enough air. It was like I was suffocating and the car was closing in around me. I felt like I was going to die right then and there. I was trembling and sweating heavily. I thought I was having a heart attack. I felt this incredible urge to escape, to just get out of the car and get away.

I somehow managed to pull the car over to the side of the road but just sat there waiting for the feelings to pass. I told myself if I was going to die, then I was going to die. I didn't know whether I'd survive long enough to get help. Somehow—I can't say how—it just passed and I sat there a long time, wondering what had just happened to me. Just as suddenly as the panic overcame me, it was gone. My breathing slowed down and my heart stopped thumping in my chest. I was alive. I was not going to die. Not until the next time, anyway.

—"The Case of Michael," from the Author's Files

WHAT IS IT LIKE TO HAVE A PANIC ATTACK? PEOPLE TEND TO USE THE WORD *PANIC* loosely, as when they say, "I panicked when I couldn't find my keys." Clients in therapy often speak of having panic attacks, though what they describe often falls in a milder spectrum of anxiety reactions. During a true panic attack, like the one Michael describes, the level of anxiety rises to the point of sheer terror. Unless you have suffered one, it is difficult to appreciate just how intense panic attacks can be. People who suffer them describe them as the most frightening experiences of their lives. Panic attacks are a feature of a severe form of anxiety disorder called *panic disorder.*

There is much to be anxious about—our health, social relationships, examinations, careers, international relations, and the condition of the environment are but a few sources of possible concern. It is normal, even adaptive, to be somewhat anxious about these aspects of life. **Anxiety** is a generalized state of apprehension or foreboding. Anxiety is useful because it prompts us to seek regular medical checkups or motivates us to study for tests. Anxiety is therefore a normal response to threats, but anxiety becomes abnormal when its level is out of proportion to a threat, or when it seems to come out of the blue—that is, when it is not in response to environmental changes. In Michael's case, panic attacks began spontaneously, without any warning or trigger. This kind of maladaptive anxiety reaction, which can cause significant emotional distress or impair the person's ability to function, is labeled an **anxiety disorder.**

This chapter explores panic disorder and other major types of anxiety disorders: phobic disorders, generalized anxiety disorder, obsessive–compulsive disorder, and traumatic stress disorders. Anxiety, the common thread that connects these disorders, can be experienced in different ways, from the intense fear associated with a panic attack to the generalized sense of foreboding or worry that we find in generalized anxiety disorder.

Anxiety encompasses myriad physical features, cognitions, and behaviors, as shown in Table 6.1. Although people with anxiety disorders don't necessarily experience all of these features, it is easy to see why anxiety is distressing.

anxiety An emotional state characterized by physiological arousal, unpleasant feelings of tension, and a sense of apprehension or foreboding.

anxiety disorders A class of psychological disorders characterized by excessive or maladaptive anxiety reactions.

TABLE 6.1

Some Features of Anxiety

Physical Features of Anxiety	Behavioral Features of Anxiety
Jumpiness, jitteriness	Avoidance behavior
Trembling or shaking of the hands or limbs	Clinging, dependent behavior
Sensations of a tight band around the forehead	Agitated behavior
Tightness in the pit of the stomach or chest	**Cognitive Features of Anxiety**
Heavy perspiration	Worrying about something
Sweaty palms	A nagging sense of dread or apprehension about the future
Light-headedness or faintness	Belief that something dreadful is going to happen, with no clear cause
Dryness in the mouth or throat	Preoccupation with bodily sensations
Difficulty talking	Keen awareness of bodily sensations
Difficulty catching one's breath	Feeling threatened by people or events that are normally of little or no concern
Shortness of breath or shallow breathing	Fear of losing control
Heart pounding or racing	Fear of inability to cope with one's problems
Tremulousness in one's voice	Thinking the world is caving in
Cold fingers or limbs	Thinking things are getting out of hand
Dizziness	Thinking things are swimming by too rapidly to take charge of them
Weakness or numbness	Worrying about every little thing
Difficulty swallowing	Thinking the same disturbing thought over and over
A "lump in the throat"	Thinking that one must flee crowded places or else pass out
Stiffness of the neck or back	Finding one's thoughts jumbled or confused
Choking or smothering sensations	Not being able to shake off nagging thoughts
Cold, clammy hands	Thinking that one is going to die, even when one's doctor finds nothing medically wrong
Upset stomach or nausea	Worrying that one is going to be left alone
Hot or cold spells	Difficulty concentrating or focusing one's thoughts
Frequent urination	
Feeling flushed	
Diarrhea	
Feeling irritable or "on edge"	

HISTORICAL PERSPECTIVES ON ANXIETY DISORDERS

The anxiety disorders, along with dissociative disorders and somatoform disorders (see Chapter 7), were classified as neuroses throughout most of the 19th century. The term *neurosis* derives from roots meaning "an abnormal or diseased condition of the nervous system." The Scottish physician William Cullen coined it in the 18th century. As the derivation implies, it was assumed neurosis had biological origins. It was seen as an affliction of the nervous system.

At the beginning of the 20th century, Cullen's organic assumptions were largely replaced by Sigmund Freud's psychodynamic views. Freud maintained that neurotic behavior stems from the threatened emergence of unacceptable anxiety-evoking ideas into conscious awareness. According to Freud, anxiety disorders, somatoform disorders, and dissociative disorders all represent ways in which the ego attempts to defend itself against anxiety. Freud's views on the *etiology*, or origins of these problems, united the disorders as neuroses. Freud's concepts were so widely accepted in the early 1900s that they formed the basis for the classification systems found in the first two editions of the *Diagnostic and Statistical Manual of Mental Disorders (DSM)*.

Since 1980, the *DSM* has not contained a category termed *neuroses*. The present *DSM* is based on similarities in observable behavior and distinctive features rather than on causal assumptions. Many clinicians continue to use the terms *neurosis* and *neurotic* in the manner in which Freud described them, however. Some clinicians use the term "neuroses" to group milder behavioral problems in which people maintain relatively good contact with reality. "Psychoses," such as schizophrenia, are typified by loss of touch with reality and by the appearance of bizarre behavior, beliefs, and hallucinations. Anxiety is not limited to the diagnostic categories traditionally termed "neuroses," moreover. People with adjustment problems, depression, and psychotic disorders may also encounter problems with anxiety.

The present version of the *DSM* system, the *DSM-IV*, recognizes the following specific types of anxiety disorders: panic disorder; phobic disorders, such as specific phobia, social phobia, and agoraphobia; generalized anxiety disorder; obsessive–compulsive disorder; and acute and posttraumatic stress disorders. Table 6.2 lists the diagnostic features of anxiety disorders. The anxiety disorders are not mutually exclusive. People frequently meet diagnostic criteria for more than one of them. Let us now consider the major forms of anxiety disorder in terms of their features or symptoms, causes, and ways of treating them.

TABLE 6.2

Diagnostic Features of Anxiety Disorders

Agoraphobia	Fear and avoidance of places or situations in which it would be difficult or embarrassing to escape, or in which help might be unavailable in the event of a panic attack or panic-type symptoms.
Panic Disorder Without Agoraphobia	Occurrence of recurrent, unexpected panic attacks in which there is persistent concern about them but without accompanying agoraphobia.
Panic Disorder with Agoraphobia	Occurrence of recurrent, unexpected panic attacks in which there is persistent concern about them and accompanying agoraphobia.
Generalized Anxiety Disorder	Persistent and excessive levels of anxiety and worry that is not tied to any particular object, situation, or activity.
Specific Phobia	Clinically significant anxiety relating to exposure to specific objects or situations, often accompanied by avoidance of these stimuli.
Social Phobia	Clinically significant anxiety relating to exposure to social situations or performance situations, often accompanied by avoidance of these situations.
Obsessive–Compulsive Disorder	Recurrent obsessions and/or compulsions.
Posttraumatic Stress Disorder	The reexperiencing of a highly traumatic event accompanied by heightened arousal and avoidance of stimuli associated with the event.
Acute Stress Disorder	Features similar to those of posttraumatic stress disorder but limited to the days and weeks following exposure to the trauma.

Note: All of these disorders are coded on Axis I in the *DSM-IV.*
Source: Adapted from *DSM-IV-TR* (APA, 2000).

panic disorder A type of anxiety disorder characterized by repeated episodes of intense anxiety or panic.

agoraphobia Excessive, irrational fear of open or public places.

Panic. Panic attacks have stronger physical components—especially cardiovascular symptoms—than other types of anxiety reactions.

PANIC DISORDER

Panic disorder is characterized by the occurrence of repeated, unexpected *panic attacks*. Panic attacks are intense anxiety reactions accompanied by physical symptoms such as a pounding heart; rapid respiration, shortness of breath, or difficulty breathing; heavy perspiration; and weakness or dizziness (Glass, 2000). There is a stronger bodily component to panic attacks than to other forms of anxiety. The attacks are accompanied by feelings of sheer terror and a sense of imminent danger or impending doom and by an urge to escape the situation. They are usually accompanied by thoughts of losing control, going crazy, or dying.

People who experience panic attacks tend to be keenly aware of changes in their heart rates (Richards, Edgar, & Gibbon, 1996). They often believe they are having a heart attack even though there is nothing wrong with their hearts. But because the symptoms of panic attacks can mimic those of heart attacks or even severe allergic reactions, a thorough medical evaluation should be performed.

As in the case of Michael, panic attacks began suddenly and spontaneously, without any warning or clear trigger. The attack builds to a peak of intensity within 10 to 15 minutes (USDHHS, 1999a). Attacks usually last for minutes, but can extend to hours and are associated with a strong urge to escape the situation in which they occur. For the diagnosis of panic disorder to be made, there must be the presence of recurrent panic attacks that begin unexpectedly—attacks that are not triggered by specific objects or situations. They seem to come out of the blue. Although the first attacks occur spontaneously or unexpectedly, over time they may become associated with certain situations or cues, such as entering a crowded department store or boarding a train or airplane. The person may associate these situations with panic attacks in the past or may perceive them as difficult to escape from in the event of another attack.

People often describe panic attacks as the worst experiences of their lives. Their coping abilities are overwhelmed. They may feel they must flee. If flight seems useless, they may freeze. There is a tendency to cling to others for help or support. Some people with panic attacks fear going out alone. Recurrent panic attacks may become so difficult to cope with that sufferers become suicidal. In many cases, people who experience panic attacks limit their activities to avoid places in which they fear attacks may occur or they are cut off from their usual supports. Consequently, panic disorder often leads to **agoraphobia**—an excessive fear of being in public places in which escape may be difficult or help unavailable (Glass, 2000).

Table 6.3 lists the diagnostic features of panic attacks. Not all of these features need to be present. Not all panic attacks are signs of panic disorder; about 10% of otherwise healthy people may experience an isolated attack in a given year (USDHHS, 1999a). For a diagnosis of panic disorder to be made, the person must have experienced repeated, unexpected panic attacks, and at least one of the attacks must be followed by one of the following: (a) at least a month of persistent fear of subsequent attacks; (b) worry about the implications or consequences of the attack (e.g., fear of losing one's mind or "going crazy" or having a heart attack); or (c) significant change in behavior (e.g., refusing to leave the house or venture into public for fear of having another attack) (APA, 2000). An estimated 1% to 4% of the population are affected by panic disorder at some point in their lives (APA, 2000; USDHHS, 1999a).

Panic disorder usually begins in late adolescence through the mid-30s (APA, 2000). Women are about twice as likely to develop panic disorder as men (USDHHS, 1999a) (see Figure 6.1). What little we know about the long-term course of panic disorder suggests it tends to follow a chronic course that waxes and wanes in severity over time (Ehlers, 1995).

TABLE 6.3

Diagnostic Features of Panic Attacks

A panic attack involves an episode of intense fear or discomfort in which at least four of the following features develop suddenly and reach a peak within 10 minutes:

1. Heart palpitations, pounding heart, tachycardia (rapid heart rate)

2. Sweating

3. Trembling or shaking

4. Shortness of breath or smothering sensations

5. Choking sensations

6. Chest pains or discomfort

7. Feelings of nausea or other signs of abdominal distress

8. Feelings of dizziness, unsteadiness, light-headedness, or faintness

9. Feelings of strangeness or unreality about one's surroundings (derealization) or detachment from oneself (depersonalization)

10. Fear of losing control or going crazy

11. Fear of dying

12. Numbness or tingling sensations

13. Chills or hot flushes

Source: Adapted from the *DSM-IV-TR* (APA, 2000).

Theoretical Perspectives

The prevailing view of panic disorder reflects a combination of cognitive and biological factors, of misattributions (misperceptions of underlying causes) on the one hand and physiological reactions on the other. Like Michael, who feared that his physical symptoms were signs of a beginning heart attack, panic-prone individuals tend to misattribute minor changes in internal bodily sensations to underlying dire causes. For example, internal sensations such as momentary dizziness, light-headedness, or heart palpitations may be taken as signs of an impending heart attack, loss of control, or "going crazy." Perceiving these bodily sensations as dire threats induces anxiety, which is accompanied by activation of the sympathetic nervous system. Under control of the sympathetic nervous system, the adrenal glands release the stress hormones epinephrine (adrenaline) and norepinephrine (noradrenaline). These hormones intensify physical sensations by inducing accelerated heart rate, rapid breathing, and sweating. These changes in bodily sensations, in turn, become misinterpreted as evidence of an impending panic attack or, worse, as a catastrophe in the making ("My God, I'm having a heart attack!"). Misattributions of bodily sensations further reinforce perceptions of threat, which further heightens anxiety, leading to yet more anxiety-related bodily symptoms and more catastrophic misinterpretations in a vicious cycle that can quickly spiral into a full-fledged panic attack.

The changes in bodily sensations that trigger a panic attack may result from many factors, such as unrecognized *hyperventilation* (rapid breathing), exertion, changes in temperature, or reactions to certain

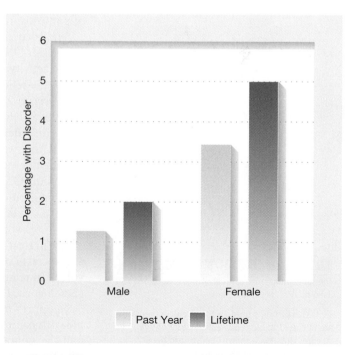

FIGURE 6.1 Prevalence of panic disorder by gender.
Panic disorder affects nearly two times as many women as men.
Source. National Comorbidity Survey (Kessler et al., 1994).

drugs or medications. Or they may be fleeting, normally occurring changes in bodily states that typically go unnoticed. But in panic-prone individuals, these bodily cues may be misattributed to dire causes, setting in motion a vicious cycle that can bring on a full-fledged attack.

Why are some people prone to develop panic disorder? Here again, a combination of biological and cognitive factors come into play.

Biological Factors Evidence suggests that genetic factors are at work in explaining proneness to panic disorder (Gorman et al., 2000; Hettema, Neale, & Kendler, 2001). Bear in mind, however, that genes can create a predisposition or likelihood, not a certainty, that a psychological disorder will develop under certain conditions (Straub et al., 2002). Other factors are also involved, especially cognitive factors. For example, people with panic disorder have a greater tendency to misinterpret bodily sensations as signs of impending catastrophe than do people without anxiety disorders or those with other types of anxiety disorders (Clark et al., 1997). Studies also show that panic-prone people have greater awareness of, and sensitivity to, their own internal physiological cues, such as heart palpitations (Pauli et al., 1997; Richards, Edgar, & Gibbon, 1996).

The strong physical components of panic disorder have led some theorists to speculate that the biological underpinnings of panic attacks involve dysfunctional alarm system in the brain (Glass, 2000). Psychiatrist Donald Klein (1994) proposed that a defect in the brain's respiratory alarm system leads to a bodily overreaction in panic-prone individuals to cues of suffocation, perhaps involving mild changes in the levels of carbon dioxide in the blood. In Klein's model, cues of suffocation from hyperventilation or other causes trigger a respiratory alarm, which in turn produces the cascading sensations involved in the classic panic attack: shortness of breath, smothering sensations, dizziness, faintness, increased heart rate or palpitations, trembling, sensations of hot or cold flashes, and feelings of nausea. Klein's intriguing proposal has met with some support in the professional community (e.g., McNally et al., 1995; Taylor & Rachman, 1994), as well as some dissenting voices (e.g., Ley, 1997). Other researchers report that episodes of traumatic suffocation (near-drownings or near-chokings) may play a role in the development of panic disorder in some patients (Bouwer & Stein, 1997).

We also need to consider the role of neurotransmitters, especially *gamma-aminobutyric acid* (GABA). GABA is an *inhibitory* neurotransmitter, which means that it tones down excess activity in the nervous system and helps quell stress responses (USDHHS, 1999a). When the action of GABA is inadequate, neurons can fire excessively, possibly bringing about seizures. In less-dramatic cases, inadequate action of GABA may heighten states of anxiety. This view of the role of GABA is supported by findings that people with panic disorder show low levels of GABA in some parts of the brain (Goddard et al., 2001). Also, we know that the group of antianxiety drugs called *benzodiazepines,* which include the well-known Valium and Xanax, make GABA receptors more sensitive, thus enhancing GABA's calming (inhibitory) effects (Zorumski & Isenberg, 1991).

Irregularities or dysfunctions in serotonin and norepinephrine receptors in the brain are also implicated in anxiety disorders (Southwick et al., 1997). This may explain why antidepressant drugs that affect these neurotransmitter systems often have beneficial effects in treating some types of anxiety disorders, including panic disorder (Glass, 2000) and social phobia (Van Ameringen et al., 2001). Investigators also suspect that genes involved in regulation of serotonin may play a role in determining anxiety-related traits (Lesch et al., 1996).

Support for a biological basis of panic disorder is found in studies showing that people with panic disorder are more likely than nonpatient controls to experience anxious, panicky symptoms in response to biological challenges such as infusion of the chemical *sodium lactate* or manipulation of carbon dioxide (CO_2) levels in the blood. CO_2 levels may be changed either via intentional hyperventilation (which reduces levels of CO_2 in the blood) or by inhalation of carbon dioxide (which increases CO_2 levels) (e.g., Gorman et al., 2001; Kent et al., 2001; Zvolensky & Eifert, 2001).

TRUTH or FICTION? *REVISITED*

The same drugs used to treat schizophrenia are also used to control panic attacks.

☑ **FALSE.** Drugs used to treat schizophrenia are not used to treat panic disorder. However, antidepressants have shown therapeutic benefits in helping to control panic attacks.

Cognitive Factors In referring to the anxiety facing the nation in the wake of the economic depression of the 1930s, President Franklin Roosevelt said in his 1932 inaugural address, "We have nothing to fear but fear itself." These words echo today in research examining whether the fear of fear itself, or *anxiety sensitivity,* plays a role in determining proneness to anxiety disorders, especially panic disorder (Zinbarg et al., 2001; Zvolensky et al., 2003). People with high levels of anxiety sensitivity fear that their emotions or the associated bodily states of arousal will get out of control, leading to harmful consequences, such as having a heart attack. They may be prone to panic whenever they experience bodily signs of anxiety, such as a racing heart or shortness of breath, because they take these symptoms to be signs of an impending catastrophe, such as a heart attack.

Anxiety sensitivity has emerged as an important risk factor in predicting the development of panic disorder (Lilienfeld, 1997). In one study, researchers used an anxiety sensitivity measure to predict which military recruits would be most likely to panic during a highly stressful period of basic training (Schmidt, Lerew, & Jackson, 1997). One in 5 recruits who scored in the top 10% on a measure of anxiety sensitivity experienced a panic attack, as compared to only 6% of the other recruits.

In other study, investigators explored the relationship between anxiety sensitivity and panic attacks in high school students (Weems et al., 2002). Students who had either high, stable levels of anxiety sensitivity or showed a pattern of escalating anxiety sensitivity were more likely than those with low, stable anxiety sensitivity to experience a panic attack.

Though investigators find linkages between anxiety sensitivity and proneness to panic attacks, the causal nature of the connection remains to be studied. It may turn out that anxiety sensitivity influences proneness to panic attacks, or that panic attacks influence the development of anxiety sensitivity. Most probably, however, the relationship is reciprocal, with anxiety sensitivity and panic attacks both influencing each other.

Ethnicity also plays a role in anxiety sensitivity. In the study of high school students, Asian and Hispanic students reported higher levels of anxiety sensitivity on the average than did Caucasian adolescents (Weems et al., 2002). Also, anxiety sensitivity was less strongly connected to panic attacks in the minority groups than in the Caucasian group. Other investigators find higher levels of anxiety sensitivity among American Indian and Alaska Native college students than among Caucasian college students (Zvolensky et al. 2001). These findings remind us to be mindful of the need to consider ethnic differences when exploring the roots of abnormal behavior.

Cognitive factors may also account for oversensitivity of panic-prone people to biological challenges, such as manipulation of the carbon dioxide levels in the blood. These challenges produce intense physical sensations that panic-prone people may misinterpret as signs of an impending heart attack or loss of control (McNally & Eke, 1996; Schmidt, Trakowski, & Staab, 1997). Perhaps these misinterpretations—not underlying biological sensitivities per se—are responsible for inducing panic. Supportive evidence for the cognitivist perspective comes from a study showing that cognitive-behavioral therapy that focused on changing faulty interpretations of bodily sensations eliminated CO_2–induced panic in a majority of panic disorder patients (Schmidt, Trakowski, & Staab, 1997). In another study, having a helper or supportive person nearby during a CO_2 infusion reduced panicky symptoms in panic-prone individuals to the same level as normal controls (Carter et al., 1995). Having a supportive person available may enable the panic-prone person to appraise the situation cognitively as less threatening, which may avert the spiraling of anxiety that leads to panic attacks. However, simply receiving reassurance about the safety of the CO_2 inhalation procedure does not seem to reduce the rate of panic (Welkowitz et al., 1999).

The fact that panic attacks often seem to come out of the blue seems to support the belief that the attacks are biologically triggered. However, the cues that set off many panic attacks may be internal, involving changes in bodily sensations, rather than external. Changes in physical cues, combined with catastrophic thinking, may lead to a spiraling of anxiety that culminates in a full-blown panic attack.

Panic Disorder:
The Case of Jerry
"I was driving on an interstate . . . And all of a sudden I got this fear."

Treatment Approaches

The most widely used forms of treatment for panic disorder are drug therapy and cognitive-behavioral therapy. Drugs commonly used to treat depression, called *antidepressant drugs,* also have antianxiety and antipanic effects (Glass, 2000; USDHHS, 1999a). Antidepressants help counter anxiety by normalizing the activity of neurotransmitters in the brain. Some antidepressants in common use for treating panic disorder include the tricyclics *imipramine* (brand name Tofranil) and *clomipramine* (brand name Anafranil) and the SSRIs *paroxetine* (brand name Paxil) and *sertraline* (brand name Zoloft). However, troublesome side effects may occur, such as heavy sweating and heart palpitations, which leads many patients to prematurely stop using the drugs. The high-potency tranquilizer *alprazolam* (Xanax), a type of benzodiazepine, is also helpful in treating panic disorder, social phobia, and generalized anxiety disorder (Barlow et al., 2000; Gould et al., 1997; van Balkom et al., 1997).

A potential problem with drug therapy is that patients may attribute clinical improvement to the drugs and not their own resources. Nor do such drugs produce cures. Relapses are common after patients discontinue the medication (Spiegel & Bruce, 1997). Reemergence of panic is likely unless cognitive-behavioral treatment is provided to help panic patients modify their cognitive overreactions to their bodily sensations (Clark, 1986).

Cognitive-behavioral therapists use a variety of techniques in treating panic disorder, including coping skills for handling panic attacks, breathing retraining and relaxation training to reduce states of heightened bodily arousal, and exposure to situations linked to panic attacks and bodily cues associated with panicky symptoms (Schmidt et al., 2000; Wilson, 1997). The therapist may help clients think differently about changes in bodily cues, such as sensations of dizziness or heart palpitations. By recognizing that these cues are fleeting sensations rather than signs of an impending heart attack or other catastrophe, clients learn to cope with them without panicking. Clients learn to replace catastrophizing thoughts and self-statements ("I'm having a heart attack") with calming, rational alternatives ("Calm down. These are panicky feelings that will soon pass."). Panic attack sufferers may also be reassured by having a medical examination to ensure that they are physically healthy and their physical symptoms are not signs of heart disease.

Breathing retraining is a technique that aims at restoring a normal level of carbon dioxide in the blood by having clients breathe slowly and deeply from the abdomen, avoiding the shallow, rapid breathing that leads to breathing off too much carbon dioxide. In some treatment programs, people with panic disorder purposefully hyperventilate in the controled setting of the treatment clinic to discover for themselves the relationship between breathing off too much carbon dioxide and cardiovascular sensations. Through these firsthand experiences, they learn to calm themselves down and cope with these sensations rather than overreacting. Some commonly used elements in cognitive-behavioral therapy (CBT) for panic disorder are shown in Table 6.4.

Michael, whom we introduced at the beginning of the chapter, was 30 when he suffered his first panic attack. Michael first sought a medical consultation with a cardiologist to rule out any underlying heart condition. He was relieved when he received a clean bill of health. Even though the attacks continued for a time, Michael learned to gain a better sense of control over them. Here he describes what the process was like:

The Case of Michael

For me, it came down to not fearing them. Knowing that I was not going to die gave me confidence that I could handle them. When I began to feel an attack coming on, I would practice relaxation and talk myself through the attack. It really seemed to take the steam out of them. At first I was having an attack every week or so, but after a few months, they whittled down to about one a month, and then they were gone completely. Maybe it was how I was coping with them, or maybe they just disappeared as mysteriously as they began. I'm just glad they're gone.

—*From the Author's Files*

TABLE 6.4

Elements of Cognitive–Behavioral Programs for Treatment of Panic Disorder

Self-monitoring	Keeping a log of panic attacks to help determine situational stimuli that might trigger them.
Exposure	A program of gradual exposure to situations in which panic attacks have occurred. During exposure trials, the person engages in self-relaxation and rational self-talk to prevent anxiety from spiraling out of control. In some programs, participants learn to tolerate changes in bodily sensations associated with panic attacks by experiencing these sensations within a controlled setting of the treatment clinic. The person may be spun around in a chair to induce feelings of dizziness, learning in the process that such sensations are not dangerous or signs of imminent harm.
Development of coping responses	Developing coping skills to interrupt the vicious cycle in which overreactions to anxiety cues or cardiovascular sensations culminate in panic attacks. Behavioral methods focus on deep, regular breathing and relaxation training. Cognitive methods focus on modifying catastrophic misinterpretations of bodily sensations. Breathing retraining may be used to help the individual avoid hyperventilation during panic attacks

Sources: Adapted from Craske, Brown, & Barlow, 1991; Rapee, 1987; Turovsky & Barlow, 1995, and other sources.

A number of well-controlled studies attest to the effectiveness of CBT in treating panic disorder (Barlow et al., 2000; Kenardy et al, 2003; Overholser, 2000; Sanderson & Rego, 2000; Tsao et al., 2002). For instance, a recent study shows that nearly 90% of panic patients treated with CBT were free of panic attacks when evaluated at a follow-up assessment (Stuart et al., 2000). Despite the common belief that panic disorder is best treated with psychiatric drugs, CBT produces about as good short-term results and even better long-term results than pharmacological approaches (Barlow et al., 2000; Otto, Pollack, & Maki, 2000). Why does CBT produce longer-lasting results? The answer seems to be that CBT helps people learn skills they can use once treatment has ended (Glass, 2000). Taking psychiatric drugs can help quell panicky symptoms, but does not help patients develop any new skills they can use once the drugs are withdrawn. However, the effectiveness of CBT may be enhanced in some cases by the addition of antidepressant drugs (van Balkom et al., 1997).

A CLOSER LOOK
Coping with a Panic Attack

People who have panic attacks usually feel their hearts pounding such that they are overwhelmed and unable to cope. They typically feel an urge to flee the situation as quickly as possible. If escape is impossible, however, they may become immobilized and "freeze" until the attack dissipates. What can you do if you suffer a panic attack or an intense anxiety reaction? Here are a few coping responses.

- Don't let your breathing get out of hand. Breathe slowly and deeply.
- Try breathing into a paper bag. The carbon dioxide in the bag may help you calm down by restoring a more optimal balance between oxygen and carbon dioxide.
- Talk yourself down: Tell yourself to relax. Tell yourself you're not going to die. Tell yourself no matter how painful the attack is, it is likely to pass soon.

- Find someone to help you through the attack. Telephone someone you know and trust. Talk about anything at all until you regain control.
- Don't fall into the trap of making yourself housebound to avert future attacks.
- If you are uncertain about whether or not sensations such as pain or tightness in the chest have physical causes, seek immediate medical assistance. Even if you suspect your attack may "only" be one of anxiety, it is safer to have a medical evaluation than to diagnose yourself.

You need not suffer recurrent panic attacks and fears about loss of control. If your attacks are persistent or frightening, consult a professional. When in doubt, see a professional. ∎

PHOBIC DISORDERS

phobia An excessive, irrational fear.

The word **phobia** derives from the Greek *phobos*, meaning "fear." The concepts of fear and anxiety are closely related. *Fear* is the feeling of anxiety and agitation in response to a threat. Phobic disorders are persistent fears of objects or situations that are disproportionate to the threats they pose. To experience a sense of gripping fear when your car is about to go out of control is normal, because you are really in danger. In phobic disorders, however, the fear exceeds any reasonable appraisal of danger. People with a driving phobia, for example, might become fearful even when they are driving well below the speed limit on a sunny day and an uncrowded highway. Or they might be so afraid that they will not drive or even ride in a car. People with phobic disorders are not out of touch with reality; they generally recognize their fears are excessive or unreasonable.

A curious thing about phobias is that they usually involve fears of the ordinary events in life, such as taking an elevator or driving on a highway, not the extraordinary. Phobias can become disabling when they interfere with such daily tasks as taking buses, planes, or trains; driving; shopping; or leaving the house.

Types of Phobias

Different types of phobias usually appear at different ages, as noted in Table 6.5. The ages of onset appear to reflect levels of cognitive development and life experiences. Fears of animals are frequent subjects of children's fantasies, for example. Agoraphobia, in contrast, often follows the development of panic attacks beginning in adulthood.

Here let us consider three types of phobic disorders classified within the *DSM* system: *specific phobia*, *social phobia*, and *agoraphobia*.

specific phobia A phobia that is specific to a particular object or situation.

Specific Phobias A **specific phobia** is a persistent, excessive fear of a specific object or situation, such as fear of heights (*acrophobia*), fear of enclosed spaces (*claustrophobia*), or fear of small animals such as mice or snakes and various other "creepy-crawlies." The person experiences high levels of fear and physiological arousal when encountering the phobic object, which prompts strong urges to avoid or escape the situation or avoid the feared stimulus, as in the following case.

> ### Carla Passes the Bar but not the Courthouse Staircase: A Case of Specific Phobia
>
> *Passing the bar exam was a significant milestone in Carla's life, but it left her terrified at the thought of entering the county courthouse. She wasn't afraid of encountering a hostile judge or losing a case, but of climbing the stairs leading to a second floor promenade where the courtrooms were located. Carla, 27, suffered from acrophobia, or fear of heights. "It's funny, you know," Carla told her therapist. "I have no problem flying or looking out the window of a plane at 30,000 feet. But the escalator at the mall throws me into a tailspin. It's just any situation where I could possibly fall, like over the side of a balcony or banister."*
>
> *People with anxiety disorders try to avoid situations or objects they fear. Carla scouted out the courthouse before she was scheduled to appear. She was relieved to find a service elevator in the rear of the building she could use instead of the stairs. She told her fellow attorneys with whom she was presenting the case that she suffered from a heart condition and couldn't climb stairs. Not suspecting the real problem, one of the attorneys said, "This is great. I never knew this elevator existed. Thanks for finding it."*
>
> —*From the Authors' Files*

(A)

(B)

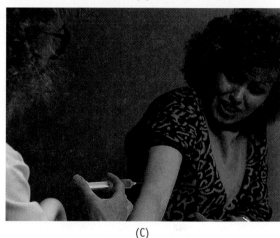

(C)

Three types of phobic disorder. The man in photo A has a specific phobia for dogs, a common phobia that may have an evolutionary origin. The young woman in photo B would like to join others but keeps to herself because of social phobia, an intense fear of social criticism and rejection. The woman in photo C has a specific phobia for injections. She does not fear the potential pain of the injection; rather, she cannot tolerate the idea of the needle sticking her.

To rise to the level of a diagnosable disorder, the phobia must significantly affect the person's lifestyle or functioning or cause significant distress. You may have a fear of snakes, but unless your fear interferes with your daily life or causes you significant emotional distress, it would not warrant a diagnosis of phobic disorder.

Specific phobias often begin in childhood. Many children develop passing fears of specific objects or situations. Some, however, go on to develop chronic clinically significant phobias (Merckelbach et al., 1996). Claustrophobia seems to develop later than most other specific phobias, with a mean age of onset of 20 years (see Table 6.5).

Specific phobias are among the most common psychological disorders, affecting about 7% to 11% of the general population at some point in their lives (APA, 2000). Specific phobias tend to persist for years or decades unless they are treated successfully (USDHHS, 1999a). Women are about twice as likely to develop specific phobias as men (APA, 2000). This gender difference may to some degree reflect cultural factors that socialize women to be dependent on men for protection from threats in the environment. Examiners also need to be aware of cultural factors when making diagnostic judgments. Fears of magic or spirits are common in some cultures and should not be considered a sign of a phobic disorder unless the fear is excessive in the culture in which it occurs and leads to significant emotional distress or impaired functioning (APA, 2000).

TABLE 6.5

Typical Age of Onset for Various Phobias

	No. of Cases	Mean Age of Onset
Animal phobia	50	7
Blood phobia	40	9
Injection phobia	59	8
Dental phobia	60	12
Social phobia	80	16
Claustrophobia	40	20
Agoraphobia	100	28

Source: Adapted from Öst (1987, 1992).

People with specific phobias will often recognize that their fears are exaggerated or unfounded. But they still are afraid, as in the case of this young woman whose fear of medical injections almost prevented her from getting married.

"This Will Sound Crazy, But . . ."

This will sound crazy, but I wouldn't get married because I couldn't stand the idea of getting the blood test. [Blood tests for syphilis were required at the time.] I finally worked up the courage to ask my doctor if he would put me out with ether or barbiturates—taken by pills—so that I could have the blood test. At first he was incredulous. Then he became sort of sympathetic but said that he couldn't risk putting me under any kind of general anesthesia just to draw some blood. I asked him if he would consider faking the report, but he said that administrative procedures made that impossible.

Then he got me really going. He said that getting tested for marriage was likely to be one of my small life problems. He told me about minor medical problems that could arise and make it necessary for blood to be drawn, or to have an IV in my arm, so his message was I should try to come to grips with my fear. I nearly fainted while he was talking about these things, so he gave it up.

The story has half a happy ending. We finally got married in [a state] where we found out they no longer insisted on blood tests. But if I develop one of those problems the doctor was talking about, or if I need a blood test for some other reason, even if it's life-threatening, I really don't know what I'll do. But maybe if I faint when they're going to [draw blood], I won't know about it anyway, right? . . .

People have me wrong, you know. They think I'm scared of the pain. I don't like pain—I'm not a masochist—but pain has nothing to do with it. You could pinch my arm till I turned black and blue and I'd tolerate it. I wouldn't like it, but I wouldn't start shaking and sweating and faint on you. But even if I didn't feel the needle at all—just the knowledge that it was in me is what I couldn't take.

—From the Authors' Files

social phobia Excessive fear of social interactions or situations.

Social Phobia (Social Anxiety Disorder):
The Case of Steve
"I imagine that people are watching me . . . stumble."

Social Phobia It is not abnormal to experience some fear of social situations such as dating, attending parties or social gatherings, or giving a talk or presentation to a class or group. Yet people with **social phobia** (also called *social anxiety disorder*) have such an intense fear of social situations that they may avoid them altogether or endure them only with great distress. Underlying social phobia is an excessive fear of negative evaluations from others. People with social phobia fear doing or saying something humiliating or embarrassing. They may feel as if a thousand eyes are scrutinizing their every move. They tend to be severely critical of their social skills and become absorbed in evaluating their own performance when interacting with others. Some even experience full-fledged panic attacks in social situations.

Stage fright and speech anxiety are common types of social phobias. A random survey of some 500 residents of Winnipeg, Manitoba, found that about 1 in 3 had experienced excessive anxiety when speaking to a large audience, which had a detrimental impact on their lives (Stein, Walker, & Forde, 1996). People with social phobias may find excuses for declining social invitations. They may lunch at their desks to avoid socializing with coworkers. Or they may find themselves in social situations and attempt a quick escape at the first sign of anxiety. Relief from anxiety negatively reinforces escape behavior, but escape prevents people with phobias from learning to cope with fear-evoking situations more adaptively. Leaving the scene before the anxiety dissipates only strengthens the association between the social situation and anxiety. Some people with social phobia are unable to order food in a restaurant for fear the server or their companions might make fun of the foods they order or how they pronounce them. Others fear meeting new people and dating.

Social phobias can severely impede daily functioning and the quality of life (Liebowitz et al., 2000; Olfson et al., 2000; Stein & Kean, 2000). They may prevent people from completing educational goals, advancing in their careers, or even holding a job in which they need to interact with others. The greater the number of feared situations, the greater the level of impairment tends to be (Stein, Torgrud, & Walker, 2000). People with social phobias often turn to tranquilizers or try to "medicate" themselves with alcohol when preparing for social interactions (see Figure 6.2). In extreme cases, they may become so fearful of interacting with others that they become essentially housebound.

Estimates of the lifetime prevalence of social phobia range from 3% to 13% (APA, 2000). The disorder appears to be more common among women than men, perhaps because of the greater social or cultural pressures placed on young women to please others and earn their approval.

Social phobia typically begins in childhood or adolescence and is often associated with a history of shyness (USDHHS, 1999a). People with social phobia typically report they were shy as children (Stemberger et al., 1995). Consistent with the *diathesis-stress model,* shyness may represent a diathesis or predisposition that makes one more vulnerable to develop social phobia in the face of stressful experiences, such as traumatic social encounters (e.g., being embarrassed in front of others). Once social phobia develops, it typically follows a chronic and persistent course throughout life.

Agoraphobia The word *agoraphobia* is derived from Greek words meaning "fear of the marketplace," which suggests a fear of being out in open, busy areas. People with agoraphobia develop a fear of places and situations from which it might be difficult or embarrassing to escape in the event of panicky symptoms or a full-fledged panic attack or of situations in which help may be unavailable if such problems should occur. People with agoraphobia may fear shopping in crowded stores; walking through crowded streets; crossing a bridge; traveling on a bus, train, or car; eating in restaurants; or even leaving the house. They may structure their lives around avoiding exposure to fearful situations and in some cases become housebound for months or even years, even to the extent of being unable to venture outside to mail a letter. Agoraphobia has the potential of becoming the most incapacitating type of phobia.

Agoraphobia is more common in women than men (USDHHS, 1999a). Frequently it begins in late adolescence or early adulthood. Approximately 6% of adult Americans have experienced agoraphobia at some point in their lives (Eaton, Dryman, & Weissman, 1991). Agoraphobia may occur with or without an accompanying panic disorder. In *panic disorder with agoraphobia,* the person may live in fear of recurrent attacks and avoid public places where attacks have occurred or might occur. Because panic attacks

---

TRUTH or FICTION? *REVISITED*

Some people are so fearful of leaving their homes that they are unable to venture outside even to mail a letter.

☑ **TRUE.** Some people with agoraphobia become literally housebound and unable to venture outside even to mail a letter.

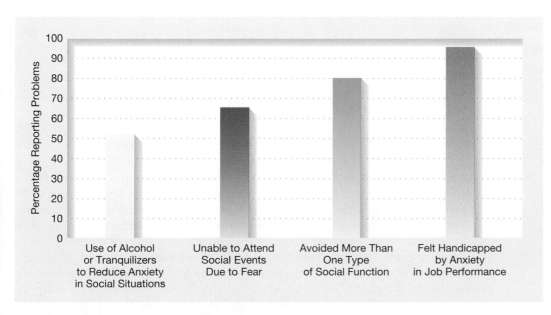

FIGURE 6.2 Percentages of people with social phobia reporting specific difficulties associated with their fears of social situations.
More than 90% of people with social phobia feel handicapped by anxiety in their jobs.
Source: Adapted from Turner & Beidel, 1989.

can descend from nowhere, some people restrict their activities for fear of making public spectacles of themselves or finding themselves without help. Others venture outside only with a companion. Still others forge ahead despite intense anxiety.

People with agoraphobia who have no history of panic disorder may experience mild panicky symptoms, such as dizziness, that lead them to avoid venturing away from places where they feel safe or secure. They too tend to become dependent on others for support. There is some evidence that people with agoraphobia without a history of panic disorder tend to function more poorly than do people who have both panic disorder and agoraphobia (Goisman et al., 1994). The following case of agoraphobia without a history of panic disorder illustrates the dependencies often associated with agoraphobia.

Helen: A Case of Agoraphobia

Helen, a 59-year-old widow, became increasingly agoraphobic after the death of her husband 3 years earlier. By the time she came for treatment, she was essentially housebound, refusing to leave her home except under the strongest urging of her daughter, Mary, age 32, and only if Mary accompanied her. Her daughter and 36-year-old son, Pete, did her shopping for her and took care of her other needs as best they could. However, the burden of caring for their mother, on top of their other responsibilities, was becoming too great for them to bear. They insisted that Helen begin treatment, and Helen begrudgingly acceded to their demands.

Helen was accompanied to her evaluation session by Mary. She was a frail-looking woman who entered the office clutching Mary's arm and insisted that Mary stay throughout the interview. Helen recounted that she had lost her husband and mother within 3 months of one another; her father had died 20 years earlier. Although she had never experienced a panic attack, she always considered herself an insecure, fearful person. Even so, she had been able to function in meeting the needs of her family until the deaths of her husband and mother left her feeling abandoned and alone. She had now become afraid of "just about everything" and was terrified of being out on her own, lest something bad would happen and she wouldn't be able to cope with it. Even at home, she was fearful that she might lose Mary and Pete. She needed continual reassurance from them that they too wouldn't abandon her.

—From the Authors' Files

Theoretical Perspectives

Theoretical approaches to understanding the development of phobias have a long history in psychology, beginning with the psychodynamic perspective.

Psychodynamic Perspectives From the psychodynamic perspective, anxiety is a danger signal that threatening impulses of a sexual or aggressive (murderous) nature are nearing the level of awareness. To fend off these threatening impulses, the ego mobilizes its defense mechanisms. In phobias, the Freudian defense mechanisms of *projection* and *displacement* come into play. A phobic reaction is a projection of the person's own threatening impulses onto the phobic object. For instance, a fear of knives or other sharp instruments may represent the projection of one's own destructive impulses onto the phobic object. The phobia serves a useful function. Avoiding contact with sharp instruments prevents these destructive wishes from becoming consciously realized or acted upon. The threatening impulses remain safely repressed. Similarly, people with acrophobia may harbor unconscious wishes to jump that are controlled by avoiding heights. The phobic object or situation symbolizes or represents these unconscious wishes or desires. The person is aware of the phobia, but not of the unconscious impulses that it symbolizes.

Learning Perspectives The classic learning perspective on phobias was offered by psychologist O. Hobart Mowrer (1948). Mowrer's **two-factor model** incorporated roles for both classical and operant conditioning in the development of phobias. The fear component of phobia is believed to be acquired through classical conditioning, as previously neutral objects and situations gain the capacity to evoke fear by being paired with noxious or aversive stimuli. A child who is frightened by a barking dog may acquire a phobia for dogs. A child who receives a painful injection may develop a phobia for hypodermic syringes. Consistent with this model, evidence shows that many cases of acrophobia, claustrophobia, and blood and injection phobias involve earlier pairings of the phobic object with aversive experiences (e.g., Kendler et al., 1992a; Merckelbach et al., 1996).

Consider the case of Phyllis, a 32-year-old writer and mother of two sons. Phyllis had not used an elevator in 16 years. Her life revolved around finding ways to avoid appointments and social events on high floors. She had suffered from a fear of elevators since the age of 8, when she had been stuck between floors with her grandmother. In conditioning terms, the unconditioned stimulus was the unpleasant experience of being stuck on the elevator, the conditioned stimulus the elevator itself.

As Mowrer pointed out, the avoidance component of phobias is acquired and maintained by operant conditioning, specifically by *negative reinforcement.* That is, relief from anxiety negatively reinforces the avoidance of fearful stimuli. In this way, Phyllis learned to relieve her anxiety over riding the elevator by opting for the stairs instead. Avoidance works to relieve anxiety, but at a significant cost. By avoiding the phobic stimulus (e.g., elevators), the fear may persist for years, even a lifetime. On the other hand, fear can be weakened and even eliminated by repeated, uneventful encounters with the phobic stimulus. In classical conditioning terms, extinction is the weakening of the conditioned response (e.g., the fear component of phobia) when the conditioned stimulus (the phobic object or stimulus) is repeatedly presented in the absence of the unconditioned stimulus (an aversive or painful stimulus).

Conditioning accounts for some, but certainly not all, phobias. In many cases, perhaps even most, people with specific phobias can't recall any aversive experiences with the objects they fear (USDHHS, 1999a). Learning theorists might counter that memories of conditioning experiences may be blurred by the passage of time or that the experience occurred too early in life to be recalled verbally. But contemporary learning theorists highlight the role of another form of learning—*observational learning*—that does not require direct conditioning of fears. In this form of learning, observing parents or significant others model a fearful reaction to a stimulus can lead to the acquisition of a fearful response. In a study of 42 people with severe phobias for spiders, observational learning apparently played a more prominent role in fear acquisition than did conditioning (Merckelbach, Arnitz, & de Jong, 1991). Moreover, simply receiving information from others, such as hearing others speak about the dangers posed by a particular stimulus—spiders, for example—can also lead to the development of phobias (Merckelbach et al., 1996).

Learning models help account for the development of phobias. But why do some people seem to acquire fear responses more readily than others? The biological and cognitive perspectives may offer some insights.

Biological Perspectives Evidence supports the view that genetic factors can predispose individuals to develop certain types of anxiety disorders, including panic disorder and phobic disorders (Gelernter et al., 2004; Hamilton et al., 2004; Hettema et al., 2003; Hook & Valentiner, 2002; Kendler et al., 2001). But how might genes affect the likelihood of developing fear responses? A recent study suggests one possible mechanism. Investigators showed links between variations of a particular gene and different patterns of brain activity when people were exposed to fearful stimuli (Hariri et al., 2002).

Unconscious defense mechanisms? For psychodynamic theorists, phobias represent the operation of unconscious defense mechanisms such as projection and displacement. In their view, a fear of heights may represent the ego's attempt to defend itself against the emergence of threatening self-destructive impulses, such as an impulse to jump from a dangerous height. By avoiding heights, the person can maintain a safe distance from such threatening impulses. Because this process occurs unconsciously, the person may be aware of the phobia, not of the unconscious impulses that it symbolizes.

two-factor model A theoretical model that accounts for the development of phobic reactions on the basis of classical and operant conditioning.

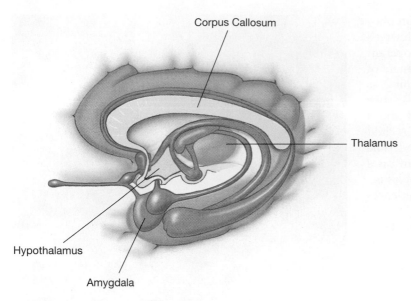

FIGURE 6.3 The amygdala and limbic system.
The amygdala is part of the limbic system, a set of interconnected structures in the brain involved in forming memories and processing emotional responses. The limbic system, which also consists of specific parts of the thalamus and hypothalamus and other nearby structures, is located in the forebrain below the cerebral cortex.

Individuals with a particular form of the gene showed greater neuronal activity in response to fearful stimuli in the amygdala, an almond-shaped structure in the limbic system of the brain (see Chapter 2). The limbic system consists of a set of structures in the brain located below the cerebral cortex that plays a key role in memory formation and processing of emotional responses. The amygdala is a kind of "emotional computer" for evaluating whether stimuli represent a threat or danger (Davidson, 2000; Öhman & Mineka, 2001) (see Figure 6.3).

Greater excitability of the amygdala may help explain why some people experience more fear and anxiety in response to threatening environmental cues. Researchers also find increased activation of the amygdala in response to faces showing expressions of anger or contempt in people with social phobia (M. B. Stein et al., 2002). This research suggests that under genetic control, the amygdala may be especially reactive to cues of threat or rejection in people with phobic disorders.

Investigators also find that a part of the prefrontal cortex in the rat's brain sends a kind of "all-clear" signal to the amygdala, quelling fearful reactions (see Figure 6.4) (Milad & Quirk, 2002). As noted in Chapter 2, the prefrontal cortex, which lies in the frontal lobes, is responsible for higher mental functions, such as problem solving and decision making. The investigators first conditioned rats to respond with fear to a tone by repeatedly pairing the tone with shock. The rats froze whenever they heard the tone. The investigators then extinguished the fear response by presenting the tone repeatedly without the shock. Following extinction, neurons in the middle of the prefrontal cortex fired up whenever the tone was sounded, sending signals through neural pathways to the amygdala. The more of these neurons that fired, the less the rats froze (NIH, 2002). The discovery that the prefrontal cortex sends a safety signal to the amygdala may eventually lead to treatments with phobic humans that can turn on the brain's "all-clear" signal.

Some investigators suggest that genetic factors also account for why people more readily acquire phobic responses to certain classes of stimuli than others (McNally, 1987; Mineka, 1991). We're more likely to develop a fear of spiders than rabbits, for example. This model, called *prepared conditioning,* suggests that evolution favored the survival of human ancestors who were genetically predisposed to acquire fears of threatening objects, such as large animals, snakes, and other "creepy-crawlers"; heights; enclosed spaces; and even strangers. This model may explain why we are more likely to develop fears of spiders or heights than of objects that appeared much later on the evolutionary scene, such as guns or knives, even though these later-appearing objects pose more direct threats today to our survival.

Cognitive Perspectives Recent research highlights the importance of cognitive factors in determining proneness to phobias, including factors such as oversensitivity to threatening cues, overpredictions of dangerousness, and self-defeating thoughts and irrational beliefs.

1. *Oversensitivity to threatening cues* (Beck & Clark, 1997). People with phobias perceive danger in situations that most people consider safe, such as riding on elevators or driving over bridges. We all possess an internal alarm system that is sensitive to cues of threat. The amygdala plays a central role in this threat-sensing system. This system may have had evolutionary advantages to ancestral humans by increasing the chances of survival in a hostile environment. Ancestral humans who responded quickly to signs of threat, such as a rustling sound in the bush that may have indicated a lurking predator about to pounce, may have

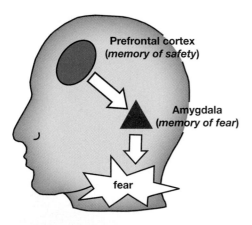

FIGURE 6.4 The "all-clear" signal quells fear in rats.
Evidence shows that "all-clear" signals from the prefrontal cortex to the amygdala inhibits fear in rats. This discovery may lead to treatments that can help quell fear reactions in humans.

Source: Milad & Quirk, 2002. Figure reprinted from "Mimicking brain's "all clear" quells fear in rats," *NIH News Release,* Posted 11/06/2002.

Snakes and spiders. According to the concept of prepared conditioning, we are genetically predisposed to more readily acquire fears of the types of stimuli that would have threatened the survival of ancestral humans—stimuli such as large animals, snakes, and other creepy-crawlers.

been better prepared to take defensive action (to fight or flee) than those with less sensitive alarm systems.

The emotion of fear is a key element in this alarm system and may have motivated our ancestors to take defensive action, which in turn may have helped them survive. People today who have specific phobias and other anxiety disorders may have inherited an acutely sensitive internal alarm that leads them to become overly sensitive to threatening cues. To cope more effectively, they may need to learn to change how they appraise cues that do not objectively pose any real danger.

2. *Overprediction of danger* (Kamphuis, Emmelkamp, & Krijn, 2002). Phobic individuals tend to overpredict how much fear or anxiety they will experience in the fearful situation. The person with a snake phobia, for example, may expect to tremble when he or she encounters a snake in a cage. People with dental phobia tend to hold exaggerated expectations of the pain they will experience during dental visits (Marks & De Silva, 1994). Typically speaking, the actual fear or pain experienced during exposure to the phobic stimulus is a good deal less than what people expect. Yet the tendency to expect the worst encourages avoidance of feared situations, which in turn prevents the individual from learning to manage and overcome anxiety.

Overprediction of dental pain and fear may also lead people to postpone or cancel regular dental visits, which can contribute to more serious dental problems down the road. On the other hand, actual exposure to fearful situations tends to promote more accurate predictions of fear levels (Rachman & Bichard, 1988). A clinical implication is that with repeated exposure, people with anxiety disorders may come to anticipate their responses to fear-inducing stimuli more accurately, leading to reductions of fear expectancies. This in turn may reduce avoidance tendencies.

3. *Self-defeating thoughts and irrational beliefs.* Self-defeating thoughts can heighten and perpetuate anxiety and phobic disorders (Meichenbaum & Deffenbacher, 1988). When faced with fear-evoking stimuli, the person may think, "I've got to get out of here," or "My heart is going to leap out of my chest." Thoughts like these intensify autonomic arousal, disrupt planning, magnify the aversiveness of stimuli, prompt avoidance behavior, and decrease self-efficacy expectancies concerning one's ability to control the situation.

TRUTH or FICTION? *REVISITED*

We may be genetically predisposed to acquire fears of objects that posed a danger to ancestral humans.

☑ TRUE. Some theorists believe that we are genetically predisposed to acquire certain fears, such as fears of large animals and snakes. The ability to readily acquire these fears may have had survival value to our early ancestors.

People with phobias also tend to hold more of the sorts of irrational beliefs catalogued by Albert Ellis than nonfearful people do. Such beliefs often involve exaggerated needs to be approved of by everyone one meets and to avoid any situation in which negative appraisal from others might arise. Consider these beliefs: "What if I have an anxiety attack in front of other people? They might think I was crazy. I couldn't stand it if they looked at me that way." Results of one early study may hit close to home: College men who believe it is awful (not just unfortunate) to be turned down when requesting a date show more social anxiety than those who are less likely to catastrophize rejection (Gormally et al., 1981).

Figure 6.5 illustrates the roles of learning models, genetic (biological) influences, and cognitive factors in the development of phobias.

Treatment Approaches

Traditional psychoanalysis fosters awareness of how clients' fears symbolize their inner conflicts, so the ego can be freed from expending its energy on repression. Modern psychodynamic therapies also foster clients' awareness of inner sources of conflict. They focus to a greater extent than traditional approaches on exploring sources of anxiety that arise from current rather than past relationships, however, and they encourage clients to develop more adaptive behaviors. Such therapies are briefer and more directed toward specific problems than traditional psychoanalysis. Though psychodynamic therapies may prove to be helpful in treating anxiety disorders, there is little compelling empirical support documenting their effectiveness (USDHHS, 1999a).

The major contemporary treatment approaches to specific phobias, as also for other anxiety disorders, derive from the learning, cognitive, and biological perspectives.

Learning-Based Approaches A substantial body of research demonstrates the effectiveness of learning-based approaches in treating a range of anxiety disorders (USDHHS, 1999a). At the core of these approaches is the effort to help individuals learn to cope more effectively with anxiety-provoking objects or situations. The major learning-based approaches are *systematic desensitization, gradual exposure,* and *flooding.*

How do self-doubts affect our performance? We are likely to feel more anxious in situations in which we doubt our ability to perform competently. Anxiety may hamper our performance, making it more difficult for us to perform successfully. Even accomplished athletes may be seized with anxiety when they are under extreme pressure, as during slumps or when competing in championship games.

Adam Learns to Overcome His Fear of Injections

Adam has a phobia for receiving injections. His behavior therapist treats him as he reclines in a comfortable padded chair. In a state of deep muscle relaxation, Adam observes slides projected on a screen. A slide of a nurse holding a needle has just been shown three times, 30 seconds at a time. Each time Adam has shown no anxiety. So now a slightly more discomforting slide is shown: one of the nurse aiming the needle toward someone's bare arm. After 15 seconds, our armchair adventurer notices twinges of discomfort and raises a finger as a signal (speaking might disturb his relaxation). The projector operator turns off the light, and Adam spends two minutes imagining his "safe scene"—lying on a beach beneath the tropical sun. Then the slide is shown again. This time Adam views it for 30 seconds before feeling anxiety.

—From Essentials of Psychology *(6th ed.) by S. A. Rathus, p. 537.*

Copyright © 2001. Reprinted with permission of Brooks/Cole, an imprint of Wadsworth Group, a division of Thomson Learning.

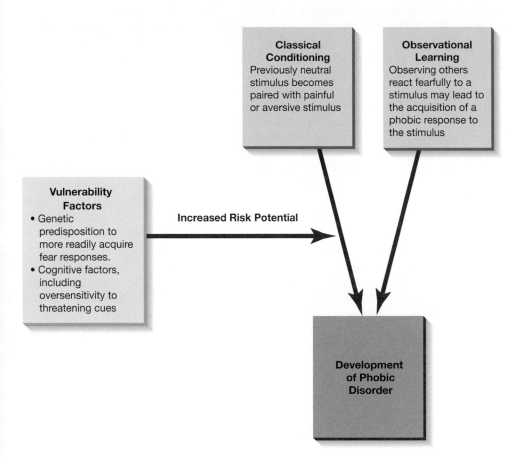

FIGURE 6.5 A multifactorial model of phobia
Learning influences play a key role in the acquisition of phobias. But whether these experiences lead to the development of phobias may depend on vulnerability factors such as a genetic predisposition and cognitive factors.

Adam is undergoing **systematic desensitization,** a fear-reduction procedure originated by psychiatrist Joseph Wolpe (1958) in the 1950s. Systematic desensitization is a gradual process in which clients learn to handle progressively more disturbing stimuli while they remain relaxed. About 10 to 20 stimuli are arranged in a sequence or hierarchy—called a **fear-stimulus hierarchy**—according to their capacity to evoke anxiety. By using their imagination or by viewing photos, clients are exposed to the items in the hierarchy, gradually imagining themselves approaching the target behavior—be it ability to receive an injection or remain in an enclosed room or elevator—without undue anxiety.

Systematic desensitization is based on the assumption that phobias are learned or conditioned responses that can be unlearned by substituting an incompatible response to anxiety in situations that usually elicit anxiety (Rachman, 2000). Muscle relaxation is generally used as the incompatible response, and followers of Wolpe usually use the method of progressive relaxation (described in Chapter 5) to help clients acquire

systematic desensitization A behavior therapy technique for overcoming phobias by means of exposure to progresively more fearful stimuli (in imagination or by viewing slides) while remaining deeply relaxed.

fear-stimulus hierarchy An ordered series of increasingly fearful stimuli.

gradual exposure In behavior therapy, a method of overcoming fears through a stepwise process of exposure to increasingly fearful stimuli in imagination or in real-life situations.

relaxation skills. For this reason, Adam's therapist is teaching Adam to experience relaxation in the presence of (otherwise) anxiety-evoking slides of needles.

Systematic desensitization creates a set of conditions that can lead to extinction of fear responses. The technique fosters extinction by providing opportunities for repeated exposure to phobic stimuli in imagination without aversive consequences.

Gradual exposure uses a stepwise approach in which phobic individuals gradually confront the objects or situations they fear. When a phobic person repeatedly encounters phobic stimuli and *nothing bad happens* as a result, the fear elicited by the phobic stimulus will eventually undergo extinction and weaken, perhaps even to the point that it is eliminated. Gradual exposure also effects cognitive changes. The person comes to perceive the previously feared object or situation as harmless.

Exposure therapy may be conducted in two forms, *imaginal exposure* (imagining oneself in the fearful situation) and *in vivo exposure* (actual encounters with phobic stimuli in real life). In vivo exposure is usually more effective than imaginal exposure (Kamphuis, Emmelkamp, & Krijn, 2002), but both techniques may be used in therapy. The effectiveness of exposure therapy for phobias is well established, making it the treatment of choice for these disorders (Barlow, Esler, & Vitali, 1998; DeRubeis & Crits-Christoph, 1998; Hoffman, 2000a, 2000b; Kamphuis, Emmelkamp, & Krijn, 2002).

In exposure therapy for social phobia, clients are instructed to enter increasingly stressful social situations (e.g., eating and conversing with coworkers in the cafeteria) and to remain in those situations until the anxiety and urge to escape lessens. The therapist may help guide them during exposure trials, gradually withdrawing direct support so that clients become capable of handling the situations on their own. Exposure therapy for agoraphobia follows a stepwise course in which the client is exposed to increasingly fearful stimulus situations, such as walking through congested streets or shopping in department stores. A trusted companion or perhaps the therapist may accompany the person during the exposure trials. The eventual goal is for the person to be able to handle each situation alone and without discomfort or an urge to escape. Gradual exposure was used in the following case of claustrophobia.

Gradual exposure. In gradual exposure, the client is exposed to a fear-stimulus hierarchy in real-life situations, often with a therapist or companion serving in a supportive role. To encourage the person to accomplish the exposure tasks increasingly on his or her own, the therapist or companion gradually withdraws direct support. Gradual exposure is often combined with cognitive techniques that focus on helping the client replace anxiety-producing thoughts and beliefs with calming, rational alternatives.

Kevin Combats His Fear of Elevators: A Case of Claustrophobia

Claustrophobia (fear of enclosed spaces) is not very unusual, though Kevin's case was. Kevin's claustrophobia took the form of a fear of riding on elevators. What made his case so unusual was his occupation: He worked as an elevator mechanic. Kevin spent his work days repairing elevators. Unless it was absolutely necessary, however, Kevin managed to complete the repairs without riding in the elevator. He would climb the stairs to the floor where an elevator was stuck, make repairs, and hit the down button. He would then race downstairs to see that the elevator had operated correctly. When his work required an elevator ride, panic would seize him as the doors closed. Kevin tried to cope by praying for divine intervention to prevent him from passing out before the doors opened.

Kevin related the origin of his phobia to an accident three years earlier in which he had been pinned in his overturned car for nearly an hour. He remembered feelings of helplessness and suffocation. Kevin developed claustrophobia—a fear of situations from which he could not escape, such as flying on an airplane, driving in a tunnel, taking public transportation, and of course, riding in an elevator. Kevin's fear had become so incapacitating that he was seriously considering switching careers, although the change would require considerable financial sacrifice. Each night he lay awake wondering whether he would be able to cope the next day if he were required to test-ride an elevator.

Kevin's therapy involved gradual exposure in which he followed a stepwise program of exposure to increasingly fearful stimuli. A typical anxiety hierarchy for helping people overcome a fear of riding on elevators might include the following steps:

1. *Standing outside the elevator*
2. *Standing in the elevator with the door open*
3. *Standing in the elevator with the door closed*
4. *Taking the elevator down one floor*
5. *Taking the elevator up one floor*
6. *Taking the elevator down two floors*
7. *Taking the elevator up two floors*
8. *Taking the elevator down two floors and then up two floors*
9. *Taking the elevator down to the basement*
10. *Taking the elevator up to the highest floor*
11. *Taking the elevator all the way down and then all the way up*

Clients begin at step 1 and do not progress to step 2 until they are able to remain calm on the first. If they become bothered by anxiety, they remove themselves from the situation and regain calmness by practicing muscle relaxation or focusing on soothing mental imagery. The encounter is then repeated as often as necessary to reach and sustain feelings of calmness. They then proceed to the next step, repeating the process.

Kevin was also trained to practice self-relaxation and talk calmly and rationally to himself to help himself remain calm during his exposure trials. Whenever he began to feel even slightly anxious, he would tell himself to calm down and relax. He was able to counter the disruptive belief that he was going to fall apart if he was trapped in an elevator with rational self-statements such as, "Just relax. I may experience some anxiety, but it's nothing that I haven't been through before. In a few moments I'll feel relieved."

Kevin slowly overcame his phobia but still occasionally experienced some anxiety, which he interpreted as a reminder of his former phobia. He did not exaggerate the importance of these feelings. Now and then it dawned on him that an elevator he was servicing had once occasioned fear. One day following his treatment, Kevin was repairing an elevator, which serviced a bank vault 100 feet underground. The experience of moving deeper and deeper underground aroused fear, but Kevin did not panic. He repeated to himself, "It's only a couple of seconds and I'll be out." By the time he took his second trip down, he was much calmer.

—From the Authors' Files

Flooding is a form of exposure therapy in which subjects are exposed to *high levels* of fear-inducing stimuli either in imagination or real-life situations. Why? The belief is that anxiety represents a conditioned response to a phobic stimulus and should dissipate if the individual remains in the phobic situation for a long enough period of time without harmful consequences. Most individuals with phobias avoid confronting phobic stimuli or beat a hasty retreat at the first opportunity if they cannot avoid them. Consequently, they lack the opportunity to unlearn the fear response. In one research example, 9 of 10 people with social phobia achieved at least moderate improvement through a flooding technique in which they directly faced fear-inducing situations, such as giving a talk before an expert audience (Turner, Beidel, & Jacob, 1994).

flooding A behavior therapy technique for overcoming fears by means of exposure to high levels of fear-inducing stimuli.

Virtual Therapy, the Next Best Thing to Being There

In the movie the *Matrix*, the lead character played by Keanu Reeves comes to realize that the world he believes is real is merely an illusion, a complex virtual environment so lifelike that people cannot tell it isn't real. The *Matrix* is science fiction, but the use of virtual reality as a therapeutic tool is science fact.

Virtual reality therapy (VRT) is a behavior therapy technique that uses computer-generated simulated environments as therapeutic tools. By donning a specialized helmet and gloves that are connected to a computer, a person with a fear of heights, for example, can encounter frightening stimuli in this virtual world, such as riding a

virtual reality therapy A form of exposure therapy involving the presentation of phobic stimuli in a virtual reality environment.

Overcoming fears with virtual reality. Virtual reality technology can be used to help people overcome phobias. Here we see a woman wearing a virtual reality helmet while participating in a fear of flying therapy program.

glass-enclosed elevator to the top floor of an imaginary hotel, peering over a railing on a balcony on the 20th floor, or crossing a virtual Golden Gate Bridge. By a process of exposure to a series of increasingly frightening virtual stimuli, while progressing only when fear at each step diminishes, people can learn to overcome fears in virtual reality in much the same way they would had they followed a program of graduated exposure in real-life situations.

Virtual therapy has been used successfully in helping people overcome various types of phobias, including fears of heights and fear of flying (Kamphuis, Emmelkamp, & Krijn, 2002; Rothbaum et al., 1995, 2000). In one recent study, virtual reality was just as effective as real-life exposure in treating fear of flying, with both treatments showing better results than an untreated (waiting list) control condition (Rothbaum et al., 2002). Ninety-two percent of VRT participants succeeded in flying on a commercial airliner in the year following treatment.

Virtual reality therapy offers some advantages over traditional exposure-based treatments. For one thing, it is often difficult or impossible to arrange in real life the types of exposure experiences that can be simulated in virtual reality, such as repeated airplane takeoffs and landings (Yancey, 2000). Virtual therapy also allows for greater control over the stimulus environment, as when the participant controls the intensity and range of stimuli used during virtual exposure sessions (Zimand et al., 2003). Individuals may also be more willing to perform certain fearful tasks in virtual reality than in real life.

In order for virtual therapy to be effective, says psychologist Barbara Rothbaum, who was an early pioneer in the use of the technique, the person must become immersed in the experience and believe at some level it is real and not like watching a videotape. "If the first person had put the helmet on and said, 'This isn't scary,' it wouldn't have worked, Dr. Rothbaum said. "But you get the same physiological changes—the racing heart, the sweat—that you would in the actual place" (cited in Goleman, 1995b, p. C11). Today, with advances in virtual reality technology, the simulated virtual environment is convincing enough to evoke intense anxiety in fearful people (Lubell, 2004).

We have only begun to explore the potential therapeutic uses of this new technology. Therapists are experimenting with virtual therapy to help people overcome many types of fears, such as fear of public speaking and agoraphobia. Therapists are experimenting

TRUTH or FICTION? *REVISITED*

Peering over a virtual ledge 20 stories up in virtual reality has helped some people overcome their fear of actual heights.

☑ **TRUE.** Virtual reality therapy has been used successfully in helping people overcome phobias, including fear of heights.

with virtual bars and crack houses to help substance abusers learn to resist drugs (Lubell, 2004). In other applications, virtual therapy may help clients work through unresolved conflicts with significant figures in their lives by allowing them to confront these "people" in a virtual environment. A family therapist envisions virtual family sessions in which participants can see things from the emotional and physical vantage points of each other member of the family (Steven, 1995).

Other potential uses of virtual therapy include treating people with depression, social phobias, and obsessive-compulsive disorder, children with attention-deficit disorders, adults with fears of intimacy or sexual aversion, and people who have problems controlling their anger or aggressive behavior (Glantz et al., 1996; Steven, 1995). Self-help "therapy" modules, consisting of compact discs and virtual reality helmets and gloves, may even begin to appear on the shelves of your neighborhood computer software store in the not-too-distant future. With these self-help modules, people may be able in their own living rooms to confront objects or situations they fear, or learn to stop smoking or lose weight, all with the help and guidance of a "virtual therapist."

Cognitive Therapy Through rational emotive behavior therapy, Albert Ellis might show people with social phobias how irrational needs for social approval and perfectionism produce unnecessary anxiety in social interactions. Eliminating exaggerated needs for social approval is apparently a key therapeutic factor (Butler, 1989).

Cognitive therapists seek to identify and correct dysfunctional or distorted beliefs. For example, people with social phobias might think no one at a party will want to talk with them and that they will wind up lonely and isolated for the rest of their lives. Cognitive therapists help clients recognize the logical flaws in their thinking and to view situations rationally. Clients may be asked to gather evidence to test out their beliefs, which may lead them to alter beliefs they find are not grounded in reality. Therapists may encourage clients with social phobias to test their beliefs that they are bound to be ignored, rejected, or ridiculed by others in social gatherings by attending a party, initiating conversations, and monitoring other people's reactions. Therapists may also help clients develop social skills to improve their interpersonal effectiveness and teach them how to handle social rejection, if it should occur, without catastrophizing. A recent clinical trial showed that cognitive therapy outperformed a combined treatment consisting of drug therapy (Prozac) and self-administered exposure training in treating the generalized form of social phobia (Clark et al., 2003).

One example of cognitive techniques is **cognitive restructuring,** a process in which therapists help clients pinpoint their self-defeating thoughts and generate rational alternatives so they learn to cope with anxiety-provoking situations. For example, Kevin learned to replace self-defeating thoughts with rational alternatives and to practice speaking rationally and calmly to himself during his exposure trials.

Cognitive-behavioral therapy (CBT) is the general term used to apply to therapeutic approaches that combine behavioral and cognitive therapy techniques. CBT practitioners incorporate behavioral techniques, such as exposure, along with techniques drawn from the cognitive therapies of Ellis, Beck, and others. For example, in treating social phobia, therapists often combine exposure treatment with cognitive restructuring techniques that help clients replace anxiety-inducing thoughts with more adjustive thoughts (Stangier et al., 2003).

Drug Therapy We noted earlier that antidepressants are helpful in treating some anxiety disorders. For example, drug therapy with antidepressants is better established for treating panic disorder and obsessive-compulsive disorder than phobias. However, recent evidence shows that antidepressant drugs *sertraline* (brand name Zoloft) and *paroxtine* (trade name Paxil) have therapeutic benefits in treating one form of phobia, social phobia (Stein et al., 2003; van Ameringen et al., 2001). A combination of psychotherapy and drug therapy may be more effective in some cases in treating social phobia than either treatment approach alone (Feldman & Rivas-Vazquez, 2003).

cognitive restructuring A cognitive therapy method that involves replacing irrational thoughts with rational alternatives.

OBSESSIVE–COMPULSIVE DISORDER

obsessive–compulsive disorder A type of anxiety disorder characterized by recurrent obsessions, compulsions, or both.

obsession A recurrring thought or image that the individual cannot control.

compulsion A repetitive or ritualistic behavior that the person feels compelled to perform.

A person is diagnosed with **obsessive–compulsive disorder** when he or she is troubled by recurrent obsessions, compulsions, or both to the extent that they cause marked distress, occupy more than an hour a day, or significantly interfere with normal routines or occupational or social functioning (APA, 2000). An **obsession** is an intrusive and recurrent thought, idea, or urge that seems beyond the person's ability to control. Obsessions can be potent and persistent enough to interfere with daily life and can engender significant distress and anxiety. They include doubts, impulses, and mental images. One may wonder endlessly whether or not one has locked the doors and shut the windows, for example. One may be obsessed with the impulse to do harm to one's spouse. One can harbor images, such as the recurrent fantasy of a young mother that her children had been run over by traffic on the way home from school.

A **compulsion** is a repetitive behavior (such as hand washing or checking door locks) or mental act (e.g., praying, repeating certain words, or counting) the person feels compelled or driven to perform (APA, 2000). Compulsions typically occur in response to obsessional thoughts and are frequent and forceful enough to interfere with daily life or cause significant distress. In the following first-person account, a man describes his obsessive concerns about having caused harm to other people (and even insects) as the result of his actions.

"Tormenting Thoughts and Secret Rituals"

My compulsions are caused by fears of hurting someone through my negligence. It's always the same mental rigmarole. Making sure the doors are latched and the gas jets are off. Making sure I switch off the light with just the right amount of pressure, so I don't cause an electrical problem. Making sure I shift the car's gears cleanly, so I don't damage the machinery. . . .

I fantasize about finding an island in the South Pacific and living alone. That would take the pressure off; if I would harm anyone it would just be me. Yet even if I were alone, I'd still have my worries, because even insects can be a problem. Sometimes when I take the garbage out, I'm afraid that I've stepped on an ant. I stare down to see if there is an ant kicking and writhing in agony. I took a walk last week by a pond, but I couldn't enjoy it because I remembered it was spawning season, and I worried that I might be stepping on the eggs of bass or bluegill.

I realize that other people don't do these things. Mainly, it's that I don't want to go through the guilt of having hurt anything. It's selfish in that sense. I don't care about them as much as I do about not feeling the guilt.

—From Osborn, 1998

Most compulsions fall into two categories: cleaning rituals and checking rituals. Rituals can become the focal point of life. A compulsive hand washer, Corinne, engaged in elaborate hand-washing rituals. She spent 3 to 4 hours daily at the sink and complained, "My hands look like lobster claws." Some people literally take hours checking and rechecking that all the appliances are off before they leave home, and still remain in doubt. Table 6.6 shows some relatively common obsessions and compulsions.

TABLE 6.6

Examples of Obsessive Thoughts and Compulsive Behaviors

Obsessive Thought Patterns	Compulsive Behavior Patterns
Thinking that one's hands remain dirty despite repeated washing.	Rechecking one's work time and time again.
Difficulty shaking the thought that a loved one has been hurt or killed.	Rechecking the doors or gas jets before leaving home.
Repeatedly thinking that one has left the door to the house unlocked.	Constantly washing one's hands to keep them clean and germ free.
Worrying constantly that the gas jets in the house were not turned off.	
Repeatedly thinking that one has done terrible things to loved ones.	

Compulsions often accompany obsessions and may at least partially relieve the anxiety created by obsessional thinking. By washing one's hands 40 or 50 times in a row each time a public doorknob is touched, the compulsive hand washer may experience some relief from the anxiety engendered by the obsessive thought that germs or dirt still linger in the folds of skin. The person may believe the compulsive act will help prevent some dreaded event, even though there is no realistic basis to the belief or the behavior far exceeds any reasonable precaution. The solution, in effect, becomes the problem (Salkovskis et al., 2003). The person gets trapped into a vicious cycle of intrusive thoughts leading to compulsive rituals and related thoughts.

Obsessive–compulsive disorder (OCD) affects between 2% and 3% of the general population at some point in their lives (APA, 2000; Taylor, 1995). A Swedish study found that although most OCD patients eventually showed some improvement, most also continued to have some symptoms of the disorder over the course of their lifetimes (Skoog & Skoog, 1999). The disorder occurs about equally often in men and women (APA, 2000; US-DHHS, 1999a). The case example below illustrates a checking compulsion.

The line between obsessions and delusions (firmly held but patently false beliefs), such as the kind we see in schizophrenia patients, is sometimes less than clear. Obsessions, such as the belief that one is contaminating other people, can, like delusions, become almost unshakable. Although adults with OCD may be uncertain at a given time about whether their obsessions or compulsions are unreasonable or excessive (Foa & Kozak, 1995), they will eventually concede that their concerns are groundless or excessive. True delusions cannot be shaken. Children with OCD may not come to recognize their concerns are groundless, however.

Theoretical Perspectives

Within the psychodynamic tradition, obsessions represent leakage of unconscious impulses into consciousness, and compulsions are acts that help keep these impulses repressed. Obsessive thoughts about contamination by dirt or germs may represent the threatened emergence of unconscious infantile wishes to soil oneself and play with feces. The compulsion (in this case, cleanliness rituals) helps keep such wishes at bay. The psychodynamic model remains largely speculative, in large part because of the difficulty (some would say impossibility) of arranging scientific tests to determine the existence of unconscious impulses and conflicts.

On the other hand, a growing body of evidence supports a genetic contribution to the development of OCD (Pato, Pato, & Pauls, 2002; Pato, Schindler, & Pato, 2001). We also know that many people with OCD, especially those who developed the disorder during childhood, have a history of tic disorders. Investigators suspect there may be a genetic link between tic disorders and OCD, or at least child-onset OCD (Eichstedt & Arnold, 2001).

An obsessive thought? One type of obsession involves recurrent, intrusive images of a calamity occurring as the result of one's own carelessness. For example, a person may not be able to shake the image of his or her house catching fire due to an electrical short in an appliance inadvertently left on.

Obsessive/Compulsive Disorder:
The Case of Dave
"I knew in my heart of hearts that the water was turned off, but I had to go back and check it anyway."

Jack's "Little Behavioral Quirks": A Case of Obsesssive–Compulsive Disorder

Jack, a successful chemical engineer, was urged by his wife Mary, a pharmacist, to seek help for "his little behavioral quirks," which she had found increasingly annoying. Jack was a compulsive checker. When they left the apartment, he would insist on returning to check that the lights or gas jets were off, or that the refrigerator doors were shut. Sometimes he would apologize at the elevator and return to the apartment to carry out his rituals. Sometimes the compulsion to check struck him in the garage. He would return to the apartment, leaving Mary fuming. Going on vacation was especially difficult for Jack. The rituals occupied the better part of the morning of their departure. Even then, he remained plagued by doubts.

Mary had also tried to adjust to Jack's nightly routine of bolting out of bed to recheck the doors and windows. Her patience was running thin. Jack realized that his behavior was impairing their relationship as well as causing himself distress. Yet he was reluctant to enter treatment. He gave lip service to wanting to be rid of his compulsive habits, but he also feared that surrendering his compulsions would leave him defenseless against the anxieties they helped ease.

—*From the Authors' Files*

Though we don't yet know how genetic factors directly influence OCD, one possibility is that the action of particular genes may affect chemical balances within the central nervous system, leading to an overarousal of brain circuitry activated during states of worry. This brain circuitry, or *worry circuit,* consists of a network of neurons in the brain involved in signaling danger. In OCD, the brain may be constantly sending messages through this worry circuit that something is wrong and requires immediate attention, leading to obsessional worrisome thoughts and repetitive compulsive behaviors. Parts of the worry circuit incorporate structures in the limbic system, including the amygdala. We noted earlier that the amygdala is a brain structure involved in processing threatening stimuli.

An intriguing possiblity requiring further study is that the compulsive aspects of OCD result from abnormalities in brain circuits that normally suppress repetitive behaviors. These abnormalities may lead people to feel compelled to perform repetitive behaviors as though they were "stuck in gear" (Leocani et al., 2001). The frontal lobes in the cerebral cortex regulate brain centers in the lower brain that control bodily movements. A recent fMRI study showed abnormal patterns of activation in parts of the frontal lobes in OCD patients (Schwartz, 1998). Perhaps a disruption in these neural pathways explains the failure of people with compulsive behavior to inhibit repetitive, ritualistic behaviors. Changes in patterns of frontal lobe activation are also found among patients who respond favorably to cognitive-behavioral treatment, which suggests that

Is this as good as it gets? In the movie, *As Good as It Gets,* Jack Nicholson plays a character with many features of OCD, including such obsessive concerns about cleanliness that he brings his own plastic utensils to dine in restaurants.

CBT may directly affect parts of the brain implicated in OCD (Ingram & Siegle, 2001; Schwartz, 1998).

Other parts of the brain, including the basal ganglia, are also implicated in OCD (Baxter, 2003). The basal ganglia are involved in controlling body movements, so it is conceivable that a dysfunction in this region might help explain the ritualistic behaviors seen in OCD patients.

Psychological models of OCD emphasize cognitive and learning-based factors. People with OCD tend to be overly focused on their thoughts (Janeck et al., 2003). They can't seem to break the mental loop in which the same intrusive, negative thoughts keep reverberating in their minds. They also tend to exaggerate the risk that unfortunate events will occur (Bouchard, Rhéaume, & Ladouceur, 1999). Because they expect terrible things to happen, people with OCD engage in rituals to prevent them. An accountant who imagines awful consequences for slight mistakes on a client's tax forms may feel compelled to repeatedly check her or his work.

Another cognitive factor linked to the development of OCD is perfectionism, or belief that one must perform flawlessly (Shafran & Mansell, 2001). People who hold perfectionist beliefs exaggerate the consequences of turning in less than perfect work and may feel compelled to redo their efforts until every detail is flawless.

From the learning perspective, compulsive behaviors are viewed as operant responses that are negatively reinforced by relief of the anxiety engendered by obsessional thoughts. Put simply, "Obsessions give rise to anxiety/distress and compulsions reduce it" (Franklin, Abramowitz et al., 2002, p. 283). If a person obsesses that dirt or foreign bodies contaminate other people's hands, shaking hands or turning a doorknob may evoke powerful anxiety. Compulsive hand washing following exposure to a perceived contaminant provides some relief from anxiety. Reinforcement, whether positive or negative, strengthens the behavior that precedes it. Thus, the person becomes more likely to repeat the compulsive ritual the next time he or she is exposed to anxiety-evoking cues, such as shaking hands or touching doorknobs.

The question remains why some people develop obsessive thoughts whereas others do not. Perhaps people who develop obsessive–compulsive disorder are physiologically sensitized to overreact to minor cues of danger. We can speculate that the brain's worry circuit may be unusually sensitive to cues of danger. Memory impairment may also play a role. Compulsive checkers may have difficulty remembering whether they have completed the task correctly, such as turning off the toaster oven before leaving for the day. Evidence shows that compulsive checkers tend to perform more poorly than others on many types of memory tasks (Woods et al., 2002). The degree to which impaired memory accounts for compulsive checking remains to be seen, however.

Treatment Approaches

Behavior therapists have achieved impressive results in treating obsessive–compulsive disorder with the technique of *exposure with response prevention* (Abramowitz, Foa, & Franklin, 2003; Abramowitz et al., 2003; McLean et al., 2001). The *exposure* component involves having clients intentionally place themselves in situations that evoke obsessive thoughts. For many people, such situations are hard to avoid. Leaving the house, for example, may trigger obsessive thoughts about whether the gas jets are turned off or the windows and doors are locked. Or clients may be instructed to purposely induce obsessive thoughts by leaving the house messy or rubbing their hands in dirt. *Response prevention* is the effort to prevent the compulsive behavior from occurring. Clients who rub their hands in dirt must avoid washing them for a designated period of time. The compulsive lock checker must avoid checking to see that the door was locked.

Through exposure with response prevention (ERP), people with OCD learn to tolerate the anxiety triggered by their obsessive thoughts while they are prevented from performing their compulsive rituals. With repeated exposure trials, the anxiety eventually subsides, and the person feels less compelled to perform the accompanying rituals. The underlying principle, yet again, is extinction. When cues that trigger obsessive

Obsessive/Compulsive Disorder:
The Case of Ed
"It was . . . awful . . . at that time . . . when the OCD started to show itself."

thoughts and accompanying anxiety are repeatedly presented but the person sees that nothing bad happens, the bonds between these cues and the anxiety response weaken. Overall, about 4 of 5 people treated with ERP show significant improvement (Abramowitz, 1996; Foa, 1996). Cognitive techniques are often combined with ERP within a cognitive–behavioral treatment program (Clark, 2004). The cognitive component involves correcting distorted ways of thinking (cognitive distortions), such as tendencies to overestimate the likelihood and severity of feared consequences.

SSRI-type antidepressant drugs also have therapeutic benefits in treating OCD (Saxena et al., 2003). This class of drugs includes *fluoxetine* (Prozac), *paroxetine* (Paxil), and *clomipramine* (Anafranil). These drugs increase the availability in the brain of the neurotransmitter serotonin (Riddle et al., 2001). The effectiveness of these drugs leads researchers to suspect that problems with serotonin transmission play an important role in the development of OCD, at least in some cases (Franklin, Abramowitz et al., 2002). Bear in mind, however, that some people with OCD fail to respond to these drugs, and among those who do respond, many experience only partial relief (Franklin, Abramowitz et al., 2002; Riddle et al., 2001).

Studies comparing cognitive–behavioral therapy (CBT) with drug therapy using SSRI-type antidepressants find that CBT produces at least as much benefit and may lead to more lasting results (Franklin, Rynn et al., 2002; Rauch & Jenike, 1998; Stanley & Turner, 1995). As with other forms of anxiety disorder, some people with OCD may benefit from a combination of psychological and pharmacological treatment (USDHHS, 1999a).

GENERALIZED ANXIETY DISORDER

generalized anxiety disorder (GAD) A type of anxiety disorder characterized by general feelings of dread and foreboding and heightened states of bodily arousal.

Generalized anxiety disorder (GAD) is characterized by persistent feelings of anxiety that are not triggered by any specific object, situation, or activity, but rather seems to be what Freud labeled "free floating." The disorder is characterized by persistent feelings of anxiety that are not triggered by any specific object, situation, or activity. The central feature of GAD is worry (Ruscio, Borkovec, & Ruscio, 2001). People with GAD are chronic worriers. They may worry excessively about their life circumstances, such as their finances, the well-being of their children, and their social relationships. They tend to worry excessively about everyday, minor things, such as getting stuck in traffic, and about unlikely future events, such as going bankrupt (Dugas, 2002). Children with generalized anxiety tend to worry about academics, athletics, and social aspects of school life.

The emotional distress associated with GAD interferes significantly with the person's daily life. GAD frequently occurs together with other disorders, such as depression or other anxiety disorders like agoraphobia and obsessive–compulsive disorder. Other related features include restlessness; feeling tense, "keyed up," or "on edge"; becoming easily fatigued; having difficulty concentrating or finding one's mind going blank; irritability; muscle tension; and disturbances of sleep, such as difficulty falling asleep, staying asleep, or having restless and unsatisfying sleep (APA, 2000).

GAD tends to be a stable disorder that initially arises in the mid-teens to mid-20s and then typically follows a lifelong course (Rapee, 1991). The lifetime prevalence of GAD in the general U.S. population is estimated to be around 5% (APA, 2000; Sheehan & Mao, 2003). The disorder is believed to be about twice as common in women as in men (APA, 2000; USDHHS, 1999a). In the following case, we find a number of features of generalized anxiety disorder:

"Worrying About Worrying": A Case of Generalized Anxiety Disorder

Earl was a 52-year-old supervisor at the automobile plant. His hands trembled as he spoke. His cheeks were pale. His face was somewhat boyish, making his hair seem grayed with worry.

He was reasonably successful in his work, although he noted that he was not a "star." His marriage of nearly three decades was in "reasonably good shape," although sexual relations were "less than exciting—I shake so much that it isn't easy to get involved." The mortgage on the house was not a burden and would be paid off within 5 years, but "I don't know what it is; I think about money all the time." The three children were doing well. One was employed, one was in college, and one was in high school. But "With everything going on these days, how can you help worrying about them? I'm up for hours worrying about them."

"But it's the strangest thing," Earl shook his head. "I swear I'll find myself worrying when there's nothing in my head. I don't know how to describe it. It's like I'm worrying first and then there's something in my head to worry about. It's not like I start thinking about this or that and I see it's bad and then I worry. And then the shakes come, and then, of course, I'm worrying about worrying, if you know what I mean. I want to run away; I don't want anyone to see me. You can't direct workers when you're shaking."

Going to work had become a major chore. "I can't stand the noises of the assembly lines. I just feel jumpy all the time. It's like I expect something awful to happen. When it gets bad like that I'll be out of work for a day or two with shakes."

Earl had been worked up "for everything; my doctor took blood, saliva, urine, you name it. He listened to everything, he put things inside me. He had other people look at me. He told me to stay away from coffee and alcohol. Then from tea. Then from chocolate and Coca-Cola, because there's a little bit of caffeine [in them]. He gave me Valium [a minor tranquilizer] and I thought I was in heaven for a while. Then it stopped working, and he switched me to something else. Then that stopped working, and he switched me back. Then he said he was 'out of chemical miracles' and I better see a shrink or something. Maybe it was something from my childhood."

—From the Authors' Files

Theoretical Perspectives

From a psychodynamic perspective, generalized anxiety represents the threatened leakage of unacceptable sexual or aggressive impulses or wishes into consious awareness. The person is aware of the anxiety but not its underlying source. The problem with speculating about unconscious origins of anxiety is that they lie beyond the reach of direct scientific tests. We cannot directly observe or measure unconscious impulses.

From a learning perspective, generalized anxiety is precisely that: generalization of anxiety across many situations. People concerned about broad life themes, such as finances, health, and family matters, are likely to experience apprehension or worry in a variety of settings. Anxiety would thus become connected with almost any environment or situation.

The cognitive perspective on GAD emphasizes the role of exaggerated or distorted thoughts and beliefs, especially beliefs that underlie worry. People with GAD tend to worry about just about everything. They tend to perceive danger at every turn and to anticipate calamitous consequences. Consequently, they feel continually on edge, as their nervous systems respond to the perception of threat or danger with activation of the sympathetic nervous system, leading to increased states of bodily arousal and the accompanying feelings of anxiety.

Though we lack a clear biological model of GAD, it is reasonable to suspect irregularities in neurotransmitter activity. We mentioned earlier that antianxiety drugs such as the benzodiazepines *diazepam* (Valium) and *alprazolam* (Xanax) increase the effects of GABA, an inhibitory neurotransmitter that tones down central nervous system arousal. Similarly, irregularities of the neurotransmitter serotonin are implicated in GAD based on evidence that GAD responds favorably to the antidepressant drug *paroxetine* (Paxil), which specifically targets serotonin (Sheehan & Mao, 2003). Neurotransmitters work on brain structures that regulate emotional states such as anxiety and worry, so it is possible that an overreactivity of these brain structures (the amygdala for example) may also be involved.

Treatment Approaches

The major forms of treatment of generalized anxiety disorder are psychiatric drugs and cognitive–behavioral therapy. Paroxetine (Paxil) is the only drug to date approved for treating GAD, though other drugs were undergoing testing as of this writing. Bear in mind, however, that although psychiatric drugs may help relieve anxiety symptoms, they cannot cure the underlying problem. Once the drugs are discontinued, the symptoms often return.

Cognitive–behavioral therapists use a combination of techniques in treating GAD, including training in relaxation skills; learning to substitute calming, adaptive thoughts for intrusive, worrisome thoughts; and learning skills of decatastrophizing (avoiding tendencies to think the worst). Evidence from controlled studies shows substantial therapeutic benefits of CBT in treating generalized anxiety disorder (Dugas et al., 2003; Heimberg, Turk, & Mennin, 2004; Ladouceur et al., 2000). In one recent study, the great majority of GAD patients treated with either behavioral or cognitive methods, or the combination of these methods, no longer met diagnostic criteria for the disorder following treatment (Borkovec et al., 2002).

TRAUMATIC STRESS DISORDERS

In adjustment disorders (discussed in Chapter 5), people have difficulty adjusting to life stressors, such as business or marital problems, chronic illness, or bereavement over a loss. Here we focus on two types of anxiety disorders that occur in response to *traumatic* events: *acute stress disorder* and *posttraumatic stress disorder*.

acute stress disorder (ASD) A traumatic stress reaction occurring during the month following exposure to a traumatic event.

Acute stress disorder (ASD) is a maladaptive reaction that occurs during the initial month following the traumatic experience. It may occur in the context of combat or exposure to natural or technological disasters. A soldier may come through a horrific battle not remembering important features of the battle and feeling numb and detached from the environment. People who are injured or who nearly lose their lives in a hurricane may walk around "in a fog" for days or weeks afterward; be bothered by intrusive images, flashbacks, and dreams of the disaster; or relive the experience as though it were happening again.

Trauma. Trauma may result from experiences in combat (left) or from terrorist violence (right), as in these survivors fleeing the World Trade Center disaster of September 11, 2001. In either case, stress-related problems may not develop until long after the experience, but may linger for years afterward in the form of posttraumatic stress disorder (PTSD).

Posttraumatic stress disorder (PTSD) is a prolonged maladaptive reaction to a traumatic experience. In contrast to ASD, PTSD may persist for months, years, or even decades and may not develop until many months or even years after the traumatic event (Zlotnick et al., 2001).

ASD is a major risk factor for PTSD, as many people with ASD later develop PTSD (Harvey & Bryant, 2000, 2002; Sharp & Harvey, 2001). We find both types of stress disorders in soldiers exposed to combat, among rape survivors, victims of motor vehicle and other accidents, and in people who have witnessed the destruction of their homes and communities by natural disasters such as floods, earthquakes, or tornadoes, or technological disasters such as railroad or airplane crashes. For Margaret, the trauma involved a horrific truck accident.

posttraumatic stress disorder (PTSD) A prolonged maladaptive reaction to a traumatic event.

"I Thought the World Was Coming to an End": A Case of PTSD

Margaret was a 54-year-old woman who lived with her husband, Travis, in a small village in the hills to the east of New York's Hudson River. Two winters earlier, in the middle of the night, a fuel truck had skidded down one of the icy inclines that led into the village center. Two blocks away, Margaret was shaken from her bed by the explosion ("I thought the world was coming to an end.") when the truck slammed into the general store. The store and the apartments above were immediately engulfed in flames. The fire spread to the church next door. Margaret's first and most enduring visual impression was of shards of red and black that rose into the air in an eerie ballet. On their way down, they bathed the centuries-old tombstones in the church graveyard in hellish light. A dozen people died, mostly those who had lived above and in back of the general store. The old caretaker of the church and the truck driver were lost as well.

Margaret shared the village's loss, took in the temporarily homeless, and did her share of what had to be done. Months later, after the general store had been leveled to a memorial park and the church was on the way toward being restored, Margaret started to feel that life was becoming strange, that the world outside was becoming a little unreal. She began to withdraw from her friends, and scenes of the night of the fire would fill her mind. At night she now and then dreamt the scene. Her physician prescribed a sleeping pill, which she discontinued because "I couldn't wake up out of the dream." Her physician turned to Valium, a minor tranquilizer, to help her get through the day. The pills helped for a while, but "I quit them because I needed more and more of the things and you can't take drugs forever, can you?"

Over the next year and a half, Margaret tried her best not to think about the disaster, but the intrusive recollections and the dreams came and went, apparently on their own. By the time Margaret sought help, her sleep had been seriously distressed for nearly two months and the recollections were as vivid as ever.

—From the Author's Files

In ASD and PTSD, the traumatic event involves either actual or threatened death or serious physical injury, or threat to one's own or another's physical safety. The person's response to the threat involves feelings of intense fear, helplessness, or a sense of horror. Children with PTSD may have experienced the threat differently, such as by showing confused or agitated behavior.

Though most people who suffer trauma experience some degree of psychological distress (Sharp & Harvey, 2001), not all trauma survivors go on to develop ASD or PTSD. Overall, investigators believe that about 8% of U.S. adults are affected by PTSD at some point in their lives (Kessler et al., 1995). About 2% of American adults currently show evidence of diagnosable PTSD. The prevalence of ASD in the general population is not known. Though exposure to combat or terrorist attacks may be most strongly linked in the public's mind to PTSD, experts believe that the type of trauma most often associated with PTSD is motor vehicle accidents (Blanchard & Hickling, 2004). More than 1% of the U.S. population experience a serious motor vehicle accident that causes personal injury each year.

Although PTSD often diminishes within a period of 6 months (USDHHS, 1999a), it can last for years, even decades (Bremmer et al., 1996; Kessler et al., 1995). Many World War II and Korean War veterans, for example, were found to meet diagnostic criteria for PTSD when evaluated decades after their combat experience ended (Schnurr, Ford, & Friedman, 2000). Veterans with PTSD often have other problem behaviors, including substance abuse, marital problems, and poor work histories (Calhoun et al., 2000). Yet there is some good news to report: People who obtain treatment for PTSD typically recover sooner than those who do not (Kessler et al., 1995). We can't say whether treatment shortens the duration of PTSD symptoms, because it is possible that people who seek out treatment differ in important ways from those who do not. Still, this finding suggests treatment has a positive influence.

Although men more often encounter traumatic experiences, women are more likely to develop PTSD in response to trauma (Ehlers, Mayou, & Bryant, 1998; Michaud, 2000). Overall, women are about twice as likely to develop PTSD during their lifetimes than men. Women who develop PTSD also tend to have an increased risk of major depression and alcohol abuse (Breslau, Davis, Peterson, & Schultz, 1997). PTSD may also occur among children exposed to traumatic experiences (Silva et al., 2000).

The *DSM-IV* loosened the criteria for PTSD to include reactions to a wide range of traumatic stressors, including receiving a diagnosis of a life-threatening illness. In breast cancer survivors, PTSD symptoms appear to be more common than would be expected in the general population (Bayer et al., 2002; Cordova et al., 1995). A recent study of patients who had experienced severe traumatic brain injuries showed a 27% rate of PTSD (Harvey & Bryant 2000).

Features of Traumatic Stress Disorders

ASD and PTSD share many of the same features or symptoms, including the following.

- *Avoidance behavior.* People with the PTSD tend to avoid cues or situations associated with the trauma. A rape survivor will avoid traveling to the part of town where she was attacked. A combat verteran will avoid reunions with soldiers or watching movies or features stories about war or combat.

- *Reexperiencing the trauma.* The trauma may be reexperienced in the form of intrusive memories, recurrent disturbing dreams, even momentary flashbacks of feeling like one is again on the battlefield or being pursued by an attacker.

- *Impaired functioning.* PTSD is often associated with psychological problems such as depression, anxiety, or alcohol or substance abuse that can make it difficult for the person to function effectively in meeting daily responsiblities.

- *Heightened arousal.* People with PTSD may be unusually tense or feel "on edge" or "keyed up" much of the time. They may become hypervigilant (always on guard) and may complain of disturbed sleep, irritability and angry outbursts, and difficulty concentrating. They may show an exaggerated startle response, such as jumping at any sudden noise.

- *Emotional numbing.* People with PTSD may feel "numb" inside and lose the ability to enjoy activities they formerly took pleasure in or to have loving feelings.

The major difference in the features of ASD and PTSD is the emphasis in ASD on *dissociation*—feelings of detachment from oneself or one's environment (Bryant, 2001; Harvey & Bryant, 2002; USDHHS, 1999a). People with acute stress disorder may feel they

---

are "in a daze" or that the world seems like a dreamlike or unreal place. People with ASD may also be unable to perform necessary tasks, such as obtaining needed medical or legal assistance (APA, 2000).

Theoretical Perspectives

The major conceptual understanding of PTSD derives from the behavioral or learning perspective. Within a classical conditioning framework, traumatic experiences are unconditioned stimuli that become paired with neutral (conditioned) stimuli such as the sights, sounds, and even smells associated with the trauma—for example, the battlefield or the neighborhood in which a person has been raped or assaulted. Consequently, anxiety becomes a conditioned response that is elicited by exposure to trauma-related stimuli.

Cues that reactivate negative arousal or anxiety are associated with thoughts, memories, or even dream images of the trauma, with overhearing someone talking about the trauma, or with visiting the scene of the trauma. Through operant conditioning, the person may learn to avoid any contact with trauma-related stimuli. Avoidance behaviors represent operant responses that are negatively reinforced by relief from anxiety. Unfortunately, by avoiding trauma-related cues, the person also avoids opportunities to overcome the underlying fear. Extinction (gradual weakening or elimination) of conditioned anxiety can occur only when the person encounters the conditioned stimuli (the cues associated with the trauma) in the absence of any troubling unconditioned stimuli.

Learning theory provides a framework for understanding the development of PTSD symptoms in trauma survivors. But bear in mind that not all people who have traumatic experiences go on to develop PTSD. Investigators have identified a number of factors relating to vulnerability to PTSD following trauma (see Table 6.7). Some relate to the event itself, such as the degree of exposure to the trauma. The more directly one is exposed to the trauma, the greater the likelihood of developing PTSD. A recent follow-up study of Vietnam veterans showed that the strongest predictor of PTSD was degree of exposure to combat situations (Koenen et al., 2003). Traumas involving violence directed against a person are more likely to lead to PTSD than other forms of trauma (Norris et al., 2003). Women who are raped are more likely to suffer PTSD than are survivors of natural disasters (Gray & Acierno, 2002).

Other vulnerability factors relate to personal characteristics. For example, people with a history of childhood sexual abuse and those lacking social support and with limited coping skills are at greater risk of suffering PTSD in response to trauma (see Table 6.7). But finding a sense of purpose or meaning in the traumatic experience, such as

Posttraumatic Stress Disorder:
The Case of Sara
"My body remembered . . . I'd go into this state of red alert."

TABLE 6.7	
Factors Predictive of PTSD in Trauma Survivors	
Factors Relating to the Event	**Factors Relating to the Person or Social Environment**
Degree of exposure to trauma	History of childhood sexual abuse
Severity of the trauma	Lack of social support
Exposure to violence	Lack of active coping responses in dealing with the traumatic stressor,
	Feelings of shame
	Symptoms of detachment or "dissociation" shortly following the trauma

Sources: Andrews et al., 2000; Brewin, Andrews, & Valentine, 2000; Koenen et al., 2003; Nishith, Mechanic, & Resick, 2000; Norris et al., 2003; Ozer et al., 2003; Prigerson et al., 2001; Regehr, Hill, & Glancy, 2000; Sharkansky et al., 2000; Silva et al., 2000.

Counseling veterans with posttraumatic stress disorder. Storefront counseling centers have been established across the country to provide supportive services to combat veterans suffering from PTSD.

believing that the war one is fighting is just, may bolster the person's ability to cope with the stressful circumstances and reduce the risk of PTSD (Sutker et al., 1995).

Treatment Approaches

Cognitive–behavioral therapy has produced impressive results in treating PTSD (Kubany et al., 2004; Resick et al., 2002; Taylor et al., 2001). The basic treatment component is repeated exposure to cues associated with the trauma. The PTSD patient may be encouraged to repeatedly talk about the traumatic experience, reexperience the emotional aspects of the trauma in imagination, view related slides or films, or visit the scene of the traumatic event. For example, survivors of serious motor-vehicle crashes who have avoided driving since the accident would be instructed to begin making short driving trips around the neighborhood (Gray & Acierno, 2002). They would also be asked to repeatedly describe the incident and their emotional reactions they experienced (Blanchard et al., 2003). For combat-related PTSD, exposure-based homework assignments might include visiting war memorials or viewing war movies (Frueh et al., 1996).

With CBT, the person gradually reexperiences the traumatic event and accompanying anxiety in a safe setting, thereby allowing extinction to take its course. Evidence shows that supplementing exposure with cognitive restructuring (challenging and replacing dysfunctional thoughts with rational alternatives) can enhance treatment gains (Bryant et al., 2003). Training in stress management skills, such as self-relaxation, may also improve the client's ability to cope with the troubling features of PTSD, such as heightened arousal and the desire to run away from trauma-related stimuli. Training in anger management skills may also be helpful, especially for combat veterans with PTSD (Frueh et al., 1996). Treatment with antidepressant drugs, such as *sertraline* (Zoloft) may also help treat the anxiety components of PTSD (Brady et al., 2000; Davidson et al., 2001).

The "Controversies in Abnormal Psychology" feature discusses a controversial form of treatment for PTSD, eye movement desensitization and reprocessing (EMDR). What is EMDR? Does it work? And if it does work, why does it work?

CONTROVERSIES IN ABNORMAL PSYCHOLOGY
EMDR: Fad or Find?

A new and controversial technique has emerged in the treatment of PTSD—**eye movement desensitization and reprocessing (EMDR)** treatment (Shapiro, 1995, 2001). In EMDR, the client is asked to picture in the mind an image associated with the trauma while the therapist rapidly moves a finger back and forth in front of the client's eyes for 20 or 30 seconds or more. While holding the image in mind, the client is asked to move his or her eyes to follow the therapist's finger. The client then relates to the therapist the images, feelings, bodily sensations, and thoughts that were experienced during the procedure. The procedure is then repeated until the client becomes desensitized to the emotional impact of this disturbing material.

Evidence from carefully controlled studies supports the therapeutic benefits of EMDR in treating PTSD (e.g., Power et al., 2002; S. Taylor et al., 2003; Wilson, Becker, & Tinker, 1997). The controversy relates to why it works and whether the key feature of the technique, the eye movements, are a necessary factor in explaining its effects.

We lack a compelling theoretical model that might explain why rapid eye movements would relieve symptoms of PTSD (Foa & Rothbaum, 1998). Critics contend that the therapeutic effects of EMDR may have nothing to do with eye movements per se (Davidson & Parker, 2001). Perhaps EMDR is effective because of factors it shares with other forms of therapy, such as creating positive expectancies of improvement or providing attention from the therapist (Goldstein et al., 2000; Herbert et al., 2000). Or perhaps EMDR works as a form of exposure therapy (Taylor et al., 2003). In this view, the effective ingredient in EMDR is repeated exposure to traumatic mental imagery, not the rapid eye movements. Though the controversy over EMDR is far from settled, the technique may turn out to be nothing more than a novel way of conducting exposure-based therapy. Meanwhile, evidence from a recent study shows that more traditional exposure therapy works better and faster in reducing avoidance behaviors than EMDR, at least among people who completed treatment (Taylor et al., 2003).

As the debate over EMDR continues, it is worthwhile to consider the famous dictum known as *Occam's razor,* or the principle of parsimony. In its most widely used form today, the principle holds that "the simpler the explanation, the better" (Carroll, 2002). In other words, if we can explain the effects of EMDR on the basis of exposure, then there is no need to posit more complex explanation involving effects of eye movements in helping the individual become desensitized to traumatic images.

Critical Thinking
- Why is it important to determine why a treatment works, not simply whether it works?
- What types of research studies would be needed to determine whether rapid eye movements are needed to account for the benefits of EMDR? ■

ETHNIC DIFFERENCES IN ANXIETY DISORDERS

Although anxiety disorders have been the subject of extensive study, little attention has been directed toward examining ethnic differences in the prevalence of these disorders. Are anxiety disorders more common in certain racial or ethnic groups? We might think that stressors that African Americans in our society are more likely to encounter, such as racism and economic hardship, might contribute to a higher rate of anxiety disorders in this population group (Neal & Turner, 1991). On the other hand, it is possible that African Americans, by dint of having to cope with these hardships in early life, develop a resiliency in the face of stress that shields them from anxiety disorders.

The National Comorbidity Survey (NCS), which was based on a sample that closely represented the general U.S. adult population, found that anxiety disorders overall and specific anxiety disorders in particular were no more common among African Americans than among non-Hispanic White Americans (Eaton et al., 1994). Moreover, panic disorder was actually less common among African Americans in the 45- to 54-year age range than among non-Hispanic White Americans. Panic disorder was also less common among Hispanics than non-Hispanic Whites among people in the 35- to 44-year age range. Trivial ethnic and racial differences were found among younger people. All in all, it appears that the rates of anxiety disorders are generally comparable across racial and ethnic groupings.

Anxiety disorders are not unique to our culture. Panic disorder, for example, is known to occur in many countries, perhaps even universally (Amering & Katschnig, 1990). A multinational study of more than 40,000 people in 10 countries (Canada, Puerto Rico, France, United States, West Germany, Italy, Lebanon, Taiwan, Korea, and New Zealand) showed that rates of panic disorder were relatively consistent, ranging between 1% and 3% in all of these countries except Taiwan, where the rate was under 1%. However, the specific features of panic attacks, such as shortness of breath or fear of dying, may vary from culture to culture (Amering & Katschnig, 1990). Some culture-bound syndromes have features similar to panic attacks, such as *ataque de nervios* (see Chapter 3).

PTSD is also found in many cultures. High rates of PTSD were found in a southwestern U.S. Indian tribe and among earthquake survivors in China, hurricane

eye movement desensitization and reprocessing (EMDR) A controversial form of therapy for PTSD that involves eye tracking of a visual target while holding images of the traumatic experience in mind.

survivors in Nicaragua, Khmer refugees who survived the "killing fields" of the 1970s Pol Pot war in Cambodia, tortured Bhutanese refugees, and survivors of the Balkan conflicts of the 1990s (Goenjian et al., 2001; Lopes et al., 2000; Mitka, 2000; Mollica et al., 2002; Mutler, 2000; Sack, Clarke, & Seeley, 1996; van Ommeren et al., 2001; Wang et al., 2000; Weine et al., 2000). Cultural factors may play a role in determining how people manage and cope with trauma as well as in their vulnerability to traumatic stress reactions and the specific form such a disorder might take (de Silva, 1993).

Overview of Anxiety Disorders

TYPES OF ANXIETY DISORDERS/PREVALENCE RATES (APPROX., IN PARENTHESES)

	Description	Features
Panic Disorder (1%–4%)	Occurrence of repeated panic attacks, which are episodes of sheer terror accompanied by strong physiological symptoms, thoughts of imminent danger or impending doom, and an urge to escape	• Fears of recurring attacks may prompt avoidance of situations in which they occur or settings in which help might not be available • Panic attacks begin unexpectedly but may become associated with certain cues or specific situations
Generalized Anxiety Disorder (5%)	Persistent anxiety that is not limited to particular situations	• Excessive worrying is the keynote feature • Associated with heightened states of bodily arousal, tenseness, being "on edge"
Phobic Disorders (specific: 7%–11%) (social: 3%–13%) (Agoraphobia: 6%)	Excessive fears of particular objects or situations	• Carries a strong avoidance component in which the individual seeks to avoid contact with the phobic stimulus or situation • Subtypes include specific phobia (e.g., acrophobia, claustrophobia, fear of insects or snakes); social phobia (excessive fear of social interactions); and agoraphobia (fear of open, public places)
Obsessive–Compulsive Disorder (2%–3%)	Recurrent obsessions (recurrent, intrusive thoughts) and/or compulsions (repetitive behaviors that the person feels compelled to perform)	• Two major types of compulsions: checking rituals and cleaning rituals • Obsessions generate anxiety that may be at least partially relieved by performance of the compulsive rituals
Traumatic Stress Disorders (8% for PTSD: unknown for ASD)	Acute maladaptive reaction in the immediate aftermath of a traumatic event (acute stress disorder) or prolonged maladaptive reaction to a traumatic event (posttraumatic stress disorder)	• Reexperiencing the traumatic event, avoidance of cues or stimuli associated with the trauma; general or emotional numbing, hyperarousal, emotional distress, and impaired functioning • Vulnerability depends on such factors as severity of the trauma, degree of exposure, coping styles, and availability of social support

CASUAL FACTORS Anxiety disorders reflect an interplay of multiple causes

Biological Factors
- Genetic predispositions
- Irregularities in neurotransmitter functioning
- Abnormalities in brain pathways signaling danger or inhibiting repetitive behaviors
- Prepared conditioning

Social–Environmental Factors
- Exposure to threatening or traumatic events
- Observing fear responses in others
- Lack of social support

Behavioral Factors
- Pairing of aversive stimuli and previously neutral stimuli (classical conditioning)
- Anxiety relief from performing compulsive rituals or avoiding phobic stimuli (operant conditioning)
- Lack of extinction opportunities due to avoidance of feared objects or situations

Emotional and Cognitive Factors
- Unresolved psychological conflicts (Freudian or psychodynamic theory)
- Cognitive factors, such as overprediction of fear, self-defeating or irrational beliefs, oversensitivity to threat, anxiety sensitivity, misattribution of bodily cues, and self-doubts or low self-efficacy

TREATMENT APPROACHES Treatment may include one or more therapeutic approaches

Drug Therapy
- To control anxiety symptoms

Cognitive–Behavioral Therapy
- To unlearn phobic reactions and develop more adaptive ways of thinking

Psychodynamic Therapy
- To gain insight into underlying conflicts that anxiety symptoms may symbolize

Humanistic Therapy
- To identify and come to accept one's genuine feelings and needs

Sources for prevalence rates: APA, 2000; Kessler, et al., 1995; Sheehan & Mao, 2003; Taylor, 1995; USDHHS, 1999a.

Tying It Together

Many psychologists believe that the origins of anxiety disorders involve a complex interplay of environmental, physiological, and psychological factors. Complicating matters further is that different causal pathways may be at work in different cases.

To illustrate, let us offer a possible causal pathway for panic disorder, which is diagrammed in Figure 6.6. Some people may inherit a genetic predisposition, or diathesis, that makes them more likely to panic in response to changes in bodily sensations. This genetic predisposition may be in the form of an overly sensitive suffocation alarm system that is triggered by mild fluctuations in blood levels of carbon dioxide, perhaps resulting from unrecognized hyperventilation. Cognitive factors may also be involved. Cues associated with changing carbon dioxide levels, such as dizziness, tingling, or numbness, may be misconstrued as signs of an impending disaster—suffocation, heart attack, or loss of control. This in turn may lead, like dominoes falling in line, to an anxiety reaction that quickly spirals into a full-fledged panic attack.

Whether this happens may depend on another vulnerability factor, the individual's level of anxiety sensitivity. People with high levels of anxiety sensitivity may be more likely to panic in response to changes in their physical sensations. In some cases, a person's anxiety sensitivity may be so high that panic ensues, even without a genetic predisposition. Over time, panic attacks may come to be triggered by exposure to internal or external cues (conditioned stimuli) that have been associated with panic attacks in the past, such as heart palpitations or boarding a train or elevator. As we saw in the case of Michael at the beginning of the chapter, changes in physical sensations can be misconstrued as signs of an impending heart attack, setting the stage for a cycle of physiological responses and catastrophic thoughts that can result in a full-blown panic attack. Helping panic sufferers develop more effective coping skills for handling anxiety symptoms without catastrophizing can help break this vicious cycle.

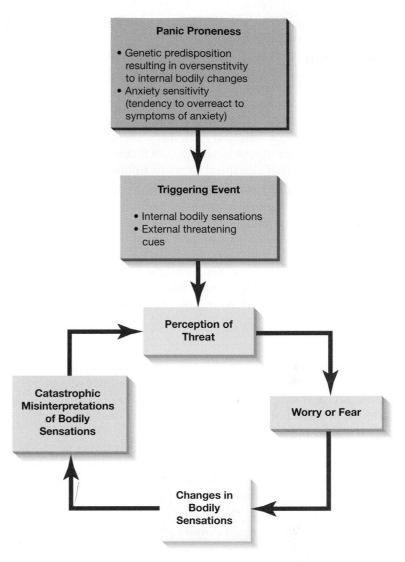

FIGURE 6.6 A cognitive/biological model of panic disorder.
In panic-prone people, perceptions of threat from internal or external cues lead to feelings of worry or fear, which are accompanied by changes in bodily sensations (for example, heart racing or palpitations). Exaggerated, catastrophic interpretations of these sensations intensifies perceptions of threat, which further heightens the perception of threat, resulting in yet more anxiety, more changes in bodily sensations, and so on in a vicious cycle that can culminate in a full-blown panic attack. Anxiety sensitivity increases the likelihood that people will overreact to bodily cues or symptoms of anxiety.

Source: Adapted from Clark, 1986, and other sources.

SUMMING UP

Historical Perspectives on Anxiety Disorders

What are anxiety disorders? Anxiety, a generalized sense of apprehension or fear, is normal and desirable under some conditions, but it can become abnormal when it is excessive or inappropriate. Disturbed patterns of behavior in which anxiety is the most prominent feature are labeled anxiety disorders.

Panic Disorder

What is panic disorder? Panic disorder is characterized by often immobilizing, repeated panic attacks, which involve intense physical features, notably cardiovascular symptoms, that may be accompanied by sheer terror and fears of losing control, losing one's mind, or dying. Panic attack sufferers often limit their outside activity in fear of recurrent attacks. This can lead to agoraphobia, the fear of venturing into public places.

How is panic disorder understood in contemporary views? The predominant model conceptualizes panic disorder in terms of a combination of biological factors (e.g., genetic proneness, increased sensitivity to bodily cues) and cognitive factors (e.g., catastrophic misinterpretation of bodily sensations, anxiety sensitivity). In this view, panic disorder involves physiological and psychological factors interacting in a vicious cycle that can spiral into a full-blown panic.

What are the major treatment approaches for panic disorder? Cognitive–behavioral treatment of panic disorder incorporates self-monitoring, exposure to panic-related cues, including bodily sensations, and development of coping responses for handling panic attacks without catastrophic misinterpretations of bodily cues. Biomedical approaches incorporate use of antidepressant drugs, which have antianxiety and antitpanic effects as well as antidepressant effects.

Phobic Disorders

What are phobic disorders? Phobias are excessive irrational fears of specific objects or situations. Phobias involve a behavioral component, avoidance of the phobic stimulus, in addition to physical and cognitive features. Specific phobias are excessive fears of particular objects or situations, such as mice, spiders, tight places, or heights. Social phobia involves an intense fear of being judged negatively by others. Agoraphobia involves fears of venturing into public places. Agoraphobia may occur with, or in the absence of, panic disorder.

How do phobias develop? Learning theorists explain anxiety disorders through conditioning and observational learning. Mowrer's two-factor model incorporates classical and operant conditioning in the explanation of phobias. Phobias, however, appear to be moderated by cognitive factors, such as oversensitivity to threatening cues, overpredictions of dangerousness, and self-defeating thoughts and irrational beliefs. Genetic factors also appear to increase proneness to development of phobias. Some investigators believe we are genetically predisposed to acquire certain types of phobias that may have had survival value for our prehistoric ancestors.

How are phobias treated? The major forms of treatment are learning-based approaches, such as systematic desensitization and gradual exposure, cognitive therapy, and drug therapy.

Obsessive–Compulsive Disorder

What is obsessive–compulsive disorder? Obsessive–compulsive disorder, or OCD, involves recurrent patterns of obsessions, compulsions, or a combination of the two. Obsessions are nagging, persistent thoughts that create anxiety and seem beyond the person's ability to control. Compulsions are apparently irresistible repetitious urges to perform certain behaviors, such as repeated elaborate washing after using the bathroom.

How is obsessive–compulsive disorder understood? Within the psychodynamic tradition, obsessions represent leakage of unconscious impulses into consciousness, and compulsions are acts that help keep these impulses repressed. Research on biological factors highlights roles for genetics and for brain mechanisms involved in signaling danger and controlling repetitive behaviors. Research evidence shows roles for cognitive factors, such as overfocusing on one's thoughts, exaggerated perceptions of risk of unfortunate events, and perfectionism, Learning theorists view compulsive behaviors as operant responses that are negatively reinforced by relief of anxiety produced by obsessional thinking.

How is obsesssive–compulsive disorder treated? The major contemporary treatment approaches include learning-based models (exposure with response prevention), cognitive therapy (correction of cognitive distortions), and use of SSRI-type antidepressants.

Generalized Anxiety Disorder

What is generalized anxiety disorder? Generalized anxiety disorder is a type of anxiety disorder involving persistent anxiety that seems to be "free floating" or not tied to specific situations.

How is generalized anxiety disorder understood? Psychodynamic theorists view anxiety disorders as attempts by the ego to control the conscious emergence of threatening impulses. Feelings of anxiety are seen as warning signals that threatening impulses are nearing awareness. Learning-based models focus on the generalization of anxiety across stimulus situations. Cognitive theorists seek to account for generalized anxiety in terms of faulty thoughts or beliefs that underlie worry. Biological models focus on irregularities in neurotransmitter functioning in the brain.

How is generalized anxiety disorder treated? The two major treatment approaches are cognitive–behavioral therapy (CBT) and drug therapy (typically *paroxetine*).

Traumatic Stress Disorders

What are the two types of traumatic stress disorders? The two types of stress disorders are acute stress disorder and posttraumatic stress disorder. Both involve maladaptive reactions to traumatic stress. Acute stress disorder occurs in the days and weeks following exposure to a traumatic event. Posttraumatic stress disorder persists for months or even years or decades after the traumatic experience and may not begin until months or years after the event.

How might we understand the development of PTSD? Learning theory provides a framework for understanding the conditioning of fear to trauma-related stimuli and the role of negative reinforcement in maintaining avoidance behavior.

However, other factors come into play in determining vulnerability to PTSD, including degree of exposure to the trauma and personal characteristics, such as a history of childhood sexual abuse and lack of social support.

How is PTSD treated? The major treatment approach is cognitive-behavioral therapy that focuses on repeated exposure to cues assciated with the trauma and may be combined with cognitive restructuring and training in stress management and anger management techniques.

Ethnic Differences in Anxiety Disorders

What relationships exist between ethnicity and the prevalence of anxiety disorders? Evidence from a nationally representative sample of U.S. adults showed that rates of anxiety disorders were generally comparable across racial and ethnic groupings.

KEY TERMS

anxiety *(p. 169)*
anxiety disorders *(p. 169)*
panic disorder *(p. 172)*
agoraphobia *(p. 172)*
phobia *(p. 178)*
specific phobia *(p. 178)*
social phobia *(p. 180)*
two-factor model *(p. 183)*

systematic desensitization *(p. 187)*
fear-stimulus hierarchy *(p. 187)*
gradual exposure *(p. 188)*
flooding *(p. 189)*
virtual reality therapy *(p. 189)*
cognitive restructuring *(p. 191)*
obsessive-compulsive disorder *(p. 192)*
obsession *(p. 192)*

compulsion *(p. 192)*
generalized anxiety disorder (GAD) *(p. 196)*
acute stress disorder (ASD) *(p. 198)*
posttraumatic stress disorder (PTSD) *(p. 199)*
eye movement desensitization and reprocessing (EMDR) *(p. 203)*

WEB TOOLS

The companion website offers tools to enrich your learning experience and help you succeed in class. Go to www.prenhall.com/nevid for the gateway to the following resources:

- **VIDEO** links to connect to the video case files on the companion CD-ROM. VIDEO icons in the margins of the chapter highlight the case examples included in the CD-ROM. You can also access the CD-ROM directly if you do not have a Web connection.

- **QUIZ** links to self-scoring quizzes corresponding to each section of the chapter. The quizzes help you review your knowledge of the content in each chapter.

- **WEB** links to direct you to related sites that enhance your learning of abnormal psychology.

Dissociative and Somatoform Disorders

"I"

"We Share a Single Body"

Elaina is a licensed clinical therapist. Connie is a nurse. Sydney is a delightful little girl who likes to collect bugs in an old mayonnaise jar. Lynn is shy and has trouble saying her l's, and Heather—Heather is a teenager trying hard to be grown-up. We are many different people, but we have one very important thing in common: We share a single body . . .

We have dozens of different people living inside us, each with our own memories, talents, dreams, and fears. Some of us "come out" to work or play or cook or sleep. Some of us only watch from inside. Some of us are still lost in the past, a tortured past full of incest and abuse. And there are many who were so damaged by this past and who have fled so deep inside, we fear we may never reach them. . . .

Many of our Alter personalities were born of abuse. Some came because they were needed, others came to protect.

Leah came whenever she heard our father say, "Come lay awhile with me." If she came, none of our other Alters would have to do those things he wanted. She could do them for us, and protect us from that part of our childhood.

Source: From "Quiet Storm," a pseudonym used by a woman who claims to have several personalities residing within herself

---

Truth or Fiction?

T❑ F❑ In some reported cases, alternate personalities within the same individual have different allergic reactions and eyeglass prescriptions. (p. 211)

T❑ F❑ The term *split personality* refers to schizophrenia. (p. 212)

T❑ F❑ Very few of us have episodes in which we feel strangely detached from our own bodies or thought processes. (p. 218)

T❑ F❑ Most people with multiple personalities do not report any history of physical or sexual abuse during childhood. (p. 221)

T❑ F❑ Some people show up repeatedly at hospital emergency rooms, feigning illness and seeking treatment for no apparent reason. (p. 227)

T❑ F❑ Some people who have lost their ability to see or move their legs become strangely indifferent toward their physical condition. (p. 228)

T❑ F❑ In China in the 1980s, more than 2,000 people fell prey to the belief that their genitals were shrinking and retracting into their bodies. (p. 232)

T❑ F❑ The term *hysteria* derives from the Greek word for *testicle*. (p. 234)

THIS IS A FIRST-HAND DESCRIPTION OF A PERSONALITY SO FRACTURED BECAUSE OF severe childhood abuse that it splinters into many different pieces. Some of the pieces bear memories of the abuse, whereas others go about their business unaware of the pain and trauma. Now imagine that these separate parts develop their own unique characteristics. Imagine too that these alter personalities become so compartmentalized that they don't know of each other's existence. Even the core personality may not know of the existence of the others.

This is a description of *dissociative identity disorder,* known popularly as "multiple personality," perhaps the most perplexing and intriguing of all psychological disorders. The diagnosis is officially recognized in the *DSM* system, although it remains controversial, with many professionals doubting its existence or ascribing it to a form of role-playing. Dissociative identity disorder is classified as a type of *dissociative disorder,* a grouping of psychological disorders characterized by changes or disturbances in the functions of self—identity, memory, or consciousness—that make the personality whole.

Normally speaking, we know who we are. We may not be certain of ourselves in an existential, philosophical sense, but we know our names, where we live, and what we do for a living. We also tend to remember the salient events of our lives. We may not recall every detail, and we may confuse what we had for dinner on Tuesday with what we had on Monday, but we generally know what we have been doing for the past days, weeks, and years. Normally speaking, there is a unity to consciousness that gives rise to a sense of self. We perceive ourselves as progressing through space and time. In people with dissociative disorders, one or more of these aspects of daily living is disturbed—sometimes bizarrely so.

In this chapter we explore the dissociative disorders as well as another class of puzzling disorders, the *somatoform disorders.* People with somatoform disorders have physical complaints that defy any medical explanation and so are believed to involve underlying psychological conflicts or issues. People with these disorders may report blindness or numbness, although no organic basis can be detected. In other cases, people may hold exaggerated beliefs about the seriousness of their physical symptoms, such as taking them to be signs of life-threatening illnesses despite medical reassurances to the contrary.

In early versions of the *DSM,* dissociative and somatoform disorders were classified with the anxiety disorders under the general category of "neurosis." This grouping was based on the psychodynamic model, which holds that dissociative and somatoform disorders, as well as the anxiety disorders discussed in Chapter 6, involve maladaptive ways of managing anxiety. In the anxiety disorders, the appearance of disturbing levels of anxiety is expressed directly in behavior, such as in a phobic reaction to an object or situation. In contrast, the role of anxiety in the dissociative and somatoform disorders is inferred rather than expressed overtly in behavior. Persons with dissociative disorders manifest psychological problems, such as loss of memory or changes in identity, that, according to the psychodynamic model, keep the underlying sources of anxiety out of awareness, such as conflicts over sexual or aggressive impulses. Likewise, people with some somatoform disorders often show a strange indifference to physical problems, such as loss of vision, that would greatly concern most of us. Here, too, it was theorized that the "symptoms" mask unconscious sources of anxiety. Some theorists interpret indifference to symptoms to mean that those symptoms have an underlying benefit; that is, they help prevent anxiety from intruding into consciousness.

The *DSM* now separates the anxiety disorders from the other categories of neuroses—the dissociative and somatoform disorders—with which they were historically linked. Yet many practitioners continue to use the broad conceptualization of neuroses as a useful framework for classifying the anxiety, dissociative, and somatoform disorders.

dissociative disorder A disorder characterized by disruption, or dissociation, of identity, memory, or consciousness.

DISSOCIATIVE DISORDERS

The major **dissociative disorders** include *dissociative identity disorder, dissociative amnesia, dissociative fugue,* and *depersonalization disorder*. In each case, there is a disruption or dissociation ("splitting off") of the functions of identity, memory, or consciousness that normally make us whole.

Dissociative Identity Disorder

The Ohio State campus dwelled in terror as four college women were seized, coerced to cash checks or get money from automatic teller machines, then raped. A cryptic phone call led to the capture of Billy Milligan, a 23-year-old drifter who had been dishonorably discharged from the Navy.

Not the Boy Next Door

Billy wasn't quite the boy next door. He tried twice to commit suicide while he was awaiting trial, so his lawyers requested a psychiatric evaluation. The psychologists and psychiatrists who examined Billy deduced that ten personalities dwelled inside of him. Eight were male and two were female. Billy's personality had been fractured by a brutal childhood. The personalities displayed diverse facial expressions, memories, and vocal patterns. They performed in dissimilar ways on personality and intelligence tests.

Arthur, a sensible but phlegmatic personality, conversed with a British accent. Danny, 14, was a painter of still lifes. Christopher, 13, was normal enough, but somewhat anxious. A 3-year-old English girl went by the name of Christine. Tommy, a 16-year-old, was an antisocial personality and escape artist. It was Tommy who had enlisted in the Navy. Allen was an 18-year-old con artist. Allen also smoked. Adelena was a 19-year-old introverted lesbian. It was she who had committed the rapes. It was probably David who had made the mysterious phone call. David was an anxious 9-year-old who wore the anguish of early childhood trauma on his sleeve. After his second suicide attempt, Billy had been placed in a straitjacket. When the guards checked his cell, however, he was sleeping with the straitjacket as a pillow. Tommy later explained that he was responsible for Billy's escape.

The defense argued that Billy was afflicted with multiple personality disorder. Several alternate personalities resided within him. The alternate personalities knew about Billy, but Billy was unaware of them. Billy, the core or dominant per-

sonality, had learned as a child that he could sleep as a way of avoiding the sexual and physical abuse of his father. A psychiatrist claimed that Billy had likewise been "asleep"—in a sort of "psychological coma"—when the crimes were committed. Therefore, Billy should be judged innocent by reason of insanity.

Billy was decreed not guilty by reason of insanity. He was committed to a mental institution. In the institution, 14 additional personalities emerged. Thirteen were rebellious and labeled "undesirables" by Arthur. The fourteenth was the "Teacher," who was competent and supposedly represented the integration of all the other personalities. Billy was released six years later.

—Adapted from Keyes, 1982

Billy was diagnosed with multiple personality disorder, which is now called **dissociative identity disorder.** In dissociative identity disorder, sometimes referred to as "split personality," two or more personalities—each with well-defined traits and memories—"occupy" one person. They may or may not be aware of one another. In some isolated cases, alternate personalities (also called *alter personalities*) may even show different EEG records, allergic reactions, responses to medication, and even different eyeglass prescriptions and pupil sizes (Birnbaum, Martin, & Thomann, 1996; Braun, 1986; S. D. Miller et al., 1991; S. D. Miller & Triggiano, 1991). Or one personality may be color blind, whereas others are not (Braun, 1986). If such patterns stand up to further scientific scrutiny, they would offer a remarkable illustration of the diversity of perceptions and somatic patterns that are possible within the same person.

Dissociative identity disorder, which is often called "multiple personality" or "split personality" by laypeople, should not be confused with schizophrenia. Schizophrenia (which comes from roots that mean "split brain") occurs much more commonly than multiple personality and involves the "splitting" of cognition, affect, and behavior. In a person with schizophrenia, there may be little agreement between the thoughts and the emotions, or between the individual's perception of reality and what is truly happening. The person with schizophrenia may become giddy when told of disturbing events or may experience

dissociative identity disorder A dissociative disorder in which a person has two or more distinct, or alter, personalities.

TRUTH or FICTION? *REVISITED*

In some reported cases, alternate personalities within the same individual have different allergic reactions and eyeglass prescriptions

☑ **TRUE.** In a few reported cases, alternate personalities were reported to have had their own allergic reactions and eyeglass prescriptions that differed from those of other personalities within the same person.

The Three Faces of Eve. In the classic film *The Three Faces of Eve,* a timid housewife, Eve White (A) harbors two alter personalities: Eve Black (B), a libidinous and antisocial personality, and Jane (C), an integrated personality who can accept her sexual and aggressive urges but still engage in socially appropriate behavior. In the film, the three personalities are successfully integrated. In real life, however, the person depicted in the film reportedly split into 22 personalities later on.

hallucinations or delusions (see Chapter 12). In people with multiple personality, the personality apparently divides into two or more personalities, but each of them usually shows more integrated functioning on cognitive, affective, and behavioral levels than is true of people with schizophrenia.

Celebrated cases of multiple personality have been depicted in the popular media. One became the subject of the 1950s film *The Three Faces of Eve*. In the film, Eve White is a timid housewife who harbors two other personalities: Eve Black, a sexually provocative, antisocial personality, and Jane, a balanced, developing personality who could balance her sexual needs with the demands of social acceptability. The three faces eventually merged into one—Jane, providing a "happy ending." The real-life Eve, whose name was Chris Sizemore, failed to maintain this integrated personality. Her personality reportedly split into 22 subsequent personalities. A second well-known case is that of Sybil. Sybil was played by Sally Field in the film of the same name and reportedly had 16 personalities.

Features In one of the largest studies on multiple personality to date, Ross, Norton, and Wozney (1989) collected 236 case reports of people with the disorder from 203 health professionals in Canada. Unlike reports of multiple personality in the 19th and early 20th centuries, in which most cases involved dual personalities, cases in the Canadian sample averaged 15 to 16 alter personalities each (Ross et al., 1989).

There are many variations. In some cases, the host (main) personality is unaware of the existence of the other identities, whereas the other identities are aware of the existence of the host (Dorahy, 2001). In other cases, the different personalities are completely unaware of one another. Sometimes two personalities vie for control of the person. Sometimes there is one dominant or core personality and several subordinate personalities. Some of the more common alter personalities include children of various ages, adolescents of the opposite gender, prostitutes, and gay males and lesbians (Ross et al., 1989). Some of the personalities may show psychotic symptoms—a break with reality expressed in the form of hallucinations and delusional thinking.

All in all, the clusters of alter personalities serve as a microcosm of conflicting urges and cultural themes. Themes of sexual ambivalence (sexual openness vs. restrictiveness) and shifting sexual orientations are particularly common. It is as if conflicting internal impulses cannot coexist or achieve dominance. As a result, each is expressed as the cardinal or steering trait of an alternate personality. The clinician can sometimes elicit alternate personalities by inviting them to make themselves known, as in asking, "Is there another part of you that wants to say something to me?" The following case illustrates the emergence of an alternate personality.

Dissociative Identity:
The Three Faces of Eve
"Let us hear the various personalitites speak . . ."

Harriet Emerges: A Case of Dissociative Identity Disorder

[Margaret explained that] she often "heard a voice telling her to say things and do things." It was, she said, "a terrible voice" that sometimes threatened to "take over completely." When it was finally suggested to [Margaret] that she let the voice "take over," she closed her eyes, clenched her fists, and grimaced for a few moments during which she was out of contact with those around her. Suddenly she opened her eyes and one was in the presence of another person. Her name, she said, was "Harriet." Whereas Margaret had been paralyzed, and complained of fatigue, headache and backache, Harriet felt well, and she at once proceeded to walk unaided around the interviewing room. She spoke scornfully of Margaret's religiousness, her invalidism, and her puritanical life, professing that she herself liked to drink and "go partying" but that Margaret was always going to church and reading the Bible. "But," she said impishly and proudly, "I make her miserable—I make her say and do things she doesn't want to." At length, at the interviewer's suggestion, Harriet reluctantly agreed to "bring Margaret back," and after more grimacing and fist clenching, Margaret reappeared, paralyzed, complaining of her headache and backache, and completely amnesiac for the brief period of Harriet's release from prison.

—From Nemiah, 1978, pp. 179–180

Like Billy Milligan, Chris Sizemore, and Margaret, the dominant personality is often unaware of the existence of the alter personalities. It thus seems that unconscious processes control the mechanism that results in dissociation. Although the dominant personality lacks insight into the existence of the other personalities, she or he may vaguely sense that something is amiss. There may even be "interpersonality rivalry" in which one personality aspires to do away with another, usually in ignorance of the fact that murdering an alternate would result in the death of all.

Although women constitute the majority of cases of multiple personality, the proportion of males diagnosed with the disorder has been on the rise (Goff & Summs, 1993). The numbers of reported alternates has also been increasing, rising to an average of 12 alternates during the 1980s from an average of 3 in earlier cases. Women with the disorder tend to have more alternate identities, averaging 15 or more, than do men, who average about 8 identities (APA, 2000). The reasons for this difference remain unknown.

The diagnostic features of dissociative identity disorder are listed in Table 7.1.

Controversies Although multiple personality is generally considered rare, the very existence of the disorder continues to arouse debate. Many professionals express profound doubts about the diagnosis (Pope et al, 1999).

Only a handful of cases worldwide were reported from 1920 to 1970, but since then the number of reported cases has skyrocketed into the thousands (Spanos, 1994). This has led some practitioners to suggest that multiple personality may be more common than was earlier believed (e.g., Bliss & Jeppsen, 1985). Others, however, believe the disorder is overdiagnosed in highly suggestible people who might simply be following suggestions that they might have the disorder (APA, 2000). Increased public attention paid to the disorder in recent years may also account for the perception that its prevalence is greater than was commonly believed.

The disorder does appear to be culture bound and largely restricted to North America (Spanos, 1994). Relatively few cases have been reported elsewhere, even in such Western countries as Great Britain and France. A recent survey in Japan failed to find even one case, and in Switzerland, 90% of the psychiatrists polled had never seen a case of the disorder (Modestin, 1992; Spanos, 1994). Even in North America, few psychologists and psychiatrists have ever encountered a case of multiple personality. Most cases are reported by a relatively small number of investigators and clinicians who strongly believe in the existence of the disorder. Critics wonder if they may be helping to manufacture that which they are seeking.

Some leading authorities, such as the late psychologist Nicholas Spanos, believe so. Spanos and others have challenged the existence of dissociative identity disorder (Reisner, 1994; Spanos, 1994). To Spanos, dissociative identity is not a distinct disorder, but a form of role-playing in which individuals first come to construe themselves as having

Dissociative Identity Disorder:
Dr. Holliday Milby

TABLE 7.1

Features of Dissociative Identity Disorder (Formerly Multiple Personality Disorder)

1. At least two distinct personalities exist within the person, with each having a relatively enduring and distinct pattern of perceiving, thinking about, and relating to the environment and the self.

2. Two or more of these personalities repeatedly take complete control of the individual's behavior.

3. There is a failure to recall important personal information too substantial to be accounted for by ordinary forgetfulness.

4. The disorder cannot be accounted for by the effects of a psychoactive substance or a general medical condition.

Source: Adapted from the *DSM-IV-TR* (APA, 2000).

multiple selves and then begin to act in ways that are consistent with their conception of the disorder. Eventually their role playing becomes so ingrained that it becomes a reality to them. Perhaps their therapists or counselors unintentionally planted the idea in their minds that their confusing welter of emotions and behaviors may represent different personalities at work. Impressionable people may have learned how to enact the role of persons with the disorder by watching others on television and in the movies. Films like *The Three Faces of Eve* and *Sybil* have given detailed examples of the behaviors that characterize multiple personalities (Spanos, Weekes, & Bertrand, 1985). Or perhaps therapists provided cues about the features of multiple personality.

Once the role is established, it is maintained through social reinforcement, such as attention from others and avoidance of accountability for unacceptable behavior. This is not to suggest that people with multiple personalities are "faking," any more than you are faking when you perform different daily roles as student, spouse, or worker. You may enact the role of a student (e.g., sitting attentively in class, raising your hand when you wish to talk) because you have learned to organize your behavior according to the nature of the role and because you have been rewarded for doing so. People with multiple personalities may have come to identify so closely with the role that it becomes real for them.

Relatively few cases of multiple personality involve criminal behavior, so the incentives for enacting a multiple personality role do not often relieve individuals of criminal responsibility for their behavior. But there still may be benefits to enacting the role of a multiple personality, such as a therapist's expression of interest and excitement at discovering a multiple personality. People with multiple personalities were often highly imaginative during childhood. Accustomed to playing games of "make believe," they may readily adopt alternate identities, especially if they learn how to enact the multiple personality role and there are external sources of validation, such as a clinician's interest and concern.

The social reinforcement model may help to explain why some clinicians seem to "discover" many more cases of multiple personality than others. These clinicians may unknowingly cue clients to enact the multiple personality role and then reinforce the performance with extra attention and concern. With the right set of cues, certain clients may adopt the role of a multiple personality to please their clinicians. Some authorities have challenged the role-playing model (for example, Gleaves, 1996), and it remains to be seen how many cases of the disorder in clinical practice the model can explain.

Whether dissociative identity disorder is a real phenomenon or a form of role-playing, there is no question that people who display this behavior have serious emotional and behavioral difficulties. Moreover, the diagnosis may not be all that unusual among some subgroups in the population, such as psychiatric inpatients. In one study of 484 adult psychiatric inpatients, at least 5% showed evidence of multiple personality (Ross et al., 1991). We have noted a tendency for claims of multiple personality to spread on inpatient units. In one case, Susan, a prostitute admitted for depression and suicidal thoughts, claimed that she could only exchange sex for money when "another person" inside her emerged and took control. Upon hearing this, another woman, Ginny—a child abuser who had been admitted for depression after her daughter had been removed from her home by social services—claimed that she only abused her daughter when another person inside of her assumed control of her personality. Susan's chart recommended that she be evaluated further for multiple personality disorder (the term used at the time to refer to the disorder), but Ginny was diagnosed with a depressive disorder and a personality disorder, not with multiple personality disorder.

Suicidal behavior is common among people with multiple personalities. Seventy-two percent of the cases in the Canadian study (Ross et al., 1989) had attempted suicide, and about 2% had succeeded.

Dissociative Amnesia

dissociative amnesia is believed to be the most common type of dissociative disorder (Maldonado, Butler, & Spiegel, 1998). *Amnesia* derives from the Greek roots *a-*, meaning "not," and *mnasthai*, meaning "to remember." In **dissociative amnesia** (formerly

dissociative amnesia A dissociative disorder in which a person experiences memory loss without any identifiable organic cause.

called *psychogenic amnesia*), the person becomes unable to recall important personal information, usually involving traumatic or stressful experiences, in a way that cannot be accounted for by simple forgetfulness. Nor can the memory loss be attributed to a particular organic cause, such as a blow to the head or a particular medical condition, or to the direct effects of drugs or alcohol. Unlike some progressive forms of memory impairment (such as dementia associated with Alzheimer's disease; see Chapter 15), the memory loss in dissociative amnesia is reversible, although it may last for days, weeks, or even years. Recall of dissociated memories may happen gradually but often occurs suddenly and spontaneously, as when the soldier who has no recall of a battle for several days afterward suddenly recalls the experience after being transported to a hospital away from the battlefield.

Amnesia is not ordinary forgetfulness, such as forgetting someone's name or where you left your car keys. Memory loss in amnesia is more profound or wide ranging. Dissociative amnesia is divided into five distinct types of memory problems.

1. *Localized amnesia.* Most cases take the form of *localized amnesia* in which events occurring during a specific time period are lost to memory. For example, the person cannot recall events for a number of hours or days after a stressful or traumatic incident, such as a battle or car accident.

2. *Selective amnesia.* In *selective amnesia,* people forget only the disturbing particulars that take place during a certain period of time. A person may recall the period of life during which he conducted an extramarital affair, but not the guilt-arousing affair itself. A soldier may recall most of the battle, but not the death of his buddy.

3. *Generalized amnesia.* In *generalized amnesia,* people forget their entire lives—who they are, what they do, where they live, whom they live with. This form of amnesia is very rare, although you wouldn't think so if you watch daytime soap operas. Persons with generalized amnesia cannot recall personal information, but they tend to retain their habits, tastes, and skills. If you had generalized amnesia, you would still know how to read, although you would not recall your elementary school teachers. You would still prefer French fries to baked potatoes—or vice versa.

4. *Continuous amnesia.* In this form of amnesia, the person forgets everything that occurred from a particular point in time up to and including the present.

5. *Systematized amnesia.* Finally, in systematized amnesia, the memory loss is specific to a particular category of information, such as memory about one's family or particular people in one's life.

People with dissociative amnesia usually forget events or periods of life that were traumatic—that generated strong negative emotions such as horror or guilt. Consider this case:

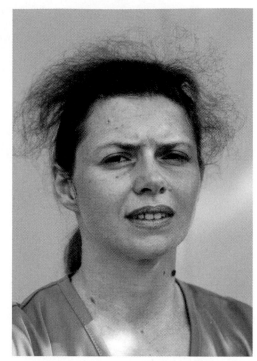

"Jane Doe." This woman, called "Jane Doe" by rescue workers, was found wandering in a Florida park in a dazed state. She reported she had no memory of her background or even who she was. She was recognized by her parents after appearing on a national TV program. She reportedly never regained her memory.

Rutger: A Case of Dissociative Amnesia

He was brought to the emergency room of a hospital by a stranger. He was dazed and claimed not to know who he was or where he lived, and the stranger had found him wandering in the streets. Despite his confusion, it did not appear that he had been drinking or abusing drugs or that his amnesia could be attributed to physical trauma. After staying in the hospital for a few days, he awoke in distress. His memory had returned. His name was Rutger and he had urgent business to attend to. He wanted to know why he had been hospitalized and demanded to leave. At the time of admission, Rutger appeared to be suffering from generalized amnesia: He could not recall his identity or the personal events of his life. But now that he was requesting discharge, Rutger showed localized amnesia for the period between entering the emergency room and the morning he regained his memory for prior events.

> *Rutger provided information about the events prior to his hospitalization that was confirmed by the police. On the day when his amnesia began, Rutger had killed a pedestrian with his automobile. There had been witnesses, and the police had voiced the opinion that Rutger—although emotionally devastated—was blameless in the incident. Rutger was instructed, however, to fill out an accident report and to appear at the inquest. Still nonplussed, Rutger filled out the form at a friend's home. He accidentally left his wallet and his identification there. After placing the form in a mailbox, Rutger became dazed and lost his memory.*
>
> *Although Rutger was not responsible for the accident, he felt awful about the pedestrian's death. His amnesia was probably connected with feelings of guilt, the stress of the accident, and concerns about the inquest.*
>
> —Adapted from Cameron, 1963, pp. 355–356

People sometimes claim they cannot recall certain events of their lives, such as criminal acts, promises made to others, and so forth. Falsely claiming amnesia as a way of escaping responsibility is called *malingering,* which refers to faking symptoms or making false claims for personal gain. Our research methods cannot guarantee that we can distinguish people with dissociative amnesia from malingerers. But experienced clinicians can make reasonably well-educated guesses.

Dissociative Fugue

dissociative fugue A dissociative disorder in which one suddenly flees from one's life situation, travels to a new location, assumes a new identity, and has amnesia for personal material.

Fugue derives from the Latin *fugere,* meaning "flight." The word *fugitive* has the same origin. Fugue is like amnesia "on the run." In **dissociative fugue** (formerly called *psychogenic fugue*), the person travels suddenly and unexpectedly from his or her home or place of work, is unable to recall past personal information, and either becomes confused about his or her identity or assumes a new identity (either partially or completely) (APA, 2000). Despite these odd behaviors, the person may appear "normal" and show no other signs of mental disturbance (Maldonado et al., 1998). The person may not think about the past, or may report a past filled with false memories without recognizing them as false.

Whereas people with amnesia appear to wander aimlessly, people in a fugue state act more purposefully. Some stick close to home. They spend the afternoon in the park or in a theater, or they spend the night at a hotel under another name, usually avoiding contact with others. But the new identity is incomplete and fleeting, and the individual's former sense of self returns in a matter of hours or a few days. Less common is a pattern in which the fugue state lasts for months or years and involves travel to distant places and assumption of a new identity. These individuals may assume an identity that is more spontaneous and sociable than their former selves, which were typically "quiet" and "ordinary." They may establish new families and successful businesses. Although these events sound rather bizarre, the fugue state is not considered psychotic because people with the disorder can think and behave quite normally—in their new lives, that is. Then one day, quite suddenly, their awareness of their past identity returns to them, and they are flooded with old memories. Now they typically do not recall the events that occurred during the fugue state. The new identity, the new life—including all its involvements and responsibilities—vanish from memory.

Fugue, like amnesia, is relatively rare and is believed to affect only about 2 people in 1,000 within the general population (APA, 2000). It is most likely to occur in wartime (Loewenstein, 1991) or in the wake of another kind of disaster or extremely stressful event. The underlying notion is that dissociation in the fugue state protects one from traumatic memories or other sources of emotionally painful experiences or conflict (Maldonado et al., 1998).

Fugue can also be difficult to distinguish from malingering. That is, persons who were dissatisfied with their former lives could claim to have amnesia when they are discovered in their new locations and new identities.

Consider the following case, in which the evidence supports a diagnosis of dissociative fugue (Spitzer et al., 1989).

Burt or Gene? A Case of Dissociative Fugue?

The man told the police that his name was Burt Tate. "Burt," a 42-year-old white male, had gotten into a fight at the diner where he worked. When the police arrived, they found that he carried no identification. He told them he had drifted into town a few weeks earlier, but could not recall where he had lived or worked before arriving in town. While no charges were pressed against him, the police prevailed upon him to come to the emergency room for evaluation. "Burt" knew the town he was in and the current date and recognized that it was somewhat unusual that he couldn't remember his past, but he didn't seem concerned about it. There was no evidence of any physical injuries, head trauma, or drug or alcohol abuse. The police made some inquiries and discovered that "Burt" fit the profile of a missing person, Gene Saunders, who had disappeared a month earlier from a city some 2,000 miles away. Mrs. Saunders was called in and confirmed that "Burt" was indeed her husband. She reported that her husband, who had worked in middle-level management in a manufacturing company, had been having difficulty at work before his disappearance. He was passed over for promotion and his supervisor was highly critical of his work. The job stress apparently affected his behavior at home. Once easygoing and sociable, he withdrew into himself and began to criticize his wife and children. Then, just before his disappearance, he had a violent argument with his 18-year-old son. His son called him a "failure" and stormed out the door. Two days later, the man disappeared. When he came face to face with his wife again, he claimed he didn't recognize her, but appeared visibly nervous.

—Adapted from Spitzer et al., 1994, pp. 254–255

Although the presenting evidence supported a diagnosis of dissociative fugue, clinicians can find it difficult to distinguish true amnesia from amnesia that is faked to allow a person to start a new life.

depersonalization Feelings of unreality or detachment from one's self or one's body.

derealization A sense of unreality about the outside world.

Depersonalization Disorder

Depersonalization is a temporary loss or change in the usual sense of our own reality. In a state of depersonalization, people feel detached from themselves and their surroundings. They may feel as though they are dreaming or acting like a robot (Guralnik, Schmeidler, & Simeon, 2000; Maldonado et al., 1998).

Derealization—a sense of unreality about the external world involving odd changes in the perception of one's surroundings or in the passage of time—may also be present. People and objects may seem to change in size or shape; they may sound different. All these feelings can be associated with feelings of anxiety, including dizziness and fears of going insane, or with depression.

Although these sensations are strange, people with depersonalization maintain contact with reality. They can distinguish reality from unreality, even during the depersonalization episode. In contrast to generalized amnesia and fugue, they know who they

Depersonalization. Episodes of depersonalization are characterized by feelings of detachment from oneself. During an episode, it may feel as if one were walking through a dream or observing the environment or oneself from outside one's body.

are. Their memories are intact and they know where they are—even if they do not like their present state. Feelings of depersonalization usually come on suddenly and fade gradually.

Note that we have thus far described only normal feelings of depersonalization. Healthy people frequently experience transient episodes of depersonalization and derealization (Hunter et al., 2003). According to the DSM, about half of all adults experience single brief episodes of depersonalization, usually during times of extreme stress (APA, 2000). About 80% to 90% of people in the general population have dissociative experiences at one time or another (Gershuny & Thayer, 1999).

Given the commonness of occasional dissociative symptoms, Richie's experience is not atypical.

"I"
Depersonalization at Disneyworld

We went to Orlando with the children after school let out. I had also been driving myself hard, and it was time to let go. We spent three days "doing" Disneyworld, and it got to the point where we were all wearing shirts with mice and ducks on them and singing Disney songs. On the third day I began to feel unreal and ill at ease while we were watching these middle-American Ivory-soap teenagers singing and dancing in front of Cinderella's Castle. The day was finally cooling down, but I broke into a sweat. I became shaky and dizzy and sat down on the cement next to the 4-year-old's stroller without giving [my wife] an explanation. There were strollers and kids and [adults'] legs all around me, and for some strange reason I became fixated on the pieces of popcorn strewn on the ground. All of a sudden it was like the people around me were all silly mechanical creatures, like the dolls in the "It's a Small World" [exhibit] or the animals on the "Jungle Cruise." Things sort of seemed to slow down, the way they do when you've smoked marijuana, and there was this invisible wall of cotton between me and everyone else.

Then the concert was over and my wife was like "What's the matter?" and did I want to stay for the Electrical Parade and the fireworks or was I sick? Now I was beginning to wonder if I was going crazy and I said I was sick, that my wife would have to take me by the hand and drive us back to the Sonesta Village [motel]. Somehow we got back to the monorail and turned in the strollers. I waited in the herd [of people] at the station like a dead person, my eyes glazed over, looking out over kids with Mickey Mouse ears and Mickey Mouse balloons. The mechanical voice on the monorail almost did me in and I got really shaky.

I refused to go back to the Magic Kingdom. I went with the family to Sea World, and on another day I dropped [my wife] and the kids off at the Magic Kingdom and picked them up that night. My wife thought I was goldbricking or something, and we had a helluva fight about it, but we had a life to get back to and my sanity had to come first.

—From the Authors' Files

Richie's depersonalization experience was limited to the one episode and would not qualify for a diagnosis of **depersonalization disorder**. Depersonalization disorder is diagnosed only when such experiences are persistent or recurrent and cause marked distress (Steinberg, 1991). The *DSM* diagnoses depersonalization disorder according to the criteria shown in Table 7.2. Note the following case example.

depersonalization disorder A disorder characterized by persistent or recurrent episodes of depersonalization.

TABLE 7.2
Diagnostic Features of Depersonalization Disorder

1. Recurrent or persistent experiences of depersonalization, which are characterized by feelings of detachment from one's mental processes or body, as if one were an outside observer of oneself. The experience may have a dreamlike quality.

2. The individual is able to maintain reality testing (i.e., distinguish reality from unreality) during the depersonalization state.

3. The depersonalization experiences cause significant personal distress or impairment in one or more important areas of functioning, such as social or occupational functioning.

4. Depersonalization experiences cannot be attributed to other disorders or to the direct effects of drugs, alcohol, or medical conditions.

Source: Adapted from the *DSM-IV-TR* (APA, 2000).

A Case of Depersonalization Disorder

A 20-year-old college student feared that he was going insane. For two years, he had increasingly frequent experiences of feeling "outside" himself. During these episodes, he experienced a sense of "deadness" in his body, and felt wobbly, frequently bumping into furniture. He was more apt to lose his balance during episodes which occurred when he was out in public, especially when he was feeling anxious. During these episodes, his thoughts seemed "foggy," reminding him of his state of mind when he was given shots of a pain-killing drug for an appendectomy five years earlier. He tried to fight off these episodes when they occurred, by saying "stop" to himself and by shaking his head. This would temporarily clear his head, but the feeling of being outside himself and the sense of deadness would shortly return. The disturbing feelings would gradually fade away over a period of hours. By the time he sought treatment, he was experiencing these episodes about twice a week, each one lasting from three to four hours. His grades remained unimpaired, and had even improved in the past several months, since he was spending more time studying. However, his girlfriend, in whom he had confided his problem, felt that he had become totally absorbed in himself and threatened to break off their relationship if he didn't change. She had also begun to date other men.

—*Adapted from Spitzer et al., 1994, pp. 270–271*

In terms of observable behavior and associated features, depersonalization may be more closely related to anxiety disorders such as phobias and panic disorder than to dissociative disorders. Unlike other forms of dissociative disorders that seem to protect the self from anxiety, depersonalization can lead to anxiety and in turn to avoidance behavior, as we saw in the case of Richie.

Culture-Bound Dissociative Syndromes

Similarities exist between the Western concept of dissociative disorder and certain culture-bound syndromes found in other parts of the world. For example, *amok* is a culture-bound syndrome occurring primarily in southeast Asian and Pacific Island cultures that describes a trancelike state in which a person suddenly becomes highly excited and violently attacks other people or destroys objects (see Chapter 3). People who "run amuck" may later claim to have no memory of the episode or recall feeling as if they were acting like a robot. Another example is *zar,* a term used in countries in North Africa and the Middle East to describe spirit possession in people who experience dissociative states. During these states, individuals engage in unusual behavior, ranging from shouting to banging their heads against the wall. The behavior itself is not deemed abnormal because it is believed to be controlled by spirits.

Theoretical Perspectives

The dissociative disorders are fascinating and perplexing phenomena. How can one's sense of personal identity become so distorted that one develops multiple personalities, blots out large chunks of personal memory, or develops a new identity? Although these disorders remain in many ways mysterious, some clues provide insights into their origins.

Psychodynamic Views   To psychodynamic theorists, dissociative disorders involve the massive use of repression, resulting in the "splitting off" from consciousness of unacceptable impulses and painful memories. Dissociative amnesia may serve an adaptive function of disconnecting or dissociating one's conscious from awareness of traumatic experiences or other sources of psychological pain or conflict (Dorahy, 2001). In dissociative amnesia and fugue, the ego protects itself from anxiety by blotting out disturbing memories or by dissociating threatening impulses of a sexual or aggressive nature. In dissociative identity disorder, people may express these

QUESTIONNAIRE
The Dissociative Experiences Scale

Brief dissociative experiences, such as momentary feelings of depersonalization, are quite common. Most of us experience them at least some of the time (Gershuny & Thayer, 1999). Dissociative disorders, by contrast, involve more persistent and severe dissociative experiences. Researchers have developed a measure, the Dissociative Experiences Scale (DES), to offer clinicians a way of measuring dissociative experiences that occur in both the general population and among people with dissociative disorders (Putnam & Carlson, 1994; Sanders & Green, 1995; Sar et al., 1996). Fleeting dissociative experiences are quite common, but those reported by people with dissociative disorders are more frequent and problematic than those in the general population (Waller & Ross, 1997).

The following is a listing of some of the types of dissociative experiences drawn from the Dissociative Experiences Scale that many people encounter from time to time. Bear in mind that transient experiences like these are reported by both normal and abnormal groups in varying frequencies. Let us also suggest that if these experiences become persistent or commonplace or cause you concern or distress, then it might be worthwhile to discuss them with a professional.

Have You Ever Experienced the Following?

1. Suddenly realizing, when you are driving the car, that you don't remember what has happened during all or part of the trip.
2. Suddenly realizing, when you are listening to someone talk, that you did not hear part or all of what the person said.
3. Finding yourself in a place and having no idea how you got there.
4. Finding yourself dressed in clothes that you don't remember putting on.
5. Experiencing a feeling that seemed as if you were standing next to yourself or watching yourself do something and actually seeing yourself as if you were looking at another person.
6. Looking in a mirror and not recognizing yourself.
7. Feeling sometimes that other people, objects, and the world around you are not real.
8. Remembering a past event so vividly that it seems like you are reliving it in the present.
9. Having the experience of being in a familiar place but finding it strange and unfamiliar.
10. Becoming so absorbed in watching television or a movie that you are unaware of other events happening around you.
11. Becoming so absorbed in a fantasy or daydream that it feels as though it were really happening to you.
12. Talking out loud to yourself when you are alone.
13. Finding that you act so differently in a particular situation compared with another that it feels almost as if you were two different people.
14. Finding that you cannot remember whether or not you have just done something or perhaps had just thought about doing it (for example, not knowing whether you have just mailed a letter or have just thought about mailing it).
15. Feeling sometimes as if you were looking at the world through a fog such that people and objects appear faraway or unclear.

Source: Bernstein, E. M., & Putnam, F. W. (1986). Development, reliability, and validity of a dissociation scale. Journal of Nervous and Mental Disease, 174, 727–735. Copyright © Williams & Wilkins, 1986. ■

unacceptable impulses through the development of alternate personalities. In depersonalization, people stand outside themselves—safely distanced from the emotional turmoil within.

Cognitive and Learning Views Learning and cognitive theorists view dissociation as a learned response that involves *not thinking* about disturbing acts or thoughts in order to avoid feelings of guilt and shame. The habit of not thinking about these matters is negatively reinforced by relief from anxiety or by removal of feelings of guilt or shame. Some social cognitive theorists, such as the late Nicholas Spanos, believe that dissociative identity disorder is a form of role-playing acquired through observational learning and reinforcement. This is not quite the same as pretending or malingering; people can honestly come to organize their behavior patterns according to particular roles they have observed. They might also become so absorbed in role playing that they "forget" they are enacting a role.

Brain Dysfunction Might dissociative behavior be connected with underlying brain dysfunction? Research along these lines is still in its infancy, but recent evidence showed differences in brain metabolic activity between people with depersonalization disorder and healthy subjects (Simeon et al., 2000). These findings, which point to a possible dysfunction in parts of the brain involved in body perception, may help account for the feeling of being disconnected from one's body that is associated with depersonalization.

Tying It Together

Although we have different conceptualizations of dissociative phenomena, psychologists recognize that a history of abuse in childhood often plays a pivotal role. The most widely held view of dissociative identity disorder is that it represents a means of coping with and surviving severe, repetitive childhood abuse, generally beginning before the age of 5 (Burton & Lane, 2001). The severely abused child may retreat into alter personalities as a psychological defense against unbearable abuse. The construction of these alter personalities allows such children to psychologically escape or distance themselves from their suffering (Burton & Lane, 2001). In the case of our opening "I" example, one alter personality, Leah, bore the worst of the abuse for all the others. Dissociation offers a means of escape when no other is available (Gershuny & Thayer, 1999). In the face of continued abuse, these alter personalities may become stabilized, making it difficult for the person to maintain a unified personality. In adulthood, people with multiple personalities may use their alter personalities to block out traumatic childhood memories and their emotional reactions to them, thus wiping the slate clean and beginning life anew in the guise of alter personalities. The alter identities or personalities may also help the person cope with stressful situations or express deep-seated resentments that the individual is unable to integrate within his or her primary personality.

Compelling evidence indicates that exposure to childhood trauma, usually by a relative or caretaker, is involved in the development of dissociative disorders, especially dissociative identity disorder. The great majority of people with dissociative identity disorder report being physically or sexually abused as children (Lewis et al., 1997; Weaver & Clum, 1995). In one sample, 83% reported a history of childhood sexual abuse, and 2 out of 3 reported both physical and sexual abuse (Putnam et al., 1986). In other samples, rates of childhood physical or sexual abuse have ranged from 76% to 95% (Ross et al., 1990; Scroppo et al., 1998). Evidence of cross-cultural similarity comes from a study in Turkey, which showed that more than 3 out of 4 of 35 dissociative identity disorder patients reported sexual or physical abuse in childhood (Sar et al., 1996). Childhood trauma or abuse is also reported more often in cases of dissociative amnesia and depersonalization disorder than in control groups (e.g., Simeon et al., 1997, 2001).

Childhood abuse is not the only source of trauma linked to dissociative disorders. Exposure to the trauma of warfare among both civilians and soldiers plays a part in some cases of dissociative fugue and dissociative amnesia. In fugue, the stress of combat and the secondary gain of leaving the battlefield seem to be important contributors (Loewenstein, 1991). The stress of coping with severe financial problems and the wish to avoid punishment for socially unacceptable behavior are other possible antecedents to episodes of fugue (Riether & Stoudemire, 1988). High levels of stress may also be linked to depersonalization disorder (Kluft, 1988).

Imaginary friends? Like the child in the photo, it is normal for children to have imaginary playmates. In the case of many multiple personalities, however, games of "make-believe" and the invention of imaginary playmates may be used as psychological defenses against abuse. Research suggests that most people who develop multiple personalities were abused as children.

Diathesis-Stress Model Despite widespread evidence of childhood trauma in cases of dissociative identity disorder, few severely abused children develop multiple personalities. Consistent with the diathesis-stress model, certain personality traits, such as proneness to fantasize, high ability to be hypnotized, and openness to altered states of consciousness, may predispose individuals to develop dissociative experiences in the face of extreme stress, such as traumatic abuse in childhood (see Figure 7.1). These personality traits themselves do not lead to dissociative disorders (Rauschenberger & Lynn, 1995). They are actually quite common in the population. However, they may increase the risk that people who experience severe trauma will develop dissociative phenomena as a survival mechanism (Butler et al., 1996). People who are low in fantasy proneness or hypnotizability may experience the kinds of anxious, intrusive thoughts characteristic of posttraumatic stress disorder (PTSD) in the aftermath of traumatic stress, rather than dissociative experiences (Kirmayer, Robbins, & Paris, 1994).

Perhaps most of us can divide our consciousness so that we become unaware of—at least temporarily—those events we normally focus on. Perhaps most of us can thrust the unpleasant from our minds and enact various roles—parent, child, lover, businessperson, soldier—that help us meet the requirements of our situations. Perhaps the marvel

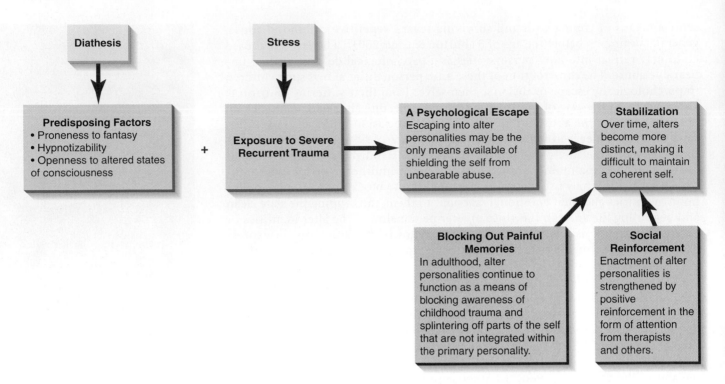

FIGURE 7.1 Diathesis-stress model of dissociative identity disorder
In this model, exposure to severe, recurrent trauma (stress), together with certain predisposing factors (diathesis), leads in some few cases to the development of alter personalities, which over time become stabilized and strengthened by social reinforcement.

is *not* that attention can be splintered, but that human consciousness is normally integrated into a meaningful whole.

Treatment of Dissociative Disorders

Dissociative amnesia and fugue are usually fleeting experiences that end abruptly. Episodes of depersonalization can be recurrent and persistent, and they are most likely to occur when people are undergoing periods of mild anxiety or depression. In such cases, clinicians usually focus on managing the anxiety or depression. Much of the attention in the research literature has focused on dissociative identity disorder and specifically on integrating the alter personalities into a cohesive personality structure (Burton & Lane, 2001).

Psychoanalysts seek to help people with dissociative identity disorder uncover and learn to cope with early childhood traumas. They often recommend establishing direct contact with alter personalities (Burton & Lane, 2001). The therapist may ask the client to close his or her eyes and wait for the alter personalities to emerge (Krakauer, 2001). Wilbur (1986) points out that the analyst can work with whatever personality dominates the therapy session. The therapist asks any and all personalities that come out to talk about their memories and dreams and assures them that the therapist will help them make sense of their anxieties, safely "relive" traumatic experiences, and make them conscious. The disclosure of abuse is considered essential to the therapeutic process (Krakauer, 2001). Wilbur enjoins therapists to keep in mind that anxiety experienced during a therapy session may lead to a switch in personalities, because alter personalities were presumably developed as a means to cope with intense anxiety. But if therapy is successful, the self will be able to work through the traumatic memories and will no longer need to escape into alternate "selves" to avoid the anxiety associated with the trauma. Thus, reintegration of the personality becomes possible.

Through the process of integration, the disparate elements or "alters" are woven into a cohesive self. Here a patient speaks about this process of "making mine" those parts of the self that had been splintered off.

"Everybody's Still Here"

... Integration made me feel alive for the first time. When I feel things now, I know I feel them. I'm slowly learning it's okay to feel all feelings, even unpleasant ones. The bonus is, I get to feel pleasurable feelings as well. I also don't worry about my sanity anymore.

It's difficult to explain even to people who try to understand what integration means to someone who has been "in parts" for a lifetime. I still talk in a "we" way sometimes. Some of my "before integration" friends assume I can now just get back to being "me"—whatever that is. They don't realize integration is like being three all over again. I don't know how to act in certain situations because "I" never did it before. Or I only know how to respond in fragmented ways. What does "sadness" mean to someone who doesn't feel it continually? I don't know sometimes when I feel sad if I really should. It's confusing and scary being responsible for me all by myself now.

The most comforting aspect of integration for me, and what I especially want other multiples to know is: Nobody died. Everybody's still here inside me, in their correct place without controlling my body independently. There was not a scene where everybody left except one. I am a remarkably different "brand new" person. I've spent months learning how to access my alters' skills and emotions—and they are mine now. I have balance and perspective that never existed before. I'm happy and content. This isn't about dying. It's about celebrating living to the fullest extent possible.

—From Olson, 1997

Wilbur describes the formation of another treatment goal in the case of a woman with dissociative identity disorder.

CONTROVERSIES IN ABNORMAL PSYCHOLOGY
Are Recovered Memories Credible?

A high-level business executive's comfortable life fell apart one day when his 19-year-old daughter accused him of having repeatedly molested her throughout her childhood. The executive lost his marriage as well as his $400,000-a-year job. But he fought back against the allegations, which he insisted were untrue. He sued his daughter's therapists, who had helped her recover these memories. A jury sided with the businessman, awarding him $500,000 in damages from the two therapists.

This case is but one of many involving adults who claim to have only recently become aware of memories of childhood sexual abuse. Hundreds of people throughout the country have been brought to trial on the basis of recovered memories of childhood abuse, with many of these cases resulting in convictions and long jail sentences, even in the absence of corroborating evidence. Such recovered memories often occur following suggestive probing by a therapist or hypnotist (Loftus, 1993). The issue of recovered memories continues to be hotly debated in psychology and the broader community. At the heart of the debate is the question, "Are recovered memories believable?" No one doubts that childhood sexual abuse is a major problem confronting our society. But should recovered memories be taken at face value?

Several lines of evidence lead us to question the validity of recovered memories. Experimental evidence shows that false memories can be created, especially under the influence of leading or suggestive questioning (Begley, 2001b; Gleaves et al., 2004; Kihlstrom, 2004; Loftus, 1997; Zoellner et al., 2000). Memory for events that never happened may be created; they may seem just as genuine as memories of real events (Zola, 1999). Moreover, although people who have experienced actual abuse in childhood may be somewhat sketchy on the details, total amnesia concerning the trauma is rare (Wakefield & Underwager, 1996). A leading memory expert, psychologist Elizabeth Loftus (1996, p. 356), writes of the dangers of taking recovered memories at face value:

After developing false memories, innumerable "patients" have torn their families apart, and more than a few innocent people have been sent to prison. This is not to say that people cannot forget horrible things that have happened to them; most certainly they can. But there is virtually no support for the idea that clients presenting for therapy routinely have extensive histories of abuse of which they are completely unaware, and that they can be helped only if the alleged abuse is resurrected from their unconscious.

Should we conclude, then, that recovered memories are bogus? Not necessarily. Both false memories and recovered true memories may exist (Gleaves et al., 2004). It is possible for adults to suddenly recover memories of long-forgotten childhood experiences (Melchert, 1996), including memories of abuse (Chu et al., 1999). All in all, some recovered memories may be true; others may not be (Brown, 1997; Gleaves et al., 2004; Rubin, 1996).

In sum, we shouldn't think of the brain as a kind of mental camera that stores snapshots of events as they actually happened in the form of memories. Memory is more of a reconstructive process in which bits of information are pieced together in ways that can sometimes lead to a distorted recollection of events, even though the person may be convinced the memory is accurate. Unfortunately we don't have the tools to distinguish the true memory from the false one (Cloitre, 2004; Loftus, 1993).

Critical Thinking

- Why should we not accept claims of recovered memories at face value?
- How does human memory work differently than a camera in recording events and experiences?

The "Children" Should Not Feel Ashamed

A 45-year-old woman had suffered from dissociative identity disorder throughout her life. Her dominant personality was timid and self-conscious, rather reticent about herself. But soon after she entered treatment, a group of "little ones" emerged, who cried profusely. The therapist asked to speak with someone in the personality system who could clarify the personalities that were present. It turned out that they included several children, all of whom were under 9 years of age and had suffered severe, painful sexual abuse at the hands of an uncle, a great-aunt, and a grandmother. The great-aunt was a lesbian with several voyeuristic lesbian friends. They would watch the sexual abuse, generating fear, pain, rage, humiliation, and shame.

It was essential in therapy for the "children" to come to understand that they should not feel ashamed because they had been helpless to resist the abuse.

—*Adapted from Wilbur, 1986, pp. 138–139*

Does therapy work? Coons (1986) followed 20 "multiples" aged from 14 to 47 at time of intake for an average of 3 1/4 years. Only 5 of the subjects showed a complete reintegration of their personalities. Other therapists report significant improvement in measures of dissociative symptoms and depressive symptoms in treated patients, even in those who failed to achieve integration. However, greater symptom improvement was reported for those who achieved integration (Ellason & Ross, 1997).

Reports of the effectiveness of psychoanalytic or of other forms of therapy, such as behavior therapy, rely on uncontrolled case studies. Controlled studies of treatments of dissociative identity disorder or other forms of dissociative disorder are yet to be reported (Maldonado et al., 1998). The relative infrequency of the disorder has hampered efforts to conduct controlled experiments that compare different forms of treatment with each other and with control groups. Nor do we have evidence showing psychiatric drugs or other biological approaches to be effective in bringing about an integration of various alternate personalities.

somatoform disorders A disorder characterized by complaints of physical problems or symptoms that cannot be explained by physical causes.

Elizabeth Loftus. Research by Loftus and others has demonstrated that false memories of events that never actually occurred can be induced experimentally. This research calls into question the credibility of reports of recovered memories.

SOMATOFORM DISORDERS

The word *somatoform* derives from the Greek *soma,* meaning "body." In the **somatoform disorders,** people have physical symptoms suggestive of physical disorders, but no organic abnormalities can be found to fully account for them. Moreover, there is evidence, or some reason to believe, that the symptoms reflect psychological factors or conflict. Some people complain of problems in breathing or swallowing, or of a "lump in the throat." Problems such as these can reflect overactivity of the sympathetic branch of the autonomic nervous system, which might result from anxiety.

There are many types of somatoform disorders. In *conversion disorder,* a person may experience "paralysis" of a hand or leg that cannot be explained medically or that is inconsistent with the workings of the nervous system. In *hypochondriasis,* people misinterpret their physical symptoms, believing them to be signs of a serious illness, despite the fact that thorough medical evaluations fail to support their concerns. In *body dysmorphic disorder,* the per-

Overview of Dissociative Disorders

TYPES OF DISSOCIATIVE DISORDERS/PREVALENCE RATES (approx., in parentheses)

	Description	Features
Dissociative Identity Disorder (unknown)	Emergence of two or more distinct personalities	• Alternates may vie for control • Some cases reported of distinct physiological characteristics of alternates
Dissociative Amnesia (unknown)	Inability to recall important personal material that cannot be accounted for by medical causes	• Information lost to memory is usually of traumatic or stressful experiences • Subtypes include localized amnesia, selective amnesia, and generalized amnesia
Dissociative Fugue (0.2 %, or 2 in 1,000 people)	Amnesia "on the run"; the person travels to a new location and is unable to remember personal information or reports a past filled with false information that is not recognized as false	• Person may be confused about his or her personal identity or assumes a new identity • Person may start a new family or business
Depersonalization Disorder (unknown)	Episodes of feeling detached from one's self or one's body or having a sense of unreality about one's surroundings (derealization)	• Person may feel as if he or she were living in a dream or acting like a robot • Episodes of depersonalization are persistent or recurrent and cause significant distress

CAUSAL FACTORS — A history of childhood trauma or abuse is implicated in many cases

Biological Factors	• Not known
Social–Environmental Factors	• Childhood sexual or physical abuse (in dissociative identity disorder) • Other traumatic experiences, such as combat trauma (in dissociative amnesia and dissociative fugue)
Behavioral Factors	• Possible reinforcement (attention) for enacting the social role of a multiple personality
Emotional and Cognitive Factors	• Relief from anxiety by psychologically distancing oneself (dissociating) from troubling emotions or memories

TREATMENT APPROACHES — Dissociative identity disorder remains a challenge to treat; dissociative amnesia and dissociative fugue tend to resolve on their own.

Psychotherapy	• For dissociative identity disorder, psychoanalytic therapy may be used to seek a reintegration of the personality

Source for prevalence rates: APA, 2000

son either has an imagined defect in appearance or exaggerates a minor physical flaw. In *pain disorder,* the person experiences pain in which psychological factors are held to play a prominent role. In *somatization disorder,* people present with many recurring physical complaints that cannot be fully explained by any known medical condition.

Somatoform disorders are not the same as **malingering,** or purposeful fabrication of symptoms for obvious gain (such as avoiding work). Feigning physical illness to avoid work or to qualify for disability benefits may be deceitful or even dishonest, but it is not a psychological disorder. Somatoform disorders also need to be distinguished from **factitious disorders,** in which people fake or manufacture their symptoms, without any apparent motive.

Because malingering is motivated by external incentives, it is not considered a mental disorder within the *DSM* framework. But in factitious disorders, the symptoms do not bring about obvious gains. The absence of external incentives in these disorders suggests that they serve a psychological need; hence, they are classified as psychological or mental disorders.

The most common form of factitious disorder is **Münchausen syndrome,** a form of feigned illness in which the person either fakes being ill or makes himself or herself ill (by ingesting toxic substances, for example) (Huffman & Stern, 2003). Although people with somatoform disorders may benefit from having physical symptoms, they do not purposefully produce them. Even if there is no medical basis to their symptoms, they do not set out to deceive others. But Münchausen syndrome is not a somatoform

malingering Faking illness in order to avoid work or duty.

factitious disorder A disorder characterized by intentional fabrication of psychological or physical symptoms for no apparent gain.

Münchausen syndrome A type of factitious disorder characterized by the fabrication of medical symptoms.

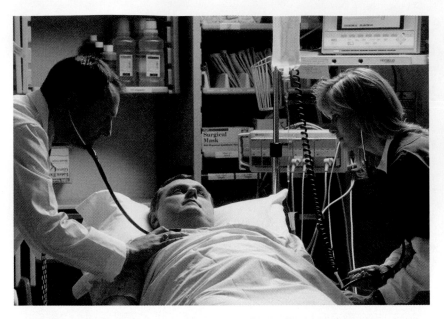

disorder. It is a factitious disorder involving the deliberate fabrication of seemingly plausible physical complaints for no obvious gain.

Münchausen syndrome was named after Baron Karl von Münchausen, one of history's great fibbers. The good baron, an 18th-century German army officer, entertained friends with tales of outrageous adventures. In the vernacular, *Münchausenism* describes tellers of tall tales. In clinical terms, Münchausen syndrome refers to patients who tell tall tales or outrageous lies to their doctors. People who have Münchausen syndrome usually suffer deep anguish as they bounce from hospital to hospital and subject themselves to unnecessary, painful, and, sometimes risky medical treatments, even surgery. The "A Closer Look" feature explores this curious disorder in more depth.

Is this patient really sick? Münchausen syndrome is characterized by the fabrication of medical complaints for no other apparent purpose than to gain admission to hospitals. Some Münchausen patients may produce life-threatening symptoms in their attempts to deceive doctors.

A CLOSER LOOK
Münchausen Syndrome

A woman staggered into the emergency room of a New York City hospital bleeding from the mouth, clutching her stomach and wailing with pain. Even in that setting, forever serving bleeders and clutchers and wailers, there was something about her, some terrible star quality that held center stage. Her pain was larger than life.

> She told a harrowing story: A man had seduced her, then tied her up, beaten her, forced her to surrender money and jewelry on threat of death. She had severe pain in her lower left side, and an unbearable headache.
>
> She was admitted, and exhaustively tested. Nothing could be found; no reason for the bleeding or the pain; the specialists were left scratching their heads.
>
> Then, one day, a hospital aide came upon these items in her bedside table: a needle, syringe, and a blood thinner called heparin. Eureka. Inject yourself with enough blood thinner and you, too, can take stage center in an emergency room.
>
> Confronted, she denied all charges. The stuff was not hers; someone was trying to frame her; if nobody believed her, she would check out of the place and find doctors who really cared. And off she went. Later, it was learned that she had recently been in two other hospitals: The same story, same symptom and same sequence of events.
>
> Diagnosis: Münchausen syndrome.
>
> Lear, 1988, p. 21. Copyright © 1988 by The New York Times Company. Reprinted by permission.

Münchausen patients may go to great lengths to seek a confirmatory diagnosis, such as agreeing to exploratory surgery, even though they know there is nothing wrong with them. Some inject themselves with drugs to produce symptoms such as skin rashes. When confronted with evidence of their deception, they may turn nasty and stick to their guns. They are also skillful enough actors to convince others that their complaints are genuine.

Why do patients with Münchausen syndrome fake illness or put themselves at risk by making themselves to be sick or injured? Perhaps enacting the sick role in the protected hospital environment provides a sense of security that was lacking in childhood. Perhaps the hospital becomes a stage on which they can act out resentments against doctors and parents that have been brewing since childhood. Perhaps they are trying to identify with a parent who was often sick. Or perhaps they learned to enact a sick role in childhood to escape from repeated sexual abuse or other traumatic experiences and continue to enact the role to escape stressors in their adult lives (Trask & Sigmon, 1997). No one is really sure, and the disorder remains one of the more puzzling forms of abnormal behavior.

Münchausen Syndrome by Proxy

In her memoir entitled *Sickened*, Julie Gregory recounts how she was subjected to numerous X-rays and operations as a child, not because there was anything wrong with her, but to find the cause of an illness that existed only in her mother's mind (Gregory, 2003). At age 13, Gregory underwent an invasive medical procedure, a heart catheterization, which her mother insisted upon to "get to the bottom of this thing." When the cardiologist informed Julie's mother that the test results were within normal limits, her mother argued for an even more invasive test involving open-heart surgery. When the doctor refused, Julie's mother confronted him in Julie's presence.

"I" Sickened

"I can't believe it? I cannot believe this! You're not going to dig into this and do the open-heart? I thought we had agreed to follow this through to the end, Michael. I thought you said you were committed to me on this."

"I'm committed to finding Julie's illness, Ms. Gregory, but Julie doesn't need heart surgery. Usually parents are thrilled to—"

"Oh, that's just it? That's all you're going to do? Just drop me like a hot potato? I mean, for crying out loud, why can't I just have a normal kid like other mothers? I mean I'm a good mom . . ."

I'm standing behind my mother's left leg, my eyes glued to the doctor, boring an SOS into his eyes: "Don't make me go, don't let her take me."

"Ms. Gregory, I didn't say you weren't a good mother. But I can't do anything else here. You need to drop the heart procedures. Period." And with that he turned on his heel.

"Well, you're the one who's going to be sorry," Mom screeches, "When this kid dies on you. That's what. 'Cause you're going to get sued out the ying-yang for being such an incompetent idiot. Can't even find out what's wrong with a thirteen-year-old girl! You are insane! This kid is sick, you hear me? She's sick!"

Source: Gregory, 2003

Julie's case highlights a most pernicious form of child maltreatment called *Münchausen syndrome by proxy* (Rosenberg, 2003; Stutts, Hickey, & Kasdan, 2003), in which people intentionally falsify or induce the physical or emotional illness or injury of a child or dependent person (Feldman, 2003).

Parents or caregivers who induce illnesses in their children or foster children may be trying to gain sympathy or experience the sense of control made possible by attending to a sick child. The disorder is controversial and remains under study by the psychiatric community. The controversy arises in large part because it appears to put a diagnostic label on abusive behavior. What is clear is that the disorder is linked to heinous crimes against children (Ayoub et al., 2002; Mart, 2003). In one sample case, a mother was suspected of purposely causing her 3-year-old's repeated bouts of diarrhea (Schreier & Ricci, 2002). Sadly, the child died before authorities could intervene. In another case, a foster mother is alleged to have brought about the deaths of three children by giving them overdoses of medicines containing potassium and sodium. The chemicals induced suffocation or heart attacks.

A review of 451 cases of Münchausen syndrome by proxy reported in the scientific literature showed that 6% of the victims died (Sheridan, 2003). Typical victims were 4 years of age or under. Mothers were perpetrators in three of four cases. Cases of Münchausen syndrome by proxy often involve mysterious high fevers in children, seizures of unknown origin, and similar symptoms. Doctors typically find the illnesses to be unusual, prolonged, and unexplained. They require some medical sophistication on the part of the perpetrator.

Let us now proceed to discuss several major types of somatoform disorder: conversion disorder, hypochondriasis, body dysmorphic disorder, pain disorder, and somatization disorder.

Conversion Disorder

Conversion disorder is characterized by a major change in or loss of physical functioning, although no medical findings are found to account for the physical symptoms or deficits (see Table 7.3). The symptoms are not intentionally produced. The person is not malingering. The physical symptoms usually come on suddenly in stressful situations. A soldier's hand may become "paralyzed" during intense combat, for example. The fact that conversion symptoms first appear in the context of, or are aggravated by, conflicts or stressors suggests that they relate to psychological factors (APA, 2000). Reported rates of the disorder in the general population range from as few as 1.1 in 10,000 people to perhaps as many as 1 in 200 people (APA, 2000). Like dissociative identity disorder, conversion disorder has been linked to childhood traumatization. A recent study found a higher frequency of childhood physical and sexual abuse among conversion disorder patients than among comparison patients diagnosed with mood disorders (Roelofs et al., 2002).

Conversion disorder is so named because of the psychodynamic belief that it represents the channeling, or *conversion*, of repressed sexual or aggressive energies into physical symptoms. Conversion disorder was formerly called *hysteria* or *hysterical neurosis*, and it played an important role in Freud's development of psychoanalysis (see Chapter 1). Hysterical or conversion disorders seem to have been more common in Freud's day than they are today.

According to the *DSM*, conversion symptoms mimic neurological or general medical conditions involving problems with voluntary motor (movement) or sensory functions. Some classic symptom patterns take the form of paralysis, epilepsy, problems in coordination, blindness and tunnel vision, loss of the sense of hearing or of smell, or loss of feeling in a limb (anesthesia). The bodily symptoms found in conversion disorders often do not match the medical conditions they suggest. For example, conversion epileptics, unlike true epileptic patients, may maintain control over their bladders during an attack. People whose vision is supposedly impaired may walk through the physician's office

conversion disorder A somatoform disorder characterized by loss or impairment of physical function in the absence of any apparent organic cause.

TRUTH or FICTION? *REVISITED*

Some people show up repeatedly at hospital emergency rooms, feigning illness and seeking treatment for no apparent reason.

☑ **TRUE.** People with Münchausen syndrome may show up repeatedly at emergency rooms, feigning illness and demanding treatment. Their motives remain a mystery.

TABLE 7.3
Diagnostic Features of Conversion Disorder
1. At least one symptom or deficit involving voluntary motor or sensory functions that suggests the presence of a physical disorder.
2. Psychological factors are judged to be associated with the disorder because the onset or exacerbation of the physical symptom is linked to the occurrence of psychosocial stressors or conflict situations.
3. The person does not purposefully produce or fake the physical symptom.
4. The symptom cannot be explained as a cultural ritual or response pattern, nor can it be explained by any known physical disorder on the basis of appropriate testing.
5. The symptom causes significant emotional distress, impairment in one or more important areas of functioning, such as social or occupational functioning, or is sufficient to warrant medical attention.
6. The symptom is not restricted to complaints of pain or problems in sexual functioning, nor can it be accounted for by another mental disorder.

Source: Adapted from the *DSM-IV-TR* (APA, 2000).

without bumping into the furniture. People who become "incapable" of standing or walking may nevertheless perform other leg movements normally. Nonetheless, hysteria may be incorrectly diagnosed in people who turn out to have underlying medical conditions. Perhaps as many as 80% of individuals given the diagnosis of conversion disorder have real neurological problems that go undiagnosed (Gould et al., 1986).

If you suddenly lost your vision, or if you could no longer move your legs, you would probably show understandable concern. But some people with conversion disorders, like those with dissociative amnesia, show a remarkable indifference to their symptoms, a phenomenon termed *la belle indifférence* ("beautiful indifference"). The *DSM* advises against relying on indifference to symptoms as a factor in making the diagnosis, however, because many people cope with real physical disorders by denying their pain or concern, which relieves anxieties—at least temporarily.

Hypochondriasis

The core feature of **hypochondriasis** is a preoccupation or fear that one's physical symptoms are due to a serious, underlying illness, such as cancer or heart disease. The fear persists despite medical reassurances that it is groundless (see Table 7.4). Hypochondriasis is believed to affect about 1% to 5% of the general population and about 5% of patients seeking medical care (APA, 2000; Barksy & Ahern, 2004).

People with hypochondriasis do not consciously fake their physical symptoms. They generally experience physical discomfort, often involving the digestive system or an assortment of aches and pains. Unlike conversion disorder, hypochondriasis does not involve the loss or distortion of physical function. Unlike people with conversion disorder, who are often indifferent toward their symptoms, people with hypochondriasis are very concerned, indeed unduly concerned, about their symptoms and what they fear they may mean. Although the underlying rates of hypochondriasis remain unknown, the disorder appears to be about equally common in men and women. It most often begins between the ages of 20 and 30, although it can begin at any age.

People with hypochondriasis may be overly sensitive to benign changes in physical sensations, such as slight changes in heartbeat and minor aches and pains (Barsky et al., 2001). Anxiety about physical symptoms can produce its own physical sensations, however—for example, heavy sweating and dizziness, even fainting. Thus, a vicious cycle

hypochondriasis A somatoform disorder characterized by the misinterpretation of physical symptoms as signs of underlying serious disease.

Hypochondriasis:
The Case of Henry
"I had a growth that I was worried about on my face."

TABLE 7.4

Diagnostic Features of Hypochondriasis

1. The person is preoccupied with a fear of having a serious illness or with the belief that one has a serious illness. The person interprets bodily sensations or physical signs as evidence of physical illness.

2. Fears of physical illness, or beliefs of having a physical illness, persist despite medical reassurances.

3. The preoccupations are not of a delusional intensity (the person recognizes the possibility that these fears and beliefs may be exaggerated or unfounded) and are not restricted to concerns about appearance.

4. The preoccupations cause significant emotional distress or interfere with one or more important areas of functioning, such as social or occupational functioning.

5. The disturbance has persisted for 6 months or longer.

6. The preoccupations do not occur exclusively within the context of another mental disorder.

Source: Adapted from the *DSM-IV-TR* (APA, 2000).

may ensue. People with hypochondriasis may become resentful when their doctors tell them that their own fears may be causing their physical symptoms. They frequently go "doctor shopping" in the hope that a competent and sympathetic physician will heed them before it is too late. Physicians, too, can develop hypochondriasis, as we see in the following case example.

The Doctor Feels Sick: A Case of Hypochondriasis

Robert, a 38-year-old radiologist, has just returned from a 10-day stay at a famous diagnostic center where he has undergone extensive testing of his entire gastrointestinal tract. The evaluation proved negative for any significant physical illness, but rather than feel relieved, the radiologist appeared resentful and disappointed with the findings. The radiologist has been bothered for several months with various physical symptoms, which he describes as symptoms of mild abdominal pain, feelings of "fullness," "bowel rumblings," and a feeling of a "firm abdominal mass." He has become convinced that his symptoms are due to colon cancer and has become accustomed to testing his stool for blood on a weekly basis and carefully palpating his abdomen for "masses" while lying in bed every several days. He has also secretly performed X-ray studies on himself. There is a history of a heart murmur that was detected when he was 13, and his younger brother died of congenital heart disease in early childhood. When the evaluation of his murmur proved it to be benign, he nonetheless began to worry that something might have been overlooked. He developed a fear that something was actually wrong with his heart, and while the fear eventually subsided, it has never entirely left him. In medical school he worried about the diseases that he learned about in pathology. Since graduating, he has repeatedly experienced concerns about his health that follow a typical pattern: noticing certain symptoms, becoming preoccupied with what the symptoms might mean, and undergoing physical evaluations that proved negative. His decision to seek a psychiatric consultation was prompted by an incident with his 9-year-old son. His son accidentally walked in on him while he was palpating his abdomen and asked, "What do you think it is this time, Dad?" He becomes tearful as he relates this incident, describing his feelings of shame and anger—mostly at himself.

—Adapted from Spitzer et al., 1994, pp. 88–90

What to take? Hypochondriasis is a persistent concern or fear that one is seriously ill, although no organic basis can be found to account for one's physical complaints. People with this disorder frequently medicate themselves with over-the-counter medications and find little if any reassurance in doctors' assertions that their health is not in jeopardy.

body dysmorphic disorder (BDD) A somatoform disorder characterized by preoccupation with an imagined or exaggerated physical defect of appearance.

People who develop hypochondriasis have more health worries, have more psychiatric symptoms, and perceive their health to be worse than do other people (Noyes et al., 1993). They are also more likely than other psychiatric patients to report having been sick as children, having missed school because of health reasons, and having experienced childhood trauma, such as sexual abuse or physical violence (Barsky et al., 1994). According to recent studies, most people who meet diagnostic criteria for hypochondriasis continue to show evidence of the disorder when reinterviewed 5 years later (Barsky et al., 1998). Most also have other psychological disorders, especially major depression and anxiety disorders (Barsky, Wyshak, & Klerman, 1992; Noyes et al., 1993).

Hypochondriasis is generally considered to be most common among elderly people. As noted by Paul Costa and Robert McCrae (1985) of the National Institute on Aging, however, authentic age-related health changes do occur, and most "hypochondriacal" complaints probably reflect these changes.

Body Dysmorphic Disorder

People with **body dysmorphic disorder (BDD)** are preoccupied with an imagined or exaggerated physical defect in their appearance (APA, 2000). They may spend hours examining themselves in the mirror and go to extreme measures to correct the perceived defect, even undergoing unnecessary plastic surgery. Others remove all mirrors from their homes so as not to be reminded of the glaring flaw in their appearance. People with BDD may believe that others view them as ugly or deformed and that their unattractive physical appearance leads others to think negatively of them (Rosen, 1996). The rates of BDD are not well established because many people with this disorder fail to seek help or try to keep their symptoms a secret (Cororve & Gleaves, 2001). People with BDD often show a pattern of compulsive grooming, washing, or styling their hair in an attempt to correct the perceived defect, as in the following case example.

"When My Hair Isn't Right, I'm Not Right": A Case of Body Dysmorphic Disorder

For Claudia, a 24-year-old legal secretary, virtually every day was a bad hair day. She explained to her therapist, "When my hair isn't right, which is like every day, I'm not right." "Can't you see it," she went on to explain, "It's so uneven. This piece should be shorter and this one just lies there. People think I'm crazy but I can't stand looking like this. It makes me look like I'm deformed. It doesn't matter if people can't see what I'm talking about. I see it. That's what counts." Several months earlier Claudia had a haircut she described as a disaster. Shortly thereafter, she had thoughts of killing herself: "I wanted to stab myself in the heart. I just couldn't stand looking at myself."

Claudia checked her hair in the mirror innumerable times during the day. She would spend two hours every morning doing her hair and still wouldn't be satisfied. Her constant pruning and checking had become a compulsive ritual. As she told her therapist, "I want to stop pulling and checking it, but I just can't help myself."

—*From the Authors' Files*

Having a "bad hair day" for Claudia meant that she would not go out with her friends and would spend every second examining herself in the mirror and fixing her hair. Occasionally she would cut pieces of her hair herself in an attempt to correct the mistakes of her last haircut. But cutting it herself inevitably made it even worse, in her view. Claudia was forever searching for the perfect haircut that would correct defects only she could perceive. Several years earlier she had what she described as a perfect haircut. "It was just right. I was on top of the world. But it began to look crooked when it grew in." Forever in search of the perfect haircut, Claudia had obtained a hard-to-get appointment with a world-renowned hair stylist in Manhattan, whose clientele included many celebrities. "People wouldn't understand paying this guy $375 for a haircut, especially on my salary, but they don't realize how important it is to me. I'd pay any amount I could." Unfortunately even this celebrated hair stylist disappointed her: "My $25 haircut from my old stylist on Long Island was better than this."

Claudia reported other fixations about her appearance earlier in life: "In high school, I felt my face was like a plate. It was just too flat. I didn't want any pictures taken of me. I couldn't help thinking what people thought of me. They won't tell you, you know. Even if they say there's nothing wrong, it doesn't mean anything. They were just lying to be polite." Claudia related that she was taught to equate physical beauty with happiness: "I was told that to be successful you had to be beautiful. How can I be happy if I look this way?"

Can't you see it? A person with body dysmorphic disorder may spend hours in front of a mirror obsessing about an imagined or exaggerated physical defect in appearance.

Pain Disorder

The major feature of **pain disorder** is pain associated with psychological factors, such as stressful life events. The psychological factors may contribute to the development, severity, or maintenance of the pain. The pain is severe enough and persistent enough to interfere with the person's daily functioning. For example, the pain may make it difficult for the person to attend school or go to work. The pain can become the major focus of the person's life and lead to disruption of normal family life. Pain disorder appears to be relatively common, although precise estimates of its prevalence are lacking (APA, 2000).

The *DSM* system does not exclude the possibility that medical conditions may help explain somatoform pain disorder; both medical conditions and psychological factors can play important roles in the disorder. But when psychological factors play little if any role in the development of pain, the condition is not classified as somatoform pain disorder.

However, the distinction between medical pain and psychiatric pain presents a problem for clinicians (Sharpe & Williams, 2002). The underlying medical cause of pain is often difficult to ascertain. Because they cannot find a physical cause, clinicians may assume that psychological factors play a prominent role. On the other hand, separating "medical pain" from "psychiatric pain" may discount the important role of psychological factors, such as coping responses, in cases of pain that involve obvious medical disease. In sum, the problem of chronic pain is widespread and involves both psychological and medical factors. However, there remains a debate in the field with respect to whether somatoform pain disorder should stand on its own as a diagnosable psychological disorder (Sullivan, 2000).

pain disorder A somatoform disorder in which psychological factors are presumed to play a significant role in the development, severity, or course of chronic pain.

Somatization Disorder

Somatization disorder, formerly known as Briquet's syndrome, is characterized by multiple and recurrent somatic complaints that begin prior to the age of 30 (but usually during the teen years), persist for at least several years, and result either in the seeking of medical attention or in significant impairment in fulfilling social or occupational roles.

Somatization disorder frustrates patients, their families, and their physicians (Holder-Perkins & Wise, 2002). Complaints usually involve different organ systems. Seldom does a year pass without some physical complaint that prompts a trip to the doctor. People

somatization disorder A somatoform disorder characterized by recurrent multiple complaints that cannot be explained by a physical cause.

with somatization disorder are heavy users of medical services. Community surveys show that virtually all (95%) of the people with somatization disorder had visited a doctor during the past year and nearly half (45%) had been hospitalized (Swartz et al., 1991). The complaints cannot be explained by physical causes or exceed what would be expected from a known physical problem. Complaints seem vague or exaggerated, and the person frequently receives medical care from a number of physicians, sometimes at the same time.

Somatization disorder usually begins in adolescence or young adulthood and appears to be a chronic or even lifelong disorder (Kirmayer, Robbins, & Paris, 1994; Smith, 1994). It often occurs together with other psychological disorders, especially anxiety disorders and depressive disorders (Holder-Perkins & Wise, 2002). Although not much is known about the childhood backgrounds of people with somatization disorder, one study reported that women with the disorder were significantly more likely to report sexual molestation in childhood than a matched comparison group of women with mood disorders (Morrison, 1989).

The essential feature of hypochondriasis is fear of disease, of what bodily symptoms may portend. Persons with somatization disorder, by contrast, are pestered by the symptoms themselves. Both diagnoses may be given to the same individual if the diagnostic criteria for both disorders are met.

Reported rates of somatization disorder vary from 0.2% to 2% in women to less than 0.2% in men (APA, 2000). The disorder is also four times more likely to occur among African Americans than other ethnic or racial groups (Swartz et al., 1991). Yet, like pain disorder, somatization disorder is controversial. Many patients, especially female patients, are misdiagnosed with psychological disorders, including somatization disorder, because modern medicine fails to identify the underlying medical basis of their physical complaints (Klonoff & Landrine, 1997).

Koro and Dhat Syndromes: Far Eastern Somatoform Disorders?

In the United States, it is common for people who develop hypochondriasis to be troubled by the idea that they have serious illnesses, such as cancer. The koro and dhat syndromes of the Far East share some clinical features with hypochondriasis. Although these syndromes may seem foreign to North American readers, each is connected with the folklore of their Far Eastern cultures.

Koro Syndrome **Koro syndrome** is a culture-bound syndrome found primarily in China and some other Far Eastern countries (Sheung-Tak, 1996). People with koro syndrome fear that their genitals are shrinking and retracting into their body, which they believe will result in death (Fabian, 1991; Goetz & Price, 1994; Tseng et al., 1992). Koro is considered a culture-bound syndrome, although some cases have been reported outside China and the Far East (e.g., Chowdhury, 1996). The syndrome has been identified mainly in young men, although some cases have also been reported in women (Tseng et al., 1992). Koro syndrome tends to be short-lived and to involve episodes of acute anxiety that one's genitals are retracting. Physiological signs of anxiety that approach panic are common, including profuse sweating, breathlessness, and heart palpitations. Men who suffer from koro have been known to use mechanical devices, such as chopsticks, to try to prevent the penis from retracting into the body (Devan, 1987).

Koro syndrome has been traced within Chinese culture as far back as 3000 B.C.E. (Devan, 1987). Epidemics involving hundreds or thousands of people have been reported in China, Singapore, Thailand, and India (Tseng et al., 1992). In Guangdong Province in China, an epidemic of koro involving more than 2,000 persons occurred during the 1980s (Tseng et al., 1992). Guangdong residents who did not fall victim to koro tended to be less superstitious, higher in intelligence, and less accepting of koro-related folk beliefs (such as the belief that shrinkage of the penis will be lethal) than those who

koro syndrome A culture-bound somatoform disorder, found primarily in China, in which people fear that their genitals are shrinking.

TRUTH or FICTION? *REVISITED*

In China in the 1980s, more than 2,000 people fell prey to the belief that their genitals were shrinking and retracting into their bodies.

☑ **TRUE.** An epidemic was reported in China in which some 2,000 people fell prey to the belief that their genitals were shrinking and retracting into their bodies. This condition, called koro, is classified by the *DSM* system as a culture-bound syndrome.

fell victim to the epidemic (Tseng et al., 1992). Medical reassurance that such fears are unfounded often quells koro episodes (Devan, 1987). Koro episodes among those who do not receive corrective information tend to pass with time but may recur. A number of investigators would like to see the koro syndrome incorporated into the *DSM* as a somatoform disorder (Bernstein & Gaw, 1990; Fishbain, 1991).

Dhat Syndrome **Dhat syndrome,** found among young Asian Indian males, involves excessive fears over the loss of seminal fluid during nocturnal emissions (Akhtar, 1988). Some men with this syndrome also believe (incorrectly) that semen mixes with urine and is excreted through urination. Men with dhat syndrome may roam from physician to physician seeking help to prevent nocturnal emissions or the (imagined) loss of semen mixed with excreted urine. There is a widespread belief within Indian culture (and other Near and Far Eastern cultures) that the loss of semen is harmful because it depletes the body of physical and mental energy (Chadda & Ahuja, 1990). Like other culture-bound syndromes, dhat must be understood within its cultural context:

> In India, attitudes toward semen and its loss constitute an organized, deep-seated belief system that can be traced back to the scriptures of the land . . . [even as far back as the classic Indian sex manual, the Kama Sutra, which was believed to be written by the sage Vatsayana between the third and fifth centuries A.D.] . . . Semen is considered to be the elixir of life, in both a physical and mystical sense. Its preservation is supposed to guarantee health and longevity.
>
> —From Akhtar, 1988, p. 71

It is a commonly held Hindu belief that it takes "forty meals to form one drop of blood; forty drops of blood to fuse and form one drop of bone marrow, and forty drops of this to produce one drop of semen" (Akhtar, 1988, p. 71). Based on the cultural belief in the life-preserving nature of semen, it is not surprising that some Indian males experience extreme anxiety over the involuntary loss of the fluid through nocturnal emissions (Akhtar, 1988). Dhat syndrome has also been associated with difficulty in achieving or maintaining erection, apparently due to excessive concern about loss of seminal fluid through ejaculation (Singh, 1985).

dhat syndrome A culture-bound somatoform disorder, found primarily among Asian Indian males, characterized by excessive fears over the loss of seminal fluid.

Dhat syndrome. Found principally in India, dhat syndrome describes men with an intense fear or anxiety over the loss of semen.

Theoretical Perspectives

Conversion disorder, or "hysteria," was known to Hippocrates, who attributed the strange bodily symptoms to a wandering uterus (*hystera* in Greek), which created internal chaos. Hippocrates noticed that these complaints were less common among married than unmarried women. He prescribed marriage as a "cure" on the basis of these observations and also on the theoretical assumption that pregnancy would satisfy uterine needs and fix the organ in place. Pregnancy fosters hormonal and structural changes that are of benefit to some women with menstrual complaints, but Hippocrates's belief in the "wandering uterus" has contributed throughout the centuries to degrading interpretations of complaints by women of physical problems. Despite Hippocrates's belief that hysteria is exclusively a female concern, it also occurs in men.

Modern theoretical accounts of the somatoform disorders, like those of the dissociative disorders, have most often sprung from psychodynamic and learning theories. Although not much is known about biological underpinnings of somatoform disorders, evidence indicates that somatization disorder tends to run in families, primarily among female members (Guze, 1993). This suggests a genetic linkage, although we cannot rule out the possibility that social influences play a part in explaining this familial association.

Psychodynamic Theory Hysterical disorders provided an arena for some of the debate between the psychological and biological theories of the 19th century. The alleviation—albeit often temporarily—of hysterical symptoms through hypnosis by Charcot, Breuer, and Freud contributed to the belief that hysteria was rooted in psychological rather than physical causes and led Freud to the development of a theory of the unconscious mind. Freud held that the ego manages to control unacceptable or threatening sexual and aggressive impulses arising from the id through defense mechanisms such as repression. Such control prevents the anxiety that would occur if the person were to become aware of these impulses. In some cases, the leftover emotion that is "strangulated," or cut off, from the threatening impulses becomes *converted* into a physical symptom, such as hysterical paralysis or blindness. Although the early psychodynamic formulation of hysteria is still widely held, empirical evidence has been lacking. One problem with the Freudian view is that it does not explain how energies left over from unconscious conflicts become transformed into physical symptoms (E. Miller, 1987).

According to psychodynamic theory, hysterical symptoms are functional: They allow the person to achieve *primary gains* and *secondary gains*. The primary gain of the symptoms is to allow the individual to keep internal conflicts repressed. The person is aware of the physical symptom but not of the conflict it represents. In such cases, the "symptom" is symbolic of, and provides the person with a "partial solution" for, the underlying conflict. For example, the hysterical paralysis of an arm might symbolize and also prevent the individual from acting out on repressed unacceptable sexual (e.g., masturbatory) or aggressive (e.g., murderous) impulses. Repression occurs automatically, so the individual remains unaware of the underlying conflicts. *La belle indifférence,* first noted by Charcot, is believed to occur because the physical symptoms help relieve rather than cause anxiety. From the psychodynamic perspective, conversion disorders, like dissociative disorders, serve a purpose.

Secondary gains from the symptoms are those that allow the individual to avoid burdensome responsibilities and to gain the support—rather than condemnation—of those around them. For example, soldiers sometimes experience sudden "paralysis" of their hands, which prevents them from firing their guns in battle. They may then be sent to recuperate at a hospital rather than face enemy fire. The symptoms in such cases are not considered contrived, as would be the case in malingering. A number of bomber pilots during World War II suffered hysterical "night blindness" that prevented them from carrying

The Wandering Uterus. The ancient Greek physician Hippocrates believed that hysterical symptoms were exclusively a female problem caused by a wandering uterus. Might he have changed his mind had he the opportunity to treat male aviators during World War II who developed "hysterical night blindness" that prevented them from carrying out dangerous nighttime missions?

out dangerous nighttime missions. In the psychodynamic view, their "blindness" may have achieved a primary gain of shielding them from guilt associated with dropping bombs on civilian areas. It may also have achieved a secondary purpose of helping them avoid dangerous missions.

Learning Theory Psychodynamic theory and learning theory concur that the symptoms in conversion disorders relieve anxiety. Psychodynamic theorists, however, seek the causes of anxiety in unconscious conflicts. Learning theorists focus on the more direct reinforcing properties of the symptom and its secondary role in helping the individual avoid or escape anxiety-evoking situations.

From the learning perspective, the symptoms in conversion and other somatoform disorders may also carry the benefits, or reinforcing properties, of the "sick role." Persons with conversion disorders may be relieved of chores and responsibilities such as going to work or performing household tasks (Miller, 1987). Being sick also usually earns sympathy and support. Figure 7.2 illustrates the psychodynamic and learning theory conceptualizations of conversion disorder.

Differences in learning experiences may explain why conversion disorders were historically more often reported among women than men. It may be that women in Western culture are more likely than men to be socialized to cope with stress by enacting a sick role (Miller, 1987). We are not suggesting that people with conversion disorders are fakers. We are merely pointing out that people may learn to adopt roles that lead to reinforcing consequences, regardless of whether they deliberately seek to enact these roles.

Some learning theorists link hypochondriasis and body dysmorphic disorder to obsessive–compulsive disorder (OCD; see Chapter 6) (e.g., Barsky et al., 1992; Buhlmann et al., 2002; Cororve & Gleaves, 2001). In hypochondriasis, people are bothered by obsessive, anxiety-inducing thoughts about their health. Running from doctor to doctor may be a form of compulsive behavior that is reinforced by the temporary relief from anxiety that patients experience when doctors assure them that their fears are unwarranted. Yet the troublesome thoughts eventually return, prompting repeated consultations. The cycle then repeats. Similarly, with body dysmorphic disorder, the constant grooming and pruning in the attempt to "fix" the perceived physical defect may offer partial relief from anxiety, but the "fix" is never quite good enough to completely erase the underlying concerns.

Cognitive Theory Cognitive theorists have speculated that some cases of hypochondriasis may represent a type of self-handicapping strategy, a way of blaming poor performance on failing health (Smith, Snyder, & Perkins, 1983). In other cases, diverting attention to physical complaints can serve as a means of avoiding thinking about other life problems.

Another cognitive explanation focuses on the role of distorted thinking. People who develop hypochondriasis have a tendency to exaggerate the significance of minor physical complaints (Barsky et al., 2001). They misinterpret benign symptoms as signs of a serious illness, which creates anxiety, which leads them to chase down one doctor after another in an attempt to uncover the dreaded disease they fear they have. The anxiety itself may lead to unpleasant physical symptoms, which are likewise exaggerated in importance, leading to more worrisome cognitions.

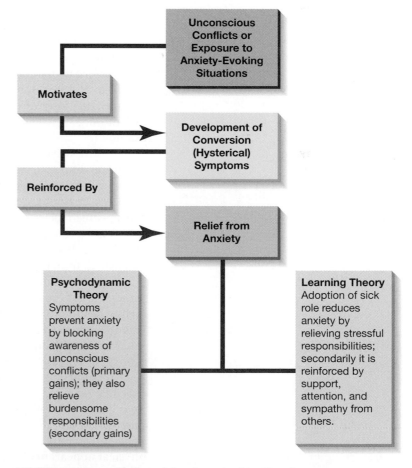

FIGURE 7.2 Conceptual models of conversion disorder
Psychodynamic and learning theory offer conceptual models of conversion disorder that emphasize the role of conversion symptoms leading to escape or relief from anxiety

Cognitive theorists speculate that hypochondriasis and panic disorder, which often occur concurrently, may share a common cause: a distorted way of thinking that leads the person to misinterpret minor changes in bodily sensations as signs of pending catastrophe (Salkovskis & Clark, 1993). Differences between the two disorders may hinge on whether the misinterpretation of bodily cues carries a perception of an imminent threat that leads to a rapid spiraling of anxiety (panic disorder) or of a longer-range threat that leads to a fear of an underlying disease process (hypochondriasis).

Research into cognitive processes in hypochondriasis deserves further study. Given the linkages that may exist between hypochondriasis and anxiety disorders such as panic disorder and OCD, it remains unclear whether hypochondriasis should be classified as a somatoform disorder or an anxiety disorder (Barsky et al., 1992).

Treatment of Somatoform Disorders

The treatment approach that Freud pioneered, psychoanalysis, began with the treatment of hysteria, which is now termed conversion disorder. Psychoanalysis seeks to uncover and bring unconscious conflicts that originated in childhood into conscious awareness. Once the conflict is aired and worked through, the symptom is no longer needed and should disappear. The psychoanalytic method is supported by case studies, some reported by Freud and others by his followers. However, the infrequent occurrence of conversion disorders in contemporary times has made it difficult to mount controlled studies of the psychoanalytic technique.

The behavioral approach to treating conversion disorders and other somatoform disorders focuses on removing sources of secondary reinforcement (or secondary gain) that may become connected with physical complaints. Family members and others, for example, often perceive individuals with somatization disorder as sickly and incapable of carrying normal responsibilities. This reinforces dependent and complaining behaviors. The behavior therapist may teach family members to reward attempts to assume responsibility and to ignore nagging and complaining. The behavior therapist may also work directly with patients, helping them learn more adaptive ways of handling stress or anxiety (through relaxation and cognitive restructuring, for example).

Cognitive-behavioral therapy has achieved good results in treating several types of somatoform disorders, including hypochondriasis and body dysmorphic disorder (Barksy & Ahern, 2004; Looper & Kirmayer, 2002; Visser & Bouman, 2001). In treating hypochondriasis, for example, the cognitive technique of restructuring distorted beliefs helps people replace exaggerated illness-related beliefs with rational alternatives. The behavioral technique of *exposure with response prevention* (see Chapter 6) helps people break the cycle of running to doctors for reassurance. People with hypochondriasis can also benefit from breaking problem habits, such as repeatedly checking the Internet for illness-related information and reading newspaper obituaries (Barksy & Ahern, 2004; "Study Finds," 2004). Unfortunately, many hypochondriasis patients drop out of treatment when they are told that their problems are psychological in nature, not physical. As one leading expert, Dr. Arthur Barksy, put it, "They'll say, 'I don't need to talk about this, I need somebody to stick a biopsy needle in my liver, I need that CAT scan repeated.'" ("Therapy and Hypochondriacs," 2004, p. A19.)

In treating body dysmorphic disorder (BDD), exposure can take the form of purposefully revealing the perceived defect in public, rather than concealing it with makeup or clothing (Cororve & Gleaves, 2001). Response prevention can involve avoiding mirror checking (for example, by covering mirrors at home) and excessive grooming. In cognitive restructuring, the therapist challenges clients' distorted beliefs about their physical appearance by encouraging them to evaluate their beliefs in the light of evidence.

Attention has recently turned to the use of antidepressants, especially fluoxetine (Prozac), in treating some types of somatoform disorder. Although we lack specific drug therapies for conversion disorder (Simon, 1998), a study of 16 patients with hypochondriasis showed significant reductions in hypochondriacal complaints over the course of a 12-week trial with *fluoxetine* (brand name Prozac) (Fallon et al., 1993). However, the lack of controlled drug-placebo studies prevents firm conclusions regarding the efficacy of drug therapy for this disorder. Recent evidence suggests that the antidepressant drug *fluvoxamine* (brand name Luvox) has therapeutic benefits in treating somatoform pain disorder (Turkington et al., 2002). Investigators also report that Prozac was significantly more effective than placebo in treating factitious disorder (Münchausen syndrome) (Phillips, Albertini, & Rasmussen, 2002).

All in all, the dissociative and somatoform disorders remain among the most intriguing and least understood patterns of abnormal behavior.

Overview of Somatoform Disorders

TYPES OF SOMATOFORM DISORDERS/PREVALENCE RATES (approx., in parentheses)

	Description	Features
Conversion Disorder (Reported rates vary, from 1.1 in 10,000 people to 1 in 200 people)	Change or loss of a physical function without medical cause	• Emerges in context of conflicts or stressful experiences, which lends credence to its psychological origins • May be associated with la belle indifférence (indifference to symptoms)
Hypochondriasis (1%–5%)	Preoccupation with the belief that one is seriously ill	• Fear persists despite medical reassurance • Tendency to interpret physical sensations or minor aches and pains as signs of serious illness
Somatization Disorder (0.2%–2% in women, less than 0.2% in men)	Recurrent, multiple complaints about physical symptoms that have no clear organic basis	• Symptoms prompt frequent medical visits or cause significant impairment of functioning
Body Dysmorphic Disorder (unknown)	Preoccupation with an imagined or exaggerated physical defect	• Person may believe that others think less of them as a person because of the perceived defect • Person may engage in compulsive behaviors, such as excessive grooming, that aim to correct the perceived defect
Pain Disorder (unknown)	Persistent physical pain believed to be associated with psychological factors.	• Pain is severe and persistent enough to interfere with daily functioning • Medical conditions and psychological factors may play important roles in accounting for the pain

CAUSAL FACTORS   Multiple causes are involved

Biological Factors	• Possible genetic influences (somatization disorder)
Social–Environmental Factors	• Socialization of women into more dependent roles, such as the "sick role," that may be expressed in the form of somatoform disorders
Behavioral Factors	• Relief from ordinary responsibilities or escape or avoidance of uncomfortable or anxiety-laden situations (secondary gain) • Reinforcing properties of enacting a "sick role" • Compulsive behaviors associated with hypochondriasis or body dysmorphic disorder may partially relieve anxiety associated with preoccupation with health concerns or perceived physical defects
Emotional and Cognitive Factors	• Misinterpretations of bodily changes or physical symptoms as signs of serious illness (hypochondriasis) • In traditional Freudian theory, psychic energy that becomes cut off from unacceptable impulses is converted into physical symptoms (conversion disorder) • Blaming poor performance on failing health may be a self-handicapping strategy (hypochondriasis)

TREATMENT APPROACHES   Treatment typically involves psychodynamic or cognitive–behavioral therapy

Biomedical Treatment	• Limited use of antidepressants in treating hypochondriasis
Cognitive–Behavioral Therapy	• May focus on removing sources of secondary reinforcement (secondary gain), promoting development of coping skills for handling stress, and correcting exaggerated or distorted beliefs about one's health or appearance
Psychodynamic Therapy	• Psychodynamic or insight-oriented therapy may be aimed at identifying and working through underlying unconscious conflicts

Source for prevalence rates: APA, 2000

SUMMING UP

Dissociative Disorders

What are dissociative disorders? Dissociative disorders involve changes or disturbances in identity, memory, or consciousness that affect the ability to maintain an integrated sense of self. Thus, the symptoms are theorized to reflect psychological rather than organic factors.

What is dissociative identity disorder? In dissociative identity disorder, two or more distinct personalities, each possessing well-defined traits and memories, exist within the person and repeatedly take control of the person's behavior.

What is dissociative amnesia? In dissociative amnesia, the person experiences a loss of memory for personal information that cannot be accounted for by organic causes.

What is dissociative fugue? In dissociative fugue, the person suddenly travels away from home or place of work, shows a loss of memory for his or her personal past, and experiences identity confusion or takes on a new identity.

What is depersonalization disorder? In depersonalization disorder, the person experiences persistent or recurrent episodes of depersonalization of sufficient severity to cause significant distress or impairment in functioning.

How do theorists explain the development of dissociative disorders? Psychodynamic theorists view dissociative disorders as involving a form of psychological defense by which the ego defends itself against troubling memories and unacceptable impulses by blotting them out of consciousness. There is increasing documentation of a link between dissociative disorders and early childhood trauma, which lends support to the view that dissociation may serve to protect the self from troubling memories. To learning and cognitive theorists, dissociative experiences involve ways of learning not to think about certain troubling behaviors or thoughts that might lead to feelings of guilt or shame. Relief from anxiety negatively reinforces this pattern of dissociation. Some social–cognitive theorists suggest that multiple personality may represent a form of role-playing behavior.

What are the major treatment approaches for dissociative identity disorder? Psychotherapy seeks a reintegration of the personality by focusing on helping persons with dissociative identity disorder uncover and integrate dissociated painful experiences from childhood. Drug therapy may help treat the anxiety and depression often associated with the disorder, but cannot bring about reintegration of the personality.

Somatoform Disorders

What are somatoform disorders? In somatoform disorders, there are physical complaints that cannot be accounted for by organic causes. Thus, the symptoms are theorized to reflect psychological rather than organic factors. Three major types

of somatoform disorders are conversion disorder, hypochondriasis, and somatization disorder.

What is Münchausen syndrome? Münchausen syndrome, a type of factitious disorder, is characterized by the deliberate fabrication of physical symptoms for no apparent reason, other than to assume a patient role.

What is conversion disorder? In conversion disorder, symptoms or deficits in voluntary motor or sensory functions occur that suggest an underlying physical disorder, but no apparent medical basis for the condition can be found to account for the condition.

What is hypochondriasis? Hypochondriasis is a preoccupation with the fear of having, or the belief that one has, a serious medical illness, although no medical basis for the complaints can be found, and fears of illness persist despite medical reassurances.

What is pain disorder? Pain disorder is a type of somatoform disorder in which psychological factors are presumed to play important roles in explaining symptoms of pain.

What is body dysmorphic disorder? In body dysmorphic disorder, people are preoccupied with an imagined or exaggerated defect in their physical appearance.

What is somatization disorder? People with somatization disorder have multiple and recurrent complaints of physical symptoms that have persisted for many years and that cannot be accounted for by organic causes.

How are somatoform disorders conceptualized within the major theoretical perspectives? The psychodynamic view holds that conversion disorders represent the conversion into physical symptoms of the leftover emotion or energy cut off from unacceptable or threatening impulses that the ego has prevented from reaching awareness. The symptom is functional, allowing the person to achieve both primary gains and secondary gains. Learning theorists focus on reinforcements that are associated with conversion disorders, such as the reinforcing effects of adopting a "sick role." One learning theory model likens hypochondriasis to obsessive–compulsive behavior. Cognitive factors in hypochondriasis include possible self-handicapping strategies and cognitive distortions.

What are the major approaches to treating somatoform disorders? Psychodynamic therapists attempt to uncover and bring to the level of awareness the unconscious conflicts, originating in childhood, believed to be at the root of the problem. Once the conflict is uncovered and worked through, the symptoms should disappear because they are no longer needed as a partial solution to the underlying conflict. Behavioral approaches focus on removing underlying sources of reinforcement that may be maintaining the abnormal behavior pattern. More generally, behavior therapists assist people with somatoform disorders to learn to handle stressful or anxiety-arousing situations more effectively. In addition, a combination of cognitive–behavioral techniques, such as exposure with response prevention and cognitive restructuring, may be used in treating hypochondriasis and body dysmorphic disorder. Antidepressant medication may also be helpful in treating some forms of somatoform disorders.

KEY TERMS

dissociative disorder *(p. 210)*
dissociative identity disorder *(p. 211)*
dissociative amnesia *(p. 214)*
dissociative fugue *(p. 216)*
depersonalization *(p. 217)*
derealization *(p. 217)*

depersonalization disorder *(p. 218)*
somatoform disorders *(p. 224)*
malingering *(p. 225)*
factitious disorder *(p. 225)*
Münchausen syndrome *(p. 225)*
conversion disorder *(p. 227)*

hypochondriasis *(p. 228)*
body dysmorphic disorder (BDD) *(p. 230)*
pain disorder *(p. 231)*
somatization disorder *(p. 231)*
koro syndrome *(p. 232)*
dhat syndrome *(p. 233)*

WEB TOOLS

The companion website offers tools to enrich your learning experience and help you succeed in class. Go to www.prenhall.com/nevid for the gateway to the following resources:

- **VIDEO** links to connect to the video case files on the companion CD-ROM. VIDEO icons in the margins of the chapter highlight the case examples included in the CD-ROM. You can also access the CD-ROM directly if you do not have a Web connection.

- **QUIZ** links to self-scoring quizzes corresponding to each section of the chapter. The quizzes help you review your knowledge of the content in each chapter.

- **WEB** links to direct you to related sites that enhance your learning of abnormal psychology.

Mood Disorders and Suicide

William Styron (1925–), the celebrated author of *The Confessions of Nat Turner* and *Sophie's Choice,* suffered at age 60 from depression that was so severe that he planned to commit suicide. In a 1990 memoir he speaks about this personal darkness and about reclaiming his commitment to life.

"I" Darkness Visible

I watched myself in mingled terror and fascination as I began to make the necessary preparation: going to see my lawyer in the nearby town—there rewriting my will—and spending part of a couple of afternoons in a muddled attempt to bestow upon posterity a letter of farewell. It turned out that putting together a suicide note, which I felt obsessed with a necessity to compose, was the most difficult task of writing that I had ever tackled. . . .

But even a few words came to seem to me too longwinded, and I tore up all my efforts, resolving to go out in silence. Late one bitterly cold night, when I knew that I could not possibly get myself through the following day, I sat in the living room of the house bundled up against the chill; something had happened to the furnace. My wife had gone to bed, and I had forced myself to watch the tape of a movie in which a young actress, who had been in a play of mine, was cast in a small part. At one point in the film, which was set in late-nineteenth-century Boston, the characters moved down the hallway of a music conservatory, beyond the walls of which, from unseen musicians, came a contralto voice, a sudden soaring passage from the Brahms Alto Rhapsody.

This sound, which like all music—indeed, like all pleasure—I had been numbly unresponsive to for months, pierced my heart like a dagger, and in a flood of swift recollection I thought of all the joys the house had known: the children who had rushed through its rooms, the festivals, the love and work, the honestly earned slumber, the voices and the nimble commotion, the perennial tribe of cats and dogs and birds. . . . All this I realized was more than I could ever abandon, even as what I had set out so deliberately to do was more than I could inflict on those memories, and upon those, so close to me, with whom the memories were bound. And just as powerfully I realized I could not commit this desecration on myself. I drew upon some last gleam of sanity to perceive the terrifying dimensions of the mortal predicament I had fallen into. I woke up my wife and soon telephone calls were made. The next day I was admitted to the hospital.

—*From* Darkness Visible *by William Styron*

Truth or Fiction?

T❑ F❑ Feeling sad or depressed is abnormal. (p. 243)

T❑ F❑ Most people who experience a major depressive episode never have another one. (p. 246)

T❑ F❑ The bleak light of winter casts some people into a diagnosable state of depression. (p. 248)

T❑ F❑ For no apparent cause, some people experience dramatic mood swings from the depths of depression to the heights of elation. (p. 252)

T❑ F❑ The most widely used remedy for depression in Germany is not a drug but an herb. (p. 274)

T❑ F❑ The ancient Greeks and Romans used a chemical to curb turbulent mood swings that is still used today. (p. 274)

T❑ F❑ Placing a powerful electromagnet on the scalp can help relieve depression. (p. 275)

T❑ F❑ People who threaten suicide are basically attention seekers. (p. 281)

A DISTINGUISHED AUTHOR STANDS AT THE PRECIPICE OF TAKING HIS OWN LIFE. THE depression that enshrouded him and that nearly cost him his life—this *darkness visible*— is an unwelcome companion for millions of people. Depression is a disturbance of mood that casts a long, deep shadow over many facets of life.

Moods are feeling states that color our psychological lives. Most of experience changes in mood. We feel elated when we have earned high grades, a promotion, or the affections of Ms. or Mr. Right. We feel down or depressed when we are rejected by a date, flunk a test, or suffer financial reverses. It is normal and appropriate to be happy about uplifting events. It is just as normal, just as appropriate, to feel depressed by dismal events. It might very well be abnormal if we did not feel down or depressed in the face of tragic or deeply disappointing events or circumstances. But people with **mood disorders** experience disturbances in mood that are unusually

mood disorders Psychological disorders characterized by disturbances of mood.

William Styron. The celebrated author William Styron suffered from severe depression—a "darkness visible" that led him to the precipice of suicide.

severe or prolonged and impair their ability to function in meeting their normal responsibilities. Some people become severely depressed even when things appear to be going well or when they encounter mildly upsetting events that others take in stride. Still others experience extreme mood swings. They ride an emotional roller coaster with dizzying heights and abysmal depths when the world around them remains largely on an even keel. Let us begin our study of these types of emotional problems by examining the different types of mood disorders.

TYPES OF MOOD DISORDERS

In this chapter we focus on several kinds of mood disorders, including two kinds of depressive disorders, major depressive disorder and dysthymic disorder, and two kinds of mood swing disorders, bipolar disorder and cyclothymic disorder (see Table 8.1). The depressive disorders are considered *unipolar* because the disturbance lies in only one emotional direction or pole—down. By contrast, mood swing disorders are considered *bipolar* because they involve states of both depression and elation, which usually appear in an alternating pattern.

Many of us, probably most of us, have periods of sadness from time to time. We may feel down in the dumps, cry, lose interest in things, find it hard to concentrate, expect the worst to happen, or even consider suicide. In a survey of college students at the University of Northern Iowa, about 30% of the students reported feeling at least mildly depressed (Wong & Whitaker, 1993). Downcast mood was greater among freshman than among seniors or graduate students, which may reflect the difficulty of adjusting to college life. For most of

TABLE 8.1

Types of Mood Disorders

Depressive Disorders (Unipolar Disorders)

Major Depressive Disorder	Occurrence of one or more periods or episodes of depression (called major depressive episodes) without a history of naturally occurring manic or hypomanic episodes. People may have one major depressive episode, followed by a return to their usual state of functioning. The majority of people with a major depressive episode have recurrences that are separated by periods of normal or perhaps somewhat impaired functioning.
Dysthymic Disorder	A pattern of mild depression (but perhaps an irritable mood in children or adolescents) that occurs for an extended period of time—in adults, typically for many years.

Mood Swing Disorders (Bipolar Disorders)

Bipolar Disorder	Disorders with one or more manic or hypomanic episodes (episodes of inflated mood and hyperactivity in which judgment and behavior are often impaired). Manic or hypomanic episodes often alternate with major depressive episodes with intervening periods of normal mood.
Cyclothymic Disorder	A chronic mood disturbance involving numerous hypomanic episodes (episodes with manic features of a lesser degree of severity than manic episodes) and numerous periods of depressed mood or loss of interest or pleasure in activities, but not of the severity to meet the criteria for a major depressive episode.

Source: Adapted from the *DSM-IV-TR* (APA, 2000).

us, mood changes pass quickly or are not severe enough to interfere with our lifestyle or ability to function. Among people with mood disorders, including depressive disorders and bipolar disorders, mood changes are more severe or prolonged and affect daily functioning.

Major Depressive Disorder

The diagnosis of **major depressive disorder** (also called *major depression*) is based on the occurrence of one or more *major depressive episodes* in the absence of a history of **mania** or **hypomania.** In a major depressive episode, the person experiences either a depressed mood (feeling sad, hopeless, or "down in the dumps") or loss of interest or pleasure in all or virtually all activities for a period of at least 2 weeks (APA, 2000). Table 8.2 lists some of the common features of depression. The diagnostic criteria for a major depressive episode are listed in Table 8.3.

Major depression is not simply a state of sadness. People with major depressive disorder (MDD) may have poor appetite, lose or gain substantial amounts of weight, have trouble sleeping or sleep too much, and become physically agitated or—at the other extreme—show a marked slowing down in their motor activity. Here, a woman recounts how depression—the "Beast" as she calls it—affects every fiber of her being.

major depressive disorder A severe mood disorder characterized by major depressive episodes.

mania A state of unusual elation, energy, and activity.

hypomania A relatively mild state of mania.

TABLE 8.2		
Common Features of Depression		
Changes in Emotional States	Changes in mood (persistent periods of feeling down, depressed, sad, or blue)	
	Evidence of tearfulness or crying	
	Increased irritability, jumpiness, or loss of temper	
Changes in Motivation	Feeling unmotivated, or having difficulty getting going in the morning or even getting out of bed	
	Reduced level of social participation or interest in social activities	
	Loss of enjoyment or interest in pleasurable activities	
	Reduced interest in sex	
	Failure to respond to praise or rewards	
Changes in Functioning and Motor Behavior	Moving about or talking more slowly than usual	
	Changes in sleep habits (sleeping too much or too little, awakening earlier than usual and having trouble getting back to sleep in early morning hours— so-called early morning awakening)	
	Changes in appetite (eating too much or too little)	
	Changes in weight (gaining or losing weight)	
	Functioning less effectively than usual at work or school	
Cognitive Changes	Difficulty concentrating or thinking clearly	
	Thinking negatively about oneself and one's future	
	Feeling guilty or remorseful about past misdeeds	
	Lack of self-esteem or feelings of inadequacy	
	Thinking of death or suicide	

When are changes in mood considered abnormal? Although changes in mood in response to the ups and downs of everyday life may be quite normal, persistent or severe changes in mood, or cycles of extreme elation and depression, may suggest the presence of a mood disorder.

TABLE 8.3

Diagnostic Features of a Major Depressive Episode

A major depressive episode is denoted by the occurrence of five or more of the following features or symptoms during a 2-week period, which represents a change from previous functioning. At least one of the features must involve either (1) depressed mood, or (2) loss of interest or pleasure in activities. Moreover, the symptoms must cause either clinically significant levels of distress or impairment in at least one important area of functioning, such as social or occupational functioning, and must not be due directly to the use of drugs or medications, to a medical condition, or be accounted for by another psychological disorder.* Further, the episode must not represent a normal grief reaction to the death of a loved one— that is, **bereavement.**

1. Depressed mood during most of the day, nearly every day. Can be irritable mood in children or adolescents.

2. Greatly reduced sense of pleasure or interest in all or almost all activities, nearly every day for most of the day.

3. A significant loss or gain of weight (more than 5% of body weight in a month) without any attempt to diet, or an increase or decrease in appetite.

4. Daily (or nearly daily) insomnia or hypersomnia (oversleeping).

5. Excessive agitation or slowing down of movement responses nearly every day.

6. Feelings of fatigue or loss of energy nearly every day.

7. Feelings of worthlessness or misplaced or excessive or inappropriate guilt nearly every day.

8. Reduced ability to concentrate or think clearly or make decisions nearly every day.

9. Recurrent thoughts of death or suicide without a specific plan, or occurrence of a suicidal attempt or specific plan for committing suicide.

*The *DSM* includes separate diagnostic categories for mood disorders due to medical conditions or use of substances such as drugs of abuse.
Source: Adapted from the *DSM-IV-TR* (APA, 2000).

Major Depression:
The Case of Everett
"You feel absolute worthlessness."

"The Beast is Back"

My body aches intermittently, in waves, as if I had malaria. I eat with no appetite, simply because the taste of food is one of my dwindling number of pleasures. I am tired, so tired. Last night I lay like a pile of old clothes, and when David came to bed I did not stir. Sex is a foreign notion. At work today I am forgetful; I have trouble forming sentences, I lose track of them halfway through, and my words keep getting tangled. I look at my list of things to do today, and keep on looking at it; nothing seems to be happening. Things are sad to me. This morning I thought of the woman who used to live in my old house, who told me she went to Sears to buy fake lace curtains. It seemed a forlorn act—having to save your pennies, not being able to afford genuine lace. (Why? A voice in my head asks. The curtains she bought looked perfectly nice.) I feel as if my brain were a lump of protoplasm with tiny circuits embedded in it, and some of the wires keep shorting out. There are tiny little electrical fires up there, leaving crispy sections of neurons smoking and ruined. . . .

I don't even know when this current siege began—a week ago? A month ago? The onset is so gradual, and these things are hard to tell. All I know is, the Beast is back.

It is called depression, and my experiences with it have shaped my life—altered my personality, affected my most intimate relationships, changed the course of my career—in ways I will probably never be fully aware of.

—From Thompson, 1995

Major depression impairs people's ability to meet the ordinary responsibility of everyday life (Judd, Akis Kal et al., 2000). People with major depression may lose interest in most of their usual activities and pursuits, have difficulty concentrating and making decisions, have pressing thoughts of death, and attempt suicide. Many people don't seem to understand that people who are clinically depressed can't simply "shake it off" or "snap out of it." Many people still view depression as a sign of weakness, not a diagnosable disorder. Even many people with major depression believe they can handle the problem themselves. These attitudes may explain why, despite the availability of safe and effective treatments, only about half of people with diagnosable major depression in a recent nationwide survey received any treatment during the preceding year, and fewer than one third of these received treatment from a mental health specialist (Kessler et al., 2003). All told, only about one in five people with MDD in the nationwide survey received adequate treatment. One factor explaining the lack of adequate care is that many depressed patients seek help from their family physicians, who often fail to treat depression aggressively (Duenweld, 2003).

Major depressive disorder is the most common type of diagnosable mood disorder, with estimates of lifetime prevalence ranging from 10% to 25% for women and from 5% to 12% for men (APA, 2000). Overall, about 16% of the population suffer from MDD at some point in their lives, and about 7% suffer from the disorder in any given year (Kessler et al., 2003). An estimated 120 million people worldwide suffer from depression (E. Olson, 2001). Depression is so common that it has been dubbed the "common cold" of psychological problems (Seligman, 1973).

The economic costs of depression are staggering, amounting to an estimated $44 billion annually in the United States in lost productive time (Stewart et al., 2003). The economic toll of depression is as great if not greater than the costs of major medical illnesses such as heart disease and diabetes (Druss, Rosenheck, & Sledge, 2000; Stewart et al., 2003). On the other hand, effective treatment for depression leads not only to psychological improvement but also to more stable employment and increased income, as people return to a more productive level of functioning (Wells et al., 2000).

Major depression, particularly in more severe episodes, may be accompanied by psychotic features, such as delusions that one's body is rotting from illness. People with severe depression may also experience hallucinations, such as "hearing" voices condemning them for perceived misdeeds.

The following case illustrates the range of features connected with major depressive disorder.

Major depression versus bereavement. Major depression is distinguished from a normal grief reaction to the death of a loved one, which is termed bereavement. Major depression may occur in people whose bereavement becomes prolonged or seriously interferes with normal functioning.

Slowly Killing Herself: A Case of Major Depressive Disorder

A 38-year-old female clerical worker has suffered from recurrent bouts of depression since she was about 13 years of age. Most recently, she has been troubled by crying spells at work, sometimes occurring so suddenly she wouldn't have enough time to run to the ladies room to hide her tears from others. She has difficulty concentrating at work and feels a lack of enjoyment from work she used to enjoy. She harbors severe pessimistic and angry feelings, which have been more severe lately since she has been recently putting on weight and has been neglectful in taking care of her diabetes. She feels guilty that she may be slowly killing herself by not taking better care of her health. She sometimes feels that she deserves to be dead. She has been bothered by excessive sleepiness for the past year and a half, and her driving license has been suspended due to an incident the previous month in which she fell asleep while driving, causing her car to hit a telephone pole. She wakes up most days feeling groggy and just "out of it," and remains sleepy throughout the day. She has never had a steady boyfriend, and lives quietly at home with her mother, with no close friends outside of her family. During the interview, she cried frequently and answered questions in a low monotone, staring downward continuously.

—Adapted from Spitzer et al., 1989, pp. 59–62

Depression:
The Case of Helen
"I had electroshock treatments every other day for two weeks."

Major depressive episodes may resolve in a matter of months or last for a year or more (APA, 2000; USDHHS, 1999a). Some people experience a single episode with a full return to previous levels of functioning. However, the great majority of people with major depression eventually have repeated occurrences (Kanai et al., 2003; Kennedy et al., 2003; Mueller et al., 1999). Over the course of a lifetime, the average person with major depression can expect to have four episodes (Judd, 1997). Relapses tend to be more frequent in people who continue to have some leftover depressive symptoms following a first depressive episode (Judd, Paulus et al., 2000). Given a pattern of repeated occurrences and long-lasting symptoms, many professionals view major depression as a chronic disorder. On the positive side, the longer the period of recovery from major depression, the lower the risk of eventual relapse (Solomon et al., 2000).

Risk Factors in Major Depression Factors that place people at increased risk of developing major depression include age (initial onset is most common among young adults); socioeconomic status (people lower down the socioeconomic ladder are at greater risk than those who are better off); and marital status (people who are separated or divorced have higher rates than married or never-married people).

Women are nearly twice as likely as men to be diagnosed with major depression (APA, 2000; Kessler et al., 1994) (see Figure 8.1). The difference in relative risk between males and females begins in early adolescence and persists through at least the mid-50s (Barefoot et al., 2001; Kessler et al., 1993). Noting the existence of a gender gap in the diagnosis of depression is one thing; explaining it is quite another (see "Controversies in Abnormal Psychology").

Major depression typically develops in young adulthood, with an average age of onset in the mid-20s (APA, 2000). However, the disorder may affect even young children, although the risks are very low through age 14 (Lewinsohn et al., 1986). A multinational study of eight countries (United States, Puerto Rico, Italy, France, Germany, Lebanon, Taiwan, and New Zealand) showed that rates of major depression have been rising in the United States and elsewhere (Cross-National Collaborative Group, 1992). In some countries, young people born after 1955 stood about three times greater likelihood of suffering major depression than did their grandparents when they were the same age (Goleman, 1992). The greatest increases were found in Florence, Italy; the least in Christchurch, New Zealand. In all countries, rates for depression were higher among women than men.

FIGURE 8.1 Prevalence of major depressive episodes by gender.
Major depressive episodes affect about twice as many women as men.

Source: Kessler et al. (1994) National Comorbidity Survey.

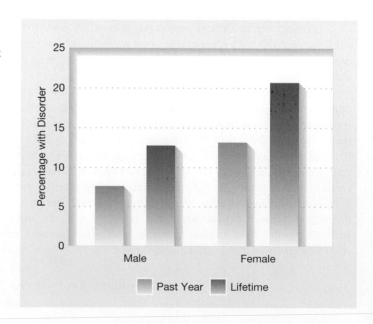

No one knows why depression has been on the rise in many cultures, but speculation focuses on social and environmental changes, such as increasing fragmentation of families due to relocations, exposure to wars and internal conflicts, and increased rates of violent crimes, as well as possible exposure to toxins or infectious agents in the environment that might affect mental as well as physical health (Cross-National Collaborative Group, 1992). One example is the dramatic increase in depression that occurred in the period 1950 to 1960 in Beirut, Lebanon. This was a period of chaotic political and demographic changes in the country. Depression dropped sharply in the following period, 1960 to 1970, a time of relative prosperity and stability, but increased again between 1970 and 1980 during a time of social upheaval and internal warfare.

Seasonal Affective Disorder   Are you glum on gloomy days? Is your temper short during the brief days of winter? Are you dismal during the long, dark winter nights and sunny when spring and summer return?

Many people report that their moods do vary with the weather. For some people, the changing of the seasons from summer into fall and winter leads to a type of major depression called *seasonal affective (mood) disorder*—SAD. SAD is not a diagnostic category in its own right in the *DSM-IV* but is a specifier of mood disorders in which major depressive episodes occur. For example, major depressive disorder that occurs seasonally would be diagnosed as major depressive disorder with seasonal pattern. The features of SAD include fatigue, excessive sleep, craving for carbohydrates, and weight gain. SAD tends to lift with the early buds of spring. It affects women more often than men and is most common among young adults. It is a subcategory of mood disorder, not a diagnostic category in its own right. For example, major depressive disorder that occurs seasonally would be diagnosed as major depressive disorder with seasonal pattern. Although the causes of SAD remain unknown, one possibility is that seasonal changes in light may alter the body's underlying biological rhythms that regulate such processes as body temperature and sleep–wake cycles (Lee et al., 1998). Another possibility is that some parts of the central nervous system may have deficiencies in transmission of the mood-regulating neurotransmitter serotonin during the winter months (Schwartz et al., 1997). Cognitive factors may play a part: People with seasonal af-

Women and depression.   Women are more likely to suffer from major depression than men. A panel convened by the APA attributed the higher rates of depression among women to factors such as unhappy marriages, physical and sexual abuse, impoverishment, single parenthood, sexism, hormonal changes, childbirth, and excessive caregiving burdens. APA panel member Bonnie Strickland expressed surprise that even more women were not clinically depressed, since they are treated as second-class citizens.

Light therapy.   Exposure to bright artificial light for a few hours a day during the fall and winter months can often bring relief from seasonal affective disorder.

CONTROVERSIES IN ABNORMAL PSYCHOLOGY
Why Are More Women Depressed?

Evidence shows that women are about twice as likely as men to suffer from clinical depression (NIMH, 2000). The gender gap is found in many other countries, including Canada, Brazil, Germany, and Japan (Gilbert, 2004). The question is, why?

Professionals continue to debate the issue. Might the gender gap be a function of biological differences between men and women? Some professionals argue that biological factors, such as hormonal fluctuations, may contribute to depression in women (Cyranowski et al., 2000).

Might the gender difference be explained, at least in part, by a reporting bias that leads men to underreport depression? In our culture, men are expected to be tough and resilient. Consequently, they are less likely to report depression or seek treatment for it. Even physicians are not immune from these social expectations. As one male physician put it, "I'm the John Wayne generation . . . I thought depression was a weakness—there was something disgraceful about it. A real man would just get over it" (cited in Wartik, 2000). The stigma associated with depression shows signs of lessening, although not disappearing. Although depression was long viewed by men as a sign of personal weakness, more men are coming forward to get help. The male ego seems to be battered by assaults from corporate downsizing and growing financial insecurity.

An expert panel convened by the American Psychological Association (APA) debated the question of gender differences in depression and concluded that they are largely the result of the greater amount of stress that women encounter in contemporary life (McGrath et al., 1990). The panel recognized that women are more likely than men to encounter such stressful life factors as physical and sexual abuse, poverty, single parenthood, and sexism.

More recently, psychologist Janet Nolen-Hoeksema proposed that differences in coping styles may also underlie women's greater proneness toward depression. Regardless of whether the factors that precipitate depression are biological, psychological, or social, one's coping responses may either exacer-

bate or reduce the severity and duration of depressive episodes. Nolen-Hoeksema and her colleagues (1991; Nolen-Hoeksema, Morrow, & Fredrickson, 1993) proposed that men are more likely to distract themselves when they are depressed, whereas women are more likely to amplify depression by ruminating about their feelings and their possible causes. Women may be more likely to sit at home when they are depressed and think about how they feel or try to understand the reasons they feel the way they do, whereas men may try to distract themselves by doing something they enjoy, such as going to a favorite hangout to get their mind off their feelings. On the other hand, men often turn to alcohol as a form of self-medication, which can lead to another set of psychological and social problems (Nolen-Hoeksema et al., 1993). Rumination is not limited to women, however (Treynor, Gonzalez, & Nolen-Hoeksema, 2003). Both men or women who ruminate more following the loss of loved ones or when feeling down or sad are more likely to become depressed and to suffer longer and more severe depression than those who ruminate less (Just & Alloy, 1997; Nolen-Hoeksema, 2000).

More research is needed to fully understand the gender gap in depression. Hopefully, research into factors such as hormonal influences, stress burdens, and ruminative styles will lead to the development of more specifically targeted interventions for treating depression in women. Likewise, by understanding the culturally instilled resistance to reporting depression among men, we can help destigmatize the disorder so that men suffering from depression will seek help rather than suffer in silence (Cochran & Rabinowitz, 2003).

Critical Thinking

- How might a theorist in the biopsychosocial tradition account for gender differences in depression?
- Give an example of how more knowledge about the causes of gender differences in depression can lead to improved treatment approaches. ■

---

fective disorder report more automatic negative thoughts throughout the year than do nondepressed controls (Rohan, Sigmon, & Dorhofer, 2003).

Whatever the underlying cause, a trial of intense light therapy, called *phototherapy,* often helps relieve depression. Phototherapy typically consists of exposure to several hours of bright artificial light a day (e.g., Terman et al., 2001). The artificial light apparently supplements the meager sunlight the person otherwise receives. Patients can generally carry out some of their daily activities (for example, eating, reading, writing) during their phototherapy sessions. Improvement typically occurs within several days of phototherapy, but treatment is apparently required throughout the course of the winter season. Light directed at the eyes tends to be more successful than light directed at the skin (Sato, 1997).

postpartum depression (PPD)
Persistent and severe mood changes that occur after childbirth.

Postpartum Depression Many, perhaps even most, new mothers experience mood changes, periods of tearfulness, and irritability following the birth of a child. These mood changes are commonly called the "maternity blues," "postpartum blues," or "baby blues." They usually last for a couple of days and are believed to be a normal response to hormonal changes that attend childbirth. Given these turbulent hormonal shifts, it would be "abnormal" for most women *not* to experience some changes in feeling states shortly following childbirth.

Some mothers, however, undergo severe mood changes that persist for months or even a year or more. These problems in mood are referred to as **postpartum depression** (PPD). *Postpartum* derives from the Latin roots *post,* meaning "after," and *papere,* meaning "to bring forth." PPD is often accompanied by disturbances in appetite and sleep, low self-esteem, and difficulties in maintaining concentration or attention. An estimated 13% of mothers suffer from some form of postpartum depression (O'Hara, 2003).

QUESTIONNAIRE
Are You Depressed?

This test, offered by the organizers of the National Depression Screening Day, can help you assess whether you are suffering from a depression. It is not intended for you to diagnose yourself, but rather to raise your awareness of concerns you may want to discuss with a professional.

	YES	NO
1. I feel downhearted, blue, and sad.	____	____
2. I don't enjoy the things that I used to.	____	____
3. I feel that others would be better off if I were dead.	____	____
4. I feel that I am not useful or needed.	____	____
5. I notice that I am losing weight.	____	____
6. I have trouble sleeping through the night.	____	____
7. I am restless and can't keep still.	____	____
8. My mind isn't as clear as it used to be.	____	____
9. I get tired for no reason.	____	____
10. I feel hopeless about the future.	____	____

Rating your responses: If you agree with at least five of the statements, including either item 1 or 2, and if you have had these complaints for at least 2 weeks, professional help is strongly recommended. If you answered "yes" to statement 3, seek consultation with a professional immediately. If you don't know whom to turn to, contact your college counseling center, neighborhood mental health center, or health provider.

Source: Adapted from J. E. Brody, "Myriad masks hide an epidemic of depression," The New York Times, *September 30, 1992, p. C12.* ■

Postpartum depression is a form of major depression in which the onset of the depressive episode begins within 4 weeks after childbirth (APA, 2000). Investigators find that postpartum depression typically is less severe than other forms of major depression and lifts relatively sooner than most (Whiffen & Gotlib, 1993). Yet some suicides are linked to postpartum depression (McQuiston, 1997). Factors associated with a heightened risk of PPD include stress, single or first-time motherhood, financial problems, a troubled marriage, social isolation, lack of support from partners and family members, a history of depression, or having an unwanted, sick, or temperamentally difficult infant (Forman et al., 2000; Ritter et al., 2000; Swendsen & Mazure, 2000). Having PPD also increases the risk that the woman will suffer future depressive episodes. Fortunately, effective treatments are available, including various forms of psychotherapy and use of antidepressant drugs (e.g., Cooper et al., 2003; Murray et al., 2003; O'Hara et al., 2000; Stuart et al., 2003; Wisner et al., 2002).

Postpartum depression is not limited to our culture. A study in an urban area in Portugal reported a similar prevalence rate (13%) (Augusto et al., 1996). Researchers have found high rates of PPD among South African women (Cooper et al., 1999) and Chinese women from Hong Kong (D. T. S. Lee et al., 2001). In the South African sample, a lack of psychological and financial support from the baby's father was associated with an increased risk of the disorder in this sample, mirroring findings with U.S. samples.

Dysthymic Disorder

Major depressive disorder is severe and marked by a relatively abrupt change from one's preexisting state. A milder form of depression seems to follow a chronic course of development that often begins in childhood or adolescence (Klein, Keller et al., 2000; Klein, Schwartz et al., 2000). Earlier diagnostic formulations of this type of chronic sadness were labeled "depressive neurosis" or "depressive personality." It was so labeled in an effort to account for several features that are traditionally connected with neurosis, such as early childhood origins, a chronic course, and generally mild levels of severity. The *DSM* classifies this form of depression **dysthymic disorder,** or *dysthymia,* which derives from Greek roots *dys-,* meaning "bad" or "hard" and *thymos,* meaning "spirit."

Persons with dysthymic disorder do feel "bad spirited" or "down in the dumps" most of the time, but they are not so severely depressed as those with major depressive disorder. Whereas major depressive disorder tends to be severe and time limited, dysthymic disorder is relatively mild and nagging, typically lasting for years (Klein, Schwartz et al., 2000). Feelings of depression and social difficulties continue even after the person makes an apparent recovery (USDHHS, 1999a). The risk of relapse is quite high (Klein, Keller et al., 2000), as is the risk of major depressive disorder: 90% of people with dysthmia eventually develop major depression (Friedman, 2002).

dysthymic disorder A mild but chronic type of depressive disorder.

Dysthymia affects about 6% of the general population at some point in their lifetimes (APA, 2000). Like major depressive disorder, dysthymic disorder is more common in women than men (see Figure 8.2).

In dysthymic disorder, complaints of depression may become such a fixture of people's lives that they seem to be intertwined with the personality structure. The persistence of complaints may lead others to perceive the person as whining and complaining. Although dysthymic disorder is less severe than major depressive disorder, persistent depressed mood and low self-esteem can affect the person's occupational and social functioning, as we see in the following case.

A Case of Dysthymic Disorder

The woman, a 28-year-old junior executive, complained of chronic feelings of depression since the age of 16 or 17. Despite doing well in college, she brooded about how other people were "genuinely intelligent." She felt she could never pursue a man she might be interested in dating because she felt inferior and intimidated. Although she had extensive therapy through college and graduate school, she could never recall a time during those years when she did not feel somewhat depressed. She got married shortly after college graduation to the man she was dating at the time, although she didn't think that he was anything "special." She just felt she needed to have a husband for companionship, and he was available. But they soon began to quarrel, and she's lately begun to feel that marrying him was a mistake. She has had difficulties at work, turning in "slipshod" work and never seeking anything more than what was basically required of her and showing little initiative. Although she dreams of acquiring status and money, she doesn't expect that she or her husband will rise in their professions because they lack "connections." Her social life is dominated by her husband's friends and their spouses, and she doesn't think that other women would find her interesting or impressive. She lacks interest in life in general and expresses dissatisfaction with all facets of her life—her marriage, her job, her social life.

—Adapted from Spitzer et al., 1994, pp. 110–112

FIGURE 8.2 Prevalence of dysthymic disorder by gender.
Like major depression, dysthymic disorder occurs in about twice as many women as men.

Source: National Comorbidity Survey (Kessler et al., 1994).

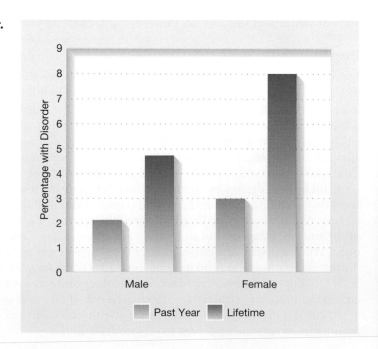

Some people are affected by both dysthymic disorder and major depression at the same time. The term **double depression** applies to those who have a major depressive episode superimposed on a longer-standing dysthymic disorder (Keller, Hirschfeld, & Hanks, 1997). People suffering from double depression generally have more severe depressive episodes than do people with major depression alone (Klein, Schwartz et al., 2000).

We have noted that major depressive disorder and dysthymic disorder are depressive disorders in the sense that the disturbance of mood is only in one direction—down. Yet people with mood disorders may have fluctuations in mood in both directions that exceed the usual ups and downs of everyday life. These types of disorders are called bipolar disorders. Here we focus on the two types of these mood-swing disorders: (1) bipolar disorder and (2) cyclothymic disorder.

Bipolar Disorder

Kay Redfield Jamison, a psychologist and leading authority on the treatment of **bipolar disorder,** herself suffers from the disorder. Within 3 months of beginning her first professional appointment as an assistant professor in the Department of Psychiatry at UCLA, she became, in her own words, "ravingly psychotic." Jamison has suffered from bipolar disorder since her teens but wasn't diagnosed until she was 28 (Ballie, 2002).

Carrie Fisher. The actress Carrie Fisher, who stared as Princess Leia in the early *Star Wars* movies, was diagnosed with bipolar disorder in her 20s.

"I" An Unquiet Mind

In her 1995 memoir, *An Unquiet Mind,* Jamison described her early and milder episodes of mania as "absolutely intoxicating states that gave rise to great personal pleasure, an incomparable flow of thoughts, and a ceaseless energy that allowed the translation of new ideas into papers and projects" (p. 5). "But then

> . . . as night inevitably goes after the day, my mood would crash, and my mind again would grind to a halt. I lost all interest in my schoolwork, friends, reading, wandering, or daydreaming. I had no idea of what was happening to me, and I would wake up in the morning with a profound sense of dread that I was going to somehow make it through another entire day. I would sit for hour after hour in the undergraduate library, unable to muster up enough energy to go to class. I would stare out the window, stare at my books, rearrange them, shuffle them around, leave them unopened, and think about dropping out of college . . . I understood very little of what was going on, and I felt as though only dying would release me from the overwhelming sense of inadequacy and blackness that surrounded me.

—From Jamison, 1995

double depression Concurrent major depressive disorder and dysthymic disorder.

bipolar disorder A psychological disorder characterized by mood swings between states of extreme elation and depression.

People with bipolar disorder ride an emotional roller coaster, swinging from the heights of elation to the depths of depression without external cause. The first episode may be either manic or depressive. Manic episodes, typically lasting from a few weeks to several months, are generally shorter in duration and end more abruptly than major depressive episodes. Some people with recurring bipolar disorder attempt suicide "on the way down" from the manic phase (Baldessarini & Tondo, 2003). They report that they would do nearly anything to escape the depths of depression they know lie ahead.

The *DSM* distinguishes between two general types of bipolar disorder, *bipolar I disorder* and *bipolar II disorder* (APA, 2000). In bipolar I disorder, the person experiences

Bipolar Disorder:
The Case of Craig
"When I'm manic . . . I have a hard time to stop talking."

manic episode A period of unrealistically heightened euphoria, extreme restlessness, and excessive activity characterized by disorganized behavior and impaired judgment.

at least one full manic episode. In many cases, the person experiences mood swings between elation and depression with intervening periods of normal mood. Some cases present with no evidence of major depressive episodes, but it is assumed that such episodes may either develop in the future or have been overlooked in the past. In a few cases, called the mixed type, a manic episode and a major depressive episode occur simultaneously.

Bipolar II disorder is associated with a milder form of mania but with more frequent depressions (Judd et al., 2003a, 2003b). In bipolar II disorder, the person has experienced one or more major depressive episodes and at least one hypomanic (mildly manic) episode. But the person has never had a full-blown manic episode. Whether bipolar I and bipolar II disorders represent qualitatively different disorders or different points along a continuum of severity of bipolar disorder remains to be determined.

Bipolar disorder is relatively uncommon, with reported lifetime prevalence rates from community surveys ranging from 0.4% to 1.6% for bipolar I disorder and about 0.5% for bipolar II disorder (APA, 2000; USDHHS, 1999a). Bipolar disorder typically develops around age 20 in both men and women and becomes a chronic, recurring condition requiring long-term treatment (Frank & Kupfer, 2003; Tohen, Zarate et al., 2003).

Unlike major depression, rates of bipolar I disorder appear about equal in men and women. In men, however, the onset of bipolar I disorder typically begins with a manic episode, whereas with women, it usually begins with a major depressive episode. The underlying reason for this gender difference remains unknown. Bipolar II disorder appears to be more common in women (APA, 2000).

In some cases, a pattern of "rapid cycling" occurs in which the individual experiences two or more full cycles of mania and depression within a year without any intervening normal periods. Rapid cycling is relatively uncommon, but occurs more often among women than men (Leibenluft, 1996). It is usually limited to a year or less, but is associated with poor social and job functioning (Coryell, Endicott, & Keller, 1992), a high rate of relapse (Keller et al., 1993), and serious suicide attempts (Coryell et al, 2003).

Many observers have noted connections between mood disorders and creativity (Jamison, 1993; McDermott, 2001; Nettle, 2001). Many distinguished writers, artists, and composers seemed to have suffered from mood disorders, including depression and bipolar disorder. The list of luminaries who suffered from mood disorders stretches from artists Michelangelo and Vincent Van Gogh, to composers William Schumann and Peter Tchaikovsky, to novelists Virginia Woolf and Ernest Hemingway, and to poets Alfred Lord Tennyson, Emily Dickinson, Walt Whitman, and Sylvia Plath. Perhaps some creative people are able to channel the seemingly boundless energy and rapid stream of thoughts associated with manic periods to enhance their productivity and ability to express themselves in novel ways. However, the great majority of writers and artists do not suffer from mood disorders, nor does creativity typically spring from psychological disturbance. Moreover, not all studies find links between psychological disorders and creativity, so it's best to reserve judgment on the nature of the relationship (Bailey, 2003).

Manic Episode Manic episodes, or periods of mania, typically begin abruptly, gathering force within days. During a manic episode, the person experiences a sudden elevation or expansion of mood and feels unusually cheerful, euphoric, or optimistic. The person seems to have boundless energy and is extremely sociable, although perhaps to the point of becoming overly demanding and overbearing toward others. Other people recognize the sudden shift in mood to be excessive in the light of the person's circumstances. It is one thing to feel elated if one has just won the state lottery. It is another to feel euphoric because it's Wednesday. Here, a young man with bipolar disorder describes what a manic episode is like for him (Behrman, 2002).

"I" Electroboy

Manic depression is about buying a dozen bottles of Heinz ketchup and all eight bottles of Windex in stock at the Food Emporium on Broadway at 4 A.M., flying from Zurich to the Bahamas and back to Zurich in three days to balance the hot and cold weather (my "sweet and sour" theory of bipolar disorder), carrying $20,000 in $100 bills in your shoes into the country on your way back to Tokyo, and picking out the person sitting six seats away at the bar to have sex with only because he or she happens to be sitting there. It's about blips and burps of madness, moments of absolute delusion, bliss, and irrational and dangerous choices made in order to heighten pleasure and excitement and to ensure a sense of control. The symptoms of manic depression come in different strengths and sizes. Most days I need to be as manic as possible to come as close as I can to destruction, to get a real good high—a $25,000 shopping spree, a four-day drug binge, or a trip around the world. Other days a simple high from a shoplifting excursion at Duane Reade for a toothbrush or a bottle of Tylenol is enough. I'll admit it: there's a great deal of pleasure to mental illness, especially to the mania associated with manic depression. It's an emotional state similar to Oz, full of excitement, color, noise, and speed—an overload of sensory stimulation—whereas the sane state of Kansas is plain and simple, black and white, boring and flat. Mania has such a dreamlike quality that often I confuse my manic episodes with dreams I've had. . . .

   Mania is about desperately seeking to live life at a more passionate level, taking second and sometimes third helpings on food, alcohol, drugs, sex, and money, trying to live a whole life in one day. Pure mania is as close to death as I think I have ever come. The euphoria is both pleasurable and frightening. My manic mind teems with rapidly changing ideas and needs; my head is cluttered with vibrant colors, wild images, bizarre thoughts, sharp details, secret codes, symbols and foreign languages. I want to devour everything—parties, people, magazines, books, music, art, movies, and television.

—From *Electroboy* by Andy Behrman

People in a manic episode tend to show poor judgment and to become argumentative, sometimes going so far as destroying property. Roommates may find them abrasive and avoid them. They may become extremely generous and make large charitable contributions they can ill afford or give away costly possessions.

People in a manic episode tend to speak very rapidly (with *pressured speech*). Their thoughts and speech may jump from topic to topic in a *rapid flight of ideas*. Others find it difficult to get a word in edgewise. They typically experience an inflated sense of self-esteem that may range from extreme self-confidence to wholesale delusions of grandeur. They may feel capable of solving the world's problems or of composing symphonies, despite a lack of any special knowledge or talent. They may spout off about matters on which they know little, such as how to eliminate world hunger or create a new world order. It soon becomes clear that they are disorganized and incapable of completing their projects. They also become highly distractible. Their attention is easily diverted by irrelevant stimuli like the sounds of a ticking clock or people talking in the next room. They tend to take on multiple tasks, more than they can handle. They may suddenly quit their jobs to enroll in law school, wait tables at night, organize charity drives on weekends, and work on the great American novel in their "spare time." They may not be able to sit still or sleep restfully. They almost always show decreased need for sleep. They tend to awaken early yet feel well rested and full of energy. They sometimes go for days without sleep and without feeling tired. Although they may have abundant stores of energy, they seem unable to organize their efforts constructively. Their elation impairs their ability to work and to maintain normal relationships.

People in manic episodes tend to exercise poor judgment and fail to weigh the consequences of their actions. They may get into trouble as a result of lavish spending, reckless driving, or sexual escapades. In severe cases, they may experience hallucinations or become grossly delusional, believing, for example, that they have a special relationship with God.

Starry, Starry Night. The famed artist Vincent Van Gogh suffered from severe bouts of depression and eventually took his own life at the age of 37, dying of a self-inflicted gunshot wound. In this self-portrait, Van Gogh strikes a melancholy pose that allows the viewer to sense the deep despair he had endured.

cyclothymic disorder A mood disorder characterized by a chronic pattern of less-severe mood swings than are found in bipolar disorder.

Cyclothymic Disorder

Cyclothymia is derived from the Greek *kyklos,* which means "circle," and *thymos* ("spirit"). The notion of a circular-moving spirit is an apt description, because this disorder represents a chronic cyclical pattern of mood disturbance characterized by mild mood swings lasting at least 2 years (1 year for children and adolescents). **Cyclothymic disorder** usually begins in late adolescence or early adulthood and persists for years. Few, if any, periods of normal mood last for more than a month or two. Neither the periods of elevated or depressed mood are severe enough to warrant a diagnosis of bipolar disorder, however. Estimates from community studies indicate lifetime prevalence rates for cyclothymic disorder of between 0.4% to 1% (4 to 10 people in 1,000), with men and women about equally likely to be affected (APA, 2000).

The periods of elevated mood are called hypomanic episodes (from the Greek prefix *hypo-,* meaning "under" or "less than"). They are less severe than manic episodes and are not accompanied by the severe social or occupational problems associated with full-blown manic episodes. During hypomanic episodes, people may have an inflated sense of self-esteem, may feel unusually charged with energy, and may be more alert, restless, and irritable than usual. They may be able to work long hours with little fatigue or need for sleep. Their projects may be left unfinished when their moods reverse, however. Then they enter a mildly depressed mood state and feel lethargic and depressed, but not to the extent typical of a major depressive episode. Social relationships may become strained by shifting moods, and work may suffer. Sexual interest waxes and wanes with the person's moods.

The boundaries between bipolar disorder and cyclothymic disorder are not yet clearly established. Some forms of cyclothymic disorder may represent a mild, early type of bipolar disorder. Approximately 33% of people with cyclothymic disorder eventually develop bipolar disorder, a figure that is about 33 times higher than the general population (USDHHS, 1999a). We presently lack the ability to distinguish persons with cyclothymia who are likely to develop bipolar disorder (Howland & Thase, 1993). The following case presents an example of the mild mood swings that typify cyclothymic disorder.

"Good Times and Bad Times": A Case of Cyclothymic Disorder

The man, a 29-year-old car salesman, reports that since the age of 14 he has experienced alternating periods of "good times and bad times." During his "bad" periods, which generally last between 4 and 7 days, he sleeps excessively and feels a lack of confidence, energy, and motivation, as if he were "just vegetating." Then his moods abruptly shift for a period of three or four days, usually upon awakening in the morning, and he feels aflush with confidence and sharpened mental ability. During these "good periods" he engages in promiscuous sex and uses alcohol, in part to enhance his good feelings and in part to help him sleep at night. The good periods may last upwards of 7–10 days at times, before shifting back into the "bad" periods, generally following a hostile or irritable outburst.

—Adapted from Spitzer et al., 1994, pp. 155–157

THEORETICAL PERSPECTIVES ON MOOD DISORDERS

Mood disorders are best understood in terms of complex interactions of biological and psychosocial influences (Cui & Vaillant, 1997). Though a full understanding of the causes of mood disorders presently lies beyond our grasp, we have begun to identify many of the important contributors to mood disorders, especially depression. Here we begin with relationships between stress and the mood disorders and then consider the psychological and biological perspectives on mood disorders.

Stress and Mood Disorders

Stressful life events such as the loss of a loved one, the breakup of a romantic relationship, prolonged unemployment, physical illness, marital or relationship problems, economic hardship, pressure at work, or racism and discrimination increase the risks of developing a mood disorder or experiencing a recurrence of a mood disorder, especially major depression (Greenberger et al., 2000; Kendler et al., 2000, 2004; Monroe et al., 2001). In one research example, investigators found that in about four of five cases, stressful life events preceded major depression (Mazure, 1998). People are also more likely to become depressed when they experience humiliating events involving key life roles (as parents, for example) and when they hold themselves responsible for undesirable events, such as school problems, financial difficulties, unwanted pregnancy, interpersonal problems, and legal problems (Hammen & de Mayo, 1982; Kendler, Hettema et al., 2003).

Yet the relationship between stress and depression may cut both ways: Stressful life events may contribute to depression, and depressive symptoms in themselves may be stressful or lead to additional sources of stress, such as divorce or loss of employment (Cui & Vaillant, 1997; Daley et al., 1997). When you're depressed, for example, you may find it more difficult to keep up with your work, which can lead to more stress as your work backs up. The stress of unemployment and financial hardship may lead to depression, but depression may also lead to unemployment and lower income (Whooley et al., 2002). Stressful events, especially traumatic events, may play important roles in the cycling of bipolar disorder, although perhaps not in the onset of the disorder (Hammen & Gitlin, 1997; Miklowitz & Alloy, 1999).

Though stress is often implicated in depression, not everyone who encounters stress becomes depressed. Factors such as coping skills, genetic endowment, and availability of social support contribute to the likelihood of depression in the face of stressful events (USDHHS, 1999a). Increased vulnerability to depression is associated with adverse experiences in early life, including parental divorce and physical abuse (Wainwright &

Stress and depression. Depression is strongly associated with major stressors, such as prolonged unemployment and economic hardship. However, whether people consider themselves responsible for the hardship affects their likelihood of becoming depressed. In addition, it may be difficult to determine whether a person becomes depressed over losing a job or loses a job because of suffering from depression.

Surtees, 2002). Consistent with the diathesis-stress model, researchers find that young women are more likely to develop depression in the face of stressful life events if they possessed a diathesis in the form of exposure to childhood adversities such as family violence or parental mental disorders or alcoholism (Hammen, Henry, & Daley, 2000). Moreover, physical or sexual abuse in childhood can disrupt the development of early attachment bonds to parents, setting the stage for later relationship problems and emotional disorders involving depression and anxiety (USDHHS, 1999a).

A strong marital relationship may provide a source of support during times of stress. Not surprisingly, people who are divorced or separated have higher rates of depression and suicide attempts than those who are married (Weissman et al., 1991). The availability of social support is also associated with quicker recoveries from episodes of both major depression and bipolar disorder (Johnson, Winett et al., 1999; Moos, Cronkite, & Moos, 1998).

People with major depression often lack skills needed to solve interpersonal problems with friends, coworkers, or supervisors (Marx, Williams, & Claridge, 1992). But those who take an active approach to solving their interpersonal problems tend to have better clinical outcomes than depressed people who assume a passive style of coping (Sherbourne, Hays, & Wells, 1995).

Psychodynamic Theories

The classic psychodynamic theory of depression of Freud (1917/1957) and his followers (e.g., Abraham, 1916/1948) holds that depression represents anger directed inward rather than against significant others. Anger may become directed against the self following either the actual or threatened loss of these important others.

Freud believed that mourning, or normal bereavement, is a healthy process by which one eventually comes to separate oneself psychologically from a person who is lost through death, separation, divorce, or other reason. Pathological mourning, however, does not promote healthy separation. Rather, it fosters lingering depression. Pathological mourning is likely to occur in people who hold powerful ambivalent feelings—a combination of positive (love) and negative (anger, hostility) feelings—toward the person who has departed or whose departure is feared. Freud theorized that when people lose, or even if they fear losing, an important figure about whom they feel ambivalent,

Social support as a buffer against depression. Social support appears to buffer the effects of stress and may reduce the risk of depression. People who lack important relationships and who rarely join in social activities are more likely to suffer from depression.

their feelings of anger turn to rage. Yet rage triggers guilt, which in turn prevents the person from venting anger directly at the lost person (called an "object").

To preserve a psychological connection to the lost object, people *introject,* or bring inward, a mental representation of the object. They thus incorporate the other person into the self. Now anger is turned inward, against the part of the self that represents the inward representation of the lost person. This produces self-hatred, which in turn leads to depression.

From the psychodynamic viewpoint, bipolar disorder represents shifting dominance of the individual's personality between the ego and superego. In the depressive phase, the superego is dominant, producing exaggerated notions of wrongdoing and flooding the individual with feelings of guilt and worthlessness. After a time, the ego rebounds and asserts supremacy, producing feelings of elation and self-confidence that characterize the manic phase. The excessive display of ego eventually triggers a return of guilt, once again plunging the individual into depression.

While also emphasizing the importance of loss, recent psychodynamic models focus more on the individual's sense of self-worth or self-esteem. One model, called the *self-focusing model,* considers how people allocate their attentional processes after a loss (death of a loved one, a personal failure, etc.) (Pyszczynski & Greenberg, 1987). According to this model, depression-prone people experience a period of intense self-examination (self-focusing) following a loss. They become preoccupied with thoughts about the lost object (loved one) or important goal and remain unable to surrender hope of somehow regaining it.

Loss and depression. Psychodynamic theorists focus on the important role of loss in the development of depression.

Consider a person who must cope with the termination of a failed romantic relationship. The self-focusing model proposes that the depression-prone individual persists in focusing attention on restoring the relationship, rather than recognizing the futility of the effort and getting on with life. Moreover, the lost partner was a source of emotional support on whom the depression-prone individual had relied to maintain self-esteem. Following the loss, the depression-prone individual feels stripped of hope and optimism because these positive feelings had depended on the lost object. The loss of self-esteem and feelings of security, not of the relationship per se, precipitates depression. Similarly, loss of a specific occupational goal may trigger self-focusing and consequent depression. Only by surrendering the object or lost goal and fostering alternate sources of identity and self-worth can the cycle be broken.

Research Evidence Psychodynamic theorists focus on the role of loss in depression. Research does show that loss of significant others (through death or divorce, for example) is often associated with the development of depression (Kendler et al., 2002; Kendler, Hettema et al., 2003). Such a loss may also lead to other psychological disorders, however. There is yet a lack of research to support Freud's view that repressed anger toward the departed loved one is turned inward in depression.

A recent meta-analysis supported the linkage between self-focusing and depression, especially with female samples (Mor & Winquist, 2002). Also supporting the model is evidence from a laboratory study that diverting attention away from the self can lift the mood of depressed people (Nix et al., 1995). On the other hand, self-focused attention is linked to disorders other than depression, including anxiety disorders, alcoholism, mania, and schizophrenia (Ingram, 1991). The general linkage between self-focused attention and psychopathology may limit the model's value as an explanation of depression.

Humanistic Theories

From the humanistic framework, people become depressed when they cannot imbue their existence with meaning and make authentic choices that lead to self-fulfillment. The world is then a drab place. People's search for meaning gives color and substance to their lives. Guilt may arise when people believe they have not lived up to their potential. Humanistic psychologists challenge us to take a long hard look at our lives. Are they worthwhile and enriching? Or are they drab and routine? If the latter, perhaps we have frustrated our needs for self-actualization. We may be settling, coasting through life. Settling can give rise to a sense of dreariness that becomes expressed in depressive behavior—lethargy, sullen mood, and withdrawal.

Like psychodynamic theorists, humanistic theorists focus on the loss of self-esteem that can arise when people lose friends or family members or suffer occupational setbacks. We tend to connect our personal identity and sense of self-worth with our social roles as parents, spouses, students, or workers. When these role identities are lost, through the death of a spouse, the departure of children to college, or loss of a job, our sense of purpose and self-worth can be shattered. Depression is a frequent consequence of such losses. It is especially likely when we base our self-esteem on our occupational role or success. The loss of a job, a demotion, or a failure to achieve a promotion are common precipitants of depression, especially when we value ourselves on the basis of occupational success.

Learning Theories

Whereas the psychodynamic perspectives focus on inner, often unconscious, causes, learning theorists dwell more on situational factors, such as the loss of positive reinforcement. We perform best when levels of reinforcement are commensurate with our efforts. Changes in the frequency or effectiveness of reinforcement can shift the balance so that life becomes unrewarding.

Reinforcement and Depression Learning theorist Peter Lewinsohn (1974) proposed that depression results from an imbalance between behavior and reinforcement. A lack of reinforcement for one's efforts can sap motivation and induce feelings of depression. Inactivity and social withdrawal reduce opportunities for reinforcement; lack of reinforcement exacerbates withdrawal. The low rate of activity typical of depression may also be a source of secondary gain or secondary reinforcement. Family members and other people may rally around people suffering from depression and release them from their responsibilities. Sympathy may thus become a source of reinforcement that helps maintain depressed behavior.

Reduction in reinforcement levels can occur for many reasons. A person who is recuperating at home from a serious illness or injury may find little that is reinforcing to do. Social reinforcement may plummet when people close to us, who were suppliers of reinforcement, die or leave us. People who suffer social losses are more likely to become depressed when they lack the social skills to form new relationships. Some first-year college students are homesick and depressed because they lack the skills to form rewarding new relationships. Widows and widowers may be at a loss as to how to start a new relationship.

Changes in life circumstances may also alter the balance of effort and reinforcement. A prolonged layoff may reduce financial reinforcements, which may in turn force painful cutbacks in lifestyle. A disability or an extended illness may also impair one's ability to ensure a steady flow of reinforcements.

Lewinsohn's model is supported by research findings that connect depression to a low level of positive reinforcement. In early work, Lewinsohn and Libet (1972) noted a correspondence between depressed moods and lower rates of participation in potentially reinforcing activities. People with depressive disorders were also found to report fewer pleasant activities than nondepressed people (MacPhillamy & Lewinsohn, 1974). However, it is conceivable that depression precedes rather than follows a reduction in reinforcement. In other words, depression may lead people to withdraw from socially reinforcing activities. Regardless of the root causes of depression, a behavioral treatment approach that encourages depressed people to increase their levels of pleasant activities and provides them with the skills to do so is often helpful in alleviating depression (DeRubeis & Crits-Christoph, 1998; Jacobson et al., 1996).

Interactional Theory Difficulties in social interactions may help explain the lack of positive reinforcement. Interactional theory, developed by psychologist James Coyne

(1976), proposes that the adjustment to living with a depressed person can become so stressful that the partner or family member becomes progressively less reinforcing.

Interactional theory is based on the concept of *reciprocal interaction.* People's behavior influences and, in turn, is influenced by the behavior of other. The theory holds that depression-prone people react to stress by demanding greater reassurance and social support from significant others. At first people who become depressed may succeed in garnering support. Over time, however, their demands and behavior begin to elicit anger or annoyance. Although loved ones may keep their negative feelings to themselves, these feelings may surface in subtle ways that spell rejection. Depressed people may react to rejection with deeper depression and greater demands, triggering a vicious cycle of further rejection and more profound depression. They may also feel guilty about distressing their family members, which can exacerbate their negative feelings about themselves.

People who become depressed tend to encounter rejection in long-term relationships (Marcus & Nardone, 1992). Family members may find it stressful to adjust to the depressed person's behavior, especially withdrawal, lethargy, despair, and constant requests for reassurance. People whose spouses are being treated for depression tend to report higher-than-average levels of emotional distress (Benazon, 2000).

All in all, research evidence generally supports Coyne's belief that people who suffer from depression elicit rejection from others. However, we lack sufficient evidence that rejection is explained by the negative emotions (anger and annoyance) that depressed people induce in others (Segrin & Dillard, 1992). Rather, evidence suggests that the depressed person's lack of effective social skills may account for the rejection (Segrin & Abramson, 1994). Depressed people tend to be unresponsive, uninvolved, and even impolite when they interact with others. For example, they tend to gaze very little at the other person, to take an excessive amount of time to respond, to show very little approval or validation of the other person, and to dwell on their problems and negative feelings (Segrin & Abramson, 1994). They even dwell on negative feelings when interacting with strangers. In effect, they turn other people off, setting the stage for rejection.

We do not yet know whether social skills deficits are a direct cause or a symptom of depression. Whatever the case, impaired social behavior likely plays an important role in determining the persistence or recurrence of depression. As we shall see, some psychological approaches to treating depression (e.g., interpersonal psychotherapy and Lewinsohn's social skills training approach—discussed later) focus on helping people with depression learn to understand and overcome their problems relating to others. This may help, in turn, alleviate depression or perhaps prevent recurrences.

Cognitive Theories

Cognitive theorists relate the origin and maintenance of depression to the ways in which people see themselves and the world around them.

Aaron Beck's Cognitive Theory One of the most influential cognitive theorists, psychiatrist Aaron Beck (Beck, 1976; Beck et al., 1979), relates the development of depression to the adoption early in life of a negatively biased or distorted way of thinking—the **cognitive triad of depression** (see Table 8.4). The cognitive triad includes negative beliefs about oneself ("I'm no good"), the environment or the world at large ("This school is awful"), and the future ("Nothing will ever turn out right for me"). Cognitive theory holds that people who adopt this negative way of thinking are at greater risk of becoming depressed in the face of stressful or disappointing life experiences, such as getting a poor grade or losing a job.

Beck views these negative concepts of the self and the world as mental templates or *cognitive schemes* that are adopted in childhood on the basis of early learning experiences. Children may find that nothing they do is good enough to please their parents or teachers. As a result, they come to regard themselves as basically incompetent and to perceive their future prospects as dim. These beliefs may sensitize them later in life to interpret any failure or disappointment as a reflection of something basically wrong or

cognitive triad of depression The view that depression derives from adopting negative views of oneself, the environment or world at large, and the future.

TABLE 8.4

The Cognitive Triad of Depression

Negative View of Oneself	Perceiving oneself as worthless, deficient, inadequate, unlovable, and as lacking the skills necessary to achieve happiness.
Negative View of the Environment	Perceiving the environment as imposing excessive demands and/or presenting obstacles that are impossible to overcome, leading continually to failure and loss.
Negative View of the Future	Perceiving the future as hopeless and believing that one is powerless to change things for the better. One expects of the future only continuing failure and unrelenting misery and hardship.

Note: According to Aaron Beck, depression-prone people adopt a habitual style of negative thinking—the so-called cognitive triad of depression.
Source: Adapted from Beck & Young, 1985; Beck et al., 1979.

inadequate about themselves. Even a minor disappointment becomes a crushing blow or a total defeat that can quickly lead to states of depression.

The tendency to magnify the importance of minor failures is an example of an error in thinking that Beck labels a *cognitive distortion.* He believes cognitive distortions set the stage for depression in the face of personal losses or negative life events. Psychiatrist David Burns (1980) enumerated a number of the cognitive distortions associated with depression:

1. *All-or-nothing thinking.* Seeing events as either all good or all bad, or as either black or white with no shades of gray For example, one may perceive a relationship that ended in disappointment as a totally negative experience, despite any positive feelings or experiences that may have occurred along the way. Perfectionism is an example of all-or-nothing thinking. Perfectionists judge any outcome other than perfect success to be complete failure. They may consider a grade of B or even A- to be tantamount to an F. Perfectionism is connected with an increased vulnerability to depression as well as to poor treatment outcomes (Blatt et al., 1998; Minarik & Ahrens, 1996).

2. *Overgeneralization.* Believing that if a negative event occurs, it is likely to occur again in similar situations in the future. One may interpret a single negative event as foreshadowing an endless series of negative events. For example, receiving a letter of rejection from a potential employer leads one to assume that all other job applications will similarly be rejected.

3. *Mental filter.* Focusing only on negative details of events, thereby rejecting the positive features of one's experiences. Like a droplet of ink that spreads to discolor an entire beaker of water, focusing only on a single negative detail can darken one's vision of reality. Beck called this cognitive distortion *selective abstraction,* meaning the individual selectively abstracts the negative details from events and ignores their positive features. One thus bases one's self-esteem on perceived weaknesses and failures, rather than on positive features or on a balance of accomplishments and shortcomings. For example, a person receives a job evaluation that contains both positive and negative comments but focuses only on the negative.

4. *Disqualifying the positive.* This refers to the tendency to snatch defeat from the jaws of victory by neutralizing or denying your accomplishments. An example is dismissal of congratulations for a job well done by thinking and saying, "Oh, it's no big deal. Anyone could have done it." By contrast, taking credit where credit is due may help people overcome depression by increasing their belief they can make changes that will lead to a positive future (Needles & Abramson, 1990).

How could he have missed that tackle? This football player missed a crucial tackle and is rehashing it. He is putting himself down and telling himself that there is nothing he can do to improve his performance. Cognitive theorists believe that a person's self-defeating or distorted interpretations of negative events can set the stage for depression.

5. *Jumping to conclusions.* Forming a negative interpretation of events, despite a lack of evidence. Two examples of this style of thinking are "mind reading" and "the fortune teller error." In *mind reading,* you arbitrarily jump to the conclusion that others don't like or respect you, as in interpreting a friend's not calling for a while as a rejection. The *fortune teller error* is the prediction that something bad is always about to happen. The person believes the prediction of calamity is factually based, even though there is no evidence to support it. For example, the person concludes that a passing tightness in the chest *must* be a sign of heart disease, discounting the possibility of more benign causes.

6. *Magnification and minimization.* Magnification, or *catastrophizing,* refers to the tendency to make mountains out of molehills—to exaggerate the importance of negative events, personal flaws, fears, or mistakes. Minimization is the mirror image, a type of cognitive distortion in which one minimizes or underestimates one's good points.

7. *Emotional reasoning.* Basing reasoning on emotions—thinking, for example, "If I feel guilty, it must be because I've done something really wrong." One interprets feelings and events based on emotions rather than on fair consideration of evidence.

8. *Should statements.* Creating personal imperatives or self-commandments— "shoulds" or "musts." For example, "I *should* always get my first serve in!" or "I *must* make Chris like me!" By creating unrealistic expectations, *musterbation*— the label given this form of thinking by Albert Ellis—can lead one to become depressed when one falls short.

9. *Labeling and mislabeling.* Explaining behavior by attaching negative labels to oneself and others. You may explain a poor grade on a test by thinking you were "lazy" or "stupid" rather than simply unprepared for the specific exam or, perhaps, ill. Labeling other people as "stupid" or "insensitive" can engender hostility toward them. Mislabeling involves the use of labels that are emotionally charged and inaccurate, such as calling yourself a "pig" because of a minor deviation from your usual diet.

10. *Personalization.* Assuming that you are responsible for other people's problems and behavior. You may assume your partner or spouse is crying because of something you have done (or not done) rather than recognizing that other causes may be involved.

Consider the errors in thinking illustrated in the following case example.

Christie's Errors in Thinking

Christie was a 33-year-old real estate sales agent who suffered from frequent episodes of depression. Whenever a deal fell through, she would blame herself: "If only I had worked harder . . . negotiated better . . . talked more persuasively . . . the deal would have been done." After several successive disappointments, each one followed by self-recriminations, she felt like quitting altogether. Her thinking became increasingly dominated by negative thoughts, which further depressed her mood and lowered her self-esteem: "I'm a loser . . . I'll never succeed . . . It's all my fault . . . I'm no good and I'm never going to succeed at anything."

Christie's thinking included cognitive errors such as the following: (1) personalization (believing herself to be the sole cause of negative events); (2) labeling and mislabeling (labeling herself to be a loser); (3) overgeneralization (predicting a dismal future on the basis of a present disappointment); and (4) mental filter (judging her personality entirely on the basis of her disappointments). In therapy, Christie learned to think more realistically about events and not to jump to conclusions that she was automatically at fault whenever a deal fell through, or to judge her whole personality on the basis of disappointments or perceived flaws in herself. In place of this self-defeating style of thinking, she began to think more realistically when disappointments occurred, like telling herself, "Okay, I'm disappointed. I'm frustrated. I feel lousy. So what? It doesn't mean I'll never succeed. Let me discover what went wrong and try to correct it the next time. I have to look ahead, not dwell on disappointments in the past."

—From the Authors' Files

Distorted thinking tends to be experienced as automatic, as if the thoughts had just popped into one's head. These automatic thoughts are likely to be accepted as statements of fact rather than as opinions or habitual ways of interpreting events.

cognitive-specificity hypothesis The belief that different emotional disorders are linked to particular kinds of automatic thoughts.

Beck and his colleagues formulated a **cognitive-specificity hypothesis,** which proposes that different disorders are characterized by different types of automatic thoughts. Beck and his colleagues showed some interesting differences in the types of automatic thoughts people with depressive and anxiety disorders reported (Beck et al., 1987) (see Table 8.5). People with diagnosable depression more often reported thoughts concerning themes of loss, self-deprecation, and pessimism. People with anxiety disorders more often reported thoughts concerning physical danger and other threats.

Research Evidence on Cognitions and Depression Evidence that depressed people show higher levels of distorted or dysfunctional thinking than nondepressed controls supports Beck's model (e.g., Clark, Cook, & Snow, 1998; Riso et al., 2003; Stader & Hokanson, 1998). Depressed people also tend to hold more pessimistic views of the future and to be more critical of themselves and others (Gara et al., 1993). Other findings indicate that dysfunctional attitudes (above a certain threshold) increase vulnerability to depression in the face of negative life events (Lewinsohn, Joiner, & Rohde, 2001). On the other hand, thinking positive thoughts may serve as a kind of buffer or shock absorber in helping people cope with negative life events without becoming depressed (Bruch, 1997; Lightsey, 1994a, 1994b).

Although dysfunctional cognitions (negative, distorted, or pessimistic thoughts) are more common among people who are depressed, the causal pathways remain unclear.

TABLE 8.5

Automatic Thoughts Associated with Depression and Anxiety

Common Automatic Thoughts Associated with Depression	Common Automatic Thoughts Associated with Anxiety
1. I'm worthless.	1. What if I get sick and become an invalid?
2. I'm not worthy of other people's attention or affection.	2. I am going to be injured.
3. I'll never be as good as other people are.	3. What if no one reaches me in time to help?
4. I'm a social failure.	4. I might be trapped.
5. I don't deserve to be loved.	5. I am not a healthy person.
6. People don't respect me anymore.	6. I'm going to have an accident.
7. I will never overcome my problems.	7. Something will happen that will ruin my appearance.
8. I've lost the only friends I've had.	8. I am going to have a heart attack.
9. Life isn't worth living.	9. Something awful is going to happen.
10. I'm worse off than they are.	10. Something will happen to someone I care about.
11. There's no one left to help me.	11. I'm losing my mind.
12. No one cares whether I live or die.	
13. Nothing ever works out for me anymore.	
14. I have become physically unattractive.	

Source: Adapted from Beck et al., 1987.

We can't yet say whether dysfunctional or negative thinking causes depression or is merely a feature of depression. Thus the central theme of cognitive theory, that negative, distorted thoughts are causally related to depression, remains to be confirmed (Cole et al., 1998; Stader & Hokanson, 1998).

Perhaps the causal linkages go both ways. Our thoughts may affect our moods, and our moods may affect our thoughts (Kwon & Oei, 1994). For example, people who become depressed may begin thinking in negative, distorted ways. The more negative and distorted their thinking becomes, the more depressed they feel, and the more depressed they feel, the more dysfunctional their thinking becomes. However, it is equally possible that dysfunctional thinking comes first in the cycle, perhaps in response to a disappointing life experience, which then leads to a downcast mood. This in turn may accentuate negative thinking, and so on. We are still faced with the old "chicken or the egg" dilemma of determining which comes first in the causal sequence, distorted thinking or depressed mood. Future research may help tease out these causal pathways. Even if it becomes clear that distorted cognitions play no direct role in causing depression, the mutual interaction between thoughts and moods may contribute to the maintenance of depressive episodes and increase the likelihood of their recurrence (Kwon & Oei, 1994). We know, for example, that people who recover from depression but continue to hold distorted cognitions tend to be at greater risk of recurrence (Rush & Weissenburger, 1994). Fortunately, evidence shows that dysfunctional attitudes tend to decrease with effective treatment for depression (Fava et al., 1994).

Learned Helplessness (Attributional) Theory The **learned helplessness** model proposes that people may become depressed because they learn to view themselves as helpless to change their lives for the better. The originator of the learned helplessness concept, Martin Seligman (1973, 1975), suggests that people learn to perceive themselves as helpless because of their experiences. The learned helplessness model therefore straddles the behavioral and the cognitive: Situational factors foster attitudes that lead to depression.

Seligman and his colleagues based the learned helplessness model on early laboratory studies of animals. In these studies, dogs exposed to an inescapable electric shock showed the "learned helplessness effect" by failing to learn to escape when escape became possible (Overmier & Seligman, 1967; Seligman & Maier, 1967). Exposure to uncontrollable forces apparently taught the animals they were helpless to change their situation. Animals who developed learned helplessness showed behaviors that were similar to those of people with depression, including lethargy, lack of motivation, and difficulty acquiring new skills (Maier & Seligman, 1976).

Seligman (1975, 1991) proposed that some forms of depression in humans might result from exposure to apparently uncontrollable situations. Such experiences can instill the expectation that future reinforcements will also be beyond the individual's control. A cruel vicious cycle may come into play in many cases of depression. A few failures may produce feelings of helplessness and expectations of further failure. Perhaps you know people who have failed certain subjects, such as mathematics. They may come to believe themselves incapable of succeeding in math. They may thus decide that studying for the quantitative section of the Graduate Record Exam is a waste of time. They then perform poorly, completing the self-fulfilling prophecy, which further intensifies feelings of helplessness, leading to lowered expectations, and so on, in a vicious cycle.

Although it stimulated much interest, Seligman's model failed to account for the low self-esteem typical of people who are depressed. Nor did it explain why depression persists in some people but not in others. Seligman and his colleagues (Abramson, Seligman, & Teasdale, 1978) offered a reformulation of the theory to meet such shortcomings. The revised theory held that perception of lack of control over reinforcement alone did not explain the persistence and severity of depression. It was also necessary to consider cognitive factors, especially the ways in which people explain their failures and disappointments to themselves.

learned helplessness A behavior pattern characterized by passivity and perceptions of lack of control.

Is it me? According to reformulated helplessness theory, the kinds of attributions we make concerning negative events can make us more or less vulnerable to depression. Attributing the breakup of a relationship to internalizing ("It's me"), globalizing ("I'm totally worthless"), and stabilizing ("Things are always going to turn out badly for me") causes can lead to depression.

Seligman and his colleagues recast helplessness theory in terms of the social psychology concept of *attributional style*. An attributional style is a personal style of explanation. When disappointments or failures occur, we may explain them in various characteristic ways. We may blame ourselves (an internal attribution), or we may blame the circumstances we face (an external attribution). We may see bad experiences as typical events (a stable attribution) or as isolated events (an unstable attribution). We may see them as evidence of broader problems (a global attribution) or as evidence of precise and limited shortcomings (a specific attribution). The reformulated helplessness theory holds that people who explain the causes of negative events (like failure in work, school, or romantic relationships) according to these three types of attributions are most vulnerable to depression:

1. Internal factors, or beliefs that failures reflect their personal inadequacies, rather than external factors, or beliefs that failures are caused by environmental factors

2. Global factors, or beliefs that failures reflect sweeping flaws in personality rather than specific factors, or beliefs that failures reflect limited areas of functioning

3. Stable factors, or beliefs that failures reflect fixed personality factors rather than unstable factors, or beliefs that the factors leading to failures are changeable

Let us illustrate these attributional styles with the example of a college student who goes on a disastrous date. Afterward he shakes his head in wonder and tries to make sense of his experience. An internal attribution for the calamity is characterized by self-blame, as in "I really messed it up." An external attribution would place the blame elsewhere, as in "Some couples just don't hit it off," or "She must have been in a bad mood." A stable attribution would suggest a problem that cannot be changed, as in "It's my personality." An unstable attribution, on the other hand, would suggest a transient condition, as in "It was probably the head cold." A global attribution for failure magnifies the extent of the problem, as in "I really have no idea what I'm doing when I'm with people." A specific attribution, in contrast, chops the problem down to size, as in "My problem is how to make small talk to get a relationship going."

The revised theory holds that each attributional dimension makes a specific contribution to feelings of helplessness. Internal attributions for negative events are linked to lower self-esteem. Stable attributions help explain the persistence—or, in medical terms, the chronicity—of helplessness cognitions. Global attributions are associated with the generality or pervasiveness of feelings of helplessness following negative events. Attributional style should be distinguished from negative thinking (Gotlib et al., 1993). Whether you think negatively (pessimistically) or positively (optimistically), you may still hold yourself to blame for your perceived failures.

Depressed people are more likely than nondepressed people to have a negative attributional style (attributing negative life events to to internal, stable, and global factors) (Riso et al., 2003; Seligman et al., 1988). A depressive attributional style also predicts how well depressed patients respond to antidepressant medication (Levitan, Rector, & Bagby, 1998). Also supporting the model are findings that negative attributional styles and dysfunctional attitudes predict higher lifetime rates of major depression (Alloy et al., 2000). Attributional style may have a stronger relationship to depression in people who tend to think more about the causes of events, however (Haaga, 1995).

Biological Factors

Evidence has accumulated pointing to the important role of biological factors, especially genetics and neurotransmitter functioning, in the development of mood disorders. Recent investigations are examining the biological roots of depression at the neurotransmitter level as well as the genetic, molecular, and even cellular level.

Genetic Factors A growing body of knowledge implicates genetic factors in mood disorders. We know that mood disorders, including major depression and especially bipolar disorder, tend to run in families (Klein et al., 2001; USDHHS, 1999a). Families, however, share environmental similarities as well as genes. Family members may share blue eyes (an inherited attribute) but also a common religion (a cultural attribute). Yet evidence pointing to a genetic basis for mood disorders comes from studies showing that the closer the genetic relationship one shares with a person with a major mood disorder (major depression or bipolar disorder), the greater the likelihood that one will also suffer from a major mood disorder (e.g., Vincent et al., 1999).

Twin studies and adoptee studies provide additional evidence of a genetic contribution. A higher concordance (agreement) rate among monozygotic (MZ) twins than dizygotic (DZ) twins for a given disorder is taken as supportive evidence of genetic factors. Both types of twins share common environments, but MZ twins share 100% of their genes as compared to 50% for DZ twins. The concordance rate for major mood disorders (major depression and bipolar disorder) between MZ twins ranges from 45% to 70%, which is more than double the rate between DZ twins (Kendler et al., 1992b, 1993). This provides strong support for a genetic component, but is short of the 100% concordance we would expect if genetics were solely responsible for these disorders. Adoptee studies, which might provide corroborating evidence of genetic factors in mood disorders, are sparse.

All in all, researchers believe that heredity plays an important role in major depression (Kendler & Prescott, 1999; Sullivan, Neale, & Kendler, 2000). However, genetics isn't the only determinant, nor is it necessarily the most important. Environmental factors, such as exposure to stressful life events, appear to play at least as great a role—if not a greater role—than genetics (Kendler & Prescott, 1999).

All in all, it appears that major depression is a complex disorder that is caused by a combination of genetic and environmental factors (Sullivan, Neale, & Kendler, 2000). Similarly, most scientists believe that there is no single cause for bipolar disorder, but that genetics plays an important role, perhaps an even more important role than in major depressive disorder (Krehbiel, 2000; McGuffin et al., 2003). As for dysthymic disorder, data from twin studies indicates that the disorder may be relatively less influenced by genetic factors than either major depression or bipolar disorder (Torgersen, 1986).

Bipolar Mood Disorder with Psychotic Features:
The Case of Ann
"When you're racing at that level you tend to alienate people."

Efforts have begun to track down specific genes involved in both major depression and bipolar disorder (e.g., Abkevich et al., 2003 Kakiuchi et al., 2003; Potash et al., 2003). For example, investigators have discovered that people who inherit a variation of a particular gene stand more than double the chance of developing depression following stressful life events than those who have another version of the gene (Caspi et al., 2003; NIMH, 2003). The gene regulates production of a protein that plays a key role in transmission of serotonin, the neurotransmitter targeted by antidepressants such as Prozac and Zoloft.

Biochemical Factors and Brain Abnormalities Early research on the biological underpinnings of depression focused on deficits in neurotransmitter levels in the brain. Neurotransmitters were first suspected of playing a role in depression back in the 1950s, when it was reported that hypertensive patients who were taking the drug *reserpine* often became depressed. Reserpine depletes the supplies of various neurotransmitters in the brain, especially norepinephrine and serotonin. Then came the discovery that drugs that increase the brain levels of these same neurotransmitters can relieve depression. These drugs, called antidepressants, include *tricyclics,* such as imipramine (trade name Tofranil) and amitriptyline (trade name Elavil); *monoamine oxidase* (MAO) *inhibitors,* such as phenelzine (trade name Nardil); and *selective serotonin-reuptake inhibitors* (SSRIs), such as fluoxetine (trade name Prozac) and sertraline (trade name Zoloft). But later research cast doubt on the belief that depression is caused simply by a lack of particular neurotransmitters in the brain. For example, although antidepressants increase availability of neurotransmitters in the brain within hours, depressed patients do not usually begin to show a response to treatment for several weeks (Jacobs, 2004; Nierenberg et al., 2000). Therefore, it is unlikely that these drugs work by simply boosting levels of neurotransmitters in the brain (Duman, Heninger, & Nestler, 1997).

More complex views of the role of neurotransmitters in depression are evolving (Bremner et al., 2003; Cravchik & Goldman, 2000). Scientists suspect underlying irregularities in the numbers of receptors on receiving neurons where neurotransmitters dock (having either too many or too few), or in the sensitivity of receptors to particular neurotransmitters (Yatham et al., 2000). Antidepressants may work by affecting either the number or sensitivity of receptors. We also need to recognize that there are several different types of receptors for each neurotransmitter. There may also be many subtypes for each type (USDHHS, 1999a). The actions of particular antidepressants may be specific to certain types or subtypes of receptors.

Another avenue of research into the biological underpinnings of mood disorders focuses on abnormalities in certain parts of the brain (Davidson et al., 2002). Brain imaging studies show lower metabolic activity of the prefrontal cortex in clinically depressed people as compared to healthy controls (e.g., Damasio, 1997; Schatzberg, 2002). The prefrontal cortex lies in the frontal lobes of the cerebral cortex and is the area of the brain responsible for higher mental functions, such as thinking, problem solving and decision making, and organizing thoughts and behaviors. The neurotransmitters serotonin and norepinephrine play important roles in regulating nerve impulses in the prefrontal cortex, so it is not surprising that evidence points to irregularities in this region of the brain. Other research reveals brain abnormalities (loss of brain cells) in people with bipolar disorder in parts of the brain involved in regulating mood states (Blumberg et al., 2003; Lopez-Larson et al., 2002; Strakowski et al., 2002) As research using brain-imaging techniques continues, we will likely learn more about how the brains of people with mood disorders may differ from those of healthy individuals.

We also find evidence of other biochemical pathways to depression, including roles for proteins that help nerve cells communicate (Kramer et al., 1998) and endocrine system activity involving the thyroid gland, the adrenal glands, and in women, fluctuations of the female sex hormones estrogen and progesterone (Daly et al., 2003; Seeman, 1997; Stahl, 2001).

A CLOSER LOOK
Something Fishy About This

You may have heard that high concentrations in the diet of certain types of fish oil, especially omega-3 fatty acids, are linked to lower rates of cardiovascular disease (Yager, 2003). But you may not know that scientists suspect that high dietary levels of fish oil are also linked to lower risks of major depression and bipolar disorder. Some scientists believe that omega-3 fatty acids are essential nutrients the brain needs to function optimally (Kalb, 2002). In a preliminary study, investigators found that adding omega-3 fatty acids in supplement form improved treatment outcomes in depressed patients receiving antidepressant medication (Warner, 2002). In a cross-national study, other investigators examined relationships between rates of bipolar disorders and consumption of seafood, which is rich in omega-3 fatty acids (Noaghiul & Hibbeln, 2003). The results showed strong relationships between high levels of seafood intake and low rates of bipolar disorders. The country consuming the most seafood, Iceland, showed low rates of bipolar disorder, whereas those with lower levels of seafood consumption, such as Germany, Switzerland, Italy, and Israel, showed higher rates.

We should caution that causal linkages cannot be ascertained from observed relationships between eating fish and lower risks of mood disorders. Nevertheless, these linkages encourage researchers to explore further whether a dietary supplement may indeed live up to its popular billing as good brain food. In the meantime, anyone for salmon? ■

Tying It Together

Depression and other mood disorders involve the interplay of multiple factors. Consistent with the *diathesis-stress model,* depression may reflect an interaction of biological factors (such as genetic factors, neurotransmitter irregularities, or brain abnormalities), psychological factors (such as cognitive distortions or learned helplessness), and social and environmental stressors (such as divorce or loss of a job).

Let us consider a possible causal pathway based on the diathesis-stress model (see Figure 8.3). Stressful life events, such as prolonged unemployment or a divorce, may have a depressing effect by reducing neurotransmitter activity in the brain. These biochemical effects may be more likely to occur or may be more pronounced in people with a genetic predisposition, or diathesis, for depression. However, a depressive disorder may not develop, or may develop in a milder form, in people with more effective coping resources for handling stressful situations. For example, people who receive emotional support from others may be better able to withstand the effects of stress than those who have to go it alone. So, too, for people who make active coping efforts to meet the challenges they face in life.

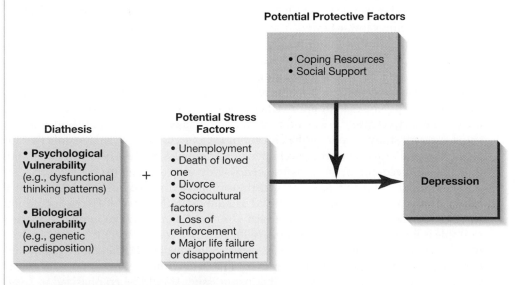

FIGURE 8.3 Diathesis-stress model of depression.

Sociocultural factors can be sources of stress that influence the development or recurrence of mood disorders (Ostler et al., 2001). These factors include poverty; overcrowding; exposure to racism, sexism, and prejudice; violence in the home or community; unequal stressful burdens placed on women; and family disintegration. Other sources of stress that can contribute to mood disorders include negative life events such as the loss of a job, the development of a serious illness, the breakup of a romantic relationship, and the loss of a loved one.

The diathesis for depression may take the form of a psychological vulnerability involving a depressive thinking style, one characterized by tendencies to exaggerate the consequences of negative events, to heap blame on oneself, and to perceive oneself as helpless to effect positive change. This cognitive diathesis may increase the risk of depression in the face of negative life events. These cognitive influences may also interact with a genetically based diathesis to further increase the risk of depression following stressful life events. Then too, the availability of social support from others may help bolster a person's resistance to stress during difficult times. People with more effective social skills may be better able to garner and maintain social reinforcement from others and thus be better able to resist depression than people lacking social skills. But biochemical changes in the brain might make it more difficult for the person to cope effectively and bounce back from stressful life events. Lingering biochemical changes and feelings of depression may exacerbate feelings of helplessness, compounding the effects of the initial stressor.

Gender-related differences in coping styles may also come into play. According to Nolen-Hoeksema, women are more likely to ruminate when facing emotional problems, and men are more likely to abuse alcohol. These or other differences in coping styles may propel women into longer and more severe bouts of depression while setting the stage for the development of drinking problems in men. As you can see, a complex web of contributing factors is likely involved in the development of mood disorders.

TREATMENT OF MOOD DISORDERS

Just as different theoretical perspectives point to many factors that may be involved in the development of mood disorders, these models have spawned. Here we focus on several of the leading contemporary approaches.

Psychodynamic Approaches

Traditional psychoanalysis aims to help people who become depressed understand their ambivalent feelings toward important people (objects) in their lives they have lost or whose loss was threatened. By working through feelings of anger toward these lost objects, people can turn anger outward—through verbal expression of feelings, for example—rather than leave it to fester and turn inward.

Traditional psychoanalysis can take years to uncover and deal with unconscious conflicts. Modern psychoanalytic approaches also focus on unconscious conflicts, but they are more direct, relatively brief, and focus on present as well as past conflicted relationships. A recent study supported the efficacy of structured, short-term dynamic therapy (Luborsky et al., 1996). Eclectic psychodynamic therapists may use behavioral methods to help clients acquire the social skills needed to develop a broader social network.

Newer models of psychotherapy for depression have emerged from the interpersonal school of psychodynamic therapy derived initially from the work of Harry Stack Sullivan (see Chapter 2) and other neo-Freudians, such as Karen Horney. One contemporary example is *interpersonal psychotherapy* (IPT) (Klerman et al., 1984). IPT is a brief form of therapy (usually no more than 9 to 12 months) that focuses on the client's current interpersonal relationships. The developers of ITP believe that depression occurs within an interpersonal context and that relationship issues should be emphasized in treatment. IPT has been shown to be an effective treatment for major depression and shows promise in treating other psychological disorders, including dysthymic disorder and bulimia (DeRubeis & Crits-Christoph, 1998; Leichsenring, 2001. Investigators find IPT effective in treating depressed patients in other parts of the world, including sub-Saharan Africa (Bolton et al., 2003).

Although IPT shares some features with traditional psychodynamic approaches (principally the belief that early life experiences and persistent personality features affect psychological adjustment), it differs from traditional psychodynamic therapy by focusing on clients' current relationships rather than on unconscious internal conflicts of childhood origins.

IPT helps clients deal with unresolved or delayed grief reactions following the death of a loved one as well as with role conflicts in present relationships (Weissman & Markowitz, 1994). The therapist also helps clients identify areas of conflict in their present relationships, understand the issues that underlie them, and consider ways of resolving them. If the problems in a relationship are beyond repair, the therapist helps the client consider ways of ending it and establishing new relationships. In the case of Sal D., a 31-year-old TV repairman's assistant, depression was associated with marital conflict.

Interpersonal psychotherapy (IPT). IPT is usually a brief, psychodynamically oriented therapy that focuses on issues in the person's current interpersonal relationships. Like traditional psychodynamic approaches, IPT assumes that early life experiences are key issues in adjustment, but IPT focuses on the present—the here and now.

Interpersonal Psychotherapy in a Case of Depression

Sal began to explore his marital problems in the fifth therapy session, becoming tearful as he recounted his difficulty expressing his feelings to his wife because of feelings of being "numb." He felt that he had been "holding on" to his feelings, which was causing him to become estranged from his wife. The next session zeroed in on the similarities between himself and his father, in particular how he was distancing himself from his wife in a similar way to how his father had kept a distance from him. By session 7, a turning point had been reached. Sal expressed how he and his wife had become "emotional" and closer to one another during the previous week and how he was able to talk more openly about his feelings, and how he and his wife had been able to make a joint decision concerning a financial matter that had been worrying them for some time. When later he was laid off from his job, he sought his wife's opinion, rather than picking a fight with her as a way of thrusting his job problems on her. To his surprise he found that his wife responded positively—not "violently" as he had expected—to times when he expressed his feelings. In his last therapy session (session 12), Sal expressed how therapy had led to a "reawakening" within himself with respect to the feelings he had been keeping to himself—an openness that he hoped to create in his relationship with his wife.

—Adapted from Klerman et al., 1984, pp. 111–113

Behavioral Approaches

Behavioral treatment approaches presume that depressive behaviors are learned and can be unlearned. Behavior therapy produces substantial benefits in treating depression both in adults and adolescents (Craighead, Craighead, & Ilardi, 1998).

Lewinsohn and his colleagues (Lewinsohn et al., 1996) developed a 12-session, 8-week group therapy program organized as a course—the *Coping With Depression (CWD) Course.* The course helps clients acquire relaxation skills, increase pleasant activities, and build social skills that enable them to obtain social reinforcement. For example, students learn how to accept rather than deny compliments and how to ask friends to join them in activities. Participants are taught to generate a self-change plan, to think more constructively, and to develop a lifetime plan for maintaining treatment gains and preventing recurrent depression. The therapist is considered a teacher; the client, a student; the session, a class. Each participant is treated as a responsible adult who is capable of learning. The structure involves lectures, activities, and homework and each session follows a structured lesson plan. Depressed adolescents who received the CWD treatment showed lower rates of depression and increased activity levels compared to control subjects (Lewinsohn et al., 1996).

Cognitive Approaches

Cognitive therapists believe that distorted thinking (cognitive distortions) play a key role in the development of depression. Depressed people typically focus on how they are feeling rather than on the thoughts that may underlie their feeling states. That is, they usually pay more attention to how bad they feel than to the thoughts that may trigger or maintain their depressed moods. Aaron Beck and his colleagues have developed a multicomponent treatment approach, called *cognitive therapy,* which focuses on helping people with depression learn to recognize and correct their dysfunctional thinking patterns. Table 8.6 shows some common examples of distorted, automatic thoughts, the types of cognitive distortions they represent, and rational alternative responses that can be used to replace these distorted thoughts.

Cognitive therapy, like behavior therapy, is relatively brief, frequently 14 to 16 weekly sessions (Butler & Beck, 1995). Therapists use a combination of behavioral and cognitive techniques to help clients identify and change dysfunctional thoughts and develop more adaptive behaviors. For example, they help clients connect thought patterns to negative moods by having them monitor the automatic negative thoughts they experience throughout the day using a thought diary or daily record. They note when and where negative thoughts occur and how they feel at the time. Then the therapist helps the client challenge the negative thoughts and replace them with more adaptive thoughts. The following case example shows how a cognitive therapist works with a client to challenge the validity of thoughts that reflect the cognitive distortion called *selective abstraction* (the tendency to judge oneself entirely on the basis of specific weaknesses or flaws in character). The client judged herself to be totally lacking in self-control because she ate a single piece of candy while she was on a diet.

Cognitive Therapy for Depression

CLIENT: *I don't have any self-control at all.*

THERAPIST: *On what basis do you say that?*

C: *Somebody offered me candy and I couldn't refuse it.*

T: *Were you eating candy every day?*

C: *No, I just ate it this once.*

T: *Did you do anything constructive during the past week to adhere to your diet?*

C: *Well, I didn't give in to the temptation to buy candy every time I saw it at the store. . . . Also, I did not eat any candy except that one time when it was offered to me and I felt I couldn't refuse it.*

T: *If you counted up the number of times you controlled yourself versus the number of times you gave in, what ratio would you get?*

C: *About 100 to 1.*

T: *So if you controlled yourself 100 times and did not control yourself just once, would that be a sign that you are weak through and through?*

C: *I guess not—not through and through (smiles).*

—Adapted from Beck et al., 1979, p. 68

A wealth of evidence supports the therapeutic effectiveness of cognitive therapy in treating major depression and reducing risks of recurrent episodes (DeRubeis et al., 2001; Hamilton & Dobson, 2002; Jarrett et al., 2001; Merrill, Tolbert, & Wade, 2003). The benefits of cognitive therapy appear to be at least equal to those of antidepressant medication in treating depression (DeRubeis et al., 1999, 2001; Jarrett et al., 1999). Might the combination of drugs and therapy be more effective still? A recent review of scientific evidence showed that the combination of antidepressant medication and psychother-

TABLE 8.6

Cognitive Distortions and Rational Responses

Automatic Thought	Kind of Cognitive Distortion	Rational Response
I'm all alone in the world.	All-or-Nothing Thinking	It may feel like I'm all alone, but there are some people who care about me.
Nothing will ever work out for me.	Overgeneralization	No one can look into the future. Concentrate on the present.
My looks are hopeless.	Magnification	I may not be perfect looking, but I'm far from hopeless.
I'm falling apart. I can't handle this.	Magnification	Sometimes I just feel overwhelmed. But I've handled things like this before. Just take it a step at a time and I'll be okay.
I guess I'm just a born loser.	Labeling and Mislabeling	Nobody is destined to be a loser. Stop talking yourself down.
I've only lost 8 pounds on this diet. I should just forget it. I can't succeed.	Negative Focusing/Minimization/Disqualifying the Positive/Jumping to Conclusions/All-or-Nothing Thinking	Eight pounds is a good start. I didn't gain all this weight overnight, and I have to expect that it will take time to lose it.
I know things must really be bad for me to feel this awful.	Emotional Reasoning	Feeling something doesn't make it so. If I'm not seeing things clearly, my emotions will be distorted too.
I know I'm going to flunk this course.	Fortune Teller Error	Give me a break! Just focus on getting through this course, not on jumping to negative conclusions.
I know John's problems are really my fault.	Personalization	Stop blaming yourself for everyone else's problems. There are many reasons why John's problems have nothing to do with me.
Someone my age should be doing better than I am.	Should Statements	Stop comparing yourself to others. All anyone can be expected to do is their best. What good does it do to compare myself to others? It only leads me to get down on myself rather than get motivated.
I just don't have the brains for college.	Labeling and Mislabeling	Stop calling yourself names like "stupid." I can accomplish a lot more than I give myself credit for.
Everything is my fault.	Personalization	There you go again. Stop playing this game of pointing blame at yourself. There's enough blame to go around. Better yet, forget placing blame and try to think through how to solve this problem.
It would be awful if Sue turns me down.	Magnification	It might be upsetting, but it needn't be awful unless I make it so.
If people really knew me, they would hate me.	Mind Reader	What evidence is there for that? More people who get to know me like me than don't like me.
If something doesn't get better soon, I'll go crazy.	Jumping to Conclusions/Magnification	I've dealt with these problems this long without falling apart. I just have to hang in there. Things are not as bad as they seem.
I can't believe I have another pimple on my face. This is going to ruin my whole weekend.	Mental Filter	Take it easy. A pimple is not the end of the world. It doesn't have to spoil my whole weekend. Other people get pimples and seem to have a good time.

apy produced slightly better outcomes as compared to either psychotherapy or medication alone (Friedman et al., 2004). Combined treatment might be especially beneficial in cases of severe, recurrent depression (Friedman et al., 2004; USDHHS, 1999a). Cognitive therapy, or cognitive–behavioral therapy, also appears to produce about the same level of benefit as interpersonal psychotherapy (Elkin et al., 1989; Leichsenring, 2001; Shapiro et al., 1995).

Psychological Treatment of Other Mood Disorders

We have little research on the psychological treatment of dysthymia, although techniques used in treating major depression, such as cognitive therapy and interpersonal psychotherapy, have shown promise (Thase et al., 1997). Large-scale investigations of the effects of psychological treatments for bipolar disorder are underway. Early studies suggest that psychosocial treatments, such as cognitive–behavioral therapy, interpersonal therapy, and family therapy, may be effective adjunctive therapies to be used along with drug therapy in the treatment of bipolar disorder (Lam et al., 2000; Otto, 2001). For example, psychological treatment can improve the level of functioning and adherence to a medication regimen in bipolar patients (Johnson & Leahy, 2003; Miklowitz et al., 2003). Moreover, a recent randomized controlled study showed that cognitive therapy reduced the rate of relapse in bipolar patients (Lam et al., 2003).

Biological Approaches

The most common biological approaches to treating mood disorders are the use of antidepressant drugs and electroconvulsive therapy for depression and lithium carbonate for bipolar disorder.

Antidepressant Drugs Drugs used to treat depression include several classes of antidepressants that increase the availability of key neurotransmitters in the brain: tricyclic antidepressants (TCAs), monoamine oxidase (MAO) inhibitors, and selective serotonin-reuptake inhibitors (SSRIs) The precise mechanisms by which they work to relieve depression remain unclear (Kupfer, 1999). Though antidepressants boost levels of neurotransmitters in the brain within a few days or even hours of use, it usually takes several weeks of treatment before a therapeutic benefit is achieved (Jacobs, 2004). Thus, the therapeutic benefits of these drugs involve more complex actions than simply increasing the availability of neurotransmitters in the brain. One possibility is that they enhance the actions or effectiveness of neurotransmitters by altering the sensitivity of postsynaptic (receiving) neurons to these chemical messengers, a process that takes time to occur. Most probably, the antidepressant effects of these drugs involve complex therapeutic actions on more than one neurotransmitter system (USDHHS, 1999a).

SSRIs not only lift mood but in many cases also eliminate delusions that may accompany severe depression (Zanardi et al., 1996). Antidepressant medication is clearly effective in many cases in helping relieve major depression and dysthmia and prevent recurrent episodes of major depression (Browne et al., 2002; Furukawa et al., 2002; Leon et al., 2003; Lépine et al., 2004). However, despite the dramatic responses to antidepressants typically seen in drug company commercials, researchers find that the magnitude of differences between antidepressant treatment and placebo (inert) drugs are modest at best, even for the newer SSRI-type drugs, such as Prozac and Zoloft (Boyles, 2002; Kirsch et al., 2002).

All antidepressants increase availability of neurotransmitters, but they do so in different ways (see Figure 8.4). The tricyclics, which include *imipramine* (trade name Tofranil), *amitriptyline* (Elavil), *desipramine* (Norpramin), and *doxepin* (Sinequan), are so named because of their three-ringed molecular structure. They increase brain levels of the neurotransmitters norepinephrine and serotonin by interfering with the reuptake (reabsorption by the transmitting cell) of these chemical messengers. The SSRIs (*fluoxextine,* trade name Prozac, is one) work in a similar fashion but have more specific effects on raising the levels of serotonin in the brain. The MAO inhibitors increase the availability of neurotransmitters by inhibiting the action of monoamine oxidase, an enzyme that normally breaks down or degrades neurotransmitters in the synaptic cleft. MAO inhibitors are used less widely than other antidepressants because of potentially serious interactions with certain foods and alcoholic beverages.

The potential side effects of tricyclics and MAO inhibitors include dry mouth, psychomotor retardation, constipation, blurred vision, sexual dysfunction, and less frequently, urinary retention, paralytic ileus (a paralysis of the intestines, which impairs the passage of intestinal contents), confusion, delirium, and cardiovascular complications, such as reduced blood pressure. Tricyclics are also highly toxic, which raises the prospect of suicidal overdoses if the drugs are used without close supervision.

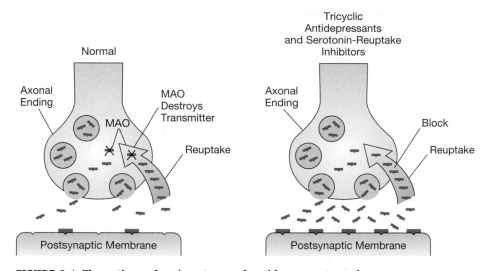
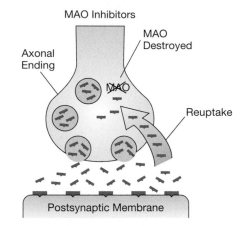

FIGURE 8.4 The actions of various types of antidepressants at the synapse.
Tricyclic antidepressants and serotonin-reuptake inhibitors both increase the availability of neurotransmitters by preventing their reuptake by the presynaptic neuron. Tricyclic antidepressants impede the reuptake of both norepinephrine and serotonin. MAO inhibitors work by inhibiting the action of monoamine oxidase, an enzyme that normally breaks down neurotransmitters in the synaptic cleft.

The SSRIs such as Prozac and Zoloft are about equal in effectiveness to the older generation of tricyclics (McGrath et al., 2000; Noonan, 2000). Yet because they hold two major advantages, they have largely replaced the earlier drugs. The first advantage is that they are less toxic and so are less dangerous in overdose. Secondly, they have fewer of the common side effects (such as dry mouth, constipation, and weight gain) associated with the tricyclics and MAO inhibitors. Still, Prozac and other SSRIs may produce side effects such as upset stomach, headaches, agitation, insomnia, lack of sexual drive, and delayed orgasm (Michelson et al., 2000).

One issue we need to address in discussing drug therapy is the high rate of relapse following discontinuation of medication. Psychologically based therapies may provide greater protection against relapse, presumably because the learning that occurs during therapy carries past the end of active treatment (Butler & Beck, 1995; Persaud, 2000). Adding cognitive–behavioral therapy to medication treatment may help reduce the risk of relapse after the drugs are withdrawn (Friedman et al., 2004).

Overall, about 50% to 70% of depressed patients treated on an outpatient basis respond favorably to either psychotherapy or antidepressant medication alone (USDHHS, 1999a). Some people who fail to respond to psychotherapy respond to antidepressants, and the opposite is the case as well: some people who fail to respond to drug therapy respond favorably to psychotherapy.

St. John's Wort—A Natural "Prozac"? Might a humble herb be a remedy for depression? The herb, called St. John's wort, or *Hypericum perforatum,* has been used for centuries to help heal wounds. Now, people are using it to relieve depression. Nowhere is it more popular than in Germany, where high-strength versions of the herb became the most widely used antidepressant on the market, outselling Prozac, its nearest competitor, by a margin of 4 to 1 (Andrews, 1997). The herb appears to increase levels of serotonin in the brain by interfering with reabsorption of the neurotransmitter, as does Prozac. Although people seeking help for depression may be attracted to the idea of using a natural product such as St. John's wort, the results of outcome studies are mixed (Kalb, 2002). More definitive studies are needed to establish its safety and effectiveness (Siegel, 2001). Hopes were lowered by the results of a 2001 study showing that St. John's wort worked no better than a placebo in treating major depression (Shelton et al., 2001;

"St. John's Wort," 2001a). However, recent evidence suggests that the herb may have therapeutic benefits in treating milder forms of depression (Lecrubier et al., 2002).

Drug Treatment for Bipolar Disorder It could be said that the ancient Greeks and Romans were among the first to use lithium as a form of chemotherapy. They prescribed mineral water that contained lithium for people with turbulent mood swings. Today, the drug *lithium carbonate,* a powdered form of the metallic element lithium, is the most widely used treatment for bipolar disorder. Lithium is effective in stabilizing moods in people with bipolar disorder and reducing the risk of recurrent manic episodes (Baldessarini & Tondo, 2000; Bowden et al., 2003; Geddes et al., 2004). However, evidence is not clear whether it reduces the risk of recurrent depressive episodes in bipolar patients (Geddes et al., 2004). On the other hand, there is general agreement that antidepressants not only fail to reduce mood cycling in bipolar patients but they may even increase risks of manic episodes (Baldessarini & Tondo, 2003; Frankle et al., 2002; Ghaemi et al., 2004).

People with bipolar disorder may need to use lithium indefinitely to control their mood swings, just as diabetics use insulin continuously to control their illness. Despite more than 40 years of use as a therapeutic drug, we still can't say how lithium works.

Yet lithium treatment is no panacea. At least 30% to 40% of patients with mania either fail to respond to the drug or cannot tolerate it (Dubovsky, 2000; Duffy et al., 1998). Among responders, about 6 in 10 eventually relapse (Goleman, 1994a).

Lithium treatment must be closely monitored because of potential toxic effects and other side effects. Lithium can also produce a mild impairment in memory, "the kind of thing that might make a productive person stop taking it," as one expert put it (Goleman, 1994a). The drug can lead to weight gain, lethargy, and grogginess, and to a general slowing down of motor functioning. It can also produce gastrointestinal distress and lead to liver problems over the long term. For a number of reasons, many patients discontinue using lithium or fail to take it reliably (Johnson & McFarland, 1996).

Though lithium is still used widely, the limitations of the drug have prompted efforts to find alternative treatments (Rivas-Vazquez et al., 2002; Tohen et al., 2003). Anticonvulsant drugs used in the treatment of epilepsy, such as *carbamazepine* (brand name Tegretol) and *divalproex* (brand name Depakote), have been shown to stabilize moods and relieve manic symptoms in people with bipolar disorder (Alao & Dewan, 2001; Baldessarini, Tohen, & Tondo, 2000; Bowden et al., 2003). Anticonvulsant drugs may benefit people with bipolar disorder who either do not respond to lithium or cannot tolerate the drug because of side effects. Anticonvulsant drugs usually cause fewer or less severe side effects than lithium. However, some patients have only a partial response to lithium or anticonvulsant drugs, and some fail to respond at all. Thus there remains the need for alternative treatments or drug strategies to be developed, perhaps involving a combination of these or other drugs (Bowden et al., 2000; Tohen et al., 2000).

For Kay Jamison, managing manic-depression involved both medication (lithium) and psychotherapy.

"I"

"Leading a Normal Life"

At this point in my existence, I cannot imagine leading a normal life without both taking lithium and having had the benefits of psychotherapy. Lithium prevents my seductive but disastrous high, diminishes my depressions, clears out the wool and webbing from my disordered thinking, slows me down, gentles me out, keeps me from ruining my career and relationships, keeps me out of a hospital, alive, and makes psychotherapy possible. But, ineffably, psychotherapy heals. It makes some sense of the confusion, reins in the terrifying thoughts and feelings, returns some control and hope and possibility of learning from it all.

—From Jamison, 1995

Electroconvulsive Therapy Electroconvulsive therapy (ECT), more commonly called *shock therapy,* continues to evoke controversy. The idea of passing an electric current through someone's brain may seem barbaric. Yet ECT is a generally safe and effective treatment for severe depression, and it can help relieve depression in many cases in which alternative treatments have failed (UK ECT Review Group, 2003).

In ECT, an electrical current of between 70 and 130 volts is applied to the head to induce a convulsion that is similar to a *grand mal* epileptic seizure. ECT is usually administered in a series of 6 to 12 treatments, given three times per week over several weeks (USDHHS, 1999a). The patient is put to sleep with a brief-acting general anesthetic and given a muscle relaxant to avoid wild convulsions that might result in injury. As a result, spasms may be barely perceptible to onlookers. The patient awakens soon after the procedure and generally remembers nothing. Although ECT had earlier been used in the treatment of a wide variety of psychological disorders, including schizophrenia and bipolar disorder, the American Psychiatric Association recommended in 1990 that ECT be used only to treat major depressive disorder in people who do not respond to antidepressant medication.

ECT leads to significant improvement in a majority of people with major depression who have failed to respond to antidepressant medication (Prudic et al., 1996, 2004; Sackeim, Prudic, & Devanand, 1990). ECT also results in shorter and less costly hospitalizations for major depression (Olfson et al., 1998). Though no one knows exactly how ECT works, one possibility is that ECT normalizes neurotransmitter activity in the brain.

Although ECT can be an effective short-term treatment of severe depression, it too is no panacea. There is an understandable concern among patients, relatives, and professionals themselves about possible risks, especially memory loss for events occurring around the time of treatment (Weiner, 2000). As noted in Chapter 4, another nagging problem with ECT is a high rate of relapse following treatment (Sackeim et al., 2001). In one recent study, about two thirds of patients whose depression had remitted following ECT experienced a relapse within 6 months (Prudic et al., 2004). Depression often returns even among patients who continue to be treated with antidepressant medication (Sackeim et al., 1994). All in all, many professionals view ECT as a treatment of last resort, to be considered only after other treatment approaches have been tried and failed.

Clinical Practice Guidelines for Depression

A government-sponsored expert panel set up to develop guidelines for treating depression found the following treatments to be effective (Depression Guideline Panel, 1993b):

- Antidepressant medication (tricyclics or selective serotonin-reuptake inhibitors)
- Three specific forms of psychotherapy: cognitive therapy, behavior therapy, and interpersonal psychotherapy
- A combination of one of the recommended forms of psychotherapy and antidepressant medication
- Other specified forms of treatment, including ECT and phototherapy for seasonal depression.

SUICIDE

Suicidal thoughts are common enough. At times of great stress, many, if not most, people have considered suicide. A recent nationally representative survey found that 13% of U.S. adults reported having experienced suicidal thoughts, and 4.6% reported making a suicide attempt (Kessler, Borges, & Walters, 1999). It is fortunate that most people who have suicidal thoughts do not act on them. Still, each year in the United States some 500,000 people are treated in hospital emergency rooms for attempted suicide, and more

electroconvulsive therapy (ECT) A method of treating severe depression by means of administering an electric current to the head.

TRUTH or FICTION? *REVISITED*

Placing a powerful electromagnet on the scalp can help relieve depression.

☑ **TRUE.** Magnetic stimulation of the head has been shown in a number of research studies to have antidepressant effects.

A CLOSER LOOK
Magnetic Stimulation Therapy for Depression

Mesmer would be proud. Franz Friedrich Mesmer (1734–1815) was the 18th-century Austrian physician from whose name the term *mesmerism* is derived (we still sometimes speak of people being "mesmerized" by things). He believed that hysteria was caused by an underlying imbalance in the distribution of a magnetic fluid in the body—a problem he believed he could correct by prodding the body with metal rods. A scientific commission of the time debunked Mesmer's claims and attributed any cures he obtained to the effects of natural recovery or self-delusion (what we might today call the power of suggestion). The chairperson of the commission was none other than our own Benjamin Franklin, who served at the time as ambassador to France from the newly independent United States. Though Mesmer's theories and practices were discredited, recent evidence into the therapeutic use of magnetism suggests that he might have been on to something.

Fast forward 200 years. Australian doctors take 60 patients with major depression who had failed to respond to different types of antidepressants (Fitzgerald et al., 2003). In a double-blind controlled design, the patients received treatment with either strong magnetic stimulation to the head (called *transcranial magnetic stimulation,* or TMS) or a fake treatment that had all the trappings of the active treatment except that the magnet was angled away to prevent magnetic stimulation of the brain. With TMS, a powerful electromagnet placed on the scalp generates a strong magnetic field that passes through the skull and affects the electrical activity of the brain.

After 2 weeks of treatment, patients receiving TMS showed clinical improvement in depression as opposed to minimal change in the sham group. Improvement was modest and did not occur in all patients. The investigators believe that longer treatment (at least 4 weeks) may be necessary to produce more meaningful therapeutic benefits. Yet this study adds to a growing body of evidence supporting the antidepressant effects of TMS (e.g., George et al., 2000; Herwig et al., 2003). The specific form and intensity of TMS needed to produce therapeutic effects remains under study. We should also note that TMS carries some potential risks, such as the possibility of seizures. However, the risk of seizures may be reduced by using low-frequency stimulation.

In sum, TMS shows promise as a new form of treatment for depression (Gershon, Dannon, & Grunhaus, 2003). It appears especially promising as an alternative to ECT in cases of major depression that fail to respond to pharmacological treatment. TMS may be particularly helpful in treating depression because the prefrontal cortex in the left cerebral hemisphere becomes less active in depressed patients, and this part of the brain can be directly affected by TMS (Henry, Pascual-Leone, & Cole, 2003). Yet investigators caution that more evidence is needed to support its efficacy and safety before it can be recommended for use in treating depression (Aarre et al., 2003; Martin et al., 2003). Recent research also indicates that TMS has therapeutic benefits in treating symptoms of posttraumatic stress disorder (Cohen et al., 2004). ■

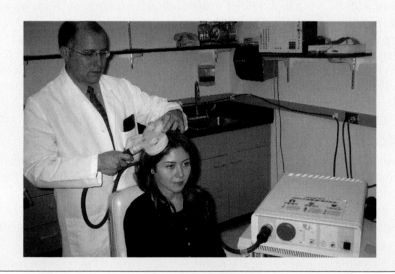

Transcranial Magnetic Stimulation Therapy TMS is a promising therapeutic approach in which powerful magnets are used to help relieve depression.

than 30,000 "succeed" in taking their lives (Lemonick, 2003a; Mokdad et al., 2004; National Strategy for Suicide Prevention, 2001). There are twice as many deaths from suicide as from HIV/AIDS (NIMH, 2003). Suicide exacts a heavy toll on the nation, as you can see in statistics reported by the U.S. Surgeon General (see Table 8.7).

Suicidal behavior is not a psychological disorder in itself. But it is often a feature or symptom of an underlying psychological disorder, usually a mood disorder, which is the reason we discuss it in this chapter. The federal government estimates that about 60% of people who commit suicide suffer from a mood disorder (National Strategy for Suicide Prevention, 2001).

Overview of Mood Disorders

TYPES OF MOOD DISORDERS/PREVALENCE RATES (approx., in parentheses)

	Description	Features
Major Depressive Disorder 10%–25% in women; 5%–12% in men)	Episodes of severe depression	• A range of features may be present, from downcast mood to appetite and sleep disturbance, to lack of interest and motivation • Seasonal affective disorder and postpartum depression are subtypes of major depression
Dysthymic Disorder 8% in women, 4%–5% in men)	Long-standing mild depression	• Feeling "down in the dumps" most of the time, but not as severely depressed as people with major depressive disorder • Double depression is characterized by major depressive episodes occurring during the course of dysthymia
Bipolar Disorder (0.4%–1.6%; or 4 to 16 people in 1,000)	Mood swings between elation and depression	• The two general subtypes are bipolar I disorder and bipolar II disorder • In rapid cycling, mania and major depression alternate without intervening periods of normal mood
Cyclothymia (0.4%–1%, or 4 to 10 people in 1,000)	Milder mood swings than bipolar disorder	• Chronic, cyclical pattern of shifting mood states from hypomanic episodes to states of mild depression • Frequent periods of depressed mood or loss of interest or pleasure in activities, but not at the level of severity of a major depressive episode

CAUSAL FACTORS   Multiple causes are involved, interacting with each other in complex ways

Biological Factors	• Genetic predispositions
	• Disturbed neurotransmitter functioning
	• Abnormalities in parts of the brain regulating mood states
	• Possible endocrine system involvement in mood states
Social–Environmental Factors	• Stressful life events, such as the loss of a loved one or prolonged unemployment
Behavioral Factors	• Lack of reinforcement
	• Negative interactions with others, leading to rejection
Emotional and Cognitive Factors	• In classic psychoanalytic theory, anger turned inward • Emotional difficulties coping with the loss of significant others
	• Lack of meaning or purpose in life
	• Negatively biased or distorted ways of thinking, or a depressive attributional style

TREATMENT APPROACHES   Treatment may include one or more therapeutic approaches

Biomedical Treatment	• Antidepressant drugs (tricyclics, MAO inhibitors, SSRIs) to control depressive symptoms by influencing the availabiliy of neurotransmitters in the brain • Lithium or anticonvulsant drugs to stabilize moods in bipolar patients • Electroconvulsive therapy (ECT) in severe cases of depression • Phototherapy for seasonal affective disorder
Cognitive–Behavioral Therapy	• To help clients correct distorted ways of thinking, develop more effective coping responses, and increase levels of positive reinforcement
Interpersonal Therapy	• To resolve interpersonal problems and lingering grief reactions

Sources for prevalence rates: APA, 2000; Kessler et al., 1994

Who Commits Suicide?

Though much attention is focused on the tragedy of youthful suicide, suicide rates are highest among adults age 65 and older, especially older White males (Bruce et al., 2004; Lambert et al., 2003; National Strategy for Suicide Prevention, 2001; see Figure 8.5). We discuss youth suicide in Chapter 14.

Despite life-extending advances in medical care, some older adults find the quality of their lives less than satisfactory. Older people are more susceptible to diseases such as cancer and Alzheimer's, which can leave them with feelings of helplessness and hopelessness that, in turn, can give rise to suicidal thinking. Many older adults also suffer a mounting accumulation of losses of friends and loved ones, leading to social isolation.

TABLE 8.7

U.S. Surgeon General's Report on Suicide: Cost to the Nation

- Every 17 minutes another life is lost to suicide. Every day, 86 Americans take their own lives and over 1,500 attempt suicide.

- Suicide is now the eighth leading cause of death in Americans.

- For every two victims of homicide in the United States, there are three deaths from suicide.

- There are now twice as many deaths due to suicide than due to HIV/AIDS.

- Between 1952 and 1995, the incidence of suicide among adolescents and young adults nearly tripled.

- In the month prior to their suicide, 75% of elderly persons had visited a physician.

- Over half of all suicides occur in adult men, ages 25 to 65.

- Many who make suicide attempts never seek professional care immediately after the attempt.

- Males are four times more likely to die from suicide than are females.

- More teenagers and young adults die from suicide than from cancer, heart disease, AIDS, birth defects, stroke, pneumonia and influenza, and chronic lung disease, combined.

- Suicide takes the lives of more than 30,000 Americans every year.

Source: Center for Mental Health Services, 2001.

These losses, as well as the loss of good health and of a responsible role in the community, may wear down the will to live. Not surprisingly, the highest suicide rates in older men are among those who are widowed or socially isolated. Society's increased acceptance of suicide in older people may also play a part. Whatever the causes, suicide has become an increased risk for elderly people. Perhaps society should focus its attention on the quality of life that is afforded our elderly, in addition to providing them the medical care that helps make longer life possible.

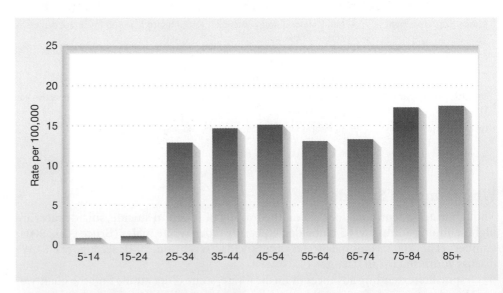

FIGURE 8.5 Suicide rates according to age.
Although adolescent suicides may be more highly publicized, adults, especially older adults, have higher suicide rates.

Source: National Vital Statistics Reports, Vol. 52, No. 5, National Center for Health Statistics, 2003

Seeds of hopelessness. Suicide rates are higher among Native Americans than other groups. Many Native Americans living in depressed areas see a bleak future ahead that offers few if any promising opportunities

More women attempt suicide, but more men "succeed" (NIMH, 2003b; Stein, Asheror et al., 2002). For every female suicide, there are four male suicides. More males "succeed" in large part because they tend to choose quicker-acting and more lethal means, such as handguns. Gender differences in suicide risk may mask the underlying factors. The common finding that men are more likely to take their own lives may be due to the fact that men are also more likely to have a history of alcohol and drug abuse and less likely to have children in the home. When these two factors were taken into account, gender differences in suicide risk disappeared (Young et al., 1994).

Overall, Whites are about twice as likely as Blacks to commit suicide. Suicide rates among adolescents are highest among White males, but they are rising at a faster rate among Black males (CDC, 2001c). Native Americans are at increased risk of suicide attempts and completed suicides (Gone, 2004). Overall, Native Americans (American Indians and Alaskan Natives) have a suicide rate that is 50% higher than other groups. As noted in Chapter 2, male Native American adolescents and young adults have the highest suicide rates in the nation (USDHHS, 1999a).

Hopelessness and exposure to others who have attempted or completed suicide may contribute to the increased risk of suicide among Native American youth. Native American youth at greatest risk tend to be reared in communities that are largely isolated from U.S. society at large. They perceive themselves as having relatively few opportunities to gain the skills necessary to join the workforce in the larger society and are also relatively more prone to substance abuse, including alcohol abuse. Knowledge that peers have attempted or completed suicide renders suicide a highly visible escape from psychological pain.

Why Do People Commit Suicide?

To many lay observers, suicide seems so extreme an act that they believe only "insane" people (meaning people who are out of touch with reality) would commit suicide. However, suicidal thinking does not necessarily imply loss of touch with reality, deep-seated unconscious conflict, or a personality disorder. Having thoughts about suicide generally reflects a narrowing of the range of options people think are available to them to

Depression/Delierate Self Harm:
The Case of Sarah
"I ended up starting to cut because the depression was so bad."

deal with their problems. That is, they are discouraged by their problems and see no other way out.

The risk of suicide is greatly elevated among people with severe mood disorders, such as major depression and bipolar disorder (Bostwick & Pankratz, 2000; Bruce et al., 2004). As many as one in five people with bipolar disorder eventually commits suicide (Cowan & Kandel, 2001). Experts believe that greater efforts toward diagnosing and treating mood disorders may result in lower suicide rates (Isacsson, 2000). Attempted or completed suicide is also linked to other psychological disorders, such as alcoholism and drug dependence, schizophrenia, panic disorder, personality disorders, posttraumatic stress disorders, borderline personality disorder, and a family history of suicide (e.g., Hufford, 2001; Moran et al, 2003; Oquendo et al., 2003; Qin, Agerbo, & Mortensen, 2003; Preuss et al, 2003; Roy, 2000, 2003; Walker et al., 2004). More than half the suicide attempters in a recent study had two or more psychological disorders (Beautrais et al., 1996).

Not all suicides are connected with psychological disorders. Some people suffering from painful and hopeless physical illness seek to escape further suffering by taking their own lives. These suicides are sometimes labeled "rational suicides" in the belief that they are based on a rational decision that life is no longer worth living in the light of continual suffering. However, in perhaps many of these cases the person's judgment and reasoning ability may be colored by an underlying and potentially treatable psychological disorder, such as depression. Other suicides are motivated by deep-seated religious or political convictions, such as in the case of people who sacrifice themselves in acts of protest against their governments or who kill themselves and others in homicide bombings in the belief that their acts will be rewarded in an afterlife.

Suicide attempts often occur in response to highly stressful life events, especially "exit events," such as the death of a spouse, close friend, or relative; divorce or separation; a family member's leaving home; or the loss of a close friend. People who consider suicide in times of stress may lack problem-solving skills and be unable to find alternative ways of coping with stressors. Underscoring the psychological impact of severe stress, researchers find suicides to be more common among survivors of natural disasters, especially severe floods (Krug et al., 1998).

Theoretical Perspectives on Suicide

The classic psychodynamic model views depression as the turning inward of anger against the internal representation of a lost love object. Suicide then represents inward-directed anger that turns murderous. Suicidal people, then, do not seek to destroy themselves. Instead, they seek to vent their rage against the internalized representation of the love object. In so doing, they destroy themselves as well, of course. In his later writings, Freud speculated that suicide may be motivated by the "death instinct," a tendency to return to the tension-free state that preceded birth. Existential and humanistic theorists relate suicide to the perception that life is meaningless and hopeless. Suicidal people report they find life duller, emptier, and more boring than nonsuicidal people (Mehrabian & Weinstein, 1985).

In the 19th century, social thinker Emile Durkheim (1958) noted that people who experienced *anomie*—who feel lost, without identity, rootless—are more likely to commit suicide. Sociocultural theorists likewise believe that alienation may play a role in suicide. In our modern, mobile society, people frequently move hundreds or thousands of miles to schools and jobs. Executives and their families may be relocated every 2 years or so. Military personnel and their families may be shifted about yet more rapidly. Many people are thereby socially isolated or cut off from their support groups. Moreover, city dwellers tend to limit or discourage informal social contacts because of crowding, overstimulation, and fear of crime. It is thus understandable that many people find few sources of support in times of crisis. In some cases, the family support is available but not helpful. Family members may be perceived as part of the problem, not part of the solution.

Learning theorists focus largely on the lack of problem-solving skills for handling significant life stress. According to Shneidman (1985), those who attempt suicide wish to escape unbearable psychological pain and may perceive no other way out. People who threaten or attempt suicide may also receive sympathy and support from loved ones and others, perhaps making future—and more lethal—attempts more likely. This is not to suggest that suicide attempts or gestures should be ignored. People who threaten suicide are *not* merely seeking attention. Although those who threaten suicide may not carry out the act, they should be taken seriously. People who commit suicide often tell others of their intentions or provide clues. Moreover, many people make aborted suicide attempts before they go on to make actual suicide attempts (Barber et al., 1998).

Social–cognitive theorists suggest that suicide may be motivated by positive expectancies and by approving attitudes toward the legitimacy of suicide (D. Stein et al., 1998). People who kill themselves may expect that they will be missed or eulogized after death, or that survivors will feel guilty for mistreating them. Suicidal psychiatric patients hold positive expectancies concerning suicide: They often express the belief that suicide will solve their problems, for example (Linehan et al., 1987). Suicide may represent a desperate attempt to deal with one's problems in one fell swoop rather than piecemeal.

Social–cognitive theorists also focus on the potential modeling effects of observing suicidal behavior in others, especially among teenagers who feel overwhelmed by academic and social stressors. A *social contagion,* or spreading of suicide in a community, may occur in the wake of suicides that receive widespread publicity. Teenagers, who seem to be especially vulnerable to these modeling effects, may even romanticize the suicidal act as one of heroic courage. The incidence of suicide among teenagers sometimes rises markedly in the period following news reports about suicide. In a study in Oregon, suicidal behavior of a friend was a risk factor in suicide attempts among adolescents (Lewinsohn, Rohde, & Seeley, 1996). Copycat suicides may be more likely to occur when reports of suicides are sensationalized, so that other teenagers expect their deaths to have broad impacts on their communities (Kessler et al., 1990).

Biological factors are also implicated in suicide. Reduced levels of the mood-regulating chemical serotonin are found in many people who attempt or commit suicide (Malone et al., 2003, Maris, 2002). Because reduced availability of serotonin is linked to depression, the relationship with suicide is not surprising. Yet serotonin acts to curb or inhibit nervous system activity, so perhaps decreased serotonin activity leads to a *disinhibition,* or release, of impulsive behavior that takes the form of a suicidal act in vulnerable individuals. Suicide also tends to run in families, which hints at genetic factors. Genes may influence susceptibility to suicide by affecting the utilization of serotonin in the brain (Lemonde et al., 2003).

Mood disorders in family members and parental suicide are also connected with suicide risk (Brent et al., 2002). But what are the causal connections? Do people who attempt suicide inherit vulnerabilities to mood disorders that are connected with suicide? Does the family atmosphere promote feelings of hopelessness? Does the suicide of one family member give others the idea of doing the same thing? Does one suicide create the impression that other family members are destined to kill themselves? These are all questions researchers need to address.

Suicide is connected with a complex web of factors, and its prediction is no simpler. Moreover, many myths about suicide abound (see Table 8.8). Yet it is clear that many suicides could be prevented if people with suicidal feelings received treatment for underlying disorders, including depression, bipolar disorder, schizophrenia, and alcohol and substance abuse. We also need strategies that emphasize the maintenance of hope during times of severe stress (Malone et al., 2000).

Predicting Suicide

"I don't believe it. I just saw him last week and he looked fine."
"She sat here just the other day, laughing with the rest of us. How were we to know what was going on inside her?"

TABLE 8.8
Myths About Suicide

Myth	Fact
People who threaten suicide are only seeking attention.	Not so. Researchers report that most people who commit suicide gave prior indications of their intentions or consulted a health provider beforehand (Luoma, Martin, & Pearson, 2002).
A person must be insane to attempt suicide.	Most people who attempt suicide may feel hopeless, but they are not insane (i.e., out of touch with reality).
Talking about suicide with a depressed person may prompt the person to attempt it.	An open discussion of suicide with a depressed person does not prompt the person to attempt it. In fact, extracting a promise that the person will not attempt suicide before calling or visiting a mental health worker may well *prevent* a suicide.
People who attempt suicide and fail aren't serious about killing themselves.	Most people who commit suicide have made previous unsuccessful attempts.
If someone threatens suicide, it is best to ignore it so as not to encourage repeated threats.	Though some people do manipulate others by making idle threats, it is prudent to treat every suicidal threat as genuine and to take appropriate action.

Source: Nevid, 2003. Reprinted with permission of Houghton Mifflin Company.

"I knew he was depressed, but I never thought he'd do something like this. I didn't have a clue."

"Why didn't she just call me?"

Friends and family members often respond to news of a suicide with disbelief or guilt that they failed to pick up signs of the impending act. Yet even trained professionals find it difficult to predict who is likely to commit suicide.

Evidence points to the pivotal role of hopelessness about the future in predicting suicidal thinking and suicide attempts (Brown et al., 2000; Kaslow et al., 2002; Malone et al., 2000). In one study, psychiatric outpatients with hopelessness scores above a certain cutoff were 11 times more likely to commit suicide than those with scores below the cutoff (Beck et al., 1990). But *when* does hopelessness lead to suicide?

People who commit suicide tend to signal their intentions, often quite explicitly, such as by telling others about their suicidal thoughts (Denneby et al., 1996). In fact, most people who commit suicide make contact beforehand with a health care provider (Luoma, Martin, & Pearson, 2002). Yet some cloak their intentions. Behavioral clues may still reveal suicidal intent, however. Edwin Shneidman, a leading researcher on suicide, found that 90% of the people who committed suicide had left clear clues, such as disposing of their possessions (Gelman, 1994). People contemplating suicide may also suddenly try to sort out their affairs, as in drafting a will or buying a cemetery plot. They may purchase guns despite lack of prior interest in firearms. When troubled people decide to commit suicide, they may seem to be suddenly at peace; they feel relieved because they no longer have to contend with life problems. This sudden calm may be misinterpreted as a sign of hope.

The prediction of suicide is not an exact science, even for experienced professionals. Many observable factors, such as hopelessness, do seem to be connected with suicide, but we cannot predict *when* a hopeless person will attempt suicide, if at all.

Suicide hotlines. Telephone hotlines provide emergency assistance and referral services to people experiencing suicidal thoughts or impulses. If you know someone experiencing suicidal thoughts or threatening suicide, speak to a mental health professional or call a suicide hotline in your community for advice.

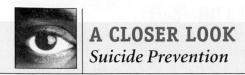

A CLOSER LOOK
Suicide Prevention

Imagine yourself having an intimate conversation with a close campus friend, Chris. You know that things have not been good. Chris's grandfather died 6 weeks ago, and the two were very close. Chris's grades have been going downhill, and Chris's romantic relationship also seems to be coming apart at the seams. Still, you are unprepared when Chris says very deliberately, "I just can't take it anymore. Life is just too painful. I don't feel like I want to live anymore. I've decided that the only thing I can do is to kill myself."

When somebody discloses that he or she is contemplating suicide, you may feel bewildered and frightened, as if a great burden has been placed on your shoulders. It has. If someone confides suicidal thoughts to you, your goal should be to persuade him or her to see a professional, or to get the advice of a professional yourself as soon as you can. But if the suicidal person declines to talk to another person and you sense you can't break away for such a conference, there are some things you can do then and there:

1. *Draw the person out.* Shneidman advises framing questions like, "What's going on?" "Where do you hurt?" "What would you like to see happen?" (1985, p. 11). Such questions may prompt people to verbalize thwarted psychological needs and offer some relief. They also grant you the time to appraise the risk and contemplate your next move.

2. *Be sympathetic.* Show that you fathom how troubled the person is. Don't say something like, "You're just being silly. You don't really mean it."

3. *Suggest that means other than suicide can be discovered to work out the person's problems, even if they are not apparent at the time.* Shneidman (1985) notes that suicidal people can usually see only two solutions to their predicaments—suicide or some kind of magical resolution. Professionals try to broaden the available alternatives.

4. *Ask how the person expects to commit suicide.* People with explicit methods who also possess the means (for example, a gun or drugs) are at greatest risk. Ask if you may hold on to the gun, drugs, or whatever, for a while. Sometimes the person agrees.

5. *Propose that the person accompany you to consult a professional right now.* Many campuses, towns, and cities have hotlines that you or the suicidal individual can call anonymously. Other possibilities include the emergency room of a general hospital, a campus health center or counseling center, or the campus or local police. If you are unable to maintain contact with the suicidal person, get professional assistance as soon as you separate.

6. *Don't say something like "You're talking crazy."* Such comments are degrading and injurious to the individual's self-esteem. Don't press the suicidal person to contact specific people, such as parents or a spouse. Conflict with them may have given rise to the suicidal thoughts.

Above all, keep in mind that your primary goal is to confer with a helping professional. Don't go it alone any longer than you have to. ∎

SUMMING UP

Types of Mood Disorders

What are mood disorders? Mood disorders are disturbances in mood that are unusually prolonged or severe and serious enough to impair daily functioning.

What are the major types of mood disorders? There are various kinds of mood disorders, including depressive (unipolar) disorders, such as major depressive disorder and dysthymic disorder, and disorders involving mood swings, such as bipolar disorder and cyclothymic disorder.

What is major depressive disorder? In major depression, people experience a profound change in mood that impairs their ability to function. There are many associated features of major depressive disorder, including downcast mood; changes in appetite; difficulty sleeping; reduced sense of pleasure in formerly enjoyable activities; feelings of fatigue or loss of energy; sense of worthlessness; excessive or misplaced guilt; difficulties concentrating, thinking clearly, or making decisions; repeated thoughts of death or suicide; attempts at suicide; and even psychotic behaviors (hallucinations and delusions).

What is dysthymic disorder? Dysthymic disorder is a form of chronic depression that is milder than major depressive disorder but may nevertheless be associated with impaired functioning in social and occupational roles.

What is bipolar disorder? In bipolar disorder, people experience fluctuating mood states that interfere with the ability to function. Bipolar I disorder is identified by one or more manic episodes. Bipolar II is characterized by the occurrence of at least one major depressive episode and one hypomanic episode, but without any full-blown manic episodes.

What are the features of a manic episode? Manic episodes are characterized by sudden elevation or expansion of mood and sense of self-importance, feelings of almost boundless energy, hyperactivity, and extreme sociability, which often takes a demanding and overbearing form. People in manic episodes tend to exhibit pressured or rapid speech, rapid "flight of ideas," and decreased need for sleep.

What is cyclothymic disorder? Cyclothymic disorder is a type of bipolar disorder characterized by a chronic pattern of mild mood swings that sometimes progresses to bipolar disorder.

Theoretical Perspectives on Mood Disorders

How is stress related to mood disorders? Exposure to life stress is associated with an increased risk of development and recurrence of mood disorders, especially major depression. Yet some people are more resilient in the face of stress, perhaps because of psychosocial factors such as social support and coping styles.

How do psychodynamic theorists conceptualize mood disorders? In classic psychodynamic theory, depression is viewed in terms of inward-directed anger. People who hold strongly ambivalent feelings toward people they have lost, or whose loss is threatened, may direct unresolved anger toward the inward representations of these people that they have incorporated or introjected within themselves, producing self-loathing and depression. Bipolar disorder is understood within psychodynamic theory in terms of the shifting balances between the ego and superego. More recent psychodynamic models, such as the self-focusing model, incorporate both psychodynamic and cognitive aspects in explaining depression in terms of the continued pursuit of lost love objects or goals that it would be more adaptive to surrender.

How do humanistic theorists view depression? Theorists working within the humanistic framework view depression as reflecting a lack of meaning and authenticity in a person's life.

How do learning theorists view depression? Learning perspectives focus on situational factors in explaining depression, such as changes in the level of reinforcement. When reinforcement is reduced, the person may feel unmotivated and depressed, which can occasion inactivity and further reduce opportunities for reinforcement. Coyne's interactional theory focuses on the negative family interactions that can lead the family members of people with depression to become less reinforcing toward them.

What are two major cognitive models of depression? Beck's cognitive model focuses on the role of negative or distorted thinking in depression. Depression-prone people hold negative beliefs toward themselves, the environment, and the future. This cognitive triad of depression leads to specific errors in thinking, or cognitive distortions, in response to negative events, which, in turn, lead to depression.

The learned helplessness model is based on the belief that people may become depressed when they come to view themselves as helpless to control the reinforcements in their environment or to change their lives for the better. A reformulated version of the theory held that the ways in which people explain events—their attributions—determine their proneness toward depression in the face of negative events. The combination of internal, global, and stable attributions for negative events renders one most vulnerable to depression.

What role do biological factors play in mood disorders? Genetics appears to play a role in mood disorders, especially in explaining major depressive disorder and bipolar disorder. Imbalances in neurotransmitter activity in the brain appear to be involved in major depression. The diathesis-stress model is used as an explanatory framework to illustrate how biological or psychological diatheses may interact with stress in the development of mood disorders.

Treatment of Mood Disorders

What approaches to treatment are represented by each of the major theoretical perspectives? Psychodynamic treatment of depression has traditionally focused on helping the depressed person uncover and work through ambivalent feelings toward the lost object, thereby lessening the anger directed inward. Modern psychodynamic approaches tend to be more direct and briefer and focus more on developing adaptive means of achieving self-worth and resolving interpersonal conflicts. Learning theory approaches have focused on helping people with depression increase the frequency of reinforcement in their lives through such means as increasing the rates of pleasant activities in which they participate and assisting them in developing more effective social skills to increase their ability to obtain social reinforcements from others. Cognitive therapists focus on helping the person identify and correct distorted or dysfunctional thoughts and learn more adaptive behaviors. Biological approaches have focused on the use of antidepressant drugs and other biological treatments, such as electroconvulsive therapy (ECT). Antidepressant drugs may help normalize neurotransmitter functioning in the brain. Bipolar disorder is commonly treated with either lithium or anticonvulsant drugs.

Suicide

What factors are linked to suicide? Mood disorders are often linked to suicide. Although women are more likely to attempt suicide, more men actually succeed, probably because they select more lethal means. The elderly—not the young—are more likely to commit suicide. People who attempt suicide are often depressed, but they are generally in touch with reality. They may, however, lack effective problem-solving skills and see no other way of dealing with life stress than suicide. A sense of hopelessness also figures prominently in suicides.

What are the major theoretical approaches to understanding suicide? These draw on the classic psychodynamic model of anger turned inward; Durkeim's theory of social alienation; and learning, social–cognitive, and biologically based perspectives.

Why should you never ignore a person's threat to commit suicide? Although certainly not all people who threaten suicide go on to commit the act, many do. People who commit suicide often signal their intentions, such as by telling others about their suicidal thoughts.

KEY TERMS

mood disorders *(p. 241)*
major depressive disorder *(p. 243)*
mania *(p. 243)*
hypomania *(p. 243)*
postpartum depression (PPD) *(p. 248)*

dysthymic disorder *(p. 249)*
double depression *(p. 251)*
bipolar disorder *(p. 251)*
manic episode *(p. 252)*
cyclothymic disorder *(p. 254)*

cognitive triad of depression *(p. 259)*
cognitive-specificity hypothesis *(p. 262)*
learned helplessness *(p. 263)*
electroconvulsive therapy (ECT) *(p. 275)*

WEB TOOLS

The companion website offers tools to enrich your learning experience and help you succeed in class. Go to www.prenhall.com/nevid for the gateway to the following resources:

- **VIDEO** links to connect to the video case files on the companion CD-ROM. VIDEO icons in the margins of the chapter highlight the case examples included in the CD-ROM. You can also access the CD-ROM directly if you do not have a Web connection.

- **QUIZ** links to self-scoring quizzes corresponding to each section of the chapter. The quizzes help you review your knowledge of the content in each chapter.

- **WEB** links to direct you to related sites that enhance your learning of abnormal psychology.

CHAPTER NINE

Substance Abuse and Dependence

CHAPTER OUTLINE

"I"

"Nothing and Nobody Comes Before My Coke"

She had just caught me with cocaine again after I had managed to convince her that I hadn't used in over a month. Of course I had been tooting (snorting) almost every day, but I had managed to cover my tracks a little better than usual. So she said to me that I was going to have to make a choice—either cocaine or her. Before she finished the sentence, I knew what was coming, so I told her to think carefully about what she was going to say. It was clear to me that there wasn't a choice. I love my wife, but I'm not going to choose anything over cocaine. It's sick, but that's what things have come to. Nothing and nobody comes before my coke.

—From Weiss & Mirin, 1987, p. 55

THESE COMMENTS FROM EUGENE, A 41-YEAR-OLD ARCHITECT, UNDERSCORE THE powerful effects that drugs like cocaine can have on people's lives. Our society is flooded with psychoactive substances that alter the mood and twist perceptions—substances that lift you up, calm you down, and turn you upside down. Many young people start using these substances because of peer pressure or because their parents and other authority figures tell them not to. For Eugene, as for many others who become addicted to drugs, the pursuit and use of drugs takes center stage in their lives and becomes even more important than family, work, or their own welfare.

In this chapter we examine the physiological and psychological effects of the major classes of drugs. We explore how mental health professionals classify substance-related disorders and where we draw the line between use and abuse. We then examine contemporary understandings of the origins of these disorders and how mental health professionals help people who struggle to combat them.

The most widely used drugs on campus (excepting caffeine) remain alcohol and nicotine (in the form of cigarette smoking). Table 9.1 shows data on reported drug use compiled from a continuing government survey of young people in the United States. The results shown here focus on college students. Respondents are asked whether they have ever used a substance or used it during the past 30 days.

For every person who smokes marijuana for the first time each year, there are about 250 people who start smoking cigarettes (Stout, 2000). But there is some good news in the offing: Teen use of illicit drugs such as marijuana and cocaine began a steady decline during the latter half of the 1990s, a trend that has continued into the early years of the new millennium ("Fewer Teens Using," 2004; Machan, 2000).

CLASSIFICATION OF SUBSTANCE-RELATED DISORDERS

Under certain conditions, the use of substances that affect mood and behavior is normal, at least as gauged by statistical frequency and social standards. It is normal to start the day with caffeine in the form of coffee or tea, to take wine or coffee with meals, to meet friends for a drink after work, and to end the day with a nightcap. Many of us take prescription drugs that calm us down or ease our pain. Flooding the bloodstream with nicotine by means of smoking is normal in the sense that about 1 in 4 Americans do it. However, some psychoactive substances are illegal and are used illicitly, such as cocaine, marijuana, and heroin. Others are available by prescription, such as minor tranquilizers and amphetamines. Still others are available without prescription or over the counter, such as tobacco (which contains nicotine, a mild stimulant) and alcohol (a depressant). Ironically, the most widely and easily accessible substances—tobacco and alcohol—cause more deaths through sickness and accidents than all illicit drugs combined.

Trends in Drug Use Among College Students During Lifetime and During Last 30 Days (in percentages)

Drug	Used . . .	1988	1992	1996	2000	2002
Marijuana	Ever	51.3	44.1	45.1	51.2	49.5
	Last 30 days	16.3	14.6	17.5	20.0	19.7
Inhalants	Ever	12.6	14.2	11.4	12.9	7.7
	Last 30 days	1.3	1.1	0.8	0.9	0.7
Hallucinogens (includes LSD)	Ever	9.2	12.0	12.6	14.4	13.6
	Last 30 days	1.7	2.3	1.9	1.4	1.2
Cocaine (includes crack)	Ever	15.8	7.9	5.0	9.1	8.2
	Last 30 days	4.2	1.0	0.8	1.4	1.6
MDMA ("ecstasy")	Ever	NA	2.9	4.3	13.1	12.7
	Last 30 days	NA	0.4	0.7	2.5	0.7
Heroin	Ever	0.3	0.5	0.7	1.7	1.0
	Last 30 days	0.1	0.0	0.0	0.2	0.0
Stimulants (other than cocaine and crystal meth)	Ever	17.7	9.5	9.5	12.3	11.9
	Last 30 days	1.8	1.1	0.9	2.9	3.0
Barbiturates	Ever	3.6	3.8	4.6	6.9	5.9
	Last 30 days	0.5	0.7	0.8	1.1	1.7
Alcohol	Ever	94.9	91.8	88.4	86.6	86.0
	Last 30 days	77.0	71.4	67.0	67.4	68.9
Cigarettes	Ever	NA	NA	NA	NA	NA
	Last 30 days	22.6	23.5	27.9	28.2	26.7

Source: Johnston, L. D., O'Malley, P. M., & Bachman, J. G. (2003). *Monitoring the Future National Survey Results on Drug Use, 1975–2002. Volume II: College students and adults ages 19–40.* (NIH Pub. No. 03-5376). Betheseda, MD: National Institute on Drug Abuse.

substance-induced disorders Disorders that can be induced by using psychoactive substances, such as intoxication.

intoxication A state of drunkenness.

substance use disorders Disorders chararacterized by maladaptive use of psychoactive substances (e.g., substance dependence).

The classification of substance-related disorders in the *DSM* system is not based on whether a drug is legal or not, but rather on how drug use impairs the person's physiological and psychological functioning. The *DSM-IV* classifies substance-related disorders into two major categories: substance use disorders and substance-induced disorders.

Substance-induced disorders are disorders induced by using psychoactive substances, such as intoxication, withdrawal syndromes, mood disorders, delirium, dementia, amnesia, psychotic disorders, anxiety disorders, sexual dysfunctions, and sleep disorders. Different substances have different effects, so some of these disorders may be induced by one, a few, or nearly all substances. Let us consider the example of intoxication.

Substance **intoxication** refers to a state of drunkenness or being "high." These effects largely reflect the chemical actions of the psychoactive substances. The particular features of intoxication depend on which drug is ingested, the dose, the user's biological reactivity, and—to some degree—the user's expectations. Signs of intoxication often include confusion, belligerence, impaired judgment, inattention, and impaired motor and spatial skills. Extreme intoxication from use of alcohol, cocaine, opioids, (narcotics) and PCP can even result in death (yes, you can die from alcohol overdoses), either because of the substance's biochemical effects or because of behavior patterns—such as suicide—that are connected with psychological pain or impaired judgment brought on by use of the drug.

Substance use disorders are patterns of maladaptive use of psychoactive substances. These disorders, which include *substance abuse* and *substance dependence,* are the major focus of our study.

Substance Abuse and Dependence

Where does substance use end and abuse begin? According to the *DSM*, **substance abuse** is a pattern of recurrent use that leads to damaging consequences. Damaging consequences may involve failure to meet one's major role responsibilities (e.g., as student, worker, or parent), putting oneself in situations where substance use is physically dangerous (e.g., mixing driving and substance use), encountering repeated problems with the law arising from substance use (e.g., multiple arrests for substance-related behavior), or having recurring social or interpersonal problems because of substance use (e.g., repeatedly getting into fights when drinking).

When people repeatedly miss school or work because they are drunk or "sleeping it off," their behavior may fit the definition of substance abuse. A single incident of excessive drinking at a friend's wedding would not qualify. Nor would regular consumption of low to moderate amounts of alcohol be considered abusive so long as it is not connected with any impairment in functioning. Neither the amount nor the type of drug ingested, nor whether the drug is illicit, is the key to defining substance abuse according to the *DSM*. Rather, the determining feature of substance abuse is whether a pattern of drug-using behavior becomes repeatedly linked to damaging consequences.

Substance abuse may continue for a long period of time or progress to **substance dependence,** a more severe disorder in which abuse is associated with physiological signs of dependence (tolerance or withdrawal syndrome) *or* compulsive use of a substance. People who become compulsive users lack control over their drug use. They may be aware of how their drug use is disrupting their lives or damaging their health, but feel helpless or powerless to stop using drugs, even though they may want to. By the time they become dependent on a given drug, they've given over much of their lives to obtaining and using it. The cocaine user whose words opened this chapter would certainly fit this definition. The diagnostic features of substance dependence are listed in Table 9.2.

Repeated use of a substance may alter the body's physiological reactions, leading to the development of tolerance or a physical withdrawal syndrome (see Table 9.2). **Tolerance** is a state of physical habituation to a drug, resulting from frequent use, such that higher doses are needed to achieve the same effect. A **withdrawal syndrome** (also called an *abstinence syndrome*) is a cluster of symptoms that occur when a dependent

substance abuse The continued use of a psychoactive drug despite the knowledge that it is causing a social, occupational, psychological, or physical problem.

substance dependence Impaired control over the use of a psychoactive substance; often characterized by physiological dependence.

tolerance Physical habituation to a drug such that with frequent use, higher doses are needed to achieve the same effects.

withdrawal syndrome A characteristic cluster of symptoms following the sudden reduction or cessation of use of a psychoactive substance after physiological dependence has developed.

Two of the many faces of alcohol use—and abuse. Alcohol is our most widely used—and abused—drug. Many people use alcohol to celebrate achievements and happy occasions, as in the photograph on the left. Unfortunately, like the man in the photograph on the right, some people use alcohol to drown their sorrows, which may only compound their problems. Where exactly does substance use end and abuse begin? According to the *DSM*, use becomes abuse when it leads to damaging consequences.

TABLE 9.2

Diagnostic Features of Substance Dependence

Substance dependence is defined as a maladaptive pattern of use that results in significant impairment or distress, as shown by the following features occurring within the same year:

1. Tolerance for the substance, as shown by either

    (a) the need for increased amounts of the substance to achieve the desired effect or intoxication, or
    (b) marked reduction in the effects of continuing to ingest the same amounts.

2. Withdrawal symptoms, as shown by either

    (a) the withdrawal syndrome that is considered characteristic for the substance, or
    (b) the taking of the same substance (or a closely related substance, as when methadone is substituted for heroin) to relieve or to prevent withdrawal symptoms.

3. Taking larger amounts of the substance or for longer periods of time than the individual intended (e.g., person had desired to take only one drink, but after taking the first, continues drinking until severely intoxicated).

4. Persistent desire to cut down or control intake of substance or lack of success in trying to exercise self-control.

5. Spending a good deal of time in activities directed toward obtaining the substance (e.g., visiting several physicians to obtain prescriptions or engaging in theft), in actually ingesting the substance, or in recovering from its use. In severe cases, the individual's daily life revolves around substance use.

6. The individual has reduced or given up important social, occupational, or recreational activities due to substance use (e.g., person withdraws from family events in order to indulge in drug use).

7. Substance use is continued despite evidence of persistent or recurrent psychological or physical problems either caused or exacerbated by its use (e.g., repeated arrests for driving while intoxicated).

Note: Not all of these features need be present for a diagnosis to be made.
Source: Adapted from the *DSM-IV-TR* (APA, 2000).

---

person abruptly stops using a particular substance following heavy, prolonged use. People who experience a withdrawal syndrome often return to using the substance to relieve the discomfort associated with withdrawal, which serves to maintain the addictive pattern. Withdrawal symptoms vary with the particular type of drug. With alcohol dependence, typical withdrawal symptoms include dryness in the mouth, nausea or vomiting, weakness, increased heart rate, anxiety, depression, headaches, insomnia, elevated blood pressure, and fleeting hallucinations.

In some cases of chronic alcoholism, withdrawal produces a state of *delirium tremens,* or DTs. The DTs are usually limited to chronic, heavy users of alcohol who dramatically lower their intake of alcohol after many years of heavy drinking. The DTs involve intense autonomic hyperactivity (profuse sweating and tachycardia) and *delirium*—a state of mental confusion characterized by incoherent speech, disorientation, and extreme restlessness. Terrifying hallucinations—frequently of creepy, crawling animals—may also be present.

Substances that may lead to withdrawal syndromes include, in addition to alcohol, opioids, cocaine, amphetamines, sedatives and barbiturates, nicotine, and antianxiety agents (minor tranquilizers). Marijuana and hallucinogens like LSD are not recognized as producing a withdrawal syndrome, because abrupt withdrawal from these substances does not produce clinically significant withdrawal effects (APA, 2000).

In the DSM system, substance dependence is often, but not always, associated with the development of physiological dependence (Langenbucher et al., 2000). In some cases it involves a pattern of compulsive use without physiological dependence. For example, people may become compulsive users of marijuana, especially when they rely on the drug to help them cope with the stresses of daily life. Yet they may not require larger amounts of the substance to get "high" or experience distressing withdrawal symptoms when they cease using it. In most cases, however, substance dependence and physiological features of dependence occur together. Despite the fact that the *DSM* considers substance abuse and dependence to be distinct diagnostic categories, the borderline between the two is not always clear.

Alcohol dependence alone affects about 1 in 7 (14%) U.S. adults (Anthony, Warner, & Kessler, 1994; Warner et al., 1995). Overall, alcohol dependence has been on the rise, due largely to increases in adolescent alcohol abuse leading eventually to outright dependence (Hill et al., 2000; Nelson, Heath, & Kessler, 1998).

About 1 in 4 U.S. adults suffer from nicotine dependence resulting from regular use of tobacco products, most usually cigarettes (Breslau et al., 2001). About 1 in 13 (7.5%) have developed a dependence on an illicit drug, inhalant, or nonprescription use of tranquilizers or other psychiatric (psychotropic) drugs. Figure 9.1 gives the lifetime prevalence of drug dependence for various types of drugs.

People may abuse or become dependent on more than one psychoactive substance at the same time. People who become dependent on heroin, for instance, may also abuse other drugs, such as alcohol, cocaine, or stimulants—either simultaneously or successively. People who abuse more than one drug face increased risk of harmful overdoses. Moreover, treatment of one form of abuse may not affect, or in some cases may even exacerbate, abuse of other drugs.

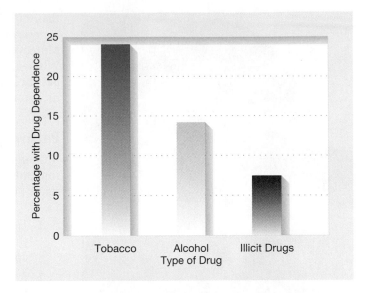

FIGURE 9.1 Lifetime prevalence of drug dependence by type of drug.
One in 4 adults in the United States suffers from tobacco dependence at some point. About 1 in 7 experiences alcohol dependence and about 1 in 13 develops a drug dependence on an illicit drug.

Source: National Comorbidity Survey (Anthony, Warner, & Kessler, 1994).

Addiction, Physiological Dependence, and Psychological Dependence

The *DSM* uses the terms *substance abuse* and *substance dependence* to classify people whose use of psychoactive substances impairs their functioning. It does not use the term *addiction* to describe these problems. Yet the concept of addiction is widespread among professionals and laypeople alike. But what does the term mean?

People define addiction in different ways. We define **addiction** as the habitual or compulsive use of a drug accompanied by evidence of physiological dependence. **Physiological dependence** means that one's body has changed as a result of the regular use of a psychoactive drug in such a way that it depends on a steady supply of the substance. The major signs of physiological dependence involve the development of tolerance or a withdrawal syndrome. **Psychological dependence** involves the compulsive use of a drug to meet a psychological need, such as relying on a drug to cope with stress. As we noted earlier, you can become psychologically dependent on a drug without developing a physiological dependence or addiction.

On the other hand, people may become physiologically dependent on a drug but not become a compulsive user or psychologically dependent. For example, people recuperating from surgery are often given narcotics derived from opium as painkillers. Some develop signs of physiological dependence, such as tolerance and a withdrawal syndrome, but do not become habitual users or show a lack of control over the use of these drugs.

addiction Impaired control over the use of a chemical substance, accompanied by physiological dependence.

physiological dependence A condition in which the drug user's body comes to depend on a steady supply of the substance.

psychological dependence Compulsive use of a substance to meet a psychological need.

TRUTH or FICTION? *REVISITED*

You cannot be psychologically dependent on a drug without also being physically dependent on it.

☑ **FALSE.** You can become psychologically dependent on a drug without developing a physiological dependence.

Racial and Ethnic Differences in Substance Dependence

Despite the popular stereotype that drug dependence is more frequent among ethnic minorities, this belief is not supported by evidence. The National Comorbidity Survey (NCS) shows that drug dependence is actually less common among African Americans

Internet addiction? Compulsive, dependent use of the Internet and other forms of compulsive behavior, such as compulsive gambling or shopping, have been likened to forms of nonchemical addiction. Whether we label such maladaptive patterns of behavior as "addictions" depends on how we define the concept of addiction.

than non-Hispanic White Americans and no more common among Hispanic Americans than among non-Hispanic White Americans (Anthony et al., 1994). Moreover, African American adolescents are much less likely than non-Hispanic White adolescents to develop substance abuse or dependence problems (Kilpatrick et al., 2000). In a later section we shall examine evidence on racial/ethnic group differences in alcohol use and abuse.

Pathways to Drug Dependence

Although the progression to substance dependence varies from person to person, one common pathway involves a progression along the following series of stages (Weiss & Mirin, 1987):

1. *Experimentation.* During the stage of experimentation, or occasional use, the drug temporarily makes users feel good, even euphoric. Users feel in control and believe they can stop at any time.

2. *Routine use.* During the next stage, a period of routine use, people begin to structure their lives around the pursuit and use of drugs. Denial plays a major role at this stage, as users mask the negative consequences of their behavior to themselves and others. Values change. What had formerly been important, such as family and work, comes to matter less than the drugs.

   The following clinical interview illustrates how denial can mask reality. This 48-year-old executive was brought for a consultation by his wife. She complained his once-successful business was jeopardized by his erratic behavior, he was grouchy and moody, and he had spent $7,000 in the previous month on cocaine.

CLINICIAN:	Have you missed many days at work recently?
EXECUTIVE:	Yes, but I can afford to, since I own the business. Nobody checks up on me.
CLINICIAN:	It sounds like that's precisely the problem. When you don't go to work, the company stays open, but it doesn't do very well.
EXECUTIVE:	My employees are well trained. They can run the company without me.
CLINICIAN:	But that's not happening.
EXECUTIVE:	Then there's something wrong with them. I'll have to look into it.
CLINICIAN:	It sounds as if there's something wrong with you, but you don't want to look into it.
EXECUTIVE:	Now you're on my case. I don't know why you listen to everything my wife says.
CLINICIAN:	How many days of work did you miss in the last two months?
EXECUTIVE:	A couple.
CLINICIAN:	Are you saying that you missed only two days of work?
EXECUTIVE:	Maybe a few.
CLINICIAN:	Only three or four days?
EXECUTIVE:	Maybe a little more.
CLINICIAN:	Ten? Fifteen?
EXECUTIVE:	Fifteen.
CLINICIAN:	All because of cocaine?
EXECUTIVE:	No.
CLINICIAN:	How many were because of cocaine?
EXECUTIVE:	Less than fifteen.
CLINICIAN:	Fourteen? Thirteen?
EXECUTIVE:	Maybe thirteen.
CLINICIAN:	So you missed thirteen days of work in the last two months because of cocaine. That's almost two days a week.
EXECUTIVE:	That sounds like a lot but it's no big deal. Like I say, the company can run itself.

CLINICIAN: How long have you been using cocaine?

EXECUTIVE: About three years.

CLINICIAN: Did you ever use drugs or alcohol before that in any kind of quantity?

EXECUTIVE: No.

CLINICIAN: Then let's think back five years. Five years ago, if you had imagined your-self missing over a third of your workdays because of a drug, and if you had imagined yourself spending the equivalent of $84,000 a year on that same drug, and if you saw your once-successful business collapsing all around you, wouldn't you have thought that that was indicative of a pretty serious problem?

EXECUTIVE: Yes, I would have.

CLINICIAN: So what's different now?

EXECUTIVE: I guess I just don't want to think about it.

—From Weiss & Mirin, 1987, pp. 79–80

As routine drug use continues, problems mount. Users devote more resources to drugs. They ravage family bank accounts, seek "temporary" loans from friends and family for trumped-up reasons, and sell family heirlooms and jewelry for a fraction of their value. Lying and manipulation become a way of life to cover up the drug use. The husband sells the TV set and forces the front door open to make it look like a burglary. The wife claims to have been robbed at knifepoint to explain the disappearance of a gold chain or engagement ring. Family relationships become strained as the mask of denial shatters and the consequences of drug abuse become apparent: days lost from work, unexplained absences from home, rapid mood shifts, depletion of family finances, failure to pay bills, stealing from family members, and missing family gatherings or children's birthday parties.

3. *Addiction or dependence.* Routine use becomes addiction or dependence when users feel powerless to resist drugs, either because they want to experience their effects or to avoid the consequences of withdrawal. Little or nothing else matters at this stage, as we saw in the case of Eugene with which we opened the chapter.

Now let us examine the effects of different types of drugs of abuse and the consequences associated with their use and abuse.

DRUGS OF ABUSE

Drugs of abuse are generally classified within three major groupings: (a) depressants, such as alcohol and opioids; (b) stimulants, such as amphetamines and cocaine; and (c) hallucinogens.

Depressants

A **depressant** is a drug that slows down or curbs the activity of the central nervous system. It reduces feelings of tension and anxiety, slows movement, and impairs cognitive processes. In high doses, depressants can arrest vital functions and cause death. The most widely used depressant, alcohol, can cause death when taken in large amounts because of its depressant effects on breathing. Other effects are specific to the particular kind of depressant. For example, some depressants, such as heroin, produce a "rush" of pleasure. Here let us consider several major types of depressants.

depressant A drug that lowers the level of activity of the central nervous system.

Alcohol   You might not think of alcohol as a drug, perhaps because it is so common, or perhaps because it is ingested by drinking rather than by smoking or injection. But alcoholic beverages—such as wine, beer, and hard liquor—contain a depressant called *ethyl alcohol* (or *ethanol*). The concentration of the drug varies with the type of beverage (wine and beer have less pure alcohol per ounce than distilled spirits such as rye, gin, or vodka). Alcohol is classified as a depressant drug because it has biochemical effects similar to those of a class of minor tranquilizers, the benzodiazepines, which includes the well-known drugs *diazepam* (Valium) and *chlordiazepoxide* (Librium). We can think of alcohol as an over-the-counter tranquilizer.

alcoholism An alcohol dependence disorder or addiction that results in serious personal, social, occupational, or health problems.

Most American adults drink alcohol at least occasionally. Most people who drink do so in moderation, but many develop significant problems with alcohol use (Garbutt et al., 1999; Miller & Brown, 1997). Alcohol is the most widely abused substance in the United States and worldwide. Alcohol dependence affects an estimated 14 million Americans, about 14% of the adult population. Many lay and professional people use the term **alcoholism** to refer to alcohol dependence. Though definitions of alcoholism vary, we use the term to refer to a physical dependence on, or addiction to, alcohol that is characterized by impaired control over the use of the drug.

The most widely held view of alcoholism is the disease model, the belief that alcoholism is a medical illness or disease. From this perspective, once a person with alcoholism takes a drink, the biochemical effects of the drug on the brain create an irresistible physical craving for more. The disease model holds that alcoholism is a chronic, permanent condition. The peer-support group Alcoholics Anonymous (AA) subscribes to this view, which is expressed in their slogan, "Once an alcoholic, always an alcoholic." AA views people suffering from alcoholism as either drinking or "recovering," never "cured." However, later in this chapter we shall see that some professionals, including the psychologists Linda and Mark Sobell, adopt a different perspective. Their research shows that some alcohol abusers can learn skills of controlled social drinking that enables them to drink moderately without "falling off the wagon." The contention that some people with alcohol problems can learn to drink moderately remains controversial.

The personal and social costs of alcoholism exceed those of all illicit drugs combined. Alcohol abuse is connected with lower productivity, loss of jobs, and downward movement in socioeconomic status. Perhaps 30% to 40% of homeless people in the United States suffer from alcoholism (McCarty et al., 1991). About one in three suicides in this country and about the same proportion of deaths due to unintentional injury (such as from motor vehicle accidents) are believed to be alcohol-related (Hingson et al., 2000). Despite increased awareness about the risks of drinking and driving, fatal alcohol-related motor vehicle accidents are on the rise (O'Donnell, 2003). All told, an estimated 100,000 people in the United States die from alcohol-related causes each year, mostly from motor vehicle crashes and diseases (Kalb, 2001a; Wood, Vinson, & Sher, 2001).

Despite the popular image of the person who develops alcoholism as a skid-row drunk, only a small minority of people with alcoholism fit the stereotype. The great majority of people with alcoholism are quite ordinary—your neighbors, coworkers, friends, and members of your own family. They are found in all walks of life and every social and economic class. Many have families, hold good jobs, and live fairly comfortably. Yet alcoholism can have just as devastating an effect on the well-to-do as on the indigent, leading to wrecked careers and marriages, to motor vehicle and other accidents, and to

QUESTIONNAIRE
Are You Hooked?

Are you dependent on alcohol? If you shake and shiver and undergo the tortures of the darned (our editor insisted on changing this word to maintain the decorum of a textbook) when you go without a drink for a while, the answer is clear enough. Sometimes the clues are more subtle, however.

The following questions, adapted from the National Council on Alcoholism's self-test, can shed some light on the question. Simply place a check mark in the "yes" or "no" column for each item. Then check the key at the end of the chapter.

	Yes	No
1. Do you sometimes go on drinking binges?		
2. Do you tend to keep away from your family or friends when you are drinking?		
3. Do you become irritated when your family or friends talk about your drinking?		

	Yes	No
4. Do you feel guilty now and then about your drinking?		
5. Do you often regret the things you have said or done when you have been drinking?		
6. Do you find that you fail to keep the promises you make about controlling or cutting down on your drinking?		
7. Do you eat irregularly or not at all when you are drinking?		
8. Do you feel low after drinking?		
9. Do you sometimes miss work or appointments because of drinking?		
10. Do you drink more and more to get drunk?		

Source: Adapted from Newsweek, *February 20, 1989, p. 52.*

severe, life-threatening physical disorders, as well as exacting an enormous emotional toll. Alcoholism is also linked to higher levels of domestic violence and greater risk of divorce (Marshal, 2003).

No single drinking pattern is exclusively associated with alcoholism. Some people with alcoholism drink heavily every day; others binge only on weekends. Others can abstain for lengthy periods of time, but periodically "go off the wagon" and engage in episodes of binge drinking that last for weeks or months.

Alcohol, not cocaine or other drugs, is the drug of choice among young people today and the leading drug of abuse. Drinking has become so integrated into college life that it is essentially normative, as much a part of the college experience as attending a weekend football or basketball game. Drinking among college students tends to be limited to weekends and to be heavier early in the semester when academic requirements are low (Del Boca et al., 2004). As a group, young adults in the 18- to 24-year age range show the highest rates of alcohol use and the highest proportions of problem drinkers (Ham & Hope, 2003). Researchers describe a continuum of alcohol-related problems among college students, ranging from mild problems, such as missing class, to extreme problem behaviors, such as arrests resulting from drinking (Ham & Hope, 2003). In the A Closer Look section, we focus on a particular form of problem drinking that has become a leading problem on college campuses today—binge drinking.

Risk Factors for Alcoholism A number of factors place people at increased risk for developing alcoholism and alcohol-related problems. These include the following.

1. *Gender.* Men are more than twice as likely as women (20% vs. 8%, respectively) to develop alcohol dependence disorder (Grant, 1997). One possible reason for this gender difference is sociocultural; perhaps tighter cultural constraints are placed on women. Yet it may also be that alcohol hits women harder, and not only because women usually weigh less than men. Alcohol seems to "go to women's heads" more rapidly than men's. This is apparently because women metabolize less alcohol in the stomach than men do. Why? It appears that women have less of an enzyme that metabolizes alcohol in the stomach than men do (Lieber, 1990). Consequently, ounce for ounce women absorb more alcohol into their

Women and alcohol. Women are less likely to develop alcoholism, in part because of greater cultural constraints on excessive drinking by women and perhaps because women absorb more pure alcohol into the bloodstream than men; thus women become more affected by the alcohol they consume than men who drink the same amount.

bloodstreams than do men. As a result, they are likely to become inebriated on less alcohol than men.

2. *Age.* The great majority of cases of alcohol dependence develops in young adulthood, typically before age 40 (Langenbucher & Chung, 1995). Although alcohol use disorders tend to develop somewhat later in women than in men, women who develop these problems experience similar health, social, and occupational problems by middle age as their male counterparts.

3. *Antisocial personality disorder.* Antisocial behavior in adolescence or adulthood increases the risk of later alcoholism. On the other hand, many people with alcoholism showed no antisocial tendencies in adolescence, and many antisocial adolescents do not abuse alcohol or other drugs as adults.

4. *Family history.* The best predictor of problem drinking in adulthood appears to be a family history of alcohol abuse. Family members who drink may act as models ("set a poor example"). Moreover, the biological relatives of people with alcohol dependence may also inherit a predisposition that makes them more likely to develop problems with alcohol.

5. *Sociodemographic factors.* A lifetime history of alcohol dependence is more common among people of lower income and educational levels and among people living alone (Anthony et al., 1994).

Ethnicity and Alcohol Use and Abuse Rates of alcohol use and alcoholism vary among American ethnic and racial groups (Beauvais, 1998; Lex, 1987; Moncher, Holden, & Trimble, 1990). Jewish Americans, for example, have relatively low rates of alcoholism (Yeung & Greenwald, 1992), perhaps because Jews tend to expose children to the ritual use of wine within a religious context and to impose strong cultural restraints on excessive and underage drinking. Asian Americans also tend to drink less heavily than other population groups (Wong, Klingle, & Price, 2004). Asian families place strong cultural constraints on excessive drinking. But a biological factor may also be involved in curbing alcohol use. Asian Americans are more likely than other groups to show a flush-

Alcohol and ethnic diversity. The damaging effects of alcohol abuse appear to be taking the heaviest toll on African Americans and Native Americans. The prevalence of alcohol-related cirrhosis of the liver is nearly twice as high among African Americans than among White Americans, even though African Americans are less likely to develop alcohol abuse or dependence disorders. Jewish Americans have relatively low incidences of alcohol-related problems, perhaps because they tend to expose children to the ritual use of wine in childhood and impose strong cultural restraints on excessive drinking. Asian Americans tend to drink less heavily than most other Americans, in part because of cultural constraints and possibly because they have less biological tolerance of alcohol, as shown by a greater flushing response to alcohol.

ing response to alcohol. Flushing is characterized by redness and feelings of warmth on the face, and, at higher doses, nausea, heart palpitations, dizziness, and headaches (Ellickson, Hays, & Bell, 1992). Genes that control the metabolism of alcohol are responsible for the flushing response (Begley, 2001b). Because people like to avoid these unpleasant experiences, flushing may serve as a natural defense against alcoholism by curbing excessive alcohol intake.

Hispanic American men and non-Hispanic White men have similar rates of alcohol consumption and alcohol-related physical problems (Caetano, 1987; Kessler et al., 1994). Hispanic American women, however, are much less likely to use alcohol and to develop alcohol use disorders than non-Hispanic White women. Why? An important factor may be cultural expectations. Traditional Hispanic American cultures place severe restrictions on the use of alcohol by women, especially heavy drinking. However, with increasing acculturation, Hispanic American women in the United States apparently are becoming more similar to Euro American women with respect to alcohol use and abuse.

Alcohol abuse is taking a heavy toll on African Americans. The prevalence of *cirrhosis,* a degenerative, potentially fatal liver disease, is nearly twice as high in African Americans as in non-Hispanic White Americans. African Americans are also much more likely to develop alcohol-related coronary heart disease and oral and throat cancers (Rogan, 1986). Yet African Americans are much less likely than non-Hispanic White Americans to develop alcohol abuse or dependence (Anthony et al., 1994; Grant et al., 1994). Why, then, do African Americans suffer more from alcohol-related problems?

Socioeconomic factors may help explain these differences. African Americans are more likely to encounter the stresses of unemployment and economic hardship, and stress may compound the damage to the body caused by heavy alcohol consumption. African Americans also tend to lack access to medical services and may be less likely to receive early treatment for the medical problems caused by alcohol abuse.

American Indians suffer more from alcohol-related problems than any other ethnic group. Though rates of drinking vary from tribe to tribe, the American Indian population has very high rates of problem drinking and alcohol-related consequences, such as cirrhosis of the liver, fetal abnormalities, and automobile and other accident fatalities (Hawkins et al., 2004; Rabasca, 2000a).

Alcoholism:
The Case of Chris
"Toughest thing I ever did was admitting I had a problem."

Many Native Americans believe the loss of their traditional culture is largely responsible for their high rates of drinking-related problems (Beauvais, 1998). The disruption of traditional Indian culture caused by the appropriation of Indian lands and by attempts by European American society to sever Native Americans from their cultural traditions while denying them full access to the dominant culture resulted in severe cultural and social disorganization (Kahn, 1982). Beset by such problems, Native American adults are also prone to child abuse and neglect. Abuse and neglect contribute to feelings of hopelessness and depression among adolescents, who then seek to escape their feelings through alcohol and other drugs (Berlin, 1987).

Psychological Effects of Alcohol   The effects of alcohol or other drugs vary from person to person. By and large they reflect the interaction of (a) the physiological effects of the substances, and (b) our interpretations of those effects. What do most people expect from alcohol? People frequently hold stereotypical expectations that alcohol will reduce tension, enhance pleasurable experiences, wash away worries, and enhance social skills. But what *does* alcohol actually do?

At a physiological level, alcohol, like the benzodiazepines (a family of antianxiety drugs; see Chapter 6), appears to heighten the sensitivity of GABA receptor sites. Because GABA is an inhibitory neurotransmitter, increasing the action of GABA reduces overall nervous system activity, producing feelings of relaxation. As people drink, their senses become clouded, and balance and coordination suffer. Still higher doses act on the parts of the brain that regulate involuntary vital functions, such as heart rate, respiration rate, and body temperature.

People may do many things when drinking that they would not do when sober, in part because of expectations concerning the drug, in part because of the drug's effects on

A CLOSER LOOK
Binge Drinking, a Dangerous College Pastime

One type of drinking problem receiving a great deal of attention is binge drinking. Many college officials consider view binge drinking—not cocaine use or ecstasy—to be the major drug problem on campuses today ("College Binge Drinking," 2001). Binge drinking is usually defined as having five or more drinks (for men) or four or more drinks (for women) on one occasion. Approximately 40% of college students today engage in binge drinking (Ham & Hope, 2003).

College officials' concerns about binge drinking are well placed. Binge drinking is linked to increased risks of serious motor vehicle and other accidents, violent and aggressive behavior, poor grades, sexual promiscuity, and development of substance abuse and dependence (Chassin et al., 2002; Naimi et al., 2003; Vik et al., 2000). Consider the tragic case of Leslie, a young college student at the University of Virginia. An art major whose work her professors found promising, Leslie had maintained a 3.67 G.P.A and was completing her senior essay on a Polish-born sculptor (Winerip, 1998). But she never finished it, because one day after binge drinking, she fell down a flight of stairs and died. We may hear more about the deaths of young people due to heroin or cocaine overdoses, but hundreds of college students, like Leslie, die from alcohol-related causes such as overdoses and accidents each year (Li et al., 2001).

In a recent review article, Lindsay Ham and Debra Hope (2003) identified two general subtypes of college students who appear most clearly at risk of becoming problem drinkers. The first type includes students who drink mostly for social or enjoyment purposes. They tend to be male, Anglo-American, and participate in Greek organizations or other social organizations in which heavy drinking is socially acceptable. The second type includes students who drink due to pressures to conform or who use alcohol to soothe negative feelings. They more often tend to be female and to be troubled by problems with anxiety or depression. Generating these profiles may help counselors and health-care providers identify young people at increased risk of developing problem drinking patterns.

Binge drinking and related drinking games (beer chugging) can place people at significant risk of death from alcohol overdose. Many students who play these games don't stop until they become too drunk or too sick to continue (Johnson, 2002). What should you do if you see a friend or acquaintance become incapacitated or pass out from heavy drinking? Should you just let the person sleep it off? Can you tell whether a person has had too much to drink? Should you just mind your own business or turn to others for help?

You cannot tell simply by looking at a person whether the person has overdosed on alcohol. But a person who becomes unconscious or unresponsive is in need of immediate medical attention. Don't assume that the person will simply "sleep it off": he or she may never wake up. Be aware of the signs of potential overdose, such as the following (adapted from Nevid, Rathus, & Rubenstein, 1998):

- Nonresponsive when talked to or shouted at
- Nonresponsive to being pinched, shaken, or poked
- Unable to stand up on his or her own
- Failure to wake up or gain consciousness
- Purplish color or clammy-feeling skin
- Rapid pulse rate or irregular heart rhythms, low blood pressure, or difficulty breathing.

If you suspect an overdose, do not leave the person alone. Summon medical help or emergency assistance and remain with the person until help arrives. Place the person on the side or have the person sit up with the head bowed. Do not give the person any food or drink or induce vomiting. If the person is responsive, find out if he or she had taken any medication or other drugs that might be interacting with the effects of the alcohol. Also, find out whether the person has an underlying illness that may contribute to the problem, such as diabetes or epilepsy.

It may be easier to just pass by without taking action. But ask yourself what you would like someone else to do if you showed signs of overdosing on alcohol. Wouldn't you want one of your friends to intervene to save your life?

A Dangerous Pastime. Beer chugging and binge drinking can quickly lead to an alcohol overdose, a medical emergency that can have lethal consequences. Many college officials cite binge drinking as *the* major drug problem on campus.

the brain. For example, they may become more flirtatious or sexually aggressive or say or do things they later regret. Their behavior may reflect their expectation that alcohol has liberating effects and provides an external excuse for questionable behavior. Later, they can claim, "It was the alcohol, not me." The drug may impair the brain's ability to curb impulsive, risk-taking, or violent behavior (Curtin et al., 2001), perhaps by interfering with information-processing functions. Investigators find strong links between alcohol use and violent behaviors (Boles & Miottoa, 2003), including domestic violence and sexual assaults (Abbey et al., 2004; Fals-Stewart, 2003; Marshal, 2003).

Although alcohol makes people feel more relaxed and self-confident, it also impairs judgment, which can lead them to make choices they would ordinarily reject, such as engaging in risky sex (Gordon & Carey, 1996). Chronic alcohol abuse can impair cognitive abilities, such as memory, problem solving, and attention (Ratti et al., 2002).

One of the lures of alcohol is that it induces short-term feelings of euphoria and elation that can drown self-doubts and self-criticism. Alcohol also makes people less capable of perceiving the unfortunate consequences of their behavior.

Alcohol in increasing amounts can dampen sexual arousal or excitement and impair sexual performance. As an intoxicant, alcohol also hampers coordination and motor ability and slurs speech. These effects help explain why alcohol use is implicated in more than 40% of the nation's fatal auto accidents, homicides, and fatal fires (see Figure 9.2).

Physical Health and Alcohol Chronic, heavy alcohol use affects virtually every organ and body system, either directly or indirectly. Heavy alcohol use is linked to increased risk of some forms of cancer, including cancer of the throat, esophagus, larynx, stomach, colon, liver, and possibly the bowels and breasts (e.g., Fuchs et al., 1995; Reichman, 1994). Heavy drinking is also linked to a wide range of other serious health concerns, including coronary heart disease, neurological disorders, and other forms of liver disease (Gordis, 1999). Two of the major forms of alcohol-related liver disease are *alcoholic hepatitis,* a serious and

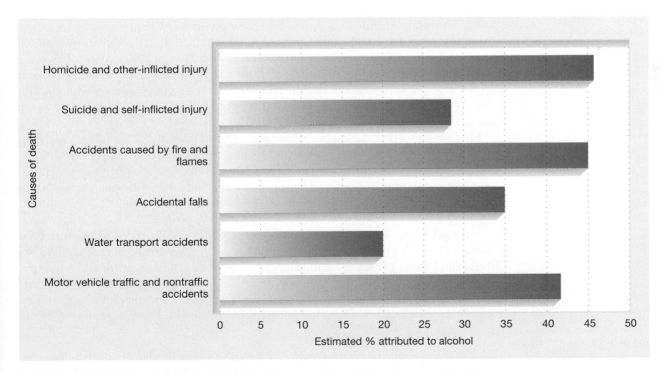

FIGURE 9.2 Alcohol use and causes of death.
Alcohol use is implicated in almost half of all homicides and in significant proportions of accidents of all types.

Source: NIAAA, 1996 (U.S. Alcohol Epidemiologic Data Reference Manual).

Alcohol and driving. Alcohol is implicated in nearly half of the nation's fatal motor vehicle accidents and about 35% of fatal falls.

potentially life-threatening inflammation of the liver, and *cirrhosis of the liver,* a potentially fatal disease in which healthy liver cells are replaced with scar tissue.

Habitual drinkers tend to be malnourished, which can put them at risk of complications arising from nutritional deficiencies. Chronic drinking is thus associated with such nutritionally linked disorders as cirrhosis of the liver (linked to protein deficiency) and *alcohol-induced persisting amnestic disorder* (connected with vitamin B deficiency). This condition, also known as *Korsakoff's syndrome,* is characterized by glaring confusion, disorientation, and memory loss for recent events (see Chapter 15).

All told, about 100,000 deaths annually in the United States result from alcohol-related diseases and motor vehicle and other accidents (Potter, 1997). After tobacco, alcohol is the second-leading cause of premature death in our society. Men who drink heavily stand nearly twice the risk of dying before the age of 65 as men who abstain; women who drink heavily are more than three times as likely to die before age 65 as are women who abstain ("NIAAA Report," 1990).

Mothers who drink during pregnancy place their fetuses at risk for infant mortality, birth defects, central nervous system dysfunctions, and later academic problems. Children whose mothers drink during pregnancy may develop *fetal alcohol syndrome* (FAS), a syndrome characterized by facial features such as a flattened nose, widely spaced eyes, and underdeveloped upper jaw, as well as mental retardation (Carroll, 2003; Wood et al., 2001). FAS affects from one to three of every 1,000 live births.

We don't know whether a minimum amount of alcohol is needed to produce FAS. Though the risk is greater among women who drank heavily during pregnancy, FAS has been found among children of mothers who drank as little as a drink and a half per week (Carroll, 2003). Although the question of whether there is any safe dose of alcohol during pregnancy continues to be debated, the fact remains that FAS is an entirely preventable birth defect. The safest course for women who know or suspect they are pregnant is not to drink. Period.

Moderate Drinking: Is There a Health Benefit? Despite this list of adverse effects associated with heavy drinking, evidence shows that moderate use of alcohol (1 to 2 drinks per day) is linked to lower risks of heart attacks and strokes, lower death rates, and lower risk of heart failure in older adults (Abramson et al., 2001; Mukamal et al., 2003; Reynolds et al., 2003). Researchers suspect that alcohol may help prevent the formation of blood clots that can clog arteries and lead to heart attacks. Alcohol also appears to increase the levels of HDL cholesterol, the so-called good cholesterol that sweeps away fatty deposits along artery walls (Goldberg et al., 2001). Although moderate use of alcohol may have a protective effect on the heart and circulatory system, public health officials have not endorsed using alcohol for this reason, based largely on concerns that such an endorsement may increase the risks of problem drinking. Health promotion efforts might be better directed toward finding safer ways of achieving the health benefits associated with moderate drinking than by encouraging alcohol consumption, such as by quitting smoking, lowering dietary intake of fat and cholesterol, and exercising more regularly.

Barbiturates Estimates indicate that about 1% of the adult population meet criteria for a substance abuse or dependence disorder involving the use of barbiturates, sleep medication (hypnotics), or antianxiety agents at some point in their lives (Anthony & Helzer, 1991). **Barbiturates** such as amobarbital, pentobarbital, phenobarbital, and secobarbital are depressants, or *sedatives.* These drugs have several medical uses, including easing anxiety and tension, dulling pain, and treating epilepsy and high blood pressure. Barbiturate use quickly leads to psychological dependence and physiological dependence in the form of both tolerance and development of a withdrawal syndrome.

Barbiturates are also popular street drugs because they are relaxing and produce a mild state of euphoria, or "high." High doses of barbiturates, like alcohol, produce drowsiness, slurred speech, motor impairment, irritability, and poor judgment—a particularly deadly combination of effects when their use is combined with operation of a motor vehicle. The effects of barbiturates last from 3 to 6 hours.

Because of synergistic effects, a mixture of barbiturates and alcohol is about four times as powerful as either drug used by itself. A combination of barbiturates and alcohol is implicated in the deaths of the entertainers Marilyn Monroe and Judy Garland. Even such widely used antianxiety drugs as Valium and Librium, which have a wide margin of safety when used alone, can be dangerous and lead to overdoses when combined with alcohol (APA, 2000).

Physiologically dependent people need to be withdrawn carefully, and only under medical supervision, from sedatives, barbiturates, and antianxiety agents. Abrupt withdrawal can produce states of delirium that may involve visual, tactile, or auditory hallucinations and disturbances in thinking processes and consciousness. The longer the period of use and the higher the doses used, the greater the risk of severe withdrawal effects. Epileptic (grand mal) seizures and even death may occur if the individual undergoes untreated, abrupt withdrawal.

Opioids Opioids are **narcotics,** a term used for addictive drugs that have pain-relieving and sleep-inducing properties. Opioids include both naturally occurring opiates (morphine, heroin, codeine) derived from the juice of the poppy plant and synthetic drugs (Demerol, Percodan, Darvon) that have opiatelike effects. The ancient Sumerians named the poppy plant *opium,* meaning "plant of joy."

Opioids produce a *rush,* or intense feelings of pleasure, which is the primary reason for their popularity as street drugs. They also dull awareness of one's personal problems, which is attractive to people seeking a mental escape from stress. Their pleasurable effects derive from their ability to directly stimulate the brain's pleasure circuits—the same brain networks responsible for feelings of sexual pleasure or pleasure from eating a satisfying meal (Begley, 2001b).

The major medical application of opioids—natural or synthetic—is the relief of pain, or *analgesia.* Medical use of opioids, however, is carefully regulated because overdoses can lead to coma and even death. Yet some prescription opioids, especially the drug OxyContin, become drugs of abuse when they are used illicitly as street drugs (Tough, 2001). Street use of opioids is associated with many fatal overdoses and accidents. In a number of American cities, young men are more likely to die of a heroin overdose than in an automobile accident (Alter, 2001).

Estimates are that about 0.7% of the adult population (7 people in 1,000) currently have or have had an opiate abuse or dependence disorder (Anthony & Helzer, 1991).

barbiturates Types of depressants that are used to reduce anxiety or to induce sleep but that are highly addictive.

narcotics Drugs that are used for pain relief and treatment of insomnia but that have strong addictive potential.

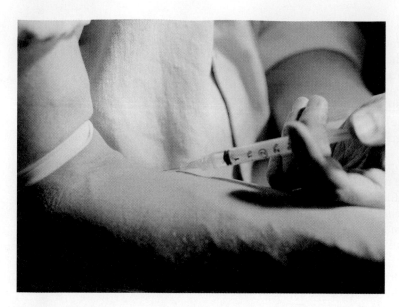

Shooting up. Heroin users often inject the substance directly into their veins. Heroin is a powerful depressant that provides a euphoric rush. Users often claim that heroin is so pleasurable that it obliterates any thought of food or sex.

endorphins Natural substances that function as neurotransmitters in the brain and are similar in their effects to morphine.

morphine A strongly addictive narcotic derived from the opium poppy that relieves pain and induces feelings of well-being.

heroin A narcotic derived from morphine that has strong addictive properties.

stimulants Psychoactive substances that increase the activity of the nervous system.

About 3 million Americans have used heroin (Krantz & Mehler, 2004). Once dependence sets in, it usually becomes chronic, relieved by brief periods of abstinence (APA, 2000).

Two discoveries made in the 1970s show that the brain produces chemicals of its own that have opiatelike effects. One was that neurons in the brain have receptor sites that opiates fit like a key in a lock. The second was that the human body produces its own opiatelike substances that dock at the same receptor sites as opiates do. These natural substances, or **endorphins,** play important roles in regulating natural states of pleasure and pain. Opioids mimic the actions of endorphins by docking at receptor sites intended for them, which in turn stimulates the brain centers that produce pleasurable sensations.

The withdrawal syndrome associated with opioids can be severe. It begins within 4 to 6 hours of the last dose. Flulike symptoms are accompanied by anxiety, feelings of restlessness, irritability, and cravings for the drug. Within a few days, symptoms progress to rapid pulse, high blood pressure, cramps, tremors, hot and cold flashes, fever, vomiting, insomnia, and diarrhea, among others. Although these symptoms can be uncomfortable, they are usually not devastating, especially when other drugs are prescribed to relieve them. Moreover, unlike withdrawal from barbiturates, the withdrawal syndrome rarely results in death.

Morphine **Morphine**—which receives its name from Morpheus, the Greek god of dreams—was introduced at about the time of the U.S. Civil War. Morphine, a powerful opium derivative, was used liberally to deaden pain from wounds. Physiological dependence on morphine became known as the "soldier's disease." There was little stigma attached to dependence until morphine became a restricted substance.

Heroin **Heroin,** the most widely used opiate, is a powerful depressant that can create a euphoric rush. Users of heroin claim that it is so pleasurable it can eradicate any thought of food or sex. Heroin was developed in 1875 during a search for a drug that would relieve pain as effectively as morphine, but without causing addiction. Chemist Heinrich Dreser transformed morphine into a new and stronger miracle drug, heroin, by means of a minor chemical change. He believed, erroneously, that heroin did not create physiological dependence.

Heroin is usually injected either directly beneath the skin (skin popping) or into a vein (mainlining). The positive effects are immediate. There is a powerful rush that lasts from 5 to 15 minutes and a state of satisfaction, euphoria, and well-being that lasts from 3 to 5 hours. In this state, all positive drives seem satisfied. All negative feelings of guilt, tension, and anxiety disappear. With prolonged usage, addiction can develop. Many physiologically dependent people support their habits through dealing (selling heroin), prostitution, or selling stolen goods. Heroin is a depressant, however, and its chemical effects do not directly stimulate criminal or aggressive behavior.

Stimulants

Stimulants are psychoactive substances that increase the activity of the nervous system. Effects vary somewhat from drug to drug, but some stimulants contribute to feelings of euphoria and self-confidence. Stimulants such as amphetamines, cocaine, and even caffeine (the stimulant found in coffee) increase the availability in the brain of the neurotransmitters norepinephrine and dopamine. High levels of these neurotransmitters therefore remain available in the synaptic gaps between neurons, maintaining high levels of nervous system activity and states of high arousal.

Amphetamines The **amphetamines** are a class of synthetic stimulants. Street names for stimulants include speed, uppers, bennies (for *amphetamine sulfate;* trade name Benzedrine), "meth" (for *methamphetamine;* trade name Methedrine), and dexies (for *dextroamphetamine;* trade name Dexedrine).

Amphetamines are used in high doses for their euphoric rush. They are often taken in pill form or smoked in a relatively pure form called "ice" or "crystal meth." The most potent form of amphetamine, liquid methamphetamine, is injected directly into the veins and produces an intense and immediate rush. Some users inject methamphetamine for days on end to maintain an extended high. Eventually such highs come to an end. People who have been on extended highs sometimes "crash" and fall into a deep sleep or depression. Some people commit suicide on the way down. High doses can cause restlessness, irritability, hallucinations, paranoid delusions, loss of appetite, and insomnia.

More than 1 million people in the United States use "meth," almost three times as many as use heroin (Bonné, 2001). Physiological dependence can develop from using amphetamines, leading to an abstinence syndrome characterized by depression and fatigue, as well as by unpleasant, vivid dreams, insomnia or hypersomnia (excessive sleeping), increased appetite, and either a slowing down of motor behavior or agitation (APA, 2000). Psychological dependence is seen most often in people who use amphetamines as a way of coping with stress or depression.

Methamphetamine abuse can cause brain damage, producing deficits in learning and memory in addition to other effects (Ernst et al., 2000; Toomey et al., 2003; Volkow et al., 2001; Zickler, 2000). Violent behavior may also occur, especially when the drug is smoked or injected intravenously (APA, 2000). The hallucinations and delusions of **amphetamine psychosis** mimic the features of paranoid schizophrenia, which has encouraged researchers to study the chemical changes induced by amphetamines as possible causes of schizophrenia.

Ecstasy The drug *ecstasy*, or MDMA (3,4-methylenedioxymethamphetamine) is a designer drug, a chemical knockoff similar in chemical structure to amphetamine (Braun, 2001). It produces mild euphoria and hallucinations and has become especially popular on college campuses and in clubs and "raves" in many cities (Hernandez, 2000; Mathias, 2000; Strote & Wechsler, 2002). On the other hand, teen use of ecstasy dropped significantly from 1998 to 2003 ("Fewer Teens," 2004). Perhaps the message about the dangers of ecstasy are beginning to get across to young people.

Ecstasy can produce adverse psychological effects, including depression, anxiety, insomnia, and even paranoia and psychosis. The drug may also impair cognitive functioning, including learning ability and attention, and may have long-lasting effects on memory (Gouzoulis-Mayfrank et al., 2000; Reneman, et al., 2001). Scientists suspect that the drug may kill dopamine-using neurons in the brain, which can have long-lasting effects on the ability to experience pleasure in everyday life experinces (Ricaurte et al., 2002). Physical side effects include higher heart rate and blood pressure, a tense or chattering jaw, and body warmth and/or chills (Braun, 2001). The drug can be lethal when taken in high doses (Kuhn & Wilson, 2001). Despite its risks, many users—including most teens—believe (mistakenly) that it is relatively safe ("Teens See Little Risk," 2003).

Cocaine It might surprise you to learn that the original formula for Coca-Cola contained an extract of **cocaine**. In 1906, however, the company withdrew cocaine from its secret formula. The drink was originally described as a "brain tonic and intellectual beverage," in part because of its cocaine content. Cocaine is a natural stimulant extracted from the leaves of the

amphetamines Types of stimulants, such as Benzedrine or Dexedrine.

amphetamine psychosis A psychotic state induced by ingestion of amphetamines.

cocaine A stimulant derived from the leaves of the coca plant.

Ecstasy. Recreational use of the drug ecstasy has become popular in many clubs catering to young people. Yet even occasional use of the drug may affect cognitive functioning, such as learning, memory, and attention. High doses can be lethal.

coca plant—the plant from which the soft drink obtained its name. Coca-Cola is still flavored with an extract from the coca plant, one that is not known to be psychoactive.

It was long believed that cocaine was not physically addicting. However, the drug produces a tolerance effect and an identifiable withdrawal syndrome, which is characterized by depressed mood and disturbances in sleep and appetite (APA, 2000). Intense cravings for the drug and loss of ability to experience pleasure may also be present. Withdrawal symptoms are usually brief in duration and may involve a "crash," or period of intense depression and exhaustion, following abrupt withdrawal.

Cocaine is usually snorted in powder form or smoked in the form of **crack,** a hardened form of cocaine that may be more than 75% pure. Crack "rocks"—so called because they look like small white pebbles—are available in small ready-to-smoke amounts and considered to be the most habit-forming street drug available. Crack produces a prompt and potent rush that wears off in a few minutes. The rush from snorting powdered cocaine is milder and takes a while to develop, but it tends to linger longer than the rush of crack.

Freebasing also intensifies the effects of cocaine. Cocaine in powder form is heated with ether, freeing the psychoactive chemical base of the drug, and then smoked. Ether, however, is highly flammable.

Next to marijuana, cocaine is the most widely used illicit drug in the United States. Nearly 3% (2.7%) of adults aged 15 to 54 have a history of cocaine dependence (Anthony et al., 1994). According to one estimate, between 10% and 15% of people who try snorting cocaine eventually develop cocaine abuse or dependence (Gawin, 1991).

The cocaine epidemic may have peaked in some respects. Although the numbers of casual users of cocaine have greatly declined, there has been no corresponding reduction in the numbers of hard-core users.

Effects of Cocaine Like heroin, cocaine directly stimulates the brain's reward or pleasure circuits (Volkow et al., 1997). It also produces a sudden rise in blood pressure, constricts blood vessels (with associated reduction of the oxygen supply to the heart), and accelerates the heart rate. Overdoses can produce restlessness, insomnia, headaches, nausea, convulsions, tremors, hallucinations, delusions, and even sudden death due to respiratory or cardiovascular collapse. Although intravenous use of cocaine carries the greatest risk of a lethal overdose, other forms of use can be fatal as well. Table 9.3 summarizes a number of the health risks of cocaine use.

Repeated use and high-dose use of cocaine can lead to depression and anxiety. Depression may be severe enough to prompt suicidal behavior. Both initial and routine users report episodes of "crashing" (feelings of depression after a binge), although crashing is more common among long-term high-dose users. Psychotic behaviors, which can be induced by cocaine use as well as by use of amphetamines, tend to become more severe with continued use. Cocaine psychosis is usually preceded by a period of heightened suspiciousness, depressed mood, compulsive behavior, faultfinding, irritability, and increasing paranoia (Weiss & Mirin, 1987). The psychosis may also include intense visual and auditory hallucinations and delusions of persecution.

Nicotine Habitual smoking is not merely a bad habit: It is also a physical addiction to a stimulant drug, nicotine, found in tobacco products including cigarettes, cigars, and smokeless tobacco (American Cancer Society, 2004). More than 400,000 lives in the United States are lost each year from tobacco-related diseases, mostly from lung cancer, cardiovascular disease, and chronic obstructive lung disease (Zickler, 2004). The World Health Organization estimates that 1 billion people worldwide smoke, and more than 3 million die each year from smoking-related causes. Largely because of health concerns, the percentage of Americans who smoke declined from 42% in 1966 to about 25% today. On the other hand, rates of teenage smoking have been on the rise, portending increasing rates of adult smoking and the consequent risks of premature deaths.

It may surprise you to learn that more women die of lung cancer than any other type of cancer, including breast cancer (Springen, 2004). More than 85% of women with

crack The hardened, smokable form of cocaine.

TABLE 9.3

Health Risks of Cocaine Use

Physical Effects and Risks

Effects	Risks
Increased heart rate	Accelerated heart rate may give rise to heart irregularities that can be fatal, such as ventricular tachycardia (extremely rapid contractions) or ventricular fibrillation (irregular, weakened contractions).
Increased blood pressure	Rapid or large changes in blood pressure may place too much stress on a weak-walled blood vessel in the brain, which can cause it to burst, producing cerebral hemorrhage or stroke.
Increased body temperature	Can be dangerous to some individuals.
Possible grand mal seizures (epileptic convulsions)	Some grand mal seizures are fatal, particularly when they occur in rapid succession or while driving a car.
Respiratory effects	Overdoses can produce gasping or shallow, irregular breathing that can lead to respiratory arrest.
Dangerous effects in special populations	Various special populations are at greater risk from cocaine use or overdose. People with coronary heart disease have died because their heart muscles were taxed beyond the capacity of their arteries to supply oxygen.

Medical Complications of Cocaine Use

Nasal problems	When cocaine is administered intranasally (snorted), it constricts the blood vessels serving the nose, decreasing the supply of oxygen to these tissues, leading to irritation and inflammation of the mucous membranes, ulcers in the nostrils, frequent nosebleeds, and chronic sneezing and nasal congestion. Chronic use may lead to tissue death of the nasal septum, the part of the nose that separates the nostrils, requiring plastic surgery.
Lung problems	Freebase smoking may lead to serious lung problems within 3 months of initial use.
Malnutrition	Cocaine suppresses the appetite so that weight loss, malnutrition, and vitamin deficiencies may accompany regular use.
Seizures	Grand mal seizures, typical of epileptics, may occur due to irregularities in the electrical activity of the brain. Repeated use may lower the seizure threshold, described as a type of "kindling" effect.
Sexual problems	Despite the popular belief that cocaine is an aphrodisiac, frequent use can lead to sexual dysfunctions, such as impotence and failure to ejaculate among males, and decreased sexual interest in both sexes. Although some people report initial increased sexual pleasure with cocaine use, they may become dependent on cocaine for sexual arousal or lose the ability to enjoy sex for extended periods following long-term use.
Other Effects	Cocaine use may increase the risk of miscarriage among pregnant women. Sharing of infected needles is associated with transmission of hepatitis, endocarditis (infection of the heart valve), and HIV. Repeated injections often lead to skin infections as bacteria are introduced into the deeper levels of the skin.

Source: Adapted from Weiss & Mirin (1987).

breast cancer are current or former smokers. Although quitting smoking clearly has health benefits for women and men, it unfortunately does not reduce the risks to normal (nonsmoking) levels. The lesson is clear: If you don't smoke, don't start; but if you do smoke, quit.

Ethnic differences in smoking rates are shown in Figure 9.3. With the exception of Native Americans (American Indian/Alaskan Native), women in each ethnic group are less likely to smoke than their male counterparts. Figure 9.4 shows relationships between smoking rates and income and educational levels. Note how smoking is disproportionately represented among the poorer and less educated segments of the population (Figure 9.4).

Nicotine is delivered to the body through the use of tobacco products. As a stimulant it increases alertness but can also give rise to cold, clammy skin, nausea and vomiting, dizziness and faintness, and diarrhea—all of which account for the discomforts of novice

TRUTH or FICTION? REVISITED

Breast cancer is the leading cause of cancer deaths among U.S. women.

☑ **FALSE.** Lung cancer has surpassed breast cancer as the leading cancer killer among women. It is also the leading cancer killer among men. Cigarette smoking is the culprit in the great majority of cases.

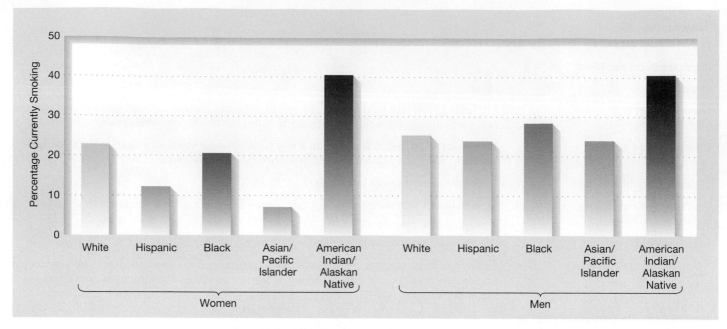

FIGURE 9.3 Ethnic and gender differences in rates of cigarette smoking among U.S. adults.

Smoking rates are highest for Native American men and women. Women in each ethnic group (with the exception of Native Americans) are less likely to smoke than their male counterparts.

Source: National Health Interview Surveys, Centers for Disease Control and Prevention, 2003.

smokers. Nicotine also stimulates the release of epinephrine, a hormone that generates a rush of autonomic activity, including rapid heartbeat and release of stores of sugar into the blood. Nicotine quells the appetite and provides a psychological "kick." Nicotine also leads to the release of endorphins, the opiatelike hormones produced in the brain. This may account for the pleasurable feelings associated with tobacco use.

Habitual use of nicotine leads to a physiological dependence on the drug. Nicotine dependence is associated with both tolerance (intake rises to a level of a pack or two a day before leveling off) and a characteristic withdrawal syndrome. The withdrawal syndrome for nicotine includes such features as lack of energy, depressed mood, irritability, frustration, nervousness, impaired concentration, lightheadedness and dizziness, drowsiness, headaches, fatigue, irregular bowels, insomnia, cramps, lowered heart rate, heart palpitations, increased appetite, weight gain, sweating, tremors, and craving for cigarettes (APA, 2000). It is nicotine dependence, not cigarette smoking per se, that is classifiable as a mental disorder in the *DSM* system. The great majority of regular smokers (80% to 90%) meet diagnostic criteria for nicotine dependence (APA, 2000).

Hallucinogens

Hallucinogens, also known as *psychedelics,* are a class of drugs that produce sensory distortions or hallucinations, including major alterations in color perception and hearing. Hallucinogens may also have additional effects, such as relaxation and euphoria or, in some cases, panic.

The hallucinogens include lysergic acid diethylamide (LSD), psilocybin, and mescaline. Psychoactive substances that are similar in effect to psychedelic drugs are marijuana (cannabis) and phencyclidine (PCP). Mescaline is derived from the peyote cactus and has been used for centuries by Native Americans in the Southwest, Mexico, and Central America in religious ceremonies, as has psilocybin, which is derived from certain mushrooms. LSD, PCP, and marijuana are the most commonly used hallucinogens in the United States.

TRUTH or FICTION? *REVISITED*

Habitual smoking is just a bad habit, not a physical addiction.

☑ **FALSE.** Habitual smoking involves physical addiction to nicotine, the stimulant drug found in tobacco.

hallucinogens Substances that cause hallucinations.

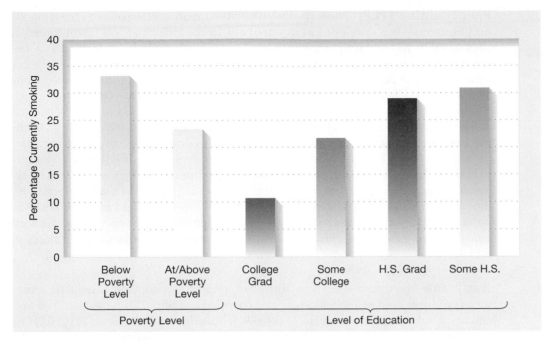

FIGURE 9.4 Cigarette smokers in the United States in relation to poverty status and level of education.
Smoking is becoming increasingly more prevalent among the poorer and less-educated members of society.

Source: Centers for Disease Control (2001a), and *Health, United States,* 2003, Centers for Disease Control and Prevention, National Center for Health Statistics, National Health Survey Interview.

Although tolerance to hallucinogens may develop, we lack evidence of a consistent or clinically significant withdrawal syndrome associated with their use (APA, 2000). Cravings following withdrawal may occur, however.

LSD LSD is the acronym for *lysergic acid diethylamide,* a synthetic hallucinogenic drug. In addition to the vivid parade of colors and visual distortions produced by LSD, users have claimed it "expands consciousness" and opens new worlds—as if they were looking into some reality beyond the usual reality. Sometimes they believe they have achieved great insights during the LSD "trip," but when it wears off they usually cannot follow through or even summon up these discoveries.

The effects of LSD are unpredictable and depend on the amount taken as well as the user's expectations, personality, mood, and surroundings. The user's prior experiences with the drug may also play a role, as users who have learned to handle the effects of the drug through past experience may be better prepared than new users.

Some users have unpleasant experiences with the drug, or "bad trips." Feelings of intense fear or panic may occur (USDHHS, 1992). Users may fear losing control or sanity. Some experience terrifying fears of death. Fatal accidents have sometimes occurred during LSD trips. *Flashbacks,* typically involving a reexperiencing of some of the perceptual distortions of the "trip," may occur days, weeks, or even years afterward. Flashbacks tend to occur suddenly and often without warning. Perceptual distortions may involve geometric forms, flashes of color, intensified colors, afterimages, or appearances of halos around objects, among others (APA, 2000). They may stem from chemical changes in the brain caused by the prior use of the drug. Triggers for flashbacks include entry into darkened environments, drug use, anxiety or fatigue states, or stress (APA, 2000). Psychological factors, such as underlying personality problems, may also explain why some users experience flashbacks. In some cases, a flashback may involve an imagined reenactment of the LSD experience.

Phencyclidine (PCP) Phencyclidine, or PCP—which is referred to as "angel dust" on the streets—was developed as an anesthetic in the 1950s but was discontinued as such when its hallucinatory side effects were discovered. A smokable form of PCP became popular as a street drug in the 1970s. By the mid-1980s, more than one in five young people in the 18 to 25 age range had used PCP (USDHHS, 1986). However, its popularity has since waned, largely because of its unpredictable effects.

The effects of PCP, like most drugs, are dose related. In addition to causing hallucinations, PCP accelerates the heart rate and blood pressure and causes sweating, flushing, and numbness. PCP is classified as a *deliriant*—a drug capable of producing states of delirium. It also has dissociating effects, causing users to feel as if there is some sort of invisible barrier between themselves and their environments. Dissociation can be experienced as pleasant, engrossing, or frightening, depending on the user's expectations, mood, setting, and so on. Overdoses can give rise to drowsiness and a blank stare, convulsions, and, now and then, coma; paranoia and aggressive behavior; and tragic accidents resulting from perceptual distortion or impaired judgment during states of intoxication.

marijuana A hallucinogenic drug derived from the leaves and stems of the plant *Cannabis sativa*.

Marijuana Marijuana is derived from the *Cannabis sativa* plant. Marijuana sometimes produces mild hallucinations, so it is regarded as a minor hallucinogen. The psychoactive substance in marijuana is delta-9-tetrahydrocannabinol, or THC. THC is found in branches and leaves of the plant but is highly concentrated in the resin of the female plant. *Hashish,* or "hash," also derived from the resin, is more potent than marijuana but has similar effects.

Use of marijuana exploded throughout the so-called swinging 1960s and the 1970s, but the drug then lost some (but not all) of its cachet. Still, marijuana remains our most widely used illegal drug, and abuse of marijuana is the most common of all the substance abuse disorders involving illicit drugs (Compton et al., 2004). That said, the prevalence of use and abuse of marijuana doesn't compare with alcohol's.

Approximately 33% of people in the United States age 12 or older, nearly 70 million people, have tried marijuana at least once in their lives, and about 4% or 5% are current users (Compton et al., 2004; USDHHS, 1993). About 1.5% of the U.S. adult population suffers from a marijuana abuse or dependence disorder (Compton et al., 2004). Males are more likely than females to develop a marijuana abuse or dependence disorder, and rates of these disorders are greatest among people age 18 to 30 (APA, 2000).

Low doses of the drug can produce relaxing feelings similar to drinking alcohol. Some users report that at low doses the drug makes them feel more comfortable in social gatherings. Higher doses, however, often lead users to withdraw into themselves. Some users believe the drug increases their capacity for self-insight or creative thinking, although the insights achieved under its influence may not seem so insightful once the drug's effects have passed. People may turn to marijuana, as to other drugs, to help them cope with life problems or to help them function when they are under stress. Strongly intoxicated people perceive time as passing more slowly. A song of a few minutes may seem to last an hour. There is increased awareness of bodily sensations, such as heartbeat. Smokers also report that strong intoxication heightens sexual sensations. Visual hallucinations may occur.

Strong intoxication can cause smokers to become disoriented. If their moods are euphoric, disorientation may be construed as harmony with the universe. Yet some smokers find strong intoxication disturbing. An accelerated heart rate and sharpened awareness of bodily sensations cause some smokers to fear their hearts will "run away" with them. Some smokers are frightened by disorientation and fear they will not "come back." High levels of intoxication now and then induce nausea and vomiting.

Cannabis dependence is associated more with patterns of compulsive use or psychological dependence than with physiological dependence. Although tolerance to many of the drug's effects may occur with chronic use, some users report reverse tolerance, or *sensitization*. Though a clear-cut withdrawal syndrome has not been reliably demonstrated, research with animals points to some disturbing similarities between marijuana and addictive drugs like heroin and cocaine. For example, investigators found that withdrawal from marijuana activated the same brain circuits involved in withdrawal from opioids, alcohol, and cocaine (Rodríguez de Fonseca et al., 1997).

College students who are heavy users of marijuana show evidence of intellectual impairment, including diminished ability in tasks requiring attention, abstraction, and mental flexibility (Pope & Yurgelun-Todd, 1996). But the question of whether regular use of marijuana causes cognitive deficits remains unsettled (Gunderson, Vosburg, & Hart, 2002; Pope, 2002). We can't yet say whether such deficits are due to the drug or to characteristics of people who become heavy users.

Evidence also links marijuana use to later use of harder drugs such as heroin and cocaine (Kandel, 2002, 2003; "Marijuana Leads, "2002). Whether marijuana use is a causal factor leading to use of harder drugs remains unclear. We should also note that marijuana use in adolescence is linked to greater risk of depression, anxiety, and even schizophrenia in young adulthood, although again we must caution that cause-and-effect relationships have not been teased out (Arseneault et al., 2002; Patton et al., 2002; Rey & Tennant, 2002; Zammit et al., 2002).

We do know that marijuana impairs perception and motor coordination and thus makes driving and the operation of other heavy machinery dangerous. It can also impair short-term memory and learning ability (Ashton, 2001; Solowij et al., 2002; Verhovek, 2000). Although marijuana use induces positive mood changes in many users, some people report anxiety and confusion; there are also occasional reports of paranoia or psychotic reactions (Johns, 2001). Marijuana elevates heart rate and blood pressure and is linked to an increased risk of heart attacks in people with heart disease ("Another Worry," 2000). Finally, marijuana smoke contains carcinogenic hydrocarbons, so chronic users risk lung cancer and other respiratory diseases (Iversen, 2000).

THEORETICAL PERSPECTIVES

People begin using psychoactive substances for various reasons. Some adolescents start using drugs because of peer pressure or because they believe drugs make them seem more sophisticated or grown up. Some use drugs as a way of rebelling against their parents or society at large. Regardless of why people get started with drugs, they continue to use them because drugs produce pleasurable effects or because they find it difficult to stop. Most adolescents drink alcohol to "get high," not to establish that they are adults. Many people smoke cigarettes for the pleasure they provide. Others smoke to help them relax when they are tense and, paradoxically, to give them a kick or a lift when they are tired. Many would like to quit but find it difficult to break their addiction.

People who are anxious about their jobs or social lives may be drawn to the calming effects of alcohol, marijuana (in certain doses), tranquilizers, and sedatives. People with low self-confidence and self-esteem may be drawn to the ego-bolstering effects of amphetamines and cocaine. Many poor young people attempt to escape the poverty, anguish, and tedium of inner-city life through using heroin and similar drugs. More well-to-do adolescents may rely on drugs to manage the transition from dependence to independence and major life changes concerning jobs, college, and lifestyles.

In the next sections we consider several major theoretical perspectives on substance abuse and dependence.

Biological Perspectives

We are beginning to learn more about the biological underpinnings of drug use and addiction. Much of the recent research has focused on neurotransmitters, especially dopamine, and on the role of genetic factors.

Neurotransmitters Many psychoactive drugs, such as nicotine, alcohol, amphetamines, heroin, cocaine, and even marijuana, produce pleasurable effects by increasing levels of dopamine in the brain's pleasure or reward circuits—the network of neurons responsible for the pleasurable feelings we experience from sexual stimulation, or

Substance Abuse:
Therapist Jean Obert
"Being addicted to heroin is one of the most difficult things to kick."

winning a sporting event, or even eating a scrumptious dessert (Friedman, 2002; Kauer, 2003; Leyton et al., 2002). The feelings of pleasure from using these drugs may range from mild happiness to euphoria.

But what of long-term use? Investigators suspect that chronic drug use damages brain circuits that produce feelings of pleasure (Begley, 2001b; "Cocaine Use," 2003). It may also reduce the brain's ability to produce dopamine on its own (Blakeslee, 1997a). Consequently, the ability to derive pleasure from activities of everyday life, such as having a good meal or attending an enjoyable movie, wanes. The chronic drug user comes to rely on drugs to produce feelings of pleasure that the brain no longer produces on its own and to avoid depression, anxiety, and other disturbing feelings. Without drugs, life may not seem to be worth living. These changes in the dopamine system may explain the intense cravings and anxiety that accompany drug withdrawal and the difficulty people have maintaining abstinence. The biochemical bases of drug use and abuse are complex and appear to involve other neurotransmitters besides dopamine. For example, researchers suspect that serotonin may also activate the brain's pleasure or reward circuits in response to cocaine, alcohol, and other drug use (Begley, 2001b; Rocha et al., 1998).

We also know that endorphins have pain-blocking properties similar to those of opioids such as heroin. Endorphins and opiates dock at the same receptor sites in the brain. Normally, the brain produces a certain level of endorphins that maintains a psychological steady state of comfort and potential to experience pleasure. However, when the body becomes habituated to a supply of opioids, it may stop producing endorphins. This makes the user dependent on opiates for comfort, relief from pain, and pleasure. When the habitual user stops using heroin or other opiates, feelings of discomfort and little aches and pains may be magnified until the body resumes adequate production of endorphins. This discomfort may account, at least in part, for the unpleasant withdrawal symptoms that opiate addicts experience. However, this model remains speculative, and more research is needed to document direct relationships between endorphin production and withdrawal symptoms.

Genetic Factors Evidence links genetic factors to various forms of substance use and abuse, including alcohol abuse and dependence, opiate addiction, and even cigarette smoking (Kendler Thornton, & Pederson, 2000; Nurnberger et al., 2001; Rhee et al., 2003; Slutske et al., 2002). Investigators have begun the hunt for specific genes involved in alcohol and drug abuse and dependence (e.g., Wall et al., 2003). We focus on alcohol dependence, because this has been the area of the greatest research interest.

Alcoholism tends to run in families (APA, 2000; Wood et al., 2001). The closer the genetic relationship, the greater the risk. Familial patterns provide only suggestive evidence of genetic factors, because families share a common environment as well as common genes. More definitive evidence comes from twin and adoptee studies.

Monozygotic (MZ) twins have identical genes, whereas fraternal or dizygotic (DZ) twins share only half of their genes. If genetic factors are involved, we would expect MZ twins to have higher concordance (agreement) rates for alcoholism than DZ twins. Evidence of higher concordance rates for alcoholism is found among MZ twins than DZ twins, although the results are more consistent for male samples than female samples (Wood et al., 2001).

A limitation of twin studies is that MZ twins may share more environmental as well as genetic similarity than DZ twins. That is, they may be treated more alike than DZ twins. However, evidence also shows that male adoptees whose biological parents suffered from alcoholism have an increased risk of developing alcoholism themselves, even if they are raised in nondrinking homes (Gordis, 1995; Schuckit, 1987). Among women, however, the rate of alcoholism in adopted-away daughters of parents with alcoholism is only slightly higher than that for adopted-away daughters of nonalcoholics, thus casting doubt on a strong genetic linkage to alcoholism in women (Svikis, Velez, & Pickens, 1994). All in all, genetic factors are believed to play a moderate role in male alcoholism and a modest role in female alcoholism (McGue, 1993).

If alcoholism or other forms of substance abuse and dependence are influenced by genetic factors, what exactly is inherited? Some clues are emerging. Researchers have linked alcoholism, nicotine dependence, and opioid addiction to genes that determine the structure of dopamine receptors in the brain (Kotler, 1997). As we've noted, dopamine is involved in regulating states of pleasure, so one possibility is that genetic factors enhance feelings of pleasure derived from alcohol. Other evidence suggests that a genetic vulnerability to alcoholism represents a combination of factors, such as reaping greater pleasure from alcohol and a capacity for greater biological tolerance for the drug (Pihl, Peterson, & Finn, 1990; Pollock, 1992). People who can tolerate larger doses of alcohol without incurring upset stomachs, dizziness, and headaches may have difficulty knowing when to stop drinking. Thus people who are better able to "hold their liquor" may be at greater risk of developing drinking problems. They may need to rely on other cues, such as counting their drinks, to limit their drinking. People whose bodies more readily "put the brakes" on excess drinking may be less likely to develop problems in moderating their drinking.

Whatever the role of heredity in alcohol and substance dependence, investigators recognize that genes interact with environmental factors (Kendler, Jacobson et al., 2003). For example, being raised in an environment free of parental alcoholism is associated with a lower risk of alcohol-related disorders in people at high genetic risk of these disorders (Jacob et al., 2003). Many researchers today believe that multiple genes acting together with social, cultural, and psychological factors contribute to the the development of alcoholism and other forms of substance dependence (e.g., Dick et al., 2001).

Learning Perspectives

Learning theorists propose that substance-related behaviors are largely learned and can, in principle, be unlearned. They focus on the roles of operant and classical conditioning and observational learning. Substance abuse problems are not regarded as symptoms of disease but rather as problem habits. Although learning theorists do not deny that genetic or biological factors may increase susceptiblity to substance abuse problems, but they emphasize the role of learning in the development and maintenance of these problem behaviors (McCrady, 1993, 1994). They also recognize that people who suffer from depression or anxiety may turn to alcohol as a way of relieving these troubling emotional states, however briefly. Evidence shows that emotional stress, such as anxiety or depression, often sets the stage for the development of substance abuse (Dixit & Crum, 2000; McGue, Slutske, & Iaono, 1999).

Drug use may become habitual because of the pleasure (positive reinforcement) or temporary relief from negative emotions like anxiety and depression, that drugs can produce. With drugs like cocaine, which appear capable of directly stimulating pleasure mechanisms in the brain, the positive reinforcement is direct and powerful.

Operant Conditioning People may initially use a drug because of social influence, trial and error, or social observation. In the case of alcohol, they learn that the drug can produce reinforcing effects, such as feelings of euphoria, and reductions in anxiety and tension. Alcohol may also reduce behavioral inhibitions. Alcohol can thus be reinforcing when it is used to combat depression (by producing euphoric feelings, even if short lived), to combat tension (by functioning as a tranquilizer), or to help people sidestep moral conflicts (for example, by dulling awareness of moral prohibitions). Substance abuse may also provide social reinforcers, such as the approval of drug-abusing companions and, in the cases of alcohol and stimulants, the (temporary) overcoming of social shyness.

Alcohol and Tension Reduction Learning theorists have long maintained that one of the primary reinforcers for using alcohol is relief from states of tension or unpleasant states of arousal (Hussong et al., 2001; Wood et al., 2001). The *tension-reduction theory* proposes that the more often one drinks to reduce tension or anxiety, the stronger or more habitual the habit becomes. Viewed in this way, alcohol use can be likened to a form of self-medication, a way of easing psychological pain, at least temporarily, as in the following case example.

"I" Taking Away the Hurt I Feel

"I use them (the pills and alcohol) to take away the hurt I feel inside." Joceyln, a 36-year-old mother of two, was physically abused by her husband, Phil. "I have no self-esteem. I just don't feel I can do anything," she told her therapist. Jocelyn had escaped from an abusive family background by getting married at age 17, hoping that marriage would offer her a better life. The first few years were free of abuse, but things changed when Phil lost his job and began to drink heavily. By then, Jocelyn had two young children and felt trapped. She blamed herself for her unhappy family life, for Phil's drinking, for her son's learning disability. "The only thing I can do is drink or do pills. At least then I don't have to think about things for awhile." Though drug use temporarily dulled her emotional pain, it came with a greater long-term cost in terms of the burden of addiction.

—From the Authors' Files

Drugs, including nicotine from cigarette smoking, may be used as a form of self-medication for depression (Breslau et al., 1998). Stimulants like nicotine temporarily elevate the mood, whereas depressants like alcohol quell anxiety. Although nicotine, alcohol, and other drugs may temporarily alleviate emotional distress, they cannot resolve underlying personal or emotional problems. Rather than learning to resolve these problems, people who use drugs as forms of self-medication often find themselves facing additional substance-related problems.

Negative Reinforcement and Withdrawal Once people become physiologically dependent, negative reinforcement comes into play in maintaining the drug habit. In other words, people may resume using drugs to gain relief from unpleasant withdrawal symptoms. In operant conditioning terms, relief from unpleasant withdrawal symptoms is a negative reinforcer for resuming drug use (Higgins, Heil, & Lussier, 2004). For example, the addicted smoker who quits cold turkey may shortly return to smoking to fend off the discomfort of withdrawal.

The Conditioning Model of Cravings Classical conditioning may help explain drug cravings. In this view, cravings reflect the body's need to restore high blood levels of the addictive substance and thus have a biological basis. But they also come to be associated

Self-medication? People who turn to other drugs or alcohol to quell disturbing emotions can compound their problems by developing a substance use disorder.

with environmental cues associated with prior use of the substance (Kilts et al., 2001, 2004). These cues, such as the sight or aroma of an alcoholic beverage or the sight of a needle and syringe, become conditioned stimuli that elicit a conditioned response: strong cravings for the drug. For example, socializing with certain companions ("drinking buddies") or even passing a liquor store may elicit conditioned cravings for alcohol. In support of this theory, alcoholic subjects show distinctive changes in brain activity in areas of the brain that regulate emotion, attention, and appetitive behavior when shown pictures of alcoholic beverages (George et al., 2001). Social drinkers, by comparison, do not show this pattern of brain activation.

Sensations of anxiety or depression that are paired with the use of alcohol or drugs may also elicit cravings. The following case illustrates conditioned cravings to environmental cues.

A Case of Conditioned Drug Cravings

A 29-year-old man was hospitalized for the treatment of heroin addiction. After four weeks of treatment, he returned to his former job, which required him to ride the subway past the stop at which he had previously bought his drugs. Each day, when the subway doors opened at this location, [he] experienced enormous craving for heroin, accompanied by tearing, a runny nose, abdominal cramps, and gooseflesh. After the doors closed, his symptoms disappeared, and he went on to work.

—From Weiss & Mirin, 1987, p. 71

Similarly, some people are primarily "stimulus smokers." They reach for a cigarette in the presence of smoking-related stimuli, such as seeing someone smoke or smelling smoke. Smoking becomes a strongly conditioned habit because it is paired repeatedly with many situational cues—watching TV, finishing dinner, driving in the car, studying, drinking or socializing with friends, sex, and, for some, using the bathroom.

The conditioning model of craving receives support from research showing that people with alcoholism tend to salivate more than others at the sight and smell of alcohol (Monti et al., 1987). Pavlov's classic experiment conditioned a salivation response in dogs by repeatedly pairing the sound of a bell (a conditioned stimulus) with the presentation of food powder (an unconditioned stimulus). Salivation among people who develop alcoholism can also be viewed as a conditioned response to alcohol-related cues. People with drinking problems who show the greatest salivary response to alcohol cues may be at highest risk of relapse. They may also profit from conditioning-based treatments designed to extinguish responses to alcohol-related cues.

One such treatment, called *cue exposure training,* holds promise in the treatment of alcohol dependence (e.g., Dawe et al., 2002). In cue exposure treatment, the person is repeatedly seated in front of alcohol-related cues, such as open alcoholic beverages, while prevented from drinking. The pairing of the cue (alcohol bottle) with nonreinforcement (by dint of preventing drinking) may lead to extinction of the conditioned craving. However, cravings often return after treatment when people return to their usual environments (Collins & Brandon, 2002; Havermans & Jansen, 2003).

Observational Learning   The role of modeling or observational learning may partly explain the increased risk of substance abuse problems in adolescents whose families show a history of similar problems (Kilpatrick et al., 2000). For example, parents who model inappropriate or excessive drinking may set the stage for alcohol use and abuse in their children. Researchers find that young men from families with a history of alcoholism are more strongly affected by exposure to others who modeled excessive drinking than are men without familial alcoholism (Chipperfield & Vogel-Sprott, 1988). When their drinking companions drink to excess, these men may be more likely to follow their lead.

Cognitive Perspectives

Evidence supports the role of cognitive factors in substance abuse and dependence, especially the role of expectancies. Expectancies about the perceived benefits of using alcohol or other drugs and smoking cigarettes clearly influence the decision to use these substances (Goldberg, Halpern-Felsher, & Millstein, 2002; Park, 2004; Wiers & Kummeling, 2004). Outcome expectancies in teens—what they expect a drug's effects will be—are strongly influenced by the beliefs of their peers. The degree to which friends hold positive attitudes toward alcohol use is an important factor in alcohol use among adolescents (Scheier, Botvin, & Baker, 1997; Wood et al., 2001). Public health campaigns appear to be having some impact in changing attitudes of young people toward cigarette smoking. In 2001, adolescents in a midwestern community had more negative attitudes toward smoking than did adolescents a generation before (Chassin et al., 2003).

Alcohol or other drug use may also boost *self-efficacy expectations*—personal expectancies we hold about our ability to successfully perform tasks. If we believe that we need a drink or two (or more) to "get out of our shell" and relate socially to others, we may come to depend on alcohol in social situations.

Expectancies may account for the "one-drink effect"—the tendency of chronic alcohol abusers to binge once they have a drink. In a classic study by Marlatt and his colleagues (1973), subjects were led to believe they were participating in a taste test. Alcohol-dependent subjects and social drinkers who were told they were sampling an alcoholic beverage (vodka) drank significantly more than counterparts who were told they were sampling a nonalcoholic beverage (the taste of vodka can be cloaked by tonic water). The expectations of both the alcohol-dependent subjects and the social drinkers were the crucial factors that predicted the amount consumed (see Figure 9.5). *The actual content of the beverages was immaterial.*

Marlatt (1978) explained the one-drink effect as a self-fulfilling prophecy. If people with alcohol-related problems believe that just one drink will cause a loss of control, they perceive the outcome as predetermined when they drink. Their drinking—even taking one drink—may thus escalate into a binge. When individuals who were formerly physiologically dependent on alcohol share this belief—which is endorsed by many groups, including Alcoholics Anonymous (AA)—they may interpret "just one drink" as "falling off the wagon." This expectation is an example of what Aaron Beck refers to as *absolutist thinking.* When we insist on seeing the world in black and white rather than shades of gray, we may interpret one bite of dessert as proof we are off our diets, or one cigarette as proof we are hooked again. Rather than telling ourselves, "Okay, I goofed, but that's it. I don't have to have more," we encode our lapses as catastrophes and transform them into relapses. Still, alcohol-dependent people who believe they may go on a drinking binge if they have just one drink are well advised to abstain.

Psychodynamic Perspectives

According to traditional psychodynamic theory, alcoholism reflects an *oral-dependent personality.* Psychodynamic theory also associates excessive alcohol use with other oral traits, such as dependence and depression, and traces the origins of these traits to fixation in the oral stage of psychosexual development. Excessive drinking or smoking in adulthood symbolizes an individual's efforts to attain oral gratification.

Research support for these psychodynamic concepts is mixed. Although people who develop alcoholism often show dependent traits, it is unclear whether dependence contributes to or stems from problem drinking. Chronic drinking, for example, is connected with loss of employment and downward movement in social status, both of which would render drinkers more reliant on others for support. Moreover, an empirical connection between dependence and alcoholism does not establish that alcoholism represents an oral fixation that can be traced to early development.

Then too, many—but certainly not all—people who suffer from alcoholism have antisocial personalities characterized by independence seeking as expressed through re-

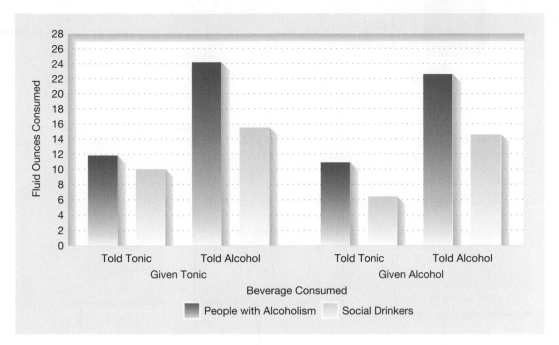

FIGURE 9.5 Must people who develop alcoholism fall off the wagon if they have one drink?
It is widely believed that people who develop alcoholism will lose control if they have just one drink. Will they? If so, why? Laboratory research by Marlatt and his colleagues suggests that the tendency of people who suffer from alcoholism to drink to excess following a first drink may be the result of a self-fulfilling prophecy rather than a craving. Like the dieter who eats a piece of chocolate, people who develop alcoholism may assume that they have lost control because they have fallen off the wagon and then go on a binge. This figure shows that people with alcoholism who participated in the Marlatt study drank more when they were led to believe that the beverage contained alcohol, regardless of its actual content. It remains unclear, however, whether binge drinking by people with alcohol-related problems in real-life settings can be explained as a self-fulfilling prophecy.

Source: Adapted from Marlatt et al. (1973).

belliousness and rejection of social and legal codes. All in all, there doesn't appear to be a single alcoholic personality (Wood et al., 2001).

Sociocultural Perspectives

Drinking is determined, in part, by where we live, whom we worship with, and the social or cultural norms that regulate our behavior. Cultural attitudes can encourage or discourage problem drinking. As we have already seen, rates of alcohol abuse vary across ethnic and religious groups. Let us note some other sociocultural factors. Church attendance, for example, is generally connected with abstinence from alcohol. Perhaps people who are more willing to engage in culturally sanctioned activities, such as churchgoing, are also more likely to adopt culturally sanctioned prohibitions against excessive drinking. Rates of alcohol use also vary across cultures.

Drug and alcohol use by peers and peer pressure are important influences in determining substance use among adolescents (Dishion & Owen, 2002; Simons-Morton et al., 2001). Kids who start drinking before age 15 stand a fivefold higher risk of developing alcohol dependence in adulthood than do teens who began drinking at a later age (Kluger, 2001). Yet studies of Hispanic and African American adolescents show that support from family members can reduce the negative influence of drug-using peers on the adolescent's use of tobacco and other drugs (Farrell & White, 1998; Frauenglass et al., 1997).

Tying It Together

Substance abuse and dependence are complex patterns of behavior that reflect an interplay of biological, psychological, and environmental factors (see Figure 9.6). These problems are best approached by investigating the distinctive constellation of factors that apply to each individual case. No single model or set of factors will explain each case, which is why we need to understand each individual's unique characteristics and personal history.

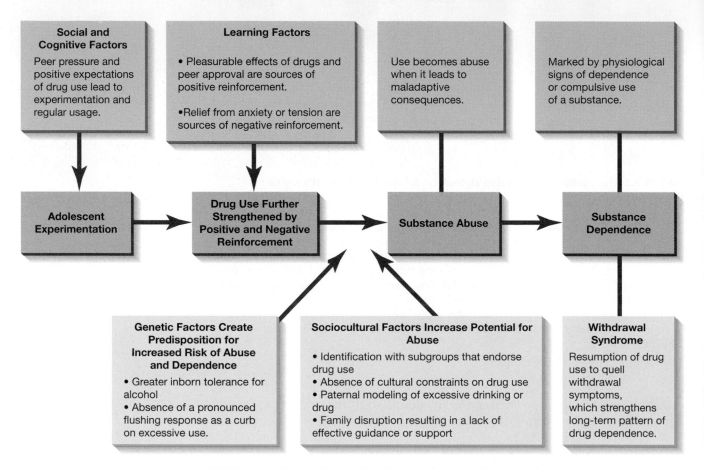

FIGURE 9.6 A biopsychosocial model of substance abuse and dependence

Genetic factors can create a predisposition or diathesis for substance abuse and dependence. Some people may be born with a greater tolerance for alcohol, which can make it difficult for them to regulate use of alcohol—to know "when to say when." Others have genetic tendencies that can lead them to become unusually tense or anxious. Perhaps they turn to alcohol or other drugs to quell their nervousness. Genetic predispositions can interact with environmental factors to increase the potential for drug abuse and dependence—factors such as pressure from peers to use drugs, parental modeling of excessive drinking or drug use, and family disruption that results in a lack of effective guidance or support. Cognitive factors, especially positive drug expectancies (e.g., beliefs that using drugs will enhance one's social skills or sexual prowess), raise the potential for alcohol or drug use problems. In adolescence and adulthood, these positive expectations, together with social pressures and a lack of cultural constraints, affect the young person's decision to begin using drugs and to continue to use them. Patterns of regular use can lead to abuse and dependence. Once physiological dependence develops, people use the substance to avoid withdrawal symptoms.

Sociocultural factors are also included in this matrix of factors: the availability of alcohol and other drugs, the presence or absence of cultural constraints, the glamorizing of drug use in popular media, and inborn tendencies (such as among Asians) to flush more readily following alcohol intake.

Learning factors also play important roles. Drug use may be *positively* reinforced by pleasurable effects (mediated perhaps by release of dopamine in the brain or by activation of endorphin receptors). It may also be *negatively* reinforced by the reduction of tension and anxiety that depressant drugs such as alcohol, heroin, and tranquilizers can produce. In a sad but ironic twist, people who become dependent on drugs may continue to use them solely because of the relief from withdrawal symptoms and cravings they encounter when they go without the drug.

TREATMENT OF SUBSTANCE ABUSE AND DEPENDENCE

There is a vast array of nonprofessional, biological, and psychological approaches to substance abuse and dependence. However, treatment has often been a frustrating endeavor. In many, perhaps most, cases, people with drug dependencies really do not want to stop and do not seek treatment on their own. When people do come for treatment, helping them through a withdrawal syndrome is usually straightforward enough, as we shall see. However, helping them pursue a life devoid of their preferred substances is more problematic. Treatment takes place in a setting—such as the therapist's office, a support group, a residential center, or a hospital—in which abstinence is valued and encouraged. Then the individual returns to the work, family, or street settings in which abuse and dependence were instigated and maintained. The problem of relapse can thus be more troublesome than the problems involved in initial treatment.

Another complication is that many people with substance abuse problems have other psychological disorders as well (McCrady & Langenbucher, 1996; Miller & Brown, 1997).

Peer pressure. Peer pressure is a major influence on alcohol and drug use among adolescents.

Most clinics and treatment programs focus on the drug or alcohol problem, or the other psychological disorders, rather than treating all these problems simultaneously, however. This narrow focus results in poorer treatment outcomes, including more frequent rehospitalizations among those with these *dual diagnoses*. It has been estimated that 20% to 70% of people who have other psychological disorders—and 50% to 70% of the young adults with other psychological disorders—merit a dual diagnosis that includes substance abuse (Polcin, 1992).

Biological Approaches

An increasing range of biological approaches is used in treating problems of substance abuse and dependence. For people with chemical dependencies, biological treatment typically begins with **detoxification**—that is, helping them through withdrawal from addictive substances.

detoxification The process of ridding the system of alcohol or other drugs under supervised conditions.

Detoxification Detoxification is often more safely carried out in a hospital setting. In the case of addiction to alcohol or barbiturates, hospitalization allows medical personnel to monitor and treat potentially dangerous withdrawal symptoms such as convulsions. Antianxiety drugs, such as the benzodiazepines Librium and Valium, may help block severe withdrawal symptoms such as seizures and delirium tremens (Mayo-Smith, 1997). Behavioral treatment using monetary rewards for abstinence (indicated by negative urine samples) can help improve outcomes during detoxification from opioids (Bickel et al., 1997). Detoxification to alcohol takes about a week. Detoxification is an important step toward staying clean, but it is only a start. Approximately half of all drug abusers relapse within a year of detoxification (Cowley, 2001b). Continuing support and structured therapy, such as behavioral counseling, plus possible use of therapeutic drugs, increase the chances of long-term success.

A number of therapeutic drugs are used in treating people with chemical dependencies, and more chemical compounds are in the testing stage (Kranzler, 2000). Here we survey some of the major drugs in use today.

Disulfiram The drug *disulfiram* (brand name Antabuse) discourages alcohol consumption because the combination of the two produces a violent response consisting of nausea, headache, heart palpitations, and vomiting (Kalb, 2001a). In some extreme cases, combining disulfiram and alcohol can produce such a dramatic drop in blood pressure that the individual goes into shock or even dies. Although disulfiram has been used widely in alcoholism treatment, its effectiveness is limited because many patients who want to continue drinking simply stop using the drug. Others stop taking the drug because they believe that they can remain abstinent without it. Unfortunately, many return to uncontrolled drinking. Another drawback is that the drug has toxic effects in people with liver disease, a frequent ailment of people who suffer from alcoholism. Little evidence supports the efficacy of the drug in the long run (Garbutt et al., 1999; Schuckit, 1996).

Antidepressants Antidepressants show promise in reducing cravings for cocaine following withdrawal. These drugs stimulate neural processes that promote feelings of pleasure derived from everyday experiences. If cocaine users can feel pleasure from nondrug-related activities, they may be less likely to return to using cocaine. However, antidepressants have yet to produce consistent results in reducing relapse rates for cocaine dependence, so it is best to withhold judgment concerning their efficacy.

Serotonin deficiencies may contribute to cravings for alcohol. Research on the use of serotonin-reuptake inhibitors, such as Prozac, to curb alcohol consumption is underway (B. A. Johnson et al., 2000; Kranzler, 2000). Because the actions of dopamine may account for the pleasurable or euphoric effects of alcohol, drugs that mimic dopamine may be helpful in blocking the pleasurably reinforcing effects of alcohol.

Nicotine Replacement Therapy Most regular smokers, perhaps the great majority, are nicotine dependent. The use of nicotine replacements in the form of prescription gum (brand name Nicorette), transdermal (skin) patches, lozenges and a recently ap-

Is the path to abstinence from smoking skin deep? Forms of nicotine replacement therapy—such as nicotine transdermal (skin) patches and chewing gum that contains nicotine—allow people to continue to take in nicotine when they quit smoking. Though nicotine replacement therapy is more effective than a placebo in helping people quit smoking, it does not address the behavioral components of addiction to nicotine, such as the habit of smoking while drinking alcohol. For this reason, nicotine replacement therapy may be more effective if it is combined with behavior therapy that focuses on changing smoking habits.

proved nasal spray can help smokers avoid unpleasant withdrawal symptoms and cravings for cigarettes ("FDA Approves," 2002; Shiffman et al., 2002; Tiffany, Cox, & Elash, 2000). After quitting smoking, ex-smokers can gradually wean themselves from the nicotine replacement.

Evidence shows that nicotine chewing gum and the nicotine patch are effective aids in quitting smoking (e.g., O'Brien & McKay, 1998; Skaar et al., 1997). The scientific jury is still out on nicotine nasal sprays. Though nicotine replacement may help quell the physiological components of withdrawal, it has no effect on the behavioral patterns of addiction, such as the habit of smoking while drinking alcohol or socializing. As a result, nicotine replacement may be ineffective in promoting long-term changes unless it is combined with behavioral therapy that focuses on fostering adaptive behavioral changes.

The antidepressant drug *bupropion* (trade name Zyban) is used to blunt cravings for nicotine in much the same way that other antidepressants are being used to reduce cocaine cravings. The drug has a modest benefit in helping people quit smoking successfully (Ahluwalia et al., 2002; Benowitz, 2002).

Methadone Maintenance Programs Methadone is a synthetic opiate that blunts cravings for heroin and helps curb the unpleasant symptoms that accompany withdrawal (P. G. O'Connor, 2000; Sees, 2000). Because methadone in normal doses does not produce a high or leave the user feeling drugged, it can help heroin addicts hold jobs and get their lives back on track (Fiellin et al., 2001; R. E. Johnson et al., 2000). However, like other opioids, methadone is highly addictive. For this reason, people treated with methadone are really substituting dependence on one drug for dependence on another. Yet because most methadone programs are publicly financed, they relieve people who are addicted to heroin of the need to engage in criminal activity to support their drug dependence. Methadone programs need to be strictly monitored because overdoses can be lethal, and the drug can become abused as a street drug (Belluck, 2003).

An estimated 200,000 heroin addicts in the U.S. participate in methadone programs, with marked public health benefits (Markel, 2002). The annual death rate from opioid dependence declined from 21 per 1,000 before the introduction of methadone maintenance to 13 per 1,000 afterward (Krantz & Mehler, 2004). Although methadone can be taken indefinitely, individuals may be weaned from it without returning to heroin. Methadone treatment produces clear benefits in improved daily functioning, but not everyone succeeds with methadone, even with counseling. Some addicts turn to other drugs such as cocaine to get high or return to using heroin. Others drop out of methadone programs.

Still another synthetic opiate drug that is chemically similar to morphine, *buprenorphine*, blocks withdrawal symptoms and cravings without producing a strong narcotic high (Clark, 2003). Many treatment providers prefer buprenorphine to methadone because it produces less of a sedative effective and can be taken in pill form only three times a week, whereas methadone is given in liquid form daily. Another synthetic antiopiate, *levomethadyl,* also lasts longer than methadone and can be dispensed three times a week (Krantz & Mehler, 2004). For maximum effectiveness, pharmacotherapy with methadone or other drugs should be combined with psychological counseling and psychosocial rehabilitation (P. G. O'Connor, 2000; E. O'Connor, 2001a; Rounsaville & Kosten, 2000).

Naltrexone Naltrexone is a drug that blocks the high produced by alcohol and by opioids, such as heroin. The drug doesn't prevent the person from taking a drink or using heroin, but seems to blunt cravings for these drugs (Kalb, 2001a). Evidence shows that naltrexone and similar drugs may be useful in preventing relapse following withdrawal from alcohol or opiates (Anton et al., 2001; Dettmer et al., 2001; Kiefer et al., 2003). By blocking the pleasure produced by alcohol, the drug can help break the vicious cycle in which one drink creates a desire for another, leading to episodes of binge drinking.

A nagging problem with drugs such as naltrexone, disulfiram, and methadone is that people with substance abuse problems may simply stop using them and return to their substance-abusing behavior. Nor do such drugs provide alternative sources of positive reinforcement that can replace the pleasurable states produced by drugs of abuse. These

methadone An artificial narcotic that is used to help people who are addicted to heroin to abstain from it without a withdrawal syndrome.

TRUTH or FICTION? *REVISITED*

A widely used treatment for heroin addiction involves substituting another addictive drug.

☑ **TRUE.** Methadone, a synthetic narcotic, is widely used in treating heroin addiction.

naltrexone A drug that blocks the high from alcohol as well as from opiates.

Culturally sensitive treatment. Culturally sensitive therapy or treatment addresses all aspects of the person, including ethnic factors and the nurturance of pride in one's cultural identity. Ethnic pride may help people resist the temptation to cope with stress through alcohol and other substances.

drugs are effective only in the context of a broader treatment program consisting of psychological counseling and life-skills components, such as job training, and stress management training. These treatments provide people with the skills they need to embark on a life in the mainstream culture and to find drug-free outlets for coping with stress (Fouquereau et al., 2003; Miller & Brown, 1997).

Culturally Sensitive Treatment of Alcoholism

Members of ethnic minority groups may resist traditional treatment approaches because they feel excluded from full participation in society. Native American women, for example, tend to respond less favorably to traditional alcoholism counseling than White women (Rogan, 1986). Hurlburt and Gade (1984) attribute this difference to the resistance of Native American women to "White man's" authority. They suggest that Native American counselors might be more successful in overcoming this resistance.

The use of counselors from the client's own ethnic group is an example of a *culturally sensitive treatment approach.* Culturally sensitive programs address all facets of the human being, including racial and cultural identity, that nurture pride and help people resist the temptation to cope with stress through chemicals (Rogan, 1986). Culturally sensitive treatment approaches have been extended to other forms of drug dependence, including programs for smoking cessation (Nevid & Javier, 1997; Nevid, Javier, & Moulton, 1996).

Treatment providers may also be more successful if they recognize and incorporate indigenous forms of healing into treatment. For example, spirituality is an important aspect of traditional Native American culture, and spiritualists have played important roles as natural healers. Seeking the assistance of a spiritualist may improve the counseling relationship. Likewise, given the importance of the church in African American and Hispanic American culture, counselors working with people with alcohol use disorders from these groups may be more successful when they draw on clergy and church members as resources.

Nonprofessional Support Groups

Despite the complexity of the factors contributing to substance abuse and dependence, these problems are frequently handled by laypeople or nonprofessionals. Such people often have or had the same problems themselves. For example, self-help group meetings are sponsored by organizations such as Alcoholics Anonymous, Narcotics Anonymous, and Cocaine Anonymous. These groups promote abstinence and provide members an opportunity to discuss their feelings and experiences in a supportive group setting. More experienced group members (sponsors) support newer members during periods of crisis or potential relapse. The meetings are sustained by nominal voluntary contributions.

The most widely used nonprofessional program, Alcoholics Anonymous (AA), is based on the belief that alcoholism is a disease, not a sin. AA assumes that people who suffer from alcoholism are never cured, regardless of how long they abstain from alcohol or how well they control their drinking. Instead of being "cured," people who suffer from alcoholism are seen as "recovering." It is also assumed that people who suffer from alcoholism cannot control their drinking and need help to stop drinking. AA has more than 50,000 chapters in North America. AA is so deeply embedded in the consciousness of helping professionals that many of them automatically refer newly detoxified people to AA as the follow-up agency. About half of AA members have problems with illicit drugs as well as alcohol.

The AA experience is in part spiritual, in part group supportive, in part cognitive. AA follows a 12-step approach that focuses on accepting one's powerlessness over alcohol and turning one's will and life over to a higher power (Cowley, 2001b). This spiritual component may be helpful to some participants but distasteful to others. (Other lay organizations, such as Rational Recovery, adopt a nonspiritual approach.) The later steps focus on examining one's character flaws, admitting one's wrongdoings, being open to a higher power for help to overcome one's character defects, making amends to others, and, in step 12, bringing the AA message to other people suffering from alcoholism (McCrady, 1994). Members are urged to pray or meditate to help them get in touch with their higher power. The meetings themselves provide group support. So does the buddy, or sponsoring, system, which encourages members to call each other for support when they feel tempted to drink.

The success rate of AA remains in question, in large part because AA does not keep records of its members and also because of an inability to conduct randomized clinical trials in AA settings (McCaul & Furst, 1994). Surely many people with alcohol dependence have been helped to achieve and maintain sobriety through AA. But the dropout rate is high: AA estimates that 50% of members drop out after 3 months ("Treatment of Alcoholism—Part II," 1996). On the other hand, investigators identify several factors associated with greater success in AA, including a commitment to abstinence, intention to avoid high-risk situations associated with alcohol use, and longer involvement with the AA program (McKellar, Stewart, & Humphreys, 2003; Moos & Moos, 2004; Morgenstern et al., 2002).

Al-Anon, begun in 1951, is a spinoff of AA that supports the families and friends of people suffering from alcoholism. Another spin-off of AA, Alateen, provides support to children whose parents have alcoholism, helping them see they are not to blame for their parents' drinking and are thus undeserving of the guilt they may feel.

Substance Abuse:
Therapist Louise Roberts
"You try to make sense out of an addiction that doesn't make sense."

Residential Approaches

A residential approach to treatment requires a stay in a hospital or therapeutic residence. Hospitalization is recommended when substance abusers cannot exercise self-control in their usual environments, cannot tolerate withdrawal symptoms, or behave self-destructively or dangerously. Less-costly outpatient treatment is indicated when withdrawal symptoms are less severe, clients are committed to changing their behavior, and support systems, such as families, can help clients make the transition to a drug-free lifestyle. The great majority (nearly 90%) of people treated for alcoholism are outpatients (McCaul & Furst, 1994).

Most inpatient programs use an extended 28-day detoxification period. For the first few days, treatment focuses on helping clients with withdrawal symptoms. Then the emphasis shifts to counseling about the destructive effects of alcohol and combating distorted ideas or rationalizations. Consistent with the disease model, abstinence is the goal.

Most people with alcohol use disorders do not require hospitalization. Studies comparing outpatient and inpatient programs reveal no overall difference in relapse rates (Miller & Hester, 1986). However, because medical insurance does not always cover outpatient treatment, many people who might benefit from outpatient treatment admit themselves for inpatient treatment instead.

A number of residential therapeutic communities are also in use. Some have part- or full-time professional staffs. Others are run entirely by laypeople. Residents are expected to remain free of drugs and take responsibility for their actions. They are often challenged to take responsibility for themselves and to acknowledge the damage caused by their drug abuse. They share their life experiences to help one another develop productive ways of handling stress.

As with AA, we lack evidence from controlled studies demonstrating the efficacy of residential treatment programs. Also like AA, therapeutic communities have high numbers of early dropouts. Moreover, many residents relapse upon returning to the world outside. A recent study suggests that a day treatment therapeutic community is as effective as a residential treatment facility (Guydish et al., 1998).

Psychodynamic Approaches

Psychoanalysts view substance abuse and dependence as symptoms of conflicts rooted in childhood experiences. The therapist attempts to resolve the underlying conflicts, assuming that abusive behavior will then subside as the client seeks more mature forms of gratification. Although there are many successful psychodynamic case studies of people with substance abuse problems, there is a dearth of controlled and replicable research studies. The effectiveness of psychodynamic methods for treating substance abuse and dependence thus remains unsubstantiated.

Behavioral Approaches

Behavioral approaches to treating substance abuse and dependence focus on modifying abusive and dependent behavior patterns. The key question to behaviorally oriented therapists is not whether substance abuse and dependence are diseases but whether abusers can learn to change their behavior when they are faced with temptation.

Self-Control Strategies *Self-control training* helps abusers develop skills they can use to change their abusive behavior. Behavior therapists focus on three components of substance abuse:

1. The *antecedent* cues or stimuli (As) that prompt or trigger abuse
2. The abusive *behaviors* (Bs) themselves
3. The reinforcing or punishing *consequences* (Cs) that maintain or discourage abuse

Table 9.4 shows the kinds of strategies used to modify the "ABCs" of substance abuse.

Contingency Management Programs Learning theorists believe that our behavior is shaped by rewards and punishments. Consider how virtually everything you do, from attending class to stopping at red lights to working for a paycheck, is influenced by the flow of rewards (money, praise, approval) and punishments (traffic tickets, rebukes). The principles of reinforcement were recently applied in the form of a *contingency management* (CM) treatment program for methadone patients (Petry & Martin, 2002). Based on a randomized controlled design, one group of patients had the opportunity to draw from a bowl and win monetary rewards (reinforcers), ranging from $1 to $100 in value. The monetary reward was contingent on submitting clean urine samples for cocaine and opioids. On average, the contingency management (reinforcement) group achieved longer periods of continual abstinence than the standard methadone treatment group. The average CM patient earned $137 in prize money. Other investigators have used the contingency management model to treat cocaine abusers (Epstein et al., 2003). These studies and others suggest that modest rewards for abstinence can help improve therapeutic outcomes in treating substance abusers (Higgins, Heil, & Lussier, 2004).

Aversive Conditioning In *aversive conditioning,* painful or aversive stimuli are paired with substance abuse or abuse-related stimuli to make abuse less appealing. In the case of problem drinking, tastes of different alcoholic beverages are usually paired with drugs that cause nausea and vomiting or with electric shock (G. T. Wilson, 1991). As a consequence, alcohol may come to elicit an aversive conditioned response. Relief from aversive responses then negatively reinforces avoidance of alcohol.

Social Skills Training Social skills training helps people develop effective interpersonal responses in social situations that prompt substance abuse. Assertiveness training, for example, may teach people fend off social pressures to drink. Behavioral marital therapy seeks to improve marital communication and problem-solving skills with the goal of relieving marital stresses that can trigger abuse. Couples may learn how to use written behavioral contracts. For example, the person with a substance abuse problem

TABLE 9.4

Self-Control Strategies for Modifying the "ABCs" of Substance Abuse

1. Controlling the As (Antecedents) of Substance Abuse

People who abuse or become dependent on psychoactive substances become conditioned to a wide range of external (environmental) and internal stimuli (bodily states). They may begin to break these stimulus-response connections by:

- Removing drinking and smoking paraphernalia from the home—all alcoholic beverages, beer mugs, carafes, ashtrays, matches, cigarette packs, lighters, etc.
- Restricting the stimulus environment in which drinking or smoking is permitted. Use the substance only in a stimulus-deprived area of their homes, such as the garage, bathroom, or basement. All other stimuli that might be connected to using the substance are removed—there is no TV, reading materials, radio, or telephone. In this way, substance abuse becomes detached from many controlling stimuli.
- Not socializing with others with substance abuse problems, by avoiding situations linked to abuse—bars, the street, bowling alleys, etc.
- Frequenting substance-free environments—lectures or concerts, a gym, museums, evening classes; and by socializing with nonabusers, sitting in nonsmoking cars of trains, eating in restaurants without liquor licenses.
- Managing the internal triggers for abuse. This can be done by practicing self-relaxation or meditation and not taking the substance when tense; by expressing angry feelings by writing them down or self-assertion, not by taking the substance; by seeking counseling for prolonged feelings of depression, not alcohol, pills, or cigarettes.

2. Controlling the Bs (Behaviors) of Substance Abuse

People can prevent and interrupt substance abuse by:

- Using response prevention—breaking abusive habits by physically preventing them from occurring or making them more difficult (e.g., by not bringing alcohol home or cigarettes to the office).
- Using competing responses when tempted; by being prepared to handle substance-related situations with appropriate ammunition—mints, sugarless chewing gum, etc; by taking a bath or shower, walking the dog, walking around the block, taking a drive, calling a friend, spending time in a substance-free environment, practicing meditation or relaxation, or exercising when tempted, rather than using the substance.
- Making abuse more laborious—buying one can of beer at a time; storing matches, ashtrays, and cigarettes far apart; wrapping cigarettes in foil to make smoking more cumbersome; pausing for 10 minutes when struck by the urge to drink, smoke, or use another substance and asking oneself, "Do I really need *this* one?"

3. Controlling the Cs (Consequences) of Substance Abuse

Substance abuse has immediate positive consequences such as pleasure, relief from anxiety and withdrawal symptoms, and stimulation. People can counter these intrinsic rewards and alter the balance of power in favor of nonabuse by:

- Rewarding themselves for nonabuse and punishing themselves for abuse.
- Switching to brands of beer and cigarettes they don't like.
- Setting gradual substance-reduction schedules and rewarding themselves for sticking to them.
- Punishing themselves for failing to meet substance-reduction goals. People with substance abuse problems can assess themselves, say, 10 cents for each slip and donate the cash to an unpalatable cause, such as a brother-in-law's birthday present.
- Rehearsing motivating thoughts or self-statements—such as writing reasons for quitting smoking on index cards. For example:
  - Each day I don't smoke adds another day to my life.
  - Quitting smoking will help me breathe deeply again.
  - Foods will smell and taste better when I quit smoking.
  - Think how much money I'll save by not smoking.
  - Think how much cleaner my teeth and fingers will be by not smoking.
  - I'll be proud to tell others that I kicked the habit.
  - My lungs will become clearer each and every day I don't smoke.

Smokers can carry a list of 20 to 25 such statements and read several of them at various times throughout the day. They can become parts of one's daily routine, a constant reminder of one's goals.

might agree to abstain from drinking or to take Antabuse, while the spouse agrees to refrain from commenting on past drinking and the probability of future lapses. Evidence suggests that social skills training and behavioral marital therapy are useful in treating alcoholism (Finney & Monahan, 1996; O'Farrell et al., 1996).

Controlled Drinking: A Viable Goal? According to the disease model of alcoholism, people who suffer from the disease who have just one drink will lose control and go on a binge. Some professionals argue that behavior modification self-control techniques can teach many people with alcohol abuse or dependence to engage in *controlled drinking*—to have a drink or two without necessarily falling off the wagon (Sobell & Sobell, 1973a, 1973b, 1984). This contention remains controversial. The proponents of the disease model of alcoholism, who wield considerable political strength, strongly oppose attempts to teach controlled social drinking.

Controlled drinking programs may actually represent a pathway to abstinence for people who would not otherwise enter abstinence-only treatment programs (Marlatt et al., 1993). That is, a controlled drinking program becomes the first step in giving up drinking completely. By offering moderation as a treatment goal, controlled drinking programs may also reach many people who refuse to participate in abstinence-only treatment programs (Marlatt et al., 1993). In the accompanying "Controversies in Abnormal Psychology," Mark and Linda Sobell speak about what it was like to be in the eye of the storm of controversy over the issue of controlled drinking.

Relapse-Prevention Training

The word *relapse* derives from Latin roots meaning "to slide back." From 50% to 90% of people who are successfully treated for substance abuse problems eventually relapse (Leary, 1996). Because of the prevalence of relapse, behaviorally oriented therapists have devised a number of methods referred to as *relapse-prevention training*. Such training helps people with substance abuse problems cope with high-risk situations and to prevent *lapses* from becoming full-blown relapses (Marlatt & Gordon, 1985). High-risk situations include negative mood states, such as depression, anger, or anxiety; interpersonal conflict (e.g., marital problems or conflicts with employers); and socially conducive situations such as "the guys getting together." Participants learn to cope with these situations, for example, by learning relaxation skills to counter anxiety and by learning to resist social pressures to drink. They also learn to avoid practices that might prompt a relapse, such as keeping alcohol on hand for friends.

Although it contains many behavioral strategies, relapse-prevention training is a cognitive-behavioral technique in that it also focuses on the person's *interpretations* of any lapses or slips that may occur, such as smoking a first cigarette or taking a first drink following quitting. Clients are taught how to avoid the *abstinence violation effect* (AVE)—the tendency to overreact to a lapse—by learning to reorient their thinking about lapses. People who have a lapse may be more likely to relapse if they attribute their slip to personal weakness, and experience shame and guilt, than if they attribute the slip to an external or transient event (Curry, Marlatt, & Gordon, 1987). For example, consider a skater who slips on the ice (Marlatt & Gordon, 1985). Whether the skater gets back up and continues to perform depends largely on whether the skater sees the slip as an isolated and correctable event or as a sign of complete failure. Lapses in ex-smokers are often associated with withdrawal symptoms (Piasecki et al., 2003), so it is important to help smokers develop ways of coping with these symptoms without resuming smoking. Participants in relapse-prevention training programs learn to view lapses as temporary setbacks that provide opportunities to learn what kinds of situations lead to temptation and to either avoid or cope with them. If they can learn to think, "Okay, I had a slip, but that doesn't mean all is lost unless I believe it is," they are less likely to relapse.

All in all, efforts to treat people with substance abuse and dependence problems have had mixed results at best. Many abusers really do not want to discontinue use of

CONTROVERSIES IN ABNORMAL PSYCHOLOGY
In the Eye of the Storm: The Controlled Drinking Controversy

Mark and Linda Sobell, in their own words

Our careers began before we had our doctorates. In 1969, we began summer jobs at Patton State Hospital (CA). Within weeks, that evolved into an unusual opportunity to conduct federally funded alcohol research. We were in the right place at the right time. The field of behavior therapy was in its infancy and witnessing some exciting advances. The scientific study of alcohol problems was also in its infancy. Early research at the hospital had demonstrated that severely dependent alcohol abusers could limit their drinking (e.g., drink just 1–3 drinks) in a supervised hospital environment. Furthermore, we found several published studies that suggested that some alcohol abusers could learn to drink moderately without losing control of their drinking. This led us to conduct our highly controversial study, "Individualized Behavior Therapy for Alcoholics" (Sobell & Sobell, 1973b).

Patients were evaluated for their eligibility for a moderate drinking goal, and those who qualified were randomly assigned either to an inpatient-based, broad-spectrum behavioral treatment program that had a controlled drinking goal or to a control group (i.e., standard hospital treatment with an abstinence goal). Those ineligible for a moderation goal were randomized to the behavioral treatment or the standard hospital treatment, both with an abstinence goal. Follow-up was conducted for 2 years (Sobell & Sobell, 1976); an independent double-blind third-year follow-up was also conducted (Caddy, Addington, & Perkins, 1978). Though both experimental groups had superior outcomes relative to their control groups, the moderate drinking group's superiority was maintained over a 3-year period, whereas differences between the abstinence goal groups were no longer significant after the 1-year follow-up. The moderate drinking group had more than twice as many "functioning well" days (i.e., not drinking or drinking just a few drinks) and twice as many abstinent days as their control group. The findings of our rigorous study challenged, as no other study had, the traditional view that only abstinence goals were effective.

In 1982 our careers almost ended when the journal *Science* published an article challenging the study's findings. Although the allegations were veiled in the article, in media interviews the authors claimed we had falsified our data (Marlatt, 1983). Fortunately, we had retained our original data (e.g., drivers' records, arrest records, tape recorded interviews with clients). When the allegations were released, they triggered a media frenzy tantamount to a witch hunt. Several investigations eventually vindicated us. The first, a blue ribbon committee in Toronto, where we were employed, examined our data and concluded, "The Committee finds the Sobell's published data to be accurate, and concludes unequivocally, that there is no evidence of fraud, deception, dishonestly or unethical behavior" (Dickens et al., 1982, p. 9). Shortly thereafter, there was a congressional investigation followed by an investigation by the National Institutes of Health and two ethics investigations by the American Psychological Association. In all instances, we were vindicated, as no investigation found evidence of fraud or deception. The allegations traveled fast among traditional alcohol treatment programs and the public, however, leading many to the unquestioning assumption that controlled drinking had been "debunked." Unfortunately, because vindications are not as newsworthy as are allegations of fraud, many still are not aware of our vindication.

Why did the attack happen? In our published response to the attack (Sobell & Sobell, 1984) we interpreted what had occurred as a reflection of a scientific revolution. The alcohol field's prevailing view that abstinence was the only legitimate treatment goal was seriously threatened, and it was defended at all costs. Our accusers' objective, as stated in media interviews, was to expunge our work from the literature. Although this did not occur, it was clear that those pursuing moderate drinking research did so at their own professional peril.

Replication is at the core of the scientific process. In the intervening years between the attack and now, many studies have demonstrated that low-risk or moderate drinking can be achieved in treating many problem drinkers (persons with low- to moderate-severity alcohol problems) (Sobell & Sobell, 1995). Interestingly, in many other countries moderate drinking treatment goals are widely accepted (e.g., Canada, England, Australia), although that is not the case in the United States (Rosenberg & Davis, 1994). Research also shows that even chronic alcohol abusers treated with behavior therapy and a moderate drinking goal did better than control patients who were treated in a traditional abstinence-oriented program (Caddy et al., 1978; Sobell & Sobell, 1973a, 1973b, 1976). That's not to say that chronic alcohol abusers treated in moderate drinking programs are problem free. Rather, we think of the outcomes of these programs in terms of *harm reduction,* meaning that participants suffer fewer negative consequences than control patients treated in traditional abstinence programs. An important legacy of our work was that it raised serious questions about the efficacy of traditional treatments, questions that remain largely unanswered.

Critical Thinking

- Do you believe that chronic alcohol abusers can learn to drink responsibly? Why or why not?
- What is the basis for determining when alcohol use becomes abuse or dependence? Have you or someone you know crossed the line between use and abuse? ■

Linda Sobell and Mark Sobell

these substances, although they would prefer, if possible, to avoid their negative consequences. Yet many treatment approaches, including 12-step and cognitive-behavioral approaches, can work well when they are well delivered and when individuals desire change (Miller & Brown, 1997; Ouimette, Finney, & Moos, 1997; Project MATCH Research Group, 1997).

Effective treatment programs involve multiple approaches that match the needs of substance abusers and the range of problems they encounter, including co-occurring psychiatric problems like depression and personality disorders (Grant, et al., 2004; Nunes & Levin, 2004; Rychtarik et al., 2000). *Comorbidity* (co-occurrence) of substance use disorders and other psychological disorders has become the rule in treatment facilities rather than the exception. Substance abusers who have comorbid disorders or more severe psychological problems typically fare more poorly in treatment for their drug or alcohol problems (Simpson et al., 1999). As noted in this first-person narrative, the co-occurrence of substance abuse greatly complicates the treatment of other psychological disorders.

"I"
"Surely They Can't Mean Beer!"

Six years ago, at the age of 24, I was diagnosed with manic-depression. Learning to live with this mental illness has been extremely difficult. I have been in a series of different hospitals. After suffering a manic episode and being hospitalized, I would attempt to recover, but within 90 days or so I would end up in a hospital again. I never really had a fair chance of recovering from my manic-depression because I had been suffering from alcoholism, another illness, at the same time. The alcoholism wasn't being treated. After being discharged from hospitals I would resume drinking and then within a matter of a few months I would be back in another hospital having suffered another manic episode. It was strongly suggested to me when I was first diagnosed with manic depression that I should stop drinking. I remember my response clearly. "Surely they can't mean beer!"

My drinking escalated when I first joined a program known as Alcoholics Anonymous. During those years I was in complete denial of what alcohol was doing to the chemical make-up of my body. I drank in order to suppress the negative feelings of mania and depression. I had to live with double trouble and the more I drank the sicker I became. I simply refused to address my alcoholism problem because alcohol had become my best friend. Denial runs deep!

It took a family crisis where my parents told me they would no longer support me emotionally or financially if I ended up in the hospital and alcohol was involved. This scared me to the point where I called Alcoholics Anonymous and began attending AA meetings. It takes time but AA seems to be working for me. I have arrested my drinking problem through total abstinence. Now the medication I take has a chance to work the way it was intended. Stopping drinking alcohol is only part of the solution. For me, working with doctors who understand my manic depressive illness and getting the proper medication is the key to a successful recovery.

—From Adam White, reprinted with permission of *New York City Voices*

Though effective treatment programs are available, as many as 80% of people in the United States with alcohol use disorders have no contact with alcohol treatment programs or self-help organizations (Institute of Medicine, 1990). A recent study in Canada echoed these findings. In a sample of more than 1,000 people in Ontario, Canada, with alcohol abuse or dependence disorders, only about one in three had ever received any treatment for their disorder (Cunningham & Breslin, 2004). Clearly more needs to be done to help people whose use of alcohol and other drugs puts them at risk.

In the case of inner-city youth who have become trapped within a milieu of street drugs and hopelessness, culturally sensitive drug counseling and job training would be of considerable benefit in helping them assume more productive social roles. The challenge is clear: to develop cost-effective ways of helping people recognize the negative effects of substances and forgo the powerful and immediate reinforcements they provide.

Overview of Substance-Related Disorders

TYPES OF SUBSTANCE-RELATED DISORDERS

Substance Use Disorders	Maladaptive use of a psychoactive substance	• **Substance Abuse Disorder:** Pattern of drug-using behavior leading to negative consequences, such as repeatedly losing time from work or aggravating an underlying physical problem • **Substance Dependence Disorder:** A more severe form of substance use disorder, it is associated with physiological dependence or compulsive use of a substance
Substance-Induced Disorders	Physiological or psychological disorders induced by the use of a psychoactive substance	• Intoxication • Dementia • Drug withdrawal syndromes • Amnesia • Mood disorders • Psychotic disorders • Delirium

CAUSAL FACTORS   Multiple factors interact in leading to problems of substance abuse and dependence

Biological Factors	• Pleasurable effects and addictive properties of drugs may depend on their effects on neurotransmitter systems in the brain • Genetic factors may create predispositions for substance-related disorders
Psychosocial Factors	• Positive reinforcement (pleasure inducing) and negative reinforcement (relief from states of tension or anxiety and avoidance or escape from unpleasant withdrawal symptoms) contribute to initiation and maintenance of drug use • Modeling of excessive drinking by family members and friends • Cravings may be conditioned responses to cues associated with prior drug use • In psychodynamic theory, alcohol and drug abuse represent forms of oral fixation and are linked to dependent personality traits
Cognitive Factors	• Positive outcome expectancies linked to drug use • Effects of drugs in boosting self-efficacy expectations • "Falling off the wagon" as a self-fulfilling prophecy
Sociocultural Factors	• Peer pressure from drug-using peers • Exposure to deviant subcultures (e.g., gang culture) in which drug use is commonplace or encouraged

TREATMENT APPROACHES   Intensive, multicomponent treatment approaches generally work best

Biological Approaches	• Detoxification to help substance abusers withdraw safely from addictive drugs • Use of drugs that cause extreme nausea when combined with alcohol (Antabuse) • Use of antidepressants to control drug cravings • Use of chemical substitutes, such as nicotine replacement in place of cigarettes or methadone in place of heroin • Use of drugs that block the high produced by opioids or alcohol (naloxone and naltrexone)
Behavioral Approaches	• To break drug-abusing patterns of behavior and strengthen more adaptive behaviors
Psychodynamic Approaches	• To help individuals with substance abuse problems identify and resolve underlying psychological conflicts
Other Treatment Approaches	• **Residential treatment approaches** and **nonprofessional support groups,** such as AA, to help individuals regain control over their lives and maintain abstinence in the community • **Relapse prevention training** to help individuals learn to resist drug temptations, to cope effectively with high-risk situations, and to prevent lapses from becoming relapses

SUMMING UP

Classification of Substance-Related Disorders

How does the DSM distinguish between substance abuse disorders and substance dependence disorders? According to the *DSM*, substance abuse disorders is a pattern of recurrent use of a substance that repeatedly leads to damaging consequences. Substance dependence disorders involve impaired control over use of a substance and often include features of physiological dependence on the substance, as manifest by the development of tolerance or an abstinence syndrome.

What do we mean by the terms addiction and psychological dependence? Although different people use the term *addiction* differently, it is used here to refer to the habitual or compulsive use of a substance combined with the development of physiological dependence. Psychological dependence is the compulsive use of a substance, with or without the development of physiological dependence.

Drugs of Abuse

What are depressants? Depressants are drugs that depress or slow down nervous system activity. They include alcohol, sedatives and minor tranquilizers, and opioids. Their effects include intoxication, impaired coordination, slurred speech, and impaired intellectual functioning. Chronic alcohol abuse is linked to alcohol-induced persisting amnestic disorder (Korsakoff's syndrome), cirrhosis of the liver, fetal alcohol syndrome, and other physical health problems. Barbiturates are depressants or sedatives that have been used medically for relief of anxiety and short-term insomnia, among other uses. Opioids such as morphine and heroin are derived from the opium poppy. Others are synthesized. Used medically for relief of pain, they are strongly addictive.

What are stimulants? Stimulants increase the activity of the nervous system. Amphetamines and cocaine are stimulants that increase the availability of neurotransmitters in the brain, leading to heightened states of arousal and pleasurable feelings. High doses can produce psychotic reactions that mimic features of paranoid schizophrenia. Habitual cocaine use can lead to a variety of health problems, and an overdose can cause sudden death. Repeated use of nicotine, a mild stimulant found in cigarette smoking, leads to physiological dependence.

What are hallucinogens? Hallucinogens are drugs that distort sensory perceptions and can induce hallucinations. They include LSD, psilocybin, and mescaline. Other drugs with similar effects are cannabis (marijuana) and phencyclidine (PCP).

There is little evidence that these drugs induce physiological dependence, although psychological dependence may occur.

Theoretical Perspectives

How do the major theoretical perspectives view the causes of substance abuse and dependence? The biological perspective focuses on uncovering the biological pathways that may explain mechanisms of physiological dependence. The biological perspective spawns the disease model, which posits that alcoholism and other forms of substance dependence are disease processes. Learning perspectives view substance abuse disorders as learned patterns of behavior, with roles for classical and operant conditioning and observational learning. Cognitive perspectives focus on roles of attitudes, beliefs, and expectancies in accounting for substance use and abuse. Sociocultural perspectives emphasize the cultural, group, and social factors that underlie drug use patterns, including the role of peer pressure in determining adolescent drug use. Psychodynamic theorists view problems of substance abuse, such as excessive drinking and habitual smoking, as signs of an oral fixation.

Treatment of Substance Abuse and Dependence

What treatment approaches are used to help people overcome problems of substance abuse and dependence? Biological approaches to substance abuse disorders include detoxification; the use of drugs such as disulfiram, methadone, naltrexone, and antidepressants; and nicotine replacement therapy. Residential treatment approaches include hospitals and therapeutic residences. Nonprofessional support groups, such as Alcoholics Anonymous, promote abstinence within a supportive group setting. Psychodynamic therapists focus on uncovering the inner conflicts originating in childhood that they believe lie at the root of substance abuse problems. Behavior therapists focus on helping people with substance-related problems change problem behaviors through such techniques as self-control training, aversive conditioning, and skills training approaches. Regardless of the initial success of a treatment technique, relapse remains a pressing problem in treating people with substance abuse problems. Relapse-prevention training employs cognitive-behavioral techniques to help recovering substance abusers cope with high-risk situations and to prevent lapses from becoming relapses by helping participants interpret lapses in less damaging ways.

KEY TERMS

substance-induced disorders *(p. 288)*
intoxication *(p. 288)*
substance use disorders *(p. 288)*
substance abuse *(p. 289)*
substance dependence *(p. 289)*
tolerance *(p. 289)*
withdrawal syndrome *(p. 289)*
addiction *(p. 291)*
physiological dependence *(p. 291)*

psychological dependence *(p. 291)*
depressant *(p. 293)*
alcoholism *(p. 294)*
barbiturates *(p. 301)*
narcotics *(p. 301)*
endorphins *(p. 302)*
morphine *(p. 302)*
heroin *(p. 302)*
stimulants *(p. 302)*

amphetamines *(p. 303)*
amphetamine psychosis *(p. 303)*
cocaine *(p. 303)*
crack *(p. 304)*
hallucinogens *(p. 306)*
marijuana *(p. 308)*
detoxification *(p. 318)*
methadone *(p. 319)*
naltrexone *(p. 319)*

Key for "Are You Hooked?" Questionnaire

Any yes answer suggests you may be dependent on alcohol. If you have answered any of these questions in the affirmative, we suggest you seriously examine what your drinking means to you.

WEB TOOLS

The companion website offers tools to enrich your learning experience and help you succeed in class. Go to www.prenhall.com/nevid for the gateway to the following resources:

- **VIDEO** links to connect to the video case files on the companion CD-ROM. VIDEO icons in the margins of the chapter highlight the case examples included in the CD-ROM. You can also access the CD-ROM directly if you do not have a Web connection.

- **QUIZ** links to self-scoring quizzes corresponding to each section of the chapter. The quizzes help you review your knowledge of the content in each chapter.

- **WEB** links to direct you to related sites that enhance your learning of abnormal psychology.

CHAPTER TEN

Eating Disorders, Obesity, and Sleep Disorders

CHAPTER OUTLINE

"I"

"What's Up with That?"

Every night that I throw up I can't help but be afraid that my heart might stop or something else happen. I just pray and hope I can stop this throwing up before it kills me. I hate this bulimia and I won't stop. It's hard for me to binge and throw up now (refrigerator is locked) and I just can't do it anymore. I just can't race through so much food so fast and then throw it up. I don't really want to. There are times that I do but not often. My new pattern is sure leaving me with an awful feeling in the morning. I eat dinner and kind of keep eating (snacking) afterwards to the point where I either feel too full or think (know) I've eaten too much, then I fall asleep (one hour or so) wake up and think I have to throw up. Half of me doesn't want to, the other half does and I always find myself throwing up. I try falling back asleep but it always seems like eventually sometime during the night I always throw up.

I feel crazy when I have a panic attack because someone I'm with is eating totally sugary foods, as though I'm afraid just being near it will somehow allow the food, or the fat, or the calories to attack me. Julie picked me up from class the other day, and she was eating dry sugar cookie mix from a bowl with a huge spoon. I panicked. I shook, perspired, had trouble taking full breaths, and couldn't focus or concentrate with all the thoughts rushing through my head. I wasn't eating it, but I could smell it and see but and heard the sugar crystals crunch as she chewed big mouthfuls of it. Then she started eating a cupcake. I couldn't handle it. She offered me some and I became severely nauseated by the mere thought of her offer. When she dropped me off, I raced into the house to gain control of this incredible binge. I was horrified and sick, saw myself gaining weight through my distorted vision, and immediately took laxatives to rid myself of all that forbidden food I felt inside, even though I hadn't eaten a thing.

After I calmed down, I realized the reality of the situation, and I felt stupid and crazy and like a total failure. Not only do I not need anyone else to abuse me, now I can do that myself. I don't even need a binge to have my purging cycle triggered to an intense degree. What's up with that?

—Costin, 1997, pp. 62–63

Truth or Fiction?

T❏ F❏ Though others see them as but "skin and bones," young women with anorexia nervosa still see themselves as too fat. (p. 334)

T❏ F❏ Dieting represents an abnormal eating pattern among American women. (p. 337)

T❏ F❏ Bulimic women induce vomiting only after binges. (p. 338)

T❏ F❏ Drugs used to treat depression may also help curb binge eating in bulimic women. (p. 343)

T❏ F❏ Obesity is one of the most common psychological disorders in the United States. (p. 344)

T❏ F❏ The excess calories consumed by Americans each day could feed a country of 80 million people. (p. 344)

T❏ F❏ When you lose weight, your body responds by slowing the rate at which it burns calories. (p. 347)

T❏ F❏ After Santa Claus, the most recognizable figure to children is Ronald McDonald. (p. 348)

T❏ F❏ Many people suffer from sleep attacks in which they suddenly fall asleep without any warning. (p. 355)

T❏ F❏ Some people literally gasp for breath hundreds of times during sleep without realizing it. (p. 356)

THE YOUNG WOMAN WHO WROTE THIS VIGNETTE HAS *BULIMIA NERVOSA*, AN EATING disorder characterized by repeated episodes of binge eating and purging. How can we explain eating disorders like *bulimia nervosa* and *anorexia nervosa*, a psychological disorder of self-starvation that can lead to serious medical consequences, even death? Eating disorders primarily affect young people of high school or college age, especially young women. Even if you don't know anyone with a diagnosable eating disorder, chances are you know people with disturbed eating behaviors such as occasional binge eating and excessive dieting. You probably also know people who suffer from obesity, a major health problem that affects increasing numbers of Americans.

This chapter explores the eating disorders of anorexia and bulimia as well as a newly proposed disorder, binge-eating disorder. We also examine the behavioral factors that contribute to obesity, a health problem that has reached epidemic proportions in our society. But our focus in this chapter extends to another set of problems that commonly affects young adults: sleep disorders. The most common form of sleep disorder, chronic insomnia, affects many young people who are making their way in the world and tend to bring their worries and concerns to bed with them.

EATING DISORDERS

In a nation of plenty, some people literally starve themselves—sometimes to death. They are obsessed with their weight and desire to achieve an exaggerated image of thinness. Others engage in repeated cycles in which they binge on food and then attempt to purge their excess eating, such as by inducing vomiting. These dysfunctional patterns are, respectively, the two major types of eating disorders, **anorexia nervosa** and **bulimia nervosa.**

anorexia nervosa An eating disorder characterized by maintenance of an abnormally low body weight, distortions of body image, intense fears of gaining weight, and in females, amenorrhea.

bulimia nervosa An eating disorder characterized by recurrent binge eating followed by self-induced purging, accompanied by overconcern with body weight and shape.

eating disorder A psychological disorder characterized by disturbed patterns of eating and maladaptive ways of controlling body weight.

Eating disorders are characterized by disturbed patterns of eating and maladaptive ways of controlling body weight. Like many other psychological disorders, anorexia and bulimia are often accompanied by other forms of psychopathology, including depression, anxiety disorders, and substance abuse disorders.

The great majority of cases of anorexia and bulimia occur among young women. Although eating disorders may develop in middle or even late adulthood, they typically begin during adolescence or early adulthood when the pressures to be thin are the strongest. As these social pressures have increased, so too have rates of eating disorders. Bulimia is believed to affect approximately 1% to 3% of women; for anorexia, the lifetime prevalence in women is estimated at .5% (1 in 200) (APA, 2000). An estimated two million college women in the United States are believed to be affected by diagnosable eating disorders (González et al., 2003). Rates of anorexia and bulimia among males are about one tenth those among females (APA, 2000; Lamberg, 2003).

Many women show anorexic or bulimic behaviors but not to the point that they would warrant a diagnosis of an eating disorder. Studies of college women indicate that perhaps 1 in 2 have binged and purged at least once (Fairburn & Wilson, 1993).

Anorexia Nervosa

The Case of Karen

Karen was the 22-year-old daughter of a renowned English professor. She had begun her college career full of promise at the age of 17, but two years ago, after "social problems" occurred, she had returned to live at home and taken progressively lighter course loads at a local college. Karen had never been overweight, but about a year ago her mother noticed that she seemed to be gradually "turning into a skeleton."

Karen spent literally hours every day shopping at the supermarket, butcher, and bakeries conjuring up gourmet treats for her parents and younger siblings. Arguments over her lifestyle and eating habits had divided the family into two camps. The camp led by her father called for patience; that headed by her mother demanded confrontation. Her mother feared that Karen's father would "protect her right into her grave" and wanted Karen placed in residential treatment "for her own good." The parents finally compromised on an outpatient evaluation.

At an even 5 feet, Karen looked like a prepubescent 11-year-old. Her nose and cheekbones protruded crisply. Her lips were full, but the redness of the lipstick was unnatural, as if too much paint had been dabbed on a corpse for the funeral. Karen weighed only 78 pounds, but she had dressed in a stylish silk blouse, scarf, and baggy pants so that not one inch of her body was revealed.

Karen vehemently denied that she had a problem. Her figure was "just about where I want it to be" and she engaged in aerobic exercise daily. A deal was struck in which outpatient treatment would be tried as long as Karen lost no more weight and showed steady gains back to at least 90 pounds. Treatment included a day hospital with group therapy and two meals a day. But word came back that Karen was artfully toying with her food—cutting it up, sort of licking it, and moving it about her plate—rather than eating it. After 3 weeks Karen had lost another pound. At that point, her parents were able to persuade her to enter a residential treatment program, where her eating behavior could be more carefully monitored.

—From the Authors' Files

The word *anorexia* derives from the Greek roots *an-*, meaning "without," and *orexis*, meaning "a desire for." *Anorexia* thus means "without desire for [food]," which is something of a misnomer, because people with anorexia nervosa rarely lose their appetite. However, they may be repelled by food and refuse to eat more than is absolutely nec-

At risk? Anorexia is most common among young women involved in ballet and modeling, in which a great emphasis is put on achieving an ultrathin body image.

essary to maintain a minimal weight for their ages and heights. Often, they starve themselves to the point where they become dangerously emaciated. Anorexia nervosa usually develops between the ages of 12 and 18, although earlier and later onsets are sometimes found.

Table 10.1 shows the clinical features used to diagnose anorexia nervosa. Although reduced body weight is the most obvious sign, the most prominent clinical feature is an intense fear of obesity. One common pattern of anorexia begins after menarche when the girl notices added weight and insists it must come off. The addition of body fat is normal in adolescent females: in an evolutionary sense, fat is added in preparation for childbearing and nursing (Angier, 1999). But anorexic women seek to rid their bodies of any additional weight and so turn to extreme dieting and, often, excessive exercise. These efforts continue unabated after the initial weight-loss goal is achieved, however—even after family and friends express concern. Another common pattern occurs when young women leave home to attend college and encounter difficulties adjusting to the demands of college life and independent living. Anorexia is also common among young women involved in ballet or modeling, both fields that place strong emphasis on maintaining an unrealistically thin body shape.

Anorexia Nervosa—Binge-Eating/ Purging Type:
The Case of Jessica
"The diet started being my only way of getting control."

TABLE 10.1
Diagnostic Features of Anorexia Nervosa

A. Refusal to maintain weight at or above the minimal normal weight for one's age and height; for example, a weight more than 15% below normal.

B. Strong fear of putting on weight or becoming fat, despite being thin.

C. A distorted body image in which one's body—or part of one's body—is perceived as fat, although others perceive the person as thin.

D. In case of females who have had menarche, absence of three or more consecutive menstrual periods.

Source: Adapted from the *DSM-IV-TR* (APA, 2000).

How do I see myself? A distorted body image is a key component of eating disorders.

Although anorexia in women is far more common than in men, an increasing number of young men are presenting with disturbed eating behavior, even anorexia. Many of the factors associated with disturbed eating behavior in young men parallel those in young women, such as perfectionism, perceived pressures from others to lose weight, and participation in sports that place a strong value on leanness (Ricciardelli & McCabe, 2004).

Adolescent girls and women with anorexia almost always deny that they are losing too much weight. They may argue that their ability to engage in stressful exercise demonstrates their fitness. Women with eating disorders are more likely than normal women to have a distorted body image (Horne, Van Vactor, & Emerson, 1991). Other people may see them as nothing but "skin and bones," but anorexic women still see themselves as too fat. Although they literally starve themselves, they may spend much of the day thinking and talking about food and even preparing elaborate meals for others (Rock & Curran-Celentano, 1996).

Subtypes of Anorexia There are two general subtypes of anorexia, a *binge-eating/purging type* and a *restrictive type*. The first type is characterized by frequent episodes of binge eating and purging; the second type is not. Although repeated cycles of binge eating and purging occur in bulimia, bulimic individuals do not reduce their weight to anorexic levels. The distinction between the subtypes of anorexia is supported by differences in personality patterns. Individuals with the eating/purging type tend to have problems relating to impulse control, which in addition to binge-eating episodes may involve substance abuse or stealing (Garner, 1993). They tend to alternate between periods of rigid control and impulsive behavior. Those with the restrictive type tend to rigidly, even obsessively, control their diet and appearance.

Medical Complications of Anorexia Anorexia can lead to serious medical complications that in extreme cases can be fatal. Losses of as much as 35% of body weight may occur, and anemia may develop. Females suffering from anorexia are also likely to encounter dermatological problems such as dry, cracking skin; fine, downy hair; even a yellowish discoloration that may persist for years after weight is regained. Cardiovascular complications include heart irregularities, hypotension (low blood pressure), and associated dizziness upon standing, sometimes causing blackouts. Decreased food ingestion can cause gastrointestinal problems such as constipation, abdominal pain, and obstruction or paralysis of the bowels or intestines. Menstrual irregularities are common, and amenorrhea (absence or suppression of menstruation) is part of the clinical definition of anorexia in females. Muscular weakness and abnormal growth of bones may occur, causing loss of height and osteoporosis.

The death rate from anorexia is estimated at 5% to 8% over a 10-year period, with most deaths due to suicide or medical complications associated with severe weight loss (Goleman, 1995g).

Bulimia Nervosa

The Case of Nicole

Nicole has only opened her eyes, but already she wishes it was time for bed. She dreads going through the day, which threatens to turn out like so many other recent days. Each morning she wonders, is this the day that she will be able to get by without being obsessed by thoughts of food? Or will she spend the day gorging herself? Today is the day she will get off to a new start, she promises herself. Today she will begin to live like a normal person. Yet she is not convinced that it is really up to her.

Nicole starts the day with eggs and toast. Then she goes to work on cookies; doughnuts; bagels smothered with butter, cream cheese, and jelly; granola; candy bars; and bowls of cereal and milk—all within 45 minutes. Then she cannot take in any more food and turns her attention to purging what she has eaten. She goes to the bathroom, ties back her hair, turns on the shower to mask any noise she will make, drinks a glass of water, and makes herself vomit. Afterward she vows, "Starting tomorrow, I'm going to change." But she suspects that tomorrow may be just another chapter of the same story.

—Adapted from Boskind-White & White, 1983, p. 29

Nicole suffers from bulimia nervosa. *Bulimia* derives from the Greek roots *bous,* meaning "ox" or "cow," and *limos,* meaning "hunger." The unpretty picture inspired by the origin of the term is one of continuous eating, like a cow chewing its cud. Bulimia nervosa is an eating disorder characterized by recurrent episodes of gorging on large quantities of food, followed by use of inappropriate ways to prevent weight gain. These may include purging by means of self-induced vomiting; use of laxatives, diuretics, or enemas; or fasting or engaging in excessive exercise (see Table 10.2). A woman with bulimia may use two or more strategies for purging, such as vomiting and laxatives (Tobin, Johnson, & Dennis, 1992). Although people with anorexia are extremely thin, bulimic individuals are usually of normal weight. However, they have an excessive concern about their shape and weight.

Bulimic individuals typically gag themselves to induce vomiting. Most attempt to conceal their behavior. Fear of gaining weight is a constant factor. Although an overconcern with body shape and weight is a cardinal feature of bulimia and anorexia, bulimic individuals do not pursue the extreme thinness characteristic of anorexia. Their ideal weights are similar to those of women who do not suffer from eating disorders.

The binge itself usually occurs in secret, most commonly at home during unstructured afternoon or evening hours (Drewnowski, 1997; Guertin, 1999). A binge typically lasts from 30 to 60 minutes and involves consumption of forbidden foods that are generally sweet and rich in fat. Binge eaters typically feel they lack control over their bingeing and may consume 5,000 to 10,000 calories at a sitting. One young woman described eating everything available in the refrigerator, even to the point of scooping out margarine from its container with her finger. The episode continues until the binger is spent or exhausted, suffers painful stomach distension, induces vomiting, or runs out of food. Drowsiness, guilt, and depression usually ensue, but bingeing is initially pleasant because of release from dietary constraints.

The average age for onset of bulimia is the late teens, when concerns about dieting and dissatisfaction with bodily shape or weight are at their height. Bulimia nervosa typically affects non-Hispanic White women in late adolescence or early adulthood (APA, 2000). Despite the widespread belief that eating disorders, especially anorexia nervosa, are most common among affluent people, available evidence shows no strong linkage between socioeconomic status and eating disorders (Wakeling, 1996). Beliefs that eating disorders are associated with high socioeconomic status may reflect the tendency

Bulimia:
The Case of Ann
"I was just afraid to go home and be around food."

TABLE 10.2
Diagnostic Features of Bulimia Nervosa

A. Recurrent episodes of binge eating (gorging) as shown by both:

  (1) Eating an unusually high quantity of food during a 2-hour period, and
  (2) Sense of loss of control over food intake during the episode.

B. Regular inappropriate behavior to prevent weight gain such as self-induced vomiting, abuse of laxatives, diuretics or enemas, or by fasting or excessive exercise.

C. A minimum average of two episodes a week of binge eating and inappropriate compensatory behavior to prevent weight gain over a period of at least 3 months.

D. Persistent overconcern with the shape and weight of one's body.

Source: Adapted from the *DSM-IV-TR* (APA, 2000).

Bingeing. People with bulimia nervosa may cram in thousands of calories during a single binge and then purge what they have consumed by forcing themselves to vomit.

for affluent patients to obtain treatment. Alternatively, it may be that the social pressures on young women to strive to achieve an ultrathin ideal have now generalized across all socioeconomic levels.

Medical Complications of Bulimia Like anorexia, bulimia is associated with many medical complications. Many of these stem from repeated vomiting: skin irritation around the mouth due to frequent contact with stomach acid, blockage of salivary ducts, decay of tooth enamel, and dental cavities. The acid from the vomit may damage taste receptors on the palate, making the person less sensitive to the taste of vomit with repeated purgings (Rodin et al., 1990). Decreased sensitivity to the aversive taste of vomit may help maintain the purging behavior. Cycles of bingeing and vomiting may cause abdominal pain, hiatal hernia, and other abdominal complaints. Stress on the pancreas may produce pancreatitis (inflammation), which is a medical emergency. Disturbed menstrual function is found in as many as 50% of normal weight women with bulimia (Weltzin et al., 1994). Excessive use of laxatives may cause bloody diarrhea and laxative dependency, so the person cannot have normal bowel movements without laxatives. In extreme cases, the bowel can lose its reflexive eliminatory response to pressure from waste material. Bingeing on large quantities of salty food may cause convulsions and swelling. Repeated vomiting or abuse of laxatives can lead to potassium deficiency, producing muscular weakness, cardiac irregularities, even sudden death—especially when diuretics are used. As with anorexia, menstruation may come to a halt.

Causes of Anorexia and Bulimia

Like other psychological disorders, anorexia and bulimia involve a complex interplay of factors (Polivy & Herman, 2002). Most significant are social pressures that lead young women to base their self-worth on their physical appearance, especially their weight.

Sociocultural Factors Sociocultural theorists point to societal pressures and expectations placed on young women in our society as contributing to the development of eating disorders (The McKnight Investigators, 2003). The pressure to achieve an unrealistic standard of thinness, combined with the importance attached to appearance in defining the female role in society, can lead young women to become dissatisfied with their bodies (Stice, 2001). These pressures are underscored by findings that among college women in one sample, one in seven (14%) reported that buying a single chocolate bar in a store would cause them to feel embarrassed (Rozin, Bauer, & Catanese, 2003). A recent study highlighted the role of peer pressure to adhere to a thin body shape as a strong predictor of bulimic behavior in young women (Young, McFatter, & Clopton, 2001).

Exposure to media images of ultrathin women can lead to the internalization of a thin ideal, setting the stage for body dissatisfaction (Blowers et al., 2003). Even in children as young as eight, girls express more dissatisfaction with their bodies than do boys (Ricciardelli & McCabe, 2001). Body dissatisfaction in young women may lead to excessive dieting and to the development of disturbed eating behaviors. Even on laboratory tasks, women with high levels of bulimic symptoms show greater attention to cues relating to body size than do other women (Viken et al., 2002). The idealization of thinness in women can be illustrated in the changes in the **body mass index** (BMI) of winners of the Miss America pageant (Rubinstein & Caballero, 2000) (see Figure 10.1). Body mass index is a measure of height-adjusted weight.

The pressure to be thin is so prevalent that dieting has become the normative pattern of eating among young American women. Four out of five young women in the United States have gone on a diet by the time they reach their eighteenth birthdays. Concerns about social pressures to be thin bring to light the idealized body images to which girls are exposed, including perhaps the most famous of all ultrathin ideals—Barbie (see "Controversies in Abnormal Psychology" feature).

In support of the sociocultural model, evidence shows that eating disorders are less common, even rare, in non-Western countries (Stice, 1994; Wakeling, 1996). Even in Western cultures, eating disorders are more prevalent in the weight-obsessed United States than in other Western countries for which data are available, such as Greece and Spain, or in the most technologically advanced nation in the Far East, Japan (Stice, 1994).

body mass index A standard measure of overweight and obesity in which height is taken into account in forming the index.

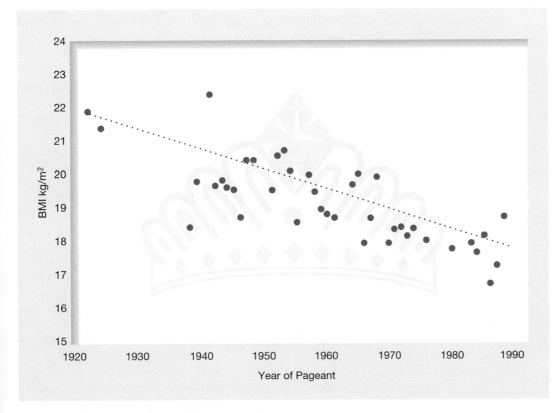

FIGURE 10.1 Thinner and thinner.
Note the downward trend in the body mass index levels (BMIs) of Miss America contest winners over time. What might these data suggest about changes in society's view of the ideal female form?
Source: Rubinstein & Caballero (2000).

Rates of disordered eating behaviors and eating disorders also vary in the United States among ethnic groups, with higher rates in Euro American adolescents than in African American and other ethnic minority adolescents (Lamberg, 2003; Striegel-Moore et al., 2003). One likely reason for this discrepancy is that body image and body dissatisfaction are less closely tied to body weight among minority women (Angier, 2000b). That said, investigators expect that the prevalence of eating disorders in young women of color will rise with increased exposure to Eurocentric concepts of feminine beauty (Gilbert, 2003).

Disturbed eating behaviors may also be more common among ethnic minority groups, including Native Americans, than is commonly believed (Shaw et al., 2004; Smith & Krejci, 1991). Likewise, investigators caution that body dissatisfaction may be more prevalent among Hispanic and Asian girls than is generally recognized and may set the stage for distorted eating behaviors in these groups (Robinson et al., 1996). There are also signs that eating disorders may increase in the future in developing countries (Grange, Telch, & Tibbs, 1998).

Psychosocial Factors Although cultural pressures to conform to an ultrathin female ideal play a major role in eating disorders, the great majority of young women exposed to these pressures do not develop eating disorders. Other factors must be involved. A pattern of overly restricted dieting is common to women with bulimia and anorexia. Women with eating disorders typically adopt very rigid dietary rules and practices about what they can eat, how much they can eat, and how often they can eat.

From a learning perspective, we can conceptualize eating disorders as a type of weight phobia. In this model, relief from anxiety acts as negative reinforcement. Bulimic women tend to have been slightly overweight before they developed bulimia, and the binge-purge cycle usually begins after a period of strict dieting to lose weight. In a typical scenario, the rigid dietary controls fail, leading to a loss of inhibitions (disinhibition), which prompts a binge-eating episode. The binge eating induces fear of weight gain, which in turn prompts self-induced vomiting or excessive exercise. Some bulimic women become so concerned about possible weight gain that they resort to vomiting after every meal (Lowe, Gleaves, & Murphy-Eberenz, 1998). Purging is negatively reinforced because it produces relief, or at least partial relief, from anxiety over gaining weight. Similarly, for women with anorexia, food-rejecting behavior (and purging in cases of the binge-eating/purging subtype) is negatively reinforced by relief from anxiety about weight gain.

Body dissatisfaction is another important factor in eating disorders. Body dissatisfaction may lead to maladaptive attempts—through self-starvation and purging—to attain a desired body weight or shape. Bulimic and anorexic women tend to be extremely concerned about their body weight and shape (Jacobi et al., 2004). Even many normal-weight children express concerns about their weight—concerns that may set the stage for the development of disturbed eating behaviors in adolescence ("Nutrition, Obesity and Perception," 2001).

Cognitive factors are also important. Young women with anorexia often have perfectionistic attitudes and high-achievement strivings (Anderluh et al., 2003; Cockell et al., 2002; Halmi et al., 2000; Shafran & Mansell, 2001). They may impose unreasonable pressures on themselves to achieve a "perfect body" and get down on themselves when they fail to meet their impossibly high standards. Their extreme dieting may give them a sense of control and independence that they feel they lack in other aspects of their lives.

Bulimic women tend to be both perfectionistic and dichotomous ("black or white") in their thinking patterns (Fairburn et al., 1997). Thus, they expect themselves to adhere perfectly to their rigid dietary rules and judge themselves as complete failures when they deviate even slightly. They also judge themselves harshly for episodes of binge eating and purging. In addition, women with bulimic tendencies tend to have a dysfunctional cognitive style that leads to exaggerated beliefs about the negative consequences of gaining weight (Poulakis & Wertheim, 1993).

TRUTH or FICTION? *REVISITED*

Bulimic women induce vomiting only after binges.

☑ **FALSE.** Some bulimic women induce vomiting after every meal.

CONTROVERSIES IN ABNORMAL PSYCHOLOGY
Should Barbie Be Banned?

We're not suggesting that Barbie and her entourage be thrown overboard in some modern-day version of the Boston Tea Party, or that stores be prohibited from selling the popular toys. But by raising such a provocative question we hope to encourage you to think critically about the effects that these anatomically incorrect figurines may have on the psyches of young women. As writer Laura Vanderkam (2003) notes in her article, "Barbie and Fat as a Feminist Issue," Barbie was designed to fit the idealized male fantasy of a bosomy but impossibly thin female form, and then sold to girls who grew up wanting to look like her. Social worker Abigail Natenshon, author of *When Your Child Has an Eating Disorder,* argues that images of Barbie and ultrathin female models and actresses create expectations in the minds of young women about how they are supposed to look. Though many factors undoubtedly contribute to eating disorders, should parents keep Barbie at bay and not bring the doll into their homes? Or should they welcome Barbie but help their daughters see that her ultrathin form is not a female ideal? Or help them understand that self-esteem should not be measured by a bathroom scale?

For that matter, should parents inform their sons that bulked-up wrestlers, muscularized movie heroes, and even action figures in video games are not exemplars of what they should aspire to? Even GI Joe-type action figures (i.e., dolls) appear more muscular today than in earlier versions. Exposure to overly masculinized male images may create pressures on boys that can lead to disturbed eating behaviors, just as young women feel pressured to look like ultrathin magazine models ("Male Eating Disorders," 2004). For either gender, regular exposure to "perfect" bodies may reinforce the idea that "normal" bodies are not acceptable.

On the other hand, Vanderkam cautions us not the throw the "Barbie" out with the bathwater (apologies for the pun). In light of the epidemic of obesity facing our society, perhaps we should champion the active, energetic lifestyle that Barbie embodies. What do you think?

Critical Thinking

- Assume you are a parent of a young boy or girl. Would you restrict the kinds of toys you buy based on considerations of appropriate body size and weight? Why or why not?
- What messages should parents convey to children regarding the overly slenderized and masculinized images that children regularly see? ■

To be like Barbie. The Barbie doll has long represented a symbol of the buxom but thin feminine form that has become idealized in our culture. If women were to be proportioned like the classic Barbie doll, they would resemble the woman in the photograph on the right. To achieve this idealized form, the average woman would need to grow nearly a foot in height, reduce her waist by 5 inches, and add 4 inches to her bustline. What message do you think the Barbie-doll figure conveys to young girls?

Is this normal? Body dissatisfaction is not limited to young women. Regular exposure to overly muscularized masculine images may reinforce the idea that "normal" bodies are not acceptable.

Anorexia Nervosa:
The Case of Tamora

"If someone had told me how ugly I looked, being that thin, I wouldn't have done it. I mean, it was . . . part beauty and . . . part power."

Psychodynamically oriented writers believe that girls with anorexia have difficulty separating from their families and consolidating separate, individuated identities (Bruch, 1973; Minuchin, Rosman, & Baker, 1978). Perhaps anorexia represents the girl's unconscious effort to remain a prepubescent child. By maintaining the veneer of childhood, pubescent girls may avoid dealing with such adult issues as increased independence and separation from their families, sexual maturation, and assumption of adult responsibilities.

Bulimia is also linked to problems in interpersonal relationships. Bulimic women tend to be shy and to have few if any close friends (Fairburn et al., 1997). Enhancing the social skills of women with bulimia may increase the quality of their relationships and perhaps reduce their tendencies to use food in maladaptive ways.

Young women with bulimia also tend to have more emotional problems and lower self-esteem than other dieters (Fairburn et al., 1997; Jacobi et al., 2004). Bulimia is often accompanied by other diagnosable disorders, such as depression, obsessive–compulsive disorder, and substance-related disorders (O'Brien & Vincent, 2003; Stice, Burton, & Shaw, 2004). This suggests that some forms of binge eating represent attempts at coping with emotional distress (Sherwood et al., 2000). Unfortunately, cycles of bingeing and purging exacerbate emotional problems rather than relieve them. Bulimic women are also more likely than other women to have experienced childhood sexual and physical abuse (Kent & Waller, 2000; Wonderlich et al., 1997). In some cases, bulimia may develop as an ineffective means of coping with abuse.

Family Factors Eating disorders frequently develop against a backdrop of family conflicts (Fairburn et al., 1997; Wonderlich et al., 1997). Some theorists focus on the brutal effect of self-starvation on parents. They suggest that some adolescents refuse to eat to punish their parents for feelings of loneliness and alienation they experience in the home. One study compared the mothers of adolescent girls with eating disorders to the mothers of other girls. Mothers of adolescents with eating disorders were more likely to be unhappy about their families' functioning, to have their own problems with eating and dieting, to believe their daughters ought to lose weight, and to regard their daughters as unattractive (Pike & Rodin, 1991). Is binge eating, as suggested by Humphrey (1986), a metaphoric effort to gain the nurturance and comfort that the mother is denying her daughter? Does purging represent the symbolic upheaval of negative feelings toward the family?

Families of young women with eating disorders tend to be more often conflicted, less cohesive and nurturing, yet more overprotective and critical than those of reference groups (Fairburn et al., 1997). The parents seem less capable of promoting independence in their daughters. Conflicts with parents over issues of autonomy are often implicated in the development of both anorexia nervosa and bulimia (Ratti, Humphrey, & Lyons, 1996). Yet it remains uncertain whether these family patterns contribute to the eating disorders or whether eating disorders disrupt family life. The truth probably lies in an interaction between the two.

From the systems perspective, families are systems that regulate themselves in ways that minimize the open expression of conflict and reduce the need for change. Within this perspective, girls who develop anorexia may be seen as helping maintain the shaky balances and harmonies found in dysfunctional families by displacing attention from family conflicts and marital tensions onto themselves (Minuchin et al., 1978). The girl may become the *identified patient,* although the family unit is actually dysfunctional.

Regardless of the factors that initiate eating disorders, social reinforcers may maintain them. Children with eating disorders may quickly become the focus of attention of their families, receiving attention from their parents that is otherwise lacking.

Biological Factors Scientists suspect that abnormalities in brain mechanisms controlling hunger and satiety are involved in bulimia, most probably involving the brain chemical serotonin. Serotonin plays a key role in regulating mood and appetite, especially appetite for carbohydrates. Low levels of the chemical, or lack of sensitivity of serotonin receptors in the brain, may prompt binge-eating episodes, especially carbohydrate binge-

QUESTIONNAIRE
The Fear of Fat Scale

The fear of becoming fat is a prime factor underlying eating disorders like anorexia and bulimia. The Goldfarb Fear of Fat Scale measures the degree to which people fear becoming fat. The scale may help identify individuals at risk of developing eating disorders. It differentiates between anorexic and normal women, and between bulimic and nonbulimic women. Dieters, however, also score higher on the scale than nondieters.

To complete the Fear of Fat Scale, read each of the following statements and write in the number that best represents your own feelings and beliefs. Then check the key at the end of the chapter.

1 = very untrue
2 = somewhat untrue
3 = somewhat true
4 = very true

1. _____ My biggest fear is of becoming fat.
2. _____ I am afraid to gain even a little weight.
3. _____ I believe there is a real risk that I will become overweight someday.
4. _____ I don't understand how overweight people can live with themselves.
5. _____ Becoming fat would be the worst thing that could happen to me.
6. _____ If I stopped concentrating on controlling my weight, chances are I would become very fat.
7. _____ There is nothing that I can do to make the thought of gaining weight less painful and frightening.
8. _____ I feel like all my energy goes into controlling my weight.
9. _____ If I can eat even a little, I may lose control and not stop eating.
10. _____ Staying hungry is the only way I can guard against losing control and becoming fat.

Source: Goldfarb, L. A., Dykens, E. M., & Gerrard, M. (1985). The Goldfarb Fear of Fat scale. Journal of Personality Assessment, 49, 329–332. Reprinted with permission.

ing (Levitan et al., 1997). This line of thinking is buttressed by evidence that antidepressants, such as Prozac, which increases serotonin activity, can decrease binge-eating episodes in bulimic women (Walsh et al., 2004). We also know that many women with eating disorders are depressed or have a history of depression, and imbalances of serotonin are implicated in depressive disorders.

Evidence also points to a role for genetic factors in eating disorders (Lamberg, 2003; Strober et al., 2000; Wade et al., 2000). Eating disorders tend to run in families, which is suggestive of a genetic component. But stronger evidence comes from a study of more than 2,000 female twins, which showed a much higher concordance rate for bulimia, 23% versus 9%, among monozygotic (MZ) twins than dizygotic (DZ) twins (Kendler et al., 1991). A greater concordance for anorexia was also found among MZ than DZ twins, 50% versus 5% (Holland, Sicotte, & Treasure, 1988). Nonetheless, genetic factors cannot fully account for the development of eating disorders. Consistent with the diathesis-stress model, perhaps a genetic predisposition affecting the regulation of neurotransmitter activity in the brain interacts with stress associated with social and family pressures to increase the risk of eating disorders.

In sum, we can conceptualize eating disorders within a multifactorial framework in which psychosocial and biological influences underlie the development of disturbed eating behaviors (see Figure 10.2). Negative reinforcement in the form of relief from anxiety about gaining weight plays a pivotal role in strengthening and maintaining maladaptive ways of controlling body weight through food-rejecting behavior and purging.

Treatment of Anorexia Nervosa and Bulimia Nervosa

Eating disorders are difficult to treat. People with anorexia may be hospitalized, especially when weight loss is severe or body weight is falling rapidly. In the hospital they are usually placed on a closely monitored refeeding regimen (Robb et al., 2002). Behavior therapy is also commonly used, with rewards made contingent on adherence to the refeeding protocol (Rock & Curran-Celentano, 1996). Commonly used reinforcers include ward privileges and social opportunities.

Psychodynamic therapy is sometimes combined with behavior therapy to probe for psychological conflicts. Family therapy may also be employed to help resolve underlying family conflicts. Behavior therapy has been shown to be effective in promoting weight gain of anorexic patients during hospitalization (Johnson, Tsoh, & Varnado, 1996). Individual or family therapy following hospitalization has also shown favorable long-term benefits (Eisler et al., 1997).

Eating Disorders:
Nutritionist Alise Thresh
"Some people are normal eaters . . . some people are concerned about their eating . . . and to an extreme, there is an eating disorder."

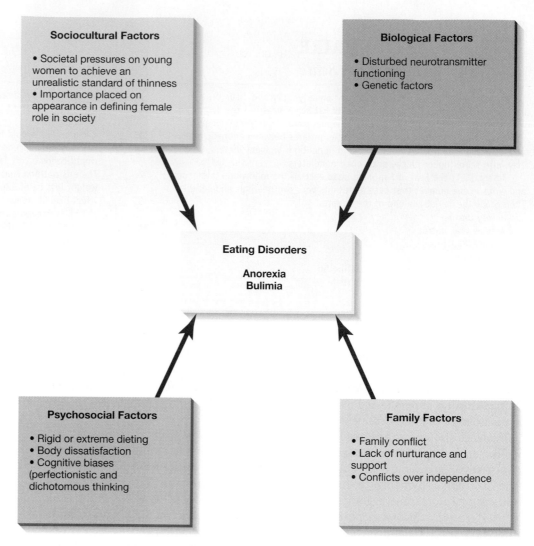

FIGURE 10.2 A multifactorial model of eating disorders (anorexia and bulimia). Psychosocial and biological influences are implicated in eating disorders, leading to disturbed eating behaviors that underlie anorexia and bulimia. Negative reinforcement in the form of temporary relief from anxiety about gaining weight strengthens food-rejecting behavior and purging, but at the cost of maintaining this maladaptive pattern.

Hospitalization may also be helpful in breaking the binge-purge cycle in bulimia, but it appears to be necessary only where eating behaviors are clearly out of control and outpatient treatment has failed, or where there are severe medical complications, suicidal thoughts or attempts, or substance abuse.

Cognitive-behavioral therapy (CBT) helps bulimic women challenge self-defeating thoughts and beliefs, such as unrealistic, perfectionistic expectations regarding dieting and body weight. Another common dysfunctional thinking pattern is dichotomous (all-or-nothing) thinking, which predisposes them to purge when they slip even a little from their rigid diets. CBT also challenges tendencies to overemphasize appearance in determining self-worth. To eliminate self-induced vomiting, therapists may use the behavioral technique of *exposure with response prevention* that was developed for treatment of people with obsessive-compulsive disorder. In this technique, the bulimic patient is exposed to eating forbidden foods while the therapist stands by to prevent vomiting until the urge to purge passes. Bulimic individuals thus learn to tolerate violations of their dietary rules without resorting to purging. Research evidence supports the effectiveness of CBT in treating bulimia (Agras et al., 2000b; Anderson & Maloney, 2001; Tuschen-Caffier, Pook, & Frank, 2001).

Interpersonal psychotherapy (IPT), a structured form of psychodynamic therapy, has also been used effectively in treating bulimia. IPT focuses on resolving interpersonal problems in the belief that more effective interpersonal functioning will lead to healthier food habits and attitudes. Although CBT appears to produce stronger and faster treatment effects (Agras et al., 2000a) IPT may be useful in cases where CBT proves unsuccessful (Wilson & Fairburn, 1998).

Antidepressant drugs, such as Prozac, also have therapeutic benefits in treating bulimia (Walsh et al., 2004). These drugs decrease the urge to binge by normalizing levels of serotonin—the brain chemical involved in regulating appetite. Antidepressant medication, especially Prozac, also appears promising in treating anorexia, perhaps because it helps relieve underlying depression (Johnson, Tsoh, & Varnado, 1996). Experimental drugs that directly target food cravings may prove to be of benefit in treating bulimia (Goode, 2003a).

All in all, investigators believe that CBT represents the most effective form of treatment for bulimia (Halmi et al., 2002). Yet drugs may prove helpful in patients who fail to respond to cognitive-behavioral treatment (Walsh et al., 2000). Studies examining whether a combination CBT/medication approach is more effective than either component alone have thus far produced inconsistent results (Johnson, Tsoh, & Varnado, 1996; Walsh et al., 1997).

Although progress has been made in treating eating disorders, there is considerable room for improvement. Even in CBT, about half of treated patients show continued evidence of bulimic behavior (Thompson-Brenner, Glass, & Westen, 2003; Wilson & Fairburn, 1998). Relapse rates are also disturbingly high, perhaps approaching 50% (Halmi et al., 2002).

Eating disorders can be tenacious and enduring problems, especially when excessive fears of body weight and distortions in body image continue beyond active treatment (Fairburn et al., 2003). A recent study reported that 10 years after an initial presentation with bulimia, approximately 30% of women still showed recurrent binge-eating or purging behaviors (Keel et al., 1999). Recovery from anorexia also tends to be a long and uncertain process (Steinhausen, 2002). A recent study of 88 German patients with anorexia showed that 50% had failed to recover 6 years after first hospitalization (Herzog, Schellberg, & Deter, 1997).

Difficulties in treating eating disorders only buttress the need to develop effective prevention programs. Recently, investigators showed positive results from an Internet-based intervention that focused on changing disordered eating behaviors and attitudes and reducing body dissatisfaction in a sample of college women (Celio et al., 2000). The intervention had a significant impact on reducing risk factors for eating disorders (i.e., disordered attitudes and behaviors) as compared to a waiting list control condition.

Binge-Eating Disorder

People with **binge-eating disorder (BED)** have recurrent eating binges but do not purge themselves of the excess food afterwards. Binge-eating disorder is classified in the *DSM* manual as a potential disorder requiring further study. We presently know too little about the characteristics of people with BED to include it as an official diagnostic category. We do know that occasional binge-eating episodes affect upwards of four million people in the U.S. ("Study Links Binge Eating," 2003). Prevalence rates for BED in community samples are believed to range from 0.7% to 4% (APA, 2000).

Though the final set of criteria that might be used in the diagnostic manual to identify the disorder remains under review, the present criteria requires evidence of bingeing at least 2 days a week for a period of 3 months (Stotland, 2000). During a binge, people with this disorder continue to eat despite feeling uncomfortably full. They are embarrassed to be seen during a binge and feel guilty afterward.

TRUTH or FICTION? REVISITED

Drugs used to treat depression may also help curb binge eating in bulimic women.

☑ **TRUE.** Antidepressants have been shown to be helpful in curbing binge eating among bulimic women.

---

binge-eating disorder (BED) A disorder characterized by recurrent eating binges without purging; classified as a potential disorder requiring further study.

The available evidence indicates that unlike bulimia, BED is commonly found among obese individuals (Spitzer et al., 1992). BED is frequently associated with depression and with a history of unsuccessful attempts at losing excess weight and keeping it off. People with BED tend to be older than those with anorexia or bulimia (Arnow, Kenardy, & Agras, 1992). Like other eating disorders, it is found more frequently among women.

People with BED are often described as "compulsive overeaters." During a binge they feel a loss of control over their eating. BED may fall within a broader domain of compulsive behaviors characterized by impaired control over maladaptive behaviors, such as pathological gambling and substance abuse disorders. A history of dieting may play a role in some cases of BED, although it appears to be a less important factor in BED than in bulimia (Howard & Porzelius, 1999). Some forms of BED may be related to the actions of particular genes (Branson et al., 2003; Farooqi et al., 2003).

Cognitive–behavioral techniques show positive effects in treating binge-eating disorder (Wilson & Fairburn, 1998). Antidepressants, especially those of the SSRI family, may also reduce the frequency of binge-eating episodes by normalizing serotonin levels in the brain (Apopolinario et al., 2003; McElroy et al., 2000; Stotland, 2000). Appetite-suppressant drugs that curb food cravings also show promise in treating binge eating in obese individuals (McElroy et al., 2003). This brings us to the problem that is closely identified with binge-eating disorder, obesity.

OBESITY: A NATIONAL EPIDEMIC

obesity A condition of excess body fat; generally defined by a BMI of 30 or higher.

The problem of **obesity** once again brings into context the complex interrelationships between the mind and body. Though obesity is classified as a medical, not a psychological, disorder, it involves psychological factors in both its development and treatment.

Obesity has reached epidemic proportions not only in the United States, but throughout the world (Kelner & Helmuth, 2003; Manson & Bassuk, 2003; Vastag, 2004). More than 120 million Americans are either overweight or obese (Hellmich, 2003). For the first time in human history, there are as many people in the world who are overweight as they are people who are underfed (Bazell, 2002). Worldwide, a billion people are either overweight or obese (Grady, 2002). Consider these other disturbing statistics:

TRUTH or FICTION? REVISITED

Obesity is one of the most common psychological disorders in the United States.

☑ **FALSE.** Obesity is a medical disorder, not a psychological disorder.

- More Americans are overweight today than at any time since the government started tracking obesity in the 1960s. Nearly two thirds of Americans are overweight, and nearly one third are obese (Grady, 2002; Mokdad et al., 2003; Vastag, 2004).

- Obesity in children and adolescents is also on the upswing, having doubled over the past 25 years (Connelly, 2003; Dietz, 2004; Parloff, 2003). All told, one in three children is overweight or at risk of becoming overweight.

- Americans consume 815 billion calories of food each day, 200 billion calories more than necessary to maintain their weight at moderate levels of activity (C. D. Jenkins, 1988). The extra calories are enough to sustain a country of 80 million people.

TRUTH or FICTION? REVISITED

The excess calories consumed by Americans each day could feed a country of 80 million people.

☑ **TRUE.** The excess calories consumed daily by Americans could feed a country of 80 million people. We, however, are paying the penalty of excess caloric intake in the form of obesity.

Health officials are concerned about obesity because it represents a major risk factor in many chronic, potentially life-threatening diseases, including heart disease, stroke, diabetes, respiratory disease, and some forms of cancer (Carmichael, 2003; Kurth et al., 2002; Manson et al., 2004; Mokdad et al., 2003). An estimated 300,000 people in the United States die prematurely because of obesity-linked diseases, such as heart disease and cancer (Hellmich, 2003; Mitka, 2003). Experts estimate that obesity shaves seven years off the average person's life span ("Being Fat," 2003).

Despite all the money and effort spent on weight-loss products and programs, our collective waistlines are getting larger—a result, government health experts believe, of consuming too many calories and exercising too little (Brody, 2002; Pollan, 2003). Americans today average 530 more calories per day than they did 30 years ago (Gorman,

Overview of Eating Disorders

TYPES OF EATING DISORDERS/PREVALENCE RATES (approx., in parentheses)

	Description	Features
Anorexia Nervosa (0.5%, or 1 in 200 women; about 1 in 2,000 men)	Self-starvation, resulting in a minimal weight for one's age and height or dangerously unhealthy weight	• Strong fears of gaining weight or becoming fat • Distorted self-image (perceiving oneself as fat despite extreme thinness) • Two general subtypes: binge-eating/purging type and restrictive type • Potentially serious, even fatal medical complications • Typically affects young, Euro American women
Bulimia Nervosa (1%–3% in women; about 0.1%–0.3% in men)	Recurrent episodes of binge eating followed by purging	• Weight is usually maintained within a normal range • Overconcern about body shape and weight • Binge–purge episodes may result in serious medical complications • Typically affects young, Euro American women
Binge-Eating Disorder (a proposed disorder requiring further study) (0.7%–4%)	Recurrent binge eating without compensatory purging	• Individuals with BED frequently are described as compulsive overeaters • Typically affects obese women who are older than those affected by anorexia or bulimia

CAUSAL FACTORS   An interplay of multiple factors are at work in eating disorders

Sociocultural Factors	• Excessive pressures on young women to adhere to unrealistic standards of thinness
Psychological Factors	• Rigid or highly restrictive dieting may set the stage for loss of control following dietary transgressions, resulting in bulimic binges • Body dissatisfaction may prompt unhealthy ways of achieving desired body weight • Perceived lack of control over other aspects of life apart from dieting • Difficulties separating from one's family and establishing an individuated identity • Psychological needs for perfectionism and tendencies to think in dichotomous or black-and-white terms
Family Factors	• Families of eating disorder patients are often characterized by conflict, lack of cohesion and nurturing, and failure to foster independence and autonomy in their daughters • From a family systems perspective, a daughter's eating disorder may serve to maintain a shaky balance within a dysfunctional family by diverting attention away from family or marital problems
Biological Factors	• Possible imbalances in neurotransmitter systems in the brain regulating mood and appetite • Possible genetic influences

TREATMENT APPROACHES   Often difficult to treat but a range of therapeutic approaches is available

Biomedical Treatment	• Hospitalization may be needed to help anorexic patients restore a healthy body weight or bulimic patients break binge–purge cycles in cases where outpatient therapy has failed • Antidepressant medication may be used to regulate appetite by altering brain chemistry or to relieve underlying depression
Psychotherapy	• Psychodynamic therapy aims at exploring and resolving underlying psychological conflicts
Cognitive–Behavioral Therapy	• To help individuals with an eating disorder challenge self-defeating thoughts and beliefs and develop healthier eating habits and thinking patterns • Behavior modification helps hospitalized anorexic patients regain weight by means of linking desired rewards to appropriate eating behaviors • Exposure with response prevention helps bulimic individuals tolerate eating forbidden foods without bingeing and purging
Family Therapy	• May be used to resolve family conflicts and improve communication among family members

Source for prevalence rates: APA, 2000.

2003). The reasons? A diet containing too much high-fat, high-calorie food and heaping portions that are growing ever larger (Wadden, Brownell, & Foster, 2002; Mitka, 2003; Smith, 2003).

Are You Obese?

The most widely used standard for determining obesity is the *body mass index,* or BMI. The BMI takes into account a person's body weight and height. It is calculated by dividing body weight (in kilograms) by the square of the person's height (in meters).

The National Institutes of Health has set a level of 25 as the cutoff for determining whether a person is overweight (see Figure 10.3). This level is associated with a weight

Hazardous waist. Obesity is indeed a hazard to health and longevity.

level about 20% above the recommended weight for a person's age and height. People with a BMI of 30 or higher are considered obese.

What Causes Obesity?

What causes obesity? Body weight varies as a function of energy balance. When caloric intake exceeds energy output, the excess calories are stored in the body in the form of fat, leading to obesity (Esparza et al., 2000; Pi-Sunyer, 2003). The key to preventing obesity is to bring energy expenditure in line with energy (caloric) intake. Unfortunately, this is easier said than done. Research suggests that a number of factors contribute to the imbalance between energy intake and expenditure that underlies obesity, including genetics, metabolic factors, lifestyle factors, and psychological factors.

Genetic Factors Increasing evidence points to a genetic contribution to obesity (Branson et al., 2003; Farooqi et al, 2003; National Institutes of Diabetes and Digestive and Kid-

All in the family? Obesity tends to run in families. The question is, *Why?*

ney Diseases, 2001). But genetics doesn't tell the whole story. Obesity experts recognize that both genetics and environmental factors (diet and exercise patterns) contribute to obesity (Wing & Polley, 2001).

Metabolic Factors When we lose weight, especially significant amounts of weight, the body reacts as if it were starving. It responds to falling weight by slowing the *metabolic rate*, the rate at which it burns calories (Pinel et al., 2000; Woods et al., 2000). This makes it difficult to continue losing more weight or even maintain the weight loss. Some theorists believe that mechanisms in the brain control the body's metabolism to keep body weight around a genetically determined *set point* (Keesey & Powley, 1986). The ability of the body to adjust the metabolic rate downward when calorie intake declines may have helped ancestral humans survive times of famine (Grady, 2002). However, this mechanism is a bane to dieters today trying to lose weight and keep it off.

You may be able to offset this metabolic adjustment by following a more vigorous exercise regimen. Vigorous exercise burns calories directly and may increase the metabolic rate by replacing fat tissue with muscle, especially if the exercise program involves weight-bearing activity. Also, ounce for ounce, muscle tissue burns more calories than fat tissue. Before starting an exercise regimen, check with your physician to determine which types of activity are best suited to your overall health condition.

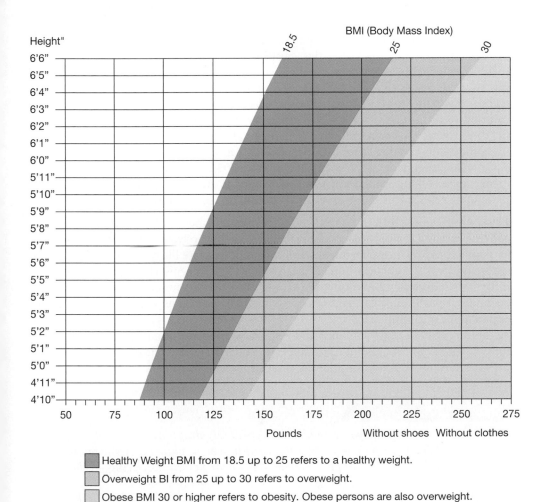

Healthy Weight BMI from 18.5 up to 25 refers to a healthy weight.

Overweight BI from 25 up to 30 refers to overweight.

Obese BMI 30 or higher refers to obesity. Obese persons are also overweight.

FIGURE 10.3 The body mass index.

Source: Report of the Dietary Guidelines Advisory Committee on the Dietary Guidelines for Americans, 2000.

Fat Cells The efforts of heavy people to keep a slender profile may be sabotaged by cells within their own bodies termed *fat cells*. No, fat cells are not cells that are fat. They are cells that store fat. Fat cells comprise fatty tissue in the body (also called *adipose tissue*). Obese people have more fat cells (Brownell & Wadden, 1992) than people who are not obese. Severely obese people may have some 200 billion fat cells, as compared to 25 or 30 billion in normal-weight individuals. Why does this matter? As time passes after eating, the blood sugar level declines, drawing out fat from these cells to supply more nourishment to the body. The hypothalamus in the brain detects the depletion of fat in these cells. The hypothalamus then signals the cerebral cortex, triggering the hunger drive, which motivates eating and thereby replenishes the fat cells.

People with more fatty tissue send more signals of fat depletion to the brain than people who are equal in weight but who have fewer fat cells. As a result, they feel food deprived sooner. Sad to say, dieters do not expel fat cells; instead, they shrink them. Many dieters who are markedly obese, even successful dieters, thus complain they are constantly hungry as they struggle to maintain normal weights. People with high levels of adipose tissue are doubly beset, because fatty tissue metabolizes food more slowly than muscle.

How is the number of fat cells in our bodies determined? Unfortunately, heredity seems to play a role. Excessive food intake in early childhood may also have an influence, however (Brownell & Wadden, 1992).

Lifestyle Factors Diet and exercise play important roles in obesity (Wing & Polley, 2001). Eating habits are changing, and not for the better. The constant bombardment of food-related cues in television commercials, print advertising, and the like, can take a toll on our individual and collective waistlines. Restaurants today are competing with each other in terms of who can pile the most food on ever-larger dinner plates. Pizzerias are using larger pans and fast-food restaurants are supersizing meals—all of which takes a toll on the waisline. That "big gulp" 64-ounce soft drink packs an incredible 800 calories! (Smith, 2003). Guess which character, after Santa Clauss, children recognize the most often? The answer: Ronald McDonald (Parloff, 2003).

Another contributing factor to our expanding waistlines is America's growing suburbs and the car-dependent culture it entails (McKee, 2003). City dwellers may burn off some extra calories hiking around town, but suburbanites must rely on their cars to get from place to place in spread-out communities in the suburban sprawl (Ewing et al., 2003).

Psychological Factors According to psychodynamic theory, eating is the cardinal oral activity. Psychodynamic theorists believe that people who were fixated in the oral stage by conflicts concerning dependence and independence are likely to regress in times of stress to excessive oral activities such as overeating. Other psychological factors connected with overeating and obesity include low self-esteem, lack of self-efficacy expectancies, family conflicts, and negative emotions. Emotions such as anger, fear, and depression can prompt excessive eating. Although connections between psychological factors and obesity affect both men and women, women most frequently seek treatment for obesity, largely because of the greater pressures they experience to adhere to social expectations of thinness. Consider the cases of Joan and Terry:

The Yo-Yo Syndrome

Joan was trapped in the yo-yo syndrome, repeatedly dropping 20 pounds, then regaining it. Whenever Joan got stuck at a certain weight plateau, or started to regain weight, her self-esteem plummeted. She'd hear herself muttering, "Who am I kidding? I'm not worthy of being thin. I should just accept being fat."

An incident with her mother revealed the trigger for her negative thinking. Joan had lost 24 pounds from an original weight of 174 and was beginning to feel good about herself. Most other people reinforced her by complimenting her on her weight loss. She called her mother, who lived in another state, to share the good news. Instead of jumping on the bandwagon, her mother cautioned her not to ex-

TRUTH or FICTION? *REVISITED*

After Santa Claus, the most recognizable figure to children is Ronald McDonald.

☑ **TRUE.** Ronald comes in Number 2. What might his popularity have to do with our fast-food-obsessed culture?

pect too much from her success. After all, her mother pointed out, she had been repeatedly disappointed in the past. The message came through loud and clear: Don't get your hopes up because you will only be more disappointed in the end. Joan's mother may have only meant to protect Joan from eventual disappointment, but her message reinforced Joan's negative view of herself: You're a loser. Don't expect too much of yourself. Don't try to change. You're a hopeless case.

As soon as she hung up the receiver, Joan rushed to the pantry. Without hesitation, she devoured three packages of chocolate chip cookies in a frenzied binge on the stairway. The next day she told her psychologist that the binge had reactivated childhood memories of bingeing on Oreo cookies while hiding in the stairwell.

—*From the Authors' Files*

Free to Be Herself

For years Terry's husband had scrutinized every morsel she consumed. "Haven't you had enough?" he would ask derisively. The more he harped on her weight, the more anger she felt, although she did not express her feelings directly. The criticism did not apply only to her weight. She also heard "You're not smart enough . . . Why don't you take better care of yourself? . . . How come you're not sexy?" After years of assault on her self-esteem, Terry petitioned for divorce, convinced the single life could be no worse than her marriage.

While separated and awaiting the final divorce decree, Terry felt free to be herself for the first time in her adult life. However, she had not expected the effect freedom would have on her weight. She ballooned from 155 pounds to 186 pounds within a few months. She identified leftover resentment from her marriage as the driving factor. "There's no one to make me diet anymore," she said. Her overeating was like saying, "See, I can eat if I want to." Without her husband, she could express her anger and outrage toward him by eating to excess. Unfortunately, her mode of expressing anger was self-defeating. Terry's lingering resentment encouraged her to act spitefully rather than constructively.

—*From the Authors' Files*

Ethnic and Socioeconomic Differences in Obesity

Obesity does not affect ethnic/racial groups in our society in equal proportions. It is more prevalent among people of color, especially among women of color (see Figure 10.4) (National Institutes of Health, 1998, 1999). The question is, why?

Socioeconomic Factors Obesity is more prevalent among poorer people (Stunkard & Sørensen, 1993). Because people of color in our society are as a group lower in socioeconomic status than (non-Hispanic) White Americans, we should not be surprised that rates of obesity are higher among people of color, at least among women of color.

Why are people on the lower rungs of the socioeconomic ladder at greater risk of obesity? For one thing, more affluent people have greater access to information about nutrition and health. They are more likely to take health education courses. They have greater access to health-care providers. Poorer people also exercise less regularly than more affluent people do. The fitness boom has been largely limited to more affluent people. They have the time, the income, and the space to exercise. Many poor people in the inner city also turn to food as a way of coping with the stresses of poverty, discrimination, crowding, and crime. And the only restaurants available in poorer communities tend to be fast-food outlets that serve only high-fat, high-sugar foods.

Acculturation Though acculturation may help immigrants adapt to their new culture, it can become a double-edged sword if it involves adopting the unhealthful dietary practices of the host culture. Consider that Japanese American men living in California

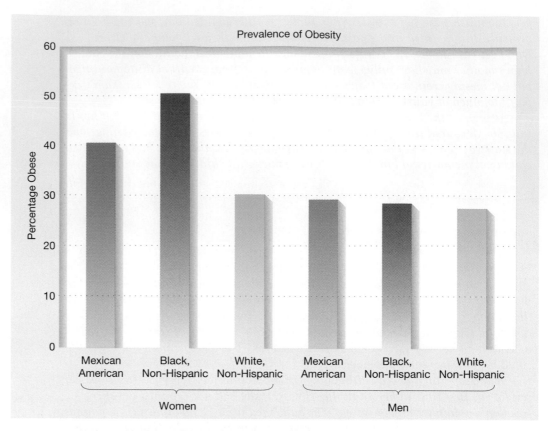

FIGURE 10.4 Rates of obesity (age 20 or higher).
This figure shows the rates of obesity among U.S. adults in relation to race and ethnicity.

Source: Health, United States, 2003, Centers for Disease Control and Prevention, National Center for Health Statistics, National Health and Nutrition Examination Survey.

and Hawaii eat a higher-fat diet than Japanese men do. Not surprisingly, the prevalence of obesity is two to three times higher among Japanese American men than among men living in Japan (Curb & Marcus, 1991).

Acculturation may also contribute to high rates of obesity among Native Americans, who are more likely than White Americans to have diseases linked to obesity, such as cardiovascular disease and diabetes (Broussard et al., 1991). A study of several hundred Cree and Ojibwa Indians in Canada found that nearly 90% of the women in the 45- to 54-year-old age group were obese (Young & Sevenhuyser, 1989). The adoption of a high-fat Western-style diet, the destruction of physically demanding native industries, and chronic unemployment combined with low levels of physical activity all contribute to obesity among Native Americans in the United States and Canada.

Metabolic Factors Biological factors, such as genetic differences in metabolic rates, may also play important roles. Researchers report that Black women had lower resting metabolic rates (the rate at which calories or food energy is burned while at rest) than did a sample of White women (Brody, 1997a).

Whatever the underlying reasons accounting for racial/ethnic differences in obesity may be, these differences may be narrowing. Though rates of obesity rose for men and women in all racial/ethnic groups during the 1980s, they rose most sharply among Whites (Burros, 1994; McMurtrie, 1994).

What Can Be Done? Preventing obesity calls for strategies that apply regardless of ethnicity or income level, such as cutting back on fat intake and sugar consumption and adopting regular exercise habits. But certain health initiatives need to be specifically targeted toward socially and economically disadvantaged groups, including the following (Jeffery, 1991):

- Increased access to health education
- Requirements for health education curricula in all public schools
- Guarantees of universal access to treatment of obesity
- Increased access to healthful foods and recreational opportunities

Facing the Challenge of Obesity

Despite their appeal, quickie diets don't work. More than 9 of 10 people who diet regain any weight they lose (Kolata, 2000b). Nor are diet drugs the answer, as they offer only temporary benefits at best and can carry significant side effects. Though drug companies are marshalling their efforts to find a "magic" pill to combat obesity, it is doubtful that they will succeed anytime soon (Grady, 2003; Stafford & Radley, 2003; Stipp, 2003).

But there is help available, the kind of help that comes through making lasting changes in diet and exercise habits. Behavior modification programs focus on helping individuals change problem eating habits by altering the "ABCs" of eating. The As are the *antecedents* of eating—cues or stimuli that trigger eating. These include environmental stimuli such as the sight and aromas of food, internal stimuli such as sensations of hunger, and emotional states such as anxiety, fatigue, anger, depression, and boredom. Controlling the As of eating takes the form of redesigning the environment so people are not continuously bombarded by food-related cues.

The Bs refer to eating *behaviors*. When you eat too quickly, your brain can't "catch up" with your stomach, because it takes about 15 minutes for feelings of satiety to register in the brain after food reaches the stomach. Therefore, you don't realize that you are full, and you keep eating. The Bs of eating extend to preparatory behaviors such as shopping for healthful foods, food storage habits, and so on.

The Cs are the *consequences* of overeating. The immediate pleasure of overeating often overshadows the long-term negative consequences of obesity and risk to health. Food is also connected to other reward systems. Food can become a substitute friend or lover. When people feel depressed, they can lift their spirits with food, if only temporarily. Because food activates the parasympathetic branch of the autonomic nervous system (through digestive processes), food also acts as a natural sedative or tranquilizer, quelling feelings of anxiety or tension and helping people relax or get to sleep. In helping people cope with the Cs of eating, behavior therapists make the long-term benefits of sensible eating more immediate. Methods commonly used to address the ABCs of eating are shown in Table 10.3.

Behavior modification leads to modest weight losses that are generally well maintained through at least a year after treatment (Brownell & Wadden, 1992). However, long-term outcomes reveal a dimmer picture (Devlin et al., 2000). As many as 90% to 95% of people who lose weight by dieting or behavior modification return to their baseline weight levels within 5 years (Kolata, 2000a; Wilson, 1994). The problem is that changes in diet, eating habits, and exercise patterns that led to initial weight loss are not carried over into changes in lifestyles that would promote long-term maintenance of weight loss. The lesson here is clear-cut: Long-term success in the "battle of the bulge" requires a lifelong commitment to a following a sensible, lower-calorie, lower-fat diet combined with regular exercise (Irwin et al., 2002; Manson et al., 2004; Wing & Polley, 2001).

Even people whose heredity may work against them can control their weight within some broad limits through adopting a sensible diet, increasing activity and exercise levels, and changing problem eating habits (Ross et al., 2000). A modest weight loss on the order of 10% or 15% of body weight can reduce the health risks associated with obesity (Lane, 1994).

SLEEP DISORDERS

Sleep is a biological function that remains in many ways a mystery. We know that sleep is restorative and that most of us need 7 or more hours of sleep a night to function at our best. Yet we cannot identify the specific biochemical changes occurring during sleep that account for its restorative function. We also know that many of us are troubled by sleep problems, although the causes of some of these problems remain obscure. Sleep

Taking it off and keeping it off. Health experts recognize that losing excess weight and keeping if off requires a lifelong commitment to adopting a sensible diet and engaging in regular exercise.

TABLE 10.3

Behavioral Techniques of Modifying the ABCs of Eating to Foster Weight Loss

Changing the As of Overeating

Change the Environmental As	Avoid settings that trigger overeating. (Eat at The Celery Stalk, not The Chocolate Gourmet.)
	Don't leave tempting treats around the house.
	Serve food on smaller plates. Use a lunch plate rather than a dinner plate.
	Don't leave seconds on the table.
	Serve preplanned portions. Do not leave open casseroles on the table.
	Immediately freeze leftovers. Don't keep them warm on the stove.
	Avoid the kitchen as much as possible.
	Disconnect eating from other stimuli, such as watching television, talking on the telephone, or reading.
	Establish food-free zones in your home. Imagine there is a barrier at the entrance to your bedroom that prevents the passage of food.
Control the Internal As	Don't bury disturbing feelings in a box of cookies or a carton of mocha delight ice cream.
	Relabel feelings of hunger as signals that you're burning calories. Say to yourself, "It's okay to feel hungry. It doesn't mean I'm going to die or pass out. Each minute I delay eating, more calories are burned."

Changing the Bs of Overeating

Slow Down the Pace of Eating	Put down utensils between bites.
	Take smaller bites.
	Chew thoroughly.
	Savor each bite. Don't wolf bites down to make room for the next.
	Take a break during the meal. Put down your utensils and converse with your family or guests for a few minutes. (Give your rising blood sugar level a chance to signal your brain.)
	When you resume eating, ask yourself whether you need to finish every bite. Leave something over to be thrown away or enjoyed later.
Modify Shopping Behavior	Shop from a list. Don't browse through the supermarket.
	Shop quickly. Don't make shopping the high point of your day.
	Treat the supermarket like enemy territory. Avoid the aisles containing junk food and snacks. If you must walk down these aisles, put on mental blinders and look straight ahead.
	Never shop when hungry. Shop after meals, not before.
Practice Competing Responses	Substitute nonfood activities for food-related activities. When tempted to overeat, leave the house, take a bath, walk the dog, call a friend, or walk around the block.
	Substitute low-calorie foods for high-calorie foods. Keep lettuce, celery, or carrots in the middle of the refrigerator so they are available when you want a snack.
	Fill spare time with non-food-related activities: volunteer at the local hospital, play golf or tennis, join exercise groups, read in the library (rather than the kitchen), take long walks.
Break the Chain	Stretch the overeating chain. Before allowing yourself to snack, wait 10 minutes. Next time wait 15 minutes, and so on.
	Break the eating chain at its weakest link. It's easier to interrupt the eating chain by taking a route home that bypasses the bakery than to exercise self-control when you're placing your order.

Changing the Cs of Overeating

Reward Yourself for Meeting Calorie/Diet Goals	One pound of body weight is equivalent to 3,500 calories. To lose 1 pound per week, you need to cut 3,500 calories per week, or 500 calories per day, from your typical calorie intake level, assuming your weight has been stable. Reward yourself for meeting weekly calorie goals. Reward yourself with gifts you would not otherwise purchase for yourself, such as a special gift for yourself, like a cashmere sweater or tickets to a show. Repeat the reward program from week to week. If during some weeks you miss your calorie goals, don't lose heart. Get back on track next week.
Use Self-Punishment	Charge yourself for deviating from your diet. Send one dollar to a political candidate you despise, or to a hated cause, each time the chocolate cake wins.

problems of sufficient severity and frequency that they lead to significant personal distress or impaired functioning in social, occupational, or other roles are classified in the *DSM* system as **sleep disorders.**

Highly specialized diagnostic facilities, called sleep disorders centers, have been established throughout the United States and Canada to provide a more comprehensive assessment of sleep problems than is possible in the typical office setting. People with sleep disorders typically spend a few nights at a sleep center, where they are wired to devices that track their physiological responses during sleep or attempted sleep—brain waves, heart and respiration rates, and so on. This form of assessment is termed *polysomnographic (PSG) recording,* because it involves simultaneous measurement of diverse physiological response patterns, including brain waves, eye movements, muscle movements, and respiration. Information obtained from physiological monitoring of sleep patterns is combined with that obtained from medical and psychological evaluations, subjective reports of sleep disturbance, and sleep diaries (i.e., daily logs compiled by the problem sleeper that track the length of time between retiring to bed and falling asleep, number of hours slept, nightly awakenings, daytime naps, and so on). Multidisciplinary teams of physicians and psychologists sift through this information to arrive at a diagnosis and suggest treatment approaches to address the presenting problem.

The *DSM* groups sleep disorders within two major categories: *dyssomnias* and *parasomnias.*

Dyssomnias

Dyssomnias are sleep disorders characterized by disturbances in the amount, quality, or timing of sleep. There are five specific types of dyssomnias: primary insomnia, primary hypersomnia, narcolepsy, breathing-related sleep disorder, and circadian rhythm sleep disorder.

Insomnia The term **insomnia** derives from the Latin *in-*, meaning "not" or "without," and, of course, *somnus,* meaning "sleep." Occasional bouts of insomnia, especially during times of stress, are not abnormal. But persistent insomnia characterized by recurrent difficulty getting to sleep or remaining asleep is an abnormal behavior pattern (Pallesen et al., 2001). Between 9% and 12% of adults in the United States suffer from

sleep disorders Persistent or recurrent sleep-related problems that cause distress or impaired functioning.

dyssomnias Sleep disorders involving disturbances in the amount, quality, or timing of sleep.

insomnia Difficulties falling asleep, remaining asleep, or achieving restorative sleep.

Sleep center. People with sleep disorders are often evaluated in sleep centers, where their physiological responses can be monitored as they sleep.

the most commonly occurring sleep disorder—primary (chronic) insomnia (Espie, 2002). Chronic insomnia lasting a month or longer is often a sign of an underlying physical problem or a psychological disorder such as depression, substance abuse, or physical illness (Kryger, Roth, & Dement, 2000; Lamberg, 2000; Morin, 2000) If the underlying problem is treated successfully, chances are that normal sleep patterns will be restored. Chronic insomnia that cannot be accounted for by another psychological or physical disorder or by the effects of drugs or medications is classified as a sleep disorder called *primary insomnia.*

Primary insomnia mostly affects people over the age 40 (Nagourney, 2001b). But many college students and other young adults are affected. People with primary insomnia have persistent difficulty falling asleep, remaining asleep, or achieving restorative sleep (sleep that leaves the person feeling refreshed and alert) for a period of a month or longer (Pallesen et al., 2001). Young people with primary insomnia usually complain it takes too long to get to sleep. Older people with insomnia are more likely to complain of waking frequently during the night or of waking too early in the morning.

Primary insomnia leads to daytime fatigue and causes significant levels of personal distress or difficulties performing usual social, occupational, student, or other roles. Not surprisingly, people with insomnia often have other psychological problems as well, especially anxiety and depression (Breslau et al., 1996; Morin & Ware, 1996).

Psychological factors can contribute to primary insomnia. People troubled by primary insomnia tend to bring their anxieties and worries to bed with them, which raises their bodily arousal to a level that prevents natural sleep. Then they worry about not getting enough sleep, which only compounds their sleep difficulties. They may try to force themselves to sleep, which tends to backfire by creating more anxiety and tension, making sleep even less likely. You cannot force yourself to fall asleep. You can only set the scene for sleep by going to bed when you are tired and relaxed and allowing sleep to occur naturally.

The principles of classical conditioning help explain the development of chronic insomnia (Pollack, 2004b). After pairing a few anxious, sleepless nights with stimuli associated with the bedroom, simply entering the bedroom for the night may be sufficient to elicit bodily arousal that impairs sleep onset. Thus, states of heightened arousal become conditioned responses elicited by the conditioned stimuli in the bedroom.

hypersomnia A pattern of excessive sleepiness during the day.

Hypersomnia The word *hypersomnia* is derived from the Greek *hyper,* meaning "over" or "more than normal," and the Latin *somnus,* meaning "sleep." Primary **hypersomnia** is a pattern of excessive sleepiness during the day that continues for a month or longer. The excessive sleepiness (sometimes referred to as "sleep drunkenness") may take the form of difficulty awakening following a prolonged sleep period (typically 8 to 12 hours). Or there may be a pattern of daytime sleep episodes, occurring virtually every day, in the form of intended or unintended napping (such as inadvertently falling asleep while watching TV). Despite the fact that daytime naps often last an hour or more, the person does not feel refreshed upon awakening. The disorder is considered primary because it cannot be accounted for by inadequate amounts of sleep during the night, by another psychological or physical disorder, or by drug or medication use.

Although many of us feel sleepy during the day from time to time, and may even drift off occasionally while reading or watching TV, the person with primary hypersomnia has persistent and severe periods of sleepiness that typically lead to difficulties in daily functioning, such as missing important meetings. Although the prevalence of the disorder is unknown, daytime sleepiness affects 0.5% to 5% of the adult population (APA, 2000).

narcolepsy A sleep disorder characterized by sudden, irresistible episodes of sleep.

Narcolepsy The word **narcolepsy** derives from the Greek *narke,* meaning "stupor" and *lepsis,* meaning "an attack." People with narcolepsy experience sleep attacks in which they suddenly fall asleep without warning at various times during the day. They remain asleep for about 15 minutes. The person can be in the midst of a conversation at one mo ment and slump to the floor fast asleep a moment later. The diagnosis is made when sleep attacks occur daily for a period of 3 months or longer and occur in conjunction with one or both of the following conditions: (a) *cataplexy* (a sudden loss of muscular control); and (b) intrusions of *REM sleep* in the transitional state between wakefulness and sleep (APA, 2000). REM, or rapid eye movement, sleep is the stage of sleep associated with dreaming. It is so named because the sleeper's eyes tend to dart about rapidly under the closed lids. Narcoleptic attacks are associated with an almost immediate transition into REM sleep from a state of wakefulness. In normal sleep, REM typically follows several stages of non-REM sleep.

Cataplexy typically follows a strong emotional reaction such as joy or anger. It can range from a mild weakness in the legs to a complete loss of muscle control that results in the person suddenly collapsing (Dahl, 1992; Siegel, 2004). People with narcolepsy may also experience *sleep paralysis,* a temporary state following awakening in which the person feels incapable of moving or talking. The person may also report frightening hallucinations, called *hypnagogic hallucinations,* which occur just before the onset of sleep and tend to involve visual, auditory, tactile, and kinesthetic (body movement) sensations.

Narcolepsy affects men and women equally and is a relatively uncommon disorder, affecting an estimated 0.02% (2 in 10,000) to 0.16% (16 in 10,000) people within the general adult population (APA, 2000). Unlike hypersomnia, in which daytime sleep episodes follow a period of increasing sleepiness, narcoleptic attacks occur abruptly, and the person awakes feeling refreshed. The attacks can be dangerous and frightening, especially if they occur when the person is driving or using heavy equipment or sharp implements. About 2 of 3 people with narcolepsy have fallen asleep while driving, and 4 of 5 have fallen asleep on the job (Aldrich, 1992). Household accidents resulting from falls are also common (Cohen, Ferrans, & Eshler, 1992). Not surprisingly, the disorder is associated with a lower quality of life in terms of general health and daily function- ing (Ferrans, Cohen, & Smith, 1992). The cause or causes of narcolepsy remain un- known, but suspicion focuses on the loss of brain cells in the hypothalamus that produce a sleep-regulating chemical (Bazell, 2000; Mignot & Thorsby, 2001; Peyron et al., 2000; Thannickal et al., 2000).

Breathing-Related Sleep Disorder

Breathing-Related Sleep Disorder People with a **breathing-related sleep dis- order** experience repeated disruptions of sleep due to respiratory problems (APA, 2000). These frequent disruptions of sleep result in insomnia or excessive daytime sleepiness.

The subtypes of the disorder are distinguished in terms of the underlying causes of the breathing problem. The most common type is *obstructive sleep apnea,* which in- volves repeated episodes of either complete or partial obstruction of breathing during sleep (Zwilich, 2000). The disorder affects as many as 18 million Americans (Bain, 2002; Smith, 2001b). The word *apnea* derives from the Greek prefix *a-,* meaning "not, with- out," and *pneuma,* meaning "breath." The breathing difficulty results from the blockage of airflow in the upper airways, which is often caused by a structural defect, such as an overly thick palate or enlarged tonsils or adenoids. In cases of complete obstruction, the sleeper may literally stop breathing for periods of from 15 to 90 seconds as many as 500 times during the night! When these lapses of breathing occur, the sleeper may suddenly sit up, gasp for air, take a few deep breaths, and fall back asleep without awakening or realizing that breathing was interrupted.

Although a biological reflex kicks in to force a gasping breath after these brief in- terruptions of breathing, the frequent disruptions of normal sleep resulting from ap- neas can leave people feeling sleepy the following day, making it difficult for them to function effectively. Obstructive sleep apnea is a relatively common problem, with es- timates indicating that the disorder affects approximately 1% to 10% of the adult pop- ulation and perhaps an even higher percentage of older adults (APA, 2000). The disorder

breathing-related sleep disorder A sleep disorder in which sleep is repeatedly disrupted by difficulty with breathing normally.

Sleep apnea. Loud snoring may be a sign of obstructive sleep apnea, a breathing-related sleep disorder in which the person may temporarily stop breathing as many as 500 times during a night's sleep. Loud snoring, described by bed partners as reaching levels of industrial noise pollution, may alternate with momentary silences when breathing is suspended.

is most common in middle age and affects men more frequently up to about the age of 50, at which point the rates are similar for men and women (Bardwell et al., 2003; Tishler et al., 2003). The disorder is more common among people who are obese, apparently because of a narrowing of the upper airways due to an enlargement of soft tissue (APA, 2000).

Not surprisingly, people who have sleep apnea report an impaired quality of life (Gall, Isaac, & Kryger, 1993). Sleep apnea is also a health concern because of its association with an increased risk of hypertension, a major risk factor for heart attacks and strokes (Arnulf et al., 2002; Peppard et al., 2000; Shahar, Whitney, & Redline, 2002).

Circadian Rhythm Sleep Disorder Most bodily functions follow a cycle or an internal rhythm—called a circadian rhythm—that lasts about 24 hours. Even when people are relieved of scheduled activities and work duties and placed in environments where they are not aware of the time of day, they usually follow relatively normal sleep–wake schedules.

In **circadian rhythm sleep disorder,** this rhythm becomes grossly disturbed because of a mismatch between the sleep schedule demands imposed on the person and the person's internal sleep–wake cycle. The disruption in normal sleep patterns can lead to insomnia or hypersomnia. For the disorder to be diagnosed, the mismatch must be persistent and severe enough to cause significant levels of distress or to impair the person's ability to function in social, occupational, or other roles. The jet lag that accompanies travel between time zones does not qualify because it is usually transient. However, frequent changes of time zones and frequent changes of work shifts (as encountered, for example, by nursing personnel) can induce more persistent or recurrent problems, resulting in a circadian rhythm sleep disorder. Treatment may include a program of gradual adjustments in the sleep schedule to allow the person's circadian system to become aligned with changes in the sleep–wake schedule (Dahl, 1992).

TRUTH or FICTION? *REVISITED*

Some people literally gasp for breath hundreds of times during sleep without realizing it.

☑ **TRUE.** People with sleep apnea may gasp for breath hundreds of times during the night without realizing it.

---

circadian rhythm sleep disorder A sleep disorder characterized by a mismatch between the body's normal sleep–wake cycle and the demands of the environment.

Parasomnias

The **parasomnias** are abnormal behavioral patterns or physiological events that take place during sleep or at the threshold between wakefulness and sleep. Among the more common parasomnias are nightmare disorder, sleep terror disorder, and sleepwalking disorder.

Nightmare Disorder **Nightmare disorder** involves recurrent awakenings from sleep because of frightening dreams (nightmares). The nightmares typically involve lengthy storylike dreams that include threats of imminent physical danger to the individual, such as being chased, attacked, or injured. The person usually recalls the nightmare vividly upon awakening. Although the person becomes alert quickly after awakening, anxiety and fear may linger and prevent a return to sleep. Perhaps half the adult population occasionally experiences nightmares, although the percentages of people having the intense, recurrent nightmares that would lead to a diagnosis of nightmare disorder remains unknown.

Nightmares are often associated with traumatic experiences and generally occur most often when the individual is under stress. Supporting the general link between trauma and nightmares, researchers report that the incidence of nightmares was greater among survivors of the 1989 San Francisco earthquake in the weeks following the quake than among comparison groups (Wood et al., 1992). An increased frequency of nightmares was also observed among children who were exposed to the 1994 Los Angeles earthquake (Kolbert, 1994).

Nightmares generally occur during REM sleep. REM periods tend to become longer and the dreams occurring during REM more intense in the latter half of sleep, so nightmares usually occur late at night or toward morning. Although nightmares may contain great motor activity, as in fleeing from an assailant, dreamers show little muscle activity. The biological processes that activate dreams—including nightmares—inhibit body movement, causing a type of paralysis. This is indeed fortunate, as it prevents the dreamer from jumping out of bed and running into a dresser or a wall in the attempt to elude the pursuing assailants from the dream.

Sleep Terror Disorder It typically begins with a loud, piercing cry or scream in the night. Even the most soundly sleeping parent will be summoned to the child's bedroom as if shot from a cannon. The child (most cases involve children) may be sitting up, appearing frightened and showing signs of extreme arousal—profuse sweating with rapid heartbeat and respiration. The child may start talking incoherently or thrash about wildly but remain asleep. If the child awakens fully, he or she may not recognize the parent or may attempt to push the parent away. After a few minutes the child falls back into a deep sleep and upon awakening in the morning remembers nothing of the experience. These terrifying attacks, called *sleep terrors,* are more intense than ordinary nightmares. Unlike nightmares, sleep terrors tend to occur during the first third of nightly sleep and during deep, non-REM sleep (Dahl, 1992).

Sleep terror disorder is characterized by repeated episodes of sleep terrors resulting in abrupt awakenings that begin with a panicky scream (APA, 2000). If awakening occurs during a sleep terror episode, the person will usually appear confused and disoriented for a few minutes. The person may feel a vague sense of terror and report some fragmentary dream images, but not the sort of detailed dreams typical of nightmares. Most of the time the person falls back asleep and remembers nothing of the experience the following morning.

Children with sleep terror disorder typically outgrow the disorder during adolescence. More boys than girls are affected, but among adults the gender ratio is about even. In adults, the disorder tends to follow a chronic course during which the frequency and intensity of the episodes waxes and wanes over time. Prevalence data on the disorder are lacking, but episodes of sleep terror are estimated to occur in 1% to 6% of children and in less than 1% of adults (APA, 2000). The cause of sleep terror disorder remains a mystery.

parasomnias Sleep disorders involving abnormal behaviors or physiological events that occur during sleep or while falling asleep.

nightmare disorder A sleep disorder characterized by recurrent awakenings due to frightening nightmares.

sleep terror disorder A sleep disorder characterized by recurrent episodes of sleep terror resulting in abrupt awakenings.

sleepwalking disorder A sleep disorder involving repeated episodes of sleepwalking.

Sleepwalking Disorder In **sleepwalking disorder,** there are repeated episodes in which the sleeper arises from bed and walks about the house while remaining fully asleep. Because these episodes tend to occur during the deeper stages of sleep in which there is an absence of dreaming, sleepwalking episodes do not seem to involve the enactment of a dream. In sleepwalking disorder, the person experiences repeated episodes of sleepwalking that are of sufficient severity to cause significant levels of personal distress or impaired functioning. Sleepwalking disorder is most common in children, affecting between 1% and 5% of children according to some estimates (APA, 2000). Between 10% and 30% of children are believed to have had at least one episode of sleepwalking. The prevalence of the disorder among adults is unknown, as are its causes. However, perhaps as many as 7% of adults have experienced occasional sleepwalking episodes (APA, 2000). Here, a man recounts a episode of sleepwalking from his childhood, which was one of many such incidents:

"I" "He's Only Sleepwalking"

All five of my sisters remember me as the family sleepwalker. Shannon [his sister] recalls helping Mom fold clothes in the den late one night when I appeared. Perhaps it was the fragrant smell of laundry, like incense, that drew me. I stopped in front of the TV in my pj's, eyes open, and began yelling. It was gibberish, Shannon remembers, but the choking anger behind it was alarming. While that behavior alone is odd, the aspect of her story I find most fascinating is my mother's reaction: unfazed, "He's only sleepwalking," she murmured, as though it were as common as the evening paperboy's late delivery. I imagine her then saying calmly, "Okay, Shannon, let's start on the towels."

—From Hayes, 2001

The causes of sleepwalking remain obscure, although both genetic and environmental factors are believed to be involved (Hublin et al., 1997). Although sleepwalkers typically avoid walking into things, accidents occasionally happen. Sleepwalkers tend to have a blank stare on their faces during these episodes. They are generally unresponsive to others and difficult to awaken. When they do awaken the following morning, they typically have little, if any, recall of the experience. If they are awakened during the episode, they may be disoriented or confused for a few minutes (as is the case with sleep terrors), but full alertness is soon restored. There is no basis to the belief that it is harmful to sleepwalkers to awaken them during episodes. Isolated incidents of violent behavior have been associated with sleepwalking, but these are rare and may well involve other forms of psychopathology.

Treatment of Sleep Disorders

The most common method for treating sleep disorders in the United States is the use of sleep medications, or **hypnotics.** However, because of problems associated with these drugs, nonpharmacological treatment approaches, principally cognitive–behavioral therapy, have come to the fore.

hypnotics Drugs with sleep-inducing properties.

Biological Approaches Antianxiety drugs are often used to treat insomnia, including a class of minor tranquilizers called benzodiazepines (for example, Valium, Librium, and Ativan) (Pallesen et al., 2001). (These drugs are also widely used in the treatment of anxiety disorders, as we saw in Chapter 6.) Another widely used drug, *zolpidem* (trade name Ambien), appears to be about as effective as the benzodiazepines but may produce fewer side effects and possibly fewer withdrawal effects (Kupfer & Reynolds, 1997). Sleep medications work by increasing the effects of GABA, a neurotransmitter that dampens the activity of the central nervous system (Pollack, 2004a).

When used for the short-term treatment of insomnia, antianxiety drugs generally reduce the time it takes to get to sleep, increase total length of sleep, and reduce nightly awakenings (Nowell et al., 1998). They work by reducing arousal and inducing feelings of calmness, thereby making the person more receptive to sleep.

A number of problems are associated with using drugs to combat insomnia (Kryger, Roth, & Dement, 2000). Sleep-inducing drugs tend to suppress REM sleep, which may interfere with some of the restorative functions of sleep. They can also lead to a carry-over or "hangover" the following day, which is associated with daytime sleepiness and reduced performance. Rebound insomnia can also follow discontinuation of the drug, causing worse insomnia than was originally the case. Rebound insomnia may be lessened, however, by tapering off the drug rather than abruptly discontinuing it. These drugs quickly lose their effectiveness at a given dosage level, so progressively larger doses must be used to achieve the same effect. High doses can be dangerous, especially if they are mixed with alcoholic beverages at bedtime.

Sleep medications can also produce chemical dependence if used regularly over time and can lead to tolerance (Pollack, 2004a). Once dependence is established, people experience withdrawal symptoms when they stop using the drugs, including agitation, tremors, nausea, headaches, and in severe cases, delusions or hallucinations.

Users can also become *psychologically* dependent on sleeping pills. That is, they can develop a psychological need for the medication and assume they will not be able to get to sleep without it. Because worry heightens bodily arousal, such self-doubts are likely to become self-fulfilling prophecies. Moreover, users may attribute their success in falling asleep to the pill and not to themselves, which strengthens reliance on the drugs and makes it harder to forgo using them.

Not surprisingly, there is little evidence of long-term benefits of drug therapy after withdrawal (Morin & Wooten, 1996). Relying on sleeping pills does nothing to resolve the underlying cause of the problem or help the person learn more effective ways of coping. If hypnotic drugs like benzodiazepines are prescribed for sleep problems, they should be used only for a brief time (a few weeks at most) and at the lowest possible dose (Dement, 1992; Kupfer & Reynolds, 1997). The aim should be to provide a temporary respite so the clinician can help the client find effective ways of handling the sources of stress and anxiety that contribute to insomnia.

Minor tranquilizers of the benzodiazepine family and tricyclic antidepressants are also used to treat the deep-sleep disorders—sleep terrors and sleepwalking. They seem to have a beneficial effect by decreasing the length of deep sleep and reducing partial arousals between sleep stages (Dahl, 1992). As with primary insomnia, use of sleep medications for these disorders incurs the risk of physiological and psychological dependence. Therefore, hypnotics should be used only in severe cases and only as a temporary means of "breaking the cycle." Other psychoactive drugs, such as stimulants, are sometimes used to help maintain wakefulness in people with narcolepsy and to combat daytime sleepiness in people with hypersomnia. Daily naps of 10 to 60 minutes and coping support from mental health professionals or self-help groups may also help people with narcolepsy (Aldrich, 1992). Sleep apnea is sometimes treated with drugs that act on brain centers that stimulate breathing. Surgery may also be used to widen the upper airways. Mechanical devices may help maintain breathing during sleep, such as a nose mask that exerts pressure to keep the upper airway passages open or a battery-powered device that continuously blows air into a mask worn over the nose, which prevents the airways from collapsing (e.g., Bain, 2002).

Psychological Approaches Psychological approaches have by and large been limited to treatment of primary insomnia. Cognitive–behavioral techniques are short term in emphasis and focus on directly lowering states of physiological arousal, modifying maladaptive sleeping habits, and changing dysfunctional thoughts. Cognitive–behavioral therapists typically use a combination of techniques, including

What's wrong with this picture? People who use their beds for many other activities, including eating, reading, and watching television, may find that lying in bed loses its value as a cue for sleeping. Behavior therapists use stimulus control techniques to help people with insomnia create a stimulus environment associated with sleeping.

stimulus control, establishment of a regular sleep-wake cycle, relaxation training, and rational restructuring.

Stimulus control involves changing the environment associated with sleeping. Under normal conditions, we learn to associate stimuli relating to lying down in bed with sleeping, so that exposure to these stimuli induces feelings of sleepiness. But when people use their beds for many other activities—such as eating, reading, and watching television—the bed may lose its association with sleepiness. Moreover, the longer the person with insomnia lies in bed tossing and turning, the more the bed becomes associated with cues related to anxiety and frustration. Stimulus control techniques attempt to strengthen the connection between the bed and sleep by restricting as much as possible the activities spent in bed to sleeping. Typically, the person is instructed to limit the time spent in bed trying to fall sleep to 10 or 20 minutes at a time. If sleep does not occur within the designated time, the person leaves the bed and goes to another room to restore a relaxed frame of mind before returning to bed, such as by sitting quietly, reading, watching TV, or practicing relaxation exercises. Moreover, the person is encouraged to establish a regular sleep–wake cycle by adopting more consistent sleeping and waking times (Riedel & Lichstein, 2001). Practicing relaxation techniques before bedtime (such as the Jacobson progressive relaxation approach described in Chapter 5), may reduce the level of physiological arousal.

A CLOSER LOOK
To Sleep, Perchance to Dream

Many of us have difficulty from time to time falling asleep or remaining asleep. Although sleep is a natural function and cannot be forced, we can develop more adaptive sleep habits that help us become more receptive to sleep (Edinger et al., 2001; Quesnel et al., 2003). However, if insomnia or other sleep-related problems persist or become associated with difficulties functioning during the day, it is worthwhile to have a professional evaluate the problem. Here are some techniques to help you acquire more adaptive sleep habits.

1. Go to bed only when you feel sleepy.
2. Limit your activities in bed as much as possible to sleeping. Avoid watching TV or reading in bed.
3. If after 10 to 20 minutes of lying in bed you are unable to fall asleep, get out of bed, go to another room, and put yourself in a relaxed mood by reading, listening to calming music, or practicing self-relaxation.
4. Establish a regular routine. Sleeping late to make up for lost sleep can throw off your body clock. Set your alarm for the same time each morning and get up, regardless of how many hours you have slept.
5. Avoid naps during the daytime. You'll feel less sleepy at bedtime if you catch *z's* during the afternoon.
6. Avoid ruminating in bed. Don't focus on problems as you attempt to sleep. Tell yourself that you'll think about tomorrow, tomorrow. Help yourself enter a more sleepful frame of mind by engaging in a mental fantasy or mind trip, or just let all thoughts slip away from consciousness. If an important idea comes to you, don't rehearse it in your mind. Jot it down on a handy pad so you won't lose it. But if thoughts persist, get up and follow them elsewhere.
7. Put yourself in a relaxed frame of mind before sleep. Some people unwind before bed by reading; others prefer watching TV or just resting quietly.

Do whatever you find most relaxing. You may find it helpful to incorporate within your regular bedtime routine the techniques for lowering your level of arousal discussed earlier in this text, such as meditation or progressive relaxation.

8. Establish a regular daytime exercise schedule. Regular exercise during the day (not directly before bedtime) can help induce sleepiness upon retiring.
9. Avoid use of caffeinated beverages, such as coffee and tea, in the evening or late afternoon. Also, avoid drinking alcoholic beverages. Alcohol can interfere with normal sleep patterns (reduced total sleep, REM sleep, and sleep efficiency), even when consumed 6 hours before bedtime (Landolt et al., 1996).
10. Practice rational restructuring. Substitute rational alternatives for self-defeating thoughts. Here are some examples:

Self-Defeating Thoughts	Rational Alternatives
"I must fall asleep right now or I'll be a wreck tomorrow."	"I may feel tired, but I've been able to get by with little sleep before. I can make up for it tomorrow by getting to bed early."
"What's the matter with me that I can't seem to fall asleep?"	"Stop blaming yourself. You can't control sleep. Just let whatever happens, happen."
"If I don't get to sleep right now, I won't be able to concentrate tomorrow on the exam (conference, meeting, etc.)."	"My concentration may be off a bit, but I'm not going to fall apart. There's no point blowing things out of proportion. I might as well get up for a while and watch a little TV rather than lie here ruminating."

Rational restructuring involves substituting rational alternatives for self-defeating, maladaptive thoughts or beliefs (see accompanying "A Closer Look" section for examples). The belief that failing to get a good night's sleep will lead to unfortunate, even disastrous, consequences the next day reduces the chances of falling asleep because it raises the level of anxiety. Most of us function reasonably well if we lose sleep or even miss a night of sleep.

Overall, cognitive–behavioral approaches have produced substantial benefits in treating chronic insomnia, as measured by the time it takes to get to asleep, wakefulness during the night, and improved ratings of sleep quality (Edinger et al., 2001; Espie, Inglis, Tessier, & Harvey, 2001; Rybarczyk et al., 2002). In one recent study, two of three treatment participants fell asleep within 30 minutes of retiring (Espie, Inglis, & Harvey, 2001). Sleep experts believe that CBT is just as effective as sleep medication in treating insomnia in the short term and more effective in the long term (Smith, 2001b). Charles Morin, a leading expert on the treatment of insomnia, notes that sleep medication may produce faster results, but behavioral treatment produces long-lasting results (cited in Pollack, 2004a, 2004b).

Overview of Sleep Disorders

TYPES OF SLEEP DISORDERS

	Description	Subtypes/Features/Prevalence Rates (in parentheses)
Dyssomnias	Disturbances in the amount, quality, or timing of sleep	• **Insomnia:** Difficulty falling asleep, remaining asleep, or getting enough restful sleep (9%–12%) • **Hypersomnia:** Excessive daytime sleepiness (unknown) • **Narcolepsy:** Sudden attacks of sleep during the day (0.2%–0.16%) • **Breathing-Related Sleep Disorder:** Sleep repeatedly interrupted due to difficulties breathing (1%–10%) • **Circadian Rhythm Sleep Disorder:** Disruption of the internal sleep–wake cycle due to time changes in sleep patterns (unknown)
Parasomnias	Disturbances occurring either during sleep or at the threshold between sleep and wakefulness	• **Nightmare Disorder:** Repeated awakenings due to nightmares (unknown) • **Sleep Terror Disorder:** Repeated experiences of sleep terrors resulting in abrupt awakenings (unknown) • **Sleepwalking Disorder:** Repeated episodes of sleepwalking (estimated 1%–5% in children)

CAUSAL FACTORS   Many causes remain unspecified, but biological and psychosocial factors are prominent contributors

Biological Factors	• Underlying physical problems (in insomnia, apnea, and narcolepsy) • Possible genetic defects disrupting brain mechanisms controlling sleep (in narcolepsy) • Drug use interfering with normal sleep
Psychological Factors	• Psychological factors, such as anxiety or depression, that interfere with getting to sleep or remaining asleep • Frequent time shifting of sleep and waking times (in circadian rhythm sleep disorder) • Exposure to trauma (in nightmare disorder)

TREATMENT APPROACHES   Sleep medication may offer short-term relief for insomnia, but cognitive–behavioral therapy helps people change unhealthy sleep habits

Drug Therapy	• May be used for short-term relief of insomnia and to treat deep-sleep disorders (sleep terrors and sleepwalking), narcolepsy, and sleep apnea
Biomedical Treatment	• Surgery or mechanical devices may be used to open airways in apnea patients
Cognitive–Behavioral Therapy	• May be used to change maladaptive sleep habits and dysfunctional thoughts or beliefs about sleep

Sources for prevalence rates: APA, 2000, Espie, 2002

Note: Prevalence rates for dyssomnias are for adults

SUMMING UP

Eating Disorders

What are the major types of eating disorders? Two major types of eating disorders are included in the *DSM:* anorexia nervosa and bulimia nervosa. Anorexia nervosa involves maintenance of weight more than 15% below normal levels, intense fears of becoming overweight, distorted body image, and in females, amenorrhea. Bulimia nervosa involves preoccupation with weight control and body shape, repeated binges, and regular purging to keep weight down, which is characterized by self-starvation and failure to maintain normal body weight. Another type of eating disorder, binge-eating disorder (BED), is presently classified as a potential disorder requiring further study.

What factors are implicated in the development of eating disorders? Eating disorders typically begin in adolescence and affect many more females than males. Anorexia and bulimia are linked to preoccupations with weight control and maladaptive ways of trying to keep weight down. Many other factors are implicated in their development, including social pressures on young women to adhere to unrealistic standards of thinness, issues of control, underlying psychological problems, and conflict within the family, especially over issues of autonomy. People with BED tend to be older than those with anorexia or bulimia and to suffer from obesity.

What are the major forms of treatment for eating disorders? Severe cases of anorexia are often treated in an inpatient setting where a refeeding regimen can be closely monitored. Behavior modification and other psychological interventions, including psychotherapy and family therapy, may also be helpful. Most cases of bulimia are treated on an outpatient basis, with evidence supporting the therapeutic benefits of cognitive–behavioral therapy, interpersonal therapy, and antidepressant medication. Cognitive–behavioral therapy and antidepressant medication have shown positive effects in treating binge-eating disorder.

Obesity: A National Epidemic

Is obesity a psychological disorder? No, obesity is classified as a chronic disease, not a psychological disorder. It is a major risk factor linked to many serious chronic diseases, including heart disease and diabetes. Rates of obesity in the United States have been rising. The causes of obesity include genetic factors, metabolic factors, fat cells, lifestyle factors, and psychological factors.

Why is obesity difficult to treat? Quickie diets and diet pills don't work because long-term success in losing weight and keeping it off depends on making lasting changes in eating habits and exercise patterns.

Sleep Disorders

What are the major types of sleep disorders? Sleep disorders are classified in two major categories, dyssomnias and parasomnias. Dyssomnias are disturbances in the amount, quality, or timing of sleep. They include five specific types: primary insomnia, primary hypersomnia, narcolepsy, breathing-related sleep disorder, and circadian rhythm sleep disorder. Parasomnias are disturbed behaviors or abnormal physiological responses occurring either during sleep or at the threshold between wakefulness and sleep. Parasomnias include three major types: nightmare disorder, sleep terror disorder, and sleepwalking disorder.

What are the major forms of treatment for sleep disorders? The most common form of treatment of sleep disorders involves the use of antianxiety drugs. However, use of these drugs should be time limited because of the potential for psychological and/or physical dependence, among other problems associated with their use. Cognitive–behavioral interventions have produced substantial benefits in helping people with chronic insomnia.

Norms for the Fear of Fat Scale

Comparative scores are available for women only. You may compare your own score on the Fear of Fat scale to those obtained by the following groups:

Group	N	Mean
Nondieting college women (women satisfied with their weight)	49	17.30
General female college population	73	18.33
College women who are dissatisfied with their weight and have been on three or more diets during the past year	40	23.90
Bulimic college women (actively bingeing and purging)	32	30.00
Anorexic women in treatment	7	35.00

Source: Goldfarb, L. A., Dykens, E. M., & Gerrard, M. (1985). The Goldfarb Fear of Fat scale. *Journal of Personality Assessment, 49,* 329–332.

Keep the following in mind as you interpret your score:

1. The Goldfarb samples are quite small.
2. A score at a certain level does not place you in that group; it merely means that you report an equivalent fear of fat. In other words, a score of 33.00 does not indicate you have bulimia or anorexia. It means that your self-reported fear of fat approximates those reported by bulimic and anorexic women in the Goldfarb study.

KEY TERMS

anorexia nervosa *(p. 331)*

bulimia nervosa *(p. 331)*

eating disorder *(p. 332)*

body mass index *(p. 337)*

binge-eating disorder (BED) *(p. 343)*

obesity *(p. 344)*

sleep disorders *(p. 353)*

dyssomnias *(p. 353)*

insomnia *(p. 353)*

hypersomnia *(p. 354)*

narcolepsy *(p. 354)*

breathing-related sleep disorder *(p. 355)*

circadian rhythm sleep disorder *(p. 356)*

parasomnias *(p. 357)*

nightmare disorder *(p. 357)*

sleep terror disorder *(p. 357)*

sleepwalking disorder *(p. 358)*

hypnotics *(p. 358)*

WEB TOOLS

The companion website offers tools to enrich your learning experience and help you succeed in class. Go to www.prenhall.com/nevid for the gateway to the following resources:

- **VIDEO** links to connect to the video case files on the companion CD-ROM. VIDEO icons in the margins of the chapter highlight the case examples included in the CD-ROM. You can also access the CD-ROM directly if you do not have a Web connection.

- **QUIZ** links to self-scoring quizzes corresponding to each section of the chapter. The quizzes help you review your knowledge of the content in each chapter.

- **WEB** links to direct you to related sites that enhance your learning of abnormal psychology.

CHAPTER ELEVEN

Disorders Involving Gender and Sexuality

CHAPTER OUTLINE

"I Know Something None Of You Will Ever Know"

Gender identity disorder (GID) is defined by the American Psychiatric Association (2000) as a "strong and persistent cross-gender identification [accompanied by] a persistent discomfort with his or her sex or sense of appropriateness in the gender role of that sex." All of my life, I harbored the strongest conviction that I was inappropriately assigned to the wrong [sex]—that of a man—when inside I knew myself to be a woman. Even so (and like so many other GIDs) I continued a life-long struggle with this deeply felt mistake; I was successful in school, became a national swimming champion, received my college degrees, married twice (fathering children in both marriages) and was respected as a competent and good man in the workplace. However, the persistently unrelenting wrongfulness of my life continued. Not until my fourth decade was I truly able to address my gender issue.

Jay Thomas, Ph.D., underwent gender reassignment and officially became Jayne Thomas, Ph.D., in November of 1985, and what has transpired in the ensuing years has been the most enlightening of glimpses into the plight of humankind. As teachers we are constantly being taught by those we purport to instruct. My students, knowing my background (I share who I am when it is appropriate to do so), find me accessible in ways that many professors are not. Granted, I am continually asked the titillating questions that one watching Geraldo might ask and we do have fun with the answers (several years ago I even appeared on a few of the Geraldo shows). My students, however, are able to take our discussions beyond the sensational and superficial, and we enter into meaningful dialogue regarding sex differences in society and the workplace, sexual harassment, power and control issues in relationships, and what it really means to be a man or a woman.

Iconoclastically, I try to challenge both the masculine and feminine. "I know something none of you women know or will ever know in your lifetime." I can provocatively address the females in my audiences as Jayne. "I once lived as a man and have been treated as an equal. You never have nor will you experience such equality." Or, when a male student once came to my assistance in a classroom, fixing an errant video playback device and then strutting peacock-like back to his seat as only a satisfied male can, I teasingly commented to a nearby female student, "I used to be able to do that."

Having once lived as a man and now as a woman, I can honestly state that I see profound differences in our social/psychological/biological being as man and woman. I have now experienced many of the ways in which women are treated as less than men. Jay worked as a consultant to a large banking firm in Los Angeles and continued in that capacity as a woman following her gender shift. Amazingly the world presented itself in a different perspective. As Jay, technical presentations to management had generally been received in a positive manner and credit for my work fully acknowledged. Jayne now found management less accessible, credit for her efforts less forthcoming and, in general, found herself working harder to be well prepared for each meeting than she ever had as a male. As a man, her forceful and impassioned presentations were an asset; as a woman they definitely seemed a liability.

On one occasion, as Jayne, when I passionately asserted my position regarding what I felt to be an important issue, my emotion and disappointment in not getting my point across (my voice showed my frustration) was met with a nearby colleague (a man) reaching to touch my arm with words of reassurance, "There, there, take it easy, it will be all right." Believe me; that never happened to Jay. There was also an occasion when I had worked most diligently on a presentation to management only to find the company vice president more interested in the fragrance of my cologne than my technical agenda.

Certainly there are significant differences in the treatment of men and women, and yet I continue to be impressed with how similar we two genders really are. Although I have made this seemingly enormous change in lifestyle (and it is immense in so many ways), I continue as the same human being, perceiving the same world through these same sensory neurons. The difference—I now find myself a more comfortable and serene being, than the paradoxical woman in a man's body, with anatomy and gender that have attained congruence . . .

Having lived as man and woman in the same lifetime one personal truth seems clear. Rather than each gender attempting to change and convert the other to their own side, as I often see couples undertaking to accomplish (women need be more logical and men more sharing of their emotions), we might more productively come together in our relationships building upon our gender uniqueness and strengths. Men and women have different perspectives, which can be used successfully to address life's issues.

—*Dr. Jayne Thomas, in her own words*[1]

[1] Dr. Thomas taught psychology at Mission College in California. Sadly, she passed away in 2002, a personal loss to your authors and to the general community.

Truth or Fiction?

T☐ F☐ Gay males and lesbians have the gender identity of the other sex. (p. 369)

T☐ F☐ Orgasm is a reflex. (p. 373)

T☐ F☐ Wearing revealing bathing suits is a form of exhibitionism. (p. 385)

T☐ F☐ People who become sexually aroused while watching their partners disrobe are voyeurs. (p. 387)

T☐ F☐ Some people cannot become sexually aroused unless they are subjected to pain or humiliation. (p. 389)

T☐ F☐ Most rapes are committed by strangers. (p. 396)

T☐ F☐ Deep down, most women desire to be raped. (p. 397)

Dr. Jayne Thomas

JAY THOMAS WAS SO UNCOMFORTABLE WITH HIS anatomical gender that he underwent a sex reassignment procedure. Imagine what it must be like to be living in a body that feels alien to you by dint of the sex to which you were born. When children are born, even before fingers and toes are counted, the obstetrician will announce, "It's a girl" (or a boy). In this chapter we explore a wide range of psychological disorders involving not only sexual identity, but also deviant or atypical patterns of sexual attraction and problems relating to lack of sexual interest or response. We will also consider a form of abnormal behavior that is not classified as a psychological disorder but that can have devastating emotional and physical effects on people it victimizes: rape.

In sexual behavior, as in other types of behavior, the lines between the normal and the abnormal are not always agreed upon or drawn precisely. Sex, like eating, is a natural function. Also like eating, sexual behavior varies greatly among individuals and cultures. Our sexual behavior is profoundly affected by cultural, religious, and moral beliefs, custom, folklore, and superstition. In the realm of sexual behavior, our conceptions of what is normal or abnormal are influenced by cultural learning imparted through the family, school, and religious institutions.

Many patterns of sexual behavior, such as masturbation, premarital intercourse, and oral–genital sex are normal in contemporary in American society, if frequency of occurrence is any indication. But frequency is not the only yardstick of normal behavior. Behavior is frequently labeled abnormal when it deviates from the norms of one's society. For example, kissing is highly popular in Western cultures but is consider deviant behavior in some preliterate societies in South America and Africa (Rathus, Nevid, & Fichner-Rathus, 2005). Members of the Thonga tribe of Africa were shocked when they first observed European visitors kissing. One man exclaimed, "Look at them—they eat each other's saliva and dirt." We will see that some sex-related activities are considered as abnormal in the eyes of mental health professionals as kissing seemed to the Thonga—for example, feeling that one is trapped in the body of the wrong sex, being more sexually aroused by articles of clothing than by one's partner, or losing interest in sex or being unable to become sexually aroused despite adequate stimulation.

We may also consider behavior to be abnormal when it is self-defeating, harms others, or causes personal distress. We shall see how psychological disorders discussed in this chapter meet one or more of these standards of abnormality. In exploring these disorders, we touch on questions that probe the boundaries between abnormality and normality. For example, is it abnormal to have difficulty becoming sexually aroused or reaching orgasm? How do mental health professionals define exhibitionism and voyeurism? When is normal to watch another person disrobe, and when is it abnormal? Where do we draw the lines?

We begin with gender identity disorder, a disorder that touches on the most basic part of our experience as a sexual being—our sense of being male or female.

GENDER IDENTITY DISORDER

gender identity One's psychological sense of being female or being male.

gender identity disorder One's psychological sense of being female or being male.

Gender identity is the psychological sense of being male or female. For most people, gender identity is consistent with a person's anatomic sex. In **gender identity disorder** (GID), however, there is a conflict between one's anatomic sex and one's gender identity.

Gender identity disorder (also referred to as *transsexualism*) may begin in childhood. Some children with the disorder find their anatomic sex to be a source of persistent and intense distress. The diagnosis is not used simply to label "tomboyish" girls and "sissyish" boys. It is applied to children who persistently repudiate their anatomic traits or who are preoccupied with clothing or activities that are stereotypical of the other sex (see Table 11.1). The diagnosis of GID applies to both children and adults who perceive

What is normal and what is abnormal? The cultural context must be considered in defining what is normal and what is abnormal in the realm of sexual and sexually related behavior. The people in these photographs—and the ways in which they cloak or expose their bodies—would be quite out of place in one another's societies.

themselves psychologically as members of the other sex and who show persistent discomfort with their anatomic sex.

Although the overall rate of GID is not known, it is believed to occur about five times more often in boys than girls (Jones & Hill, 2002). GID takes many paths. It can end by adolescence, with the child's becoming more accepting of her or his gender identity. Or it may persist into adolescence or adulthood (Cohen-Kettenis, 2001). The child sometimes develops a gay male or lesbian sexual orientation (Bailey, 2003a, 2003b).

TABLE 11.1

Clinical Features of Gender Identity Disorder

(A) A strong, persistent identification with the other gender. At least four of the following features are required to make the diagnosis in children:

(1) Repeated expression of the desire to be a member of the other sex (or expression of the belief that one actually belongs to the other sex).

(2) Preference for wearing clothing stereotypical of members of the other sex.

(3) Persistent fantasies about being a member of the other sex, or assumption of roles played by members of the other sex in make-believe play.

(4) Desire to participate in activities and games considered stereotypical of the other sex.

(5) Preference for playmates that belong to the other sex at ages when children typically prefer playmates of their own sex.

Adolescents and adults typically express the wish to be of the other sex, frequently "pass" as a member of the other sex, or believe that their emotions and behavior typify the other sex.

(B) A strong, persistent sense of discomfort with one's anatomic sex or with the stereotypical gender role of one's sex.

In children, these features are commonly present: Boys state that their external genitals are repugnant or that it would be better not to have them, show aversion to masculine-typed toys, games, and rough-and-tumble play. Girls prefer not to urinate while sitting, express the wish not to grow breasts or to menstruate, or show an aversion to feminine-typed clothing.

Adolescents and adults typically state that they were born the wrong sex and express the wish for medical intervention (e.g., hormone treatments, surgery, or both) to rid them of their own sex characteristics and simulate the characteristics of the other sex.

(C) There is no "intersex condition," such as ambiguous sexual anatomy, that might give rise to the individual's feelings.

(D) The features cause serious distress or impair key areas of occupational, social, or other functioning.

Source: Adapted from the *DSM-IV-TR* (APA, 2000)

Gender Identity Disorder:
The Case of Denise
"My earliest memories, back when I was about 4 years old . . . I remember cross-dressing back then, all the way until really around my puberty."

Transsexual adults typically showed cross-gender preferences in play and dress in early childhood. Some report feeling that they belonged to the opposite sex for as long as they could remember. Some male transsexuals recall that, as children, they preferred playing with dolls, enjoyed wearing frilly dresses, and disliked rough-and-tumble play. Some female transsexuals report that as children they disliked dresses and acted like tomboys. They preferred playing "boys' games" and playing with boys. Female transsexuals appear to have an easier time adjusting than male transsexuals (Selvin, 1993). Tomboys generally find acceptance more easily than "sissy boys." Even in adulthood, it may be easier for a female transsexual to wear male clothes and "pass" as a slightly built man than it is for a brawny man to pass for a large woman.

The prevalence of GID is unknown, but the disorder is certainly uncommon. Fewer than 20,000 people are known to have undergone sex-reassignment surgery (Jones & Hill, 2002). However, not all people with GID seek reassignment surgery. For those who do, surgeons attempt to construct external genital organs that closely resemble those of the opposite sex. Male-to-female surgery is generally more successful than female-to-male. Hormone treatments promote the development of secondary sex characteristics of the reassigned sex, such as growth of fatty tissue in the breasts in male-to-female cases and the growth of the beard and body hair in female-to-male cases. People who undergo sex-reassignment surgery can participate in sexual activity and even reach orgasm, but they cannot conceive or bear children because they lack the internal reproductive organs of their newly reconstructed sex. Investigators generally find positive psychological outcomes following sex-reassignment surgery (e.g., Cohen-Kettenis & van Goozen, 1997), especially when surgical treatment is restricted to the most appropriate candidates. In one study, 14 male-to-female and 5 female-to-male individuals were found to be functioning well socially and psychologically postoperatively. None expressed regrets (Cohen-Kettenis & van Goozen, 1997). Another study found that none of 20 adolescents who underwent sex reassignment surgery later expressed regrets (Smith et al., 2001).

Dr. Jayne Thomas, whom we introduced at the beginning of the chapter, spoke about the psychological adjustment and shift in gender roles she experienced following sex-reassignment surgery.

"Everybody Is Born Unique, But Most of Us Die Copies"

Does the shifting of gender role create difficulties in the GID's life? Most assuredly it does. Family and intimate relationships rank highest among those issues most problematic for the transitioning individual to resolve. When one shifts gender role the effects of such a change are global; as ripples in a pond, the transformation radiates outward impacting all that have significantly touched the GID's life. My parents had never realized that their eldest son was dealing with such a lifelong problem. Have they accepted or do they fully understand the magnitude of my issue? I fear not. After almost fifteen years of having lived as a female, my father continues to call me by my male name. I do not doubt my parents' or children's love for me, but so uninformed are we of the true significance of gender identity that a clear understanding seems light-years away. Often I see my clients losing jobs, closeness with family members, visitation rights with children, and generally becoming relegated to the role of societal outcast. Someone once stated that "Everybody is born unique, but most of us die copies"—a great price my clients often pay for personal honesty and not living their lives as a version of how society deems they should.

—Dr. Jayne Thomas

Men seeking sex-reassignment outnumber women by perhaps 3 or 4 to 1. Most female-to-male individuals with GID do not seek complete sex-reassignment surgery. Instead, they may remove their internal sex organs (ovaries, fallopian tubes, uterus) along with the fatty tissue in their breasts. Testosterone (male sex hormone) treatments increase muscle mass and growth of the beard. But only a few female-to-male transsexuals have the series of operations necessary to construct an artificial penis, largely because the constructed penises do not work very well, and the surgery is expensive. Therefore, most female-to-male transsexuals limit their physical alteration to hysterectomies, mastectomies, and testosterone treatment (Bailey, 2003b).

Gender identity should not be confused with sexual orientation. Gay males and lesbians have erotic interests in members of their own sex, but their gender identity (sense of being male or female) is consistent with their anatomic sex. They do not desire to become members of the other sex or despise their own genitalia, as we find in many people with GID. Though homosexuality is not classified as a mental disorder, questions remain about whether *homophobia,* or hatred and fear of gay men and lesbians, is a form of psychopathology (see the "A Closer Look" feature).

Theoretical Perspectives

The origins of GID remain unclear (van Goozen et al., 2002). Psychodynamic theorists point to extremely close mother–son relationships, empty relationships with parents, and fathers who were absent or detached (Stoller, 1969). These family circumstances may foster strong identification with the mother in young males, leading to a reversal of expected gender roles and identity. Girls with weak, ineffectual mothers and strong masculine fathers may overly identify with their fathers and develop a psychological sense of themselves as "little men."

Learning theorists similarly point to father absence in the case of boys—to the unavailability of a strong male role model. Children who were reared by parents who had wanted children of the other gender and who strongly encouraged cross-gender dressing and patterns of play may learn socialization patterns and develop a gender identity associated with the opposite sex.

TRUTH or FICTION? *REVISITED*

Gay males and lesbians have the gender identity of the other sex.

☑ **FALSE.** Gender identity should not be confused with sexual orientation. Gay males and lesbians have erotic interest in members of their own gender but their gender identity is consistent with their anatomic sex.

Nonetheless, the great majority of people with the types of family histories described by psychodynamic and learning theorists do not develop GID. Perhaps these family factors play a role in combination with a biological predisposition. We know that people with GID often showed cross-gender preferences in toys, games, and clothing very early in childhood. If there are critical early learning experiences in GID, they most probably occur very early in life.

GID may develop as the result of an interaction in utero between the developing brain and the release of male sex hormones (Dennis, 2004). Investigators suspect that the release of male sex hormones during prenatal development has an organizing effect on the brain, sculpting it in a masculine direction if sufficient amounts of the hormone are present, or in a feminine direction if the hormone is absent (as is normally the case with female fetuses) (van Goozen et al., 2002). Perhaps a disturbance in the endocrine (hormonal) environment during gestation leads the brain to become differentiated with respect to gender identity in one direction while the genitals develop normally in the other direction. However, we lack direct evidence of abnormal hormonal balances during prenatal development that could explain the development of transsexualism (Gooren & Kruijver, 2002). Even if such hormonal factors were demonstrated, they are unlikely to be the sole cause of transsexualism.

Investigators are also actively exploring possible genetic underpinnings of transsexualism (Dennis, 2004). As with many psychological disorders, biological factors, such as genetic and hormonal influences, may create a disposition that interacts with early life experiences to result in GID. Yet speculations about the origins of gender identity disorder remain unsubstantiated by hard evidence.

homophobia Hatred and fear of lesbians and gay males.

heterosexism The culturally based belief system that holds that only reproductive sexuality between men and women is psychologically healthy and morally correct.

A CLOSER LOOK
Homophobia: Social Prejudice or Personal Psychopathology?

George Weinberg (1972) coined the term **homophobia** to describe the persistent, irrational fear of lesbians and gay men. Homophobia is deemed irrational because is usually based on beliefs that are of questionable validity or have been overwhelmingly disputed. For example, homophobes may believe, falsely, that gay men are more likely to become child molesters than heterosexual men, that lesbians and gay men wish to be members of the other gender, that they do not make good parents, that their children will become lesbian or gay, that they are sexually promiscuous or indiscriminate in their sexual attractions, that their relationships are transitory and focused only on sex, that they are responsible for the AIDS epidemic, and so on. People who hold such beliefs may use them to justify prejudical acts against lesbians and gay men, ranging from personal rudeness or hostility to vandalism, harassment, and even violent physical attacks (Freiberg, 1995; Katz, 1995). As these attacks have become commonplace in many parts of the United States, they have created a climate of terror for lesbians and gay men.

But do the roots of homophobia lie within the individual or the society? Many theoreticians use the term **heterosexism** (Herek, 1996) to describe a broader cultural ideology and resulting pattern of institutional discrimination

Gay bashing. In a heinous case that brought gay bashing into the national spotlight in 1998, a gay 21-year-old University of Wyoming student, Matthew Shepard, was pistol-whipped, tied to a fencepost, and left to die by a group of assailants.

against lesbians and gay men. They suggest that the antigay feelings of individuals are only part of a broader pattern that is based on a cultural assumption that reproductive sexuality is the only outcome of healthy and morally correct psychosexual development. They go on to suggest that antigay sentiments are rewarded in our society more than they are punished and so are not widely considered to be abnormal or pathological.

Others believe that homophobia represents a form of personal psychopathology because it involves irrational beliefs that persist in the face of evidence to the contrary. Marvin Kantor (1998) views homophobia as an emotional disorder in which the false beliefs about lesbians and gay men and the anxiety associated with them resemble a paranoid delusion. In this view, homophobic beliefs represent people's underlying fears or anxieties about their own underlying homosexual attractions or insecurity about their own masculinity or femininity.

Violent physical and verbal attacks against lesbians and gay men are referred to as gay bashing and are considered a form of hate crime. According to Kantor, many people who engage in gay bashing are really attempting to reassure themselves that they do not have such feelings or attractions. By punishing those who express these forbidden wishes, the gay basher may be seeking to prove to himself and others that he is not one of them.

Research on homophobes suggests that they tend to have rigid personalities and are intolerant of anything that deviates from their personal view of appropriate behavior (Kantor, 1998). Often they have not, to their knowledge, had direct contact with lesbians or gay men (Herek, 1996). Their beliefs are selectively drawn from a larger culture that has historically created demeaning images of lesbians and gay men, depicting them as dangerous, perverted, depressed, or comical. Ignorance about lesbians and gay men, maintained by negative portrayals in the media, fuels homophobic attitudes.

Because of the harm that homophobia and heterosexism do to lesbians and gay men and because of adverse effects on their mental health, these phenomena are worthy of our serious attention and understanding. The question remains, do heterosexism and homophobia constitute a form of social or personal pathology, or both? ∎

SEXUAL DYSFUNCTIONS

Sexual dysfunctions are persistent problems with sexual interest, arousal, or response. Prevalences of sexual dysfunctions are not well established and vary across surveys. Table 11.2 shows frequencies of reports of sexual difficulties based on a national survey called the National Health and Social Life Survey or NHSLS (Laumann et al., 1994). The results showed that sexual problems were widespread in our society, affecting 43% of women and 31% of men (Laumann, Paik, & Rosen, 1999; Rosen & Laumann, 2003). Women more often reported painful sex, lack of pleasure, inability to attain orgasm, and lack of sexual desire. Men were more likely to report reaching orgasm too quickly (premature ejaculation) and anxiety about their performance. Table 11.3 shows several common features of different types of sexual dysfunctions.

Sexual dysfunctions may be classified according to two general categories, lifetime versus acquired and situational versus generalized. Cases of sexual dysfunction that have existed for the individual's lifetime are called *lifelong dysfunctions. Acquired dysfunctions* begin following a period of normal functioning. In *situational dysfunctions,* the problems occur in some situations (for example, with one's spouse), but not in others (for example, with a lover or when masturbating), or at some times but not others. *Generalized dysfunctions* occur in all situations and at every time the individual engages in sexual activity.

Table 11.4 shows differences in the incidences of sexual dysfunctions between European Americans and African Americans, according to the NHSLS study (Laumann et al., 1994). African American men report a higher incidence of sexual dysfunctions than European American men. African American women report a higher incidence of most sexual dysfunctions, with the exceptions of painful sex and trouble lubricating.

sexual dysfunctions Persistent or recurrent problems with sexual interest, arousal, or response.

Types of Sexual Dysfunctions

The *DSM-IV-TR* groups most sexual dysfunctions within the following categories:

1. Sexual desire disorders
2. Sexual arousal disorders
3. Orgasm disorders
4. Sexual pain disorders

TABLE 11.2

Sexual Dysfunctions Reported within the Past Year, According to the NHSLS Study

	Men (%)	Women (%)
Pain during sex	3.0	14.4
Sex not pleasurable	8.1	21.2
Unable to reach orgasm	8.3	24.1
Lack of interest in sex	15.8	33.4
Anxiety about performance*	17.0	11.5
Reaching climax too early	28.5	10.3
Unable to keep an erection**	10.4	—
Having trouble lubricating	—	18.8

Source: Adapted from Tables 10.8A and 10.8B, pages 370 and 371, in Laumann, E. O., Gagnon, J. H., Michael, R. T., & Michaels, S. (1994). *The social organization of sexuality: Sexual practices in the United States.* Chicago: University of Chicago Press.

*Anxiety about performance is not itself a sexual dysfunction. However, it figures prominently in sexual dysfunctions.

**Incidence increases with age, and the NHSLS figures may be an underestimate.

TABLE 11.3

Common Features of Sexual Dysfunctions

Fear of failure	Fears relating to failure to achieve or maintain erection or failure to reach orgasm
Assumption of a spectator role rather than a performer role	Monitoring and evaluating your body's reactions during sex
Diminished self-esteem	Thinking less of yourself for failure to meet your standard of normality
Emotional effects	Guilt, shame, frustration, depression, anxiety
Avoidance behavior	Avoiding sexual contacts for fear of failure to perform adequately; making excuses to your partner

hypoactive sexual desire disorder
Persistent or recurrent lack of sexual interest or sexual fantasies.

Sexual Desire Disorders Sexual desire disorders are disturbances in sexual appetite or an aversion to genital sexual activity. People with **hypoactive sexual desire disorder** have an absence or lack of sexual interest or desire. Typically there is either a complete or virtual absence of sexual fantasies. Lack of desire is more common among women than men (Bancroft, Loftus, & Long, 2003; Laumann et al., 1994). Nevertheless, the belief that men are always eager for sex is a myth.

Clinicians do not necessarily agree on criteria for determining the level of sexual desire considered "normal." They may weigh various factors in reaching a diagnosis of hypoactive sexual desire disorder, such as the client's lifestyle (for example, parents contending with the demands of young children may lack energy for interest in sex), sociocultural factors (culturally restrictive attitudes may restrain sexual desire or interest), the quality of the relationship (problems in a relationship may contribute to lack of interest in sex), and the client's age (desire normally declines with age) (Ghizzani, 2003; Kingsberg, 2002).

The literature on sex differences supports the view that women are generally less interested in sex than are men (Baumeister, Catanese, & Vohs, 2001; Peplau, 2003). Some researchers argue that labeling the lack of sexual desire among women as a dysfunction imposes a male model of what is normal on women (Bean, 2002). Researchers continue to debate whether female sexual dysfunction should be determined by lack or desire or difficulty achieving orgasm or by the woman's perception of these experience as causing distress (Smith, 2003b). Keep in mind that lack of desire usually does not come to

TABLE 11.4

Differences Between European Americans and African Americans in the Incidence of Current Sexual Problems (Respondents Reporting the Problem Within the Past Year)

	European American Men (%)	African American Men (%)	European American Women (%)	African American Women (%)
Pain during sex	3.0	3.3	14.7	11.5
Sex not pleasurable	7.0	15.2	19.7	30.0
Unable to reach orgasm	7.4	9.9	23.2	29.2
Lack of interest in sex	14.7	20.0	30.9	44.5
Anxiety about performance	16.8	23.7	10.5	14.5
Reaching climax too early	27.7	33.8	7.5	20.4
Unable to keep an erection	9.9	14.5	—	—
Having trouble lubricating	—	—	20.7	13.0

Source: Adapted from Tables 10.8A and 10.8B, pages 370 and 371, in Laumann, E. O., Gagnon, J. H., Michael, R. T., & Michaels, S. (1994). *The social organization of sexuality: Sexual practices in the United States.* Chicago: University of Chicago Press.

the health practitioner's attention unless one partner is more interested in sex than the other. That is when the less-interested partner may be labeled with a dysfunction. But questions remain about where to draw the line between "normal" and "abnormal" levels of sexual drive or interest.

People with **sexual aversion disorder** have a strong aversion to genital sexual contact and avoid all or nearly all genital contact with a partner. They may, however, desire and enjoy affectionate contact or nongenital sexual contact. Disgust with any form of genital contact may stem from childhood sexual abuse, rape, or other traumatic experiences. In other cases, deep-seated feelings of sexual guilt or shame may impair sexual response. In men, the diagnosis is often connected with a history of erectile failure, which may lead men to associate sexual opportunities with feelings of failure and shame. Their partners may also develop aversions to sexual contact because their sexual contacts have been so frustrating or emotionally painful.

Sexual Arousal Disorders Disorders of sexual arousal are characterized by an inability to achieve or maintain the physiological responses involved in sexual arousal or excitement—vaginal lubrication in the woman or erection in the man—that are needed to complete sexual activity to the point of genital intercourse.

In women, sexual arousal is characterized by lubrication of the vaginal walls that makes entry by the penis possible. In men, sexual arousal is characterized by erection. Almost all women now and then have difficulty becoming or remaining lubricated. Almost all men have occasional difficulty attaining or maintaining an erection through intercourse. The diagnoses of **female sexual arousal disorder** and **male erectile disorder** (also called erectile dysfunction) are reserved for persistent or recurrent problems in becoming genitally aroused. People with sexual arousal disorders may also lack the feelings of sexual pleasure or excitement that normally accompany sexual arousal (APA, 2000).

Erectile disorder affects as many as 30 million men in the United States to some degree (Goldstein, 1998). The occurrence of erectile disorder increases with age (Ghizzani, 2003). A recent study found that about 3% of men in their 50s and 35% of men in their 70s reported difficulty obtaining or maintaining erections (Blanker et al., 2001).

Occasional problems in achieving or maintaining erection are common enough, due to factors such as fatigue, alcohol, or anxiety with a new partner. The more concerned the man becomes about his sexual ability, the more likely he is to suffer *performance anxiety*. As we will explore further, performance anxiety can contribute to repeated failure, and a vicious cycle of anxiety and failure may develop.

Orgasm Disorders Orgasm or sexual climax is an involuntary reflex that results in rhythmic contractions of the pelvic muscles and is usually accompanied by feelings of intense pleasure. In men, these contractions are accompanied by expulsion of semen. There are three types of disorders involving problems with achieving orgasm: **female orgasmic disorder, male orgasmic disorder,** and **premature ejaculation.**

In male and female orgasmic disorder, there is a persistent or recurrent delay in reaching orgasm, or the absence of orgasm, following a normal level of sexual interest and arousal. The clinician needs to make a judgment about whether there is an "adequate" amount and type of stimulation needed to achieve orgasm, taking into consideration the wide variation in normal sexual response. Many women, for example, require direct clitoral stimulation (by her own hand or her partner's) in order to achieve orgasm during vaginal intercourse. This should not be considered abnormal because it is the *clitoris*, not the *vagina*, that is the woman's most erotically sensitive organ.

Male orgasmic disorder is relatively rare and has received little attention in the clinical literature (Dekker, 1993; Rosen & Leiblum, 1995). Men with this problem can usually reach orgasm through masturbation but not through intercourse.

Premature ejaculation is defined as a recurrent or persistent pattern of ejaculation with minimal sexual stimulation. Most men with the disorder ejaculate either just prior to or

sexual aversion disorder A type of sexual dysfunction characterized by aversion to, and avoidance, of genital sexual contact.

female sexual arousal disorder A type of sexual dysfunction in women involving difficulty becoming sexually aroused or lack of sexual excitement or pleasure during sexual activity.

male erectile disorder A sexual dysfunction in males characterized by difficulty in achieving or maintaining erection during sexual activity.

female orgasmic disorder A type of sexual dysfunction involving persistent difficulty achieving orgasm despite adequate stimulation.

male orgasmic disorder Persistent or recurrent delay in achieving orgasm or inability to achieve orgasm despite a normal level of sexual interest and arousal.

premature ejaculation A type of sexual dysfunction involving a pattern of unwanted rapid ejaculation during sexual activity.

TRUTH or FICTION? *REVISITED*

Orgasm is a reflex.

✓ **TRUE.** People cannot will or force an orgasm. Nor can they will or force other sexual reflexes, such as erection and vaginal lubrication. However, they can expose themselves to sexual stimulation and let these reflexes occur naturally.

immediately upon penetration or following a few penile thrusts (Byers & Grenier, 2003). In making the diagnosis, the clinician weighs the man's age, the novelty of the partner, and the frequency of sexual activity. Occasional experiences of rapid ejaculation, such as when the man is with a new partner, has had infrequent sexual contacts, or is very highly aroused, are not considered abnormal.

dyspareunia Persistent or recurrent pain experienced during or following sexual intercourse.

vaginismus Persistent or recurrent pain experienced during or following sexual intercourse.

Sexual Pain Disorders In **dyspareunia,** sexual intercourse is associated with recurrent pain in the genital region. The pain cannot be explained fully by an underlying medical condition and so is believed to have a psychological component. However, many and perhaps even most cases of pain during intercourse are traceable to an underlying medical condition, such as insufficient lubrication or a urinary tract infection. The *DSM* classifies these cases under a different diagnostic label, "Sexual Dysfunction Due to Medical Condition."

Vaginismus is the involuntary spasm of the muscles surrounding the vagina when vaginal penetration is attempted, making sexual intercourse painful or impossible. Vaginismus is not a medical condition, but a conditioned response in which penile contact with the woman's genitals elicits an involuntary response of the vaginal musculature, preventing penetration.

Theoretical Perspectives

Many factors are implicated in the development of sexual dysfunctions, including factors representing psychological, biological, and sociocultural perspectives.

Psychological Perspectives The major contemporary psychological views emphasize the roles of anxiety, lack of sexual skills, irrational beliefs, self-focused attributional styles, and relationship problems in the development and maintenance of sexual dysfunctions.

Physically or psychologically painful sexual experiences may lead the person to respond to sexual cues with anxiety rather than sexual arousal or pleasure. Conditioned anxiety resulting from a history of sexual trauma or rape plays a role in many women with sexual arousal disorder, sexual aversion disorder, orgasmic disorder, and vaginismus. Men or women who have been sexually traumatized earlier in life may find it difficult to respond sexually when they develop intimate relationships. Along with anxiety, they may be flooded with feelings of helplessness, unresolved anger, or misplaced guilt. They may also experience flashbacks of the abusive experiences when they engage in sexual relations, preventing them from becoming sexually aroused or achieving orgasm. Other psychological problems, such as depression, can also result in impaired sexual interest, arousal, or response.

Another principal form of anxiety in sexual dysfunctions is *performance anxiety,* which represents an excessive concern about the ability to perform successfully. Performance anxiety can develop when people experience problems performing sexually and begin to doubt their abilities. People troubled by performance anxiety become spectators during sex, rather than performers. Their attention is focused on how their bodies are responding (or not responding) to sexual stimulation. They are plagued by disruptive thoughts about the anticipated negative consequences of failing to perform adequately ("What will she think of me?") rather than focusing on their erotic experiences. Men with performance anxiety may have difficulty achieving or maintaining an erection or may ejaculate prematurely; women may fail to become adequately aroused or have difficulty achieving orgasm. A vicious cycle may ensue in which each failure experience instills deeper doubts, which leads to more anxiety during sexual encounters, which occasions repeated failure, and so on (see Figure 11.1).

In Western cultures, there is a deeply ingrained connection between a man's sexual performance and his sense of manhood. The man who repeatedly fails to perform sexually may suffer a loss of self-esteem, become depressed or feel he is no longer a man (Carey, Wincze, & Meisler, 1998). He may see himself as a total failure, despite other accomplishments in life. Sexual opportunities are construed as tests of his manhood, and he may respond to them by bearing down and trying to will (force) an erection. Willing an erection may backfire because erection is a reflex that cannot be forced. With so much of his self-esteem riding on the line whenever he makes love, it is little wonder that performance anxiety may mount to a point that it inhibits erection. The erectile reflex is controlled by the parasympathetic branch of the autonomic nervous system. Activation of the sympathetic nervous system, which occurs when we are anxious or under stress, can block parasympathetic control, preventing the erectile reflex from occurring. Ejaculation, in contrast, is under sympathetic nervous system control, so heightened levels of arousal, as in the case of performance anxiety, can trigger premature ejaculation. The relationship between performance anxiety and sexual dysfunction can become a vicious cycle, as represented in Figure 11.1.

One client who suffered from erectile dysfunction described his feelings of sexual inadequacy this way:

> I always felt inferior, like I was on probation, having to prove myself. I felt like I was up against the wall. You can't imagine how embarrassing this was. It's like you walk out in front of an audience that you think is a nudist convention and it turns out to be a tuxedo convention.
> —The Authors' Files

Another client described how performance anxiety led him to prepare for sexual relations as though he were psyching himself up for a big game:

"I" "Paralyzed with Anxiety"

At work I have control over what I do. With sex, you don't have control over your sex organ. I know that my mind can control what my hands do. But the same is not true of my penis. I had begun to view sex as a basketball game. I used to play in college. When I would prepare for a game, I'd always be thinking, "Who was I guarding that night?" I'd try to psych myself up, sketching out in my mind how to play this guy, thinking through all possible moves and plays. I began to do the same thing with sex. If I were dating someone, I'd be thinking the whole evening about what might happen in bed. I'd always be preparing for the outcome. I'd sketch out in my mind how I was going to touch her, what I'd ask her to do. But all the time, right through dinner or the movies, I'd be worrying that I wouldn't get it up. I kept picturing her face and how disappointed she'd be. By the time we did go to bed, I was paralyzed with anxiety.

—The Authors' Files

Women, too, may equate their self-esteem with their ability to reach frequent and intense orgasms. Yet when men and women try to will arousal or lubrication, or to force an orgasm, they may find that the harder they try, the more these responses elude them. Several generations ago the pressures concerning sex often revolved around the issue "Should I or shouldn't I?" Today, however, the pressures for both men and women are often based more on achieving performance goals relating to reaching orgasm and satisfying one's partner's sexual needs.

Sexual fulfillment is also based on learning sexual skills. Sexual skills or competencies, like other types of skills, are acquired through opportunities for new learning. We learn about how our bodies and our partner's respond sexually in various ways, in-

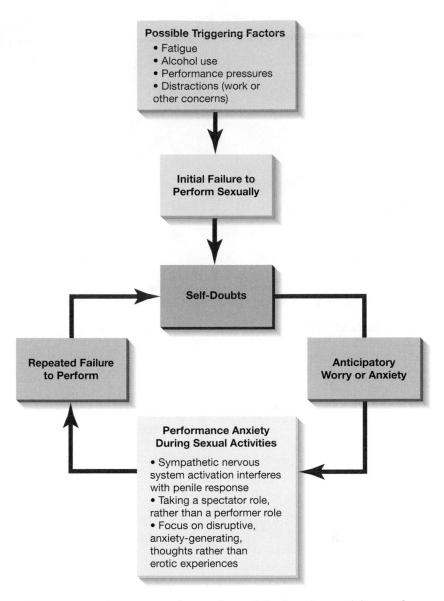

FIGURE 11.1 Performance anxiety and sexual dysfunction: a vicious cycle.

When a source of pleasure becomes a source of misery. Sexual dysfunctions can be a source of intense personal distress and lead to friction between partners. Lack of communication is a major contributor to the development and maintenance of sexual dysfunctions.

cluding trial and error with our partners, by learning about our own sexual response through self-exploration (as in masturbation), by reading about sexual techniques, and perhaps by talking to others or viewing sex films or videotapes. Yet children who are raised to feel guilty or anxious about sex may have lacked such opportunities to develop sexual knowledge and skills and so remain ignorant of the types of stimulation they need to achieve sexual gratification. They may also respond to sexual opportunities with feelings of anxiety and shame rather than arousal and pleasure.

Cognitive theorists, such as Albert Ellis (1977b), point out that underlying irrational beliefs and attitudes can contribute to sexual dysfunctions. Consider two such irrational beliefs: (a) we must have the approval at all times of everyone who is important to us; and (b) we must be thoroughly competent at everything we do. If we cannot accept the occasional disappointment of others, we may catastrophize the significance of a single frustrating sexual episode. If we insist that every sexual experience be perfect, we set the stage for inevitable failure.

How we appraise situations in terms of the perceived causes of events also plays a role. Attributing the cause for erectile difficulty to oneself ("What's wrong with me?") rather than to the situation ("It was the alcohol . . . I was tired. . . .") can undermine future sexual functioning (Weisberg et al., 2001).

Relationship problems can also contribute to sexual dysfunctions. "It takes two to tango," to coin a phrase. The quality of our sexual relations is usually no better than other facets of our relationships or marriages. Couples who harbor resentments toward one another may choose the sexual arena for combat. Communication problems, moreover, are linked to general marital dissatisfaction. Couples who find it difficult to communicate their sexual desires may lack the means to help each other become more effective lovers.

The following case illustrates how sexual arousal disorder may be connected with problems in the relationship.

The Case of Paul and Petula

After living together for six months, Paul and Petula are contemplating marriage. But a problem has brought them to a sex therapy clinic. As Petula puts it, "For the last two months he hasn't been able to keep his erection after he enters me." Paul is 26 years old, a lawyer; Petula, 24, is a buyer for a large department store. They both grew up in middle-class, surburban families, were introduced through mutual friends and began having intercourse, without difficulty, a few months into their relationship. At Petula's urging, Paul moved into her apartment, although he wasn't sure he was ready for such a step. A week later he began to have difficulty maintaining his erection during intercourse, although he felt strong desire for his partner. When his erection waned, he would try again, but would lose his desire and be unable to achieve another erection. After a few times like this, Petula would become so angry that she began striking Paul in the chest and screaming at him. Paul, who at 200 pounds weighed more than twice as much as Petula, would just walk away, which angered Petula even more. It became clear that sex was not the only trouble spot in their relationship. Petula complained that Paul preferred to spend time with his friends and go to baseball games than to spend time with her. When together at home, he would become absorbed in watching sports events on television, and showed no interest in activities she enjoyed—attending the theater, visiting museums, etc. Because there was no evidence that the sexual difficulty was due to either organic problems or depression, a diagnosis of male erectile disorder was given. Neither Paul or Petula was willing to discuss their nonsexual problems with a therapist. Although the sexual problem was treated successfully with a form of sex therapy modeled after techniques developed by Masters and Johnson, and the couple later married, Paul's ambivalences continued, even well into their marriage, and there were future recurrences of sexual problems as well.

—Adapted from Spitzer et al., 1994, pp. 198–200

Biological Perspectives Biological factors such as low testosterone levels and disease can dampen sexual desire and reduce responsiveness. The male sex hormone testosterone plays a pivotal role in energizing sexual desire and sexual activity in both men and women (Tuiten et al., 2000; Yates, 2000). Both men and women produce testosterone in their bodies, although women produce smaller amounts. Men with deficient production of testosterone in the testes may lose sexual interest and the capacity for erections (Kresin, 1993). The adrenal glands and ovaries are the sites where testosterone is produced in women. Women who have these organs surgically removed because of invasive disease no longer produce testosterone and may gradually lose sexual interest and the capacity for sexual response. However, most men and women with sexual dysfunctions have normal hormone levels (Spark, 1991).

Circulatory problems that impair the flow of blood to and through the penis can cause erectile disorder—a problem that becomes more common as men age (Goldstein, 1998, 2000). Erectile disorder is also common among men with *diabetes mellitus,* a disease that can damage blood vessels and nerves, including those serving the penis. Erectile disorder and male orgasmic disorder may also result from multiple sclerosis (MS), a disease in which nerve cells lose the protective coatings that facilitate transmission of neural messages. Chronic kidney disease, cancer, and emphysema can also impair erectile response, as can endocrine disorders that impair testosterone production (Ralph & McNicholas, 2000).

Eric Rimm (2000) of the Harvard School of Public Health studied 2,000 men and found that erectile dysfunction was associated with having a large waist, physical inactivity, and drinking too much alcohol (or not drinking at all!). The common link among these factors may be high levels of cholesterol. Cholesterol can impede blood flow to the penis, just as it can impede blood flow to the heart. Exercise, weight loss, and one or two drinks a day all help lower cholesterol levels, but we are not recommending that abstainers begin drinking to avert or treat erectile problems. However, the findings of the Massachusetts Male Aging Study suggest that regular exercise may reduce the risk of erectile dysfunction (Derby, 2000). In this study, men who burned 200 calories or more a day in physical activity, an amount that can be achieved by taking a brisk walk for two miles, had about half the risk of erectile dysfunction than did more sedentary men. Exercise may help prevent clogging of arteries, keeping them clear for the flow of blood into the penis.

Women also develop vascular or nervous disorders that impair genital blood flow, reducing lubrication and sexual excitement, rendering intercourse painful, and reducing their ability to reach orgasm. As with men, these problems become more likely as women age.

Before we move on to discuss psychological factors, we need to note that prescription drugs and psychoactive drugs account for many cases of erectile disorder. Antidepressant medication and antipsychotic drugs may impair erectile functioning and cause orgasmic disorders (Ashton et al., 2000; Michelson et al., 2000). Tranquilizers such as Valium and Xanax may cause orgasmic disorder in either men or women. Some drugs used to treat high blood pressure can interfere with erectile response (Ralph & McNicholas, 2000). Other medicinal drugs, such as adrenergic blockers, diuretics, cholesterol-lowering drugs, and anticonvulsants, can also cause erectile problems (Ralph & McNicholas, 2000).

Depressant drugs such as alcohol, heroin, and morphine can reduce sexual desire and impair sexual arousal. Narcotics, such as heroin, also depress testosterone production, which can diminish sexual desire and lead to erectile failure. Regular use of cocaine can cause erectile disorder or male orgasmic disorder and reduce sexual desire in both women and men (Rawson et al., 2002). Some people report increased sexual pleasure from initial use of cocaine, but repeated use can lead to dependency on the drug for sexual arousal, and long-term use may lessen sexual pleasure.

Sociocultural Perspectives At around the turn of the 20th century, an Englishwoman was quoted as saying she would "close her eyes and think of England" when her husband approached her to perform her marital duties. This old-fashioned stereotype suggests how sexual pleasure was once considered exclusively a male preserve—that sex, for women, was primarily a duty. Mothers usually informed their daughters of the conjugal duties before the wedding, and girls encoded sex as just one of the ways in which women serviced the needs of others. Women who harbor such stereotypical attitudes toward female sexuality are unlikely to become aware of their sexual potentials. In addition, sexual anxieties may transform negative expectations into self-fulfilling prophecies. Sexual dysfunctions in men, too, may be linked to severely restricted sociocultural beliefs and sexual taboos.

Psychologist Rafael Javier (1993) takes note of the idealization within many Hispanic cultures of the *marianismo* stereotype, which derives its name from the Virgin Mary. From this sociocultural perspective, the ideal virtuous woman "suffers in silence" as she submerges her needs and desires to those of her husband and children. She is the provider of joy, even in the face of her own pain or frustration. It is not difficult to imagine that women who adopt these stereotypical expectations find it difficult to assert their own needs for sexual gratification or express resistance to this cultural ideal by becoming sexually unresponsive.

Sociocultural factors play an important role in erectile dysfunction as well. Investigators find a greater incidence of erectile dysfunction in cultures with more restrictive sexual attitudes toward premarital sex among females, toward sex in marriage, and toward extramarital sex (Welch & Kartub, 1978). Men in these cultures may be prone to develop sexual anxiety or guilt that interferes with sexual performance.

In India, cultural beliefs that link the loss of semen to a draining of the man's life energy underlie the development of Dhat syndrome, an irrational fear of loss of semen. Men with this condition sometimes develop erectile dysfunction because their fears about wasting precious seminal fluid interfere with their ability to perform sexually (Shukla & Singh, 2000).

Treatment of Sexual Dysfunctions

Until the groundbreaking research of the famed sex researchers William Masters and Virginia Johnson in the 1960s, there was no effective treatment for most sexual dysfunctions. Psychoanalytic therapy approached sexual dysfunctions indirectly, for example. It was assumed that sexual dysfunctions represented underlying conflicts, so treatment focused on resolving those conflicts through psychoanalysis. A lack of evidence that about the efficacy of this approach led to development of methods that focus more directly on the sexual problems.

Most contemporary sex therapists assume sexual dysfunctions can be treated by directly modifying the couple's sexual interactions. Pioneered by Masters and Johnson (1970), sex therapy employs cognitive–behavioral techniques that focus on enhancing self-confidence, improving communication, enhancing sexual competencies (sexual knowledge and skills), and reducing performance anxiety. Therapists may also help couples iron out problems in the relationship that impair sexual functioning. When feasible, both partners are involved in therapy. In some cases, however, individual therapy may be preferable, as we shall see.

Significant changes have occurred in the treatment of sexual dysfunctions in the past 20 years. Clinicians increasingly emphasize the role of biological or organic factors in the development of sexual problems and use of medical treatments, such as the drug *Viagra*, to treat male erectile dysfunction (Leiblum & Rosen, 2000). But even men whose erectile problems can be traced to physical causes can benefit from sex therapy along with

Masters & Johnson Sex therapists William Masters and Virginia Johnson.

medical intervention (Carey, Wincze, & Meisler, 1998). Let us survey some of the more common sex therapy techniques for particular types of disorders.

Sexual Desire Disorders Sex therapists may try to help people with low sexual desire kindle their sexual appetite through the use of self-stimulation (masturbation) exercises together with erotic fantasies. When working with couples, therapists prescribe mutual pleasuring exercises the couple could perform at home or encourage them to expand their sexual repertoire to add novelty and excitement to their sex life. When a lack of sexual desire is connected with depression, the treatment focuses on treating the underlying depression. Lack of sexual desire may reflect problems in the relationship, in which case couple therapy might be in order. When problems of low sexual desire or sexual aversion appear to stem from deep-seated causes, sex therapist Helen Singer Kaplan (1987) recommends insight-oriented approaches to help uncover and resolve underlying issues.

Some cases of hypoactive sexual desire in men and women are associated with hormonal deficiencies, especially lack of the male sex hormone testosterone (Rabkin et al., 2000). Treatment with testosterone shows promise in heightening sexual desire in such cases (Munarriz et al., 2002; Tuiten et al., 2000).

Disorders of Arousal Sexual arousal results in the pooling of blood in the genital region, causing erection in the male and vaginal lubrication in the female. These changes in blood flow occur as a reflexive response to sexual stimulation; they cannot be willed. Women who have difficulty becoming sexually aroused and men with erectile problems are first educated to the fact that they need not "do" anything to become aroused. As long as their problems are psychological, not organic, they need only expose themselves to sexual stimulation under relaxed, unpressured conditions, so that disruptive thoughts and anxiety do not inhibit reflexive responses.

Masters and Johnson have a couple counter performance anxiety by engaging in *sensate focus exercises*. These are nondemand sexual contacts—sensuous exercises that do not demand sexual arousal in the form of vaginal lubrication or erection. Partners begin by massaging one another without touching the genitals. The partners learn to "pleasure" each other and to "be pleasured" by following and giving verbal instructions and by guiding each other's hands. The method fosters both communication and sexual skills and countermands anxiety because there is no demand for sexual arousal. After several sessions, direct massage of the genitals is included in pleasuring. Even when obvious signs of sexual excitement are produced (lubrication or erection), the couple does not straightaway engage in intercourse, because intercourse might create performance demands. After excitement is achieved consistently, the couple engages in a relaxed sequence of other sexual activities, culminating eventually in intercourse.

Success rates in treating individual cases of erectile disorder with sex therapy techniques are variable, and we still lack methodologically sound studies that support the overall effectiveness of the technique (Leiblum & Rosen, 2000; O'Donohue et al., 1999). The following case example illustrates sex therapy techniques for treating erectile dysfunction.

A Case of Erectile Dysfunction

Victor P., a 44-year-old concert violinist, was eager to show the therapist reviews of his concert tour. A solo violinist with a distinguished orchestra, Victor's life revolved around practice, performances, and reviews. He dazzled audiences with his technique and the energy of his performance. As a concert musician, Victor had exquisite control over his body, especially his hands. Yet he could not control his erectile response in the same way. Since his divorce seven years earlier, Victor had been troubled by recurrent episodes of erectile failure. Time and time again he had become involved in a new relationship, only to find himself unable to perform sexually. Fearing repetition, he would sever the relationship. He was unable to face an audience of only one. For a while he dated casually, but then he met Michelle.

Michelle was a writer who loved music. They were a perfect match because Victor, the musician, loved literature. Michelle, a 35-year-old divorcée, was exciting, earthy, sensual, and accepting. The couple soon grew inseparable. He would practice while she would write—poetry mostly, but also short magazine pieces. Unlike some women Victor met who did not know Bach from Bartok, Michelle held her own in conversations with Victor's friends and fellow musicians over late night dinner at Sardi's. They kept their own apartments; Victor needed his own space and solitude for practice.

In the nine months of their relationship, Victor was unable to perform on the stage that mattered most to him—his canopied bed. It was just so frustrating, he said. "I would become erect and then just as I approach her to penetrate, pow! It collapses on me." Victor's history of nocturnal erections and erections during light petting suggested that he was basically suffering from performance anxiety. He was bearing down to force an erection, much as he might try to learn the fingering of a difficult violin piece. Each night became a command performance in which Victor served as his own severest critic. Rather than focus on his partner, his attention was riveted on the size of his penis. As noted by the late great pianist Vladimir Horowitz, the worst thing a pianist can do is watch his fingers. Perhaps the worst thing a man with erectile problems can do is watch his penis.

To break the vicious cycle of anxiety, erectile failure, and more anxiety, Victor and Michelle followed a sex therapy program (Rathus & Nevid, 1977) modeled after the Masters-and-Johnson-type treatment. The aim was to restore the pleasure of sexual activity, unfettered by anxiety. The couple was initially instructed to abstain from attempts at intercourse to free Victor from any pressure to perform. The couple progressed through a series of steps:

1. *Relaxing together in the nude without any touching, such as when reading or watching TV together.*
2. *Sensate focus exercises.*
3. *Genital stimulation of each other manually or orally to orgasm.*
4. *Nondemand intercourse (intercourse performed without any pressure on the man to satisfy his partner). The man may afterward help his partner achieve orgasm by using manual or oral stimulation.*
5. *Resumption of vigorous intercourse (intercourse involving more vigorous thrusting and use of alternative positions and techniques that focus on mutual satisfaction). The couple is instructed not to catastrophize occasional problems that may arise.*

The therapy program helped Victor overcome his erectile disorder. Victor was freed of the need to prove himself by achieving erection on command. He surrendered his post as critic. Once the spotlight was off the bed, he became a participant and not a spectator.

—From the Authors' Files

Disorders of Orgasm Women with orgasmic disorder often harbor underlying beliefs that sex is dirty or sinful. They may have been taught not to touch themselves. They feel anxious about sex and have not learned, through trial and error, what kinds of sexual stimulation will arouse them and help them reach orgasm. Treatment in these cases includes modification of negative attitudes toward sex. When orgasmic disorder reflects the woman's feelings about or relationship with her partner, treatment also involves enhancing the relationship.

In either case, Masters and Johnson worked with the couple and first used sensate focus exercises to lessen performance anxiety, open channels of communication, and help the couple acquire sexual skills. The woman directs her partner to use caresses and techniques that stimulate her. By taking charge, the woman becomes psychologically freed from the stereotype of the passive, submissive female role.

Masters and Johnson preferred working with the couple in cases of female orgasmic dysfunction, but other sex therapists prefer to work with the woman individually by directing her to practice masturbation in private (Leiblum & Rosen, 2000). Directed masturbation provides women opportunities to learn about their own bodies at their own pace and has a success rate of 70% to 90% (Leiblum & Rosen, 2000). It frees women of the need to rely on or please partners. Once women can reliably masturbate to orgasm, couple-oriented treatment may facilitate transfer of training to orgasm with a partner.

Little attention has focused on male orgasmic disorder in the scientific literature. The standard treatment, barring underlying organic problems, focuses on increasing sexual stimulation and reducing performance anxiety (Leiblum & Rosen, 2000).

The most widely used behavioral approach to treating premature ejaculation, called the *stop-start* or *stop-and-go* technique, was introduced in 1956 by a urologist with the intriguing name of James Semans. The partners suspend sexual activity when the man is about to ejaculate and then resume stimulation when his sensations subside. Repeated practice enables him to regulate ejaculation by sensitizing him to the cues that precede the ejaculatory reflex, making him more aware of his "point of no return," the point at which the ejaculatory reflex is triggered. Therapists have reported success rates as high as 95% in treating premature ejaculation with the stop-start method, but relapse rates tend to be high (Segraves & Althof, 1998).

Vaginismus and Dyspareunia Vaginismus is a conditioned reflex involving the involuntary constriction of the vaginal opening. It represents a psychologically based fear of penetration, rather than a physical problem (LoPiccolo & Stock, 1986). Treatment for vaginismus may include a combination of relaxation techniques and the use of vaginal dilators to gradually desensitize the vaginal musculature. The woman herself regulates the insertion of dilators (plastic rods) of increasing diameter, always proceeding at her own pace to avoid any discomfort (LoPiccolo & Stock, 1986). The method is generally successful as long as it is unhurried. Reported success rates in treating vaginismus with gradual desensitization have ranged as high as 80% (Hawton & Catalan, 1990) to 100% (Masters & Johnson, 1970). Because many women with vaginismus and dyspareunia have histories of rape or sexual abuse, psychotherapy may be part of the treatment program in order to deal with the psychological consequences of traumatic experiences.

Viagra Viagra and other erectile disorder drugs are advertised widely on television and even on billboards. Do you believe these drugs should be advertised so heavily in popular media? Why or why not?

Biological Treatments of Sexual Dysfunction   Erectile disorder frequently has organic causes, so it is not surprising that treatment is becoming more medicalized (Kleinplatz, 2003).

Biological treatments focus on the use of drugs to either induce erections or delay ejaculation. The most widely known examples are *Viagra, Levitra,* and *Cialis,* all of which increase blood flow to the penis and can produce erections in the majority of men. These drugs work by relaxing blood vessels in the genitals, allowing them to expand and carry more blood to the penis. *Cialis* has been dubbed the "weekender" because of its long-lasting effects—upwards of 36 hours (Naughton, 2004; Walker, 2004). Table 11.5 summarizes the kinds of biological treatments currently available for men with erectile disorder.

Investigators are actively exploring biomedical therapies for female sexual dysfunctions (Berman et al, 2003; Kleinplatz, 2003). Sexual arousal in both men and women depends on engorgement of blood in the genitals. Drugs that increase blood flow to the genitals, such as Viagra, hold promise for treating sexual dysfunctions in women as well as men. For example, Viagra appears to increase sexual arousal in women (O'Connor, 2004). Many women also report greater vaginal lubrication and stronger orgasms after using Viagra (e.g., Berman, 2000; Berman et al., 2001).

The male sex hormone testosterone has also been used successfully to increase sexual drive in both premenopausal women (Goldstat et al., 2003) and older women (Munarriz et al., 2002). A cream form of testosterone is applied to the thighs. However, questions remain about the safety and side effects of these hormonal treatments, such as possible growth of facial hair and acne.

As we noted earlier, testosterone hormone may also help men with low levels of male sex hormones (Rakic et al., 1997). Because testosterone treatments can have side effects, such as liver damage and prostate cancer, they are undertaken cautiously. Surgery may be effective in rare cases in which blocked blood vessels prevent blood flow to the penis, or in which the penis is structurally defective.

TABLE 11.5
Biological Treatments of Erectile Problems

Surgery	
Vascular Surgery	Helps when blood vessels that supply the penis are blocked.
Penile Implants	May be used when other treatments fail due to biological problems.
Medication	
Hormone Therapy	Helps men with abnormally low levels of male sex hormones.
Injections	Muscle relaxants such as *alprostadil* and *phentolamine* are injected into the penis, relaxing the muscles that surround the arteries in the penis, allowing the vessels to dilate and blood to flow more freely.
Suppository	Alprostadil is inserted into the tip of the penis in gel form.
Oral Medication	Oral forms of several compounds—sildenafil (*Viagra*), vardenafil (*Levitra*), and tadalafil (*Cialis*)—relax the muscles that surround the small blood vessels in the penis, allowing them to dilate so that blood can flow into them more freely. Apomorphine (*Uprima*) increases brain levels of the neurotransmitter dopamine. (Parkinson's disease is caused by the death of dopamine-producing cells and often accompanied by erectile dysfunction. Men who use drugs that treat Parkinson's disease by increasing dopamine levels often have erections as side effects.)
Vacuum Pump	
Vacuum Pump	A *vacuum constriction device* creates a vacuum when it is held over the penis. The vacuum induces erection by increasing the flow of blood into the penis. Rubber bands around the base of the penis maintain the erection

Source: Adapted from Rathus, Nevid, & Fichner-Rathus, 2005. Reprinted with permission of Allyn & Bacon, Inc.

Overview of Sexual Dysfunctions

TYPES OF SEXUAL DYSFUNCTIONS	Problems with sexual interest, arousal, or response
Sexual Desire Disorders	• **Hypoactive sexual desire disorder:** Lack of sexual interest or desire • **Sexual aversion disorder:** Aversion to, and avoidance of, genital sexual contact
Sexual Arousal Disorders	• **Female sexual arousal disorder:** Difficulty becoming aroused or maintaining sexual arousal or excitement during sexual activity • **Male erectile disorder:** Difficulty achieving or maintaining erection during sexual activity
Orgasm Disorders	• **Female orgasmic disorder:** Difficulty achieving orgasm • **Male orgasmic disorder:** Difficulty achieving orgasm
Sexual Pain Disorders	• **Dyspareunia:** Pain during or following sexual intercourse not explainable by an underlying medical condition • **Vaginismus:** Involuntary contraction of the vaginal musculature, making penile penetration painful or impossible

CAUSAL FACTORS	
Biological Factors	• Disease or deficient sex hormone production may disrupt sexual desire, arousal, or response
Psychodynamic Factors	• Psychodynamic theorists speculate that unconscious conflicts dating from childhood may lie at the root of problems with sexual arousal or response
Psychosocial Factors	• Performance anxiety arising from excessive concerns about one's ability to perform sexually • History of sexual trauma or abuse • Lack of opportunity to acquire sexual skills • Exposure to negative attitudes and beliefs toward sexuality, especially female sexuality
Cognitive Factors	• Adoption of irrational beliefs, such as the belief that one should be perfectly competent at all times, may engender performance anxiety • In premature ejaculation, failure to gauge rising levels of sexual tension preceding ejaculation • Interfering cognitions, such as fears of failure, may impair normal sexual response
Relationship Factors	• Relationship problems and failure to communicate sexual needs

TREATMENT APPROACHES	Most cases of sexual dysfunction can be treated successfully
Biomedical Treatment	• Primarily involves use of drugs to treat erectile dysfunction or premature ejaculation
Cognitive–Behavioral Therapy	• Sex therapy—brief, cognitive-behavioral techniques that help individuals and couples develop more satisfying sexual relations and reduce performance anxiety

Selective serotonin reuptake inhibitors (SSRIs), such as the antidepressants fluoxetine (Prozac), paroxetine (Paxil), and sertraline (Zoloft), work by increasing the action of the neurotransmitter serotonin. Increased availability of serotonin in the brain can have the side effect of delaying ejaculation, which can be helpful to men with premature ejaculation (Meston & Frohlich, 2000; Waldinger et al., 2001).

The medicalization of treatments for sexual dysfunctions holds great promise, but no pill or biomechanical device will enhance the quality of a relationship. If people have serious problems with their partners, popping a pill or applying a cream is unlikely to solve them. All in all, the success rates reported for treating sexual dysfunctions through psychological or biological approaches are quite encouraging, especially when we remember that only a few generations ago, there were no effective treatments.

PARAPHILIAS

The word *paraphilia* was coined from the Greek roots *para*, meaning "to the side of," and *philos*, meaning "loving." People with **paraphilias** show sexual arousal ("loving") in response to atypical stimuli ("to the side of" normally arousing stimuli). According to the *DSM-IV-TR*, paraphilias are recurrent, powerful sexual urges and fantasies lasting 6 months or longer that center on either (a) nonhuman objects such as underwear, shoes, leather, or silk; (b) humiliation or experience of pain in oneself or one's partner; or (c)

paraphilias Sexual deviations or types of sexual disorders in which the person experiences recurrent sexual urges and sexually arousing fantasies involving nonhuman objects (such as articles of clothing), inappropriate or nonconsenting partners (for example, children), or situations producing humiliation or pain to oneself or one's partner.

Exhibitionism. Exhibitionism is a type of paraphilia that characterizes people who seek sexual arousal or gratification through exposing themselves to unsuspecting victims. People with this disorder are usually not interested in actual sexual contact with their victims.

children and other persons who do not or cannot grant consent. Diagnosis of a paraphilia may be given even in the absence of overt paraphiliac behavior. In these cases, there must be evidence that the urges are a source of personal distress or cause other significant problems.

Some persons who receive the diagnosis can function sexually in the absence of paraphiliac stimuli or fantasies. Others resort to paraphiliac stimuli under stress. Still others cannot become sexually aroused unless these stimuli are used, in actuality or in fantasy. For some individuals, the paraphilia is their exclusive means of attaining sexual gratification. Though the prevalence rates of paraphilias are unknown, we do know that except for sexual masochism and some isolated cases of other disorders, these disorders are almost never diagnosed in women (Seligman & Hardenburg, 2000). Even with masochism, it is estimated that men receiving the diagnosis outnumber women by a ratio of 20 to 1 (APA, 2000).

Types of Paraphilias

Some paraphilias are relatively harmless and victimless. Among these are fetishism and transvestic fetishism. Others, such as exhibitionism and pedophilia, have unwilling victims. A most harmful paraphilia is sexual sadism when acted out with a nonconsenting partner. Voyeurism falls somewhere in between because the victim does not typically know he or she is being watched.

exhibitionism A type of paraphilia almost exclusively occurring in males, in which the man experiences persistent and recurrent sexual urges and sexually arousing fantasies involving the exposure of his genitals to a stranger and either has acted upon these urges or feels strongly distressed by them.

Exhibitionism Exhibitionism—or "flashing"—involves recurrent, powerful urges to expose one's genitals to an unsuspecting stranger to surprise, shock, or sexually arouse the victim. The person may masturbate while fantasizing about or actually exposing himself (almost all cases involve men). The victims are almost always women.

Studies in England, Guatemala, the United States, and Hong Kong showed that fewer than one in five cases of exhibitionism were reported to the police (Cox, 1988). The prevalence of exhibitionism in the general population is unknown, but a survey of 846 college women at nine randomly selected universities in the U.S. found it to be widespread. A third of the women said they had encountered a "flasher" at one time or another (Cox, 1988). Few of the women had reported these incidents to the police.

The person diagnosed with exhibitionism usually does not seek sexual contact with the victim. Nevertheless, some exhibitionists progress to more serious crimes of sexual aggression (Price et al., 2002). Whether or not the exhibitionist seeks physical contact, the victim may believe herself to be in danger and be traumatized by the act. Victims are probably best advised to show no reaction to exhibitionists, but to just continue on their way, if possible. It would be unwise to insult the exhibitionist, lest it provoke a violent reaction. Nor do we recommend an exaggerated show of shock or fear, which tends to reinforce the behavior.

Some researchers view exhibitionism as a means of indirectly expressing hostility toward women, perhaps because of perceptions of having been wronged by women in the past or of not being noticed or taken seriously by them (Geer, Heiman, & Leitenberg, 1984). Men with this disorder tend to be shy, dependent, lacking in social and sexual skills, and socially inhibited (Dwyer, 1988). Some doubt their masculinity and harbor feelings of inferiority. Their victims' revulsion or fear boosts their sense of mastery of the situation and heightens their sexual arousal. Consider the following case example of exhibitionism.

The Case of Michael

Michael was a 26-year-old, handsome, boyish-looking married male with a 3-year-old daughter. He had spent about one quarter of his life in reform schools and in prison. As an adolescent he had been a fire-setter. As a young adult, he had begun to expose himself. He came to the clinic without his wife's knowledge because he was exposing himself more and more often—up to three times a day—and he was afraid that he would eventually be arrested and thrown into prison again.

Michael said he liked sex with his wife, but it wasn't as exciting as exposing himself. He couldn't prevent his exhibitionism, especially now, when he was between jobs and worried about where the family's next month's rent was coming from. He loved his daughter more than anything and couldn't stand the thought of being separated from her.

Michael's method of operation was as follows: He would look for slender adolescent females, usually near the junior high school and the senior high school. He would take his penis out of his pants and play with it while he drove up to a girl or a small group of girls. He would lower the car window, continuing to play with himself, and ask them for directions. Sometimes the girls didn't see his penis. That was okay. Sometimes they saw it and didn't react. That was okay, too. When they saw it and became flustered and afraid, that was best of all. He would start to masturbate harder, and now and then he managed to ejaculate before the girls had departed.

Michael's history was unsettled. His father had left home before he was born, and his mother had drunk heavily. He was in and out of foster homes throughout his childhood. Before he was 10 years old he was involved in sexual activities with neighborhood boys. Now and then the boys also forced neighborhood girls into petting, and Michael had mixed feelings when the girls got upset. He felt bad for them, but he also enjoyed it. A couple of times girls seemed horrified at the sight of his penis, and it made him "really feel like a man. To see that look, you know, with a girl, not a woman, but a girl—a slender girl, that's what I'm after."

—*The Authors' Files*

Virtually all people diagnosed with exhibitionism are men, and they are motivated by the wish to shock and dismay unsuspecting observers, not to show off the attractiveness of their bodies. Therefore, wearing skimpy bathing suits or other revealing clothing is not a form of exhibitionism in the clinical sense of the term. Nor do professional strippers typically meet the clinical criteria for exhibitionism. They are generally not motivated by the desire to expose themselves to unsuspecting strangers in order to arouse them or shock them. The chief motive of the exotic dancer, of course, may simply be to earn a living.

Fetishism   The French word *fétiche* is thought to derive from the Portuguese *feitico*, referring to a "magic charm." In this case, the "magic" lies in the object's ability to arouse sexually. The chief feature of **fetishism** is recurrent, powerful sexual urges and arousing fantasies involving inanimate objects, such as an article of clothing (bras, panties, hosiery, boots, shoes, leather, silk, and the like). It is normal for men to like the sight, feel, and smell of their lovers' undergarments. Men with fetishism, however, may prefer the object to the person and may not be able to become sexually aroused without it. They often experience sexual gratification by masturbating while fondling the object, rubbing it, or smelling it; or by having their partners wear it during sexual activity.

The origins of fetishism can be traced to early childhood in many cases. Most individuals with a rubber fetish in one research sample were able to recall first experiencing a fetishistic attraction to rubber sometime between the ages of 4 and 10 (Gosselin & Wilson, 1980).

TRUTH or FICTION? *REVISITED*

Wearing revealing bathing suits is a form of exhibitionism.

☑ **FALSE.** Wearing revealing bathing suits is not a form of exhibitionism in the clinical sense of the term. Virtually all people diagnosed with the disorder are men, and they are motivated by the wish to shock and dismay unsuspecting observers, not to show off the attractiveness of their bodies.

fetishism A type of paraphilia in which a person uses an inanimate object or a body part (*partialism*) as a focus of sexual interest and as a source of arousal.

transvestic fetishism A type of paraphilia in heterosexual males involving sexual urges and sexually arousing fantasies involving dressing in female clothing. Also termed *transvestism*.

Transvestic Fetishism The chief feature of **transvestic fetishism** is recurrent, powerful urges and related fantasies involving cross-dressing for purposes of sexual arousal. Other men with fetishes can be satisfied by handling objects such as women's clothing while they masturbate; men with transvestic fetishism want to wear them. They may wear full feminine attire and makeup or favor one particular article of clothing, such as women's stockings. Although some transvestites are gay, transvestic fetishism is usually reported among heterosexual men. The man typically cross-dresses in private and imagines himself to be a woman whom he is stroking as he masturbates. Some frequent transvestite clubs or become involved in a transvestic subculture. Some transvestites are sexually stimulated by fantasies that their own bodies are female (Bailey, 2003b).

Men with GID may cross-dress to "pass" as women or because they are not comfortable dressing in male clothing. Some gay men also cross-dress, perhaps to make a statement about overly rigid gender roles, but not because they seek to become sexually aroused. Because cross-dressing among gay men and men with GID is performed for reasons other than sexual arousal or gratification, their behavior is not classified as transvestic fetishism. Nor are female impersonators who cross-dress for theatrical purposes considered to have a form of transvestism. For these reasons, the diagnosis is usually limited to heterosexuals.

Most men with transvestic fetishism are married and engage in sexual activity with their wives, but they seek additional sexual gratification through dressing as women, as in the following case.

A Case of Transvestic Fetishism

Archie was a 55-year-old plumber who had been cross-dressing for many years. There was a time when he would go out in public as a woman, but as his prominence in the community grew, he became more afraid of being discovered in public. His wife Myrna knew of his "peccadillo," especially since he borrowed many of her clothes, and she also encouraged him to stay at home, offering to help him with his "weirdness." For many years his paraphilia had been restricted to the home.

The couple came to the clinic at the urging of the wife. Myrna described how Archie had imposed his will on her for 20 years. Archie would wear her undergarments and masturbate while she told him how disgusting he was. (The couple also regularly engaged in "normal" sexual intercourse, which Myrna enjoyed.) The cross-dressing situation had come to a head because a teenaged daughter had almost walked into the couple's bedroom while they were acting out Archie's fantasies.

With Myrna out of the consulting room, Archie explained that he grew up in a family with several older sisters. He described how underwear had been perpetually hanging all around the one bathroom to dry. As an adolescent Archie experimented with rubbing against articles of underwear, then with trying them on. On one occasion a sister walked in while he was modeling panties before the mirror. She told him he was a "dredge to society" and he straightaway experienced unparalleled sexual excitement. He masturbated when she left the room, and his orgasm was the strongest of his young life.

Archie did not think that there was anything wrong with wearing women's undergarments and masturbating. He was not about to give it up, regardless of whether his marriage was destroyed as a result. Myrna's main concern was finally separating herself from Archie's "sickness." She didn't care what he did anymore, so long as he did it by himself. "Enough is enough," she said.

That was the compromise the couple worked out in marital therapy. Archie would engage in his fantasies by himself. He would choose times when Myrna was not at home, and she would not be informed of his activities. He would also be very, very careful to choose times when the children were not around.

Six months later the couple were together and content. Archie had replaced Myrna's input into his fantasies with transvestic-sadomasochistic magazines. Myrna said, "I see no evil, hear no evil, smell no evil." They continued to have sexual intercourse. After a while, Myrna even forgot to check to see which underwear had been used.

—The Authors' Files

Voyeurism The chief feature of **voyeurism** is either acting on or being strongly distressed by recurrent, powerful sexual urges and fantasies of watching unsuspecting people, generally strangers, who are undressed, disrobing, or engaging in sexual activity. The purpose of watching, or "peeping," is to attain sexual excitement. The person who engages in voyeurism does not typically seek sexual activity with the person or persons being observed.

Are acts of watching your partner disrobe or viewing sexually explicit films forms of voyeurism? The answer is no. The people who are observed know they are being observed by their partners or will be observed by film audiences. Nor is attending a strip club for purposes of sexual stimulation considered abnormal, as it does not involve seeking sexual arousal by watching unsuspecting persons. People may also frequent strip clubs for other reasons than sexual gratification, such as bonding experiences with friends (Montemurro et al., 2003).

The voyeur usually masturbates while watching or while fantasizing about watching. Peeping may be the voyeur's only sexual outlet. Some people engage in voyeuristic acts in which they place themselves in risky situations. The prospects of being discovered or injured apparently heighten their excitement.

Frotteurism The French word *frottage* refers to the artistic technique of making a drawing by rubbing against a raised object. The chief feature of the paraphilia of **frotteurism** is recurrent, powerful sexual urges and related fantasies involving rubbing against or touching a nonconsenting person. Frotteurism, also called "mashing," often occurs in crowded places, such as subway cars, buses, or elevators. The rubbing or touching, not the coercive aspect of the act, sexually arouses the man. He may imagine himself enjoying an exclusive, affectionate sexual relationship with the victim. Because the physical contact is brief and furtive, people who commit frotteurism stand only a small chance of being caught by authorities. Even victims may not realize at the time what has happened or register much protest. In the following case, a man victimized about 1,000 women over several years but was arrested only twice.

voyeurism A type of paraphilia involving sexual urges and sexually arousing fantasies focused on acts of watching unsuspecting others who are naked, in the act of undressing, or engaging in sexual activity.

frotteurism A type of paraphilia involving sexual urges or sexually arousing fantasies involving bumping and rubbing against nonconsenting persons for sexual gratification.

A Case of Frotteurism

A 45-year old man was seen by a psychiatrist following his second arrest for rubbing against a woman in the subway. He would select as his target a woman in her 20s as she entered the subway station. He would then position himself behind her on the platform and wait for the train to arrive. He would then follow her into the subway car and when the doors closed would begin bumping against her buttocks, while fantasizing that they were enjoying having intercourse in a loving and consensual manner. About half of the time he would reach orgasm. He would then continue on his way to work. Sometimes when he hadn't reached orgasm, he would change trains and seek another victim. While he felt guilty for a time after each episode, he would soon become preoccupied with thoughts about his next encounter. He never gave any thought to the feelings his victims might have about what he had done to them. Although he was married to the same woman for 25 years, he appears to be rather socially inept and unassertive, especially with women.

—Adapted from Spitzer et al., 1994, pp. 164–165

pedophilia A type of paraphilia involving sexual attraction to children.

Pedophilia The word **pedophilia** derives from the Greek *paidos*, meaning "child." The chief feature of pedophilia is recurrent, powerful sexual urges and related fantasies involving sexual activity with prepubescent children (typically 13 years old or younger). Molestation of children may or may not occur. To be diagnosed with pedophilia, the person must be at least 16 years of age and at least 5 years older than the child or children toward whom the person is sexually attracted or has victimized. In some cases of pedophilia, the person is attracted only to children. In other cases, the person is attracted to adults as well.

Although some persons with pedophilia restrict their pedophilic activity to looking at or undressing children, others engage in exhibitionism, kissing, fondling, oral sex, and anal intercourse and, in the case of girls, vaginal intercourse (Knudsen, 1991). Not being worldly wise, children are often taken advantage of by molesters, who inform them they are "educating" them, "showing them something," or doing something they will "like."

Some men with pedophilia limit their sexual activity with children to incestuous relations with family members; others only molest children outside the family. Not all child molesters have pedophilia, however. The clinical definition of pedophilia is brought to bear only when sexual attraction to children is recurrent and persistent. Some molesters engage in these acts or experience pedophilic urges only occasionally or during times of opportunity.

Despite the stereotype, most cases of pedophilia do not involve "dirty old men" who hang around schoolyards in raincoats. Men with this disorder (virtually all cases involve men) are usually (otherwise) law-abiding, respected citizens in their 30s or 40s. Most are married or divorced and have children of their own. They are usually well acquainted with their victims, who are typically either relatives or friends of the family. Many cases of pedophilia are not isolated incidents. They often begin when children are very young and continue for years until they are discovered or the relationship is broken off (Finkelhor et al., 1990).

The origins of pedophilia are complex and varied. Some cases fit the stereotype of the weak, shy, socially inept, and isolated man who is threatened by mature relationships and turns to children for sexual gratification because children are less critical and demanding (Ames & Houston, 1990). In other cases, it may be that childhood sexual experiences with other children were so enjoyable that the man, as an adult, is attempting to recapture the excitement of earlier years. In some cases, men who were sexually abused in childhood reverse the situation in an effort to establish feelings of mastery. Men whose pedophilic acts involve incestuous relationships with their own children tend to fall at one extreme or the other on the dominance spectrum, either being very dominant or very passive (Ames & Houston, 1990).

Childhood Sexual Abuse:
The Case of Karen
"He started when I was six years old . . . He would always get one bed in motel rooms because he said he needed to save money."

Effects of Sexual Abuse on Children An estimated 50,000 children in the United States suffer sexual abuse each year (Villarosa, 2002). The typical abuser is not the proverbial stranger lurking in the shadows, but a relative or step-relative of the child, a family friend, or a neighbor—someone who has held and then abused the child's trust. Sexual abuse can inflict great psychological harm, whether it is perpetrated by a family member, acquaintance, or stranger. Abused children may suffer from a litany of short- and long-term psychological problems, including anger, anxiety, depression, eating disorders, inappropriate sexual behavior, aggressive behavior, drug abuse, suicide attempts, posttraumatic stress disorder, low self-esteem, sexual dysfunction, and feelings of detachment (Edwards et al., 2003). But the psychological effects of sexual abuse on children are variable, and no one single pattern emerges (Resick, 2003; Saywitz et al., 2000). Sexual abuse may also cause genital injuries and psychosomatic problems such as stomachaches and headaches.

Younger children sometimes react with tantrums or aggressive or antisocial behavior. Older children often develop substance abuse problems (Herrera & McCloskey, 2003; Kendler, Bulik et al., 2000). Some abused children become socially withdrawn and retreat into fantasy or refuse to leave the house. Abused children may also show regressive behaviors, such as thumb sucking, fear of the dark, and fear of strangers. Many survivors of childhood sexual abuse develop posttraumatic stress disorder (see Chapter 6). They suffer flashbacks, nightmares, emotional numbing, and feel alienated from other people (Herrera & McCloskey, 2003).

The sexual development of abused children may veer off in dysfunctional directions. For example, abused children may become prematurely sexually active or promiscuous in adolescence and adulthood (Browning, 2002; Herrera & McCloskey, 2003; Kendler, Bulik et al., 2000). Adolescent girls who have been sexually abused tend to be more sexually active than their peers (Browning, 2002; Herrera & McCloskey, 2003).

The effects of childhood sexual abuse are similar in boys and girls (Edwards et al., 2003). Both tend to become fearful and have trouble sleeping. But there are some sex differences. The most pronounced is that boys more often externalize their problems, often through physical aggression. Girls more often internalize their difficulties, as by becoming depressed (Edwards et al., 2003).

Psychological problems may continue into adulthood in the form of PTSD, anxiety, depression, substance abuse, and relationship problems (Bradley & Follingstad, 2001; Kendler, Bulik et al., 2000; Read et al., 2001). Late adolescence and early adulthood are particularly difficult times for survivors of child sexual abuse, because unresolved feelings of anger and guilt and a deep sense of mistrust can prevent the development of intimate relationships (Jackson et al., 1990). Women who blame themselves for the abuse show relatively lower self-esteem and greater depression than those who do not (Edwards et al., 2003). Childhood sexual abuse is also linked to later development of borderline personality disorder (Murray, 1993; Weaver & Clum, 1995). (See Chapter 13.)

Sexual Masochism

Sexual masochism derives its name from the Austrian novelist Ritter Leopold von Sacher Masoch (1835–1895), who wrote stories and novels about men who sought sexual gratification from women by inflicting pain on them, often in the form of flagellation (being beaten or whipped). Sexual masochism involves strong, recurrent urges and fantasies relating to sexual acts that involve being humiliated, bound, flogged, or made to suffer in other ways. The urges are either acted on or cause significant personal distress. In some cases of sexual masochism, the person cannot attain sexual gratification in the absence of pain or humiliation.

In some cases, sexual masochism involves binding or mutilating oneself during masturbation or sexual fantasies. In others, a partner is engaged to restrain (bondage), blindfold (sensory bondage), paddle, or whip the person. Some partners are prostitutes; others are consensual partners who are asked to perform the sadistic role. In some cases, the person may desire, for purposes of sexual gratification, to be urinated or defecated upon or subjected to verbal abuse.

A most dangerous expression of masochism is **hypoxyphilia,** in which participants are sexually aroused by being deprived of oxygen—for example, by using a noose, plastic bag, chemical, or pressure on the chest during a sexual act, such as masturbation. The oxygen deprivation is usually accompanied by fantasies of asphyxiating or being asphyxiated by a lover. People who engage in this activity generally discontinue it before they lose consciousness, but occasional deaths due to suffocation occur (Blanchard & Hucker, 1991).

Sexual Sadism

Sexual sadism is named after the infamous Marquis de Sade, the 18th-century Frenchman who wrote stories about the pleasures of achieving sexual gratification by inflicting pain or humiliation on others. Sexual sadism is the flip side of sexual masochism. It is characterized by recurrent, powerful urges and related fantasies to engage in acts in which the person is sexually aroused by inflicting physical suffering or humiliation on another person. People with this paraphilia either act out their fantasies with nonconsenting others, or the urges and related fantasies cause significant personal distress or difficulties with others. People with sexually sadistic fantasies do sometimes recruit consenting partners, who may be lovers or wives with masochistic interests, or prostitutes, who are paid to play a masochistic role. But some sexual sadists stalk and assault nonconsenting victims and become aroused by inflicting pain or suffering on them.

sexual masochism A type of paraphilia characterized by sexual urges and sexually arousing fantasies involving receiving humiliation or pain.

TRUTH or FICTION? *REVISITED*

Some people cannot become sexually aroused unless they are subjected to pain or humiliation.

☑ **TRUE.** These people have a form of paraphilia called sexual masochism.

hypoxyphilia A paraphilia in which a person seeks sexual gratification by being deprived of oxygen by means of using a noose, plastic bag, chemical, or pressure on the chest.

sexual sadism A type of paraphilia or sexual deviation characterized by recurrent sexual urges and sexually arousing fantasies involving inflicting humiliation or physical pain on sex partners.

sadomasochism Sexual activities between partners involving the attainment of gratification by means of inflicting and receiving pain and humiliation.

Sadistic rapists fall into this last group. Let us note, however, that most rapists do not become sexually aroused by inflicting pain; many even lose sexual interest when they see their victims in pain.

Many people have occasional sadistic or masochistic fantasies or engage in sex play involving simulated or mild forms of **sadomasochism** (or *S&M*) with their partners. Sadomasochism describes a mutually gratifying sexual interaction involving both sadistic and masochistic acts. Stimulation may take the form of using a feather brush to strike one's partner, so that no actual pain is administered. People who engage in sadomasochism frequently switch roles. The clinical diagnosis of sexual masochism or sadism is not brought to bear unless such people become distressed by their behavior or fantasies, or these urges and fantasies lead to problems with other people.

Other Paraphilias   There are many other paraphilias. These include making obscene phone calls ("telephone scatologia"), necrophilia (sexual urges or fantasies involving contact with corpses), partialism (sole focus on part of the body), zoophilia (sexual urges or fantasies involving contact with animals), and sexual arousal associated with feces (coprophilia), enemas (klismaphilia), and urine (urophilia).

In the "Controversies in Abnormal Psychology" feature, we discuss what may be a new psychological disorder—cybersex addiction.

Theoretical Perspectives

As in the case of so many psychological disorders, approaches to understanding the causes of paraphilias emphasize psychological and biological factors.

Psychological Perspectives   Psychodynamic theorists see many of the paraphilias as defenses against leftover *castration anxiety* from the phallic period period of early childhood (see Chapter 2). In Freudian theory, the young boy develops a sexual desire for his mother and perceives his father as a rival. Castration anxiety—the unconscious fear that the father will retaliate by removing the organ that has become associated with sexual pleasure through masturbation—motivates the boy to give up his incestuous yearnings for his mother and identify with the aggressor, his father. But a failure to successfully resolve the conflict may lead to leftover castration anxiety in adulthood. The adult man now unconsciously equates the disappearance of the penis during genital intercourse with adult women with the risk of castration. Castration anxiety motivates the man to displace his sexual arousal onto sexual activities that are unconsciously perceived as safer, such as sexual contact with undergarments, viewing others, or having sex with children. Psychodynamic views of the origins of paraphilias remain speculative and controversial. We lack any direct evidence that men with paraphilias are handicapped by unresolved castration anxiety.

Learning theorists explain paraphilias in terms of conditioning and observational learning. Some object or activity becomes inadvertently associated with sexual arousal. The object or activity then gains the capacity to elicit sexual arousal. For example, sex researcher June Reinisch (1990) speculates that the earliest awareness of sexual arousal or response (such as erection) may have been connected with rubber pants or diapers. The person makes an association between the two, setting the stage for the development of a rubber fetish. Or a boy who glimpses his mother's stockings on the towel rack while he is masturbating goes on to develop a fetish for stockings (Breslow, 1989). Orgasm in the presence of the object reinforces the erotic connection, especially when it occurs repeatedly. Yet if fetishes were acquired by mechanical association, we might expect people to develop fetishes to stimuli that are inadvertently and repeatedly connected with sexual activity, such as bed sheets, pillows, even ceilings. But they do not. The *meaning* of the stimulus plays a primary role. The development of fetishes may depend on eroticizing certain types of stimuli (like women's undergarments) by incorporating them within sexual fantasies and masturbation rituals.

Family relationships may play a role. Some transvestite men report a history of "petticoat punishment" during childhood. That is, they were humiliated by being dressed in girl's attire. Some authorities have speculated that the adult transvestite is attempting psy-

Origins of fetishism? The conditioning model of the origins of fetishism suggests that men who develop fetishisms involving women's undergarments may have had experiences in childhood in which sexual arousal was paired with exposure to their mother's undergarments. The developing fetish may have been strengthened by eroticizing the meaning of these stimuli by incorporating them within erotic fantasies or masturbatory activity.

CONTROVERSIES IN ABNORMAL PSYCHOLOGY
"Cybersex Addiction"—A New Psychological Disorder?

Internet use has exploded in recent years, and cybersex is a major factor accounting for this growth (Greenspan, 2003). People are logging on to view adult sites on the Internet, engaging in online sex with people in Internet chat rooms, and sometimes progressing to real-life sexual encounters with people they meet online. There are now more than four million pornographic Web sites, which account for more than 10% of the total number of Web sites worldwide. Nearly 40 million Americans regularly visit adult Web sites and about one quarter of all search engine requests are for pornographic online material.

For some, the attraction to cybersex is a relatively harmless recreational pursuit. But experts express concern that for others, easy access to cybersex is feeding a new type of psychological disorder called *cybersex addiction* (Brody, 2000). An estimated 6% of adult users of the Internet show evidence of sexual compulsiveness in their online behavior, such as experiencing withdrawal symptoms when they are away from the Internet for a length of time (Bailey, 2003a).

Writing in the journal *Sexual Addiction and Compulsivity*, psychologist Al Cooper and his colleagues (2000) report that many heavy users of Internet pornography deny that they have a problem and refuse to seek help until their marriages begin to suffer. Dr. Mark Schwartz of the Masters and Johnson Institute compares sex on the Internet to heroin: "It grabs them and takes over their lives. And it's very difficult to treat because the people affected don't want to give it up" (cited in Brody, 2000). It is not unusual for people who become hooked on cybersex to spend hours a day masturbating while viewing online pornography or interacting with online hosts and hostesses who, for a fee, titillate them in private online sessions. According to Schwartz, a major reason cybersex is so attractive to so many people is that is easily accessible with just a few keystrokes, is relatively inexpensive, and provides access to a virtually unlimited range of fantasized encounters with idealized partners. Some heavy users of Internet pornography develop a conditioned response to the computer, becoming sexually excited by the machine even before they turn it on (Brody, 2000).

Cooper and his colleagues (1999, 2000) conducted the largest and most detailed survey of online sex. In a survey of more than 9,000 men and women who reported using Internet sex sites, they found at least 1% of the respondents showed clear signs of cybersex addiction. To Cooper, the Internet represents "the crack cocaine of sexual compulsivity." He believes that cybersex represents a hidden public health hazard that is exploding because heavy users of sexually oriented sites fail to recognize they have a problem or don't take it seriously until it creates marital strain or their activities are inadvertently discovered by their children.

In another survey, Tucson physician Jennifer Schneider polled 94 family members who reported they were affected by cybersex addiction (Brody, 2000). Schneider found that problems arose even within secure, loving marriages in which sexual opportunities were available. She points out that people can easily get hooked on cybersex before they even know it. Schneider argues that cybersex addiction is a true addiction in the sense that the person loses control over their cybersex behavior and continues to pursue these activities, even when they begin having adverse consequences on the person's closest relationships. Schneider's survey showed that partners of people addicted to cybersex often reported feeling betrayed, deceived, and abandoned, and unable to compete with the idealized world of online sexuality. One married woman who discovered that her husband was a compulsive user of Internet porn sites questioned how she could compete with the hundreds of anonymous strangers who she feared were in her husband's head. Where once she had felt an intimate connection with her husband, she now feels as though her bed is "crowded with countless faceless strangers" (cited in Brody, 2000).

As in other patterns of addictive behavior, people who become addicted to online pornography may begin taking more risks, such as surfing porn sites while at work or while the children or spouse are nearby. Visiting pornographic sites on the job has led to people being fired, as companies are now monitoring the online activities of their employees.

Cybersex addiction is not yet recognized as an official diagnostic category. Nor can we clearly determine where recreational use of sexual material on the Internet ends and sexual compulsion begins. Yet the problem of cybersex compulsion continues to grow and may enter yet another phase as increased availability of broadband allows for the streaming of explicit sexual video programming to computer screens around the world.

Critical Thinking

- What criteria would you apply to determine that pursuit of sexual explicit content on the Internet represents a psychological disorder?
- What the similarities between cybersex addiction and drug addiction? What are the differences?   ■

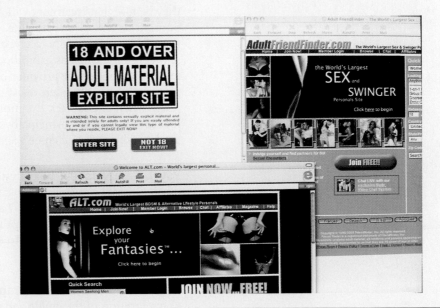

Cybersex addiction. Easy access to cybersex may be feeding a new psychological disorder called cybersex addiction. Many compulsive users of online sexual content deny that they have a problem, even though their behavior can seriously disrupt their work and home lives.

chologically to convert humiliation into mastery by achieving an erection and engaging in sexual activity despite being attired in female clothing (Geer et al., 1984).

Biological Perspectives Researchers are investigating the possible role of biological factors in paraphiliac behavior, involving, for example, the endocrine system (organs that release hormones) and the nervous system. Because the male sex hormone testosterone is linked to sex drive, researchers have focused on differences in testosterone levels between people with paraphilias and people without them. Investigators find evidence of higher-than-average sex drives in men with paraphilias, as evidenced by a higher frequency of sexual fantasies and urges and a shorter *refractory period* after orgasm by masturbation (i.e., length of time needed to become rearoused) (Haake et al., 2003; Kafka, 2003). Kafka (2003) refers to this heightened sex drive as *hypersexual desire*—the opposite of hypoactive sexual desire disorder (see the section on sexual dysfunctions). Other investigators find differences in the electrical response patterns in the brain to paraphiliac (fetishistic and sadomasochistic) images and control images (nude women, genital intercourse, oral sex) between paraphiliac men and male control subjects (Waismann et al., 2003). The meaning of these differences is not yet clear, but they suggest that the brains of paraphiliac and other men may respond differently to different types of sexual stimuli.

Psychologist J. Michael Bailey (2003a) believes that with time, we will learn more about the biological underpinnings of paraphiliac behavior. Like other sexual patterns, paraphilias may have multiple biological, psychological, and sociocultural origins (Seligman & Hardenburg, 2000). Might our understanding of them thus be best approached from a theoretical framework that incorporates multiple perspectives? Sex researcher John Money (2000), for example, traces the origins of paraphilias to childhood. He suggests that childhood experiences etch a pattern in the brain, which he calls a lovemap. A lovemap determines the types of stimuli and activities that become sexually arousing. In the paraphilias, lovemaps may become distorted or "vandalized" by early traumatic experiences. Evidence does tie early childhood emotional or sexual trauma to later development of paraphilias in many cases (Lee et al., 2002).

Treatment of Paraphilias

A major problem with treating paraphilias is that many people who engage in these behaviors are not motivated to change. They may not want to alter their behavior unless they believe that treatment will relieve them from serious punishment, such as imprisonment or loss of a family life. Consequently, they don't typically seek treatment on their own. They usually receive treatment in prison after they have been convicted of a sexual offense, such as exhibitionism, voyeurism, or child molestation. Or they are referred to a treatment provider by the courts. Under these circumstances it is not surprising that sex offenders resist treatment. Therapists recognize that treatment may be futile when clients lack the motivation to change their behavior. Nonetheless, some forms of treatment, principally cognitive–behavioral therapy, may be helpful to sex offenders who seek to change their behavior (Abracen & Looman, 2004).

Psychoanalysis Psychoanalysts attempt to bring childhood sexual conflicts (typically of an Oedipal nature) into awareness so they can be resolved in the light of the individual's adult personality (Laws & Marshall, 2003). Favorable results from individual case studies appear in the literature from time to time, but there is a dearth of controlled investigations to support the efficacy of psychodynamic treatment of paraphilias.

Cognitive–Behavioral Therapy Traditional psychoanalysis involves a lengthy process of exploration of the childhood roots of the problem. Cognitive–behavioral therapy is briefer and focuses directly on changing problem behavior. Cognitive–behavioral therapy includes a number of specific techniques to help eliminate paraphiliac behaviors and strengthen appropriate sexual behaviors, such as aversion therapy, covert sensitization, and social skills training (Krueger & Kaplan, 2002). In many cases a combination of methods is used.

The goal of *aversion therapy* is to induce a negative emotional response to paraphiliac stimuli or fantasies. In this technique, a stimulus that elicits sexual arousal (for example, a mental image of a nude child) is paired repeatedly with an aversive stimulus (for example, electric shock) in the hope that the person will develop a conditioned aversion toward the paraphiliac stimulus.

Covert sensitization is a variation of aversion therapy in which paraphiliac fantasies are paired with an aversive stimulus in imagination. In one study of 38 pedophiles and 62 exhibitionists, more than half of whom were court-referred, subjects paired imagined aversive odors with fantasies of the problem behavior (Maletzky, 1980). They were instructed to fantasize pedophiliac or exhibitionistic scenes. Then,

> At a point . . . when sexual pleasure is aroused, aversive images are presented. . . . Examples might include a pedophiliac fellating a child, but discovering a festering sore on the boy's penis, an exhibitionist exposing to a woman but suddenly being discovered by his wife or the police, or a pedophiliac laying a young boy down in a field, only to lie next to him in a pile of dog feces. (Maletzky, 1980, p. 308)

In a 25-year follow-up study of 7,275 sex offenders who received similar treatment, Maletzky and Steinhauser (2002) found that benefits were maintained for many men with exhibitionism but few with pedophilia. However, fewer than 50% of the original participants could be contacted after this amount of time elapsed.

Social skills training helps the individual improve his ability to develop and maintain relationships with adult partners. The therapist might first model a desired behavior, such as asking a woman out on a date or handling rejection. The client might then rehearse the behavior with the therapist playing the woman's role. The therapist provides feedback and additional guidance and modeling to help the client further improve his social skills.

Research on the effectiveness of cognitive–behavioral techniques is limited by the absence of untreated control groups. Consequently, we cannot discount the possibility that other factors, such as fears of legal consequences, influenced the outcomes.

Biomedical Therapies   There is no magic pill or other medical cure for paraphilias. Yet progress has been made in treating exhibitionism, voyeurism, and fetishism with selective serotonin reuptake inhibitor (SSRI) antidepressants, such as Prozac (Bradford, 2001; Roesler & Witztum, 2000). Why SSRIs? We noted in Chapter 6 that SSRIs are often helpful in treating obsessive–compulsive disorder, a psychological disorder characterized by recurrent obsessions and compulsions. Paraphilias appear to mirror these behavioral patterns, which suggests that they may fall within an obsessive–compulsive spectrum of behaviors. People with paraphilias often experience obsessive thoughts or images of the paraphiliac object or stimulus, such as intrusive and recurrent mental images of young children. Many also feel compelled to repeatedly carry out the paraphiliac acts.

Antiandrogen drugs reduce levels of testosterone in the bloodstream (Bradford, 2001). Testosterone energizes sexual drives, so use antiandrogens can reduce sexual desires, including paraphiliac urges and fantasies (Roesler & Witztum, 2000). The most widely used antiandrogen is *medroxyprogesterone acetate* (MPA) (trade name: Depo-Provera), which is usually administered in weekly injections. Antiandrogens do not completely eliminate paraphiliac urges, nor do they change the types of erotic stimuli to which the man is attracted. Yet they may help curb impulses to act out on these urges. Evidence

Overview of Paraphilias

MAJOR TYPES OF PARAPHILIAS	Atypical or deviant patterns of sexual gratification; excepting masochism, these disorders occur almost exclusively among males
Exhibitionism	Sexual gratification from exposing one's genitals in public
Voyeurism	Sexual gratification from observing unsuspecting others who are naked, undressing, or engaging in sexual arousal
Sexual Masochism	Sexual gratification associated with the receipt of humiliation or pain
Fetishism	Sexual attraction to inanimate objects or particular body parts
Frotteurism	Sexual gratification associated with acts of bumping or rubbing against nonconsenting strangers
Sexual Sadism	Sexual gratification associated with inflicting humiliation or pain on others
Transvestic Fetishism	Sexual gratification associated with cross-dressing
Pedophilia	Sexual attraction to children

CAUSAL FACTORS	Multiple causes may be involved
Learning Perspective	• Atypical stimuli become conditioned stimuli for sexual arousal as the result of prior pairing with sexual activity • Atypical stimuli may become eroticized by incorporating them within erotic and masturbatory fantasies
Psychodynamic Perspective	• Unresolved castration anxiety from childhood leads to sexual arousal being displaced onto safer objects or activities
Multifactorial Perspective	• Sexual or physical abuse in childhood may corrupt normal sexual arousal patterns

TREATMENT APPROACHES	Results remain questionable
Biomedical Treatment	• Drugs to help individuals control deviant sexual urges or reduce sexual drives
Cognitive–Behavioral Therapy	• Including aversive conditioning (pairing deviant stimuli with aversive stimuli), covert sensitization (pairing the undesirable behavior with an aversive stimulus in imagination), and nonaversive methods that help individuals acquire more adaptive behaviors

suggests that antiandrogens are helpful in controlling paraphiliac urges, especially when they are used in combination with psychological treatment (Roesler & Witztum, 2000).

RAPE

Ann, a college student who met a young man at a party, offered the following account of a rape.

"I Never Thought It Would Happen to Me"

I first met him at a party. He was really good looking and he had a great smile. I wanted to meet him but I wasn't sure how. I didn't want to appear too forward. Then he came over and introduced himself. We talked and found we had a lot in common. I really liked him. When he asked me over to his place for a drink, I thought it would be OK. He was such a good listener, and I wanted him to ask me out again.

When we got to his room, the only place to sit was on the bed. I didn't want him to get the wrong idea, but what else could I do? We talked for a while and then he made his move. I was so startled. He started by kissing. I really liked him so the kissing was nice. But then he pushed me down on the bed. I tried to get up and I told him to stop. He was so much bigger and stronger. I got scared and I started to cry. I froze and he raped me.

It took only a couple of minutes and it was terrible, he was so rough. When it was over he kept asking me what was wrong, like he didn't know. He had just forced himself on me and he thought that was OK. He drove me home and said he wanted to see me again. I'm so afraid to see him. I never thought it would happen to me.

—The Authors' Files

Rape, especially date rape, is a pressing concern on college campuses, where thousands of women have been raped by dates or acquaintances. College men frequently perceive their dates' protests as part of an adversarial sex game (Bernat et al., 1999). Consider the comments of Jim, the man who raped Ann.

Misreading cues? Many date rapists misperceive social cues, such as assuming that women who frequent singles bars and similar places are signaling their willingness to have sex.

"I" "Why Did She Put Up Such A Big Struggle?"

I first met her at a party. She looked really hot, wearing a sexy dress that showed off her great body. We started talking right away. I knew that she liked me by the way she kept smiling and touching my arm while she was speaking. She seemed pretty relaxed so I asked her back to my place for a drink. . . . When she said yes, I knew that I was going to be lucky!

When we got to my place, we sat on the bed kissing. At first, everything was great. Then, when I started to lay her down on the bed, she started twisting and saying she didn't want to. Most women don't like to appear too easy, so I knew that she was just going through the motions. When she stopped struggling, I knew that she would have to throw in some tears before we did it.

She was still very upset afterwards, and I just don't understand it! If she didn't want to have sex, why did she come back to the room with me? You could tell by the way she dressed and acted that she was no virgin, so why she had to put up such a big struggle I don't know.

—The Authors' Files

Rape is not classified as a mental disorder in the *DSM* system, and rapists do not necessarily suffer from any diagnosable disorder. However, its violent nature and the often devastating effects it has on its victims' place rape and other forms of sexual assault squarely within the framework of abnormal behavior. Moreover, rape survivors often experience a range of health problems, both psychological and physical.

Many survivors are traumatized by the experience (Koss et al., 2002, 2003). They have trouble sleeping and cry frequently. They report eating problems, cystitis, headaches, irritability, mood changes, anxiety and depression, and menstrual irregularity. Survivors may become withdrawn, sullen, and mistrustful. Women who are raped may at least partly blame themselves, which can lead to feelings of guilt and shame. Emotional distress tends to peak by about 3 weeks following the attack and generally remains high for a month or so, before beginning to decline (Koss et al., 2002, 2003). But many survivors encounter lasting problems. A study of women in the military who had survived rape and physical abuse found psychological and health-related problems a decade after the assault (Sadler et al., 2000). Some survivors suffer physical injuries and sexually transmitted infections, even HIV/AIDS.

rape Forced sexual intercourse with a nonconsenting person. Note that the legal definition of rape varies from state to state.

The government's National Crime Victimization Survey (U.S. Department of Justice, 2003) estimates that 225,320 women were sexually assaulted in a recent year. This figure includes 76,850 rapes and 62,620 attempted rapes. Men were also victimized by rape—6,770 of them. Such surveys, which are based on crime statistics, underreport the incidence of rape, because the majority of rapes are not reported or prosecuted (Fisher et al., 2003; Watts & Zimmerman, 2002). Many women do not report rape because they fear being humiliated by the criminal justice system. Some fear reprisal from their families or the rapist himself. Many women mistakenly believe that coercive sex is rape only when the rapist is a stranger or uses a weapon (Watts & Zimmerman, 2002). In sum, the best estimates indicate that between one in seven and one in four women in the United States is raped during her lifetime (Koss & Kilpatrick, 2001). Women aged 16 to 24 are two to three times more likely to be raped than older women (U.S. Department of Justice, 2003).

Types of Rape

The main types of rape include stranger rape, acquaintance rape, marital rape, and male rape. *Stranger rape* is committed by an assailant (or assailants) who is not acquainted with the victim. The stranger rapist tends to select targets who appear to be vulnerable— women who live alone, who are walking deserted or dimly lit streets, or who are asleep or drugged.

According to the U.S. Department of Justice (2003), about two thirds of rapes are *acquaintance rapes*—rapes committed by people known by the victim. Survivors of rape may not perceive sexual assaults by acquaintances as rapes. Only about one quarter of the women in a national college survey who had been sexually assaulted saw themselves as victims of rape (Koss et al., 1987; Koss & Kilpatrick, 2001; Rozee & Koss, 2001).

Figure 11.2 shows the relationship patterns of rapist and victim based on a large national survey of college women (Koss, Gidycz, & Wisniewski, 1987). This survey revealed a disturbingly high percentage of college women reporting they had experienced rape (15.4%) or attempted rape (11.1%) (Koss et al., 1987). In nearly 90% of the rapes in the college sample, the woman was acquainted with the assailant (Koss, 1988). In any given year, about 3% of college women in the United States suffer a rape or attempted rape (Fisher et al, 2003).

Date rape is a kind of acquaintance rape. Surveys of college women find that 10% to 20% have been forced into sexual intercourse by dates (Koss & Kilpatrick, 2001; Tang et al., 1995). Date rape is more likely to occur when the couple has been drinking and then park in the man's car or return to his room. Men tend to perceive a date's willingness to go home with him as a sign of willingness to have sexual relations. Most men who engage in date rape overcome the women's protests by force.

Some date rapists believe that acceptance of a date implies willingness to engage in sexual relations. They may believe that a woman they take out to dinner should pay with sex. Men may think that women who frequent singles bars and similar places are automatically willing to have sex. Some date rapists believe that women who resist advances are simply trying not to look "easy." These men misinterpret resistance as a ploy in the "battle of the sexes." Like Jim, who raped Ann in his dorm room, they may believe that when a woman says no, she means yes, especially when a sexual relationship has already begun (Monson et al., 2000; Osman, 2003).

Marital rapes may be even more common than date rapes because the sexual relationship has already been established in the context of marriage (Monson et al., 2000; Osman, 2003). A traditional-minded husband may think he is entitled to have sex with his wife whenever he wishes. He may see sex as his wife's duty, even when she is unwill-

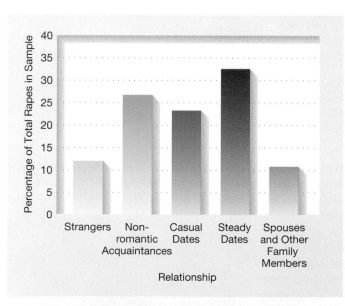

FIGURE 11.2 Relative Percentages of Stranger Rapes and Acquaintance Rapes

According to a large-scale survey of more than 3,000 college women at 32 colleges, the great majority of rapes of college women were committed by men whom the women were acquainted with, including dates, nonromantic acquaintances, and family members.

Source: Adapted from Koss (1988).

ing. But rape is rape, regardless of the woman's marital status. Men who are better educated and less accepting of traditional stereotypes about relationships between men and women are less likely to commit marital rape (Basile, 2002).

Gang rapists seek to exercise power over their victims and typically try to impress their friends by conforming to the stereotype of the tough "he-man." Consider the case of Kurt, who committed multiple rapes with his friend, Pete.

"I Couldn't Chicken Out"

I always looked up to Pete and felt second-class to him. I felt I owed him and couldn't chicken out on the rapes. I worshiped him. He was the best fighter, lover, water-skier, motorcyclist I knew. Taking part in the sexual assaults made me feel equal to him. . . . I didn't have any friends and felt like a nobody. . . . He brought me into his bike club. He made me a somebody.

I'd go to a shopping center and find a victim. I'd approach her with a knife or a gun and then bring her to him. He'd rape her first and then I would. . . . We raped about eight girls together over a four-month period.

—Groth & Birnbaum, 1979, p. 113

The U.S. Department of Justice (2003) estimates that 1 in 10 rape survivors is a man. Most men who engage in *male rape* are heterosexual. Their motives often include domination and control, revenge and retaliation, sadism and degradation, and—when the rape is carried out by a gang member—status and affiliation. Sexual motives are often minimal or absent.

Theoretical Perspectives

Many motives underlie rape. Feminists see rape as an expression of men's desire to dominate and degrade women, to establish unquestioned power and superiority over them (Gebhard et al., 1965; Groth & Birnbaum, 1979). Other theorists argue that sexual motivation plays a key role in many kinds of rape, particularly acquaintance rape, date rape, and marital rape (Baumeister et al., 2002; Bushman et al., 2003). In such cases the motive may be largely sexual, but make no mistake—coerced sex in any form is an act of violence. For some rapists, violent cues appear to enhance sexual arousal, so they are motivated to combine sex with aggression (Barbaree & Marshall, 1991). College men who report having used force or threat of force to gain sexual favors showed greater penile arousal in a laboratory study in response to depictions of rape scenes than did noncoercive men (Lohr, Adams, & Davis, 1997). Some rapists who were abused as children may humiliate women as a way of expressing anger and power over women and of taking revenge.

Social attitudes, myths, and cultural factors also contribute to the high incidence of rape. Many people believe myths about rape, such as "Women say no when they mean yes" (Maxwell et al., 2003; Osman, 2003). Yet another myth is that deep down inside, women want to be raped. Certainly the popular media contribute to this belief when they portray a woman as first resisting a man's advances but then yielding to his overpowering masculinity. These myths have the effect of blaming the victim for the assault and legitimizing rape in the eyes of the public. Although both women and men believe some rape myths, researchers find that college men are more likely than college women to do so (Maxwell et al., 2003; Van Wie & Gross, 2001). The nearby questionnaire will afford you insight as to whether you believe in myths that have the effect of legitimizing rape.

Although some rapists show evidence of psychopathology on psychological tests, especially psychopathic traits, many do not (Brown & Forth, 1997; Herkov et al., 1996). The very normality of many rapists on psychological instruments suggests that socialization of young men plays an important role in creating a climate of sexual aggression.

Perhaps, as some researchers contend, our society breeds rapists by socializing men into socially and sexually dominant roles (Davis & Liddell, 2002; Holcomb et al., 2002). Males are often reinforced from childhood for aggressive and competitive behavior.

TRUTH or FICTION? REVISITED

Deep down, most women desire to be raped.

☑ **FALSE.** This is an example of a rape myth. Holding such a belief can lead to victim blaming and excusing perpetrators of sexual violence.

QUESTIONNAIRE
Cultural Myths That Create a Climate That Supports Rape

Read each of the following statements and indicate whether you believe it to be true or false by circling the T or the F. Then look at the scoring key at the end of the chapter to evaluate your beliefs.

1. T F Women who dress provocatively in public places are just "asking for it."
2. T F A woman who accompanies a man home from a club or a bar deserves whatever she gets.
3. T F Women who claim they were raped are just looking for excuses for having engaged in sex.
4. T F Any physically healthy woman could resist a man's advances if she really wanted to.
5. T F If a woman allows a man to touch her in a sexual way, it means she wants to have intercourse.

6. T F Most women who are raped probably did something to lead the man on.
7. T F If a woman initiates touching or petting with a man, it's her own fault if things go too far.
8. T F Women may not admit it, but they truly want to be overpowered by men.
9. T F If a woman has too much to drink at a party, it's her fault if men take advantage of her.
10. T F Rape results from a misunderstanding that gets out of hand.

Source: Adapted from Burt (1980). Reprinted from Nevid & Rathus, 2005, with permission of John Wiley & Sons, Inc.

They may learn to "score" at all costs, whether they are on the ball field or in the bedroom. Such socialization influences may also lead men to reject "feminine" traits such as tenderness and empathy that might restrain aggression (Davis & Liddell, 2002; Shultz et al., 2000). A rapist may be just like the boy next door; in fact, he may be the boy next door. We end with two questions that we hope will provoke some thoughtful discussion: What are we teaching our sons? How can we teach them differently?

SUMMING UP

Gender Identity Disorder

What is gender identity disorder? People with GID find their anatomic gender to be a source of persistent and intense distress. People with the disorder may seek to change their sex organs to resemble those of the other sex, and many undergo hormone treatments and/or surgery to achieve this end.

How does gender identity disorder differ from sexual orientation? In GID, as defined in the *DSM* system, there is a mismatch between one's psychological sense of being male or female and one's anatomic sex. Sexual orientation relates to the direction of one's sexual attraction—toward members of one's own sex or the other sex. Unlike people with GID, the great majority of people with a gay male or lesbian sexual orientation have a gender identity that is consistent with their anatomic sex.

Sexual Dysfunctions

What are sexual dysfunctions? Sexual dysfunctions involve persistent or recurrent patterns of lack of sexual desire, problems in becoming sexually aroused, and/or problems in reaching orgasm.

What types of sexual dysfunctions are there? Sexual dysfunctions include sexual desire disorders (hypoactive sexual desire disorder and sexual aversion disorder), sexual arousal disorders (female sexual arousal disorder and male erectile disorder), orgasm disorders (female and male orgasmic disorders and premature ejaculation), and sexual pain disorders (dyspareunia and vaginismus).

What are the causes of sexual dysfunctions? Sexual dysfunctions can stem from biological factors (such as fatigue, disease, the effects of aging, or the effects of alcohol and other drugs), psychological factors (such as performance anxiety, lack of sexual skills, disruptive cognitions, relationship problems), and sociocultural factors (such as sexually restrictive cultural learning).

What is sex therapy? Sex therapy is a cognitive–behavioral approach that helps people overcome sexual dysfunctions by enhancing self-efficacy expectancies, teaching sexual skills, improving communication, and reducing performance anxiety.

What biologically based treatments are available to help treat sexual dysfunctions? These include hormone treatments, vascular surgery, mechanical devices, and most commonly, the use of drugs to facilitate blood flow to the genital region (sildenafil and its cousins) or delay ejaculation (SSRIs).

Paraphilias

What are paraphilias? Paraphilias are sexual deviations involving patterns of arousal to stimuli such as nonhuman objects (for example, shoes or clothes), humiliation or the experience of pain in oneself or one's partner, or children.

What are the major types of paraphilia? Paraphilias include exhibitionism, fetishism, transvestic fetishism, voyeurism, frotteurism, pedophilia, sexual masochism, and sexual sadism. Although some paraphilias are essentially harmless (such as fetishism), others, such as pedophilia and sexual sadism, often harm nonconsenting victims.

What are the causes of paraphilias? Psychoanalysts see many paraphilias as defenses against castration anxiety. Learning theorists attribute paraphilias to early learning experiences. Researchers are also investigating the roles of the endocrine system and the nervous system in paraphilias, Many people with paraphilias have higher-than-normal sex drives.

Rape

What are the effects of rape? Many survivors of rape suffer physical and/or psychological trauma, such as PTSD. They have trouble sleeping, cry frequently, may become sullen and mistrustful, and may blame themselves. There may be injuries to the genital organs and other parts of the body, and the victim may be infected with disease organisms.

What are the major types of rape? The main types of rape include stranger rape, acquaintance rape, date rape, marital rape, and male rape.

What motivates rape? Men rape women as a way of dominating them and as a way of coercing them into sexual activity. Cultural myths about rape have the effects of blaming the victim and creating a climate that legitimizes rape. For some rapists, sexual arousal and violence become fused together.

Scoring the Rape Myths Scale

Each of the items on this scale represents a rape myth. For example, a rapist who believes that women truly desire to be overpowered by men may think he was just giving the woman what she wanted. But how can anyone know what someone else truly wants unless that person reveals it? Such beliefs are often used as self-serving justifications to explain away unacceptable behavior. Let's be entirely clear about this: When it comes to sex, *no* means *no*. Not *maybe*. Not *sometimes*. Not *in a few minutes*. Just *no*. Moreover, consenting to one sexual act (fondling, kissing, oral sex, etc.) does not imply consent for any other sexual act. Anyone has a right to say *no* at any time or to place limits on what they are willing to do. If you endorsed any of these items, apply your critical thinking skills to reexamine your beliefs.

KEY TERMS

gender identity *(p. 366)*
gender identity disorder *(p. 366)*
homophobia *(p. 370)*
heterosexism *(p. 370)*
sexual dysfunctions *(p. 371)*
hypoactive sexual desire disorder *(p. 372)*
sexual aversion disorder *(p. 373)*
female sexual arousal disorder *(p. 373)*
male erectile disorder *(p. 373)*

female orgasmic disorder *(p. 373)*
male orgasmic disorder *(p. 373)*
premature ejaculation *(p. 373)*
dyspareunia *(p. 374)*
vaginismus *(p. 374)*
paraphilias *(p. 383)*
exhibitionism *(p. 384)*
fetishism *(p. 385)*
transvestic fetishism *(p. 386)*

voyeurism *(p. 387)*
frotteurism *(p. 387)*
pedophilia *(p. 388)*
sexual masochism *(p. 389)*
hypoxyphilia *(p. 389)*
sexual sadism *(p. 389)*
sadomasochism *(p. 390)*
rape *(p. 395)*

WEB TOOLS

The companion website offers tools to enrich your learning experience and help you succeed in class. Go to www.prenhall.com/nevid for the gateway to the following resources:

- **VIDEO** links to connect to the video case files on the companion CD-ROM. VIDEO icons in the margins of the chapter highlight the case examples included in the CD-ROM. You can also access the CD-ROM directly if you do not have a Web connection.

- **QUIZ** links to self-scoring quizzes corresponding to each section of the chapter. The quizzes help you review your knowledge of the content in each chapter.
- **WEB** links to direct you to related sites that enhance your learning of abnormal psychology.

Schizophrenia and Other Psychotic Disorders

Schizophrenia typically develops in late adolescence or early adulthood, at the very time that young people are making their way from the family into the outside world. For Lori Schiller, an active speaker who shares her personal experience with schizophrenia, the first psychotic episode ("first break") came during her last year at summer camp.

66 I 99

"I Hear Something You Can't Hear"

It was a hot night in August 1976, the summer of my seventeenth year, when, uninvited and unannounced, the Voices took over my life.

I was going into my senior year in high school, so this was to be my last year at summer camp. College, a job, adulthood, responsibility—they were all just around the corner. But for the moment I wasn't prepared for anything more than a summer of fun. I certainly wasn't prepared to have my life change forever . . .

"You must die!" Other Voices joined in. "You must die! You will die!"

At first I didn't realize where I was. Was I at the lake? Was I asleep? Was I awake? Then I snapped back to the present. I was here at camp, alone. My summertime fling was long gone, two years gone. That long-ago scene was being played out in my mind, and in my mind alone. But as soon as I realized that I was in my bunk, and awake—and that my roommate was still sleeping peacefully—I knew I had to run. I had to get away from these terrible, evil Voices . . .

Since that time, I have never been completely free of those Voices. At the beginning of that summer, I felt well, a happy healthy girl—I thought—with a normal head and heart. By summer's end, I was sick, without any clear idea of what was happening to me or why. And as the Voices evolved into a full-scale illness, one that I only later learned was called schizophrenia, it snatched from me my tranquility, sometimes my self-possession, and very nearly my life.

Along the way I have lost many things: the career I might have pursued, the husband I might have married, the children I might have had. During the years when my friends were marrying, having their babies and moving into the houses I once dreamed of living in, I have been behind locked doors, battling the Voices who took over my life without even asking my permission.

—*From Schiller & Bennett, 1994*

SCHIZOPHRENIA IS PERHAPS THE MOST PUZZLING AND DISABLING PSYCHOLOGICAL disorder. It is the condition that best corresponds to popular conceptions of madness or lunacy. Although researchers are probing the psychological and biological foundations of schizophrenia, the disorder remains a mystery. In this chapter we consider what we know about schizophrenia and what remains to be learned. But schizophrenia is not the only type of psychotic disorder in which the person experiences a break with reality. In this chapter we also consider other psychotic disorders, including brief psychotic disorder, schizophreniform disorder, schizoaffective disorder, and delusional disorder. But we begin with the most common of these disorders, schizophrenia.

SCHIZOPHRENIA

Schizophrenia is a chronic, debilitating disorder that touches every facet of the affected person's life. People who develop schizophrenia become increasingly disengaged from society. They fail to function in the expected roles of student, worker, or spouse, and their families and communities grow intolerant of their deviant behavior. Acute episodes of schizophrenia are characterized by delusions, hallucinations, illogical thinking, incoherent speech, and bizarre behavior. Between acute episodes, people with schizophrenia may still be unable to think clearly and may lack an appropriate emotional response to the people and events in their lives. They may speak in a flat tone and show little if any facial expressiveness (Gur et al., 2002). They also tend to have difficulty perceiving emotions in other people's facial expressions (Edwards, Jackson, & Pattison, 2002; Kohler et al., 2003).

schizophrenia A chronic psychotic disorder characterized by disturbed behavior, thinking, emotions, and perceptions.

401

A Beautiful Mind. In the movie *A Beautiful Mind,* Russell Crowe portrayed Nobel Prize winner John Nash, a brilliant mathematician whose mind captured the beautiful intricacies of mathematical formulations but was also twisted by the delusions and hallucinations of schizophrenia.

Schizophrenia often elicits fear, misunderstanding, and condemnation rather than sympathy and concern. It strikes at the heart of the person, stripping the mind of the intimate connections between thoughts and emotions and filling it with distorted perceptions, false ideas, and illogical conceptions, as in the following case example.

Angela's "Hellsmen"

Angela, 19, was brought to the emergency room by her boyfriend, Jaime, because she had cut her wrists. When she was questioned, her attention wandered. She seemed transfixed by creatures in the air, or by something she might be hearing. It seemed as though she had an invisible earphone.

Angela explained that she had slit her wrists at the command of the "hellsmen." Then she became terrified. Later she related that the hellsmen had cautioned her not to disclose their existence. Angela feared that the hellsmen would punish her for her indiscretion.

Jaime related that Angela and he had been living together for nearly a year. They had initially shared a modest apartment in town. But Angela did not like being around other people and persuaded Jaime to rent a cottage in the country. There Angela spent much of her days making fantastic sketches of goblins and monsters. She occasionally became agitated and behaved as though invisible beings were issuing directions. Her words would become jumbled.

Jaime would try to persuade her to go for help, but she would resist. Then, about nine months ago, the wrist-cutting began. Jaime believed that he had made the bungalow secure by removing all knives and blades. But Angela always found a sharp object.

Then he would bring Angela to the hospital against her protests. Stitches would be put in, she would be held under observation for a while, and she would be medicated. She would recount that she cut her wrists because the hellsmen had

> *informed her that she was bad and had to die. After a few days in the hospital, she would disavow hearing the hellsmen and insist on discharge.*
> *Jaime would take her home. The pattern would repeat.*
>
> —*From the Authors' Files*

Course of Development

Schizophrenia typically develops during a person's late teens or early 20s, a time when the brain is reaching full maturation (Cowan & Kandel, 2001; Harrop & Trower, 2001). In about three of four cases, the first signs of schizophrenia appear by the age of 25. In some cases, the onset of the disorder is acute, as it was in the case of Lori Schiller. It occurs suddenly, within a few weeks or months. The individual may have been well adjusted and shown few signs of behavioral disturbance. Then a rapid transformation in personality and behavior leads to an acute psychotic episode.

In most cases, there is a slower, more gradual decline in functioning, as was the case with Ian Chovil, a young man who has been living with schizophrenia since the age of 17. He shares his story with the hope that the next generation of people affected by this debilitating disorder will be spared some of the experiences he has endured.

"I and I, Dancing Fool, Challenge You the World to a Duel"

Insidious is an appropriate word to describe the onset of schizophrenia I experienced. I gradually lost all my human relationships, first my girlfriend, then my immediate family, then friends and coworkers. I experienced a lot emotional turmoil and social anxiety. Somehow I graduated from Trent University in Peterborough, Ontario, Canada, but the last year I was smoking marijuana almost every day. I was creative but found it increasingly difficult to actually read anything. My career aspirations were to become a Rastafarian sociobiologist. I had become incapable of long term romantic relationships after the demise of my first one. At graduate school in Halifax I was hospitalized for a couple for weeks, a nervous breakdown I thought. Even though I was prescribed chlorpromazine and then trifluoperazine, no one mentioned schizophrenia to me or my father, a family physician. I tried to complete my year, but some courses went unfinished and I was kicked out of graduate school.

Within two years I was one of the homeless in Calgary, sleeping in a city park or the single men's hostel, hungry because I didn't get to eat very often. A World War II hero wanted to hurt me because I had discovered the war was caused by the influenza of 1918. Tibetan Buddhists read my mind everywhere I went because I had caused the Mount Saint Helens eruption for them earlier that year with my natural tantric abilities. For 10 years I lived more or less like that, in abject poverty, without any friends, quite delusional. At first I was going to be a Buddhist saint, then I was a pawn in a secret war between the sexuals and the antisexuals that would determine the fate of humanity, then I realized I was in contact with aliens of the future. There was going to be a nuclear holocaust that would break up the continental plates, and the oceans would evaporate from the lava. The aliens had come to collect me and one woman. All life here was about to be destroyed. My future wife and I were going to become aliens and have eternal life.

My actual situation by then was a sharp contrast. I was living in a downtown Toronto rooming house with only cockroaches for friends, changing light bulbs as they burnt out in a large department store. It was a full time job I could do, but I hated it intensely. I worried about my enemies who were trying to turn me into a homosexual, and I was in constant telepathic conversation with my future wife, listening to rock and roll songs for messages from aliens in my spare time. I ran into trouble with the law one night after becoming furious with the aliens for not transferring my mind to another body. The judge sentenced me to 3 years of probation with the condition I see a psychiatrist for that time.

. . . I wrote a poem as an undergraduate that was published in the student newspaper. The first line was "I and I, dancing fool, challenge you the world to a duel." I intend to challenge the world to the best of my ability, until people like me have the quality of life possible with the most effective treatment strategies available.

From Chovil, 2000 Reprinted with permission of the National Institute of Mental Heath

prodromal phase In schizophrenia, the period of decline in functioning that precedes the first acute psychotic episode.

residual phase In schizophrenia, the phase that follows an acute phase, characterized by a return to the level of functioning of the prodromal phase.

As in this case, psychotic behaviors may emerge gradually over several years, although early signs of deterioration may be observed. This period of deterioration is called the **prodromal phase.** It is characterized by waning interest in social activities and increasing difficulty in meeting the responsibilities of daily living. At first, such people seem to take less care of their appearance. They fail to bathe regularly or they wear the same clothes repeatedly. Over time, their behavior may become increasingly odd. There are lapses in job performance or schoolwork. Their speech becomes vague and rambling. At first these changes in personality may be so gradual that they raise little concern among friends and families. They may be attributed to "a phase" that the person is passing through. But as behavior becomes more bizarre—such as hoarding food, collecting garbage, or talking to oneself on the street—the acute phase of the disorder begins. Frankly psychotic symptoms develop, such as wild hallucinations, delusions, and increasingly bizarre behavior.

Following acute episodes, some people with schizophrenia enter the **residual phase,** in which their behavior returns to the level of the prodromal phase. Flagrant psychotic behaviors are absent, but the person is still impaired by significant cognitive, social, and emotional deficits, such as a deep sense of apathy and difficulties thinking or speaking clearly, and by harboring unusual ideas, such as beliefs in telepathy or clairvoyance (Docherty et al., 2003; Roth et al., 2004). These cognitive and social deficits can impede the ability of schizophrenia patients to function effectively in social and occupational roles even more severely than the severe hallucinations and delusions of the psychotic episode (Barch, 2003). Here, in his first-person account, Ian Chovil observes that despite improvement following treatment with the antipsychotic drug *olanzapine*, his functioning was still impaired by these deficits—the "poverties" as he calls them.

"I"

"The Poverties"

My life has been improving a little each year, and noticeably on olanzapine, but I am still quite unsure of myself. I still have what I call "the poverties," like poverty of thought, emotion, friends, and hard cash. My social life seems to be the slowest to improve. I have three or four recreational friends, only one without a mental illness, only one that I see fairly often. I lived for awhile with Rosemary, whom I still see often, in a two bedroom apartment until the government changed its regulations on cohabitation and we had to separate or lose almost $400 a month in income. Now I'm in a very nice subsidized apartment, fairly happy on my own for the first time thanks to olanzapine and my position at the Homewood, which brings me into contact with a lot of people.

From Chovil, 2000 Reprinted with permission of the National Institute of Mental Health

Though schizophrenia is a chronic disorder, as many as one half to two thirds of schizophrenia patients improve significantly over time (USDHHS, 1999a). Full return to normal behavior is uncommon but does occur in some cases. Typically, patients develop a chronic pattern characterized by occasional acute episodes and continued cognitive, emotional, and motivational impairment between psychotic episodes (Walker et al., 2004).

Prevalence

About 1% of the adult population in the United States is affected by schizophrenia, more than 2 million people in total (Cowan & Kandel, 2001; Freedman, 2003). According to the results of the World Health Organization (WHO) multinational study reported in Chapter 1, the rate of schizophrenia appears to be similar in both developed and developing cultures (Jablensky et al., 1992). The WHO estimates that about 24 million people worldwide suffer from schizophrenia (Olson, 2001). Nearly 1 million people in the United States receive treatment for schizophrenia each year, with about a third of these requiring hospitalization (Grady, 1997). The costs for treating schizophrenia are estimated at $30 billion annually and account for 75% of all expenditures in the

United States for mental health treatment (Cowan & Kandel, 2001; "Schizophrenia Update—Part I," 1995).

Men tend to have a slightly higher risk of developing schizophrenia than women (Aleman, Kahn, & Selten, 2003). Women tend to develop the disorder somewhat later than men do, with onset occurring most commonly between age 25 and the mid-30s in women and between age 18 and 25 in men (APA, 2000). Women also tend to achieve a higher level of functioning before the onset of the disorder and to have a less severe course of illness than do men (Häfner et al., 1998; USDHHS, 1999a).

Though we believe schizophrenia occurs universally across cultures, the course of the disorder and its particular symptoms can vary from culture to culture (Thakker & Ward, 1998). For example, visual hallucinations appear to be most common in some non-Western cultures (Ndetei & Singh, 1983). In a study conducted in an English hospital in Kenya, researchers found that people of African, Asian, or Jamaican background with schizophrenia were about twice as likely to experience visual hallucinations as those of European background (Ndetei & Vadher, 1984).

Diagnostic Features

Schizophrenia is a pervasive disorder that affects a wide range of psychological processes involving cognition, affect, and behavior (Arango, Kirkpatrick, & Buchanan, 2000).

The *DSM-IV* criteria for schizophrenia require that psychotic behaviors be present at some point during the course of the disorder and that signs of the disorder be present for at least 6 months. People with briefer forms of psychosis received other diagnoses, such as brief psychotic disorder (discussed later in the chapter). Table 12.1 lists the major diagnostic criteria for schizophrenia.

People with schizophrenia show a marked decline in occupational and social functioning. They may have difficulty holding a conversation, forming friendships, holding a job, or taking care of their personal hygiene. Yet no one behavior pattern is unique to schizophrenia. People with schizophrenia may exhibit delusions, problems with associative thinking, and hallucinations at one time or another, but not necessarily all at once. There are also different kinds or types of schizophrenia, characterized by different behavior patterns.

TRUTH or FICTION? *REVISITED*

Schizophrenia exists in the same form in every culture that has been studied.

☑ **FALSE.** Both the course of schizophrenia and its features can vary among cultures.

TABLE 12.1

Major Clinical Features of Schizophrenia

A. Two or more of the following must be present for a significant portion of time over the course of a 1-month period:

   (1) Delusions

   (2) Hallucinations

   (3) Speech that is either incoherent or characterized by marked loosening of associations

   (4) Disorganized or catatonic behavior

   (5) Negative features (e.g., flattened affect)

B. Functioning in such areas as social relations, work, or self-care during the course of the disorder is markedly below the level achieved prior to the onset of the disorder. If the onset develops during childhood or adolescence, there is a failure to achieve the expected level of social development.

C. Signs of the disorder have occurred continuously for a period of at least 6 months. This 6-month period must include an active phase lasting at least a month in which psychotic symptoms (listed in A), which are characteristic of schizophrenia, occur.

D. The disorder cannot be attributed to the effects of a substance (e.g., substance abuse or prescribed medication) or to a general medical condition.

Source: Adapted from the *DSM-IV-TR* (APA, 2000).

Men and women with schizophrenia differ in several ways. Men tend to show an earlier age of onset, have a poorer level of adjustment before showing signs of the disorder, and have more cognitive impairment, behavioral deficits, and a poorer response to drug therapy than do women (Gorwood et al., 1995; Ragland et al., 1999). These differences have led researchers to speculate that men and women may tend to develop different forms of schizophrenia. Perhaps schizophrenia affects different areas of the brain in men and women, which may explain differences in the form or features of the disorder.

Here let us consider how schizophrenia affects thinking, speech, attentional and perceptual processes, emotional processes, and voluntary behavior.

Disturbed Thought and Speech   Schizophrenia is characterized by disturbances in thinking and expression of thoughts through coherent, meaningful speech. Aberrant thinking may be found in both the content and form of thought.

Aberrant Content of Thought   *Delusions* represent disturbed content of thought. These are false beliefs that remain fixed in the person's mind despite their illogical bases and lack of evidence to support them. They tend to remain unshakable even in the face of disconfirming evidence. Delusions may take many forms. Some of the most common are

- *Delusions of persecution* (e.g., "The CIA is out to get me")
- *Delusions of reference* ("People on the bus are talking about me," or "People on TV are making fun of me," or "The neighbors hear everything I say. They've put bugs in the walls of my house")
- *Delusions of being controlled* (believing that one's thoughts, feelings, impulses, or actions are controlled by external forces, such as agents of the devil)
- *Delusions of grandeur* (believing oneself to be Jesus or believing one is on a special mission, or having grand but illogical plans for saving the world)

Other delusions include beliefs that one has committed unpardonable sins, is rotting away from a horrible disease, that the world or oneself does not really exist, or, as in the following case, that one desperately needs to help people.

The Hospital at the North Pole

Though people with schizophrenia may feel hounded by demons or earthly conspiracies, Mario's delusions had a messianic quality. "I need to get out of here," he said to his psychiatrist. "Why do you need to leave?" the psychiatrist asked. Mario responded, "My hospital. I need to get back to my hospital." "Which hospital?" he was asked. "I have this hospital. It's all white and we find cures for everything wrong with people." Mario was asked where his hospital was located. "It's all the way up at the North Pole," he responded. His psychiatrist asked, "But how do you get there?" Mario responded, "I just get there. I don't know how. I just get there. I have to do my work. When will you let me go so I can help the people?"

—From the Authors' Files

Other commonly occurring delusions include *thought broadcasting* (believing one's thoughts are somehow transmitted to the external world so that others can overhear them), *thought insertion* (believing one's thoughts have been planted in one's mind by an external source), and *thought withdrawal* (believing that thoughts have been removed from one's mind). Mellor (1970) offers the following examples.

- *Thought Broadcasting:* A 21-year-old student reported, "As I think, my thoughts leave my head on a type of mental ticker-tape. Everyone around has only to pass the tape through their mind and they know my thoughts." (p. 17)
- *Thought Insertion:* A 29-year-old housewife reported that when she looks out of the window, she thinks, "The garden looks nice and the grass looks cool, but the

thoughts of [a man's name] come into my mind. There are no other thoughts there, only his. . . . He treats my mind like a screen and flashes his thoughts on it like you flash a picture." (p. 17)

- *Thought Withdrawal:* A 22-year-old woman experienced the following: "I am thinking about my mother, and suddenly my thoughts are sucked out of my mind by a phrenological vacuum extractor, and there is nothing in my mind, it is empty." (pp. 16–17)

Aberrant Forms of Thought   Unless we are engaged in daydreaming or purposely letting our thoughts wander, our thoughts tend to be tightly knit together. The connections (or associations) between our thoughts tend to be logical and coherent. In contrast, people with schizophrenia tend to think in a disorganized, illogical fashion. In schizophrenia, the form or structure of thought processes as well as their content is often disturbed. Clinicians label this type of disturbance a **thought disorder.**

Thought disorder is recognized by the breakdown in the organization, processing, and control of thoughts. Looseness of associations is a cardinal sign of thought disorder. The speech pattern of people with schizophrenia is often disorganized or jumbled, with parts of words combined incoherently or words strung together to make meaningless rhymes. Their speech may jump disconnectedly from one topic to another. People with thought disorder are usually unaware that their thoughts and behavior appear abnormal. In severe cases their speech may become completely incoherent or incomprehensible.

Another common sign of thought disorder is *poverty of speech* (speech that is coherent but so slow, limited in production, or vague that little information is conveyed). Less commonly occurring signs include *neologisms* (made-up words that have little or no meaning to others), *perseveration* (inappropriate but persistent repetition of the same words or train of thought), *clanging* (stringing together of words or sounds on the basis of rhyming, such as, "I know who I am but I don't know Sam"), and *blocking* (involuntary, abrupt interruption of speech or thought). Disconnected speech is more common and more severe among younger patients, whereas poverty of speech is found more often and is more severe among older patients (Harvey et al., 1997).

Many but not all people with schizophrenia show evidence of thought disorder. Some appear to think and speak coherently but have disordered content of thought, as seen by the presence of delusions. Nor is disordered thought unique to schizophrenia; it is even found in milder form among people without psychological disorders, especially when they are tired or under stress. Disordered thought is also found among other diagnostic groups, such as persons with mania. Thought disorders in people experiencing a manic episode tend to be short lived and reversible, however. In those with schizophrenia, thought disorder tends to be more persistent or recurrent. Thought disorder occurs most often during acute episodes, but may linger into residual phases.

Attentional Deficiencies   To read this book you must screen out background noises and other environmental stimuli. Attention, the ability to focus on relevant stimuli and ignore irrelevant ones, is basic to learning and thinking. People with schizophrenia appear to have difficulty filtering out irrelevant stimuli, which makes it nearly impossible to focus their attention, organize their thoughts, and filter out unessential information (Asarnow et al., 1991; Braff, 1993). Scientists have discovered a genetic defect tied to a brain abnormality that may explain this filtering deficit (Grady, 1997). The mother of a son who had schizophrenia described her son's difficulties in filtering out extraneous sounds:

thought disorder   A disturbance in thinking characterized by the breakdown of logical associations between thoughts.

Filtering out extraneous stimuli.   You probably have little difficulty filtering out unimportant stimuli, such as street sounds. But people with schizophrenia may be distracted by irrelevant stimuli and be unable to filter them out. Consequently, they may have difficulty focusing their attention and organizing their thoughts.

His hearing is different when he's ill. One of the first things we notice when he's deteriorating is his heightened sense of hearing. He cannot filter out anything. He hears each and every sound around him with equal intensity. He hears the sounds from the street, in the yard, and in the house, and they are all much louder than normal.

Anonymous, 1985, p. 1; as cited in Freedman et al., 1987, p. 670

People with schizophrenia also appear to be *hypervigilant,* or acutely sensitive to extraneous sounds, especially during the early stages of the disorder. During acute episodes, they may become flooded by these stimuli, overwhelming their ability to make sense of their environments. Through measuring brain waves, researchers find that the brains of people with schizophrenia are less able than those of other people to inhibit or screen out responses to distracting sounds (Braff, 1993). Scientists suspect there may be a "gating" mechanism in the brain for filtering extraneous stimuli (Leonard et al., 2002).

Links between attentional deficits and schizophrenia are supported by various studies focusing on the psychophysiological aspects of attention. Here we review some of this research.

Schizophrenia:
The Case of Larry
"I have all kinds of voices."

Eye Movement Dysfunction   About one in three chronic schizophrenia patients shows evidence of eye movement dysfunction (Ross, 2000). Patients with *eye movement dysfunction* (also called *eye tracking dysfunction*) show abnormal movements of the eyes as they track a target that moves across the field of vision. Rather than steadily tracking the target, the eyes fall back and then catch up in a kind of jerky movement. Eye movement dysfunctions appear to involve a defect in the brain's involuntary attentional processes responsible for visual attention.

Eye movement dysfunctions are common among people with schizophrenia and among their first-degree relatives (parents, children, and siblings), which suggests it might be a genetically transmitted trait, or *marker,* that is associated with genes involved in the development of schizophrenia (Holzman et al., 1997; Ross, 2000).

The role of eye movement dysfunction as a biological marker for schizophrenia is clouded, however, because it is not unique to schizophrenia; many people with bipolar disorder show similar types of dysfunction (Sweeney et al., 1994). Research is needed to identify markers that are more specific to schizophrenia. We should also note that not all people with schizophrenia or their family members show eye movement dysfunctions. This suggests there may be different underlying genetic pathways associated with schizophrenia.

Deficiencies in Event-Related Potentials   Researchers have also studied brain wave patterns, called *event-related potentials,* or ERPs, that occur in response to external stimuli. ERPs can be broken down into components that emerge at various intervals following the presentation of a stimulus such as a flash of light or an auditory tone. Early components (brain wave patterns occurring within the first 250 milliseconds [ms], or one quarter of a second, of exposure to a stimulus) are involved in registering the stimulus in the brain. Later components, such as the P300 component (a brain wave pattern that typically occurs about 300 ms, or three tenths of a second, after a stimulus) may be involved in focusing attention on the stimulus.

People with schizophrenia often have early ERP components of greater than expected magnitude in response to touch (Holzman, 1987). This pattern of brain wave activity suggests that abnormally high levels of sensory information are reaching higher brain centers in people with schizophrenia, producing a condition called *sensory overload.* This may help explain the difficulty that people with schizophrenia have in filtering out distracting stimuli. We also have evidence of lower than expected levels of P300 brain wave patterns in parts of the brain that process auditory stimulation (e.g., van der Stelt et al., 2004; Winterer et al., 2004). This evidence points to attentional deficits that may at least partly explain why people with schizophrenia have difficulty extracting meaningful information from stimuli such as lights, sounds, and touch.

Studies of ERPs are consistent with the view that people with schizophrenia are flooded with high levels of sensory information and have great difficulty extracting useful information from it. As a result, they may be confused and find it difficult to filter out irrelevant stimuli. Although ERP research is promising, more research is needed to determine what role these abnormalities play in schizophrenia.

In sum, several lines of evidence point to underlying physiological deficits in the ability to attend to relevant stimuli and ignore distracting stimuli among people with schizophrenia (O'Leary et al., 1996). Although the search continues for biological markers for schizophrenia, no unique biological pattern has yet been found. Recent evidence indicates that training in attention skills may help reduce attentional deficits in schizophrenia patients (Medalia et al., 1998).

Perceptual Disturbances

Voices, Devils, and Angels

Every so often during the interview, Sally would look over her right shoulder in the direction of the office door and smile gently. When asked why she kept looking at the door, she said that the voices were talking about the two of us just outside the door and she wanted to hear what they were saying. "Why the smile?" Sally was asked. "They were saying funny things," she replied, "like maybe you thought I was cute or something."

Tom was flailing his arms wildly in the hall of the psychiatric unit. Sweat seemed to pour from his brow, and his eyes darted about with agitation. He was subdued and injected with haloperidol (brand name Haldol) to reduce his agitation. When he was about to be injected he started shouting, "Father, forgive them for they know not . . . forgive them . . . father . . ." His words became jumbled. Later, after he had calmed down, he reported that the ward attendants had looked to him like devils or evil angels. They were red and burning, and steam issued from their mouths.

—From the Authors' Files

Hallucinations Hallucinations, the most common form of perceptual disturbance in schizophrenia, are images perceived in the absence of external stimulation. They are difficult to distinguish from reality. For Sally, the voices coming from outside the consulting room were real enough, even though no one was there. Hallucinations can involve any of the senses. Auditory hallucinations ("hearing voices") are most common, affecting about three of four schizophrenia patients (Goode, 2003b). Tactile hallucinations (such as tingling, electrical, or burning sensations) and somatic hallucinations (such as feeling like snakes are crawling inside one's belly) are also common. Visual hallucinations (seeing things that are not there), gustatory hallucinations (tasting things that are not present), and olfactory hallucinations (sensing odors that are not present) are rarer.

People with schizophrenia may experience auditory hallucinations as female or male and as originating inside or outside their head (Asaad & Shapiro, 1986). Hallucinators may hear voices conversing about them in the third person, debating their virtues or faults. Some voices are experienced as supportive and friendly, but most are critical or even terrorizing.

Some people with schizophrenia experience *command hallucinations,* voices that instruct them to perform certain acts, such as harming themselves or others (Rogers et al., 1990). Angela, for example, was instructed by the "hellsmen" to commit suicide. People with schizophrenia who experience command hallucinations are often hospitalized for fear they may harm themselves or others. There is a good reason for this. A recent study found that four of five people with command hallucinations reported obeying them, with nearly half reporting they had obeyed commands to harm themselves during the past month (Kasper, Rogers, & Adams, 1996). Yet command

hallucinations Perceptions occurring in the absence of external stimuli that become confused with reality.

TRUTH or FICTION? *REVISITED*

Visual hallucinations ("seeing things") are the most common type of hallucination in people with schizophrenia.

☑**FALSE.** Auditory, not visual, hallucinations are the most common type of hallucinations among people with schizophrenia.

A painting by a man with schizophrenia.
This picture was painted by a young man who reported monsters—apparent hallucinations—like the one pictured here crawling on the floor. He also reported that the chairs next to his bed had turned into devils.

TRUTH or FICTION? *REVISITED*

It is normal for people to hallucinate nightly.

☑ **TRUE.** Hallucinations—perceptual experiences such as visual images, smells, etc., in the absence of external stimulation—occur nightly in the form of dreams.

---

hallucinations often go undetected by professionals, because patients deny them or are unwilling to discuss them.

Hallucinations are not unique to schizophrenia. People with major depression and mania sometimes experience hallucinations. Nor are hallucinations invariably a sign of psychopathology. They are common and socially valued in some cultures (Bentall, 1990). Even in developed countries like the United States, about 5% of respondents in nonpatient samples report experiencing hallucinations during the preceding year, mostly auditory hallucinations (Honig et al., 1998). Hallucinations in people without psychiatric conditions are often triggered by unusually low levels of sensory stimulation (lying in the dark in a soundproof room for extended time) or low levels of arousal (Teunisse et al., 1996). Unlike psychotic individuals, these people realize that their hallucinations are not real and feel in control of them.

People who are free of psychological disorders sometimes experience hallucinations during the course of a religious experience or ritual (Asaad & Shapiro, 1986). Participants in such experiences may report fleeting trancelike states with visions or other perceptual aberrations. All of us hallucinate nightly, if we consider dreams to be a form of hallucination (perceptual experience in the absence of external stimuli).

Hallucinations in waking states also occur in response to hallucinogenic drugs, such as LSD, and can occur during grief reactions, when images of the deceased may appear, and in other stressful conditions. The hallucinations of psychiatric patients are different from those of mourners because those with psychiatric disorders typically cannot distinguish between real and imaginary events (Bentall, 1990).

Drug-induced hallucinations tend to be visual and often involve abstract shapes such as circles or stars or flashes of light. Schizophrenic hallucinations, in contrast, tend to be more fully formed and complex. Hallucinations (for example, of bugs crawling on one's skin) may also arise during delirium tremens (the DTs), which often occur as part of the withdrawal syndrome for chronic alcoholism. Hallucinations may also occur as side effects of medications or in neurological disorders, such as Parkinson's disease.

The causes of psychotic hallucinations remain unknown, but speculations abound. Disturbances in brain chemistry are suspected. The neurotransmitter dopamine is implicated, largely because antipsychotic drugs that block dopamine activity also tend to reduce hallucinations. Conversely, drugs that lead to increased production of dopamine tend to induce hallucinations. Because hallucinations resemble dreamlike states, they may be connected to a failure of brain mechanisms that normally prevent dream images from intruding on waking experiences.

Hallucinations may also represent a type of inner speech (silent self-talk) (Cleghorn et al., 1992). Many of us talk to ourselves from time to time, although we usually keep our mutterings beneath our breaths (subvocal) and recognize the voice as our own. Might auditory hallucinations that occur among people with schizophrenia be projections of their own internal voices, or self-speech, onto external sources? In one experiment, 14 of 18 hallucinators who suffered from schizophrenia reported that the voices disappeared when they engaged in a procedure that prevented them from talking to themselves under their breath (Bick & Kinsbourne, 1987). Similar results were obtained for 18 of 21 normal subjects who reportedly experienced hallucinations in response to hypnotic suggestions.

Researchers find that brain activity in Broca's area, a part of the brain involved in controlling speech, is greater in men with schizophrenia when they hear voices than when they are no longer hallucinating (McGuire, Shah, & Murray, 1993). This same area is active when people engage in inner speech (Paulesu, Frith, & Frackowisk, 1993). Researchers also find evidence of similar electrical activity in the auditory cortex of the brain during auditory hallucinations and in response to hearing real sounds (Tiihonen et al., 1992). This supports the view that auditory hallucinations may be a form of inner speech that for some unknown reason is attributed to external sources rather than to one's own thoughts (Ford et al., 2001; Hoffman et al., 1999). This line of research has led to treatments in which behavior therapists attempt to teach hallucinators to reattribute their voices to themselves (Bentall, Haddock, & Slade, 1994). Hallucinators are also trained to recognize the situational cues associated with their hallucinations. For example,

> . . . one patient . . . recognized that her voices tended to become worse following family arguments. She became aware that the content of her voices reflected the things that she was feeling and thinking about her family but that she was unable to express. Specific targets and goals were then set to allow her to address these difficulties with her family, and techniques such as rehearsal, problem solving and cognitive restructuring were employed to help her work towards these goals.
>
> —Bentall, Haddock, & Slade, 1994, p. 58

Although cognitive–behavioral approaches to treating hallucinations are still in their infancy, the early results are promising (e.g., Messari & Hallam, 2003; Wiersma et al., 2001). But even if theories linking inner speech to auditory hallucinations stand up to further scientific inquiry, they cannot account for hallucinations in other sensory modalities, such as visual, tactile, or olfactory hallucinations.

The brain mechanisms responsible for hallucinations probably involve a number of interconnected systems. One intriguing possibility is that defects in deeper brain structures may lead the brain to create its own reality. This alternative reality goes unchecked because the higher thinking centers in the brain, located in the frontal lobes of the cerebral cortex, fail to perform a reality check on these images to determine whether they are real, imagined, or hallucinated (Begley, 1995). Consequently, people may misattribute their own internally generated voices to outside sources. As we'll see later, evidence from other brain-imaging studies points to abnormalities in the frontal lobes in people with schizophrenia.

Emotional Disturbances Disturbances of affect or emotional response in schizophrenia are typified by blunted affect—also called *flat affect*—and by inappropriate affect. Flat affect is inferred from the absence of emotional expression in the face and voice. People with schizophrenia may speak in a monotone and maintain an expressionless face, or "mask." They may not experience a normal range of emotional response to people and events. Or their emotional responses may be inappropriate, such as giggling at bad news.

It is not clear, however, whether emotional blunting in people with schizophrenia is a disturbance in their ability to express emotions, to report the presence of emotions, or to actually experience emotions (Berenbaum & Oltmanns, 1990). Recent laboratory-based evidence shows that schizophrenia patients experience more intense negative emotions, but less intense positive emotions, than controls (Myin-Germeys, Delespaul, & deVries, 2000). In other words, schizophrenia patients may experience strong emotions (especially negative emotions), even if their experiences are not communicated to the world outside through their facial expressions or behavior. People with schizophrenia may lack the capacity to express their emotions outwardly (Kring & Neale, 1996).

Other Types of Impairment People who suffer from schizophrenia may become confused about their personal identities—the cluster of attributes and characteristics that define themselves as individuals and give meaning and direction to their lives. They may fail to recognize themselves as unique individuals and be unclear about how much of what they experience is part of themselves. In psychodynamic terms, this phenomenon is sometimes referred to as loss of *ego boundaries*. They may also have difficulty adopting a third-party perspective: they fail to perceive their own behavior and verbalizations as socially inappropriate in a given situation because they cannot see things from another person's point of view (Carini & Nevid, 1992). They also have difficulty recognizing or perceiving emotions in others (Penn et al., 2000).

Disturbances of volition are most often seen in the residual or chronic state. These disturbances are characterized by loss of initiative to pursue goal-directed activities. People with schizophrenia may be unable to carry out plans and may lack interest or drive. Apparent ambivalence toward choosing courses of action may block goal-directed activities.

Schizophrenia:
The Case of Georgiana
"Then it got out of hand, where I couldn't control coming and going, back and forth, and in my body, out of my body, it was no longer under my control."

A young man diagnosed with disorganized schizophrenia. One of the characteristic features of disorganized schizophrenia is grossly inappropriate affect, as shown by this patient, who continually giggles and laughs for no apparent reason.

disorganized type The subtype of schizophrenia characterized by disorganized behavior, bizarre delusions, and vivid hallucinations.

People with schizophrenia may show highly excited or wild behavior or may slow to a state of *stupor*. They may exhibit odd gestures and bizarre facial expressions or become unresponsive and curtail spontaneous movement. In extreme cases, as in catatonic schizophrenia, the person seems unaware of the environment or maintains a rigid posture. Or the person moves about in an excited but seemingly purposeless manner.

People with schizophrenia also show significant impairment in their interpersonal relationships. They withdraw from social interactions and become absorbed in private thoughts and fantasies. Or they cling so desperately to others that they make them uncomfortable. They may become so dominated by their own fantasies that they essentially lose touch with the outside world. They also tend to have been introverted and peculiar even before the appearance of psychotic behavior (Berenbaum & Fujita, 1994). These early signs may be associated with a vulnerability to schizophrenia, at least in people with a genetic risk of developing the disorder.

Subtypes of Schizophrenia

The *DSM-IV* lists three specific types of schizophrenia: *disorganized, catatonic,* and *paranoid*. People with schizophrenia who display active psychotic features, such as hallucinations, delusions, incoherent speech, or confused or disorganized behavior, but who do not meet the specifications of the other types, are considered to be of an *undifferentiated type*. Others who have no prominent psychotic features at the time of evaluation but have some residual features (for example, social withdrawal, peculiar behavior, blunted or inappropriate affect, strange beliefs or thoughts) would be classified as having a *residual type* of schizophrenia.

Here let us consider the specific types of schizophrenia recognized by the *DSM* system.

Disorganized Type The **disorganized type** of schizophrenia is associated with such features as confused behavior, incoherent speech, silly irrelevant laughter, vivid and frequent hallucinations, flattened or inappropriate affect, and disorganized delusions that often involve sexual or religious themes. Social impairment is common. People with disorganized schizophrenia display silliness and giddiness of mood, giggling and talking nonsensically. They often neglect their appearance and hygiene and lose control of their bladders and bowels. Consider the following case example.

A Case of Schizophrenia, Disorganized Type

A 40-year-old man who looks more like 30 is brought to the hospital by his mother, who reports that she is afraid of him. It is his twelfth hospitalization. He is dressed in a tattered overcoat, baseball cap, and bedroom slippers, and sports several medals around his neck. His affect ranges from anger (hurling obscenities at his mother) to giggling. He speaks with a childlike quality and walks with exaggerated hip movements and seems to measure each step very carefully. Since stopping his medication about a month ago, his mother reports, he had been hearing voices and looking and acting more bizarrely. He tells the interviewer he has been "eating wires" and lighting fires. His speech is generally incoherent and frequently falls into rhyme and clanging associations. His history reveals a series of hospitalizations since the age of 16. Between hospitalizations, he lives with his mother, who is now elderly, and often disappears for months at a time, but is eventually picked up by the police for wandering in the streets.

—Adapted from Spitzer et al., 1994, pp. 189–190

Catatonic Type The **catatonic type** of schizophrenia is characterized by markedly impaired motor behavior and a slowing down of activity that progresses to a stupor but may switch abruptly into an agitated phase. People with catatonic schizophrenia may show unusual mannerisms or grimacing or maintain bizarre, apparently strenuous postures for hours, even though their limbs become stiff or swollen. A striking but less common feature is *waxy flexibility,* which involves adopting a fixed posture into which they have been positioned by others. They will not respond to questions or comments during these periods, which can last for hours. Later they may report they heard what others were saying at the time, however.

> ### A Case of Schizophrenia, Catatonic Type
>
> *A 24-year-old man had been brooding about his life. He professed that he did not feel well but could not explain his bad feelings. While hospitalized, he initially sought contact with people but a few days later was found in a statuesque position, his legs contorted awkwardly. He refused to talk to anyone and acted as if he couldn't see or hear. His face was an expressionless mask. A few days later, he began to talk, but in an echolalic or mimicking way. For example, he would respond to the question, "What is your name?" by saying, "What is your name?" He could not care for his needs and had to be fed.*
>
> *—Adapted from Arieti, 1974, p. 40*

Catatonia is not unique to schizophrenia. It occurs in other disorders, including brain disorders, drug intoxication, and metabolic disorders. In fact, it is found more often in people with mood disorders than those with schizophrenia (Taylor & Fink, 2003).

Paranoid Type The **paranoid type** of schizophrenia is characterized by preoccupations with one or more delusions or with the presence of frequent auditory hallucinations (APA, 2000). The behavior and speech of someone with paranoid schizophrenia does not show the marked disorganization typical of the disorganized type, nor is there a prominent display of flattened or inappropriate affect or catatonic behavior. The delusions often involve themes of grandeur, persecution, or jealousy. The patient may believe, for example, that the spouse or lover is unfaithful despite a lack of evidence. Patients may become highly agitated, confused, and fearful.

> ### A Case of Schizophrenia, Paranoid Type
>
> *The 25-year-old woman was visibly frightened. She was shaking badly and had the look of someone who feared that she might be attacked at any moment. The night before she had been found cowering in a corner of the local bus station, mumbling incoherently to herself, having arrived in town minutes earlier on a bus from Philadelphia. The station manager had called the police, who took her to the hospital. She told the interviewer that she had to escape Philadelphia because the Mafia was closing in on her. She was a schoolteacher, she explained, at least until the voices started bothering her. The voices would tell her she was bad and had to be punished. Sometimes the voices were in her head, sometimes they spoke to her through the electrical wires in her apartment. The voices told her how someone from the Mafia would come to kill her. She felt that one of her neighbors, a shy man who lived down the hall, was in league with the Mafia. She felt the only hope she had was to escape. To go somewhere, anywhere. So she hopped on the first bus leaving town, heading nowhere in particular, except away from home.*
>
> *—From the Authors' Files*

catatonic type The subtype of schizophrenia characterized by gross disturbances in motor activity, such as catatonic stupor.

paranoid type The subtype of schizophrenia characterized by hallucinations and systematized delusions, commonly involving themes of persecution.

positive symptoms Flagrant symptoms of schizophrenia, such as hallucinations, delusions, bizarre behavior, and thought disorder.

negative symptoms Behavioral deficiencies associated with schizophrenia, such as social skills deficits, social withdrawal, flattened affect, poverty of speech and thought, psychomotor retardation, and failure to experience pleasure.

Type I versus Type II Schizophrenia Some investigators have gone beyond the *DSM* typology in proposing other ways of typing schizophrenia. One alternative typology distinguishes between two basic types of schizophrenia, Type 1 and Type II (Crow, 1980a, 1980b, 1980c). Type I schizophrenia is characterized by the more flagrant symptoms, called **positive symptoms,** such as hallucinations, delusions, and looseness of associations, as well as by an abrupt onset, preserved intellectual ability, and a more favorable response to antipsychotic medication (Penn, 1998; Roth et al., 2004; Walker et al., 2004). Type II schizophrenia corresponds to a pattern consisting largely of the deficit, or **negative symptoms,** of schizophrenia. These involve a loss or reduction of normal functions, such as lack of emotional expression, low or absent levels of motivation, loss of pleasure in activities, social withdrawal, and poverty of speech, as well as by a more gradual onset, intellectual impairment, and poorer response to antipsychotic drugs (USDHHS, 1999a).

One intriguing possibility is that Type I and Type II schizophrenia represent different pathological processes. The Type I pattern may involve a defect in the inhibitory (blocking) mechanisms in the brain that normally control excessive or distorted behaviors. Underlying this malfunction may be a disturbance in the supply or regulation of dopamine in the brain, because antipsychotic drugs that regulate dopamine levels generally have a favorable impact on positive symptoms. The negative symptoms associated with Type II schizophrenia represent the more enduring or persistent characteristics of schizophrenia. The Type II pattern is associated with poorer functioning before the person developed schizophrenia (*premorbid functioning*) and with a more progressive decline in functioning leading to enduring disability (Earnst & Kring, 1997; McGlashan & Fenton, 1992). One possibility is that the negative symptoms associated with Type II schizophrenia are caused by structural damage in the brain.

The Type I–Type II distinction remains controversial. Some investigators (e.g., Kay, 1990) find that only a minority of people with schizophrenia can be classified as exhibiting either predominantly positive or negative symptoms. Positive and negative symptoms may not define distinct subtypes of schizophrenia but rather separate dimensions that can coexist in the same individual.

Perhaps, as recent research suggests, a three-dimensional model is most appropriate for grouping schizophrenic symptoms (Arango et al., 2000; USDHHS, 1999a). One dimension, a *psychotic dimension,* consists of delusional thinking and hallucinations. A *negative dimension* comprises negative symptoms, such as flat affect and poverty of speech and thought. The third dimension, labeled a *disorganized dimension,* includes inappropriate affect and thought disorder (disordered thought and speech). Although schizophrenic symptoms seem to cluster into these three dimensions, there is considerable overlap among the dimensions. Thus, although the three-factor model may have clinical value in representing particular clusters of symptoms, these dimensions do not appear to represent distinct subtypes of schizophrenia.

A person diagnosed with catatonic schizophrenia. People with catatonic schizophrenia remain in unusual, difficult positions that can last for hours, even though their limbs become stiff or swollen. They seem oblivious to their environment during these episodes, even to people who are talking about them. Some sufferers later say that they heard what was being said. Periods of stupor commonly alternate with periods of agitation.

Theoretical Perspectives

Schizophrenia has been approached from each of the major theoretical perspectives. Though the underlying causes of schizophrenia remain elusive, they are presumed to involve biological abnormalities in combination with psychosocial and environmental influences (USDHHS, 1999a).

Psychodynamic Perspectives According to the psychodynamic perspective, schizophrenia represents the overwhelming of the ego by primitive sexual or aggressive drives or impulses arising from the id. These impulses threaten the ego and give rise to intense intrapsychic conflict. Under such a threat, the person regresses to an early period in the oral stage, referred to as *primary narcissism.* In this period, the infant has not yet learned that the world is distinct from itself. Because the ego mediates the relationship between the self and the outer world, this breakdown in ego functioning accounts for the detachment from reality that is typical of schizophrenia. Input from the id causes fantasies to become mistaken for reality, giving rise to hallucinations and delusions. Primitive impulses may also carry more weight than social norms and be expressed in bizarre, socially inappropriate behavior.

Freud's followers, such as Erik Erikson and Harry Stack Sullivan, placed more emphasis on interpersonal than intrapsychic factors. Sullivan (1962), for example, who devoted much of his life's work to schizophrenia, emphasized that impaired mother–child relationships can set the stage for gradual withdrawal from other people. In early childhood, anxious and hostile interactions between the child and parent lead the child to take refuge in a private fantasy world. A vicious cycle ensues: The more the child withdraws, the less opportunity there is to develop a sense of trust in others and the social skills necessary to establish intimacy. Then the weak bonds between the child and others prompt social anxiety and further withdrawal. This cycle continues until young adulthood. Then, faced with increasing demands at school or work and in intimate relationships, the person becomes overwhelmed with anxiety and withdraws completely into a world of fantasy.

Critics of Freud's views point out that schizophrenic behavior and infantile behavior are different, so schizophrenia cannot be explained by regression. Critics of Freud and modern psychodynamic theorists note that psychodynamic explanations are post hoc, or retrospective. Early child–adult relationships are recalled from the vantage point of adulthood rather than observed longitudinally. Psychoanalysts have not been able to demonstrate that hypothesized early childhood experiences or family patterns lead to schizophrenia.

Paranoid schizophrenia. People with paranoid schizophrenia hold systematized delusions that commonly involve themes of persecution and grandeur. They usually do not show the degree of confusion, disorganization, or disturbed motor behavior seen in people with catatonic or disorganized schizophrenia. Unless they are discussing the areas in which they are delusional, their thought processes can appear to be relatively intact.

Learning Perspectives Though learning theory does not offer a complete explanation of schizophrenia, the development of some forms of schizophrenic behavior can be understood in terms of the roles of conditioning and observational learning. From this perspective, people with schizophrenia learn to exhibit certain bizarre behaviors when these are more likely to be reinforced than normal behaviors.

Support for this view is found in operant conditioning studies in which bizarre behavior is shaped by reinforcement. Experiments involving individuals with schizophrenia show, for example, that reinforcement affects the frequency of bizarre versus normal verbalizations and that hospital patients can be shaped into performing odd behaviors. In a classic case example, Haughton and Ayllon (1965) conditioned a 54-year-old woman with chronic schizophrenia to cling to a broom. A staff member gave her the broom to hold, and when she did, another staff member gave her a cigarette. This pattern was repeated several times. Soon the woman could not be parted from the broom. But the fact that reinforcement can influence people to engage in peculiar behavior does not demonstrate that the bizarre behaviors characteristic of schizophrenia are shaped by reinforcement.

Social–cognitive theorists suggest that modeling of schizophrenic behavior can occur within the mental hospital, where patients may begin to model themselves after fellow patients who act strangely. Hospital staff may also inadvertently reinforce schizophrenic behavior by paying more attention to patients who exhibit bizarre behavior. This understanding is consistent with the observation that schoolchildren who disrupt the class garner more attention from their teachers than well-behaved children do.

Perhaps some types of of schizophrenic behavior can be explained by the principles of modeling and reinforcement. However, many people display schizophrenic behavior

TRUTH or FICTION? *REVISITED*

A 54-year-old hospitalized woman diagnosed with schizophrenia was conditioned to cling to a broom by being given cigarettes as reinforcers.

✓ **TRUE.** A 54-year-old hospitalized woman with schizophrenia was in fact conditioned to cling to a broom by being given cigarettes as reinforcers. The issue is the extent to which principles of learning can account for the bizarre behavior patterns shown by people with schizophrenia.

Withdrawing into oneself? Harry Stack Sullivan and some other psychodynamic theorists see individuals with schizophrenia as withdrawing into private fantasy worlds, largely because of severely disturbed relationships with their mothers.

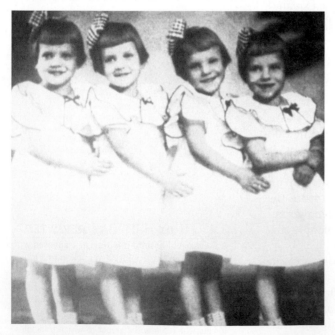

The Genain quadruplets. Schizophrenia is more likely to affect individuals who have family members with the disorder. Here we see a photo of the Genain quadruplets, each of whom developed schizophrenia.

patterns without prior exposure to other people with schizophrenia. In fact, the onset of schizophrenic behavior patterns is more likely to lead to hospitalization than to result from hospitalization.

Biological Perspectives Although we still have much to learn about the biological underpinnings of schizophrenia, most investigators today recognize that biological factors play a determining role.

Genetic Factors We now have compelling evidence that schizophrenia is strongly influenced by genetic factors (Freedman, 2003; Gottesman, 2001; Sullivan, Kendler, & Neale, 2003; Tienari et al., 2003). Cross-cultural evidence from studies in Sweden, Iceland, and Ireland, as well as the United States, shows an increased risk of schizophrenia in people who have biological relatives with the disorder (Erlenmeyer-Kimling et al., 1997; Kendler & Diehl, 1993). Overall, first-degree relatives of people with schizophrenia (parents, children, or siblings) have about a ten-fold greater risk of developing schizophrenia than do members of the general population (APA, 2000; Kendler & Diehl, 1993).

Further supporting a genetic linkage, the closer the genetic relationship between people diagnosed with schizophrenia and their family members, the greater the likelihood (or *concordance rate*) of schizophrenia in their relatives (Gottesman, 2001). Figure 12.1 shows the pooled results of European studies on family incidence of schizophrenia conducted from 1920 to 1987. However, the fact that families share common environments as well as common genes requires that we dig deeper to examine the genetic underpinnings of schizophrenia.

More direct support for a genetic contribution to schizophrenia is found in twin studies, which show concordance rates for the disorder among identical or monozygotic (MZ) twins of about 48%, more than twice the rate found among fraternal or dizygotic (DZ) twins (about 17%) (Gottesman, 1991; Plomin et al., 1994). A twins study in Norway found an even greater spread: 48% concordance in MZ twins versus 3.6% in DZ twins (Onstad et al., 1991).

We should be cautious, however, not to overinterpret the results of twin studies. MZ twins not only share 100% genetic similarity, but they may also be treated more alike than DZ twins. Thus environmental factors may help explain the higher concordance rates found among MZ twins. To help sort out environmental from genetic factors, investigators have turned to adoption studies in which high-risk (HR) children (children of one or more biological parents with schizophrenia) were adopted away shortly after birth and reared apart from their biological parents.

Adoption studies provide the strongest evidence to date for a genetic contribution to schizophrenia. In perhaps the best-known example, researchers in Denmark examined official registers and found 39 HR adoptees who had been reared apart from their biological mothers who had schizophrenia (Rosenthal et al., 1968, 1975). Three of the 39 HR adoptees (8%) were diagnosed with schizophrenia, as compared to 0% of a reference group of 47 adoptees whose biological parents had no psychiatric history.

Other investigators have approached the question of heredity from the opposite direction. U.S. researcher Seymour Kety and Danish colleagues (Kety et al., 1975, 1978) used official records to find 33 index cases of children in Copenhagen, Denmark, who had been adopted early in life and were later diagnosed with schizophrenia. They compared the rates of diagnosed schizophrenia in the biological and adoptive relatives of the index cases with those of the relatives of a matched

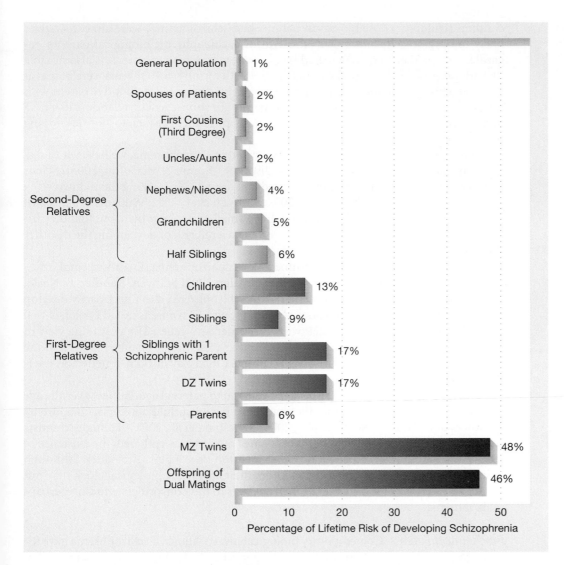

FIGURE 12.1 The familial risk of schizophrenia.
Generally speaking, the more closely one is related to people who have developed schizophrenia, the greater the risk of developing schizophrenia for oneself. Monozygotic (MZ) twins, whose genetic heritages are identical, are much more likely than dizygotic (DZ) twins, whose genes overlap by 50%, to be concordant for schizophrenia.

Source: Adapted from Gottesman et al. (1987).

reference group of adoptees with no psychiatric history. The results strongly supported the genetic explanation. The incidence of diagnosed schizophrenia was greater among the biological relatives of the adoptees who had schizophrenia than among the biological relatives of the control adoptees. Adoptive relatives of both the index cases and control cases showed similar, *low* rates of schizophrenia. Similar results were found in later research that extended the scope of the investigation to the rest of Denmark (Kety et al., 1994). It thus appears that family linkages in schizophrenia follow shared genes, not shared environments (Kinney et al., 1997; Moldin, 1994).

Still another approach, the *cross-fostering study,* has yielded additional evidence of genetic factors in schizophrenia. In this approach, investigators compare the incidence of schizophrenia among children whose biological parents either had or didn't have schizophrenia and who were reared by adoptive parents who either had or didn't have schizophrenia. In a classic study conducted in Denmark, Wender and his colleagues (Wender et al., 1974) found the risk of schizophrenia related to the presence of schizophrenia in the children's biological parents, but not in their adoptive parents. High-risk children (children whose biological parents had schizophrenia) were almost twice as likely to develop schizophrenia as those of nonschizophrenic biological parents, regardless of whether they were reared by a parent with schizophrenia. It is also notable that adoptees whose biological parents did not suffer from schizophrenia were placed at no greater risk of developing schizophrenia by being reared by an adoptive parent with schizophrenia than by a nonschizophrenic parent. In sum, a genetic relationship with a person with schizophrenia seems to be the most prominent risk factor for developing the disorder.

Although genetic factors are clearly implicated in schizophrenia, we have yet to discover the particular genes involved in the disorder (Plomin & McGuffin, 2003). Scientists believe that multiple genes are involved and are actively tracking them down (e.g., Bunney et al., 2003; Kromkamp et al., 2003; Shifman et al., 2002; Williams et al., 2004). Scientists suspect that each of these genes has a small effect on its own, but that they influence each other in contributing to raising the overall risk of developing the disorder (Wilcox et al., 2002).

Yet genetics alone does not determine risk of schizophrenia. Environmental influences also play an important role (Sawa & Snyder, 2002; Sullivan, Kendler, & Neale, 2003). People who carry a high genetic risk of schizophrenia don't necessarily develop the disorder. In fact, the rate of concordance among MZ twins, as noted earlier, is well below 100%, even though identical twins carry identical genes. The prevailing view of schizophrenia, the diathesis-stress model (discussed later in the chapter) holds that the development of schizophrenia involves a complex interplay of both genetic and environmental factors.

Some cases of schizophrenia appear to be linked to paternal age. Fathers over the age of 50 in one study had three times the chances of having a child develop schizophrenia as fathers under the age of 25 (Lewin, 2001; Malaspina et al., 2001). Though scientists remain skeptical of the link to paternal age until more data is gathered, the existence of such a link would raise the possibility that men too have a biological clock. Although older men may be capable of siring children, their advancing biological clock may put them at greater risk of transmitting genetic defects to their offspring, including perhaps schizophrenia.

dopamine hypothesis The prediction that schizophrenia involves overactivity of dopamine receptors in the brain.

Biochemical Factors Contemporary biological investigations of schizophrenia have focused on the role of the neurotransmitter dopamine. The leading biochemical model of schizophrenia, the **dopamine hypothesis,** posits that schizophrenia involves an overreactivity of dopamine transmission in the brain. Increasing evidence supports the view that schizophrenia involves an irregularity in dopamine transmission in the brain (McGowan et al., 2004).

The major source of evidence for the dopamine model is found in the effects of antipsychotic drugs called major tranquilizers or *neuroleptics.* The most widely used neuroleptics belong to a class of drugs called *phenothiazines,* which includes such drugs as Thorazine, Mellaril, and Prolixin. Neuroleptic drugs block dopamine receptors, thereby reducing the level of dopamine activity (Gründer, Carlsson, & Wong, 2002). As a consequence, neuroleptics inhibit excessive transmission of neural impulses that may give rise to schizophrenic behavior.

Another source of evidence supporting the role of dopamine in schizophrenia is based on the actions of amphetamines, a class of stimulant drugs. These drugs increase the concentration of dopamine in the synaptic cleft by blocking its reuptake by presynaptic neurons. When given in large doses to normal people, these drugs cause symptoms that mimic paranoid schizophrenia.

Overall, evidence points to irregularities in schizophrenia patients in the neural pathways in the brain that utilize dopamine (McGowan et al., 2004). The specific nature of this abnormality remains under study. We can't yet say whether there is an overreactivity of particular dopamine pathways, an excess number of dopamine receptors, or yet more complex interactions among dopamine systems. One possibility is that overreactivity of dopamine receptors is involved in producing positive symptoms, and decreased dopamine reactivity is connected with negative symptoms (Earnst & Kring, 1997; Okubo et al., 1997). Other neurotransmitters, such as norepinephrine, serotonin, and GABA, also appear to be involved in schizophrenia (Walker et al., 2004).

Viral Infections Might schizophrenia be caused by a slow-acting virus that attacks the developing brain of a fetus or newborn child? Prenatal rubella (German measles), a viral infection, is a cause of later mental retardation. Could another virus give rise to schizophrenia?

Viral infections are most prevalent in the winter months. The viral theory could account for the fact that a higher-than-expected number of people who later develop schizophrenia were born in the winter (Mortensen et al., 1999). However, we have yet to identify a viral agent we can link to schizophrenia. Thus we must consider the viral theory of schizophrenia to be intriguing but inconclusive. Even if a viral basis for schizophrenia were discovered, it would probably account for but a small fraction of cases.

Brain Abnormalities Using modern brain-imaging techniques, investigators are trying to track down the abnormalities in the brain that result in schizophrenia. We now have compelling evidence of both structural changes (loss of brain tissue) and functional disturbance (abnormalities of functioning) in the brains of schizophrenia patients (e.g., Bagary et al., 2003; Kuperberg et al., 2003). However, we have yet to discover any one source of pathology in the brain that is specific to schizophrenia or present in all cases of schizophrenia (Walker et al., 2004).

Perhaps the most prominent finding of pathology is a loss of brain tissue (gray matter) of about 5% on the average in schizophrenia patients as compared to normal controls (Cowan & Kandel, 2001). In Figure 12.2 we can see a visual representation of the loss of brain tissue in the brain of adolescents with early-onset (childhood) schizophrenia (Thompson et al., 2001). We see evidence of a loss of brain tissue in perhaps three of four adult schizophrenia patients as shown by the presence of enlarged brain ventricles (hollow spaces in the brain) (Coursey, Alford, & Safarjan, 1997) (see Figure 12.3). Enlarged ventricles are signs of loss of brain tissue (cell loss).

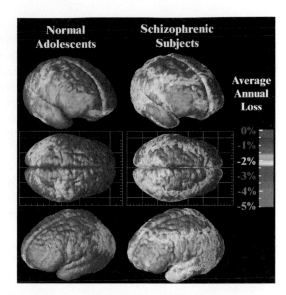

FIGURE 12.2 Loss of brain tissue in adolescents with early-onset schizophrenia.
The brains of adolescents with early-onset schizophrenia (right image) show a substantial loss of gray matter. Some shrinkage of gray matter occurs normally during adolescence (left image), but the loss is more pronounced in adolescents with schizophrenia.

Source: Thompson et al. (2001).

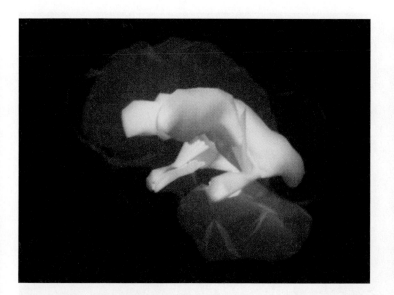
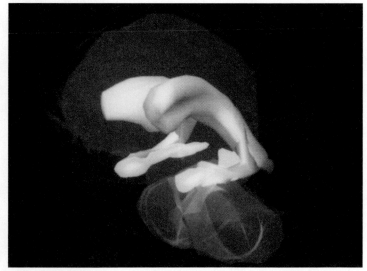

FIGURE 12.3 Structural changes in the brain of a person with schizophrenia as compared with that of a normal subject.
The magnetic resonance imaging (MRI) of the brain of a person with schizophrenia (left) shows a relatively shrunken hippocampus (yellow) and relatively enlarged, fluid-filled ventricles (gray) when compared to the structures of the normal subject (right). The MRI was conducted by schizophrenia researcher Nancy C. Andreasen.

Source: Gershon, E. S., & Rieder, R. O. (1992). Major disorders of mind and brain. *Scientific American, 267*(No. 3), p. 128.

What is the underlying cause of the loss of brain tissue? Scientists can't yet say, but they suspect that the brains of schizophrenia patients may have been damaged or failed to develop normally as the result of early influences such as prenatal factors (e.g., viral infections, inadequate fetal nutrition, genetic defects) or birth traumas or complications (McGlashan & Hoffman, 2000; Sørensen et al., 2003; Wahlbeck et al., 2001; Walker et al, 2004). Bear in mind, however, that not all people with schizophrenia show evidence of structural damage to brain tissue. This finding leads researchers to suspect that there may be several forms of schizophrenia that have different causal processes.

One area of the brain showing prominent signs of both abnormal functioning and loss of brain tissue is the prefrontal cortex (Cahn et al., 2002; Gur, Cowell et al., 2000; Winterer et al., 2004). The prefrontal cortex is the thinking and organizing center of the brain. It is the area of the frontal lobes of the cerebral cortex that lies in front of the motor cortex (the part of the brain that controls voluntary body movements).

Evidence of functional impairment comes from studies showing reduced brain wave activity in the prefrontal cortex in many schizophrenia patients (Callicott et al., 2003; Ragland et al., 2001; Walker et al, 2004) (see Figure 12.4). For example, schizophrenia patients show less activation in this part of the brain than do healthy controls during mental arithmetic tasks (Hugdahl et al., 2004). Functional impairment may result from underlying structural damage (loss of brain tissue) (Karp et al., 2001; Mathalno et al., 2001; Selemon et al., 2002).

The prefrontal cortex controls many cognitive and emotional functions, the kinds of functions that are often impaired in people with schizophrenia. The prefrontal cortex serves as a kind of mental clipboard for holding information needed to guide organized behavior. Prefrontal abnormalities may explain why people with schizophrenia have difficulty with working memory—the ability to temporarily hold information in mind and mull it over (Barch, 2003; Silver et al., 2003). The prefrontal cortex is also responsible for other higher-order (or "executive") functions, such as as regulating attention, organizing thoughts and behavior, prioritizing information, and formulating goals—the very types of deficits often found in people with schizophrenia (Barch, 2003; Barch et al.,

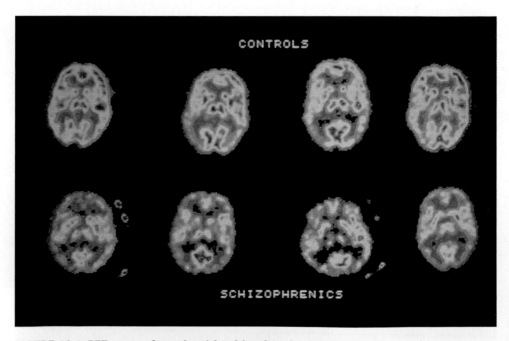

FIGURE 12.4 PET scans of people with schizophrenia versus normals.
Positron emission tomography (PET) scan evidence of the metabolic processes of the brain shows relatively less metabolic activity (indicated by less yellow and red) in the frontal lobes of the brains of people with schizophrenia. PET scans of the brains of four normal people are shown in the top row, and PET scans of the brains of four people with schizophrenia are shown below.

2001; Goldberg et al., 2003). These are intriguing findings that may provide clues as to the biological bases of schizophrenia as well as lead to new treatment approaches. For example, cognitive training efforts have recently been found to help schizophrenia patients improve their working memory (Bell et al., 2003).

We have yet other evidence of structural differences in the brains of schizophrenia patients in subcortical regions of the brain—structures in the brain lying beneath the cortex that are involved in regulating emotions, attention, and memory formation (e.g., Byne et al., 2001; Csernansky et al., 2002, 2004; Gaser et al., 2004; Gur, Turetsky et al., 2000). Disturbances in brain physiology in subcortical regions, perhaps involving neurotransmitter imbalances or faulty connections (wiring) between neurons, may contribute to disturbances in thinking, attention, and emotions associated with schizophrenia (Hazlett et al., 2004). Though evidence of the biological underpinnings of schizophrenia continues to mount, a long-standing debate is whether disordered behavior of the kind we see in schizophrenia patients is necessarily a sign of a biological disease process. We review this controversy in the "Controversies in Abnormal Psychology" feature, "Is Mental Illness a Myth?"

Family Theories Disturbed family relationships have long been regarded as playing a role in the development and course of schizophrenia (Miklowitz, 1994). Early family theories of schizophrenia focused on the role of the *schizophrenogenic mother* (Fromm-Reichmann, 1948, 1950). In what some feminists view as historic psychiatric sexism, the schizophrenogenic mother was described as cold, aloof, overprotective, and domineering. She was characterized as stripping her children of self-esteem, stifling their independence, and forcing them into dependency on her. Children reared by such mothers were believed to be at special risk for developing schizophrenia if their fathers were passive and failed to counteract the mother's pathogenic influences. Thankfully, the concept of the "schizophrenogenic mother" was discredited as investigators showed that mothers of people who develop schizophrenia do not fit this stereotypical pattern (e.g., Hirsch & Leff, 1975).

More promising were efforts begun in the 1950s to examine the role of disturbed communications in the family. One of the more prominent theories, put forth by Gregory Bateson and his colleagues (1956), was that **double-bind communications** contribute to the development of schizophrenia. A double-bind communication transmits two mutually incompatible messages. For example, a mother freezes up when her child approaches her and then scolds the child for keeping a distance. Whatever the child does is wrong. With repeated exposure to such double binds, the child's thinking may become disorganized and chaotic. The double-binding mother prevents discussion of her inconsistencies, because she cannot admit to herself that she is unable to tolerate closeness. Note this vignette:

double-bind communications A communication pattern involving contradictory or mixed messages without acknowledging the inherent conflict.

A Case Example of Double-Bind Communication

A young man who had fairly well recovered from an acute schizophrenic episode was visited in the hospital by his mother. He was glad to see her and impulsively put his arm around her shoulders whereupon she stiffened. He withdrew his arm and she asked, "Don't you love me anymore?" He then blushed and she said, "Dear, you must not be so easily embarrassed and afraid of your feelings." The patient was able to stay with her only a few minutes more and following her departure he assaulted an aide.

—From Bateson et al., 1956, p. 251

Perhaps double-bind communications serve as a source of family stress that increases the risk of schizophrenia in genetically vulnerable individuals. In more recent years, investigators have broadened the investigation of family factors in schizophrenia by viewing the family as a system of relationships among the members rather than singling out

CONTROVERSIES IN ABNORMAL PSYCHOLOGY
Is Mental Illness A Myth?

In 1961 the psychiatrist Thomas Szasz shocked the psychiatric establishment by making a bold claim that mental illness does not exist. In his controversial book, *The Myth of Mental Illness,* Szasz argued that mental illness is a myth, a convenient fiction society uses to stigmatize and subjugate people whose behavior it finds to be deviant, odd, or bizarre. To Szasz, "mental illnesses" are really "problems in living," not diseases in the same sense that influenza, hypertension, and cancer are diseases. Szasz does not dispute that the behavior of people diagnosed with schizophrenia or other mental disorders is peculiar or disturbed. Nor does he deny that these individuals suffer emotional problems or have difficulties adjusting to society. But he challenges the conventional view that strange or eccentric behavior is a product of an underlying disease. Szasz argues that treating problems as "diseases" empowers psychiatrists to put socially deviant people away in medical facilities. To Szasz, involuntary hospitalization is a form of tyranny disguised as therapy. It deprives people of human dignity and strips them of the most essential human right—liberty.

Are the myriad problems of people with schizophrenia—the deluded thoughts and hallucinations and incoherent speech—merely "problems in living," or are they symptoms of an underlying disease process? The belief that mental illness is a myth or a social construction is difficult to reconcile with a large body of evidence showing structural and functional differences in the brains of schizophrenia patients and of genetic factors that increase the risk of developing the disorder.

We've learned a great deal about the biological underpinnings of mental or psychological disorders since Szasz claimed that mental illness doesn't exist, although we still have much to learn. Our knowledge of the causes of many diseases, including cancer and Alzheimer's disease, is also incomplete, but a lack of knowledge does not make them any less of a disease. Many professionals believe that radical theorists like Szasz go too far in arguing that mental illness is merely a fabrication invented by society to stigmatize social deviants.

Evidence supports a prominent role for biological factors in many abnormal behavior patterns, including schizophrenia, mood disorders, and autism. But how far should we extend the disease model? Is antisocial personality disorder an illness? Or attention-deficit hyperactivity disorder? Or specific phobias, such as fear of flying? What are the implications of treating abnormal behavioral patterns as diseases versus viewing them as problems in living?

The *DSM* itself does not take a position on which mental disorders, if any, are biologically based. It recognizes that causes of most mental disorders remain uncertain: Some disorders may have purely biological causes. Some may have psychological causes. Still others, probably most, involve an interaction of biological, psychological, and social/environmental causes.

All in all, the views of Szasz and other critics of the mental health establishment have helped bring about much needed improvements in the protection of the rights of mental patients in psychiatric institutions. They have also directed our attention to the social and political implications of our responses to deviant behavior. Perhaps most importantly, they have challenged us to examine our assumptions when we label and treat undesirable behaviors as signs of illness rather than as problems of adjustment.

Thomas Szasz. Psychiatrist Thomas Szasz has waged a long-standing battle with institutional psychiatry. Arguing that mental illness is a myth, Szasz believes that mental health problems are problems in living, not medical diseases.

Critical Thinking

- What would it mean to say that schizophrenia is a problem of living rather than a disease? What would be the implications for treatment? For the way society responds to people who behave in unusual ways?
- Based on knowledge that has accumulated since Szasz wrote his book, which mental illnesses should be classified as problems of living? Which as diseases?

mother–child or father–child interactions. Research has begun to identify stressful factors in the family that may interact with a genetic vulnerability to lead to the development of schizophrenia. Two principal sources of family stress that have been studied are deviant communications patterns and negative emotional expression.

Communication Deviance Communication deviance (CD) is a pattern of unclear, vague, disruptive, or fragmented communication that is often found among parents and family members of schizophrenia patients. CD is characterized by speech that is hard to follow and from which it is difficult to extract any shared meaning (Wahlberg et al., 2001). High CD parents also have difficulty focusing on what their children are saying (Miklowitz, 1994). They tend to verbally attack their children rather than offer constructive criticism and may subject them to double-bind communications. They also tend to interrupt the child with intrusive, negative comments. They are prone to telling the child what she or he "really" thinks rather than allowing the child to formulate her or his own thoughts and feelings. Parents of people with schizophrenia show higher levels of communication deviance than parents of people without schizophrenia (Miklowitz, 1994).

Communication deviance may be one of the stress-related factors that increases the risk of development of schizophrenia in genetically vulnerable individuals (Goldstein, 1987). Then too, the causal pathway may work in the opposite direction. Perhaps communication deviance is a parental reaction to the behavior of disturbed children. Parents may learn to use odd language as a way of coping with children who continually interrupt and confront them. Or perhaps parents and children share genetic traits that become expressed as disturbed communications and increased vulnerability toward schizophrenia, without there being a casual link between the two.

Expressed Emotion Another form of disturbed family communication, *expressed emotion* (EE), is a pattern of responding to the schizophrenic family member in hostile, critical, and unsupportive ways (Barrowclough & Hooley, 2003). Schizophrenia patients from high EE families stand a higher risk of relapsing than those with more supportive (low EE) families (Cutting & Docherty, 2000; Van Humbeeck et al., 2002). High EE relatives typically show less empathy, tolerance, and flexibility than low EE relatives (Hooley & Hiller, 2000). They also tend to believe that schizophrenia patients can exercise greater control over their behavior than do low EE relatives of the same patients (Weisman et al., 2000). Expressed emotion in relatives is also associated with a greater risk of relapse from other disorders, such as major depression and eating disorders (Van Humbeeck et al., 2002).

Low EE families may actually protect, or buffer, the family member with schizophrenia from the adverse impact of outside stressors and help prevent recurrent episodes (see Figure 12.5). Yet family interactions are a two-way street. Family members and patients influence each other and are influenced in turn. Disruptive behaviors by the schizophrenic family member frustrate other members of the family, prompting them to respond to the person in a less-supportive and more critical and hostile way. This in turn can exacerbate the schizophrenia patient's disruptive behavior.

Though high EE families can be found in all cultures, high EE families tend to be more prevalent in industrialized countries, such as the United States and Canada, than in developing countries, such as India (Barrowclough & Hooley, 2003). In the United States, Anglo families of schizophrenia patients are more likely to be high in EE than are those of Mexican American patients. But high levels of expressed emotion also predicts higher relapse rates among schizophrenia patients from Mexican American families (Karno et al., 1987). Both Mexican American families and Anglo American families with high levels of

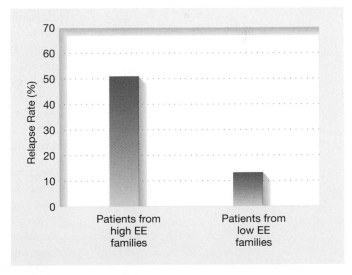

FIGURE 12.5 Relapse rates of people with schizophrenia in high and low EE families.
People with schizophrenia whose families are high in expressed emotion (EE) are at greater risk of relapse than those whose families are low in EE. Whereas low-EE families may help protect the family member with schizophrenia from environmental stressors, high-EE families may impose additional stress.

Source: Adapted from King & Dixon, 1999, based upon data provided in two seminal British studies.

expressed emotion are more likely than low EE families to view the psychotic behavior of a schizophrenic family member as within the person's control (Weisman et al., 1993, 1998). The anger and criticism of high EE family members may stem from the perception that patients can and should exert greater control over their aberrant behavior.

The extended family structure often found in traditional cultures may offer an emotional and financial buffer against the hardships imposed by the behavioral excesses and deficiencies of people with schizophrenia. In Western cultures, these burdens are more likely to be borne by the nuclear family (Lefley, 1990). Such differences remind us of the need to take cultural factors into account when examining relationships between family factors and schizophrenia.

Families of people with schizophrenia tend to have little if any preparation for coping with the stress of caring for them (Winefield & Harvey, 1994). Rather than focusing so much attention on the negative influence of high EE family members, perhaps we should seek to help family members learn more constructive ways of relating to one another. Evidence shows that families can be helped to reduce their level of expressed emotion (Dixon, Adams, & Lucksted, 2000; Penn & Mueser, 1996).

Family Factors in Schizophrenia: Causes or Sources of Stress? No evidence supports the belief that family factors, such as negative family interactions, lead to schizophrenia in children who do not have a genetic vulnerability. What then is the role of family factors in schizophrenia? Within the diathesis-stress model, disturbed patterns of emotional interaction and communication in the family represent a source of potential stress that may increase the risks of developing schizophrenia among people with a genetic predisposition for the disorder. Perhaps these increased risks could be minimized or eliminated if families are taught to handle stress and to be less critical and more supportive of the members of their families with schizophrenia. Family intervention programs have been developed to help family members develop more cooperative, less-confrontational ways of relating to their family members with schizophrenia. Family intervention programs can reduce the risks of relapse and subsequent hospitalization of schizophrenia patients as compared to routine care (Pilling et al., 2002; Pitschel-Walz, et al., 2001).

How families conceptualize mental disorders also has a bearing on how they relate to relatives who suffer from them. For example, the term *schizophrenia* carries a stigma in our society and comes with the expectation that the disorder is enduring (Jenkins & Karno, 1992). In contrast, to many Mexican Americans, a person with schizophrenia is perceived as suffering from *nervios* ("nerves"), a cultural label attached to a wide range of troubled behaviors, including anxiety, schizophrenia, and depression, and one that carries less stigma and more positive expectations than the label of schizophrenia (Jenkins, 1988; Jenkins & Karno, 1992). Researchers believe the label *nervios* may have the effect of destigmatizing the person with schizophrenia:

> Since severe cases of *nervios* are not considered blameworthy or under an individual's control, the person who suffers its effects is deserving of sympathy, support, and special treatment. Moreover, severe cases of *nervios* are potentially curable. It is interesting to note that Mexican-descent relatives do not adopt another possible cultural label for craziness, *loco*. As a *loco*, the individual would be much more severely stigmatized and considered to be out of control with little chance for recovery. . . .
>
> Defining the problem as *nervios*, a common condition that in its milder forms afflicts nearly everyone, provides them a way of identifying with and minimizing the problem by claiming that the ill relative is "just like me, only more so." (Jenkins & Karno, 1992, pp. 17–18)

Family members may respond differently to relatives who have schizophrenia if they ascribe aspects of their behavior to a temporary or curable condition, which they believe can be altered by willpower, than if they believe the behavior is caused by a permanent brain abnormality. The degree to which relatives perceive family members with schizophrenia as having control over their disorders may be a critical factor in how they respond to them. Families may cope better with a family member with schizophrenia if they take a balanced view, believing on the one hand that people with schizophrenia can maintain some control over their behavior, while allowing that some of their odd or disruptive behavior is a product of their underlying disorder (Weisman et al., 1993). It remains to be seen whether these different ways in which family members conceptualize schizophrenia are connected with differences in the rates of recurrence of the disorder among affected family members.

Tying It Together: The Diathesis-Stress Model

In 1962, psychologist Paul Meehl proposed an integrative model for schizophrenia that led to the development of the diathesis-stress model. Meehl suggested that certain people possess a genetic predisposition to schizophrenia that is expressed behaviorally only if they are reared in stressful environments (Meehl, 1962, 1972).

Later, Zubin and Spring (1977) formulated the diathesis-stress model, which views schizophrenia in terms of the interaction or combination of a *diathesis,* in the form of a genetic predisposition to develop the disorder, with environmental stress that exceeds the individual's stress threshold or coping resources. Environmental stressors may include psychological factors, such as family conflict, child abuse, emotional deprivation, or loss of supportive figures, as well as physical environmental influences, such as early brain trauma or injury. On the other hand, if environmental stress remains below the person's stress threshold, schizophrenia may never develop, even in persons at genetic risk (see Figure 12.6).

But what is the biological basis for the diathesis? No one has yet been able to find any specific brain abnormality present in all individuals who receive a schizophrenia diagnosis (Powchik et al., 1998; Stevens, 1997). Perhaps it shouldn't surprise us that a "one-size-fits-all" model doesn't apply. Schizophrenia is a complex disorder characterized by different subtypes and symptom complexes. Different causal processes in the brain may explain different forms of schizophrenia. What we now call *schizophrenia* may turn out to be more than one disorder (Buchanan & Carpenter, 1997; Knoll et al., 1998).

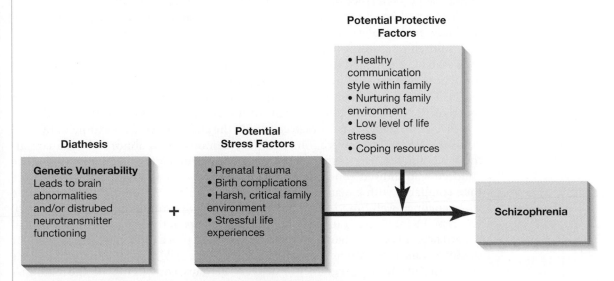

FIGURE 12.6 Diathesis-stress model of schizophrenia.

We noted two possible causal processes for schizophrenia, one involving structural damage to brain tissue, the other involving disturbed neurotransmitter functioning. These factors, or perhaps a combination of the two, result in disrupted brain circuits between the prefrontal cortex and lower brain regions responsible for organizing our thoughts, perceptions, emotions, and attentional processes. These neural networks are involved in processing information efficiently and turning it into meaningful thoughts and behavior. Defects in this circuitry may be involved in explaining the positive features of schizophrenia, such as hallucinations, delusions, and thought disorder.

Research Evidence Supporting the Diathesis-Stress Model Several lines of evidence support the diathesis-stress model. One is the fact that schizophrenia tends to develop in late adolescence or early adulthood, around the time that young people typically face the increased stress associated with establishing independence and finding a role in life. Other evidence shows that psychosocial stress, such as harping criticisms from family members, worsens symptoms in people with schizophrenia, increasing risks of relapse (King & Dixon, 1995). However, the question of whether stress directly triggers the initial onset of schizophrenia in genetically vulnerable individuals still remains open to debate (Walker & Diforio, 1997).

Other sources of stress that may contribute to the development of schizophrenia in genetically vulnerable individuals involve sociocultural factors associated with poverty, such as overcrowding, poor diet and sanitation, impoverished housing, and inadequate health care (Kety, 1980). Other support for the diathesis-stress model comes from longitudinal studies of high-risk (HR) children who are at increased genetic risk of developing the disorder by virtue of having one or both parents with schizophrenia. Longitudinal studies of HR children support the central tenet of the diathesis-stress model that heredity interacts with environmental influences in determining vulnerability to schizophrenia. Longitudinal studies track individuals over extended periods of time. Ideally they begin before the emergence of the disorder or behavior pattern in question and follow its course. In this way, investigators may identify early characteristics that predict the later development of a disorder. These studies require a commitment of many years and substantial cost. Because schizophrenia occurs in only about 1% of the general population, researchers have focused on HR children. Children with one parent with schizophrenia have about a 10% to 25% chance of developing schizophrenia, and those with two parents have about a 45% risk (Erlenmeyer-Kimling et al., 1997; Gottesman, 1991). Still, even children with two biological parents with schizophrenia stand a slightly better than even chance of not developing the disorder themselves.

The best-known longitudinal study of HR children was undertaken by Sarnoff Mednick and his colleagues in Denmark. In 1962, the Mednick group identified 207 HR children (children whose mothers had schizophrenia) and 104 reference subjects who were matched for such factors as gender, social class, age, and education but whose mothers did not have schizophrenia (Mednick, Parnas, & Schulsinger, 1987). The children from both groups ranged in age from 10 to 20 years, with a mean of 15 years. None showed signs of disturbance when first interviewed.

Five years later, at an average age of 20, the children were reexamined. By then 20 of the HR children were found to have demonstrated abnormal behavior, although not necessarily a schizophrenic episode (Mednick & Schulsinger, 1968). The children who showed abnormal behavior, referred to as the HR "sick" group, were then compared with a matched group of 20 HR children from the original sample who remained well functioning (an HR "well" group) and a matched group of 20 low-risk (LR) subjects. It turned out that the mothers of the HR "well" offspring had experienced easier pregnancies and deliveries than those of the HR "sick" group or the LR group. Seventy percent of the mothers of the HR "sick" children had serious complications during pregnancy or delivery. Perhaps, consistent with the diathesis-stress model, complications during pregnancy, childbirth, or shortly after birth cause brain damage (a stress factor) that, in combination with a genetic vulnerability, leads to severe mental disorders in later life. Finnish researchers also find links between fetal and post-natal abnormalities and the development of schizophrenia in adulthood (Jones et al., 1998). The low rate of complications during pregnancy and birth in the HR "well" group in the Danish study suggests that normal pregnancies and births may actually help protect HR children from developing abnormal behavior patterns (Mednick et al., 1987).

Evaluation of these same HR subjects in the late 1980s, when they averaged 42 years of age and had passed through the period of greatest risk for development of schizophrenia, showed a significantly higher percentage of schizophrenia in the HR group than the LR comparison group, 16% versus 2%, respectively (Parnas et al., 1993).

Certain environmental factors, such as good parenting, may help prevent the disorder in people at increased genetic risk. In support of the role of early environmental influences, Mednick and his colleagues found that HR children who developed schizophrenia had poorer relationships with their parents than did HR children who did not (Mednick et al., 1987). The presence of childhood behavior problems may also be a marker for the later development of schizophrenia-related disorders in HR children (Amminger et al., 1999).

Protective factors in high-risk children. A supportive and nurturing environment may reduce the likelihood of developing schizophrenia among high-risk children.

Treatment Approaches

There is no cure for schizophrenia. Treatment is generally multifaceted, incorporating pharmacological, psychological, and rehabilitative approaches. Most people treated for schizophrenia in organized mental health settings receive some form of antipsychotic medication, which is intended to control symptoms such as hallucinations and delusions and decrease the risk of recurrent episodes.

Biological Approaches The advent in the 1950s of antipsychotic drugs—also referred to as major tranquilizers or neuroleptics—revolutionized the treatment of schizophrenia and provided the impetus for large-scale releases of mental patients to the community (deinstitutionalization). Antipsychotic medication helped control the more flagrant behavior patterns of schizophrenia and reduced the need for long-term hospitalization when taken on a maintenance or continuing basis after an acute episode (Kane, 1996; Sheitman et al., 1998). Yet for many patients with chronic schizophrenia, entering a hospital is like going through a revolving door: they are repeatedly admitted and discharged. Many are simply discharged to the streets once they are stabilized on medication and receive little if any follow-up care. This often leads to a pattern of chronic homelessness punctuated by brief stays in the hospital. Only a small proportion of people with schizophrenia who are discharged from long-term care facilities are successfully reintegrated into the community (Bellack & Mueser, 1990).

Commonly used antipsychotic drugs include the phenothiazines *chlorpromazine* (Thorazine), *thioridazine* (Mellaril), *trifluoperazine* (Stelazine), and *fluphenazine* (Prolixin). *Haloperidol* (Haldol), which is chemically distinct from the phenothiazines, produces similar effects.

Though we can't say with certainty how these drugs work, it appears they derive their therapeutic effect from blocking dopamine receptors in the brain. This reduces dopamine activity, which seems to quell the symptoms such as hallucinations and delusions. The effectiveness of antipsychotic drugs has been repeatedly demonstrated in double-blind,

tardive dyskinesia (TD) A disorder characterized by involuntary movements of the face, mouth, neck, trunk, or extremities and caused by long-term use of antipsychotic medication.

placebo-controlled studies (Kane, 1996). Yet a substantial minority of people with schizophrenia receive little benefit from traditional neuroleptics, and no clear-cut factors exist to help clinicians determine who will best respond (Kane & Marder, 1993).

The major risk of long-term treatment with neuroleptic drugs (possibly excluding clozapine) is a potentially disabling side effect called **tardive dyskinesia (TD)** (Suzuki et al., 2002). TD can take different forms, the most common of which is frequent eye blinking. Common signs of the disorder include involuntary chewing and eye movements, lip smacking and puckering, facial grimacing, and involuntary movements of the limbs and trunk. In some cases, the movement disorder is so severe that patients have difficulty breathing, talking, or eating. Overall, about one in four people receiving long-term treatment with neuroleptics eventually develops TD (Jeste & Caligiuri, 1993). In many cases the disorder persists even when the neuroleptic medication is withdrawn.

TD is most common among older people and among women. Although TD tends to improve gradually or stabilize over a period of years, many people with TD remain persistently and severely disabled. We presently lack an effective and safe treatment for this very troubling side effect, although some promising treatments are being tested (e.g. Richardson et al., 2003).

The risk of this potentially disabling side effect requires physicians to weigh carefully the risks and benefits of long-term drug treatment. Investigators have altered drug regimens in the attempt to reduce the risk of TD, such as by stopping medication in stable outpatients and starting it again when early symptoms reappear. However, intermittent medication schedules are associated with a twofold increase in the risk of relapse and have not been shown to lower the risk of TD (Kane, 1996).

A new generation of drugs, commonly referred to as *atypical antipsychotic drugs* (*clozapine, risperidone,* and *olanzapine* are examples) has been introduced in clinical treatment of schizophrenia in recent years. These "atypicals" are at least as effective as the first generation of antipsychotics but carry fewer neurological side effects (Davis, Chen, & Glick, 2003; Kapur & Remington, 2000; Rosenheck et al., 2003, 2004). Early evidence indicates that these atypicals also carry a lower risk of tardive dyskinesia than the first generation of antipsychotic drugs (Correll, Leucht, & Kane, 2004). We also have evidence that these drugs produce a modest reduction in the risk of relapse as compared to conventional antipsychotics (Leucht et al., 2003) and can help schizophrenia patients who have failed to respond to the older drugs (Essock et al., 2000; Geddes et al., 2000). It remains to be seen whether the atypical drugs improve negative symptoms better than conventional antipsychotics.

One of these atypical antipsychotics, clozapine, is the only known drug that carries a minimal risk of TD (Conley & Buchanan, 1997). However, other side effects limit its use, especially the risk of a potentially lethal disorder in which the body produces inadequate supplies of white blood cells. Because of this risk, patients receiving the drug must receive frequent blood monitoring (USDHHS, 1999a). In another promising finding, olanzapine may reduce the risk of TD relative to conventional antipsychotics (e.g., Rosenheck et al., 2003), but more research is needed.

For Lori Schiller, the woman who experienced her first psychotic break during summer camp, the voices became softer when she was treated with clozapine.

"I" *The Voices Grow Softer*

It was as if it [my brain] were draining out from the inside. My head had been filled with sticky stuff, like melted rubber or motor oil. Now all that sticky stuff was dripping out, leaving only my brain behind. Slowly I was beginning to think more clearly.

And the Voices? The Voices were growing softer. Were the Voices growing softer? They were growing softer! They began moving around, from outside my skull, to inside, to outside again. But their decibel level was definitely falling.

It was happening. I was being set free. I had prayed to find some peace, and my prayers were finally being answered . . . I want to live. I want to live.

—From Schiller & Bennett, 1994

Over time the voices receded into the background and then disappeared. Lori needed to learn to live without the voices and to build a life for herself. She began venturing beyond the confines of the hospital. She entered a halfway house and began to move toward a more independent life. Lori spent 3 ½ years at a halfway house and is now living independently.

Antipsychotic drugs help control the more flagrant or bizarre features of schizophrenia but are not a cure. People with chronic schizophrenia typically receive maintenance doses of antipsychotic drugs once their acute symptoms abate. However, many patients, perhaps 15% to 20% per year, relapse even if they keep taking medication (Kane, 1996). Estimates are that 75% of patients with schizophrenia who have been in remission for a year or more will relapse within 12 to 18 months if their medication is withdrawn (Kane, 1996). Still, not all people with schizophrenia require antipsychotic medication to live independently. Unfortunately, no one can yet predict which patients can manage effectively without continued medication.

Medication alone is insufficient to meet the multifaceted needs of people with schizophrenia. For example, a recent drug trial failed to find any substantial benefit from the antipsychotic drug clozapine in improving either social skills or problem-solving ability of schizophrenia patients (Bellack et al., 2004). Drug therapy needs to be supplemented with psychoeducational programs that help schizophrenia patients develop better social skills and adjust to demands of community living. A wide array of treatment components are needed within a comprehensive model of care, including such elements as antipsychotic medication, medical care, family therapy, social skills training, crisis intervention, rehabilitation services, and housing and other social services (Penn & Mueser, 1996; USDHHS, 1999a). Treatment programs must also ensure a continuity of care between the hospital and the community.

Sociocultural Factors in Treatment Investigators find that response to psychiatric medications and dosage levels varies with patient ethnicity (USDHHS, 1999a). Asians and Hispanics, for example, may require lower doses of neuroleptics than do Caucasians. Asians also tend to experience more side effects from the same dosage. But racial disparities also exist in how schizophrenia patients are treated. For example, African American patients are less likely to receive the newer generation of atypical antipsychotics than are White patients (Kuno & Rothbard, 2002).

Ethnicity may also play a role in the family's involvement in treatment. In a study of 26 Asian Americans and 26 non-Hispanic White Americans with schizophrenia, family members of the Asian American patients were more frequently involved in the treatment program (Lin et al., 1991). For example, family members were more likely to accompany the Asian American patients to their medication evaluation sessions. The authors believe that the greater family involvement among Asian Americans represents the relatively stronger sense of family responsibility in Asian cultures. Non-Hispanic White Americans are more likely to emphasize individualism and self-responsibility.

Maintaining connections between the person with schizophrenia and the family and larger community is part of the cultural tradition in many Asian cultures, as well as in other parts of the world, such as Africa. The seriously mentally ill of China, for instance, retain strong supportive links to their families and workplaces, which helps increase their chances of being reintegrated into community life (Liberman, 1994). In traditional healing centers for the treatment of schizophrenia in Africa, the strong support that patients receive from the family and community members, together with a community centered lifestyle, are important elements of successful care (Peltzer & Machleidt, 1992).

There is clear value in working with the family in treating schizophrenia in Asian Americans, as well as in other groups. Researchers find that failure to include the family often compromises the value of therapy for Asian Americans and causes them to drop out of therapy prematurely (Lin et al., 1978). Researchers in a British hospital reported that living with family members was among the factors that might explain the lower relapse and rehospitalization rates found among Asian people with schizophrenia as compared to White or Afro-Caribbean people (Birchwood et al., 1992). Family interactions are not necessarily harmonious or conducive of better outcomes, however, as

---

TRUTH or FICTION? *REVISITED*

We now have drugs that not only treat schizophrenia but also can cure it in many cases.

☑ **FALSE.** Antipsychotic drugs help control the symptoms of schizophrenia but cannot cure the disorder.

research on expressed emotion makes clear. Neglect or rejection of the person with schizophrenia within the family may play an important role in premature treatment termination and poorer outcomes.

Psychodynamic Therapy Freud did not believe that traditional psychoanalysis was well suited to the treatment of schizophrenia. The withdrawal into a fantasy world that typifies schizophrenia prevents the individual with schizophrenia from forming a meaningful relationship with the psychoanalyst. The techniques of classical psychoanalysis, Freud wrote, must "be replaced by others; and we do not know yet whether we shall succeed in finding a substitute" (as cited in Arieti, 1974, p. 532).

Other psychoanalysts, such as Harry Stack Sullivan and Frieda Fromm-Reichmann, adapted psychoanalytic techniques specifically for the treatment of schizophrenia. However, research has failed to demonstrate the effectiveness of psychoanalytic or psychodynamic therapy for schizophrenia. In the light of negative findings, some critics have argued that further research on the use of psychodynamic therapies for treating schizophrenia is not warranted (e.g., Klerman, 1984). However, promising results are reported for a form of individual psychotherapy called *personal therapy* that is grounded in the diathesis-stress model. Personal therapy helps patients cope with stress and helps them build social skills, such as learning how to deal with criticism from others. Preliminary evidence suggests that personal therapy may reduce relapse rates and improve social functioning, at least among schizophrenia patients living with their families (Bustillo et al., 2001; Hogarty et al., 1997a, 1997b).

Learning-Based Therapies Although few behavior therapists believe that faulty learning causes schizophrenia, learning-based interventions have been shown to be effective in modifying schizophrenic behavior and helping people with the disorder develop behaviors that can help them adjust more effectively to living in the community. Therapy methods include the following:

1. *Selective reinforcement of behavior,* such as providing attention for appropriate behavior and extinguishing bizarre verbalizations through withdrawal of attention
2. *The token economy,* in which individuals on inpatient units are rewarded for appropriate behavior with tokens, such as plastic chips, that can be exchanged for tangible reinforcers such as desirable goods or privileges
3. *Social skills training,* in which clients are taught conversational skills and other appropriate social behaviors through coaching, modeling, behavior rehearsal, and feedback

Intensive learning-based approaches in hospital settings show promising results. A classic study by Paul and Lentz (1977) showed that a psychosocial treatment program based on a token-economy system improved adaptive behavior in the hospital, decreased need for medication, and lengthened community tenure following release, compared with a traditional, custodial-type treatment and a *milieu* treatment approach in which the social environment (milieu) of the hospital unit was changed to allow patients greater participation in decision making.

Overall, token economies have proven to be more effective than intensive milieu treatment and traditional custodial treatment in improving social functioning and reducing psychotic behavior (Glynn & Mueser, 1992; Mueser & Liberman, 1995). However, these programs have many prerequisites, such as strong administrative support, skilled treatment leaders, extensive staff training, and continuous quality control, that limit their practicality (Glynn & Mueser, 1986).

Recently, cognitive–behavioral therapy (CBT) has shown promise in reducing hallucinations and delusions in medication-resistant schizophrenia patients (Bouchard et al., 1996; Bustillo et al., 2001). More research is needed to demonstrate the clinical utility of CBT to treat psychotic symptoms in general clinical practice.

Social skills training (SST) programs help individuals acquire a range of social and vocational skills. People with schizophrenia are often deficient in basic social skills needed for community living, such as assertiveness, interviewing skills, and general conversational skills. SST can improve social functioning of schizophrenia patients in clinical settings (Hogan et al., 2003; Penn, 1998). The effectiveness of SST is not limited to our culture; it was recently demonstrated to be of benefit in treating Chinese schizophrenia patients in Hong Kong (Tsang, 2001). However, it remains unclear whether SST can reduce the relapse rate or improve community functioning (Bustillo et al., 2001; Walker et al., 2004).

The basic model for social skills training uses role-playing exercises within a group format. Participants practice skills such as starting or maintaining conversations with new acquaintances and receive feedback and reinforcement from the therapist and other group members. The first step might be a dry run in which the participant role-plays the targeted behavior, such as asking strangers for bus directions. The therapist and other group members then praise the effort and provide constructive feedback. Role-playing is augmented by techniques such as modeling (observation of the therapist or other group members enacting the desired behavior), direct instruction (specific directions for enacting the desired behavior), shaping (reinforcement for successive approximations to the target behavior), and coaching (use of verbal or nonverbal prompts to elicit a particular desired behavior in the role play). Participants are given homework assignments to practice the behaviors in the settings in which they live, such as on the hospital ward or in the community. The aim is to generalize the training or transfer it to other settings. Training sessions may also be run in stores, restaurants, schools, and other real-life settings.

Psychosocial Rehabilitation People with schizophrenia typically have difficulties functioning in social and occupational roles. These problems limit their ability to adjust to community life, even in the absence of overt psychotic behavior.

A number of self-help clubs (commonly called clubhouses) and rehabilitation centers have sprung up to help people with schizophrenia find a place in society. Many centers were launched by nonprofessionals or by people with schizophrenia themselves, largely because mental health agencies often failed to provide comparable services (Anthony & Liberman, 1986). The clubhouse movement began in 1948 with the founding of Fountain House by a group of formerly hospitalized people with schizophrenia (Foderaro, 1994). There are now more than 200 clubhouses modeled after Fountain House across the country, and some 50 or more in other countries including Sweden, Japan, and Australia. The clubhouse is not a home; rather, it serves as a self-contained community that provides members with social support and help in finding educational opportunities and paid employment.

Multiservice rehabilitation centers typically offer housing as well as job and educational opportunities. These centers often make use of skills training approaches to help clients learn how to handle money, resolve disputes with family members, develop friendships, take buses, cook their own meals, shop, and so on.

Family Intervention Programs Family conflicts and negative family interactions can heap stress on family members with schizophrenia, increasing the risk of recurrent episodes (Marsh & Johnson, 1997). Researchers and clinicians have worked with families of people with schizophrenia to help them cope with the burdens of care and assist them in developing more cooperative, less-confrontational ways of relating to others. The specific components of family interventions vary, but they usually share some common features, such as a focus on the practical aspects of everyday living, educating family members about schizophrenia, teaching them how to relate in a less-hostile way to family members with schizophrenia, improving communication, and fostering effective problem-solving and coping skills. Structured family intervention programs can reduce friction in the family, improve social functioning in schizophrenia patients, and even reduce relapse rates (Bustillo et al., 2001; Mueser et al., 2001). However, the benefits appear to be modest, and questions remain about whether relapses are prevented or merely delayed.

In sum, no single treatment approach meets all the needs of people with schizophrenia. The conceptualization of schizophrenia as a lifelong disability underscores the need for long-term treatment interventions that incorporate antipsychotic medication, family therapy, supportive or cognitive–behavioral forms of therapy, vocational training, and housing and other social support services (Bustillo et al., 2001; Huxley, Rendall, & Sederer, 2000; Sensky et al., 2000; Tarrier et al., 2000). To help the individual reach maximal social adjustment, these interventions should be coordinated and integrated within a comprehensive model of treatment (Coursey et al., 1997).

OTHER FORMS OF PSYCHOSIS

DSM-IV recognizes several other types of psychotic disorders beside schizophrenia. Here we focus on several of these disorders: brief psychotic disorder, schizophreniform disorder, delusional disorder, and schizoaffective disorder.

Brief Psychotic Disorder

brief psychotic disorder A psychotic disorder lasting from a day to a month that often follows exposure to a major stressor.

Some brief psychotic episodes do not progress to schizophrenia. The *DSM-IV* category of **brief psychotic disorder** applies to a psychotic disorder that lasts from a day to a month and is characterized by at least one of the following features: delusions, hallucinations, disorganized speech, or disorganized or catatonic behavior. Eventually there is a full return to the individual's prior level of functioning. Brief psychotic disorder is often linked to a significant stressor or stressors, such as the loss of a loved one or exposure to brutal traumas in wartime. Women sometimes experience the disorder after childbirth.

Schizophreniform Disorder

schizophreniform disorder A psychotic disorder lasting less than 6 months in duration, with features that resemble schizophrenia.

Schizophreniform disorder consists of abnormal behaviors identical to those in schizophrenia that have persisted for at least 1 month but less than 6 months. They thus do not yet justify the diagnosis of schizophrenia. Although some cases have good outcomes, in others the disorder persists beyond 6 months and may be reclassified as schizophrenia or perhaps another form of psychotic disorder, such as schizoaffective disorder. Questions remain about the validity of the diagnosis, however (Strakowski, 1994). It may be more appropriate to diagnose people who show psychotic features of recent origin with a classification such as *psychotic disorder of an unspecified type* until additional information clearly indicates the specific type of disorder involved.

Delusional Disorder

delusional disorder A type of psychosis characterized by persistent delusions, often of a paranoid nature, that do not have the bizarre quality of the type found in paranoid schizophrenia.

Many of us, perhaps even most of us, feel suspicious of other people's motives at times. We may feel others have it in for us or believe others are talking about us behind our backs. For most of us, however, paranoid thinking does not take the form of outright delusions. The diagnosis of **delusional disorder** applies to people who hold persistent, clearly delusional beliefs, often involving paranoid themes. Delusional disorder is uncommon, affecting an estimated 5 to 10 people in 10,000 during their lifetimes (APA, 2000).

In delusional disorders, the delusional beliefs concern events that may possibly occur, such as the infidelity of a spouse, persecution by others, or attracting the love of a famous person. The apparent plausibility of these beliefs may lead others to take them seriously and check them out before concluding they are unfounded. Apart from the delusion, the individual's behavior does not show evidence of obviously bizarre or odd behavior, as we see in the following case example.

Is someone out to get you? People with delusional disorder often weave paranoid fantasies in their minds such that they confuse with reality.

Mr. Polsen's Hit Men

Mr. Polsen, a married 42-year-old postal worker, was brought to the hospital by his wife because he had been insisting that there was a contract out on his life. Mr. Polsen told the doctors that the problem had started some four months ago when his supervisor accused him of tampering with a package, an offense that could have cost him his job. When he was exonerated at a formal hearing, his su-

pervisor was "furious" and felt publicly humiliated, according to Mr. Polsen. Shortly afterwards, Mr. Polsen reported, his coworkers began avoiding him, turning away from him when he walked by, as if they didn't want to see him. He then began to think that they were talking about him behind his back, although he could never clearly make out what they were saying. He gradually became convinced that his coworkers were avoiding him because his boss had put a contract on his life. Things remained about the same for two months, when Mr. Polsen began to notice several large white cars cruising up and down the street where he lived. This frightened him, and he became convinced there were hit men in these cars. He then refused to leave his home without an escort and would run home in panic when he saw one of these cars approaching. Other than the reports of his belief that his life was in danger, his thinking and behavior appeared entirely normal on interview. He denied experiencing hallucinations and showed no other signs of psychotic behavior, except for the queer beliefs about his life being in danger. The diagnosis of Delusional Disorder, Persecutory type seemed the most appropriate, since there was no evidence that a contract had been taken on his life (hence, a persecutory delusion) and there were no other clear signs of psychosis that might support a diagnosis of a schizophrenic disorder.

—*Adapted from Spitzer et al., 1994, pp. 177–179*

erotomania A delusional disorder characterized by the belief that one is loved by someone of high social status.

A CLOSER LOOK
The Love Delusion

Erotomania, or the love delusion, is a rare delusional disorder in which the individual believes he or she is loved by someone else, usually someone famous or of high social status (Kennedy et al., 2002). In reality, the individual has only a passing or nonexistent relationship with the alleged lover (R. L. Goldstein, 1986). People with erotomania are often unemployed and socially isolated (Kennedy et al., 2002). Although the love delusion was once thought to be predominantly a female disorder, recent reports suggest it may not be a rarity among men. Although women with erotomania may have a potential for violence when their attentions are rebuffed, men with this condition appear more likely to threaten or commit acts of violence in the pursuit of the objects of their unrequited desires (Goldstein, 1986). Antipsychotic medications may reduce the intensity of the delusion but do not appear to eliminate it (Kelly, Kennedy, & Shanley, 2000; Segal, 1989). Nor is there evidence that psychotherapy helps people with erotomania. The prognosis is thus bleak, and people with erotomania may harass their love objects for many years. Mental health professionals also need to be aware of the potential for violence in the management of people who possess these delusions of love (Mullen, 2000; Segal, 1989). The following cases provide some examples of the love delusion.

Three Cases of Erotomania

Mr. A., a 35-year-old man, was described as a "love-struck" suitor of a daughter of a former President of the United States. He was arrested for repeatedly harassing the woman in an attempt to win her love, although they were actually perfect strangers. Refusing to adhere to the judge's warnings to stop pestering the woman, he placed numerous phone calls to her from prison and was later transferred to a psychiatric facility, still declaring they were very much in love.

Mr. B. was arrested for breaching a court order to stop pestering a famous pop singer. A 44-year-old farmer, Mr. B. had followed his love interest across the country, constantly bombarding her with romantic overtures. He was committed to a psychiatric hospital, but maintained the belief that she'd always wait for him.

Then there was Mr. C., a 32-year-old businessman, who believed a well-known woman lawyer had fallen in love with him following a casual meeting. He constantly called and sent flowers and letters, declaring his love. While she repeatedly rejected his advances and eventually filed criminal charges for harassment, he felt that she was only testing his love by placing obstacles in his path. He abandoned his wife and business and his functioning declined. When the woman continued to reject him, he began sending her threatening letters and was committed to a psychiatric facility.

—*Adapted from Goldstein, 1986, p. 802* ■

Mr. Polsen's delusional belief that "hit teams" were pursuing him was treated with antipsychotic medication in the hospital and faded in about 3 weeks. His belief that he had been the subject of an attempted "hit" stuck in his mind, however. A month following admission, he stated, "I guess my boss has called off the contract. He couldn't get away with it now without publicity" (Spitzer et al., 1994, p. 179).

Although delusions frequently occur in schizophrenia, delusional disorder is believed to be distinct from schizophrenia. Persons with delusional disorder do not exhibit confused or jumbled thinking. Hallucinations, when they occur, are not as prominent. Delusions in schizophrenia are embedded within a larger array of disturbed thoughts, perceptions, and behavior. In delusional disorders, the delusion itself may be the only clear sign of abnormality.

Delusional disorder is relatively uncommon and should also be distinguished from another disorder in which paranoid thinking is present—*paranoid personality disorder* (discussed in Chapter 13). People with paranoid personality disorder may hold exaggerated or unwarranted suspicions of others, but not the outright delusions that are found among people with delusional disorders or paranoid schizophrenia.

Various types of delusional disorder are described in Table 12.2. Like other forms of psychosis, delusional disorders often respond to antipsychotic medication (Morimoto et al., 2002). However, once the delusion is established, it may persevere, although the individual's concern about it may wax and wane over the years. In other cases, the delusion may disappear entirely for periods of time and then recur. Sometimes the disorder permanently disappears.

Schizoaffective Disorder

Schizoaffective disorder is sometimes referred to as a "mixed bag" of symptoms because it includes psychotic features such as hallucinations and delusions along with disturbances of mood, such as mania or major depression. Like schizophrenia, schizoaffective disorder tends to follow a chronic course that is characterized by persistent difficulties adjusting to the demands of adult life (Marneros, 2003). Also like schizophrenia, the psychotic features of schizoaffective disorder respond to antipsychotic drugs (Jaffe & Levine, 2003; Woerner et al., 2003).

TRUTH or FICTION? REVISITED

Some people have delusions that they are loved by a famous person.

☑ **TRUE.** Some people do suffer from the delusion that they are loved by a famous person. They are said to have a delusional disorder, erotomanic type.

---

schizoaffective disorder A type of psychotic disorder in which individuals experience both severe mood disturbance and features associated with schizophrenia.

TABLE 12.2

Types of Delusional Disorder

Type	Description
Erotomanic Type	Delusional beliefs that someone else, usually someone of higher social status, such as a movie star or political figure, is in love with you; also called *erotomania*.
Grandiose Type	Inflated beliefs about your worth, importance, power, knowledge, or identity, or beliefs that you hold a special relationship to a deity or a famous person. Cult leaders who believe they have special mystical powers of enlightenment may have delusional disorders of this type.
Jealous Type	Delusions of jealousy in which the person may become convinced, without due cause, that his or her lover is unfaithful. The delusional person may misinterpret certain clues as signs of unfaithfulness, such as spots on the bedsheets.
Persecutory Type	The most common type of delusional disorder, persecutory delusions involve themes of being conspired against, followed, cheated, spied upon, poisoned or drugged, or otherwise maligned or mistreated. Persons with such delusions may repeatedly institute court actions, or even commit acts of violence, against those who they perceived are responsible for their mistreatment.
Somatic Type	Delusions involving physical defects, disease, or disorder. Persons with these delusions may believe that foul odors are emanating from their bodies, or that internal parasites are eating away at them, or that certain parts of their body are unusually disfigured or ugly, or not functioning properly despite evidence to the contrary.
Mixed Type	Delusions typify more than one of the other types; no single theme predominates.

Source: Adapted from *DSM-IV-TR* (APA, 2000).

Schizoaffective disorder and schizophrenia appear to share a genetic link (Bramon & Sham, 2001). Consistent with a common genetic basis, researchers find a greater than average incidence of schizoaffective disorders among the relatives of people with schizophrenia and a greater than average incidence of schizophrenia among the relatives of people with schizoaffective disorder (Kendler, Gruenberg, & Tsuang, 1985; Maj et al., 1991). If schizoaffective disorders and schizophrenia share a common genetic substrate, we need to discover why this genetic predisposition leads to one disorder and not the other.

Schizoaffective Disorder:
The Case of Josh
"I looked out the window and saw this guy with a machete chasing one of the psychiatrists."

Overview of Schizophrenia

CLINICAL FEATURES OF SCHIZOPHRENIA

Disturbed Thought Processes	• Delusions (fixed false ideas) and thought disorder (disorganized thinking and incoherent speech)
Attentional Deficiencies	• Difficulty attending to relevant stimuli and screening out irrelevant stimuli
Perceptual Disturbances	• Hallucinations (sensory perceptions in the absence of external stimulation)
Emotional Disturbances	• Flat (blunted) or inappropriate emotions
Other Impairments	• Confusion about personal identity, lack of volition, excitable behavior or states of stupor, odd gestures or bizarre facial expressions, and impaired ability to relate to others

MAJOR SUBTYPES OF SCHIZOPHRENIA*

Disorganized Type	• Confused and bizarre behavior, incoherent speech, vivid hallucinations, flat or inappropriate affect, and disorganized delusions
Catatonic Type	• Gross disturbances in motor activity in which behavior may slow to a stupor but abruptly shift to a highly agitated state
Paranoid Type	• Delusions (typically of themes of grandeur, persecution, or jealousy) and frequent auditory hallucinations

*Variations of schizophrenia distinguished in terms of specific subtypes. Another way of subtyping schizophrenia is based on distinguishing between Type I schizophrenia, characterized by more flagrant symptoms (positive symptoms), and Type II schizophrenia, characterized by deficit symptoms (negative symptoms).

CAUSAL FACTORS*

Biological Factors	• Strong evidence of a major genetic contribution
	• Irregularities in neurotransmitter systems in the brain, especially in brain circuits that utilize the neurotransmitter dopamine
	• Underlying brain abnormalities in many cases, such as structural damage or deterioration of brain tissue or disturbed brain circuitry in parts of the brain regulating cognitive and emotional functioning
	• Possible role of viral infections affecting the developing brain prenatally or during early life
Psychosocial Factors	• Stressful experiences may contribute to the development of schizophrenia in genetically vulnerable individuals.

*The specific causes remain unknown, but most researchers believe they reflect an interaction of genetic and stress-related factors, as represented by the diathesis-stress model.

TREATMENT APPROACHES

A comprehensive treatment approach incorporating biomedical, psychosocial, and family interventions is recommended.

Biomedical Treatment	• Antipsychotic drugs are used to control psychotic symptoms.
Psychosocial Treatment	• Learning-based approaches, such as the token economy system and social skills training, can help schizophrenia patients develop more adaptive behaviors.
Psychosocial Rehabilitation	• Self-help clubs and structured residential programs can help schizophrenia patients adjust to community living.
Family Intervention Programs	• Family interventions are used to improve communication in the family and reduce levels of family conflict and stress.

SUMMING UP

Schizophrenia

What is schizophrenia and how prevalent is it? Schizophrenia is a chronic psychotic disorder characterized by acute episodes involving a break with reality, as manifest by such features as delusions, hallucinations, illogical thinking, incoherent speech, and bizarre behavior. Residual deficits in cognitive, emotional, and social areas of functioning persist between acute episodes. Schizophrenia is believed to affect about 1% of the population.

What are the major phases of schizophrenia? Schizophrenia usually develops in late adolescence or early adulthood. Its onset may be abrupt or gradual. Gradual onset is preceded by a prodromal phase, a period of gradual deterioration that precedes the onset of acute symptoms. Acute episodes, which may occur periodically throughout life, are typified by clear psychotic symptoms, such as hallucinations and delusions. Between acute episodes the disorder is characterized by a residual phase in which the person's level of functioning is similar to that which was present during the prodromal phase.

What are the most prominent features of schizophrenia? Among the more prominent features of schizophrenia are disorders in the content of thought (delusions) and the form of thought (thought disorder), as well as the presence of often severe perceptual distortions (hallucinations) and emotional disturbances (flattened or inappropriate affect). There are also dysfunctions in brain processes regulating attention to the external world.

What are the specific subtypes of schizophrenia? The disorganized type is associated with grossly disorganized behavior and thought processes. The catatonic type is associated with grossly impaired motor behaviors, such as maintenance of fixed postures and muteness for long periods. The paranoid type is characterized by paranoid delusions and frequent auditory hallucinations. The undifferentiated type is a catchall category applying to cases in which schizophrenic episodes don't clearly fit the other types. The residual type applies to individuals with schizophrenia who do not have prominent psychotic behaviors at the time of evaluation. Researchers have also distinguished between two general types of schizophrenia: Type I, characterized by positive symptomatology, more abrupt onset, better response to antipsychotic medication, and better preserved intellectual ability, and Type II, characterized by negative symptomatology, more gradual onset, poorer response to antipsychotic medication, and greater cognitive impairment.

How is schizophrenia conceptualized within traditional psychodynamic theory and learning perspectives? In the traditional psychodynamic model, schizophrenia represents a regression to a psychological state corresponding to early infancy in which the proddings of the id produce bizarre, socially deviant behavior and give rise to hallucinations and delusions. Learning theorists propose that some form of schizophrenic behavior may result from lack of social reinforcement, which leads to gradual detachment from the social environment and increased attention to an inner world of fantasy. Modeling and selective reinforcement of bizarre behavior may explain some schizophrenic behaviors in the hospital setting.

What do we know about the biological bases of schizophrenia? Compelling evidence for a strong genetic component in schizophrenia comes from studies of family patterns of schizophrenia, twin studies, and adoption studies. The mode of genetic transmission remains unknown. Most researchers believe the neurotransmitter dopamine plays a role in schizophrenia, especially in the more flagrant features of the disorder. Viral factors may also be involved, but definite proof of viral involvement is lacking. Evidence of brain dysfunctions and structural damage in schizophrenia is accumulating, but researchers are uncertain about causal pathways.

How is schizophrenia conceptualized within the diathesis-stress model? The diathesis-stress model posits that schizophrenia results from an interaction of a genetic predisposition (the diathesis) and environmental stressors (e.g., family conflict, child abuse, emotional deprivation, loss of supportive figures, early brain trauma).

How are family factors related to the development and course of schizophrenia? Family factors such as communication deviance and expressed emotion may act as sources of stress that increase the risk of development or recurrence of schizophrenia among people with a genetic predisposition.

How does the treatment of schizophrenia involve a multifaceted approach? Contemporary treatment approaches tend to be multifaceted, incorporating pharmacological and psychosocial approaches. Antipsychotic medication is not a cure but tends to stem the more flagrant aspects of the disorder and to reduce the need for hospitalization and the risk of recurrent episodes.

What types of psychosocial interventions have shown promising results? These are principally learning-based approaches, such as token economy systems and social skills training. They help increase adaptive behavior of schizophrenia patients. Psychosocial rehabilitation approaches help people with schizophrenia adapt more successfully to occupational and social roles in the community. Family intervention programs help families cope with the burdens of care, communicate more clearly, and learn more helpful ways of relating to the patient.

Other Forms of Psychosis

What are other forms of psychotic disorders besides schizophrenia? These include brief psychotic disorder (a psychotic disorder lasting less than a week that may be reactive to a significant stressor), schizophreniform disorder (symptoms identical to those of schizophrenia that lasting for a month to less than 6 months), delusional disorder (denoted by delusions that are apparently plausible and less bizarre than those in schizophrenia), and schizoaffective disorder (combination of psychotic symptoms and significant mood disturbance).

KEY TERMS

schizophrenia *(p. 401)*
prodromal phase *(p. 404)*
residual phase *(p. 404)*
thought disorder *(p. 407)*
hallucinations *(p. 409)*
disorganized type *(p. 412)*

catatonic type *(p. 413)*
paranoid type *(p. 413)*
positive symptoms *(p. 414)*
negative symptoms *(p. 414)*
dopamine hypothesis *(p. 418)*
double-bind communications *(p. 421)*

tardive dyskinesia (TD) *(p. 428)*
brief psychotic disorder *(p. 432)*
schizophreniform disorder *(p. 432)*
delusional disorder *(p. 432)*
erotomania *(p. 433)*
schizoaffective disorder *(p. 434)*

WEB TOOLS

The companion website offers tools to enrich your learning experience and help you succeed in class. Go to www.prenhall.com/nevid for the gateway to the following resources:

* **VIDEO** links to connect to the video case files on the companion CD-ROM. VIDEO icons in the margins of the chapter highlight the case examples included in the CD-ROM. You can also access the CD-ROM directly if you do not have a Web connection.

* **QUIZ** links to self-scoring quizzes corresponding to each section of the chapter. The quizzes help you review your knowledge of the content in each chapter.

* **WEB** links to direct you to related sites that enhance your learning of abnormal psychology.

Personality Disorders

"I"

My Dark Place

There are times in my life when I go to a dark place. I find it hard to run or hide from this symptom that feels like it controls my life. It's called self-mutilation or cutting. It's part of my and other's diagnosis called borderline personality disorder (BPD). Cutting is when you feel an urge to cut different places on your body. In my case, it's my arms and legs. I remember being depressed at a very young age. At age eight-years-old, I cut myself for the first time. I was very alone in my pain and no one noticed my scar. But, even at that very young age, after I cut, I felt a sense of relief. For a while I was able to block out everything and just feel free. Even today, I still feel a need to comfort myself. Now that I'm older I must find other outlets for my pain. It's something that's going to take a lot of work and therapy.

Source: New York City Voices. *Reprinted with permission*

LIKE THIS PERSON, PEOPLE WITH BORDERLINE PERSONALITY DISORDER ARE OFTEN severely depressed and turn to self-mutilation in a twisted attempt to escape from emotional pain. But their problems lie deeper than depression. They involve the kinds of rigid, inflexible and maladaptive behavior patterns that clinicians classify as *personality disorders.* These maladaptive patterns of behavior have far-reaching consequences for the person's psychological adjustment and relationships with others.

All of us have particular styles of behavior and ways of relating to others. Some of us are orderly, others sloppy. Some of us prefer solitary pursuits; others are more social. Some of us are followers; others are leaders. Some of us seem immune to rejection by others, whereas others avoid social initiatives for fear of getting shot down. When behavior patterns become so inflexible or maladaptive that they cause significant personal distress or impair people's social or occupational functioning, they may be classified as personality disorders.

TYPES OF PERSONALITY DISORDERS

> In most of us by the age of thirty, the character has set like plaster, and will never soften again.
>
> —William James

Personality disorders are excessively rigid patterns of behavior or ways of relating to others. The rigidity prevents people from adjusting to external demands; thus the patterns ultimately become self-defeating. The disordered personality traits or characteristics become evident by adolescence or early adulthood and continue through much of adult life, becoming so deeply ingrained that they are highly resistant to change. The warning signs of personality disorders may be detected during childhood, even in the troubled behavior of preschoolers. Children with psychological disorders or problem behaviors in childhood, such as conduct disorder, depression, anxiety, and immaturity, are at greater than average risk of later developing personality disorders (Bernstein et al., 1996; Kasen et al., 2001). Personality disorders appear to be quite common: a recent community survey of adults in Oslo, Norway, found that 13.4% of community residents showed evidence of one or more personality disorders (Torgersen, Kringlen, & Cramer, 2001).

Despite the self-defeating consequences of their behavior, people with personality disorders do not generally perceive a need to change. Using psychodynamic terms, the *DSM* notes that people with personality disorders tend to perceive their traits as **ego syntonic**—as natural parts of themselves. Consequently, people with personality disorders are more likely to be brought to the attention of mental health professionals by others than to seek services themselves. In contrast, people with anxiety disorders (Chapter 6) or mood disorders (Chapter 8) tend to view their disturbed behaviors as **ego dystonic.** They do not see their behaviors as parts of their self-identities and are thus more likely to seek help to relieve the distress caused by them.

Truth or Fiction?

T☐ F☐ People with schizoid personalities may have deeper feelings for animals than they do for people. (p. 442)

T☐ F☐ People with antisocial personalities inevitably run afoul of the law. (p. 445)

T☐ F☐ Many notable figures in history, from Lawrence of Arabia to Adolf Hitler and even Marilyn Monroe, shown signs of borderline personality. (p. 447)

T☐ F☐ Some people with dependent personality disorder have so much difficulty making independent decisions that they allow their parents to decide whom they will marry. (p. 453)

T☐ F☐ Despite a veneer of self-importance, people with narcissistic personalities may harbor deep feelings of insecurity. (p. 458)

T☐ F☐ Recent research supports the popular image of psychopathic murderers as "cold-blooded" killers. (p. 461).

T☐ F☐ People with antisocial personalities tend to remain unduly calm in the face of impending pain. (p. 462)

T☐ F☐ Personality disorders can be successfully treated with psychiatric drugs. (p. 466)

personality disorders Excessively rigid behavior patterns, or ways of relating to others, that ultimately become self-defeating.

ego syntonic Referring to behaviors or feelings that are perceived as natural parts of the self.

ego dystonic Referring to behaviors or feelings that are perceived to be alien to one's self-identity.

The *DSM* groups clinical syndromes (such as mood disorders and anxiety disorders) on Axis I and personality disorders on Axis II. The personality disorders are classified separately from the clinical syndromes because they typically involve more enduring and rigid patterns of behavior. But clinical syndromes and personality disorders often occur together, or *comorbidly.* For example, a person may have an Axis I mood disorder, such as major depression, as well as an Axis II personality disorder, such as borderline personality disorder.

The *DSM* groups personality disorders into three clusters:

Cluster A: People who are perceived as odd or eccentric. This cluster includes paranoid, schizoid, and schizotypal personality disorders.
Cluster B: People whose behavior is overly dramatic, emotional, or erratic. This grouping consists of antisocial, borderline, histrionic, and narcissistic personality disorders.
Cluster C: People who often appear anxious or fearful. This cluster includes avoidant, dependent, and obsessive–compulsive personality disorders.

Personality Disorders Characterized by Odd or Eccentric Behavior

This group of personality disorders includes paranoid, schizoid, and schizotypal disorders. People with these disorders often have difficulty relating to others or show little or no interest in developing social relationships.

Paranoid Personality Disorder The defining trait of the **paranoid personality disorder** is pervasive suspiciousness—the tendency to interpret other people's behavior as deliberately threatening or demeaning. People with the disorder are excessively mistrustful of others, and their relationships suffer for it. Though they may be suspicious of coworkers and supervisors, they can generally maintain employment.

The following case illustrates the unwarranted suspicion and reluctance to confide in others that typifies people with paranoid personalities.

paranoid personality disorder A personality disorder characterized by undue suspiciousness of others' motives, but not to the point of delusion.

> ### A Case of Paranoid Personality Disorder
>
> *An 85-year-old retired businessman was interviewed by a social worker to determine health care needs for himself and his infirm wife. The man had no history of treatment for a mental disorder. He appeared to be in good health and mentally alert. He and his wife had been married for 60 years, and it appeared that his wife was the only person he'd ever really trusted. He had always been suspicious of others. He would not reveal personal information to anyone but his wife, believing that others were out to take advantage of him. He had refused offers of help from other acquaintances because he suspected their motives. When called on the telephone, he would refuse to give out his name until he determined the nature of the caller's business. He'd always involved himself in "useful work" to occupy his time, even during his 20 years of retirement. He spent a good deal of time monitoring his investments and had altercations with his stockbroker when errors on his monthly statement prompted suspicion that his broker was attempting to cover up fraudulent transactions.*
>
> *—Adapted from Spitzer et al., 1994, pp. 211–213*

People who have paranoid personality disorder tend to be overly sensitive to criticism, whether real or imagined. They take offense at the smallest slight. They are readily angered and hold grudges when they think they have been mistreated. They are unlikely to confide in others because they believe that personal information may be used against them. They question the sincerity and trustworthiness of friends and associates. A smile or a glance may be viewed with suspicion. As a result, they have few friends and intimate relationships. When they do form an intimate relationship, they may suspect infidelity, even without evidence. They tend to remain hypervigilant, as if they must be on the lookout against harm. They deny blame for misdeeds, even when warranted, and are perceived by others as cold, aloof, scheming, devious, and humorless. They tend to be argumentative and may launch repeated lawsuits against those who they believe have mistreated them.

Clinicians need to weigh cultural and sociopolitical factors when arriving at a diagnosis of paranoid personality disorder. For example, members of immigrant or ethnic minority groups, political refugees, or people from other cultures may seem guarded or defensive, but this behavior may reflect unfamiliarity with the language, customs, or rules and regulations of the majority culture or a cultural mistrust arising from a history of neglect or oppression. Such behavior should not be confused with paranoid personality disorder.

Although people with paranoid personality disorder harbor exaggerated and unwarranted suspicions, they do not have the outright paranoid delusions that characterize the thought patterns of people with paranoid schizophrenia (for example, believing the FBI is out to get them). People who have paranoid personalities are unlikely to seek treatment; they see others as causing their problems. The reported prevalence of paranoid personality disorder in the general population ranges from 0.5% to 2.5% (APA, 2000). The disorder is diagnosed in people receiving mental health treatment more often in men than women.

Schizoid personality. It is normal to be reserved about displaying one's feelings, especially when one is among strangers. But people with schizoid personalities rarely express emotions and are distant and aloof. Yet the emotions of people with schizoid personalities are not as shallow or blunted as they are in people with schizophrenia.

Schizoid Personality Disorder Social isolation is the cardinal feature of **schizoid personality disorder.** Often described as a loner or an eccentric, the person with a schizoid personality lacks interest in social relationships. The person's emotions usually appear shallow or blunted, but not to the degree found in schizophrenia (see Chapter 12). People with this disorder rarely, if ever, experience strong anger, joy, or sadness. They look distant and aloof. Their faces tend to show no emotional expression, and they rarely exchange social smiles or nods. They seem indifferent to criticism or praise and appear to be wrapped up in abstract ideas rather than in thoughts about people. Although they prefer to remain distant from others, they maintain better contact with reality than do people with schizophrenia. The prevalence of the disorder in the general population remains unknown. Men with this disorder rarely date or marry. Women with the disorder are more likely to accept romantic advances passively and to marry, but they seldom initiate relationships or develop strong attachments to their partners.

Akhtar (1987, 2003) claims that there may be discrepancies between outer appearances and the inner lives of people with schizoid personalities. Although they may appear to have little appetite for sex, for example, they may harbor voyeuristic wishes and become attracted to pornography. Akhtar also suggests that the distance and social aloofness of people with schizoid personalities may be somewhat superficial. They may also harbor exquisite sensitivity, deep curiosities about people, and wishes for love that they cannot express. In some cases, sensitivity is expressed in deep feelings for animals rather than people.

schizoid personality disorder A personality disorder characterized by persistent lack of interest in social relationships, flattened affect, and social withdrawal.

A Case of Schizoid Personality Disorder

John, a 50-year-old retired police officer, sought treatment a few weeks after his dog was hit by a car and died. Since the dog's death, John has felt sad and tired. He has had difficulty concentrating and sleeping. He lives alone and prefers to be by himself, limiting his contacts with others to a passing "Hello" or "How are you?" He feels that social conversation is a waste of time and feels awkward when others try to initiate a friendship. Though he avidly reads newspapers and keeps abreast of current events, he has no real interest in people. He works as a security guard and is described by his coworkers as a "loner" and a "cold fish." The only relationship he had was with his dog, with which he felt he could exchange more sensitive and loving feelings than he could share with people. At Christmas, he would "exchange gifts" with his dog, buying presents for the dog and wrapping a bottle of Scotch for himself as a gift from the animal. The only event that ever saddened him was the loss of his dog. In contrast, the loss of his parents failed to evoke an emotional response. He considers himself to be different from other people and is bewildered by the displays of emotionality that he sees in others.

—*Adapted from Spitzer et al., 1989, pp. 249–250*

TRUTH or FICTION? REVISITED

People with schizoid personalities may have deeper feelings for animals than they do for people.

☑ **TRUE.** People with a schizoid personality may show little or no interest in people but develop strong feelings for animals.

schizotypal personality disorder A personality disorder characterized by eccentricities of thought and behavior, but without clearly psychotic features.

Schizotypal Personality Disorder   The diagnosis of **schizotypal personality disorder** applies to people who have difficulties forming close relationships and whose behavior, mannerisms, and thought patterns are peculiar or odd, but not disturbed enough to merit a diagnosis of schizophrenia. They may be especially anxious in social situations, even when interacting with familiar people. Their social anxieties seem to be associated with paranoid thinking (e.g., fears that others mean them harm) rather than with concerns about being rejected or evaluated negatively by others (APA, 2000).

Schizotypal personality disorder may be slightly more common in males than in females and is believed to affect about 3% of the general population (APA, 2000). Investigators also find higher rates of the disorder among African Americans than among Caucasians or Hispanic Americans (Chavira et al., 2003). However, clinicians need to be careful not to label as schizotypal certain behavior patterns that reflect culturally determined beliefs or religious rituals, such as beliefs in voodoo and other magical beliefs.

The eccentricity associated with the schizoid personality is limited to a lack of interest in social relationships. In paranoid personality disorder, unusual beliefs are limited to undue suspiciousness of others. But in schizotypal personality disorder, there is a wider range of odd behaviors, beliefs, and perceptions. Persons with the disorder may experience unusual perceptions or illusions, such as feeling the presence of a deceased family member in the room. They realize, however, that the person is not actually there. They may become unduly suspicious of others or paranoid in their thinking. They may develop *ideas of reference,* such as the belief that other people are talking about them. They may engage in *magical thinking,* such as believing they possess a "sixth sense" (i.e., can foretell the future) or that others can sense their feelings. They may attach unusual meanings to words. Their own speech may be vague or unusually abstract, but it is not incoherent or filled with the loose associations that characterize schizophrenia. They may appear unkempt, display unusual mannerisms, and engage in unusual behaviors, such as talking to themselves in the presence of others. Their faces may register little emotion. Like people with schizoid personalities, they may fail to exchange smiles with, or nod at, others. Or they may appear silly and smile and laugh at the wrong times. They tend to be socially withdrawn and aloof, with few if any close friends or confidants. They seem to be especially anxious around unfamiliar people. We can see evidence of the social aloofness and illusions that are often associated with schizotypal personality disorder in this case.

A Case of Schizotypal Personality Disorder

Jonathan, a 27-year-old auto mechanic, had few friends and preferred science fiction novels to socializing with other people. He seldom joined in conversations. At times, he seemed to be lost in his thoughts, and his coworkers would have to whistle to get his attention when he was working on a car. He often showed a "queer" expression on his face. Perhaps the most unusual feature of his behavior was his reported intermittent experience of "feeling" his deceased mother standing nearby.

These illusions were reassuring to him, and he looked forward to their occurrence. Jonathan realized they were not real. He never tried to reach out to touch the apparition, knowing it would disappear as soon as he drew closer. It was enough, he said, to feel her presence.

—From the Authors' Files

Despite the *DSM*'s grouping of "schizotypal" behaviors with personality disorders, the schizotypal behavior pattern may fall within a spectrum of schizophrenia-related disorders that includes paranoid and schizoid personality disorders and schizoaffective disorder (discussed in Chapter 12) as well as schizophrenia itself. Schizotypal personality disorder may actually share a common genetic basis with schizophrenia (Kendler & Walsh, 1995; Siever & Davis, 2004). Let us note, however, that schizotypal personality disorder tends to follow a chronic course, and relatively few people diagnosed with the disorder go on to develop schizophrenia or other psychotic disorders (APA, 2000). Perhaps the emergence of schizophrenia in persons with this shared genetic predisposition is determined by such factors as stressful early family relationships.

Personality Disorders Characterized by Dramatic, Emotional, or Erratic Behavior

This cluster of personality disorders includes the antisocial, borderline, histrionic, and narcissistic types. People with these disorders exhibit behavior patterns that are excessive, unpredictable, or self-centered; they also have difficulty forming and maintaining relationships.

Antisocial Personality Disorder   People with **antisocial personality disorder** are *antisocial* in the sense that they often violate the rights of others, disregard social norms and conventions, and, in some cases, break the law. They are not "antisocial" in the colloquial sense of seeking to avoid people. People with antisocial personalities also tend to be impulsive and fail to live up to their commitments to others. Yet they often show a superficial charm and possess at least average intelligence (Cleckley, 1976). They frequently show low levels of anxiety when faced with threatening situations and lack feelings of guilt or remorse following wrongdoing. Punishment seems to have little if any effect on their behavior. Although parents and others have usually punished them for their misdeeds, they persist in leading irresponsible and impulsive lives.

antisocial personality disorder A personality disorder characterized by antisocial and irresponsible behavior and lack of remorse for misdeeds.

Men are more likely than women to receive diagnoses of antisocial personality disorder (Cale & Lilienfeld, 2002). The prevalence rates for the disorder in community samples range from about 3% to 6% in men and about 1% in women (APA, 2000; Kessler et al., 1994; see Figure 13.1). For the diagnosis of antisocial personality disorder to be applied, the person must be at least 18 years of age. The alternative diagnosis of conduct disorder is used with younger people (see Chapter 14). Many children with conduct disorders do not continue to show antisocial behavior as adults.

We once used terms such as *psychopath* and *sociopath* to refer to people who today are classified as having antisocial personalities, people whose behavior is amoral and asocial, impulsive, and lacking in remorse and shame. Some clinicians continue to use these terms interchangeably with *antisocial personality*. The roots of the word *psychopath* focus on the idea that there is something amiss (pathological) in the individual's psychological functioning. The roots of *sociopath* center on the person's social deviance.

The pattern of behavior that characterizes antisocial personality disorder begins in childhood or adolescence and extends into adulthood. However, the antisocial and criminal behavior

Antisocial personality. Mass murderer Henry Lee Lucas, a drifter and violent career criminal, fits the stereotype of an antisocial personality.

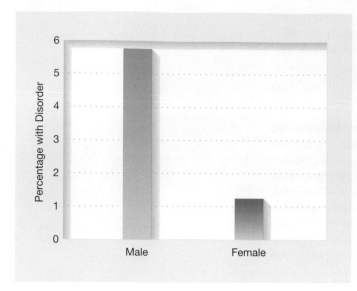

FIGURE 13.1 Lifetime prevalences of antisocial personality disorder by gender.
Antisocial personality disorder is more than five times as common among men than women. However, the disorder has been rising more rapidly among women in recent years.

Source: National Comorbidity Survey (Kessler et al., 1994).

associated with the disorder tends to decline with age and may disappear by the time the person reaches the age of 40. Not so for the underlying personality traits associated with the disorder—traits such as egocentricity; manipulativeness; lack of empathy, guilt, or remorse; and callousness toward others. These appear to be relatively stable even with increasing age (Harpur & Hare, 1994).

Much of our attention in this chapter focuses on antisocial personality disorder. Historically it is the personality disorder that has been most extensively studied by scholars and researchers.

Sociocultural Factors and Antisocial Personality Disorder Antisocial personality disorder cuts across all racial and ethnic groups. Researchers find no evidence of either ethnic or racial differences in the rates of the disorder (Robins, Tipp, & Przybeck, 1991). The disorder is most common, however, among people in lower socioeconomic groups. One explanation is that people with antisocial personality disorder drift downward occupationally, perhaps because their antisocial behavior makes it difficult for them to hold steady jobs or progress upward. People from lower socioeconomic levels may also be more likely to have parents who modeled antisocial behavior. However, the diagnosis may also be misapplied to people living in hard-pressed communities who engage in seemingly antisocial behaviors as a survival strategy (APA, 2000).

Antisocial Behavior and Criminality We tend to think of antisocial behavior as synonymous with criminal behavior. Although a strong relationship exists between the two, not all criminals show signs of antisocial personality, and not all people with this disorder become criminals (Lilienfeld & Andrews, 1996). Many are law abiding and successful, even though they exhibit a callous disregard of the interests and feelings of others.

Investigators have begun to view antisocial personality as composed of two somewhat independent dimensions. The first is a *personality dimension*. It consists of such traits as superficial charm, selfishness, lack of empathy, callous and remorseless use of others, and disregard for their feelings and welfare. This type of psychopathic personality applies to people who have these kinds of psychopathic traits but don't become lawbreakers.

The second dimension is a *behavioral dimension*. It is characterized by the adoption of a generally unstable and antisocial lifestyle, including frequent problems with the law, poor employment history, and unstable relationships (Brown & Forth, 1997; Cooke & Michie, 1997). These two dimensions are not entirely separate; many antisocial individuals show evidence of both sets of traits.

We should also note that some people do not become criminals or delinquents because of a disordered personality but because they were reared in environments or subcultures that rewarded criminal behavior. Although criminal behavior is deviant to society at large, it is normal by the standards of the subculture. Also, lack of remorse, which is a cardinal feature of antisocial personality disorder, does not characterize all criminals. Some criminals regret their crimes, and judges and parole boards consider evidence of remorse when passing sentence or recommending a prisoner for parole.

Criminality or antisocial personality disorder? It is likely that many prison inmates could be diagnosed with antisocial personality disorder; however, people may become criminals or delinquents not because of a disordered personality but because they were raised in environments or exposed to subcultures that both encouraged and rewarded criminal behavior.

Only about half of prison inmates could be diagnosed with antisocial personality disorder (Robins et al., 1991). Conversely, fewer than half of the people with antisocial personality disorder run afoul of the law (Robins et al., 1991). Many fewer still fit (thankfully!) the stereotype of the psychopathic killer popularized in such films as *The Silence of the Lambs.*

Profile of the Antisocial Personality Hervey Cleckley (1941) showed that the characteristics that define the psychopathic or antisocial personality—self-centeredness, irresponsibility, impulsivity, and insensitivity to the needs of others—exist not only among criminals but also among many respected members of the community, including doctors, lawyers, politicians, and business executives. Other common traits of people with antisocial personality disorder include failure to conform to social norms, irresponsibility, aimlessness and lack of long-term goals or plans, impulsive behavior, outright lawlessness, violence, chronic unemployment, marital problems, lack of remorse or empathy, substance abuse or alcoholism, and a disregard for the truth and for the feelings and needs of others (Patrick, Cuthbert, & Lang, 1994; Robins et al., 1991). Irresponsibility may be seen in a personal history dotted by repeated, unexplained absences from work, abandonment of jobs without having other job opportunities to fall back on, or long stretches of unemployment. Irresponsibility extends to financial matters, where there may be repeated failure to repay debts, to pay child support, or to meet other financial responsibilities to one's family and dependents. The diagnostic features of antisocial personality disorder, as defined in the DSM, are shown in Table 13.1.

Antisocial Personality Disorder:
The Case of Paul
"I went to prison for kicking down my wife's door."

TABLE 13.1

Diagnostic Features of Antisocial Personality Disorder

(a) The person is at least 18 years old.

(b) There is evidence of a conduct disorder prior to the age of 15, as shown by such behavior patterns as truancy, running away, initiating physical fights, use of weapons, forcing someone into sexual activities, physical cruelty to people or animals, deliberate destruction of property or fire setting, lying, stealing, or mugging.

(c) Since the age of 15, there has been general indifference to and violation of the rights of other people, as shown by several of the following:

   (1) Lack of conformity to social norms and legal codes, as shown by law-breaking behavior that may or may not result in arrest, such as destruction of property, engaging in unlawful occupations, stealing, or harassing others.

   (2) Aggressive and highly irritable style of relating to others, as shown by repeated physical fights and assaults with others, possibly involving abuse of one's spouse or children.

   (3) Consistent irresponsibility, as shown by failure to maintain employment due to chronic absences, lateness, abandonment of job opportunities or extended periods of unemployment despite available work; and/or by failure to honor financial obligations, such as failing to maintain child support or defaulting on debts; and/or by lack of a sustained monogamous relationship.

   (4) Failure to plan ahead or impulsivity, as shown by traveling around without prearranged employment or clear goals.

   (5) Disregard for the truth, evidenced by repeated lying, conning others, or use of aliases for personal gain or pleasure.

   (6) Recklessness with regard to personal safety or the safety of other people, as shown by driving while intoxicated or repeated speeding.

   (7) Lack of remorse for misdeeds, as shown by indifference to the harm done to others, and/or by rationalizing that harm.

Source: Adapted from the *DSM-IV-TR* (APA, 2000).

The following case represents a number of antisocial characteristics.

A Case of Antisocial Behavior

The 19-year-old male is brought by ambulance to the hospital emergency room in a state of cocaine intoxication. He's wearing a T-shirt with the imprint "Twisted Sister" on the front, and he sports a punk-style haircut. His mother is called and sounds groggy and confused on the phone; the doctors must coax her to come to the hospital. She later tells the doctors that her son has arrests for shoplifting and for driving while intoxicated. She suspects that he takes drugs, although she has no direct evidence. She believes that he is performing fairly well at school and has been a star member of the basketball team.

It turns out that her son has been lying to her. In actuality, he never completed high school and never played on the basketball team. A day later, his head cleared, the patient tells his doctors, almost boastfully, that his drug and alcohol use started at the age of 13, and that by the time he was 17, he was regularly using a variety of psychoactive substances, including alcohol, speed, marijuana, and cocaine. Lately, however, he has preferred cocaine. He and his friends frequently participate in drug and alcohol binges. At times they each drink a case of beer in a day along with downing other drugs. He steals car radios from parked cars and money from his mother to support his drug habit, which he justifies by adopting a (partial) "Robin Hood" attitude—that is, taking money only from people who have lots of it.

—Adapted from Spitzer et al., 1994, pp. 81–83

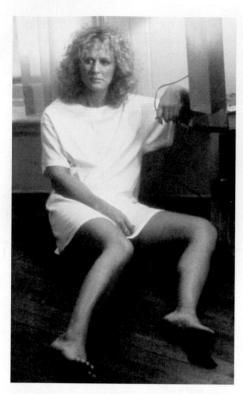

Borderline personality. In the movie *Fatal Attraction,* the actress Glenn Close played a character who exhibited many of the characteristics associated with borderline personality disorder, including impulsivity, extreme mood swings, and unstable relationships.

borderline personality disorder (BPD) A personality disorder characterized by abrupt shifts in mood, lack of a coherent sense of self, and unpredictable, impulsive behavior.

Although this case is suggestive of antisocial personality disorder, the diagnosis was maintained as provisional because the interviewer could not determine that the deviant behavior (lying, stealing, skipping school) began before the age of 15.

Borderline Personality Disorder Borderline personality disorder (BPD) is characterized by a range of behavioral, emotional, and personality features (Sanislow, Grilo, & McGlashan, 2000). At the core is a pervasive pattern of instability in relationships, self-image, and mood and a lack of control over impulses. People with borderline personality disorder tend to be uncertain about their personal identities—their values, goals, careers, and perhaps even their sexual orientations. This instability in self-image or personal identity leaves them with nagging feelings of emptiness and boredom. They cannot tolerate being alone and will make desperate attempts to avoid feelings of abandonment (Gunderson, 1996). Fear of abandonment renders them clinging and demanding in their social relationships, but their clinging often pushes away the people on whom they depend. Signs of rejection may enrage them, straining their relationships further. Their feelings toward others are consequently intense and shifting. They alternate between extremes of adulation (when their needs are met) and loathing (when they feel scorned). They tend to view other people as all good or all bad, shifting abruptly from one extreme to the other. As a result, they may flit from partner to partner in a series of brief and stormy relationships. People they had idealized are treated with contempt when relationships end or when they feel the other person fails to meet their needs (Gunderson, 2001).

BPD is believed to occur in about 2% of the general population (APA, 2000). Although it is diagnosed more often (about 75% of the time) in women, gender differences in prevalence rates for BPD in the general population remain undetermined. Recent evidence indicates higher rates of the disorder among Hispanics than among Caucasians and African Americans (Chavira et al., 2003). The factors accounting for these differences require further investigation.

Many notable figures have been described as having personality features associated with borderline personality disorder, including Marilyn Monroe, Lawrence of Arabia,

A CLOSER LOOK
Did Samson Have Antisocial Personality Disorder?

Did Samson, the biblical figure who fought the Philistines but lost his great strength when his long hair was shorn by the wily Delilah, have antisocial personality disorder? We noted in Chapter 1 that case studies have been reported on deceased individuals, even historical figures who died several hundred years ago. Applying modern diagnostic criteria to individuals from biblical times requires quite a leap of faith. Yet four psychiatrists writing in a respected professional journal argue that Samson's behavior nearly 3,000 years ago clearly meets many of the criteria for antisocial personality disorder (Altschuler et al., 2001). The biblical account of his behavior shows that Samson broke the law, lied repeatedly, acted impulsively and without regard for the safety of himself and others, initiated many physical fights, and lacked remorse for his actions—patterns of behavior that today are recognized as signs of antisocial personality disorder (Goode, 2001). As an example of his reckless disregard of his own safety, the authors point to Samson's revelation to Delilah that the secret of his strength lay in his uncut locks, even after she had tried three times to pry the secret from him. The biblical account also relates that 3,000 Israelites—Samson's own people!—captured him and turned him over the Philistines. This may indicate that his brutal behavior was not viewed as acceptable conduct in the time in which he lived. However, it cannot be determined based on the biblical record whether Samson showed evidence of conduct disorder prior to the age of 15, as the diagnostic criteria for antisocial personality disorder require.

On a broader level, the authors argue that modern diagnostic concepts may help us better understand the behavior of historical figures. Then again, others who read the same biblical or historical record may reach different conclusions. For example, was Samson truly reckless in divulging the secret of his strength to Delilah? Perhaps he was "playing a lover's game as lovers do," in the words of another commentator on the Samson legend (Ryan, 2002). Or perhaps he had no reason to suspect that she had hidden motives. In any event, historical analysis makes for interesting conjecture but falls short of the evidence needed to establish a clear diagnosis by modern standards. ■

Samson: A case of antisocial personality disorder? The actor Victor Mature portrayed Samson in the 1949 film *Samson and Delilah*. Recently, several psychiatrists have claimed that the biblical record of Samson's behavior indicates that he met many of the criteria for antisocial personality disorder.

Adolf Hitler, and the philosopher Sören Kierkegaard. Some theorists believe we live in highly fragmented and alienating times that tend to create the problems in forming cohesive identities and stable relationships that characterize borderline personality disorder (Sass, 1982). "Living on the edge," or border, can be seen as a metaphor for an unstable society.

The term *borderline personality* was originally used to refer to individuals whose behavior appeared on the border between neuroses and psychoses. People with borderline personality disorder generally maintain better contact with reality than people with psychoses, although they may show fleeting psychotic behaviors during times of stress. Generally speaking, they are more severely impaired than most people with neuroses but not as dysfunctional as those with psychotic disorders. Instability of moods is a central characteristic of borderline personality disorder (Sanislow et al., 2000). Moods run the gamut from anger and irritability to depression and anxiety (Koenigsberg et al., 2002). Mood shifts tends to be frequent and abrupt. Other features of BPD include chronic anger, loneliness, boredom, a deep sense of emptiness, and impulsivity (Hochhausen, Lorenz, & Newman, 2002; Zanarini et al., 2003). People with BPD have difficulty controlling anger and are prone to fights or smashing things. They often act on impulse, such as eloping with someone they have just met. This impulsive and unpredictable behavior is often self-destructive, involving such behaviors as self-mutilation and suicidal gestures and actual attempts (e.g., Sanislow et al., 2000). Suicide attempts and nonsuicidal self-injuries may be motivated by the desire to escape from troubling emotions (Brown, Comtois, & Linehan, 2002). Impulsive behavior in BPD patients may also include spending sprees, gambling, drug abuse, unsafe sexual activity, reckless driving, binge eating, or shoplifting. Among young adults, borderline personality features such as emotional

Borderline Personality Disorder:
The Case of Liz
"I have problems with anger management."

Over the top? Not all people who dress outrageously or flamboyantly have histrionic personalities. What other personality features characterize people with histrionic personality disorder?

splitting An inability to reconcile the positive and negative aspects of the self and others, resulting in sudden shifts between positive and negative feelings.

histrionic personality disorder A personality disorder characterized by excessive need for attention, praise, reassurance, and approval.

instabilty and impulsivity are associated with poor performance in school and social maladjustment (Bagge et al., 2004). We also have evidence of greater impulsivity among female prison inmates with borderline personality disorder than other female inmates (Hochhausen, Lorenz, & Newman, 2002). A saving grace perhaps is that impulsivity tends to "burn out" with age, as investigators find that impulsivity decreases among older BPD patients (Stevenson et al., 2003). Impulsive acts of self-mutilation, such as the self-inflicted cutting described at the opening of this chapter, may also involve such acts as scratching the wrists or even touching burning cigarettes on the arms. The following dialogue illustrates this type of behavior.

CLIENT: I've got such repressed anger in me; what happens is . . . I can't *feel* it; I get anxiety attacks. I get very nervous, smoke too many cigarettes. So what happens to me is I tend to *explode*. Into tears or hurting myself or whatever . . . because I don't know how to contend with all those mixed up feelings.

INTERVIEWER: What was the more recent example of such an "explosion"?

CLIENT: I was alone at home a few months ago; I was frightened! I was trying to get in touch with my boyfriend and I couldn't . . . He was nowhere to be found. All my friends seemed to be busy that night and I had no one to talk to . . . I just got more and more nervous and more and more agitated. Finally, *bang!* . . . I took out a cigarette and lit it and stuck it into my forearm. I don't know why I did it because I didn't really care for him all that much. I guess I felt I had to do something dramatic . . .

—Adapted from Stone, 1980, p. 400

Self-mutilation is sometimes an expression of anger or a means of manipulating others. Such acts may be intended to counteract self-reported feelings of "numbness," particularly in times of stress. Not surprisingly, frequent self-mutilation among people with BPD is associated with an increased risk of suicidal thinking (Dulit et al., 1994).

Individuals with BPD tend to have very troubled relationships with their families and with others. They often had traumatic childhood experiences, such as parental losses or separations, abuse, neglect, or witnessing violence (Liotti et al., 2000). They tend to view their relationships as rife with hostility and to perceive others as rejecting and abandoning (Benjamin & Wonderlich, 1994). They also tend to be difficult to work with in psychotherapy, demanding a great deal of support from therapists, calling them at all hours or acting suicidally to elicit support, or dropping out of therapy prematurely. Their feelings toward therapists, as toward other people, undergo rapid alterations between idealization and outrage. Psychoanalysts interpret these abrupt shifts in feelings as signs of **splitting,** or inability to reconcile the positive and negative aspects of one's experience of oneself and others.

Histrionic Personality Disorder **Histrionic personality disorder** is characterized by excessive emotionality and an overwhelming need to be the center of attention. The term is derived from the Latin *histrio*, which means "actor." People with histrionic personality disorder tend to be dramatic and emotional, but their emotions seem shallow, exaggerated, and volatile. The disorder was formerly called *hysterical personality*. The following case example illustrates the excessively dramatic behaviors typical of someone with histrionic personality disorder.

A Case of Histrionic Personality Disorder

Marcella was a 36-year-old, attractive, but overly made up woman who was dressed in tight pants and high heels. Her hair was in a bird's nest of the type that had been popular when she was a teenager. Her social life seemed to bounce from relationship to relationship, from crisis to crisis. Marcella sought help from the psychologist at this time because her 17-year-old daughter, Nancy, had just been hospitalized for cutting her wrists. Nancy lived with Marcella and Marcella's current boyfriend, Morris, and there were constant arguments in the apartment. Marcella recounted the disputes that took place with high drama, waving her hands, clanging the bangles that hung from her bracelets, and then clutching her breast. It was difficult having Nancy live at home because Nancy had expensive tastes, was "always looking for attention," and flirted with Morris as a way of "flaunting her youth." Marcella saw herself as a doting mother and denied any possibility that she was in competition with her daughter.

Marcella came for a handful of sessions, during which she basically ventilated her feelings and was encouraged to make decisions that might lead to a reduction of some of the pressures on her and her daughter. At the end of each session she said, "I feel so much better" and thanked the psychologist profusely. At termination of "therapy," she took the psychologist's hand and squeezed it endearingly. "Thank you so much, Doctor," she said and made her exit.

—From the Authors' Files

The supplanting of *hysterical* with *histrionic* and the associated exchange of the roots *hystera* (meaning "uterus") and *histrio* allow professionals to distance themselves from the notion that the disorder is intricately bound up with being female. The disorder is diagnosed more frequently in women than men (Hartung & Widiger, 1998), although some studies using structured interview methods find similar rates of occurrence among men and women (APA, 2000). Whether the gender discrepancy in clinical practice reflects true differences in the underlying rates of the disorder, diagnostic biases, or unseen factors remains an open question (Corbitt & Widiger, 1995).

People with histrionic personalities may become unusually upset by news of a sad event and exude exaggerated delight at a pleasant occurrence. They may faint at the sight of blood or blush at a slight faux pas. They tend to demand that others meet their needs for attention and to play the victim when others fall short. They tend to be self-centered and intolerant of delays of gratification: They want what they want when they want it. They grow quickly restless with routine and crave novelty and stimulation. They are drawn to fads. Others may see them as putting on airs or playacting, although they may evince a certain charm. They tend to be flirtatious and seductive but are too wrapped up in themselves to develop intimate relationships or have deep feelings toward others. As a result, their associations tend to be stormy and ultimately ungratifying. They tend to use their physical appearance as a means of drawing attention to themselves. Men with the disorder may act and dress in an overly "macho" way, and women may choose very frilly, feminine clothing. Glitter supercedes substance.

People with histrionic personalities may be attracted to professions like modeling or acting, where they can hog the spotlight. Despite outward successes, they lack self-esteem and strive to impress others to boost their self-worth. If they suffer setbacks or lose their place in the limelight, depressing inner doubts may emerge.

Narcissistic Personality Disorder *Narkissos* was a handsome youth who, according to Greek myth, fell in love with his reflection in a spring. Because of his excessive self-love, the gods transformed him into the flower we know as the narcissus.

Persons with **narcissistic personality disorder** have an inflated or grandiose sense of themselves and an extreme need for admiration. They brag about their accomplishments and expect others to shower them with praise. They expect others to notice their special qualities, even when their accomplishments are ordinary, and they enjoy basking in the light of adulation. They are self-absorbed and lack empathy for others. Although they share certain features with histrionic personalities, such as demanding to be the center of attention, they have a much more inflated view of themselves and are less melodramatic than people with histrionic personality disorder. The label of borderline personality disorder (BPD) is sometimes applied to them, but people with narcissistic personality disorder are generally better able to organize their

narcissistic personality disorder A personality disorder characterized by adoption of an inflated self-image and demands for attention and admiration.

A person with a narcissistic personality? People with narcissistic personalities are often preoccupied with fantasies of success and power, ideal love, or recognition for their brilliance or beauty. They may pursue careers that provide opportunities for public recognition and adulation, such as acting, modeling, or politics. They may become deeply wounded by any hint that they are not as special as they believe themselves to be.

thoughts and actions. They tend to be more successful in their careers and are better able to rise to positions of status and power. Their relationships also tend to be more stable than those of people with BPD.

Narcissistic personality disorder is found among less than 1% of the general population (APA, 2000). Although more than half of the people diagnosed with the disorder are men, we cannot say whether there is an underlying gender difference in prevalence rates in the general population. A certain degree of narcissism may represent a healthful adjustment to insecurity, a shield from criticism and failure, or a motive for achievement (Goleman, 1988). Excessive narcissistic qualities can become unhealthful, especially when the cravings for adulation are insatiable. Table 13.2 compares "normal" self-interest with self-defeating extremes of narcissism. Up to a point, self-interest fosters success and happiness. In more extreme cases, as with narcissism, it can compromise relationships and careers.

People with narcissistic personalities tend to be preoccupied with fantasies of success and power, ideal love, or recognition for brilliance or beauty. Like people with histrionic personalities, they may gravitate toward careers in modeling, acting, or politics. Although they tend to exaggerate their accomplishments and abilities, many people with narcissistic personalities are quite successful in their occupations. But they envy those who achieve even greater success. Insatiable ambition may prompt them to devote themselves tirelessly to work. They are driven to succeed, not so much for money as for the adulation that attends success.

Interpersonal relationships are invariably strained by the demands that people with narcissistic personality impose on others and by their lack of empathy with, and concern for, other people. They seek the company of flatterers and, although they are often superficially charming and friendly, their interest in people is one-sided: They seek people who will serve their interests and nourish their sense of self-importance (Goleman, 1988). They have feelings of entitlement that lead them to exploit others. They tend to adopt a game-playing style in romantic relationships rather than seek true intimacy, apparently because of their needs for power and autonomy (Campbell, Foster, & Finkel, 2002). They treat sex partners as devices for their own pleasure or to brace their self-esteem, as in the case of Bill.

A Case of Narcissistic Personality Disorder

Most people agreed that Bill, a 35-year-old investment banker, had a certain charm. He was bright, articulate, and attractive. He possessed a keen sense of humor that drew people to him at social gatherings. He would always position himself in the middle of the room, where he could be the center of attention. The topics of conversation invariably focused on his "deals," the "rich and famous" people he had met, and his outmaneuvering of opponents. His next project was always bigger and more daring than the last. Bill loved an audience. His face would light up when others responded to him with praise or admiration for his business successes, which were always inflated beyond their true measure. But when the conversation shifted to other people, he would lose interest and excuse himself to make a drink or to call his answering machine. When hosting a party, he would urge guests to stay late and feel hurt if they had to leave early; he showed no sensitivity to, or awareness of, the needs of his friends.

TABLE 13.2

Features of Normal Self-Interest Compared with Self-Defeating Narcissism

Normal Self-Interest	Self-Defeating Narcissism
Appreciating acclaim, but not requiring it in order to maintain self-esteem.	Craving adoration insatiably; requiring acclaim in order to feel momentarily good about oneself.
Being temporarily wounded by criticism.	Being inflamed or crushed by criticism and brooding about it extensively.
Feeling unhappy but not worthless following failure.	Having enduring feelings of mortification and worthlessness triggered by failure.
Feeling "special" or uncommonly talented in some way.	Feeling incomparably better than other people, and insisting upon acknowledgment of that preeminence.
Feeling good about oneself, even when other people are being critical.	Needing constant support from other people in order to maintain one's feelings of well-being.
Being reasonably accepting of life's setbacks, even though they can be painful and temporarily destabilizing.	Responding to life's wounds with depression or fury.
Maintaining self-esteem in the face of disapproval or denigration.	Responding to disapproval or denigration with loss of self-esteem.
Maintaining emotional equilibrium despite lack of special treatment.	Feeling entitled to special treatment and becoming terribly upset when one is treated in an ordinary manner.
Being empathic and caring about the feelings of others.	Being insensitive to other people's needs and feelings; exploiting others until they become fed up.

Source: Based on Goleman, 1988, p. C1.

The few friends he had maintained over the years had come to accept Bill on his own terms. They recognized that he needed to have his ego fed or that he would become cool and detached.

Bill had also had a series of romantic relationships with women who were willing to play the adoring admirer and make the sacrifices that he demanded—for a time. But they inevitably tired of the one-sided relationship or grew frustrated by Bill's inability to make a commitment or feel deeply toward them. Lacking empathy, Bill was unable to recognize other people's feelings and needs. His demands for constant attention from willing admirers did not derive from selfishness, but from a need to ward off underlying feelings of inadequacy and diminished self-esteem. It was sad, his friends thought, that Bill needed so much attention and adulation from others and that his many achievements were never enough to calm his inner doubts.

—From the Authors' Files

Personality Disorders Characterized by Anxious or Fearful Behavior

This cluster of personality disorders includes the avoidant, dependent, and obsessive–compulsive types. Although the features of these disorders differ, they share a component of fear or anxiety.

Avoidant Personality Disorder Persons with **avoidant personality disorder** are so terrified of rejection and criticism that they are generally unwilling to enter relationships without ardent reassurances of acceptance. As a result, they may have few close relationships outside their immediate families. They also tend to avoid group

avoidant personality disorder A personality disorder characterized by avoidance of social relationships due to fears of rejection.

A person with an avoidant personality? People with avoidant personalities often keep to themselves because of fear of rejection.

occupational or recreational activities for fear of rejection. They prefer to lunch alone at their desks. They shun company picnics and parties, unless they are perfectly sure of acceptance. Avoidant personality disorder, which appears to be equally common in men and women, is believed to affect between 0.5% and 1.0% of the general population (APA, 2000).

Unlike people with schizoid qualities, with whom they share the feature of social withdrawal, individuals with avoidant personalities have interest in, and feelings of warmth toward, other people. However, fear of rejection prevents them from striving to meet their needs for affection and acceptance. In social situations, they tend to hug the walls and avoid conversing with others. They fear public embarrassment, the thought that others might see them blush, cry, or act nervously. They tend to stick to their routines and exaggerate the risks or effort involved in trying new things. They may refuse to attend a party that is an hour away on the pretext that the late drive home would be too taxing. Consider the following case example.

A Case of Avoidant Personality Disorder

Harold, a 24-year-old accounting clerk, had dated but a few women, and he had met them through family introductions. He never felt confident enough to approach a woman on his own. Perhaps it was his shyness that first attracted Stacy. Stacy, a 22-year-old secretary, worked alongside Harold and asked him if he would like to get together sometime after work. At first Harold declined, claiming some excuse, but when Stacy asked again a week later, Harold agreed, thinking she must really like him if she were willing to pursue him. The relationship developed quickly, and soon they were dating virtually every night. The relationship was strained, however. Harold interpreted any slight hesitation in her voice as a lack of interest. He repeatedly requested reassurance that she cared about him, and he evaluated every word and gesture for evidence of her feelings. If Stacy said that she could not see him because of fatigue or illness, he assumed she was rejecting him and sought further reassurance. After several months, Stacy decided she could no longer accept Harold's nagging, and the relationship ended. Harold assumed that Stacy had never truly cared for him.

—From the Authors' Files

There is a good deal of overlap between avoidant personality disorder and social phobia, particularly a severe subtype of social phobia involving a generalized pattern of social phobia (excessive, irrational fear of most social situations) (Turner, Beidel, & Townsley, 1992; Widiger, 1992). Although many cases of generalized social phobia occur in the absence of avoidant personality disorder (Holt, Heimberg, & Hope, 1992), relatively fewer cases of avoidant personality occur in the absence of generalized social phobia (Widiger, 1992). Thus avoidant personality disorder may represent a more severe form of social phobia (Hoffman et al., 1995). Still, the scientific jury is out on the question of whether avoidant personality disorder should be considered a severe form of generalized social phobia or a distinct diagnostic category.

dependent personality disorder A personality disorder characterized by difficulty making independent decisions and overly dependent behavior.

Dependent Personality Disorder **Dependent personality disorder** describes people who have an excessive need to be taken care of by others. This leads them to be overly submissive and clinging in their relationships and extremely fearful of separation. People with this disorder find it very difficult to do things on their own. They seek advice in making even the smallest decision. Children or adolescents with the problem may look to their parents to select their clothes, diets, schools or colleges, even their friends.

Adults with the disorder allow others to make important decisions for them. Sometimes they are so dependent on others that they allow their parents to determine whom they will marry, as in the case of Matthew.

A Case of Dependent Personality Disorder

Matthew, a 34-year-old single accountant who lives with his mother, sought treatment when his relationship with his girlfriend came to an end. His mother had objected to marriage because his girlfriend was of a different religion, and—because "blood is thicker than water"—Matthew acceded to his mother's wishes and ended the relationship. Yet he is angry with himself and at his mother because he feels that she is too possessive to ever grant him permission to get married. He describes his mother as a domineering woman who "wears the pants" in the family and is accustomed to having things her way. Matthew alternates between resenting his mother and thinking that perhaps she knows what's best for him.

Matthew's position at work is several levels below what would be expected of someone of his talent and educational level. Several times he has declined promotions in order to avoid increased responsibilities that would require him to supervise others and make independent decisions. He has maintained close relationships with two friends since early childhood and has lunch with one of them on every working day. On days his friend calls in sick, Matthew feels lost. Matthew has lived his whole life at home, except for one year away at college. He returned home because of homesickness.

—Adapted from Spitzer et al., 1994, pp. 179–180

After marriage, people with dependent personality disorder may rely on their spouses to make decisions such as where they should live, which neighbors they should cultivate, how they should discipline the children, what jobs they should take, how they should budget money, and where they should vacation. Like Matthew, individuals with dependent personality disorder avoid positions of responsibility. They turn down challenges and promotions and work beneath their potential. They tend to be overly sensitive to criticism and preoccupied with fears of rejection and abandonment. They may be devastated by the end of a close relationship or by the prospect of living on their own. Because of fear of rejection, they often subordinate their wants and needs to those of others. They may agree with outlandish statements about themselves and do degrading things to please others.

Before going further, we should note that dependence needs to be examined through the lens of culture. Arranged marriages are the norm in some traditional cultures, so people from those cultures who let their parents decide whom they will marry would not be classified as having dependent personality disorder. Similarly, in strongly patriarchal cultures, women may be expected to defer to their fathers and husbands in making many life decisions, even small everyday decisions.

But we needn't look beyond our own society to consider the role of culture. Evidence shows that dependent personality disorder in our culture is diagnosed more frequently in women than in men (APA, 2000; Bornstein, 1997). The diagnosis is often applied to women who, for fear of abandonment, tolerate husbands who openly cheat on them, abuse them, or gamble away the family's resources. Underlying feelings of inadequacy and helplessness discourage them from taking effective action. In a vicious cycle, their passivity encourages further abuse, leading them to feel yet more inadequate and helpless. Applying the diagnosis to women with this pattern is controversial and may be seen as unfairly "blaming the victim," because women in our society are often socialized to dependent roles. Women typically encounter greater stress than men in contemporary life as well as greater social pressures to be passive, demure, or deferential. Therefore, dependent behaviors in women may reflect cultural influences rather than an underlying personality disorder.

Dependent personality disorder has been linked to other psychological disorders, including major depression, bipolar disorder, and social phobia, and to physical problems,

TRUTH or FICTION? *REVISITED*

Some people with dependent personality disorder have so much difficulty making independent decisions that they allow their parents to decide whom they will marry.

☑ **TRUE.** People with dependent personality disorder in our culture may be so dependent on others for making decisions that they allow their parents to determine whom they will marry.

such as hypertension, cancer, and gastrointestinal disorders like ulcers and colitis (Bornstein, 1999b; Loranger, 1996; Reich, 1996). There also appears to be a link between dependent personality and what psychodynamic theorists refer to as "oral" behavior problems, such as smoking, eating disorders, and alcoholism (Bornstein, 1993, 1999b). Psychodynamic writers trace dependent behaviors to the utter dependence of the newborn baby and the baby's seeking of nourishment through oral means (suckling). Food may come to symbolize love, and persons with dependent personalities may overeat to ingest love symbolically. People with dependent personalities often attribute their problems to physical rather than emotional causes and seek support and advice from medical experts rather than psychologists or counselors (Greenberg & Bornstein, 1988a, 1988b).

obsessive–compulsive personality disorder A personality disorder characterized by rigid ways of relating to others, perfectionistic tendencies, lack of spontaneity, and excessive attention to detail.

Obsessive–Compulsive Personality Disorder The defining features of **obsessive–compulsive personality disorder** include excessive orderliness, perfectionism, rigidity, difficulty coping with ambiguity, difficulty expressing feelings, and meticulousness in work habits. About 1% of people in community samples are diagnosed with the disorder (APA, 2000). The disorder is about twice as common in men than women. Unlike obsessive–compulsive anxiety disorder, people with obsessive–compulsive personality disorder do not necessarily experience outright obsessions or compulsions. If they do, both diagnoses may be deemed appropriate.

Persons with obsessive–compulsive personality disorder are so preoccupied with the need for perfection that they cannot complete work on time. Their efforts inevitably fall short of their expectations, so they redo their work. Or they ruminate about how to prioritize their work and never seem to start working. They focus on details that others perceive as trivial. As the saying goes, they fail to see the forest for the trees. Their rigidity impairs their social relationships; they insist on doing things their way rather than compromising. Their zeal for work keeps them from participating in, or enjoying, social and leisure activities. They tend to be stingy with money. They find it difficult to make decisions and postpone or avoid them for fear of making the wrong choice. They tend to be inflexible and overly rigid in issues of morality and ethics, to be overly formal in relationships, and to find it difficult to express feelings. It is hard for them to relax and enjoy pleasant activities; they worry about the costs of such diversions. Consider the following case example.

A Case of Obsessive–Compulsive Personality Disorder

Jerry, a 34-year-old systems analyst, was perfectionistic, overly concerned with details, and rigid in his behavior. Jerry was married to Marcia, a graphics artist. He insisted on scheduling their free time hour by hour and became unnerved when they deviated from his agenda. He would circle a parking lot repeatedly in search of just the right parking spot to ensure that another car would not scrape his car. He refused to have the apartment painted for over a year because he couldn't decide on the color. He had arranged all the books in their bookshelf alphabetically and insisted that every book be placed in its proper position.

Jerry never seemed to relax. Even on vacation, he was bothered by thoughts of work that he had left behind and by fears that he might lose his job. He couldn't understand how people could lie on the beach and let all their worries evaporate in the summer air. Something can always go wrong, he figured, so how can people let themselves go?

—From the Authors' Files

Problems with the Classification of Personality Disorders

Questions remain about the reliability and validity of the diagnostic categories for personality disorders in the DSM system (Farmer, 2000). Here we focus on major concerns that clinicians and researchers have raised about how these patterns of behavior are diagnosed or classified. In the accompanying feature, Controversies in Abnormal Psychology, we focus on a running debate in the field concerning whether some diagnostic categories of personality disorders have sexist underpinnings.

Problems Distinguishing Personality Disorders from Mood and Stress Disorders

Some reviewers question whether personality disorders can be reliably differentiated from Axis I clinical syndromes such as anxiety or mood disorders (Farmer, 2000; Livesley et al., 1994). For example, clinicians often have difficulty distinguishing between obsessive–compulsive disorder and obsessive–compulsive personality disorder. Clinical syndromes are believed to be variable over time, whereas personality disorders are held to be generally more enduring patterns of disturbance. Yet features of personality disorders may vary over time with changes in circumstances. On the other hand, some Axis I clinical syndromes (dysthymia, for example) follow a more or less chronic course.

Overlap Among Disorders

There is also a high degree of overlap among diagnostic criteria for the personality disorders (Westen & Shedler, 1999). Although some personality disorders have distinct features, many appear to share common traits, such as problems in romantic relationships (Daley, Burge, & Hammen, 2000). Moreover, the same person may have traits suggestive of dependent personality disorder (inability to make decisions or initiate activities independently) as well as avoidant personality disorder (extreme social anxiety and heightened sensitivity to criticism). Overall, about two in three people with personality disorders meet diagnostic criteria for more than one personality disorder (Widiger, 1991). This suggests that the personality disorders included in the *DSM* system may not be sufficiently distinct from one another (Westen & Schedler, 1999). Some so-called disorders may thus represent different aspects of the same disorder, not separate diagnostic categories.

"A place for everything, and everything in its place"? People with obsessive–compulsive personalities may have invented this maxim. Many such people have excessive needs for orderliness in their environment, as suggested in this Laurie Simmons photograph, Red Library #2.

Difficulty in Distinguishing Between Normal and Abnormal Behavior

Another problem with the diagnosis of personality disorders is that they involve personality traits which, in lesser degrees, describe the behavior of most normal individuals. Feeling suspicious now and then does not mean you have a paranoid personality disorder. The tendency to exaggerate your own importance does not mean you are narcissistic. You may avoid social interactions for fear of embarrassment or rejection without having an avoidant personality disorder, and you may be especially conscientious in your work without having an obsessive–compulsive personality disorder. Because the defining attributes of these disorders are common personality traits, clinicians should only apply these diagnostic labels when the patterns are so pervasive that they interfere with the individual's functioning or cause significant personal distress. Yet it can be difficult to draw the line between normal behavior and personality disorders. We lack data to guide us in determining the precise point at which a trait becomes sufficiently inflexible or maladaptive to justify a personality disorder diagnosis (Widiger & Costa, 1994).

Confusing Labels with Explanations

It may seem obvious that we should not confuse diagnostic labels with explanations, but in practice the distinction is sometimes clouded. If we confuse labeling with explanation, we may fall into the trap of circular reasoning. What is wrong, for example, with the logic of the following statements?

1. John's behavior is antisocial.
2. Therefore, John has an antisocial personality disorder.
3. John's behavior is antisocial because he has an antisocial personality disorder.

The statements demonstrate circular reasoning because they (a) use behavior to make a diagnosis, and then (b) use the diagnosis as an explanation for the behavior. We may be guilty of circular reasoning in our everyday speech. Consider: "John never gets his work in on time; therefore, he is lazy. John doesn't get his work in because he's lazy." The label may be acceptable in everyday conversation, but it lacks scientific rigor. For a construct such as *laziness* to have scientific rigor, we need to understand the causes of laziness and the factors that help maintain it. We should not confuse the label we attach to behavior with the cause of the behavior.

Moreover, labeling people with disturbing behavior as having personality disorders overlooks the social and environmental contexts of the behavior. The impact of traumatic life events, which may occur with a greater range or intensity among members of particular gender or cultural group, is an important underlying factor in maladaptive behavior. However, the conceptual underpinnings of the personality disorders do not consider cultural differences, social inequalities, or power differences between genders or cultural groups. For example, many women diagnosed with personality disorders have a history of childhood physical and sexual abuse (Brown, 1992; Walker, 1988). The ways in which people cope with abuse may come to be viewed as flaws in their character rather than as reflections of the dysfunctional societal factors that underlie abusive relationships.

Personality disorders are convenient labels for identifying common patterns of ineffective and self-defeating behavior, but labels do not explain the behaviors they name. Still, the development of an accurate descriptive system is an important step toward scientific explanation. The establishment of reliable diagnostic categories sets the stage for valid research into causation and treatment.

THEORETICAL PERSPECTIVES

In this section we consider theoretical perspectives on the personality disorders. Many theoretical accounts of disturbed personality derive from the psychodynamic model. We thus begin with a review of traditional and modern psychodynamic models.

Psychodynamic Perspectives

Traditional Freudian theory focused on problems arising from the Oedipus complex as the foundation for abnormal behaviors, including personality disorders. Freud believed that children normally resolve the Oedipus complex by forsaking incestuous wishes for the parent of the opposite gender and identifying with the parent of the same gender. As a result, they incorporate the parent's moral principles in the form of a personality structure called the *superego.* Many factors may interfere with appropriate identification and sidetrack the normal developmental process, preventing children from developing moral constraints and the feelings of guilt or remorse that normally follow antisocial behavior. Freud's account of moral development focused mainly on the development of males. He has been criticized for failing to account for the moral development of females.

More recent psychodynamic theories have generally focused on the earlier, pre-Oedipal period of about 18 months to 3 years, during which infants begin to develop identities separate from those of their parents. These theories focus on the development of the sense of self in explaining such disorders as narcissistic and borderline personality disorders.

Hans Kohut One of the principal shapers of modern psychodynamic concepts is Hans Kohut, whose theory is labeled *self-psychology* because of its emphasis on processes in the development of a cohesive sense of self. Freud believed that the resolution of the Oedipus complex was central to the development of adult personality. Kohut disagreed, arguing that what matters most is how the self develops—whether the person is able to develop self-esteem, values, and a cohesive and realistic sense of self as opposed to a narcissistic personality (Anderson, 2003; Goldberg, 2003).

Kohut (1966) believed that people with narcissistic personalities might mount a facade of self-importance to cover up deep feelings of inadequacy. The narcissist's self-esteem is like a reservoir that needs to be constantly replenished with a steady stream of

CONTROVERSIES IN ABNORMAL PSYCHOLOGY
Are Personality Disorders Sexist?

Is the *DSM* classification of personality disorders biased against women? This is a broad charge, but the conceptualization of at least some types of personality disorders appears to have sexist underpinnings. The diagnostic criteria seem to label stereotypical feminine behaviors as pathological with greater frequency than stereotypical masculine behaviors. Take the example of histrionic personality, which seems a caricature of the traditional stereotype of the feminine personality: flighty, emotional, shallow, seductive, attention-seeking.

But if the feminine stereotype corresponds to a mental disorder, shouldn't we also have a diagnostic category that reflects the masculine stereotype of the "macho male"? We can argue that overly masculinized traits are associated with significant distress or impairment in social or occupational functioning in certain males. For example, highly masculinized males often get into fights and experience difficulties working for female bosses. Yet there is no personality disorder that corresponds to the "macho male" stereotype.

Does the diagnosis of dependent personality disorder unfairly stigmatize women who have been socialized into dependent roles by attaching to them a label of a personality disorder? Women may be at greater risk of receiving diagnoses of histrionic or dependent personality disorders simply because clinicians perceive these patterns as common among women or because women are more likely than men to be socialized into these behavior patterns.

Are some personality disorders more likely to be diagnosed in men or in women because of societal expectations rather than because of real underlying pathology? Clinicians tend to show a bias in favor of perceiving women as having histrionic personality disorder and men as having antisocial personality disorder, even when they demonstrate the same symptoms (Garb, 1997). Additional evidence of gender bias is found in a study that examined diagnoses of borderline personality disorder. Researchers presented a hypothetical case example to 311 psychologists, social workers, and psychiatrists (Becker & Lamb, 1994). Half of the sample was presented with a case identified as a female; the other half read the identical case, except that it was identified as male. Clinicians more often diagnosed the case identified as female as having borderline personality disorder.

Is the *DSM* classification of personality disorders gender biased or gender free? Should it be more evenly balanced in its characterizations of disordered

Are there sexist biases in the conception of personality disorders? The concept of the histrionic personality disorder seems to be a caricature of the highly stereotyped feminine personality. Why, then, is there not also something akin to a macho male personality disorder, which caricatures the highly stereotyped masculine personality?

personality? What do you think? Consider your own attitudes: Have you ever assumed that women are "just dependent or hysterical" or that men are "just narcissists or antisocial"?

Critical Thinking

- What are the roots of sexist biases in determining where to draw the line between normal and abnormal behavior? How does culture enter in the problem of bias?
- How can clinicians avoid bias when making diagnostic judgments? ■

---

praise and attention lest it run dry. A sense of grandiosity helps people with a narcissistic personality mask their underlying feelings of worthlessness. Failures or disappointments threaten to expose these feelings and drive the person into a state of depression, so as a defense against despair, the person attempts to diminish the importance of disappointments or failures.

People with narcissistic personalities may become enraged by others whom they perceive have failed to protect them from disappointment or have declined to shower them with reassurance, praise, and admiration. They may become infuriated by even the slightest criticism, no matter how well intentioned. They may mask feelings of rage and humiliation by adopting a facade of cool indifference. They can make difficult psychotherapy clients because they may become enraged when therapists puncture their inflated self-images to help them develop more realistic self-concepts.

To Kohut, early childhood involves a normal stage of "healthful narcissism." Infants feel powerful, as though the world revolves around them. Infants also normally perceive their parents as idealized towers of strength and wish to be one with them and to share their power (Edmundson, 2001; Strozier, 2001). Empathic parents reflect their children's inflated perceptions by making them feel that anything is possible and by nourishing their self-esteem (e.g., telling them how terrific and precious they are). Even empathic parents are critical from time to time, however, and puncture their children's grandiose sense of self. Or they fail to measure up to their children's idealized views of them. Gradually, unrealistic expectations dissolve and are replaced by more realistic appraisals of oneself and others. In adolescence, childhood idealization is transformed into realistic admiration for parents, teachers, and friends. In adulthood, these ideas develop into a set of internal ideals, values, and goals.

Lack of parental empathy and support, however, sets the stage for pathological narcissism. Children who are not prized by their parents fail to develop a sturdy sense of self-esteem. They develop damaged self-concepts and feel incapable of being loved and admired. Pathological narcissism involves the construction of a grandiose facade of self-perfection that cloaks perceived inadequacies. The facade always remains on the brink of crumbling, however, and it must be shored up by a constant flow of reassurance that one is special and unique. This leaves the person vulnerable to painful blows to self-esteem following failure to achieve social or occupational goals.

Kohut's approach to therapy provides clients who have a narcissistic personality with an initial opportunity to express their grandiose self-images and to idealize the therapist. Over time, however, the therapist helps them explore the childhood roots of their narcissism and gently points out imperfections in both client and therapist to encourage clients to form more realistic images of the self and others.

Otto Kernberg Otto Kernberg (1975), a leading psychodynamic theorist, views borderline personality in terms of a failure in early childhood to develop a sense of constancy and unity in one's image of oneself and others. From this perspective, borderline individuals cannot synthesize contradictory (positive and negative) elements of themselves and others into complete, stable wholes. Rather than viewing important people in their lives as sometimes loving and sometimes rejecting, they shift back and forth between pure idealization and utter hatred. This rapid shifting back and forth between viewing others as either "all good" or "all bad" is referred to as splitting.

Kernberg tells of a woman in her 30s whose attitude toward him vacillated in such a way. The woman would respond to him in one session as the most wonderful therapist and feel that all her problems were solved. But several sessions later she would turn against him and accuse him of being unfeeling and manipulative, become dissatisfied with treatment, and threaten to drop out (Sass, 1982).

In Kernberg's view, parents, even excellent parents, invariably fail to meet all their children's needs. Infants therefore face the early developmental challenge of reconciling images of the nurturing, comforting "good mother" with those of the withholding, frustrating "bad mother." Failure to reconcile these opposing images into a realistic, unified, and stable parental image may psychologically fixate children in the pre-Oedipal period. As adults, then, they may retain these rapidly shifting attitudes toward their therapists and others.

Separation-individuation. According to the influential psychodynamic theorist Margaret Mahler, young children undergo a process of separation-individuation by which they learn to differentiate their own identities from their mothers. She believed that a failure to successfully master this developmental challenge may lead to the development of a borderline personality.

Margaret Mahler Margaret Mahler, another influential modern psychodynamic theorist, explained borderline personality disorder in terms of childhood separation from the mother figure. Mahler and her colleagues (Mahler & Kaplan, 1977; Mahler, Pine, & Bergman, 1975) believed that during the first year infants develop a symbiotic attachment to their mothers. *Symbiosis,* or interdependence, is a biological term derived from Greek roots meaning "to live together." In psychology, symbiosis is a state of oneness in which the child's identity is fused with the mother's. Normally, children gradually differentiate their own identities or senses of self from their mothers. The process, *separation-individuation,* is the development of a separate psychological and biological identity from the mother (separation) and recognition of personal characteristics that define one's self-identity (individuation). Separation-individuation may be a stormy process. Children may vacillate between seeking greater independence and moving closer to, or "shadowing," the mother, which is seen as a wish for reunion. The mother may disrupt normal separation-individuation by refusing to let go of the child or by too quickly pushing the child toward independence. The tendencies of people with borderline personalities to react to others with ambivalence and to alternate between love and hate is suggestive of earlier ambivalences during the separation-individuation process. Borderline personality disorder may arise from the failure to master this developmental challenge.

Psychodynamic theory provides insights for understanding the development of several personality disorders. But a limitation of the theory is that it is based largely on inferences drawn from behavior and retrospective accounts of adults rather than on observations of children. We may also question whether it is valid to compare normal childhood experiences with abnormal behaviors in adulthood. For example, the ambivalences that characterize the adult borderline personality may bear only a superficial relationship, if any, to children's vacillations between closeness and separation during separation-individuation.

Links between abuse in childhood and later development of personality disorders suggest that failure to form close-bonding relationships with parental caretakers in childhood plays a critical role in the development of personality disorders. We will explore the links between abuse and personality disorders later in this chapter.

Learning Perspectives

Learning theorists focus on maladaptive behaviors rather than disorders of personality. They are interested in identifying the learning histories and environmental factors that give rise to maladaptive behaviors associated with diagnoses of personality disorders and the reinforcers that maintain them.

Learning theorists suggest that childhood experiences shape the pattern of maladaptive habits of relating to others that constitute personality disorders. For example, children who are regularly discouraged from speaking their minds or exploring their environments may develop a dependent behavior pattern. Excessive parental discipline may lead to obsessive–compulsive behaviors. Theodore Millon (1981) suggests that children whose behavior is rigidly controlled and punished by parents, even for slight transgressions, may develop inflexible, perfectionistic standards. As these children mature, they strive to develop themselves in an area in which they excel, such as schoolwork or athletics, as a way of avoiding parental criticism or punishment. But because of overattention to a single area of development, they do not become well rounded. Thus they squelch expressions of spontaneity and avoid risks. They may also place perfectionistic demands on themselves to avoid punishment or rebuke, or develop other behaviors associated with the obsessive-compulsive personality pattern.

Millon suggests that histrionic personality disorder may be rooted in childhood experiences in which social reinforcers, such as parental attention, are connected to the child's appearance and willingness to perform for others, especially when reinforcers are dispensed inconsistently. Inconsistent attention teaches children not to take approval for granted and to strive for it continually. People with histrionic personalities may also identify with parents who are dramatic, emotional, and attention-seeking. Extreme sibling rivalry would further heighten motivation to perform for attention from others.

Social–cognitive theories emphasize the role of reinforcement in explaining the origins of antisocial behaviors. Ullmann and Krasner (1975) proposed, for example, that people with antisocial personalities failed to learn to respond to other people as potential reinforcers. Most children learn to treat others as reinforcing agents because others reinforce them with praise for good behavior and punishment for bad. Reinforcement and punishment provide feedback that helps children modify their behavior to maximize the chances of future rewards and minimize the risks of future punishments. As a consequence, children become sensitive to the demands of powerful others, usually parents and teachers, and learn to regulate their behavior accordingly. They thus adapt to social expectations. They learn what to do and what to say, how to dress and how to act to obtain social reinforcement.

People with antisocial personalities, by contrast, may not have become socialized in this way because their early learning experiences lacked consistency and predictability. Perhaps they were sometimes rewarded for doing the "right thing," but just as often not. They may have borne the brunt of harsh physical punishments, delivered at random. As adults, they do not place much value on what other people expect, because as children, they saw no connection between their own behavior and reinforcement. Although Ullmann and Krasner's views may account for some features of antisocial personality dis-

What are the origins of antisocial personality disorder? Are youth who develop antisocial personalities largely "unsocialized" because their early learning experiences lack the consistency and predictability that help other children connect their behavior with rewards and punishments? Or are they very "socialized," but socialized to imitate the behavior of other antisocial youth? To what extent does criminal behavior or membership in gangs overlap with antisocial personality disorder?

order, they may not adequately address the development of the "charming" type of antisocial personality; people in this group are skillful at reading the social cues of others and in using them for personal advantage.

Social–cognitive theorist Albert Bandura has studied the role of observational learning in aggressive behavior, a common component of antisocial behavior. In a classic study, he and his colleagues (e.g., Bandura, Ross, & Ross, 1963) showed that children acquire skills, including aggressive skills, by observing the behavior of others. Exposure to aggression may come from watching violent television programs or observing parents who behave violently. Bandura does not believe children and adults display aggressive behaviors in a mechanical way, however. Rather, people usually do not imitate aggressive behavior unless they are provoked and believe they are more likely to be rewarded than punished for it. Children are most likely to imitate violent role models who get their way with others by acting aggressively. Children may also acquire antisocial behaviors such as cheating, bullying, or lying by direct reinforcement if they find that those behaviors help them avoid blame or manipulate others.

Social–cognitive psychologists have also shown that the ways in which people with personality disorders interpret their social experiences influence their behavior. Evidence shows that antisocial (psychopathic) individuals tend to have difficulty "reading" emotions in other people's faces (Kosson et al., 2002) and even in certain vocal expressions, especially vocal expressions of fear (Blair et al., 2002). Antisocial adolescents also tend to have hostile cognitive biases—they incorrectly interpret other people's behavior as threatening (Dodge et al., 2002). Often, perhaps because of their family and community experiences, they presume that others intend them ill when they do not. A method of therapy called *problem-solving therapy* helps aggressive, antisocial children and adolescents reconceptualize conflict situations as problems to be solved rather than as threats to be responded to aggressively (Kazdin & Whitley, 2003). Children learn to generate nonviolent solutions to social confrontations and, like scientists, test the most promising ones. In the section on biological perspectives we also see that the antisocial personality's failure to profit from punishment is connected with a cognitive factor: the *meaning* of the aversive stimulus.

All in all, learning approaches to personality disorders, like the psychodynamic approaches, have their limitations. They are grounded in theory rather than in observations of family interactions that presage the development of personality disorders. Research is needed to determine whether childhood experiences proposed by psychodynamic and learning theorists actually lead to the development of particular personality disorders as hypothesized.

Family Perspectives

Many theorists have argued that disturbances in family relationships underlie the development of personality disorders. Consistent with psychodynamic formulations, researchers find that people with borderline personality disorder (BPD) *remember* their parents as having been more controlling and less caring than do reference subjects with other psychological disorders (Zweig-Frank & Paris, 1991). When people with BPD recall their earliest memories, they are more likely than other people to paint significant others as malevolent or evil. They portray their parents and others close to them as likely to injure them or fail to protect them (Nigg et al., 1992).

A number of researchers link childhood physical or sexual abuse or neglect to the development of personality disorders, including BPD (e.g., Golier et al., 2003; McLean & Gallop, 2003; Trull, 2001; Wilkinson-Ryan & Westen, 2000). Perhaps the "splitting" observed in people with the disorder is a function of having learned to cope with unpredictable and harsh behavior from parental figures or other caregivers.

Again consistent with psychodynamic theory, family factors such as parental overprotection and authoritarianism (a "do what I said because I said so" style of parenting) are implicated in the development of dependent personality traits (Bornstein, 1992).

Extreme fears of abandonment may also be involved, perhaps resulting from a failure to develop secure bonds with parental attachment figures in childhood due to parental neglect, rejection, or death. Subsequently, these individuals develop a chronic fear of abandonment by significant others, leading to the clinginess that typifies dependent personality disorder. Theorists also suggest that obsessive–compulsive personality disorder may emerge within a strongly moralistic and rigid family environment, which does not permit even minor deviations from expected roles or behavior (e.g., Oldham, 1994).

As with BPD, researchers find that childhood abuse or neglect is a risk factor in the development of antisocial personality disorder (APD) in adulthood (Luntz & Widom, 1994). In a view that straddles the psychodynamic and learning theories, the McCords (McCord & McCord, 1964) focus on the role of parental rejection or neglect in the development of APD. They suggest that children normally learn to associate parental approval with conformity to parental practices and values and disapproval with disobedience. When tempted to transgress, children feel anxious about losing parental love. Anxiety signals the child to inhibit antisocial behavior. Eventually, the child identifies with parents and internalizes these social controls in the form of a conscience. When parents do not show love for their children, this identification does not occur. Children do not fear loss of love, because they have never had it. The anxiety that might have served to restrain antisocial and criminal behavior is absent.

Children who are rejected or neglected by their parents may not develop warm feelings of attachment to others. They may lack the ability to empathize with the feelings and needs of others, developing instead an attitude of indifference. Or perhaps they retain a wish to develop loving relationships but lack the ability to experience genuine feelings.

Although family factors may be implicated in some cases of antisocial personality disorder, many neglected children do not later show antisocial or other abnormal behaviors. We are left to develop other explanations to predict which deprived children will develop antisocial personalities or other abnormal behaviors, and which will not.

Biological Perspectives

Little is known about biological factors in most personality disorders. Although many theorists see personality disorders as the expression of maladaptive personality traits, the biological components of such traits remain unknown. Much of the work in this area has focused on antisocial personality disorder, which is also the focus of much of our discussion.

Genetic Factors   Evidence suggests a role for genetic factors in the development of personality disorders. For example, we know that first-degree biological relatives (parents and

A CLOSER LOOK
"In Cold Blood": Peering into the Minds of Psychopathic Murderers

The popular image we hold of the psychopathic murderer is of a "cold-blooded" killer, someone motivated by external goals in carrying out calculating, premeditated murder. But is this image supported by hard evidence?

Canadian researchers compared homicides committed by psychopathic offenders with those committed by nonpsychopathic offenders in a sample of 125 incarcerated murderers (Woodworth & Porter, 2002). They expected that the homicides committed by the psychopathic offenders would fit the profile of a cold-blooded killing, whereas those committed by nonpsychopathic offenders would be "crimes of passion" (impulsive, "hot-headed," angry reactions to provocative situations). The sample was drawn from two Canadian federal institutions, one in British Columbia and the other in Nova Scotia. The investigators administered a widely used and well-validated measure of psychopathy to classifying offenders as psychopathic. The results supported the hypothesis that psychopathic offenders were more likely to have committed cold-blooded homicides—intentional acts motivated by such goals as obtain-

ing drugs, money, sex or revenge without any emotional triggering situation. More than 90% (93%) of the homicides committed by the psychopathic offenders fit this profile, as compared to 48% of the murders committed by nonpsychopathic offenders.

Interestingly, the image of the "cold-blooded" psychopathic killer does not square with the long-recognized belief that psychopathic personalities often engage in impulsive, acting-out behavior. The investigators suggest that psychopathic offenders may engage in *selective impulsivity* by constraining their impulses to perform such an extreme act as murder. With such high stakes involved (e.g., lifetime incarceration if convicted), the psychopathic offender may adopt a more calculated role when carrying out these acts.

However chilling the results of this study, they help us better understand the psychological aspects of homicide. In that respect, they may help homicide investigators narrow the scope of their investigations by focusing on personality profiles of offenders who are likely to commit particular types of crimes. ■

siblings) of people with certain personality disorders, especially antisocial, schizotypal, and borderline types, are more likely to be diagnosed with these disorders than are members of the general population (APA, 2000; Battaglia et al., 1995; Nigg & Goldsmith, 1994).

Studies of familial transmission are limited because family members share common environments as well as genes. Hence researchers have turned to twin and adoption studies to tease out genetic and environmental effects. Evidence from these studies supports a genetic contribution to antisocial behavior (Rhee & Waldman, 2002) and narcissism (Livesley et al., 1993). Bear in mind that these studies drew on twins and adoptees from the general population, not people with diagnosed personality disorders. Therefore, the results may not be generalizable to people with diagnosable disorders. Still, the findings suggest that genetics plays a role in the development of antisocial and narcissistic patterns of behavior that are associated with personality disorders. That said, environmental factors also play a contributing role in the development of personality disorders (Krueger et al., 2002). For example, people may be more vulnerable to developing personality disorders if they encounter certain environmental influences, such as being reared in a dysfunctional family. Investigators also find that a variant on a particular gene is associated with antisocial behavior in adult men, but only in those who were maltreated in childhood (Caspi et al, 2002). Here again, we see that the development of antisocial personality disorder, like many other abnormal behavior patterns, represents an interaction of genetic factors and life experiences.

Lack of Emotional Responsiveness According to a leading theorist, Hervey Cleckley (1976), people with antisocial personalities can maintain their composure in stressful situations that would induce anxiety in most people. Lack of anxiety in response to threatening situations may help explain the failure of punishment to induce antisocial people to relinquish antisocial behavior. For most of us, the fear of getting caught and being punished is sufficient to inhibit antisocial impulses. People with antisocial personalities, however, often fail to inhibit behavior that has led to punishment in the past (Arnett, Smith, & Newman, 1997), perhaps because they experience little if any fear or anticipatory anxiety about being caught and punished.

When people get anxious, their palms tend to sweat. This skin response, called the *galvanic skin response* (GSR), is a sign of activation of the sympathetic branch of the autonomic nervous system (ANS). In an early study, Hare (1965) showed that people with antisocial personalities had lower GSR levels when they were expecting painful stimuli than did normal controls. Apparently, the people with antisocial personalities experienced little anxiety in anticipation of impending pain.

Hare's findings of a weaker GSR response in people with antisocial personalities has been replicated a number of times (e.g., Arnett, 1997; Patrick, Cuthbert, & Lang, 1994). Other research generally supports the view that people with antisocial personalities are generally less aroused than others, both at times of rest and in stressful situations (Fowles, 1993). This lack of emotional responsivity may help explain why the threat of punishment seems to have so little effect on deterring their antisocial behavior. It is conceivable that the autonomic nervous system (ANS) of people with antisocial personalities is underresponsive to threatening stimuli.

The Craving-for-Stimulation Model Other investigators have attempted to explain the antisocial personality's lack of emotional response in terms of the levels of stimulation necessary to maintain an optimum level of arousal. Your optimum level of arousal is the degree of arousal at which you feel best and function most efficiently.

People with antisocial or psychopathic personalities appear to have exaggerated cravings for stimulation (Arnett et al., 1997). Perhaps they require a higher-than-normal threshold of stimulation to maintain an optimum state of arousal. In other words, they may need more stimulation than other people to maintain interest and function normally.

A need for higher levels of stimulation may explain why people with antisocial personality traits tend to become bored easily and gravitate to stimulating but potentially dangerous activities, like the use of intoxicants such as drugs or alcohol, motorcycling, skydiving, high-stakes gambling, or sexual adventures. A higher-than-normal thresh-

TRUTH or FICTION? *REVISITED*

People with antisocial personalities tend to remain unduly calm in the face of impending pain.

☑ **TRUE.** People with antisocial personalities tend to show little anxiety in anticipation of impending pain. This lack of emotional responsivity may help explain why the threat of punishment seems to have so little effect on deterring their antisocial behavior.

old for stimulation would not directly cause antisocial or criminal behavior; after all, astronauts, soldiers, police officers, and firefighters must also exhibit this trait to some respect. However, the threat of boredom and inability to tolerate monotony may influence some sensation seekers to drift into crime or reckless behavior (R. J. Smith, 1978).

Brain Abnormalities Studies utilizing sophisticated brain-imaging techniques link antisocial personality disorder to abnormalities in the prefrontal cortex of the frontal lobes (Damasio, 2000; Raine et al., 2000). The prefrontal cortex is the part of the brain responsible for inhibiting impulsive behavior, weighing the consequences of our actions, solving problems, and planning for the future (Angier, 2000a; Duncan et al., 2000). Brain abnormalities could help account for many features of antisocial personality disorder, including lack of conscience, failure to inhibit impulsive behavior, low arousal states, poor problem-solving efforts, and failure to think about the consequences of one's behavior (Raine et al., 2000). Nevertheless, we do not know how many people with APD have underlying brain abnormalities.

Sociocultural Perspectives

Social conditions may contribute to the development of personality disorders. Because antisocial personality disorder is reported most frequently among people from lower socioeconomic classes, the kinds of stressors encountered by disadvantaged families may contribute to antisocial behavior patterns. Many inner-city neighborhoods are beset by social problems such as alcohol and drug abuse, teenage pregnancy, and disorganized and disintegrating families. These stressors are associated with an increased likelihood of child abuse and neglect, which may in turn contribute to lower self-esteem and breed feelings of anger and resentment in children. Neglect and abuse may become translated into the lack of empathy and a callous disregard for the welfare of others that are associated with antisocial personalities.

Children reared in poverty are also more likely to be exposed to deviant role models, such as neighborhood drug dealers. Maladjustment in school may lead to alienation and frustration with the larger society, leading to antisocial behavior (Siegel, 1992). Addressing the problem of antisocial personality may thus require attempts at a societal level to redress social injustice and improve social conditions.

Little information is available about the rates of personality disorders in other cultures. One initiative in this direction involved a joint program sponsored by the World Health Organization (WHO) and the U.S. Alcohol, Drug Abuse, and Mental Health Administration (ADAMHA). The goal of the program was to develop and standardize diagnostic instruments that could be used to arrive at psychiatric diagnoses worldwide. One result of this effort was the development of the International Personality Disorder Examination (IPDE), a semistructured interview protocol for diagnosing personality disorders (Loranger et al., 1994). The IPDE was pilot-tested by psychiatrists and clinical psychologists in 11 countries (India, Switzerland, the Netherlands, Great Britain, Luxembourg, Germany, Kenya, Norway, Japan, Austria, and the United States). The interview protocol diagnoses personality disorders reasonably reliably among the different languages and cultures that were sampled. Although more research is needed to determine the rates of particular personality disorders in other countries, investigators found the borderline and avoidant types to be the most frequently diagnosed. Perhaps the characteristics associated with these personality disorders reflect some dimensions of personality disturbance that are common throughout the world.

Tying It Together

Throughout the text we've endorsed the value of a multifactorial model of abnormal behavior, the view that psychological disorders result from a complex web of psychological, sociocultural, and biological factors. Our understanding of per-

A high need for sensation-seeking? The actor Jason Priestly, whose interests in thrill-seeking extended to motorcycles, racing boats, and bungee jumping, nearly died when the racing car he was driving at 186 miles an hour crashed into a wall of race track. Priestly reported that he had suffered 14 concussions in his life. Looking back at the accident, he admitted to an interviewer that he was never the brightest bulb in the bunch.

sonality disorders is no exception. A history of childhood abuse, neglectful or punitive parents, and learning experiences that bred fear of social interactions rather than self-confidence underlie the development of personality disorders. Social–cognitive factors, such as the effects of modeling aggressive behavior and cognitive biases that predispose people to misconstrue other people's behavior as threatening, also influence the development of maladaptive ways of relating to others that become identified with personality disorders. Evidence also suggests a genetic contribution to several types of personality disorders, including antisocial, schizotypal, and borderline types. Other biological factors implicated in antisocial personality disorder include a lack of emotional responsiveness to threatening cues, excessive need for stimulation, and underlying brain abnormalities. Sociocultural factors, such as social stressors associated with poverty and living in a disintegrating, crime-ridden neighborhood, are linked to a greater likelihood of child abuse and neglect, which in turn sets the stage for lingering resentments and lack of empathy for others that typify the antisocial personality.

How are these factors linked together? Typically, we find common themes in the development of specific personality disorders, such as harsh or punitive parenting in the case of antisocial personality. However, we need to allow for different combinations of factors and causal pathways to come into play. For example, some people with antisocial personality disorder were raised in economically deprived conditions and lacked consistent parenting. Others were raised in middle-class families but experienced neglectful or harsh parenting. Clinicians need to evaluate how each person's developmental history may have shaped his or her way of relating to others.

Figure 13.2 illustrates a potential causal pathway. Poor models and harsh or neglectful parenting contribute to poor socialization. In young people with predisposing cognitive or biological factors, poor socialization may lead to the development of callous, impulsive, and criminal or aggressive behaviors associated with a pattern of antisocial behavior.

QUESTIONNAIRE
The Sensation-Seeking Scale

Do you crave stimulation or seek sensation? Are you satisfied by reading or in watching television, or must you ride the big wave or bounce your motorbike over desert dunes? Zuckerman (1980) finds four factors related to sensation seeking: (a) pursuit of thrill and adventure, (b) *disinhibition* (that is, tendency to express impulses), (c) pursuit of experience, and (d) susceptibility to boredom. Although some sensation seekers use drugs or have trouble with the law, many are law abiding and limit their sensation seeking to sanctioned activities. Thus sensation seeking should not be interpreted as criminal or antisocial in itself.

Zuckerman developed several sensation-seeking scales that assess the levels of stimulation people seek to feel at their best and function efficiently. A brief one follows. To assess your own sensation-seeking tendencies, pick the choice, A or B, that best depicts you. Then compare your responses to those in the key at the end of the chapter.

1. a. I would like a job that requires a lot of traveling.
   b. I would prefer a job in one location.
2. a. I am invigorated by a brisk, cold day.
   b. I can't wait to get indoors on a cold day.
3. a. I get bored seeing the same old faces.
   b. I like the comfortable familiarity of everyday friends.
4. a. I would prefer living in an ideal society in which everyone is safe, secure, and happy.
   b. I would have preferred living in the unsettled days of our history.
5. a. I sometimes like to do things that are a little frightening.
   b. A sensible person avoids activities that are dangerous.
6. a. I would not like to be hypnotized.
   b. I would like to have the experience of being hypnotized.
7. a. The most important goal in life is to live it to the fullest and experience as much as possible.
   b. The most important goal in life is to find peace and happiness.
8. a. I would like to try parachute jumping.
   b. I would never want to try jumping out of a plane, with or without a parachute.
9. a. I enter cold water gradually, giving myself time to get used to it.
   b. I like to dive or jump right into the ocean or a cold pool.
10. a. When I go on a vacation, I prefer the change of camping out.
    b. When I go on a vacation, I prefer the comfort of a good room and bed.
11. a. I prefer people who are emotionally expressive even if they are a bit unstable.
    b. I prefer people who are calm and even-tempered.
12. a. A good painting should shock or jolt the senses.
    b. A good painting should give one a feeling of peace and security.
13. a. People who ride motorcycles must have some kind of unconscious need to hurt themselves.
    b. I would like to drive or ride a motorcycle.

Source: From Zuckerman, M. Sensation seeking. In H. London & J. Exner (Eds.), Dimensions of personality. *New York: John Wiley & Sons. Copyright © 1980 by John Wiley & Sons. This material is used by permission of John Wiley & Sons, Inc.*

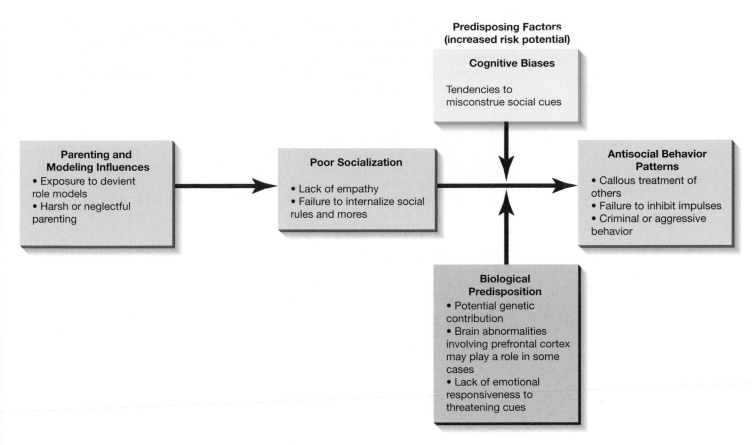

FIGURE 13.2 A multifactorial model of antisocial personality disorder.

TREATMENT OF PERSONALITY DISORDERS

We began the chapter with a quote from the eminent psychologist William James, who suggested that people's personalities seem to be "set in plaster" by a certain age. James's view is applicable to many people with personality disorders, who are typically highly resistant to change.

People with personality disorders usually see their behaviors, even maladaptive, self-defeating behaviors, as natural parts of themselves. Even when unhappy and distressed, they are unlikely to perceive their own behavior as causative. Like Marcella, whom we described as showing features of a histrionic personality disorder, they may condemn others for their problems and believe others, not they, need to change. Thus they usually do not seek help on their own. Or they begrudgingly acquiesce to treatment at the urging of others but drop out or fail to cooperate with the therapist. Even if they go for help, they commonly feel overwhelmed by anxiety or depression and terminate treatment as soon as they find some relief, rather than probe more deeply for the underlying causes of their problems. People with personality disorders also tend to respond poorly to treatment of other problems, like depression, perhaps because of the negative influence of their maladaptive behavioral patterns (Shea, Widiger, & Klein, 1992). Despite these obstacles, evidence supports the effectiveness of both psychodynamic therapy and cognitive behavior therapy in treating personality disorders (Leichsenring & Leibing, 2003; Salekin, 2002).

Psychodynamic Approaches

Psychodynamic approaches are often used to help people diagnosed with personality disorders become aware of the roots of their self-defeating behavior patterns and learn more adaptive ways of relating to others. However, people with personality disorders, especially those with borderline and narcissistic personality disorders, often present particular challenges to the therapist. For example, people with borderline personality disorder have turbulent relationships with therapists, sometimes idealizing them, sometimes denouncing them as uncaring.

Promising results have been reported using psychodynamically oriented therapies in treating personality disorders (Bateman & Fonagy, 2001; Perry & Bond, 2000; Svartberg, Stiles, & Seltzer, 2004). One example involves a brief, structured form of psychodynamic therapy pioneered at New York's Beth Israel Medical Center (Winston et al., 1991). There, a relatively brief form of therapy—an average of 40 weeks of treatment—resulted in significant improvement both in symptom complaints and the social adjustment of people with personality disorders (Winston et al., 1994). The treatment emphasized interpersonal behavior and used a more active, confrontational style in addressing the client's defenses than is the case in traditional psychoanalysis.

Behavioral Approaches

Behavior therapists see their task as changing clients' behaviors rather than their personality structures. Many behavioral theorists do not think in terms of clients' "personalities" at all, but rather in terms of acquired maladaptive behaviors that are maintained by reinforcement contingencies. Behavior therapists therefore focus on attempting to replace maladaptive behaviors with adaptive behaviors through techniques such as extinction, modeling, and reinforcement. If clients are taught behaviors that are likely to be reinforced by other people, the new behaviors may well be maintained.

Despite difficulties in treating borderline personality disorder (BPD), two groups of therapists headed by Aaron Beck (e.g., Beck et al, 2003) and Marsha Linehan (Koerner & Linehan, 2002; Linehan, 1993) report promising results using cognitive–behavioral techniques. Beck's approach focuses on helping the individual correct cognitive distortions that underlie tendencies to see oneself and others as either all good or all bad. Linehan's technique, called *dialectical behavior therapy* (DBT), is a form of cognitive–behavioral and supportive therapy techniques specifically designed for treating people with borderline personality disorder. Behavioral techniques are used to help clients develop more effective social skills and problem-solving skills, which can help improve their relationships with others and their ability to cope with negative events. Because people with BPD tend to be overly sensitive to even the slightest cues of rejection, therapists provide continuing acceptance and support, even when clients become manipulative or overly demanding. Although early results are promising, more research is needed to support the efficacy of dialectical behavior therapy in treating this challenging disorder (Scheel, 2000; Turner, 2000).

Some antisocial adolescents have been placed, often by court order, in residential and foster-care programs that contain numerous behavioral treatment components. These programs have concrete rules and clear rewards for obeying them. At Achievement Place, for example, which was founded in Kansas in the 1960s and has been reproduced elsewhere, prosocial behaviors such as completing homework are systematically reinforced; antisocial behaviors, such as using profanity, are extinguished (Kirigin & Wolf, 1998). Some residential programs rely on *token economies,* in which prosocial behaviors are rewarded with tokens such as plastic chips that can be exchanged for privileges. Although participants in such programs often show improved behavior, it remains unclear whether such programs reduce the risk that adolescent antisocial behavior will continue into adulthood.

Biological Approaches

Drug therapy does not directly treat personality disorders. Antidepressants or antianxiety drugs are sometimes used to treat associated depression or anxiety, especially in people with borderline personality disorder (Rinne et al., 2002; Sansone, Rytwinski, & Gaither, 2003). Antidepressants of the SSRI class (e.g., Prozac) may also help temper anger and rage in people with borderline personality disorder and help them control anger and impulsive and aggressive behaviors, including self-mutilation (Rivas-Vazquez & Blais, 2002). Researchers suspect that impulsive and aggressive behavior may be related to serotonin deficiencies. Prozac and similar drugs increase the availability of serotonin in the synap-

TRUTH or FICTION? *REVISITED*

Personality disorders can be successfully treated with psychiatric drugs.

☑ **FALSE.** Drugs can be used to relieve anxiety or depression associated with some personality disorders, but they do not change the underlying maladaptive and inflexible patterns of behavior that typify these disorders.

Overview of Personality Disorders

TYPES OF PERSONALITY DISORDERS/PREVALENCE RATES (approx., in parentheses)
Personality Disorders Characterized by Odd or Eccentric Behavior

Paranoid Personality Disorder (0.5%–2.5%)	• Pervasive suspiciousness of the motives of others but without outright paranoid delusions
Schizoid Personality Disorder (unknown)	• Social aloofness and shallow or blunted emotions
Schizotypal Personality Disorder (3%)	• Persistent difficulty forming close social relationships and odd or peculiar beliefs and behaviors without clear psychotic features

Personality Disorders Characterized by Dramatic, Emotional, or Erratic Behavior

Antisocial Personality Disorder (3%–6% in men, 1% in women)	• Chronic antisocial behavior, callous treatment of others, irresponsible behavior, and lack of remorse for wrongdoing
Borderline Personality Disorder (2%)	• Tumultuous moods and stormy relationships with others, unstable self-image, and lack of impulse control
Histrionic Personality Disorder (est. 2%–3%)	• Overly dramatic and emotional behavior; demands to be the center of attention; excessive needs for reassurance, praise, and approval
Narcissistic Personality Disorder (under 1%)	• Grandiose sense of self; extreme needs for admiration

Personality Disorders Characterized by Anxious or Fearful Behavior

Avoidant Personality Disorder (0.5%–1%)	• Chronic pattern of avoiding social relationships due to fears of rejection
Dependent Personality Disorder (unknown)	• Excessive dependence on others and difficulty making independent decisions
Obsessive–Compulsive Personality Disorder (1%)	• Excessive needs for orderliness and perfectionism, excessive attention to detail, rigid ways of relating to others

THEORETICAL PERSPECTIVES

Psychodynamic Perspectives	• To Kohut, the failure to replace childhood narcissism with more realistic appraisals of self and others underlies the development of narcissistic personality • To Kernberg, the failure in early childhood to develop a cohesive sense of self and others leads to the development of borderline personality • To Mahler, the failure to master the developmental challenge of separation-individuation early in life underlies the development of borderline personality
Learning Perspectives	• Behavioral features of personality disorders relate to learning experiences in childhood, including observational learning of deviant or aggressive behavior • Lack of opportunity in childhood to learn explorative or independent behaviors may lead to dependent personality traits • Excessive parental discipline or overcontrol may lead to obsessive–compulsive personality traits • Inconsistent attention and reinforcement for attention-getting behaviors may lead to histrionic personality traits • Lack of predictable and consistent reinforcement for socially approved behavior may lead to antisocial personality traits
Family Perspectives	• For antisocial personality disorder, parental rejection or neglect may lead to a failure to internalize parental values and failure to develop empathy • Parental overprotection and authoritarianism may lead to the development of dependent personality traits
Sociocultural Perspectives	• Social or economic disadvantage and exposure to deviant role models may lead to the failure to develop properly socialized behaviors • Physical or sexual abuse may underlie the development of borderline personality traits
Biological Perspectives	• Genetic influences on personality traits underlying certain personality disorders • For antisocial personality disorder, possible lack of emotional responsiveness in threatening situations • For antisocial personality disorder, possible needs for higher levels of stimulation to maintain optimum levels of arousal • For antisocial personality disorder, abnormalities in brain centers controlling impulsive behavior

TREATMENT APPROACHES
Despite difficulties working therapeutically with individuals with personality disorders, promising results are emerging based on psychodynamic and cognitive–behavioral approaches

Drug Therapy	• Antidepressants or antianxiety drugs may be used to control symptoms but do not alter underlying patterns of behavior
Cognitive–Behavioral Therapy	• To help foster more adaptive behavior, to develop more effective social skills and problem-solving skills, and to replace faulty thinking with rational alternatives
Psychodynamic Therapy	• To help people understand the childhood roots of their problems and learn more effective ways of relating to others

Sources for prevalence rates: APA, 2000; Kessler et al., 1994.

tic connections in the brain. However, drugs do not target long-standing patterns of maladaptive behavior that are the defining features of personality disorders.

Much remains to be learned about working with people who have personality disorders. The major challenges involve recruiting people who do not see themselves as being disordered into treatment and prompting them to develop insight into their self-defeating or injurious behaviors. Current efforts to help such people are too often reminiscent of the old couplet:

> He that complies against his will,
> Is of his own opinion still.

—Samuel Butler, *Hudibras*

SUMMING UP

Types of Personality Disorders

What are personality disorders? Personality disorders are maladaptive or rigid behavior patterns or personality traits associated with states of personal distress that impair the person's ability to function in social or occupational roles. People with personality disorders do not generally recognize a need to change themselves.

What are the classes of personality disorders within the DSM system? The *DSM* classifies personality disorders on Axis II and categorizes them according to the following clusters of characteristics: odd or eccentric behavior; dramatic, emotional, or erratic behavior; or anxious or fearful behavior.

What are the features of personality disorders characterized by odd or eccentric behavior? People with paranoid personality disorder are unduly suspicious and mistrustful of others, to the point that their relationships suffer. But they do not hold the more flagrant paranoid delusions typical of schizophrenia. Schizoid personality disorder describes people who have little if any interest in social relationships, show a restricted range of emotional expression, and appear distant and aloof. People with schizotypal personalities appear odd or eccentric in their thoughts, mannerisms, and behavior, but not to the degree found in schizophrenia.

What are the features of personality disorders characterized by dramatic, emotional, or erratic behavior? Antisocial personality disorder describes people who persistently engage in behavior that violates social norms and the rights of others and who tend to show no remorse for their misdeeds. Borderline personality disorder is defined in terms of instability in self-image, relationships, and mood. People with borderline personality disorder often engage in impulsive acts, which are frequently self-destructive. People with histrionic personality disorder tend to be highly dramatic and emotional in their behavior, whereas people diagnosed with narcissistic personality disorder have an inflated or grandiose sense of self, and like those with histrionic personalities, they demand to be the center of attention.

What are the features of personality disorders characterized by anxious or fearful behavior? Avoidant personality disorder describes people who are so terrified of rejection and criticism that they are generally unwilling to enter relationships without unusually strong reassurances of acceptance. People with dependent personality disorder are overly dependent on others and have extreme difficulty acting independently or making even the smallest decisions on their own. People with obsessive–compulsive personality disorder have various traits such as orderliness, perfectionism, rigidity, and overattention to detail, but are without the true obsessions and compulsions associated with obsessive–compulsive (anxiety) disorder.

What are some problems associated with the classification of personality disorders? Various controversies and problems attend the classification of personality disorders, including lack of demonstrated reliability and validity, too much overlap among the categories, difficulty in distinguishing between variations in normal behavior and abnormal behavior, confusion of labels with explanations, and possible underlying sexist biases.

Theoretical Perspectives

How do traditional Freudian concepts of disturbed personality development compare with more recent psychodynamic approaches? Earlier Freudian theory focused on unresolved Oedipal conflicts in explaining normal and abnormal personality development. More recent psychodynamic theorists have focused on the pre-Oedipal period in explaining the development of such personality disorders as narcissistic and borderline personality.

How do learning theorists view personality disorders? Learning theorists view personality disorders in terms of maladaptive patterns of behavior rather than personality traits. Learning theorists seek to identify the early learning experiences and present reinforcement patterns that explain the development and maintenance of personality disorders.

What is the role of family relationships in personality disorders? Many theorists argue that disturbed family relationships play formative roles in the development of personality disorders. For example, theorists have connected antisocial personality to parental rejection or neglect and parental modeling of antisocial behavior.

How do antisocial adolescents interpret social cues? Antisocial adolescents are more likely to interpret social cues as provocations or intentions of ill will. This cognitive bias may lead them to be confrontational in their relationships with peers.

What roles might biological factors play in antisocial personality disorder? People with antisocial personalities may lack emotional responsiveness to physically threatening stimuli and have reduced levels of autonomic reactivity. People with antisocial personalities may also require higher levels of stimulation to maintain optimal levels of arousal.

What role do sociocultural factors play in the development of personality disorders? The effects of poverty, urban blight, and drug abuse can lead to family disorganization and disintegration, making it less likely that children will receive the nurturance and support they need to develop more socially adaptive behavior patterns. Sociocultural theorists believe that such factors may underlie the development of personality disorders, especially antisocial personality disorder.

Treatment of Personality Disorders

How do therapists approach the treatment of personality disorders? Therapists from different schools of therapy help people with personality disorders become aware of their self-defeating behavior patterns and learn more adaptive ways of relating to others. Despite difficulties in working therapeutically with people with personality disorders, promising results have emerged from the use of relatively short-term psychodynamic therapy and cognitive–behavioral treatment approaches.

KEY TERMS

personality disorders *(p. 439)*
ego syntonic *(p. 439)*
ego dystonic *(p. 439)*
paranoid personality disorder *(p. 440)*
schizoid personality disorder *(p. 441)*
schizotypal personality disorder *(p. 442)*

antisocial personality disorder *(p. 443)*
borderline personality disorder (BPD) *(p. 446)*
splitting *(p. 448)*
histrionic personality disorder *(p. 448)*
narcissistic personality disorder *(p. 449)*

avoidant personality disorder *(p. 451)*
dependent personality disorder *(p. 452)*
obsessive-compulsive personality disorder *(p. 454)*

KEY FOR SENSATION-SEEKING SCALE

Because this is an abbreviated version of a questionnaire, no norms are applicable. However, answers that agree with the following key are suggestive of sensation seeking:

1. A
2. A
3. A
4. B
5. A

6. B
7. A
8. A
9. B
10. A
11. A
12. A
13. B

WEB TOOLS

The companion website offers tools to enrich your learning experience and help you succeed in class. Go to www.prenhall.com/nevid for the gateway to the following resources:

- **VIDEO** links to connect to the video case files on the companion CD-ROM. VIDEO icons in the margins of the chapter highlight the case examples included in the CD-ROM. You can also access the CD-ROM directly if you do not have a Web connection.

- **QUIZ** links to self-scoring quizzes corresponding to each section of the chapter. The quizzes help you review your knowledge of the content in each chapter.
- **WEB** links to direct you to related sites that enhance your learning of abnormal psychology.

CHAPTER FOURTEEN

Abnormal Behavior in Childhood and Adolescence

CHAPTER OUTLINE

An autistic woman, Donna Williams, reflects on what it is like to be an autistic child. In this excerpt from her memoir *Nobody Nowhere*, she speaks about her need to keep the world out. She was about three when her parents took her to a doctor out of concern that she appeared malnourished.

"I"

"A World of My Own Creation"

My parents thought I had leukemia and took me for a blood test. The doctor took some blood from my earlobe. I cooperated. I was intrigued by a multicolored cardboard wheel the doctor had given me. I also had hearing tests because, although I mimicked everything, it appeared that I was deaf. My parents would stand behind me and make sudden loud noises without my so much as blinking in response. "The world" simply wasn't getting in . . . The more I became aware of the world around me, the more I became afraid. Other people were my enemies, and reaching out to me was their weapon, with only a few exceptions—my grandparents, my father, and my Aunty Linda . . .

Donna also recalled how, for her, people became things and things existed to offer her protection and shield her from a fear of vulnerability:

I collected scraps of colored wool and crocheted bits and would put my fingers through the holes so that I could fall asleep securely. For me, the people I liked were their things, and those things (or things like them) were my protection from the things I didn't like—other people.

The habits I adopted of keeping and manipulating these symbols were my equivalent of magic spells cast against the nasties who could invade me if I lost my cherished objects or had them taken away. My strategies were not the result of insanity or hallucination, but simply harmless imagination made potent by my overwhelming fear of vulnerability . . .

People were forever saying that I had no friends. In fact my world was full of them. They were far more magical, reliable, predictable, and real than other children, and they came with guarantees. It was a world of my own creation where I didn't need to control myself or the objects, animals, and nature, which were simply being in my presence.

—*Williams, 1992, pp. 5, 6, 9*

PSYCHOLOGICAL DISORDERS OF CHILDHOOD AND ADOLESCENCE OFTEN HAVE A special poignancy, perhaps none more than autism. These disorders affect children at ages when they have little capacity to cope. Some of these problems, such as autism and mental retardation, prevent children from fulfilling their developmental potentials. Some psychological problems in childhood and adolescents mirror those found in adults— problems such as mood disorders and anxiety disorders. In some cases, the problems are unique to childhood, such as separation anxiety; in others, such as ADHD, or attention-deficit hyperactivity disorder, the problem manifests itself differently in childhood than in adulthood.

NORMAL AND ABNORMAL BEHAVIOR IN CHILDHOOD AND ADOLESCENCE

To determine what is normal and abnormal among children and adolescents, we consider, in addition to the criteria outlined in Chapter 1, the child's age and cultural background (USDHHS, 1999a). Many problems are first identified when the child enters school. They may have existed earlier but been tolerated or not seen as problems in the home. Sometimes the stress of starting school contributes to their onset. Keep in mind, however, that what is socially acceptable at one age, such as intense fear of strangers at about 9 months, may be socially unacceptable at more advanced ages. Many behavior patterns that would be considered abnormal among adults—such as intense fear of strangers and lack of bladder control—are perfectly normal for children at certain ages.

Cultural Beliefs About What Is Normal and Abnormal

Cultural beliefs help determine whether people view behavior as normal or abnormal. Because children rarely label their own behavior as abnormal, definitions of normality depend largely on how a child's behavior is filtered through the family's cultural lenses. Cultures vary with respect to the types of behaviors they classify as unacceptable as well as the threshold for labeling child behaviors as deviant.

Parents judge the unusualness of children's behavior from their own cultural perspective (Lambert et al., 1992). In one study, researchers posed the question, "When a child has psychological problems, what determines whether adults will consider the problem serious or whether they will seek professional help?" (Weisz et al., 1988, p. 601). To explore this question, researchers presented vignettes to Thai and American parents, teachers, and clinical psychologists. The vignettes depicted two children, one with problems characterized by "overcontrol" (for example, shyness and fears) and one with problems characterized by undercontrol (for example, disobedience and fighting). The Thai parents rated *both* sets of problems as less serious and worrisome than American parents (see Figure 14.1) and as more likely to improve without treatment as time passed. Such an interpretation is embedded within traditional Thai-Buddhist beliefs and values, which tolerate broad variations in children's behavior. They assume that change is inevitable and that children's behavior will eventually change for the better. Differences be-

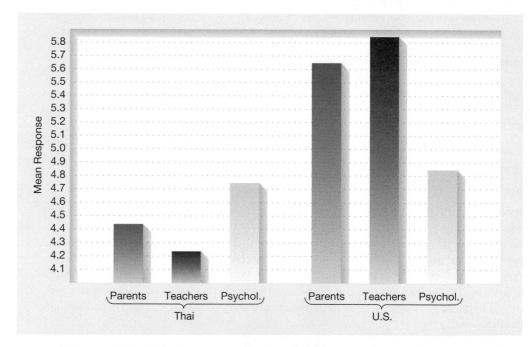

FIGURE 14.1 Ratings by Thai and U.S. parents of the seriousness of children's behavioral problems.
Researchers presented vignettes of children with problems characterized by overcontrol (for example, shyness and fears) and undercontrol (for example, disobedience and fighting) to Thai and American parents. The Thai parents rated both sets of problems as less serious and worrisome than American parents and as more likely to improve without treatment. The Thai parents apparently assume that people change and that their children's behavior will eventually change for the better.
Source: Weisz, J. R., et al., (1988). Thai and American perspectives on over- and undercontrolled child behavior problem: Exploring the threshold model among parents, teachers, and psychologists. *Journal of Consulting and Clinical Psychology, 56,* 601–609. Copyright © 2001 by the American Psychological Association. Reprinted with permission.

tween cultural groups were greater for parents and teachers than for psychologists, which suggests that professional training in a common scientific tradition might offset cultural differences.

Like definitions of abnormality, methods of treatment differ for children. Children may not have the verbal skills to express their feelings through speech or the attention span required to sit through a typical therapy session. Therapy methods must be tailored to the level of the child's cognitive, physical, social, and emotional development. For example, psychodynamic therapists have developed techniques of *play therapy* in which children enact family conflicts symbolically through their play activities, such as by play acting with dolls or puppets. Or they might be given drawing materials and asked to draw pictures, in the belief that their drawings will reflect their underlying feelings.

As with other forms of therapy (see Chapter 4), child therapy needs to be offered in a culturally sensitive framework. Therapists need to tailor their interventions to the cultural backgrounds and social and linguistic needs of children in order to establish effective therapeutic relationships.

How serious is this problem? Thai parents might judge the behavior shown by these children to be less serious than American parents would. Thai-Buddhist values tolerate broad variations in children's behavior and assume that it will change for the better.

Prevalence of Mental Health Problems in Children and Adolescents

Just how common are mental health problems among America's children and adolescents? Unfortunately, quite common.

According to a recent report from the U.S. Surgeon General, 1 in 10 children suffers from a mental disorder severe enough to impair development ("A Children's Mental Illness 'Crisis,'" 2001). Three million American teenagers have either attempted suicide or have thought seriously about taking their own lives ("Three Million Teens," 2002). A recent telephone survey based on a national probability sample of American youth ages 12 to 17 found that 7% of the boys and 14% of the girls had suffered from major depression in the 6-month period preceding the survey (Kilpatrick et al., 2003). Major depression is etimated to affect 5% of preteens (Beardslee & Goldman, 2003). Overall, more American children suffer from mental disorders than from diabetes, AIDS, and leukemia combined (Chamberlin, 2001). Yet 60% to 80% of children with mental health disorders fail to get the treatment they need (Goldberg, 2001). Children who have *internalized* problems, such as anxiety and depression, are at higher risk of going untreated than are children with *externalized* problems (problems involving acting out or aggressive behavior) that are disruptive or annoying to others.

Risk Factors for Childhood Disorders

Many factors contribute to increased risk of developmental disorders, including genetic susceptibility, environmental stressors (such as living in decaying neighborhoods), and family factors (such as inconsistent or harsh discipline, neglect, or physical or sexual abuse). Gender is yet another predictive factor. Boys are at greater risk for developing many childhood disorders, ranging from autism to hyperactivity to elimination disorders. Problems of anxiety and depression also affect boys more often than girls. In adolescence, however, anxiety and mood disorders become more common among girls and remain so throughout adulthood (USDHHS, 1999a).

Child abuse and neglect figure prominently in the developmental histories of children and adolescents with psychological disorders. (Effects of childhood sexual abuse are discussed in Chapter 11.) Physically abused or neglected children often

Play therapy. In play therapy, children may enact scenes with dolls or puppets that symbolically represent conflicts occurring within their own families.

pervasive developmental disorders (PDDs) A class of developmental disorders characterized by significantly impaired behavior or functioning in multiple areas of development.

autism A pervasive developmental disorder characterized by failure to relate to others, lack of speech, disturbed motor behaviors, intellectual impairment, and demands for sameness in the environment.

Asperger's disorder A pervasive developmental disorder characterized by social deficits and stereotyped behavior but without the significant language or cognitive delays associated with autism.

Rett's disorder A pervasive development disorder characterized by a range of physical, behavioral, motor, and cognitive abnormalities that begin after a few months of apparently normal development.

childhood disintegrative disorder A pervasive developmental disorder involving loss of previously acquired skills and abnormal functioning following a period of apparently normal development during the first 2 years of life.

have difficulty forming healthy peer relationships and healthy attachments to others. They may lack the capacity for empathy or fail to develop a sense of conscience or concern about the welfare of others. They may act out in ways that mirror the cruelty they've experienced in their lives, such as by torturing or killing animals, setting fires, or picking on smaller, more vulnerable children. Other common psychological effects of neglect and abuse include lowered self-esteem, depression, immature behaviors such as bed-wetting or thumb-sucking, suicide attempts and suicidal thinking, poor school performance, behavior problems, and failure to venture beyond the home to explore the outside world (Golden, 2000; Saywitz et al., 2000; Shonk & Cicchetti, 2001; Wolfe et al., 2001). The behavioral and emotional consequences of child abuse often extend into adulthood (Briere & Elliott, 2003).

Child abuse is hardly an isolated problem. Each year more than 1.5 million children in the United States are victims of child abuse or neglect (Gershater-Molko, Lutzker, & Sherman, 2002). More than 1,000 children in the United States die each year as the result of abuse or neglect. As horrific as these numbers are, they greatly understate the problem, as most incidents of child maltreatment are never publicly identified.

We now turn to consider the specific types of psychological disorders of childhood and adolescence. We will examine the features of these disorders, their causes, and the treatments used to help children who suffer from them.

PERVASIVE DEVELOPMENTAL DISORDERS

Children with **pervasive developmental disorders (PDDs)** show markedly impaired behavior or functioning in multiple areas of development. These disorders generally become evident in the first few years of life and are often associated with mental retardation. They were generally classified as forms of psychoses in early editions of the *DSM*. They were thought to reflect childhood forms of adult psychoses like schizophrenia because they share features such as social and emotional impairment, oddities of communication, and stereotyped motor behaviors. Research has shown that they are distinct from schizophrenia and other psychoses, however. Only very rarely in these children is there evidence of the prominent hallucinations or delusions that would justify a diagnosis of schizophrenia.

Autism (*autistic disorder*) is the major type of pervasive developmental disorder and the focus of our discussion. But first let us note some other types of pervasive developomental disorders. **Asperger's disorder,** a milder form of pervasive developmental disorder, is characterized by poor social interactions and development of narrow, obsessive or repetitive behavior (Murphy et al., 2002). The narrowing of behavior may take the form of fixations with obscure topics or interests (Corcoran, 2002). For example, one Asperger child became obsessed with vacuum cleaners (Osborne, 2002). However, in contrast to autism, Asperger's children are not impaired by significant intellectual or language deficits (APA, 2000; Szatmari et al., 2000). Other, less-common types of pervasive developmental disorder include **Rett's disorder,** a disorder reported only in females; and **childhood disintegrative disorder,** a rare condition that appears to be more common among males.

Though the rate of PDDs remains unclear, a recent community study of preschool children in England showed that 0.6% of the children (6 in 1,000) met criteria for one or another PDD, most commonly autism (Chakrabarti & Fombonne, 2001). The diagnostic features of autistic disorder are found in Table 14.1. Table 14.2 lists the diagnostic features of other types of pervasive developmental disorders.

Autism

A Case of Autism

Peter nursed eagerly, sat and walked at the expected ages. Yet some of his behavior made us vaguely uneasy. He never put anything in his mouth. Not his fingers nor his toys—nothing. . . .

More troubling was the fact that Peter didn't look at us, or smile, and wouldn't play the games that seemed as much a part of babyhood as diapers. He rarely

TABLE 14.1

Diagnostic Features of Autistic Disorder

A. Diagnosis requires a combination of features from the following groups. Not all of the features from each group need be present for a diagnosis to be made.

Impaired Social Interactions

1. Impairment in the nonverbal behaviors such as facial expressiveness, posture, gestures, and eye contact that normally regulate social interaction

2. Does not develop age-appropriate peer relationships

3. Failure to express pleasure in the happiness of other people

4. Does not show social or emotional reciprocity (give and take)

Impaired Communication

1. Delay in development of spoken language (nor is there an effort to compensate for this lack through gestures)

2. When speech development is adequate, there is nevertheless lack of ability to initiate or sustain conversation

3. Shows abnormalities in form or content of speech (e.g., stereotyped or repetitive speech, as in echolalia; idiosyncratic use of words; speaking about the self in the second or third person—using "you" or "he" to mean "I")

4. Does not show spontaneous social or imaginative (make-believe) play

Restricted, repetitive, and stereotyped behavior patterns

1. Shows restricted range of interests

2. Insists on routines (e.g., always uses same route to go from one place to another)

3. Shows stereotyped movements (e.g., hand flicking, head banging, rocking, spinning)

4. Shows preoccupation with parts of objects (e.g., repetitive spinning of wheels of toy car) or unusual attachments to objects (e.g., carrying a piece of string)

B. Onset occurs prior to the age of 3 through display of abnormal functioning in at least one of the following: social behavior, communication, or imaginative play.

Source: Adapted from the *DSM-IV-TR* (APA, 2000).

laughed, and when he did, it was at things that didn't seem funny to us. He didn't cuddle, but sat upright in my lap, even when I rocked him. But children differ and we were content to let Peter be himself. We thought it hilarious when my brother, visiting us when Peter was 8 months old, observed that "That kid has no social instincts, whatsoever." Although Peter was a first child, he was not isolated. I frequently put him in his playpen in front of the house, where the schoolchildren stopped to play with him as they passed. He ignored them, too.

It was Kitty, a personality kid, born two years later, whose responsiveness emphasized the degree of Peter's difference. When I went into her room for the late feeding, her little head bobbed up and she greeted me with a smile that reached from her head to her toes. And the realization of that difference chilled me more than the wintry bedroom.

Peter's babbling had not turned into speech by the time he was 3. His play was solitary and repetitious. He tore paper into long thin strips, bushel baskets of it every day. He spun the lids from my canning jars and became upset if we tried to divert him. Only rarely could I catch his eye, and then saw his focus change from me to the reflection in my glasses. . . .

[Peter's] adventures into our suburban neighborhood had been unhappy. He had disregarded the universal rule that sand is to be kept in sandboxes, and the

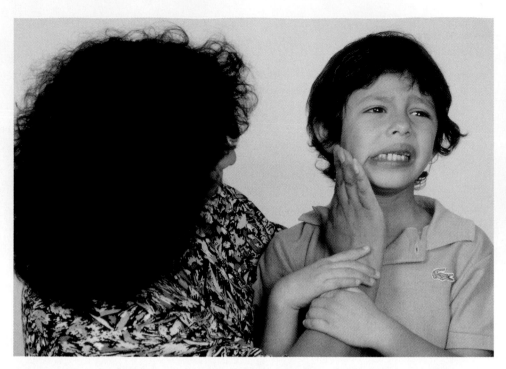

Autism. Autism, one of the most severe childhood disorders, is characterized by pervasive deficits in the ability to relate to and communicate with others and by a restricted range of activities and interests. Children with autistic disorder lack the ability to relate to others and seem to live in their own private worlds.

children themselves had punished him. He walked around a sad and solitary figure, always carrying a toy airplane, a toy he never played with. At that time, I had not heard the word that was to dominate our lives, to hover over every conversation, to sit through every meal beside us. That word was autism.

—Adapted from Eberhardy, 1967

Autism is one of the severest disorders of childhood. It is a chronic, lifelong condition. Children with autism, like Peter, seem utterly alone in the world, despite parental efforts to bridge the gulf that divides them.

The word *autism* derives from the Greek *autos,* meaning "self." The term was first used in 1906 by the Swiss psychiatrist Eugen Bleuler to refer to a peculiar style of thinking among people with schizophrenia. Autistic thinking is the tendency to view oneself as the center of the universe, to believe that external events somehow refer to oneself. In 1943, another psychiatrist, Leo Kanner, applied the diagnosis "early infantile autism" to a group of disturbed children who seemed unable to relate to others, as if they lived in their own private worlds. Unlike children suffering from mental retardation, these children seemed to shut out any input from the outside world, creating a kind of "autistic aloneness" (Kanner, 1943).

Scientists today face a baffling mystery: What accounts for the nearly 10-fold rise in reported cases of autism over the past decade (Goode, 2004a)? The causes remain unclear, though improved diagnostic practices and greater awareness of the disorder among physicians probably contributes to some of the increase. Scientists are actively investigating whether other factors, such as prenatal or childhood infections or exposure environmental toxins, play a role. Presently, no one really knows (Ault, 2004). Suspicion has also focused on possible contamination from a preservative in the widely used MMR (measles, mumps, rubella) vaccine. However, scientists have thus far failed to find any

TABLE 14.2

Diagnostic Features of Other Pervasive Developmental Disorders

Disorder	Diagnostic Features
Asperger's Disorder	• Markedly impaired social interactions (e.g., failure to maintain eye contact or to develop age-appropriate peer relationships, or failure to seek out others to share enjoyable activities or interests)
	• Development of narrow, repetitive, and stereotyped behaviors, interests, and activities (e.g., twisting hands or fingers; rigidly adhering to fixed routines or rituals that lack any clear purpose; fascination with train schedules)
	• No clinically significant delay in language or cognitive development or in development of self-help skills or adaptive behaviors apart from social interactions
Rett's Disorder	After apparently normal development during the first few months of life, the following abnormalities develop:
	• Slowing of head growth
	• Deteriorating motor skills (loss of purposeful hand skills)
	• Development of stereotyped hand movements, typically resembling hand-wringing or hand washing
	• Development of poorly coordinated gait or movement of whole body
	• Loss of social interest
	• Severe deficits in language development
	• Typically associated with profound or severe mental retardation
Childhood Disintegrative Disorder	After apparently normal development for at least the first 2 years of life:
	• Significant loss of previously acquired skills in such areas as understanding or using language, social or adaptive functioning, bowel or bladder control, play, or motor skills
	• Abnormal functioning as shown by impaired social interactions or communication, and development of narrow, stereotyped, and repetitive behaviors, interests, or activities

Source: Adapted from the DSM-IV-TR (APA, 2000).

association between autism and vaccines (Madsen et al., 2002. Dr. Fred Volkmar, an autism expert at the Yale Child Study Center, says, "hard scientific evidence to support any specific environmental cause has been lacking" (quoted in Goode, 2004b, p. A 17).

The prevalence of autism is estimated at about 30 children per 10,000 (Goode, 2004a; Yeargin-Allsopp et al., 2003). The rates are even higher, perhaps even double, if you take into account children falling within a broader autistic sprectrum of disorders, which includes Asperger's syndrome (Fombonne, 2003a, 2003b).

Autism occurs in four times as many boys as girls (Cowley, 2003). The disorder generally becomes evident in toddlers between 18 and 30 months of age (Rapin, 1997), but the average child is not diagnosed until about age 6 (Fox, 2000). Delays in diagnosis can be detrimental, as children with autism generally do better the earlier they are diagnosed and treated (Fox, 2000).

Autism seems always to have been with Peter. However, in the following case example, the disorder apparently developed between the ages of 12 and 24 months.

Children with autism are often described by their parents as having been "good babies" early in infancy. This generally means they were not demanding. As they develop, however, they begin to reject physical affection, such as cuddling, hugging, and kissing. Their speech development begins to fall behind the norm. Although Eric did quite well through his first 16 months, signs of social detachment often begin during the first year of life, such as failure to look at other people's faces. The clinical features of the disorder appear prior to 3 years of age (APA, 2000).

The Case of Eric

"People used to say to me they hoped they [would have] a baby just like mine," Sarah said of Eric, 3 years old at the time. As an infant, Eric smiled endearingly, laughed, and hugged. He uttered a dozen words by his first birthday. By 16 months he had memorized the alphabet and could read some signs. "People were very impressed," Sarah said.

Gradually, things changed, but it took months for Sarah to realize that Eric had a problem. At the age of 2, other members of Eric's play group bubbled with conversation. Eric had abandoned words completely. Instead, Eric combined letters and numbers in idiosyncratic ways, such as "B–T–2–4–6–Z–3."

Eric grew increasingly withdrawn. His diet was essentially self-limited to peanut butter and jelly sandwiches. He spent hour after hour arranging letters and numbers on a magnetic board. But the "symptom" that distressed Sarah most was impossible to measure: when she gazed into Eric's eyes, she no longer saw a "sparkle."

—Adapted from Martin, 1989

Autism:
The Case of Xavier
"He'll watch a DVD, same scene over and over and over again."

Features of Autism Perhaps the most poignant feature of autism is the child's utter aloneness (see Table 14.1). Other features include language and communication problems and ritualistic or stereotyped behavior. The child may also be mute, or if some language skills are present, they may be characterized by peculiar usage, as in *echolalia* (parroting back what the child has heard in a high-pitched monotone); pronoun reversals (using "you" or "he" instead of "I"); use of words that have meaning only to those who have intimate knowledge of the child; and tendencies to raise the voice at the end of sentences, as if asking a question. Nonverbal communication may also be impaired or absent. For example, children with autistic disorder may not engage in eye contact or display facial expressions. They are also slow to respond to adults who try to grab their attention, if they attend at all (Leekam & López, 2000). Although they may be unresponsive to others, they display strong emotions, especially strong negative emotions such as anger, sadness, and fear (Capps et al., 1993; Kasari et al., 1993).

A primary feature of autism is repeated purposeless stereotyped movements—interminably twirling, flapping the hands, or rocking back and forth with the arms around the knees. Some children with autism mutilate themselves, even as they cry out in pain. They may bang their heads, slap their faces, bite their hands and shoulders, or pull out their hair. They may also throw sudden tantrums or panics. Another feature of autism is aversion to environmental changes—a feature termed *preservation of sameness*. When familiar objects are moved even slightly from their usual places, children with autism may throw tantrums or cry continually. Like Eric, children with autistic disorder may insist on eating the same food every day.

Children with autism are bound by ritual. The teacher of a 5-year-old girl with autistic disorder learned to greet her every morning by saying, "Good morning, Lily, I am very, very glad to see you" (Diamond, Baldwin, & Diamond, 1963). Although Lily would not respond to the greeting, she would shriek if the teacher omitted even one of the *very*s.

Like Donna Williams, the woman whose childhood experiences opened this chapter, autistic children often view people as a threat. Reflecting back on his childhood, a high-functioning autistic young man speaks about his needs for sameness and for performing repetitive, stereotyped behaviors. For this young man, people were a threat because they were not always the same and were made up of pieces that didn't quite fit together:

❝I❞
"I Didn't Know What They Were For"

I loved repetition. Every time I turned on a light I knew what would happen. When I flipped the switch, the light went on. It gave me a wonderful feeling of security because it was exactly the same each time. Sometimes there were two switches on one plate, and I like those even better; I really liked wondering which light would go on from which switch. Even when I knew, it was thrilling to do it over and over. It was always the same.

People bothered me. I didn't know what they were for or what they would do to me. They were not always the same and I had no security with them at all. Even a person who was always nice to me might be different sometimes. Things didn't fit together to me with people. Even when I saw them a lot, they were still in pieces, and couldn't connect them to anything. . . .

From Barron & Barron, 2002, pp. 20–21

Autistic children appear to have failed to develop a differentiated self-concept, a sense of themselves as distinct individuals. Despite their unusual behavior, they are often quite attractive and have an "intelligent look" about them. However, as measured by scores on standardized tests, their intellectual development tends to lag below the norm. Though some autistic children have normal I.Qs, three of four of them show evidence of mental retardation (Noonan, 2003; Rapin, 1997). Even those without intellectual impairment have difficulty acquiring the ability to symbolize, such as recognizing emotions, engaging in symbolic play, and solving problems conceptually. They also display difficulty in performing tasks that require interaction with other people. The relationship between autism and intelligence is clouded, however, by difficulties in administering standardized IQ tests to these children. Testing requires cooperation, a skill that is dramatically lacking in children with autism. At best, we can only estimate their intellectual ability.

Theoretical Perspectives   The causes of autism remain unknown, but are presumed to include underlying brain abnormalities. Early, discredited views of autism viewed the child's aloofness as a reaction to parents who were cold and detached—"emotional refrigerators" who lacked the ability to establish warm relationships with their children. Research failed to support the assumption—so devastating to many parents—that they are frosty and remote (Hoffmann & Prior, 1982).

Psychologist O. Ivar Lovaas and his colleagues (1979) offered a cognitive-learning perspective on autism. They suggest that children with autism have perceptual deficits that limit them to processing only one stimulus at a time. As a result, they are slow to learn by means of classical conditioning (association of stimuli). From the learning theory perspective, children become attached to their primary caregivers through associations with primary reinforcers such as food and hugging. Autistic children, however, attend either to the food or to the cuddling and do not connect it with the parent.

Research on cognitive deficits shows that autistic children often have difficulty integrating information from various senses (e.g., Toichi et al., 2002). At times they seem unduly sensitive to stimulation. At other times they become so insensitive that an observer might wonder whether they are deaf. Perceptual and cognitive deficits seem to diminish their capacity to make use of information—to comprehend and apply social rules.

Autism:
Dr. Kathy Pratt

But what is the basis of these perceptual and cognitive deficits? The many impairments associated with autism, including mental retardation, language deficits, bizarre motor behavior, even seizures, suggest an underlying neurological basis involving brain abnormalities (Courchesne, Carper, & Akshoomoff, 2003; Herbert et al., 2002; Stokstad, 2001). Evidence from MRI and PET scan studies show abnormalities in the brains of boys and men with autistic disorder, including disturbances in the development of neural pathways in the brain and enlarged ventricles that suggest a loss of brain cells (Allen & Courchesne, 2003; Haznedar et al., 2000; Kates et al., 2004; Müller et al., 2003). Most investigators believe that the development of autism is strongly influenced by genetic factors (Goode, 2004a, 2004b).

Autism may stem from multiple causes involving more than one type of brain abnormality. Many scientists suspect that the underlying causes of brain abnormalities involve genetic factors or prenatal exposure to toxic agents or a combination of these

Establishing contact. One of the principal therapeutic tasks in working with children with autism is the establishment of interpersonal contact. Behavior therapists use reinforcers to increase adaptive social behaviors, such as paying attention to the therapist and playing with other children. Behavior therapists may also use punishments to suppress self-mutilative behavior.

mental retardation A generalized delay or impairment in the development of intellectual and adaptive abilities.

factors (O'Connor, 2001b; Stokstad, 2001; Yu et al., 2002). Scientists are searching for specific genes that increase susceptibility to autism (Auranen et al., 2002; Shao et al., 2003) Still, the underlying causes of autism remain a mystery.

Treatment Although there is no cure for autism, 30 years of research support the efficacy of intensive behavioral treatment programs that apply learning principles to improve learning and communication skills and reduce disturbed behaviors (USD-HHS, 1999a). No other treatment approach has yielded comparable results (Gill, 2001). Using operant conditioning methods, therapists and parents systematically use rewards and punishments to increase the child's ability to attend to others, to play with other children, to develop academic skills, and to eliminate self-mutilative behavior.

The most effective behavioral treatment programs are highly intensive and structured, offering a great deal of individual, one-to-one instruction (Rapin, 1997). In a classic study, psychologist O. Ivar Lovaas of UCLA demonstrated impressive gains in autistic children who received more than 40 hours of one-to-one behavior modification each week for at least 2 years (Lovaas, 1987). Unfortunately, intensive one-to-one treatment is expensive, and parents seeking these programs are often put on long waiting lists (Gross, 2004). Also, although long-term follow-ups remain to be reported, some children make great progress and others do not (Smith, 1999). Children who are better functioning at the start of treatment typically gain the most.

Biomedical treatments have been limited largely to the use of psychiatric drugs to control disruptive behavior. For example, antipsychotic drugs normally used to treat schizophrenia have been used to help control tantrums, aggression, or self-injurious behavior in autistic children (e.g., McCracken et al., 2002). But drugs have not produced consistent improvement in cognitive and language development.

Autistic traits generally continue into adulthood to one degree or another. Yet some autistic children do go on to earn college degrees and function independently (Rapin, 1997). Others need continuing treatment throughout their lives, even institutionalized care. Even the highest functioning adults with the disorder manifest deficient social and communication skills and a highly limited range of interests and activities (APA, 2000).

MENTAL RETARDATION

About 1% of the general population is affected by **mental retardation,** a broad-ranging impairment in the development of cognitive and social functioning (APA, 2000). The course of mental retardation is variable. Many children with mental retardation improve over time, especially if they receive support, guidance, and enriched educational opportunities. Those who are reared in impoverished environments may fail to improve or may deteriorate further.

Mental retardation is diagnosed by a combination of three criteria: (a) low scores on formal intelligence tests (an IQ score of approximately 70 or below); (b) impaired functioning in performing life tasks expected of someone of the same age in a given cultural setting; and (c) development of the disorder before the age of 18 (APA, 2000; Kanaya, Scullin, & Ceci, 2003; Robinson, Zigler, & Gallagher, 2001).

The *DSM* classifies mental retardation according to level of severity, as shown in Table 14.3. Most children with mental retardation (about 85%) fall into the mildly retarded range. These children are generally capable of meeting basic academic demands, such as learning to read simple passages. As adults they are generally capable of independent functioning, although they may require some guidance and support. Table 14.4 provides a description of the deficits and abilities associated with various degrees of mental retardation.

TABLE 14.3

Levels of Mental Retardation

Degree of Severity	Approximate IQ Range	Percentage of People with Mental Retardation within the Range
Mild mental retardation	50–55 to approximately 70	Approximately 85%
Moderate mental retardation	35–40 to 50–55	10
Severe mental retardation	20–25 to 35–40	3–4
Profound mental retardation	Below 20 or 25	1–2

Source: Adapted from the *DSM-IV-TR* (APA, 2000).

Causes of Mental Retardation

The causes of mental retardation include biological factors, psychosocial factors, or a combination of these factors (APA, 2000). Biological causes include chromosomal and genetic disorders, infectious diseases, and maternal alcohol use during pregnancy. Psychosocial causes include exposure to an impoverished home environment marked by the lack of intellectually stimulating activities during childhood.

Down Syndrome and Other Chromosomal Abnormalities The most frequently identified cause of mental retardation is **Down syndrome** (formerly called Down's syndrome), which is characterized by an extra chromosome on the 21st pair of chromosomes, resulting in 47 chromosomes rather than the normal complement of 46 (Wade, 2000; Yang, Rasmussen, & Friedman, 2002). Down syndrome occurs in about 1 in 800 births. It usually occurs when the 21st pair of chromosomes in either the egg or the sperm fails to divide normally, resulting in an extra chromosome. Chromosomal abnormalities become more likely as parents age, so expectant couples in their mid-30s or

Down syndrome A condition caused by the presence of an extra chromosome on the 21st pair and characterized by mental retardation and various physical anomalies.

TABLE 14.4

Levels of Retardation, Typical Ranges of IQ Scores, and Types of Adaptive Behaviors Shown

Approximate IQ Score Range	Preschool Age 0–5 Matuation and Development	School Age 6–21 Training and Education	Adult 21 and Over Social and Vocational Adequacy
Mild 50–70	Often not noticed as retarded by casual observer, but is slower to walk, feed self, and talk than most children.	Can acquire practical skills and useful reading and arithmetic to a 3rd- to 6th- grade level with special education. Can be guided toward social conformity.	Can usually achieve social and vocational skills adequate to self-maintenance; may need occasional guidance and support when under unusual social or economic stress.
Moderate 35–49	Noticeable delays in motor development, especially in speech; responds to training in various self-help activities.	Can learn simple communication, elementary health and safety habits, and simple manual skills; does not progress in functional reading or arithmetic.	Can perform simple tasks under sheltered conditions; participates in simple recreation; travels alone in familiar places; usually incapable of self-maintenance.
Severe 20–34	Marked delay in motor development; little or no communication skill; may respond to training in elementary self-help—e.g., self-feeding.	Usually walks, barring specific disability; has some understanding of speech and some response; can profit from systematic habit training.	Can conform to daily routines and repetitive activities; needs continuing direction and supervision in protective environment.
Profound Below 20	Gross retardation; minimal capacity for functioning in sensorimotor areas; needs nursing care.	Obvious delays in all areas of development; shows basic emotional responses; may respond to skillful training in use of legs, hands, and jaws; needs close supervision.	May walk, may need nursing care, may have primitive speech; will usually benefit from regular physical activity; incapable of self-maintenance.

Source: From *Essentials of Psychology* (Sixth Edition) by S.A. Rathus (1996). Copyright © 2001. Reprinted with permission of Brooks/Cole, an imprint of the Wadsworth Group, a division of Thomson Learning. FAX 800-730-2215.

Striving to achieve. Most children with Down syndrome can learn basic academic skills if they are afforded opportunities to learn and are provided with the right encouragement.

fragile X syndrome An inherited form of mental retardation caused by a mutated gene on the X chromosome.

older often undergo prenatal genetic tests to detect Down syndrome and other genetic abnormalities. Down syndrome can be traced to a defect in the mother's chromosomes in about 95% of cases (Antonarakas et al., 1991), with the remainder attributable to defects in the father's sperm.

People with Down syndrome are recognizable by distinctive physical features: a round face, broad, flat nose, and small, downward-sloping folds of skin at the inside corners of the eyes that gives the impression of slanted eyes. A protruding tongue, small, squarish hands and short fingers, a curved fifth finger, and disproportionately small arms and legs in relation to their bodies also characterize children with Down syndrome. Nearly all of these children have mental retardation, and many suffer from physical problems, such as malformations of the heart and respiratory difficulties. Sadly, the average age of death of Down syndrome patients is only 49 years (Yang, Rasmussen, & Friedman, 2002). In their later years, people with Down syndrome tend to suffer memory losses and experience childish emotions that represent a form of senility.

Children with Down syndrome suffer various deficits in learning and development. They tend to be uncoordinated and to lack proper muscle tone, which makes it difficult for them to carry out physical tasks and play like other children. Down syndrome children suffer memory deficits, especially for information presented verbally, which makes it difficult for them to learn in school. They also have difficulty following instructions from teachers and expressing their thoughts or needs clearly in speech. Despite their disabilities, most can learn to read, write, and perform simple arithmetic, if they receive appropriate schooling and encouragement.

Although less common than Down syndrome, chromosomal abnormalities on the sex chromosome may also result in mental retardation, such as in Klinefelter's syndrome and Turner's syndrome. *Klinefelter's syndrome,* which only occurs among males, is characterized by the presence of an extra X chromosome, resulting in an XXY chromosomal pattern rather than the normal XY pattern. Estimates of the prevalence of Klinefelter's syndrome range from 1 in 500 to 1 in 1,000 male births (Brody, 1993). These men fail to develop appropriate secondary sex characteristics, resulting in small, underdeveloped testes, low sperm production, enlarged breasts, poor muscular development, and infertility. Mild retardation or learning disabilities are also common. Men with Klinefelter's syndrome often don't discover they have the condition until they undergo tests for infertility.

Turner's syndrome, found only among females, is characterized by the presence of a single X sex chromosome instead of the normal two. Although such girls develop normal external genitals, their ovaries remain poorly developed, producing reduced amounts of estrogen. As women, they tend to be shorter than average and infertile. They also tend to show evidence of mild retardation, especially in skills relating to math and science.

Fragile X Syndrome and Other Genetic Abnormalities Fragile X syndrome is the most common type of inherited (genetic) mental retardation (Kwon et al., 2001). It is the second most common form of retardation overall, after Down syndrome (Plomin et al., 1994). The disorder is believed to be caused by a mutated gene on the X chromosome (Huber et al., 2002). The defective gene is located in an area of the chromosome that appears fragile, hence the name. Fragile X syndrome causes mental retardation in 1 out of 1,000 to 1,500 males and (generally less severe) mental handicaps in 1 out of 2,000 to 2,500 females (Angier, 1991b; Rousseau et al., 1991). The effects of fragile X syndrome range from mild learning disabilities to retardation so profound that those affected can hardly speak or function.

Females normally have two X chromosomes, whereas males have only one. For females, having two X chromosomes seems to provide some protection against the disorder if the defective gene turns up on one of the two chromosomes. This may explain why the disorder usually has more profound effects on males than on females. Yet the mutation does not always manifest itself. Many males and females carry the fragile X mutation without showing any clinical signs, yet they can pass the syndrome to their offspring.

A genetic test that can detect the mutation by direct DNA analysis may help prospective parents in genetic counseling. Prenatal testing of the fetus is also possible. Although there is no treatment for fragile X syndrome, genetic research focused on identifying the molecular cause of the disorder may lead to effective treatments (Huber et al., 2002).

Phenylketonuria (PKU) is a genetic disorder that occurs in 1 in 10,000 births (Plomin et al., 1994). It is caused by a recessive gene that prevents the child from metabolizing the amino acid phenylalanine, which is found in many foods. Consequently, phenylalanine and its derivative, phenylpyruvic acid, accumulate in the body, causing damage to the central nervous system that results in mental retardation and emotional disturbance. PKU can be detected in newborns by analyzing blood or urine samples. Although there is no cure for PKU, children with the disorder may suffer less damage or develop normally if they are placed on a diet low in phenylalanine soon after birth (Brody, 1990). Such children receive protein supplements that compensate for their nutritional loss.

Today, various prenatal tests can detect chromosomal abnormalities and genetic disorders. In *amniocentesis,* which is usually conducted about 14 to 15 weeks following conception, a sample of amniotic fluid is drawn with a syringe from the amniotic sac that contains the fetus. Cells from the fetus can then be separated from the fluid, allowed to grow in a culture, and examined for abnormalities, including Down syndrome. Blood tests are used to detect carriers of other disorders.

Prenatal Factors Some cases of mental retardation are caused by maternal infections or substance abuse during pregnancy. Rubella (German measles) in the mother, for example, can be passed along to the unborn child, causing brain damage that results in retardation, and it may play a role in autism. Although the mother may experience mild symptoms or none at all, the effects on the fetus can be tragic. Other maternal infections that may cause retardation in the child include syphilis, cytomegalovirus, and genital herpes.

Widespread programs that immunize women against rubella before pregnancy and tests for syphilis during pregnancy have reduced the risk of transmission of these infections to children. Most children who contract genital herpes from their mothers do so during delivery by coming into contact with the herpes simplex virus in the birth canal. Therefore, delivery by caesarean section (C-section) can prevent viral transmission during childbirth.

Drugs that the mother ingests during pregnancy may pass through the placenta to the child. Some can cause severe birth deformities and mental retardation. Children whose mothers drink alcohol during pregnancy are often born with fetal alcohol syndrome (described in Chapter 9), one of the most prominent causes of mental retardation. Maternal smoking during pregnancy has also been linked to the development of attention-deficit hyperactivity disorder in children (Milberger et al., 1996).

Birth complications, such as oxygen deprivation or head injuries, place children at increased risk for neurological disorders, including mental retardation. Prematurity also places children at risk of retardation and other developmental problems. Brain infections, such as encephalitis and meningitis, or traumas during infancy and early childhood can cause mental retardation and other health problems. Children who ingest toxins, such as paint chips containing lead, may also suffer brain damage that produces mental retardation.

Cultural–Familial Causes Most children with mental retardation are mildly disabled and have no apparent biological cause or distinguishing physical feature. Psychosocial factors, such as an impoverished home or social environment that is intellectually unstimulating or parental neglect or abuse may play a causal or contributing role in the development of mental retardation. A study in Atlanta that showed that mothers who failed to finish high school were four times more likely than better-educated mothers to have children with mild retardation supports an environmental linkage (Drews et al., 1995).

phenylketonuria (PKU) A genetic disorder that prevents the metabolization of phenylpyruvic acid, leading to mental retardation unless the diet is strictly controlled.

Environmental hazards. Children who are exposed to environmental hazards, such as paint chips containing lead-based paint, may suffer brain damage that can lead to mental retardation.

cultural–familial retardation A mild form of mental retardation that is influenced by impoverishment of the home environment.

These cases are considered **cultural–familial retardation.** Children in impoverished families may lack toys, books, or opportunities to interact with adults in intellectually stimulating ways. Consequently, they may not develop appropriate language skills or acquire any motivation to learn. Economic burdens, such as the need to hold multiple jobs, may prevent their parents from spending time reading to them, talking to them at length, and exposing them to creative play or activities. They may spend most of their days glued to the TV set. The parents, most of whom were also reared in poverty, may lack the reading or communication skills to help develop these skills in their children. A vicious cycle of poverty and impoverished intellectual development is repeated from generation to generation.

Children with this form of retardation may respond dramatically when provided with enriched learning experiences, especially at an early age. Social programs like Head Start, for example, have helped children at risk of cultural-familial retardation to function within the normal range of ability (e.g., Barnett & Escobar, 1990).

Intervention

The services that children with mental retardation need depend on the level of severity and type of retardation (Dykens & Hodapp, 1997; Snell, 1997). With appropriate training, children with mild retardation may approach a sixth-grade level of competence. They can acquire vocational skills and support themselves minimally through meaningful work. Many such children can be mainstreamed in regular classes. At the other extreme, children with severe or profound mental retardation may need institutional care or placement in a residential care facility in the community, such as a group home. Placement in an institution is often based on the need to control destructive or aggressive behavior, not because of severity of the individual's intellectual impairment. Consider the case of a child with moderate retardation.

A Case of Moderate Mental Retardation

The mother pleaded with the emergency room physician to admit her 15-year-old son, claiming that she couldn't take it anymore. Her son, a Down syndrome patient with an IQ of 45, had alternated since the age of 8 between living in institutions and at home. Each visiting day he pleaded with his mother to take him home, and after about a year at each placement, she would bring him home but find herself unable to control his behavior. During temper tantrums, he would break dishes and destroy furniture and had recently become physically assaultive toward his mother, hitting her on the arm and shoulder during a recent scuffle when she attempted to stop him from repeatedly banging a broom on the floor.

—Adapted from Spitzer et al., 1989, pp. 338–340

Educators sometimes disagree about whether children with mental retardation should be mainstreamed in regular classes or placed in special education classes. Although some children with mild retardation achieve better when they are mainstreamed, others do not. They may find these classes overwhelming and withdraw from their schoolmates. There has also been a trend toward deinstitutionalization of people with more severe mental retardation, motivated in large part by public outrage over the appalling conditions that formerly existed in many institutions serving this population. The Developmentally Disabled Assistance and Bill of Rights Act, which Congress passed in 1975, provided that persons with mental retardation have the right to receive appropriate treatment in the least-restrictive treatment setting. Nationwide, the population of institutions for people with mental retardation shrunk by nearly two thirds from the 1970s to the 1990s.

People with mental retardation who are capable of functioning in the community have the right to receive less-restrictive care than is provided in large institutions. Many are capable of living outside the institution and have been placed in supervised group homes. Residents typically share household responsibilities and are encouraged to participate in meaningful daily activities, such as training programs or sheltered workshops. Others live with their families and attend structured day programs. Adults with mild retardation often work in outside jobs and live in their own apartments or share apartments with other persons with mild retardation. Although the large-scale dumping of mental patients in the community from psychiatric institutions resulted in massive social problems and swelled the ranks of America's homeless population, deinstitutionalization of people with mental retardation has largely been a success story that has been achieved with rare dignity (Winerip, 1991).

People with mental retardation (MR) stand a high risk of developing other psychiatric disorders (Glidden, 2002). Unfortunately, the emotional life of people with MR has received little attention in the literature (Ross & Oliver, 2003). Many professionals even assumed (wrongly) that people with mental retardation were somehow immune from psychological problems or that they lacked the verbal skills needed to benefit from psychotherapy (Bütz, Bowlling, & Bliss, 2000; Nezu, 1994). However, evidence shows that people with mental retardation can benefit from psychotherapy (Bütz et al., 2000). People with MR may need psychological help dealing with problems of anxiety or depression or adjustment to life in the community. Many have difficulty making friends and become socially isolated. Problems with self-esteem are also common, especially because people who have mental retardation are often demeaned and ridiculed. Psychological counseling may be supplemented with behavioral techniques that help people acquire skills in areas such as personal hygiene, work, and social relationships. Structured behavioral approaches can be used to teach persons with more severe retardation such basic hygienic behaviors as toothbrushing, self-dressing, and hair combing.

Other behavioral treatment techniques include social skills training, which focuses on increasing the individual's ability to relate effectively to others, and anger management training to help individuals develop effective ways of handling conflicts without acting out (Huang & Cuvo, 1997; Rose, 1996).

Imparting skills. In 1975, Congress enacted legislation that requires public schools to provide children with disabilities with educational programs that meet their individual needs.

LEARNING DISORDERS

Nelson Rockefeller served as governor of New York State and as vice-president of the United States. He was brilliant and well educated. However, despite the best of tutors, he always had trouble reading. Rockefeller suffered from **dyslexia,** a term derived from the Greek roots *dys-*, meaning "bad," and *lexikon,* meaning "of words." Dyslexia is the most common type of **learning disorder** (also called a *learning disability*), accounting for perhaps 80% of cases. People with dyslexia have trouble reading despite possessing at least average intelligence (Miller-Medzon, 2000).

People with learning disorders show poor development in reading, math, or writing skills to a point that it impairs their school performance or daily functioning. Today, about one in eight children (about 12%) is placed in a program for the learning disabled, and the percentage of children participating in such programs is growing (Levine, 2000).

Learning disorders are typically chronic disorders that affect development well into adulthood. Children with learning disorders tend to perform poorly in school. Their teachers and families often view them as failures. It is not surprising that children with learning disorders often have other psychological problems, such as low self-esteem. They are also more likely than their peers to be diagnosed with attention-deficit hyperactivity disorder (Faraone et al., 2000; Swanson et al., 1999).

Types of Learning Disorders

Types of learning disorders include *mathematics disorder, disorder of written expression,* and *reading disorder.*

dyslexia A learning disorder characterized by impaired reading ability.

learning disorder A deficiency in a specific learning ability in the context of normal intelligence and exposure to learning opportunities.

TRUTH or FICTION? *REVISITED*

A former vice-president of the United States had such difficulty with arithmetic that he could never balance a checkbook.

☑ **FALSE.** Vice-President Rockefeller suffered from dyslexia and struggled with reading, not arithmetic.

A CLOSER LOOK
The Savant Syndrome

Got a minute? Try the following:

1. Without referring to a calendar, calculate the day of the week that March 15, 2079, will fall on.
2. List the prime numbers between 1 and 1 billion. (Hint: the list starts 1, 2, 3, 5, 7, 11, 13, 17 . . .)
3. Repeat verbatim the newspaper stories you read over coffee this morning.
4. Sing accurately every note played by the first violin in Beethoven's Ninth Symphony.

Give up? Don't feel badly about yourself, for very few people can perform such mental feats. Ironically, the people most likely to be able to accomplish these tasks suffer from autism, mental retardation, or both. Clinicians use the label *savant syndrome* to refer to someone with severe mental deficiencies who possesses some remarkable mental abilities (Miller, 1999). Commonly, these people are called *savants* (the term *savant* is derived from the French *savoir*, meaning "to know"). People with the savant syndrome have shown remarkable though circumscribed mental skills, such as calendar calculating, rare musical talent, even accomplished poetry (Dowker, Hermelin, & Pring, 1996)—all of which stand in contrast to their limited general intellectual abilities. People with the savant syndrome also have prodigious memories. Just as we learn about health by studying illness, we may be able to learn more about normal mechanisms of memory by studying people in whom memory stands apart from other aspects of mental functioning (e.g., Kelly, Macaruso, & Sokol, 1997).

The savant syndrome phenomenon occurs more frequently in males by a ratio of about 6 to 1. The special skills of people with the savant syndrome tend to appear out of the blue and may disappear as suddenly. Some people with the syndrome engage in lightning calculations. A 19th-century enslaved person in Virginia, Thomas Fuller, "was able to calculate the number of seconds in 70 years, 17 days, and 12 hours in a minute and one half, taking into account the 17 leap years that would have occurred in the period" (Smith, 1983). There are also cases of persons with the syndrome who were blind but could play back any musical piece, no matter how complex, or repeat long passages of foreign languages without losing a syllable. Some people with the syndrome make exact estimates of elapsed time. One could reportedly repeat verbatim the contents of a newspaper he had just heard; another could repeat backward what he had just read (Tradgold, 1914, cited in Treffert, 1988).

Many theories have been proposed to explain the savant syndrome, but scientists have yet to reach a consensus. One theory is that people with savant syndrome may inherit two sets of hereditary factors, one for retardation and the other for special memory abilities. Other theorists speculate that the brains of savants are wired with specialized circuitry that allows them to perform concrete and narrowly defined tasks, such as perceiving number relationships (Treffert, 1988). An environment that reinforces savant abilities and provides opportunities for practice and concentration would give further impetus to the development of these unusual abilities. Still the savant syndrome remains a mystery. ■

Savant syndrome. Leslie Lemke, a blind autistic savant musician, played music he heard verbatim and composed his own music, even though he had no music education. One day when he was about 14, he played flawlessly the entirety of Tchaikovsky's Piano Concerto No. 1 after having heard it once the night before.

Mathematics Disorder *Mathematics disorder* describes children with deficiencies in arithmetic skills. They may have problems understanding basic mathematical terms or operations, such as addition or subtraction; decoding mathematical symbols (+, =, etc.); or learning multiplication tables. The problem may become apparent as early as the first grade (age 6) but is not generally recognized until about the second or third grade.

Disorder of Written Expression *Disorder of written expression* refers to children with grossly deficient writing skills. The deficiency may be characterized by errors in spelling, grammar, or punctuation, or by difficulty in composing sentences and paragraphs. Severe writing difficulties generally become apparent by age 7 (second grade), although milder cases may not be recognized until the age of 10 (fifth grade) or later.

Reading Disorder Reading disorder—*dyslexia*—characterizes children who have poorly developed skills in recognizing words and comprehending written text. Dyslexia is estimated to affect about 4% of school-age children (APA, 2000) and is much more common in boys than girls (Rutter et al., 2004). Boys with dyslexia are also more likely than girls to show disruptive behavior in class and so are more likely to be referred for evaluation.

Children with dyslexia may read slowly and with great difficulty and may distort, omit, or substitute words when reading aloud. They have trouble decoding letters and letter combinations and translating them into the appropriate sounds (Miller-Medzon, 2000). They may also misperceive letters as upside down (for example, confusing *w* for *m*) or in reversed images (*b* for *d*). Dyslexia is usually apparent by the age of 7, coinciding with the second grade, although it is sometimes recognized in 6-year-olds. Children and adolescents with dyslexia are prone to depression, low self-worth, and attention-deficit hyperactivity disorder (Boetsch, Green, & Pennington, 1996).

Rates of dyslexia vary with respect to native language. Rates of dyslexia are high in English-speaking and French-speaking countries, where the language contains a large number of ways to spell words containing the same meaningful sounds (e.g., the same "o" sound in the words "toe" and "tow"). They are low in Italy, where the language has a smaller ratio of sounds to letter combinations ("Dyslexia," 2001; Paulesu et al., 2001).

Understanding and Treating Learning Disorders

Much of the research on learning disorders focuses on dyslexia, with mounting evidence pointing to underlying abnormalities in the way dyslexic children's brains process visual and auditory information (Corina et al., 2001; Habib, 2000; Helmuth, 2001; Paulesu et al., 2001). The brains of many children with dyslexia are not efficient at decoding written characters into corresponding sounds (e.g., seeing an *f* or a *ph* or a *gh* and saying or hearing in our minds an *f* sound) and distinguishing among speech sounds as those of normal readers. In one recent study, investigators found that the normally dominant speech centers in the left hemisphere of the brain were not as active in dyslexic children as they were in children without reading problems (Breier et al., 2003). These underlying brain deficits may have a genetic basis, as evidence connects genetic factors with a greater risk of dyslexia (Nagourney, 2001a; Plomin, 2001; Raskind, 2001).

Recently, scientists speculated that dyslexia may take two general forms, one more genetically influenced and the other more environmentally influenced (Morris, 2003; Shaywitz et al., 2003). The predominant genetic type appears to involve defects in the neural circuitry in the brain that normal readers use to process speech sounds. These people learn to compensate for these defects by relying on other brain capabilities, although they continue to read slowly. In the more environmentally influenced type, neural circuity is intact but people rely more on memory than on decoding strategies to understand written words. This second type may be more prevalent in children from disadvantaged educational backgrounds and is associated with more persistent reading disability (Kersting, 2003).

Linking learning disorders to defects in brain circuitry responsible for processing sensory (visual and auditory) information may point toward development of treatment programs that help children adjust to their sensory capabilities. Therapists need to design strategies tailored to each child's particular type of disability and educational needs (Levine, 2000; Morris, 2003). For example, a child who retains auditory information better than visual information might be taught verbally, by using tape recordings rather than written materials. Other intervention approaches focus on evaluating children's learning competencies and designing strategies to help them acquire skills needed to perform basic academic tasks, such as arithmetic skills. In addition, language specialists can help dyslexic children grasp the structure and use of words (Rashotte et al., 2001; Torgesen et al., 2001).

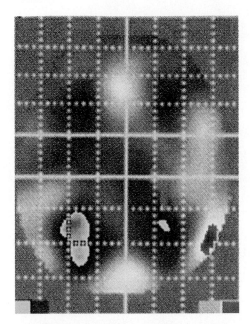

Brain Imaging Study of Dyslexic Adults. Brain scans taken during a reading task show that stronger activation of the reading systems in the left hemisphere (shown here by areas tinted in yellow) is associated with better reading skills in nondyslexic readers. By contrast, more competent dyslexic readers rely more on the right hemisphere (as shown by blue-tinted areas). More capable dyslexic readers seem to rely on different neural pathways than normal readers. By examining differences in activation of particular areas of the brain, scientists hope to learn more about the neurological underpinnings of dyslexia.

COMMUNICATION DISORDERS

Communication disorders are persistent difficulties in understanding or using language. The categories of communication disorders include expressive language disorder, mixed receptive/expressive language disorder, phonological disorder, and stuttering. Each of these disorders interferes with academic or occupational functioning or ability

communication disorders A class of psychological disorders characterized by difficulties in understanding or using language.

to communicate socially. Table 14.5 lists the *DSM-IV* classification of learning disorders and communication disorders.

Expressive language disorder is a persistent impairment in the use of spoken language, such as slow vocabulary development, errors in tense, difficulties recalling words, and problems producing sentences of appropriate length and complexity for the individual's age. Affected children may also have a phonological (articulation) disorder, compounding their speech problems.

Mixed receptive/expressive language disorder refers to difficulties both understanding and producing speech. There may be difficulty understanding words or sentences. In some cases, children have difficulty understanding certain word types (such as words expressing differences in quantity—*large, big,* or *huge*), spatial terms (such as *near* or *far*), or sentence types (such as sentences that begin with the word *unlike*). Other cases are marked by difficulties understanding simple words or sentences.

Phonological disorder is a persistent difficulty articulating the sounds of speech in the absence of defects in the oral speech mechanism or neurological impairment. Children with the disorder may omit, substitute, or mispronounce certain sounds—especially *ch, f, l, r, sh,* and *th,* which most children articulate properly by the time they reach the early school years. It may sound as if they are uttering "baby talk." Children with more severe cases have problems articulating sounds usually mastered during the preschool years: *b, m, t, d, n,* and *h.* Speech therapy is often helpful, and mild cases often resolve themselves by the age of 8.

Stuttering is a disturbance in the ability to speak fluently with appropriate timing of speech sounds. The lack of normal fluency must be inappropriate for the person's age in order to justify the diagnosis. Stuttering usually begins between 2 and 7 years of age and affects about 1 child in 100 before puberty (APA, 2000). The disorder is characterized by one or more of the following characteristics: (a) repetitions of sounds and syllables; (b) prolongations of certain sounds; (c) interjections of inappropriate sounds; (d) broken words, such as pauses occurring within a spoken word; (e) blocking of speech; (f) circumlocutions (substitutions of alternative words to avoid problematic words); (g) displaying an excess of physical tension when emitting words; and (h) repetitions of monosyllabic whole words (for example, "I-I-I-I am glad to meet you") (APA, 2000).

Stuttering occurs in three times as many males as females. Stuttering remits in upward of 80% of children, typically before age 16. As many as 60% of cases show remission without any treatment. Stuttering is believed to involve an interaction of genetic and environmental influences (Shugart et al., 2004; Starkweather, 2002). Brain scans reveal disturbed neural activation patterns in certain regions of the brain (Ingham, 2003; Neumann et al., 2003). Underlying social anxiety or social phobias may also contribute to problems with fluency (Kraaimaat, Vanryckeghem, & Van Dam-Baggen, 2002; Schneier, Wexler, & Liebowitz, 1997). Treatment of communication disorders is generally ap-

TABLE 14.5	
DSM-IV Classification of Learning Disorders and Communication Disorders	
Learning Disorders	Reading Disorder
	Mathematics Disorder
	Disorder of Written Expression
Communication Disorders	Expressive Language Disorder
	Mixed Receptive/Expressive Language Disorder
	Phonological Disorder
	Stuttering

Source: Adapted from the *DSM-IV-TR* (APA, 2000).

proached with specialized speech therapy or fluency training and with psychological counseling for social anxiety or other emotional problems.

ATTENTION-DEFICIT AND DISRUPTIVE BEHAVIOR DISORDERS

Attention-deficit and disruptive behavior disorders are a diverse range of problem behaviors, including attention-deficit hyperactivity disorder (ADHD), conduct disorder (CD), and oppositional defiant disorder (ODD). These disorders are socially disruptive and usually more upsetting to other people than to the children who are diagnosed with these problems. The rate of comorbidity (co-occurrence) among these disorders is very high (Jensen, Martin, & Cantwell, 1997).

Attention-Deficit Hyperactivity Disorder

Many parents believe that their children are not attentive toward them—that they run around on whim and do things their own way. Some inattention, especially in early childhood, is normal enough. In **attention-deficit hyperactivity disorder (ADHD),** however, children display impulsivity, inattention, and **hyperactivity** that are inappropriate to their developmental levels.

ADHD is divided into three subtypes: (a) a predominantly inattentive type; (b) a predominantly hyperactive or impulsive type, and (c) a combination type characterized by high levels of both inattention and hyperactivity–impulsivity (APA, 2000). The disorder is usually first diagnosed during elementary school, when problems with attention or hyperactivity–impulsivity make it difficult for the child to adjust to school. Although signs of hyperactivity are often observed earlier, many overactive toddlers do not go on to develop ADHD.

ADHD is the most commonly diagnosed psychological disorder in children today (Bradley & Golden, 2001). The disorder is estimated to affect between 3% and 7% of school-age children, or some two million American youngsters (APA, 2000; Shute, Locy, & Pasternak, 2000; Wingert, 2000). ADHD is diagnosed two to nine times more often in boys than girls (APA, 2000). Although inattention appears to be the basic problem, associated problems include inability to sit still for more than a few moments, bullying, temper tantrums, stubbornness, and failure to respond to punishment (see Table 14.6). Boys with ADHD tend to be judged by their teachers as showing more inattention and hyperactivity in the classroom than are girls with ADHD (Hartung et al., 2002).

Children with ADHD have great difficulty in school. They seem incapable of sitting still. They fidget and squirm in their seats, butt into other children's games, have outbursts of temper, and may engage in dangerous behavior, such as running into the street without looking. All in all, they can drive parents and teachers to despair.

Where does "normal" age-appropriate overactivity end and hyperactivity begin? Assessment of the degree of hyperactive behavior is crucial, because many normal children are called "hyper" from time to time. Some critics of the ADHD diagnosis argue that it merely labels children who are difficult to control as mentally disordered or sick. Most children, especially boys, are highly active during the early school years. Proponents of the diagnosis counter that there is a difference in quality between normal overactivity and ADHD. Normally overactive children are usually goal directed and can exert voluntary control over their behavior. But children with ADHD appear hyperactive without reason and seem unable to conform their behavior to the demands of teachers and parents. Put another way: Most children can sit still and concentrate for a while when they want to; children who are hyperactive seemingly cannot.

attention-deficit hyperactivity disorder (ADHD) A behavior disorder characterized by excessive motor activity and inability to focus one's attention.

hyperactivity An abnormal behavior pattern characterized by difficulty in maintaining attention and extreme restlessness.

Attention-deficit hyperactivity disorder (ADHD). ADHD is more common in boys than girls and is characterized by attentional difficulties, restlessness, impulsivity, excessive motor behavior (continuous running around or climbing), and temper tantrums.

TABLE 14.6

Diagnostic Features of Attention-Deficit Hyperactivity Disorder (ADHD)

Kind of Problem	Specific Behavior Pattern
Lack of attention	Fails to attend to details or makes careless errors in schoolwork, etc.
	Has difficulty sustaining attention in schoolwork or play
	Doesn't appear to pay attention to what is being said
	Fails to follow through on instructions or to finish work
	Has trouble organizing work and other activities
	Avoids work or activities that require sustained attention
	Loses work tools (e.g., pencils, books, assignments, toys)
	Becomes readily distracted
	Is forgetful in daily activities
Hyperactivity	Fidgets with hands or feet or squirms in his or her seat
	Leaves seat in situations such as the classroom in which remaining seated is required
	Is constantly running around or climbing on things
	Has difficulty playing quietly
Impulsivity	Frequently "calls out" in class
	Fails to wait his/her turn in line, games, etc.

To receive a diagnosis of ADHD, the disorder must begin by the age of 7; must have significantly impaired academic, social, or occupational functioning; and must be characterized by a designated number of clinical features shown in this table occurring over a 6-month period in at least two settings such as at school, at home, or at work.

Source: Adapted from the *DSM-IV-TR* (APA, 2000).

Attention-Deficit/Hyperactivity Disorder (ADHD):
The Case of Jimmy
"Sometimes I just drift off."

Although children with ADHD tend to be of average or above-average intelligence, they often underachieve in school. They are frequently disruptive in the classroom and tend to get into fights (especially the boys). They may fail to follow or remember instructions or complete assignments. Compared to children not diagnosed with ADHD, they are more likely to have learning disabilities, to repeat grades, to suffer physical injuries, and to be placed in special education classes (Faraone et al., 1993; Leibson et al., 2001). They are also more likely to have mood disorders, anxiety disorders, and problems getting along with family members (Biederman et al., 1996a, 1996b). Compared to their peers, ADHD boys tend to lack empathy, or awareness of other people's feelings (Braaten & Rosén, 2000). Not surprisingly, children with ADHD tend to be unpopular with their classmates.

ADHD symptoms tend to decline with age, but the disorder often persists in milder form into adolescence and adulthood (Faraone, 2003a, 2003b; Wilens et al., 2003; Volkmar, 2003). Adult forms of ADHD primarily involve problems of inattention and distractabilty rather than hyperactivity. Teenagers with ADHD are more likely than their peers to use alcohol, tobacco, and illicit drugs ("Attention Disorder," 2003; Lambert et al., 1987; Molina & Pelham, 2003).

Theoretical Perspectives Evidence points to an important role for genetics in the development of ADHD (Bradley & Golden, 2001; Faraone et al., 2001). We know that ADHD tends to run in families, which suggests a genetic contribution (Faraone et al., 2000). But more direct evidence comes from findings of a higher concordance rate for the disorder among monozygotic (MZ) twins than among DZ (dizygotic) twins (Sherman et al., 1997). Researchers recognize that genetics doesn't operate in a vacuum; they believe that environmental factors and the interaction of genes and environment play important roles in ADHD (Bradley & Golden, 2001). For example, ADHD is much more common in children whose mothers smoked during pregnancy than in other children

(Milberger et al., 1996). Maternal smoking may cause defects in the brain during pre-natal development. Investigators continue to track down other possible environmental factors, such as a high level of family conflict, emotional stress during pregnancy, and poor parenting skills in handling children's misbehavior. Scientists are also seeking to track down the specific genes involved in ADHD (Langley et al., 2002; Wigg et al., 2002).

One prominent view of ADHD today is that it involves problems with the "executive control" centers in the prefrontal cortex, the part of the cerebral cortex responsible for inhibiting impulsive behavior and maintaining self-control (Barkley, 2001; Nigg, 2001). One possibility under study is that a genetically determined pattern of underactivity of the prefrontal cortex leads to a breakdown in the ability to maintain control over im-pulsive, hyperactive behavior. Supporting this view is evidence from brain-imaging stud-ies showing subtle abnormalities in children and adolescents with ADHD in areas of the brain involved in regulating attention, arousal, control of motor (movement) be-havior, and communication between the left and right hemispheres (e.g., Castellanos et al., 2001, 2003; Murray, 2000a, 2000b; Semrud-Clikeman et al., 2000).

Treatment It may seem odd that most prescription drugs used to help ADHD children calm down and attend better in school are actually stimulants, such as the widely used drug Ritalin and longer-acting stimulants, including the once-daily drug, Concerta (Rug-ino & Copley, 2001; Schonwald & Rappaport, 2003). Concerta has become the most commonly prescribed drug for treating ADHD (Bauchner, 2003). Stimulant drugs in-crease the availability of the neurotransmitters dopamine and norepinephrine in the prefrontal cortex of the brain (Faraone, 2003b; Keating et al., 2001; Nigg, 2001). In-creasing the availability of these neurotransmitters appears to enhance the brain's abil-ity to regulate attention and maintain control over impulsive, acting-out behavior.

Stimulant drugs not only reduce disruptive, hyperactive behavior but also improve attention spans of ADHD children (Biederman, 2003; Pelham et al., 2002). Stimulant drugs are even being used with preschoolers as young as 3 to 5 years of age (Stolberg, 2002). Although use of stimulants is not without critics, these drugs can help many chil-dren with ADHD calm down and concentrate better on tasks and schoolwork, perhaps for the first times in their lives.

Although stimulant medication can help reduce restlessness and increase attention in school, it is unclear whether these gains translate into improved academic performance (Stein et al., 2003). However, combining stimulant medication with behavior modifica-tion boosts academic performance in teenagers with ADHD, including performance on such measures as quiz scores and daily assignments (Carpenter, 2001a; Evans et al., 2001). One problem with stimulant medication, as with many other uses of psychotropic drugs, is a high rate of relapse once the child stops taking the medication (Greenhill, 1998). Also, the range of effectiveness is limited, as in the following case example.

Eddie Hardly Ever Sits Still

Nine-year-old Eddie is a problem in class. His teacher complains that he is so rest-less and fidgety that the rest of the class cannot concentrate on their work. He hardly ever sits still. He is in constant motion, roaming the classroom, talking to other children while they are working. He has been suspended repeatedly for out-rageous behavior, most recently swinging from a fluorescent light fixture and un-able to get himself down. His mother reports that Eddie has been a problem since he was a toddler. By the age of 3 he had become unbearably restless and demand-ing. He has never needed much sleep and always awakened before anyone else in the family, making his way downstairs and wrecking things in the living room and kitchen. Once, at the age of 4, he unlocked the front door and wandered into traf-fic, but was rescued by a passerby.

Psychological testing shows Eddie to be average in academic ability but to have a "virtually nonexistent" attention span. He shows no interest in television or in games or toys that require concentration. He is unpopular with peers and prefers to ride his bike alone or to play with his dog. He has become disobedient at home and at school and has stolen small amounts of money from his parents and classmates.

Eddie has been treated with methylphenidate (Ritalin), but it was discontinued because it had no effect on his disobedience and stealing. However, it did seem to reduce his restlessness and increase his attention span at school.

—Adapted from Spitzer et al., 1989, pp. 315–317

Then there's the matter of side effects. Although short-term side effects (e.g., loss of appetite or insomnia) usually subside within a few weeks or may be eliminated by lowering the dose, stimulant drugs may lead to other effects, including a slowdown of physical growth (Wingert, 2000). Fortunately, children taking stimulant medication eventually catch up to their peers in physical stature (Gittelman-Klein & Mannuzza, 1990; Gorman, 1998).

The first nonstimulant drug approved for use in treating ADHD is Strattera (Caballero & Nahata, 2003). Strattera works differently than stimulant medication. It is a *selective norepinephrine reuptake inhibitor,* which means that it increases the availability of the neurotransmitter norepinephrine in the brain by interfering with the reuptake of the chemical by transmitting neurons. Though we don't know precisely how the drug works on ADHD, the increased availability of norepinephrine may enhance the brain's ability to regulate impulsive behavior and attention.

Whatever the benefits of ADHD medication may be, drugs cannot teach new skills. So researchers are focusing on whether a combination of stimulant medication and behavioral or cognitive–behavioral techniques can produce greater benefits than either approach alone (e.g., Arnold et al., 2003).

Cognitive–behavioral therapy (CBT) combines behavior modification, which typically includes reinforcement for appropriate behaviors (for example, a teacher praising the child for sitting quietly), and cognitive modification (for example, training the child to silently talk himself or herself through the steps involved in solving challenging academic problems). Cognitive–behavioral therapists can help train ADHD children to "stop and think" before giving in to angry impulses and acting out aggressively (Miranda & Presentacion, 2000). Though evidence on combining medication and CBT is mixed (Braswell & Kendall, 2001), some children may do well with therapeutic drugs alone, others with CBT alone, and still others with a combination of both treatments (Abikoff, 2001; Greene & Ablon, 2001).

Attention-Deficit/Hyperactivity Disorder (ADHD):
Dr. Raun Melmed

conduct disorder A psychological disorder in childhood and adolescence characterized by disruptive, antisocial behavior.

Conduct Disorder

Although it also involves disruptive behavior, **conduct disorder** differs in important ways from ADHD. Whereas children with ADHD seem literally incapable of controlling their behavior, children with conduct disorder purposefully engage in patterns of antisocial behavior that violate social norms and the rights of others. Whereas children with ADHD throw temper tantrums, children diagnosed as conduct disordered are intentionally aggressive and cruel. Like antisocial adults, many conduct-disordered children are callous and apparently do not experience guilt or remorse for their misdeeds. As children, they steal or destroy property; as adolescents they commit rape, armed robbery, even homicide. They may cheat in school—when they bother to attend—and lie to cover their tracks. They frequently engage in substance abuse and sexual activity.

Rates of conduct disorder in adolescence range from about 2% to 16% in boys and from less than 1% to 9% in girls (Loeber et al., 2000). Conduct disorder is not only more common among boys than girls, it also takes a somewhat different form. In boys, conduct disorder is more likely to be manifested by stealing, fighting, vandalism, or disciplinary problems at school, whereas in girls it is more likely to involve lying, truancy, running away, substance use, and prostitution. Children with conduct disorder often present with other disorders or problem behaviors, including ADHD, social withdrawal, and major depression (Decker et al., 2001; Lahey et al., 2003; Lambert et al., 2001).

Conduct disorder is typically a chronic or persistent disorder (Lahey et al., 1995). Longitudinal studies show that elementary school children with conduct disorder are more likely than other children to engage in delinquent acts as early adolescents (Tremblay et al., 1992). Antisocial behavior in the form of delinquent acts (stealing, truancy, vandalism, fighting or threatening others, and so on) during early adolescence (ages 14 to 15) has also been found to predict alcohol and substance abuse in late adolescence, especially among boys (Boyle et al., 1992). Another form of conduct disorder may involve a cluster of personality traits that have different origins than antisocial behavior (Wootton et al., 1997). These include callousness (uncaring, mean, cruel) and an unemotional way of relating to others (Barry et al., 2000).

Oppositional Defiant Disorder

Conduct disorder (CD) and **oppositional defiant disorder (ODD)** are often combined under the general heading of "conduct problems." Though the disorders may be related, evidence suggests that ODD is a separate diagnostic category, not merely a milder form of CD (Greene et al., 2002; Silverthorn, 2001). ODD is more closely related to non-delinquent (negativistic or oppositional) conduct disturbance, whereas conduct disorder involves more outright delinquent behavior, such as truancy, stealing, lying, and aggression. Yet oppositional defiant disorder, which typically develops earlier than CD, may lead to the development of antisocial behavior and conduct disorder at later ages.

Children with ODD tend to be negativistic or oppositional. They defy authority by arguing with parents and teachers and refusing to follow requests or directives. They may deliberately annoy other people, become easily angered or lose their temper, become touchy or easily annoyed, blame others for their mistakes or misbehavior, feel resentful toward others, or act in spiteful or vindictive ways toward others (Angold & Costello, 1996; APA, 2000). The disorder typically begins before age 8 and develops gradually over a period of months or years. It typically starts in the home environment but may extend to other settings, such as school.

ODD is one of the most common diagnoses among children. The disorder is believed to affect between 6% and 12% of school-age children and upwards of 15% of adolescents (Frick & Silverthorn, 2001). ODD is more common overall among boys than girls. However, this overall effect masks a gender shift that occurs with age. Among children age 12 or younger, ODD appears to be more than twice as common among boys. Among adolescents, prevalence is higher among girls (Rey, 1993). By contrast, most studies find conduct disorder to be more common in boys than girls across all age groups.

Theoretical Perspectives on ODD and CD The causal factors in ODD remain obscure. Some theorists believe that oppositionality is an expression of an underlying temperament described as the "difficult–child" type (Rey, 1993). Others believe that unresolved parent–child conflicts or overly strict parental control lie at the root of the disorder. Psychodynamic theorists look at ODD as a sign of fixation at the anal stage of psychosexual development, when conflicts between the parent and child emerge over toilet training. Leftover conflicts may later become expressed in the form of rebelliousness against parental wishes (Egan, 1991). Learning theorists view oppositional behaviors as arising from parental use of inappropriate reinforcement strategies. In this view, parents may inappropriately reinforce oppositional behavior by giving in when the child refuses to comply with their wishes, which can become a pattern.

Family factors are also implicated in the development of conduct disorder. Some forms of conduct disorder appear to be linked to ineffective parenting styles, such as failure to provide positive reinforcement for appropriate behavior and use of harsh and inconsistent discipline for misbehavior. Families of children with CD tend to be characterized by negative, coercive interactions (Dadds et al., 1992). Children with CD are often very demanding and noncompliant with their parents and other family members. Family members often reciprocate by using negative behaviors, such as threatening or yelling at the child or using physical means of coercion. Parental aggression

oppositional defiant disorder (ODD)
A psychological disorder in childhood and adolescence characterized by excessive oppositionality or tendencies to refuse requests from parents and others.

Oppositional defiant disorder (ODD). ODD is characterized by negativistic and oppositional behavior in response to directives from parents, teachers, or other authority figures. Children with ODD may act spitefully or vindictively toward others, but do not typically show the cruelty, aggressivity, and delinquent behavior associated with conduct disorder. Yet questions remain about whether the two disorders are truly distinct or are variations of a common underlying disorder involving disruptive behavior patterns.

against children with conduct behavior problems commonly includes pushing, grabbing, slapping, spanking, hitting, or kicking (Jouriles et al., 1997). Parents of children with oppositional defiant disorders or severe conduct disorder display high rates of antisocial personality disorder and substance abuse (Frick et al., 1992). It's not too much of a stretch to speculate that parental modeling of antisocial behaviors can lead to antisocial conduct in children.

Conduct disorders often occur in a context of parental distress, such as marital conflict (Curtner-Smith, 2000). Coercive parental discipline and poor parental monitoring are also linked to increased risk of conduct disorders (Kilgore et al., 2002). Poor parenting behaviors such as harsh discipline and lack of monitoring may foster the lack of empathy for others and the poor control over disruptive behavior we find in conduct disordered children.

Some investigations focus on the ways in which children with disruptive behavior disorders process information. For example, children who are overly aggressive in their behavior tend to be biased in their processing of social information: They assume that others intend them ill when they do not (Lochman, 1992). They usually blame others for the scrapes they get into. They believe that they are misperceived and treated unfairly. They may believe that aggression leads to favorable results (Dodge et al., 1997). They are also less able than their peers to generate alternative, nonviolent, responses to social conflicts (Lochman & Dodge, 1994).

Genetic factors are also implicated in the development of conduct disorder (APA, 2000; Hudziak, 2001). For example, investigators find more evidence of antisocial behavior in the biological parents of adopted-away children with conduct disorder than in the adoptive parents (Langbehn & Cadoret, 2001). Genetic factors may also be involved in the development of oppositional defiant disorder.

Treatment   Parent training programs are used widely in treating conduct problems (Kazdin, 2003; Silverthorn, 2001). Parents are trained in behavioral techniques to alter the child's aggressive and oppositional behavior in the home and increase the child's adaptive behavior. Treatment generally targets several goals, including helping parents develop more consistent and effective discipline strategies, increasing the use of positive reinforcement for rewarding compliant behavior, and increasing the frequency of positive interactions between the parent and child. Parents must learn not only how to alter disruptive behaviors in their children but also to pay attention to their children and reward them when they act appropriately (Cavell, 2001).

The following example illustrates the involvement of the parents in the behavioral treatment of a child with oppositional defiant disorder.

A Case of Oppositional Defiant Disorder

Billy was a 7-year-old second grader referred by his parents. The family was relocated frequently because the father was in the navy. Billy usually behaved when his father was taking care of him, but he was noncompliant with his mother and yelled at her when she gave him instructions. His mother was incurring great stress in the effort to control Billy, especially when her husband was at sea.

Billy had become a problem at home and in school during the first grade. He ignored and violated rules in both settings. Billy failed to carry out his chores and frequently yelled at and hit his younger brother. When he acted up, his parents would restrict him to his room or the yard, take away privileges and toys, and spank him. But all of these measures were used inconsistently. He also played on the railroad tracks near his home, and twice the police had brought him home after he had thrown rocks at cars.

A home observation showed that Billy's mother often gave him inappropriate commands. She interacted with him as little as possible and showed no verbal praise, physical closeness, smiles, or positive facial expressions or gestures. She paid attention to him only when he misbehaved. When Billy was noncompliant, she would yell back at him and then try to catch him to force him to comply. Billy would then laugh and run from her.

Billy's parents were informed that the child's behavior was a product of inappropriate cueing techniques (poor directions), a lack of reinforcement for appropriate behavior, and lack of consistent sanctions for misbehavior. They were taught the appropriate use of reinforcement, punishment, and time out. The parents then charted Billy's problem behaviors to gain a clearer idea of what triggered and maintained them. They were shown how to reinforce acceptable behavior and use time out as a contingent punishment for misbehavior. Billy's mother was also taught relaxation training to help desensitize her to Billy's disruptions. Biofeedback was used to enhance the relaxation response.

During a 15-day baseline period, Billy behaved in a noncompliant manner about four times per day. When treatment was begun, Billy showed an immediate drop to about one instance of noncompliance every two days. Follow-up data showed that instances of noncompliance were maintained at a bearable level of about one per day. Fewer behavioral problems in school were also reported, even though they had not been addressed directly.

—Adapted from Kaplan, 1986, pp. 227–230

Children with conduct disorder are sometimes placed in residential treatment programs that establish explicit rules with clear rewards and mild punishments (e.g., withdrawal of privileges). Many children with conduct disorders, especially boys, display aggressive behavior and have problems controlling their anger. Many can benefit from programs designed to help them develop skills to manage conflict without resorting to aggressive behavior (Webster-Stratton et al., 2001).

Cognitive–behavioral therapy is also used to teach aggressive children to reconceptualize social provocations as problems to be solved rather than as challenges to answer with violence. These children learn to use calming self-talk to inhibit impulsive behavior and control anger and to find and use nonviolent solutions to social conflicts.

CHILDHOOD ANXIETY AND DEPRESSION

Anxieties and fears are a normal feature of childhood, just as they are a normal feature of adult life. Childhood fears—of the dark or of small animals—are common, and most children outgrow them naturally. Anxiety is abnormal, however, when it is excessive and interferes with normal academic or social functioning or becomes troubling or persistent. Children, like adults, may suffer from different types of diagnosable anxiety disorders, including specific phobias, social phobias, generalized anxiety disorder (GAD), and posttraumatic stress disorder (PTSD). Although these disorders may develop at any age, we consider further a type of disorder that typically develops during early childhood: separation anxiety disorder.

Some children show the more general pattern of avoidance of social interactions that characterizes avoidant personality disorder. Although children who are socially avoidant or have social anxiety disorder (also called social phobia) may have warm relationships with family members, they tend to be shy and withdrawn around others. This interferes with their development of social relationships with their peers. Such problems tend to develop after normal fear of strangers

Social avoidance. Socially avoidant children tend to be excessively shy and withdrawn and have difficulty interacting with other children.

Separation anxiety. In separation anxiety disorder, a child shows persistent anxiety when separated from her or his parents that is inconsistent with her or his developmental level. Such children tend to cling to their parents and resist even brief separations.

separation anxiety disorder A childhood disorder characterized by extreme fear of separation from parents or other caretakers.

fades, at age 2 ½ or later. Their distress at being around other children at school can also affect their academic progress. Having a social anxiety disorder during adolescence or young adulthood also increases the likelihood of later developing a depressive disorder (Stein et al., 2001).

Separation Anxiety Disorder

It is normal for young children to show anxiety when they are separated from their caregivers. Mary Ainsworth (1989) chronicled the development of attachment behaviors and found that separation anxiety normally begins during the first year. The sense of security normally provided by bonds of attachment apparently encourages children to explore their environments and become progressively independent of their caregivers (Bowlby, 1988).

Separation anxiety disorder is diagnosed when separation anxiety is persistent and excessive or inappropriate for the child's developmental level. That is, 3-year-olds ought to be able to attend preschool without nausea and vomiting brought on by anxiety. Six-year-olds ought to be able to attend first grade without persistent dread that something awful will happen to them or their parents. Children with this disorder tend to cling to their parents and follow them around the house. They may voice concerns about death and dying and insist that someone stay with them while they are falling asleep. Other features of the disorder include nightmares, stomachaches, nausea and vomiting when separation is anticipated (as on school days), pleading with parents not to leave, or throwing tantrums when parents are about to depart. Children may refuse to attend school for fear that something will happen to their parents while they are away.

Separation anxiety disorder affects an estimated 4% to 5% of children and young adolescents (American Psychiatric Association, 2000; Masi et al., 2001). The disorder occurs most often in girls and is associated with school refusal in about 75% of cases. The disorder may persist into adulthood, leading to an exaggerated concern about the well-being of one's children and spouse and difficulty tolerating any separation from them.

In previous years, separation anxiety disorder was usually referred to as *school phobia*. Separation anxiety disorder may occur at preschool ages, however. In young children, refusal to attend school is usually viewed as separation anxiety. In adolescents, however, refusal to attend school is frequently connected with academic and social concerns, so the label of separation anxiety disorder would not apply.

The development of separation anxiety disorder frequently follows a stressful life event, such as illness, the death of a relative or pet, or a change of schools or homes. Alison's problems followed the death of her grandmother.

Alison's Fear of Death

Alison's grandmother died when Alison was 7 years old. Her parents decided to permit her request to view her grandmother in the open coffin. Alison took a tentative glance from her father's arms across the room, then asked to be taken out of the room. Her 5-year-old sister took a leisurely close-up look, with no apparent distress.

Alison had been concerned about death for two or three years by this time, but her grandmother's passing brought on a new flurry of questions: "Will I die?", "Does everybody die?", and so on. Her parents tried to reassure her by saying, "Grandma was very, very old, and she also had a heart condition. You are very young and in perfect health. You have many, many years before you have to start thinking about death."

Alison could not be alone in any room in her house. She pulled one of her parents or her sister along with her everywhere she went. She also reported nightmares about her grandmother and, within a couple of days, insisted on sleeping in the same room with her parents. Fortunately, Alison's fears did not extend to school. Her teacher reported that Alison spent some time talking about her grandmother, but her academic performance was apparently unimpaired.

Alison's parents decided to allow Alison time to "get over" the loss. Alison gradually talked less and less about death, and by the time 3 months had passed, she was able to go into any room in her house by herself. She wanted to continue to sleep in her parents' bedroom, however. So her parents "made a deal" with her. They would put off the return to her own bedroom until the school year ended (a month away), if Alison would agree to return to her own bed at that time. As a further incentive, a parent would remain with her until she fell asleep for the first month. Alison overcame the anxiety problem in this fashion with no additional delays.

—From the Authors' Files

Understanding and Treating Childhood Anxiety Disorders

Theoretical perspectives on anxiety disorders in children parallel to some degree explanations of anxiety disorders in adults. Psychoanalytic theorists argue that childhood anxieties and fears, like their adult counterparts, symbolize unconscious conflicts. Cognitive theorists focus on the role of cognitive biases: Anxious children tend to show the types of cognitive distortions found in adults with anxiety disorders, including interpreting ambiguous situations as threatening and expecting negative outcomes (e.g., Kazdin, 2003; Weems et al., 2001). They also tend to engage in negative and doubting self-talk. Expecting the worst, combined with having low self-confidence, encourages avoidance of feared activities—with friends, in school, and elsewhere. Negative expectations also heighten feelings of anxiety to the point where they impair performance in the classroom or the athletic field.

Learning theorists suggest that generalized anxiety may arise from fears of rejection or failure that carry across situations. Underlying fears of rejection or feelings of inadequacy generalize to most areas of social interaction and achievement. Genetics may also play a role in explaining susceptiblity to separation anxiety and other anxiety disorders (Coyle, 2001).

Whatever the causes, overanxious children can benefit from the same cognitive–behavioral techniques for treating anxiety that we discussed in Chapter 6, such as gradual exposure to phobic stimuli and relaxation training. Cognitive techniques can help children test their anxiety-generating thoughts and replace them with adaptive alternative thoughts. Cognitive–behavioral therapy has shown good results in treating childhood anxiety disorders (Barrett et al., 2001; Kazdin, 2003; Kendall et al., 2004; Velting, Setzer, & Albano, 2004). The drug *fluvoxamine* (brand name Luvox), a selective serotonin-reuptake inhibitor, also shows good therapeutic effects in treating children and adolescents with various types of anxiety disorders, including social phobia, separation anxiety disorder, and generalized anxiety disorder (Coyle, 2001; Pine et al., 2001; Riddle et al., 2001; Walkup et al., 2001).

Childhood Depression

We may think of childhood as the happiest time of life. Most children are protected by their parents and are unencumbered by adult responsibilities. From the perspective of aging adults, their bodies seem made of rubber and free of aches. They have apparently boundless energy. However, children and adolescents can suffer from diagnosable mood disorders, including bipolar disorder and major depression (Geller & DelBello, 2003; Geller et al., 2002; McClure, Kubisyn, & Kaslow, 2002). An estimated three million adolescents in the United States suffer from major depression (Wright & Kantrowitz, 2002). Estimates indicate that perhaps 8% to 9% of children age 10 to 13 experience major depression during any given 1 year period (Goleman, 1994a). Major depression even occurs among preschoolers, although it is rare. During childhood there is no discernible gender difference in the risk of depression, but after age 15, girls are about twice as likely to become depressed as boys (Hankin et al., 1998; Lewinsohn, Rohde, & Seeley, 1994).

Is this child too young to be depressed? Although we tend to think of childhood as the happiest and most carefree time of life, depression is actually quite common among older children and adolescents. Depressed children may report feelings of sadness and lack of interest in previously enjoyable activities. Many, however, do not report or are not aware of feelings of depression, even though they may look depressed to observers. Depression may also be masked by other problems, such as conduct or school-related problems, physical complaints, and overactivity.

Like depressed adults, depressed children and adolescents typically have feelings of hopelessness; distorted thinking patterns and tendencies to blame themselves for negative events; and lower self-esteem, self-confidence, and perceptions of competence (Kovacs, 1996; Lewinsohn et al., 1994). They report episodes of sadness and crying, feelings of apathy, as well as insomnia, fatigue, and poor appetite. They may also experience suicidal thoughts or even attempt suicide. Yet depression in children is also associated with some distinctive features, such as refusal to attend school, fears of parents' dying, and clinging to parents. Depression may also be masked by behaviors that appear unrelated. Conduct disorders, academic problems, physical complaints, and even hyperactivity may stem from unrecognized depression. Among adolescents, aggressive and sexual acting out may also be signs of depression.

Depressed children or adolescents may not label what they are feeling as depression. They may not report feeling sad even though they appear sad to others. Part of the problem is cognitive-developmental. Children are not usually capable of recognizing internal feeling states until about the age of 7. They may not be able to identify negative feeling states in themselves, including depression, until adolescence (Larson et al., 1990). Even adolescents may not recognize what they are experiencing as depression.

Depressed children may lack academic, athletic, and social skills. They may find it hard to concentrate in school and may suffer from impaired memory, making it difficult for them to keep their grades up. They often keep their feelings to themselves, which may prevent their parents from recognizing the problem and seeking help. The child may express negative feelings in the form of anger, sullenness, or impatience, leading to conflicts with parents that in turn can accentuate and prolong the depression.

The average length of a major depressive episode in childhood or adolescence is about 11 months, but an individual episode may last for as long as 18 months (Goleman, 1994a). Moderate levels of depression, however, may persist for years, severely impairing school performance and social functioning (Nolen-Hoeksema & Girgus, 1994). Adolescent depression is associated with an increased risk of major depressive episodes and suicide attempts in adulthood (Fergusson & Woodward, 2002; Weissman, 1999). About three of four children who become depressed from ages 8 to 13 have a recurrence later in life (Goleman, 1994a).

Childhood depression rarely occurs by itself. Depressed children typically experience other psychological disorders, especially anxiety disorders and conduct or oppositional defiant disorders (Hammen & Compas, 1994). Eating disorders are also common among depressed adolescent girls (Rohde, Lewinsohn, & Seeley, 1991). Overall, childhood depression increases the chances that a child will develop another psychological disorder by at least 20-fold (Angold & Costello, 1993). A sizable percentage of depressed adolescents (between 20% and 40%) later develop bipolar disorder (USDHHS, 1999a).

Understanding and Treating Childhood Depression

Depression and suicidal behavior in childhood are frequently related to family problems and conflicts. Children who are exposed to stressful life events affecting the family, such as parental conflict or unemployment, stand an increased risk of depression, especially younger children (Nolen-Hoeksema, Girgus, & Seligman, 1992; Rudolph et al., 2001). Rejection and lack of social support from friends and family members contribute to depression in adolescents (Lewinsohn et al., 1994; Nolan, Glynn, & Garber, 2003). Depression in adolescents can also be triggered by such stressful life events as conflicts with parents and dissatisfaction with school grades. In girls, disturbed eating behaviors and body dissatisfaction after puberty often predict the development of major depression during adolescence (Stice et al., 2000). Interestingly, the relationship between loss of a parent in childhood and later depression during childhood or adolescence is not consistent; some studies show a connection whereas others do not (Lewinsohn et al., 1994).

As children mature and their cognitive abilities develop, cognitive factors, such as negative thinking styles, appear to play a stronger role in the development of depression (Garber, Keiley, & Martin, 2002). Like their adult counterparts, children and adolescents

TRUTH or FICTION? *REVISITED*

Difficulties at school, problem behaviors and physical complaints may actually be signs of depression in children.

☑ **TRUE.** Children may not label what they are feeling as depression or be able to put into words how they feel. Depression is often masked by conduct problems, academic problems, and physical complaints.

with depression tend to adopt a cognitive style characterized by negative attitudes toward themselves and the future (Garber, Weiss, & Shanley, 1993). They also tend to adopt a more helpless or pessimistic attributional style than their nondepressed peers (Lewinsohn et al., 1994). This means that they attribute negative events to internal, stable, and global causes and positive events to external, unstable, and specific causes.

Investigators find distorted thinking patterns in depressed children in other cultures. For example, a study of 582 Chinese children in secondary schools in Hong Kong linked feelings of depression to distorted thinking patterns involving tendencies to minimize accomplishments and blow failures and shortcomings out of proportion (Leung & Poon, 2001). European researchers linked several thinking patterns to depression in young people, including blaming onself for things that were not one's fault, ruminating about one's problems (mulling over them again and again in one's mind), and blowing problems out of proportion (Garnefski et al., 2001).

All in all, the distorted cognitions of depressed children include the following:

1. Expecting the worst (pessimism)
2. Catastrophizing the consequences of negative events
3. Assuming personal responsibility for negative outcomes, even when it is unwarranted
4. Minimizing accomplishments and focusing only on negative aspects of events

Although there are links between cognitive factors and depression, we do not know which comes first: whether children become depressed because of a depressive mind-set or whether depression leads to distorted, negative thoughts. Quite possibly the relationship is reciprocal, with depression affecting thinking patterns and thinking patterns affecting emotional states. Genetic factors also appear to play a role in explaining depressive symptoms in adolescents (O'Connor et al., 1998).

Adolescent girls tend to show greater levels of depressive symptoms than do adolescent boys (Stewart et al., 2004), a finding that mirrors the gender gap in depression among adults. The trajectory of depressive symptoms also differs in boys and girls. Boys, on the average, show no increase in depressive symptoms from ages 8 through 16; for the average girl, however, depressive symptoms remain fairly steady from ages 8 to 11 but then increase between ages 12 and 16 (Twenge & Nolen-Hoeksema, 2002). The greater level of depression of the average adolescent girl may reflect the greater social challenges that girls tend to face, such as pressures to narrow their interests and pursue feminine-typed activities (Nolen-Hoeksema & Girgus, 1994). Girls who adopt a passive, ruminative coping style may be at greatest risk of becoming depressed.

Cognitive–behavioral therapy (CBT) produces impressive results in the treatment of depressed children and adolescents (Berman et al., 2000; Braswell & Kendall, 2001; Lewinsohn & Clarke, 1999). Although individual approaches vary, CBT usually involves social skills training (e.g., learning how to start a conversation or make friends) to increase the likelihood of obtaining social reinforcement. CBT typically also includes training in problem-solving skills and ways of increasing the frequency of rewarding activities and countering depressive styles of thinking. In addition, family therapy may help families resolve underlying conflicts and reorganize their relationships so that members can become more supportive of each other.

The antidepressant drug *fluoxetine* (brand name Prozac) shows promise in treating depression in both children and adolescents (Harris, 2004; Mitka, 2003). Recent research also supports the benefits of *sertraline* (Zoloft) with children and adolescents (Wagner et al., 2003). However, critics of this study comment that the benefits of sertraline over inert placebos may not be large enough to produce clinically meaningful effects in treating depressed youth (Price, 2004; Speilmans, 2004).

Lithium is also used with generally favorable results in children and adolescents with bipolar disorder (USDHHS, 1999a). But concerns that stimulants and antidepressants are being prescribed too widely in treating childhood disorders has prompted a heated debate, as we examine in the "Controversies in Abnormal Psychology" feature.

CONTROVERSIES IN ABNORMAL PSYCHOLOGY
Are We Overmedicating Our Kids?

The use of the stimulant drug Ritalin for treating ADHD in children nearly tripled during the 1990s (Shute, Locy, & Pasternak, 2000). As the new millennium began, physicians were writing nearly 20 million prescriptions monthly for stimulant medication for children (Zernike & Petersen, 2001). Increasing numbers of young people are also receiving psychiatric drugs used widely in treating adults, including antidepressants, mood stabilizers, antianxiety drugs, sleep medications, and even antipsychotic drugs (Kluger, 2003; Zito et al., 2000).

With so many children receiving powerful psychiatric drugs, critics claim that we are too ready to seek a "quick fix" for problem behavior rather than examine contributing factors, such as family conflicts, that may take more effort and time to treat. As one pediatrician put it, "It takes time for parents and teachers to sit down and talk to kids. . . . It takes less time to get a child a pill" (Hancock, 1996, p. 52).

The two sides of the debate are clearly drawn. Critics contend that we are overusing psychiatric drugs, especially Ritalin (Pear, 2000). They point to the risk of potentially troubling side effects, such as weight loss and sleeplessness from Ritalin, and to concerns about what stimulant drugs may be doing to still-developing brains (Kluger, 2003). Critics also contend that alternative treatments, such as cognitive–behavioral therapy, are available for treating many of these problems, but are underused in comparison with the prescription pad.

On the other hand, increasing evidence points to the therapeutic effectiveness of psychiatric drugs in treating ADHD and childhood depression. Stimulant drugs like Ritalin help calm down hyperactive children and improve concentration. That said, the scientific jury is still out on the question of the long-term effectiveness of stimulant medication and whether use of such drugs results in significant improvement in academic performance.

What about antidepressants? We know that the earlier generation of tricyclic antidepressants proved ineffective in treating childhood depression (Brody, 2002). However, as noted earlier, the newer generation of SSRI-type antidepressants (Prozac and Zoloft, for example) shows promise in treating childhood depression, although lingering doubts remain about whether the therapeutic benefits are clinically meaningful.

Clouding the picture further was the concern expressed in 2004 by a Food and Drug Administration advisory panel that antidepressants increase the risk of suicidal behavior in children and adolescents (Dooren, 2004; Harris, 2004). On the other hand, drug therapy advocates express concerns about the consequences of failing to medicate children and teens who have psychiatric problems. They contend that failure to treat depression can increase the risk for suicide, whereas leaving ADHD untreated or undertreated may lead to serious substance abuse and academic problems down the road (Kluger, 2003).

One thing both sides seem to agree on is that drug therapy alone is not sufficient treatment for psychological problems in children and adolescents. The child with academic difficulties, problems at home, and low self-esteem needs more than a pill. Clearly, the use of therapeutic drugs needs to be supplemented by psychological interventions that help children develop more adaptive behaviors. Perhaps drug therapy should be considered a second-line treatment when nonpharmacological approaches prove ineffective. Combination approaches may also be of benefit. A recent study of depressed adolescents showed that treatment with Prozac was superior to cognitive–behavioral therapy alone, but that the combination of therapy and drugs was more effective than either treatment alone (Harris, 2004).

Critical Thinking

- Why is the prescription of stimulant drugs and antidepressants in treating childhood disorders controversial?
- In many comparable countries drugs are prescribed much less frequently for childhood disorders than they are in the United States. What does this suggest?

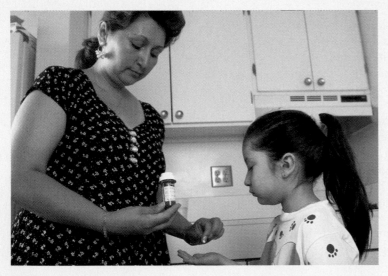

Should this child be medicated? The use of psychiatric drugs in children has skyrocketed in recent years. Do you know any children who have benefited from psychiatric drugs? What concerns does the use of these drugs pose? What alternatives are available?

Suicide in Children and Adolescents

Suicide is rare among children and early adolescents but becomes more common in later adolescents and young adults (Pelkonen & Marttunen, 2003). Suicide is the third most common cause of death among young people age 15 to 24, after accidents and homicides (NIMH, 2003b; Winerman, 2004). Approximately 1 per 10,000 people in this age range commit suicide (.01%). Among 10- to 14-year-olds, the suicide rate is much lower, about one eighth as high as it among the 15- to 24-year-olds. Teenage suicide rates rose sharply in the early 1990s but headed downward in recent years (Goode, 2003c; Gould et al., 2003). Even so, youth suicide remains a major public health problem in the United States and Canada (Koplin & Agathen, 2002; Langlois & Morrison, 2002). Official statistics only account for reported suicide; some apparent accidental deaths, such as those due to falling from a window, may be suicides as well.

Despite the commonly held view that children and adolescents who talk about suicide are only venting their feelings, most young people who kill themselves send out signals beforehand (Bongar, 2002; Hendin et al., 2001). In fact, those who discuss their plans are the ones most likely to carry them out. Unfortunately, parents tend not to take their children's suicidal talk seriously.

In addition to increasing age, other factors associated with heightened risk of suicide in children and adolescents include the following (Fergusson & Woodward, 2002; Lewinsohn et al., 2001; Miller et al., 2000; NIMH, 2003b; Pelkonen & Marttunen, 2003; Wu et al., 2001; USDHHS, 1991, 1999a):

- *Gender.* Girls, like women, are three times more likely than boys to attempt suicide. Boys, like men, are more likely to succeed, however, perhaps because boys, like men, are more apt to use lethal means such as guns.
- *Geography.* Adolescents in less-populated areas are more likely to commit suicide. Adolescents in the rural western regions of the United States have the highest suicide rate.
- *Ethnicity.* The suicide rates for African American, Asian American, and Hispanic American youth are about 30% to 60% lower than that of (non-Hispanic) White youth. Yet, the suicide rate among Native American young adults (age 15 to 24) is nearly twice that of young White adults.
- *Depression and hopelessness.* Depression figures prominent in youth suicide as it does in suicide in adults, especially when it is combined with feelings of hopelessness and low self-esteem.
- *Previous suicidal behavior.* One quarter of adolescents who attempt suicide are repeaters. More than 80% of adolescents who take their lives have talked about it before doing so. Suicidal teenagers may carry lethal weapons, talk about death, make suicide plans, or engage in risky or dangerous behavior. A family history of suicide also increases the risk of teenage suicide (Mann et al., 1996).
- *Prior sexual abuse.* In an Australian sample, young people with a history of childhood sexual abuse had more than 10 times higher rates of suicide than the national average (Plunkett et al., 2001). Moreover, about one third of young people who had been abused had attempted suicide, compared to none in a nonabused control group.
- *Family problems.* Family problems contribute to an increased risk of suicide attempts and actual suicides. These problems include family instability and conflict, physical or sexual abuse, loss of a parent due to death or separation, and poor parent–child communication.
- *Stressful life events.* Many suicides among young people are directly preceded by stressful or traumatic events, such as breaking up with a girlfriend or boyfriend, having an unwanted pregnancy, getting arrested, having problems at school, moving to a new school, or having to take an important test.
- *Substance abuse.* Addiction in the adolescent's family, or by the adolescent, is a factor.
- *Social contagion.* Adolescent suicides sometimes occur in clusters, especially when a suicide or a group of suicides receives widespread publicity. Adolescents may romanticize suicide as a heroic act of defiance. There are often suicides or attempts among the siblings, friends, parents, or adult relatives of suicidal adolescents. Adolescent suicides may occur in bunches in a community, especially when adolescents are subjected to mounting academic pressures, such as competing for admission to college. Perhaps the suicide of a family member or schoolmate renders suicide a more "real" option for managing stress or punishing others. Perhaps the other person's suicide gives the adolescent the impression that he or she is "doomed" to commit suicide. Note the case of Pam.

> ### Pam, Kim, and Brian
>
> *Pam was an exceptionally attractive 17-year-old who was hospitalized after cutting her wrists. "Before we moved to [an upper-middle-class town in suburban New York]," she told the psychologist, "I was the brightest girl in the class. Teachers loved me. If we had had a yearbook, I'd have been the most likely to succeed. Then we moved, and suddenly I was hit with it. Everybody was bright, or tried to be. Suddenly I was just another ordinary student planning to go to college.*
>
> *"Teachers were good to me, but I was no longer special, and that hurt. Then we all applied to college. Do you know that 90 percent of the kids in the high school go on to college? I mean four-year colleges? And we all knew—or suspected—that the good schools had quotas on kids from here. I mean you can't have 30 kids from our senior class going to Yale or Princeton or Wellesley, can you? You're better off applying from Utah.*
>
> *"Then Kim got her early-acceptance rejection from Brown. Kim was number one in the class. Nobody could believe it. Her father'd gone to Brown and Kim had almost 1500 SATs. Kim was out of commission for a few days—I mean she didn't come to school or anything—and then, boom, she was gone. She offed herself, kaput, no more, the end. Then Brian was rejected from Cornell. A few days later, he was gone, too. And I'm like, 'These kids were better than me.' I mean their grades and their SATs were higher than mine, and I was going to apply to Brown and Cornell. I'm like, 'What chance do I have? Why bother?' "*
>
> —*From the Authors' Files*

You can see how catastrophizing thoughts play a role in such tragic cases. Consistent with the literature on suicide among adults, young people who attempt suicide do not use active problem-solving strategies in handling stressful situations. They may see no other way out of their perceived failures or stresses. As with adults, one approach to working with suicidal children helps them challenge distorted thinking and generate alternative strategies for handling problems and stressors. Promising prevention programs, including school-based skills training programs, have been developed, but evidence supporting their effectiveness remains to be demonstrated (Gould et al., 2003).

ELIMINATION DISORDERS

Fetuses and newborn children eliminate waste products reflexively. As children develop, they are trained to inhibit the natural reflexes that govern urination and bowel movements. In the classic *Patterns of Child Rearing*, Robert Sears and his colleagues (1957) reported that American children were toilet trained, on the average, at 18 months. However, nighttime bladder accidents occurred frequently until about 24 months. Today, most children in the United States achieve bladder control between the ages of 2 and 3. Many continue to have nighttime accidents for another year or so, however. Enuresis and encopresis are disorders involving problems with elimination that are not due to organic causes.

Enuresis

Enuresis derives from the Greek roots *en-*, meaning "in," and *ouron*, meaning "urine." **Enuresis** is failure to control urination after one has reached the "normal" age for attaining such control. Conceptions of what age is normal for achieving control vary among clinicians. *DSM-IV* standards are shown in Table 14.7. Enuresis, like so many other developmental disorders, is more common among boys. Enuresis is estimated to affect 7% of boys and 3% of girls by age 5. Bed-wetting affects upwards of 7 million children age 6 and over in the United States (Lim, 2003). The disorder usually resolves itself by adolescence if not earlier, although in about 1% of cases the problem continues into adulthood (APA, 2000).

enuresis Failure to control urination after one has reached the "normal" age for attaining such control.

Enuresis may occur during nighttime sleep only, during waking hours only, or during both nighttime sleep and waking hours. Nighttime-only enuresis is the most common type, and accidents occurring during sleep are referred to as *bed-wetting*. Achieving bladder control at night is more difficult than achieving daytime control. When asleep at night, children must learn to wake up when they feel the pressure of a full bladder and then go to the bathroom to relieve themselves. The younger the "trained" child is, the more likely she or he is to wet the bed at night. It is perfectly normal for children who have acquired daytime control over their bladders to have nighttime accidents for a year or more. Bed-wetting usually occurs during the deepest stage of sleep and may reflect immaturity of the nervous system. The diagnosis of enuresis applies in cases of repeated bed-wetting or daytime wetting of clothes by children of at least 5 years of age.

Theoretical Perspectives Psychodynamic explanations of enuresis suggest that it represents the expression of hostility toward children's parents because of harsh toilet training. It may represent regression in response to the birth of a sibling or some other stressor or life change, such as starting school or suffering the death of a parent or relative. Learning theorists point out that enuresis occurs most commonly in children whose parents attempted to train them early. Early failures may have connected anxiety with efforts to control the bladder. Conditioned anxiety, then, induces rather than curbs urination.

Evidence from a 1995 Danish study strongly suggests that *primary enuresis,* the most prevalent form of the disorder, which characterizes children who have persistent bed-wetting and have never established urinary control, is genetically transmitted (Eiberg, Berendt, & Mohr, 1995). We don't yet understand the genetic mechanism in enuresis, but one possibility implicates the genes that regulate the rate of development of motor control over eliminatory reflexes by the cerebral cortex. Although genetic factors appear to be involved in the transmission of primary enuresis, it is likely that environmental and behavioral factors also come into play in determining the development and course of the disorder. The other type of enuresis, *secondary enuresis,* characterizes children who develop the problem after having established urinary control and is associated with occasional bed-wetting. Genetic factors are apparently not involved in this type of enuresis (Goleman, 1995a).

Treatment Enuresis usually resolves itself as children mature. Behavioral methods have been shown to be helpful when enuresis endures or causes parents or children great distress, however. Such methods condition children to wake up when their bladders are full. One dependable example is the use of a urine alarm method, a variation on a technique introduced by psychologist O. Hobart Mowrer in the 1930s.

The problem in bed-wetting is that children with enuresis continue to sleep despite bladder tension that awakens most other children. As a consequence, they reflexively urinate in bed. Mowrer pioneered the use of the urine alarm, which in its present form involves a moisture-activated alarm that is placed beneath the sleeping child. A sensor sounds the alarm when the child wets the bed, which awakens the child (Lim, 2003). After several repetitions, most children learn to awaken in response to bladder tension—*before* the alarm is sounded. The technique is usually explained through principles of classical conditioning. Tension in children's bladders is paired repeatedly with a stimulus (an alarm) that wakes them up. The bladder tension (conditioned stimulus, or CS) comes to elicit the same response (waking up—the conditioned response, or CR) that is elicited by the alarm (the unconditioned stimulus, or US).

Psychological treatment, generally involving the urine alarm technique, or drug therapy are often helpful in treating enuresis (Fitz et al., 2004). Various drugs have shown therapeutic benefits, including tricyclics and *fluvoxamine* (brand name Luvox), a SSRI-type antidepressant that

TABLE 14.7

Diagnostic Features of Enuresis

The child repeatedly wets bedding or clothes (whether intentional or involuntary).

The child's chronological age is at least 5 (or child is at an equivalent developmental level).

The behavior occurs at least twice a week for 3 months or causes significant impairment in functioning or distress.

The disorder does not have an organic basis.

Source: Adapted from the *DSM-IV-TR* (APA, 2000).

TRUTH or FICTION? *REVISITED*

Techniques of classical conditioning can help children with persistent bed-wetting learn to stay dry.

☑ **TRUE.** The use of a urine alarm can help condition the enuretic child to awaken to the pressure of a full bladder. In this paradigm, what is the unconditioned stimulus and what is the conditioned stimulus?

Urine alarm. The urine alarm method is widely used in the treatment of nighttime enuresis. How does the method illustrate the principles of classical conditioning?

Overview of Disorders of Childhood and Adolescence

TYPES OF DISORDERS

	Description	Major Types/Prevalence Rates (%)	Features
Pervasive Developmental Disorder	Marked impairment in multiple areas of development	• Autistic Disorder (0.3%) • Asperger's Disorder	• **Autism:** Major deficits in relating to others, impaired language and cognitive functioning, and restricted range of activities and interests • **Asperger's Disorder:** Poor social interactions and stereotyped behavior but without the significant language or cognitive deficits of autism
Mental Retardation	A broad-based delay in the development of cognitive and social functioning	• Deficits vary with level of severity from mild to profound (1%)	• Diagnosed on the basis of low IQ score and poor adaptive functioning
Learning Disorders	Deficiencies in specific learning abilities in the context of at least average intelligence and exposure to learning opportunities	• Mathematics Disorder • Disorder of Written Expression • Reading Disorder (Dyslexia) (4%)	• **Mathematics Disorder:** Difficulty understanding basic mathematical operations • **Disorder of Written Expression:** Grossly deficient writing skills • **Reading Disorder:** Difficulty recognizing words and comprehending written text
Communication Disorders	Difficulties in understanding or using language	• Expressive Language Disorder • Mixed Receptive/Expressive Language Disorder • Phonological Disorder • Stuttering (1%)	• **Expressive Language Disorder:** Difficulty using spoken language • **Mixed Receptive/Expressive Disorder:** Difficulty understanding and producing speech • **Phonological Disorder:** Difficulty articulating the sounds of speech • **Stuttering:** Difficulty speaking fluently without interruption
Attention-Deficit and Disruptive Behavior Disorders	Patterns of disturbed behavior that are generally disruptive to others and to adaptable social functioning	• Attention-Deficit Hyperactivity Disorder (3%–7%) • Conduct Disorder (2%–16% adolescent boys; < 1%–9% adolescent girls) • Oppositional Defiant Disorder (6%–12%)	• **ADHD:** Problems of impulsivity, inattention, and hyperactivity • **CD:** Antisocial behavior that violates social norms and the rights of others • **ODD:** Pattern of noncompliant, negativistic, or oppositional behavior
Anxiety and Mood Disorders	Emotional disorders affecting children and adolescents	• Separation Anxiety Disorder (4%–5%) • Specific Phobia • Social Phobia • Generalized Anxiety Disorder • Major Depression • Bipolar Disorder	• Anxiety and depression often have similar features in children as in adults, but some differences exist • Children may suffer from school phobia as a form of separation anxiety • Depressed children may fail to label their feelings as depression or may show behaviors that mask depression, such as conduct problems and physical complaints
Elimination Disorders	Persistent problems with controlling urination or defecation that cannot be explained by organic causes	• Enuresis (lack of control over urination) (7% boys; 3% girls) • Encopresis (lack of control over defecation) (1%)	• **Enuresis:** Nighttime-only enuresis (bed-wetting) is the most common type • **Encopresis:** Occurs most often during daytime hours

Sources for prevalence rates: APA, 2000; Frick & Silverthorn, 2001; Loeber et al., 2000; Masi et al., 2001; Shute et al., 2000; Wingert, 2000; Yeargin-Allsopp et al., 2003.

works on brain systems that control urination (Horrigan, & Barnhill, 2000; Kano & Arisaka, 2000). However, the urine alarm technique has the highest cure rates and the lowest relapse rates among available treatments (Glazener, Evans, & Peto, 2000; Thiedke, 2003). The lower relapse rate of psychological treatment shows that therapeutic drugs by themselves do not teach any new skills or adaptive behaviors that can be retained beyond the active treatment period.

Encopresis

encopresis Lack of control over bowel movements that is not caused by an organic problem in a child who is at least 4 years old.

Encopresis derives from the Greek roots *en-* and *kopros,* meaning "feces." **Encopresis** is lack of control over bowel movements that is not caused by an organic problem. The child must have a chronological age of at least 4, or in children with intellectual impairment, a mental age of at least 4 years. About 1% of 5-year-olds have encopresis (APA,

CAUSAL FACTORS

- **Autism:** Causes unknown, but are presumed to involve underlying brain abnormalities, possibly resulting from genetic defects or prenatal exposure to toxic agents

- Chromosomal abnormalities, such as Down syndrome
- Genetic abnormalities, such as fragile X syndrome
- Prenatal infections or maternal substance abuse
- Cultural-familial causes

- Causes unclear, but may involve abnormalities in brain circuits for processing visual and auditory information (in dyslexia)
- Genetic factors are also implicated in dyslexia

- **Stuttering:** Causes unclear, but may involve a combination of genetic and environmental influences

- Family factors, such as unresolved parent–child conflict; negative marital conflict; and coercive parent–child interactions
- Poor parenting behaviors, such as lack of reinforcement for appropriate behavior
- Possible genetic component and subtle brain abnormalities associated with ADHD

- Cognitive factors, such as dysfunctional thinking patterns, are observed in depressed and anxious children as well as adults
- Stressful life events, family conflicts and problems, and lack of social support
- Genetic factors may also play a role, especially in adolescent depression

- **Enuresis:** Psychological conflicts, conditioned anxiety, and biological factors (genetic) may be involved
- **Encopresis:** Causes may involve a combination of such factors as constipation, inconsistent or incomplete toilet training, psychosocial stressors, and anxiety or other psychological factors

TREATMENT APPROACHES

- **Autism:** Intensive, long-term behavioral treatment to improve adaptive behavior and communication skills

- Psychoeducational interventions to foster development of academic skills and adaptive behaviors; institutional care may be needed in more severe cases

- Interventions based on one or more of the following theoretical models:
  - —Psychoeducational model
  - —Behavioral model
  - —Medical model
  - —Neuropsychological model
  - —Linguistic model
  - —Cognitive model

- Speech therapy and possible additional psychological counseling for social anxiety associated with speech impairment

- **ADHD:** Drug therapy (Ritalin or other drugs), cognitive-behavioral therapy to help develop more appropriate behaviors and attentional skills
- Parent training to assist parents in use of more appropriate reinforcement
- **CD:** Residential treatment programs, anger management programs, and parent training programs to help conduct-disordered children develop more appropriate social behaviors

- Cognitive–behavioral therapy to help anxious and depressed children develop healthier thinking patterns and coping skills
- SSRI-type antidepressants, such as Prozac, may be helpful, but more research examining their effectiveness and safety is needed

- **Enuresis:** Some variation of the urine alarm method is commonly used
- **Encopresis:** Operant conditioning methods may be employed (rewards for successful efforts at self-control, mild punishment for continued accidents)

2000). Like enuresis, this condition is most common among boys. Encopresis is rare, except among teens who are profoundly or severely retarded. Soiling may be voluntary or involuntary and is not caused by an organic problem, except in cases in which constipation is involved. Among the possible predisposing factors are inconsistent or incomplete toilet training and psychosocial stressors, such as the birth of a sibling or beginning school.

Soiling, unlike enuresis, is more likely to happen during the day than at night. It can thus be keenly embarrassing to the child. Classmates often avoid or ridicule soilers. Because feces have a strong odor, teachers may find it hard to act as though nothing has happened. Parents, too, are eventually galled by recurrent soiling and may increase their demands for self-control and employ powerful punishments for failure. As a result, children may hide soiled underwear, distance themselves from classmates, or feign sickness to stay at home. Their levels of anxiety concerning soiling increase. Because anxiety (arousal of the sympathetic branch of the autonomic nervous system) promotes bowel movements, control may become yet more elusive.

When soiling is involuntary, it is often associated with constipation, impaction, or retention that results in subsequent overflow. Constipation may be related to psychological factors, such as fears associated with defecating in a particular place or with a more general pattern of negativistic or oppositional behavior. Or constipation may be related to physiological factors, such as complications from an illness or from medication. Much less frequently, encopresis is deliberate or intentional.

Soiling often appears to follow harsh punishment for an accident or two, particularly in children who are already highly stressed or anxious. Harsh punishment may rivet children's attention on soiling. They may then ruminate about soiling, raising their level of anxiety so that self-control is impaired.

Behavior therapy techniques are helpful in treating encopresis (Loening-Baucke, 2002). Treatment generally involves the parents rewarding (by praise and other means) successful attempts at self-control and using mild punishments for continued accidents (for example, gentle reminders to attend more closely to bowel tension and having the child clean her or his own underwear). When encopresis persists, thorough medical and psychological evaluation is recommended to determine possible causes and appropriate treatments.

SUMMING UP

Normal and Abnormal Behavior in Childhood and Adolescence

What factors do we need to consider in distinguishing normal and abnormal behavior in childhood and adolescence? In addition to the criteria described in Chapter 1, we need to take into account the child's age and cultural background.

What are the effects of child abuse? The effects of child abuse range from physical injuries, even death, to emotional consequences, such as difficulties forming healthy attachments, low self-esteem, suicidal thinking, depression, and failure to explore the outside world, among other problems. The emotional and behavioral consequences of child abuse and neglect often extend into adulthood.

Pervasive Developmental Disorders

What are pervasive developmental disorders? Pervasive developmental disorders involve marked deficiencies in multiple areas of development. They develop within the first years of life and are often associated with mental retardation. Autistic disorder is the most prominent pervasive developmental disorder.

What are the clinical features of autism? Children with autism shun affectionate behavior, engage in stereotyped behavior, attempt to preserve sameness, and tend to have peculiar speech habits such as echolalia, pronoun reversals, and idiosyncratic speech. The causes of autism remain unknown, but gains in academic and social functioning have been obtained through the use of intensive behavior therapy.

Mental Retardation

What is mental retardation and how is it assessed? Mental retardation involves impaired development of intellectual and adaptive abilities. It is assessed by intelligence tests and measures of functional ability. Most cases fall in the mildly retarded range.

What are the causes of mental retardation? Mental retardation is caused by chromosomal abnormalities, such as Down syndrome; genetic disorders, such as fragile X syndrome and phenylketonuria; prenatal factors, such as maternal diseases and alcohol use; and familial/cultural factors associated with intellectually impoverished home environments.

Learning Disorders

What are learning disorders? Learning disorders (also called learning disabilities) are specific deficits in the development of arithmetic, writing, or reading skills.

What are the causes of learning disorders and approaches to treatment? The causes remain under study but probably involve underlying brain dysfunctions that make it difficult to process or decode visual and auditory information. Intervention focuses mainly on attempts to remediate specific skill deficits.

Communication Disorders

What are communications disorders? These disorders are characterized by impaired understanding or use of language. The specific types of communication disorders include expressive language disorder, mixed receptive/expressive language disorder, phonological disorder, and stuttering.

Attention-Deficit and Disruptive Behavior Disorders

What are attention-deficit and disruptive behavior disorders? This category includes attention-deficit hyperactivity disorder (ADHD), conduct disorder, and oppositional defiant disorder (ODD). ADHD is characterized by impulsivity, inattention, and hyperactivity. Children with conduct disorders intentionally engage in antisocial behavior. Children with ODD show negativistic or oppositional behavior but not outright delinquent or antisocial behavior characteristic of conduct disorder. However, ODD may lead to the development of conduct disorder.

How are these disorders treated? Stimulant medication is generally effective in reducing hyperactivity, but it has not led to general academic gains. Behavior therapy may help ADHD children adapt better to school. Behavior therapy may also be helpful in modifying behaviors of children with conduct disorders and oppositional defiant disorder.

Childhood Anxiety and Depression

What types of anxiety disorders affect children? Anxiety disorders that occur commonly among children and adolescents include specific phobias, social phobia, and generalized anxiety disorder. Children may also show separation anxiety disorder, which involves excessive anxiety at times when they are separated from their parents. Cognitive biases, such as expecting negative outcomes, negative self-talk, and interpreting ambiguous situations as threatening, figure prominently in anxiety disorders in children and adolescents, as they often do among adults.

What are the distinguishing features of depression in childhood and adolescence? Depressed children, especially younger children, may not report or be aware of feeling depressed. Depression may also be masked by seemingly unrelated behaviors, such as conduct disorders. Depressed children also tend to show cognitive biases associated with depression in adulthood, such as adoption of a pessimistic explanatory style and distorted thinking. Although rare, suicide in children does occur and threats should be taken seriously. Risk factors for adolescent suicide include gender, age, geography, race, depression, past suicidal behavior, strained family relationships, stress, substance abuse, and social contagion.

Elimination Disorders

What are elimination disorders? These are problems of impaired control over urination (enuresis) and bowel movements (encopresis) that cannot be accounted for by organic causes. Both disorders are more common in boys.

What is the urine alarm method for treating enuresis? The urine alarm method conditions children with enuresis to respond to bladder tension by awakening before urinating.

KEY TERMS

pervasive developmental disorders (PDDs) *(p. 474)*
autism *(p. 174)*
Asperger's disorder *(p. 474)*
Rett's disorder *(p. 474)*
childhood disintegrative disorder *(p. 474)*
mental retardation *(p. 480)*
Down syndrome *(p. 481)*

fragile X syndrome *(p. 482)*
phenylketonuria (PKU) *(p. 483)*
cultural-familial retardation *(p. 484)*
dyslexia *(p. 485)*
learning disorder *(p. 485)*
communication disorders *(p. 487)*
attention-deficit hyperactivity disorder (ADHD) *(p. 489)*

hyperactivity *(p. 489)*
conduct disorder *(p. 492)*
oppositional defiant disorder (ODD) *(p. 493)*
separation anxiety disorder *(p. 496)*
enuresis *(p. 502)*
encopresis *(p. 504)*

WEB TOOLS

The companion website offers tools to enrich your learning experience and help you succeed in class. Go to www.prenhall.com/nevid for the gateway to the following resources:

- **VIDEO** links to connect to the video case files on the companion CD-ROM. VIDEO icons in the margins of the chapter highlight the case examples included in the CD-ROM. You can also access the CD-ROM directly if you do not have a Web connection.

- **QUIZ** links to self-scoring quizzes corresponding to each section of the chapter. The quizzes help you review your knowledge of the content in each chapter.

- **WEB** links to direct you to related sites that enhance your learning of abnormal psychology.

CHAPTER FIFTEEN

Cognitive Disorders and Disorders Related to Aging

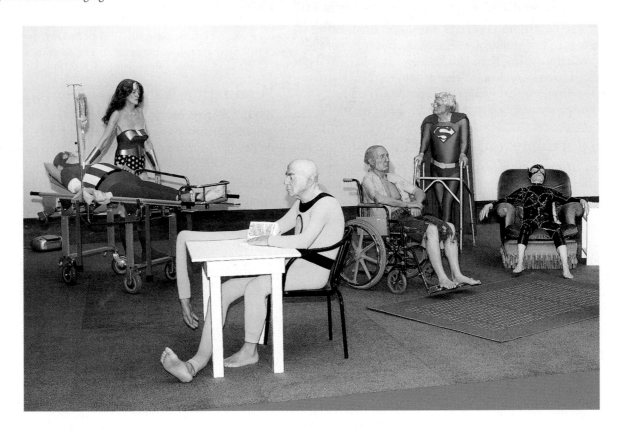

> "You should pray for a sound mind in a sound body."
> —Juvenal, Roman poet, 55 AD - 127 AD

"I"

"Now Is The Last Best Time"

The disease [Alzheimer's disease] works slowly, destroying the mind, stealing life in a tedious, silent dance of death. Slowly the memory is impaired, and then you wander in a world without certainty and names. Yesterdays disappear, except those long ago. Eventually there is a descent into silence and a dependence on caretakers. Hands other than yours feed and bathe you. A cipher takes your place amid the tubes and tragedy. By the end, Alzheimer's leaves its victims silent, quivering in their flesh, awaiting the last rites. Some common illness often takes credit on the death certificate . . .

I am alone and I can hear water running somewhere in the house. I don't remember going to the bathroom. Who else turned on the water?

Writing sometimes becomes difficult. Words vanish before they reach the page. Most of the time the biggest drawback is my plummeting typing accuracy. So far there are few words the spell checker cannot correct . . .

I do not want to succumb to this illness, but I am powerless in its clutches. Words come when I sit down to write, but they dance away seductively, and meaning and substance disappear quickly. Of course, this is not new; such things happen many times, but before they were retrievable and now they are not . . .

There are many days of tears now. Some mornings I wake and my eyes are wet. I cry, choked with emotion I cannot express. I am having trouble reading the writing I do with a pencil or pen. It used to be clear and sharp; now it wobbles and is full of uncertainty. The words come normally but the letters are sometimes not in the proper order. I spend valuable time deciphering the meaning in each letter of the alphabet until the word's meaning becomes clear. Progress is slow and I am losing time. A few months ago I had no trouble writing. I have to be careful to spell correctly but sometimes . . .

I am aware of the loss of language more than ever before. I am afraid to write because watching the words come out distorted is painful and it reveals the destructive power of the disease over which I have no control.

Now is the last best time.

—From DeBaggio, 2002

HAVING A "SOUND MIND IN A SOUND BODY" IS AN ANCIENT PRESCRIPTION FOR A healthy and happy life. However, brain diseases and injuries can make us unsound in both body and mind. When damage to the brain results from an injury or stroke, the deterioration in cognitive, social, and occupational functioning can be rapid and severe. In the case of a more gradual but progressive form of deterioration, such as in Alzheimer's disease, the decline of mental functioning is more gradual but leads eventually to a state of virtual helplessness. Sadly, people with Alzheimer's may come to realize that each day is their last best time.

In this chapter, we focus on the class of psychological disorders called *cognitive disorders*. These disorders arise from injuries or diseases that affect the brain.

Some of these diseases, including Alzheimer's disease, primarily affect older adults. Consequently we focus in this chapter on the types of psychological problems that often affect people in late adulthood.

COGNITIVE DISORDERS

Cognitive disorders are disturbances of thinking or memory that represent a marked change from the individual's prior level of functioning (APA, 2000). Cognitive disorders are not psychologically based; they are caused by physical or medical conditions, including drug use or withdrawal, that affect the functioning of the brain. In some cases

cognitive disorders A class of psychological disorders characterized by impairment in cognitive abilities and daily functioning in which biological causation is either known or presumed.

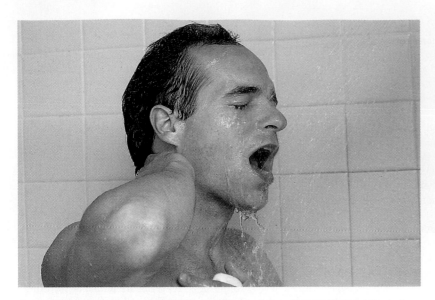

Does this man's singing help him coordinate his actions? In a celebrated case study, Dr. Oliver Sacks discussed the case of "Dr. P.," who was discovered to be suffering from a brain tumor that impaired his ability to interpret visual cues. Yet he could continue to eat meals and wash and dress himself so long as he could sing to himself.

the specific cause of the cognitive disorder can be pinpointed; in others, it cannot. Although these disorders are biologically based, psychological and environmental factors play key roles in determining the impact and range of disabling symptoms as well as the individual's ability to cope with them.

Our ability to perform cognitive functions—to think, reason, and store and recall information—depends on the functioning of the brain. Cognitive disorders arise when the brain is either damaged or impaired in its ability to function due to injury, illness, exposure to toxins, or use or abuse of psychoactive drugs. The more widespread the damage to the brain, the greater and more extensive the impairment in functioning. The extent and location of brain damage largely determine the range and severity of impairment. The location of the damage is also critical because many brain structures or regions perform specialized functions. Damage to the temporal lobe, for example, is associated with defects in memory and attention, whereas damage to the occipital lobe may result in visual–spatial deficits, such as in the famous case of Dr. P, a distinguished musician and teacher who lost the ability to visually recognize objects, including faces.

In *The Man Who Mistook His Wife for a Hat,* the neurologist Oliver Sacks (1985) recounts how Dr. P. failed to recognize the faces of his students at the music school. When a student spoke, however, Dr. P. immediately recognized his or her voice. Not only did the professor fail to discriminate faces visually, but sometimes he perceived faces where none existed. He patted the heads of fire hydrants and parking meters, which he took to be children. He warmly addressed the rounded knobs on furniture. Dr. P. and his colleagues generally dismissed these peculiarities as jokes—after all, Dr. P. was well known for his oddball humor and jests. His music remained as accomplished as ever, and his general health seemed fine, so these misperceptions seemed little to be concerned about.

Not until 3 years later did Dr. P. seek a neurological evaluation. His ophthalmologist had found that although Dr. P.'s eyes were healthy, he had problems interpreting visual stimulation. So he made the referral to Dr. Sacks, a neurologist. When Sacks engaged Dr. P. in conversation, Dr. P.'s eyes fixated oddly on miscellaneous features of Dr. Sack's face—his nose, then his right ear, then his chin, sensing parts of his face but apparently not connecting them in a meaningful pattern. When Dr. P. sought to put on his shoe after a physical examination, he confused his foot with the shoe. When preparing to leave, Dr. P. looked around for his hat, and then . . .

> [Dr. P.] reached out his hand, and took hold of his wife's head, tried to lift it off, to put it on. He had apparently mistaken his wife for a hat! His wife looked as if she was used to such things.

(Sacks, 1985, p. 10)

Dr. P.'s peculiar behavior may seem amusing to some, but his loss of visual perception was tragic. Although Dr. P. could identify abstract forms and shapes—a cube, for example—he no longer recognized the faces of his family, or his own. Some features of particular faces would strike a chord of recognition. For example, he could recognize a picture of Einstein from the distinctive hair and mustache and a picture of his own brother from the square jaw and big teeth. But he was responding to isolated features, not grasping the facial patterns as wholes.

Sacks recounts a final test:

> It was still a cold day, in early spring, and I had thrown my coat and gloves on the sofa.
> "What is this?" I asked, holding up a glove.

"May I examine it?" he asked, and, taking it from me, he proceeded to examine it as he had examined the geometrical shapes.

"A continuous surface," he announced at last, "infolded on itself. It appears to have"— he hesitated—"five outpouchings, if this is the word."

"Yes," I said cautiously. "You have given me a description. Now tell me what it is."

"A container of some sort?"

"Yes," I said, "and what would it contain?"

"It would contain its contents!" said Dr. P., with a laugh. "There are many possibilities. It could be a change-purse, for example, for coins of five sizes. It could . . ."

I interrupted the blarney flow. "Does it not look familiar? Do you think it might contain, might fit, a part of your body?"

No light of recognition dawned on his face.

No child would have the power to see and speak of "a continuous surface . . . infolded on itself," but any child, any infant, would immediately know a glove as a glove, see it as familiar, as going with a hand. Dr. P. didn't. He saw nothing as familiar. Visually, he was lost in a world of lifeless abstractions.

(Sacks, 1985, p. 13)

Later, we might add, Dr. P. accidentally put the glove on his hand, exclaiming, "My God, it's a glove!" (Sacks, 1985, p. 13). His brain immediately seized the pattern of tactile information, although his visual brain centers were powerless to interpret the shape as a whole. Dr. P., that is, showed lack of visual knowledge—a symptom referred to as visual **agnosia,** derived from Greek roots meaning "without knowledge." Still, Dr. P.'s musical abilities and verbal skills remained intact. He was able to function, to dress himself, take a shower, and eat his meals by singing various songs to himself—for example, eating songs and dressing songs—that helped him coordinate his actions. However, if his dressing song was interrupted while he was dressing himself, he would lose his train of thought and be unable to recognize not only the clothes his wife had laid out but also his own body. When the music stopped, so did his ability to make sense of the world. Sacks later learned that Dr. P. had a massive tumor in the area of the brain that processes visual information. Dr. P. was apparently unaware of his deficits, having filled his visually empty world with music in order to function and imbue his life with meaning and purpose.

Dr. P.'s case is unusual in the peculiarity of his symptoms, but it illustrates the universal dependence of psychological functioning on an intact brain. The case also shows how some people adjust—sometimes so gradually that the changes are all but imperceptible—to developing physical or organic problems. Dr. P.'s visual problems might have been relatively more debilitating in a person who was less talented or who had less social support to draw on. The tragic case of Dr. P. illustrates how psychological and environmental factors determine the impact and range of disabling symptoms as well as the individual's ability to cope with them.

People who suffer from cognitive disorders may become completely dependent on others to meet basic needs in feeding, toileting, and grooming. In other cases, although some assistance in meeting the demands of daily living may be required, people are able to function at a level that permits them to live semi-independently. The cognitive deficit that Dr. P developed, *agnosia,* is often a feature of dementia, a type of cognitive disorder involving a general deterioration of mental functioning. Dementia, along with delirium and amnestic disorders, are three major types of cognitive disorders (see Table 15.1).

Dementia

Dementia is a profound deterioration in mental functioning characterized by severe problems with memory and by one or more of the cognitive deficits listed in Table 15.2 (APA, 2000). There are many causes of dementia, including brain diseases, such as Alzheimer's disease (AD) and Pick's disease, and infections or disorders that affect the functioning of the brain, such as meningitis, HIV infection, and encephalitis. In some cases, the dementia can be halted or reversed, especially when it is caused by certain types of tumors, seizures, metabolic disturbances, and treatable infections, or when it

agnosia A disturbance of sensory perception, usually affecting visual perception.

TRUTH or FICTION? *REVISITED*

A man with a brain tumor patted the heads of fire hydrants and parking meters in the belief that they were children.

☑ **TRUE.** A man with a brain tumor patted the heads of fire hydrants and parking meters in the belief that they were children. The tumor caused dysfunction in the parts of his brain that processed visual information.

dementia Profound deterioration of mental functioning, characterized by impaired memory, thinking, judgment, and language use.

TABLE 15.1

Major Types of Delirium, Dementia, and Amnestic Disorder

Delirium	Delirium due to a general medical condition
	Substance intoxication delirium
	Substance withdrawal delirium
Dementia	Dementia of the Alzheimer's type
	Vascular dementia
	Dementia due to HIV disease
	Dementia due to head trauma
	Dementia due to Parkinson's disease
	Dementia due to Huntington's disease
	Dementia due to Pick's disease
	Dementia due to Creutzfeldt-Jakob disease
	Dementia due to other general medical conditions (e.g., hypothyroidism or brain tumor)
	Substance-induced persisting dementia
Amnestic disorder	Amnestic disorder due to a general medical condition
	Substance-induced persisting amnestic disorder

Source: Adapted from *DSM–IV-TR* (APA, 2000).

senile dementias Forms of dementia that begin after age 65.

presenile dementias Forms of dementia that begin at or before age 65.

results from depression or substance abuse. But the great majority of dementias are progressive and irreversible, including the most common form, dementia associated with AD (Kasl-Godley & Gatz, 2000). AD accounts for most cases of dementia in older adults (Wilson & Bennett, 2003).

Dementias usually occur in people over the age of 80. Those that begin after age 65 are called late-onset or **senile dementias.** Those that begin at age 65 or earlier are termed early-onset or **presenile dementias.** Though the risk of dementia is greater in later life,

TABLE 15.2

Cognitive Deficits in Dementia

Cognitive Deficit	Definition	Description
Aphasia	Impaired ability to comprehend and/or produce speech.	There are several types of aphasia. In sensory or receptive aphasia, people have difficulty understanding written or spoken language, but retain the ability to express themselves through speech. In motor aphasia, the ability to express thoughts through speech is impaired, but the person can understand spoken language. A person with a motor aphasia may not be able to summon up the names of familiar objects or may scramble the normal order of words.
Apraxia	Impaired ability to perform purposeful movements despite an absence of any defect in motor functioning.	There may be an inability to tie a shoelace or button a shirt, although the person can describe how these activities should be performed and despite the fact that there is nothing wrong with the person's arm or hand. The person may have difficulty pantomiming the use of an object (e.g., combing one's hair).
Agnosia	Inability to recognize objects despite an intact sensory system.	Agnosias may be limited to specific sensory channels. A person with a visual agnosia may not be able to identify a fork when shown a picture of the object, although he or she has an intact visual system and may be able to identify the object if allowed to touch it and manipulate it by hand. Auditory agnosia is marked by impairment in the ability to recognize sounds; in tactile agnosia, people are unable to identify objects (such as coins or keys) by holding them or touching them.
Disturbance in Executive Functioning	Deficits in planning, organizing, or sequencing activities or in engaging in abstract thinking.	An office manager who formerly handled budgets and scheduling loses the ability to manage the flow of work in the office or adapt to new demands. An English teacher loses the ability to extract meaning from a poem or story.

Source: Adapted from *DSM-IV-TR* (APA, 2000).

dementia is not a consequence of normal aging. It is a sign of a degenerative brain disease, such as Alzheimer's disease.

Delirium

Delirium derives from the Latin roots *de-*, meaning "from," and *lira,* meaning "line" or "furrow." It means straying from the line, or the norm, in perception, cognition, and behavior. **Delirium** is a state of extreme mental confusion in which people have difficulty concentrating and speaking clearly and coherently (see Table 15.3). People suffering from delirium may find it difficult to tune out irrelevant stimuli or to shift their attention to new tasks. They may speak excitedly, but their speech carries little if any meaning. Disorientation as to time (not knowing the current date, day of the week, or time) and place (not knowing where you are) is common. Disorientation to person (the identities of oneself and others) is not. People in a state of delirium may experience terrifying hallucinations, especially visual hallucinations.

Disturbances in perceptions often occur, such as misinterpretations of sensory stimuli (for example, confusing an alarm clock for a fire bell) or illusions (for instance, feeling as if the bed has an electrical charge passing through it). There can be a dramatic slowing down of movement into a state resembling catatonia. There may be rapid fluctuations between restlessness and stupor. Restlessness is characterized by insomnia, agitated, aimless movements, even bolting out of bed or striking out at nonexistent objects. This may alternate with periods in which victims have to struggle to stay awake.

Delirium can result from a variety of medical conditions (Lichtenberg & Duffy, 2000). These include head trauma; metabolic disorders, such as hypoglycemia (low blood sugar); fluid or electrolyte imbalances; seizure disorders (epilepsy); deficiencies of the B vitamin thiamine; brain lesions; and various diseases that affect the functioning of the central nervous system, including Parkinson's disease, AD, viral encephalitis (a type of brain infection), liver disease, and kidney disease (APA, 2000). Delirium may also occur due to exposure to toxic substances (such as eating certain poisonous mushrooms), as a side effect of using certain medications, or during states of drug or alcohol intoxication. The most common cause is abrupt withdrawal from psychoactive drugs, especially alcohol (Freemon, 1981). People with chronic alcoholism who abruptly stop drinking may experience a form of delirium called *delirium tremens* or DTs. During an acute episode of the DTs, the person may be terrorized by wild and frightening hallucinations, such as "bugs crawling down walls" or on the skin. The DTs can last for a week or more and are best treated in a hospital, where the patient can be carefully monitored and the symptoms treated with mild tranquilizers and environmental support. Although there are many known causes of delirium, in many cases the specific cause cannot be identified.

Whatever the cause, delirium is a generalized disturbance of the brain's metabolic processes and imbalance in the levels of neurotransmitters. As a result, the ability to

delirium A state of mental confusion, disorientation, and inability to focus attention.

TABLE 15.3

Features of Delirium

Domain	Level of Severity		
	Mild	**Moderate**	**Severe**
Emotion	Apprehension	Fear	Panic
Cognition and perception	Confusion, racing thoughts	Disorientation, delusions	Meaningless mumbling, vivid hallucinations
Behavior	Tremors	Muscle spasms	Seizures
Autonomic activity	Abnormally fast heartbeat (tachycardia)	Perspiration	Fever

Source: Adapted from Freemon (1981), p. 82.

process information is impaired and confusion reigns. The abilities to think and speak clearly, to interpret sensory stimuli accurately, and to attend to the environment decline. Delirium may occur abruptly, as in cases resulting from seizures or head injuries, or gradually over hours or days, as in cases involving infections, fever, or metabolic disorders. During the course of delirium, the person's mental state will often fluctuate between periods of clarity ("lucid intervals"), which are most common in the morning, and periods of confusion and disorientation. Delirium is generally worse in the dark and following sleepless nights.

Unlike dementia, in which there is a steady deterioration of mental ability, states of delirium often clear up spontaneously when the underlying organic or drug-related cause is resolved. The course of delirium is relatively brief, usually lasting about a week, but rarely longer than a month. However, if the underlying cause persists or leads to further deterioration, delirium may progress to coma or death.

Amnestic Disorders

amnestic disorders Disturbances of memory associated with inability to learn new material or recall past events.

Amnestic disorders (commonly called amnesias) are characterized by a dramatic decline in memory functioning that is not connected with states of delirium or dementia. Amnesia is an inability to learn new information (deficits in short-term memory) or to recall previously accessible information or past events from one's life (deficits in long-term memory). Problems with short-term memory may be revealed by an inability to remember the names of, or to recognize, people whom the person met 5 or 10 minutes earlier. Immediate memory, as measured by ability to repeat back a series of numbers, seems to be unimpaired in states of amnesia. The person is unlikely to remember the number series later, however, no matter how often it is rehearsed.

Unlike the memory disorders of dissociative amnesia and dissociative fugue discussed in Chapter 7, amnestic disorder results from a physical cause. Amnestic disorders frequently follow a traumatic event, such as a blow to the head, an electric shock, or an operation. A head injury may prevent people from remembering events that occurred shortly before the accident. The automobile accident victim may not remember anything that transpired after getting into the car. The football player who is rendered amnestic from a blow to the head during the game may not remember anything after leaving the locker room. In some cases, people retain memories for the remote past but

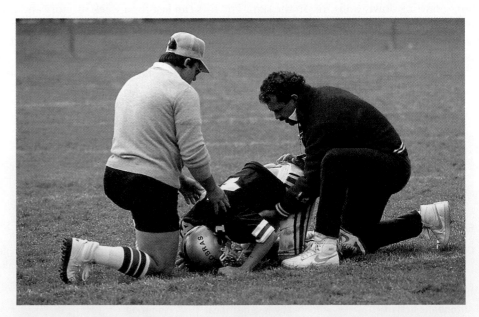

Amnestic disorder. An amnestic disorder syndrome can follow a traumatic injury such as a blow to the head. This football player may not be able to recall the events that happened just prior to his being tackled, nor the collision itself.

lose those for recent events. People with amnesia may be more likely to remember events from their childhood than last evening's dinner, for example. Consider the following case.

> ### Who Is She?
>
> *A medical student was rushed to the hospital after he was thrown from a motorcycle. His parents were with him in his hospital room when he awakened. As his parents were explaining what had happened to him, the door suddenly flew open and his flustered wife, whom he had married a few weeks earlier, rushed into the room, leaped onto his bed, began to caress him, and expressed her great relief that he was not seriously injured. After several minutes of expressing her love and reassurance, his wife departed and the flustered student looked at his mother and asked: "Who is she?"*
>
> —Adapted from Freemon, 1981, p. 96

The medical student's long-term memory loss included memories dating not only to the accident but also further back to the time before he was married or had met his wife. Like most victims of posttraumatic amnesia, the medical student recovered his memory fully.

People with an amnestic disorder may experience disorientation, more commonly involving disorientation to place (not knowing where one is at the time) and time (not knowing the day, month, and year) than disorientation as to self (not knowing one's own name). They may not be aware of their memory loss or attempt to deny or mask their memory deficits even when evidence of their impairment is presented to them. They may attempt to fill the gaps in their memories with imaginary events. Or they may admit they have a memory problem but appear apathetic about it, showing a kind of emotional blandness.

Although people with amnestic disorder may suffer profound memory losses, their general intelligence tends to remain within a normal range. In contrast, in progressive dementias like AD, memory and intellectual functioning both deteriorate. Early detection and diagnosis of the causes of memory problems are vital to many sufferers, because 20% to 30% of them are correctable (Cohen, 1986).

Other causes of amnesia include brain surgery; **hypoxia,** or sudden loss of oxygen to the brain; brain infection or disease; **infarction,** or blockage of the blood vessels supplying the brain; and chronic, heavy use of certain psychoactive substances, most commonly alcohol.

Alcohol-Induced Persisting Amnestic Disorder (Korsakoff's Syndrome) A common cause of amnestic disorder is thiamine deficiency linked to chronic abuse of alcohol. Alcohol abusers tend to take poor care of their nutritional needs and may not follow a diet rich enough in vitamin B_1, or thiamine. Thiamine deficiencies may produce an irreversible form of memory loss called *alcohol-induced persisting amnestic disorder,* commonly known as **Korsakoff's syndrome.** The word *persisting* is used because the memory deficits persist even years after the person stops drinking (APA, 2000). Korsakoff's syndrome is not limited to people with chronic alcoholism, however. It has been reported in other groups who experience thiamine deficiencies during times of deprivation, such as prisoners of war.

People with Korsakoff's syndrome have major gaps in their memory of past experiences (Phaf, Geurts, & Eling, 2000). Their memory deficits are believed to result from the loss of brain tissue due to bleeding in the brain. Despite their memory losses, patients with Korsakoff's syndrome may retain their general level of intelligence. They are often described as being superficially friendly but lacking in insight, unable to discriminate between actual events and wild stories they invent to fill the gaps in their memories. They sometimes become grossly disoriented and confused and require custodial care.

Korsakoff's syndrome often follows an acute attack of **Wernicke's disease,** another brain disorder caused by thiamine deficiency. Wernicke's disease is characterized by confusion and disorientation, difficulty maintaining balance while walking (**ataxia),** and

hypoxia Decreased supply of oxygen to the brain or other organs.

infarction The development of an infarct, or area of dead or dying tissue, resulting from the blocking of blood vessels normally supplying the tissue.

Korsakoff's syndrome A syndrome associated with chronic alcoholism that is characterized by memory loss and disorientation (also called *alcohol-induced persisting amnestic disorder*).

Wernicke's disease A brain disorder, associated with chronic alcoholism, characterized by confusion, disorientation, and difficulty maintaining balance while walking.

ataxia Loss of muscle coordination.

paralysis of the muscles that control eye movements. These symptoms may pass, but the person is often left with Korsakoff's syndrome and enduring memory impairment. If, however, Wernicke's disease is treated promptly with major doses of vitamin B_1, Korsakoff's syndrome may not develop. Once Korsakoff's syndrome has set in, it is usually permanent, although slight improvement is possible with treatment.

PSYCHOLOGICAL DISORDERS RELATED TO AGING

Many physical changes occur with aging. Changes in calcium metabolism cause the bones to grow brittle and heighten the risk of breaks from falls. The skin grows less elastic, creating wrinkles and folds. The senses become less keen, so older people see and hear less acutely. Older people need more time (called *reaction time*) to respond to stimuli, whether they are driving or taking intelligence tests. For example, older drivers require more time to react to traffic signals and other cars. The immune system functions less effectively with increasing age, so people become more vulnerable to illness.

Cognitive changes occur as well. It is normal for people in later life to experience some decline in memory functioning and general cognitive ability, as measured by tests of intelligence, or IQ tests. The decline is sharpest on timed items, such as the performance scales of the Wechsler Adult Intelligence Scale. Although some declines in cognitive ability (reading comprehension, spatial ability as in map reading, or basic mathematical reasoning) in later life is common, it is not universal. Studies show that 20% to 30% of people in their 80s perform about as well on intelligence tests as those in their 30s and 40s (Goleman, 1994b). Some abilities, such as vocabulary and accumulated store of knowledge, hold up well. However, people typically experience some reduction in memory as they age, especially memory for names or recent events. But apart from the occasional social embarrassment resulting from forgetting a person's name, cognitive declines do not significantly interfere with most people's ability to meet their social or occupational responsibilities. Declines in cognitive functioning may also be offset to a certain extent by increased knowledge and experience.

The important point here is that dementia, or senility, is not the result of normal aging (USDHHS, 1999a). It is a sign of degenerative brain disease. Screening and testing on neurological and neuropsychological tests can help distinguish dementias from normal aging processes. Generally speaking, the decline in intellectual functioning in dementia is more rapid and severe.

Let us now turn to consider relationships between various psychological disorders and aging, beginning with anxiety disorders, the most common mental disorder of older adults.

Anxiety Disorders and Aging

Though anxiety disorders may develop at any point in life, they tend to be less prevalent among older adults than their younger counterparts. Still, anxiety disorders are the most common mental disorder affecting older adults and are about twice as common as mood disorders, such as depression ("Anxiety," 2000). Approximately 1 in 10 adults over the age of 55 suffers from a diagnosable anxiety disorder (USDHHS, 1999a). Older women are more likely to be affected than older men, by a ratio of two to one (Stanley & Beck, 2000). The most frequently occurring anxiety disorders among older adults are generalized anxiety disorder (GAD) and phobic disorders. Panic disorder is rare. Most cases of agoraphobia affecting older adults tend to be of recent origin and may involve the loss of social support systems due to the death of a spouse or close friends. Then again, some older individuals who are frail may have realistic fears of falling on the street and may be misdiagnosed

What changes take place as we age? How do they affect our moods? Although some declines in cognitive and physical functioning are connected with aging, older adults who remain active and engage in rewarding activities can be highly satisfied with their lives.

as agoraphobic if they refuse to leave the house alone. Generalized anxiety disorder may arise from the perception that one lacks control over one's life, which may be the case for older people contending with infirmity, loss of friends and loved ones, and lessened economic opportunities. Mild tranquilizers, such as the benzodiazepines (Valium is one), are commonly used to quell anxiety in older adults. Psychological interventions, such as cognitive–behavior therapy, show therapeutic benefits in treating anxiety in older adults and do not carry the risk of side effects or potential dependence (Nordhus & Pallesen, 2003; Stanley & Beck, 2000).

Depression and Aging

Though the risks of major depression also decline with age, many older adults experience depression (Karel & Hinrichsen, 2000). In some cases, depression is a continuation of a lifelong pattern; in other cases, it first arises in later life. Between 8% and 20% of older adults experience some symptoms of depression (USDHHS, 1999a), with perhaps about 3% of them suffering from major depressive disorder (Rimer, 1999; Steffens et al., 2000). Rates of depression are higher still among residents of nursing homes. Though fewer older adults suffer from major depression than do younger adults, suicide is more frequent among older adults, especially older males (Bruce et al., 2004; USDHHS, 1999a).

Depression in later life is associated with a faster rate of physical decline and a higher mortality rate (Brenda et al., 1998; Zubenko et al., 1997). Depression may be linked to a higher mortality rate because of coexisting medical conditions or perhaps because of a lack of compliance with taking necessary medications.

Older people of color often carry an especially heavy stress burden. In one recent study, a sample of 127 elderly African Americans recruited from senior citizens programs in two large urban centers in the northeastern United States were administered measures of race-related stress, satisfaction with life, and health concerns (Utsey et al., 2002). The investigators found that men reported higher levels of institutional and collective forms of racism than did women. The investigators commented that they weren't surprised by these findings, as African American men have traditionally been subjected to harsher experiences of societal racism and oppression. Going further, the investigators reported that institutional racism-related stress was associated with poorer psychological well-being. Many of the elderly men in this sample had experienced institutional racism (i.e., government-sanctioned discrimination in housing, education, employment, health care, and public policy) during their early and middle life. This study contributes to a growing body of literature showing links between race-related stress and mental health functioning of African Americans.

Other investigators have examined the role of acculturative stress in elderly people from immigrant groups. A study of Mexian American older adults showed that those who were minimally acculturated to U.S. society had greater rates of depression than either highly acculturated or bicultural individuals (Zamanian et al., 1992).

Depressive disorders occur commonly in people suffering from various brain disorders, several of which, like AD and stroke, disproportionately affect older people (Teri & Wagner, 1992). Researchers estimate that depressive disorders occur in as many as half of stroke victims and about a third to a half of people affected by AD or Parkinson's disease (e.g., Chemerinski et al., 2001; Heun et al., 2001; Lyketsos et al., 2000). In the case of Parkinson's disease, depression may result not only from coping with the disease but also from neurobiological changes in the brain caused by the disease (Rao, Huber, & Bornstein, 1992). Coping with a depressed spouse can lead to an increased risk of depression in the caretaking spouse (Tower & Kasl, 1996).

Agoraphobia? Or a need for support? Some older adults may refuse to venture away from home on their own because of realistic fears of falling in the street. They may be in need of social support, not therapy.

Elder stress. Older people of color may experience similar stresses as other older adults, but they are also more likely to have been exposed to additional social stresses, such as discrimination and poverty.

Social support can help buffer the effects of stress, bereavement, and illness, thereby reducing the risk of depression. Social support is especially important to older people who are challenged because of physical disability. Evidence shows that participation in volunteer organizations and religious institutions is associated with a lower risk of depression among older people (Palinkas, Wingard, & Barrett-Connor, 1990). These forms of social participation may provide not only a sense of meaning and purpose but also a needed social outlet.

Older people may be especially vulnerable to depression because of the stress of coping with life changes—retirement; physical illness or incapacitation; placement in a residential facility or nursing home; the deaths of a spouse, siblings, lifetime friends, and acquaintances; or the need to care for a spouse whose health is declining. Retirement, whether voluntary or forced, may lead to a loss of role identity. Deaths of relatives and friends induce grief and remind older people of their own advanced age as well as reduce the availability of social support. Older adults may feel incapable of forming new friendships or finding new goals in life. The chronic strain of coping with a family member with dementia can lead to depression in the caregiver, even without any prior vulnerability to depression (Mittelman et al., 2004). Nearly half of Alzheimer's caregivers become clinically depressed (Small et al., 1997).

Despite the prevalence of depression in older people, physicians often fail to recognize it or to treat it appropriately (Bruce et al., 2002). In one study of more than 500 elderly people in Ontario who committed suicide, nearly 9 of 10 were found to have gone untreated (Duckworth & McBride, 1996). Health-care providers may be less likely to recognize depression among older people than in middle-aged or young people for several reasons: They tend to focus on the older patient's physical complaints or depression in older people is often masked by physical complaints and sleeping problems.

Most older people with memory deficits do not suffer from Alzheimer's disease. They are more likely to have memory losses due to depression or other factors like chronic alcohol use or the effects of small strokes (Bäckman & Forsell, 1994). The good news is that the memory impairment that can accompany depression often lifts when the underlying depression is resolved.

Treatments used widely in young people with major depression, such as antidepressant medication, cognitive–behavioral therapy, and interpersonal psychotherapy, are also effective in treating depression in older adults (Bondareff et al., 2000; Ciechanowski et al., 2004; Karel & Hinrichsen, 2000). In fact, older adults benefit as much, although perhaps more slowly, from pharmacological and psychological interventions as midlife or younger adults (Reynolds et al., 1996; Scogin & McElreath, 1994). These findings should help put to rest the belief that psychotherapy is not appropriate for older people. We lack evidence, however, showing whether any particular form of psychotherapy is clearly superior in treating depression in older people.

Sleep Problems and Aging

Sleep problems, especially insomnia, are common among older people (Lichstein et al., 2001). Insomnia in late adulthood is actually more prevalent than depression (Morgan, 1996). Sleep problems reflect age-related changes in sleep physiology, such as tendencies to wake up earlier in the morning (Martin, Shochat, & Ancoli-Israel, 2000). However, sleep problems may be a feature of other psychological disorders, such as depression, dementia, and anxiety disorders, as well as medical illness (Lamberg, 2000). Psychosocial factors, such as loneliness and the related difficulty of sleeping alone after the loss of a spouse, may also be involved. Dysfunctional thoughts, such as excessive concerns about lack of sleep and perceptions of hopelessness and helplessness about controlling sleep, may contribute to insomnia in older people.

Mild tranquilizers are often used in treating late-life insomnia, but long-term use of these drugs can cause dependence and withdrawal symptoms. Fortunately, behavioral approaches, similar to those described in Chapter 10, are effective in treating insomnia in later life (Lichstein, Wilson, & Johnson, 2000; Martin, Shochat, & Ancoli-Israel, 2000). Moreover, older adults are as capable of benefiting from the treatment as younger adults.

A study of sleep apnea (temporary cessation of breathing during sleep) in a geriatric population showed that between 25% and 42% of the people studied had five or more apneas per hour of sleep (Ancoli-Israel et al., 1991). Apnea may involve more than a sleep problem; it is also linked to an increased risk of dementia and of cardiovascular disorders (Strollo & Rogers, 1996).

Dementia of the Alzheimer's Type

Alzheimer's disease (AD) is a degenerative brain disease that leads to progressive and irreversible dementia, characterized by loss of memory and other cognitive functions (Thompson et al., 2003). As noted earlier, AD accounts for more than half of the cases of dementia in the general population. AD affects about 4.5 million Americans and is the fourth leading cause of death among adults (Cowan & Kandel, 2001; Grady, 2004). An estimated 10% of American over the age of 65, and about half of those in the 75 to 84-year age range, are believed to suffer from AD (Herbert et al., 2003; Lemonick & Park, 2001). As the U.S. population ages, the disease is expected to affect increasing numbers of Americans, perhaps as many as 16 million by the year 2050 (Fackelmann, 2003).

The great majority of cases of AD occur in people over the age of 65, most typically in those in their late 70s and 80s (Plomin & McGuffin, 2003; see Figure 15.1). Women are at higher risk of developing the disease than men, though this may be a consequence of women tending to live longer. Economic costs of AD are estimated at more than $90 billion a year in the United States (Cowan & Kandel, 2001). But let us note that although AD is strongly connected with aging, it is a disease and not a consequence of normal aging (Butler, 2001).

The dementia associated with AD takes the form of a progressive deterioration of mental abilities involving memory, language, and problem solving. Occasional memory loss or forgetfulness in middle life (e.g., forgetting where one put one's glasses) is normal and not a sign of the early stages of Alzheimer's disease. People in later life (and some of us not quite that advanced in years) complain of not remembering names as well as they used to or of forgetting names that were once well known to them. Although mild forgetfulness may concern people, it need not impair their social or occupational functioning.

Suspicions of AD are raised when cognitive impairment is more severe and pervasive, affecting the individual's ability to meet the ordinary responsibilities of daily work and social roles. Over the course of the illness, people with AD may get lost in parking lots or in stores, or even in their own homes. The wife of an AD patient describes how AD has affected her husband: "With no cure, Alzheimer's robs the person of who he is. It is painful to see Richard walk around the car several times because he can't find the door" (Morrow, 1998, p. D4). Agitation, wandering behavior, depression, and aggressive behavior are common as the disease progresses (Chen et al., 1999; Slone & Gleason, 1999).

People with AD may become confused or delusional in their thinking and may sense that their mental ability is slipping away but not understand why. Bewilderment and fear may lead to paranoid delusions or beliefs that their loved ones have betrayed them, robbed them, or don't care about them. They may forget the names of their loved ones or fail to recognize them. They may even forget their own names.

Psychotic features such as delusions and hallucinations occur in in about one in three people with AD (Jeste et al., 1992). Psychotic symptoms appear to be connected with greater cognitive impairment and more rapid deterioration. People with AD are frequently depressed or even suicidal (Wilson et al., 2002). However, their doctors often overlook the danger signs of severe depression or disregard them.

AD was first described in 1907 by the German physician Alois Alzheimer (1864–1915). During an autopsy of a 56-year-old woman who had suffered

Alzheimer's disease (AD) A progressive brain disease characterized by gradual loss of memory and intellectual functioning, personality changes, and eventual loss of ability to care for oneself.

TRUTH or FICTION? REVISITED

People who become occasionally forgetful as they age are probably suffering from the early stages of Alzheimer's disease.

☑ **FALSE.** Occasional memory loss or forgetfulness is a normal consequence of the aging process.

Alzheimer's disease. Alzheimer's disease (AD) has struck a number of notable people, including former President Ronald Reagan, here shown with his wife, Nancy, at his first public appearance after being diagnosed with AD. Reagan died of the disease in June 2004.

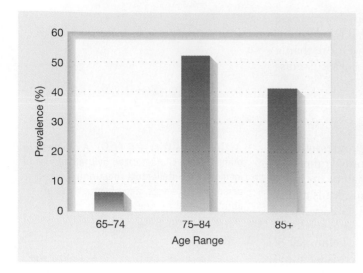

FIGURE 15.1 Prevalence of Alzheimer's disease among older adults.

Among older adults, the risk of Alzheimer's disease is much greater among people over the age of 75 than among those 65 to 74.

Source: Herbert et al., 2003

from severe dementia, he found two brain abnormalities now regarded as signs of the disease: plaques (portions of degenerative brain tissue) and neurofibrillary tangles (twisted bundles of nerve cells) (Näslund et al., 2000) (see Figure 15.2). The darkly shaded areas in the photo to the right in Figure 15.2 show the diminished brain activity associated with AD.

Diagnosis   There is no definitive diagnostic test for AD. The diagnosis is generally based on a clinical evaluation and given only when other possible causes of dementia are eliminated. Other medical and psychological conditions may mimic AD, such as severe depression resulting in memory loss and impaired cognitive functioning. Consequently, misdiagnoses may occur, especially in the early stages of the disease. A confirmatory diagnosis of AD can be made only upon inspection of brain tissue by biopsy or autopsy. However, biopsy is rarely performed because of the risk of hemorrhage or infection, and autopsy, of course, occurs too late to help the patient.

Features of Alzheimer's Disease   Alzheimer's disease develops gradually but progresses steadily, leading to dementia in about 3 years following onset (Skoog, 2000). Earlier age of onset is associated with poorer cognitive functioning, even when the duration of the illness is taken into account. AD that strikes earlier in life may involve a more severe form of the disease.

The early stages of the disease are marked by limited memory problems and subtle personality changes. People may at first have trouble managing their finances; remembering recent events or basic information such as telephone numbers, area codes, zip codes, and the names of their grandchildren; and performing numerical computations. A business executive who once managed millions of dollars may become unable to perform simple arithmetic. There may be subtle personality changes, such as signs of with-

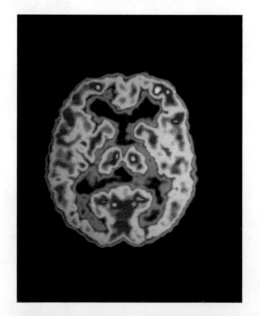 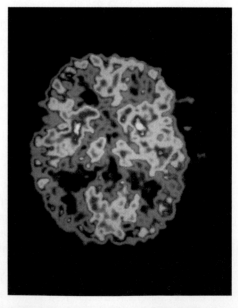

FIGURE 15.2 PET scans of brains from a healthy aged adult (left) and a patient with Alzheimer's disease (right).

The darkly shaded areas in the photo to the right suggest how the neurological changes associated with Alzheimer's disease (as marked by the excess of dark shading) impair brain activity.

Source: Friedland, R. P., Case Western Reserve University, courtesy of *Clinical Neuroimaging.* Copyright © 1988 by John Wiley and Sons, Inc.

Do you know my name? Alzheimer's disease can devastate patients' families. Spouses usually provide the bulk of daily care. This man has been caring for his wife for several years, and he believes that his hugs and kisses sometimes prompt his wife to murmur his name.

drawal in people who had been outgoing or irritability in people who had been gentle. In these early stages, people with AD generally appear neat and well groomed and are generally cooperative and socially appropriate.

Some people with AD are not aware of their deficits. Others deny them. At first they may attribute their problems to other causes, such as stress or fatigue. Denial may protect people with AD in the early or mild stages of the disease from recognition that their intellectual abilities are in decline (Reisberg et al., 1986). Or the recognition that one's mental abilities are slipping away may lead to depression.

In moderately severe AD, people require assistance in managing everyday tasks. At this stage, people may be unable to select appropriate clothes or recall their addresses or names of family members. When they drive, they begin making mistakes, such as failing to stop at stop signs or accelerating when they should be braking. They may encounter difficulties in toileting and bathing themselves. There often make mistakes in recognizing themselves in mirrors. They may no longer be able to speak in full sentences. Verbal responses may become limited to a few words.

Movement and coordination functions deteriorate further. People with AD at the moderately severe level may begin walking in shorter, slower steps. They may no longer be able to sign their names, even when assisted by others. They may have difficulty handling a knife and fork. Agitation becomes a prominent feature at this stage, and victims may act out in response to the threat of having to contend with an environment that no longer seems controllable. They may pace or fidget or display aggressive behavior such as yelling, throwing, or hitting. Patients may wander off because of restlessness and be unable to find their way back.

People with advanced AD may start talking to themselves or experience visual hallucinations or paranoid delusions. They may believe someone is attempting to harm them or is stealing their possessions, or that their spouses are unfaithful to them. They may believe their spouses are actually other people.

At the most severe stage, cognitive functions decline to the point where people become essentially helpless. They may lose the ability to speak or control body movement (Fuchs, 2001). They become incontinent; are unable to communicate, walk, or even sit

Alzheimer's Disease:
The Case of Wilburn "John"
"You kinda have hope whenever you have cancer . . . but then, [with] Alzheimer's . . . you die, just a little each day."

up; and require assistance in toileting and feeding. In the end state, seizures, coma, and death result.

The following case illustrates the major features of Alzheimer's disease, such as memory loss, disorientation, and behavior problems.

A Case of Dementia of the Alzheimer's Type

A 65-year-old draftsman began to have problems remembering important details at work; at home he began to have difficulty keeping his financial records up-to-date and remembering to pay bills on time. His intellectual abilities progressively declined, forcing him eventually to retire from his job. Behavioral problems began to appear at home, as he grew increasingly stubborn and even verbally and physically abusive toward others when he felt thwarted.

On neurological examination, he displayed disorientation as to place and time, believing that the consultation room was his place of employment and that the year was "1960 or something," when it was actually 1982. He had difficulty with even simple memory tests, failing to remember any of six objects shown to him ten minutes earlier, not recalling the names of his parents or siblings, or the name of the president of the United States. His speech was vague and filled with meaningless phrases. He couldn't perform simple arithmetical computations, but he could interpret proverbs correctly.

Shortly following the neurological consultation, the man was placed in a hospital since his family was no longer able to control his increasingly disruptive behavior. In the hospital, his mental abilities continued to decline, while his aggressive behavior was largely controlled by major tranquilizers (antipsychotic drugs). He was diagnosed as suffering from a primary degenerative dementia of the Alzheimer type. He died at age 74, some 8 years following the onset of his symptoms.

—Adapted from Spitzer et al., 1989, pp. 131–132

AD wreaks havoc not only on the affected person but also on the entire family. Families who helplessly watch their loved ones slowly deteriorate have been described as attending a "funeral that never ends" (Aronson, 1988). The symptoms of advanced AD, such as wandering away, aggressiveness, destructiveness, incontinence, screaming, and remaining awake at night, cause high levels of stress imposed in caregivers. Living with a person with advanced AD may seem like living with a stranger, so profound are the changes in personality and behavior. Not surprisingly, caregivers experience more health problems and higher levels of stress hormone than do noncaregivers (Vitaliano, Zhang, & Scanlan, 2003). Typically, the caretaking burden falls disproportionately on the daughters in the family, who are often middle-aged women feeling "sandwiched" between their responsibilities to their children and to their affected parents. Here is one woman's story.

"I"
"A Daughter's Dilemma"

Mom is eighty-six years old and is in the third stage of Alzheimer's disease. I first recognized a change in Mom about ten years ago when she became emotionally volatile. My dilemma is: How much responsibility do I have for Mom's care while maintaining my own family life?

I am a fifty-two-year-old married woman raising three teenage boys. My career is in clinical psychology, and I have a Ph.D. in gerontology. I seem to be the logical one to coordinate her care, since I am her only daughter and have the knowledge of Alzheimer's disease. But I left my parents' home in Brooklyn, New York, long ago and now live in Colorado. How do I manage Mom's care long distance? . .

In an effort to help, I suggested that Mom spend time in my home in Colorado . . . I accompanied Mom on the plan trip to Colorado, and that trip brought me into the stark, cold reality that Mom had Alzheimer's. She did not know where she was or where she was going. Upon arrival, she did not recognize my home, although she had visited me numerous times in the past.

She tried sleeping in the bathtub the first night. She said that she was trying to find her bed. She stayed for two months, and during that time she rarely found the bathroom, which was adjacent to her bedroom . . .

During our first month together, I was feeling good about forgetting myself and serving her. I told her that I loved her and wanted to give her the care that she deserved. But I began to burn out during the second month. I stopped looking forward to the weekends when she was in my constant care. At work, I was helping other caretakers keep a balance in their lives, yet I found myself always putting Mom first. Many of my personal, marital, and family's needs went unmet.

—Source: Smoller, 1997, pp. 23. 28, 33, 36

Causal Factors AD is a brain disease of unknown origin. We do know that plaques, the steel-wool-like clumps that form in the brains of people with Alzheimer's disease, are composed of a material called *beta amyloid*, which consists of fibrous protein fragments (Iwata et al., 2001; Skoog, 2000). For some unknown reason, possibly involving a genetic mutation, these fragments break off from a larger protein during metabolism and cluster together in strings that attract remnants of other nerve cells, forming plaques. These plaques may be responsible for destroying adjacent brain tissue, leading to the death of brain cells across a large area of the brain, which in turn may lead to the memory loss, confusion, and other symptoms of the disease.

Increasing evidence points to genetics playing an important role in AD (Mattson, 2003; Plomin & McGuffin, 2003). Late-onset AD is linked to genes that regulate production of a protein called *apolipoprotein E* (APOe) (Voelker, 2000). This protein transports cholesterol through the bloodstream. People with defects in these genes may begin to show signs of brain deterioration even before memory symptoms appear ("New Use of Brain Scan," 2000). Their brains also appear to work harder when performing a memory task, which suggests that the brain is trying to compensate for underlying abnormalities (Bookheimer et al., 2000). Other genes may also be involved in AD, including genes involved in cell metabolism (the process of converting food into energy) and in the production of beta amyloid (Bertram et al., 2000; Ertekin-Taner et al., 2000; Li, 2000).

Treatment and Prevention The presently available drugs to treat AD produce at best modest effects in slowing cognitive decline and boosting cognitive functioning (Grady, 2004; Reisberg et al., 2003; Trinh et al., 2003). None is a cure. One widely used drug, *donepezil* (brand name Aricept), increases levels of the neurotransmitter acetylcholine (ACh). AD patients show reduced levels of ACh, possibly because of the death of brain cells in ACh-producing areas of the brain. Another drug, *memantine* (brand name Axura) blocks the neurotransmitter glutamate, a brain chemical found in abnormally high concentrations in AD patients. High levels of glutamate may damage brain cells. *Memantine* is the first drug designed to tackle moderate to severe AD and appears helpful when used alone or in combination with donepezil (Reisberg et al., 2003; Tariot et al., 2004). Psychosocial interventions, such as memory training programs, can also help AD patients make optimal use of their remaining abilities (Kasl-Godley & Gatz, 2000).

Some promising strides are reported on the prevention front. Preliminary evidence suggests that anti-inflammatory drugs (e.g., the widely used pain reliever *ibuprofen*) might help reduce the risk of AD (Etminan et al., 2003; in Veld et al., 2001). That said, we need more definitive research on the preventive effects of these drugs to reach any firm conclusions (Breitner & Zandi, 2001; Launer, 2003). Scientists are also testing naturally occurring substances, such as certain vitamins and plant materials, to see if they can curb the progression of the disease or prevent its development (Carmichael, 2002; Morris et al., 2002). Investigators also report that participation in intellectually challenging tasks in older adults may delay or even prevent the development of AD (Verghese et al., 2003).

Researchers report initial success with an experimental vaccine in reducing or preventing buildup of plaques in the brains of laboratory mice ("Alzheimer's Vaccine," 2001). Although it has not yet been tested in humans, the vaccine offers hope that we may one day be able to prevent Alzheimer's disease or stem its progess (Check, 2003).

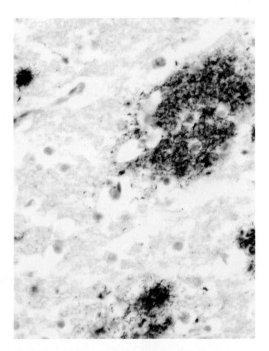

Plaques linked to Alzheimer's disease. In Alzheimer's disease, nerve tissue in the brain degenerates, forming steel-wool-like clumps or plaques composed of beta-amyloid protein fragments, shown here as blue-stained areas in a section of the cerebral cortex.

Boosting memory. Memory training programs are not a cure, but they may help Alzheimer's patients make the best use of their remaining abilities.

Vascular Dementia

cerebrovascular accident (CVA) A stroke, or brain damage resulting from a rupture or blockage of a blood vessel supplying oxygen to the brain.

The brain, like other living tissues, depends on the bloodstream to supply it with oxygen and glucose and to carry away its metabolic wastes. A stroke, also called a **cerebrovascular accident (CVA),** occurs when part of the brain becomes damaged because of a disruption in its blood supply, usually as the result of a blood clot that becomes lodged in an artery that services the brain and obstructs circulation (Adler, 2004). Areas of the brain may be damaged or destroyed, leaving the victim with disabilities in motor,

QUESTIONNAIRE
Examining Your Attitudes Toward Aging

What are your assumptions about late adulthood? Do you see older people as basically different from the young in their behavior patterns and their outlooks, or just as more mature?

To evaluate the accuracy of your attitudes toward aging, mark each of the following items true (T) or false (F). Then turn to the answer key at the end of the chapter.

	True	False
1. By age 60 most couples have lost their capacity for satisfying sexual relations.	____	____
2. Older people cannot wait to retire.	____	____
3. With advancing age people become more externally oriented, less concerned with the self.	____	____
4. As individuals age, they become less able to adapt satisfactorily to a changing environment.	____	____
5. General satisfaction with life tends to decrease as people become older.	____	____
6. As people age they tend to become more homogeneous—that is, all old people tend to be alike in many ways.	____	____
7. For the older person, having a stable intimate relationship is no longer highly important.	____	____

	True	False
8. The aged are susceptible to a wider variety of psychological disorders than young and middle-aged adults.	____	____
9. Most older people are depressed much of the time.	____	____
10. Church attendance increases with age.	____	____
11. The occupational performance of the older worker is typically less effective than that of the younger adult.	____	____
12. Most older people are just not able to learn new skills.	____	____
13. Compared to younger persons, older people tend to think more about the past than the present or the future.	____	____
14. Most people in later life are unable to live independently and reside in nursing-home-like institutions.	____	____

Source. Adapted from Rathus, S. A., & Nevid, J. S. (1995). Adjustment and growth: The challenges of life (6th ed.), p. 440. Reprinted with permission of Brooks/Cole, an imprint of Wadsworth Group, a division of Thomson Learning. FAX 800-730-2215.

speech, and cognitive functions. Death may also occur. **Vascular dementia** (formerly called *multi-infarct dementia*) is a form of dementia that results from repeated strokes (Vermeer et al., 2003). (An *infarct* refers to the death of tissue caused by insufficient blood supply.) Vascular dementia, the second most common form of dementia, most often affects people in later life but at somewhat earlier ages than dementia due to Alzheimer's disease (APA, 2000; Wilkinson et al., 2003). The disease affects more men than women and accounts for about one in five cases of dementia. Unlike AD, heredity does not appear to play a major role in vascular dementia (Bergem et al., 1997).

Single strokes may produce gross impairments in specific functions, such as **aphasia,** but single strokes do not typically cause the more generalized cognitive declines that characterize dementia. Vascular dementia generally results from multiple strokes that occur at different times and that have cumulative effects on a wide range of mental abilities.

Features of Vascular Dementia The symptoms of vascular dementia are similar to those of dementia of the Alzheimer's type, including impaired memory and language ability, agitation and emotional instability, and loss of ability to care for one's own basic needs. However, AD is characterized by an insidious onset and a gradual decline of mental functioning, whereas vascular dementia typically occurs abruptly and follows a stepwise course of deterioration involving rapid declines in cognitive functioning that are believed to reflect the effects of additional strokes (e.g., Kasl-Godley & Gatz, 2000). Some cognitive functions in people with vascular dementia remain relatively intact in the early course of the disorder, leading to a pattern of patchy deterioration in which islands of mental competence remain while other abilities suffer gross impairment, depending on the particular areas of the brain that have been damaged by multiple strokes.

DEMENTIAS DUE TO GENERAL MEDICAL CONDITIONS

We have examined relationships between aging and psychological disorders such as dementia and depression. Next we consider a number of physical disorders that affect psychological functioning in various ways.

Dementia Due to Pick's Disease

Pick's disease causes a progressive dementia that is symptomatically similar to AD. Symptoms include memory loss and social inappropriateness, such as a loss of modesty or the display of flagrant sexual behavior. Diagnosis is confirmed only upon autopsy by the *absence* of the neurofibrillary tangles and plaques that are found in AD and by the presence of other abnormal structures—Pick's bodies—in nerve cells. Pick's disease is believed to account for perhaps 5% of dementias. Unlike AD, it becomes evident most often between the ages of 50 and 60, although it can occur at later ages (APA, 2000). The risk declines with advancing age after 70. Men are more likely than women to suffer from Pick's disease.

Pick's disease appears to run in families, and a genetic component is suspected in its etiology (Brun, 1996; Hutton, 2001). It has been estimated that members of the immediate family of victims of Pick's disease have an overall risk of 17% of contracting the disease by age 75 (Heston, White, & Mastri, 1987).

Dementia Due to Parkinson's Disease

Parkinson's disease is a slowly progressing neurological disease that affects between one half million and one million people in the United States, including the former heavyweight champion Muhammad Ali and the actor Michael J. Fox (Carroll, 2004; Cowan & Kandel, 2001). The disease affects men and women about equally and most often strikes between the ages of 50 and 69. Dementia occurs in perhaps 20% to as many as 75% or more of Parkinson's patients over the course of the illness (APA, 2000; Aarsland et al., 2003).

vascular dementia Dementia resulting from a number of strokes in the brain.

aphasia Impaired ability to understand or express speech.

Pick's disease A form of dementia, similar to Alzheimer's disease, but distinguished by specific abnormalities (Pick's bodies) in nerve cells and absence of neurofibrillary tangles and plaques.

Parkinson's disease A progressive disease of the basal ganglia characterized by muscle tremor and shakiness, rigidity, difficulty walking, poor control of fine motor movements, lack of facial muscle tone, and in some cases, cognitive impairment.

Battling Parkinson's disease. Actor Michael J. Fox has been waging a personal battle against Parkinson's disease and has brought national attention to the need to fund research efforts to develop more effective treatments for this degenerative brain disease.

Parkinson's disease is characterized by uncontrollable shaking or tremors, rigidity, disturbances in posture (leaning forward), and lack of control over body movements. People with Parkinson's disease may be able to control their shaking or tremors, but only briefly. Some cannot walk at all. Others walk laboriously, in a crouch. Some execute voluntary body movements with difficulty, have poor control over fine motor movements, such as finger control, and have sluggish reflexes. They may look expressionless, as if they are wearing masks, a symptom that apparently reflects the degeneration of brain tissue that controls facial muscles. It is particularly difficult for patients to engage in sequences of complex movements, such as those required to sign their names. People with Parkinson's disease may be unable to coordinate two movements at the same time, as seen in this description of a Parkinson's patient who had difficulty walking and reaching for his wallet at the same time.

> ### Motor Impairment in a Case of Parkinson's disease
>
> *A 58-year-old man was walking across the hotel lobby in order to pay his bill. He reached into his inside jacket pocket for his wallet. He stopped walking instantly as he did so and stood immobile in the lobby in front of strangers. He became aware of his suspended locomotion and resumed his stroll to the cashier; however, his hand remained rooted in his inside pocket, as though he were carrying a weapon he might display once he arrived at the cashier.*
>
> —*Adapted from Knight, Godfrey, & Shelton, 1988*

Despite the severity of motor disability, cognitive functions seem to remain intact during the early stages of the disease. Dementia is more common in the later stages or among those with more severe forms of the disease (APA, 2000). The form of dementia associated with Parkinson's disease typically involves a slowing down of thinking processes, impaired ability to think abstractly or plan or organize a series of actions, and difficulty retrieving memories. Overall, the cognitive impairments associated with Parkinson's disease tend to be more subtle than those associated with AD. People with Parkinson's disease often become socially withdrawn and stand a greater-than-average risk of depression, either because of difficulty coping with the disease or biochemical changes that are part and parcel of the disease (Rao et al., 1992).

Parkinson's disease is caused by the destruction or impairment of dopamine-producing nerve cells in the *substantia nigra* ("black substance"), an area of the brain that helps regulate body movement. The causes of the disease remain unknown, but most scientists suspect an interaction between a genetic predisposition and environmental factors, such as exposure to certain toxins (Bonifati et al., 2003; Carroll, 2004; Nussbaum & Ellis, 2003; Pankratz et al., 2002). According to one expert, "Dopamine is like the oil in the engine of a car . . . If the oil is there, the car runs smoothly. If not, it seizes up" (cited in Carroll, 2004, p. F5).

Whatever the underlying cause, the symptoms of the disease—the uncontrollable tremors, shaking, rigid muscles, and difficulty walking—are tied to deficiencies in the amount of dopamine in the brain. The drug L-dopa, which increases dopamine levels, brought hope to Parkinson's patients when it was introduced in the 1970s. L-dopa is converted in the brain into dopamine.

L-dopa helps control the symptoms of the disease and slows its progress, but it does not cure it (Kaiser et al., 2003; Parkinson Study Group, 2000). About 80% of people with Parkinson's disease show significant improvement in their tremors and motor symptoms following treatment with L-dopa. After a few years, however, L-dopa begins to lose its effectiveness, and the disease continues to progress. Several other drugs are in the experimental stage, offering hope for further advances in treatment. Another source of hope comes from experimental use of electrical stimulation of deep-brain structures (Krack et al., 2003) and from genetic studies that may one day lead to an effective gene therapy for the disease (Kordower et al., 2000; Olson, 2000). Investigators suspect that non-aspirin-type anti-inflammatory drugs (such as *ibuprofen*) may help protect brain cells and perhaps lower the risk of developing Parkinson's disease (Chen et al., 2003; Schiess, 2003; Zhang et al., 2003). However, more definitive research is needed to see if these drugs truly have preventive effects.

Dementia Due to Huntington's Disease

Huntington's disease, also known as *Huntington's chorea,* was first recognized by the neurologist George Huntington in 1872. In Huntington's disease, there is progressive deterioration of the basal ganglia, a part of the brain that helps regulate body movement and posture.

The most prominent physical symptoms of the disease are involuntary, jerky movements of the face (grimaces), neck, limbs, and trunk—in contrast to the poverty of movement that typifies Parkinson's disease. These twitches are termed *choreiform,* which derives from the Greek *choreia,* meaning "dance." Unstable moods, alternating with states of apathy, anxiety, and depression, are common in the early stages of the disease. As the disease progresses, paranoia may develop, and people may become suicidally depressed. Difficulties retrieving memories in the early course of the disease may develop later into dementia. Eventually, there is loss of control of bodily functions, leading to death occurring within about 15 years after onset of the disease.

Huntington's disease, which afflicts about 1 in 10,000 people, typically begins in the prime of adulthood, between the ages of 30 and 45 ("Researchers Gain Insight," 2001). Men and women are equally likely to develop the disease (APA, 2000). One of the victims of the disease was the folksinger Woody Guthrie, who gave us the beloved song "This Land Is Your Land," among many others. He died of Huntington's disease in 1967, after 22 years of battling the malady. Because of the odd, jerky movements associated with the disease, Guthrie, like many other Huntington's victims, was misdiagnosed as suffering from alcoholism. He spent several years in mental hospitals before the correct diagnosis was made.

Huntington's disease is caused by a genetic defect on a single defective gene (Cowan & Kandel, 2001; Nucifora et al., 2001). It is transmitted genetically from either parent to children of either gender. People who have a parent with Huntington's disease stand a 50% chance of inheriting the gene. People who inherit the gene eventually contract the disease.

Dementia Due to HIV Disease

The human immunodeficiency virus (HIV), which causes AIDS, can invade the central nervous system and cause a cognitive disorder—dementia due to HIV disease. The most typical signs of dementia due to HIV disease include forgetfulness and impaired concentration and problem-solving ability (APA, 2000). Common behavioral features of the dementia are apathy and social withdrawal. As AIDS progresses, the dementia grows more severe, taking the form of delusions, disorientation, further impairments in memory and thinking processes, and perhaps even delirium. In its later stages, the dementia may resemble the profound deficiencies found among people with advanced Alzheimer's disease.

Dementia is rare in persons with HIV who have not yet developed full-blown AIDS. Yet one in four people with AIDS develops a cognitive impairment that may progress to dementia (Center for Mental Health Services, 1994). Signs of intellectual impairment short of full-blown dementia may also occur earlier than the onset of AIDS (Baldeweg et al., 1997). People with HIV who show early signs of intellectual impairment appear to be at greater risk of early death from AIDS ("Cognitive Impairment," 1996; Wilkie et al., 1998).

Dementia Due to Creutzfeldt-Jakob Disease

Creutzfeldt-Jakob disease is a rare and fatal brain disease (Cowley, 2001a; Spencer et al., 2002). It is characterized by the formation of small cavities in the brain that resemble the holes in a sponge. Dementia is a common feature of the disease. The disease typically affects people in the 40- to 60-year-old age range, although it may develop in adults at any age (APA, 2000). There are no treatments for the disease, and death usually results within months of onset of symptoms. In about 5% to 15% of cases there is evidence

Huntington's disease An inherited degenerative disease that is characterized by jerking and twisting movements, paranoia, and mental deterioration.

TRUTH or FICTION? *REVISITED*

A famous folksinger and songwriter was misdiagnosed with alcoholism and spent several years in mental hospitals until the correct diagnosis was made.

☑ **TRUE.** The folksinger and songwriter was Woody Guthrie, whose Huntington's disease went misdiagnosed for years.

CONTROVERSIES IN ABNORMAL PSYCHOLOGY
Genetic Testing: Should People at Risk Be Tested?

Until recently, children of patients with Huntington's disease had to wait until they developed symptoms themselves—usually in midlife—to know whether they had inherited the disease. Today, a genetic test is available that can detect carriers of the defective gene, those who will eventually develop the disease should they live long enough (Timman et al., 2004). Eventually, perhaps, genetic engineering may provide a means of modifying the defective gene or its effects. Because researchers have not yet developed ways to cure or control Huntington's disease, some potential carriers, like the folksinger Arlo Gurthie, son of the famed folksinger Woody Guthrie who died from the disease, preferred not knowing whether they had inherited the gene. Now in his late 50s, Arlo seems to have escaped his father's fate.

If you were in Arlo's position, would you want to undergo genetic testing to see if you are a carrier? Would you want to know? Or would you prefer keeping yourself in the dark and living your life as best as you could? In thinking critically about this question, you may wish to challenge some common assumptions, such as that knowledge is necessarily better than ignorance. Gaining knowledge about one's genetic risk is valued when it can be used to help stave off or limit the impact of disease. But what if knowledge carried no health benefits? Might ignorance be better than knowledge? Though evidence on the psychological effects of genetic disclosure is limited, investigators in Holland found increasing pessimism among carriers as their age of onset grew nearer (Timman et al., 2004).

Deciding upon genetic testing is a personal choice. But controversy arises over whether people who may be potential carriers of genetic diseases have an ethical or moral responsibility to determine their genetic risk before deciding whether to bear children. We pose the question to encourage you to examine the issue critically. Do you believe people at genetic risk have an obligation to determine their genetic risk before becoming parents? Going further, should people who discover they are carrying a potentially lethal or disabling gene be morally (or perhaps legally) obliged not to bear children? How might you look at this question differently if you a fundamentalist Christian, an orthodox Jew, or a practicing Buddhist or Muslim?

Genetics plays an important role in many diseases discussed in this chapter, such as Parkinson's disease and Alzheimer's disease. Genes are also implicated in many physical conditions, such as Tay-Sachs disease, sickle-cell disease, and cystic fibrosis. As we gain more knowledge and the ability to determine whether people carry many different conditions, insurance companies might require expectant parents to undergo genetic testing. Knowledge about the genetic causes of devastating disease has deep ramifications for society.

Would you want to know? Folksinger Arlo Guthrie decided no. What do you think you would do if you had been in Arlo's place?

Critical Thinking

- Should people be required to be tested for genetic defects?
- Should we be required to reveal our relative risk of developing a wide range of diseases as a condition for obtaining health insurance or for getting a job? What are the effects of requiring such disclosure? Of not requiring it?

of familial transmission, which suggests that a genetic component contributes to determining susceptibility to the disease. The human form of mad-cow disease, a fatal illness spread by eating infected beef, is a variant of Creutzfeldt-Jakob disease (Cowan & Kandel, 2001; McNeil, 2001).

Dementia Due to Head Trauma

Head trauma resulting from jarring, banging, or cutting brain tissues, usually because of accident or assault, can injure the brain, sometimes severely so (Teasdale & Engberg, 2003). Progressive dementia due to head trauma is more likely to result from multiple head traumas (as in the case of boxers who receive multiple blows to the head during their careers) than from a single blow or head trauma (APA, 2000; Guskiewicz et al., 2003; McCrea et al., 2003). Yet even a single head trauma can have psychological effects, and if severe enough, can lead to physical disability or death. Specific changes in personality following traumatic injury to the brain vary with the site and extent of the injury, among other factors (Prigatano, 1992). Damage to the frontal lobe, for example, is

TRUTH or FICTION? *REVISITED*

A form of dementia is linked to mad-cow disease.

☑ **TRUE.** A form of dementia is caused by the human form of mad-cow disease.

Overview of Cognitive Disorders

TYPES OF COGNITIVE DISORDERS/PREVALENCE RATES (approx., in parentheses)

	Description	Features
Delirium (unknown)	States of extreme mental confusion interfering with concentration and ability to speak coherently	• Difficulty filtering out irrelevant stimuli or shifting attention • Excited speech that conveys little meaning • Disorientation as to time and place • Frightening hallucinations or other perceptual distortions • Motor behavior may slow to a stupor or fluctuate between states of restlessness and stupor • Mental states may fluctuate between lucid intervals and periods of confusion
Dementia (Alzheimer's disease: 10% over age 65)	Profound deterioration of mental functioning, including memory	• Most forms are irreversible and progressive, such as dementia of the Alzheimer's type • Associated with specific cognitive deficits, such as aphasia, apraxia, agnosia, and disturbance in executive functioning • Types of dementias are grouped by age of onset into senile dementias (beginning after age 65) and presenile dementias (beginning at age 65 or earlier)
Amnestic Disorder (unknown)	Profound deficit in memory not associated with delirium or dementia	• May affect short-term memory and/or long-term memory • Person may be disoriented, especially as to place and time

CASUAL FACTORS

Delirium	• Medical conditions, such as head trauma, metabolic disorders, low blood sugar, fluid or electrolyte imbalances, epilepsy, vitamin B deficiencies, and brain lesions • Brain diseases, such as Parkinson's disease and Alzheimer's disease • Abrupt withdrawal from alcohol in cases of chronic alcoholism (called delirium tremens, or DTs)
Dementia	• Brain diseases, such as Alzheimer's disease, Pick's disease, Parkinson's disease, Huntington's disease, HIV disease, and Creutzfeldt-Jakob disease • Neurosyphilis • Multiple strokes (vascular dementia) • Brain tumors • Head trauma • Brain infections such as meningitis and encephalitis • Causes of Alzheimer's disease remain unknown, but evidence points to a genetic contribution
Amnestic Disorder	• Physical causes such as a blow to the head • Complications from brain surgery • Brain infection • Blockage of blood supply to the brain • Heavy use of certain psychoactive substances (as in Korsakoff's syndrome)

TREATMENT APPROACHES

Delirium	• May clear up spontaneously or when the underlying medical condition is treated successfully • Monitoring in hospital setting may be needed, especially for the DTs
Dementia	• Available treatments for dementia of the Alzheimer's type are limited to drugs that may slow the progression of the disease but are not a cure
Amnestic Disorder	• Memory may return spontaneously or with effective treatment of underlying conditions

Sources for prevalence rates: APA, 2000; Herbert et al., 2003.

associated with a range of emotional changes involving alterations of mood and personality.

Neurosyphilis

General paresis (from the Greek *parienai,* meaning "to relax") is a form of dementia—or "relaxation" of the brain in its most negative connotation—that results from neurosyphilis, a form of syphilis in which the disease organism, in a late stage of infection, directly attacks the brain and central nervous system. General paresis is of historical significance to abnormal psychology. The 19th-century discovery of the connection between this form of dementia and a concrete physical illness, syphilis, strengthened the medical model and held out the promise that organic causes would eventually be found

general paresis A form of dementia resulting from neurosyphilis.

Heading toward brain damage? Multiple blows to the head may lead to a progressive form of dementia.

for other abnormal behavior patterns. Syphilis is a sexually transmitted disease caused by the bacterium *Treponema pallidum*.

General paresis is associated with physical symptoms such as tremors, slurred speech, impaired motor coordination, and, eventually, paralysis—all of which are suggestive of relaxed control over the body. Psychological signs include shifts in mood states, blunted emotional responsiveness, and irritability; delusions; changes in personal habits, such as suspension of personal grooming and hygiene; and progressive intellectual deterioration, including impairments of memory, judgment, and comprehension. Some people with general paresis grow euphoric and entertain delusions of grandiosity. Others become lethargic and depressed. Eventually, people with general paresis lapse into a state of apathy and confusion, characterized by the inability to care for themselves or to speak intelligibly. Death results either from renewed infection or the damage caused by the existing infection.

Late-stage syphilis once accounted for 10% to 30% of admissions to psychiatric hospitals. However, advances in detection and the development of antibiotics that cure the infection have sharply reduced the incidence of late-stage syphilis and the development of general paresis. The effectiveness of treatment depends on when antibiotics are introduced and the extent of central nervous system damage. In cases where extensive tissue damage has occurred, antibiotics can stem the infection and prevent further damage, producing some improvement in intellectual performance. They cannot restore people to their original levels of functioning, however.

SUMMING UP

Cognitive Disorders

What are cognitive disorders? Cognitive disorders are disturbances of thinking or memory that represent a marked decline in intellectual or memory functioning. They are caused by physical or medical conditions or drug use or withdrawal affecting the functioning of the brain.

What is delirium? Delirium is a state of mental confusion characterized by symptoms such as impaired attention, disorientation, disorganized thinking and rambling speech, reduced level of consciousness, and perceptual disturbances. Delirium is most commonly caused by alcohol withdrawal, as in the form of delirium tremens (DTs).

What is dementia? Dementia is a cognitive deterioration or impairment, as evidenced by memory deficits, impaired judgment, personality changes, and disorders of higher cognitive functions such as problem-solving ability and abstract thinking.

Is dementia a normal part of aging? No, dementia is not a normal consequence of aging but a sign of a degenerative brain disorder. There are various causes of dementias, including Alzheimer's disease and Pick's disease, and brain infections or disorders.

What are amnestic disorders? Amnestic disorders represent persistent deficits in short-term or long-term memory. The most common cause of amnestic syndrome is alcohol-induced persisting amnestic disorder, or Korsakoff's syndrome, which involves a thiamine deficiency typically associated with patterns of chronic alcohol abuse.

Psychological Disorders Related to Aging

What types of psychological problems affect people in later life? Generalized anxiety disorder and phobic disorders are the most commonly occurring anxiety disorders among older people. Depression to varying degrees is common among people in later life and may be associated with memory deficits that may lift as the depression clears. Dementia of the Alzheimer's type and vascular dementia primarily affect people in later life. They involve irreversible and progressive memory impairment. Certain sleep disorders, such as insomnia and sleep apnea, are also common among older people.

What are Alzheimer's disease and vascular dementia? Alzheimer's disease (AD) is a progressive brain disease characterized by progressive loss of memory and cognitive ability, as well as deterioration in personality functioning and self-care skills. There is no cure or effective treatment for AD. Research into its causes has focused on genetic factors and imbalances in neurotransmitters, especially acetylcholine. Vascular dementia results from multiple strokes (blood clots that block the supply of blood to parts of the brain, damaging or destroying brain tissue).

Dementias Due to General Medical Conditions

What other general medical conditions can lead to dementia? Various other medical conditions can lead to dementia, including Pick's disease, Parkinson's disease, Huntington's disease, Creutzfeldt-Jakob disease, HIV disease, head trauma, and neurosyphilis.

Scoring Key for Attitudes Toward Aging Scale

1. False. Most healthy couples continue to engage in satisfying sexual activities into their 70s and 80s.
2. False. This is too general a statement. Those who find their work satisfying are less desirous of retiring.
3. False. In late adulthood, we tend to become more concerned with internal matters—our physical functioning and our emotions.
4. False. Adaptability remains reasonably stable throughout adulthood.
5. False. Age itself is not linked to noticeable declines in life satisfaction. Of course, we may respond negatively to disease and losses, such as the death of a spouse.
6. False. Although we can predict some general trends for older adults, we can also do so for younger adults. Older adults, like their younger counterparts, are heterogeneous in personality and behavior patterns.
7. False. Older adults with stable intimate relationships are more satisfied.
8. False. We are susceptible to a wide variety of psychological disorders at all ages.
9. False. Only a minority are depressed.
10. False. Actually, church attendance declines, but not verbally expressed religious beliefs.
11. False. Although reaction time may increase and general learning ability may undergo a slight decline, older adults usually have little or no difficulty at familiar work tasks. In most jobs, experience and motivation are more important than age.
12. False. Learning may just take a bit longer.
13. False. Older adults do not direct a higher proportion of thoughts toward the past than do younger people. Regardless of our age, we may spend more time daydreaming at any age if we have more time on our hands.
14. False. Fewer than 10% of older adults require some form of institutional care.

KEY TERMS

cognitive disorders *(p. 509)*
agnosia *(p. 511)*
dementia *(p. 511)*
senile dementias *(p. 512)*
presenile dementias *(p. 512)*
delirium *(p. 513)*
amnestic disorders *(p. 514)*

hypoxia *(p. 515)*
infarction *(p. 515)*
Korsakoff's syndrome *(p. 515)*
Wernicke's disease *(p. 515)*
ataxia *(p. 515)*
Alzheimer's disease (AD) *(p. 519)*
cerebrovascular accident (CVA) *(p. 524)*

vascular dementia *(p. 525)*
aphasia *(p. 525)*
Pick's disease *(p. 525)*
Parkinson's disease *(p. 525)*
Huntington's disease *(p. 527)*
general paresis *(p. 529)*

WEB TOOLS

The companion website offers tools to enrich your learning experience and help you succeed in class. Go to www.prenhall.com/nevid for the gateway to the following resources:

- **VIDEO** links to connect to the video case files on the companion CD-ROM. VIDEO icons in the margins of the chapter highlight the case examples included in the CD-ROM. You can also access the CD-ROM directly if you do not have a Web connection.

- **QUIZ** links to self-scoring quizzes corresponding to each section of the chapter. The quizzes help you review your knowledge of the content in each chapter.
- **WEB** links to direct you to related sites that enhance your learning of abnormal psychology.

Abnormal Psychology and the Law

"I"

"Please Look Into Your Heart"

Dear Jodie,

There is a definite possibility that I will be killed in my attempt to get Reagan. It is for this very reason that I am writing you this letter now.

As you well know by now I love you very much. Over the past seven months I've left you dozens of poems, letters and love messages in the faint hope that you could develop an interest in me . . .

Jodie, I would abandon this idea of getting Reagan in a second if I could only win your heart and live out the rest of my life with you, whether it be in total obscurity or whatever.

I will admit to you that the reason I'm going ahead with this attempt now is because I just cannot wait any longer to impress you. I've got to do something now to make you understand, in no uncertain terms, that I am doing all of this for your sake! By sacrificing my freedom and possibly my life, I hope to change your mind about me. This letter is being written only an hour before I leave for the Hilton Hotel. Jodie, I'm asking you to please look into your heart and at least give me the chance, with this historical deed, to gain your respect and love.

—*John Hinckley's letter to actress Jodie Foster, written on March 31, 1980, shortly before he attempted to assassinate President Ronald Reagan*

Source: Linder, 2004, "The John Hinckley Trial"

GUNSHOTS RANG OUT AS PRESIDENT RONALD REAGAN STEPPED OUT OF THE Washington Hilton that cold day in March 1981. Secret Service agents formed a human shield around the president; one shoved him into a waiting limousine, which sped to a hospital. Agents seized the gunman, John Hinckley, a 25-year-old drifter. The president had been wounded; James Brady, his press secretary, was hit by a stray bullet that shattered his spine and left him partially paralyzed; and a Secret Service agent was shot.

The letter Hinckley left in his hotel room, parts of which are cited above, revealed his hope that his assassination of the president would impress a young actress, Jodie Foster. Hinckley had never met Foster but had a crush on her.

At Hinckley's trial, there was never any question whether Hinckley had fired the wounding bullets, but the prosecutor was burdened to demonstrate beyond a reasonable doubt that Hinckley had the capacity to control his behavior and appreciate its wrongfulness. The defense presented testimony that portrayed Hinckley as an incompetent schizophrenic who suffered under the delusion that he would achieve a "magic union" with Foster as a result of killing the president. The prosecutor claimed that Hinckley made a conscious and willful choice to kill the president and that, whatever mental disorder Hinckley might have, it did not prevent him from controlling his behavior. The jury sided with the defense and found Hinckley not guilty by reason of insanity (Janofsky, 2003). He was remanded to a federal psychiatric facility, St. Elizabeth's Hospital in Washington, D.C., where he has remained ever since.

Fast-forward 22 years. In 2003, Hinckley, then 48, petitioned the courts to allow him to leave the grounds of the hospital for day trips in the company of his parents (Sokolove, 2003). A federal judge granted his request for unsupervised daytime visits with his parents (Arena & Frieden, 2003). Eventually, perhaps by the time this book reaches your hands, Hinckley may be permitted overnight trips, perhaps even a full release. Hinckley's doctors argue that his psychiatric condition (a combination of psychosis and depression) is "in full remission." The idea that Hinckley might one day be released is an unsettling thought to many people. Should someone who has committed such grievous acts have been found "not guilty" at all, even by "reason of insanity"? Shouldn't he have been imprisoned rather than treated in a mental hospital? How should society treat mentally disturbed individuals who commit crimes?

Truth or Fiction?

T❑ F❑ People can be committed to psychiatric facilities because of odd behavior. (p. 535)

T❑ F❑ Psychologists and other mental health professionals can accurately predict whether people they evaluate will become dangerous. (p. 536)

T❑ F❑ Therapists are not obligated to breach client confidentiality even to warn intended victims of threats of violence made against them by their clients. (p. 540)

T❑ F❑ Patients in mental hospitals may be required to perform general housekeeping duties in a facility. (p. 543)

T❑ F❑ An attempt to assassinate the president of the United States was seen by millions of television viewers, but the would-be assassin was found not guilty by a court of law. (p. 544)

T❑ F❑ The insanity defense is used in a large number of trials, usually successfully. (p. 545)

T❑ F❑ People who are found not guilty of a crime by reason of insanity may remain confined to a mental hospital for many years longer than they would have been sentenced to prison, if they had been found guilty. (p. 548)

T❑ F❑ It is possible for a defendant to be held competent to stand trial but still be judged not guilty of a crime by reason of insanity. (p. 549)

Not guilty by reason of insanity. In 1981, John Hinckley Jr. attempted to assassinate President Ronald Reagan outside a Washington hotel. Hinckley was later found not guilty by reason of insanity. Here we see President Reagan at the moment he was struck by a bullet from the gun fired by Hinckley.

civil commitment The legal process of placing a person in a mental institution, even against his or her will.

criminal commitment The legal process of confining a person found not guilty by reason of insanity in a mental institution.

The Hinckley case provides an example of the interface of society and abnormal behavior. In this chapter we will discuss the insanity defense, its history in U.S. law, and the legal and moral arguments that underlie its use. We will also examine the legal rights of mental patients and the legal responsibility that falls on mental health-care providers to warn third parties of threats made by patients. We will address questions that touch on the general issue of how to balance the rights of the individual with the rights of society. Do people who are obviously mentally disturbed have the right to refuse treatment? Do psychiatric institutions have the right to administer antipsychotic and other drugs to patients against their will? Should mental patients with a history of disruptive or violent behavior be hospitalized indefinitely or permitted to live in supervised residences in the community once their conditions are stabilized? When severely disturbed people break the law, should society respond to them with the criminal justice system or with the mental health system?

We begin with psychiatric commitment, the process by which individuals are involuntarily confined in mental hospitals because they are deemed to be mentally ill and a danger to either themselves or others. As with other issues we consider in this chapter, the practice of psychiatric commitment brings into focus the interface between the rights of individuals and the rights of society.

PSYCHIATRIC COMMITMENT AND PATIENTS' RIGHTS

Legal placement of people in psychiatric institutions against their will is called **civil commitment** (also called *psychiatric commitment*). Through civil commitment, individuals who are judged to be mentally ill and a threat to themselves or others can be involuntarily confined to psychiatric institutions to provide them with treatment and help ensure their own safety and that of others (Failer, 2002; Glenn, 2003).

Civil commitment should be distinguished from *voluntary hospitalization*, in which an individual voluntarily seeks treatment in a psychiatric institution and can, with adequate notice, leave the institution when she or he so desires. Even in such cases, however, when the hospital staff believes that a voluntary patient presents a threat to her or his own welfare or to others, they may petition the court to change the patient's legal status from voluntary to involuntary.

Civil commitment should also be distinguished from **criminal commitment,** in which an individual who is acquitted of a crime by reason of insanity is placed in a psychiatric institution for treatment. In criminal commitment, a defendant's unlawful act is judged by a court of law to result from a mental disorder or defect, and the defendant is committed to a psychiatric hospital where treatment can be provided rather than incarcerated in a prison.

Civil commitment in a psychiatric hospital usually requires that a relative or professional file a petition with the court, which empowers psychiatric examiners to evaluate the person. Finally, a judge hears psychiatric testimony and decides whether or not to commit the individual. In the event of commitment, the law usually requires periodic legal review and recertification of the patient's involuntary status. The legal process is intended to ensure that people are not indefinitely "warehoused" in psychiatric hospitals. Hospital staff must demonstrate the need for continued inpatient treatment.

Legal safeguards protect people's civil rights in commitment proceedings. Defendants have the right to due process and to be assisted by an attorney, for example. But when individuals are deemed to present a clear and imminent threat to themselves or others, the court may order immediate hospitalization until a formal commitment hearing can be held. Such emergency powers are usually limited to a specific period, usually 72 hours (Failer, 2002). If a formal commitment petition is not filed with the court during this time, the individual has a right to be discharged.

Standards for psychiatric commitment have been tightened over the past generation, and the rights of individuals who are subject to commitment proceedings are more strictly protected. In the past, psychiatric abuses were more common. People were often committed without clear evidence that they posed a threat. Not until 1979, in fact, did the U.S. Supreme Court rule, in *Addington* v. *Texas,* that in order for individuals to be hospitalized involuntarily, they must be judged both to be "mentally ill" and to present a clear and present danger to themselves or others. Thus people cannot be committed because of their eccentricity.

Few would argue that contemporary tightening of civil commitment laws protects the rights of the individual. Even so, some critics of the psychiatric system have called for the abolition of psychiatric commitment on the grounds that commitment deprives the individual of liberty in the name of therapy, and that such a loss of liberty cannot be justified in a free society. Perhaps the most vocal and persistent critic of the civil commitment statutes is psychiatrist Thomas Szasz (Szasz, 1970, 2003a, 2003b). Szasz argued that the label of *mental illness* is a societal invention that transforms social deviance into medical illness. In Szasz's view, people should not be deprived of their liberty because their behavior is perceived to be socially deviant or disruptive. Szasz likens involuntary hospitalization to institutional slavery (Szasz, 2003b). According to Szasz, people who violate the law should be prosecuted for criminal behavior, not confined to a psychiatric hospital. Although psychiatric commitment may prevent some individuals from acting violently, it does violence to many people who are innocent of any crime by depriving them of the fundamental right of liberty:

> The mental patient, we say, *may be* dangerous: he may harm himself or someone else. But we, society, *are* dangerous: we rob him of his good name and of his liberty, and subject him to tortures called "treatments." (Szasz, 1970, p. 279)

> It is a fundamental principle of English and American law that only persons charged with and convicted of certain crimes are subject to imprisonment. Persons who respect other people's rights to life, liberty, and property have an inalienable right to their own life, liberty, and property. (Szasz, 2003a, p. 228).

Szasz's strident opposition to institutional psychiatry and his condemnation of psychiatric commitment focused attention on abuses in the mental health system. Many patients who have experienced psychiatric commitment rail against the practice. A recent survey in Germany showed that most patients believed that their court-mandated commitment was not justified and could have been avoided (Langle et al., 2003).

Szasz was effective in persuading many professionals to question the legal, ethical, and moral bases of coercive psychiatric treatment in the forms of involuntary hospitalization and forced medication. Many caring and concerned professionals draw the line at abolishing psychiatric commitment, however. They argue that people may not be acting in their considered best interests when they threaten suicide or harm to others, or when their behavior becomes so disorganized that they cannot meet their basic needs (McMillan, 2003; Sayers, 2003). Most countries, including the United States and Canada, have laws that permit commitment of dangerous, mentally ill people (Appelbaum, 2003). Yet the issue of psychiatric commitment continues to rouse debate. In the feature "Controversies in Abnormal Psychology," we frame the issue by looking more closely at two celebrated cases, that of the so-called Wild Man of West 96th Street and that of a psychiatrically disturbed homeless woman, Joyce Brown.

Predicting Dangerousness

Mental health professionals are often called on to judge whether patients are a danger to themselves or others as part of the legal proceedings to determine whether people should be involuntarily hospitalized or maintained involuntarily in the hospital. But how accurate are the judgments of professionals when predicting dangerousness? Do professionals have special skills or clinical wisdom that renders their predictions accurate, or are their predictions no more accurate than those of laypeople?

Unfortunately, psychologists and other mental health professionals who rely on their clinical judgments are not very accurate when it comes to predicting dangerousness of

Should she be committed to a psychiatric institution? People must be judged as dangerous in order to be psychiatrically hospitalized against their wills. This photograph of emergency workers pulling a woman away from a ledge after she threatened to jump leaves little doubt about the dangerousness of her behavior. But professionals have not demonstrated that they can reliably predict future dangerousness.

the people they treat. Mental health professionals tend to overpredict dangerousness— that is, to label many individuals as dangerous when they are not. Clinicians tend to err on the side of caution in predicting the potential for dangerous behavior, perhaps because they believe that failure to predict violence may have more serious consequences than overprediction. Overprediction of dangerousness does deprive many people of liberty. According to Szasz and other critics of the practice of psychiatric commitment, the commitment of the many to prevent the violence of the few is a form of preventive detention that violates basic constitutional principles.

The leading professional organizations, the American Psychological Association (1978) and the American Psychiatric Association (1998), have both gone on record as stating that neither psychologists nor psychiatrists, respectively, can reliably predict violent behavior. As a leading authority in the field, John Monahan of the University of Virginia, said, "When it comes to predicting violence, our crystal balls are terribly cloudy" (Rosenthal, 1993, p. A1).

Clinician predictions are generally also less accurate than predictions based on evidence of past violent behavior (Gardner et al., 1996; Mossman, 1994). Basically, clinicians do not possess any special knowledge or ability for predicting violence beyond that of the average person. In fact, a layperson supplied with information concerning an individual's past violent behavior may predict the individual's potential for future violence more accurately than the clinician, who bases a prediction solely on a clinical interview (Mossman, 1994). Unfortunately, although past violent behavior is the best predictor of future violence, hospital staff may not be permitted access to criminal records or may lack the time or resources to track down these records. The prediction problem has been cited by some as grounds for abandoning dangerousness as a criterion for civil commitment.

Why is predicting dangerousness so difficult? Investigators have identified a number of factors that lead to inaccurate predictions, including the following.

The Post Hoc Problem Recognizing violent tendencies after a violent incident occurs (post hoc) is easier than predicting it beforehand. It is often said that hindsight is 20/20. Like Monday morning quarterbacking, it is easier to piece together fragments of people's prior behaviors as evidence of violent tendencies *after* they have committed acts of violence. Predicting a violent act before the fact is a more difficult task, however.

TRUTH or FICTION? *REVISITED*

Psychologists and other mental health professionals can accurately predict whether people they evaluate will become dangerous.

☑ **FALSE.** Psychologists and other mental health professionals who rely on their clinical judgments are not very accurate when it comes to predicting the dangerousness of the people they treat. The best predictor of future violence is a history of past violence.

CONTROVERSIES IN ABNORMAL PSYCHOLOGY
What Should We Do About the "Wild Man of West 96th Street"?

We first learned about Larry Hogue—the "wild man" of West 96th Street—in the early 1990s. Hogue was a homeless Vietnam War veteran who inhabited the alleyways and doorways of Manhattan's affluent Upper West Side. He went barefoot in winter, ate from garbage cans, and muttered to himself (Dugger, 1992). A reporter characterized Hogue as conducting a personal war of terror on the neighborhood (Kolker, 2002). He reportedly stalked a teacher and threatened to cook and eat her fawn-colored Akita. He also became violent when he smoked crack and was once arrested for pushing a schoolgirl in front of a school bus (Shapiro, 1992). (Miraculously, she escaped injury.)

Hogue was shuttled in and out of state psychiatric hospitals and prisons more than 40 times (Wickenhaver, 1992). For Hogue, the criminal justice, social services, and mental health systems were nothing but revolving doors. Typically, Hogue would improve during a brief hospital stay and be released, only to return to using crack instead of his psychiatric medication. His behavior would then deteriorate (Dugger, 1994). For many people, Larry Hogue became a national symbol of the many cracks in the system.

Then there was the celebrated case of Joyce Brown, a middle-aged woman who also lived on the streets of New York. At one time she slept above a hot air vent on the sidewalk on the Upper East Side of Manhattan, in the midst of some of the most expensive real estate in the world. Sometimes she was observed defecating in her clothes or on the sidewalk. She hurled insults at strangers and refused to go to a shelter, preferring to live in the streets, despite the obvious dangers of potential attack and the risks of exposure to the elements.

In New York, a program was begun to provide outreach services to homeless people in need of psychological treatment. Teams of specialists, each consisting of a nurse, a social worker, and a psychiatrist, were charged with identifying and monitoring behaviorally disordered homeless people, helping them obtain services, bringing them soup and sandwiches, and taking them to the hospital if they were deemed to represent an immediate threat to themselves or others under the authority provided by state laws governing psychiatric commitment, even if it was against the individual's will.

Brown had been picked up and brought against her will to a city hospital for evaluation, where she was diagnosed with paranoid schizophrenia and judged to be in need of treatment. She resisted treatment and claimed that she had a right to live her life as she saw fit, even if it offended other people. As long as she committed no crime, what right did society have to deprive her of her liberty? Yes, she admitted, she had defecated in the streets. But there were no public restrooms available, and establishments such as restaurants had refused her access.

Brown sued for her release, and while her case meandered through the courts, she remained in the hospital, although her doctors were prevented from medicating her against her will. Because she refused medication, the doctors released her, claiming there was little they could do for her. Although we've lost track of Joyce Brown, Larry Hogue turned up a few years later in his old haunts on the Upper West Side of Manhattan, where he was seen panhandling. Local residents expressed fears that he would return to terrorizing them (Holloway, 1998).

It may seem obvious that people like Hogue and Brown need care and that it is the responsibility of a humane society to provide that care, whether through an outpatient clinic or a locked psychiatric facility. But critics of the mental health system, such as Thomas Szasz, argue that by the very nature of a free society, people should be free to make their own decisions, even when those decisions are not in the best interests of their health or welfare. Others argue that society has a duty to protect such people from themselves, as well as to protect citizens from the dangers they pose to others. Now extend the argument: If society has an obligation to protect individuals like Joyce Brown from themselves, or to protect citizenry from individuals like Hogue—does it not have obligations to protect individuals whose behavior is harmful in other ways, such as those who smoke cigarettes, drink alcohol to excess, or become obese? Where would you draw that line?

What should society do about the "Larry Hogue's" and "Joyce Browns" of our cities and towns? What do you think should be done? The cases of Larry Hogue and Joyce Brown touch on the more general issue of how to balance the rights of the individual with the rights of society. Cases like these prompt us to consider a number of questions about the rights of individuals in society to act in ways that offend others—questions that challenge us to think critically about these issues.

Critical Thinking

- Do people in a free society have the right to live on the streets under unsanitary conditions?
- Do people who are obviously mentally disturbed have the right to refuse treatment?
- Should mental patients with a history of disruptive or violent behavior be hospitalized indefinitely or permitted to live in supervised residences in the community once their conditions are stabilized?
- Do people have a right to be mentally ill and be left alone, so long as they do not break any laws? Or do you agree with psychiatrist E. Fuller Torrey and attorney Mary Zdanowicz (1999) that ". . . . for individuals whose brain is impaired by severe mental illness, defending their right to remain mentally ill is mindless"?
- When severely disturbed people do break the law, should society respond to them with the criminal justice system or with the mental health system?

"The Wild Man of West 96th Street." Larry Hogue, the so-called Wild Man of West 96th Street in New York City, has become a symbol of the cracks in the mental health, criminal justice, and social services systems.

Is he suicidal? One reason clinicians have difficulty predicting violent behaviors such as suicide or murder is that they are relatively infrequent acts. Clinicians often err on the side of caution and so have a tendency toward overpredicting dangerousness.

The Problem in Leaping from the General to the Specific Generalized perceptions of violent tendencies may not predict specific acts of violence. Most people who have "general tendencies" toward violence never act on them. Nor is a diagnosis associated with aggressive or dangerous behavior, such as antisocial personality disorder, a sufficient basis for predicting specific violent acts in individuals (Bloom & Rogers, 1987).

Problems in Defining Dangerousness One difficulty in predicting dangerousness is the lack of agreement over what types of behavior are violent or dangerous. Most people would agree that crimes such as murder, rape, and assault are acts of violence. There is less agreement, even among authorities, for labeling other acts—for example, driving recklessly, harshly criticizing one's spouse or children, destroying property, selling drugs, shoving into people at a tavern, or stealing cars—as violent or dangerous. Consider, also, the behavior of business owners and corporate executives who produce and market cigarettes despite widespread knowledge of the death and disease these substances cause. Clearly, the determination of which behaviors are regarded as dangerous involves moral and political judgments within a given social context (Monahan, 1981).

Base-Rate Problems The prediction of dangerousness is complicated by the fact that violent acts such as murder, assault, or suicide are infrequent within the general population, even if newspaper headlines sensationalize them regularly. Other rare events—such as earthquakes—are also difficult to predict with any degree of certainty concerning when or where they will strike.

The relative difficulty of making predictions about infrequent or rare events is known as the *base-rate problem*. Consider as an example the problem of suicide prediction. If the suicide rate in a given year has a low base rate of about 1% of a clinical population, the likelihood of accurately predicting that any given person in this population will commit suicide is very small. You would be correct 99% of the time if you predicted that any given individual in this population would *not* commit suicide in a given year. But if you predicted the nonoccurrence of suicide in every case, you would fail to predict the relatively few cases in which suicide does occur, even though virtually all your predictions would likely be correct. Yet predicting the one likely case of suicide among those 100 people is likely to be tricky. When clinicians make predictions, they weigh the relative risks of incorrectly failing to predict the occurrence of a behavior (a *false negative*) against the consequences of incorrectly predicting it (a *false positive*). Clinicians often err on the side of caution by overpredicting dangerousness. From the clinician's perspective, erring on the side of caution might seem like a no-lose situation. Yet many people committed to an institution under such circumstances are denied their liberty when they would not actually have acted violently against themselves or others.

The Unlikelihood of Disclosure of Direct Threats of Violence How likely is it that truly dangerous people will disclose their intentions to a health professional who is evaluating them or to their own therapist? The client in therapy is not likely to inform a therapist of a clear threat, such as "I'm going to kill _____ next Wednesday morning." Threats are more likely to be vague and nonspecific, as in "I'm so sick of _____; I could kill her," or "I swear he's driving me to murder." In such cases, therapists must infer dangerousness from hostile gestures and veiled threats. Vague, indirect threats of violence are less-reliable indicators of dangerousness than specific, direct threats.

The Difficulty of Predicting Behavior in the Community from Behavior in the Hospital Mental health professionals fall well short of the mark when making long-term predictions of dangerousness (Buchanan, 1999). They are often wrong when predicting whether patients will become dangerous following release from the hospital. One reason is that they often base their predictions on patients' behavior in the hospital. But violent or dangerous behavior may be situation specific. A model patient who is able to adapt to a structured environment like that of a psychiatric hospital may be unable to cope with the pressures of independent communal life. Clinicians are generally more accurate when their predictions are based on the patient's past behavior in the community than on behavior in the hospital setting (Klassen & O'Connor, 1988).

Overall, clinician predictions of dangerousness are significantly better than predictions based on chance alone, but they are still often inaccurate (Kaplan, 2000). Although their crystal balls may be cloudy, mental health professionals who work in institutional settings continue to be called on to make predictions—deciding whom to commit and whom to discharge based largely on how they appraise the potential for violence (McNiel et al., 2003). Rather than expecting clinicians to rely on clinical judgment, investigators are developing better decision-based tools, such as structured screening methods, to guide assessment of violence risk (e.g., McNiel et al., 2002, 2003; Swets, Dawes, & Monahan, 2000).

These efforts are helping to improve the ability to predict the likelihood of violent behavior, at least with respect to short-term predictions (e.g., McNiel et al., 2003). Clinicians may be more successful in predicting violence by basing predictions on a composite of factors, including evidence of past violent behavior, than on any single factor (Shaffer, Waters, & Adams, 1994). Another promising method is a decision-tree model (Lehmann, 2002). In this branching technique, clinicians ask specific questions based on the patient's previous responses to determine the likelihood of future violence (Monahan et al., 2001). All told, however, professionals still lack valid instruments for assessing the risk of dangerousness (Bauer et al., 2003).

Not surprisingly, the accuracy of clinician predictions of violence tends to be greatest when clinicians agree with one another than when they disagree (McNiel, Lam, & Binder, 2000). Accuracy is also improved when clinicians make short-term predictions of dangerousness, such as predictions of imminent violence (Binder, 1999).

An important variable in predicting violence is substance abuse. The potential for violence is heightened in people with serious psychiatric disorders when they use alcohol, crack, or other drugs (Tardiff et al., 1997). A recent large-scale study of 951 mental patients found that patients who did not abuse drugs were no more likely than controls to engage in violent behavior (Monahan et al., 2001). However, psychiatric patients who abused alcohol or drugs were twice as likely as control subjects with substance abuse problems to engage in violent acts. The likelihood of violence is also heightened among schizophrenia patients who experience command hallucinations—voices commanding them to harm themselves or others (McNiel, Lam, & Binder, 2000).

As we explore in the "A Closer Look" section, the problem of predicting dangerousness also arises when therapists need to evaluate the seriousness of threats made by their patients against others. Do therapists have a "duty to warn"—a legal obligation to warn the intended targets of these threats? The "duty to warn" is one of many legal issues arising from society's response to problems of abnormal behavior. In the following sections, we discuss such major legal issues as patients' rights, the insanity defense, and the right of mental patients to refuse treatment. Table 16.1 contains a listing of the landmark court cases that underpin our discussion of these issues.

Patients' Rights

We have considered society's right to hospitalize involuntarily people who are judged to be mentally ill and to pose a threat to themselves or others. But what happens after commitment? Do involuntarily committed patients have the right to receive or demand treatment? Or can society just

What are the rights of mental patients? Popular books and films, such as *One Flew Over the Cuckoo's Nest* starring Jack Nicholson, have highlighted many of the abuses of mental hospitals. In recent years, a tightening of standards of care and the adoption of legal safeguards have led to better protection of the rights of patients in mental hospitals.

TABLE 16.1

Mental Health and the Law

Case	Year	Legal Issue
Durham v. *United States*	1954	Insanity defense
Wyatt v. *Stickney*	1972	Minimum standard of care
O'Connor v. *Donaldson*	1975	Patients' rights
Jackson v. *Indiana*	1972	Competency to stand trial
Tarasoff v. *the Regents of the University of California*	1976	Duty to warn
Rogers v. *Okin*	1979	Right to refuse treatment
Youngberg v. *Romeo*	1982	Right to confinement in less-restrictive conditions
Jones v. *United States*	1983	Length of criminal commitment
Medina v. *California*	1992	Burden of proof for determining mental competency
Sell v. *United States*	2003	Forced medication of mentally ill defendants

warehouse them in psychiatric facilities indefinitely without treating them? Consider the opposite side of the coin as well: May people who are involuntarily committed refuse treatment? Such issues—which have been brought into public light by landmark court cases—fall under the umbrella of *patients' rights.* Generally speaking, the history of abuses in the mental health system, as highlighted in such popular books and movies as *One Flew Over the Cuckoo's Nest,* have led to a tightening of standards of care and adoption of legal guarantees to protect patients' rights. The legal status of some issues, such as the right to treatment, remains unsettled, however.

Right to Treatment We might assume that mental health institutions that accept people for treatment would provide them with treatment. Not until the 1972 landmark federal court case of *Wyatt* v. *Stickney,* however, did a federal court establish a minimum standard of care to be provided by hospitals. The case was a class action suit against Stickney, the commissioner of mental health for the State of Alabama, brought on behalf of Ricky Wyatt, a mentally retarded young man, and other patients at a state hospital and school in Tuscaloosa.

The federal district court in Alabama held both that the hospital had failed to provide treatment to Wyatt and others and that living conditions at the hospital were inadequate and dehumanizing. The court described the hospital dormitories as "barnlike structures" that afforded no privacy to the residents. The bathrooms had no partitions between stalls, the patients were outfitted with shoddy clothes, the wards were filthy and crowded, the kitchens were unsanitary, and the food was substandard. In addition, the staff was inadequate in numbers and poorly trained. The case of *Wyatt* v. *Stickney* established certain patient rights, including the right not to be required to perform work that is performed for the sake of maintaining the facility. The court held that mental hospitals must, at a minimum, provide the following:

1. A humane psychological and physical environment,
2. Qualified staff in numbers sufficient to administer adequate treatment, and
3. Individualized treatment plans (*Wyatt* v. *Stickney,* 1972).

The court established that the state was obliged to provide adequate treatment for people who were involuntarily confined to psychiatric hospitals. The court further ruled that to commit people to hospitals for treatment involuntarily, and then not to provide treatment, violated their rights to due process under the law.

TRUTH or FICTION? *REVISITED*

Therapists are not obligated to breach client confidentiality even to warn intended victims of threats of violence made against them by their clients.

☑ **FALSE.** Therapists are obligated under some state laws to breach client confidentiality to warn people when threats of violence are made against them by their clients.

---

duty to warn The therapist's obligation to warn third parties of threats made against them by clients.

One of the most difficult dilemmas a therapist faces is whether to disclose confidential information that may protect third parties from harm. Part of the difficulty lies in determining whether the client has made a bona fide threat. The other part is that information a client discloses in psychotherapy is generally protected as privileged communication, which carries a right to confidentiality. But this right is not absolute. State courts have determined that a therapist is obligated to breach confidentiality under certain conditions, such as when there is clear and compelling evidence that an individual poses a serious threat to others.

A 1976 court ruling in California in the case of *Tarasoff* v. *the Regents of the University of California* established the legal basis for the therapist's **duty to warn** (Jones, 2003). In 1969, a graduate student at the University of California at Berkeley, Prosenjit Poddar, a native of India, became depressed when his romantic overtures toward a young woman, Tatiana Tarasoff, were rebuffed. Poddar entered psychotherapy with a psychologist at a student health facility and informed the psychologist that he intended to kill Tatiana when she returned from her summer vacation. The psychologist, concerned about Poddar's potential for violence, first consulted with his colleagues and then notified the campus police that Poddar was dangerous, recommending that he be taken to a facility for psychiatric treatment.

The campus police interviewed Poddar. They believed he was rational and released him after he promised to keep away from Tatiana. Poddar then terminated treatment with the psychologist and shortly afterward killed Tatiana. Poddar was found guilty of the lesser sentence of voluntary manslaughter rather than murder, based on testimony of three psychiatrists that he suffered from diminished mental capacity and paranoid schizophrenia. Under California law, his diminished capacity prevented the finding of malice that was necessary for a murder conviction. Following a prison term, Poddar returned to India, where he reportedly made a new life for himself (Schwitzgebel & Schwitzgebel, 1980).

Tatiana's parents, however, sued the university. They claimed that the university health center had failed in its responsibility to warn Tatiana of the threat made against her by Poddar. The California Supreme Court agreed with the parents. They ruled that a therapist who has reason to believe that a client poses a serious threat to another person is obligated to warn the potential victim, not merely to notify police. This ruling imposed on therapists a duty-to-warn obligation when their clients show the potential for violence by making threats against others.

The ruling recognized that the rights of the intended victim outweigh the rights of confidentiality. Under *Tarasoff,* the therapist does not merely have a *right* to breach confidentiality and warn potential victims of danger, but is *obligated* by law to divulge such confidences to the victim.

The duty-to-warn provision poses ethical and practical dilemmas for clinicians. Under *Tarasoff,* therapists may feel obliged to protect their personal interests and those of others by breaching confidentiality on the mere suspicion that their clients harbor violent intentions. Because clients' threats are seldom carried out, the *Tarasoff* ruling may deny many clients their rights to confidentiality in order to prevent such rare instances. Although some clinicians may "overreact" to *Tarasoff* and breach confidentiality without sufficient cause, it can be argued that the interests of the few potential victims outweigh the interests of the many who may suffer a loss of confidentiality.

Another problem with applying the *Tarasoff* standard is the lack of any special ability on the therapist's part to predict dangerousness. Nevertheless, the *Tarasoff* ruling obliges therapists to judge whether or not their clients' disclosures indicate an imminent intent to harm others (VandeCreek & Knapp 2001). In the *Tarasoff* case, the threat was obvious. In most cases, however, threats are not so clear cut. We have no clear criteria for determining whether a therapist "should have known" that a client was dangerous before a violent act occurs. In the absence of guidelines that specify the criteria therapists should use to fulfill their duty to warn, they must rely on their best subjective judgments.

The ethical issues become even murkier when therapists treat HIV-infected patients who put their sexual partners at risk by concealing their HIV status. Therapists must balance their duty-to-warn obligations with their ethical responsibility to protect patient confidentiality. Presently, we lack a clear set of professional standards that therapists can follow to resolve these dilemmas (Huprich, Fuller, & Schneider, 2003). Psychologists must follow the laws of the states in which they practice regarding the requirements for maintaining confidentiality of their clients' HIV status and become aware of any exceptions that might exist for breaching confidentiality (APA, 2003).

Although the intent of the *Tarasoff* decision was to protect potential victims, it may inadvertently increase the risks of violence when applied to clinical practice (Stone, 1976; Weiner, 2003). For example,

1. *Clients may be less willing to confide in their therapists,* making it more difficult for therapists to help them diffuse violent feelings.
2. *Potentially violent people may be less likely to enter therapy,* fearing that disclosures made to a therapist will be revealed.
3. *Therapists may be less likely to probe violent tendencies,* seeking to avoid legal complications. Therapists may avoid asking clients about potential violence or may avoid treating patients who are believed to have violent tendencies.

It remains unclear whether *Tarasoff* has done more good than harm (Herbert, 2002;Weiner, 2003). It is clear, however, that *Tarasoff* has raised concerns for clinicians who are trying to meet their legal responsibilities under *Tarasoff* and their clinical responsibilities to their clients.

A survey of psychiatric residents in San Francisco showed that nearly half had issued Tarasoff-type warnings (Binder & McNiel, 1996). In most cases, the intended victim was already aware of the threat. Most of the therapists told their patients about the warnings. Though issuing a warning produced no clear effects on the therapeutic relationship in most cases, negative effects were reported in some cases.

The *Tarasoff* case was brought in California, and the decision applied only to that state (Weiner, 2003). Other states have different statutes (Schaffer, 2000). Some states permit therapists to breach confidentiality to warn third parties of a patient's threats against them, but do not impose an obligation on therapists to do so (Herbert & Young, 2002). Therapists must be aware of local statutes and legal precedents. Therapists must also not lose sight of the primary therapeutic responsibility to their clients when legal issues arise. They must balance the obligation to meet their responsibilities under duty-to-warn provisions with the need to help their clients resolve the feelings of rage and anger that give rise to violent threats.

Tatiana Tarasoff and Prosenjit Poddar. Poddar, Tatiana's killer, was a rejected suitor who had made threats against her to his therapist at a university health center. Poddar was subsequently convicted of voluntary manslaughter in her death. A suit brought by Tatiana's parents against the university led to a landmark court ruling that established an obligation on therapists to warn third parties of threats made against them by their clients.

A listing of some of the rights granted institutionalized patients under the court's ruling is shown in Table 16.2. Although the ruling of the court was limited to Alabama, many other states have revised their mental hospital standards to ensure that involuntarily committed patients are not denied basic rights.

Other court cases have further clarified patients' rights.

O'Connor v. Donaldson The 1975 case of Kenneth Donaldson is another landmark in patients' rights. Donaldson, a former patient at a state hospital in Florida, sued two hospital doctors on the grounds that he had been involuntarily confined without receiving treatment for 14 years, despite the fact that he posed no serious threat to himself or others. Donaldson had been originally committed on the basis of a petition filed by his father, who had perceived him as delusional. Despite the fact that Donaldson received no treatment during his confinement and was denied grounds privileges and occupational training, his repeated requests for discharge were denied. He was finally released when he threatened to sue the hospital. Once discharged, Donaldson did sue his doctors and was awarded damages of $38,500 from O'Connor, the superintendent of the hospital. The case was eventually argued before the U.S. Supreme Court.

Court testimony established that although the hospital staff had not perceived Donaldson to be dangerous, they had refused to release him. The hospital doctors argued that continued hospitalization had been necessary because they had believed Donaldson was unlikely to

Kenneth Donaldson. Donaldson points to the U.S. Supreme Court decision that ruled that people who are considered mentally ill but not dangerous cannot be confined against their will if they can be maintained safely in the community.

TABLE 16.2

Partial Listing of the Patient's Bill of Rights Under *Wyatt* v. *Stickney*

1. Patients have rights to privacy and to be treated with dignity.

2. Patients shall be treated under the least restrictive conditions that can be provided to meet the purposes that commitment was intended to serve.

3. Patients shall have rights to visitation and telephone privileges unless special restrictions apply.

4. Patients have the right to refuse excessive or unnecessary medication. In addition, medication may not be used as a form of punishment.

5. Patients shall not be kept in restraints or isolation except in emergency conditions in which their behavior is likely to pose a threat to themselves or others and less-restrictive restraints are not feasible.

6. Patients shall not be subject to experimental research unless their rights to informed consent are protected.

7. Patients have the right to refuse potentially hazardous or unusual treatments, such as lobotomy, electroconvulsive shock, or aversive behavioral treatments.

8. Unless it is dangerous or inappropriate to the treatment program, patients shall have the right to wear their own clothing and keep possessions.

9. Patients have rights to regular exercise and to opportunities to spend time outdoors.

10. Patients have rights to suitable opportunities to interact with the opposite gender.

11. Patients have rights to humane and decent living conditions.

12. No more than six patients shall be housed in a room, and screen or curtains must be provided to afford a sense of privacy.

13. No more than eight patients shall share one toilet facility, with separate stalls provided for privacy.

14. Patients have a right to nutritionally balanced diets.

15. Patients shall not be required to perform work that is performed for the sake of maintenance of the facility.

adapt successfully to community living. The doctors had prescribed antipsychotic medications, but Donaldson had refused to take them because of his Christian Science beliefs. As a result, he received only custodial care.

The Supreme Court held that "mental illness [alone] cannot justify a State's locking a person up against his will and keeping him indefinitely in simple custodial confinement. There is still no constitutional basis for confining such persons involuntarily if they are dangerous to no one and can live safely in freedom" (*O'Connor* v. *Donaldson,* 1975, p. 2493). The ruling addressed patients who are not considered dangerous. It is not yet clear whether the same constitutional rights would be applied to committed patients who are judged to be dangerous.

In its ruling in *O'Connor* v. *Donaldson,* the Supreme Court did not deal with the larger issue of the rights of patients to receive treatment. The ruling does not directly obligate state institutions to treat involuntarily committed, nondangerous people, because the institutions may elect to release them instead.

The Supreme Court did touch on the larger issue of society's rights to protect itself from individuals who are perceived as offensive. In delivering the opinion of the Court, Justice Potter Stewart wrote,

> May the State fence in the harmless mentally ill solely to save its citizens from exposure to those whose ways are different? One might as well ask if the State, to avoid public uneasiness, could incarcerate all who are physically unattractive or socially eccentric. Mere public intolerance or animosity cannot constitutionally justify the deprivation of a person's physical liberty. (*O'Connor* v. *Donaldson,* 1975)

Youngberg v. Romeo In a 1982 case, *Youngberg v. Romeo,* the U.S. Supreme Court more directly addressed the issue of the patient's right to treatment. Even so, it seemed to retreat somewhat from the patients' rights standards established in *Wyatt* v. *Stickney.* Nicholas Romeo, a 33-year-old man with profound retardation who was unable to talk or care for himself, had been institutionalized in a state hospital and school in Pennsylvania. While in the state facility he had a history of injuring himself through his violent behavior and was often kept in restraints. The case was brought by the patient's mother, who alleged that the hospital was negligent in not preventing his injuries and in routinely using physical restraints for prolonged periods while not providing adequate treatment.

The Supreme Court ruled that involuntarily committed patients, like Nicholas, have a right to be confined in less-restrictive conditions, such as being freed from physical restraints whenever it is reasonable to do so. The Supreme Court ruling also included a limited recognition of the committed patient's right to treatment. The Court held that institutionalized patients have a right to minimally adequate training to help them function free of physical restraints, but only to the extent that such training can be provided in reasonable safety. Reasonableness, the Court held, should be determined on the basis of the judgment of qualified professionals. The federal courts should not interfere with the internal operations of the facility, the Court held, because "there's no reason to think judges or juries are better qualified than appropriate professionals in making such decisions" (*Youngberg* v. *Romeo,* 1982, p. 2462). The courts should only second guess the judgments of qualified professionals when such judgments depart from professional standards of practice. But the Supreme Court did not address the broader issues of the rights of committed patients to receive training that might eventually enable them to function independently outside the hospital.

The related issue of whether people with severe psychological disorders who reside in the community have a constitutional right to receive mental health services (and whether states are obliged to provide these services) continues to be argued in the courts at both the state and federal levels (Perlin, 1994).

Right to Refuse Treatment Consider the following scenario. A person, John Citizen, is involuntarily committed to a mental hospital for treatment. The hospital staff

Should he be released? In 2003, some 22 years after he shot President Ronald Reagan, John Hinckley, Jr. was permitted unsupervised daytime visits with his parents. If his psychiatric condition remains "in remission," should Hinckley be released?

determines that John suffers from a psychotic disorder, paranoid schizophrenia, and should be treated with antipsychotic medication. John, however, decides not to comply with treatment. He claims that the hospital has no right to treat him against his will. The hospital staff seeks a court order to mandate treatment, arguing it makes little sense to commit people involuntarily unless the hospital is empowered to treat them as the staff deems fit.

Does an involuntary patient, like John, have the right to refuse treatment? If so, does this right conflict with states' rights to commit people to mental institutions to receive treatment? One might also wonder whether people who are judged in need of involuntary hospitalization are competent to make decisions about which treatments are in their best interests.

The rights of committed patients to refuse psychotropic medications was tested in the 1979 case, *Rogers* v. *Okin,* in which a Massachusetts federal district court imposed an injunction on a Boston state hospital prohibiting the forced medication of patients except in emergency situations. The court ruled that committed patients could not be forcibly medicated, except in the case of emergency—for example, when patients' behaviors pose a significant threat to themselves or others. The court recognized that a patient may be unwise to refuse medication, but it held that a patient with or without a mental disorder has the right to exercise bad judgment so long as the effects of the "error" do not impose "a danger of physical harm to himself, fellow patients, or hospital staff" (*Rogers* v. *Okin,* 1979).

Despite the concerns some mental health professionals raised that patients who refused medications would be "rotting with their rights on" (Gutheil, 1980), legal protections ensuring patients' rights to refuse psychiatric treatments do not appear to have had seriously damaging or disruptive effects on mental health services or on the people receiving these services (Kapp, 1994).

Although statutes and regulations vary from state to state, cases in which hospitalized patients refuse medications are often first brought before an independent review panel. If the panel rules against the patient, the case may then be brought before a judge, who makes the final decision about whether the patient is to be forcibly medicated. In practice, only about 10% of patients refuse medication. Furthermore, between 70% and 90% of refusals that reach the review process are eventually overridden. Hospitalized patients in a recent study who refused medication tended to be more assaultive, were more likely to require seclusion and restraint, and had longer hospitalizations than did compliant patients (Kasper et al., 1997). However, the refusal episodes tended to be brief, about 3 days on the average, and all initial refusers were eventually treated.

Our discussion of legal issues and abnormal behavior now turns to the controversy concerning the insanity defense.

TRUTH or FICTION? *REVISITED*

An attempt to assassinate the president of the United States was seen by millions of television viewers, but the would-be assassin was found not guilty by a court of law.

☑ **TRUE.** A man who was seen by millions of TV viewers attempting to assassinate President Reagan was found "not guilty by reason of insanity" by a court of law.

THE INSANITY DEFENSE

John Hinckly, a man who was seen by millions of TV viewers attempting to assassinate President Reagan, was found "not guilty by reason of insanity." The verdict led to a public outcry, with many calling for the abolition of the insanity defense. Public opinion polls taken several days after the Hinckley verdict was returned showed the public had little confidence in the psychiatric testimony offered at the trial (Slater & Hans, 1984). One objection focused on the fact that once the defense presented evidence to support a plea of insanity, the federal prosecutor had the responsibility of proving *beyond a reasonable doubt* that the defendant was sane. It can be difficult enough to demonstrate that someone is sane or insane in the present, so imagine the problems that attend proving someone was sane at the time a criminal act was committed.

In the aftermath of the Hinckley verdict, the federal government and many states changed their statutes to shift the burden of proof to the defense to prove insanity (Ogloff, Roberts, & Roesch, 1993). Even the American Psychiatric Association went on record as stating that psychiatric expert witnesses should not be called on to render opinions about whether defendants can control their behavior. In the opinion of the psychiatric association, these are not medical judgments that psychiatrists are trained to provide.

Perceptions of the use of the **insanity defense** tend to stray far from the facts. The public grossly overestimates the number of cases in which the insanity defense is used and how often it succeeds. The public estimates that the insanity defense is used in about 1 in 3 felony cases, but in actuality it is used in fewer than 1% of cases (Silver, Cirincione, & Steadman, 1994; Steadman et al., 1993). A study in Baltimore showed that the insanity defense plea was used in 1/100th of 1% of indictments brought to trial (Janofsky et al., 1996). Whereas the public believes that 44% of defendants who claim insanity are acquitted, the actual figure (based on a review of the records in eight states) was 26% (Silver et al., 1994; Steadman et al., 1993). In practice, out of 1,000 felony cases, there are fewer than 10 in which the insanity defense is used, and only about 2 or 3 in which it succeeds. Thus despite public perceptions, the use of the insanity defense is rare, and the rate of acquittals is rarer still ("Insanity," 1992).

The public also overestimates the proportion of defendants acquitted on the basis of insanity who are set free rather than confined to mental health institutions and underestimates the length of hospitalization of those who are confined (Silver et al., 1994). People found not guilty on the basis of insanity are often confined to mental hospitals for longer periods of time than they would have served in prison (Lymburner & Roesch, 1999). The net result is that although changes in the insanity defense, or its abolition, may prevent a few flagrant cases of abuse, they will not afford the public much broader protection.

In the wake of the Hinckley acquittal, a number of states adopted a new type of verdict, the "guilty-but-mentally-ill" (GBMI) verdict (Boudouris, 2000; Maeder, 1985). The GBMI verdict offers juries the option of finding that the defendant is mentally ill but that the mental illness did not cause the defendant to commit the crime. People convicted under a GBMI statute go to prison but receive treatment while incarcerated.

Fourteen states have permitted GMBI verdicts (Melville & Naimark, 2002). However, the verdict has sparked controversy. Although GBMI was intended to reduce the number of NGRI (not guilty by reason of insanity) verdicts, it has failed to do so (Melville & Naimark, 2002). All in all, the GBMI verdict is a social experiment that has thus far failed to prove its usefulness (Palmer & Hazelrigg, 2000). Critics argue that the verdict merely stigmatizes defendants who are found guilty as also being mentally ill (Maeder, 1985). Some even call for the abolition of the verdict (Melville & Naimark, 2002).

In a celebrated case, John E. du Pont, an heir to the du Pont family fortune, was found guilty but mentally ill following trial for the 1996 murder of Olympic gold medalist wrestler David Schultz ("Du Pont Heir Found Guilty," 1997). Du Pont was subsequently remanded to a state psychiatric hospital for treatment rather than to prison. At trial, it was reported that du Pont exhibited bizarre behavior and suffered from delusions of being spied on by Nazis and of having his body inhabited by bugs.

Although the public outrage over the Hinckley and other celebrated insanity verdicts has led to a reexamination of the insanity defense, society has long held to the doctrine of free will as a basis for determining responsibility for wrongdoing. The doctrine of free will, as applied to criminal responsibility, requires that people can be held guilty of a crime only if they are judged to have been in control of their actions at the time. Not only must a court of law determine, beyond a reasonable doubt, that a defendant had committed a crime, but the individual's state of mind must be considered as well in determining guilt. The court must thus rule not only on whether a crime was committed but also on whether an individual is morally responsible and deserving of punishment. The insanity defense is based on the belief that when a criminal act derives from a distorted state of mind, and not from the exercise of free will, the individual should not be punished but rather treated for the underlying mental disorder. The insanity defense has a long legal history.

insanity defense A legal defense in which a defendant in a criminal case pleads innocent on the basis of insanity.

TRUTH or FICTION? *REVISITED*

The insanity defense is used in a large number of trials, usually successfully.

☑ **FALSE.** The insanity defense is rarely used in felony cases, and the rate of acquittals based on the defense is even rarer.

Legal Bases of the Insanity Defense

Three major modern court rulings bear on the insanity defense. The first was an 1834 case in Ohio that was ruled that people could not be held responsible if they are compelled to commit criminal actions because of impulses they are unable to resist.

The second major legal test of the insanity defense is referred to as the M'Naghten rule, based on a case in England in 1843 of a Scotsman, Daniel M'Naghten, who had intended to assassinate the prime minister of England, Sir Robert Peel. Instead, he killed Peel's secretary, whom he had mistaken for the prime minister. M'Naghten claimed that the voice of God had commanded him to kill Peel. The English court acquitted M'Naghten on the basis of insanity, finding that the defendant had been ". . . labouring under such a defect of reason, from disease of the mind, as not to know the nature and quality of the act he was doing; or, if he did know it, that he did not know he was doing what was wrong." The M'Naghten rule holds that people do not bear criminal responsibility if, by reason of a mental disease or defect, they either have no knowledge of their actions or are unable to tell right from wrong.

The third major case that helped lay the foundation for the modern insanity defense was *Durham* v. *United States* of 1954. This case held that the "accused [person] is not criminally responsible if his unlawful act was the product of mental disease or mental defect" (pp. 874–875). Under the *Durham* rule, juries were expected to decide not only whether the accused suffered from a mental disease or defect but also whether this mental condition was causally connected to the criminal act. The court recognized that criminal intent is a precondition of criminal responsibility:

> The legal and moral traditions of the western world require that those who, of their own free will and with evil intent . . . commit acts which violate the law, shall be criminally responsible for those acts. Our traditions also require that where such acts stem from and are the product of a mental disease or defect . . . moral blame shall not attach, and hence there will not be criminal responsibility. (*Durham* v. *United States,* 214 F2d 862, D.C. circ. 1954)

The intent of the *Durham* rule was to reject as outmoded the two earlier standards of legal insanity, the irresistible impulse rule and the "right–wrong" principle. The court argued that the "right–wrong test" was outmoded because the concept of "mental disease" is broader than the ability to recognize right from wrong. The legal basis of insanity should thus not be judged on just one feature of a mental disorder, such as deficient reasoning ability. The irresistible impulse test was denied because the court recognized that in certain cases, criminal acts arising from "mental disease or defect" might occur in a cool and calculating manner rather than in the manner of a sudden, irresistible impulse. Defendants may have known they were committing criminal acts, but were not driven to do so by an irresistible impulse (Sokolove, 2003).

The *Durham* rule, however, has proved to be unworkable for several reasons, such as a lack of precise definitions of such terms as *mental disease* or *mental defect* (Maeder, 1985). Courts were confused, for example, about whether a personality disorder (e.g., antisocial personality disorder) constituted a "disease." Also, juries found it difficult to draw conclusions about whether an individual's "mental disease" was causally connected to the criminal act. Without clear or precise definitions of terms, juries came to rely increasingly on expert psychiatric testimony, their verdicts simply endorsing the testimony of expert witnesses (Maeder, 1985).

By 1972, the *Durham* rule was replaced in many jurisdictions by legal guidelines formulated by the American Law Institute (ALI) to define the legal basis of insanity (Van Susteren, 2002). These guidelines, which essentially combine the M'Naghten principle with the irresistible impulse principle, include the following provisions:

1. A person is not responsible for criminal conduct if at the time of such conduct as a result of mental disease or defect he lacks substantial capacity either to appreci-

Guilty but mentally ill? John du Pont, an heir to the du Pont family fortune, was tried for the 1996 murder of Olympic gold medalist wrestler David Schultz. Du Pont was found guilty but mentally ill, a verdict that remains controversial in part because it is seen by some people as merely a way of stigmatizing defendants who are found guilty as also being mentally ill.

ate the criminality (wrongfulness) of his conduct or to conform his conduct to the requirements of law.

2. . . . the terms "mental disease or defect" do not include an abnormality manifested only by repeated criminal or otherwise antisocial conduct. (American Law Institute, 1962, p. 66)

The first guideline incorporates aspects of the M'Naghten test (being unable to appreciate right from wrong) and the irresistible impulse test (being unable to conform one's behavior to the requirements of law) of insanity. The second guideline asserts that repeated criminal behavior (such as a pattern of drug dealing) is not sufficient in itself to establish a mental disease or defect that might relieve the individual of criminal responsibility. Although many legal authorities believe the ALI guidelines are an improvement over earlier tests, questions remain as to whether a jury composed of ordinary citizens can be expected to make complex judgments about the defendant's state of mind, even on the basis of expert testimony. Under the ALI guidelines, juries must determine whether defendants lack substantial capacity to be aware of, or capable of, conforming their behavior to the law. By adding the term *substantial capacity* to the legal test, the ALI guidelines broaden the legal basis of the insanity defense, implying that defendants need not be completely incapable of controlling their actions to meet the legal test of not guilty by reason of insanity.

Under our system of justice, juries must struggle with the complex question of determining criminal responsibility, not merely criminal actions. But what of those individuals who successfully plead not guilty by reason of insanity? Should they be committed to a mental institution for a fixed sentence, as they might have been had they been incarcerated in a penal institution? Or should their commitments be of an indeterminate term and their release depend on their mental status? The legal basis for answering such questions was decided in the case of a man named Michael Jones.

Determining the Length of Criminal Commitment

The issue of determinate versus indeterminate commitment was addressed in the case of Michael Jones (*Jones* v. *United States*), who was arrested in 1975 and charged with petty larceny for attempting to steal a jacket from a Washington, D.C., department store. Jones was first committed to a public mental hospital, St. Elizabeth's Hospital (the same hospital where John Hinckley remains committed as of this writing). Jones was diagnosed as suffering from paranoid schizophrenia and was kept hospitalized until he was judged competent to stand trial, about 6 months later. Jones offered a plea of not guilty by reason of insanity, which the court accepted without challenge, remanding him to St. Elizabeth's. Despite the fact that Jones's crime carried a maximum sentence of 1 year in prison, Jones's repeated attempts to obtain release were denied in subsequent court hearings.

The U.S. Supreme Court eventually heard his appeal *7 years* after Jones was hospitalized and reached its decision in 1983. It ruled against Jones's appeal and affirmed the decision of the lower courts that he was to remain in the hospital. The Supreme Court thereby established a principle that individuals who are acquitted by reason of insanity "constitute a special class that should be treated differently" than civilly committed individuals (Morris, 2002). They may be committed for an indefinite period to a mental institution under criteria that require a less stringent level of proof of dangerousness than is ordinarily applied in cases of civil commitment. Thus people found not guilty by reason of insanity may remain confined to a mental hospital for many years longer than they would have been sentenced to prison had they been found guilty.

Among other things, the Supreme Court ruling in *Jones* v. *United States* provides that the usual and customary sentences that the law provides for particular crimes have no bearing on criminal commitment. In the words of the Court,

> different considerations underlie commitment of an insanity acquittee. As he was not convicted, he may not be punished. His confinement rests on his continuing illness and

dangerousness. There simply is no necessary correlation between severity of the offense and length of time necessary for recovery. (*Jones* v. *United States*, 103 S.Ct. 3043, 1983)

The ruling held that a person who is criminally committed may be confined "to a mental institution until such time as he has regained his sanity or is no longer a danger to society" (p. 3053). As in the case of Michael Jones, people who are acquitted on the basis of insanity may remain confined for much longer than they would have been sentenced to prison. They may also be released earlier than they might have been released from prison, if their "mental condition" improves. However, public outrage over a speedy release, especially for a major crime, might prevent rapid release.

The indeterminateness of criminal commitment raises various questions. Is it reasonable to deny people like Michael Jones their liberty for an indefinite and possibly lifelong term for a relatively minor crime, such as petty larceny? On the other hand, is justice served by acquitting perpetrators of heinous crimes by reason of insanity and then releasing them early if they are deemed by professionals to be able to rejoin society?

The Supreme Court's ruling in *Jones* v. *United States* seems to imply that we must separate the notion of legal sentencing from that of legal or criminal commitment. Legal sentencing rests on the principle that the punishment should fit the crime: the more serious the crime, the longer the punishment. In criminal commitment, however, persons acquitted of their crimes by reason of insanity are guiltless in the eyes of the law, and their length of confinement is determined by their mental state.

Perspectives on the Insanity Defense

The insanity defense places special burdens on juries. In assessing criminal responsibility, the jury must determine not only that the accused committed a crime but also the defendant's state of mind at the time. In rejecting the *Durham* decision, courts have relieved psychiatrists and other expert witnesses from responsibility for determining whether the defendant's behavior is a product of a "mental disease or defect." But is it reasonable to assume that juries are better able to assess defendants' states of mind than mental health professionals? In particular, how can a jury evaluate the testimony of expert conflicting witnesses? The jury's task imposed is made even more difficult by the mandate to decide whether the defendant was mentally incapacitated *at the time of the crime.* The defendant's courtroom behavior may bear little resemblance to his or her behavior during the crime.

Thomas Szasz and others who deny the existence of mental illness have raised another challenge to the insanity defense. If mental illness does not exist, then the insanity defense becomes groundless. Szasz argues that the insanity defense is ultimately degrading because it strips people of personal responsibility for their behavior. People who break laws are criminals, Szasz argues, and should be prosecuted and sentenced accordingly. Acquittal of defendants by reason of insanity treats them as nonpersons, as unfortunates who are not deemed to possess the basic human qualities of free choice, self-determination, and personal responsibility. We are each responsible for our behavior, Szasz contends, and we should each be held accountable for our misdeeds.

Szasz argues that the insanity defense has historically been invoked in crimes that were particularly heinous or perpetrated against persons of high social rank. When persons of low social rank commit crimes against persons of higher status, Szasz argues, the insanity defense directs attention away from the social ills that may have motivated the crime. Despite Szasz's contention, however, the insanity defense is invoked in many cases of less-shocking crimes or in cases involving persons from similar social classes.

How, then, are we to evaluate the insanity defense? To abolish it would reverse hundreds of years of legal tradition that recognizes that people are not to be held responsible for their criminal behavior when their ability to control themselves is impaired by a mental disorder or defect.

TRUTH or FICTION? *REVISITED*

People who are found not guilty of a crime by reason of insanity may remain confined to a mental hospital for many years longer than they would have been sentenced to prison, if they had been found guilty.

☑ TRUE. People who are found not guilty of a crime by reason of insanity may remain confined to a mental hospital indefinitely.

Consider a hypothetical example. John Citizen commits a crime, say a heinous crime like murder, while acting on a delusional belief that the victim was intent on assassinating him. The accused claims that voices from his TV set informed him of the identity of the assailant and commanded him to kill the assailant to save himself and other potential victims. Cases like this are thankfully rare. Few mentally disturbed persons, even few people with psychotic features, commit violent crimes, and even fewer commit murder.

In reaching a judgment on the insanity plea, we need to consider whether the law should apply special standards in cases like John Citizen's, or whether one standard of criminal responsibility should apply to all. If we assert the legitimacy of the insanity defense in some cases, we still need a standard of insanity that can be interpreted and applied by juries of ordinary citizens. The furor over the Hinckley verdict suggests that issues concerning the insanity plea remain unsettled.

Competency to Stand Trial

There is a basic rule of law that those who stand accused of crimes must be able to understand the charges and proceedings brought against them and be able to participate in their own defense. The concept of **competency to stand trial** should not be confused with the insanity defense. A defendant can be held competent to stand trial but still be judged not guilty of a crime by reason of insanity. A clearly delusional person, for example, may understand the court proceedings and be able to confer with defense counsel, but still be acquitted by reason of insanity. On the other hand, a person may be incapable of standing trial at a particular time, but be tried at a later time when competency is restored.

Far more people are confined to mental institutions on the basis of a determination that they lack the mental competence to stand trial than on the basis of the insanity verdict (Roesch et al., 1999). There may be 45 people committed under the mental competency to stand trial criteria for every one committed following a verdict of not guilty by reason of insanity (Steadman, 1979).

People declared incompetent to stand trial are generally confined to a mental institution until they are deemed competent or it is determined that they are unlikely to regain competency. Abuses may occur, however, if the accused are kept incarcerated for indefinite periods awaiting trial. In 1972, the U.S. Supreme Court ruled, in the case of *Jackson* v. *Indiana,* that a person could not be kept in a mental hospital awaiting trial longer than it would take to determine whether treatment was likely to restore competency. Under *Jackson,* psychiatric examiners must determine whether there exists a substantial probability that the defendant would regain competency through treatment within the foreseeable future (Hubbard, Zapf, & Ronan, 2003). If it does not seem the person would ever become competent, even with treatment, the individual must either be released or committed under the procedures for civil commitment. However, compliance with the *Jackson* standard has been inconsistent, with some states imposing a minimum length of treatment (e.g., 5 years) before acknowledging that a defendant is deemed permanently incompetent (Morris, 2002).

A 1992 ruling by the U.S. Supreme Court, in the case of *Medina* v. *California,* held that the burden of proof for determining competency to stand trial lies with the defendant, not the state (Greenhouse, 1992). Then, in 2003, the U.S. Supreme Court held in the case of *Sell* v. *United States* that mentally ill defendants could be forcibly medicated to render them competent to stand trial in limited circumstances. The decision allows a defendant to be involuntarily medicated if it is deemed medically appropriate and would not cause side effects that would compromise the fairness of the trial (Greenhouse, 2003). The effect of the *Sell* decision may be to bring to trial many people whose trials were delayed due to a lack of mental competence.

We opened this book by noting that despite the public impression that abnormal behavior affects only the few, it actually affects every one of us in one way or another. Let us close by suggesting that if we all work together to foster research into the causes,

competency to stand trial The ability of criminal defendants to understand the charges and proceedings brought against them and to participate in their own defense.

TRUTH or FICTION? REVISITED

It is possible for a defendant to be held to be competent to stand trial but still be judged not guilty of a crime by reason of insanity.

☑ **TRUE.** A defendant can be held competent to stand trial but still be judged not guilty of a crime by reason of insanity.

treatment, and prevention of abnormal behavior, perhaps we can meet the multifaceted challenges that abnormal behavior poses to so many of us and to our society at large.

SUMMING UP

Psychiatric Commitment and Patients' Rights

What is the difference between civil commitment and criminal commitment? The legal process by which people are placed in psychiatric institutions against their will is called civil or psychiatric commitment. Civil commitment is intended to provide treatment to people who are deemed to suffer from mental disorders and to pose a threat to themselves or others. Criminal commitment, by comparison, involves the placement of a person in a psychiatric institution for treatment who has been acquitted of a crime by reason of insanity. In voluntary hospitalization, people voluntarily seek treatment in a psychiatric facility and can leave of their own accord unless a court rules otherwise.

How successful are mental health professionals in predicting the dangerousness of patients they evaluate? Although people must be judged dangerous to be placed involuntarily in a psychiatric facility, mental health professionals have not demonstrated any special ability to predict dangerousness. Factors that may account for the failure to predict dangerousness include (a) recognizing violent tendencies post hoc is easier than predicting it; (b) generalized perceptions of violent tendencies may not predict specific acts of violence; (c) lack of agreement in defining violence or dangerousness; (d) base-rate problems; (e) unlikelihood of direct threats of violence; and (f) predictions based on hospital behavior may not generalize to community settings.

What is meant by the duty to warn? Although information disclosed by a client to a therapist generally carries a right to confidentiality, the California *Tarasoff* ruling held that therapists have a duty or obligation to warn third parties of threats made against them by their clients.

What landmark court cases dealt with the rights of patients in psychiatric facilities? In *Wyatt* v. *Stickney*, a court in Alabama imposed a minimum standard of care. In *O'Connor* v. *Donaldson*, the U.S. Supreme Court ruled that nondangerous mentally ill people could not be held in psychiatric facilities against their will if such people could be maintained safely in the community. In *Youngberg* v. *Romeo*, the Supreme Court ruled that involuntarily confined patients have a right to less-restrictive types of treatment and to receive training to help them function. Court rulings, such as that of *Rogers* v. *Okin* in Massachusetts, have established that patients have a right to refuse medication, except in case of emergency.

The Insanity Defense

What are the legal bases of the insanity defense? Three court cases established legal precedents for the insanity defense. In 1834, a court in Ohio applied a principle of irresistible impulse as the basis of an insanity defense. The M'Naghten rule, based on a case in England in 1843, treated the failure to appreciate the wrongfulness of one's action as the basis of legal insanity. The *Durham* rule was based on a case in the United States in 1954 in which it was held that persons did not bear criminal responsibility if their criminal behavior was the product of "mental disease or mental defect." Another set of standards developed by the American Law Institute that combines the M'Naghten and irresistible impulse principles. People who are criminally committed may be hospitalized for an indefinite period of time, with their eventual release dependent on a determination of their mental status.

What is meant by the legal concept of competency to stand trial? People who are accused of crimes but are incapable of understanding the charges against them or assisting in their own defense can be found incompetent to stand trial and remanded to a psychiatric facility. In the case of *Jackson* v. *Indiana*, the U.S. Supreme Court placed restrictions on the length of time a person judged incompetent to stand trial could be held in a psychiatric facility.

KEY TERMS

civil commitment (*p. 534*)
criminal commitment (*p. 534*)

duty to warn (*p. 540*)
insanity defense (*p. 545*)

competency to stand trial (*p. 549*)

WEB TOOLS

The companion website offers tools to enrich your learning experience and help you succeed in class. Go to www.prenhall.com/nevid for the gateway to the following resources:

- **VIDEO** links to connect to the video case files on the companion CD-ROM. VIDEO icons in the margins of the chapter highlight the case examples included in the CD-ROM. You can also access the CD-ROM directly if you do not have a Web connection.

- **QUIZ** links to self-scoring quizzes corresponding to each section of the chapter. The quizzes help you review your knowledge of the content in each chapter.
- **WEB** links to direct you to related sites that enhance your learning of abnormal psychology.

A

Abnormal psychology. The branch of psychology that deals with the description, causes, and treatment of abnormal behavior patterns.

Abstinence violation effect (AVE). The tendency to overreact to a minor lapse with feelings of guilt and resignation that may trigger a relapse.

Acculturation. The process of adapting to a new culture.

Acquired immunodeficiency syndrome (AIDS). An immunological disease caused by HIV.

Acrophobia. Excessive, irrational fear of heights.

Acute stress disorder (ASD). A traumatic stress reaction occurring in the days and weeks following exposure to a traumatic event.

Addiction. Impaired control over the use of a chemical substance, accompanied by physiological dependence.

Adjustment disorder. A maladaptive reaction to an identified stressor, which is characterized by impaired functioning or signs of emotional distress that exceed what would normally be expected.

Adoptee studies. Studies that compare the traits and behavior patterns of adopted children to those of their biological parents and their adoptive parents.

Affect. Emotional responsiveness.

Agnosia. A disturbance of sensory perception, usually affecting visual perception.

Agoraphobic. Relating to excessive, irrational fear of open places.

Al-Anon. An organization that sponsors support groups for family members of people with alcoholism.

Alarm reaction. The first stage of the GAS, characterized by heightened sympathetic activity.

Alcoholism. An alcohol dependence disorder or addiction that results in serious personal, social, occupational, or health problems.

Alcohol-induced persisting amnestic disorder. A form of brain damage associated with chronic thiamine deficiency and alcoholism; characterized by memory loss, disorientation, and confabulation.

Alzheimer's disease (AD). A progressive brain disease characterized by gradual loss of memory and intellectual functioning, personality changes, and eventual loss of ability to care for oneself.

Ambivalent. Holding conflicting feelings toward another person or a goal.

Amenorrhea. Absence of menstruation.

Amnestic disorders. Disturbances of memory associated with inability to learn new material or recall past events.

Amphetamine psychosis. A psychotic state induced by ingestion of amphetamines.

Amphetamines. Types of stimulants, such as Benzedrine or Dexedrine.

Amygdala. Limbic system structure involved in processing threatening stimuli.

Anal stage. The psychosexual stage during toddlerhood in which pleasure is sought primarily through anal activities.

Analgesia. Relief from pain without loss of consciousness.

Analogue measure. A measure taken in a contrived situation meant to simulate a real-life situation.

Analogue. Something that resembles something else.

Analytical psychology. Jung's theory, emphasizing the collective unconscious, archetypes, and the self as the unifying force of personality.

Anomie. A feeling of rootlessness.

Anorexia nervosa. An eating disorder characterized by maintenance of an abnormally low body weight, distortions of body image, intense fears of gaining weight, and in females, amenorrhea.

Antianxiety drugs. Drugs that combat anxiety and reduce states of muscle tension.

Antibodies. Substances produced by white blood cells that identify and target antigens for destruction.

Antidepressants. Drugs used to treat depression.

Antigens. Substances that trigger an immune response.

Antipsychotic drugs. Drugs used to treat schizophrenia or other psychotic disorders.

Antisocial personality disorder. A personality disorder characterized by antisocial and irresponsible behavior and lack of remorse for misdeeds.

Anxiety. An emotional state characterized by physiological arousal, unpleasant feelings of tension, and a sense of apprehension or foreboding.

Anxiety disorder. A type of mental disorder whose most prominent feature is anxiety.

Anxiety sensitivity. A fear of anxiety and anxiety-related symptoms.

Apnea. Temporary cessation of breathing.

Archetypes. Primitive images or concepts that reside in the collective unconscious.

Arteriosclerosis. A disease involving thickening and hardening of the arteries.

Asperger's disorder. A pervasive developmental disorder characterized by social deficits and stereotyped behavior but without the significant language or cognitive delays associated with autism.

Associations. Relationships among thoughts.

Ataxia. Loss of muscle coordination.

Atherosclerosis. The buildup of fatty deposits along artery walls that leads to the formation of artery-clogging plaque.

Attention-deficit hyperactivity disorder (ADHD). A behavior disorder characterized by excessive motor activity and inability to focus one's attention.

Attributional style. A personal style for explaining cause-and-effect relationships between events.

Autism. Withdrawal into a private fantasy world.

Automatic thoughts. Thoughts that seem to pop into one's mind.

Autonomic nervous system. The division of the peripheral nervous system that regulates the activities of the glands and involuntary functions.

Aversive conditioning. A behavior therapy technique in which a maladaptive response is paired with exposure to an aversive stimulus to develop a conditioned aversion.

Avoidant personality disorder. A personality disorder characterized by avoidance of social relationships due to fears of rejection.

Axon. The long, thin part of a neuron along which nerve impulses travel.

B

Barbiturates. Types of depressants that are used to reduce anxiety or to induce sleep but that are highly addictive.

Basal ganglia. An assemblage of neurons located between the thalamus and cerebrum, involved in coordinating motor (movement) processes.

Baseline. The rate at which a behavior occurs before treatment.

Behavior therapy. The therapeutic application of learning-based techniques.

Behavioral assessment. The approach to clinical assessment that focuses on the objective recording and description of the problem behavior.

Behavioral interview. Clinical interview that focuses on relating the problem behavior to antecedent stimuli and reinforcement consequences.

Behavioral rating scale. A scale used to record the frequency of occurrence of target behaviors.

Behaviorism. The school of psychology that defines psychology as the study of observable behavior.

Benzodiazepines. The class of antianxiety drugs that includes Valium and Xanax.

Bereavement. The experience of grief suffering following the death of a loved one.

Binge-eating disorder (BED). A disorder characterized by recurrent eating binges without purging; classified as a potential disorder requiring further study.

Biofeedback training (BFT). A method of feeding back to the individual information about bodily functions so that the person can gain some degree of control over these functions.

Bipolar. Characterized by opposite ends of a dimension or continuum, as in bipolar disorder.

Bipolar disorder. A disorder characterized by mood swings between states of extreme elation and severe depression.

Blind. A state of being unaware of whether one has received an experimental treatment.

Blocking. An involuntary interruption of speech.

Borderline personality disorder (BPD). A personality disorder characterized by abrupt shifts in mood, lack of a coherent sense of self, and unpredictable, impulsive behavior.

Brain electrical activity mapping (BEAM). Imaging technique involving computer analysis of data from multiple electrodes to reveal areas of the brain with relatively high or low levels of activity.

Breathing-related sleep disorder. A sleep disorder in which sleep is repeatedly disrupted by difficulty with breathing normally.

Brief psychotic disorder. A psychotic disorder lasting from a day to a month that often follows exposure to a major stressor.

Bulimia nervosa. An eating disorder characterized by recurrent binge eating followed by self-induced purging, accompanied by overconcern with body weight and shape.

C

Cardiovascular disease. A disease or disorder of the cardiovascular system, such as coronary heart disease or hypertension.

Case study. A carefully drawn biography based on clinical interviews, observations, and psychological tests.

Castration anxiety. The young boy's unconscious fear that he will be castrated as punishment for his incestuous desire for his mother.

Cataplexy. A brief, sudden loss of muscle control.

Catastrophize. To exaggerate the negative consequences of events.

Catatonic type. The subtype of schizophrenia characterized by gross disturbances in motor activity, such as catatonic stupor.

Catharsis. The discharge of states of tension associated with repression of threatening impulses or material; the purging or free expression of feelings.

Central nervous system. The brain and spinal cord.

Cerebellum. A structure in the hindbrain involved in coordination and balance.

Cerebral cortex. The wrinkled surface area of the cerebrum, it is responsible for processing sensory stimuli and controlling higher mental functions, such as thinking and use of language.

Cerebrovascular accident (CVA). Damage to part of the brain because of a disruption in its blood supply, usually as the result of a blood clot.

Cerebrum. The large mass of the forebrain, consisting of the two cerebral hemispheres.

Childhood disintegrative disorder. A pervasive developmental disorder involving loss of previously acquired skills and abnormal functioning following a period of apparently normal development during the first two years of life.

Choleric. Having or showing bad temper.

Chromosomes. The structures found in the nuclei of cells that carry the units of heredity, or genes.

Circadian rhythm sleep disorder. A sleep disorder characterized by a mismatch between the body's normal sleep–wake cycle and the demands of the environment.

Civil commitment. The legal process of placing a person in a mental institution, even against his or her will.

Clanging. The tendency to string words together because they rhyme or sound alike.

Claustrophobia. Excessive, irrational fear of small, enclosed spaces.

Client-centered therapy. Another term for *person-centered therapy.*

Closed-ended questions. Questionnaire or test items with a limited range of response options.

Cocaine. A stimulant derived from the leaves of the coca plant.

Cognitive disorders. Mental disorders characterized by impaired cognitive abilities and daily functioning in which biological causation is either known or presumed.

Cognitive restructuring. A cognitive therapy method that involves replacing irrational thoughts with rational alternatives.

Cognitive therapy. Aaron Beck's form of therapy that helps clients recognize and correct distorted patterns of thinking.

Cognitive triad of depression. The view that depression derives from adopting negative views of oneself, the environment or world at large, and the future.

Cognitive-behavioral therapy (CBT). A learning-based approach to therapy incorporating cognitive and behavioral techniques.

Cognitive-specificity hypothesis. The belief that different emotional disorders are linked to particular kinds of automatic thoughts.

Collective unconscious. The storehouse of archetypes and racial memories.

Communication disorders. A class of psychological disorders characterized by difficulties in understanding or using language.

Compulsion. A repetitive or ritualistic behavior that the person feels compelled to perform.

Compulsion to utter. The urge to verbally express repressed material.

Computed tomography (CT scan). Computer-enhanced imaging of the internal structures of the brain by passing a narrow X-ray beam through the head.

Concordance. Agreement.

Concurrent validity. A type of test validity based on the statistical relationship between the test and a criterion measure taken at the same time.

Conditional positive regard. Valuing other people on the basis of whether their behavior meets one's approval.

Conditioned response. In classical conditioning, a learned response to a previously neutral stimulus.

Conditioned stimulus. A previously neutral stimulus that evokes a conditioned response after repeated pairings with an unconditioned stimulus that had previously evoked that response.

Conditions of worth. Standards by which one judges the worth or value of oneself or others.

Conduct disorder. A psychological disorder in childhood and adolescence characterized by disruptive, antisocial behavior.

Confidentiality. Protection of the identity of participants by keeping records secure and not disclosing their identities.

Congruence. The fit between one's thoughts, behaviors, and feelings.

Conscious. To Freud, the part of the mind that corresponds to our present awareness.

Construct validity. The degree to which treatment effects can be accounted for by the theoretical mechanisms (constructs) represented in the independent variables; the degree to which a test measures the hypothetical construct that it purports to measure.

Content validity. The degree to which the content of a test covers a representative sample of the content it is designed to measure.

Control subjects. In an experiment, subjects who do not receive the experimental treatment.

Controlled drinking. An approach to treating problem drinkers that has as its goal to moderate social drinking rather than abstinence.

Conversion disorder. A type of somatoform disorder characterized by loss or impairment of physical function in the absence of any apparent organic cause.

Corpus callosum. A thick bundle of fibers that connects the two cerebral hemispheres.

Correlation. A relationship or association between variables.

Countertransference. The transfer of feelings or attitudes that the analyst holds toward other persons onto the client.

Couple therapy. Therapy that focuses on resolving conflicts in distressed couples.

Crack. The hardened, smokable form of cocaine.

Creative self. To Adler, the self-aware part of the personality that strives to achieve its potential.

Criterion validity. The degree to which a test correlates with an independent, external criterion or standard.

Critical thinking. Adoption of a questioning attitude and careful scrutiny of claims and arguments in the light of evidence.

Cross-fostering study. A method of determining heritability of a trait or disorder by examining differences in prevalence among adoptees reared by either adoptive or biological parents who possessed the trait or disorder in question.

Cultural-familial retardation. A mild form of mental retardation that is influenced by impoverishment of the home environment.

Culture-bound syndromes. Patterns of abnormal behavior found within only one or a few cultures.

Cyclothymic disorder. A mood disorder characterized by a chronic pattern of mild mood swings that is not sufficiently severe to be classified as bipolar disorder.

Cytomegalovirus. A source of infection that, in pregnant women, carries a risk of mental retardation to the unborn child.

D

Debriefed. To be fully informed about an experiment after it takes place.

Defense mechanisms. The reality-distorting strategies used by the ego to shield the self from awareness of anxiety-provoking materials.

Deinstitutionalization. The policy of shifting care for patients with severe or chronic mental health problems from inpatient facilities to community-based facilities; the practice of discharging hospitalized mental patients into the community and of reducing the need for new admissions through alternative treatment approaches.

Delirium. A state of mental confusion, disorientation, and extreme difficulty focusing attention.

Delirium tremens. A withdrawal syndrome that occurs following sudden decrease of drinking in people with chronic alcoholism.

Delta-9-tetrahydrocannabinol (THC). The active ingredient in marijuana.

Delusion. A firmly held but inaccurate belief that persists despite evidence that it has no basis in reality.

Delusional disorder. A type of psychosis characterized by persistent delusions, often of a paranoid nature, that do not have the bizarre quality of the type often found in paranoid schizophrenia.

Dementia. Deterioration of mental functioning, involving impaired memory, thinking, judgment, and language use.

Dementia praecox. The term given by Kraepelin to the disorder now called schizophrenia.

Demonological model. The model that explains abnormal behavior in terms of supernatural forces.

Demonology. The idea that abnormal behavior is caused by supernatural forces.

Dendrites. The rootlike structures at the ends of neurons that receive nerve impulses from other neurons.

Dependent personality disorder. A personality disorder characterized by difficulty making independent decisions and overly dependent behavior.

Dependent variables. Outcomes of an experiment believed to be dependent on the effects of an independent variable.

Depersonalization disorder. A disorder characterized by persistent or recurrent episodes of depersonalization.

Depersonalization. Feelings of unreality or detachment from one's self or one's body.

Depressant. A drug that lowers the level of activity of the central nervous system.

Derealization. Loss of the sense of reality of one's surroundings, experienced in terms of strange changes in the environment or in the passage of time.

Description. The representation of observations without making interpretations or drawing inferences.

Detoxification. The process of ridding the system of alcohol or other drugs under supervised conditions.

Deviation IQ. An intelligence quotient obtained by determining the deviation between the person's score and the norm (mean).

Dhat syndrome. A culture-bound somatoform disorder, found primarily among Asian Indian males, characterized by excessive fears over the loss of seminal fluid.

Diathesis. A vulnerability or predisposition to a particular disorder.

Diathesis-stress model. A model that posits that abnormal behavior problems involve the interaction of a vulnerability or predisposition and stressful life events or experiences.

Disorganized type. The subtype of schizophrenia characterized by disorganized behavior, bizarre delusions, and vivid hallucinations.

Disorientation. A state of mental confusion and lack of awareness of time, place, or the identity of oneself or others.

Displacement. A defense mechanism in which one transfers sexual or aggressive impulses toward less threatening or safer objects or persons.

Displacing. Transferring impulses toward threatening or unacceptable objects onto more acceptable or safer objects.

Dissociative amnesia. A dissociative disorder in which a person experiences memory loss without any identifiable organic cause.

Dissociative disorder. Any of a group of disorders characterized by a disruption, or dissociation, of the functions of identity, memory, or consciousness.

Dissociative fugue. A dissociative disorder in which a person suddenly flees from his or her life situation, travels to a new location, assumes a new identity, and has amnesia for personal material.

Dissociative identity disorder. A dissociative disorder in which a person has two or more distinct, or alter, personalities.

Distress. A state of physical or emotional pain or suffering.

Dizygotic (DZ) twins. Twins that develop from separate fertilized eggs.

Dopamine hypothesis. The theory that proposes that schizophrenia involves overactivity of dopamine receptors in the brain.

Double depression. A diagnosis of both major depressive disorder and dysthymic disorder.

Double-bind communications. A communication pattern involving contradictory or mixed messages without acknowledging the inherent conflict.

Down syndrome. A condition caused by the presence of an extra chromosome on the 21st pair and characterized by mental retardation and various physical anomalies.

Downward drift hypothesis. The theory that explains the linkage between low socioeconomic status and behavior problems by suggesting that problem behaviors lead people to drift downward in social status.

Duty to warn. The therapist's obligation to warn third parties of threats made against them by clients.

Dyslexia. A learning disorder characterized by impaired reading ability.

Dyspareunia. Persistent or recurrent pain experienced during or following sexual intercourse.

Dyssomnias. Sleep disorders involving disturbances in the amount, quality, or timing of sleep.

Dysthymic disorder. A mild but chronic type of depressive disorder.

E

Eating disorder. A psychological disorder characterized by disturbed patterns of eating and maladaptive ways of controlling body weight.

Eclectic therapy. An approach to psychotherapy that incorporates principles or techniques from various systems or theories.

Ego. The psychic structure that corresponds to the concept of the self, governed by the reality principle and characterized by the ability to tolerate frustration.

Ego analysts. Psychodynamically oriented therapists who are influenced by ego psychology.

Ego dystonic. Referring to behaviors or feelings that are perceived to be alien to one's self-identity.

Ego identity. The achievement of a firm sense of personal identity.

Ego psychology. Modern psychodynamic approach that focuses more on the conscious strivings of the ego than on the hypothesized unconscious functions of the id.

Ego syntonic. Referring to behaviors or feelings that are perceived as natural parts of the self.

Electra complex. The conflict that occurs during the phallic stage of development, in which the young girl desires her father and perceives her mother as a rival.

Electroconvulsive therapy (ECT). A method of treating severe depression by administering electrical shock to the head.

Electroencephalograph (EEG). An instrument for measuring the electrical activity of the brain.

Electromyograph (EMG). An instrument for measuring muscle tension.

Emotion-focused coping. A coping style that attempts to minimize emotional responsiveness rather than deal with the stressor directly.

Empathy. The ability to understand someone's experiences and feelings from that person's point of view.

Encopresis. Lack of control over bowel movements that is not caused by an organic problem in a child who is at least 4 years old.

Endocrine system. The system of ductless glands that secrete hormones directly into the bloodstream.

Endorphins. Natural substances that function as neurotransmitters in the brain and are similar in their effects to morphine.

Enuresis. Failure to control urination after one has reached the "normal" age for attaining such control.

Epidemiological study. A method of research that involves tracking the rates of occurrence of a disorder among different groups.

Erogenous zone. A part of the body that is sensitive to sexual stimulation.

Eros. Freud's concept of the basic life instinct that seeks to preserve and perpetuate life.

Erotomania. A delusional disorder characterized by the belief that one is loved by someone of high social status.

Etiology. A cause or origin.

Exhaustion stage. The third stage of the GAS, characterized by lowered resistance, increased parasympathetic activity, and possible physical deterioration.

Exhibitionism. A paraphilia in which one is sexually aroused by exposing one's genitals to a stranger.

Exorcism. A ritual intended to expel demons from a person believed to be possessed.

Expectancies. Beliefs about expected outcomes.

Experimental method. A scientific method that aims to discover cause-and-effect relationships by manipulating independent variables and observing the effects on the dependent variables.

Experimental subjects. In an experiment, subjects who receive the experimental treatment.

External attribution. A belief that the cause of an event involved factors outside oneself.

External validity. The degree to which experimental results can be generalized to other settings and conditions.

F

Factitious disorder. A disorder characterized by intentional fabrication of psychological or physical symptoms for no apparent gain.

False negative. An incorrect appraisal that a person is free of a disorder, when in fact he or she has the disorder.

False positive. An incorrect appraisal that a person has a particular disorder.

Family therapy. Therapy in which the family, not the individual, is the unit of treatment.

Fat cells. Body cells specialized to store fat.

Fear-stimulus hierarchy. An ordered series of increasingly fearful stimuli.

Female orgasmic disorder. A sexual dysfunction in women involving difficulty reaching orgasm or inability to reach orgasm following a normal level of sexual interest and arousal.

Female sexual arousal disorder. A sexual dysfunction in women involving difficulty becoming sexually aroused or lack of sexual excitement or pleasure during sexual activity.

Fetishism. A paraphilia in which one uses an inanimate object or body part as a focus of sexual interest and arousal.

Fight-or-flight reaction. The inborn tendency to respond to a threat by either fighting or fleeing.

Fixation. Arrested development in the form of attachment to objects of an earlier developmental stage.

Flashbacks. The experience of sensory distortions or hallucinations occurring after use of LSD or other hallucinogenic drugs.

Flooding. A form of exposure therapy in which subjects are exposed to high levels of fear-inducing stimuli.

Forcible rape. Forced sexual intercourse with a nonconsenting person.

Fragile X syndrome. An inherited form of mental retardation caused by a mutated gene on the X chromosome.

Free association. The method of verbalizing thoughts as they occur without a conscious attempt to edit or censure them.

Freebasing. A method of ingesting cocaine by heating it with ether to separate its most potent component (its "free base") and then smoking the extract.

Frotteurism. A paraphilia characterized by recurrent sexual urges involving bumping or rubbing against nonconsenting others for sexual gratification.

Functional analysis. Analysis of behavior in terms of antecedent stimuli and reinforcement consequences.

Functional magnetic resonance imaging (fMRI). Type of MRI used to identify parts of the brain that become active when people engage in particular tasks.

G

Galvanic skin response (GSR). A measure of the change in electrical activity of the skin that accompanies sympathetic nervous system arousal.

Gamma-aminobutyric acid (GABA). An inhibitory neurotransmitter believed to play a role in anxiety.

Gender identity disorder. A disorder in which the individual believes that her or his anatomical gender is inconsistent with her or his gender identity.

Gender identity. One's psychological sense of being female or male.

Gender roles. The characteristic ways in which males and females are expected to behave in a given culture.

General adaptation syndrome (GAS). The body's three-stage response to states of prolonged or intense stress.

Generalized anxiety disorder (GAD). A type of anxiety disorder characterized by general feelings of dread and foreboding and heightened states of bodily arousal.

Genes. The units, found on chromosomes, that carry heredity.

Genetics. The science of heredity.

Genital stage. The final stage of psychosexual development, characterized by expression of libido through sexual intercourse with an adult of the opposite sex.

Genotype. The set of traits specified by an individual's genetic code.

Genuineness. The ability to recognize and express one's true feelings.

Global attribution.   A belief that the cause of an event involved generalized, rather than specific, factors.

Gradual exposure.   A behavior therapy technique for overcoming fears through direct exposure to increasingly fearful stimuli.

Group therapy.   Therapy method in which a group of clients meet together with a therapist.

H

Halfway houses   Supervised community residences that provide a bridge between institutional facilities and independent community living.

Hallucination.   A perception that occurs in the absence of an external stimulus and that is confused with reality.

Hallucinogens.   Substances that cause hallucinations.

Hashish.   A drug derived from the resin of the plant *Cannabis sativa.*

Health psychologist.   A psychologist who studies the relationships between psychological factors and physical illness.

Heroin.   A narcotic derived from morphine that has strong addictive properties.

Heterosexism.   The culturally based belief system that holds that only reproductive sexuality is psychologically healthy and morally correct.

Histrionic personality disorder.   A personality disorder characterized by excessive need for attention, praise, reassurance, and approval.

Homophobia.   Hatred and fear of lesbians and gay males.

Homosexuality.   A sexual orientation characterized by erotic interest in, and development of romantic relationships with, members of one's own gender.

Hormones.   Substances secreted by endocrine glands that regulate body functions and promote growth and development.

Human immunodeficiency virus (HIV).   The virus that causes AIDS.

Humors.   According to the ancient Hippocratic belief system, the vital bodily fluids (phlegm, black bile, blood, yellow bile).

Huntington's disease.   An inherited degenerative disease that is characterized by jerking and twisting movements, psychotic behavior, and mental deterioration.

Hyperactivity.   An abnormal behavior pattern characterized by difficulty in maintaining attention and extreme restlessness.

Hypersomnia.   A pattern of excessive sleepiness during the day.

Hyperventilation.   A pattern of overly rapid breathing associated with states of anxiety.

Hypnosis.   A trancelike state, induced by suggestion, in which the individual responds to the commands of the hypnotist.

Hypnotics.   Drugs, including anesthetics and sedatives, that induce partial or complete unconsciousness and are used to treat sleep disorders.

Hypoactive sexual desire disorder.   Persistent or recurring lack of sexual interest or sexual fantasies.

Hypomanic.   Referring to a mild state of mania, or elation.

Hypothalamus.   A structure in the forebrain involved in regulating body temperature, emotion, and motivation.

Hypothesis.   An assumption that is tested through experimentation.

Hypothyroidism.   A physical condition, caused by deficiency of the hormone thyroxin, characterized by sluggishness and lowered metabolism.

Hypoxia.   Decreased supply of oxygen to the brain or other organs.

Hypoxyphilia.   A paraphilia in which a person seeks sexual gratification by being deprived of oxygen.

I

Id.   The unconscious psychic structure, present at birth, that contains primitive instincts and is regulated by the pleasure principle.

Ideas of persecution.   A form of delusional thinking characterized by false beliefs that one is being persecuted or victimized by others.

Ideas of reference.   A form of delusional thinking in which a person reads personal meaning into the behavior of others or external events.

Identification.   The process of incorporating the personality or behavior of others.

Immune system.   The body's system of defense against disease.

Incidence.   The number of new cases of a disorder that occurs within a specific period of time.

Independent variables.   Factors that are manipulated in experiments.

Individual psychology.   Adler's psychodynamic theory.

Individual response specificity.   The belief that people respond to the same stressor in different ways.

Infarction.   The development of an infarct, or area of dead or dying tissue, resulting from the blocking of blood vessels normally supplying the tissue.

Inference.   A conclusion that is drawn from data.

Inferiority complex.   The feelings of inferiority that Adler believed to be a central source of motivation.

Informed consent.   The principle that subjects should receive enough information about an experiment beforehand to decide freely whether to participate.

Insanity defense.   A legal defense in which a defendant in a criminal case pleads innocent on the basis of insanity.

Insight.   The attainment of awareness and understanding of one's true motives and feelings.

Insomnia.   Difficulties falling asleep, remaining asleep, or achieving restorative sleep.

Instinct.   A fixed, inborn pattern of behavior that is specific to members of a particular species.

Intelligence.   (1) The capacity to understand the world and respond to its challenges; (2) the trait measured by intelligence tests.

Intelligence quotient (IQ).   A measure of intelligence based on scores on an intelligence test; the ratio between a respondent's mental age and actual age.

Internal attribution.   A belief that the cause of an event involved factors within oneself.

Internal consistency.   Cohesiveness or interrelationships of items on a test or scales.

Internal locus of control.   Perception of one's ability to control reinforcements or affect outcomes.

Internal validity.   The degree to which manipulation of the independent variables can be causally related to changes in the dependent variables.

Interpersonal psychotherapy (IPT).   A brief form of psychodynamic therapy that focuses on the client's current interpersonal relationships.

Interrater reliability.   Consistency of or agreement between raters.

Intoxication.   A state of drunkenness.

Introject.   To unconsciously incorporate features of another person's personality into one's own ego structure.

Involuntary.   Automatic or without conscious direction.

K

Knobs.   The swollen endings of axon terminals.

Koro syndrome.   A culture-bound somatoform disorder, found primarily in China, in which people fear that their genitals are shrinking.

Korsakoff's syndrome.   A syndrome associated with chronic alcoholism that is characterized by memory loss and disorientation (also called alcohol persisting amnestic disorder).

L

La belle indifference   A French expression ("beautiful indifference" in English) describing the lack of concern over one's symptoms displayed by some people with conversion disorder.

Latency stage.   The psychosexual stage in middle childhood characterized by repression of sexual impulses.

Latent content.   The underlying or symbolic content of dreams.

Learned helplessness.   A behavior pattern characterized by passivity and perceptions of lack of control.

Learning disorder.   A deficiency in a specific learning ability in the context of normal intelligence and exposure to learning opportunities.

Legal commitment.   The legal process of confining a person found not guilty by reason of insanity in a mental institution.

Leukocytes.   White blood cells.

Libido.   The energy of Eros; sexual drive or energy.

Limbic system.   A group of forebrain structures involved in learning, memory, and basic drives.

Longitudinal study.   A research study in which subjects are followed over time.

Lysergic acid diethylamide (LSD).   A type of hallucinogen.

M

Magnetic resonance imaging (MRI).   A computer-generated image of the brain formed by measuring the signals emitted when the head is placed in a strong magnetic field.

Major depressive disorder.   A severe mood disorder characterized by major depressive episodes.

Male erectile disorder.   A sexual dysfunction in men characterized by difficulty achieving or maintaining erection during sexual activity.

Male orgasmic disorder.   A sexual dysfunction in males involving difficulty achieving orgasm following a normal pattern of sexual interest and excitement.

Malingering.   Faking illness.

Managed care systems.   Health care delivery systems that impose limits on the number of treatment sessions they will approve for payment and the fees they will allow for reimbursement.

Manic episode.   A period of unrealistically heightened euphoria, extreme restlessness, and excessive activity characterized by disorganized behavior and impaired judgment.

Manic.   Relating to mania, as in the manic phase of bipolar disorder.

Manifest content.   The reported content or apparent meaning of dreams.

Mantra.   A word or phrase that is repeated to induce a state of relaxation and narrowing of consciousness.

Marijuana.   A hallucinogenic drug derived from the leaves and stems of the plant *Cannabis sativa.*

Medical model.   A biological perspective in which abnormal behavior is viewed as symptomatic of underlying illness.

Medulla.   An area of the hindbrain involved in regulation of heartbeat and respiration.

Melancholia.   A state of severe depression.

Mental age.   The age equivalent that corresponds to a person's level of intelligence as measured by the Stanford-Binet Intelligence Scale.

Mental retardation.   A generalized delay or impairment in the development of intellectual and adaptive abilities.

Mental status examination.   A structured clinical assessment to determine various aspects of the client's mental functioning.

Meta-analysis.   A statistical technique for combining the results of different studies into an overall average.

Metabolic rate.   The rate at which energy is used in the body.

Methadone.   An artificial narcotic that is used to help people who are addicted to heroin to abstain from it without a withdrawal syndrome.

Modeling.   Learning by observing and imitating the behavior of others; a behavior therapy technique for helping an individual acquire a new behavior by means of having a therapist or another individual demonstrate a target behavior that is then imitated by the client.

Monoamine oxidase (MAO) inhibitors.   A group of antidepressant drugs that increase the availability of neurotransmitters in the brain by inhibiting the actions of an enzyme that breaks down neurotransmitters.

Monozygotic (MZ) twins.   Twins that develop from the same fertilized egg and therefore share identical genes.

Mood disorder.   A type of disorder characterized by disturbances of mood.

Mood.   The pervasive quality of an individual's emotional experience.

Moral principle.   The principle that governs the superego to set and enforce moral standards.

Moral therapy.   A 19th-century treatment approach that emphasized treating hospitalized patients with care and understanding.

Morphine.   A strongly addictive narcotic derived from the opium poppy that relieves pain and induces feelings of well-being.

Mourning.   Normal feelings of grief following a loss.

Münchausen syndrome.   A type of factitious disorder characterized by the feigning of medical symptoms.

Musterbation.   A rigid thought pattern characterized by the tendency to impose excessive, unrealistic demands on oneself or personal imperatives.

Myocardial infarction.   A breakdown of heart tissue due to an obstruction in the blood vessels that supply blood to the heart.

N

Naltrexone.   A drug that blocks the high from alcohol as well as from opiates.

Narcissistic personality disorder.   A personality disorder characterized by adoption of an inflated self-image and demands for attention and admiration.

Narcolepsy.   A sleep disorder characterized by sudden, irresistible episodes of sleep.

Narcotics.   Drugs that are used for pain relief and treatment of insomnia but that have strong addictive potential.

Naturalistic-observation method.   A research method in which subjects' behavior is observed and measured in their natural environments.

Negative correlation.   A statistical relationship between two variables such that increases in one are associated with decreases in the other.

Negative reinforcers.   Reinforcers that on removal increase the frequency of behavior.

Negative symptoms.   Behavioral deficiencies associated with schizophrenia, such as social skills deficits, social withdrawal, flattened affect, poverty of speech and thought, psychomotor retardation, and failure to experience pleasure.

Neo-Freudians.   Theorists, such as Jung, Adler, Horney, and Sullivan, who, in comparison with Freud, placed greater emphasis on the importance of cultural and social influences and lesser emphasis on sexual impulses.

Neologisms.   New words.

Neuroleptics.   A group of antipsychotic drugs (the "major tranquilizers") used in the treatment of schizophrenia, such as the phenothiazines (Thorazine, Mellaril, etc.).

Neurons.   Nerve cells.

Neuropsychological.   Pertaining to the relationships between the brain and behavior.

Neurosis.   A nonpsychotic form of disturbed behavior characterized by problems involving anxiety.

Neuroticism.   A trait that involves characteristics such as anxious behavior, apprehension about the future, and avoidance behavior.

Neurotransmitters.   Chemical substances that transmit messages from one neuron to another.

Nightmare disorder.   A sleep disorder characterized by recurrent awakenings due to frightening nightmares.

Nonspecific factors.   Factors not specific to any one form of psychotherapy, such as therapist attention and support, and the engendering of positive expectancies of change.

O

Obesity.   A condition of excessive body fat; generally defined by a body mass index (BMI) of 30 or higher.

Object relations.   The person's relationships to the internalized representations, or "objects," of others' personalities that have been introjected within the person's ego structure.

Object-relations theory.   The psychodynamic viewpoint that focuses on the influences of internalized representations of the personalities of parents and other strong attachment figures (called objects).

Objective tests.   Tests that allow a limited range of response options and can therefore be scored objectively.

Obsession.   A recurrring thought or image that the individual cannot control.

Obsessive–compulsive personality disorder.   A personality disorder characterized by rigid ways of relating to others, perfectionistic tendencies, lack of spontaneity, and excessive attention to detail.

Oedipus complex.   The conflict that occurs during the phallic stage of development, in which the young boy desires his mother and perceives his father as a rival.

Open-ended questions.   Questions that provide an unlimited range of response options.

Opioids.   Natural or synthetic drugs with strong addictive properties; natural opioids, referred to as opiates, are derived from the opium poppy.

Oppositional defiant disorder (ODD).   A psychological disorder in childhood and adolescence characterized by excessive oppositionality, or tendencies to refuse requests from parents and others.

Optimum level of arousal.   The level of arousal associated with peak performance and optimal feelings of well-being.

Oral stage.   The psychosexual stage during infancy in which pleasure is sought primarily through oral activities.

Osteoporosis.   A physical disorder caused by calcium deficiency and characterized by brittle bones.

P

Panic disorder.   A type of anxiety disorder characterized by repeated episodes of intense anxiety or panic.

Paranoid personality disorder.   A personality disorder characterized by suspiciousness of others' motives, but not to the point of delusion.

Paranoid.   Referring to irrational suspicions.

Paranoid type.   The subtype of schizophrenia characterized by hallucinations and system-

atized delusions, commonly involving themes of persecution.

Paraphilias.   Sexual disorders in which the person experiences recurrent sexual urges and fantasies involving nonhuman objects, inappropriate or nonconsenting partners, or painful or humiliating situations.

Parasomnias.   Sleep disorders involving abnormal behaviors or physiological events that occur during sleep or while falling asleep.

Parasympathetic.   Pertaining to the division of the autonomic nervous system whose activity reduces states of arousal and regulates bodily processes that replenish energy reserves.

Parkinson's disease.   A progressive disease of the basal ganglia characterized by muscle tremor and shakiness, rigidity, difficulty walking, poor control of fine motor movements, lack of facial muscle tonus, and in some cases, cognitive impairment.

Pathogens.   Disease-causing organisms.

Pedophilia.   A paraphilia involving recurrent, powerful sexual urges and related fantasies involving sexual activity with prepubescent children.

Performance anxiety.   Fear relating to the threat of failure to perform adequately.

Peripheral nervous system.   The somatic and autonomic nervous systems.

Perseveration.   The persistent repetition of the same thought or response.

Person-centered therapy.   The establishment of a warm, accepting therapeutic relationship that frees clients to engage in self-exploration and achieve self-acceptance.

Personality disorders.   Excessively rigid behavior patterns, or ways of relating to others, that ultimately become self-defeating.

Pervasive developmental disorders.   A class of developmental disorders characterized by significantly impaired behavior or functioning in multiple areas of development.

Phallic stage.   A psychosexual stage in early childhood during which pleasure is sought primarily through the phallic region and the child develops incestuous desires for the parent of the opposite sex.

Phenothiazines.   A group of antipsychotic drugs (major tranquilizers) used to treat schizophrenia.

Phenotype.   An individual's actual or expressed traits.

Phenylketonuria (PKU).   A genetic disorder that prevents the metabolization of phenylpyruvic acid, leading to mental retardation unless the diet is strictly controlled.

Phlegmatic.   Slow and solid.

Phrenologist.   Someone who studies the bumps on a person's head to determine the person's underlying traits.

Physiological dependence.   A condition in which the drug user's body comes to depend on a steady supply of the substance.

Pick's disease.   A form of dementia, similar to Alzheimer's disease, but distinguished by specific abnormalities (Pick's bodies) in nerve cells and absence of neurofibrillary tangles and plaques.

Placebo.   An inert medication or bogus treatment that is intended to control for expectancy effects.

Play therapy.   A form of psychodynamic therapy in which play activities and objects are used to help children symbolically enact conflicts or express underlying feelings.

Pleasure principle.   The governing principle of the id, involving demands for immediate gratification of needs.

Polysomnographic (PSG) recording.   Simultaneous measurement of multiple physiological responses during sleep or attempted sleep.

Pons.   A structure in the hindbrain involved in respiration.

Population.   A total group of people, other organisms, or events.

Positive correlation.   A statistical relationship between two variables such that increases in one are associated with increases in the other.

Positive reinforcers.   Reinforcers that, introduced, increase with the frequency of behavior.

Positive symptoms.   Flagrant symptoms of schizophrenia, such as hallucinations, delusions, bizarre behavior, and thought disorder.

Positron emission tomography (PET scan).   An imaging technique that forms a computer-generated image by tracing the amount of glucose used in various regions of the brain.

Possession.   A superstitious belief in which abnormal behavior is taken as a sign that the person is possessed by demons or the devil.

Postpartum depression (PPD).   Persistent and severe mood changes that occur after childbirth.

Posttraumatic stress disorder (PTSD).   A prolonged maladaptive reaction to a traumatic event.

Preconscious.   To Freud, the part of the mind whose contents lie outside present awareness but can be brought into awareness by focusing attention.

Predictive validity.   The degree to which a test score is predictive of some future behavior or outcome.

Prefrontal lobotomy.   A form of psychosurgery, no longer in use, in which certain neural pathways in the brain are severed in order to control disturbed behavior.

Pregenital.   Referring to characteristics typical of psychosexual stages that precede the genital stage.

Premature ejaculation.   A sexual dysfunction in men characterized by ejaculation following minimal sexual stimulation.

Premorbid functioning.   The level of functioning before the person developed schizophrenia.

Prepared conditioning.   The belief that people are genetically prepared to acquire fear responses to certain stimuli, such as snakes or large animals.

Presenile dementia.   Dementia that begin at age 65 or earlier.

Pressured speech.   An outpouring of speech in which words seem to surge urgently for expression.

Prevalence.   The overall number of cases of a disorder in a population within a specific period of time.

Primary gains.   Relief from underlying anxiety gained through the development of neurotic symptoms.

Primary prevention.   Efforts designed to prevent problems from arising.

Primary process thinking.   In infancy, the mental process by which the id seeks gratification by imagining that it possesses what it desires; thinking that is illogical or magical.

Primary reinforcers.   Reinforcers that fulfill basic needs, such as water, food, warmth, and relief from pain.

Proband.   The case first diagnosed of a given disorder.

Problem-focused coping.   A coping style that attempts to confront the stressor directly.

Problem-solving therapy.   A form of therapy that focuses on helping people develop more effective problem-solving skills.

Prodromal phase.   In schizophrenia, the period of decline in functioning that precedes the first acute psychotic episode.

Projection.   A defense mechanism in which one's own sexual or aggressive impulses are attributed to another person.

Projective tests.   Psychological tests that present ambiguous stimuli onto which the examinee is thought to project his or her personality and unconscious motives.

Psychiatrist.   A physician who specializes in the diagnosis and treatment of emotional disorders.

Psychic.   Relating to mental phenomena.

Psychoactive.   Referring to chemical substances that have psychological effects.

Psychoanalysis.   The method of psychotherapy developed by Sigmund Freud.

Psychoanalytic theory.   The theoretical model of personality developed by Sigmund Freud; also called psychoanalysis.

Psychodynamic model.   The theoretical model of Freud and his followers, in which abnormal behavior is viewed as the product of clashing forces within the personality.

Psychodynamic therapy.   Therapy that helps individuals gain insight into, and resolve, unconscious conflicts.

Psychological dependence.   Compulsive use of a substance to meet a psychological need.

Psychological disorders.   Abnormal behavior patterns that involve a disturbance of psychological functioning or behavior.

Psychological hardiness.   A cluster of stress-buffering traits characterized by commitment, challenge, and control.

Psychologist.   A person with advanced graduate training in psychology.

Psychoneuroimmunology.   The study of relationships between psychological factors and immunological functioning.

Psychopharmacology.   The field of study that examines the effects of therapeutic or psychiatric drugs.

Psychosexual.   Pertaining to Freud's stages of development, in which libido becomes expressed through different erogenous zones during different stages.

Psychosis.   A severe form of disturbed behavior characterized by impaired ability to interpret reality and difficulty meeting the demands of daily life.

Psychosomatic.   Pertaining to a physical disorder in which psychological factors play a causal or contributing role.

Psychotherapy.   A structured form of treatment derived from a psychological framework which consists of one or more verbal interactions or treatment sessions between a client and a therapist.

Punishments.   Unpleasant stimuli that reduce the frequency of the behaviors they follow.

R

Random sample.   A sample that is drawn in such a way that every member of a population has an equal chance of being included.

Rapid flight of ideas.   A characteristic of manic behavior involving rapid speech and changes of topics.

Rational-emotive behavior therapy (REBT).   A therapeutic approach that focuses on helping clients replace irrational, maladaptive beliefs with alternative, more adaptive beliefs.

Reactivity.   The tendency for the behavior being observed to be influenced by the way in which it is measured.

Reality principle.   The governing principle of the ego, which involves considerations of social acceptability and practicality.

Reality testing.   The ability to perceive the world accurately and to distinguish between reality and fantasy.

Rebound anxiety.   The experiencing of strong anxiety following withdrawal from a tranquilizer.

Receptor site.   A part of a dendrite on a receiving neuron that is structured to receive a neurotransmitter.

Reinforcement.   A stimulus or event that increases the frequency of the response that it follows.

Relapse.   A recurrence of a problem behavior or disorder.

Relapse-prevention training.   A cognitive–behavioral technique involving the use of behavioral and cognitive strategies for resisting temptations and preventing relapses.

Reliable.   In psychological assessment, the consistency of a measure or diagnostic instrument or system.

REM sleep.   The stage of sleep associated with dreaming and characterized by rapid eye movements under the closed eyelids.

Repression.   A defense mechanism involving the unconscious ejection of anxiety-provoking ideas, images, or impulses.

Residual phase.   In schizophrenia, the phase that follows an acute phase, characterized by a return to the level of functioning of the prodromal phase.

Resistance stage.   The second stage of the GAS, involving the body's attempt to withstand prolonged stress and preserve resources.

Resistance.   The blocking of thoughts or feelings that would evoke anxiety if they were consciously experienced.

Reticular activating system.   Brain structure involved in processes of attention, sleep, and arousal.

Rett's disorder.   A pervasive development disorder characterized by a range of physical, behavioral, motor, and cognitive abnormalities that begin after a few months of apparently normal development.

Reversal design.   An experimental design that consists of repeated measurement of a subject's behavior through a sequence of alternating baseline and treatment phases.

Reward.   A pleasant stimulus or event that increases the frequency of the response that it follows.

Role diffusion.   A state of confusion, aimlessness, and heightened susceptibility to the suggestions of others, associated with failure to acquire a firm sense of identity during adolescence.

S

Sadomasochism.   Sexual activities involving the attainment or gratification by means of inflicting and receiving pain and humiliation.

Sample.   Part of a population.

Sanguine.   Having a cheerful disposition.

Sanism.   The negative stereotyping of people who are identified as mentally ill.

Schizoaffective disorder.   A type of psychotic disorder in which individuals experience both severe mood disturbance and features associated with schizophrenia.

Schizoid personality disorder.   A personality disorder characterized by persistent lack of interest in social relationships, flattened affect, and social withdrawal.

Schizophrenia.   An enduring psychotic disorder that involves disturbed behavior, thinking, emotions and perceptions.

Schizophreniform disorder.   A psychotic disorder lasting less than six months in duration with features that resemble schizophrenia.

Schizophrenogenic mother.   The since-discarded concept of a cold but overprotective mother who it was believed was capable of causing schizophrenia in her children.

Schizotypal personality disorder.   A personality disorder characterized by eccentricities of thought and behavior, but without clearly psychotic features.

Scientific method.   A method of conducting scientific research in which theories or assumptions are examined in the light of evidence.

Secondary gains.   Side benefits associated with neurotic or other disorders, such as expressions of sympathy, increased attention, and release from responsibilities.

Secondary prevention.   Efforts to ameliorate existing problems at an early stage.

Secondary process thinking.   The reality-based thinking processes and problem-solving activities of the ego.

Secondary reinforcers.   Stimuli that gain reinforcement value through their association with established reinforcers, such as money and social approval.

Sedatives.   Types of depressants that reduce states of tension and restlessness and induce sleep.

Selection factor.   A type of bias in which differences between experimental and control groups result from differences in the subjects placed in the groups, not from the independent variable.

Selective abstraction.   A cognitive distortion involving the tendency to focus only on the negative parts of experiences or events.

Selective serotonin-reuptake inhibitors (SSRIs).   A group of antidepressant drugs that increase the availability of serotonin in the brain by interfering with its reuptake by the transmitting neuron.

Self-actualization.   In humanistic psychology, the tendency to strive to become all that one is capable of being. The motive that drives one to reach one's full potential and express one's unique capabilities.

Self-monitoring.   The process of observing or recording one's own behaviors, thoughts, or emotions.

Self-psychology.   A theory that describes processes that normally lead to achievement of a cohesive sense of self.

Self-report personality test.   A structured personality test in which individuals give information about themselves by responding to items that require a limited type of response, such as "yes–no" or "agree–disagree."

Self-spectatoring.   The tendency to observe one's behavior as if one were a spectator.

Semistructured interview.   Interview in which the clinician follows a general outline of questions designed to gather essential information but is free to ask them in any order and to branch off in other directions.

Senile dementias.   Forms of dementia that begin after age 65.

Sensate focus exercises.   Mutual pleasuring activities focused on the partners taking turns giving and receiving physical pleasure.

Sensitivity.   The ability of a diagnostic instrument to correctly identify people who have the disorder the test is intended to detect.

Separation anxiety disorder.   A childhood disorder characterized by extreme fear of separation from parents or other caretakers.

Separation-individuation.   The process by which an infant develops a separate identity from that of the mother.

Set point.   A value, such as body weight, that the body's regulatory mechanisms attempt to maintain.

Sexual aversion disorder.   A type of sexual dysfunction characterized by aversion to and avoidance of genital sexual contact.

Sexual dysfunctions.   Persistent problems with sexual interest, arousal, or response.

Sexual harassment.   Speech, gestures, demands, or physical contact of a sexual nature that is unwelcomed by the person to whom such actions are directed.

Sexual masochism.   A paraphilia characterized by recurrent, powerful sexual urges and fantasies involving receiving humiliation or pain.

Sexual sadism.   A paraphilia characterized by recurrent, powerful sexual urges and fantasies involving inflicting humiliation or pain.

Significant.   In statistics, a magnitude of difference that is taken as indicating meaningful differences between groups.

Single-case experimental design.   A type of case study in which the subject is used as his or her own control.

Sleep disorders.   Persistent or recurrent sleep-related problems that cause distress or impaired functioning.

Sleep terror disorder.   A sleep disorder characterized by recurrent episodes of sleep terror resulting in abrupt awakenings.

Sleepwalking disorder.   A sleep disorder involving repeated episodes of sleepwalking.

Social phobia.   Excessive fear of social interactions or situations.

Social-cognitive theory.   A learning-based theory that emphasizes observational learning and incorporates roles for both situational and cognitive variables in determining behavior.

Sociobiology.   Biological perspective that explains psychological traits as behavioral tendencies that increased our ancestors' chances of survival and were passed down genetically.

Soma.   A cell body.

Somatic nervous system.   The division of the peripheral nervous system that relays information from the sense organs to the brain and transmits messages from the brain to the skeletal muscles.

Somatization disorder.   A type of somatoform disorder involving recurrent multiple complaints that cannot be explained by any physical cause.

Somatoform disorders.   A group of disorders characterized by complaints of physical problems or symptoms that cannot be explained by physical causes.

Specific attribution.   A belief that the cause of an event involved specific, rather than generalized, factors.

Specific phobia.   A persistent and excessive fear of a specific object or situation.

Specificity.   The ability of a diagnostic instrument to avoid classifying people as having a characteristic or disorder when they truly do not have the characteristic or disorder.

Splitting.   An inability to reconcile the positive and negative aspects of the self and others, resulting in sudden shifts between positive and negative feelings.

Stable attribution.   A belief that the cause of an event involved stable, rather than changeable, factors.

Standard scores.   Scores that indicate the relative standing of raw scores in relation to the distribution of normative scores.

Steroids.   A group of hormones that includes testosterone, estrogen, progesterone, and corticosteroids.

Stress.   A demand made on an organism to adapt or adjust.

Stressor.   A source of stress.

Stroke.   Blocking of a blood vessel that supplies the brain due to a blood clot.

Structural hypothesis.   The belief that the clashing forces within the personality can be divided into three structures: id, ego, and superego.

Structured interview.   Interview that follows a preset series of questions in a particular order.

Stupor.   A state of relative or complete unconsciousness in which a person is not aware of or responsive to the environment.

Substance abuse.   The continued used of a psychoactive drug despite the knowledge that it is causing a social, occupational, psychological, or physical problem.

Substance dependence.   Impaired control over the use of a psychoactive substance; often characterized by physiological dependence.

Substance use disorders.   Disorders that involve maladaptive use of psychoactive substances, such as substance abuse and substance dependence.

Substance-induced disorders.   Disorders that can be induced by using psychoactive substances, such as intoxication.

Superego.   The psychic structure that incorporates the values of the parents and important others and that is governed by the moral principle; consists of two parts, the conscience and the ego ideal.

Survey method.   A research method in which large samples of people are questioned by means of a survey instrument.

Symbiotic.   The state of oneness that normally exists between mother and infant.

Sympathetic.   Pertaining to the division of the autonomic nervous system whose activity leads to heightened states of arousal.

Synapse.   The junction between the terminal knob of one neuron and the dendrite or soma of another through which nerve impulses pass.

Syndromes.   Clusters of symptoms that are characteristic of particular disorders.

Systematic desensitization.   A behavior therapy technique for overcoming phobias by means of exposure to progressively more fearful stimuli while one remains deeply relaxed.

Systems perspective.   The view that problems reflect the systems (family, social, school ecological, etc.) in which they occur.

T

Tachycardia.   Abnormally rapid heartbeat.

Tactile.   Pertaining to the sense of touch.

Taijin-kyofu-sho.   A psychiatric syndrome, found in Japan, involving excessive fear of offending or embarrassing others.

Tardive dyskinesia (TD).   A disorder characterized by involuntary movements of the face, mouth, neck, trunk, or extremities and caused by long-term used of antipsychotic medication.

Temporal stability.   The consistency of test responses over time, as measured by test–retest reliability.

Terminals.   The small branching structures at the tips of axons.

Test–retest reliability.   A method of measuring the reliability of a test by means of comparing the scores of the same subjects on different occasions.

Thalamus.   A structure in the forebrain involved in relaying sensory information to the cortex and in processes related to sleep and attention.

Theory.   A formulation of the relationships underlying observed events.

Thermistor.   A device for registering body temperature.

Thought disorder.   A disturbance in thinking characterized by the breakdown of logical associations between thoughts.

Time-out.   A behavioral technique in which a person who behaves in an undesirable way is removed from a reinforcing environment and placed in an unreinforcing environment for a short time.

Token economy.   Behavioral treatment program in which a controlled environment is constructed such that people are reinforced for desired behaviors by receiving tokens that may be exchanged for desired rewards.

Tolerance.   Physical habituation to use of a drug; habituation to a drug such that, with frequent use, higher doses are needed to achieve the same effects.

Transcendental meditation (TM).   A form of meditation that focuses on repeating a mantra to induce a meditative state.

Transference relationship.   The client's transfer onto the analyst of feelings or attitudes the client holds toward important figures in his or her life.

Transvestic fetishism.   A paraphilia in heterosexual males characterized by recurrent sexual urges involving dressing in female clothing.

Trephination.   A harsh, prehistoric practice of cutting a hole in a person's skull, possibly in an attempt to release demons.

Tricyclics.   A group of antidepressant drugs that increase the activity of norepinephrine and serotonin by interfering with the reuptake of these neurotransmitters.

Two-factor model.   A theoretical model that accounts for the development of phobic reactions on the basis of classical and operant conditioning.

Type A behavior pattern (TABP).   A behavior pattern characterized by a sense of time urgency, competitiveness, and hostility.

U

Unconditional positive regard.   The expression of unconditional acceptance of another person's basic worth as a person.

Unconditioned response.   An unlearned response.

Unconditioned stimulus.   A stimulus that elicits an unlearned response.

Unconscious.   To Freud, the part of the mind that lies outside the range of ordinary awareness and that contains instinctual urges.

Unipolar.   Pertaining to a single pole, or direction.

Unobtrusive.   Not interfering or conspicuous.

Unstable attribution.   A belief that the cause of an event involved changeable, rather than stable, factors.

Unstructured interview.   Interview in which the clinician adopts his or her own style of questioning rather than following any standard format.

V

Vaginismus.   A sexual dysfunction characterized by persistent or recurring contraction of the muscles surrounding the vaginal opening, making intercourse difficult or impossible.

Validity scales.   Groups of test items that are used to detect whether the results of a test are valid.

Validity.   The degree to which a test or diagnostic system measures the traits or constructs it purports to measure.

Variables.   Conditions that are measured (dependent variables) or manipulated (independent variables) in experiments.

Voyeurism.   A paraphilia characterized by recurrent sexual urges involving watching unsuspecting others in sexual situations.

W

Waxy flexibility.   A feature of catatonic schizophrenia in which a person's limbs are moved into a certain posture or position, which the person then rigidly maintains.

Weaning.   The process of accustoming a child to eat solid food.

Wernicke's disease.   A brain disorder, associated with chronic alcoholism, characterized by confusion, disorientation, and difficulty maintaining balance while walking.

Withdrawal syndrome.   A characteristic cluster of symptoms following the sudden reduction or cessation of use of a psychoactive substance after physiological dependence has developed.

Worldview.   The prevailing view of the times (English translation of German term *Weltanschaung*).

A

A children's mental illness "crisis": Report: 1 in 10 children suffers enough to impair development. (2001, January 3). *Associated Press Web Posting*. Retrieved January 5, 2001, from http://www.msnbc.com/news/510934.asp.

Aarre, T. F., Dahl, A. A., Johansen, J. B., Kjonniksen, I., & Neckelmann, D. (2003). Efficacy of repetitive transcranial magnetic stimulation in depression: A review of the evidence. *Nordic Journal of Psychiatry, 57,* 227–232.

Aarsland, D., Andersen, K., Larsen, J. P., Lolk, A., & Kragh-Sorensen, P. (2003). Prevalence and characteristics of dementia in Parkinson disease: An 8-year prospective study. *Archives of Neurology, 60,* 387–392.

Abbey, A., Zawackia, T., Bucka, O., Clinton, A. M., & McAuslan, P. (2004). Sexual assault and alcohol consumption: What do we know about their relationship and what types of research are still needed? *Aggression and Violent Behavior, 9,* 271–303.

Abikoff, H. (2001). Tailored psychosocial treatments for ADHD: The search for a good fit. *Journal of Clinical Child Psychology, 30*(1), 122–125.

Abkevich, V., Camp, N. J., Hensel, C. H., Neff, C. D., Russell, D. L., Hughes, D. C., et al. (2003). Predisposition locus for major depression at chromosome 2q22-12q23.2 *American Journal of Human Genetics, 73,* 1271–1281.

Abracen, J., & Looman, J. (2004). Issues in the treatment of sexual offenders: Recent developments and directions for future research. *Aggression and Violent Behavior, 9,* 229–246.

Abraham, K. (1948). The first pregenital stage of the libido (1916). In D. Bryan & A. Strachey (Eds.), *Selected papers of Karl Abraham, M. D.* London: The Hogarth Press.

Abramowitz, J. S. (1996). Variants of exposure and response prevention in the treatment of obsessive-compulsive disorder: A meta-analysis. *Behavior Therapy, 27,* 583–600.

Abramowitz, J.S., Foa, E. B., & Franklin, M. E. (2003). Exposure and ritual prevention for obsessive–compulsive disorder: Effects of intensive versus twice-weekly sessions. *Journal of Consulting and Clinical Psychology, 71,* 394–398.

Abramowitz, J. S., Franklin, M. E., Schwartz, S. A., & Furr, J. M. (2003). Symptom presentation and outcome of cognitive-behavioral therapy for obsessive-compulsive disorder. *Journal of Consulting and Clinical Psychology, 71,* 1049–1057.

Abramson, J. L., Williams, S. A., Krumholz, H. M., & Vaccarino, V. (2001). Moderate alcohol consumption and risk of heart failure among older persons. *Journal of the American Medical Association, 285,* 1971–1977.

Achenbach, T. M., & Dumenci, L. (2001). Levent advances in empirically based assessment: Revised cross-informant syndromes and new DSM-oriented scales for the CBCL, YSR, and TRF: Comment on Lengua, Sadowski, Friedrich, and Fisher (2001). *Journal of Consulting and Clinical Psychology, 69,* 699–702.

Achenbach, T. M., & Edelbrock, C. S. (1979). The Child Behavior Profile: I. Boys aged 12–16 and girls aged 6–11 and 12–16. *Journal of Consulting and Clinical Psychology, 47,* 223–233.

Ackerman, S. J., & Hilsenroth, M. J. (2003). A review of therapist characteristics and techniques positively impacting the therapeutic alliance. *Clinical Psychology Review, 23,* 1–33.

Acklin, M. W., et al. (2000). Interobserver agreement, intraobserver reliability, and the Rorschach comprehensive system. *Journal of Personality Assessment, 74,* 15–47.

Addis, M. E. (2002). Methods for disseminating research products and increasing evidence-based practice: Promises, obstacles, and future directions. *Clinical Psychology: Science and Practice, 9,* (pp. 367–378).

Ader, R., Felten, D. L., & Cohen, N. (2001). *Psychoneuroimmunology* (3rd ed.). New York: Academic Press.

Adler, J. (2004, March 8). The war on strokes. *Newsweek,* 42–48.

Agras, W. S., et al. (2000a). A multicenter comparison of cognitive-behavioral therapy and interpersonal psychotherapy for bulimia nervosa. *Archives of General Psychiatry, 57,* 459–466.

Agras, W. S., et al. (2000b). Outcome predictors for the cognitive behavior treatment of bulimia nervosa: Data from a multisite study. *American Journal of Psychiatry, 157,* 1302–1308.

Ahluwalia, J. S., Harris, K. J., Catley, D., Okuyemi, K. S., & Mayo, M. S. (2002). Sustained release bupropion for smoking cessation in African Americans: A randomized controlled trial. *Journal of the American Medical Association, 288,* 468–474.

Ainsworth, M. D. S. (1989). Attachments beyond infancy. *American Psychologist, 44,* 709–716.

Akhtar, A. (1987). Schizoid personality disorder: A synthesis of developmental, dynamic, and descriptive features. *American Journal of Psychotherapy, 41,* 499–517.

Akhtar, S. (1988). Four culture-bound psychiatric syndromes in India. *The International Journal of Social Psychiatry, 34,* 70–74.

Akhtar, S. (2003). Things: Developmental, psychopathological, and technical aspects of inaminate objects. *Canadian Journal of Psychoanalysis, 11,* 1–44.

Alao, A. O., & Dewan, M. J. (2001). Evaluating the tolerability of the newer mood stabilizers. *Journal of Nervous & Mental Disease, 189,* 60–63.

Aldrich, M. S. (1992). Narcolepsy. *Neurology, 42* (7, Suppl. 6), 34–43.

Aleman, A., Kahn, R. S., & Selten, J.-P. (2003). Sex differences in the risk of schizophrenia: Evidence from meta-analysis. *Archives of General Psychiatry, 60,* 565–571.

Allderidge, P. (1979). Hospitals, madhouses and asylums: Cycles in the care of the insane. *British Journal of Psychiatry, 134,* 1476–1478.

Allen, G., & Courchesne, E. (2003). Differential effects of developmental cerebellar abnormality on cognitive and motor functions in the cerebellum: An fMRI study of autism. *American Journal of Psychiatry, 160,* 262–273.

Alloy, L. B., et al. (2000). The Temple-Wisconsin cognitive vulnerability to depression project: Lifetime history of Axis I psychopathology in individuals at high and low cognitive risk for depression. *Journal of Abnormal Psychology, 109,* 403–418.

Alter, J. (2001, February 12). The war on addiction. *Newsweek,* pp. 36–39.

Altman, L. K. (1994, February 22). Stomach microbe offers clues to cancer as well as ulcers. *The New York Times,* p. C3.

Altschuler, E. L., Haroun, A., Ho, B., & Weimer, A. (2001). Did Samson have antisocial personality disorder? *Archives of General Psychiatry, 58,* 202.

Alzheimer's vaccine passes key test. (2001, July 23). *CNN Web Posting.* Retrieved July 25, 2001, from http://www.cnn.com/2001/HEALTH/07/23/alzheimers.vaccine/index.html.

American Cancer Society. (2004). *Questions about smoking, tobacco, and health.* Retrieved May 5, 2004, from http://www.cancer.org/docroot/PED/content/PED_10_2x_Questions_About_Smoking_Tobacco_and_Health.asp

American Law Institute. (1962). Model penal code: Proposed official draft. Philadelphia: Author.

American Psychiatric Association. (1994). *DSM-IV: Diagnostic and statistical manual of mental disorders* (4th ed.). Washington, DC: Author.

American Psychiatric Association. (1998). *Fact sheet: Violence and mental illness.* Washington, DC: Author.

American Psychiatric Association. (2000). *DSM-IV-TR: Diagnostic and statistical manual of mental disorders* (4th ed., Text Revision). Washington, DC: Author.

American Psychological Association. (1978). Report of the Task Force on the Role of Psychology in the Criminal Justice System. *American Psychologist, 33,* 1099–1113.

American Psychological Association (APA) (2002). Ethical principles of psychologists and code of conduct. *American Psychologist, 57,* 1060–1073.

American Psychological Association (2003). A guide for including information on HIV/AIDS in graduate courses in psychology. *APA Online,* Retrieved January 14, 2004 from http://www.apa.org/pi/aids/toc.html.

Amering, M., & Katschnig, H. (1990). Panic attacks and panic disorder in cross-cultural perspective. *Psychiatric Annals, 20,* 511–516.

Ames, M. A., & Houston, D. A. (1990). Legal, social, and biological definitions of pedophilia. *Archives of Sexual Behavior, 19,* 333–342.

Amminger, G. P., Pape, S., Rock, D., Roberts, S. A., Ott, S. L., Squires-Wheeler, E., et al. (1999). Relationship between childhood behavioral disturbance and later schizophrenia in the New York High-Risk Project. *American Journal of Psychiatry, 156,* 525–530.

Ancoli-Israel, S., Klauber, M. R., Butters, N., Parker, L., & Kripke, D. F. (1991). Dementia in institutionalized elderly: Relation to sleep apnea. *Journal of the American Geriatrics Society, 39,* 258–263.

Anderluh, M. B., Tchanturia, K., Rabe-Hesketh, S., & Treasure, J. (2003). Childhood obsessive–compulsive personality traits in adult women with eating disorders: Defining a broader eating disorder phenotype. *American Journal of Psychiatry, 160,* 242–247.

Andersen, B. L. (1992). Psychological interventions for cancer patients to enhance the quality of life. *Journal of Consulting and Clinical Psychology, 60,* 552–568.

Andersen, B. L. (2002). Biobehavioral outcomes following psychological interventions for cancer patients. *Journal of Consulting and Clinical Psychology, 70,* 590–610.

Andersen, B. L., Golden-Kreutz, D. M., & DiLillo, V. (2001). Cancer. In A. Baum, T. A. Revenson, & J. E. Singer (Eds.), *Handbook of health psychology* (pp. 709–726). Mahwah, NJ: Lawrence Erlbaum Associates.

Anderson, D. Q., & Maloney, K. C. (2001). The efficacy of cognitive–behavioral therapy on the core symptoms of bulimia nervosa. *Clinical Psychology Review, 21,* 971–988.

Anderson, E. M., & Lambert, M. J. (1995). Short-term dynamically oriented psychotherapy: A review and meta-analysis. *Clinical Psychology Review, 15,* 503–514.

Anderson, E. M., & Lambert, M. J. (2001). A survival analysis of clinically significant change in outpatient psychotherapy. *Journal of Clinical Psychology, 57,* 875–888.

Anderson, J. W. (2003). "Mr. Psychoanalysis" breaks with Freud. *Contemporary Psychology: APA Review of Books, 48,* 855–857.

Anderson, L. P. (1991). Acculturative stress: A theory of relevance to Black Americans. *Clinical Psychology Review, 11,* 685–702.

Andreasen, A. (2003). From molecule to mind: Genetics, genomics, and psychiatry. *American Journal of Psychiatry, 160,* 613. [Editorial]

Andrews, B., Brewin, C. R., Rose, S., & Kirk, M. (2000). Predicting PTSD symptoms in victims of violent crime: The role of shame, anger, and childhood abuse. *Journal of Abnormal Psychology, 109,* 69–73.

Andrews, E. L. (1997, September 9). In Germany, humble herb is a rival to Prozac. *The New York Times,* pp. C1, C7.

Angier, N. (1991b, August 4). Kids who can't sit still. *The New York Times,* Section 4A, pp. 30–33.

Angier, N. (1999). *Woman: An intimate geography.* Boston: Houghton Mifflin.

Angier, N. (2000a, July 21). Study finds region of brain may be key problem solver. *The New York Times,* pp. C1, C4.

Angier, N. (2000b, November 7). Who is fat? It depends on culture. *The New York Times,* pp. F1–F2.

Angier, N. (2003, February 25). Not just genes: Moving beyond nature vs. nurture. *The New York Times*, pp. F1, F10.

Angold, A., & Costello, E. J. (1993). Depressive comorbidity in children and adolescents: Empirical, theoretical, and methodological issues. *American Journal of Psychiatry, 150*, 1779–1791.

Angold, A., & Costello, J. (1996). Toward establishing an empirical basis for the diagnosis of oppositional defiant disorder. *Journal of the American Academy of Child and Adolescent Psychiatry, 35*, 1205–1212.

Anonymous. (1985, June 13). Schizophrenia—A mother's agony over her son's pain. *Chicago Tribune*, Section 5, pp. 1–3.

Another worry for aging baby boomers—pot and their hearts. (2000, March 3). *CNN Web Posting*. Retrieved March 13, 2000, from www.canoe.ca/Health0003/03_pot.html.

Ansell, B. J. (2001, January 9). Fearing one fate, women ignore a killer. *The New York Times*, p. F8.

Anthony, J. C., & Helzer, J. E. (1991). Syndromes of drug abuse and dependence. In L. N. Robins & D. A. Regier (Eds.), *Psychiatric disorders in America: The Epidemiologic Catchment Area Study* (pp. 116–154). New York: The Free Press.

Anthony, J. C., Warner, L. A., & Kessler, R. C. (1994). Comparative epidemiology of dependence on tobacco, alcohol, controlled substances, and inhalants: Basic findings from the National Comorbidity Survey. *Experimental and Clinical Psychopharmacology, 2*, 244–268.

Anthony, W. A., & Liberman, R. P. (1986). The practice of psychiatric rehabilitation: Historical, conceptual, and research base. *Schizophrenia Bulletin, 12*, 542–559.

Anton, R. F., Moak, D. H., Latham, P., K., Waid, L. R., Malcolm, R. J., Dias, J. K., et al. (2001). Posttreatment results of combining naltrexone with cognitive-behavior therapy for the treatment of alcoholism. *Journal of Clinical Psychopharmacology, 21*, 72–77.

Antonarakas, S. E., et al. (1991). Prenatal origin of the extra chromosome trisomy 21 as indicated by analysis of DNA polymorphisms. *The New England Journal of Medicine, 324*, 872–876.

Antoni, M. H., Levine, J., Tischer, P., Green, C., & Millon, T. (1986). Refining personality assessments by combining MCMI high-point profiles and MMPI codes: IV. MMPI 89/98. *Journal of Personality Assessment, 50*, 65–72.

Anxiety: Most common mental health problem. (2000, February 2). *CNN Web Posting*. Retrieved February 4, 2000, from www.cnn.com/2000/HEALTH/02/02/mental.health.wmd/

Apopolinario, J. C., Bacaltchuk, J., Sichieri, R., Claudino, A. M., Godoy-Matos, A., Morgan, C., et al. (2003). A randomized, double-blind, placebo-controlled study of sibutramine in the treatment of binge-eating disorder. *Archives of General Psychiatry, 60*, 1109–1116.

Appelbaum, P. S. (2003). Dangerous persons, moral panic, and the uses of psychiatry. *Psychiatric Services, 54*, 441–442.

Arango, C., Kirkpatrick, B., &. Buchanan, R. W. (2000). Neurological signs and the heterogeneity of schizophrenia. *American Journal of Psychiatry, 157*, 566–572.

Arbisi, P. A., Ben-Porath, Y., S., & McNulty, J. A. (2002). A comparison of MMPI-2 validity in African American and Caucasian psychiatric inpatients. *Psychological Assessment, 14*, 3–15.

Arena, K., & Frieden, T. (2003, December 17). Judge grants Hinckley unsupervised visits with his parents. CNN Web Posting, Retrieved December 17, 2003, from http://www.cnn.com/2003/LAW/12/17/hinckley.decision/index.html.

Arieti, S. (1974). *Interpretation of schizophrenia* (2nd ed.). New York: Basic Books.

Arnett, P. A. (1997). Autonomic responsivity in psychopaths: A critical review and theoretical proposal. *Clinical Psychology Review, 17*, 903–936.

Arnett, P. A., Smith, S. S., & Newman, J. P. (1997). Approach and avoidance motivation in psychopathic criminal offenders during passive avoidance. *Journal of Personality and Social Psychology, 72*, 1413–1428.

Arnold, L. E., Elliott, M., Sachs, L., Bird, H., Kraemer, H. C., Wells, K. C., et al. (2003). Effects of ethnicity on treatment attendance, stimulant response/dose, and 14-month outcome in ADHD. *Journal of Consulting and Clinical Psychology, 71*, 713–727.

Arnow, B., Kenardy, J., & Agras, W. S. (1992). Binge eating among the obese: A descriptive study. *Journal of Behavioral Medicine, 15*, 155–170.

Arnulf, I., Merino-Andreu, M., Perrier, A., Birolleau, S., Similowski, T., Derenne, J.-P., et al. (2002). Obstructive sleep apnea and venous thromboembolism. *Journal of the American Medical Association, 287.*

Aronson, M. K. (1988). Patients and families: Impact and long-term-management implications. In M. K. Aronson (Ed.), *Understanding Alzheimer's disease* (pp. 74–78). New York: Charles Scribners Sons.

Arseneault, L, et al. (2002). Cannabis use in adolescence and risk for adult psychosis: Longitudinal prospective study. *British Medical Journal, 325*, 1212–1213.

Asaad, G., & Shapiro, B. (1986). Hallucinations: Theoretical and clinical overview. *American Journal of Psychiatry, 143*, 1088–1097.

Asarnow, R. F., et al. (1991). Span of apprehension in schizophrenia. In J. Zubin, S. Steinhauer, & J. Gruzelier (Eds.), *Handbook of schizophrenia: Vol. 5. Neuropsychology, psychophysiology, and information-processing* (pp. 353–370). Amsterdam: Elsevier Science.

Ashton, A. K., Ahrens, K., Gupta, S., & Masand, P. S. (2000). Antidepressant-induced sexual dysfunction and ginkgo biloba. *American Journal of Psychiatry, 157*, 836–837.

Ashton, C. H. (2001). Pharmacology and effects of cannabis: A brief review. *British Journal of Psychiatry, 178*, 101–106.

Attention disorder linked with drug abuse. (2003, August 18). *CNN Web Posting*, Retrieved September 12, 2003, from http://www.cnn.com/2003/HEALTH/parenting/08/18/adhd.study.reut/index.html August 18, 2003 Posted: 2:27 PM EDT (1827 GMT).

Augusto, A., et al. (1996). Post-natal depression in an urban area of Portugal: Comparison of childbearing women and matched controls. *Psychological Medicine, 26*, 135–141.

Ault, A. (2004, February 10). Federal panel hears testimony on vaccinations and autism. *The New York Times*, p. A20.

Auranen, M., Vanhala, R., Varilo, T., Ayers, K., Kempas, E., A, Ylisaukko-oja, T., et al. (2002). Genomewide screen for autism-spectrum disorders: evidence for a major susceptibility locus on chromosome 3q25–27. *American Journal of Human Genetics, 71*, 777–790.

Ayoub, C. C., Alexander, R., Beck, D., et al., & the APSAC Taskforce on Münchausen by Proxy, Definitions Working Group. (2002). Position paper: definitional issues in Münchausen by proxy. *Child Maltreatment, 7*, 105–112.

Azrin, N. H., & Peterson, A. L. (1989). Reduction of an eye tick by controlled blinking. *Behavior Therapy, 20*, 467–473.

B

Bäckman, L., & Forsell, Y. (1994). Episodic memory functioning in a community-based sample of old adults with major depression: Utilization of cognitive support. *Journal of Abnormal Psychology, 103*, 361–370.

Baer, L., Rauch, S. L., Ballantine, H. T., Jr., Martuza, R., Cosgrove, R., Cassem, E., et al. (1995). Cingulotomy for intractable obsessive–compulsive disorder: Prospective long-term follow-up of 18 patients. *Archives of General Psychiatry, 52*, 384–392.

Baer, R. A. (2003). Mindfulness training as a clinical intervention: A conceptual and empirical review. *Clinical Psychology: Science and Practice, 10*, 125–143.

Bagary, M. S., Symms, M. R., Barker, G. J., Mutsatsa, S. H., Joyce, E. M., & Ron, M. A. (2003). Gray and white matter brain abnormalities in first-episode schizophrenia inferred from magnetization transfer imaging. *Archives of General Psychiatry, 60*, 779–788.

Bagby, R. M., Nicholson, R., & Buis, T. (1998). Effectiveness of the MMPI-2 validity indicators. *Journal of Personality Assessment, 70*, 405–415.

Bagge, C., Nickell, A., Steppp, S., Durrett, C., Jackson, K., & Trull, T. J. (2004). Borderline persoanlity disorder features predict negative outcomes 2 years later. *Journal of Abnormal Psychology, 113*, 279–288.

Bagley, C., & D'Augelli, A. R. (2000). Suicidal behaviour in gay, lesbian, and bisexual youth. *British Medical Journal, 320*, 1617–1618.

Bailar, J. C., III. (2001). The powerful placebo and the wizard of Oz. *The New England Journal of Medicine, 344*, 1630–1632.

Bailey, D. S. (2003). The "Sylvia Plath" effect. *Monitor on Psychology, 34*, 42–43.

Bailey, J. M. (1999). Homosexuality and mental illness. *Archives of General Psychiatry, 56*, 883–884.

Bailey, J. M. (2003a). Personal communication.

Bailey, J. M. (2003b). *The man who would be queen: The science of gender-bending and transsexualism*. Washington, DC: Joseph Henry Press.

Bain, J. (2002, April 30). New treatments may help control sleep apnea. *New York Times Online*, Retrieved May 3, 2002, from http://www.nytimes.com/2002/04/30/health/30APNE.html.

Baity, M. R., & Hilsenroth, M. J. (2002). Rorschach aggressive content (AgC) variable: A study of criterion validity. *Journal of Personality Assessment, 78*, 275–287.

Baker, R. C., & Kirschenbaum, D. S. (1993). Self-monitoring may be necessary for successful weight control. *Behavior Therapy, 24*, 377–394.

Baldessarini, R. J., Tohen, M., & Tondo, L. (2000). Maintenance treatment in bipolar disorder. *Archives of General Psychiatry, 57*, 490–492.

Baldessarini, R. J., & Tondo, L. (2000). Does lithium treatment still work? Evidence of stable responses over three decades. *Archives of General Psychiatry, 57*, 187–190.

Baldessarini, R. J., & Tondo, M. D. (2003). Suicide risk and treatments for patients with bipolar disorder. *Journal of the American Medical Association, 290*, 1517–1519.

Baldeweg, T., et al. (1997). Neurophysiological changes associated with psychiatric symptoms in HIV-infected individuals without AIDS. *Biological Psychiatry, 41*, 474–487.

Ballie, R. (2002, January). Kay Redfield Jamison receives $500,000 "genius award." *Monitor on Psychology*, Retrieved March, 15, 2003, from http://www.apa.org/monitor/jan02/redfield.html.

Baltimore, D. (2000, June 25). 50,000 genes, and we know them all (almost). *The New York Times*, Section 4, p. 17.

Bancroft, J., Loftus, J., & Long, J. S. (2003). Distress about sex: A national survey of women in heterosexual relationships. *Archives of Sexual Behavior, 32*, 193–208.

Bandura, A. (1982). Self-efficacy mechanism in human agency. *American Psychologist, 37*, 122–147.

Bandura, A. (1986). *Social foundations of thought and action: A social-cognitive theory*. Englewood Cliffs, NJ: Prentice Hall.

Bandura, A. (2001). Social cognitive theory: An agentic perspective. *Annual Review of Psychology, 52*, 1–26.

Bandura, A. (2004). Swimming against the mainstream: The early years from chilly tributary to transformative mainstream. *Behaviour Research and Therapy, 42*, 613–630.

Bandura, A., Barr-Taylor, C., Williams, S. L., Mefford, I. N., & Barchas, J. D. (1985). Catecholamine secretion as a function of perceived coping self-efficacy. *Journal of Consulting and Clinical Psychology, 53*, 406–414.

Bandura, A., Jeffery, R. W., & Wright, C. L. (1974). Efficacy of participant modeling as a function of response induction aids. *Journal of Abnormal Psychology, 83*, 56–64.

Bandura, A., Ross, S. A., & Ross, D. (1963). Imitation of film-mediated aggressive models. *Journal of Abnormal and Social Psychology, 66*, 3–11.

Barbaree, H. E., & Marshall, W. L. (1991). The role of male sexual arousal in rape: Six models. *Journal of Consulting and Clinical Psychology, 59*, 621–631.

Barber, J., Connolly, M. B., Crits-Christoph, P., Gladis, L., & Siqueland, L. (2000). Alliance predicts patients' outcome beyond in-treatment change in symptoms. *Journal of Consulting and Clinical Psychology, 68*, 1027–1032.

Barber, M. E., et al. (1998). Aborted suicide attempts: A new classification of suicidal behavior. *American Journal of Psychiatry, 155*, 385–389.

Barch, D. M. (2003). Cognition in schizophrenia: does working memory work? *Current Directions in Psychological Science, 12*, 146–150.

Barch, D. M., Carter, C. S., Braver, T. S., Sabb, F. W., MacDonald, A. 3rd, Noll, D. C., et al. (2001). Selective deficits in prefrontal cortex function in medication-naive patients with schizophrenia. *Archives of General Psychiatry, 58*, 280–288.

Bardwell, W. A., Moore, P., Ancoli-Israel, S., & Dimsdale, J. E. (2003). Fatigue in obstructive sleep apnea: Driven by depressive symptoms instead of apnea severity? *American Journal of Psychiatry, 160*, 350–355.

Barefoot, J. C., Mortensen, E. L., Helms, M. J., Avlund, K., & Schroll, M. (2001). A longitudinal study of gender differences in depressive symptoms from age 50 to 80. *Psychology and Aging, 16*, 342–345.

Barkham, M., Rees, A., Stiles, W. B., Shapiro, D. A., Hardy, G. E., & Reynolds, S. (1996). Dose-effect relations in limited psychotherapy for depression. *Journal of Consulting and Clinical Psychology, 64*, 927–935.

Barkley, R. A. (2001). Executive function and ADHD: A reply. *Journal of the American Academy of Child & Adolescent Psychiatry, 40*, 501–502.

Barlow, D. H., Esler, J. L., & Vitali, A. E. (1998). Psychosocial treatments for panic disorders, phobias, and generalized anxiety disorder. In P. E. Nathan & J. M. Gorman (Eds.), *A guide to treatments that work* (pp. 288–318). New York: Oxford University Press.

Barlow, D. H., Gorman, J. M., Shear, K., & Woods, S. W. (2000). Cognitive-behavioral therapy, imipramine, or their combination for panic disorder: A randomized controlled trial. *Journal of the American Medical Association, 283*, 2529–2536.

Barnett, W. S., & Escobar, C. M. (1990). Economic costs and benefits of early intervention. In S. J. Meisels & J. P. Shonkoff (Eds.), *Handbook of early childhood intervention* (pp. 560–582). New York: Cambridge University Press.

Barrett, P. M., et al. (2001). Cognitive-behavioral treatment of anxiety disorders in children: Long-term (6-year) follow-up. *Journal of Consulting and Clinical Psychology, 69*, 135–141.

Barron, J., & Barron, S. (2002). *There's a boy in here.* Arlington, TX: Future Horizons.

Barrowclough, C., Tarrier, N., Humphreys, L., Ward, J., Gregg, L., & Andrews, B. (2003). Self-esteem in schizophrenia: relationships between self-evaluation, family attitudes, and symptomatology. *Journal of Abnormal Psychology, 112*, 92–99.

Barry, C. T., et al. (2000). The importance of callous–unemotional traits for extending the concept of psychopathy to children. *Journal of Abnormal Psychology, 109*, 335–340.

Barry, D. T., & Grilo, C. M. (2002). Cultural, psychological, and demographic correlates of willingness to use psychological services among East Asian immigrants. *Journal of Nervous & Mental Disease, 190*, 32–39.

Barsky, A. J., & Ahern, D. K. (2004). Cognitive behavior therapy for hypochondriasis: A randomized controlled trial. *Journal of the American Medical Association, 291*, 1464–1470.

Barsky, A. J., Ahern, D. K., Bailey, E. D., Saintfort, R., Liu, E. B., & Peekna, H. M. (2001). Hypochondriacal patients'

appraisal of health and physical risks. *American Journal of Psychiatry, 158*, 783 787.

Barsky, A. J., Fama, J. M., Bailey, E. D., & Ahern, D. K. (1998). A prospective 4- to 5-year study of *DSM-III-R* hypochondriasis. *Archives of General Psychiatry, 55*, 737–744.

Barsky, A. J., Wool, C., Barnett, M. C., & Cleary, P. D. (1994). Histories of childhood trauma in adult hypochondriacal patients. *American Journal of Psychiatry, 151*, 397–401.

Barsky, A. J., Wyshak, G., & Klerman, G. L. (1992). Psychiatric comorbidity in *DSM-III-R* hypochondriasis. *Archives of General Psychiatry, 49*, 101–108.

Basch, M. F. (1980). *Doing psychotherapy.* New York: Basic Books.

Basile, K. C. (2002). Attitudes toward wife rape: Effects of social background and victim status. *Violence & Victims, 17*(3), 341–354.

Bateman, A. B., & Fonagy, P. (2001). Treatment of borderline personality disorder with psychoanalytically oriented partial hospitalization: An 18-month follow-up. *American Journal of Psychiatry, 158*, 36–42.

Bateson, G. D., Jackson, D., Haley, J., & Weakland, J. (1956). Toward a theory of schizophrenia. *Behavioral Science, 1*, 251–264.

Battaglia, M., Bernardeschi, L., Franchini, L., Bellodi, L., & Smeraldi, E. (1995). A family study of schizotypal disorder. *Schizophrenia Bulletin, 21*, 33–45.

Bauchner, H. (2003, December 23). Response to medication differs for ADHD subtypes. *Journal Watch Psychiatry,* Retrieved December 24, 2003, from http://psychiatry.jwatch.org/cgi/content/full/2003/1223/10?q=etoc.

Bauer, A. Rosca, P., Khawalled, R., Gruzniewski, A., & Grinshpoon, A. (2003). Dangerousness and risk assessment: the state of the art. *Israeli Journal of Psychiatry and Related Sciences, 40*, 182–190.

Baumeister, R. F., Catanese, K. R., & Vohs, K. D. (2001). Is there a gender difference in strength of sex drive? Theoretical views, conceptual distinctions, and a review of relevant evidence. *Personality & Social Psychology Review, 5*(3), 242–273.

Baumeister, R. F., Catanese, K. R., & Wallace, H. M. (2002). Conquest by force: A narcissistic reactance theory of rape and sexual coercion. *Review of General Psychology, 6*, 92–135.

Baxter, L. R., Jr. (2003). Basal ganglia systems in ritualistic social displays: Reptiles and humans; function and illness. *Physiology and Behavior, 79*, 451–460.

Bayer, B. A., Bubel, D., Jacobs, S. R., Knolls, M. L., Harwell, V. D., et al. (2002). Posttraumatic stress in women with breast cancer and their daughters. *American Journal of Family Therapy, 30*, 323–338.

Bazell, R. (2000, August 29). Cause of narcolepsy pinpointed. *MSNBC Web Posting.* Retrieved August 29, 2000, from http://www.msnbc.com/news/452884.asp.

Bazell, R., The Associated Press, & Reuters (2002, August 7). Hunger hormone may fight obesity: Natural chemical shown to make people feel full in buffet experiment. *MSNBC Web Posting.* Retrieved August 9, 2002, from http://www.msnbc.com/news/791118.asp.

Bean, J. L. (2002). Expressions of female sexuality. *Journal of Sex & Marital Therapy, 28*(Suppl 1), 29–38.

Beardslee, W. R., & Goldman, S. (2003, September 22). Living beyond sadness. *Newsweek,* 70.

Beauvais, F. (1998). American Indians and alcohol. *Alcohol Health and Research World, 22*, 253–259.

Bechtoldt, H., Norcross, J. C., Wyckoff, L. A., Pokrywa, M. L., Campbell, L. F., et al. (2001, Winter). Theoretical orientations and employment settings of clinical and counseling psychologists: A comparative study. *The Clinical Psychologist, 54*, 3–6.

Beck, A. T. (1976). *Cognitive therapy and the emotional disorders.* New York: International Universities Press.

Beck, A. T., & Clark, D. A. (1997). An information processing model of anxiety: Automatic and strategic processes. *Behaviour Research and Therapy, 35*, 49–58.

Beck, A. T., Brown, G., Steer, R. A., Eidelson, J. I., & Riskind, J. H. (1987). Differentiating anxiety and depression: A test of the cognitive content-specificity hypothesis. *Journal of Abnormal Psychology, 96*, 179–183.

Beck, A. T., et al. (1990). Relationship between hopelessness and ultimate suicide: A replication with psychiatric outpatients. *American Journal of Psychiatry, 147*, 190–195.

Beck, A. T., Freeman, A., Davis, D. D., & Associates. (2003). *Cognitive therapy of personality disorders.* (2nd ed.). New York: Guilford.

Beck, A. T., Rush, A. J., Shaw, B. F., & Emery, G. (1979). *Cognitive therapy of depression.* New York: Guilford Press.

Beck, A. T., & Young, J. E. (1985). Depression. In D. H. Barlow (Ed.), *Clinical handbook of psychological disorders* (pp. 206–244). New York: Guilford Press.

Becker, D., & Lamb, S. (1994). Sex bias in the diagnosis of borderline personality disorder and posttraumatic stress disorder. *Professional Psychology: Research and Practice, 25*, 55–61.

Begley, S. (1995, November 20). Lights of madness. *Newsweek,* pp. 76–77.

Begley, S. (2001b, June 11). How it all starts inside your brain. *Newsweek,* pp. 40–42.

Behrman, A. (2002). *Electroboy: A memoir of mania.* New York: Random House.

Being fat at 40 cuts years off life (2003, January 6). *CNN Web Posting,* Retrieved January 8, 2003, from http://www.cnn.com/2003n/HEALTH/diet.fitness/01/-06/obesity.mortality/index.html.

Beitman, B. D., Goldfried, M. R., & Norcross, J. C. (1989). The movement toward integrating the psychotherapies: An overview. *American Journal of Psychiatry, 146*, 138–147.

Bell, A. P., & Weinberg, M. S. (1978). *Homosexualities: A study of diversity among men and women.* New York: Simon & Schuster.

Bell, M., Bryson, G., Wexler, B. E. (2003). Cognitive remediation of working memory deficits: durability of training effects in severely impaired and less severely impaired schizophrenia. *Acta Psychiatrica Scandinavica, 108*, 101–109.

Bellack, A. S., & Mueser, K. T. (1990). Schizophrenia. In A. S. Bellack, M. Hersen, & A. E. Kazdin (Eds.), *International handbook of behavior modification and therapy* (2nd ed., pp. 353–370). New York: Plenum Press.

Bellack, A. S., & Mueser, K. T. (1993). Psychosocial treatment for schizophrenia. *Schizophrenia Bulletin, 19*, 317–336.

Bellack, A. S., Schooler, N. R., Marder, S. R., Kane, J. M., Brown, C. H., & Yang, Y. (2004). Do clozapine and risperidone affect social competence and problem solving? *American Journal of Psychiatry, 161*, 364–367.

Belluck, P. (2003, February 9). Methadone, once the way out, suddenly grows as a killer drug. *The New York Times,* pp. A1, A30.

Benazon, N. R. (2000). Predicting negative spousal attitudes toward depressed persons: A test of Coyne's interpersonal model. *Journal of Abnormal Psychology, 109*, 500–554.

Bender, L. (1938). A visual motor gestalt test and its clinical use. *Research Monograph of the American Orthopsychiatric Association, 3, XI*, 176.

Benjamin, L., & Wonderlich, S. A. (1994). Social perceptions and borderline personality disorder: The relation to mood disorders. *Journal of Abnormal Psychology, 103*, 610–624.

Bennett, D. (1985). Rogers: More intuition in therapy. *APA Monitor, 16*, p. 3.

Benowitz, N. L. (2002). Smoking cessation trials targeted to racial and economic minority groups. *New England Journal of Medicine, 344*, 1351–1357.

Benson, H. (1975). *The relaxation response.* New York: Morrow.

Benson, H., Manzetta, B. R., & Rosner, B. (1973). Decreased systolic blood pressure in hypertensive subjects who practiced meditation. *Journal of Clinical Investigation, 52*, 8.

Bentall, R. P. (1990). The illusion of reality: A review and integration of psychological research on hallucinations. *Psychological Bulletin, 107,* 82–95.

Bentall, R. P., Haddock, G., & Slade, P. (1994). Cognitive behavior therapy for persistent auditory hallucinations: From theory to therapy. *Behavior Therapy, 25,* 51–66.

Berenbaum, H., & Fujita, F. (1994). Schizophrenia and personality: Exploring the boundaries and connections between vulnerability and outcome. *Journal of Abnormal Psychology, 103,* 148–158.

Berenbaum, H., & Oltmanns, T. F. (1990). Emotional experience and expression in schizophrenia and depression. *Journal of Abnormal Psychology, 101,* 37–44.

Bergem, A. L. M., et al. (1997). Heredity in late-onset Alzheimer's disease and vascular dementia. *Archives of General Psychiatry, 54,* 264–270.

Bergner, R. M. (1997). What is psychopathology? And so what? *Clinical Psychology: Science and Practice, 4,* 235–248.

Berlin, I. N. (1987). Effects of changing Native American cultures on child development. *Journal of Community Psychology, 15,* 299–306.

Berman, J. R., Berman, L. A., Lin, H., Flaherty, E., Lahey, N., Goldstein, I., & Cantey-Kiser, J. (2001). Effect of sildenafil on subjective and physiologic parameters of the female sexual response in women with sexual arousal disorder. *Journal of Sex & Marital Therapy, 27*(5), 411–420.

Berman, J. R., Berman, L. A., Toler, S. M., Gill, J., Haughie, S., & Sildenafil Study Group. (2003). Safety and efficacy of sildenafil citrate for the treatment of female sexual arousal disorder: A double-blind, placebo controlled study. *Journal of Urology, 170,* 2333–2338.

Berman, L. A. (2000). Cited in "Women, too, may benefit from Viagra." (2000, May 1). *CNN Web Posting.* Retrieved February 23, 2004, from http://www.cnn.com/2000/HEALTH/women/05/01/women.sex.function/

Berman, S. L., et al. (2000). Predictors of outcome in exposure-based cognitive and behavioral treatments for phobic and anxiety disorders in children. *Behavior Therapy, 31,* 713–731.

Bernstein, D. P., et al. (1996). Childhood antecedents of adolescent personality disorders. *American Journal of Psychiatry, 153,* 907–913.

Bernstein, E. M., & Putnam, F. W. (1986). Development, reliability, and validity of a dissociation scale. *The Journal of Nervous and Mental Disease, 174,* 727–735.

Bernstein, R. L., & Gaw, A. C. (1990). Koro: Proposed classification for *DSM-IV. American Journal of Psychiatry, 147,* 1670–1674.

Bertram, L., Blacker, D., Mullin, K., Keeney, D., Jones, J., Basu, S., Yhu, S., et al. (2000). Evidence for genetic linkage of Alzheimer's disease to chromosome 10q. *Science, 290,* 2302–2303.

Beutler, L. E., Harwood, T. M., & Caldwell, R. (2001). Cognitive-behavioral therapy and psychotherapy integration. In K. S. Dobson (Ed.), *Handbook of cognitive-behavioral therapies* (2nd ed., pp. 138–170). New York: Guilford Press.

Bick, P. A., & Kinsbourne, M. (1987). Auditory hallucinations and subvocal speech in schizophrenic patients. *American Journal of Psychiatry, 144,* 222–225.

Bickel, W. K., et al. (1997). Effects of adding behavioral treatment to opioid detoxification with buprenorphine. *Journal of Consulting and Clinical Psychology, 65,* 803–810.

Biederman, J. (2003, August). *Current concepts on the pharmacotherapy of ADHD.* Paper presented at the meeting of the American Psychological Association, Toronto, CA.

Biederman, J., Faraone, S., Milberger, S., Guite, J., Mick, E., Chen, L., & Mennin, D. (1996b). A prospective 4-year follow-up study of attention-deficit hyperactivity and related disorders. *Archives of General Psychiatry, 53,* 437–446.

Biederman, J., Faraone, S., Milberger, S., Jetton, J. G., Chen, L., Mick, E. et al. (1996a). Is childhood oppositional de-fiant disorder a precursor to adolescent conduct disorder? Findings from a four-year follow-up study of children with ADHD. *Journal of the American Academy of Child and Adolescent Psychiatry, 35,* 1193–1204.

Biever, J. L., Castaño, M. T., de las Fuentes, C., González, C., Servín-López, S., Sprowls, C., et al. (2002). The role of language in training psychologists to work with Hispanic clients. *Professional Psychology: Research and Practice, 33,* 330–336.

Bigler, E. D., & Ehrenfurth, J. W. (1981). The continued inappropriate singular use of the Bender Visual Motor Gestalt Test. *Professional Psychology, 12,* 562–569.

Binder, R. L. (1999). Are the mentally ill dangerous? *Journal of the American Academy of Psychiatry and the Law, 27,* 189–201.

Binder, R. L., & McNiel, D. E. (1996). Application of the Tarasoff ruling and its effect on the victim and the therapeutic relationship. *Psychiatric Services, 47,* 1212–1215.

Biran, M. (1988). Cognitive and exposure treatment for agoraphobia: Re-examination of the outcome research. *Journal of Cognitive Psychotherapy: An International Quarterly, 2,* 165–178.

Birchwood, M., Cochrane, R., Macmillan, F., Copestake, S., Kucharska, J., & Carriss, M. (1992). The influence of ethnicity and family structure on relapse in first-episode schizophrenia: A comparison of Asian, Afro-Caribbean, and White patients. *British Journal of Psychiatry, 161,* 783–790.

Birnbaum, M. H., Martin, H., & Thomann, K. (1996). Visual function in multiple personality disorder. *Journal of the American Optometric Association, 67,* 327–334.

Blackman, S. J. (1996). Has drug culture become an inevitable part of youth culture? A critical assessment of drug education. *Educational Review, 48,* 131–142.

Blair, R. J. R., Mitchell, D. G. V., Richell, R., Kelly, S., Leonard, A., Newman, C., et al. (2002). Turning a deaf ear to fear: Impaired recognition of vocal affect in psychopathic individuals. *Journal of Abnormal Psychology, 111,* 682–686.

Blais, M. A., et al. (2001). Predicting *DSM-IV* cluster B personality disorder criteria from MMPI-2 and Rorschach data: A test of incremental validity. *Journal of Personality Assessment, 76,* 150–168.

Blakeslee, S. (1997a, June 27). Brain studies tie marijuana to other drugs. *The New York Times,* p. A16.

Blanchard, E. B., Appelbaum, K. A., Radnitz, C. L. & Morrill, B. et al. (1990). A controlled evaluation of thermal biofeedback and thermal feedback combined with cognitive therapy in the treatment of vascular headache. *Journal of Consulting and Clinical Psychology, 58,* 216–224.

Blanchard, E. B., & Diamond, S. (1996). Psychological treatment of benign headache disorders. *Professional Psychology, 27,* 541–547.

Blanchard, E. B., & Hickling, E. J. (2004). *After the crash: Psychological assessment and treatment of survivors of motor vehicle accidents* (2nd ed.). Washington, DC: American Psychological Association.

Blanchard, E. B., Hickling, E. J., Devineni, T., Veazey, C. H., & Galovski, T. E. (2003). A controlled evaluation of cognitive behavioral therapy for posttraumatic stress in motor vehicle accident survivors. *Behavior Research and Therapy, 41,* 79–96.

Blanchard, R., & Hucker, S. J. (1991). Age, transvestism, bondage, and concurrent paraphilic activities in 117 fatal cases of autoerotic asphyxia. *British Journal of Psychiatry, 159,* 371–377.

Blanker, M. H., Bosch, J. L., Groeneveld, E. P., Bohnen, A. M., Prins, A., Thomas, S., et al. (2001). Erectile and ejaculatory dysfunction in a community-based sample of men 50 to 78 years old: prevalence, concern, and relation to sexual activity. *Urology, 57,* 763–768.

Blankstein, K. R., & Segal, Z. V. (2001). Cognitive assessment: Issues and methods. In K. S. Dobson (Ed.), *Handbook of cognitive-behavioral therapies* (2nd ed., pp. 40–85). New York: Guilford Press.

Blatt, S. J., et al. (1998). When and how perfectionism impedes the brief treatment of depression: Further analyses of the National Institute of Mental Health Treatment of Depression Collaborative Research Program. *Journal of Consulting and Clinical Psychology, 66,* 423–428.

Bliss, E. L., & Jeppsen, E. A. (1985). Prevalence of multiple personality among inpatients and outpatients. *American Journal of Psychiatry, 142,* 250–251.

Bloom, J. D., & Rogers, J. L. (1987). The legal basis of forensic psychiatry: Statutorily mandated psychiatric diagnosis. *American Journal of Psychiatry, 144,* 847–853.

Blowers, L. C., Loxton, N. J., Grady-Flesser, M., Occhipinti, S., & Dawe, S. (2003). The relationship between sociocultural pressure to be thin and body dissatisfaction in preadolescent girls. *Eating Behaviors, 4,* 229–244.

Blumberg, H. P., Kaufman, J., Martin, A., Whiteman, R., Zhang, J. H., Gore, J. C., et al. (2003). Amygdala and hippocampal volumes in adolescents and adults with bipolar disorder. *Archives of General Psychiatry, 60,* 1201–1208.

Boles, S. M., & Miottoa, K. (2003). Substance abuse and violence: A review of the literature. *Aggression and Violent Behavior, 8,* 155–174.

Bolton, P. (2001). Cross-cultural validity and reliability testing of a standard psychiatric assessment instrument without a gold standard. *Journal of Nervous & Mental Disease, 189,* 238–242.

Bolton, P., Bass, J., Neugebauer, R., Verdeli, H., Clougherty, K. F., Wickramaratne, P., Speelman, L., et al. (2003). Group interpersonal psychotherapy for depression in rural Uganda: A randomized controlled trial. *Journal of the American Medical Association, 289,* 3117–3124.

Bondareff, W., Alpert, M., Friedhoff, A. J., Richter, E. M., Clary, C. M., & Batzar, E. (2000). Comparison of sertraline and nortriptyline in the treatment of major depressive disorder in late life. *American Journal of Psychiatry, 157,* 745–750.

Bongar, B. (2002). *The suicidal patient: Clinical and legal standards of care* (2nd ed.). Washington, DC: American Psychological Association.

Bonifati, V., Rizzu, P., van Baren, M. J., Schaap, O., Breedveld, G. J., Krieger, E. et al. (2003). Mutations in the DJ-1 Gene associated with autosomal recessive early-onset Parkinsonism. *Science, 299,* 256–258.

Bonné, J. (2001, February 6). Meth's deadly buzz. *MSNBC.com Special Report.* Retrieved February 8, 2001, from http://www.msnbc.com/news/510835.asp?bt=nm&btu=http://www.msnbc.com/tools/newstools/d/news_menu.asp&cp1=1.

Bookheimer, S. Y., Strojwas, M. H., Cohen, M. S., Saunders, A. M., Pericak-Vance, M. A., Mazziotta, J. C., et al. (2000). Patterns of brain activation in people at risk for Alzheimer's disease. *The New England Journal of Medicine, 343,* 450–456.

Boren, T., Faulk, P., Roth, K. A., Larson, G., & Normark, S. (1993). Attachment of *Helicobacter pylori* to human gastric epithelium mediated by blood group antigens. *Science, 262,* 1892–1895.

Borkovec, T. D., Newman, M. G., Pincus, A. L., & Lytle, R. (2002). A component analysis of cognitive-behavioral therapy for generalized anxiety disorder and role of interpersonal problems. *Journal of Consulting and Clinical Psychology, 70,* 288–298.

Bornstein, R. F. (1992). The dependent personality: Developmental, social, and clinical perspectives. *Psychological Bulletin, 112,* 3–23.

Bornstein, R. F. (1993). *The dependent personality.* New York: The Guilford Press.

Bornstein, R. F. (1997). Dependent personality disorder in the *DSM-IV* and beyond. *Clinical Psychology: Science and Practice, 4,* 175–187.

Bornstein, R. F. (1999). Dependent and histrionic personality disorders. In T. Millon, et al. (Eds.), *Oxford textbook of psychopathology. Oxford textbooks in clinical psychology, Vol. 4* (pp. 535–554). New York: Oxford University Press.

Boskind-White, M., & White, W. C. (1983). *Bulimarexia: The binge-purge cycle.* New York: W. W. Norton.

Bostwick, J. M., & Pankratz, V. S. (2000). Affective disorders and suicide risk: A reexamination. *American Journal of Psychiatry,* 157, 1925–1932.

Botelho, R. J., & Richmond, R. (1996). Secondary prevention of excessive alcohol use: Assessing the prospects of implementation. *Family Practice, 13,* 182–193.

Bouchard, C., Rhéaume, J., & Ladouceur, R. (1999). Responsibility and perfectionism in OCD: An experimental study. *Behaviour Research & Therapy, 37,* 239–248.

Bouchard, S., et al. (1996). Cognitive restructuring in the treatment of psychotic symptoms in schizophrenia: A critical analysis. *Behavior Therapy, 27,* 257–277.

Boudouris, J. (2000). The insanity defense in Polk County, Iowa. *American Journal of Forensic Psychology, 18,* 41–79.

Bouwer, C., & Stein, D. J. (1997). Association of panic disorder with a history of traumatic suffocation. *American Journal of Psychiatry, 154,* 1566–1570.

Bowden, C. L., Calabrese, J. R., Sachs, G., Yatham, L. N., Asghar, S. A., Hompland, M., et al. (2003). A placebo-controlled 18-month trial of lamotrigine and lithium maintenance treatment in recently manic or hypomanic patients with bipolar I disorder. *Archives of General Psychiatry, 60,* 392–400.

Bowden, C. L., Calabrese, J. R., McElroy, S. L., Gyulai, L., Wassef, A., Petty, F, et al. (2000). A randomized, placebo-controlled 12-month trial of divalproex and lithium in treatment of outpatients with bipolar I disorder. *Archives of General Psychiatry, 57,* 481–489.

Bowers, T. G., & Clum, G. A. (1988). Relative contribution of specific and nonspecific treatment effects: Meta-analysis of placebo-controlled behavior therapy research. *Psychological Bulletin, 103,* 315–323.

Bowlby, J. (1988). *A secure base.* New York: Basic Books.

Boyd-Franklin, N. (1989). *Black families in therapy: A multisystems approach.* New York: Guilford Press.

Boyle, M. H., Offord, D. R., Racine, Y. A., Szatmari, P., Fleming, J. E., & Links, P. S. (1992). Predicting substance use in late adolescence: Results from the Ontario Child Health Study Follow-up. *American Journal of Psychiatry, 149,* 761–767.

Boyles, S. (2002, July 10). Are antidepressants effective? *WebMD Web Posting,* Retrieved July 12, 2002, from http://my.webmd.com/condition_center_content/mhl/article/1663.53542.

Braaten, E. B., & Rosén, L. E. (2000). Self-regulation of affect in attention deficit–hyperactivity disorder (ADHD) and non-ADHD boys: Differences in empathic responding. *Journal of Consulting and Clinical Psychology, 68,* 313–321.

Braddock, D. (1992). Community mental health and mental retardation services in the United States: A comparative study of resource allocation. *American Journal of Psychiatry, 149,* 175–183.

Bradford, J. M. W. (2001). The neurobiology, neuropharmacology, and pharmacological treatment of the paraphilias and compulsive sexual behaviour. *Canadian Journal of Psychiatry, 46(1)* 26–34.

Bradley, J. D. D., & Golden, C. J. (2001). Biological contributions to the presentation and understanding of attention-deficit/hyperactivity disorder: A review. *Clinical Psychology Review, 21,* 907–929.

Bradley, R. G., & Follingstad, D. R. (2001). Utilizing disclosure in the treatment of the sequelae of childhood sexual abuse. A theoretical and empirical review. *Clinical Psychology Review, 21,* 1–32.

Brady, K., Pearlstein, T., Asnis, G. M., Baker, D., Rothbaum, B., Sikes, C. R., & Farfel, G. M. (2000). Efficacy and safety of sertraline treatment of posttraumatic stress disorder: A randomized controlled trial. *Journal of the American Medical Association, 283,* 1837–1844.

Braff, D. L. (1993). Information processing and attention dysfunction in schizophrenia. *Schizophrenia Bulletin, 19,* 233–259.

Bramon, E., & Sham, P. C. (2001). The common genetic liability between schizophrenia and bipolar disorder: A review. *Current Psychiatry Reports, 3,* 332–337.

Branson, R., Potoczna, N., Kral, J. G., Lentes, K-U., Hoehe, M. R., et al. (2003). Binge eating as a major phenotype of melanocortin 4 receptor gene mutations. *New England Journal of Medicine, 348,* 1096–1103.

Braswell, L., & Kendall, P. C. (2001). Cognitive-behavioral therapy with youth. In K. S. Dobson (Ed.), *Handbook of cognitive-behavioral therapies* (2nd ed., pp. 246–294). New York: The Guilford Press.

Braun, B. G. (Ed.). (1986). *Treatment of multiple personality disorder.* Washington, DC: American Psychiatric Press.

Braun, S. (2001, Spring). Seeking insight by prescription. *Cerebrum,* pp. 10–21.

Breaux, C., Matsuoka, J. K., & Ryujin, D. H. (1995, August). *National utilization of mental health services by Asian/ Pacific Islanders.* Paper presented at the meeting of the American Psychological Association, New York, NY.

Breier, J. I., Simos, P. G., Fletcher, J. M., Castillo, E. M., Zhang, W., & Papanicolaou, A. C. (2003). Abnormal activation of temporoparietal language areas during phonetic analysis in children with dyslexia. *Neuropsychology, 17,* 610–621.

Breitner, J. C. S., & Zandi, P. P. (2001). Do nonsteroidal antiinflammatory drugs reduce the risk of Alzheimer's disease? *New England Journal of Medicine, 345,* 1567–1568.

Bremmer, J. D., Southwick, S., M., Darnell, A., & Charney, D. S. (1996). Chronic PTSD in Vietnam combat veterans: Course of illness and substance abuse. *American Journal of Psychiatry, 153,* 369–375.

Bremmer, J. D., Vythilingam, M., Ng, C. K., Vermetten, E., Nazeer, A., Oren, D. A., et al. (2003). Regional brain metabolic correlates of -methylparatyrosine–induced depressive symptoms implications for the neural circuitry of depression. *Journal of the American Medical Association, 289,* 3125–3134.

Brenda, W. J. H., et al. (1998). Depressive symptoms and physical decline in community-dwelling older persons. *Journal of the American Medical Association, 279,* 1720–1726.

Brent, D. A., Oquendo, M., Birmaher, B., Greenhill, L., Kolko D, Stanley, B. et al. (2002). Familial pathways to early-onset suicide attempt: Risk for suicidal behavior in offspring of mood-disordered suicide attempters. *Archives of General Psychiatry, 59,* 801–807.

Breslau, N., Johnson, E. O, Hiripi, E., & Kessler, R. (2001). Nicotine dependence in the United States: Prevalence, trends, and smoking persistence. *Archives of General Psychiatry, 58,* 810–816.

Breslau, N., Peterson, E. L., Schultz, L. R., Chilcoat, H. D., & Andreski, P. (1998). Major depression and stages of smoking: A longitudinal investigation. *Archives of General Psychiatry, 55,* 161–166.

Breslau, N., Roth, T, Rosenthal, L., & Andreski, P. (1996). Sleep disturbance and psychiatric disorders: A longitudinal epidemiological study of young adults. *Biological Psychiatry, 39,* 411–418.

Breslow, N. (1989). Sources of confusion in the study and treatment of sadomasochism. *Journal of Social Behavior and Personality, 4,* 263–274.

Brewin, C. R., Andrews, B., & Valentine, J. D. (2000). Meta-analysis of risk factors for posttraumatic stress disorder in trauma-exposed adults. *Journal of Consulting and Clinical Psychology, 68,* 748–766.

Brody, J. E. (1990, June 7). A search to bar retardation in a new generation. *The New York Times,* p. B9.

Brody, J. E. (1993, December 15). Living with a common genetic abnormality. *The New York Times,* p. C17.

Brody, J. E. (1996, November 20). Controlling anger is good medicine for the heart. *The New York Times,* p. C15.

Brody, J. E. (1997, March 26). Race and weight. *The New York Times,* p. C8.

Brody, J. E. (2000, May 16). Cybersex gives birth to a psychological disorder. *The New York Times,* pp. F7, F11.

Brody, J. E. (2002, December 24). Adolescent angst or a deeper disorder? Tips for spotting serious symptoms. *The New York Times,* p. F5.

Broussard, B. A., Johnson, A., Himes, J. H., Story, M., Fichtner, R., Hauck, F., et al. (1991). Prevalence of obesity in American Indians and Alaska Natives. *American Journal of Clinical Nutrition, 53* (6 Suppl.), 1535S–1542S.

Brown, D. R., Ahmed, F., Gary, L. E., & Milburn, N. G. (1995). Major depression in a community sample of African Americans. *American Journal of Psychiatry,* 373–378.

Brown, G. K., Beck, A. T., Steer, R. A., & Grisham, J. R. (2000). Risk factors for suicide in psychiatric outpatients: A 20-year prospective study. *Journal of Consulting and Clinical Psychology, 68,* 371–377.

Brown, K. W., & Ryan, R. M. (2003). The benefits of being present: Mindfulness and its role in psychological well-being. *Journal of Personality and Social Psychology, 84,* 822–848.

Brown, L. S. (1992). A feminist critique of the personality disorders. In L. Brown & M. Balou (Eds.), *Personality and psychopathology: Feminist reappraisals* (pp. 206–228). New York: Guilford Press.

Brown, L. S. (1997, November). Recovered memories of abuse: Research and clinical update. *Clinician's Research Digest, Supplemental Bulletin, 17,* 1–2.

Brown, M. Z., Comtois, K. A., & Linehan, M. M. (2002). Reasons for suicide attempts and nonsuicidal self-injury in women with borderline personality disorder. *Journal of Abnormal Psychology, 111,* 198–202.

Brown, S. L., & Forth, A. E. (1997). Psychopathy and sexual assault: Static risk factors, emotional precursors, and rapist subtypes. *Journal of Consulting and Clinical Psychology, 65,* 848–857.

Brown, T. A., Di Nardo, P. A., Lehman, C. L., & Campbell, L. A. (2001). Reliability of *DSM–IV* anxiety and mood disorders: Implications for the classification of emotional disorders. *Journal of Abnormal Psychology, 110,* 49–58.

Brownell, K. D., & Wadden, T. A. (1992). Etiology and treatment of obesity: Understanding a serious, prevalent, and refractory disorder. *Journal of Consulting and Clinical Psychology, 60,* 505–517.

Bruce, M. L., McAvay, G J., Raue, P. J., Brown, E. L., Meyers, B. S., Keohane, D. J., et al. (2002). Major depression in elderly home health care patients. *American Journal of Psychiatry, 159,* 1367–1374.

Bruce, M. L., Ten Have, T. R., Reynolds, C. F., III, Katz, I. I., Schulberg, H. C., Mulsant, B. H., Brown, G. K., et al. (2004). Reducing suicidal ideation and depressive symptoms in depressed older primary care patients: A randomized controlled trial. *Journal of the American Medical Association, 291,* 1081–1091.

Bruch, H. (1973). *Eating disorders: Obesity, anorexia and the person within.* New York: Basic Books.

Bruch, M. A. (1997). Positive thoughts or cognitive balance as a moderator of the negative life events–dysphoria relationship: A reexamination. *Cognitive Therapy and Research, 21,* 25–38.

Brun, A. (1996). Frontal lobe degeneration of non-Alzheimer type. *Acta Neurologica Scandinavica Supplementum, 168,* 28–30.

Bryant, R. A. (2001). Posttraumatic stress disorder and traumatic brain injury: Can they co-exist? *Clinical Psychology Review, 21,* 931–948.

Bryant, R. A., Moulds, M. L., Guthrie, R. M., Dang, S. T., & Nixon , R. D. V. (2003). Imaginal exposure alone and imaginal exposure with cognitive restructuring in treatment of posttraumatic stress disorder. *Journal of Consulting and Clinical Psychology, 71,* 706–712.

Buchanan, A. (1999). Risk and dangerousness. *Psychological Medicine, 29,* 465–473.

Buchanan, R. W., & Carpenter, W. T., Jr. (1997). The neuroanatomies of schizophrenia. *Schizophrenia Bulletin, 23,* 367–372.

Buchanan, T., (2002). Online assessment: Desirable or dangerous? *Professional Psychology: Research and Practice, 33,* No. 2, 148–154.

Buhlmann, U., McNally, R. J., Wilhelm, S., & Florin, I. (2002). Selective processing of emotional information in body dysmorphic disorder. *Journal of Anxiety Disorders, 16,* 289–298.

Bunney, W. E., Bunney, B. G., Vawter, M. P., Tomita, H., Li, J., Evans, S. J., et al. (2003). Microarray technology: A review of new strategies to discover candidate vulnerability genes in psychiatric disorders. *American Journal of Psychiatry, 160,* 657–666.

Buriel, R., Calzada, S., & Vazquez, R. (1982). The relationship of traditional Mexican American culture to adjustment and delinquency among three generations of Mexican American male adolescents. *Hispanic Journal of Behavioral Sciences, 4,* 41–55.

Burns, D. D. (1980). *Feeling good: The new mood therapy.* New York: Morris.

Burns, D. D., & Beck, A. T. (1978). Modification of mood disorders. In J. P. Foreyt & D. P. Rathjen (Eds.), *Cognitive behavior therapy: Research and application* (pp. 109–134). New York: Plenum Press.

Burns, D. D., & Nolen-Hoeksema, S. (1992). Therapeutic empathy and recovery from depression in cognitive-behavioral therapy: A structural equation model. *Journal of Consulting and Clinical Psychology, 60,* 441–449.

Burros, M. (1994, July 17). Despite awareness of risks, more in U.S. are getting fat. *The New York Times,* pp. A1, A8.

Burton, N., & Lane, R. C. (2001). The relational treatment of dissociative identity disorder. *Clinical Psychology Review, 21,* 301–320.

Bushman, B. J., Bonacci, A. M., van Dijk, M., & Baumeister, R. F. (2003). Narcissism, sexual refusal, and aggression: Testing a narcissistic reactance model of sexual coercion. *Journal of Personality and Social Psychology, 84,* 1027–1040.

Busseri, M. A., & Tyler, J. D. (2003). Interchangeability of the Working Alliance Inventory and Working Alliance Inventory, Short Form. *Psychological Assessment, 15,* 193–197.

Bustillo, J. R., Lauriello, J., Horan, W., & Keith, S. (2001). The psychosocial treatment of schizophrenia: An update. *American Journal of Psychiatry, 158,* 163–175.

Butcher, J., Derksen, J., Sloore, H., & Sirigatti, S. (2003). Objective personality assessment of people in diverse cultures: European adaptations of the MMPI-2. *Behaviour Research and Therapy, 41,* 819–840.

Butler, A. C., & Beck, A. T. (1995, Summer). Cognitive therapy for depression. *The Clinical Psychologist, 48,* 3–5.

Butler, G. (1989). Issues in the application of cognitive and behavioral strategies to the treatment of social phobia. *Clinical Psychology Review, 9,* 91–106.

Butler, L. D., et al. (1996). Hypnotizability and traumatic experience: A diathesis-stress model of dissociative symptomatology. *American Journal of Psychiatry, 153*(Suppl.), 42–63.

Butler, R. N. (2001, Fall/Winter). The myth of old age. *Newsweek Special Issue,* p. 33.

Bütz, M. R., Bowlling, J. B., & Bliss, C. A. (2000). Psychotherapy with the mentally retarded: A review of the literature and the implications. *Professional Psychology: Research and Practice, 31,* 42–47.

Byers, E. S., & Grenier, G. (2003). Premature or rapid ejaculation: Heterosexual couples' perceptions of men's ejaculatory behavior. *Archives of Sexual Behavior, 32*(3), 261–270.

Byne, W., Buchsbaum, M. S., Kemether, E. Hazlett, E. A., Shinwari, A., Mitropoulou, V., et al. (2001). Magnetic resonance imaging of the thalamic mediodorsal nucleus and pulvinar in schizophrenia and schizotypal personality disorder. *Archives of General Psychiatry, 58,* 133–140.

C

Caddy, G. R., Addington, H. J., Jr., & Perkins, D. (1978). Individualized behavior therapy for alcoholics. A third year independent double-blind follow-up, *Behaviour Research & Therapy, 16,* 345–362.

Caetano, R. (1987). Acculturation and drinking patterns among U.S. Hispanics. *British Journal of Addiction, 82,* 789–799.

Cahn, W., Pol, H. E. H., Lems, E. B. T., van Haren, N. E. M., Schnack, H. G., van der Linden, J. A., et al. (2002). Brain volume changes in first-episode schizophrenia: a 1-year follow-up study. *Archives of General Psychiatry, 59,* 1002–1010.

Cale, E. M., & Lilienfeld, S. O. (2002). Sex differences in psychopathy and antisocial personality disorder. A review and integration. *Clinical Psychology Review, 22,* 1179–1207.

Calhoon, S. K. (1996). Confirmatory factor analysis of the Dysfunctional Attitude Scale in a student sample. *Cognitive Therapy and Research, 20,* 81–91.

Calhoun, P. S., et al. (2000). Drug use and validity of substance use self-reports in veterans seeking help for posttraumatic stress disorder. *Journal of Consulting and Clinical Psychology, 68,* 923–927.

Callicott, J. H., Mattay, V. S., Verchinski, B. A., Marenco, S., Egan, M. F., & Weinberger, D. R. (2003). Complexity of prefrontal cortical dysfunction in schizophrenia: More than up or down. *American Journal of Psychiatry, 160,* 2209–2215.

Cameron, N. (1963). *Personality development and psychopathology: A dynamic approach.* Boston: Houghton Mifflin.

Campbell, T. (2000). First person account: Falling on the pavement. *Schizophrenia Bulletin, 26,* 507–509.

Campbell, W. K., Foster, C. A., & Finkel, E. J. (2002). Does self-love lead to love for others? A story of narcissistic game playing. *Journal of Personality and Social Psychology, 83,* 340–354.

Capps, L., et al. (1993). Parental perception of emotional expressiveness in children with autism. *Journal of Consulting and Clinical Psychology, 61,* 475–484.

Cardemil, E. V., & Battle, C. L. (2003). Guess who's coming to therapy? Getting comfortable with conversations about race and ethnicity in psychotherapy. *Professional Psychology: Research and Practice, 34,* 278–286.

Carey, G., & DiLalla, D. L. (1994). Personality and psychopathology: Genetic perspectives. *Journal of Abnormal Psychology, 103,* 32–43.

Carey, M. P., Carey, K. B., Maisto, S. A., Gordon, C. M., Schroder, K. E. E., & Vanable, P. A. (2004). Reducing HIV-risk behavior among adults receiving outpatient psychiatric treatment: Results from a randomized controlled trial. *Journal of Consulting and Clinical Psychology, 72,* 252–268.

Carey, M. P., Wincze, J. P., & Meisler, A. W. (1998). Sexual dysfunction: Male erectile disorder. In D. H. Barlow (Ed.), *Clinical handbook for psychological disorders* (pp. 442–480). New York: Guilford Press.

Carini, M. A., & Nevid, J. S. (1992). Social appropriateness and impaired perspective in schizophrenia. *Journal of Clinical Psychology, 48,* 170–177.

Carmichael, M. (2002, December 2). *Ginkgo on your mind? Newsweek,* p. 59.

Carmichael, M. (2003, May 5). The fat factor. *Newsweek,* p. 69.

Carney, R. M., Freedland, K. E., & Jaffe, A. S. (2001). Depression as a risk factor for coronary heart disease mortality. *Archives of General Psychiatry, 58.*

Carpenter, S. (2000, September). Psychologists tackle neuroimaging at APA-sponsored Advanced Training Institute. *Monitor on Psychology,* pp. 42–43.

Carpenter, S. (2001a, May). Stimulants boost achievement in ADHD teens. *Monitor on Psychology,* pp. 26–27.

Carroll, L. (2003, November 4). Fetal brains suffer badly from effects of alcohol. *New York Times Online,* retrieved November 4, 2003, from http://www.nytimes.com/2003/11/04/health/04FETA.html?th.

Carroll, L. (2004, February 10). Parkinson's research focuses on links to genes and toxins. *The New York Times,* p. F5.

Carroll, R. T. (2002). *Occam's razor.* From the "Skeptic's Dictionary" by Robert T. Carroll. Retrieved January 12, 2004, from http://skepdic.com/occam.html.

Carter, M. M., Hollon, S. D., Carson, R., & Shelton, R. C. (1995). Effects of a safe person on induced distress following a biological challenge in panic disorder with agoraphobia. *Journal of Abnormal Psychology, 104,* 156–163.

Carver, C. S., & Gaines, J. G. (1987). Optimism, pessimism, and postpartum depression. *Cognitive Therapy & Research, 11,* 449–462.

Caspi, A., McClay, J., Moffitt, T. E., Mill, J., Martin, J., Craig, I. W., et al. (2002). Role of genotype in the cycle of violence in maltreated children. *Science, 297,* 851–854.

Caspi, A., Sugden, K., Moffitt, T. E., Taylor, A., Craig, I. W., Harrington, H. L., McClay, J., et al. (2003). Influence of life stress on depression: Moderation by a polymorphism in the 5-HTT Gene. *Science, 301,* 386–389.

Castellanos, F. X., Giedd, J. N., Berquin, P. C., Walter, J. M., Sharp, W., Tran, T., et al. (2001). Quantitative brain magnetic resonance imaging in girls with attention-deficit/hyperactivity disorder. *Archives of General Psychiatry, 58,* 289–295.

Castellanos, F. X., Sharp, W. S., Gottesman, R. F., Greenstein, D. K., Giedd, J. N., & Rapoport, J. L. (2003). Anatomic brain abnormalities in monozygotic twins discordant for attention deficit hyperactivity disorder. *American Journal of Psychiatry, 160,* 1693–1696.

Catz, S. L., & Kelly, J. A. (2001). Living with HIV disease. In A. Baum, T. A. Revenson, & J. E. Singer (Eds.), *Handbook of health psychology* (pp. 841–850). Mahwah, NJ: Erlbaum.

Cavell, T. A. (2001). Updating our approach to parent training. I: The case against targeting noncompliance. *Clinical Psychology: Science & Practice, 8*(3), 299–318.

Celio, A. A., Winzelberg, A. J.,Wilfley, D. E., Eppstein-Herald, D., Springer, E. A., Dev, P., et al. (2000). Reducing risk factors for eating disorders: comparison of an Internet- and a classroom-delivered psychoeducational program. *Journal of Consulting and Clinical Psychology, 68,* 650–657.

Center for Mental Health Services (CMHS). (1994). *Mental health statistics.* Office of Consumer, Family and Public Information, Center for Mental Health Services, U.S. Department of Health and Human Services. Rockville, MD: Author.

Center for Mental Health Services (2001, May). *National Strategy for Suicide Prevention: Goals and objectives for action: Summary. A joint effort of SAMHS, CDC, NIH, and HRSA.* Washington, DC: Author.

Centers for Disease Control (CDC). (2000). Tobacco use among middle and high school students—United States, 1999. *Morbidity and Mortality Weekly Report, 49,* 49–53.

Centers for Disease Control (CDC). (2001a, October 12). Cigarette smoking among adults—United States, 1999. *Morbidity and Mortality Weekly Report, 50*(40). Retrieved November 15, 2001, from http://www.cdc.gov/tobacco/research_data/adults_prev/mm5040.htm.

Centers for Disease Control (CDC). (2001c). *Suicide in the United States.* National Center for Injury Prevention and Control, Centers for Disease Control. Atlanta: Author.

Chadda, R. K., & Ahuja, N. (1990). Dhat syndrome: A sex neurosis of the Indian subcontinent. *British Journal of Psychiatry, 156,* 577–579.

Chakrabarti, S., & Fombonne, E. (2001). Pervasive developmental disorders in preschool children. *Journal of the American Medical Association, 285,* 3093–3099.

Chamberlin, J. (2001, July/August). Putting a face on child mental illness. *Monitor on Psychology,* pp. 28–29.

Chambless, D. L., & Ollendick, T. H. (2001). Empirically supported psychological interventions: Controversies and evidence. *Annual Review of Psychology, 52,* 685–716.

Chan, D. W. (1991). The Beck Depression Inventory: What difference does the Chinese version make? *Psychological Assessment, 3,* 616–622.

Chang, D. F. (2002). Understanding the rates and distribution of mental disorders. In K. S. Kurasaki, S. Okazaki, & S. Sue (Eds.), *Asian American mental health: Assessment, theories, and methods.* (pp. 9–28). New York: Kluwer Academic/Plenum Publishers.

Chang, S. C. (1984). Review of I. Yamashita "Taijin-kyofu." *Transcultural Psychiatric Research Review, 21,* 283–288.

Charney, D. S., Nemeroff, C. B., Lewis, L., Laden, S. K., Gorman, J. M., Laska, E. M. (2002). National depressive and manic-depressive association consensus statement on the use of placebo in clinical trials of mood disorders. *Archives of General Psychiatry, 59,* 262–270.

Chassin, L., Pitts, S. C., & Prost, J. (2002). Binge drinking trajectories from adolescence to emerging adulthood in a high-risk sample: Predictors and substance abuse outcomes. *Journal of Consulting and Clinical Psychology, 70,* 67–78.

Chassin, L., Presson, C. C., Sherman, S. J., & Kim, K. (2003). Historical changes in cigarette smoking and smoking-related beliefs after 2 decades in a Midwestern community. *Health Psychology, 22,* 347–353.

Chavira, D. A., Grilo, C., Carlos, M., Shea, M. T., Yen, S., Gunderson, J. G., et al. (2003). Ethnicity and four personality disorders. *Comprehensive Psychiatry, 44,* 483–491.

Check, E. (2003). Battle of the mind. *Nature, 422,* 370–372.

Chemerinski, E., et al. (2001). The specificity of depressive symptoms in patients with Alzheimer's disease. *American Journal of Psychiatry, 158,* 68–72.

Chen, E., Bloomberg, G. R., Fisher, E. B., Jr., & Strunk, R. C. (2003). Predictors of repeat hospitalizations in children with asthma: The role of psychosocial and socioenvironmental factors. *Health Psychology, 22,* 12–18.

Chen, H., Zhang, S. M., Hernan, M. A., Schwarzchild, M. A., Willett, W. C., Colditz, G. A., et al. (2003). Nonsteroidal anti-inflammatory drugs and the risk of Parkinson disease. *Archives of Neurology, 60,* 1059–1064.

Chen, J., Rathore, S. S., Radford, M. J., Wang, Y., Krumholz, H. M., et al. (2001). Racial differences in the use of cardiac catheterization after acute myocardial infarction. *The New England Journal of Medicine, 344,* 1443–1449.

Chen, P., Ganguli, M., Mulsant, B. H., & DeKosky, S. T. (1999). The temporal relationship between depressive symptoms and dementia: A community-based prospective study. *Archives of General Psychiatry, 56,* 261–266.

Cheung, F. M. (1991). The use of mental health services by ethnic minorities. In H. F. Myers et al. (Eds.), *Ethnic minority perspectives on clinical training and services in psychology* (pp. 23–31). Washington, DC: American Psychological Association.

Cheung, F. M., & Ho, R. M. (1997). Standardization of the Chinese MMPI-A in Hong Kong: A preliminary study. *Psychological Assessment, 9,* 499–502.

Cheung, F. M., Kwong, J. Y. Y., & Zhang, J. (2003). Clinical validation of the Chinese Personality Assessment Inventory. *Psychological Assessment, 15,* 89–100.

Cheung, F. M. Song, W., & Butcher, J. N. (1991). An infrequency scale for the Chinese MMPI. *Psychological Assessment, 3,* 648–653.

Ching, J. W. J., McDermott, J.F., Fukunaga, C. & Yanagida, E. (1995). Perceptions of family values and roles among Japanese Americans: Clinical considerations. *American Journal of Orthopsychiatry, 65,* 216–224.

Chipperfield, B., & Vogel-Sprott, M. (1988). Family history of problem drinking among young male social drinkers: Modeling effects on alcohol consumption. *Journal of Abnormal Psychology, 97,* 423–428.

Chobanian, A. V., Bakris, G. L., Black, H. R., Cushman, W. C., Green, L. A., Izzo, J. L. Jr., Jones, D. W. et al. (2003). The seventh report of the Joint National Committee on Prevention, Detection, Evaluation, and Treatment of High Blood Pressure: The JNC 7 report. *Journal of the American Medical Association, 289,* 2560–2572.

Chorpita, B. F., Yim, L. M., Donkervoet, J. C., Arensdorf, A., Amundsen, M. J., McGee, C., Serrano, A., et al. (2002). Toward large-scale implementation of empirically supported treatments for children: A review and observations by the Hawaii Empirical Basis to Services Task Force. *Clinical Psychology: Science and Practice, 9,* 165–190.

Chovil, I. (2000). First person account: I and i, dancing fool, challenge you the world to a duel. *Schizophrenia Bulletin, 26 (3),* 745–747.

Chowdhury, A. N. (1996). The definition and classification of Koro. *Culture, Medicine and Psychiatry, 20,* 41–65.

Christensen, A., Atkins, D. C., Berns, S., Wheeler, J., Baucom, D. H., & Simpson, L. E. (2004). Traditional versus integrative behavioral couple therapy for significantly and chronically distressed married couples. *Journal of Consulting and Clinical Psychology, 72,* 176–191.

Chu, J. A., Frey, L. M., Ganzel, B. L., & Matthews, J. A. (1999). Memories of childhood abuse: Dissociation, amnesia, and corroboration. *American Journal of Psychiatry, 156,* 749–755.

Ciechanowski, P., Wagner, E., Schmaling, K., Schwartz, S., Williams, B., Diehr, P., et al. (2004). Community-integrated home-based depression treatment in older adults: A randomized controlled trial. *Journal of the American Medical Association, 291,* 1569–1577.

Clark, D. A., (2004). *Cognitive-behavioral therapy for OCD.* New York: Guilford.

Clark, D. A., Cook, A., & Snow, D. (1998). Depressive symptom differences in hospitalized, medically ill, depressed psychiatric inpatients and nonmedical controls. *Journal of Abnormal Psychology, 107,* 38–48.

Clark, D. M. (1986). A cognitive approach to panic. *Behaviour Research and Therapy, 24,* 461–470.

Clark, D. M., Ehlers, A., McManus, F., Hackmann, A., Fennell, M., Campbell, H., et al. (2003). Cognitive therapy versus fluoxetine in generalized social phobia: a randomized placebo-controlled trial. *Journal of Consulting and Clinical Psychology, 71,* 1058–1067.

Clark, D. M., Salkovskis, P. M., Ost, L. G., Breitholtz, E., Koehler, K. A., Westling, B. E., et al. (1997). Misinterpretation of body sensations in panic disorder. *Journal of Consulting and Clinical Psychology, 65,* 203–213.

Clark, H. W. (2003). Office-based practice and opioid-use disorders. *New England Journal of Medicine, 349,* 928–930.

Clark, S. E., & Loftus, E. F. (1996). The construction of space alien abduction memories. *Psychological Inquiry, 7,* 140–143.

Clay, R. A. (2001a, January). Bringing psychology to cardiac care. *Monitor on Psychology,* pp. 46–49.

Clay, R. A. (2001b, January). To the heart of the matter. *Monitor on Psychology,* pp. 42–45.

Cleckley, H. (1976). *The mask of sanity* (5th ed.). St. Louis: Mosby.

Cleghorn, J. M., Franco, S., Szechtman, B., Kaplan, R. D., Szechtman, H., Brown, G. M., et al. (1992). Toward a brain map of auditory hallucinations. *American Journal of Psychiatry, 149,* 1062–1069.

Clemetson, L. (2003, January 21). Hispanics now largest minority, census shows. *The New York Times,* pp. A 1, A17.

Cloitre, M. (2004). Aristotle revisited: The case of recovered memories. *Clinical Psychology: Science and Practice, 11,* 42–46.

CNS Spectrums, 7, 585–587

Cocaine use tied to loss of pleasure sense. (2003, January 7). *The New York Times,* p. F10.

Cochran, S. D., Sullivan, J. G., & Mays, V. M. (2003). Prevalence of mental disorders, psychological distress, and mental health services use among lesbian, gay, and bisexual adults in the United States. *Journal of Consulting and Clinical Psychology, 71,* No. 1, 53–61.

Cochran, S. V., & Rabinowitz, F. E. (2003). Gender-sensitive recommendations for assessment and treatment of depression in men. *Professional Psychology: Research and Practice, 34,* 132–140.

Cockell, S. J., Hewitt, P. L., Seal, B., Sherry, S., Goldner, E. M., Flett, G. L., et al. (2002). Trait and self-presentational dimensions of perfectionism among women with anorexia nervosa. *Cognitive Therapy and Research, 26,* 745–758.

Cognitive impairment linked to early death in HIV-infected patients. (1996, March 29). *Reuters News Service.*

Cohen, A. C., Gold, D. P., Shulman, K. I., Wortley, J. T., McDonald, G., & Wargon, M. (1993). Factors determining the decision to institutionalize dementing individuals: A prospective study. *The Gerontologist, 22,* 714–720.

Cohen, D. (1986). Psychopathological perspectives: Differential diagnosis of Alzheimer's disease and related disorders. In L. W. Poon (Ed.), *Handbook for clinical memory assessment of older adults* (pp. 81–88). Washington, DC: American Psychological Association.

Cohen, F. L., Ferrans, C. E., & Eshler, B. (1992). Reported accidents in narcolepsy. *Loss, Grief and Care, 5,* 71–80.

Cohen, H., Kaplan, Z., Kotler, M., Kouperman, I., Moisa, R., & Grisaru, N. (2004). Repetitive transcranial magnetic stimulation of the right dorsolateral prefrontal cortex in posttraumatic stress disorder: A double-blind, placebo-controlled study. *American Journal of Psychiatry, 161,* 515–524.

Cohen, J. A., & Mannarino, A. P. (1997). A treatment study for sexually abused preschool children: Outcome during a one-year follow-up. *Journal of the American Academy of Child and Adolescent Psychiatry, 36,* 1228–1235.

Cohen, S., Frank, E., Doyle, W. J., Skoner, D. P., Rabin, B. S., & Gwaltney, J. M., Jr. (1998). Types of stressors that increase susceptibility to the common cold in healthy adults. *Health Psychology, 17,* 214–223.

Cohen, S., Tyrrell, D. A. J., & Smith, A. P. (1991). Psychological stress and susceptibility to the common cold. *The New England Journal of Medicine, 325,* 606–612.

Cohen-Kettenis, P. T., & van Goozen, S. H. M. (1997). Sex reassignment of adolescent transsexuals: A follow-up study. *Journal of the American Academy of Child and Adolescent Psychiatry, 36,* 263–271.

Cohen-Kettens, P. T. (2001). Gender identity disorder in *DSM? Journal of American Academy of Child & Adolescent Psychiatry, 40,* 391.

Cole, D. A., et al. (1998). A longitudinal look at the relation between depression and anxiety in children and adolescents. *Journal of Consulting and Clinical Psychology, 66,* 451–460.

Cole, S. W., Naliboff, B. D., Kemeny, M. E., Griswold, M. P., Fahey, J. l., & Zack, J. A. (2002). Impaired response to HAART in HIV-infected individuals with high autonomic nervous system activity. *Proceedings of the National Academy of Science, 98,* 12695–12700.

Coleman, D., & Baker, F. M. (1994). Misdiagnosis of schizophrenia in older, Black veterans. *Journal of Nervous and Mental Disease, 182,* 527–528.

College binge drinking worries (1999, August 27). *Associated Press, NewsReal, Inc.*

Collins, B. N., & Brandon, T. H. (2002). Effects of extinction context and retrieval cues on alcohol cue reactivity among nonalcoholic drinkers. *Journal of Consulting and Clinical Psychology, 70,* 390–397.

Collins, P. H. (1990). *Black feminist thought: Knowledge, consciousness, and the politics of empowerment.* Boston: Unwin Hyman.

Comas-Diaz, L., & Griffith, E. (1988). Introduction: On culture and psychotherapeutic care. In L. Comas-Diaz & E. Griffith (Eds.), *Clinical guidelines in cross-cultural mental health.* New York: Wiley.

Compton, W. M., Grant, B. F., Colliver, J. D., Glantz, M. D., & Stinson, F. S. (2004). Prevalence of marijuana use disorders in the United States: 1991–1992 and 2001–2002. *Journal of the American Medical Association, 291,* 2114–2121.

Conley, R. R., & Buchanan, R. W. (1997). Evaluation of treatment-resistant schizophrenia. *Schizophrenia Bulletin, 23,* 663–674.

Cooke, D. J., & Michie, C. (1997). An item response theory analysis of the Hare Psychopathy Checklist—Revised. *Psychological Assessment, 9,* 3–14.

Coons, P. M. (1986). Treatment progress in 20 patients with multiple personality disorder. *Journal of Nervous and Mental Disease, 174,* 715–721.

Cooper, A., Delmonico, D. L., & Burg, R. (2000). Cybersex users, abusers, and compulsives: New findings and implications. *Sexual Addiction & Compulsivity, 7(1–2),* 5–29.

Cooper, A., Scherer, C. R., Boies, S. C., & Gordon, B. L. (1999). Sexuality on the Internet: From sexual exploration to pathological expression. *Professional Psychology: Research & Practice, 30*(2), 154–164.

Cooper, P. J., Murray, L., Wilson, A., & Romaniuk, H. (2003). Controlled trial of the short- and long-term effect of psychological treatment of post-partum depression: 1. Impact on maternal mood. *British Journal of Psychiatry, 182,* 412–419.

Cooper, P. J., Tomlinson, M., Swartz, L., Woolgar, M., Murray, L., & Molteno, C. (1999). Post-partum depression and the mother-infant relationship in a South African peri-urban settlement. *British Journal of Psychiary, 175,* 554–558.

Corbitt, E. M., & Widiger, T. A. (1995). Sex differences among the personality disorders: An exploration of the data. *Clinical Psychology: Science and Practice, 2,* 225–238.

Corcoran, D. (2002, December 3). What's normal? A look at Asperger Syndrome. *The New York Times,* p. F6.

Cordova, M. J., Andrykowski, M. A., Kenady, D. E., McGrath, P. C., Sloan, D. A, & Redd, W. H. (1995). Frequency and correlates of posttraumatic-stress-disorder-like symptoms after treatment for breast cancer. *Journal of Consulting and Clinical Psychology, 63,* 981–986.

Corina, D. P., Richards, T. L., Serafini, S., Richards, A. L., Steury, K., Abbott, R. D., Echelard, D. R., et al. (2001). fMRI auditory language differences between dyslexic and able reading children. *Neuroreport: For Rapid Communication of Neuroscience Research, 12*(6), 1195–1201.

Coronado, S. F., & Peake, T. H. (1992). Culturally sensitive therapy: Sensitive principles. *Journal of College Student Psychotherapy, 7,* 63–72.

Cororve, M. B., & Gleaves, D. H. (2001). Body dysmorphic disorder: A review of conceptualizations, assessment, and treatment strategies. *Clinical Psychology Review, 21,* 949–970.

Correll, C. U., Leucht, S., & Kane, J. M. (2004). Lower risk for tardive dyskinesia associated with second-generation antipsychotics: a systematic review of 1-year studies. *American Journal of Psychiatry, 161,* 414–425.

Coryell, W., Endicott, J., & Keller, M. (1992). Rapidly cycling affective disorder: Demographics, diagnosis, family history, and course. *Archives of General Psychiatry, 49,* 126–131.

Coryell, W., Solomon, D., Turvey, C., Keller, M., Leon, A. C., Endicott, J., et al. (2003). The long-term course of rapid-cycling bipolar disorder. *Archives of General Psychiatry, 60,* 914–920.

Costa, P. T., Jr., & McCrae, R. R. (1985). Hypochondriasis, neuroticism, and aging: When are somatic complaints unfounded? *American Psychologist, 40,* 19–28.

Costello, E. J., Compton, S. N., Keele, G., & Angold, A. (2003). Relationships between poverty and psychopathology: A natural experiment. *Journal of the American Medical Association, 290,* 2023–2029.

Costin, C. (1997). *Your dieting daughter: Is she dying for attention?* New York: Brunner/Mazel.

Courchesne, E., Carper, R., & Akshoomoff, N. (2003). Evidence of brain overgrowth in the first year of life in autism. *Journal of the American Medical Association, 290,* 337–344.

Coursey, R. D., Alford, J., & Safarjan, B. (1997). Significant advances in understanding and treating serious mental illness. *Professional Psychology: Research and Practice, 28,* 205–216.

Cowan, W. M., & Kandel, E. R. (2001). Prospects for neurology and psychiatry. *Journal of the American Medical Association, 285,* 594–600.

Cowley, G. (2001a, March 12). Cannibals to cows: The path of a deadly disease. *Newsweek,* pp. 53–61.

Cowley, G. (2001b, February 12). New ways to stay clean. *Newsweek,* pp. 45–47.

Cowley, G. (2003, September 8). Girls, boys, and autism. *Newsweek,* pp. 42–46.

Coyle, J. T. (2001). Drug treatment of anxiety disorders in children. *The New England Journal of Medicine, 344,* 1326–1327.

Coyne, J. C. (1976). Toward an interactional description of depression. *Psychiatry, 39,* 14–27.

Craighead, W. E., Craighead, L. W., & Ilardi, S. S. (1998). Psychosocial treatments for major depressive disorder. In P. E. Nathan & J. M. Gorman (Eds.), *A guide to treatments that work* (pp. 226–239). New York: Oxford University Press.

Cramer, P. (2000). Defense mechanisms in psychology today: Further processes for adaptation. *American Psychologist, 55,* 637–646.

Craske, M. G., Brown, T. A., & Barlow, D. H. (1991). Behavioral treatment of panic disorder: A two-year follow-up. *Behavior Therapy, 22,* 289–304.

Cravchik, A., & Goldman, D. (2000). Neurochemical individuality: Genetic diversity among human dopamine and serotonin receptors and transporters. *Archives of General Psychiatry, 57,* 1105–1114.

Crits-Christoph, P. (1992). The efficacy of brief dynamic psychotherapy: A meta-analysis. *American Journal of Psychiatry, 149,* 151–158.

Cross-National Collaborative Group. (1992). The changing rate of major depression: Cross-national comparisons. *Journal of the American Medical Association, 268,* 3098–3105.

Csernansky, J. G., Schindler, M. K., Splinter, N. R., Wang, L., Gado, M., Selemon, L. D., et al. (2004). Abnormalities of thalamic volume and shape in schizophrenia. *American Journal of Psychiatry, 161,* 896–902.

Cui, X-J., & Vaillant, G. E. (1997). Does depression generate negative life events? *Journal of Nervous and Mental Disease, 185,* 145–150.

Cunningham, J. A., & Breslin, F. C. (2004). Links Only one in three people with alcohol abuse or dependence ever seek treatment. *Addictive Behaviors, 29,* 221–223.

Curb, J. D., & Marcus, E. B. (1991). Body fat and obesity in Japanese-Americans. *American Journal of Clinical Nutrition, 53,* 1552S–1555S.

Curry, S., Marlatt, G. A., & Gordon, J. R. (1987). Abstinence violation effect: Validation of an attributional construct with smoking cessation. *Journal of Consulting and Clinical Psychology, 55,* 145–149.

Curtin, J. J., Patrick, C. J., Lang, A. R, Cacioppo, J. T., & Birbaumer, N. (2001). Alcohol affects emotion through cognition. *Psychological Science, 12,* 527–531.

Curtner-Smith, M. E. (2000). Mechanisms by which family processes contribute to school-age boy's bullying. *Child Study Journal, 30*(3), 169–186.

Cutrona, C. E., Russell, D. W., Hessling, R. M., Brown, P. A., & Murry, V. (2000). Direct and moderating effects of community context on the psychological well-being of African American women. *Journal of Personality and Social Psychology, 79,* 1088–1101.

Cutting, L. P., & Docherty, N. M. (2000). Schizophrenia outpatients' perceptions of their parents: Is expressed emotion a factor? *Journal of Abnormal Psychology, 109,* 266–272.

Cyranowski, J. M., Frank, E., Young, E., & Shear, M. K. (2000). Adolescent onset of the gender difference in lifetime rates of major depression: a theoretical model. *Archives of General Psychiatry, 57,* 21–27.

D

Dadds, M. R., Sanders, M. R., Morrison, M., & Rebgetz, M. (1992). Childhood depression and conduct disorder: II. An analysis of family interaction patterns in the home. *Journal of Abnormal Psychology, 101,* 505–513.

Dahl, R. E. (1992). The pharmacologic treatment of sleep disorders. *Psychiatric Clinics of North America, 15,* 161–178.

Daley, S. E., Burge, D., & Hammen, C. (2000). Borderline personality disorder symptoms as predictors of 4-year romantic relationship dysfunction in young women: Addressing issues of specificity. *Journal of Abnormal Psychology, 109,* 451–460.

Daley, S. E., Hammen, C., Burge, D., Davila, J., Paley, B., Lindberg, N., et al. (1997). Predictors of the generation of episodic stress: A longitudinal study of late adolescent women. *Journal of Abnormal Psychology, 106,* 251–259.

Daly, R. C., Danaceau, M.A., Rubinow, D. R., & Schmidt, P. J. (2003). Concordant restoration of ovarian function and mood in perimenopausal depression. *American Journal of Psychiatry, 160,* 1842–1846.

Damasio, A. R. (1997). Towards a neuropathology of emotion and mood. *Nature, 386,* 769–770.

Damasio, R. (2000). A neural basis for sociopathy. *Archives of General Psychiatry, 57,* 128–129.

Dana, R. H. (Ed.) (2000). *Handbook of cross-cultural and multicultural personality assessment.* Mahwah, NJ: Lawrence Erlbaum Associates.

Davidson, J. R. T., Rothbaum, B. O., van der Kolk, B. A., Sikes, C. R., & Farfel, G. M. (2001). Multicenter, double-blind comparison of sertraline and placebo in the treatment of posttraumatic stress disorder. *Archives of General Psychiatry, 58,* 485–492.

Davidson, P. R., & Parker, K. C. H. (2001). Eye movement desensitization and reprocessing (EMDR): A meta-analysis. *Journal of Consulting and Clinical Psychology, 69,* 305–316.

Davidson, R. J. (2000). Affective style, psychopathology, and resilience: Brain mechanisms and plasticity. *American Psychologist, 55,* 1196–1214.

Davidson, R. J., Pizzagalli, D., Nitschke, J. B., & Putnam, K. (2002). Depression: Perspectives from affective neuroscience. *Annual Review of Psychology, 53,* 545–574.

Davis, J. M., Chen, N, & Glick, I. D. (2003). A meta-analysis of the efficacy of second-generation antipsychotics. *Archives of General Psychiatry, 60,* 553–564.

Davis, T. L., & Liddell, D. L. (2002). Getting inside the house: The effectiveness of a rape prevention program for college fraternity men. *Journal of College Student Development, 43*(1), 35–50.

Daw, J. (2001, April). Survey uncovers communication breakdown in the treatment of depression. *Monitor on Psychology,* p. 69.

Dawe, S., Rees, V. W., Mattick, R., Sitharthan, T., & Heather, N. (2002). Efficacy of moderation-oriented cue exposure for problem drinkers: A randomized controlled trial. *Journal of Consulting and Clinical Psychology, 70,* 1045–1050.

De La Cancela, V., & Guzman, L. P. (1991). Latino mental health service needs: Implications for training psychologists. In H. F. Myers et al. (Eds.), *Ethnic minority perspectives on clinical training and services in psychology* (pp. 59–64). Washington, DC: American Psychological Association.

de Moor, C., Sterner, J., Hall, M., Warneke, C., Gilani, Z. Amato, R. et al. (2003). A pilot study of the effects of expressive writing on psychological and behavioral adjustment in patients enrolled in a Phase II trial of vaccine therapy for metastatic renal cell carcinoma. *Health Psychology, 21,* 615–619.

De Silva, P. (1993). Post-traumatic stress disorder: Cross-cultural aspects. *International Review of Psychiatry, 5,* 217–229.

DeAngelis, T. (2002, June). How do mind-body interventions affect breast cancer? *Monitor on Psychology, 33,* pp. 51–53.

DeBaggio, T. (2002). *Losing my mind. An intimate look at life with Alzheimer's.* New York: The Free Press.

Decker, S. L., McIntosh, D. E., Kelly, A. M., Nicholls, S. K., & Dean, R. S. (2001). Comorbidity among individuals classified with attention disorders. *International Journal of Neuroscience, 110*(1–2), 43–54.

Deegear, J., & Lawson, D. M. (2003). The utility of empirically supported treatments. *Professional Psychology: Research and Practice, 34,* 271–277.

Deffenbacher, J. L., et al. (2000). An application of Beck's cognitive therapy to general anger reduction. *Cognitive Therapy & Research, 24,* 689–697.

Dekker, J. (1993). Inhibited male orgasm. In W. O'Donohue & J. H. Geer (Eds.), *Handbook of sexual dysfunctions: As-*

sessment and treatment (pp. 279–301). Boston: Allyn & Bacon.

Del Boca, F. K., Darkes, J., Greenbaum, P. E., & Goldman, M. S. (2004). Up close and personal: Temporal variability in the drinking of individual college students during their first year. *Journal of Consulting and Clinical Psychology, 72,* 155–164.

Delahanty, D. L., & Baum, A. (2001). Stress and breast cancer. In A. Baum, T. A. Revenson, & J. E. Singer (Eds.), *Handbook of health psychology* (pp. 747–756). Mahwah, NJ: Erlbaum.

Dement, W. C. (1992). The proper use of sleeping pills in the primary care setting. *Journal of Clinical Psychiatry, 53*(12, Suppl.), 50–56.

Denneby, J. A., Appleby, L., Thomas, C. S., Faragher, E. B., et al. (1996). Case-control study of suicide by discharged psychiatry patients. *British Medical Journal, 312,* 1580.

Dennis, C. (2004, January 29). Brain development: The most important sexual organ. *Nature, 427,* 390–392.

Denollet, J., et al. (1996). Personality as independent predictor of long-term mortality in patients with coronary heart disease. *Lancet, 347,* 417–421.

Depression Guideline Panel. (1993b). *Depression in primary care: Vol. 2. Treatment of major depression.* Clinical Practice Guideline No. 5. Rockville, MD: U.S. Department of Health and Human Services, Public Health Service, Agency for Health Care Policy and Research (AHCPR Pub. No. 93–0551).

Derby, C. A. (2000, October 2). Cited in, "Study finds exercise reduces the risk of impotence." *CNN.com.* Retrieved November 12, 2002, from http://www.cnn.com/2000/HEALTH/men/10/02/fitness.impotence.ap/.

DeRubeis, R. J., & Crits-Christoph, P. (1998). Empirically supported individual and group psychological treatments for adult mental disorders. *Journal of Consulting and Clinical Psychology, 66,* 37–52.

DeRubeis, R. J., Gelfand, L. A., Tang, T. Z., & Simons, A. D. (1999). Medications versus cognitive behavior therapy for severely depressed outpatients: Meta-analysis of four randomized comparisons. *American Journal of Psychiatry, 156,* 1007–1013.

DeRubeis, R. J., Tang, T. Z., & Beck, A. T. (2001). Cognitive therapy. In K. S. Dobson (Ed.), *Handbook of cognitive-behavioral therapies* (2nd ed., pp. 349–392). New York: Guilford Press.

Dettmer, K., Saunders, B., & Strang, J. (2001). Take home naloxone and the prevention of deaths from opiate overdose: Two pilot schemes. *British Medical Journal, 322,* 895–896.

Devan, G. S. (1987). Koro and schizophrenia in Singapore. *British Journal of Psychiatry, 150,* 106–107.

Devlin, M. J., Yanovski, S. Z., & Wilson, G. T. (2000). Obesity: What mental health professionals need to know. *American Journal of Psychiatry, 157,* 854–866.

Diamond, S., Baldwin, R., & Diamond, R. (1963). *Inhibition and choice.* New York: Harper & Row.

Dick, D. M., Rose, R. J., Viken, R. J., Kaprio, J., & Koskenvuo, M. (2001). Exploring gene-environment interactions: Socioregional moderation of alcohol use. *Journal of Abnormal Psychology, 110,* 625–632.

Dickens, B. M., Doob, A. N., Warwick, O. H., & Winegard, W. C. (1982). *Report of the Committee of Enquiry into Allegations Concerning Drs. Linda and Mark Sobell.* Toronto: Addiction Research Foundation.

Dishion, T. J., & Owen, L. D. (2002). A longitudinal analysis of friendships and substance use: Bidirectional influence from adolescence to adulthood. *Developmental Psychology, 38,* 480–491.

Dittmann, M. (2003, February). Psychology's first prescribers. *Monitor on Psychology,* pp. 36–37.

Dixit, A. R., & Crum, R. M. (2000). Prospective study of depression and the risk of heavy alcohol use in women. *American Journal of Psychiatry, 157,* 801–807.

Dixon, L, Adams, C., & Lucksted, A. (2000). Update on family psychoeducation for schizophrenia. *Schizophrenia Bulletin, 26* (1), 5–20.

Dixon, L., Weiden, P., Torres, M., & Lehman, A. (1997). Assertive community treatment and medication compliance in the homeless mentally ill. *American Journal of Psychiatry, 154,* 1302–1304.

Dobson, K. S., & Dozois, D. J. A. (2001). Historical and philosophical bases of the cognitive-behavioral therapies. In K. S. Dobson (Ed.), *Handbook of cognitive-behavioral therapies* (2nd ed., pp. 3–40). New York: Guilford Press.

Docherty, N. M., Cohen, A. S., Nienow, T. M., Dinzeo, T. J., & Dangelmaier, R. E. (2003). Stability of formal thought disorder and referential communication disturbances in schizophrenia. *Journal of Abnormal Psychology, 112,* 469–475.

Dodge, K. A., Laird, R., Lochman, J. E., & Zelli, A. (2002). Multidimensional latent-construct analysis of children's social information processing patterns. *Psychological Assessment, 14,* 60–73.

Dodge, K. A., Lochman, J. E., Harnish, J. D., Bates, J. E., & Pettit, G. S. (1997). Reactive and proactive aggression in school children and psychiatrically impaired chronically assaultive youth. *Journal of Abnormal Psychology, 106,* 37–51.

Donker, F. J. S. (2000). Cardiac rehabilitation: A review of current developments. *Clinical Psychology Review, 20,* 923–943.

Dooren, J. C. (2004, September 14). FDA panel says antidepressants increase children suicide risk. *Wall Street Journal Online,* Retrieved September 15, 2004, from http://online.wsj.com/search.

Dorahy, M. J. (2001). Dissociative identity disorder and memory dysfunction: The current state of experimental research and its future directions. *Clinical Psychology Review, 21,* 771–795.

Dougall, A. L., & Baum, A. (2001). Stress, health, and illness. In A. Baum, T. A. Revenson, & J. E. Singer (Eds.), *Handbook of health psychology* (pp. 339–348). Mahwah, NJ: Erlbaum.

Dowker, A., Hermelin, B., & Pring, L. (1996). A savant poet. *Psychological Medicine, 26,* 913–924.

Draguns, J. G., & Tanaka-Matsumi, J. (2003). Assessment of psychopathology across and within cultures: Issues and findings *Behaviour Research and Therapy, 41,* 755–776.

Drake, R. E., Wallach, M. A., Teague, G. B., Freeman, D. H., Paskus, T. S., & Clark, T. A. (1991). Housing instability and homelessness among rural schizophrenic patients. *American Journal of Psychiatry, 148,* 211–215.

Drewnowski, A. (1997). Taste preferences and food intake. *Annual Review of Nutrition, 17,* 237–253.

Drews, C. D., Yeargin-Allsopp, M., Decoufle, P., & Murphy, C. C. (1995). Variation in the influence of selected sociodemographic risk factors for mental retardation. *American Journal of Public Health, 85,* 329–334.

Druss, B. G., Miller, C. L., Rosenheck, R. A., Shih, S. C., & Bost, J. E. (2002). Mental health care quality under managed care in the United States: A view from the Health Employer Data and Information Set (HEDIS). *American Journal of Psychiatry, 159,* 567–572.

Druss, B. G., Rosenheck, R. A., & Sledge, W. H. (2000). Health and disability costs of depressive illness in a major U.S. corporation. *American Journal of Psychiatry, 157,* 1274–1278.

Dryden, W., & Ellis, A. (2001). Rational emotive behavior therapy. In K. S. Dobson (Ed.), *Handbook of cognitive-behavioral therapies* (2nd ed., pp. 295–348). New York: Guilford Press.

Du Pont heir found guilty of murder but mentally ill. (1997, February 26). *The New York Times,* p. A10.

Dubovsky, S. (2000, September). Lithium: The oldest specific psychotropic medication. *Journal Watch for Psychiatry,* pp. 73, 76.

Duckworth, K., & McBride, H. (1996). Suicide in old age: A tragedy of neglect. *Canadian Journal of Psychiatry, 41,* 217–222.

Duenweld, M. (2003, June 18). More Americans seeking help for depression. *The New York Times,* pp. A1, A22.

Duffy, A., Alda, M., Kutcher, S., Fusee, C., & Grof, P. (1998). Psychiatric symptoms and syndromes among adolescent children of parents with lithium-responsive or lithium-nonresponsive bipolar disorder. *American Journal of Psychiatry, 155,* 431–433.

Duffy, F. H. (1994). The role of quantified electroencephalography in psychological research. In G. Dawson & K. W. Fischer (Eds.), *Human behavior and the developing brain* (pp. 93–132). New York: Guilford Press.

Dugas, M. J. (2002). Generalized anxiety disorder. In M. Hersen (Ed.), *Clinical behavior therapy: Adults and children* (pp. 125–143). New York: Wiley.

Dugas, M. L., Ladouceur, R., Léger, E., Freeston, M. H., Langlis, F., Provencher, M. D., et al. (2003). Group cognitive–behavioral therapy for generalized anxiety disorder: Treatment outcome and long-term follow-up. *Journal of Consulting and Clinical Psychology, 71,* 821–825.

Dugger, C. W. (1992, September 3). Threat only when on crack, homeless man foils system. *The New York Times,* pp. A1, B4.

Dugger, C. W. (1994, July 15). Larry Hogue is arrested in Westchester. *The New York Times,* pp. B1, B2.

Dulit, R. A., Fyer, M. R., Leon, A. C., Brodsky, B. S., & Frances, A. J. (1994). Clinical correlates of self-mutilation in borderline personality disorder. *American Journal of Psychiatry, 151,* 1305–1311.

Duman, R. S., Heninger, G. R., & Nestler, E. J. (1997). A molecular and cellular theory of depression. *Archives of General Psychiatry, 54,* 597–606.

Duncan, J., Seitz, R. J., Kolodny, J., Bor, D., Herzog, H., Ahmed, A., et al. (2000). A neural basis for general intelligence. *Science, 289,* 457–460.

Durham v. United States, 214 F. 2d 862 (DC Circ 1954).

Durkheim, E. (1958). *Suicide* (J. A. Spaulding & G. Simpson, Trans.). New York: Free Press. (Original work published 1897).

Dwyer, M. (1988). Exhibitionism/voyeurism. *Journal of Social Work and Human Sexuality, 7,* 101–112.

Dykens, E. M., & Hodapp, R. M. (1997). Treatment issues in genetic mental retardation syndromes. *Professional Psychology: Research and Practice, 28,* 263–270.

Dyslexia: The interaction of culture and biology. (2001, March 15). *CNN Web Posting.* Retrieved March 16, 2001, from http://www.cnn.com/2001/fyi/teachers.ednews/03/15/dyslexia.reading.ap.

E

Earnst, K. S., & Kring, A. M. (1997). Construct validity of negative symptoms: An empirical and conceptual review. *Clinical Psychology Review, 17,* 167–189.

Eaton, W. W., Dryman, A., & Weissman, M. M. (1991). Panic and phobia. In L. N. Robins & D. A. Regier (Eds.), *Psychiatric disorders in America: The Epidemiologic Catchment Area Study* (pp. 155–179). New York: Free Press.

Eaton, W. W., Kessler, R. C., Wittchen, H. U., & Magee, W. J. (1994). Panic and panic disorder in the United States. *American Journal of Psychiatry, 151,* 413–420.

Eberhardy, F. (1967). The view from "the couch." *Journal of Child Psychological Psychiatry, 8,* 257–263.

Ebigbo, P. O. (1993). Situation analysis of child abuse and neglect in Nigeria. *Journal of Psychology in Africa, 1,* 159–178.

Edelson, E. (1998, March 9). Migraines come into focus. *Newsday,* p. C7.

Edinger, J. D., Wohlgemuth, W. K., Radtke, R. A., Marsh, G. R., & Quillian, R. E. (2001). Cognitive behavioral therapy for treatment of chronic primary insomnia: A randomized controlled trial. *Journal of the American Medical Association, 285,* 1856–1864.

Edman, J. L., & Johnson, R. C. (1999). Filipino American and Caucasian American beliefs about the causes and treatment of mental problems. *Cultural Diversity and Ethnic Minority Psychology, 5,* 380–386.

Edmundson, M. (2001, June 3). I'm O.K, and then some. *The New York Times Book Review,* p. 33.

Edwards, J., Jackson, H. R., & Pattison, P. E. (2002). Emotion recognition via facial expression and affective prosody in schizophrenia: A methodological review. *Clinical Psychology Review, 22,* 789–832.

Edwards, V. J., Holden, G. W., Felitti, V. J., & Anda, R. F. (2003). Relationship between multiple forms of childhood maltreatment and adult mental health in community respondents: Results from the Adverse Childhood Experiences Study. *American Journal of Psychiatry, 160,* 1453–1460.

Egan, J. (1991). Oppositional defiant disorder. In J. M. Wiener (Ed.), *Textbook of child and adolescent psychiatry.* Washington, DC: American Psychiatric Press.

Ehlers, A. (1995). A 1-year prospective study of panic attacks: Clinical course and factors associated with maintenance. *Journal of Abnormal Psychology, 104,* 164–172.

Ehlers, A., Clark, D. M., Hackmann, A., McManus, F., Fennell, M., Herbert, C., & Mayou, R. (2003). A randomized controlled trial of cognitive therapy, a self-help booklet, and repeated assessments as early interventions for posttraumatic stress disorder. *Archives of General Psychiatry, 60,* 1024–1032.

Ehlers, A., Mayou, R. A., & Bryant, B. (1998). Psychological predictors of chronic posttraumatic stress disorder after motor vehicle accidents. *Journal of Abnormal Psychology, 107,* 508–519.

Eiberg, H., Berendt, I., & Mohr, J. (1995). Assignment of dominant inherited nocturnal euresis (ENUR1) to chromosome 13q. *Nature Genetics, 10,* 354–356.

Eichstedt, J. A., & Arnold, S. L. (2001). Childhood-onset obsessive-compulsive disorder. A tic-related subtype of OCD? *Clinical Psychology Review, 21,* 137–157.

Eisenbruch, M. (1992). Toward a culturally sensitive DSM: Cultural bereavement in Cambodian refugees and the traditional healer as taxonomist. *Journal of Nervous and Mental Disease, 180,* 8–10.

Eisler, I., Dare, C., Hodes, M., Russell, G., Dodge, E., & Le Grange, D. (1997). Family and individual therapy in anorexia nervosa: A 5-year follow-up. *Archives of General Psychiatry, 54,* 1025–1030.

El Nasser, H. (2003, June 19). 39 million make Hispanics largest minority group. *USA Today,* pp. 1, 3.

Elkin, I., Shea, M. T., Watkins, J. T., Imber, S. D., Sotsky, S. M., Collins, J. F., et al. (1989). National Institute of Mental Health treatment of depression collaborative research program: General effectiveness of treatments. *Archives of General Psychiatry, 46,* 971–982.

Ellason, J. W., & Ross, C. A. (1997). Two-year follow-up of inpatients with dissociative identity disorder. *American Journal of Psychiatry, 154,* 832–839.

Ellickson, P. L., Hays, R. D., & Bell, R. M. (1992). Stepping through the drug use sequence: Longitudinal scalogram analysis of initiation and regular use. *Journal of Abnormal Psychology, 101,* 441–451.

Elliott, A. J., Uldall, K. K., Bergam, K., Russo, J., Claypoole, K., & Roy-Byrne, P. P. (1998). Randomized, placebo-controlled trial of paroxetine versus imipramine in depressed HIV-positive outpatients. *American Journal of Psychiatry, 155,* 367–372.

Ellis, A. (1977b). The basic clinical theory of rational-emotive therapy. In A. Ellis & R. Grieger (Eds.), *Handbook of rational-emotive therapy.* (pp. 3–34) New York: Springer.

Ellis, A. (1993). Reflections on rational-emotive therapy. *Journal of Consulting and Clinical Psychology, 61,* 199–201.

Ellis, A. (1997). Using rational emotive behavior therapy techniques to cope with disability. *Professional Psychology: Research and Practice, 28,* 17–22.

Ellis, A. (2001). *Overcoming destructive beliefs, feelings, and behaviors: New directions for rational emotive behavior therapy.* Amherst, NY: Prometheus Books.

Ellis, A., & Dryden, W. (1987). *The practice of rational emotional therapy.* New York: Springer.

Ellis, L., & Bonin, S. L. (2003). Genetics and occupation-related preferences. Evidence from adoptive and non-adoptive families. *Personality and Individual Differences, 35,* 929–937.

Epping-Jordan, J. E., Compas, B. E., & Howell, D. C. (1994). Predictors of cancer progression in young adult men and women: Avoidance, intrusive thoughts, and psychological symptoms. *Health Psychology, 13,* 539–547.

Epstein, D. H., Hawkins, W. E, Covia, L., Umbrichtc, A., & Preston, K. L. (2003). Cognitive–behavioral therapy plus contingency management for cocaine use: Findings during treatment and across 12-month follow-up. *Psychology of Addictive Behaviors, 17,* 73–82.

Epstein, H. (2003, October 12). Enough to make you sick? *The New York Times Magazine,* pp. 75–81, 98, 102–108.

Erlenmeyer-Kimling, L., et al. (1997). The New York high-risk project: Prevalence and comorbidity of Axis I disorders in offspring of schizophrenic parents at 25-year follow-up. *Archives of General Psychiatry, 54,* 1096–1102.

Ernst, T., Chang, L., Leonido-Yee, M., & Speck, O. (2000). Evidence for long-term neurotoxicity associated with methamphetamine abuse: A 1HMRS study. *Neurology, 54,* 1344–1349.

Ertekin-Taner, N., Graff-Radford, N., Younkin, L. H., Eckman, C., Baker, M., Adamson, J., et al. (2000). Linkage of plasma A42 to a quantitative locus on chromosome 10 in late-onset Alzheimer's disease pedigrees. *Science, 290,* 2303–2304.

Escobar, J. I. (1998). Immigration and mental health: Why are immigrants better off? *Archives of General Psychiatry, 55,* 781–782.

Esparza, J., Fox, C., Harper, I. T., Bennett, P. H., Schulz, L. O., Valencia, M. E., et al. (2000). Daily energy expenditure in Mexican and USA Pima Indians: Low physical activity as a possible cause of obesity. *International Journal of Obesity and Related Metabolic Disorders, 24,* 55–59.

Espie, C. A. (2002). Insomnia. *Annual Review of Psychology, 53,* 215–243.

Espie, C. A., Inglis, S. J., & Harvey, L. (2001). Predicting clinically significant response to cognitive behavior therapy for chronic insomnia in general medical practice: Analyses of outcome data at 12 months posttreatment. *Journal of Consulting and Clinical Psychology, 69,* 58–66.

Espie, C. A., Inglis, S. J., Tessier, S., & Harvey, L. (2001). The clinical effectiveness of cognitive behaviour therapy for chronic insomnia: Implementation and evaluation of a sleep clinic in general medical practice. *Behaviour Research and Therapy, 39,* 45–60.

Essock, S. M., et al. (2000). Cost-effectiveness of clozapine compared with conventional antipsychotic medication for patients in state hospitals. *Archives of General Psychiatry, 57,* 987–994.

Esterling, B. A., L'Abate, L., Murray, E. J., & Pennebaker, J. W. (1999). Empirical foundations for writing in prevention and psychotherapy: Mental and physical health outcomes. *Clinical Psychology Review, 19,* 79–96.

Etminan, M., Gill, S., & Samii, A. (2003). Effect of nonsteroidal anti-inflammatory drugs on risk of Alzheimer's disease: Systematic review and meta-analysis of observational studies. *British Medical Journal, 327,* 128–131.

Evans, S. W., Pelham, W. E., Smith, B. H., Bukstein, O., Gnagy, E. M., Greiner, A. R., et al. (2001). Dose-response effects of methylphenidate on ecologically valid measures of academic performance and classroom behavior in adolescents with ADHD. *Experimental and Clinical Psychopharmacology, 9,* 163–175.

Ewing, R., Schmid, T., Killingsworth, R., Zlot, A., & Raudenbush, S. (2003). Relationship between urban sprawl and physical activity, obesity and morbidity. *American Journal of Health Promotion, 18* (1), 47–57.

Exner, J. E. (1991). *The Rorschach: A comprehensive system: Vol. 2. Interpretation.* New York: Wiley.

Exner, J. E. (1993). *The Rorschach: A comprehensive system: Vol. 1. Basic foundations* (3rd ed.). New York: Wiley.

Exner, J. E., Jr. (2002). Early development of the Rorschach test. *Academy of Clinical Psychology Bulletin, 8,* 9–24.

F

Fabian, J. L. (1991). "Koro: Proposed classification for *DSM-IV*": Comment. *American Journal of Psychiatry, 148,* 1766.

Fabrega, H., Jr. (1990). Hispanic mental health research: A case for cultural psychiatry. *Journal of Behavioral Sciences, 12,* 339–365.

Fabrega, H., Jr. (1992). Diagnosis interminable: Toward a culturally sensitive *DSM-IV. Journal of Nervous and Mental Disease, 180,* 5–7.

Fackelmann, K. (2003, August 19). Alzheimer's cases expected to rise at a more rapid rate. *USA Today,* p. 7D.

Failer, J. L. (2002). *Who qualifies for rights? Homelessness, mental illness, and civil commitment.* Ithaca, NY: Cornell University Press.

Fairburn, C. G., & Wilson, G. T. (Eds.). (1993). *Binge eating: Nature, assessment, and treatment.* New York: Guilford Press.

Fairburn, C. G., Stice, E., Cooper, Z., Doll, H. A., Norman, P. A., & O'Connor, E. E. (2003). Understanding persistence in bulimia nervosa: A 5-year naturalistic study. *Journal of Consulting and Clinical Psychology, 71,* 103–109.

Fairburn, C. G., Welch, S. L., Doll, H. A., Davies, B. A., & O'Connor, M. E. (1997). Risk factors for bulimia nervosa: A community-based case-control study. *Archives of General Psychiatry, 54,* 509–517.

Fallon, B. A., et al. (1993). Fluoxetine for hypochondriacal patients without major depression. *Journal of Clinical Psychopharmacology, 13,* 438–441.

Fals-Stewart, W. (2003). The occurrence of partner physical aggression on days of alcohol consumption: A longitudinal diary study. *Journal of Consulting and Clinical Psychology, 71,* 41–52.

Faraone, S. V. (2003a, August). *ADHD: Facts and fiction.* Paper presented at the meeting of the American Psychological Association, Toronto, CA.

Faraone, S. V. (2003b, August). *The persistence of attention-deficit/hyperactivity disorder through adolescence and adulthood.* Paper presented at the meeting of the American Psychological Association, Toronto, CA.

Faraone, S. V., Biederman, J., Feighner, J. A., & Monuteaux, M. C. (2000). Assessing symptoms of attention deficit hyperactivity disorder in children and adults: Which is more valid? *Journal of Consulting and Clinical Psychology, 68,* 830–842.

Faraone, S. V., Biederman, J., Mick, E., Williamson, S., Wilens, T., Spencer, T., et al. (2000). Family study of girls with attention deficit hyperactivity disorder. *American Journal of Psychiatry, 157*(7), 1077–1083.

Faraone, S. V., Doyle, A. E., Mick, E., & Biederman, J. (2001). Meta-analysis of the association between the 7-repeat allele of the dopamine d4 receptor gene and attention deficit hyperactivity disorder. *American Journal of Psychiatry, 158,* 1052–1057.

Faraone, S. V., et al. (1993). Intellectual performance and school failure in children with attention deficit hyperactivity disorders and their siblings. *Journal of Abnormal Psychology, 102,* 616–623.

Farber, B. A., Brink, D. C., & Raskin, P. M. (1996). *The psychotherapy of Carl Rogers: Cases and commentary* (pp. 74–75). New York: The Guilford Press.

Farmer, R. F. (2000). Issues in the assessment and conceptualization of personality disorders. *Clinical Psychology Review, 20,* 823–851.

Farooqi, I. S., Keogh, J. M., Yeo, G. S. H., Lank, E. J., Cheetham, T., et al. (2003). Clinical spectrum of obesity and mutations in the melanocortin 4 receptor gene. *New England Journal of Medicine, 348,* 1085–1095.

Farr, C. B. (1994). Benjamin Rush and American psychiatry. *American Journal of Psychiatry, 151*(Suppl.), 65–73.

Farrell, A. D., Camplair, P. S., & McCullough, L. (1987). Identification of target complaints by computer interview: Evaluation of the Computerized Assessment System for Psychotherapy Evaluation and Research. *Journal of Consulting and Clinical Psychology, 55,* 691–700.

Farrell, A. D., & White, K. S. (1998). Peer influences and drug use among urban adolescents: Family structure and parent/adolescent relationship as protective factors. *Journal of Consulting and Clinical Psychology, 66,* 248–258.

Fava, M., Bless, E., Otto, M. W., Pava, J. A., & Rosenbaum, J. F. (1994). Dysfunctional attitudes in major depression: Changes with pharmacotherapy. *Journal of Nervous and Mental Disease, 182,* 45–49.

FDA approves nicotine lozenge. (2002, November 1). *CNN Web Posting,* Retrieved November 1, 2002, from http://www.cnn.com/2002/HEALTH/11/01/tobacco.lozenge.ap/index.html.

Feldman, L. B., & Rivas-Vazquez, R. A. (2003). Assessment and treatment of social anxiety disorder *Professional Psychology: Research and Practice, 34,* 396–405.

Feldman, M. D. (2003). Foreword to "*Sickened, the memoir of a Munchausen by proxy childhood*" (pp. v–ix). New York: Bantam.

Fensterheim, H., & Kantor, J. S. (1980). Behavioral approach to sexual disorders. In B. Wolman & J. Money (Eds.), *Handbook of human sexuality.* Englewood Cliffs, NJ: Prentice Hall.

Ferguson-Peters, M. (1985). Racial socialization of young black children. In H. & J. L. McAdoo (Eds.), *Black children* (pp. 159–173). Beverly Hills, CA: Sage Publications.

Fergusson, D. M., & Woodward, L. J. (2002). Mental health, educational, and social role outcomes of adolescents with depression. *Archives of General Psychiatry, 59,* 225–231.

Fergusson, D. M., Horwood, L. J., & Meautrais, A. L. (1999). Is sexual orientation related to mental health problems and suicidality in young people? *Archives of General Psychiatry, 56,* 876–880.

Ferketich, A. K., Schwartzbaum, J. A., Frid, D. J., & Moeschberger, M. L. (2000). Depression as an antecedent to heart disease among women and men in the NHANES I Study. *Archives of Internal Medicine, 160,* 1261–1268.

Ferrans, C. E., Cohen, F. L., & Smith, K. M. (1992). The quality of life of persons with narcolepsy. *Loss, Grief and Care, 5,* 23–32.

Fewer teens using drugs. (2004). *CNN Web Posting,* Retrieved March 3, 2004, from http://www.cnn.com/2004/HEALTH/parenting/02/25/teen.drug/index.html

Fiellin, D. A., O'Connor, P. G., Chawarski, M., Pakes, J. P. Pantalon, M. V., & Schottenfeld, R. S. (2001). Methadone maintenance in primary care: A randomized controlled trial. *Journal of the American Medical Association, 286,* 1724–1731.

Fieve, R. R. (1975). *Moodswings: The third revolution in psychiatry.* New York: Morrow.

Fiez, J. A. (2001). Bridging the gap between neuroimaging and neuropsychology: Using working memory as a case-study. *Journal of Clinical & Experimental Neuropsychology, 23,* 19–31.

Finkelhor, D., Hotaling, G., Lewis, I. A., & Smith, C. (1990). Sexual abuse in a national survey of adult men and women: Prevalence, characteristics, and risk factors. *Child Abuse and Neglect, 14,* 19–28.

Finney, J. W., & Monahan, S. C. (1996). The cost-effectiveness of treatment for alcoholism: A second approximation. *Journal of Studies on Alcohol, 57,* 229–243.

Fishbain, D. A. (1991). "Koro: Proposed classification for *DSM-IV*": Comment. *American Journal of Psychiatry, 148,* 1765–1766.

Fisher, B. S., Daigle, L. E., Cullen, F. T., & Turner, M. G. (2003). Reporting sexual victimization to the police and others: Results from a national-level study of college women. *Criminal Justice & Behavior, 30*(1), 6–38.

Fisher, J. D., Fisher, W. A., Bryan, A. D., & Misovich, S. J. (2002). Information-motivation-behavioral skills model-based HIV risk behavior change intervention for inner-city high school youth. *Health Psychology, 21,* 177–186.

Fitzgerald, P. B., Brown, T. L., Marston, N. A. U., Daskalakis, J., de Castella, A., & Kulkarni, J. (2003). Transcranial magnetic stimulation in the treatment of depression: A double-blind, placebo-controlled trial. *Archives of General Psychiatry, 60,* 1002–1008.

Foa, E. B. (1996). The efficacy of behavioral therapy with obsessive-compulsives. *The Clinical Psychologist, 49,* 19–21.

Foa, E. B., & Kozak, M. J. (1995). *DSM-IV* field trial: Obsessive-compulsive disorder. *American Journal of Psychiatry, 152,* 90–96.

Foa, E. B., & Rothbaum, B. O. (1998). *Treating the trauma of rape: Cognitive-behavioral therapy for PTSD.* New York: Guilford Press.

Foderaro, L. W. (1994, November 8). "Clubhouse" helps mentally ill find the way back. *The New York Times,* p. B1.

Fombonne, E. (2003a). The prevalence of autism. *Journal of the American Medical Association, 287,* 87–89.

Fombonne, E. (2003b). Epidemiological surveys of autism and other pervasive developmental disorders: An update. *Journal of Autism and Developmental Disorders, 33,* 365–382.

Food and Drug Administration (FDA) (2004, March). Antidepressant use in children, adolescents, and adults. *FDA/Center for Drug Evaluation and Research Online Posting.* Retrieved April 23, 2004, from http://www.fda.gov/cder/drug/antidepressants/default.htm.

Ford, J. M., Mathalon, D. H., Kalba, S., Whitfield, S., Faustman, W. O., & Roth, W. T. (2001). Cortical responsiveness during inner speech in schizophrenia: An event-related potential study. *American Journal of Psychiatry, 158,* 1914–1916.

Forman, D. N., et al. (2000). Postpartum depression: Identification of women at risk. *British Journal of Obstetrics and Gynaecology, 107,* 1210–1217.

Foster, S. E., Vaughan, R. D., Foster, W. H., & Califano, J. A., Jr. (2003). Alcohol consumption and expenditures for underage drinking and adult excessive drinking. *Journal of the American Medical Association, 289,* 989–995.

Fouquereau, E., Fernandez, A., Mullet, E., & Sorum, P. C. (2003). Stress and the urge to drink. *Addictive Behaviors, 28,* 669–685.

Fowles, D. C. (1993). Electrodermal activity and antisocial behavior: Empirical findings and theoretical issues. In J. C. Roy, et al. (Eds.), *Psychological theories of drinking and alcoholism* (pp. 181–226). New York: Guilford Press.

Fox, M. (2000, August 21). Autism checks urged for all babies. *Reuters Limited, MSNBC Web Posting.* Retrieved August 23, 2000, from http://www. msnbc.com/news/449244.asp.

Foxhall, K. (2001, March). Study finds marital stress can triple women's risk of recurrent coronary event. *Monitor on Psychology, 32,* p. 14.

Frackiewicz, E. J., Sramek, J. J., Herrera, J. M., & Cutler, N. R. (1999). Review of neuroleptic dosage in different ethnic groups. In J. M. Herrera et al. (Eds.), *Cross cultural psychiatry* (pp. 107–130). Chichester, England: Wiley.

Frank, E., & Kupfer, D. J. (2000). Peeking through the door to the 21st century. *Archives of General Psychiatry, 57,* 83–85.

Frank, E., & Kupfer, D. J. (2003). Progress in the therapy of mood disorders: Scientific support. *American Journal of Psychiatry, 160,* 1207–1208.

Frankle, W. G., Perlis, R. H., Deckersbach, T., Grandin, L. D., Gray, S. M., Sachs, G. S., et al. (2002). Bipolar depression: Relationship between episode length and antidepressant treatment. *Psychological Medicine, 32,* 1417–23.

Fraser, J. S. (1996). All that glitters is not always gold: Medical offset effects and managed behavioral health care. *Professional Psychology: Research & Practice, 27,* 335–344.

Frauenglass, S., et al. (1997). Family support decreases influence of deviant peers on Hispanic adolescent's substance use. *Journal of Clinical Child Psychology, 26,* 15–23.

Fredrickson, B. L., Tugade, M. M., Waugh, C. E., & Larkin, G. R. (2003). What good are positive emotions in crises? A prospective study of resilience and emotions following the terrorist attacks on the United States on September 11th, 2001. *Journal of Personality and Social Psychology, 84,* 365–376.

Freedman, R. (2003). Schizophrenia. *New England Journal of Medicine, 349,* 1738–1749.

Freedman, R., et al. (1987). Neurobiological studies of sensory gating in schizophrenia. *Schizophrenia Bulletin, 13,* 669–678.

Freemon, F. R. (1981). *Organic mental disease.* Jamaica, NY: Spectrum.

Freiberg, P. (1995, June). Psychologists examine attacks on homosexuals. *APA Monitor, 26*(6), 30–31.

Freud, S. (1957). Mourning and melancholia. (1917). In J. Rickman (Ed.), *A general selection from the works of Sigmund Freud.* Garden City, NY: Doubleday.

Freud, S. (1964). New introductory lectures. In *Standard edition of the complete psychological works of Sigmund Freud* (Vol. 22). London: Hogarth. (Original work published in 1933) (pp. 3–182)

Frick, P. J., & Silverthorn, P. (2001). Psychopathology in children and adolescents. In H. E. Adams (Ed.), *Comprehensive handbook of psychopathology* (3rd ed., 879–919). New York: Plenum Press.

Frick, P. J., Lahey, B. B., Loeber, R., Stouthamer-Loeber, M., Christ, M. A., & Hanson, K. (1992). Familial risk factors to oppositional defiant disorder and conduct disorder: Parental psychopathology and maternal parenting. *Journal of Consulting and Clinical Psychology, 60,* 49–55.

Friedman, M. A., Detweiler-Bedell, J. B., Leventhal, H. E., Horne, R., Keitner, G. I., & Miller, I. W. (2004). Combined psychotherapy and pharmacotherapy for the treatment of major depressive disorder. *Clinical Psychology: Science and Practice, 11,* 47–68.

Friedman, M., & Ulmer, D. (1984). *Treating Type A behavior and your heart.* New York: Fawcett Crest.

Friedman, M., et al. (1986). Alteration of type A behavior and its effect on cardiac recurrences in postmyocardial infarction patients: Summary results of the recurrent coronary prevention project. *American Heart Journal, 112,* 653–665.

Friedman, R. A. (2002, December 31). Born to be happy, through a twist of human hard wire. *The New York Times,* p F5.

Frueh, B. C., et al. (1996). Trauma management therapy: A preliminary evaluation of a multicomponent behavioral treatment for chronic combat-related PTSD. *Behaviour Research and Therapy, 34,* 533–543.

Fuchs, C. S., Stampfer, M. J., Colditz, G. A., Giovannucci, E. L., Manson, J. E., Kawachi, I., et al. (1995). Alcohol consumption and mortality among women. *The New England Journal of Medicine, 332,* 1245–1250.

Fuchs, M. (2001, June 9). For Alzheimer's patients, some solace, if not hope. *The New York Times,* pp. B1, B6.

Fuertes, J. N., & Brobst, K. (2002). Clients' ratings of counselor multicultural competency. *Cultural Diversity and Ethnic Minority Psychology, 8,* 214–223.

Furlong, M., & Oei, T. P. S. (2002). Changes to automatic thoughts and dysfuntional attitudes in group: CBT for depression. *Behavioural and Cognitive Psychotherapy, 30,* 351–360.

Furukawa, T. A., McGuire, H., & Barbui, C. (2002). Meta-analysis of effects and side effects of low dosage tricyclic antidepressants in depression: Systematic review. *British Medical Journal, 325,* 991–995.

G

Gabbard, G. O., et al. (1997). The economic impact of psychotherapy: A review. *American Journal of Psychiatry, 154,* 147–155.

Galea, S., Vlahov, D., Resnick, H., Kilpatrick, D., Bucuvalas, M. J., & Morgan, M. D. An investigation of the psychological effects of the September 11, 2001, attacks on New York City: developing and implementing research in the acute postdisaster period.

Gall, R., Isaac, L., & Kryger, M. (1993). Quality of life in mild obstructive sleep apnea. *Sleep, 16*(Suppl.), S59–S61.

Gallant, J. E. (2000). Strategies for long-term success in the treatment of HIV infection. *Journal of the American Medical Association, 283,* 1329–1334.

Ganellen, R. J. (1996). Comparing the diagnostic efficiency of the MMPI, MCMI-II, and Rorschach: A review. *Journal of Personality Assessment, 67,* 219–243.

Gara, M. A., Woolfolk, R. L., Cohen, B. D, Goldston, R. B., Allen, L. A., & Novalany, J. (1993). Perceptions of self and other in major depression. *Journal of Abnormal Psychology, 102,* 93–100.

Garb, H. N. (1997). Race bias, social class bias, and gender bias in clinical judgment. *Clinical Psychology: Science and Practice, 4,* 99–120.

Garb, H. N. (2000). Computers will become increasingly important for psychological assessment: Not that there's anything wrong with that! *Psychological Assessment, 12,* 31–39.

Garb, H. N. (2003). Incremental validity and the assessment of psychopathology in adults. *Psychological Assessment, 15,* 508–520.

Garb, H. N., Wood, J. M., Lilienfeld, S. O., & Nezworski, M. T. (2002). Effective use of projective techniques in clinical practice: Let the data help with selection and interpretation. *Professional Psychology: Research and Practice, 33,* 454–463.

Garber, J. Keiley, M. K., & Martin, N. C. (2002). Developmental trajectories of adolescents' depressive symptoms: Predictors of change. *Journal of Consulting & Clinical Psychology, 70,* 79–95.

Garber, J., Weiss, B., & Shanley, N. (1993). Cognitions, depressive symptoms, and development in adolescents. *Journal of Abnormal Psychology, 102,* 47–57.

Garbutt, J. C., West, S. L., Carey, T. S., Lohr, K. N., & Crews, F. T. (1999). Pharmacological treatment of alcohol dependence. *Journal of the American Medical Association, 281,* 1318–1325.

Gardner, W., Lidz, C. W., Mulvey, E. P., & Shaw, E. C. (1996). Clinical versus actuarial predictions of violence in patients with mental illnesses. *Journal of Consulting and Clinical Psychology, 64,* 602–609.

Garfield, S. L. (1994). Eclecticism and integration in psychotherapy: Developments and issues. *Clinical Psychology: Science and Practice, 1,* 123–137.

Garlick, D. (2003). Integrating brain science research with intelligence research. *Current Directions in Psychological Science, 12,* 185–189.

Garnefski, N., Kraaij, V., & Spinhoven, P. (2001). De relatie tussen cognitieve copingstrategieen en symptomen van depressie, angst en suiecidaliteit. *Gedrag & Gezondheid: Tijdschrift voor Psychologie & Gezondheid, 29,* 148–158.

Garner, D. M. (1993). Binge eating in anorexia nervosa. In C. G. Fairburn & G. T. Wilson (Eds.), *Binge eating: Nature, assessment, and treatment* (pp. 50–76). New York: Guilford.

Gaser, C., Nenadic, I., Buchsbaum, B. R., Hazlett, E. A., & Buchsbaum, M.S. (2004). Ventricular enlargement in schizophrenia related to volume reduction of the thalamus, striatum, and superior temporal cortex. *American Journal of Psychiatry, 161,* 154–156.

Gatchel, R. J. (2001). Biofeedback and self-regulation of physiological activity: A major adjunctive treatment modality in health psychology. In A. Baum, T. A. Revenson, & J. E. Singer (Eds.), *Handbook of health psychology* (pp. 95–104). Mahwah, NJ: Erlbaum.

Gauthier, J. G., Ivers, H., & Carrier, S. (1996). Nonpharmacological approaches in the management of recurrent headache disorders and their comparison and combination with pharmacotherapy. *Clinical Psychology Review, 16,* 543–571.

Gawin, F. H. (1991). Cocaine addiction: Psychology and neurophysiology. *Science, 251,* 1581.

Gebhard, P. H., Gagnon, J. H., Pomeroy, W. B., & Christenson, C. V. (1965). *Sex offenders: An analysis of types.* New York: Harper & Row.

Geddes, J. R., Burgess, S., Hawton, K., Jamison, K., & Goodwin, G. M. (2004). Long-term lithium therapy for bipolar disorder: Systematic review and meta-analysis of randomized controlled trials. *American Journal of Psychiatry, 161,* 217–222.

Geddes, J., Freemantle, N., Harrison, P., & Bebbington, P. (2000). Atypical antipsychotics in the treatment of schizophrenia: Systematic overview and meta-regression analysis. *British Medical Journal, 321,* 1371–1376.

Geer, J., Heiman, J., & Leitenberg, H. (1984). *Human sexuality.* Englewood Cliffs, NJ: Prentice Hall.

Geller, B., Craney, J. L., Bolhofner, K., Nickelsburg, M. J., Williams, M., & Zimerman, B. (2002). Two-year prospective follow-up of children with a prepubertal and early adolescent bipolar disorder phenotype. *American Journal of Psychiatry, 159,* 927–933.

Geller, B., & DelBello, M. P. (2003). (Eds.). *Bipolar disorder in childhood and early adolescence.* New York: Guilford.

Gelman, D. (1994, April 18). The mystery of suicide. *Newsweek,* pp. 44–49.

George, M. S., Anton, R. F., Bloomer, C., Teneback, C., Drobes, D. J., Lorberbaum, J. P., et al. (2001). Activation of prefrontal cortex and anterior thalamus in alcoholic subjects on exposure to alcohol-specific cues. *Archives of General* Psychiatry, *58,* 345–352.

George, M. S. Nahas, Z., Molloy, M., Speer, A. M., Oliver, N. C., Li, X. B., et al. (2000). A controlled trial of daily left prefrontal cortex TMS for treating depression. *Biological Psychiatry, 48,* 382–389.

Gershater-Molkoa, R. M., Lutzker, J. R., & Sherman, J. A. (2002). Intervention in child neglect: An applied behavioral perspective. *Aggression and Violent Behavior, 7,* 103–124.

Gershon, A. A., Dannon, P. N., & Grunhaus, L. (2003). Transcranial magnetic stimulation in the treatment of depression. *American Journal of Psychiatry, 160,* 835–845.

Gershon, E. S., & Rieder, R. O. (1992). Major disorders of mind and brain. *Scientific American, 267*(3), 126–133.

Gershuny, B. S., & Thayer, J. F. (1999). Relations among psychological trauma, dissociative phenomena, and trauma-related distress: A review and integration. *Clinical Psychology Review, 19,* 631–657.

Ghaemi, S. N., Rosenquist, K. J., Ko, J. Y., Baldassano, C. F., Kontos, N. J., &. Baldessarini, R. J. (2004). Antidepressant treatment in bipolar versus unipolar depression. *American Journal of Psychiatry, 161,* 163–165.

Ghizzani, A. (2003). Aging and male sexuality. *Archives of Sexual Behavior, 32*(3), 294–295.

Gidron, Y., & Davidson, K. (1996). Development and preliminary testing of a brief intervention for modifying CHD-predictive hostility components. *Journal of Behavioral Medicine, 19,* 203–220.

Gidron, Y., Davidson, K., & Bata, I. (1999). The short-term effects of a hostility-reduction intervention on male coronary heart disease patients. *Health Psychology, 18,* 416–420.

Giembycz, M. A., & O'Connor, B. J. (2000). *Asthma: Epidemiology, anti-inflammatory therapy and future trends.* Boston: Birkhauser.

Gil, K. M., Williams, D. A., Keefe, F. J., & Beckham, J. C. (1990). The relationship of negative thoughts to pain and psychological distress. *Behavior Therapy, 21,* 349–362.

Gilbert, S. (1997b, June 25). Social ties reduce risk of a cold. *The New York Times,* p. C11.

Gilbert, S. (2004, March 16). New clues to women veiled in black. *The New York Times, Science Times,* pp. F1, F7.

Gilbert, S. C. (2003). Eating disorders in women of color. *Clinical Psychology: Science and Practice, 10,* 444–455.

Gill, A. R. (2001). Interventions for autism. In reply. *Journal of the American Medical Association, 286,* 670–671. [Letter]

Gist, R., & Devilly, G. J. (2002). Post-trauma debriefing: The road too frequently travelled. *Lancet, 360,* 741–742.

Gittelman-Klein, R., & Mannuzza, S. (1990). Hyperactive boys almost grown up. *Archives of General Psychiatry, 45,* 1131–1134.

Glantz, K., et al. (1996). Virtual reality (VR) for psychotherapy: From the physical to the social environment. *Psychotherapy, 33,* 464–473.

Glaser, R., Kiecolt-Glaser, J. K., Speicher, C. E., & Holliday, J. E. (1985). Stress, loneliness, and changes in herpes virus latency. *Journal of Behavioral Medicine, 8,* 249–260.

Glaser, R., Rice, J., Sheridan, J., Fertel, R., Stout, J., Speicher, C., Pinsky, D., et al. (1987). Stress-related immune suppression: Health implications. *Brain, Behavior, and Immunity, 1,* 7–20.

Glass, R. M. (2000). Panic disorder—It's real and it's treatable. *Journal of the American Medical Association, 283,* 2573–2574. [Editorial]

Glass, R. M. (2001). Electroconvulsive therapy: Time to bring it out of the shadows. *Journal of the American Medical Association, 285,* 1346–1348. [Editorial]

Glazener, C. M., Evans, J. H., & Peto, R. E. (2000). Tricyclic and related drugs for nocturnal enuresis in children. *Cochrane Database Systems Review, 3,* CD002117.

Gleaves, D. H. (1996). The sociocognitive model of dissociative identity disorder: A reexamination of the evidence. *Psychological Bulletin, 120,* 42–59.

Gleaves, D. H., Smith, S. M., Butler, L. D., & Spiegel, D. (2004). False and recovered memories in the laboratory and clinic: A review of experimental and clinical evidence. *Clinical Psychology: Science and Practice, 11,* 3–28.

Glenn, D. (2003, January 27). Liberty, sanity, equality. *The Chronicle of Higher Education,* Retrieved November 14, 2003, from http://www.alternet.org/story.html?StoryID=15034.

Glidden, L. M. (2002). *International review of research in mental retardation* (Vols. 24 & 25). San Francisco: Academic Press.

Glueckauf, R. L., Pickett, T. C., Ketterson, T. U., Loomis, J. S., & Rozensky, R. H. (2003). Preparation for the delivery of telehealth services: A self-study framework for expansion of practice. *Professional Psychology: Research and Practice, 34,* 159–163.

Glynn, S., & Mueser, K. T. (1986). Social learning for chronic mental inpatients. *Schizophrenia Bulletin, 12,* 648–668.

Glynn, S., & Mueser, K. T. (1992). Social learning. In R. P. Liberman (Ed.), *Handbook of psychiatric rehabilitation* (pp. 127–152). New York: Macmillan.

Goddard, A. W., Mason, G. F., Almai, A., Rothman, D. L., Behar, K. L., et al. (2001). Reductions in occipital cortex GABA levels in panic disorder detected with 1h-magnetic spectroscopy. *Archives of General Psychiatry, 58,* 556–561.

Goenjian, A. K., Molina, L., Steinberg, A. M., Fairbanks, L. A., Alvarez, M. L., Goenjian, H. A., et al. (2001). Posttraumatic stress and depressive reactions among Nicaraguan adolescents after Hurricane Mitch. *American Journal of Psychiatry, 158,* 788–794.

Goetz, K. L., & Price, T. R. P. (1994). The case of koro: Treatment response and implications for diagnostic classification. *Journal of Nervous and Mental Disease, 182,* 590–591.

Goff, D. C., & Summs, C. A. (1993). Has multiple personality disorder remained consistent over time? A comparison of past and recent cases. *Journal of Nervous and Mental Disease, 181,* 595–600.

Goisman, R. M., et al. (1994). Panic, agoraphobia, and panic disorder with agoraphobia: Data from a multicenter anxiety disorders study. *Journal of Nervous and Mental Disease, 182,* 72–79.

Goldberg, A. (2003). Heinz Kohut, 1913–1981. *American Journal of Psychiatry, 160,* 670.

Goldberg, C. (2001, July 9). Children trapped by mental illness. *The New York Times,* pp. A1, A11.

Goldberg, I. J., et al. (2001). Wine and your heart: A science advisory for healthcare professionals from the Nutrition Committee, Council on Epidemiology and Prevention, and Council on Cardiovascular Nursing of the American Heart Association. *Circulation, 103,* 472–475.

Goldberg, J. H., Halpern-Felsher, B. L., & Millstein, S. G. (2002). Beyond invulnerability: The importance of benefits in adolescents' decision to drink alcohol. *Health Psychology, 21,* 477–484.

Goldberg, T. E., Egan, M. F., Gscheidle, T., Coppola, R., Weickert, T., Kolachana, B. S., et al. (2003). Executive subprocesses in working memory. *Archives of General Psychiatry, 60,* 889–896.

Golden, O. (2000). The federal response to child abuse and neglect. *American Psychologist, 55,* 1050–1053.

Goldfarb, L. A., Dynens, E. M., & Gerrard, M. (1985). The Goldfarb fear of fat scale. *Journal of Personality Assessment, 49,* 329–332.

Goldstat, R., Briganti, E., Tran, J., Wolfe, R., & Davis, S. R. (2003). Transdermal testosterone therapy improves well-being, mood, and sexual function in premenopausal women. *Menopause, 10,* 390–8.

Goldstein, A. J., de Beurs, E. E., Chambless, D. L., & Wilson, K. A. (2000). EMDR for panic disorder with agoraphobia: Comparison with waiting list and credible attention-placebo control conditions. *Journal of Consulting and Clinical Psychology, 68,* 947–956.

Goldstein, I., et al. (1998). Oral sildenafil in the treatment of erectile dysfunction. *The New England Journal of Medicine, 338,* 1397–1404.

Goldstein, R. L. (1986). Erotomania. *American Journal of Psychiatry, 143,* 802.

Goleman, D. (1988, November 1). Narcissism looming larger as root of personality woes. *The New York Times,* pp. C1, C16.

Goleman, D. (1992, December 8). A rising cost of modernity: Depression. *The New York Times,* pp. C1, C13.

Goleman, D. (1993, December 7). Stress and isolation tied to a reduced life span. *The New York Times,* p. C5.

Goleman, D. (1994a, January 11). Childhood depression may herald adult ills. *The New York Times,* pp. C1, C10.

Goleman, D. (1994b, April 26). Mental decline in aging need not be inevitable. *The New York Times,* p. C1, C10.

Goleman, D. (1995, October 4). Eating disorder rates surprise the experts. *The New York Times,* C11.

Goleman, D. (1995a, July 13). A genetic clue to bedwetting is located. *The New York Times,* p. A8.

Goleman, D. (1995b, June 21). "Virtual reality" conquers fear of heights. *The New York Times,* p. C11.

Golier, J. A., Yehuda, R., Bierer, L. M., Mitropoulou, V., New, A. S., Schmeidler, J., et al. (2003). The relationship of borderline personality disorder to posttraumatic stress disorder and traumatic events. *American Journal of Psychiatry, 160,* 2018–2024.

Gone, J. (2004). Mental health services for Native Americans in the 21st century United States. *Professional Psychology: Research and Practice, 35,* 10–18.

González, B., Huerta-Sánchez, E., Ortiz-Nieves, A., Vázquez-Alvarez, T., & Kribs-Zaleta, C. (2003). Am I too fat? Bulimia as an epidemic. *Journal of Mathematical Psychology, 47,* 515–526.

Goode, E. (2001, February 20). Samson diagnosis: Antisocial personality disorder, with muscles. *The New York Times,* p. F7.

Goode, E. (2003a, April 15). To curb cravings, and maybe more. *The New York Times,* p. F5.

Goode, E. (2003b, May 6). Experts see mind's voices in new light. *The New York Times Online,* Retrieved July 18, 2003, from http://notes.utk.edu/bio/greenberg.nsf/0/611983b95a021f7985256d1f003e1949?OpenDocument.

Goode, E. (2003c, October 14). Study links prescriptions to decrease in suicides. *The New York Times,* p. F5.

Goode, E. (2003d, December 11) British warning on antidepressant use for youth. *The New York Times,* pp. A1, A6.

Goode, E. (2004a). Lifting the veils of autism, one by one by one. *The New York Times,* pp. F1, F4.

Goode, E. (2004b, January 26). Autism cases up; cause is unclear. *The New York Times,* A1, A17.

Goodstein, L., & Connelly, M. (1998, April 30). Teen-age poll finds a turn to the traditional. *The New York Times,* p. A20.

Goodwin, P. J., Leszcz, M., Ennis, M., Koopmans, J., Vincent, L., Guther, H., et al. (2001). The effect of group psychosocial support on survival in metastatic breast cancer. *New England Journal of Medicine, 345,* 1719–1726.

Gooren, L. J. G., & Kruijver, P. M. (2002). Androgens and male behavior. *Molecular and Cellular Endocrinology, 198,* 31–40.

Gordis, E. (1995). The National Institute on Alcohol Abuse and Alcoholism. *Alcohol Health & Research World, 19,* 5–11.

Gordis, E. (1999, May 5). *What we know: Conceptual advances in alcohol research.* National Institute on Alcohol Abuse and Alcoholism (NIAAA). Retrieved July 13, from http://www.niaaa.nih.gov/about/conceptual.htm.

Gordon, C. M., & Carey, M. P. (1996). Alcohol's effects on requisites for sexual risk reduction in men: An initial experimental investigation. *Health Psychology, 15,* 56–60.

Gormally, J., Sipps, G., Raphael, R., Edwin, D., & Varvil-Weld, D. (1981). The relationship between maladaptive cognitions and social anxiety. *Journal of Consulting and Clinical Psychology, 49,* 300–301.

Gorman, C. (1998, November 30). How does it work? *Time,* p. 92.

Gorman, C. (2003, October 20). How to eat smarter. *Time,* pp. 48–59.

Gorman, J. M., Kent, J., Martinez, J., Browne, S., Coplan, J., & Papp, L. A. (2001). Physiological changes during carbon dioxide inhalation in patients with panic disorder, major depression, and premenstrual dysphoric disorder: Evidence for a central fear mechanism. *Archives of General Psychiatry, 58,* 125–131.

Gorman, J. M., Kent, J. M., Sullivan, G. M., & Coplan, J. D. (2000). Neuroanatomical hypothesis of panic disorder, revised. *American Journal of Psychiatry, 57,* 493–505.

Gorwood, P., Leboyer, M., Jay, M., Payan, C., & Feingold, J. (1995). Gender and age at onset in schizophrenia: Impact of family history. *American Journal of Psychiatry, 152,* 208–212.

Gosselin, C., & Wilson, G. (1980). *Sexual variations.* New York: Simon & Schuster.

Gottesman, I. I. (1991). *Schizophrenia genetics: The origins of madness.* New York: Freeman.

Gottesman, I. I., & Gould, T. D. (2003). The endophenotype concept in psychiatry: Etymology and strategic intentions. *American Journal of Psychiatry, 160,* 636–645.

Gottesman, I. I., McGuffin, P., & Farmer, A. E. (1987). Clinical genetics as clues to the "real" genetics of schizophrenia. *Schizophrenia Bulletin, 13,* 23–47.

Gottesman, I. J. (2001). Psychopathology through a life span-genetic prism. *American Psychologist, 56,* 867–878.

Gould, M. S., Greenberg, T., Velting, D. M., & Shaffer, D. (2003). Youth suicide risk and preventive interventions: A review of the past 10 years. *Journal of the American Academy of Child and Adolescent Psychiatry; 42,* 386–405.

Gould, M. S., Greenberg, T., Velting, D. M., & Shaffer, D. (2003). Youth suicide risk and preventive interventions: A review of the past 10 years. *Evidence Based Mental Health, 6,* 121.

Gould, R. A., et al. (1997). Cognitive-behavioral and pharmacological treatment for social phobia: A meta-analysis. *Clinical Psychology: Science and Practice, 4,* 291–306.

Gould, R., Miller, B. L., Goldberg, M. A., & Benson, D. F. (1986). The validity of hysterical signs and symptoms. *The Journal of Nervous and Mental Disease, 174,* 593–597.

Gouzoulis-Mayfrank, E., et al. (2000). Impaired cognitive performance in drug free users of recreational ecstasy (MDMA). *Journal of Neurology, Neurosurgery, & Psychiatry, 68,* 719–725.

Grady, D. (1997, January 21). Brain-tied gene defect may explain why schizophrenics hear voices. *The New York Times,* pp. C1, C3.

Grady, D. (2002, November 26). Why we eat (and eat and eat). *The New York Times,* pp. F 1, F 4.

Grady, D. (2003, April 15). Quest for weight-loss drug takes an unusual turn. *The New York Times,* p. F. 5

Grady, D. (2004, April 7). Minimal benefit is seen in drugs for Alzheimer's. *The New York Times,* pp. A1, A16.

Graham, J. R. (2000). *MMPI-2: Assessing personality and psychopathology.* New York: Oxford University Press.

Grange, D., Telch, C. F., & Tibbs, J. (1998). Eating attitudes and behaviors in 1,435 South African caucasian and non-caucasian college students. *American Journal of Psychiatry, 155,* 250–254.

Grant, B. F. (1997). Prevalence and correlates of alcohol use and *DSM-IV* alcohol dependence in the United States: Results of the National Longitudinal Alcohol Epidemiologic Survey. *Journal of Studies on Alcohol, 58,* 464–473.

Grant, B. F., et al. (1994). Prevalence of *DSM-IV* alcohol abuse and dependence: United States, 1992. *Alcohol Health & Research World, 18,* 243–248.

Grant, B. F., Stinson, F. S., Dawson, D. A., Chou, P., Ruan, W. J., & Pickering, R. P. (2004). Co-occurrence of 12-month alcohol and drug use disorders and personality disorders in the United States: Results from the national epidemiologic survey on alcohol and related conditions. *Archives of General Psychiatry, 61,* 361–368.

Gray, M. J., & Acierno, R. (2002) Posttraumatic stress disorder. In M. Hersen (Ed.), *Clinical behavior therapy: Adults and children* (pp. 106–124). New York: Wiley.

Gray-Little, B., & Hafdahl, A. R. (2000). Factors influencing racial comparisons of self-esteem: A quantitative review. *Psychological Bulletin, 126,* 26–54.

Greenberg, R. P., & Bornstein, R. F. (1988a). The dependent personality: I. Risk for physical disorders. *Journal of Personality Disorders, 2,* 126–135.

Greenberg, R. P., & Bornstein, R. F. (1988b). The dependent personality: II. Risk for psychological disorders. *Journal of Personality Disorders, 2,* 136–143.

Greenberg, R. P., et al. (1994). A meta-analysis of fluoxetine outcome in the treatment of depression. *Journal of Nervous and Mental Disease, 182,* 547–551.

Greenberger, E., Chen, C., & Tally, S. R. (2000). Family, peer, and individual correlates of depressive symptomatology among U.S. and Chinese adolescents. *Journal of Consulting and Clinical Psychology, 68,* 209–219.

Greene, B. A. (1985). Considerations in the treatment of Black patients by White therapists. *Psychotherapy, 22,* 389–393.

Greene, B. A. (1986). When the therapist is White and the patient is Black: Considerations for psychotherapy in the feminist heterosexual and lesbian communities. *Women & Therapy, 5,* 41–65.

Greene, B. A. (1990). Sturdy bridges: The role of African American mothers in the socialization of African American children. *Women & Therapy, 10,* 205–225.

Greene, B. A. (1992a). Black feminist psychotherapy. In E. Wright (Ed.), *Psychoanalysis and feminism: A critical dictionary* (pp. 34–35). Oxford, UK: Basil Blackwell.

Greene, B. A. (1992b). Still here: A perspective on psychotherapy with African American women. In J. Chrisler & D. Howard (Eds.), *New directions in feminist psychology* (pp. 13–25). New York: Springer.

Greene, B. A. (1993a). African American women. In L. Comas-Diaz & B. Greene (Eds.), *Women of color and mental health.* (pp. 13-25) New York: Guilford Press.

Greene, B. A. (1993b, Spring). Psychotherapy with African American women: The integration of feminist and psychodynamic approaches. *Journal of Training and Practice in Professional Psychology, 7,* 49–66.

Greene, R. L., Robin, R. W., Albaugh, B., Caldwell, A., & Goldman, D. (2003). Use of the MMPI-2 in American Indians: II. Empirical correlates. *Psychological Assessment, 5,* 360–369.

Greene, R. W., & Ablon, J. S. (2001). What does the MTA study tell us about effective psychosocial treatment for ADHD? *Journal of Clinical Child Psychology, 30*(1), 114–121.

Greene, R. W., Biederman, J., Zerwas, S., Monuteaux, M. C., Goring, J. G., & Faraone, S. V., (2002). Psychiatric comorbidity, family dysfunction, and social impairment in referred youth with oppositional defiant disorder. *American Journal of Psychiatry, 159,* 1214–1224.

Greengrass, M. (2002, September). Psychological aspects of asthma: 10 years of research. *Monitor on Psychology,* p. 13.

Greenhill, L. L. (1998). Childhood attention deficit hyperactivity disorder: Pharmacological treatments. In P. E. Nathan & J. M. Gorman (Eds.), *A guide to treatments that work* (pp. 42–64). New York: Oxford University Press.

Greenhouse, L. (1992, June 23). Defendants must prove incompetency. *The New York Times,* p. A17.

Greenhouse, L. (2003, July 1). In a momentous term, justices remake the law, and the court. *The New York Times,* pp. A1, A18, A19.

Greenspan, R. (2003, September 25). Porn pages reach 260 million. *ClickZ Network Web Posting*, Retrieved April 23, 2004, from http://www.clickz.com/stats/big_picture/traffic_patterns/article.php/3083001.

Gregory, J. (2003). *Sickened, the memoir of a Münchausen by proxy childhood*. New York: Bantam.

Griffith, J. (1983). Relationship between acculturation and psychological impairment in adult Mexican-Americans. *Hispanic Journal of Behavioral Sciences, 5*, 431–459.

Grissom, R. J. (1996). The magical number .7 + −.2: Meta-meta-analysis of the probability of superior outcome in comparisons involving therapy, placebo, and control. *Journal of Consulting and Clinical Psychology, 64*, 973–982.

Grob, G. N. (1983). *Mental illness and American society, 1875–1940*. Princeton, NJ: Princeton University Press.

Grob, G. N. (1994). *The mad among us: A history of the care of America's mentally ill*. New York: Free Press.

Grof, P., & Alda, M. (2000). Discrepancies in the efficacy of lithium. *Archives of General Psychiatry, 57*, 191.

Gross, J. (2004, January 30). As autism cases rise, parent run frenzied race to get help. *The New York Times*, pp. A1, B7.

Grossman, L. (2003, January 20). Can Freud get his job back? *Time*, pp. 48–51.

Groth, A. N., & Birnbaum, H. J. (1979). *Men who rape: The psychology of the offender*. New York: Plenum Press.

Grunder, G., Carlsson, A., & Wong, D. F. (2002). Mechanism of new antipsychotic medications: Occupancy is not just antagonism. *Archives of General Psychiatry, 60*, 974–977.

Guarnaccia, P. J., & Rodriguez, O. (1996). Concepts of culture and their role in the development of culturally competent mental health services. *Hispanic Journal of Behavioral Sciences, 18*, 419–443.

Guertin, T. L. (1999). Eating behavior of bulimics, self-identified binge eaters, and noon-eating disordered individuals: What differentiates these populations? *Clinical Psychology Review, 19*, 1–24.

Gullette, E. C. D., et al. (1997). Effects of mental stress on myocardial ischemia during daily life. *Journal of the American Medical Association, 277*, 1521–1526.

Gunderson, E. W., Vosburg, S. K., & Hart, C. L. (2002). Does marijuana use cause long-term cognitive deficits? *Journal of the American Medical Association, 287*, 2652. [Letter]

Gunderson, J. G. (1996). The borderline patient's intolerance of aloneness: Insecure attachments and therapist availability. *American Journal of Psychiatry, 153*, 752–758.

Gunderson, J. G. (2001). *Borderline personality disorder: A clinical guide*. Washington DC: American Psychiatric Press.

Gupta, S. (2003, January 20). If everyone were on Prozac. *Time*, p. 49.

Gur, R. E., Cowell, P. E., Latshaw, A., Turetsky, B. I., Grossman, R. I., Arnold, S. E., et al. (2000). Reduced dorsal and orbital prefrontal gray matter volumes in schizophrenia. *Archives of General Psychiatry, 57*, 761–768.

Gur, R. E., Turetsky, B. I., Cowell, P. E., Finkelman, C., Maany, V., Grossman, R. I., et al (2000). Temporolimbic volume reductions in schizophrenia. *Archives of General Psychiatry, 57*, 769–775.

Guralnik, O., Schmeidler, J., & Simeon, D. (2000). Feeling unreal: Cognitive processes in depersonalization. *American Journal of Psychiatry, 157*, 103–109.

Guskiewicz, K. M., McCrea, M., Marshall, S. W., Cantu, R. C., Randolph, C., Barr, W., et al. (2003). Cumulative effects associated with recurrent concussion in collegiate football players: The NCAA concussion study. *Journal of the American Medical Association, 290*, 2549–2555.

Gutheil, T. G. (1980). In search of true freedom: Drug refusal, involuntary medication, and "rotting with your rights on." *American Journal of Psychiatry, 137*, 327–328.

Guthrie, P. C., & Mobley, B. D. (1994). A comparison of the differential diagnostic efficiency of three personality dis-

order inventories. *Journal of Clinical Psychology, 50*, 656–665.

Guydish, J., Werdegar, D., Sorensen, J. L., Clark, W., & Acampora, A. (1998). Drug abuse day treatment: A randomized clinical trial comparing day and residential treatment programs. *Journal of Consulting and Clinical Psychology, 66*, 280–289.

Guze, S. B. (1993). Genetics of Briquet's syndrome and somatization disorder: A review of family, adoption, and twin studies. *Annals of Clinical Psychiatry, 5*, 225–230.

H

Haaga, D. A. F. (1995). Metatraits and cognitive assessment: Application to attributional style and depressive symptoms. *Cognitive Therapy and Research, 19*, 121–142.

Haake, P., Schedlowski, M., Exton, M. S., Giepen, C., Hartmann, U., et al. (2003). Acute neuroendocrine response to sexual stimulation in sexual offenders. *Canadian Journal of Psychiatry, 48*(4), 265–271.

Habib, M. (2000). The neurological basis of developmental dyslexia: An overview and working hypothesis. *Brain, 123*(12), 2373–2399.

Häfner, H., an der Heiden, W., Behrens, S., Gattaz, W. F., Hambrecht, M., Loffler, W., et al. (1998). Causes and consequences of the gender difference in age at onset of schizophrenia. *Schizophrenia Bulletin, 24*, 99–113.

Hagen, S., & Carouba, M. (2002). *Women at Ground Zero: Stories of courage and compassion*. Indianapolis, IN: Alpha Books.

Hall, G. N. (2003). Cultual competence in clinical psychology research. *Clinical Psychologist, 56*, 11–16.

Halmi, K. A., et al. (2000). Perfectionism in anorexia nervosa: Variation by clinical subtype, obsessionality, and pathological eating behavior. *American Journal of Psychiatry, 157*, 1799–1805.

Halmi, K., Agras, W. S., Mitchell, J., Wilson, G. T., Crow, S., Bryson, S. W., et al. (2002). Relapse predictors of patients with bulimia nervosa who achieved abstinence through cognitive behavioral therapy. *American Journal of Psychiatry, 59*, 1105–1109.

Ham, L. S., & Hope, D. A. (2003). College students and problematic drinking: A review of the literature. *Clinical Psychology Review, 23*, 719–759.

Hamel, M., Shafer, T. W., & Erdberg, P. (2003). A study of nonpatient preadolescent Rorschach protocols. *Journal of Personality Assessment, 75*, 280–294.

Hamilton, K. E., & Dobson, K. S. (2002). Cognitive therapy of depression: Pretreatment patient predictors of outcome. *Clinical Psychology Review, 22*, 875–893.

Hamilton, S. P., Slager, S. L., De Leon, A. B., Heiman, G. A., Klein, D. F., Hodge, S. E., et al. (2004). Evidence for genetic linkage between a polymorphism in the adenosine 2A receptor and panic disorder. *Neuropsychopharmacology, 29*, 558–565.

Hammen, C., & Compas, B. E. (1994). Unmasking unmasked depression in children and adolescents: The problem of comorbidity. *Clinical Psychology Review, 14*, 585–603.

Hammen, C., & de Mayo, R. (1982). Cognitive correlates of teacher stress and depressive symptoms: Implications for attributional models of depression. *Journal of Abnormal Psychology, 91*, 96–101.

Hammen, C., & Gitlin, M. (1997). Stress reactivity in bipolar patients and its relation to prior history of disorder. *American Journal of Psychiatry, 154*, 856–857.

Hammen, C., Henry, R., & Daley, S. E. (2000). Depression and sensitization to stressors among young women as a function of childhood adversity. *Journal of Consulting and Clinical Psychology, 68*, 782–787.

Hancock, L. (1996, March 18). Mother's little helper. *Newsweek*, pp. 51–56.

Hankin, B. L., Abramson, L. Y., Moffitt, T. E., Silva, P. A., McGee, R., & Angell, K. E. (1998). Development of depression from preadolescence to young adulthood:

Emerging gender differences in a 10-year longitudinal study. *Journal of Abnormal Psychology, 107*, 128–140.

Hanna, F. J. (2003). Confronting the controversy. *Contemporary Psychology: APA Review of Books, 48*, 835–836.

Hansen, N. B., Lambert, M. J., & Forman, E. M. (2002). The psychotherapy dose-response effect and its implication for treatment delivery services. *Clinical Psychology: Science and Practice, 9*, 329–343.

Hare, R. D. (1965). Temporal gradient of fear arousal in psychopaths. *Journal of Abnormal Psychology, 70*, 442–445.

Hariri, A. R., Mattay, V. S., Tessitore, A., Kolachana, B., Fera, F., Goldman, D. (2002). Serotonin transporter genetic variation and the response of the human amygdala. *Science, 19*, 400–403.

Harmer, C. J., Bhagwagar, Z., Perrett, D. I., Vollm, B. A., Cowen, P. J., et al. (2003). Acute SSRI administration affects the processing of social cues in healthy volunteers. *Neuropsychopharmacology, 28*, 148–152.

Harpur, T. J., & Hare, R. D. (1994). Assessment of psychopathy as a function of age. *Journal of Abnormal Psychology, 103*, 604–609.

Harris, A. E., & Curtin, L. (2002). Parental perceptions, early maladaptive schemas, and depressive symptoms in young adults. *Cognitive Therapy and Research, 26*, 405–416.

Harris, G. (2004, June 2). Antidepressants seen as effective for adolescents. *The New York Times*, pp. A1, A16.

Harris, G. (2004, September 16). Doctors say they will cut antidepressant use. *The New York Times*, p.A18.

Harrop, C., & Trower, P. (2001). Why does schizophrenia develop at late adolescence? *Clinical Psychology Review, 21*, 241–266.

Hartung, C. M., & Widiger, T. A. (1998). Gender differences in the diagnosis of mental disorders: Conclusions and controversies of the *DSM-IV*. *Psychological Bulletin, 123*, 260–278.

Hartung, C. M., Willcutt, E. G., Lahey, B. B., Pelham, W. E., Loney, J., et al. (2002). Sex differences in young children who meet criteria for attention deficit hyperactivity disorder. *Journal of Clinical Child and Adolescent Psychology, 31*, 453–464.

Harvey, A. G., & Bryant, R. A. (2000). Two-year prospective evaluation of the relationship between acute stress disorder and posttraumatic stress disorder following mild traumatic brain injury. *American Journal of Psychiatry, 157*, 629–631.

Harvey, P. D., et al. (1997). Age-related differences in formal thought disorder in chronically hospitalized schizophrenic patients: A cross-sectional study. *American Journal of Psychiatry, 154*, 205–210.

Haughton, E., & Ayllon, T. (1965). Production and elimination of symptomatic behavior. In L. P. Ullmann & L. Krasner (Eds.), *Case studies in behavior modification*. (pp. 94–98) New York: Holt, Rinehart and Winston.

Havermans, R. C., &. Jansen, A. T. M. (2003). Increasing the efficacy of cue exposure treatment in preventing relapse of addictive behavior. *Addictive Behaviors, 28*, 989–994.

Hawkins, E. H., Cummins, L. H., & Marlatt, G. A. (2004). Preventing substance abuse in American Indian and Alaska Native Youth: Promising strategies for healthier communities. *Psychological Bulletin, 130*, 304–323.

Hawton, K., & Catalan, J. (1990). Sex therapy for vaginismus: Characteristics of couples and treatment outcomes. *Sexual and Marital Therapy, 5*, 39–48.

Hayes, B. (2001). *Sleep demons: An insomniac's memoir*. New York: Washington Square Press.

Hayes, S. C., & Wilson, K. G. (2003). Mindfulness: Method and process. *Clinical Psychology: Science and Practice, 10*, 161–165.

Hazlett, E. A., Buchsbaum, M. S., Kemether, E., Bloom, R., Platholi, J., et al. (2004). Abnormal glucose metabolism in the mediodorsal nucleus of the thalamus in schizophrenia. *American Journal of Psychiatry, 161*, 305–314.

Haznedar, M. M., Buchsbaum, M. S., Wei, T. C., Hof, P. R., Cartwright, C., Bienstock, C. A., et al. (2000). Limbic circuitry in patients with autism spectrum disorders studied with positron emission tomography and magnetic resonance imaging. *American Journal of Psychiatry, 157,* 1994–2001.

Headache coping strategies depend on the cause. (2000, August 14). *CNN Web Posting.* Retrieved August 20, 2000, from http://www.cnn.com/2000/HEALTH/08/14/headache.redux/index.html

Heckman, T. G., Anderson, E. S., Sikkema, K. J., Kochman, A., Kalichman, S. C., & Anderson, T. (2004). Emotional distress in nonmetropolitan persons living with HIV disease enrolled in a telephone-delivered, coping improvement group intervention. *Health Psychology, 23,* 94–100.

Heidrich, S. M., Forsthoff, C. A., & Ward, S. E. (1994). Psychological adjustment in adults with cancer: The self as mediator. *Health Psychology, 13,* 346–353.

Heimberg, R. G., Turk, C. L., & Mennin, D. S. (2004). (Eds.). *Generalized anxiety disorder.* New York: Guilford.

Hellmich, N. (2003, April 24). Being overweight linked to dying of cancer. *USA Today,* p. 1A.

Helmuth, L. (2001). Commentary: Dyslexia: Same brains, different languages. *Science, 291,* 2064.

Hendin, H., Maltsberger, J. T., Lipschitz, A., Pollinger H., & Kyle, J. (2001). Recognizing and responding to a suicide crisis. *Suicide & Life-Threatening Behavior, 31*(2), 115–128.

Henkin, W. A. (1985). Toward counseling the Japanese in America: A cross-cultural primer. *Journal of Counseling and Development, 63,* 500–503.

Henry, M., Pascual-Leone, A., & Cole, J. (2003). Electromagnetic stimulation shows promise for treatment-resistant depression. *HealthPlace.com Depression Community,* Retrieved November 14, 2003, from http://www.healthyplace.com/communities/depression/treatment/tms/index.asp.

Herbert, J. D., et al. (2000). Science and pseudoscience in the development of eye movement desensitization and reprocessing. *Clinical Psychology Review, 20,* 945–972.

Herbert, L. E., Scherr, P. A., Bienias, J. L., Bennett, D. A., & Evans, D. A. (2003). Alzheimer's disease in the U.S. population: Prevalence estimates using the 2000 census. *Archives of Neurology, 60,* 1119–1122.

Herbert, M. R., Harris, G. J., Adrien, K. T., Ziegler, D. A., Makris, N., Kennedy, D. N., et al. (2002). Abnormal asymmetry in language association cortex in autism. *Annals of Neurology, 52,* 588–96.

Herbert, P. B. (2002). The duty to warn: A reconsideration and critique. *The Journal of the American Academy of Psychiatry and the Law, 30,* 417–424.

Herbert, P. B., & Young, K. A. (2002). *Tarasoff* at twenty-five. *The Journal of the American Academy of Psychiatry and the Law, 30,* 275–281.

Herek, G. M. (1996). Heterosexism and homophobia. In R. P. Cabaj & T. S. Stein (Eds.), *Textbook of homosexuality and mental health* (pp. 101–113). Washington, DC: American Psychiatric Association Press.

Herkov, M. J., Gynther, M. D., Thomas, S., & Myers, W. C. (1996). MMPI differences among adolescent inpatients, rapists, sodomists, and sexual abusers. *Journal of Personality Assessment, 66,* 81–90.

Hernandez, R. (2000, August 2). In new drug battle, use of ecstasy among young soars. *The New York Times,* p. A21.

Herrera, V. M., & McCloskey, L. A. (2003). Sexual abuse, family violence, and female delinquency: Findings from a longitudinal study. *Violence & Victims, 18,* 319–334.

Hertz, M. R. (1986). Rorschach bound: A 50-year memoir. *Journal of Personality Assessment, 50,* 396–416.

Herwig, U., Lampe, Y., Juengling, F. D., Wunderlich, A., Walter, H., Spitzer, M., et al. (2003). Add-on rTMS for treatment of depression: A pilot study using stereotaxic coil-navigation according to PET data. *Journal of Psychiatric Research, 37,* 267–275.

Herzog, W., Schellberg, D., & Deter, H. C. (1997). First recovery in anorexia nervosa patients in the long-term course: A discrete-time survival analysis. *Journal of Consulting and Clinical Psychology, 65,* 169–177.

Heston, L. L., White, J. A., & Mastri, A. R. (1987). Pick's disease: Clinical genetics and natural history. *Archives of General Psychiatry, 44,* 409–411.

Hettema, J. M., Annas, P., Neale, M. C., Kendler, K. S., & Fredrikson, M. (2003). A twin study of the genetics of fear conditioning. *Archives of General Psychiatry, 60,* 702–708.

Hettema, J. M., Neale, M. C., & Kendler, K. S. (2001). A review and meta-analysis of the genetic epidemiology of anxiety disorders. *American Journal of Psychiatry, 158,* 1568–1578.

Heun, R., Papassotiropoulos, A., Jessen, F., Maier, W., & Breitner, J. C. (2001). A family study of Alzheimer disease and early- and late-onset depression in elderly patients. *Archives of General Psychiatry, 58,* 190–196.

Higgins, S. T., Heil, S. H., & Lussier, J. P. (2004). Clinical implications of reinforcement as a determinant of substance use disorders *Annual Review of Psychology, 55,* 431–461.

Hilchey, T. (1994, November 11). High anxiety raises risk of heart failure in men, study finds. *The New York Times,* p. A17.

Hill, K. G., et al. (2000). Early adult outcomes of adolescent binge drinking: Person- and variable-centered analyses of binge drinking trajectories. *Alcohol: Clinical Experimental Research, 24,* 892–901.

Hingson, R. W., Heeren, T., Jamanka, A., & Howland, J. (2000). Age of drinking onset and unintentional injury involvement after drinking. *Journal of the American Medical Association, 284,* 1527–1533.

Hirsch, S. R., & Leff, J. P. (1975). *Abnormalities in parents of schizophrenics.* Oxford, U.K.: Oxford University Press.

Hochhausen, N. M., Lorenz, A. R., & Newman, J. P. (2002). Specifying the impulsivity of female inmates with borderline personality disorder. *Journal of Abnormal Psychology, 111,* 495–501.

Hoffman, R. E., Rapaport, J., Mazure, C. M., & Quinlan, D. M. (1999). Selective speech perception alterations in schizophrenic patients reporting hallucinated "voices." *American Journal of Psychiatry, 156,* 393–399.

Hoffman, S. G. (2000a). Self-focused attention before and after treatment of social phobia. *Behavior Research and Therapy, 38,* 717–725.

Hoffman, S. G. (2000b). Treatment of social phobia: Potential mediators and moderators. *Clinical Psychology: Science and Practice, 7*(1), 3–16.

Hoffman, S. G., Newman, M. G., Ehlers, A., & Roth, W. T. (1995). Psychophysiological differences between subgroups of social phobia. *Journal of Abnormal Psychology, 104,* 224–231.

Hoffman, W., & Prior, M. (1982). Neuropsychological dimensions of autism in children: A test of the hemispheric dysfunction hypothesis. *Journal of Clinical Neuropsychology, 4,* 27–42.

Hogan, B. E., Linden, W., & Najarian, B. (2002). Social support interventions. Do they work? *Clinical Psychology Review, 22,* 381–440.

Hogarty, G. E., et al. (1997). Three-year trials of personal therapy among schizophrenic patients living with or independent of family, II: Effects on adjustment of patients. *American Journal of Psychiatry, 154,* 1514–1524.

Hogarty, G. E., Schroeder, N. R., Ulrich, R., Mussare, N., Peregino, F., & Herron, E. (1979). Fluphenazine and social therapy in the aftercare of schizophrenic patients. *Archives of General Psychiatry, 36,* 1283–1294.

Holcomb, D. R., Savage, M. P., Seehafer, R., & Waalkes, D. M. (2002). A mixed-gender date rape prevention intervention targeting freshman college athletes. *College Student Journal, 36*(2), 165–179.

Holland, A. J., Sicotte, N., & Treasure, J. (1988). Anorexia nervosa: Evidence of a genetic basis. *Journal of Psychosomatic Research, 32,* 561–571.

Hollingshead, A. B., & Redlich, F. C. (1958). *Social class and mental illness: A community study.* New York: Wiley.

Hollon, S. D., & Kendall, P. C. (1980). Cognitive self-statements in depression: Development of an automatic thoughts questionnaire. *Cognitive Therapy and Research, 4,* 383–395.

Holloway, J. D. (2003, December). Snapshot from the therapy room. *Monitor on Psychology,* p. 31.

Holloway, J. D. (2004, June). Gaining prescriptive knowledge. *Monitor on Psychology,* pp. 22–24.

Holloway, L. (1998, February 12). A mental patient skips care and West Siders worry again. *The New York Times,* p. B5.

Holroyd, K. A. (2002). Assessment and psychological management of recurrent headache disorders. *Journal of Consulting and Clinical Psychology, 70,* 656–677.

Holroyd, K. A., et al. (2001). Management of chronic tension-type headache with tricyclic antidepressant medication, stress management therapy, and their combination: A randomized controlled trial. *Journal of the American Medical Association, 285,* 2208–2215.

Holt, C. S., Heimberg, R. G., & Hope, D. A. (1992). Avoidant personality disorder and the generalized subtype of social phobia. *Journal of Abnormal Psychology, 101,* 318–325.

Holzman, P. S. (1987). Recent studies of psychophysiology in schizophrenia. *Schizophrenia Bulletin, 13,* 49–75.

Holzman, P. S., Levy, D. L., Matthysse, S. W., & Abel, L. A. (1997). Smooth pursuit eye tracking in twins: A critical commentary. *Archives of General Psychiatry, 54,* 429–431.

Honig, A., et al. (1998). Auditory hallucinations: A comparison between patients and nonpatients. *Journal of Nervous and Mental Disease, 186,* 646–651.

Hook, J. N., & Valentiner, D. P. (2002). Are specific and generalized social phobias qualitatively distinct? *Clinical Psychology: Science and Practice, 9,* 379–395.

Hooley, J. M., & Hiller, J. B. (2000). Personality and expressed emotion. *Journal of Abnormal Psychology, 109,* 40–44.

Horne, L. R., Van Vactor, J. C., & Emerson, S. (1991). Disturbed body image in patients with eating disorders. *American Journal of Psychiatry, 148,* 211–215.

Horrigan, J. P., & Barnhill, J. L. J. (2000). "Fluvoxamine and enuresis." Comment. *Journal of the American Academy of Child & Adolescent Psychiatry, 39,* 1465–1466.

Houston, T. K., Cooper, L. A., & Ford, D. E. (2002). Internet support groups for depression: A 1-year prospective cohort study. *American Journal of Psychiatry, 159,* 2062–2068.

Howard, C. E., & Porzelius, L. K. (1999). The role of dieting in binge eating disorder: Etiology and treatment implications. *Clinical Psychology Review, 19,* 25–44.

Howard, K. I., Kopta, S. M., Krause, M. S., & Orlinksy, D. E. (1986). The dose-effect relationship in psychotherapy. *American Psychologist, 41,* 159–164.

Howland, R. H., & Thase, M. E. (1993). A comprehensive review of cyclothymic disorder. *Journal of Nervous and Mental Disease, 18,* 485–493.

Hrobjartsson, A., & Gotzsche, P. C. (2001). Is the placebo powerless? An analysis of clinical trials comparing placebo with no treatment. *The New England Journal of Medicine, 344,* 1594–1602.

Hu, F. B., & Willett, W. C. (2002). Optimal diets for prevention of coronary heart disease. *Journal of the American Medical Association, 288,* 2569–2578.

Huang, L. H. (1994). An integrative approach to clinical assessment and intervention with Asian-American adolescents. *Journal of Clinical Child Psychology, 23,* 21–31.

Huang, W., & Cuvo, A. J. (1997). Social skills training for adults with mental retardation in job-related settings. *Behavior Modification, 21,* 3–44.

Hubbard, K. L., Zapf, P. A., & Ronan, K. A. (2003). Competency restoration: An examination of the differences between defendants predicted restorable and not restorable to competency. *Law and Human Behavior, 27,* 127–139.

Huber, K. M., Gallagher, S. M., Warren, S. T., & Bear, M. F. (2002). Altered synaptic plasticity in a mouse model of fragile X mental retardation. *Proceedings of the National Academy of Sciences of the United States of America, 99,* 7746–7750.

Hublin, C., et al. (1997). Prevalence and genetics of sleepwalking: A population-based twin study. *Neurology, 48,* 177–181.

Hudson, J. I., Mangweth, B., Pope, H. G., Jr., De Col, C., Hausmann, A., Gutweniger, S., et al. (2003). Family study of affective spectrum disorder. *Archives of General Psychiatry, 60,* 170–177.

Hudziak, J. J. (2001). Latent class analysis of ADHD and comorbid symptoms in a population sample of adolescent female twins. *Journal of Child Psychology & Psychiatry & Allied Disciplines, 42,* 933–942.

Huffman, J. C., & Stern, T. A. (2003). The diagnosis and treatment of Munchausen' s. *General Hospital Psychiatry, 25,* 358–363.

Hufford, M. R. (2001). Alcohol and suicidal behavior. *Clinical Psychology Review, 21,* 797–811.

Hugdahl, K., Rund, B. R., Lund, A., Asbjørnsen, A., Egeland, J., Ersland, L., et al. (2004). Brain activation measured with fmri during a mental arithmetic task in schizophrenia and major depression. *American Journal of Psychiatry, 161,* 286–293.

Humphrey, L. L. (1986). Family dynamics in bulimia. In S. C. Feinstein et al. (Eds.), *Adolescent psychiatry* (pp. 315–332). Chicago: University of Chicago Press.

Hunsley, J., & Bailey, J. M. (2001). Whither the Rorschach? An analysis of the evidence *Psychological Assessment, 13,* 472–485.

Hunter, E. C., M., Phillips, M. L., Chalder, T., Sierra, M., & David, A. S. (2003). Depersonalisation disorder: A cognitive–behavioural conceptualization. *Behaviour Research and Therapy, 41,* 1451–1467.

Huprich, S. K., Fuller, K. M., & Schneider, R. B. (2003). Divergent ethical perspectives on the duty-to-warn principle with HIV patients. *Ethics Behav, 13,* 263–278.

Hurlburt, G., & Gade, E. (1984). Personality differences between Native American and Caucasian women alcoholics: Implications for alcoholism counseling. *White Cloud Journal, 3,* 35–39.

Hussong, A. M., et al. (2001). Specifying the relations between affect and heavy alcohol use among young adults. *Journal of Abnormal Psychology, 110,* 449–461.

Hutton, M. (2001). Missense and splice site mutations in tau associated with FTDP-17: Multiple pathogenic mechanisms. *Neurology, 56*(Suppl. 4), S21–S25.

Huxley, N. A., Rendall, M., & Sederer, L. (2000). Psychosocial treatments in schizophrenia: A review of the past 20 years. *Journal of Nervous & Mental Disease, 188,* 187–201.

I

Ickovics, J. R., et al. (2001). Mortality, CD4 cell count decline, and depressive symptoms among HIV-seropositive women: Longitudinal analysis from the HIV Epidemiology Research Study. *Journal of the American Medical Association, 285,* 1466–1474.

Ilardi, S. S., & Craighead, W. E. (1994). The role of nonspecific factors in cognitive-behavior therapy for depression. *Clinical Psychology: Science and Practice, 1,* 138–156.

in 't Veld, B. A., Ruitenberg, A., Hofman, A., Launer, L. J., van Duijn, C. M., et al. (2001). Nonsteroidal antiinflammatory drugs and the risk of Alzheimer's disease. *New England Journal of Medicine, 345,* 1515–1521.

Ingham, R. J. (2003). Brain imaging and stuttering: Some reflections on current and future developments. *Journal of Fluency Disorders, 28,* 411–420.

Ingram, R. E. (1991). Tilting at windmills: A response to Pyszczynski, Greenberg, Hamilton, and Nix. *Psychological Bulletin, 110,* 544–550.

Ingram, R. E., & Siegle, G. J. (2001). Cognition and clinical science: From revolution to evolution. In K. S. Dobson (Ed.), *Handbook of cognitive-behavioral therapies* (2nd ed., pp. 111–137). New York: Guilford Press.

Insanity: A defense of last resort. (1992, February 3). *Newsweek,* p. 49.

Institute of Medicine. (1990). *Broadening the base of treatment for alcohol problems.* Washington, DC: National Academy Press.

International Human Genome Sequencing Consortium (2001). Initial sequencing and analysis of the human genome. *Nature 409,* 860–921.

Ioannidis, J. P. A., & Karassa, P. (2001). Comparison of evidence of treatment effects in randomized and nonrandomized studies. *Journal of the American Medical Association, 286,* 821–830.

Irle, E., Exner, C., Thielen, K., Weniger, G., & Ruether, E. (1998). Obsessive-compulsive disorder and ventromedial frontal lesions: Clinical and neuropsychological findings. *American Journal of Psychiatry, 155,* 255–263.

Ironson, G., Wynings, C., Schneiderman, N., Baum, A., Rodriguez, M., Greenwood, D., et al. (1997). Posttraumatic stress symptoms, intrusive thoughts, loss, and immune function after hurricane Andrew. *Psychosomatic Medicine, 59,* 128–141.

Irwin, M. L., Yasui, Y., Ulrich, C. M., Bowen, D., Rudolph, R. E., Schwartz, R. S., et al. (2002). Effect of exercise on total and intra-abdominal body fat in postmenopausal women: A randomized controlled trial. *Journal of the American Medical Association, 289,* 323–330.

Isacsson, G. (2000). Suicide prevention—A medical breakthrough? *Acta Psychiatrica Scandinavica, 102,* 113–117.

Iversen, L. L. (2000). *The science of marijuana.* New York: Oxford University Press.

Iwamasa, G. Y, Soroccco, K. H., & Koonce, D. A. (2002). Ethnicity and clinical psychology: A content analysis of the literature. *Clinical Psychology Review, 22,* 931–944.

Iwata, N., Tsubuki, S., Takaki Y., Shirotani, K., Lu, B., Gerard, N. P., et al. (2001). Metabolic regulation of brain abeta by neprilysin. *Science, 292,* 1550–1552.

J

Jablensky, A., Sartorius, N., Ernberg, G., & Anker, M. (1992). Schizophrenia: Manifestations, incidence and course in different cultures: A World Health Organization ten-country study [Monograph Suppl.]. *Psychological Medicine, 20*(Monograph Suppl.), 1–97.

Jackson, J., Calhoun, K. S., Amick, A. E., Maddever, H. M., & Habifm V. L. (1990). Young adult women who report childhood intrafamilial sexual abuse: Subsequent adjustment. *Archives of Sexual Behavior, 19,* 211–221.

Jacobi, C., Hayward, C., de Zwaan, M., Kraemer, H. C., & Agras, W. S. (2004). Coming to terms with risk factors for eating disorders: Application of risk terminology and suggestions for a general taxonomy. *Psychological Bulletin, 130,* 19–65.

Jacobs, B. L. (2004). Depression: The brain finally gets into the act. *Current Directions in Psychological Science, 13,* 103–106.

Jacobs, M. K., Christensen, A., Snibbe, J. R., Dolezal-Wood, S., Huber, A., & Polterok, A. (2001). A comparison of computer-based versus traditional individual psychotherapy. *Professional Psychology: Research and Practice, 32,* 92–96.

Jacobs, W., Newman, G. H., & Burns, J. C. (2001). The Homeless Assessment Program: A service-training model for providing disability evaluations for homeless, mentally ill individuals. *Professional Psychology: Research and Practice, 32,* 319–323.

Jacobson, N. S., Dobson, K. S., Truax, P. A., Addis, M. E., Koerner, K., Gollan, J. K., et al. (1996). A component analysis of cognitive-behavioral treatment for depression. *Journal of Consulting and Clinical Psychology, 64,* 295–304.

Jaffe, A. B., & Levine, J. (2003). Efficacy and effectiveness of first- and second-generation antipsychotics in schizophrenia. *Clinical Psychiatry, 64, Suppl 17,* 3–6.

James, S., & Prilleltensky, I. (2002). Cultural diversity and mental health: Towards integrative practice. *Clinical Psychology Review, 22,* 1133–1154.

Jamison, K. R. (1993). *Touched with fire.* New York: Free Press.

Jamison, K. R. (1995). *An unquiet mind.* New York: Knopf.

Janeck, A. S., Calamari, J. E., Riemann, B. C., & Heffelfinger, S. K. (2003). Too much thinking about thinking? Metacognitive differences in obsessive-compulsive disorder. *Journal of Anxiety Disorders, 17,* 181–195.

Janofsky, J. S., Dunn, M. H., Roskes, E. J., Briskin, J. K., & Rudolph, M. S. (1996). Insanity defense pleas in Baltimore City: An analysis of outcome. *American Journal of Psychiatry, 153,* 1464–1468.

Janofsky, M. (2003, December 18). Man who shot Reagan allowed to visit parents unsupervised. *The New York Times,* pp. A1, A38.

Januzzi, J., & DeSanctis, R. (1999). Looking to the brain to save the heart. *Cerebrum, 1,* 31–43.

Jarrett, R. B., Kraft, D., Doyle, J., Foster, B. M., Eaves, G. G., & Silver, P. C. (2001). Preventing recurrent depression using cognitive therapy with and without a continuation phase: A randomized clinical trial. *Archives of General Psychiatry, 58,* 381–388.

Jarrett, R. B., Schaffer, M., McIntire, D., Witt-Browder, A., Kraft, D., & Risser, R. C. (1999). Treatment of atypical depression with cognitive therapy or phenelzine. *Archives of General Psychiatry, 56,* 431–437.

Javier, R. A. (1993). Cited in Rathus, S. A. (1993). *Psychology* (5th ed.). Fort Worth, TX: Harcourt Brace Jovanovich.

Jaycox, L. H., Reivich, K. J., Gillham, J., & Seligman, M. E. P. (1994). Prevention of depressive symptoms in school children. *Behaviour Research and Therapy, 32,* 801–816.

Jeffery, R. W. (1991). Population perspectives on the prevention and treatment of obesity in minority populations. *American Journal of Clinical Nutrition, 53* (6 Suppl.), 1621A–1624S.

Jemmott, J. B., et al. (1983, June 25). Academic stress, power motivation, and decrease in secretion rate of salivary secretory immunoglobin A. *Lancet,* 1400–1402.

Jenkins, C. D. (1988). Epidemiology of cardiovascular diseases. *Journal of Consulting and Clinical Psychology, 56,* 324–332.

Jenkins, J. H. (1988). Ethnopsychiatric interpretations of schizophrenic illness: The problem of nervios within Mexican-American families. *Culture, Medicine, and Psychiatry, 12,* 301–329.

Jenkins, J. H., & Karno, M. (1992). The meaning of expressed emotion: Theoretical issues raised by cross-cultural research. *American Journal of Psychiatry, 149,* 9–21.

Jensen, P. S., Martin, D., & Cantwell, D. P. (1997). Comorbidity in ADHD: Implications for research practice, and DSM-V. *Journal of the American Academy of Child and Adolescent Psychiatry, 36,* 1065–1079.

Jerome, L. W., et al. (2000). The coming of age in telecommunications in psychological research and practice. *American Psychologist, 55,* 507–421.

Jeste, D. V., & Caligiui, M. P. (1993). Tardive dyskinesia. *Schizophrenia Bulletin, 19,* 303–315.

Jeste, D. V., Lindamer, L. A., Evans, J., & Lacro, J. P. (1996). Relationship of ethnicity and gender to schizophrenia and pharmacology of neuroleptics. *Psychopharmacology Bulletin, 32,* 243–251.

Jeste, D. V., Wragg, R. E., Salmon, D. P., Harris, M. J., & Thal, L. J. (1992). Cognitive deficits of patients with Alzheimer's disease with and without delusions. *American Journal of Psychiatry, 149,* 184–188.

Johnson, B. A., Roache, J. D., Javors, M. A., DiClemente, C. C., Cloninger, C. R., Prihoda, T. J., et al. (2000). Ondansetron for reduction of drinking among biologically predisposed alcoholic patients: A randomized controlled trial. *Journal of the American Medical Association, 284,* 963–971.

Johnson, R. E., Chutuape, M. A., Strain, E. C., Walsh, S. L., Stitzer, M. L., & Bigelow, G. E. (2000). A comparison of levomethadyl acetate, buprenorphine, and methadone for opioid dependence. *The New England Journal of Medicine, 343,* 1290–1297.

Johnson, R. J., & McFarland, B. H. (1996). Lithium use and discontinuation in a health maintenance organization. *American Journal of Psychiatry, 153,* 993–1000.

Johnson, S. L., & Leahy, R. L. (2003) (Eds). *Psychological treatment of bipolar disorder.* New York: Guilford.

Johnson, S., Winett, C. A., Meyer, B., Greenhouse, W. J., & Miller, I. (1999). Social support and the course of bipolar disorder. *Journal of Abnormal Psychology, 108,* 558–566.

Johnson, T. J., (2002). College students' self-reported reasons for why drinking games end. *Addictive Behaviors, 27,* 145–153.

Johnson, W. G., Tsoh, J. Y., & Varnado, P. J. (1996). Eating disorders: Efficacy of pharmacological and psychological interventions. *Clinical Psychology Review, 16,* 457–478.

Johnston, T. D., & Edwards, L. (2002). Genes, interactions, and the development of behavior. *Psychological Review, 109,* 26–34.

Jones v. United States, 103 S. Ct. 3043 (1983).

Jones, B. E., & Hill, M. J. (2002). *Mental health issues in lesbian, gay, bisexual, and transgender communities: Review of Psychiatry, Volume 21.* Washington, DC: American Psychiatric Publishing.

Jones, C. (2003). Tightropes and tragedies: 25 years of Tarasoff. *Medicine, Science, and the Law, 43,* 13–22.

Jones, E. (1953). *The life and work of Sigmund Freud.* New York: Basic Books.

Jones, P. B., et al. (1998). Schizophrenia as a long-term outcome of pregnancy, delivery, and perinatal complications: A 28-year follow-up of the 1966 North Finland general population birth cohort. *American Journal of Psychiatry, 155,* 355–364.

Jouriles, E. N., et al. (1997). Psychometric properties of family members' reports of parental physical aggression toward clinic-referred children. *Journal of Consulting and Clinical Psychology, 65,* 309–318.

Judd, L. J. (1997). The clinical course of unipolar major depressive disorders. *Archives of General Psychiatry, 54,* 989–991.

Judd, L. L., Akiskal, H. S., Schettler, P. J., Coryell, W., Endicott, J., Maser, J. D., et al. (2003b). A prospective investigation of the natural history of the long-term weekly symptomatic status of bipolar II disorder. *Archives of General Psychiatry, 60,* 261–269.

Judd, L. L., Akiskal, H. S., Schettler, P. J., Coryell, W., Maser, J., Rice, J. A., et al. (2003a). The comparative clinical phenotype and long term longitudinal episode course of bipolar I and II. *Journal of Affective Disorders, 73,* 19–32.

Judd, L. L., Akiskal, H. S., Zeller, P. J., Paulus, M., Leon, A. C., Maser, J. D., et al. (2000). Psychosocial disability during the long-term course of unipolar major depressive disorder. *Archives of General Psychiatry, 57,* 375–380.

Judd, L. L., Paulus, M. J., Schettler, P. J., Akiskal, H. S., Endicott, J., Leon, A. C., et al. (2000). Does incomplete recovery from first lifetime major depressive episode herald a chronic course of illness? *American Journal of Psychiatry, 157,* 1509–1511.

Just, N., Abramson, L. Y., & Alloy, L. B. (2001). Remitted depression studies as tests of the cognitive vulnerability hypotheses of depression onset. A critique and conceptual analysis. *Clinical Psychology Review, 21,* 63–83.

Just, N., & Alloy, L. B. (1997). The response styles theory of depression: Tests and an extension of the theory. *Journal of Abnormal Psychology, 106,* 221–229.

K

Kabat-Zinn, J. (2003). Mindfulness-based interventions in context: Past, present, and future. *Clinical Psychology: Science and Practice, 10,* 144–156.

Kafka, M. P. (2003). Sex offending and sexual appetite: The clinical and theoretical relevance of hypersexual desire.

International Journal of Offender Therapy & Comparative Criminology, 47(4) 439–451.

Kahn, M. W. (1982). Cultural clash and psychopathology in three aboriginal cultures. *Academic Psychology Bulletin, 4,* 553–561.

Kaiser, R., Hofer, A., Grapengiesser, A., Gasser, T., Kupsch, A., Roots, I., & Brockmoller, J. (2003). L-Dopa-induced adverse effects in PD and dopamine transporter gene polymorphism. *Neurology, 60,* 1750–1755.

Kakiuchi, C., et al. (2003). Impaired feedback regulation of XBP1 as a genetic risk factor for bipolar disorder. *Nature Genetics, 35,* 171–175.

Kalb, C. (2001a). Can this pill stop you from hitting the bottle? *Newsweek,* pp. 46–48.

Kalb, C. (2001b, January 22). Seeing a virtual shrink. *Newsweek,* pp. 34–37.

Kalb, C. (2002, December 2). How to life the mind. *Newsweek,* pp. 67–70.

Kalichman, S. C. (2000). HIV transmission risk behaviors of men and women living with HIV-AIDS: Prevalence, predictors, and emerging clinical intervention. *Clinical Psychology: Science and Practice, 7,* 32–47.

Kamphuis, J. H., Emmelkamp, P. M. G., & Krijn, M. U. (2002). Specific phobia. In M. Hersen (Ed.), *Clinical behavior therapy: Adults and children* (pp. 75–89). New York: Wiley.

Kanai, T., Takeuchi, H., Furukawa, T. A., Yoshimura, R., Imaizumi, T., & Kitamura, T. (2003). Time to recurrence after recovery from major depressive episodes and its predictors. *Psychological Medicine, 33,* 839–845.

Kanaya, T., Scullin, M. H., & Ceci, S. J. (2003). The Flynn Effect and U.S. policies: The impact of rising IQ scores on American society via mental retardation diagnoses. *American Psychologist, 58,* 778–790.

Kandel, D. B. (Ed.). (2002). *Stages and pathways of drug involvement: Examining the gateway hypothesis.* Cambridge, England: Cambridge University Press.

Kandel, D. B. (2003). Does marijuana use cause the use of other drugs? *Journal of the American Medical Association, 289,* 482–483.

Kane, J. M. (1996). Drug therapy: Schizophrenia. *The New England Journal of Medicine, 334,* 34–41.

Kane, J. M., & Marder, S. R. (1993). Psychopharmalogic treatment of schizophrenia. *Schizophrenia Bulletin, 19,* 287–302.

Kanner, A. D., Coyne, J. C., Schaefer, C., & Lazarus, R. S. (1981). Comparison of two modes of stress measurement: Daily hassles and uplifts versus major life events. *Journal of Behavioral Medicine, 4,* 1–39.

Kanner, L. (1943). Autistic disturbances of affective content. *Nervous Child, 2,* 217–240.

Kano, K., & Arisaka, O. (2000). Fluvoxamine and enuresis. *Journal of the American Academy of Child & Adolescent Psychiatry, 39,* 1464–1465.

Kantor, M. (1998). *Homophobia: Description, development and dynamics of gay bashing.* Westport, CT: Praeger.

Kaplan, H. S. (1987). *Sexual aversion, sexual phobias, and panic disorder.* New York: Brunner/Mazel.

Kaplan, R. M. (2000). Two pathways to prevention. *American Psychologist, 55,* 382–396.

Kapp, M. B. (1994). Treatment and refusal rights in mental health: Therapeutic justice and clinical accommodation. *American Journal of Orthopsychiatry, 64,* 223–234.

Kaptchuk, R., Eisenberg, D., & Komaroff, A. (2002, December 2). Pondering the placebo effect. *Newsweek,* pp. 71–73.

Kapur, S., & Remington, G. (2000). Atypical antipsychotics: Patients value the lower incidence of extrapyramidal side effects. *British Medical Journal, 321,* 1360–1361.

Karel, J. J., & Hinrichsen, G. (2000). Treatment of depression in late life: Psychotherapeutic interventions. *Clinical Psychology Review, 20,* 707–729.

Karno, M., et al. (1987). Expressed emotions and schizophrenic outcome among Mexican-American Families. *Journal of Nervous and Mental Disease, 175,* 143–151.

Karp, B. I., Garvey, M., Jacobsen, L. K., Frazier, J. A., Hamburger, S. D., Bedwell, J. S., et al. (2001). Abnormal neurologic maturation in adolescents with early-onset schizophrenia. *American Journal of Psychiatry, 158,* 118–122.

Kasari, D., et al. (1993). Affective development and communication in children with autism. In A. P. Kaiser & D. B. Gray (Eds.), *Enhancing children's communication: Research foundation for intervention* (pp. 201–222). New York: Brookes.

Kasen, S., Cohen, P., Skodol, A. E., Johnson, J. G., Smailes, E., & Brook, J. S. (2001). Childhood depression and adult personality disorder: Alternative pathways of continuity. *Archives of General Psychiatry, 58,* 231–236.

Kasl-Godley, J., & Gatz, M. (2000). Psychosocial interventions for individuals with dementia: An integration of theory, therapy, and a clinical understanding of dementia. *Clinical Psychology Review, 20,* 755–782.

Kaslow, N. J., Thompson, M. P., Okun, A., Price, A., Young, S., Bender, M., et al. (2002). Risk and protective factors for suicidal behavior in abused African American women. *Journal of Consulting and Clinical Psychology, 70,* 311–319.

Kasper, J. A., Hoge, S. K., Feucht-Haviar, T., Cortina, J., & Cohen, B. (1997). Prospective study of patients' refusal of antipsychotic medication under a physician discretion review procedure. *American Journal of Psychiatry, 154,* 483–489.

Kasper, M. E., Rogers, R., & Adams, P. A. (1996). Dangerousness and command hallucinations: An investigation of psychotic inpatients. *Bulletin of the American Academy of Psychiatry and the Law, 24,* 219–224.

Kates, W. R., Burnette, C. P., Eliez, S., Strunge, L. A., Kaplan, D., Landa, R., et al. (2004). Neuroanatomic variation in monozygotic twin pairs discordant for the narrow phenotype for autism. *American Journal of Psychiatry, 161,* 539–546.

Katz, J. N. (1995). *The invention of heterosexuality.* New York: Dutton.

Kauer, J. A. (2003). Addictive drugs and stress trigger a common change at VTA synapses. *Neuron, 37,* 549–550.

Kawachi, I., Colditz, G. A., Ascherio, A., Rimm, E. B., Giovannucci, E., Stampfer, M. J., & Willett, W. C. (1994). Prospective study of phobic anxiety and risk of coronary heart disease in men. *Circulation, 89,* 1992–1997.

Kay, S. R. (1990). Significance of the positive-negative distinction in schizophrenia. *Schizophrenia Bulletin, 16,* 635–652.

Kaysen, S. (1994). *Girl, interrupted.* New York: Random House.

Kazdin, A. E. (1992). *Research design in clinical psychology* (2nd ed.). Boston: Allyn & Bacon.

Kazdin, A. E. (2003). Psychotherapy for children and adolescents. *Annual Review of Psychology, 54,* 253–276.

Kazdin, A. E., & Whitley, M. K. (2003). Treatment of parental stress to enhance therapeutic change among children referred for aggressive and antisocial behavior. *Journal of Consulting and Clinical Psychology, 71,* 504–515.

Keating, G. M., McClellan, K., & Jarvis, B. (2001). Methylphenidate (OROS(R) formulation). *CNS Drugs, 15*(6), 495–500.

Keel, P. K., Mitchell, J. E., Miller, K. B., Davis, T. L., & Crow, S. J. (1999). Long-term outcome of bulimia nervosa. *Archives of General Psychiatry, 56,* 63–69.

Keesey R. E., & Powley, T. L. (1986). The regulation of body weight. *Annual Review of Psychology, 37,* 109–133.

Kelly, B. D., Kennedy, N., & Shanley, D. (2000). Delusion and desire: erotomania revisited. *Acta Psychiatrica Scandinavica, 102,* 74–75.

Kelly, J. A., & Kalichman, S. C. (2002). Behavioral research in HIV/AIDS primary and secondary prevention: Recent advances and future directions. *Journal of Consulting and Clinical Psychology, 70,* 626–639.

Kelly, S. J., Macaruso, P., & Sokol, S. M. (1997). Mental calculation in an autistic savant: A case study. *Journal of Clinical and Experimental Neuropsychology, 19,* 172–184.

Kelner, K., & Helmuth, L. (2003). Obesity—What is to be done? *Science, 299,* 845.

Kemeny, M. E. (2003). The psychobiology of stress. *Current Directions in Psychological Science, 12,* 124–129.

Kenardy, J. A., Dow, M. G. T., Johnston, D. W., Newman, M. G., Thomson, A., & Taylor, C. B. (2003). A comparison of delivery methods of cognitive–behavioral therapy for panic disorder: An international multicenter trial. *Journal of Consulting and Clinical Psychology, 71,* 1068–1075.

Kendall, P. C., Safford, S., Flannery-Schroeder, E., & Webb, A. (2004). Child anxiety treatment: Outcomes in adolescence and impact on substance use and depression at 7.4-year follow-up. *Journal of Consulting and Clinical Psychology, 72,* 276–287.

Kendell, R., & Jablensky, A. (2003). Distinguishing between the validity and utility of psychiatric diagnoses. *American Journal of Psychiatry, 160,* 4–12.

Kendler, K. S., et al. (1997). Resemblance of psychotic symptoms and syndromes in affected sibling pairs from the Irish study of high-density schizophrenia families: Evidence for possible etiologic heterogeneity. *American Journal of Psychiatry, 154,* 191–198.

Kendler, K. S. (1994). Twin studies of psychiatric illness: Current status and future directions. *Archives of General Psychiatry, 50,* 905–918.

Kendler, K. S. (2001). A psychiatric dialogue on the mind-body problem. *American Journal of Psychiatry, 158,* 989–1000.

Kendler, K. S., & Diehl, S. R. (1993). The genetics of schizophrenia: A current, genetic-epidemiologic perspective. *Schizophrenia Bulletin, 19,* 261–295.

Kendler, K. S., Bulik, C. M., Silberg, J., Hettema, J. M., Myers, J., & Prescott, C. A. (2000). Childhood sexual abuse and adult psychiatric and substance use disorders in women: An epidemiological and co-twin control analysis. *Archives of General Psychiatry, 57*(10), 953–959.

Kendler, K. S., et al. (1991). The genetic epidemiology of bulimia nervosa. *American Journal of Psychiatry, 148,* 1627–1637.

Kendler, K. S., et al. (1992a). The genetic epidemiology of phobias in women: The interrelationship of agoraphobia, social phobia, situational phobia, and simple phobia. *Archives of General Psychiatry, 49,* 273–281.

Kendler, K. S., et al. (1993). The lifetime history of major depression in women: Reliability of diagnosis and heritability. *Archives of General Psychiatry, 50,* 863–870.

Kendler, K. S., et al. (2001). The genetic epidemiology of irrational fears and phobias in men. *Archives of General Psychiatry, 58,* 257–265.

Kendler, K. S., & Gardner, C. O. (1998). Boundaries of major depression: An evaluation of *DSM-IV* criteria. *American Journal of Psychiatry, 155,* 172–177.

Kendler, K. S., Gardner, C. O., & Prescott, C. A. (2002). Toward a comprehensive developmental model for major depression in women. *American Journal of Psychiatry, 159,* 1133–1145.

Kendler, K. S., Gruenberg, A. M., & Tsuang, M.T. (1985). Psychiatric illness in first-degree relatives of schizophrenic and surgical control patients, a family study using *DSM-III* criteria. *Archives of General Psychiatry, 42,* 770–779.

Kendler, K. S., Hettema, J. M., Butera, F., Gardner, C. O., & Prescott, C. A., (2003). Life event dimensions of loss, humiliation, entrapment, and danger in the prediction of onsets of major depression and generalized anxiety. *Archives of General Psychiatry, 60,* 789–796.

Kendler, K. S., Jacobson, K. C., Prescott, C. A., & Neale, M. C. (2003). Specificity of genetic and environmental risk factors for use and abuse/dependence of cannabis, cocaine, hallucinogens, sedatives, stimulants, and opiates in male twins. *American Journal of Psychiatry, 160,* 687–695.

Kendler, K. S., Kuhn, J., & Prescott, C. A. (2004). The interrelationship of neuroticism, sex, and stressful life events in the prediction of episodes of major depression. *American Journal of Psychiatry, 161,* 631–636.

Kendler, K. S., & Prescott, C. A. (1999). A population-based twin study of lifetime major depression in men and women. *Archives of General Psychiatry, 56,* 39–44.

Kendler, K. S., & Thornton, L. M., & Gardner, C. O. (2000). Stressful life events and previous episodes in the etiology of major depression in women: An evaluation of the "kindling" hypothesis. *American Journal of Psychiatry, 157,* 1243–1251.

Kendler, K. S., & Walsh, D. (1995). Schizotypal personality disorder in parents and the risk for schizophrenia in siblings. *Schizophrenia Bulletin, 21,* 47–52.

Kendler, K. S., Thornton, L. M., & Pedersen, N. L. (2000). Tobacco consumption in Swedish twins reared apart and reared together. *Archives of General Psychiatry, 57,* 886–892.

Kennedy, N., Abbott, R., & Paykel, E. S. (2003). Remission and recurrence of depression in the maintenance era: Long-term outcome in a Cambridge cohort. *Psychological Medicine, 33,* 827–838.

Kennedy, N., McDonough, M., Kelly, B., & Berrios, G. E. (2002). Erotomania revisited: Clinical course and treatment. *Comprehensive Psychiatry, 43,* 1–6.

Kent, A., & Waller, G. (2000). Childhood emotional abuse and eating psychopathology. *Clinical Psychology Review, 20,* 887–903.

Kent, J. M., Papp, L. A., Martinez, J. M., Browne, S. T., Coplan, J. D., Klein, D. F., et al. (2001). Specificity of panic response to CO2 inhalation in panic disorder: A comparison with major depression and premenstrual dysphoric disorder. *American Journal of Psychiatry, 158,* 58–67.

Kernberg, O. F. (1975). *Borderline conditions and pathological narcissism.* New York: Jason Aronson.

Kersting, K. (2003, November). Study shows two types of reading disability. *Monitor on Psychology,* Retrieved February 3, 2004, from http://www.apa.org/monitor/nov03/study.html.

Kessler, R. C., Berglund, P., Demler, O., Jin, R., Koretz, D., Merikangas, K. R., et al. (2003). The epidemiology of major depressive disorder: Results from the National Comorbidity Survey Replication (NCS-R). *Journal of the American Medical Association, 289,* 3095–3105.

Kessler, R. C., Borges, G., & Walters, E. E. (1999). Prevalence of and risk factors for lifetime suicide attempts in the National Comorbidity Survey. *Archives of General Psychiatry, 56,* 617–626.

Kessler, R. C., Crum, R. M., Warner, L. A., Nelson, C. B., Schulenberg, J., & Anthony, J. C. (1997b). Lifetime co-occurrence of *DSM-III-R* alcohol abuse and dependence with other psychiatric disorders in the National Comorbidity Survey. *Archives of General Psychiatry, 54,* 313–321.

Kessler, R. C., Downey, G., Milavsky, J. R., & Stipp, H. (1990). Clustering of teenage suicides after television news stories about suicides: A reconsideration. *American Journal of Psychiatry, 145,* 1379–1383.

Kessler, R. C., McGonagle, K. A., Swartz, M., Blazer, D. G., & Nelson, C. B. (1993). Sex and depression in the National Comorbidity Survey I: Lifetime prevalence, chronicity and recurrence. *Journal of Affective Disorders, 29,* 85–96.

Kessler, R. C., McGonagle, K. A., Zhao, S., Nelson, C. B., Hughes, M., Eshleman, S., et al. (1994). Lifetime and 12-month prevalence of *DSM-III-R* psychiatric disorders in the United States: Results from the National Comorbidity Survey. *Archives of General Psychiatry, 51,* 8–19.

Kessler, R. C., Sonnega, A., Bromet, E., Hughes, M., & Nelson, C. B. (1995). Posttraumatic stress disorder in the National Comorbidity Survey. *Archives of General Psychiatry, 52,* 1048–1060.

Kety, S. S. (1980). The syndrome of schizophrenia: Unresolved questions and opportunities for research. *British Journal of Psychiatry, 136,* 421–436.

Kety, S. S., Rosenthal, D., Wender, P. H., Schulsinger, F., & Jacobsen, B. (1975). Mental illness in the biological and adoptive families of adoptive individuals who have be-

come schizophrenic: A preliminary report based on psychiatric interviews. In R. R. Fieve, D. Rosenthal, & H. Brill (Eds.), *Genetic research in psychiatry* (pp. 147–165). Baltimore: The Johns Hopkins University Press.

Kety, S. S., Rosenthal, D., Wender, P. H., Schulsinger, F., & Jacobsen, B. (1978). The biological and adoptive families of adopted individuals who become schizophrenic. In C. Wynne, R. L. Cromwell, & S. Mathysse (Eds.), *The nature of schizophrenia* (pp. 25–37). New York: Wiley.

Kety, S., Wender, P. H., Jacobsen, B., Ingraham, L. J., Jansson, L., Faber, B., et al. (1994). Mental illness in the biological and adoptive relatives of schizophrenic adoptees: Replication of the Copenhagen study in the rest of Denmark. *Archives of General Psychiatry, 51,* 442–455.

Keyes, D. (1982). *The minds of Billy Milligan.* New York: Bantam Books.

Kiecolt-Glaser, J. K., et al. (1987). Marital quality, marital disruption, and immune function. *Psychosomatic Medicine, 49,* 13–34.

Kiecolt-Glaser, J. K., Kennedy, S., Malkoff, S., Fisher, L., Speicher, C. E., & Glaser, R. (1988). Marital discord and immunity in males. *Psychosomatic Medicine, 50,* 213–229.

Kiecolt-Glaser, J. K., Marucha, P. T., Malarkey, W. B., Mercado, A. M., & Glaser, R. (1995). Slowing of wound healing by psychological stress. *Lancet, 346,* 1194–1196.

Kiecolt-Glaser, J. K., McGuire, L., Robles, T. F., & Glaser, R. (2002). Emotions, morbidity, and mortality: New perspectives from psychoneuroimmunology. *Annual Review of Psychology, 53,* 83–107.

Kiecolt-Glaser, J. K., Preacher, K. J., MacCallum, R. C., Atkinson, C., Malarkey, W. B., & Glaser, R. (2003). Chronic stress and age-related increases in the proinflammatory cytokine IL-6. *Proceedings of the National Academy of Sciences, 100,* 9090–9095.

Kiecolt-Glaser, J. K., Speicher, C. E., Holliday, J. E., & Glaser, R. (1984). Stress and the transformation of lymphocytes in Epstein-Barr virus. *Journal of Behavioral Medicine, 7,* 1–12.

Kiefer, F., Jahn, H., Tarnaske, T., Helwig, H., Briken, P., Holzbach, R., et al. (2003). Comparing and combining naltrexone and acamprosate in relapse prevention of alcoholism: A double-blind, placebo-controlled study. *Archives of General Psychiatry, 60,* 92–99.

Kiesler, C. A., & Sibulkin, A. E. (1987). *Mental hospitalization: Myths and facts about a national crisis.* Newbury Park, CA: Sage.

Kiesler, D. J. (1999). *Beyond the disease model of mental disorders.* Westport, CT: Praeger Publishers.

Kihlstrom, J. F. (2004). An unbalanced balancing act: Blocked, recovered, and false memories in the laboratory and clinic. *Clinical Psychology: Science and Practice, 11,* 34–39.

Kilgore, K., Snyder, J., & Lentz, C. (2000). The contribution of parental discipline, parental monitoring, and school risk to early-onset conduct problems in African American boys and girls. *Developmental Psychology, 36*(6), 835–845.

Kilpatrick, D. G., et al. (2000). Risk factors for adolescent substance abuse and dependence: Data from a national sample. *Journal of Consulting and Clinical Psychology, 68,* 19–30.

Kilpatrick, D. G., Ruggiero, K. J., Acierno, R., Saunders, B. E., Resnick, H. S., & Best, C. L. (2003). Violence and risk of PTSD, major depression, substance abuse/dependence, and comorbidity: Results from the National Survey of Adolescents. *Journal of Consulting & Clinical Psychology, 71,* 692–700.

Kilts, C. D., et al. (2001). Neural activity related to drug craving in cocaine addiction. *Archives of General Psychiatry, 58,* 334–341.

King, S., & Dixon, M. J. (1995). Expressed emotion, family dynamics, and symptom severity in a predictive model of social adjustment for schizophrenic young adults. *Schizophrenia Research, 14,* 121–132.

King, S., & Dixon, M. J. (1999). Expressed emotion and relapse in young schizophrenia outpatients. *Schizophrenia Bulletin, 25,* 377–386.

Kingsberg, S. A. (2002). The impact of aging on sexual function in women and their partners. *Archives of Sexual Behavior, 31*(5), 431–437.

Kinney, D. K., Holzman, P. S., Jacobsen, B., Jansson, L., Faber, B., Hildebrand, W., Kasell, E., et al. (1997). Thought disorder in schizophrenic and control adoptees and their relatives. *Archives of General Psychiatry, 54,* 475–479.

Kirmayer, L. J., Robbins, J. M., & Paris, J. (1994). Somatoform disorders: Personality and the social matrix of somatic distress. *Journal of Abnormal Psychology, 103,* 125–136.

Kirsch, I., Moore, T. J., Scoboria, A., & Nicholls, S. S. (2002). The emperor's new drugs: An analysis of antidepressant medication data submitted to the U.S. Food and Drug Administration. *Prevention & Treatment, 5,* Posted July 15, 2002. Retrieved July 16, 2003, from http://journals. apa.org/preveniton/volume5/pre0050023a.html.

Klassen, D., & O'Connor, W. A. (1988). Predicting violence in schizophrenic and non-schizophrenic patients: A prospective study. *Journal of Community Psychology, 16,* 217–227.

Klein, D. F. (1994). "Klein's suffocation theory of panic": Reply. *Archives of General Psychiatry, 51,* 506.

Klein, D. N., Lewinsohn, P. M., Seeley, J. R., & Rohde, P. (2001). A family study of major depressive disorder in a community sample of adolescents. *Archives of General Psychiatry, 58,* 13–20.

Klein, D. N., Schwartz, J. E., Santiago, J. J., Vivian, D., Vocisano, C., Castonguay, L. G., et al. (2003). Therapeutic alliance in depression treatment: Controlling for prior change and patient characteristics. *Journal of Consulting and Clinical Psychology, 71,* 997–1006.

Kleinman, A. (1987). Anthropology and psychiatry: The role of culture in cross-cultural research on illness. *British Journal of Psychiatry, 151,* 447–454.

Kleinplatz, P. J. (2003). What's new in sex therapy? From stagnation to fragmentation. *Sexual & Relationship Therapy, 18*(1), 95–106.

Klerman, G. L. (1984). Ideology & science in the individual psychotherapy of schizophrenia. *Schizophrenia Bulletin, 10,* 608–612.

Klerman, G. L., Weissman, M. M., Rounsaville, B. J., & Chevron, E. S. (1984). *Interpersonal psychotherapy of depression.* New York: Basic Books.

Klonoff, E. A., & Landrine, H. (1997). *Preventing misdiagnosis of women: A guide to physical disorders that have psychiatric symptoms.* Thousand Oaks, CA: Sage.

Kluft, R. P. (1988). The dissociative disorders. In J. Talbott, R. Hales, & S. Yudofsky (Eds.), *Textbook of psychiatry.* Washington, DC: American Psychiatric Press.

Kluger, J. (2001, June 18). How to manage teen drinking (the smart way). *Time,* pp. 42–44.

Kluger, J. (2003, October 26). Medicating young minds. *Time Magazine Online,* Retrieved October 27, 2003, from http://www.time.com/time/magazine/article/ 0,9171,1101031103-526331,00.html.

Knight, R. G., Godfrey, H. P. D., & Shelton, E. J. (1988). The psychological deficits associated with Parkinson's disease. *Clinical Psychology Review, 8,* 391–410.

Knoll, J. L., IV, Garver, D. L., Ramberg, J. E., Kingsbury, S. J., Croissant, D., & McDermott, B. (1998). Heterogeneity of the psychoses: Is there a neurodegenerative psychosis? *Schizophrenia Bulletin, 24,* 365–379.

Knudsen, D. D. (1991). Child sexual coercion. In E. Grauerholz & M. A. Koralewski (Eds.), *Sexual coercion: A sourcebook on its nature, causes, and prevention* (pp. 17–28). Lexington, MA: Lexington Books.

Kobak, K. A., Greist, J. H., Jefferson, J. W., & Katzelnick, D. J. (1996). Computer-administered clinical rating scales: A review. *Psychopharmacology, 127,* 291–301.

Kobak, K. A., Taylor, L. H., Dottl, S. L., Greist, J. H., Jefferson, J. W., Burroughs, D., et al. (1997). A computer-administered telephone interview to identify mental

disorders. *Journal of the American Medical Association, 278,* 905–910.

Kobasa, S. C. (1979). Stressful life events, personality, and health: An inquiry into hardiness. *Journal of Personality and Social Psychology, 37,* 1–11.

Kobasa, S. C., Maddi, S. R., & Kahn, S. (1982). Hardiness and health: A prospective study. *Journal of Personality and Social Psychology, 42,* 168–177.

Koenen, K. C., Stellman, J. M., & Stellman, S. D. (2003). Risk factors for course of posttraumatic stress disorder among Vietnam veterans: A 14-year follow-up of American Legionnaires. *Journal of Consulting and Clinical Psychology, 71,* 980–986.

Koenigsberg, H. W., Harvey, P. D., Mitropoulou, V., Schmeidler, J., New, A. S., Goodman, M., et al. (2002). Characterizing affective instability in borderline personality disorder. *American Journal of Psychiatry, 159,* 789–796.

Koerner, K., & Linehan, M. M. (2002). Dialectical behavior therapy for borderline personality disorder. In S. G. Hofmann & M. Tompson (Eds.), *Treating chronic and severe mental disorders: A handbook of empirically supported interventions* (pp. 317–342). New York: Guilford Press.

Kohler, C. G., Turner, T. H., Bilker, W. B., Brensinger, C. M., Siegel, S. J., Kanes, S. J., et al. (2003). Facial emotion recognition in schizophrenia: intensity effects and error pattern. *American Journal of Psychiatry, 160,* 1768–1774.

Kohler, C. G., Turner, T. H., Bilker, W. B., Brensinger, C. M., Siegel, S. J., et al. (2003). Facial emotion recognition in schizophrenia: intensity effects and error pattern. *American Journal of Psychiatry, 160,* 1768–1774.

Kolata, G. (2000a, October 18). Days off are not allowed, experts argue. *The New York Times,* pp. A1, A20.

Kolata, G. (2000b, October 17). How the body knows when to gain or lose. *The New York Times,* pp. F1, F8.

Kolbert, E. (1994, January 21). Demons replace dolls and bicycles in world of children of the quake. *The New York Times,* p. A19.

Kolker, R. (2002, January 14). *Quality-of-life control. New York Magazine Online.* Retrieved November 14, 2003, from http://www.newyorkmetro.com/nymetro/news/ politics/newyork/features/5581/.

Kolko, D. J., & Rickard-Figueroa, J. L. (1985). Effects of video games on the adverse corollaries of chemotherapy in pediatric oncology patients: A single-case analysis. *Journal of Consulting and Clinical Psychology, 53,* 223–228.

Koplin, B., & Agathen, J. (2002). Suicidality in children and adolescents: A review. *Current Opinions in Pediatrics, 14,* 713–717.

Kordower, J. H., Emborg, M. E., Bloch, J., Ma, S. Y., Chu, Y., Leventhal, L., McBride, J., & Chen, E. Y. (2000). Neurodegeneration prevented by lentiviral vector delivery of GDNF in primate models of Parkinson's disease. *Science, 290,* 767–773.

Koss, M. P. (1988). Stranger and acquaintance rape: Are there differences in the victim's experience? *Psychology of Women Quarterly, 12,* 1–24.

Koss, M. P., & Kilpatrick, D. G. (2001). Rape and sexual assault. In E. Gerrity, et al. (Eds.), *The mental health consequences of torture.* Plenum series on stress and coping (pp. 177–193). Dordrecht, Netherlands: Kluwer Academic Publishers.

Koss, M. P., Bailey, J. A., Yuan, N. P., Herrera, V. M., & Lichter, E. L. (2003). Depression and PTSD in survivors of male violence: Research and training initiatives to facilitate recovery. *Psychology of Women Quarterly, 27*(2), 130–142.

Koss, M. P., Figueredo, A. J., & Prince, R. J. (2002). Cognitive mediation of rape's mental, physical and social health impact: Tests of four models in cross-sectional data. *Journal of Consulting & Clinical Psychology, 70*(4), 926–941.

Koss, M. P., Gidycz, C. A., & Wisniewski, N. (1987). The scope of rape: Incidence and prevalence of sexual aggression and victimization in a national sample of higher education students. *Journal of Consulting and Clinical Psychology, 55,* 162–170.

Kosson, D. S., Suchy, Y., Mayer, A. R., & Libby, J. (2002). Facial affect recognition in criminal psychopaths. *Emotion, 4,* 398–411.

Kotler, M. (1997). Excess dopamine D4 receptor (D4DR) exon III seven repeat allele in opioid-dependent subjects. *Molecular Psychiatry, 2,* 251–254.

Kouyoumdjian, H., Zamboanga, B. L., & Hansen, D. J. (2003). Barriers to community mental health services for Latinos: Treatment considerations. *Clinical Psychology: Science and Practice, 10,* 394–422.

Kovacs, M. (1996). Presentation and course of major depressive disorder during childhood and later years of the life span. *Journal of the American Academy of Children and Adolescent Psychiatry, 35,* 705–715.

Kraaimaat, F. W., Vanryckeghem, M., & Van Dam-Baggen, R. (2002). Stuttering and social anxiety. *Journal of Fluency Disorders, 27,* 319–330.

Krack, P., Batir, A., Van Blercom, N., Chabardes, S., Fraix, V., Ardouin, C., et al. (2003). Five-Year follow-up of bilateral stimulation of the subthalamic nucleus in advanced Parkinson's disease. *New England Journal of Medicine, 349,* 1925–1934.

Kraepelin, E. (1909–1913). *Psychiatrie* (8th ed.). Leipzig: J. A. Barth.

Krakauer, S. Y. (2001). *Treating dissociative identity disorder: The power of the collective heart.* Philadelphia: Brunner-Routledge.

Kramer, M. S., et al. (1998, September 11). Distinct mechanism for antidepressant activity by blockade of central substance P receptors. *Science,* pp. 1640–1645.

Krantz, D. S., Contrada, R. J., Hills, D. R., & Friedler, E. (1988). Environmental stress and biobehavioral antecedents of coronary heart disease. *Journal of Consulting and Clinical Psychology, 56,* 333–341.

Krantz, M. J., & Mehler, P. S. (2004). Treating opioid dependence: Growing implications for primary care. *Archives of Internal Medicine, 164,* 277–288.

Kranzler, H. R. (2000). Medications for alcohol dependence: New vistas. *Journal of the American Medical Association, 284,* 1016–1017. [Editorial]

Krehbiel, K. (2000, October). Diagnosis and treatment of bipolar disorder. *Monitor on Psychology,* p. 22.

Kremer, T. G., & Gesten, E. L. (2003). Managed mental health care: The client's perspective. *Professional Psychology: Research & Practice, 34,* 187–196.

Kring, A. M., & Neale, J. M. (1996). Do schizophrenic patients show a disjunctive relationship among expressive, experiential, and psychophysiological components of emotion? *Journal of Abnormal Psychology, 105,* 249–257.

Kristof, N. D. (2002, December 5). Love and race. *The New York Times Online.* Retrieved July 23, 2003, from http://www.racematters.org/loveandrace.htm

Kromkamp, M, Uylings, H. B., Smidt, M. P., Hellemons, A. J., Burbach, J. P., & Kahn, R. S. (2003). Decreased thalamic expression of the homeobox gene DLX1 in psychosis. *Archives of General Psychiatry, 60,* 869–874.

Krueger, R. B., & Kaplan, M. S. (2002). Behavioral and psychopharmacological treatment of the paraphilic and hypersexual disorders. *Journal of Psychiatric Practice, 8*(1), 21–32.

Krueger, R. F., Hicks, B. M., Patrick, C. J., Carlson, S. R., Iacono, W. G., & McGue, M. (2002). Etiologic connections among substance dependence, antisocial behavior, and personality: Modeling the externalizing spectrum. *Journal of Abnormal Psychology, 111,* 411–424.

Krug, E., Kresnow, M., Peddicord, J. P., Dahlberg, L. L., Powell, K. E., Crosby, A. E., & Annest, J. L. (1998). Suicide after natural disasters. *The New England Journal of Medicine, 338,* 373–378.

Kryger, M. H., Roth, T., & Dement, W. C. (Eds.). (2000). *Principles and practice of sleep medicine* (3rd ed.). Philadelphia: W. B. Saunders.

Kubany, E. S., Hill, E. E., Owens, J. A., Iannce-Spencer, C., McCaig, M. A., et al. (2004). Cognitive trauma therapy for battered women with PTSD (CTT-BW). *Journal of Consulting and Clinical Psychology, 72,* 3–18.

Kubisyzn, T. W., et al. (2000). Empirical support for psychological assessment in clinical health care settings. *Professional Psychology: Research and Practice, 31,* 119–130.

Kuhn, C. M., & Wilson, W. A. (2001, Spring). Our dangerous love affair with ecstasy. *Cerebrum,* pp. 22–33.

Kuno, E., & Rothbard, A. B. (2002). Racial disparities in antipsychotic prescription patterns for patients with schizophrenia. *American Journal of Psychiatry, 159,* 567–572.

Kuperberg, G. R., Broome, M.R., McGuire, P., K., David, A. S., Eddy, M., Ozawa, F., et al. (2003). Regionally localized thinning of the cerebral cortex in schizophrenia. *Archives of General Psychiatry, 60,* 878–888.

Kupfer, D. J. (1999). Research in affective disorders comes of age. *American Journal of Psychiatry, 156,* 165–167. [Editorial]

Kupfer, D. J., & Reynolds, C. F. (1997). Current concepts: Management of insomnia. *The New England Journal of Medicine, 336,* 341–346.

Kurth, T., Gaziano, J.M., Berger, K., Kase, C. S., Rexrode, K. M., Cook, N. R., et al. (2002). Body mass index and the risk of stroke in men. *Archives of Internal Medicine, 162,* 2557–2562.

Kwon, H., Menon, V., Eliez, S., Warsofsky, I. S., White, C. D., Dyer-Friedman, J. J., et al. (2001). Functional neuroanatomy of visuospatial working memory in Fragile X syndrome: Relation to behavioral and molecular measures. *American Journal of Psychiatry, 158,* 1040–1051.

Kwon, S., & Oei, T. P. S. (1994). The roles of two levels of cognitions in the development, maintenance, and treatment of depression. *Clinical Psychology Review, 14,* 331–358.

L

La Roche, M. J., & Maxie, A. (2003). Ten considerations in addressing cultural differences in psychotherapy. *Professional Psychology: Research and Practice, 34,* 180–186.

Ladouceur, R., Dugas, M. J., Freeston, M. H., Leger, E., Gagnon, F., & Thibodeau, N. (2000). Efficacy of a cognitive–behavioral treatment for generalized anxiety disorder: Evaluation in a controlled clinical trial. *Journal of Consulting and Clinical Psychology, 68,* 957–964.

Lahey, B. B., et al. (1995). Four-year longitudinal study of conduct disorder in boys: Patterns and predictors of persistence. *Journal of Abnormal Psychology, 104,* 83–93.

Lahey, B. B., Loeber, R., Burke, J., Rathouz, P. J., & McBurnett, K. (2003). Waxing and waning in concert: Dynamic comorbidity of conduct disorder with other disruptive and emotional problems over 7 years among clinic-referred boys. *Journal of Abnormal Psychology, 111,* 556–567.

Lam, D. H., Watkins, E. R., Hayward, P., Bright, J., Wright, K., Kerr, N., et al.. (2000). Cognitive therapy for bipolar illness: A pilot study of relapse prevention. *Cognitive Therapy & Research, 24,* 503–520.

Lam, D. H., Watkins, E. R., Hayward, P., Bright, J., Wright, K., Kerr, N., et al. (2003). A randomized controlled study of cognitive therapy for relapse prevention for bipolar affective disorder: Outcome of the first year. *Archives of General Psychiatry, 60,* 145–152.

Lamb, H. R. (2001). A century and a half of psychiatric rehabilitation in the United States. In H. R. Lamb & L. E. Weinberger (Eds.), *Deinstitutionalization: Promise and problems. New directions for mental health services* (pp. 99–110). San Francisco. Jossey-Bass/Pfeiffer.

Lamb, H. R., & Weinberger L. (2001). (Eds.). *Deinstitutionalization: Promise and problems. New directions for mental health services* San Francisco: Jossey-Bass/Pfeiffer.

Lamberg, L. (2000). Sleep disorders, often unrecognized, complicate many physical illnesses. *Journal of the American Medical Association, 284,* 2173–2175.

Lamberg, L. (2003). Advances in eating disorders offer food for thought. *Journal of the American Medical Association, 290,* 1437–1442.

Lambert, E. W., Wahler, R. G., Andrade, A. R., & Bickman, L. (2001). Looking for the disorder in conduct disorder. *Journal of Abnormal Psychology, 110,* 110–123.

Lambert, G., Johansson, M., Agren, H., & Friberg, P. (2000). Reduced brain norepinephrine and dopamine release in treatment-refractory depressive illness: Evidence in support of the catecholamine hypothesis of mood disorders. *Archives of General Psychiatry, 57,* 787–793.

Lambert, G., Reid, C., Kaye, D., Jennings, G., & Esler, M. (2003). Increased suicide rate in the middle-aged and its association with hours of sunlight. *American Journal of Psychiatry, 160,* 793–795.

Lambert, M. C., Weisz, J. R, Knight, F., Desrosiers, M. F., Overly, K., & Thesiger, C. (1992). Jamaican and American adult perspectives on child psychopathology: Further exploration of the threshold model. *Journal of Consulting and Clinical Psychology, 60,* 146–149.

Lambert, N. M., Hartsough, C. S., Sassone, D., & Sandoval, J. (1987). Persistence of hyperactivity symptoms from childhood to adolescence and associated outcomes. *American Journal of Orthopsychiatry, 57,* 22–32.

Landerman, L. R., Burns, B. J., Swartz, M. S., Wagner, H. R., & George, K. K. (1994). The relationship between insurance coverage and psychiatric disorder in predicting use of mental health services. *American Journal of Psychiatry, 151,* 1785–1790.

Landolt, H. P., Roth, C., Dijk, D. J., & Borbely, A. A.. (1996). Late-afternoon ethanol intake affects nocturnal sleep and the sleep EEG in middle-aged men. *Journal of Clinical Psychopharmacology, 16,* 428–436.

Lane, E. (1994, December 6). Losing weight isn't enough. *New York Newsday,* p. A6.

Langbehn, D. R., & Cadoret, R. J. (2001). The adult antisocial syndrome with and without antecedent conduct disorder: Comparisons from an adoption study. *Comprehensive Psychiatry, 42(4),* 272–282.

Lange, A., Rietdijk, D., Hudcovicova, M., van de Ven, J.-P., Schrieken, B., &. Emmelkamp, P. M. G. (2003). Interapy: A controlled randomized trial of the standardized treatment of posttraumatic stress through the Internet. *Journal of Consulting and Clinical Psychology, 71,* 901–909.

Langenbucher, J. W., & Chung, T. (1995). Onset and staging of *DSM-IV* alcohol dependence using mean age and survival-hazard methods. *Journal of Abnormal Psychology, 104,* 346–354.

Langenbucher, J. W., Martin, C. S., Labouvie, E., Sanjuan, P. M., Bavly, L., & Pollock, N. K. (2000). Toward the DSM–V: The withdrawal-gate model versus the DSM-IV in the diagnosis of alcohol abuse and dependence. *Journal of Consulting and Clinical Psychology, 68,* 799–809.

Langle, G., Renner, G., Gunthner, A., Stuhlinger, M., Eschweiler, G., U'Ren, R., et al. (2003). Psychiatric commitment: patients' perspectives. *Med Law, 22,* 39–53.

Langlois, S., & Morrison, P. (2002) Suicide deaths and suicide attempts. *Health Reports, 13(2),* 9–22.

Lara, M. E., Leader, J., & Klein, D. N. (1997). The association between social support and course of depression: Is it confounded with personality? *Journal of Abnormal Psychology, 106,* 478–482.

Largo-Marsh, L., & Spates, C. R. (2002). The effects of writing therapy in comparison to EMDR on traumatic stress: The relationship between hypnotizability and client expectancy to outcome. *Professional Psychology: Research and Practice, 33,* 581–586.

Lauerman, C. (2000, November 7). *Psychological counseling is now just a computer click away.* Retrieved November 21, 2000, from http://www.psycport.com/news/2000/11/07/Knigt/3822-0076-MEDE-.

Laumann, E. O., Gagnon, J. H., Michael, R. T., & Michaels, S. (1994). *The social organization of sexuality: Sexual practices in the United States.* Chicago: University of Chicago Press.

Laumann, E. O., Paik, A., & Rosen, R. C. (1999). Sexual dysfunction in the United States: Prevalence and predic-

tors. *Journal of the American Medical Association, 281,* 537–544.

Launer, L. J. (2003). Nonsteroidal anti-inflammatory drugs and Alzheimer disease: What's next? *Journal of the American Medical Association, 289,* 2865.

Lawrence, J., Mayers, D. L., Hullsiek, K. H., Collins, G., Abrams, D. I., Reisler, R. B. et al. (2003). Structured treatment interruption in patients with multidrug-resistant human immunodeficiency virus. *New England Journal of Medicine, 349,* 837–846.

Laws, D. R., & Marshall, W. L. (2003). A brief history of behavioral and cognitive behavioral approaches to sexual offenders: Part 1. Early developments. *Sexual Abuse: Journal of Research & Treatment, 15(2),* 75–92.

Lawson, W. B. (1986). Racial and ethnic factors in psychiatric research. *Hospital and Community Psychiatry, 37,* 50–54.

Lawson, W. B. (1996). Clinical issues in the pharmacotherapy of African-Americans. *Psychopharmacology Bulletin, 32,* 275–281.

Lawson, W. B., Helper, N., Holladay, J., & Cuffel, B. (1994). Race as a factor in inpatient and outpatient admissions and diagnosis. *Hospital and Community Psychiatry, 45,* 72–74.

Lazarus, A. A. (1992). Multimodal therapy: Technical eclecticism with minimal integration. In J. C. Norcross & M. R. Goldfried (Eds.), *Handbook of psychotherapy integration* (pp. 231–263). New York: Basic Books.

Lazarus, R. S., & Folkman, S. (1984). *Stress, appraisal, and coping.* New York: Springer.

Leary, W. E. (1996, December 18). Responses of alcoholics to therapies seem similar. *The New York Times,* p. A17.

Leber, P. (2000). Placebo controls: No news is good news. *Archives of General Psychiatry, 57,* 319–320.

Lechner, S. C., Antonia, M. H., Lydstona, D., LaPerrierea, A., Ishiia, M., Devieuxa, J., et al. (2003). Cognitive–behavioral interventions improve quality of life in women with AIDS. *Journal of Psychosomatic Research, 54,* 253–261.

Lecrubier, Y., Clerc, G., Didi, R., & Kieser, M. (2002). Efficacy of St. John's Wort extract vs 5570 in major depression: A double-blind, placebo-controlled trial. *American Journal of Psychiatry, 159,* 1361–1366.

Lee, C. C., & Richardson, B. L. (1991). *Multicultural issues in counseling: New approaches to diversity.* Alexandria, VA: AACD.

Lee, D. T. S., et al. (2001). A psychiatric epidemiological study of postpartum Chinese women. *American Journal of Psychiatry, 158,* 220–226.

Lee, J. K. P., Jackson, H. J., Pattison, P., & Ward, T. (2002). Developmental risk factors for sexual offending. *Child Abuse & Neglect, 26,* 73–92.

Lee, T. M. C., et al. (1998). Seasonal affective disorder. *Clinical Psychology: Science and Practice, 5,* 275–290.

Leekam, S. R., & López, B. (2000). Attention and joint attention in preschool children with autism. *Developmental Psychology, 36,* 261–273.

Lefley, H. P. (1990). Culture and chronic mental illness. *Hospital and Community Psychiatry, 41,* 277–286.

Lehmann, C. (2002, June). Computer program helps identify violent patients. *Psychiatric News, 87(12),* 4.

Lehrer, M., et al. (1994). Relaxation and music therapies for asthma among patients prestabilized on asthma medication. *Journal of Behavioral Medicine, 17,* 1–24.

Lehrer, P. M., Sargunaraj, D., & Hochron, S. (1992). Psychological approaches to the treatment of asthma. *Journal of Consulting and Clinical Psychology, 60,* 639–643.

Lehrer, P. M., Feldman, J., Giardino, N., Song, H.-S., & Schmaling, K. (2002). Psychological aspects of asthma. *Journal of Consulting and Clinical Psychology, 70,* 691–711.

Leibenluft, E. (1996). Women with bipolar illness: Clinical and research issues. *American Journal of Psychiatry, 153,* 163–173.

Leiblum, S. R., & Rosen, R. C. (Ed.). (2000). *Principles and practice of sex therapy (3rd ed.).* New York: Guilford Press.

Leibson, C. L., et al. (2001). Use and costs of medical care for children and adolescents with and without attention-deficit/hyperactivity disorder. *Journal of the American Medical Association, 285,* 60–66.

Leichsenring, F. (2001). Comparative effects of short-term psychodynamic psychotherapy and cognitive–behavioral therapy in depression: A meta-analytic approach. *Clinical Psychology Review, 21,* 401–419.

Leichsenring, F., & Leibing, E. (2003). The effectiveness of psychodynamic therapy and cognitive behavior therapy in the treatment of personality disorders: A meta-analysis. *American Journal of Psychiatry, 160,* 1223–1232.

Lemonde, S., Turecki, G., Bakish, D., Du, L., Hrdina, P. D., Bown, C. D., Sequeira, A., et al. (2003). Impaired repression at a 5-hydroxytryptamine 1A receptor gene polymorphism associated with major depression and suicide. *Journal of Neuroscience, 23,* 8788–8799.

Lemonick, M. D. (2003a, January 20). The power of mood. *Time,* pp. 36–41.

Lemonick, M. D. (2003b, January 20). Your mind your body. *Time,* p. 35.

Lemonick, M. D., & Park, A. (2001, May 14). Alzheimer's: The nun study. *Time,* pp. 54–64.

Leocani, L., et al. (2001). Abnormal pattern of cortical activation associated with voluntary movement in obsessive-compulsive disorder: An EEG study. *American Journal of Psychiatry, 158,* 140–142.

Leon, A. C. (2000). Placebo protects subjects from nonresponse: A paradox of power. *Archives of General Psychiatry, 57,* 329–330.

Leon, A. C., Solomon, D. A., Mueller, T. L., Endicott, J., Rice, J. P., Maser, J. D., et al. (2003). A 20-year longitudinal observational study of somatic antidepressant treatment effectiveness. *American Journal of Psychiatry, 160,* 727–733.

Leonard, S., Gault, J., Hopkins, J., Logel, J., Vianzon, R., Short, M., Drebing, C., et al. (2002). Association of promoter variants in the 7 nicotinic acetylcholine receptor subunit gene with an inhibitory deficit found in schizophrenia. *Archives of General Psychiatry, 59,* 1085–1096.

Lépine, J.-P., Caillard, V., Bisserbe, J.-C., Troy, S., Hotton, J.-M., & Boyer, P. (2004). A randomized, placebo-controlled trial of sertraline for prophylactic treatment of highly recurrent major depressive disorder. *American Journal of Psychiatry, 161,* 836–842.

Lesch, K. P., et al. (1996). Association of anxiety-related traits with a polymorphism in the serotonin transporter gene regulatory region. *Science, 274,* 1527–1531.

Leserman, J., Petitto, J. M., Golden, R. N., Gaynes, B. N., Gu, H., Perkins, D. O., et al. (2000). Impact of stressful life events, depression, social support, coping, and cortisol on progression to AIDS. *American Journal of Psychiatry, 157,* 1221–1228.

Lesser, I. (1992, December). *Ethnic differences in response to psychotropic drugs.* Paper presented at a symposium, Anxiety Disorders in African Americans, presented by the State University of New York Health Science Center at Brooklyn, Brooklyn, NY.

Leucht, S., Barnes, T. R., Kissling, W., Engel, R. R., Correll, C., & Kane, J. M. (2003). Relapse prevention in schizophrenia with new-generation antipsychotics: a systematic review and exploratory meta-analysis of randomized, controlled trials. *American Journal of Psychiatry, 160,* 1209–1222.

Leung, P. W. L., & Poon, M. W. L. (2001). Dysfunctional schemas and cognitive distortions in psychopathology: A test of the specificity hypothesis. *Journal of Child Psychology & Psychiatry & Allied Disciplines, 42(6),* 755–765.

Levenson, J. L., & Bemis, C (1991). The role of psychological factors in cancer onset and progression. *Psychosomatics, 32,* 124–132.

Levenstein, S., Ackerman, S., Kiecolt-Glaser, J. K., & Dubois, A. (1999). Stress and peptic ulcer disease. *Journal of the American Medical Association, 281,* 10–11.

Levine, A. (2000, December 22). Tomorrow's education, made to measure. *The New York Times,* p. A 33.

Levitan, R. D., Kaplan, A. S., Joffe, R. T., Levitt, A. J., & Brown, G. M. (1997). Hormonal and subjective responses to intravenous metachlorophenylpiperazine in bulimia nervosa. *Archives of General Psychiatry, 54,* 521–527.

Levitan, R. D., Rector, N. A., & Bagby, R. M. (1998). Negative attributional style in seasonal and nonseasonal depression. *American Journal of Psychiatry, 155,* 428–430.

Lewin, T. (2001, April 15). Ask not for whom the clock ticks. *The New York Times Week in Review,* p. 4.

Lewinsohn, P. M. (1974). A behavioral approach to depression. In R. J. Friedman & M. M. Katz (Eds.), *The psychology of depression: Contemporary theory and research.* Washington, DC: Winston-Wiley.

Lewinsohn, P. M., & Clarke, G. N. (1999). Psychosocial treatments for adolescent depression. *Clinical Psychology Review, 19,* 329–342.

Lewinsohn, P. M., Clarke, G. N., Rhode, P., Hops, H., & Seely, J. (1996). A course in coping: A cognitive–behavioral approach to the treatment of adolescent depression. In D. Hibbs & P. S. Jensen (Eds.), *Psychosocial treatments for child and adolescent disorders: Empirically based strategies for clinical practice* (pp. 109–135). Washington, DC: American Psychological Association.

Lewinsohn, P. M., Duncan, E. M., Stanton, A. K., & Hautzinger, M. (1986). Age at first onset for nonpolar depression. *Journal of Abnormal Psychology, 95,* 378–383.

Lewinsohn, P. M., et al. (1994). Adolescent psychopathology: II. Psychosocial risk factors for depression. *Journal of Abnormal Psychology, 103,* 302–315.

Lewinsohn, P. M., & Libet, J. M. (1972). Pleasant events, activity schedules and depression. *Journal of Abnormal Psychology, 79,* 291–295.

Lewinsohn, P. M., Joiner, T. E., & Rohde, P. (2001). Evaluation of cognitive diathesis-stress models in predicting major depressive disorder in adolescents. *Journal of Abnormal Psychology, 110,* 203–215.

Lewinsohn, P. M., Rohde, P., & Seeley, J. R. (1994). Psychosocial risk factors for future adolescent suicide attempts. *Journal of Consulting and Clinical Psychology, 62,* 297–305.

Lewinsohn, P. M., Rohde, P., & Seeley, J. R. (1996). Adolescent suicidal ideation and attempts: Prevalence, risk factors, and clinical implications. *Clinical Psychology: Science and Practice, 3,* 25–46.

Lewinsohn, P. M., Rohde, P., Seeley, J. R., & Baldwin, C. L. (2001). Gender differences in suicide attempts from adolescence to young adulthood. *Journal of American Academy of Child & Adolescent Psychiatry, 40,* 427–434.

Lewis, D. O., et al. (1997). Objective documentation of child abuse and dissociation in 12 murderers with dissociative identity disorder. *American Journal of Psychiatry, 154,* 1703–1710.

Lewis-Hall, F. (1992, December). *Overview of DSM-III-R: Focus on panic disorder and obsessive-compulsive disorder.* Paper presented at a symposium, Anxiety Disorders in African Americans, presented by the State University of New York Health Science Center at Brooklyn, Brooklyn, NY.

Lex, B. W. (1987). Review of alcohol problems in ethnic minority groups. *Journal of Consulting and Clinical Psychology, 55,* 293–300.

Ley, R. (1997). The Ondine curse, false suffocation alarms, trait-state suffocation fear, and dyspnea-suffocation fear in panic attacks. *Archives of General Psychiatry, 54,* 677.

Leyton, M., Boileau, I., Benkelfat, C., Diksic, M., Baker, G., & Dagher, A. (2002). Amphetamine-induced increases in extracellular dopamine, drug wanting, and novelty seeking: A PET/[11C]raclopride study in healthy men. *Neuropsychopharmacology, 27,* 1027–1035.

Li, G., Baker, S. P., Smialek, J. E., & Soderstrom, C. A. (2001). Use of alcohol as a risk factor for bicycling injury. *Journal of the American Medical Association, 284,* 893–896.

Li, Y. M., Xu, M., Lai, M. T., Huang, Q., Castro, J. L., DiMuzio-Mower, J., et al. (2000). Photoactivated-secretase inhibitors directed to the active site covalently label presenilin, 1. *Nature, 405,* 689–693.

Liberman, R. P. (1994). Treatment and rehabilitation of the seriously mentally ill in China: Impressions of a society in transition. *American Journal of Orthopsychiatry, 64,* 68–77.

Lichstein, K. L., Durrence, H. H., Bayen, U. J., & Riedel, B. W. (2001). Primary versus secondary insomnia in older adults: Subjective sleep and daytime functioning. *Psychology and Aging, 16,* 264–271.

Lichstein, K. L., Wilson, N. M., & Johnson, C. T. (2000). Psychological treatment of secondary insomnia. *Psychology and Aging, 15,* 232–240.

Lichtenberg, P. A., & Duffy, M. (2000). Psychological assessment and psychotherapy in long-term care. *Clinical Psychology: Science and Practice,* 317–328.

Lieber, C. S. (1990, January 14). Cited in "Barroom biology: How alcohol goes to a woman's head." *The New York Times,* p. E24.

Liebowitz, M. R., Heimberg, R. G., Fresco, D. M., Travers, J., & Stein, M. B. (2000). Social phobia or social anxiety disorder: What's in a name? *Archives of General Psychiatry, 57,* 191–192.

Liebowitz, M. R., Stein, M. B., Tancer, M., Carpenter, D., Oakes, R., & Pitts, C. D. (2002). A randomized, double-blind, fixed-dose comparison of paroxetine and placebo in treatment of generalized social anxiety disorder. *Journal of Clinical Psychiatry, 63,* 66–74.

Lightsey, O. W., Jr. (1994a). Positive automatic cognitions as moderators of the negative life event-dysphoria relationship. *Cognitive Therapy and Research, 18,* 353–365.

Lightsey, O. W., Jr. (1994b). "Thinking positive" as a stress buffer: The role of positive automatic cognitions in depression and happiness. *Journal of Counseling Psychology, 41,* 325–334.

Lilienfeld, S. O. (1997). The relation of anxiety sensitivity to higher and lower order personality dimensions: Implications for the etiology of panic attacks. *Journal of Abnormal Psychology, 106,* 539–544.

Lilienfeld, S. O., & Andrews, B. P. (1996). Identifying noncriminal psychopaths. *Journal of Personality Assessment, 66,* 488–524.

Lilienfeld, S. O., Fowler, K. A, & Lohr, J. M. (2003). And the band played on: Science, pseudoscience, and the Rorschach Inkblot Method. *The Clinical Psychologist, 56(1),* 6–7.

Lilienfeld, S. O., & Marino, L. (1995). Mental disorder as a Roschian concept: A critique of Wakefield's "harmful dysfunction" analysis. *Journal of Abnormal Psychology, 104,* 411–420.

Lilienfeld, S. O., Wood, J. M., & Garb, H. N. (2000). The scientific status of projective techniques. *Psychological Science in the Public Interest, 1,* 27–66.

Lim, S. (2003, September 2). Beating the bed-wetting blues. *MSNBC Online.* Retrieved September 3, 2003, from http://www.msnbc.com/news/954846.asp

Lin, K., et al. (1991). Ethnicity and family involvement in the treatment of schizophrenic patients. *Journal of Nervous & Mental Disease, 179,* 631–633.

Lin, T. Y., et al. (1978). Ethnicity and patterns of help-seeking. *Culture, Medicine, and Psychiatry, 2,* 3–14.

Linder, D. (2004). *The John Hinckley Trial (Hinkley's Communications with Jodie Foster).* Retrieved April 24, 2004, from http://www.law.umkc.edu/faculty/projects/ftrials/hinckley/hinckleytrial.html.

Lindsey, K. P., & Paul, G. L. (1989). Involuntary commitments to public mental institutions: Issues involving the overrepresentation of blacks and assessment of relevant functioning. *Psychological Bulletin, 106,* 171–183.

Linehan, M. M. (1993). *Cognitive-behavioral treatment of borderline personality disorder.* New York: Guilford Press.

Linehan, M. M., Camper, P., Chiles, J. A., Strosahl, K., & Shearin, E. (1987). Interpersonal problem solving and parasuicide. *Cognitive Therapy and Research, 11,* 1–12.

Liotti, G., et al. (2000). Predictive factors for borderline personality disorder. *Acta Psychiatrica Scandinavica, 102,* 282–289.

Lipsey, M. W., & Wilson, D. B. (1993). The efficacy of psychology, educational, and behavioral treatment:

Confirmation from meta-analysis. *American Psychologist, 48,* 1181–1209.

Lipsey, M. W., & Wilson, D. B. (1995). Reply to comments on Lispey and Wilson (1993). *American Psychologist, 50,* 113–115.

Lipton, R. B., et al. (1998). Efficacy and safety of acetaminophen, aspirin, and caffeine in alleviating migraine headache pain. *Archives of Neurology, 55,* 210–217.

Lipton, R. B., Stewart, W. F., Stone, A. M., Láinez, M. J., & Sawyer, J. P. (2000). Stratified care vs step care strategies for migraine: The disability in strategies of Care (DISC) Study: A randomized trial. *Journal of the American Medical Association, 284,* 2599–2605.

Little, S. J., Holte, S., Routy, J. P., Daar, E. S., Markowitz, M., Collier, A. C., et al. (2002). Antiretroviral-drug resistance among patients recently infected with HIV. *New England Journal of Medicine, 347,* 385–394.

Livesley, W. J., et al. (1993). Genetic and environmental contributions to dimensions of personality disorder. *American Journal of Psychiatry, 150,* 1826–1831.

Livesley, W. J., Schroeder, M. L., Jackson, D. N., & Jang, K. L. (1994). Categorical distinctions in the study of personality disorder: Implications for classification. *Journal of Abnormal Psychology, 103,* 6–17.

Lobel, M., DeVincent, C. J., Kaminer, A., & Meyer, B. A. (2000). The impact of prenatal maternal stress and optimistic disposition on birth outcomes in medically high-risk women. *Health Psychology, 19,* 544–553.

Lochman, J. E. (1992). Cognitive-behavioral intervention with aggressive boys: Three-year follow-up and preventive effects. *Journal of Consulting and Clinical Psychology, 60,* 426–432.

Lochman, J. E., & Dodge, K. A. (1994). Social-cognitive processes of severely violent, moderately aggressive, and nonaggressive boys. *Journal of Consulting and Clinical Psychology, 62,* 366–374.

Loeber, R., Burke, J. D., Lahey, B. B., Winters, A., & Zera, M. (2000). Oppositional defiant and conduct disorder: A review of the past 10 years. *Journal of the American Academy of Child and Adolescent Psychiatry, 39,* 1468–1484.

Loening-Baucke, V. (2002). Encopresis. *Current Opinions in Pediatrics, 14,* 570–575.

Loewenstein, R. J. (1991). Psychogenic amnesia and psychogenic fugue: A comprehensive review. *Annual Review of Psychiatry, 10,* 223–247.

Loftus, E. F. (1993). The reality of repressed memories. *American Psychologist, 48,* 518–537.

Loftus, E. F. (1996). The myth of repressed memory and the realities of science. *Clinical Psychology: Science and Practice, 3,* 356–365.

Loftus, E. F. (1997). Creating childhood memories. *Applied Cognitive Psychology, 11,* S75–S86.

Logsdon-Conradsen, S. (2002). Using mindfulness meditation to promote holistic health in individuals with HIV/AIDS. *Cognitive and Behavioral Practice, 9,* 67–71.

Lohman, J. J. H. M. (2001). Treatment strategies for migraine headache. *Journal of the American Medical Association, 285,* 1014.

Lohr, B. A., Adams, H. E., & Davis, J. M. (1997). Sexual arousal to erotic and aggressive stimuli in sexually coercive and noncoercive men. *Journal of Consulting and Clinical Psychology, 106,* 230–242.

Looper, K. J., & Kirmayer, L. J. (2002). Behavioral medicine approaches to somatoform disorders. *Journal of Consulting and Clinical Psychology, 70,* 810–827.

Lopes, C. L., Vergara, A., Agani, F., & Gotway, C. A. (2000). Mental health, social functioning, and attitudes of Kosovar Albanians following the war in Kosovo. *Journal of the American Medical Association, 284,* 569–577.

López-Larson, M. P., DelBello, M. P., Zimmerman, M. E., Schwiers, M. L., & Strakowski, S. M. (2002). Regional prefrontal gray and white matter abnormalities in bipolar disorder. *Biological Psychiatry, 52,* 93–100.

LoPiccolo, J., & Stock, W. E. (1986). Treatment of sexual dysfunction. *Journal of Consulting and Clinical Psychology, 54,* 158–167.

Loranger, A. W. (1996). Dependant personality disorder: Age, sex, and Axis I comorbidity. *Journal of Nervous and Mental Disease, 184,* 17–21.

Loranger, A. W., Sartorius, N., Andreoli, A., Berger, P. Buchheim, P., Channabasavanna, S. M., et al. (1994). The international personality disorder examination: The World Health Organization/ Alcohol, Drug, Abuse and Mental Health Administration International Pilot Study of Personality Disorders. *Archives of General Psychiatry, 51,* 215–224.

Lovaas, O. I. (1987). Behavioral treatment and normal educational and intellectual functioning in young autistic children. *Journal of Consulting and Clinical Psychology, 55,* 3–9.

Lovaas, O. I., Koegel, R. L., & Schreibman, L. (1979). Stimulus overselectivity in autism: A review of the research. *Psychological Bulletin, 86,* 1236–1254.

Lowe, M. R., Gleaves, D. H., Murphy-Eberenz, K. P. (1998). On the relation of dieting and bingeing in bulimia nervosa. *Journal of Abnormal Psychology, 107,* 263–271.

Lowenstein, L. F. (2002). Recent research into dealing with the problem of malingering. *Medico Legal Journal, 70,* 38–49.

Lubell, S. (2004, February 19). On the therapist's couch, a jolt of virtual reality. *The New York Times,* p. G5.

Luborsky, I., et al. (1996). Factors in outcomes of short-term dynamic psychotherapy for chronic vs. nonchronic major depression. *Journal of Psychotherapy: Practice and Research, 5,* 152–159.

Luborsky, L., et al. (1988). *Who will benefit from psychotherapy? Predicting therapeutic outcomes.* New York: Basic Books.

Luntz, B. K., & Widom, C. S. (1994). Antisocial personality disorder in abused and neglected children grown up. *American Journal of Psychiatry, 151,* 670–674.

Luoma, J. B., Martin, C. E., & Pearson, J. L. (2002). Contact with mental health and primary care providers before suicide: A review of the evidence. *American Journal of Psychiatry, 159,* 909–916.

Lutgendorf, S. K., Antoni, M. H., Ironson, G., Klimas, N., Kumar, M., Starr, K., et al. (1997). Cognitive-behavioral stress management decreases dysphoric mood and herpes simplex virus-type 2 antibody titer in symptomatic HIV-seropositive gay men. *Journal of Consulting and Clinical Psychology, 65,* 31–43.

Lyketsos C. G., Sheppard, J. M., Steele, C. D., Kopunek, S., Steinberg, M., Baker, A. S., et al. (2000). Randomized, placebo-controlled, double-blind clinical trial of sertraline in the treatment of depression complicating Alzheimer's disease: Initial results from the Depression in Alzheimer's Disease Study. *American Journal of Psychiatry, 157,* 1686–1689.

Lymburner, J. A., & Roech, R. (1999). The insanity defense: Five years of research (1993–1997). *International Journal of Law and Psychiatry, 22,* 213–240.

M

Ma, S. H., & Teasdale, J. D. (2004). Mindfulness-based cognitive therapy for depression: Replication and exploration of differential relapse prevention effects. *Journal of Consulting and Clinical Psychology, 72,* 31–40.

Machan, D. (2000, December). Forget the champagne. *Forbes,* pp. 118–120.

MacPhillamy, D. J., & Lewinsohn, P. M. (1974). Depression as a function of levels of desired and obtained pleasure. *Journal of Abnormal Psychology, 83,* 651–657.

Maddi, S. R., & Kobasa, S. C. (1984). *The hardy executive: Health under stress.* Homewood, IL: Dow Jones-Irwin.

Madsen, K. M., Hviid, A., Vestergaard, M., Schendel, D., Wohlfahrt, J., Thorsen, P., et al. (2002). A population-based study of measles, mumps, and rubella vaccination and autism. *New England Journal of Medicine, 347,* 1477–1482.

Maeder, T. (1985). *Crime and madness: The origins and evolution of the insanity defense.* New York: Harper & Row.

Maher, W. B., & Maher, B. A. (1985). Psychopathology: I. From ancient times to the eighteenth century. In G. A. Kimble & K. Schlesinger (Eds.), *Topics in the history of psychology* (Vol. 2). Hillsdale, NJ: Erlbaum. (pp. 251–294)

Mahler, M., & Kaplan, L. (1977). Developmental aspects in the assessment of narcissistic and so-called borderline personalities. In P. Hartocollis (Ed.), *Borderline personality disorders: The concept, the syndrome, the patient* (pp. 71–85). New York: International Universities Press.

Mahler, M. S., Pine, F., & Bergman, A. (1975). The borderline syndrome: The role of the mother in the genesis and psychic structure of the borderline personality. *International Journal of Psychoanalysis, 56,* 163–177.

Maier, S. F., & Seligman, M. E. P. (1976). Learned helplessness: Theory and evidence. *Journal of Experimental Psychology (General), 105,* 3–46.

Maier, S. F., Watkins, L. R., & Fleshner, M. (1994). Psychoneuroimmunology; The interface between behavior, brain, and immunity. *American Psychologist, 49,* 1004–1017.

Maj, M., Starace, F., & Pirozzi, R. (1991). A family study of *DSM–III–R* schizoaffective disorder, depressive type, compared with schizophrenia and psychotic and nonpsychotic major depression. *American Journal of Psychiatry, 148,* 612–616.

Malaspina, D., Harlap, S., Fennig, S., Heiman, D., Nahon, D., Feldman, D., & Susser, E. S. (2001). Advancing paternal age and the risk of schizophrenia. *Archives of General Psychiatry, 58,* 361–367.

Maldonado, J. R., Butler, L. D., & Spiegel, D. (1998). Treatments for dissociative disorders. In P. E. Nathan & J. M. Gorman (Eds.), *A guide to treatments that work* (pp. 423–446). New York: Oxford University Press.

Male eating disorders on rise, experts say (2004, May 12). *CNN Web Posting.* Retrieved May 26, 2004, from http://www.cnn.com/2004/HEALTH/diet.fitness/05/12/male.eating.disorder.ap/index.html

Maletzky, B. M. (1980). Self-referred vs. court-referred sexually deviant patients: Success with assisted covert sensitization. *Behavior Therapy, 11,* 306–314.

Maletzky, B. M., & Steinhauser, C. (2002). A 25-year follow-up of cognitive/behavioral therapy with 7,275 sexual offenders. *Behavior Modification, 26(2),* 123–147.

Malone, K. M., Oquendo, M. A., Haas, G. L., Ellis, S. P., Li, S., & Mann, J. J. (2000). Protective factors against suicidal acts in major depression: Reasons for living. *American Journal of Psychiatry, 157,* 1084–1088.

Malone, K. M., Waternaux, C., Haas, G. L., Cooper, T. B., Li, S., & Mann, J. J. (2003). Cigarette smoking, suicidal behavior, and serotonin function in major psychiatric disorders. *American Journal of Psychiatry, 160,* 773–779.

Mann, J. J., et al. (1996). Postmortem studies of suicide victims. In S. J. Watson (Ed.), *Biology of schizophrenia and affective disease* (pp. 179–221). Washington, DC: American Psychiatric Press.

Manson, J. E., & Bassuk, S. S. (2003). Obesity in the United States: A fresh look at its high toll. *Journal of the American Medical Association, 289,* 229–230.

Manson, J. E., Skerrett, P. J., Greenland, P., & VanItallie, T. B. (2004). The escalating pandemics of obesity and sedentary lifestyle a call to action for clinicians. *Archives of Internal Medicine, 164,* 249–258.

Marcus, D. K., & Nardone, M. E. (1992). Depression and interpersonal rejection. *Clinical Psychology Review, 12,* 433–449.

Marijuana leads to hard drugs. (2002, January 21). *MSNBC Web Posting.* Retrieved January 22, 2002, from http://www.msnbc.com/news/862289.asp

Maris, R. W. (2002). Suicide. *Lancet, 360,* 1892.

Mark, D. H. (1998). Editor's Note. *Journal of the American Medical Association, 279,* 151.

Markel, H. (2002, October 27). For addicts, relief may be an office visit away. *The New York Times Week in Review,* pp. 14.

Markovitz, J. H., et al. (1993). Psychological predictors of hypertension in the Framingham Study: Is there tension in hypertension? *Journal of the American Medical Association, 270,* 2439–2443.

Marks, M., & De Silva, P. (1994). The "match/mismatch" mode of fear: Empirical status and clinical implications. *Behaviour Research and Therapy, 32,* 759–770.

Marlatt, G. A. (1978). Craving for alcohol, loss of control, and relapse: A cognitive-behavioral analysis. In P. E. Nathan, G. A. Marlatt, & T. Loberg (Eds.), *Alcoholism: New directions in behavioral research and treatment* (pp. 271–314). New York: Plenum Press.

Marlatt, G. A. (1983). The controlled drinking controversy: A commentary. *American Psychologist, 38,* 1097–1110.

Marlatt, G. A., Baer, J. S., Kivlahan, D. R., Dimeff, L. A., Larimer, M. E., Quigley, L. A., et al. (1998). Screening and brief intervention for high-risk college student drinkers: Results from a 2-year follow-up assessment. *Journal of Consulting and Clinical Psychology, 66,* 604–615.

Marlatt, G. A., Demming, B., & Reid, J. B. (1973). Loss of control drinking in alcoholics: An experimental analogue. *Journal of Abnormal Psychology, 81,* 233–241.

Marlatt, G. A., & Gordon, J. R. (1985). *Relapse prevention: Maintenance strategies in the treatment of addictive behaviors.* New York: Guilford Press.

Marlatt, G. A., Somers, J. M., & Tapert, S. F. (1993). Harm reduction: Application to alcohol abuse problems. *NIDA Research Monographs, 137,* 147–166.

Marneros, A. (2003). The schizoaffective phenomenon: The state of the art. *Acta Psychiatrica Scandinavica,* Suppl, 418, 29–33.

Marsh, D. T., & Johnson, D. L. (1997). The family experience of mental illness: Implications for intervention. *Professional Psychology: Research & Practice, 28,* 229–237.

Marshal, M. P. (2003). For better or for worse? The effects of alcohol use on marital functioning. *Clinical Psychology Review, 23,* 959–997.

Mart, E. G. (2003). Munchausen's syndrome by proxy reconsidered. *Child Maltreatment: Journal of the American Professional Society of the Abuse of Children, 8,* 72–73.

Martin, D. (1989, January 25). Autism: Illness that can steal a child's sparkle. *The New York Times,* p. B1.

Martin, D. J., Garske, J. P., & Davis, M. K. (2000). Relation of the therapeutic alliance with outcome and other variables: A meta-analytic review. *Journal of Consulting and Clinical Psychology, 68,* 438–450.

Martin, J. L., Barbanoj, M. J., Schlaepfer, T. E., Thompson, E., Perez, V., & Kulisevsky, J. (2003). Repetitive transcranial magnetic stimulation for the treatment of depression. Systematic review and meta-analysis. *British Journal of Psychiatry, 182,* 480–491.

Martin, J., Shochat, T., & Ancoli-Israel, S. (2000). Assessment and treatment of sleep disturbances in older adults. *Clinical Psychology Review, 20,* 783–805.

Martin, P. R., & Seneviratne, H. M. (1997). Effects of food deprivation and a stressor on head pain. *Health Psychology, 16,* 310–318.

Marx, E. M., Williams, J. M. G., & Claridge, G. C. (1992). Depression and social problem solving. *Journal of Abnormal Psychology, 101,* 78–86.

Masi, G., Mucci, M., & Millepiedi, S. (2001). Separation anxiety disorder in children and adolescents: Epidemiology, diagnosis, and management. *CNS Drugs, 15*(2), 93–104.

Mason, M. (1994, September). Why ulcers run in families. *Health,* pp. 44, 48.

Masters, W. H., & Johnson, V. E. (1970). *Human sexual inadequacy.* Boston: Little, Brown.

Mathalno, D. H., et al. (2001). Progressive brain volume changes and the clinical course of schizophrenia in men: A longitudinal magnetic resonance imaging study. *Archives of General Psychiatry, 58,* 148–157.

Mathias, R. (2000). Cocaine, marijuana, and heroin abuse up, methamphetamine abuse down. *NIDA Notes, 15*(3), 4–5.

Mattson, M. P. (2003). Neurobiology: Ballads of a protein quartet. *Nature, 422,* 385–387.

Maxwell, C. D., Robinson, A. L., & Post, L. A. (2003). The nature and predictors of sexual victimization and offending among adolescents. *Journal of Youth & Adolescence, 32*(6) 465–477.

Mayo-Smith, M. F. (1997). Pharmacological management of alcohol withdrawal. A meta-analysis and evidence-based practice guideline. American Society of Addiction Medicine Working Group on Pharmacological Management of Alcohol Withdrawal. *Journal of the American Medical Association, 278,* 144–151.

Mays, V. M. (1985). The Black American and psychotherapy: The dilemma. *Psychotherapy, 22,* 379–388.

Mazure, C. M. (1998). Life stressors as risk factors in depression. *Clinical Psychology: Science and Practice, 5,* 291–313.

McCarty, D., et al. (1991). Alcoholism, drug abuse, and the homeless. *American Psychologist, 46,* 1139–1148.

McCaul, M. E., & Furst, J. (1994). Alcoholism treatment in the United States. *Alcohol Health & Research World, 18,* 253–260.

McClure, E. B., Kubiszyn, T., & Kaslow, N. J. (2002). Advances in the diagnosis and treatment of childhood mood disorders. *Professional Psychology: Research and Practice, 33,* 125–134.

McCord, W., & McCord, J. (1964). *The psychopath: An essay on the criminal mind.* New York: D. Van Nostrand.

McCracken, J. T., McGough, J., Shah, B., Cronin, P., Hong, D., Aman, M. G., et al. (2002). Risperidone in children with autism and serious behavioral problems. *New England Journal of Medicine, 347,* 314–321.

McCrady, B. S. (1993). Alcoholism. In D. H. Barlow (Ed.), *Clinical handbook of psychological disorders* (2nd ed., pp. 362–393). New York: Guilford Press.

McCrady, B. S. (1994). Alcoholics Anonymous and behavior therapy: Can habits be treated as diseases? Can diseases be treated as habits? *Journal of Consulting and Clinical Psychology, 62,* 1159–1166.

McCrady, B. S., & Langenbucher, J. W. (1996). Alcohol treatment and health care system reform. *Archives of General Psychiatry, 53,* 737–746.

McCrea, M., Guskiewicz, K. M., Marshall, S. W., Barr, W., Randolph, C., Cantu, R. C., et al. (2003). Acute effects and recovery time following concussion in collegiate football players: The NCAA Concussion Study. *Journal of the American Medical Association, 290,* 2556–2563.

McDermott, J. F. (2001). Emily Dickinson revisited: A study of periodicity in her work. *American Journal of Psychiatry, 158,* 686–690.

McDermut, W., Miller, I. W., & Brown, R. A. (2001). The efficacy of group psychotherapy for depression: A meta-analysis and review of the empirical research. *Clinical Psychology: Science and Practice, 8,* 98–116.

McElroy, S. L., Casuto, L. S., Nelson, E. B., Lake, K. A., Soutullo, C. A., Keck, P. E., Jr., & Hudson, J. I. (2000). Placebo-controlled trial of sertraline in the treatment of binge eating disorder. *American Journal of Psychiatry, 157,* 1004–1006.

McElroy, S. L., Hudson, J. I., Malhotra, S., Welge, J. A., Nelson, E. B, & Keck, P.E. Jr. (2003). Citalopram in the treatment of binge-eating disorder: A placebo-controlled trial. *Journal of Clinical Psychiatry, 64,* 807–813.

McGinn, L. K., & Sanderson, W. C. (2001). What allows cognitive behavioral therapy to be brief: Overview, efficacy, and crucial factors facilitating brief treatment. *Clinical Psychology: Science and Practice, 8,* 23–37.

McGlashan, T. H., & Fenton, W. S. (1992). The positive-negative distinction in schizophrenia: Review of natural history validators. *Archives of General Psychiatry, 49,* 63–72.

McGlashan, T. H., & Hoffman, R. E. (2000). Schizophrenia as a disorder of developmentally reduced synaptic connectivity. *Archives of General Psychiatry, 57,* 637–648.

McGovern, P. G., Pankow, J. S., Shahar, E., Doliszny, K. M., Folsom, A. R., Blackburn, H., et al. (1996). Recent trends in acute coronary heart disease. *The New England Journal of Medicine, 334,* 884–890.

McGowan, S., Lawrence, A. D., Sales, T., Quested, D., & Grasby, P. (2004). Presynaptic Dopaminergic dysfunction in schizophrenia: A positron emission tomographic [18f]fluorodopa study. *Archives of General Psychiatry, 61,* 134–142.

McGrath, E., Keita, G. P., Strickland, B. R., & Russo, N. F. (1990). *Women and depression: Risk factors and treatment issues.* Washington DC: American Psychological Association.

McGrath, P. J., Stewart, J. W., Janal, M. N., Petkova, E., Quitkin, F. M., & Klein, D. F. (2000). A placebo-controlled study of fluoxetine versus imipramine in the acute treatment of atypical depression. *American Journal of Psychiatry, 157,* 344–350.

McGrath, R. E, Pogge, D. L., & Stokes, J. M. (2002). Incremental validity of selected MMPI—A content scales in an inpatient setting. *Psychological Assessment, 14,* 401–409.

McGrath, R. E., Wiggins, J. G., Sammons, M. T., Levant, R. F., Brown, A., & Stock, W. (2004). Professional issues in pharmacotherapy for psychologists. *Professional Psychology: Research and Practice, 35,* 158–163.

McGue, M. (1993). From proteins to cognitions: The behavioral genetics of alcoholism. In R. Plomin & G. E. McClearn (Eds.), *Nature, nurture & psychology* (pp. 245–268). Washington, DC: American Psychological Association.

McGue, M., Slutske, W., & Iaono, W. G. (1999). Personality and substance use disorders: II. Alcoholism versus drug use disorders. *Journal of Consulting and Clinical Psychology, 67,* 394–404.

McGuffin, P., Rijsdijk, F., Andrew, M., Sham, P., Katz, R., & Cardno, A. (2003). The heritability of bipolar affective disorder and the genetic relationship to unipolar depression. *Archives of General Psychiatry, 60,* 497–502.

McGuire, P. K., Shah, G. M. S., & Murray, R. M. (1993). Increased blood flow in Broca's area during auditory hallucinations in schizophrenia. *The Lancet, 342,* 703–706.

McKee, B. (2003, September 4). As suburbs grow, so do waistlines. *The New York Times,* pp. F1, F 13.

McKellar, J., Stewart, E., & Humphreys, K. (2003). Alcoholics Anonymous involvement and positive alcohol-related outcomes: Cause, consequence, or just a correlate? A prospective 2-year study of 2,319 alcohol-dependent men. *Journal of Consulting and Clinical Psychology, 71,* 302–308.

McKenna, M. C., Zevon, M. A., Corn, B., & Rounds, J. (1999). Psychosocial factors and the development of breast cancer: A meta-analysis. *Health Psychology, 18,* 520–531.

McLean, L. M., & Gallop, R. (2003). Implications of childhood sexual abuse for adult borderline personality disorder and complex posttraumatic stress disorder. *American Journal of Psychiatry, 160,* 369–371.

McLean, P. D., et al. (2001). Cognitive versus behavior therapy in the group treatment of obsessive-compulsive disorder. *Journal of Consulting and Clinical Psychology, 69,* 205–214.

McLeod, B. D., & Weisz, J. R. (2004). Using dissertations to examine potential bias in child and adolescent clinical trials. *Journal of Consulting and Clinical Psychology, 72,* 235–251.

McMillan, J. R. (2003). Dangerousness, mental disorder, and responsibility. *Journal of Medical Ethics, 29,* 232–235.

McMurtrie, B. (1994, July 19). Overweight fatten ranks. *New York Newsday,* p. A26.

McNally, R. (1987). Preparedness and phobias: A review. *Psychological Bulletin, 101,* 283–303.

McNally, R. J., Bryant, R. A., & Ehlers, A. (2003). Does early psychological intervention promote recovery from posttraumatic stress? *Psychological Science in the Public Interest, 4*(2), 45–79.

McNally, R. J., Cassiday, K. L., & Calamari, J. E. (1990). Taijin-kyofu-sho in a Black American woman: Behavioral treatment of a "culture-bound" anxiety disorder. *Journal of Anxiety Disorders, 4,* 83–87.

McNally, R. J., & Eke, M. (1996). Anxiety sensitivity, suffocation fear, and breath-holding duration as predictors of response to carbon dioxide challenge. *Journal of Abnormal Psychology, 105,* 146–149.

McNally, R. J., et al. (1995). Clinical versus nonclinical panic: A test of suffocation false alarm theory. *Behaviour Research & Therapy, 33,* 127–131.

McNeil, D. E., Borum, R., Douglas, K. S., Hart, S. D., Lyon, D., Sullivan, L. E., & Hemphill, J. F. (2002). Risk assessment. In J. P. Ogloff (Ed.), *Taking psychology and law into the 21st century: Reviewing the discipline—A bridge to the future* (pp. 147–170). New York: Plenum.

McNeil, D. G., Jr. (2001, February 4). Epidemic errors. *The New York Times Week in Review,* pp. 1, 5.

McNiel, D. E., Gregory, A. L., Lam, J. N., Binder, R. L., Sullivan, G. R. (2003). Utility of decision support tools for assessing acute risk of violence *Journal of Consulting and Clinical Psychology, 71,* 945–53.

McNiel, D. E., Lam, J. N., & Binder, R. L. (2000). Relevance of interrater agreement to violence risk assessment. *Journal of Consulting and Clinical Psychology, 68,* 6, 1111–1115.

McNulty, J. L., Graham, J. R., Ben-Porath, Y. S., & Stein, L. A. R. (1997). Comparative validity of MMPI-2 scores of African American and Caucasian mental health center clients. *Psychological Assessment, 9,* 464–470.

McQuiston, J. T. (1997, February 5). New mother on Long Island suffering from depression is found, apparently a suicide. *The New York Times,* p. B5.

Meacham, J. (2000, September 18). The new face of race. *Newsweek,* pp. 38–41.

Mead, M. (1935). *Sex and temperament in three primitive societies.* New York: Morrow.

Medalia, A., Aluma, M., Tryon, W., & Merriam, A. E. (1998). Effectiveness of attention training in schizophrenia. *Schizophrenia Bulletin, 24,* 147–152.

Mednick, S. A., Parnas, J., & Schulsinger, F. (1987). The Copenhagen High-Risk project, 1962–86. *Schizophrenia Bulletin, 13,* 485–495.

Mednick, S. A., & Schulsinger, F. (1968). Some premorbid characteristics related to breakdown in children with schizophrenic mothers. In D. Rosenthal & S. S. Kety (Eds.), *The transmission of schizophrenia* (pp. 267–291). New York: Pergamon Press.

Meehl, P. E. (1962). Schizotaxia, schizotypy, schizophrenia. *American Psychologist, 17,* 827–838.

Meehl, P. E. (1972). A critical afterword. In I. I. Gottesman & J. Shields (Eds.), *Schizophrenia and genetics: A twin study vantage point* (pp. 367–415). New York: Academic Press.

Mehrabian, A., & Weinstein, L. (1985). Temperament characteristics of suicide attempters. *Journal of Consulting and Clinical Psychology, 53,* 544–546.

Meichenbaum, D. (1993). Changing conceptions of cognitive behavior modification: Retrospect and prospect. *Journal of Consulting and Clinical Psychology, 61,* 202–204.

Meichenbaum, D., & Deffenbacher, J. L. (1988). Stress inoculation training. *The Counseling Psychologist, 16*(1), 69–90.

Melani, D. (2001, January 17). Emotions can pull trigger on heart attack. *Evansville Courier & Press, Scripps Howard News Service.* Retrieved January 19, 2001, from http://www.psycport.com/news/2001/01/17/eng-courier press_features/eng-courierpress_features_134435_74_ 9803814571351.html

Melchert, T. P. (1996). Childhood memory and a history of different forms of abuse. *Professional Psychology: Research and Practice, 27,* 438–446.

Mellor, C. S. (1970). First rank symptoms of schizophrenia. *British Journal of Psychiatry, 177,* 15–23.

Melville, J. D., & Naimark, D. (2002). Punishing the insane: The verdict of guilty but mentally ill. *Journal of the American Academy of Psychiatry and the Law, 30,* 553–55.

Merckelbach, H., Arntz, A., & de Jong, P. (1991). Conditioning experiences in spider phobics. *Behaviour Research and Therapy, 29,* 301–304.

Merckelbach, H., et al. (1996). The etiology of specific phobias: A review. *Clinical Psychology Review, 16,* 337–361.

Merikangas, K. R., & Risch, N. (2003). Will the genomics revolution revolutionize psychiatry? *American Journal of Psychiatry, 160,* 625–635.

Merrill, K. A., Tolbert, V. E., & Wade, W. A. (2003). Effectiveness of cognitive therapy for depression in a community mental health center: A benchmarking study. *Journal of Consulting and Clinical Psychology, 71,* 404–409.

Messari, S., & Hallam, R. (2003). CBT for psychosis: a qualitative analysis of clients' experiences. *British Journal of Clinical Psychology, 42,* 171–188.

Messer, S. B. (2001a). Empirically supported treatments: What's a nonbehaviorist to do? In B. D. Slife & R. N. Williams (Eds.), *Critical issues in psychotherapy: Translating new ideas into practice* (pp. 3–19). Thousand Oaks, CA: Sage.

Messer, S. B. (2001b). What makes brief psychodynamic therapy time efficient? *Clinical Psychology: Science and Practice, 8,* 5–22.

Meston, C. M., & Frohlich, P. F. (2000). The neurobiology of sexual function. *Archives of General Psychiatry, 57,* 1012–1030.

Meston, C. M., & Heiman, J. R. (2000). Sexual abuse and sexual function: An examination of sexually relevant cognitive processes. *Journal of Consulting and Clinical Psychology, 68*(3), 399–406.

Meyer, B., Pilkonis, P. A., Krupnick, J. L., Egan, M. K., Simmens, S., J., & Sotksy, S. M. (2002). Treatment expectancies, patient alliance, and outcome: Further analyses from the National Institute of Mental Health treatment of depression collaborative research program. *Journal of Consulting and Clinical Psychology, 70,* 1051–1055.

Meyer, G. J. (1997). Assessing reliability: Critical corrections for a critical examination of the Rorschach comprehensive system. *Psychological Assessment, 9,* 480–489.

Meyer, G. J. (2000). Incremental validity of the Rorschach Prognostic Rating Scale over the MMPI Ego Strength Scale and IQ. *Journal of Personality Assessment, 74,* 365–370.

Meyer, G. J., (2001). To the final special section in the special series on the utility of the Rorschach for clinical assessment. *Psychological Assessment, 13,* 419–422.

Meyer, G. J., & Archer, R. P. (2001). The hard science of Rorschach research: What do we know and where do we go? *Psychological Assessment, 13,* 486–502.

Meyer, G. J., et al. (2001). Psychological testing and psychological assessment: A review of evidence and issues. *American Psychologist, 56,* 128–165.

Meyer, G. J., Hilsenroth, M. J., Baxter, D., Exner, J. E., Jr., et al. (2002). An examination of interrater relaibilty for scoring the Rorschach comprehensive system in eight data sets. *Journal of Personality Assessment, 78,* 219–274.

Meyer, I. H. (2003). Prejudice, social stress, and mental health in lesbian, gay, and bisexual populations: Conceptual issues and research evidence. *Psychological Bulletin, 129,* 674–697.

Meyer, J. H., McMain, S., Kennedy, S. H., Korman, L., Brown, G. M., DaSilva, J. N., et al. (2003). Dysfunctional attitudes and 5-HT2 receptors during depression and self-harm. *American Journal of Psychiatry, 160,* 90–99.

Michaud, E. (2000, October). Women's secret terror. *Prevention,* pp. 118–127.

Michelson, D., Bancroft, J., Targum, S., Kim, Y., & Tepner, R. (2000). Female sexual dysfunction associated with antidepressant administration: A randomized, placebo-controlled study of pharmacologic intervention. *American Journal of Psychiatry, 157,* 239–243.

Michelson, D., Bancroft, J., Targum, S., Kim, Y., & Tepner, R. (2000). Female sexual dysfunction associated with antidepressant administration: A randomized, placebo-controlled study of pharmacologic intervention. *American Journal of Psychiatry, 157,* 239–243.

Mignot, E., & Thorsby, E. (2001). Narcolepsy and the HLA System. *The New England Journal of Medicine, 344,* 692.

Miklowitz, D. J. (1994). Family risk indicators in schizophrenia. *Schizophrenia Bulletin, 20,* 137–149.

Miklowitz, D. J., & Alloy, L. B. (1999). Psychosocial factors in the course and treatment of bipolar disorder: Intro-

duction to the special section. *Journal of Abnormal Psychology, 108,* 555–557.

Miklowitz, D. J., George, E. L., Richards, J. A., Simoneau, T. L., & Suddath, R. L. (2003). A randomized study of family-focused psychoeducation and pharmacotherapy in the outpatient management of bipolar disorder. *Archives of General Psychiatry, 60,* 904–912.

Milad, R. R., & Quirk, G. J. (2002). Neurons in medial prefrontal cortex signal memory for fear extinction. *Nature 420,* 70–74.

Milberger, S., et al. (1996). Is maternal smoking during pregnancy a risk factor for attention deficit hyperactivity disorder in children? *American Journal of Psychiatry, 153,* 1138–1142.

Miller, A. L., Wyman, S. E., Huppert, J. D., Glassman, S. L., & Rathus, J. H. (2000). Analysis of behavioral skills utilized by suicidal adolescents receiving dialectical behavior therapy. *Cognitive & Behavioral Practice, 7*(2), 183–187.

Miller, E. (1987). Hysteria: Its nature and explanation. *British Journal of Clinical Psychology, 26,* 163–173.

Miller, G. E., & Cohen, S. (2001). Psychological interventions and the immune system: A meta-analytic review and critique. *Health Psychology, 20,* 47–63.

Miller, L. K. (1999). The savant syndrome: Intellectual impairment and exceptional skills. *Psychological Bulletin, 125,* 31–46.

Miller, S. D., Blackburn, R., Scholes, G., White, G. L., & Mamalis, N. (1991). Optical differences in multiple personality disorder: A second look. *Journal of Nervous & Mental Disease, 179,* 132–135.

Miller, S. D., & Triggiano, P. (1991). The psychophysiolgocal investigation of multiple personality disorder: Review and update. *American Journal of Clinical Hypnosis, 35,* 47–61.

Miller, T. Q., Turner, C. W., Tindale, R. S., Posavac, E. J., & Dugoni, B. L. (1991). Reasons for the trend toward null findings in research on Type A Behavior. *Psychological Bulletin, 110,* 469–485.

Miller, W. R., & Brown, S. A., (1997). Why psychologists should treat alcohol and drug problems. *American Psychologist, 52,* 1269–1279.

Miller, W. R., & Hester, R. K. (1986). Inpatient alcoholism treatment: Who benefits? *American Psychologist, 41,* 794–805.

Miller-Medzon, K. (2000, August 20). Early dyslexia detection leads to normal learning. *Boston Herald,* pp. 1, 11.

Millon, T. (1981). *Disorders of personality DSM-III: Axis II.* New York: Wiley.

Millon, T. (1982). *Millon Clinical Multiaxial Inventory manual* (3rd ed.). Minneapolis: National Computer Systems.

Millon, T. (2003). It's time to rework the blueprints: Building a science for clinical psychology. *American Psychologist, 58,* 949–961.

Minarik, M. L., & Ahrens, A. H. (1996). Relations of eating and symptoms of depression and anxiety to the dimensions of perfectionism among undergraduate women. *Cognitive Research & Therapy, 20,* 155–169.

Mineka, S. (1991, August). Paper presented at the annual meeting of the American Psychological Association, San Francisco. (Cited in Turkington, C. [1991]). Evolutionary memories may have phobia role. *APA Monitor, 22*(11), 14.

Minuchin, S., Rosman, B. L., & Baker, L. (1978). *Psychosomatic families: Anorexia nervosa in context.* Cambridge, MA: Harvard University Press.

Miranda, A., & Presentacion, M. J. (2000). Efectos de un tratamiento cognitivo-conductual en ninos con trastorno por deficit de atencion con hiperactividad, agresivos y no agresivos. *Infancia y Aprendizaje, 92,* 51–70.

Mitka, M. (2000). Psychiatrists help survivors in the Balkans. *Journal of the American Medical Association, 283,* 1277–1278.

Mitka, M. (2003, November 19). FDA alert on antidepressants for youth. *Journal of the American Medical Association, 290,* 2354–2355.

Mittelman, M. S., Roth, D. L., Coon, D. W., & Haley, W. E. (2004). Sustained benefit of supportive intervention for depressive symptoms in caregivers of patients with Alzheimer's disease. *American Journal of Psychiatry, 161*, 850–856.

Mixed progress on cancer front. (2003, September 3). *MSNBC Web Posting*. Retrieved September 4, 2003, from http://www.msnbc.com/news/960534.asp.

Modestin, J. (1992). Multiple personality disorder in Switzerland. *American Journal of Psychiatry, 149*, 88–92.

Mokdad, A. H., Ford, E. S., Bowman, B. A., Dietz, W. H., Vinicor, F., Bales, V. S., et al. (2003). Prevalence of obesity, diabetes, and obesity-related health risk factors, 2001. *Journal of the American Medical Association, 289*, 76–79.

Mokdad, A. H., Marks, J. S., Stroup, D. F., & Gerberding, J. L. (2004). Actual causes of death in the United States, 2000. *Journal of the American Medical Association, 291*, 1238, 1241.

Mokuau, N. (1990). The impoverishment of native Hawaiians and the social work challenge. *Health and Social Work, 15*, 235–242.

Moldin, S. O. (1994). Indicators of liability to schizophrenia: Perspectives from genetic epidemiology. *Schizophrenia Bulletin, 20*, 169–184.

Mollica R. F., Henderson, D. C., & Tor, S. (2002). Psychiatric effects of traumatic brain injury events in Cambodian survivors of mass violence. *British Journal of Psychiatry, 181*, 339–347.

Monahan, J. (1981). *A clinical prediction of violent behavior.* DHHS Publication, Adm. 81–921. Rockville, MD: National Institutes of Mental Health.

Monahan, J., Steadman, H. J., Silver, E., Appelbaum, P. S., Robbins, P. C., Mulvey, E. P., Roth, L. H., et al. (2001). *Rethinking risk assessment: The MacArthur Study of Mental Disorder and Violence.* New York: Oxford University Press.

Moncher, M. S., Holden, G. W., & Trimble, J. E. (1990). Substance abuse among Native-American youth. *Journal of Consulting and Clinical Psychology, 58*, 408–415.

Money, J. (2000). Reflections of a gender biographer. *Men & Masculinities, 3*, 209–216.

Monroe, S. M., Harkness, K., Simons, A. D., & Thase, M. E. (2001). Life stress and the symptoms of major depression. *Journal of Nervous & Mental Disease, 189*, 168–175.

Monson, C. M., Langhinrichsen-Rohling, J., & Binderup, T. (2000). Does "no" really mean "no" after you say "yes"? Attributions about date and marital rape. *Journal of Interpersonal Violence, 15*, 1156–1174.

Montemurro, B., Bloom, C., & Madell, K. (2003). Ladies night out: A typology of women patrons of a male strip club. *Deviant Behavior, 24* 333–352.

Monti, P. M., et al. (1987). Reactivity of alcoholics and non-alcoholics to drinking cues. *Journal of Abnormal Psychology, 96*, 122–126.

Mooney, M., White, T., & Hatsukami, D. (2004). The blind spot in the nicotine replacement therapy literature: Assessment of the double-blind in clinical trials. *Addictive Behaviors, 29*, 673–684.

Moos, R. H., Cronkite, R. C., & Moos, B. S. (1998). Family and extrafamily resources and the 10-year course of treated depression. *Journal of Abnormal Psychology, 107*, 450–460.

Moos, R. H., McCoy, L., & Moos, B. S. (2000). Global Assessment of Functioning (GAF) ratings: Determinants and roles as predictors of one-year treatment outcomes. *Journal of Clinical Psychology, 56*, 449–461.

Moos, R. H., & Moos, B. S. (2004). Long-term influence of duration and frequency of participation in alcoholics anonymous on individuals with alcohol use disorders. *Journal of Consulting and Clinical Psychology, 72*, 81–90.

Mor, N., & Winquist, J. (2002). Self-focused attention and negative affect: A meta-analysis. *Psychological Bulletin, 128*, 638–662.

Moran, P., Walsh, E., Tyrer, P., Burns, T., Creed, F., & Fahy, T. (2003). Does co-morbid personality disorder increase the risk of suicidal behaviour in psychosis? *Acta Psychiatrica Scandinavica, 107*, 441–448.

Morgan, D. L., & Morgan, R. K. (2001). Single-participant research design: Bringing science to managed care. *American Psychologist, 56*, 119–127.

Morgan, K. (1996). Mental health factors in late-life insomnia. *Reviews in Clinical Gerontology, 6*, 75–83.

Morgenstern, J., Bux, D. A., Labouvie, E., Morgan, T., Blanchard, K. A., & Muench, F., et al. (2002). Examining mechanisms of action in 12-step treatment: The role of 12-step cognitions. *Journal of Studies on Alcohol, 63*, 665–672.

Morimoto, K., Miyatake, R., Nakamura, M., Watanabe, T., Hirao, T., & Suwaki, H. (2002). Delusional disorder: Molecular genetic evidence for dopamine psychosis. *Neuropsychopharmacology, 26*, 794–801.

Morin, C. M. (2000). The nature of insomnia and the need to refine our diagnostic criteria. *Psychosomatic Medicine, 62*, 483–485.

Morin, C. M., Stone, J., Trinkle, D., Mercer, J., & Remsberg S. (1993). Dysfunctional beliefs and attitudes about sleep among older adults with and without insomnia complaints. *Psychology and Aging, 8*, 463–467.

Morin, C. M., & Ware, J. C. (1996). Sleep and psychopathology. *Applied and Preventive Psychology, 5*, 211–224.

Morin, C. M., & Wooten, V. (1996). Psychological and pharmacological approaches to treating insomnia: Critical issues in assessing their separate and combined effects. *Clinical Psychology Review, 16*, 521–542.

Morris, B. R. (2003, July 8). Two types of brain problems are found to cause dyslexia. *The New York Times*, p. F5.

Morris, G. H. (2002). Commentary: Punishing the unpunishable—the abuse of psychiatry to confine those we love to hate. *Journal of the American Academy of Psychiatry and the Law, 30*, 556–562.

Morris, M. C., Evans, D. A., Bienias, J. L., Tangney, C. C., & Wilson, R. S. (2002). Vitamin E and cognitive decline in older persons. *Archives of Neurology, 59*, 1125–1132.

Morrison, J. (1989). Childhood sexual histories of women with somatization disorder. *American Journal of Psychiatry, 146*, 239–241.

Morrison, M. F., Petitto, J. M., Have, T. T., Gettes, B. S., Chiappini, M. S., Weber, A. L., et al. (2002). Depressive and anxiety disorders in women with HIV infection. *American Journal of Psychiatry, 159*, 860–862.

Morrow, D. J. (1998, March 5). Stumble on the road to market. *The New York Times*, p. D1.

Mortensen, P. B., Pedersen, C. B., Westergaard, T., Wohlfahrt, J., Ewald, H., Mors, O., et al. (1999). Effects of family history and place and season of birth on the risk of schizophrenia. *New England Journal of Medicine, 340*, 603–608.

Mossman, D. (1994). Assessing predictions of violence: Being accurate about accuracy. *Journal of Consulting and Clinical Psychology, 62*, 783–792.

Mowrer, O. H. (1948). Learning theory and the neurotic paradox. *American Journal of Orthopsychiatry, 18*, 571–610.

Mueller, T. I., Leon, A. C., Keller, M. B., Solomon, D. A., Endicott, J., Coryell, W., et al. (1999). Recurrence after recovery from major depressive disorder during 15 years of observational follow-up. *The American Journal of Psychiatry, 156*, 1000–1006.

Mueser, K. T., & Liberman, R. P. (1995). Behavior therapy in practice. In B. Bongar & L. E. Beutler (Eds.), *Comprehensive textbook of psychotherapy: Theory and practice* (pp. 84–110). New York: Oxford.

Mueser, K. T., Sengupta, A., Schooler, N. R., Bellack, A. S., Xie, H., Glick, I. D., & Keith, S. J., et al. (2001). Family treatment and medication dosage reduction in schizophrenia: Effects on patient social functioning, family attitudes, and burden. *Journal of Consulting and Clinical Psychology, 69*, 3–12.

Mukamal, K. J, Conigrave, K. M., Mittleman, M. A., Camargo, C. A., Jr., Stampfer, M. J., Willett, W. C., et al. (2003). Roles of drinking pattern and type of alcohol consumed in coronary heart disease in men. *New England Journal of Medicine, 348*, 109–118.

Mullen, A. (2000). Risperidone and tardive dyskinesia: a case of blepharospasm. *Australian and New Zealand Journal of Psychiatry, 34*, 879–880.

Müller, R. A., Kleinhans, N., Kemmotsu, N., Pierce, K., & Courchesne, E. (2003). Abnormal variability and distribution of functional maps in autism: an fMRI study of visuomotor learning. *American Journal of Psychiatry, 160*, 1847–1862.

Munarriz, R., Talakoub, L., Flaherty, E., Gioia, M., Hoag, L., Kim, N. N. et al. (2002). Androgen replacement therapy with dehydroepiandrosterone for androgen insufficiency and female sexual dysfunction: Androgen and questionnaire results. *Journal of Sex & Marital Therapy, 28*(Suppl1), 165–173.

Muñoz, R. F., Mrazek, P. J., & Haggerty, R. J. (1996). Institute of Medicine Report on Prevention of Mental Disorders: Summary and commentary. *American Psychologist, 51*, 1116–1121.

Murphy, D. G. M., Critchley, H. D., Schmitz, N., McAlonan, G., van Amelsvoort, T., Robertson, D., et al. (2002). A proton magnetic resonance spectroscopy study of brain. *Archives of General Psychiatry, 59*, 885–891.

Murray, B. (2000a). From brain scan to lesson plan. *Monitor on Psychology, 31*, pp. 22–28.

Murray, B. (2000b, July/August). Psychology seeks to replicate groundbreaking research on the success of drug/psychotherapy treatment. *Monitor on Psychology*, p. 13.

Murray, B. (2003, October). A brief history of RxP. *Monitor on Psychology, 34*, 66–67.

Murray, H. A. (1943). *Thematic Apperception Test: Pictures and manual.* Cambridge, MA: Harvard University Press.

Murray, J. B. (1993). Relationship of childhood sexual abuse to borderline personality disorder, posttraumatic stress disorder, and multiple personality disorder. *Journal of Psychology, 127*, 657–676.

Murray, L., Cooper, P. J., Wilson, A., & Romaniuk, H. (2003). Controlled trial of the short- and long-term effect of psychological treatment of post-partum depression: 2. Impact on the mother-child relationship and child outcome. *British Journal of Psychiatry, 182*, 420–427.

Murstein, B. I., & Mathes, S. (1996). Projection on projective techniques & pathology: The problem that is not being addressed. *Journal of Personality Assessment, 66*, 337–349.

Murtagh, D. R. R., & Greenwood, K. M. (1995). Identifying effective psychological treatments for insomnia: A meta-analysis. *Journal of Consulting and Clinical Psychology, 63*, 79–89.

Mutler, A. (2000, August 3). One-fourth of Kosovo's population suffering mental anguish in the aftermath of war. *Associated Press Web Listing*. Copyrighted by Associated Press. Retrieved August 3, 2000, from http://psycport.com/news/2000/08/03/wstm-/2537-2706-Kosovo-StillatWar.html

Myin-Germeys, I., Delespaul, P. A. E. G., & deVries, M. W. (2000). Schizophrenia patients are more emotionally active than is assumed based on their behavior. *Schizophrenia Bulletin, 26*, 847–853.

N

Nabel, E. G. (2003). Cardiovascular disease. *New England Journal of Medicine, 349*, 60–72.

Naglieri, J. A., Drasgow, F., Schmit, M., Handler, L., Prifitera, A., Margolis, A., et al. (2004). Psychological testing on the Internet: New problems, old issues. *American Psychologist, 59*, 150–162.

Nagourney, E. (2001a, April 10). Geography of dyslexia is explored. *The New York Times*, p. F7.

Nagourney, E. (2001b, April 24). A good night's sleep, without the pills. *The New York Times*, p. F8.

Naimi, T. S., Brewer, R. D., Mokdad, A., Denny, C., Serdula, M. K., & Marks, J. S. (2003). Binge drinking among US adults. *Journal of the American Medical Association, 289*, 70–75.

Narrow, W. E., Rae, D. S., Robins, L. N., & Regier, D. A. (2002). Revised prevalence estimates of mental disorders in the United States: Using a clinical significance criterion to reconcile 2 surveys' estimates. *Archives of General Psychiatry, 59,* 115–123.

Näslund, J., et al. (2000). Correlation between elevated levels of amyloid-peptide in the brain and cognitive decline. *Journal of the American Medical Association, 283,* 1571–1577.

Nathan, P. E., Stuart, S. P., & Dolan, S. L. (2000). Research on psychotherapy efficacy and effectiveness: Between Scylla and Charybdis? *Psychological Bulletin, 126,* 964–981.

National Institute of Mental Health (NIMH) (2000). *Depression Research at the National Institute of Mental Health.* (2000). NIH Publication No. 00-4501, Retrieved from http://www.nimh.nih.gov/publicat/depresfact.cfm

National Institute of Mental Health (NIMH) (2003a, July 17). Gene more than doubles risk of depression following life stresses. *NIMH Press Office.* Retrieved July 19, 2003, from http://www.nih.gov/news/pr/jul2003/nimh-17.htm

National Institute of Mental Health (NIMH) (2003b, December 23). *Suicide facts.* Retrieved February 12, 2004, from http://www.nimh.nih.gov/research/suifact.cfm

National Institutes of Diabetes and Digestive and Kidney Diseases (NIDDK). (2001, Summer). New obesity gene discovered. *WIN Notes,* p. 2.

National Institutes of Health (NIH) (2003). *HIV/AIDS, severe mental illness and homelessness.* Retrieved March 24, 2004, from http://grants.nih.gov/grants/guide/pafiles/PA-04-024.html

National Institutes of Health, National Heart, Lung, and Blood Institute. (1998). *Clinical guidelines on the identification, evaluation, and treatment of overweight and obesity in adults:* Bethesda, MD: Author.

National Institutes of Health, Office of Research on Women's Health, Office of the Director. (1999). *Women of color health data book: Adolescents to seniors.* NIH Publication 99–4247. Bethesda, MD: Author.

National Strategy for Suicide Prevention. (2001, May). *Goals and Objectives for Action: Summary.* A joint effort of SAMHSA, CDC, NIH, and HRSA. The Center for Mental Health Services. Rockville, MD: Author.

Naughton, K. (2004, February 2). *The soft sell.* Newsweek, pp. 46–47.

Navarro, M. (2004, January 17). Blacks and Latinos try to find balance in touchy new math. *The New York Times,* pp. A1, B2.

Ndetei, D. M., & Singh, A. (1983). Hallucinations in Kenyan schizophrenic patients. *Acta Psychiatrica Scandinavica, 67,* 144–147.

Ndetei, D. M., & Vadher, A. (1984). A comparative cross-cultural study of the frequencies of hallucination in schizophrenia. *Acta Psychiatrica Scandinavica, 70,* 545–549.

Neal, A. M., & Turner, S. M. (1991). Anxiety disorders research with African Americans: Current status. *Psychological Bulletin, 109,* 400–410.

Needles, D. J., & Abramson, L. Y. (1990). Positive life events, attributional style, and hopefulness: Testing a model of recovery from depression. *Journal of Abnormal Psychology, 99,* 156–165.

Negy, C., & Snyder, D. K. (1997). Ethnicity and acculturation: Assessing Mexican American couples' relationships using the marital satisfaction inventory—revised. *Psychological Assessment, 9,* 414–421.

Neighbors, H. (1992, December). *The help seeking behavior of black Americans: A summary of the National Survey of Black Americans.* Paper presented at a symposium, Anxiety Disorders in African Americans, presented by the State University of New York Health Science Center at Brooklyn, Brooklyn, NY.

Nelson, C. B., Heath, A. C., & Kessler, R. C. (1998). Temporal progression of alcohol dependence symptoms in the U.S. household population: Results from the National Comorbidity Survey. *Journal of Consulting and Clinical Psychology, 66,* 474–483.

Nemiah, J. C. (1978). Psychoneurotic disorders. In A. M. Nicholi (Ed.), *Harvard guide to modern psychiatry.* Cambridge, MA: Harvard University Press.

Nestadt, G., et al. (2000). A family study of obsessive-compulsive disorder. *Archives of General Psychiatry, 57,* 358–363.

Nettle, D. (2001). *Strong imagination: Madness, creativity, and human nature.* New York: Oxford University Press.

Neugebauer, R. (1979). Medieval and early modern theories of mental illness. *Archives of General Psychiatry, 36,* 477–484.

Neumann, K., Euler, H. A., von Gudenberg, A. W., Giraud, A. L., Lanfermann, H., Gall, V., et al. (2003). The nature and treatment of stuttering as revealed by fMRI A within- and between-group comparison. *Journal of Fluency Disorders, 28,* 381–409.

Nevid, J. S., & Javier, R. A. (1997). Preliminary investigation of a culturally-specific smoking cessation intervention for Hispanic smokers. *American Journal of Health Promotion, 11,* 198–207.

Nevid, J. S., Javier, R.A., & Moulton, J. (1996). Factors predicting participant attrition in a community-based culturally-specific smoking cessation program for Hispanic smokers. *Health Psychology, 15,* 226–229.

Nevid, J. S., Rathus, S. A., & Rubenstein, H. R. (1998). *Health in the new millennium.* New York: Worth.

Neville, H. A., et al. (1996). The impact of multicultural training on white racial identity attitudes and therapy competencies. *Professional Psychology: Research & Practice, 27,* 83–89.

New use of brain scan may yield delays in Alzheimer's symptoms. (2000, May 15). *CNN Web Posting.* Retrieved May 16, 2000, from http://www.cnn.com/2000/HEALTH/aging/05/15/alzheimers.diagnosis/

Nezu, A. M. (1994). Introduction to special section: Mental retardation and mental illness. *Journal of Consulting and Clinical Psychology, 62,* 4–5.

NIAAA report links drinking and early death. (1990, October). *The Addiction Letter, 6,* p. 5.

Niaura, R., Todaro, J. F., Stroud, L., Spiro III, A., Ward, K. D., & Weiss, S. (2002). Hostility, the metabolic syndrome, and incident coronary heart disease. *Health Psychology, 21,* 588–593.

Nicholson, R. A., et al. (1997). Utility of MMPI-2 indicators of response distortion: Receiver operating characteristic analysis. *Psychological Assessment, 9,* 471–479.

Nickerson, K. J., Helms, J. E., & Terrell, F. (1994). Cultural mistrust, opinions about mental illness, and Black students' attitudes toward seeking psychological help from White counselors. *Journal of Counseling Psychology, 41,* 378–385.

Nierenberg, A. A., et al. (2000). Timing of onset of antidepressant response with fluoxetine treatment. *American Journal of Psychiatry, 157,* 1429–1435.

Nigg, J. T. (2001). Is ADHD a disinhibitory disorder? *Psychological Bulletin, 127*(5), 571–598.

Nigg, J. T., et al. (1992). Malevolent object representations in borderline personality disorder and major depression. *Journal of Abnormal Psychology, 101,* 61–67.

Nigg, J. T., & Goldsmith, H. H. (1994). Genetics of personality disorders: Perspectives from personality and psychopathology research. *Psychological Bulletin, 115,* 346–380.

NIH (National Institutes of Health). (2002). Mimicking brain's "all clear" quells fear in rats. *NIH News Release,* Posted 11/06/2002.

Nishith, P., Mechanic, M. B., & Resick, P. A. (2000). Prior interpersonal trauma: The contribution to current PTSD symptoms in female rape victims. *Journal of Abnormal Psychology, 109,* 20–25.

Nix, G., Watson, C., Pyszczynski, T., & Greenberg, J. (1995). Reducing depressive affect through external focus of attention. *Journal of Social and Clinical Psychology, 14,* 36–52.

Noaghiul, S., & Hibbeln, J. R. (2003). Cross-national comparisons of seafood consumption and rates of bipolar disorders. *American Journal of Psychiatry, 160,* 2222–2227.

Nock, M. K. (2002). A multiple-baseline evaluation of the treatment of food phobia in a young boy. *Journal of Behavior Therapy and Experimental Psychiatry, 33,* 217–225.

Nolan, S. A., Glynn, C., & Garber, J. (2003). Prospective relations between rejection and depression in young adolescents, *Journal of Personality and Social Psychology, 85,* 745–755.

Nolen-Hoeksema, S. (1991). Responses to depression and their effects on the duration of depressive episodes. *Journal of Abnormal Psychology, 100,* 569–582.

Nolen-Hoeksema, S. (2000). The role of rumination in depressive disorders and mixed anxiety/depressive symptoms. *Journal of Abnormal Psychology, 109,* 504–511.

Nolen-Hoeksema, S., & Girgus, J. S. (1994). The emergence of gender differences in depression during adolescence. *Psychological Bulletin, 115,* 424–443.

Nolen-Hoeksema, S., Girgus, J. S., & Seligman, M. E. P. (1992). Predictors and consequences of childhood depressive symptoms: A 5-year longitudinal study. *Journal of Abnormal Psychology, 101,* 405–422.

Nolen-Hoeksema, S., Morrow, J., & Fredrickson, B. L. (1993). Response styles and the duration of episodes of depressed mood. *Journal of Abnormal Psychology, 102,* 20–28.

Noonan, D. (2000, September 25). Why drugs cost so much. *Newsweek,* pp. 22–30.

Noonan, D. (2003, September 8). "Allowed to be odd." *Newsweek,* p. 50.

Nordhus, I. H., & Pallesen, S. (2003). Psychological treatment of late-life anxiety: An empirical review. *Journal of Consulting and Clinical Psychology, 71,* 643–651.

Norris, F. N., Murphy, A. D., Baker, C. K., Perilla, J. L., Rodriguez, F. G., & Rodriguez, J. de J. (2003). Epidemiology of trauma and posttraumatic stress disorder in Mexico. *Journal of Abnormal Psychology, 112,* 646–656.

North, C. S., & Pfefferbaum, B. (2002). Research on the mental health effects of terrorism. *Journal of the American Medical Association, 288,* 633–636.

Nowell, P. D., et al. (1998). Effective treatments for selected sleep disorders. In P. E. Nathan & J. M. Gorman (Eds.), *A guide to treatments that work* (pp. 531–543). New York: Oxford University Press.

Noyes, R., et al. (1993). The validity of *DSM-III-R* hypochondriasis. *Archives of General Psychiatry, 50,* 961–970.

Nucifora, F. C., Jr., Sasaki, M., Peters, M. F., Huang, H., Cooper, J. K., Yamada, M., et al. (2001). Interference by Huntington and atrophin-1 with cbp-mediated transcription leading to cellular toxicity. *Science, 291,* 2423–2428.

Nunes, E. V., & Levin, F. R. (2004). Treatment of depression in patients with alcohol or other drug dependence: A meta-analysis. *Journal of the American Medical Association, 291,* 1887–1896.

Nurnberger, J. I., et al. (2001). Evidence for a locus on chromosome 1 that influences vulnerability to alcoholism and affective disorder. *American Journal of Psychiatry, 158,* 718–724.

Nussbaum, R. L., & Ellis, C. E. (2003). Alzheimer's disease and Parkinson's disease. *New England Journal of Medicine, 348,* 1356–64.

Nutrition, obesity and perception. (2001, January 9). *CNN Web Posting.* Retrieved January 11, 2001, from http://www.cnn.com/2001/HEALTH/children/01/09/overweight.kids/index.html

O

O'Brien, C. P., & McKay, J. (1998). Psychopharmacological treatments of substance use disorders. In P. E. Nathan & J. M. Gorman (Eds.), *A guide to treatments that work* (pp. 127–155). New York: Oxford University Press.

O'Brien, K. M., & Vincent, N. K. (2003). Psychiatric co-morbidity in anorexia and bulimia nervosa: nature, prevalence, and causal relationships. *Clinical Psychology Review, 23,* 57–74.

O'Connor v. Donaldson, 95 S. Ct. 2486 (1975).

O'Connor, A. (2004, March 16). In sex, brain studies show, "la difference" still holds. *The New York Times, Science Times,* p. F5.

O'Connor, E. (2001a, January). Law sanctions new treatment for heroin addiction—and recommends psychological counseling. *Monitor on Psychology,* p. 18.

O'Connor, E. (2001b, February). Researchers pinpoint potential cause of autism. *Monitor on Psychology,* p. 13.

O'Connor, P. G. (2000). Treating opioid dependence—new data and new opportunities. *The New England Journal of Medicine, 343,* 1332–1334. [Editorial]

O'Connor, T. G., McGuire, S., Reiss, D., Hetherington, E. M., & Plomin, R. (1998). Co-occurrence of depressive symptoms and antisocial behavior in adolescence: A common genetic liability. *Journal of Abnormal Psychology, 107,* 27–37.

O'Donnell, J. (2003, April 24). Traffic deaths rise to 12-year high. *USA Today,* p. 1D.

O'Donohue, W., McKay, J. S., & Schewe, P. A. (1996). Rape: The roles of outcome expectancies and hypermasculinity. *Sexual Abuse Journal of Research and Treatment, 8,* 133–141.

O'Farrell, T. J., et al. (1996). Cost-benefit and cost-effectiveness analyses of behavioral marital therapy as an addition to outpatient alcoholism treatment. *Journal of Substance Abuse, 8,* 145–166.

O'Hara, M. W. (2003, November). *Clinician's Research Digest, Supplemental Bulletin 29.* 1–2.

O'Hara, M. W., Stuart, S., Gorman, L. L., & Wenzel, A. (2000). Efficacy of interpersonal psychotherapy for postpartum depression. *Archives of General Psychiatry, 57,* 1039–1045.

O'Leary, A. (1990). Stress, emotion, and human immune functions. *Psychological Bulletin, 108,* 382–383.

O'Leary, D. S., Andreasen, N. C., Hurtig, R. R., Kesler, M. L., Rogers, M., Arndt, S., et al. (1996). Auditory attentional deficits in patients with schizophrenia: A positron emission tomography study. *Archives of General Psychiatry, 53,* 633–641.

Oei, T. P. S., & Shuttlewood, G. J. (1996). Specified and nonspecific factors in psychotherapy: A case of cognitive therapy for depression. *Clinical Psychology Review, 16,* 83–103.

Ogloff, J. R. P., Roberts, C. F., & Roesch, R. (1993). The insanity defense: Legal standards and clinical assessment. *Applied & Preventive Psychology, 2,* 163–178.

Öhman, A., & Mineka, S. (2001). Fears, phobias, and preparedness: Toward an evolved module of fear and fear learning. *Psychological Review, 108,* 483–522.

Okubo, Y., et al. (1997). Decreased prefrontal dopamine D1 receptors in schizophrenia revealed by PET. *Nature, 385,* 634–636.

Oldham, J. M. (1994). Personality disorders: Current perspectives. *Journal of the American Medical Association, 272,* 213–220.

Olesen, J. (1994). Understanding the biologic basis of migraine. *New England Journal of Medicine, 331,* 1713–1714.

Olfson, M., Guardino, M., Struening, E., Schneier, F. R., Hellman, F., & Klein, D. F. (2000). Barriers to the treatment of social anxiety. *American Journal of Psychiatry, 157,* 542–548.

Olfson, M., Marcus, S., Sackeim, H. A., Thompson, J., & Pincus, H. A. (1998). Use of ECT for the inpatient treatment of recurrent major depression. *American Journal of Psychiatry, 155,* 22–29.

Olson, E. (2001, October 7). Countries lag in treating mental illness, W. H. O. says. *The New York Times,* p. A24.

Olson, L. (2000). Combating Parkinson's disease—Step three. *Science, 290,* 721–724.

Olson, S. E. (1997). *Becoming one: A story of triumph over multiple personality disorder.* Pasadena, CA: Trilogy Books.

Onstad, S., Skre, I., Torgensen, S., & Kringlen, E. (1991). Twin concordance for *DSM-III-R* schizophrenia. *Acta Psychiatrica Scandinavica, 83,* 395–401.

Oquendo, M. A., Friend, J. M., Halberstam, B., Brodsky, B. S., Burke, A. K., Grunebaum, M. F., Malone, K. M., & Mann, J. J. (2003). Association of comorbid posttraumatic stress disorder and major depression with greater risk for suicidal behavior. *American Journal of Psychiatry, 160,* 580–582.

Ormel, J., Oldehinkel, A. J., & Brilman, E. I. (2001). The interplay and etiological continuity of neuroticism, difficulties, and life events in the etiology of major and subsyndromal, first and recurrent depressive episodes in later life. *American Journal of Psychiatry, 158,* 885–891.

Ortega, A. N., Rosenheck, R., Alegria, M., & Desai, R. A. (2000). Acculturation and the lifetime risk of psychiatric and substance use disorders among Hispanics. *Journal of Nervous & Mental Disease, 188,* 728–735.

Orth-Gomér, K., Wamala, S. P., Horsten, M., Schenck-Gustafsson, K., Schneiderman, N., & Mittleman, M. A. (2000). Marital stress worsens prognosis in women with coronary heart disease: The Stockholm Female Coronary Risk Study. *Journal of the American Medical Association, 284,* 3008–3014.

Osborn, I. (1998). *The hidden epidemic of obsessive-compulsive disorder.* New York: Random House.

Osborne, L. (2001, May 6). Regional disturbances. *The New York Times,* p. A17.

Osborne, L. (2002). *American normal: The hidden world of Asperger Syndrome.* Copernicus Books.

Osman, S. L. (2003). Predicting men's rape perceptions based on the belief that "No" really means "Yes." *Journal of Applied Social Psychology, 33*(4), 683–692.

Öst, L. (1987). Age of onset in different phobias. *Journal of Abnormal Psychology, 96,* 223–229.

Öst, L. (1992). Blood and injection phobia: Background and cognitive, physiological, and behavioral variables. *Journal of Abnormal Psychology, 101,* 68–74.

Öst, L-G., Svensson, L., Hellström, K., & Lindwall, R. (2001). One-session treatment of specific phobias in youths: A randomized clinical trial. *Journal of Consulting and Clinical Psychology, 69,* 814–824.

Ostler, K., Thompson, C., Kinmonth, A. L., Peveler, R. C., Stevens, L., & Stevens, A. (2001). Influence of socio-economic deprivation on the prevalence and outcome of depression in primary care. *British Medical Journal, 178,* 12–17.

Otto, M. W. (2001, February). A pilot study of CBT for bipolar disorders. *Journal Watch Psychiatry, 7,* 9.

Otto, M. W., Pollack, M. H., & Maki, K. M. (2000). Empirically supported treatments for panic disorder: Costs, benefits, and stepped care. *Journal of Consulting and Clinical Psychology, 68,* 556–563.

Ouellette, S. C., & DiPlacido, J. (2001). Personality's role in the protection and enhancements of health: Where the research has been, where it is stuck, how it might move. In A. Baum, T. A. Revenson, & J. E. Singer (Eds.), *Handbook of health psychology* (pp. 3–318). Mahwah, NJ: Lawrence Erlbaum Associates.

Ouimette, P. C., Finney, J. W., & Moos, R. H. (1997). Twelve-step and cognitive-behavioral treatment for substance abuse: A comparison of treatment effectiveness. *Journal of Consulting and Clinical Psychology, 65,* 230–240.

Overholser, J. C. (2000). Cognitive-behavioral treatment of panic disorder. *Psychotherapy: Theory, Research, Practice, Training, 37,* 247–256.

Overmier, J. B. L., & Seligman, M. E. P. (1967). Effect of inescapable shock upon subsequent escape and avoidance learning. *Journal of Comparative and Physiological Psychology, 63,* 28–33.

Ozer, E. J., Best, S. R., Lipsey, T. L, & Weiss, D. S. (2003). Predictors of posttraumatic stress disorder and symptoms in adults: A meta-analysis. *Psychological Bulletin, 129,* 52–73.

P

Palinkas, L. A., Wingard, D. L., & Barrett-Connor, E. (1990). The biocultural context of social networks and depression among the elderly. *Social Science and Medicine, 4,* 441–447.

Pallesen, S., Hilde, I. N., Havik, O. E., & Nielsen, G. H. (2001). Clinical assessment and treatment of insomnia. *Professional Psychology: Research and Practice, 32,* 115–124.

Palmer, C. A., & Hazelrigg, M. (2000). The guilty but mentally ill verdict: a review and conceptual analysis of intent and impact. *Journal of the American Academy of Psychiatry and the Law, 28,* 47–54.

Palmiter, D. Jr., & Renjilian, D. (2003). Clinical Web pages: Do they meet expectations? *Professional Psychology: Research and Practice, 34,* 164–169.

Panek, R. (2002, November 24). Hmm, what did you mean by all that, Dr. Freud? *The New York Times, Section AR,* p. 36.

Pankratz, N., Nichols, W. C., Uniacke, S. K., Halter, C., Rudolph, A., Shults, C., et al. (2002). Genome screen to identify susceptibility genes for Parkinson disease in a sample without Parkinson mutations. *American Journal of Human Genetics, 71,* 124–135.

Park, C. L. (2004). Positive and negative consequences of alcohol consumption in college students. *Addictive Behaviors, 29,* 311–321.

Parker, G., Gladstone, G., & Chee, K. T. (2001). Depression in the planet's largest ethnic group: The Chinese. *American Journal of Psychiatry, 158,* 857–864.

Parkinson Study Group. (2000). Pramipexole vs. levodopa as initial treatment for Parkinson disease: A randomized controlled trial. *Journal of the American Medical Association, 284,* 1931–1938.

Parloff, R. (2003, February 3). Is fat the next tobacco? *Fortune,* pp. 51–54.

Parnas, J., et al. (1993). Lifetime *DSM-III-R* diagnostic outcomes in the offspring of schizophrenic mothers: Results from the Copenhagen High-Risk Study. *Archives of General Psychiatry, 50,* 707–714.

Pato, M. T., Pato, C. N., & Pauls, D. L. (2002). Recent findings in the genetics of OCD. *Clinical Psychiatry, 63,* Suppl 6: 30–33.

Pato, M. T., Schindler, K. M., & Pato, C. N (2001). The genetics of obsessive-compulsive disorder. *Currrent Psychiatry Reports, 3,* 163–168.

Patrick, C. J., Cuthbert, B. N., & Lang, P. J. (1994). Emotion in the criminal psychopath: Fear image processing. *Journal of Abnormal Psychology, 103,* 523–534.

Patton, G. C., Coffey, C., Carlin, J. B., Degenhardt, L., Lynskey, M., Hall, W., et al. (2002). Cannabis use and mental health in young people: Cohort study. *British Medical Journal, 325,* 1195–1198.

Paul, G. L., & Lentz, R. J. (1977). *Psychosocial treatment of chronic mental patients: Milieu versus social-learning programs.* Cambridge, MA: Harvard University Press.

Paulesu, E., Demonet, J. F., Fazio, F., McCrory, E., Chanoine, V., Brunswick, N., et al. (2001). Dyslexia: Cultural diversity and biological unity. *Science, 291,* 2165–2167.

Paulesu, E., Frith, C. D., & Frackowisk, R. S. J. (1993). The neural correlates of the verbal component of working memory. *Nature, 362,* 342–344.

Pauli, P., Dengler, W., Wiedemann, G., Montoya, P., Flor, H., Birbaumer, N., et al. (1997). Behavioral and neurophysiological evidence for altered processing of anxiety-related words in panic disorder. *Journal of Abnormal Psychology, 106,* 213–220.

Pear, R. (2000, March 20). White House seeks to curb pills used to calm young. *The New York Times online.*

Pelham, W. E., Hoza, B., Pillow, D. R., Gnagy, E. M., Kipp, H. L., Greiner, A. R., et al. (2002). Effects of Methylphenidate and expectancy on children with ADHD: Behavior, academic performance, and attributions in a summer treatment program and regular classroom settings. *Journal of Consulting and Clinical Psychology, 70,* 320–335.

Pelkonen, M., & Marttunen, M. (2003). Child and adolescent suicide: Epidemiology, risk factors, and approaches to prevention. *Paediatric Drugs, 5,* 243–65.

Peltzer, K., & Machleidt, W. (1992). A traditional (African) approach towards the therapy of schizophrenia and its comparison with Western models. *Therapeutic Communities International Journal for Therapeutic and Supportive Organizations, 13,* 229–242.

Penn, D. L. (1998, June). Assessment and treatment of social dysfunction in schizophrenia. *Clinician's Research Digest, Supplemental Bulletin 18.*

Penn, D. L., Combs, D. R., Ritchie, M., Francis, J., Cassisi, J., Morris, S., et al. (2000). Emotion recognition in schizophrenia: Further investigation of generalized versus specific deficit models. *Journal of Abnormal Psychology, 109,* 555–558.

Penn, D. L., & Mueser, K. T. (1996). Research update on the psychosocial treatment of schizophrenia. *American Journal of Psychiatry, 153,* 607–617.

Penninx, B. W., Guralnik, J. M., Bandeen-Roche, K., Kasper, J. D., Simonsick, E. M., Ferrucci, L., et al. (2000). The protective effect of emotional vitality on adverse health outcomes in disabled older women. *Journal of the American Geriatrics Society, 48,* 1359–1366.

Peplau, L. A. (2003). Human sexuality: How do men and women differ? *Current Directions in Psychological Science, 12,* 37–40.

Peppard, P. E., Young, T., Palta, M., & Skatrud, J. (2000). Prospective study of the association between sleep-disordered breathing and hypertension. *The New England Journal of Medicine, 342,* 1378–1384.

Perlin, M. L. (1994). Law and the delivery of mental health services in the community. *American Journal of Orthopsychiatry, 64,* 194–208.

Perry, J. C., & Bond M. (2000). Empirical studies of psychotherapy for personality disorders. In J. G. Gunderson & G. O. Gabbard, *Psychotherapy for personality disorders* (pp. 1–31). Washington, DC: American Psychiatric Press.

Perry, W. (2003). Let's call the whole thing off: A response to Dawes (2001). *Psychological Assessment, 15,* 582–585.

Persaud, R. (2000). Recurrent depression and stressful life events: In reply. *Archives of General Psychiatry, 57,* 617. [Letter]

Peterson, E. D., Shaw, L. K., DeLong, E. R., Pryor, D. B., Califf, R. M., & Mark, D. B. (1997). Racial variation in the use of coronary-revascularization procedures—Are the differences real? Do they matter? *The New England Journal of Medicine, 336,* 480–486.

Petrie, K. J., Booth, R. J., & Pennebaker, J. W. (1998). The immunological effects of thought suppression. *Journal of Personality and Social Psychology, 75,* 1264–1272.

Petry, N. M., & Martin, B. (2002). Low-cost contingency management for treating cocaine- and opioid-abusing methadone patients. *Journal of Consulting and Clinical Psychology, 70,* 398–405.

Petticrew, M., Bell, R., & Hunter, D. (2002). Influence of psychological coping on survival and recurrence in people with cancer: Systematic review. *British Medical Journal, 325,* 1066–1069.

Pettingale, K. W. (1985). Towards a psychobiological model of cancer: Biological considerations. Special issue: Cancer and the mind. *Social Science and Medicine, 20,* 779–787.

Peyron, C., Faraco, J., Rogers, W., Ripley, B., Overeem, S., & Charnay, Y. (2000). A mutation in a case of early onset narcolepsy and a generalized absence of hypocretin peptides in human nacroleptic brains. *Nature Medicine, 6,* 991–997.

Phaf, R. H., Geurts, H., & Eling, P. A. T. M. (2000). Word frequency and word stem completion in Korsakoff patients. *Journal of Clinical & Experimental Neuropsychology, 22,* 817–829.

Phillips, K. A., Albertini, R. S., & Rasmussen, S. A. (2002). A randomized placebo-controlled trial of fluoxetine in body dysmorphic disorder. *Archives of General Psychiatry, 59,* 381–388.

Phinney, J. (1989). Stages of ethnic identity in minority group adolescents. *Journal of Early Adolescence, 9,* 34–49.

Phinney, J., Lochner, B., & Murphy, R. (1990). Ethnic identity development and psychological adjustment in adolescence. In A. Stiffman & L. Davis (Eds.), *Ethnic issues in adolescent mental health.* (pp. 53–72). Newbury Park. CA: Sage.

Pianta, R. C., & Egeland, B. (1994). Relation between depressive symptoms and stressful life events in a sample of disadvantaged mothers. *Journal of Consulting and Clinical Psychology, 62,* 1229–1234.

Piasecki, T. M., Jorenby, D. E., Smith, S. S., Fiore, M. C., & Baker, T. B. (2003). Smoking withdrawal dynamics: I. Abstinence distress in lapsers and abstainers. *Journal of Consulting and Clinical Psychology, 112,* 3–13.

Pickering, T. G., (2003). Lifestyle modification and blood pressure control: Is the glass half full or half empty? *Journal of the American Medical Association, 289,* 2131–2132.

Pihl, R. O., Peterson, J., & Finn, P. (1990). Inherited predisposition to alcoholism: Characteristics of sons of male alcoholics. *Journal of Abnormal Psychology, 99,* 291–301.

Pike, K. M., & Rodin, J. (1991). Mothers, daughters, and disordered eating. *Journal of Abnormal Psychology, 101,* 198–204.

Pilling, S., Bebbington, P., Kuipers, E., Garety, P, Geddes, J., Orbach, G., et al. (2002) Psychological treatments in schizophrenia: I. Meta-analysis of family intervention and cognitive behaviour therapy. *Psychological Medicine, 32,* 763–82.

Pinderhughes, E. (1989). *Understanding race, ethnicity and power: Keys to efficacy in clinical practice.* New York: Free Press.

Pine, D. S., and the Research Unit on Pediatric Psychopharmacology Anxiety Study Group (2001). Fluvoxamine for the treatment of anxiety disorders in children and adolescents. *New England Journal of Medicine, 344*(17), 1279–1285.

Pinel, J. P. J., Assanand, S., & Lehman, D. R. (2000). Hunger, eating, and ill health. *American Psychologist, 55,* 1105–1116.

Pi-Sunyer, X. (2003). A clinical view of the obesity problem. *Science, 299,* 859–860.

Pitschel-Walz, G., Leucht, S., Bauml, J., Kissling, W., & Engel, R. R. (2001). The effect of family interventions on relapse and rehospitalization in schizophrenia—a meta-analysis. *Schizophrenia Bulletin, 27*(1), 73–92.

Plomin, R. (2001). Genetic factors contributing to learning and language delays and disabilities. *Child & Adolescent Psychiatric Clinics of North America, 10*(2), 259–277.

Plomin, R. (2003, April). 65 years of DNA. *APS Observer, 16*(4), 7–8.

Plomin, R., & Crabbe, J. C. (2001). DNA. *Psychological Bulletin, 126,* 806–828.

Plomin, R., & McGuffin, P. (2003). Psychopathology in the postgenomic era. *Annual Review of Psychology, 54,* 205–228.

Plomin, R., DeFries, J. C., Craig, I. W., & McGuffin, P. (Eds.). (2003). *Behavioral genetics in the postgenomic era.* Washington, DC: APA Books.

Plomin, R., Owen, M. J., & McGuffin, P. (1994). The genetic basis of complex human behaviors. *Science, 264,* 1733–1739.

Plunkett, A., O'Toole, B., Swanston, H., Oates, R. K., Shrimpton, S., & Parkinson, P. (2001). Suicide risk following child sexual abuse. *Ambulatory Pediatrics, 5,* 262–266.

Polcin, D. L. (1992). Issues in the treatment of dual diagnosis clients who have chronic mental illness. *Professional Psychology: Research and Practice, 23,* 30–37.

Polivy, J., & Herman, C. P. (2002). Causes of eating disorders. *Annual Review of Psychology, 53,* 187–213.

Pollack, A. (2004a, January 13). Putting a price on a good night's sleep. *The New York Times,* pp. CF1, F8.

Pollack, A. (2004b, January 13). Sleep experts debate root of insomnia: Body, mind or a little of each. *The New York Times,* p. F8.

Pollock, V. E. (1992). Meta-analysis of subjective sensitivity to alcohol in sons of alcoholics. *American Journal of Psychiatry, 149,* 1534–1538.

Pollan, M. (2003, October 12). The (Agri)cultural contradictions of obesity. *The New York Times Magazine,* pp. 41, 48.

Pope, H. G., Jr. (2002). Cannabis, cognition, and residual confounding. *Journal of the American Medical Association, 287,* 1172–1174.

Pope, H. G., Oliva, P. S., Hudson, J. I., Bodkin, J. A., & Gruber, A. J. (1999). Attitudes towards DSM-IV dissociative disorders diagnoses among board-certified American psychiatrists. *American Journal of Psychiatry, 156,* 321–323.

Pope, H. G., Jr., & Yurgelun-Todd, D. (1996). The residual cognitive effects of heavy marijuana use in college students. *Journal of the American Medical Association, 275,* 521–527.

Potash, J. B., Zandi, P. P., Willour, V. L., Lan, T.-H., Huo, Y., Avramopoulos, D., et al. (2003). Suggestive linkage to chromosomal regions 13q31 and 22q12 in families with psychotic bipolar disorder. *American Journal of Psychiatry, 160,* 680–686.

Potter, J. D. (1997). Hazards and benefits of alcohol. *The New England Journal of Medicine, 337,* 1763–1764.

Poulakis, Z., & Wertheim, E. H. (1993). Relationships among dysfunctional cognitions, depressive symptoms, and bulimic tendencies. *Cognitive Therapy and Research, 17,* 549–559.

Powchik, P., et al. (1998). Postmortem studies in schizophrenia. *Schizophrenia Bulletin, 24,* 325–341.

Power, K., McGoldrick, T., Brown, K., Buchanan, R., Sharp, D., Swanson, V., & Karatzias, A. (2002). A controlled comparison of eye movement desensitization and reprocessing versus exposure plus cognitive restructuring versus wait list in the treatment of post-traumatic stress disorder. *Clinical Psychology and Psychotherapy, 9,* 299–318.

PracticeNet (2003, Summer). Survey results—clinical practice patterns. *American Psychological Association Online,* Retrieved December 11, 2003, from www.apapracticenet.net/results/Summer2003/13.asp

Preuss, U. W., Schuckit, M. A., Smith, T. L., Danko, G. P., Bucholz, K. K., Hesselbrock, M. N., et al. (2003). Predictors and correlates of suicide attempts over 5 years in 1,237 alcohol-dependent men and women. Suicide attempts over 5 years. *American Journal of Psychiatry, 160,* 56–63.

Price, D. (2004). Efficacy of sertraline in the treatment of children and adolescents with major depressive disorder. *Journal of the American Medical Association, 291,* 40–41.

Prigatano, G. P. (1992). Personality disturbances associated with traumatic brain injury. *Journal of Consulting and Clinical Psychology, 60,* 360–368.

Prigerson, H. G., Maciejewski, P. K., & Rosenheck, R. A. (2001). Combat trauma: Trauma with highest risk of delayed onset and unresolved posttraumatic stress disorder symptoms, unemployment, and abuse among men. *Journal of Nervous & Mental Disease, 189,* 99–108.

Project MATCH Research Group. (1997). Matching alcoholism treatments to client heterogeneity: Project MATCH posttreatment drinking outcomes. *Journal of Studies on Alcohol, 58,* 7–29.

Prudic, J., et al. (1996). Resistance to antidepressant medications and short-term clinical response to ETC. *American Journal of Psychiatry, 153,* 985–992.

Pumariega, A. J. (1986). Acculturation and eating attitudes in adolescent girls: A comparative correlational study. *Journal of the American Academy of Child Psychiatry, 25,* 276–279.

Prudic, J., Olfson, M., Marcus, S. C., Fuller, R. B., & Sackeim, H. A. (2004). Effectiveness of electroconvulsive therapy in community settings. *Biological Psychiatry, 55,* 301–312.

Purdum, T. S. (2001, March 30). Non-Hispanic whites a minority, California census figures show. *The New York Times,* pp. A1, A18.

Purisch, A. D. (2001). Misconceptions about the Luria-Nebraska Neuropsychological Battery. *NeuroRehabilitation, 16,* 275–280.

Putnam, F. W., & Carlson, E. B. (1994). "Screening for multiple personality disorder with the Dissociative Experiences Scale": A reply. *American Journal of Psychiatry, 151,* 1249–1250.

Putnam, F. W., Guroff, J. J., Silberman, E. K., Barban, L., & Post, R. M. (1986). The clinical phenomenology of multiple personality disorder: Review of 100 recent cases. *Journal of Clinical Psychiatry, 47,* 285–293.

Pyszczynski, T., & Greenberg, J. (1987). Self-regulatory perseveration and the depressive self-focusing style: A self-awareness theory of reactive depression. *Psychological Bulletin, 102,* 122–138.

Q

Qin, P., Agerbo, E., & Mortensen, P. B. (2003). Suicide risk in relation to socioeconomic, demographic, psychiatric, and familial factors: A national register–based study of all suicides in Denmark, 1981–1997. *American Journal of Psychiatry, 160,* 765–772.

Quesnel, C., Savard, J., Simard, S., Ivers, H., & Morin, C. M. (2003). Efficacy of cognitive–behavioral therapy for insomnia in women treated for nonmetastatic breast cancer. *Journal of Consulting and Clinical Psychology, 71,* 189–200.

R

Rabasca, L. (2000a, March). Listening instead of preaching. *Monitor on Psychology, 31,* pp. 50–51.

Rabkin, J. G., Wagner, G. J., & Rabkin R. (2000). A double-blind, placebo-controlled trial of testosterone therapy for HIV-positive men with hypogonadal symptoms. *Archives of General Psychiatry, 57,* 141–147.

Rachman, S. J. (2000). Joseph Wolpe (1915–1997). *American Psychologist, 55,* 431.

Rachman, S. J., & Bichard, S. (1988). The overprediction of fear. *Clinical Psychology Review, 8,* 303–312.

Ragland, J. D., et al. (1999). Neuropsychological laterality indices of schizophrenia: Interactions with gender. *Schizophrenia Bulletin, 25,* 79–89.

Ragland, J. D., et al. (2001). Effect of schizophrenia on frontotemporal activity during word encoding and recognition: A PET cerebral blood flow study. *American Journal of* Psychiatry, *158,* 1114–1125.

Räikkönen. K., et al. (1999). Effects of hostility on ambulatory blood pressure and mood during daily living in healthy adults. *Health Psychology, 18,* 44–53.

Raine, A., et al. (2000). Reduced prefrontal gray matter volume and reduced autonomic activity in antisocial personality disorder. *Archives of General Psychiatry, 57,* 119–127.

Rakic, Z., Starcevic, V., Starcevic, V. P., & Marinkovic, J. (1997). Testosterone treatment in men with erectile disorder and low levels of total testosterone in serum. *Archives of Sexual Behavior, 26,* 495–504.

Ralph, D., & McNicholas, T. (2000). UK management guidelines for erectile dysfunction. *British Medical Journal, 321,* 499–503.

Rao, K., DiClemente, R. J., & Ponton, L. E. (1992). Child sexual abuse of Asians compared with other populations. *Journal of the American Academy of Child and Adolescent Psychiatry, 31,* 880–886.

Rao, S. M., Huber, S. J., & Bornstein, R. A. (1992). Emotional changes with multiple sclerosis and Parkinson's disease. *Journal of Consulting and Clinical Psychology, 60,* 369–378.

Rapee, R. M. (1987). The psychological treatment of panic attacks: Theoretical conceptualization and review of evidence. *Clinical Psychology Review, 7,* 427–438.

Rapee, R. M. (1991). Generalized anxiety disorder: A review of clinical features and theoretical concepts. *Clinical Psychology Review, 11,* 419–440.

Raphael, A., J., Golden, C., & Cassidy-Feltgen, S. (2002). The Bender-Gestalt Test (BGT) in forensic assessment. *Journal of Forensic Psychology Practice, 2,* 93–106.

Rapin, I. (1997). Autism. *The New England Journal of Medicine, 337,* 97–104.

Rashotte, C. A., MacPhee, K., & Torgesen, J. K. (2001). The effectiveness of a group reading instruction program with poor readers in multiple grades. *Learning Disability Quarterly, 24*(2), 119–134.

Raskind, W. H. (2001). Current understanding of the genetic basis of reading and spelling disability. *Learning Disability Quarterly, 24*(3), 141–157.

Rathus, S. A., & Nevid, J. S. (1977). *Behavior therapy.* Garden City, NY: Doubleday.

Rathus, S. A., Nevid, J. S., & Fichner-Rathus, L. (2005). *Human sexuality in a world of diversity* (6th ed.). Boston: Allyn & Bacon.

Ratti, L. A., Humphrey, L. L., & Lyons, J. S. (1996). Structural analysis of families with a polydrug-dependent, bulimic, or normal adolescent daughter. *Journal of Consulting & Clinical Psychology, 64,* 1255–1262.

Ratti, M. T., Bo, P., Giardini, A., & Soragna, D. (2002). Chronic alcoholism and the frontal lobe: Which executive functions are impaired? *Acta Neurology Psychiatrica Scandinavica, 105,* 276–281.

Rauch, S. L., & Jenike, M. A. (1998). Pharmacological treatment of obsessive complusive disorder. In P. E. Nathan & J. M. Gorman (Eds.), *A guide to treatments that work* (pp. 358–376). New York: Oxford University Press.

Rauschenberger, S. L., & Lynn, S. J. (1995). Fantasy proneness, *DSM-III-R* Axis I psychopathology, and dissociation. *Journal of Abnormal Psychology, 104,* 373–380.

Rawson, R. A., Washton, A., Domier, C. P., & Reiber, C. (2002). Drugs and sexual effects: Role of drug type and gender. *Journal of Substance Abuse Treatment, 22,* 103–108.

Read, J., et al. (2001). Assessing suicidality in adults: Integrating childhood trauma as a major risk factor. *Professional Psychology: Research and Practice, 32,* 367–372.

Ready, T. (2000, June 7). Meditation apparently good for the heart as well as the mind. *CNN Web Posting.* Retrieved June 8, 2000, from http://www.cnn.com/2000/HEALTH/06/07/minding.heart.wmd/

Redd, W. H. (1995). Behavioral research in cancer as a model for health psychology. *Health Psychology, 14,* 99–100.

Redd, W. H., & Jacobsen, P. (2001). Behavioral intervention in comprehensive cancer care. In A. Baum, T. A. Revenson & J. E. Singer (Eds.), *Handbook of health psychology* (pp. 757–776). Mahwah, NJ: Erlbaum.

Reed, G. M., McLaughlin, C. J., & Milholland, K. (2000). Ten interdisciplinary principles for professional practice in telehealth: Implications for psychology. *Professional Psychology: Research and Practice, 31,* 170–178.

Regehr, C., Hill, J., & Glancy, G. D. (2000). Individual predictors of traumatic reactions in firefighters. *Journal of Nervous & Mental Disease, 188,* 333–339.

Reich, J. (1996). The morbidity of *DSM-III-R* dependent personality disorder. *Journal of Nervous & Mental Disease, 184,* 22–26.

Reichman, M. E. (1994). Alcohol and breast cancer. *Alcohol Health and Research World, 18,* 182–183.

Reinisch, J. M. (1990). *The Kinsey Institute new report on sex: What you must know to be sexually literate.* New York: St. Martin's Press.

Reisberg B., Doody, R., Stoffler, A., Schmitt, F., Ferris, S., Mobius, H. J., & Memantine Study Group. (2003). Memantine in moderate-to-severe Alzheimer's disease. *New England Journal of Medicine, 348,* 1333–1341.

Reisberg, B., et al. (1986). Assessment of presenting symptoms. In L. W. Poon (Ed.), *Handbook for clinical memory assessment of older adults* (pp. 108–128). Washington, DC: American Psychological Association.

Reisner, A. D. (1994). Multiple personality disorder diagnosis: A house of cards? *American Journal of Psychiatry, 151,* 629.

Reitan, R. M., & Wolfson, D. (2000). The neuropsychological similarities of mild and more severe head injury. *Archives of Clinical Neuropsychology, 15,* 433–442.

Reneman, L., Lavalaye, J., Schmand, B., de Wolff, F. A., van den Brink, W., den Heeten, G. J., et al. (2001). Cortical serotonin transporter density and verbal memory in individuals who stopped using 3,4-methylenedioxymethamphetamine (MDMA or "Ecstasy"): Preliminary findings. *Archives of General Psychiatry, 58,* 901–906.

Renfrey, G. S. (1992). Cognitive-behavior therapy and the Native American client. *Behavior Therapy, 23,* 321–340.

Researchers gain insight into Huntington's. (2001, March 22). *CNN Web Posting.* Retrieved March 24, 2001, from http://www.cnn.com/2001/HEALTH/conditions/03/22/huntingtons.gene/index.html

Resick, P. A. (2003). Post hoc reasoning in possible cases of child sexual abuse: Just say no. *Clinical Psychology: Science & Practice, 10*(3), 349–351.

Resick, P. A., Nishith, P., Weaver, T. L., Astin, M. C., & Feuer, C. A. (2002). A comparison of cognitive-processing therapy with prolonged exposure and a waiting condition for the treatment of chronic posttraumatic stress disorder in female rape victims. *Journal of Consulting and Clinical Psychology, 70,* 867–879.

Rey, J. M. (1993). Oppositional defiant disorder. *American Journal of Psychiatry, 150,* 1769–1778.

Rey, J. M, & Tennant, C. C. (2002). Cannabis and mental health: More evidence establishes clear link between use of cannabis and psychiatric illness, *British Medical Journal, 325,* 1183–1184.

Reynolds, C. F., III, et al. (1996). Treatment outcome in recurrent major depression: A post hoc comparison of elderly ("Young Old") and midlife patients. *American Journal of Psychiatry, 153,* 1288–1292.

Reynolds, K., Lewis, L. B., Nolen, J. D. L., Kinney, G. L., Sathya, B., He, J., et al. (2003). Alcohol consumption and risk of stroke. *Journal of the American Medical Association, 289,* 579–588.

Rhee, S. H., Hewitt, J. K.,Young, S. E., Corley, R. P., Crowley, T. J., & Stallings, M. C. (2003). Genetic and environmental influences on substance initiation, use, and problem use in adolescents. *Archives of General Psychiatry, 60,* 1256–1264.

Rhee, S. H., & Waldman, I. D. (2002). Genetic and environmental influences on antisocial behavior: A meta-analysis of twin and adoption studies. *Psychological Bulletin, 128,* 490–529.

Ribisl, K. M., et al. (2000). English language use as a risk factor for smoking initiation among Hispanic and Asian American Adolescents: Evidence for mediation by tobacco-related beliefs and social norms. *Health Psychology, 19,* 403–410.

Ricaurte G. A., Yuan, J., Hatzidimitriou, G., Cord, B. J., & McCann, U. D. (2002). Severe dopaminergic neurotoxicity in primates after a common recreational dose regimen of MDMA ("ecstasy"). *Science, 297,* 2260–2263.

Ricciardelli, L. A., & McCabe, M. P. (2001). Children's body image concerns and eating disturbance: A review of the literature. *Clinical Psychology Review, 21,* 325–344.

Ricciardelli, L. A., & McCabe, M. P. (2004). A biopsychosocial model of disordered eating and the pursuit of muscularity in adolescent boys. *Psychological Bulletin, 130,* 179–205.

Rice, N., & O'Donohue, W. (2002). Cultural sensitivity: A critical examination. *New Ideas in Psychology, 20,* 35–48.

Richard, D. C. S., & Bobicz, K. (2003, January). Computers and behavioral assessment: 6 years later. *The Behavior Therapist,* pp. 219–223.

Richards, J. C., Edgar, L. V., & Gibbon, P. (1996). Cardiac acuity in panic disorder. *Cognitive Therapy and Research, 20,* 361–376.

Richardson, M. A., Bevans, M. L., Read, L. L., Chao, H. M., Clelland, J. D., et al. (2003). Efficacy of the branched-chain amino acids in the treatment of tardive dyskinesia in men. *American Journal of Psychiatry, 160,* 1117–1124.

Riddle, M. A., Reeve E. A., Yaryura-Tobias, J. A, Yang, H. M., Claghorn, J. L., Gaffney, G., et al. (2001). Fluvoxamine for children and adolescents with obsessive-compulsive disorder: A randomized controlled, multicenter trial. *Journal of the American Academy of Child and Adolescent Psychiatry, 40*, 222–229.

Ridley, C. R. (1984). Clinical treatment of the nondisclosing Black client: A therapeutic paradox. *American Psychologist, 39*, 1234–1244.

Ridley, M. (2003). *Nature via nurture genes, experience, and what makes us human.* New York: HarperCollins.

Riedel, B. R. W., & Lichstein, K. L. (2001). Strategies for evaluating adherence to sleep restriction treatment for insomnia. *Behaviour Research and Therapy, 39*, 201–212.

Riether, A. M., & Stoudemire, A. (1988). Psychogenic fugue states: A review. *Southern Medical Journal, 81*, 568–571.

Riley, V. (1981). Psychoneuroendocrine influences on immunocompetence and neoplasia. *Science, 212*, 1100–1109.

Rimer, S. (1999, September 5). Gaps seen in treating depression in elderly. *The New York Times*, pp. 1, 18.

Rimm, E. (2000, May). *Lifestyle may play role in potential for impotence.* Paper presented to the annual meeting of the American Urological Association, Atlanta, GA.

Rinne, T., van den Brink, W., Wouters, L., & van Dyck, R. (2002). SSRI treatment of borderline personality disorder: A randomized, placebo-controlled clinical trial for female patients with borderline personality disorder. *American Journal of Psychiatry, 159*, 2048–2054.

Riso, L. P., duToit, P. L., Blandino, J. A., Penna, S., Dacey, S., Duin, J. S., et al. (2003). Cognitive aspects of chronic depression. *Journal of Abnormal Psychology, 112*, 72–80.

Ritter, C., et al. (2000). Stress, psychosocial resources, and depressive symptomatology during pregnancy in low-income, inner-city women. *Health Psychology, 19*, 576–585.

Ritterband, L. M., Cox, D. J., Walker, L. S., Kovatchev, B., McKnight, L., Patel, K., et al. (2003). An Internet intervention as adjunctive therapy for pediatric encopresis. *Journal of Consulting and Clinical Psychology, 71*, 910–917.

Rivas-Vazquez, R. A., & Blais, M. A. (2002). Pharmacologic treatment of personality disorder. *Professional Psychology: Research and Practice, 33*, 104–107.

Rivas-Vazquez, R. A., Johnson, S. L., Rey, G. J., Blais, M. A., & Rivas-Vazquez, A. (2002). Current treatments for bipolar disorder: A review and update for psychologists. *Professional Psychology: Research and Practice, 33*, 212–223.

Robb, A. S., Silber, T. J., Orrell-Valente, J. K., Valadez-Meltzer, A., Ellis, N., & Dadson, M. J. (2002). Supplemental nocturnal nasogastric refeeding for better short-term outcome in hospitalized adolescent girls with anorexia nervosa. *American Journal of Psychiatry, 159*, 1347–1353.

Robin, R. W., Greene, R. L., Albaugh, B., Caldwell, A., & Goldman, D. (2003). Use of the MMPI-2 in American Indians: I. Comparability of the MMPI-2 between two tribes and with the MMPI-2 normative group. *Psychological Assessment, 15*, 351–359.

Robins, L. N., Locke, B. Z., & Reiger, D. A. (1991). An overview of psychiatric disorders in America. In L. N. Robins & D. A. Regier (Eds.), *Psychiatric disorders in America: The Epidemiologic Catchment Area Study* (pp. 328–366). New York: Free Press.

Robins, L. N., Tipp, J., & Przybeck, T. (1991). Antisocial personality. In L. N. Robins & D. A. Regier (Eds.), *Psychiatric disorders in America: The Epidemiologic Catchment Area Study* (pp. 258–290). New York: Free Press.

Robinson, N. M., Zigler, E., & Gallagher, J. J. (2001). Two tails of the normal curve: Similarities and differences in the study of mental retardation and giftedness. *American Psychologist, 55*, 1413–1424.

Robinson, T., et al. (1996). Ethnicity and body dissatisfaction: Are Hispanic and Asian girls at increased risk of eating disorders. *Journal of Adolescent Health, 19*, 384–393.

Rocha, B. A., Scearce-Levie, K., Lucasm J. J., Hiroi, N., Castanon, N., Crabbe, J. C., et al. (1998). Increased vulnerability to cocaine in mice lacking the serotonin-1 B receptor. [Letter]. *Nature, 393*, 175.

Rock, C. L., & Curran-Celentano, J. (1996). Nutritional management of eating disorders. *The Psychiatric Clinics of North America, 19*, 701–713.

Rodin, J., Bartoshuk, L., Peterson, C., & Schank, D. (1990). Bulimia and taste: Possible interactions. *Journal of Abnormal Psychology, 99*, 32–39.

Rodríguez de Fonseca, F., Carrera, M. R., Navarro, M., Koob, G. F., & Weiss, R. (1997). Activation of corticotropin-releasing factor in the limbic system during cannabinoid withdrawal. *Science, 276*, 2050–2054.

Roelofs, K., Keijsers, G. P. J., Hoogduin, K. A. L., Näring, G. W. B., & Moene, F. C. (2002). Childhood abuse in patients with conversion disorder. *American Journal of Psychiatry, 159*, 1908–1913.

Roemer, L., & Orsillo, S. M. (2003). Mindfulness: A promising intervention strategy in need of further study. *Clinical Psychology: Science and Practice, 10*, 172–178.

Roesch, R., Zapf, P. A., Golding, S. L., & Skeem, J. L. (1999). Defining and assessing competence to stand trial. In A. K. Hess, I. B. Weiner, et al. (Eds.), *The handbook of forensic psychology* (2nd ed., pp. 327–349). New York: Wiley.

Roesler, A., & Witztum, E. (2000). Pharmacotherapy of paraphilias in the next millennium. *Behavioral Sciences & the Law, 18*(1), 43–56.

Rogan, A. (1986, Fall). Recovery from alcoholism: Issues for black and Native American alcoholics. *Alcohol Health and Research World, 10*, 42–44.

Rogers v. Okin, 478 F.Supp. 1242 (D.Mass. 1979).

Rogers, C. R. (1951). *Client-centered therapy.* Boston: Houghton Mifflin.

Rogers, R., Gillis, J. R., Turner, R. E., & Frise-Smith, T. (1990). The clinical presentation of command hallucinations in a forensic population. *American Journal of Psychiatry, 147*, 1304–1307.

Rogler, L. H., Cortes, D. E., & Malgady, R. G. (1991). Acculturation and mental health status among Hispanics: Convergence and new directions for research. *American Psychologist, 46*, 584–597.

Rohan, K. J., Sigmon, S. T., & Dorhofer, D. M. (2003). Cognitive-behavioral factors in seasonal affective disorder. *Journal of Consulting and Clinical Psychology, 71*, 22–30.

Rohde, P., Lewinsohn, P. M., & Seeley, J. R. (1991). Comorbidity of unipolar depression: II. Comorbidity with other mental disorders in adolescents and adults. *Journal of Abnormal Psychology, 101*, 214–222.

Rose, J. (1996). Anger management: A group treatment program for people with mental retardation. *Journal of Developmental and Physical Disabilities, 8*, 133–149.

Rosen, J. C. (1996). Body dysmorphic disorder: Assessment and treatment. In J. K. Thompson (Ed.), *Body image, eating disorders, and obesity* (pp. 149–170). Washington, DC: American Psychological Association.

Rosen, R. C., & Laumann, E. O. (2003). The prevalence of sexual problems in women: How valid are comparisons across studies? Commentary on Bancroft, Loftus, and Long's (2003) "Distress about sex: A national survey of women in heterosexual relationships." *Archives of Sexual Behavior, 32*(3), 209–211.

Rosen, R. C., & Leiblum, S. R. (1995). Treatment of sexual disorders in the 1990s: An integrated approach. *Journal of Consulting and Clinical Psychology, 63*, 877–890.

Rosenberg, D. A. (2003). Münchausen syndrome by proxy: Medical diagnostic criteria. *Child Abuse and Neglect, 27*, 421–430.

Rosenberg, H., & Davis, L. A. (1994). Acceptance of moderate drinking by alcohol treatment services in the United States. *Journal of Studies on Alcohol, 55*, 167–172.

Rosenheck, R. (2000). Cost-effectiveness of services for mentally ill homeless people: The application of research to policy and practice. *American Journal of Psychiatry, 157*, 1563–1570.

Rosenheck, R., Kasprow, W., Frisman, L., & Liu-Mares, W. (2003). Cost-effectiveness of supported housing for homeless persons with mental illness. *Archives of General Psychiatry, 60*, 940–951.

Rosenheck, R., Perlick, D., Bingham, S., & Collins, J. (2004). In reply. *Journal of the American Medical Association, 291*, 1065–1066.

Rosenheck, R., Perlick, D., Bingham, S., Liu-Mares, W., Collins, J., Warren, S., et al. (2003). Effectiveness and cost of olanzapine and haloperidol in the treatment of schizophrenia: A randomized controlled trial. *Journal of the American Medical Association, 26*, 2693–2702.

Rosenthal, D., et al. (1968). Schizophrenics' offspring reared in adoptive homes. In D. Rosenthal & S. S. Kety (Eds.), *The transmission of schizophrenia*. Oxford: Pergamon Press.

Rosenthal, D., et al. (1975). Parent-child relationships and psychopathological disorder in the child. *Archives of General Psychiatry, 32*, 466–476.

Rosenthal, E. (1993, April 9). Who will turn violent? Hospitals have to guess. *The New York Times*, pp. A1, C12.

Ross, C. A., Anderson, G., Fleisher, W. P., & Norton, & G. R. (1991). The frequency of multiple personality disorder among psychiatric inpatients. *American Journal of Psychiatry, 148*, 1717–1720.

Ross, C. A., Miller, S. D., Reagor, P., Bjornson, L., Fraser, G. A., & Anderson, G. (1990). Structured interview data on 102 cases of multiple personality disorder from four centers. *American Journal of Psychiatry, 147*, 596–601.

Ross, C. A., Norton, G. R., & Wozney, K. (1989). Multiple personality disorder: An analysis of 236 cases. *Canadian Journal of Psychiatry, 34*, 413–418.

Ross, D. E. (2000). The deficit syndrome and eye tracking disorder may reflect a distinct subtype within the syndrome of schizophrenia. *Schizophrenia Bulletin, 26*, 855–866.

Ross, E., & Oliver, C. (2003). The assessment of mood in adults who have severe or profound mental retardation. *Clinical Psychology Review, 23*, 225–245.

Ross, R., Dagnone, D., Jones, P. J., Smith, H., Paddags, A., & Hudson, R. (2000). Reduction in obesity and related comorbid conditions after diet-induced weight loss or exercise-induced weight loss in men: A randomized, controlled trial. *Annals of Internal Medicine, 133*, 92–103.

Roth, R. M., Flashman, L. A., Saykin, A. J., McAllister, T. W., & Vidaver, R. (2004). Apathy in schizophrenia: Reduced frontal lobe volume and neuropsychological deficits. *American Journal of Psychiatry, 161*, 157–159.

Rothbaum, B. O., Hodges, L., Anderson, P. L., Price, L., & Smith, S. (2002). Twelve-month follow-up of virtual reality and standard exposure therapies for the fear of flying. *Journal of Consulting and Clinical Psychology, 70*, 428–432.

Rotter, J. B. (1966). Generalized expectancies for internal vs. external control of reinforcement. *Psychological Monographs, 1*, 210–609.

Rounsaville, B. J., & Kosten, T. R. (2000). Treatment for opioid dependence: Quality and access. *Journal of the American Medical Association, 283*, 1337–1339. [Editorial]

Rousseau, F., et al. (1991). Direct diagnosis by DNA analysis of the fragile X syndrome of mental retardation. *New England Journal of Medicine, 325*, 1673–1681.

Roy A. (2003). Characteristics of HIV patients who attempt suicide. *Acta Psychiatrica Scandinavica 107*, 41–44.

Roy, E. (2000). Relation of family history of suicide to suicide attempts in alcoholics. *American Journal of Psychiatry, 157*, 2050–2051.

Rozee, P. D., & Koss, M. P. (2001). Rape: A century of resistance. *Psychology of Women Quarterly, 25*(4), 295–311.

Rozin, P., Bauer, R., & Catanese, D. (2003). Food and life, pleasure and worry, among American college students: gender differences and regional similarities. *Journal of Personality and Social Psychology, 85*, 132–141.

Rubin, L. J. (1996). Childhood sexual abuse: False accusations of "false memory"? *Professional Psychology: Research and Practice, 27*, 447–451.

Rubinstein, S., & Caballero, B. (2000). Is Miss America an undernourished role model? *Journal of the American Medical Association, 283,* 1569.

Rudolph, K. D., Kurlakowsky, K. D., & Conley, C. S. (2001). Developmental and social-contextual origins of depressive control-related beliefs and behavior. *Cognitive Therapy & Research, 25*(4), 447–475.

Rugino, T., & Copley, T. C. (2001). Effects of modafinil in children with attention-deficit/hyperactivity disorder: An open-label study. *Journal of American Academy of Child & Adolescent Psychiatry, 40,* 230–235.

Ruscio, A. M., Borkovec, T. D., & Ruscio, J. (2001). A taxometric investigation of the latent structure of worry. *Journal of Abnormal Psychology, 110,* 413–422.

Rush, A. J., & Weissenburger, J. E. (1994). Do thinking patterns predict depressive symptoms? *Cognitive Therapy and Research, 10,* 225–236.

Rutledge, T., & Hogan, B. E. (2002). A quantitative review of prospective evidence linking psychological factors with hypertension development. *Psychosomatic Medicine, 64,* 758–66.

Rutter, M. (2003). Poverty and child mental health: Natural experiments and social causation. *Journal of the American Medical Association, 290,* 2063–2064.

Rutter, M., Caspi, A., Fergusson, D., Horwood, L. J., Goodman, R., Maughan, B., et al. (2004). Sex differences in developmental reading disability: New findings from 4 epidemiological studies. *Journal of the American Medical Association, 291,* 2007–2012.

Ryan, R. (2002). Samson was heroic, exhausted, depressed, and in love, but he does not have antisocial personality disorder. *Archives of General Psychiatry, 59,* 564–565.

Rybarczyk, B., Lopez, M., Benson, R., Alsten, C., & Stepanski, E. (2002). Efficacy of two behavioral treatment programs for comorbid geriatric insomnia. *Psychology and Aging, 17,* 288–298.

Rychtarik, R. G., et al. (2000). Treatment settings for persons with alcoholism: Evidence for matching clients to inpatient versus outpatient care. *Journal of Consulting and Clinical Psychology, 68,* 277–289.

Ryder, A. G., Alden, L. E., & Paulhus, D. L. (2000). Is acculturation unidimensional or bidimensional? A head-to-head comparison in the prediction of personality, self-identity, and adjustment. *Journal of Personality and Social Psychology, 79*(1), 49–65.

S

Sachdev, P., & Hay, P. (1996). Site and size of lesion and psychosurgical outcome in obsessive-compulsive disorder: A magnetic resonance imaging study. *Biological Psychiatry, 39,* 739–742.

Sack, W. H., Clarke, G. N., & Seeley, J. (1996). Multiple forms of stress in Cambodian adolescent refugees. *Child Development, 67,* 107–116.

Sackeim, H. A., Haskett, R. F., Mulsant, B. H., Thase, M. E., Mann, J. J., Pettinati, H. M., et al. (2001). Continuation pharmacotherapy in the prevention of relapse following electroconvulsive therapy. *Journal of the American Medical Association, 285,* 1299–1307.

Sackheim, H. A., et al. (1994). Effects of stimulus intensity and electrode placement on the efficacy and cognitive effects of electroconvulsive therapy. *New England Journal of Medicine, 328,* 839–846.

Sackheim, H. A., Prudic, J., & Devanand, D. P. (1990). Treatment of medication-resistant depression with electroconvulsive therapy. In A. Tasman, et al. (Eds.), *Review of psychiatry* (Vol. 9). Washington, DC: American Psychiatric Press.

Sacks, O. (1985). *The man who mistook his wife for a hat and other clinical tales.* New York: Summit.

Sadler, A. G., Booth, B. M., Nielson, D., & Doebbeling, B. N. (2000). Health-related consequences of physical and sexual violence: Women in the military. *Obstetrics & Gynecology, 96*(3), 473–480.

Safran, J. D., & Messer, S. B. (1997). Psychotherapy integration: A postmodern critique. *Clinical Psychology: Science and Practice, 4,* 140–152.

Salekin, R. T. (2002). Psychopathy and therapeutic pessimism: Clinical lore or clinical reality? *Clinical Psychology Review, 22,* 79–112.

Salekin, R. T., Ziegler, T. A., Larrea, M. A., Anthony, V. L., et al. (2003). Predicting dangerousness with two million Adolescent Clinical Inventory psychopathy scales: The important of egocentric and callous traits. *Journal of Personality Assessment, 80,* 154–163.

Salgado de Snyder, V. N. (1987). Factors associated with acculturative stress and depressive symptomatology among married Mexican immigrant women. *Psychology of Women Quarterly, 11,* 475–488.

Salgado de Snyder, V. N., Cervantes, R. C., & Padilla, A. M. (1990). Gender and ethnic differences in psychosocial stress and generalized distress among Hispanics. *Sex Roles, 22,* 441–453.

Salkovskis, P. M., & Clark, D. M. (1993). Panic disorder and hypochondriasis. Special issue: Panic, cognitions and sensations. *Advances in Behaviour Research and Therapy, 15,* 23–48.

Salkovskis, P. M., Thorpe, S. J., Wahl, K., Wroe, A. L., & Forrester, E. (2003). Neutralizing increases discomfort associated with obsessional thoughts: an experimental study with obsessional patients. *Journal of Abnormal Psychology, 112,* 709–715.

Sammons, M. T., & Brown, A. B. (1997). The Department of Defense psychopharmacology demonstration project: An evolving program for postdoctoral education in psychology. *Professional Psychology: Research and Practice, 28,* 107–112.

Sanders, B., & Green, J. A. (1995). The factor structure of the Dissociative Experiences Scale in college students. *Dissociation Progress in the Dissociative Disorders, 7,* 23–27.

Sanders Thompson, V. L., Bazile, A., & Akbar, M. (2004). African Americans' perceptions of psychotherapy and psychotherapists. *Professional Psychology: Research and Practice, 35,* 19–26.

Sanderson, W. C., & Rego, S. A. (2000). Empirically supported treatment for panic disorder: Research, theory, and application of cognitive behavioral therapy. *Journal of Cognitive Psychotherapy, 14,* 219–244.

Sanislow, C. A., Grilo, C. M., & McGlashan, T. H. (2000). Factor analysis of the *DSM-III-R* borderline personality disorder criteria in psychiatric inpatients. *American Journal of Psychiatry, 157,* 1629–1633.

Sansone, R. A., Rytwinski, D., & Gaither, G. A. (2003). Borderline personality and psychotropic medication prescription in an outpatient psychiatry clinic. *Comprehensive Psychiatry, 44,* 454–458.

Sapolsky, R. M. (2000, April 10). It's not "all in the genes." *Newsweek, 68,* 43–44.

Sapolsky, R. M. (2003). Gene therapy for psychiatric disorders. *American Journal of Psychiatry, 160,* 208–220.

Sar, V., Yargic, L. I., & Tutkun, H. (1996). Structured interview data on 35 cases of dissociative identity disorder in Turkey. *American Journal of Psychiatry, 153,* 1329–1333.

Sass, L. (1982, August 22). The borderline personality. *The New York Times Magazine,* pp. 12–15, 66–67.

Satcher, D. (2000). Mental health: A report of the Surgeon General—Executive summary. *Professional Psychology: Research and Practice, 31,* 5–13.

Sato, T. (1997). Seasonal affective disorder and phototherapy: A critical review. *Professional Psychology: Research and Practice, 28,* 164–169.

Sawa, A., & Snyder, S. H. (2002). Schizophrenia: Diverse approaches to a complex disease Science, 00, 692–695.

Sayers, G. M. (2003). Psychiatry and the control of dangerousness: A comment. *Journal of Medical Ethics, 29,* 235–236.

Saywitz, K. J., Mannarino, A. P., Berliner, L., & Cohen, J. A. (2000). Treatment for sexually abused children and adolescents. *American Psychologist, 55,* 1040–1049.

Schaffer, S. J. (2000, November/December). New NY Tarasoff/confidentiality ruling. *NYSPA Notebook,* p. 5.

Schatzberg, A. F. (2002). Brain imaging in affective disorders: More questions about causes versus effects. *American Journal of Psychiatry, 159,* 1807–1808.

Scheel, K. R. (2000). The empirical basis of dialectical behavior therapy: Summary, critique, and implications. *Clinical Psychology: Science and Practice, 7,* 68–86.

Scheier, L. M., Botvin, G. J., & Baker, E. (1997). Risk and protective factors as predictors of adolescent alcohol involvement and transitions in alcohol use: A prospective analysis. *Journal of Studies on Alcohol, 58,* 652–767.

Scheier, M. F., & Carver, C. S. (1985). Optimism, coping, and health: Assessment and implications of generalized outcome expectancies. *Health Psychology, 4,* 219–247.

Scheier, M. F., & Carver, C. S. (1992). Effects of optimisim on psychological and physical well-being: Theoretical overview and empirical update. Special issue: Cognitive perspectives in health psychology. *Cognitive Therapy and Research, 16,* 201–228.

Scheier, M. F., Matthews, K. A., Owens, J. F., Schulz, R., Bridges, M. W., Magovern, G. J., et al. (1999). Optimism and rehospitalization after coronary artery bypass graft surgery. *Archives of Internal Medicine, 159,* 829–935.

Schiess, M. (2003). Nonsteroidal anti-inflammatory drugs protect against Parkinson neurodegeneration: Can an NSAID a day keep Parkinson disease away? *Archives of Neurology, 60,* 1043–1044.

Schiller, L., & Bennett, A. (1994). *The quiet room: A journey out of the torment of madness.* New York: Warner Books, Inc.

Schizophrenia Update—Part I (1995, June). *The Harvard Mental Health Letter, 11,* 1–4.

Schlenger, W. E., Caddell, J. M., Ebert, L., Jordan, B. K., Rourke, K. M., Wilson, D. et al. (2002). Psychological reactions to terrorist attacks: Findings from the National Study of Americans' Reactions to September 11. *Journal of the American Medical Association, 288,* 581–588.

Schmidt, N. B., Lerew, D. R., & Jackson, R. J. (1997). The role of anxiety sensitivity in the pathogenesis of panic: Prospective evaluation of spontaneous panic attacks during acute stress. *Journal of Abnormal Psychology, 106,* 355–364.

Schmidt, N. B., Trakowski, J. H., & Staab, J. P. (1997). Extinction of panicogenic effects of a 35% CO₂ challenge in patients with panic disorder. *Journal of Abnormal Psychology, 106,* 630–638.

Schmidt, N. B., Woolaway-Bickel, K., Trakowski, J., Santiago, H., Storey, J., Koselka, M., et al. (2000). Dismantling cognitive–behavioral treatment for panic disorder: Questioning the utility of breathing retraining. *Journal of Consulting and Clinical Psychology, 68,* 417–424.

Schmitt, E. (2001a, April 1). U.S. now more diverse, ethnically and racially. *The New York Times,* p. A20.

Schmitt, E. (2001b, March 13). For 7 million people in census, one race category isn't enough. *The New York Times,* pp. A1, A14.

Schneiderman, N., Antoni, M. H., Saab, P. G., & Ironson, G. (2001). Health psychology: Psychosocial and biobehavioral aspects of chronic disease management. *Annual Review of Psychology, 52,* 555–580.

Schneier, F. R., Wexler, K. B., & Liebowitz, M. R. (1997). Social phobia and stuttering. *American Journal of Psychiatry, 154,* 131.

Schnurr, P. P., Ford, J. D., & Friedman, M. J. (2000). Predictors and outcomes of posttraumatic stress disorder in World War II veterans exposed to mustard gas. *Journal of Consulting and Clinical Psychology, 68,* 258–268.

Schoenman, T. J. (1984). The mentally ill witch in text books of abnormal psychology: Current status and implications of a fallacy. *Professional Psychiatry, 15,* 299–314.

Schonwald, A. D., & Rappaport, L. (2003, September 22). New options for ADHD. *Newsweek,* 77.

Schreier, H., & Ricci, L. R. (2002). Follow-up of a case of Münchausen by proxy syndrome. *Journal of the*

American Academy of Child and Adolescent Psychiatry, 41, 1395–1396.

Schteingart, J. S., et al. (1995). Homeless and child functioning in the context of risk and protective factors moderating child outcomes. *Journal of Clinical Child Psychology, 24*, 320–331.

Schuckit, M. A. (1987). Biological vulnerability to alcoholism. *Journal of Consulting and Clinical Psychology, 55*, 301–309.

Schuckit, M. A. (1996). Recent developments in the pharmacotherapy of alcohol dependence. *Journal of Consulting and Clinical Psychology, 64*, 669–676.

Schwartz, B. S., Stewart, W. F., Simon, D., & Lipton, R. B. (1998). Epidemiology of tension-type headache. *Journal of the American Medical Association, 279*, 381–383.

Schwartz, C. E., Wright, C. I., Shin, L. M., Kagan, J., & Rauch, S. L. (2003). Inhibited and uninhibited infants "grown up": Adult amygdalar response to novelty. *Science, 300*, 1952–1953.

Schwartz, J. M. (1998). Neuroanatomical aspects of cognitive- behavior therapy response in obsessive–compulsive disorder. *British Journal of Psychiatry, 173*, 38–44.

Schwitzgebel, R. L., & Schwitzgebel, R. K. (1980). *Law and psychological practice.* New York: Wiley.

Scientists discover migraine gene. (2003, January 21). *MSNBC Web Posting.* Retrieved February 2, 2003, from http://www.msnbc.com/news/862298.asp

Scientists learn why stress can kill. (2003, June 30). *MSNBC Web Posting.* Retrieved July 1, 2003 from http://www.msnbc.com/news/933118.asp?cp1=1

Scogin, F., & McElreath, L. K. (1994). Efficacy of psychosocial treatments for geriatric depression: A quantitative review. *Journal of Consulting and Clinical Psychology, 62*, 69–74.

Scroppo, J. C., Drob, S. L., Weinberger, J. L., & Eagle, P. (1998). Identifying dissociative identity disorder: A self-report and projective study. *Journal of Abnormal Psychology, 107*, 272–284.

Sears, M. R., Greene, J. M., Willan, A. R., Wiecek, E. M., Taylor, D. R., Flannery, E. M., et al. (2003). A longitudinal, population-based, cohort study of childhood asthma followed to adulthood. *New England Journal of Medicine, 349*, 1414–1422.

Sears, R. R., Maccoby, E. E., & Levin, H. (1957). *Patterns of child rearing.* New York: Harper & Row.

See, L. (1999, November). My face doesn't match my race. *Self,* pp. 60–61.

Seeman, M. V. (1997). Psychopathology in women and men: Focus on female hormones. *American Journal of Psychiatry, 154*, 1641–1647.

Sees, K. L., et al. (2000). Methadone maintenance vs. 180-day psychosocially enriched detoxification for treatment of opioid dependence. *Journal of the American Medical Association, 283*, 1303–1310.

Segal, J. H. (1989). Erotomania revisited: From Kraepelin to *DSM-III-R. American Journal of Psychiatry, 146*, 1261–1266.

Segal, S. P., Bola, J. R., & Watson, M. A. (1996). Race, quality of care, and antipsychotic prescribing practices in psychiatric emergency services. *Psychiatric Services, 47*, 282–286.

Segraves, R. T., & Althof, S. (1998). Psychotherapy and pharmacotherapy of sexual dysfunctions. In P. E. Nathan & J. M. Gorman (Eds.), *A guide to treatments that work* (pp. 447–471). New York: Oxford University Press.

Segrin, C., & Abramson, L. Y. (1994). Negative reactions to depressive behaviors: A communication theories analysis. *Journal of Abnormal Psychology, 103*, 655–668.

Segrin, C., & Dillard, J. P. (1992). The international theory of depression: A meta-analysis of the research literature. *Journal of Social and Clinical Psychology, 11*, 43–70.

Selemon, L. D., Kleinman, J. E., Herman, M. M., & Goldman-Rakic, P. S. (2002). Smaller frontal gray matter volume in postmortem schizophrenic brains. *American Journal of Psychiatry, 159*, 1983–1991.

Seligman, L., & Hardenburg, S. A. (2000). Assessment and treatment of paraphilias. *Journal of Counseling & Development, 78*(1), 107–113.

Seligman, M. E. P. (1973). Fall into helplessness. *Psychology Today, 7*, 43–48.

Seligman, M. E. P. (1975). *Helplessness: On depression, development, and death.* San Francisco: Freeman.

Seligman, M. E. P. (1991). *Learned optimism.* New York: Knopf.

Seligman, M. E. P. (1998, August). *Prevention of depression and positive psychology.* Paper presented at the meeting of the American Psychological Association, San Francisco.

Seligman, M. E. P., Castellon, C., Cacciola, J., Schulman, P., Luborsky, L., Ollove, M., et al. (1988). Explanatory style change during cognitive therapy for unipolar depression. *Journal of Abnormal Psychology, 97*, 13–18.

Seligman, M. E. P., & Maier, S. F. (1967). Failure to escape traumatic shock. *Journal of Experimental Psychology, 74*, 1–9.

Selvin, B. W. (1993, June 1). Transsexuals are coming to terms with themselves and society. *New York Newsday,* pp. 55, 58, 59.

Selye, H. (1976). *The stress of life* (rev. ed.) New York: McGraw-Hill.

Semrud-Clikeman, M., et al. (2000). Using MRI to examine brain-behavior relationships in males with attention deficit disorder with hyperactivity. *Journal of the American Academy of Child & Adolescent Psychiatry, 39*, 477–484.

Sensky, T., et al. (2000). A randomized controlled trial of cognitive-behavioral therapy for persistent symptoms in schizophrenia resistant to medication. *Archives of General Psychiatry, 57*, 165–172.

Seppa, N. (1997, June). Children's TV remains steeped in violence. *APA Monitor, 28*(6), 36.

Shadish, W. R., Lurigio, A. J., & Lewis, D. A. (1989). After deinstitutionalization: The present and future of mental health long-term care policy. *Journal of Social Issues, 45*, 1–15.

Shadish, W. R., Matt, G. E., Navarro, A. M., & Phillips, G. (2000). The effects of psychological therapies under clinically representative conditions: A meta-analysis. *Psychological Bulletin, 126*, 512–529.

Shaffer, C. E., Jr., Waters, W. F., & Adams, S. G., Jr. (1994). Dangerousness: Assessing the risk of violent behavior. *Journal of Consulting and Clinical Psychology, 62*, 1064–1068.

Shafran, R., & Mansell, W. (2001). Perfectionism and psychopathology: A review of research and treatment. *Clinical Psychology Review, 21*, 879–906.

Shahar, E., Whitney, C. W., Redline, S., et al. (2002). Sleep-disordered breathing and cardiovascular disease: cross-sectional results of the Sleep Heart Health Study. *American Journal of Respiratory Critical Care Medicine, 163*, 19–25.

Shao, Y., Cuccaro, M. L., Hauser, E. R., Raiford, K. L., Menold, M. M., Wolpert, C. M., et al. (2003). Fine mapping of autistic disorder to chromosome 15q11-q13 by use of phenotypic subtypes. *American Journal of Human Genetics, 72*, 539–548.

Shapiro, D. A., Rees, A., Barkham, M., Hardy, G., Reynolds, S., & Startup, M. (1995). Effects of treatment duration and severity of depression on the maintenance of gains after cognitive-behavioral and psychodynamic interpersonal psychotherapy. *Journal of Consulting and Clinical Psychology, 63*, 378–387.

Shapiro, E. (1992, August 22). Fear returns to sidewalks of West 96th Street. *The New York Times,* pp. B3–B4.

Sharkansky, E. J., King, D. W., King, L. A., & Wolfe, J. (2000). Coping with Gulf War combat stress: Mediating and moderating effects. *Journal of Abnormal Psychology, 109*, 188–197.

Sharp, T. J., & Harvey, A. G. (2001). Chronic pain and posttraumatic stress disorder: Mutual maintenance? *Clinical Psychology Review, 21*, 857–877.

Sharpe, M., & Williams, A. C. de-C. (2002). Treating patients with somatoform pain disorder and hypochondriasis. Turk, D. C., & Gatchel, R. J. (Eds.), *Psychological approaches to pain management: A practitioner's handbook* (2nd ed.), (pp. 515–533). New York: Guilford Press.

Shaw, H., Ramirez, L., Trost, A., Randall, P., & Stice, E. (2004). Body image and eating disturbances across ethnic groups: More similarities than differences. *Psychology of Addictive Behaviors, 18*, 12–18.

Shaw, R., Cohen, F., Doyle, B., & Palesky, J. (1985). The impact of denial and repressive style on information gain and rehabilitation outcomes in myocardial infarction patients. *Psychosomatic Medicine, 47*, 262–273.

Shaywitz, S. E., Shaywitz, B. A., Fulbright, R. K., Skudlarski, P., Mencl, W. E., et al. (2003). Neural systems for compensation and persistence: Young adult outcome of childhood reading disability. *Biological Psychiatry, 54*, 25–33.

Shea, M. T., Widiger, T. A., & Klein, M. H. (1992). Comorbidity of personality disorders and depression: Implications for treatment. *Journal of Consulting and Clinical Psychology, 60*, 857–868.

Sheehan, D. V., & Mao, C. G. (2003). Paroxetine treatment of generalized anxiety disorder. *Psychopharmacology Bulletin, 37,* Suppl 1: 64–75.

Sheitman, B. B., et al. (1998). Pharmacological treatments of schizophrenia. In P. E. Nathan & J. M. Gorman (Eds.). *A guide to treatments that work* (pp. 167–189). New York: Oxford University Press.

Shelton, R. C., et al. (2001). Effectiveness of St. John's Wort in major depression: A randomized controlled trial. *Journal of the American Medical Association, 285*, 1978–1986.

Sherbourne, C. D., Hays, R D., Fleishman, J. A., Vitiello, B., Magruder, K. M., Bing, E. G., et al. (2000). Impact of psychiatric conditions on health-related quality of life in persons with HIV infection. *American Journal of Psychiatry, 157*, 248–254.

Sherbourne, C. D., Hays, R. D., & Wells, K. B. (1995). Personal and psychosocial risk factors for physical and mental health outcomes and course of depression among depressed patients. *Journal of Consulting and Clinical Psychology, 63*, 345–355.

Sheridan, M. S. (2003). The deceit continues: An updated literature review of Münchausen syndrome by proxy. *Child Abuse and Neglect, 27*, 431–451.

Sherman, D. K., McGue, M. K., & Iacono, W. G. (1997). Twin concordance for attention deficit hyperactivity disorder: A comparison of teachers' and mothers' reports. *American Journal of Psychiatry, 154*, 532–535.

Sherwood, N. E., et al. (2000). The perceived function of eating for bulimic, subclinical bulimic, and non-eating disordered women. *Behavior Therapy, 31*, 777–793.

Sheung-Tak, C. (1996). A critical review of Chinese koro. *Culture, Medicine and Psychiatry, 20*, 67–82.

Shiffman, S., Dresler, C. M., Hajek, P., Gilburt, S. J. A., Targett, D. A., & Strahs, K. R. (2002). Efficacy of a nicotine lozenge for smoking cessation. *Archives of Internal Medicine, 162*, 1267–1276.

Shneidman, E. S. (1985). *Definition of suicide.* New York: Wiley.

Shnek, Z. M., et al. (2001). Psychological factors and depressive symptoms in ischemic heart disease. *Health Psychology,* 141–145.

Shonk, S. M., & Cicchetti, D. (2001). Maltreatment, competency deficits, and risk for academic and behavioral maladjustment. *Developmental Psychology, 37*, 3–17.

Shugart, Y. Y., Mundorff, J., Kilshaw, J., Doheny, K., Doan, B., Wanyee, J., et al. (2004). Results of a genome-wide linkage scan for stuttering. *American Journal of Medical Genetics, 124A*, 133–135.

Shukla, P. R., & Singh, R. H. (2000). Supportive psychotherapy in Dhat syndrome patients. *Journal of Personality & Clinical Studies, 16*, 49–52.

Shultz, S. K., Scherman, A., & Marshall, L. J. (2000). Evaluation of a university-based date rape prevention program: Effect on attitudes and behavior related to rape. *Journal of College Student Development, 41*(2), 193–201.

Shute, N., Locy, T., & Pasternak, D. (2000, March 6). The perils of pills. *U.S. News & World Report,* pp. 44–50.

Siegel, J. (2001, January 18). St. John's Wort: Nature's antidepressant? *HealthGate Web Posting. NBCI.com.* Retrieved January 28, 2001, from http://healthgate. nbci.com/getcontent.asp?siteid=nbci&docid=/healthy/ alternative/2000/johnwort/index

Siegel, J. M. (2004). Hypocretin (orexin): role in normal behavior and neuropathology. *Annual Review of Psychology, 55,* 125–148.

Siegel, L. J. (1992). *Criminology* (4th ed.). St. Paul, MN: West.

Siever, L. J., & Davis, K. L. (2004). The pathophysiology of schizophrenia disorders: perspectives from the spectrum. *American Journal of Psychiatry, 161,* 398–413.

Silberstein, R. B., Farrow, M. M., Levy, F., Pipingas, A., Hay, D. A., & Jarman, F. C. (1998). Functional brain electrical activity mapping in boys with attention-deficit/ hyperactivity disorder. *Archives of General Psychiatry, 55,* 1105–1112.

Silberstein, S. D., Massiou, H., Le Jeunne, C., Johnson-Pratt, L., McCarroll, K. A., & Lines, C. R. (2000). Rizaptriptan in the treatment of menstrual migraine. *Obstetrics & Gynecology, 96,* 237–242.

Silva, R. R., Alpert, M., Munoz, D. M., Singh, S., Matzner, F., & Dummit, S. (2000). Stress and vulnerability to posttraumatic stress disorder in children and adolescents. *American Journal of Psychiatry, 157,* 1229–1235.

Silver, E., Cirincione, C., & Steadman, H. J. (1994). Demythologizing inaccurate perceptions of the insanity defense. *Law and Human Behavior, 18,* 63–70.

Silver, H., Feldman, P., Bilker, W., & Gur, R. C. (2003). Working memory deficit as a core neuropsychological dysfunction in schizophrenia. *American Journal of Psychiatry, 160,* 1809–1816.

Silverthorn, P. (2001). Oppositional defiant disorder. In H. Orvaschel, et al. (Eds.), *Handbook of conceptualization and treatment of child psychopathology* (pp. 41–56). Amsterdam, Netherlands: Pergamon/Elsevier Science.

Simeon, D., Greenberg, J., Knutelska, M., Schmeidler, J., & Hollander, E. (2003). Peritraumatic reactions associated with the World Trade Center disaster. *American Journal of Psychiatry, 160,* 1702–1705.

Simeon, D., Gross, S., Guralnik, O., Stein, D. J., Schmeidler, J. & Hollander, E. (1997). Feeling unreal: 30 Cases of *DSM-III-R* depersonalization disorder. *American Journal of Psychiatry, 154,* 1107–1113.

Simeon, D., Guralnik, O., Hazlett, E. A., Spiegel-Cohen, J., Hollander, E., & Buchsbaum, M. S. (2000). Feeling unreal: A PET study of depersonalization disorder. *American Journal of Psychiatry, 157,* 1782–1788.

Simeon, D., Guralnik, O., Schmeidler, J., Sirof, B., & Knutelska, M. (2001). The role of childhood interpersonal trauma in depersonalization disorder. *American Journal of Psychiatry, 158,* 1027–1033.

Simon, G. E. (1998). Management of somatoform and factitious disorders. In P. E. Nathan & J. M. Gorman (Eds.), *A guide to treatments that work* (pp. 408–422). New York: Oxford University Press.

Simonsen, G., Blazina, C., & Watkins, C. E., Jr. (2000). Gender role conflict and psychological well-being among gay men. *Journal of Counseling Psychology, 47*(1), 85–89.

Simons-Morton, B., Haynie, D. L., Crump, A. D., Eitel, S. P., & Saylor, K. E. (2001). Peer and parent influences on smoking and drinking among early adolescents. *Health Education & Behavior, 28,* 95–107.

Simpson, D. D., Joe, G. W., Fletcher, B. W., Hubbard, R. L., & Anglin, M. D. (1999). A national evaluation of treatment outcomes for cocaine dependence. *Archives of General Psychiatry, 57,* 507–514.

Singh, G. (1985). Dhat syndrome revisited. *Indian Journal of Psychiatry, 27,* 119–122.

Skaar, K. L., et al. (1997). Smoking cessation 1: An overview of research. *Behavioral Medicine, 23,* 5–13.

Skegg, K., Nada-Raja, S., Dickson, N., Paul, C., & Williams, S. (2003). Sexual orientation and self-harm in men and women. *American Journal of Psychiatry, 160,* 541–546.

Skinner, B. F. (1938). *The behavior of organisms: An experimental analysis.* New York: Appleton.

Skoog, G., & Skoog, I. (1999). A 40-year follow-up of patients with obsessive–compulsive disorder. *Archives of General Psychiatry, 56,* 121–127.

Skoog, I. (2000). Detection of preclinical Alzheimer's disease. *The New England Journal of Medicine, 343,* 502–503.

Slater, D., & Hans, V. P. (1984). Public opinion of forensic psychiatry following the Hinckley verdict. *American Journal of Psychiatry, 141,* 675–679.

Sloan, D. M., & Marx, B. P. (2004). A closer examination of the structured written disclosure procedure. *Journal of Consulting and Clinical Psychology, 72,* 165–175.

Slone, D. G., & Gleason, C. E. (1999). Behavior management planning for problem behaviors in dementia: A practical model. *Professional Psychology: Research and Practice, 30,* 27–36.

Slutske, W. S., Heath, A. C., Madden, P. A. F., Bucholz, K. K., Statham, D. J., & Martin, N. G. (2002). Personality and the genetic risk for alcohol dependence. *Journal of Abnormal Psychology, 111,* 124–133.

Small, J. G., et al. (1997). Quetiapine in patients with schizophrenia: A high- and low-dose double-blind comparison with placebo. *Archives of General Psychiatry, 54,* 549–557.

Smith, D. (2001b, October). Sleep psychologists in demand. *Monitor on Psychology,* pp. 36–38.

Smith, D. (2003a, March). Hostility associated with immune function. *Monitor on Psychology,* p. 47.

Smith, G. R. (1994). The course of somatization and its effects on utilization of health care resources. *Psychosomatics, 35,* 263–267.

Smith, J. E., & Krejci, J. (1991). Minorities join the majority: Eating disturbances among Hispanic and Native American youth. *International Journal of Eating Disorders, 10,* 179–186.

Smith, M. L., & Glass, G. V. (1977). Meta-analysis of psychotherapy otucome studies. *American Psychologist, 32,* 752–760.

Smith, M. L., Glass, G. V., & Miller, T. I. (1980). *The benefits of psychotherapy.* Baltimore: Johns Hopkins University Press.

Smith, R. E., Smoll, F. L., & Ptacek, J. T. (1990). Conjunctive moderator variables in vulnerability and reliency research: Life stress, social support and coping skills, and adolescent sport injuries. *Journal of Personality and Social Psychology, 58,* 360–370.

Smith, S. C. (1983). *The great mental calculators.* New York: Columbia University Press.

Smith, T. (1999). Outcome of early intervention for children with autism. *Clinical Psychology: Science and Practice, 6,* 33–49.

Smith, T. K. (2003, February). We've got to stop eating like this. *Fortune,* pp. 58–70.

Smith, T. W., & Ruiz, J. M. (2002). Psychosocial influences on the development and course of coronary heart disease: Current status and implications for research and practice. *Journal of Consulting and Clinical Psychology, 70,* 548–568.

Smith, T. W., Snyder, C. R., & Perkins, S. C. (1983). The self-serving function of hypochondriacal complaints: Physical symptoms as self-handicapping strategies. *Journal of Personality and Social Psychology, 44,* 787–797.

Smith, Y. L. S., et al. (2001). Adolescents with gender identity disorder who were accepted or rejected for sex reassignment surgery: A prospective follow-up study. *Journal of American Academy of Child & Adolescent Psychiatry, 40,* 472–481.

Smoller, E. S. (1997). *I can't remember: Family stories of Alzheimer's disease.* Philadelphia: Temple University Press.

Smyth, J. M., et al. (1999). Effects of writing about stressful experiences on symptom reduction in patients with asthma or rheumatoid arthritis. *Journal of the American Medical Association, 281,* 1304–1309.

Smyth, J. M., & Pennebaker, J. W. (2001). What are the health effects of disclosure? In A. Baum, T. A. Revenson, & J. E. Singer (Eds.), *Handbook of health psychology* (pp. 339–348). Mahwah, NJ: Erlbaum.

Snell, M. E. (1997). Teaching children and young adults with mental retardation in school programs: Current research. *Behaviour Change, 14,* 73–105.

Snyder, S. H. (2002). Forty years of neurotransmitters: A personal account. *Archives of General Psychiatry, 59,* 983–994.

Sobell, M. B., & Sobell, L. C. (1973a). Alcoholics treated by individualized behavior therapy: One year treatment outcome, *Behaviour Research and Therapy, 11,* 599–618.

Sobell, M. B., & Sobell, L. C. (1973b). Individualized behavior therapy for alcoholics, *Behavior Therapy, 4,* 49–72.

Sobell, M. B., & Sobell, L. C. (1976). Second year treatment outcome of alcoholics treated by individualized behavior therapy: Results, *Behaviour Research and Therapy, 14,* 195–215.

Sobell, M. B., & Sobell, L. C. (1984). The aftermath of heresy: A response to Pendery et al.'s (1982) critique of "Individualized behavior therapy for alcoholics," *Behaviour Research and Therapy, 22,* 413–440.

Sobell, M. B., & Sobell, L. C. (1995). Controlled drinking after 25 years: How important was the great debate? *Addiction, 90,* 1149–1153.

Sokolove, M. (2003, November 16). Should John Hinckley go free? *The New York Times Magazine,* pp. 54–57.

Solomon, D. A., et al. (1997). Recovery from major depression: A 10-year prospective follow-up across multiple episodes. *Archives of General Psychiatry, 54,* 1001–1006.

Solomon, D. A., et al. (2000). Multiple recurrences of major depressive disorder. *American Journal of Psychiatry, 157,* 229–233.

Solowij, N., Stephens, R. S., Roffman, R. A., Babor, T., Kadden, R., Miller, M., et al. (2002). Cognitive functioning of long-term heavy cannabis users seeking treatment. *Journal of the American Medical Association, 287,* 1123–1131.

Sørensen, H. J. Mortensen, E. L., Reinisch, J. M., & Mednick, S. A. (2003). Do hypertension and diuretic treatment in pregnancy increase the risk of schizophrenia in offspring? *American Journal of Psychiatry, 160,* 464–468.

Southwick, S. M., et al. (1997). Noradrenergic and serotonergic function in posttraumatic stress disorder. *Archives of General Psychiatry, 54,* 749–758.

Spanos, N. P. (1978). Witchcraft in histories of psychiatry: A critical analysis and an alternative conceptualization. *Psychological Bulletin, 85,* 417–439.

Spanos, N. P. (1994). Multiple identity enactments and multiple personality disorder: A sociocognitive perspective. *Psychological Bulletin, 116,* 143–165.

Spanos, N. P., Weekes, J. R., & Bertrand, L. D. (1985). Multiple personality: A social psychological perspective. *Journal of Abnormal Psychology, 94,* 362–376.

Spechler, S. J., Fischbach, L., & Feldman, M. (2000). Clinical aspects of genetic variability in *Helicobacter pylori. Journal of the American Medical Association, 283,* 1264–1266.

Spencer, D. J. (1983). Psychiatric dilemmas in Australian aborigines. *International Journal of Social Psychiatry, 29*(3), 208–214.

Spencer, M. D., Knight, R. S., & Will, R. G. (2002). First hundred cases of variant Creutzfeldt-Jakob disease: Retrospective case note review of early psychiatric and neurological features. *British Medical Journal, 324,* 1479–1482.

Spiegel, D. A., & Bruce, T. J. (1997). Benzodiazepines and exposure-based cognitive behavior therapies for panic disorder: Conclusions from combined treatment trials. *American Journal of Psychiatry, 154,* 773–781.

Spielmans, G. I. (2004). To the editor. *Journal of the American Medical Association, 291,* 41. [Letter]

Spitzer, R. L., et al. (1992). Binge eating disorder: A multi-site field trial of the diagnostic criteria. *International Journal of Eating Disorders, 11,* 191–203.

Spitzer, R. L., et al. (1994). *DSM-IV case book* (4th ed.). Washington, DC: American Psychiatric Press.

Spitzer, R. L., Gibbon, M., Skodol, A. E., Williams, J. B. W., & First, M. B. (1989). *DSM-III-R casebook.* Washington, DC: American Psychiatric Press.

Springen, K. (2004, May 10). Women, cigarettes and death. *Newsweek,* p. 69.

Squier, L. H., & Domhoff, G. W. (1998). The presentation of dreaming and dreams in introductory psychology textbooks: A critical examination with suggestions for textbook authors and course instructors. *Dreaming, 8,* 149–168.

St. John's wort doesn't help with major depression. (2001a, June). *Tufts University Health & Nutrition Letter,* p. 2.

Staddon, J. E., R., & Cerutti, D. T. (2003). Operant conditioning. *Annual Review of Psychology, 4,* 115–144.

Stader, S. R., & Hokanson, J. E. (1998). Psychosocial antecedents of depressive symptoms: An evaluation using daily experiences methodology. *Journal of Abnormal Psychology, 107,* 17–26.

Stafford, R. S., & Radley, D. C. (2003). National trends in antiobesity medication use. *Archives of Internal Medicine, 163,* 1046–50.

Stahl, S. M. (2001). Sex and psychopharmacology: Is natural estrogen a psychotropic drug in women? *Archives of General Psychiatry, 58,* 537–538. [Letter]

Stamm, B. H., & Perednia, D. A. (2000). Evaluating psychosocial aspects of telemedicine and telehealth systems. *Professional Psychology: Research and Practice, 31,* 184–189.

Stangier, U., Heidenreicha, T., Peitza, M., Lauterbach, W., & Clark, D. M. (2003). Cognitive therapy for social phobia: Individual versus group treatment. *Behaviour Research and Therapy, 41,* 991–1007.

Stanley, M. A., & Beck, J. G. (2000). Anxiety disorders. *Clinical Psychology Review, 20,* 731–754.

Stanley, M. A., & Turner, S. M. (1995). Current status of pharmacological and behavioral treatment of obsessive-compulsive disorder. *Behavior Therapy, 26,* 163–186.

Starkweather, C. W. (2002). The epigenesis of stuttering. *Journal of Fluency Disorders, 27,* 269–287.

Steadman, H. J. (1979). *Beating a rap: Defendants found incompetent to stand trial.* Chicago: University of Chicago Press.

Steadman, H. J., et al. (1993). *Before and after Hinckley: Evaluating insanity defense reform.* New York: Guilford Press.

Steffens, D. C., Skoog, I., Norton, M. C., Hart, A. D., Tschanz, J. T., Plassman, B.L., et al. (2000). Prevalence of depression and its treatment in an elderly population: The Cache County Study. *Archives of General Psychiatry, 57,* 601–607.

Stein, D., Asherov, J., Lublinksy, E., Sobol-Havia, D., et al. (2002). Sociodemographic factors associated with attempted suicide in two Israeli cities between 1990 and 1998. *Journal of Nervous & Mental Disease, 190,* 115–118.

Stein, D., Brom, D., Elizur, A., & Witztum, E. (1998). The association between attitudes toward suicide and suicidal ideation in adolescents. *Acta Psychiatrica Scandinavia, 97,* 195–201.

Stein, M. A. Sarampote, C. S., Waldman, I. D., Robb, A. S., Conlon, C., Pearl, P. L., et al. (2003). A dose-response study of OROS methylphenidate in children with attention-deficit/hyperactivity disorder. *Pediatrics, 112,* 404–413.

Stein, M. B., Fuetsch, M., Muller, N., Hofler, M., Lieb, R., & Wittchen, H. U. (2001). Social anxiety disorder and the risk of depression: A prospective community study of adolescents and young adults. *Archives of General Psychiatry, 58,* 251–256.

Stein, M. B., Goldin, P. R., Sareen, J., Zorrilla, L. T. E., & Brown, G. G. (2002). Increased amygdala activation to angry and contemptuous faces in generalized social phobia. *Archives of General Psychiatry, 59,* 1027–1034.

Stein, M. B., & Kean, Y. M. (2000). Disability and quality of life in social phobia: Epidemiologic findings. *American Journal of Psychiatry, 157,* 1606–1613.

Stein, M. B., Torgrud, L. J., & Walker, J. R. (2000). Social phobia symptoms, subtypes, and severity: Findings from a community survey. *Archives of General Psychiatry, 57,* 1046–1052.

Stein, M. B., Walker, J. R., & Forde, D. R. (1996). Public-speaking fears in a community sample: Prevalence, impact on functioning, and diagnostic classification. *Archives of General Psychiatry, 53,* 169–174.

Steinberg, M. (1991). The spectrum of depersonalization: Assessment and treatment. *Annual Review of Psychiatry, 10,* 223–247.

Steinhausen, H.-C. (2002). The outcome of anorexia nervosa in the 20th century. *American Journal of Psychiatry, 159,* 1284–1293.

Stemberger, R. R., et al. (1995). Social phobia: An analysis of possible developmental factors. *Journal of Abnormal Psychology, 194,* 526–531.

Stenson, J. (2001a, August 26). Burden of mental illness in America falls on minorities. *MSNBC Web Posting.* Retrieved August 26, 2001, from http://www.msnbc.com/news/619545.asp

Stern, E., & Silbersweig, D. A. (2001). Advances in functional neuroimaging methodology for the study of brain system underlying human neuropsychological function and dysfunction. *Journal of Clinical & Experimental Neuropsychology, 23,* 3–18.

Steven, J. E. (1995, January 30). Virtual therapy. *The Boston Globe,* pp. 25, 29.

Stevens, J. R. (1997). Anatomy of schizophrenia revisited. *Schizophrenia Bulletin, 23,* 373–383.

Stevens, S. E., Hynan, M. T., & Allen, M. (2000). A meta-analysis of common factor and specific treatment effects across the outcome domains of the phase model of psychotherapy. *Clinical Psychology: Science and Practice, 7,* 273–290.

Stevenson, J., Meares, R., & Comerford, A. (2003). Diminished impulsivity in older patients with borderline personality disorder. *American Journal of Psychiatry, 160,* 165–166.

Stewart, M. W., et al. (1994). Differential relationships between stress and disease activity for immunologically distinct subgroups of people with rheumatoid arthritis. *Journal of Abnormal Psychology, 1103,* 251–258.

Stewart, S. M., Kennard, B. D., Lee, P. W. H., Hughes, C. W., Mayes, T. L., Emslie, G. J, et al. (2004). A cross-cultural investigation of cognitions and depressive symptoms in adolescents. *Journal of Abnormal Psychology, 113,* 248–257.

Stewart, W. F., Ricci, J. A., Chee, E., Hahn, S. R., & Morganstein, D. (2003). Cost of lost productive work time among US workers with depression. *Journal of the American Medical Association, 289,* 3135–3141.

Stice, E. (1994). Review of the evidence for a sociocultural model of bulimia nervosa and an exploration of the mechanisms of action. *Clinical Psychology Review, 14,* 633–661.

Stice, E. (2001). A prospective test of the dual-pathway model of bulimic pathology: Mediating effects of dieting and negative affect. *Journal of Abnormal Psychology, 110,* 124–135.

Stice, E., Burton, E. M., & Shaw, H. (2004). Prospective relations between bulimic pathology, depression, and substance abuse: unpacking comorbidity in adolescent girls. *Journal of Consulting and Clinical Psychology, 72,* 62–71.

Stice, E., Hayward, C., Cameron, R. P., Killen, J. D., & Taylor, C. B. (2000). Body-image and eating disturbances predict onset of depression among female adolescents: A longitudinal study. *Journal of Abnormal Psychology, 109,* 438–444.

Stipp, D. (2003, February). The quest for the antifat pill. *Fortune,* pp. 66–67.

Stokstad, E. (2001). New hints into the biological basis of autism. *Science, 294,* pp. 34–37.

Stolberg, S. G. (1998a, March 13). New cancer cases decreasing in U.S. as deaths do, too. *The New York Times,* p. A1, A14.

Stolberg, S. G. (2001, May 10). Blacks found on short end of heart attack procedure. *The New York Times,* p. A20.

Stolberg, S. G. (2002, November 17). Preschool meds. *The New York Times Magazine,* pp. 58–61.

Stoller, R. J. (1969). Parental influences in male transsexualism. In R. Green & J. Money (Eds.), *Transsexualism and sex reassignment.* Baltimore: Johns Hopkins University Press.

Stone, A. (1976). The *Tarasoff* decisions: Suing psychotherapists to safeguard society. *Harvard Law Review, 90,* 358–378.

Stone, A. A. et al. (2000). Structured writing about stressful events: Exploring potential psychological mediators of positive health effects. *Health Psychology, 19,* 619–624.

Stone, A. A., Neale, J. M., Cox, D. S., & Napoli, A., et al. (1994). Daily events are associated with a secretory immune response to an oral antigen in men. *Health Psychology, 13,* 440–446.

Stone, M. H. (1980). *The borderline syndromes: Constitution, personality, and adaptation.* New York: McGraw-Hill.

Stoney, C. M. (2003). Gender and cardiovascular disease: a psychobiological and integrative approach. *Current Directions in Psychological Science, 12,* 129–133.

Stotland, N. L. (2000, July 26). Sertraline: An effective treatment for binge-eating disorder? *Journal Watch Women's Health,* pp. 1, 4.

Stout, D. (2000, September 1). Use of illegal drugs is down among young, survey finds. *The New York Times,* p. A18.

Stover, E. S., et al. (1996). Perspectives from the National Institute of Mental Health: Preventing or living with AIDS. *Annals of Behavioral Medicine, 18,* 58–60.

Strakowski, S. M., DelBello, M. P., Zimmerman, M. E., Getz, G. E., Mills, N. P., Ret, J., et al. (2002). Ventricular and periventricular structural volumes in first- versus multiple-episode bipolar disorder. *American Journal of Psychiatry, 159,* 1841–1847.

Straub, R. E., Jiang, Y., MacLean, C. J., Ma, Y., Webb, B. T., Myakishev, M. V., et al. (2002). Genetic variation in the 6p22.3 gene DTNBP1, the human ortholog of the mouse dysbindin gene, is associated with schizophrenia. *American Journal of Human Genetics, 71,* 337–348.

Stricker, G. (2003). Is this the right book at the wrong time? *Contemporary Psychology, 48,* 726–728.

Stricker, G., & Gold, J. R. (1999). The Rorschach: Toward a nomothetically based, idiographically applicable configurational model. *Psychological Assessment, 11,* 240–250.

Stricker, G., & Gold, J. R. (2001, January). An introduction to psychotherapy integration. *NYS Psychologist, 13,* 7–12.

Striegel-Moore, R. H., Dohm, F. A., Kraemer, H. C., Taylor, C. B., Daniels, S. D., Crawford, P. B., et al. (2003). Eating disorders in white and black women. *American Journal of Psychiatry, 160,* 1326–1331.

Strober, M., Freeman, R., Lampert, C., Diamond, J., & Kaye, W. (2000). Controlled family study of anorexia nervosa and bulimia nervosa: Evidence of shared liability and transmission of partial syndromes. *American Journal of Psychiatry, 157,* 393–401.

Strollo, P. J., & Rogers, R. M. (1996). Obstructive sleep apnea. *The New England Journal of Medicine, 334,* 99–104.

Ström, L., Pettersson, R., & Andersson, G. (2004). Internet-based treatment for insomnia: A controlled evaluation. *Journal of Consulting and Clinical Psychology, 72,* 113–120.

Strote, J., Lee, J. E., & Wechsler, H. (2002). Increasing MDMA use among college students: Results of a national survey. *Journal of the American Academy of Child & Adolescent Psychiatry, 41,* 1215.

Strozier, C. B. (2001). *Heinz Kohut: The making of a psychoanalyst.* New York: Farrar, Straus & Giroux.

Stuart, G. L., Treat, T. A., & Wade, W. A., (2000). Effectiveness of an empirically based treatment for panic disorder delivered in a service clinic setting: 1-year follow-up. *Journal of Consulting and Clinical Psychology, 68*, 506–512.

Stuart, R. B. (2004). Twelve practical suggestions for achieving multicultural competence. *Professional Psychology: Research and Practice, 35*, 3–9.

Stuart, S., O'Hara, M. W., & Gorman, L. L. (2003). The prevention and treatment of postpartum depression. *Archives of Women's Mental Health, 6* (Suppl. 2), S57–S69.

Study finds psychotherapy can treat those with disease fears. (2004, March 23). *CNN Web Posting*, Retrieved March 23, 2004, from http://www.cnn.com/2004/HEALTH/03/23/hypochondria.treatment.ap/index.html

Study links binge eating to mutation in a gene. (2003, March 20). *The New York Times*, p. A27.

Stunkard, A. J., & Sørensen, T. I. A. (1993). Obesity and socioeconomic status—A complex relation. *New England Journal of Medicine, 329*, 1036–1037.

Stutts, J. T., Hickey, S. E., & Kasdan, M. L. (2003) Malingering by proxy: A form of pediatric condition falsification. *Journal of Developmental and Behavioral Pediatrics, 24*, 276–278.

Styron, W. (1990). *Darkness visible*. New York: Random House.

Sue, S. (2003). In defense of cultural competency in psychotherapy and treatment. *American Psychologist, 58*, 964–970.

Suinn, R. M. (2001). The terrible twos—Anger and anxiety: Hazardous to your health. *American Psychologist, 56*, 27–36.

Sullivan, H. S. (1962). *Schizophrenia as a human process*. New York: Norton.

Sullivan, M. D., (2000). DSM-IV pain disorder: A case against the diagnosis. *International Review of Psychiatry, 12*, 91–98.

Sullivan, P. F., Neale, M. C., & Kendler, K. S. (2000). Genetic epidemiology of major depression: Review and meta-analysis. *American Journal of Psychiatry, 157*, 1552–1562.

Sullivan, P. F., Neale, M. C., & Kendler, K. S. (2000). Genetic epidemiology of major depression: Review and meta-analysis. *American Journal of Psychiatry, 157*, 1552–1562.

Sulloway, F. J. (1983). *Freud: Biologist of the mind*. New York: Basic Books.

Suls, J., Wan, C. K., & Blanchard, E. B. (1994). A multilevel data-analytic approach for evaluation of relationships between daily life stressors and symptomatology: Patients with irritable bowel syndrome. *Health Psychology, 13*, 103–113.

Sutker, P. B., Davis, J., M., Uddo, M., & Ditta, S. R. (1995). War zone stress, personal resources, and PTSD in Persian Gulf War returnees. *Journal of Abnormal Psychology, 104*, 444–452.

Svartberg, M., Stiles, T. C., & Seltzer, M. H. (2004). Randomized, controlled trial of the effectiveness of short-term dynamic psychotherapy and cognitive therapy for Cluster C personality disorders. *American Journal of Psychiatry, 161*, 810–817.

Svikis, D. S., Velez, M. L., & Pickens, R. W. (1994). Genetic aspects of alcohol use and alcoholism in women. *Alcohol Health & Research World, 18*, 192–196.

Swanson, H. L., Mink, J., & Bocian, K. M. (1999). Cognitive processing deficits in poor readers with symptoms of reading disabilities and ADHD: More alike than different? *Journal of Educational Psychology, 91*(2), 321–333.

Swartz, M., et al. (1991). Somatization disorder. In L. N. Robins & D. A. Regier (Eds.), *Psychiatric disorders in America: The Epidemiologic Catchment Area Study* (pp. 220–257). New York: Free Press.

Sweeney, J. A., Clementz, B. A., Haas, G. L., Escobar, M. D., Drake, K., & Frances, A. J. (1994). Eye tracking dysfunction in schizophrenia: Characterization of component eye movement abnormalities, diagnostic specificity, and the role of attention. *Journal of Abnormal Psychology, 103*, 222–230.

Swendsen, J. D., & Mazure, C. M. (2000). Life stress as a risk factor for postpartum depression: Current research and methodological issues. *Clinical Psychology: Science and Practice, 7*, 17–31.

Swets, J. A., Dawes, R. M., & Monahan, J. (2000). Psychological science can improve diagnostic decisions. *Psychological Science in the Public Interest, 1*, 1–26.

Szasz, T. S. (1961). *The myth of mental illness*. New York: Harper & Row.

Szasz, T. S. (1970). *Ideology and insanity: Essays on the psychiatric dehumanization of man*. New York: Doubleday Anchor.

Szasz, T. S. (2000). Second commentary on "Aristotle's function argument." *Philosophy, Psychiatry, & Psychology, 7*(1), 3–16.

Szasz, T. (2003a). Psychiatry and the control of dangerousness: On the apotropaic function of the term "mental illness." *Journal of Medical Ethics, 29*, 227–230.

Szasz, T. (2003b). Response to: Comments on psychiatry and the control of dangerousness: On the apotropaic function of the term "mental illness." *Journal of Medical Ethics, 29*, 237.

Szatmari, P., Bryson, S. E., Streiner, D. L., Wilson, F., Archer, L., & Ryerse, C. (2000). Two-year outcome of preschool children with autism or Asperger's syndrome. *American Journal of Psychiatry, 157*, 1980–1987.

T

Takahashi, C. (2001, April 8). Selling to Gen Y: A far cry from Betty Crocker. *The New York Times Week in Review*, p. 3.

Tanasescu, M., Leitzmann, M. F., Rimm, E. B., Willett, W. C., Stampfer, M. J., & Hu, F. B. (2002). Exercise type and intensity in relation to coronary heart disease in men. *Journal of the American Medical Association, 288*, 1994–2000.

Tang, C. S., Critelli, J. W., & Porter, J. F. (1995). Sexual aggression and victimization in dating relationships among Chinese college students. *Archives of Sexual Behavior, 24*, 47–53.

Tardiff, K., Marzuk, P. M., Leon, A. C., Portera, L., & Weiner, C. (1997). Violence by patients admitted to a private psychiatric hospital. *American Journal of Psychiatry, 154*, 88–93.

Tariot, P. N., Farlow, M. R., Grossberg, G. T., Graham, S. M., McDonald, S., Gergel, I., et al. (2004). Memantine treatment in patients with moderate to severe Alzheimer disease already receiving donepezil: A randomized controlled trial. *Journal of the American Medical Association, 291*, 317–324.

Tarrier, N., Kinney, C., McCarthy, E., Humphreys, L., Wittkowski, A., & Morris, J. (2000). Two-year follow-up of cognitive-behavioral therapy and supportive counseling in the treatment of persistent symptoms in chronic schizophrenia. *Journal of Consulting and Clinical Psychology, 68*, 917–922.

Tate, D. F., Wing, R. R., & Winett, R. A. (2001). Internet technology to deliver a behavioral weight loss program. *Journal of the American Medical Association, 285*, 1172–1177.

Taylor, C. B., & Luce, K. H. (2003). Computer- and Internet-based psychotherapy interventions. *Current Directions in Psychological Science, 12*, 18–22.

Taylor, K. L., Lamdan, R. M., Siegel, J. E., Shelby, R., Moran-Klimi, K., & Hrywna, M. (2003). Psychological adjustment among African American breast cancer patients: One-year follow-up results of a randomized psychoeducational group intervention. *Health Psychology, 22*, 316–323.

Taylor, M. A., & Fink, M. (2003). Catatonia in psychiatric classification: a home of its own. *American Journal of Psychiatry, 160*, 1233–1241.

Taylor, S. (1995). Assessment of obsessions and compulsions: Reliability, validity, and sensitivity to treatment effects. *Clinical Psychology Review, 15*, 261–296.

Taylor, S., & Rachman, S. J. (1994). Klein's suffocation theory of panic. *Archives of General Psychiatry, 51*, 505–506.

Taylor, S., Fedoroff, I. C., Koch, W. J., Thordarson, D. S., Fecteau, G., & Nicki, R. M. (2001). Posttraumatic stress disorder arising after road traffic collisions: Patterns of response to cognitive–behavior therapy. *Journal of Consulting and Clinical Psychology, 69*, 541–551.

Taylor, S., Thordarson, D. S., Maxfield, L., Fedoroff, I. C., Lovell, K., & Ogrodniczuk, J. (2003). Comparative efficacy, speed, and adverse effects of three PTSD treatments: Exposure therapy, EMDR, and relaxation training. *Journal of Consulting and Clinical Psychology, 71*, 330–338.

Teasdale, T. W., & Engberg, A. W. (2003). Cognitive dysfunction in young men following head injury in childhood and adolescence: A population study. *Journal of Neurology and Neurosurgical Psychiatry, 74*, 933–936.

Tecott, L. H. (2003). The genes and brains of mice and men. *American Journal of Psychiatry, 160*, 646–656.

Teens see little risk in ecstasy. (2003, February 11). *CNN Web Posting*. Retrieved February 15, 2003, from http://www.cnn.com/2003/HEALTH/parenting/02/11/drug.survey/index.html.

Teri, L., & Wagner, A. (1992). Alzheimer's disease and depression. *Journal of Consulting and Clinical Psychology, 60*, 379–391.

Terman, J. S., et al. (2001). Circadian time of morning light administration and therapeutic response in winter depression. *Archives of General Psychiatry, 58*, 69–75.

Teunisse, R. J., Cruysberg, J. R., Hoefnagels, W. H., Verbeek, A. L., & Zitman, F. G., (1996). Visual hallucinations in psychologically normal people: Charles Bonnet's syndrome. *Lancet, 347*, 794–797.

Thakker, J., & Ward, T. (1998). Culture and classification: The cross-cultural application of the *DSM-IV*. *Clinical Psychology Review, 18*, 501–529.

Thannickal, T. C., et al. (2000). Reduced number of hypocretin neurons in human narcolepsy. *Neuron, 17*, 469–474.

Thase, M. E., et al. (1997). Treatment of major depression with psychotherapy or psychotherapy-pharmacotherapy combinations. *Archives of General Psychiatry, 54*, 1009–1015.

The McKnight Investigators. (2003). Risk factors for the onset of eating disorders in adolescent girls: Results of the McKnight Longitudinal Risk Factor Study. *American Journal of Psychiatry, 160*, 248–254.

Theorell, T. (1992). Critical life changes. A review of research. *Psychotherapy and Psychoomatics, 57*, 108–117.

Therapy and hypochondriacs often make poor mix, study says. (2004, March 25). *The New York Times*, p. A19.

Thiedke, C. C. (2003). Nocturnal enuresis. *American Family Physician, 67*, 1509–1510.

Thoits, P. A. (1983). Dimensions of life events as influences upon the genesis of psychological distress and associated conditions: An evaluation and synthesis of the literature. In H. B. Kaplan (Ed.), *Psychosocial stress: Trends in theory and research*. (pp. 33–103). New York: Academic Press.

Thompson, P. M, Vidal, C., Gledd, J. N., Gochman, P., Blumenthal, J., Nicolson, R., et al. (2001). Mapping adolescent brain change reveals dynamic wave of accelerated gray matter loss in very early-onset schizophrenia. *Proceedings of the National Academy of Science, 98*, 11650–11655.

Thompson, T. (1995). *The beast: A journey through depression*. New York: Putnam.

Thompson-Brenner, H., Glass, S., & Westen, D. (2003). A multidimensional meta-analysis of psychotherapy for bulimia nervosa. *Clinical Psychology: Science and Practice, 10*, 269–287.

Three million teens think suicide. (2002, July 15). *MSNBC Web Posting*. Retrieved July 15 from http://www.msnbc.com/news/780187.asp

Tienari, P, Wynne, L. C., Läksy, K., Moring, J., Nieminen, P., Sorri, A., et al. (2003). Genetic boundaries of the schizophrenia spectrum: Evidence from the Finnish adoptive family study of schizophrenia. *American Journal of Psychiatry, 160*, 1587–1594.

Tiffany, S. T., Cox, L. S., & Elash, C. A. (2000). Effects of transdermal nicotine patches on abstinence-induced and cue-elicited craving in cigarette smokers. *Journal of Consulting and Clinical Psychology, 68,* 233–240.

Tiihonen, J., et al. (1992). Modified activity of the human auditory cortex during auditory hallucinations. *American Journal of Psychiatry, 149,* 255–257.

Tillfors, M., Furmark, T., Ekselius, L., & Fredrikson, M. (2001). Social phobia and avoidant personality disorder as related to parental history of social anxiety: A general population study. *Behaviour Research and Therapy, 39,* 289–298.

Time capsule. (2000, November). *Monitor on Psychology,* p. 10.

Timman, R., Roos, R., Maat-Kievit, A., & Tibben, A. (2004). Adverse effects of predictive testing for Huntington Disease underestimated: Long-term effects 7–10 years after the test. *Health Psychology, 23,* 189–197.

Timpson, J., et al. (1988). Depression in a Native Canadian in Northwestern Ontario: Sadness, grief or spiritual illness? *Canada's Mental Health, 36*(2–3), 5–8.

Tishler, P. V., Larkin, E. K., Schluchter, M. D., & Redline, S. (2003). Incidence of sleep-disordered breathing in an urban adult population: The relative importance of risk factors in the development of sleep-disordered breathing. *Journal of the American Medical Association, 289,* 2230–2237.

Tobin, D. L., Johnson, C. L., & Dennis, A. B. (1992). Divergent forms of purging behavior in bulimia nervosa patients. *International Journal of Eating Disorders, 11,* 17–24.

Tohen, M., Jacobs, T. G., Grundy, S. L., McElroy, S. L., Banov, M. C., Janicak, P. G., et al. (2000). Efficacy of olanzapine in acute bipolar mania: A double-blind, placebo-controlled study. *Archives of General Psychiatry, 57,* 841–849.

Tohen, M., Ketter, T. A., Zarate, C. A., Suppes, T., Frye, M., Altshuler, L., et al. (2003). Olanzapine versus divalproex sodium for the treatment of acute mania and maintenance of remission: A 47-week study. *American Journal of Psychiatry, 160,* 1263–1271.

Tohen, M., Zarate, C. A., Hennen, J., Khalsa, H.-M. K., Strakowski, S. M., Gebre-Medhin, P., et al. (2003). The McLean-Harvard First-Episode Mania Study: Prediction of recovery and first recurrence. *American Journal of Psychiatry, 160,* 2099–2107.

Toichi, M. Kamio, Y., Okada, T., Sakihama, M., Youngstrom, E. A., Findling, R. F., & Yamamoto, K. (2002). A lack of self-consciousness in autism. *American Journal of Psychiatry, 159,* 1422–1424.

Tolomiczenko, G. S., Sota, T., & Goering, P. N. (2000). Personality assessment of homeless adults as a tool for service planning. *Journal of Personality Disorders, 14,* 152–161.

Toomey, R., Lyons, M. J., Eisen, S. A., Xian, H., Chantarujikapong, S., Seidman, L. J., et al. (2003). A twin study of the neuropsychological consequences of stimulant abuse. *Archives of General Psychiatry, 60,* 303–310.

Torgersen, S. (1986). Genetic factors in moderately severe and mild affective disorder. *Archives of General Psychiatry, 43,* 222–226.

Torgersen, S., Kringlen, E., & Cramer, V. (2001). The prevalence of personality disorders in a community sample. *Archives of General Psychiatry, 58,* 590–596.

Torgesen, J. K., et al. (2001). Intensive remedial instruction for children with severe reading disabilities: Immediate and long-term outcomes from two instructional approaches. *Journal of Learning Disabilities, 34*(1), 33–58.

Torrey, E. F., & Zdanowicz, M. (1999, May 28). A right to mental illness? *PsychLaws.Org.* Retrieved November 14, 2003, from http://www.psychlaws.org/GeneralResources/article14.htm.

Tough, P. (2001, July 29). The alchemy of OxyContin. *The New York Times Magazine,* pp. 32–37, 52, 62–63.

Tower, R. B., & Kasl, S. V. (1996). Depressive symptoms across older spouses: Longitudinal influences. *Psychology and Aging, 11,* 683–697.

Tradgold, A. F. (1914). *Mental deficiency.* New York: Wainwood.

Trask, P. C., & Sigmon, S. T. (1997). Munchausen syndrome: A review and new conceptualization. *Clinical Psychology: Science and Practice, 4,* 346–358.

Traven, N. D., Kuller, L. H., Ives, D. G., Rutan, G. H., & Perper, J. A. (1995). Coronary heart disease mortality and sudden death: Trends and patterns in 35- to 44-year-old white males, 1970–1990. *American Journal of Epidemiology, 142,* 45–52.

Treatment of alcoholism—Part II. (1996, September). *The Harvard Mental Health Letter, 13,* 1–5.

Treffert, D. A. (1988). The idiot savant: A review of the syndrome. *American Journal of Psychiatry, 145,* 563–572.

Tremblay, R. E., et al. (1992). Early disruptive behavior, poor school achievement, delinquent behavior, and delinquent personality: Longitudinal analyses. *Journal of Consulting and Clinical Psychology, 60,* 64–72.

Treynor, W., Gonzalez, R., & Nolen-Hoeksema, S. (2003). Rumination reconsidered: A psychometric analysis. *Cognitive Therapy & Research, 27,* 247–259.

Trimble, J. E. (1991). The mental health service and training needs of American Indians. In H. F. Myers, et al. (Eds.), *Ethnic minority perspectives on clinical training and services in psychology* (pp. 43–48). Washington, DC: American Psychological Association.

Trinh, N.-H., Hoblyn, J., Mohanty, S., & Yaffe, K. (2003). Efficacy of cholinesterase inhibitors in the treatment of neuropsychiatric symptoms and functional impairment in Alzheimer Disease: A meta-analysis. *Journal of the American Medical Association, 289,* 210–216.

Trull, T. J. (2001). Structural relations between borderline personality disorder features and putative etiological correlates. *Journal of Abnormal Psychology, 110,* 471–481.

Trunzo, J. J., & Pinto, B. M. (2003). Social support as a mediator of optimism and distress in breast cancer survivors. *Journal of Consulting and Clinical Psychology, 71,* 805–811.

Tsang, H. W.-H. (2001). Applying social skills training the context of vocational rehabilitation for people with schizophrenia. *Journal of Nervous & Mental Disease, 189,* 90–98.

Tsao, J. C. I., Lewin, M. R., & Craske, M. G. (2002). Effects of cognitive–behavior therapy for panic disorder on comorbid conditions: Replication and extension. *Behavior Therapy, 33,* 493–509.

Tseng, W., Mo, K. M., Li, L. S., Chen, G. Q., Ou, L. W., & Zheng, H. B. (1992). Koro epidemics in Guangdong, China: A questionnaire survey. *Journal of Nervous & Mental Disease, 180,* 117–123.

Tuiten, A., Van Honk, J., Koppeschaar, H., Bernaards, C., Thijssen, J., & Verbaten, R. (2000). Time course of effects of testosterone administration on sexual arousal in women. *Archives of General Psychiatry, 57,* 149–153.

Turkington, D., Grant, J. B. F., Rao, N., Sanjay, K., Linsley, K. R., & Young, A. H. (2002). A randomized controlled trial of fluvoxamine in prostatodynia, a male somatoform pain disorder. *Journal of Clinical Psychiatry, 63,* 778–781.

Turner, J., & Reid, S. (2002). Munchausen's syndrome. *Lancet, 359,* 346–349.

Turner, R. M. (2000). Understanding dialectical behavior therapy. *Clinical Psychology: Science and Practice, 7,* 95–98.

Turner, S. M., & Beidel, D. C. (1989). Social phobia: Clinical syndrome, diagnosis, and comorbidity. *Clinical Psychology Review, 9,* 3–18.

Turner, S. M., Beidel, D. C., & Jacob, R. G. (1994). Social phobia: A comparison of behavior therapy and atenolol. *Journal of Consulting and Clinical Psychology, 62,* 350–358.

Turner, S. M., Beidel, D. C., & Townsley, R. M. (1992). Social phobia: A comparison of specific and generalized subtypes and avoidant personality disorder. *Journal of Abnormal Psychology, 101,* 326–331.

Turner, S. M., McCann, B. S., Beidel, D. C., & Mezzich, J. E. (1986). DSM-III classification of the anxiety disorders: A psychometric study. *Journal of Abnormal Psychology, 95,* 168–172.

Turovksy, J., & Barlow, D. H. (1995, Summer). Albany Panic Control Treatment (PCT) for panic disorder and agoraphobia. *The Clinical Psychologist, 48*(3), 5–6.

Tuschen-Caffier, B., Pook, M., & Frank, M. (2001). Evaluation of manual-based cognitive-behavioral therapy for bulimia nervosa in a service setting. *Behaviour Research and Therapy, 39,* 299–308.

Twenge, J. M., & Nolen-Hoeksema, S. (2002). Age, gender, race, socioeconomic status, and birth cohort differences on the Children's Depression Inventory: A meta-analysis. *Journal of Abnormal Psychology, 111,* 578–588.

U

U.N. AIDS deaths, infections at new highs (2003, November 25). *CNN Web Posting.* Retrieved January 14, 2004, from http://www.cnn.com/2003/HEALTH/conditions/11/25/aids.reut/

U.S. Department of Health and Human Services (USDHHS). (1986). *NIDA capsules: Heroin.* No. 11. Rockville, MD: U.S. Department of Health and Human Services, Public Health Service, Alcohol, Drug Abuse, and Mental Health Administration, National Institute on Drug Abuse.

U.S. Department of Health and Human Services (USDHHS). (1991). *Vital statistics of the United States 1988.* (Vol. 2. Part A. Mortality.) Washington, DC: U.S. Government Printing Office. (DHHS Pub. No. PHS 91–1101).

U.S. Department of Health and Human Services (USDHHS). (1992). *NIDA capsules: LSD (lysergic acid diethylamide)* No. 39. Rockville, MD: U.S. Department of Health and Human Services, Public Health Service, Alcohol, Drug Abuse, and Mental Health Administration, National Institute on Drug Abuse, National Institute on Drug Abuse.

U.S. Department of Health and Human Services (USDHHS). (1993). *National household survey on drug abuse: Highlights 1991.* (DHHS Publication No. (SMA) 93–1979). Washington, DC: U.S. Government Printing Office.

U.S. Department of Health and Human Services (USDHHS). (1999a). *Mental health: A report of the Surgeon General.* Rockville, MD: U.S. Department of Health and Human Services, Substance Abuse and Mental Health Services Administration, Center for Mental Health Services, National Institutes of Health, National Institute of Mental Health.

U.S. Department of Health and Human Services (USDHHS). (1999b). *Mental health: A report of the Surgeon General—Executive summary.* Rockville, MD: U.S. Department of Health and Human Services, Substance Abuse and Mental Health Services Administration, Center for Mental Health Services, National Institutes of Health, National Institute of Mental Health.

U.S. Department of Health and Human Services (USDHHS). (2001). *Mental health: Culture, race, and ethnicity: A supplement to mental health: A report of the Surgeon General—Executive summary.* Rockville, MD: U.S. Department of Health and Human Services, Substance Abuse and Mental Health Services Administration, Center for Mental Health Services, National Institutes of Health, National Institute of Mental Health.

U.S. Department of Justice (2003). National Crime Victimization Survey. Washington, DC: U.S. Department of Justice.

Uhl, G. R., & Grow, R. W. (2004). The burden of complex genetics in brain disorders. *Archives of General Psychiatry, 61,* 223–229.

UK ECT Review Group. (2003). Efficacy and safety of electroconvulsive therapy in depressive disorders: A systematic review and meta-analysis. *Lancet, 361,* 799–808.

Ullmann, L. P., & Krasner, L. (1975). *A psychological approach to abnormal behavior* (2nd ed.). Englewood Cliffs, NJ: Prentice Hall.

Unger, J. B., Cruz, T. B., & Rohrbach, L. A. (2000). English language use as a risk factor for smoking initiation among Hispanic and Asian American adolescents: Evidence for mediation by tobacco-related beliefs and social norms. *Health Psychology, 19,* 403–410.

Utsey, S. O., Chae, M. H., Brown, C. F., & Kelly, D. (2002). Effect of ethnic group membership on ethnic identity, race-related stress, and quality of life. *Cultural Diversity and Ethnic Minority Psychology, 8,* 366–377.

Utsey, S. O., Payne, Y. A., Jackson, E. S., & Jones, M. A. (2002). Race-related stress, quality of life indicators, and life satisfaction among elderly African Americans. *Cultural Diversity and Ethnic Minority Psychology, 8,* 224–233.

V

Van Ameringen, M. A., et al. (2001). Sertraline treatment of generalized social phobia: A 20-week, double-blind, placebo-controlled study. *American Journal of Psychiatry, 158,* 275–281.

Van Balkom, A. J. L. M., Bakker, A., Spinhoven, P., Blaauw, B. M., Smeenk, S., & Ruesink, B. (1997). A meta-analysis of the treatment of panic disorder with or without agoraphobia: A comparison of psychopharmacological, cognitive-behavioral, and combination treatments. *Journal of Nervous & Mental Disease, 185,* 510–516.

van der Stelt, O., Frye, J., Lieberman, J. A., & Belger, A. (2004). Impaired P3 generation reflects high-level and progressive neurocognitive dysfunction in schizophrenia. *Archives of General Psychiatry, 61,* 237–248.

Van Eerdewegh, P., Little, R. D., Dupuis, J., Del Mastro, R. G., Falls, K., Simon, J., et al. (2002). Association of the ADAM33 gene with asthma and bronchial hyperresponsiveness. *Nature, 418,* 426–430.

van Emmerik, A. A. P., Kamphuis, J. H., Hulsbosch, A. M., & Emmelkamp, P. M. (2002). Single session debriefing after psychological trauma: A meta-analysis. *Lancet, 360,* 766–771.

van Goozen, S. H. M., Slabbekoorn, D., Gooren, L. J. G., Sanders, G., & Cohen-Kettenis, P. T. (2002). Organizing and activating effects of sex hormones in homosexual transsexuals. *Behavioral Neuroscience, 116,* 982–988.

Van Humbeeck, G., Van Audenhove, Ch., De Hert, M., Pieters, G., & Storms, G. (2002). Expressed emotion: A review of assessment instruments *Clinical Psychology Review, 22,* 321–341.

Van Ommeren, M., de Jong, J. T., Sharma, B., Komproe, I., Thapa, S. B., & Cardena, E. (2001). Psychiatric disorders among tortured Bhutanese refugees in Nepal. *Archives of General Psychiatry, 58,* 475–482.

Van Susteren, L. (2002). The insanity defense, continued. *The Journal of the American Academy of Psychiatry and the Law, 30,* 474–475. [Editorial]

Van Wie, V. E., & Gross, A. M. (2001). The role of woman's explanations for refusal on men's ability to discriminate unwanted sexual behavior in a date rape scenario. *Journal of Family Violence, 16,* 331–344.

VandeCreek, L., & Knapp, S. (2001). *Tarasoff and beyond: Legal and clinical considerations in the treatment of life-endangering patients.* Sarasota, FL: Professional Resource Press.

VandenBos, G. R., & Williams, S. (2000). The Internet versus the telephone: What is telehealth, anyway? *Professional Psychology: Research and Practice, 31,* 490–492.

Vanderkam, L. (2003). *Barbie and fat as a feminist issue.* Retrieved November 19, 2003, from http://www.shethinks.org/articles/an00208.cfm.

Vastag, B. (2004b). Obesity is now on everyone's plate. *Journal of the American Medical Association, 291,* 1186–1188.

Vega, W. A., et al. (1998). Lifetime prevalence of *DSM-III-R* psychiatric disorders among urban and rural Mexican Americans in California. *Archives of General Psychiatry, 55,* 771–778.

Velting, O. N., Setzer, N. J., & Albano, A. M. (2004). Update on and advances in assessment and cognitive–behavioral treatment of anxiety disorders in children and adolescents. *Professional Psychology: Research and Practice, 35,* 42–54.

Verghese, A. (2004, February 22). Hope and clarity: Is optimism a cure? *The New York Times Magazine,* pp. 11–12.

Verghese, J., Lipton, R. B., Katz, M. J., Hall, C. B., Derby, C. A., Kuslansky, G., et al. (2003). Leisure activities and the risk of dementia in the elderly. *New England Journal of Medicine, 348,* 2508–2516.

Verhovek, S. H. (2000). What is the matter with Mary Jane? *The New York Times Week in Review,* p. 3.

Vermeer, S. E., Prins, N. D., den Heijer, T., Hofman, A., Koudstaal, P. J., & Breteler, M. M. B. (2003). Silent brain infarcts and the risk of dementia and cognitive decline. *New England Journal of Medicine, 348,* 1215–1222.

Viglione, D. J. (1999). A review of recent research addressing the utility of the Rorschach. *Psychological Assessment, 11,* 251–265.

Vik, P. W., Carrello, P., Tate, S. R., & Field, C. (2000). Progression of consequences among heavy-drinking college students. *Psychology of Addictive Behaviors, 14,* 91–101.

Viken, R. J., Treat, T. A., Nosofsky, R. M., McFall, R. M., & Palmeri, T. J. (2002). Modeling individual differences in perceptual and attentional processes related to bulimic symptoms. *Journal of Abnormal Psychology, 111,* 598–609.

Villarosa, L. (2002, December 3). To prevent sexual abuse, abusers step forward. *The New York Times,* p. F5.

Vincent, J. B., Masellis, M., Lawrence, J., Choi, V., Gurling, H. M., Parikh, S. V., et al. (1999). Genetic association analysis of serotonin system genes in bipolar affective disorder. *American Journal of Psychiatry, 156,* 136–138.

Visser, S., & Bouman, T. K. (2001). The treatment of hypochondriasis: Exposure plus response prevention vs. cognitive therapy. *Behaviour Research and Therapy, 39,* 423–442.

Vitaliano, P. P., Zhang, J., & Scanlan, J. M. (2003). Is caregiving hazardous to one's physical health? A meta-analysis. *Psychological Bulletin, 129,* 946–972.

Voelker, R. (2000). Recessive Alzheimer gene? *Journal of the American Medical Association, 284,* 1777.

Volkmar, F. R. (2003). Changing perspectives on ADHD. *American Journal of Psychiatry, 160,* 1025–1007.

Volkow, N. D., Chang, L., Wang, G. J., Fowler, J. S., Leonido-Yee, M., Franceschi, D., et al. (2001). Association of dopamine transporter reduction with psychomotor impairment in methamphetamine abusers. *American Journal of Psychiatry, 158,* 377–382.

Volkow, N. D., Wang, G. J., Fischman, M. W., Foltin, R. W., Fowler, J. S., Abumrad, N. N., et al. (1997). Relationship between subjective effects of cocaine and dopamine transporter occupancy. *Nature, 386,* 827–830.

W

Wadden, T. A., Brownell, K. D., & Foster, G. D. (2002). Obesity: Responding to the global epidemic. *Journal of Consulting and Clinical Psychology, 70,* 510–525.

Wade, N. (2000, May 9). Scientists decode Down syndrome chromosome. *The New York Times,* pp. C1, C3.

Wade, N. (2003a, June 3). Gene sweepstakes ends, but winner may well be wrong. *The New York Times,* pp. F1, F. 2.

Wade, N. (2003b, April 15). Once again, scientists say human genome is complete. *The New York Times,* p. F1.

Wade, T. D., Bulik, C. M., Neale, M., & Kendler, K. S. (2000). Anorexia nervosa and major depression: Shared genetic and environmental risk factors. *American Journal of Psychiatry, 157,* 469–471.

Wagner, K. D., Ambrosini, P., Rynn, M., Wohlberg, C., Yang, R., Greenbaum, M. S., et al. (2003). Efficacy of sertraline in the treatment of children and adolescents with major depressive disorder: Two randomized controlled trials. *Journal of the American Medical Association, 290,* 1033–1041.

Wahlbeck, K., Forsen, T., Osmond, C., Barker, D. J., & Eriksson, J. G. (2001). Association of schizophrenia with low maternal body mass index, small size at birth, and thinness during childhood. *Archives of General Psychiatry, 58,* 48–52.

Wahlberg, K. E., et al. (2001). Long-term stability of communication deviance. *Journal of Abnormal Psychology, 110,* 443–448.

Wainwright, N. W. J., & Surtees, P. G. (2002). Childhood adversity, gender and depression over the life-course. *Journal of Affective Disorders, 72,* 33–44.

Wakefield, H., & Underwager, R. (1996). Commentary on Kenneth Pope's review. *Clinical Psychology: Science and Practice, 3,* 366–371.

Wakefield, J. C. (1992a). The concept of mental disorder: On the boundary between biological facts and social values. *American Psychologist, 47,* 373–388.

Wakefield, J. C. (1992b). Disorder as harmful dysfunction: A conceptual critique of *DSM-III-R's* definition of mental disorder. *Psychological Review, 99,* 232–247.

Wakefield, J. C. (1997). Normal inability versus pathological disability: Why Ossorio's definition of mental disorder is not sufficient. *Clinical Psychology: Science and Practice, 4,* 249–258.

Wakefield, J. C. (2001). Evolutionary history versus current causal role in the definition of disorder: Reply to McNally. *Behaviour Research and Therapy, 39,* 347–366.

Wakeling, A. (1996). Epidemiology of anorexia nervosa. *Psychiatry Research, 62,* 3–9.

Waldinger, M. D., Zwinderman, A. H., & Olivier, B. (2001). Antidepressants and ejaculation: A double-blind, randomized, placebo-controlled, fixed-dose study with paroxetine, sertraline and nefazodone. *Journal of Clinical Psychopharmacology, 21*(3), 293–297.

Walker, E. F., & Diforio, D. (1997). Schizophrenia: A neural diathesis-stress model. *Psychological Review, 104,* 667–685.

Walker, E., Kestler, L., Bollini, A., & Hochman, K. M. (2004). Schizophrenia: Etiology and course. *Annual Review of Psychology, 55,* 401–430.

Walker, L. E. (1988). The battered woman syndrome. In G. T. Hotaling, D. Finkelhor, J. T. Kirkpatrick, & M. A. Straus (Eds.), *Family abuse and its consequences: New directions in research* (pp. 139–148). Newbury Park, CA: Sage.

Walker, R. (2004, February 8). Cialis. *The New York Times Magazine,* p. 26.

Walkup, J. T., et al. (2001). Fluvoxamine for the treatment of anxiety disorders in children and adolescents. The Research Unit on Pediatric Psychopharmacology Anxiety Study Group. *The New England Journal of Medicine, 344,* 1279–1285.

Wall, T. L., Carr, L. G., & Ehlers, C. L. (2003). Protective association of genetic variation in alcohol dehydrogenase with alcohol dependence in Native American Mission Indians. *American Journal of Psychiatry, 160,* 41–46.

Waller, N. G., & Ross, C. A. (1997). The prevalence of biometric structure of pathological dissociation in the general population: Taxometric and behavior genetic findings. *Journal of Abnormal Psychology, 106,* 499–510.

Walsh, B. T., Agras, W. W., Devlin, M. J., Fairburn, C. G., Wilson, G. T., Kahn, C., et al. (2000). Fluoxetine for bulimia nervosa following poor response to psychotherapy. *American Journal of Psychiatry, 157,* 1332–1334.

Walsh, B. T., Fairburn, C. G., Mickley, D., Sysko, R., & Parides, M. K. (2004). Treatment of bulimia nervosa in a primary care setting. *American Journal of Psychiatry, 161,* 556–561.

Walsh, B. T., Wilson, G. T., Loeb, K. L., Devlin, M. J., Pike, K. M., Roose, S. P., et al. (1997). Medication and psychotherapy in the treatment of bulimia nervosa. *American Journal of Psychiatry, 154,* 523–531.

Wampold, B. E. (2001). *The great psychotherapy debate: Models, methods, and findings.* Mahwah, NJ: Erlbaum.

Wampold, B. E., et al. (1997b). The flat earth as a metaphor for the evidence for uniform efficacy of bona fide psychotherapies: Reply to Crits-Christoph (1997) and Howard et al. (1997). *Psychological Bulletin, 122,* 226–230.

Wang, X., Gao, L., Shinfuku, N., Zhang, H., Zhao, C., & Shen, Y. (2000). Longitudinal study of earthquake-related PTSD in a randomly selected community sample in North China. *American Journal of Psychiatry, 157,* 1260–1266.

Warheit, G. J., Vega, W. A., Auth, J., & Meinhardt, K. (1985). Psychiatric symptoms and dysfunctions among Anglos and Mexican Americans: An epidemiological study. In J. R. Greenley (Ed.), *Research in community and mental health* (pp. 3–32). London: JAI Press.

Warner, J. (2002, October 18). Fish oil eases depression. Retrieved October 20, 2002, from http://my.webmd.com/condition_center_content/mhl/article/1663.54436?z=2950_00000_0000_ f1_06

Warner, L. A., Kessler, R. C., Hughes, M., Anthony, J. C., & Nelson, C. B. (1995). Prevalence and correlates of drug use and dependence in the United States. *Archives of General Psychiatry, 52,* 219–229.

Wartik, N. (2000, June 25). Depression comes out of hiding. *The New York Times,* pp. MH1, MH4.

Wassertheil-Smoller, S., Shumaker, S., Ockene, J., Talavera, G. A., Greenland, P., Cochrane, B., et al. (2004). Depression and cardiovascular sequelae in postmenopausal women: The Women's Health initiative (WHI). *Archives of Internal Medicine, 164,* 289–298.

Waterworth, D. M., Bassett, A. S., & Brzustowicz, L. M. (2002). Recent advances in the genetics of schizophrenia. *Cellular and Molecular Life Sciences, 59,* 331–348.

Watts, C., & Zimmerman, C. (2002). Violence against women: Global scope and magnitude. *Lancet, 359* (9313), 1232–1237.

Weaver, T. L., & Clum, G. A. (1995). Psychological distress associated with interpersonal violence: A meta-analysis. *Clinical Psychology Review, 15,* 115–140.

Webster-Stratton, C., Reid, J., & Hammond, M. (2001). Social skills and problem-solving training for children with early-onset conduct problems: Who benefits? *Journal of Child Psychology & Psychiatry & Allied Disciplines, 42*(7), 943–952.

Wechsler, D. (1975). Intelligence defined and undefined: A relativistic appraisal. *American Psychologist, 30,* 135–139.

Weed, W. S. (2003, December 14). Questions for Raymond Damadian: Scanscam? *The New York Times Online.* Retrieved January 8, 2004, from www.nytimes.com/2003/12/14/magazine/14QUESTIONS.html

Weems, C. F., Berman, S. L., Silverman, W. K., & Saavedra, L. M. (2001). Cognitive errors in youth with anxiety disorders: The linkages between negative cognitive errors and anxious symptoms. *Cognitive Therapy & Research, 25,* 559–575.

Weems, C. F., Hayward, C., Killen, J., & Taylor, C. B. (2002). A longitudinal investigation of anxiety sensitivity in adolescence. *Journal of Abnormal Psychology, 111,* 471–477.

Weich, S., Churchill, R., & Lewis, G. (2003). Dysfunctional attitudes and the common mental disorders in primary. *Journal of Affective Disorders, 75,* 269–278.

Weinberg, G. (1972). *Society and the healthy homosexual.* New York: St. Martin's Press.

Weine, S. M., Razzano, L., Brkic, N., Ramic, A., Miller, K., Smajkic, A., et al. (2000). Profiling the trauma related symptoms of Bosnian refugees who have not sought mental health services. *Journal of Nervous & Mental Disease, 188,* 416–421.

Weiner, I. B. (2001). Advancing the science of psychological assessment: The Rorschach Inkblot Method as exemplar. *Psychological Assessment, 13,* 423–432.

Weiner, I. B., Spielberger, C. D., & Abeles, N. (2002). Scientific psychology and the Rorschach Inkblot Method. *The Clinical Psychologist, 55,* 7–12.

Weiner, I. B., Spielberger, C. D., & Abeles, N. (2003). Once more around the park: Correcting misinformation

about Rorschach assessment. *The Clinical Psychologist, 56,* 8–9.

Weiner, J. R. (2003). *Tarasoff* warnings resulting in criminal charges: Two case reports. *The Journal of the American Academy of Psychiatry and the Law, 31,* 239–241.

Weiner, R. D. (2000). Retrograde amnesia with electroconvulsive therapy characteristics and implications. *Archives of General Psychiatry, 57,* 591–592.

Weisberg, R. B., Brown, T. A., Wincze, J. P., & Barlow, D. H. (2001). Causal attributions and male sexual arousal: The impact of attributions for a bogus erectile difficulty on sexual arousal, cognitions, and affect. *Journal of Abnormal Psychology, 110,* 324–334.

Weisman, A., et al. (1993). An attributional analysis of expressed emotion in Mexican-American families with schizophrenia. *Journal of Abnormal Psychology, 102,* 601–606.

Weisman, A. G., et al. (1998). Expressed emotion, attributions, and schizophrenia symptom dimensions. *Journal of Abnormal Psychology, 107,* 355–359.

Weisman, A. G., et al. (2000). Controllability perceptions and reactions to symptoms of schizophrenia: A within-family comparison of relatives with high and low expressed emotion. *Journal of Abnormal Psychology, 109,* 167–171.

Weiss, R. D., & Mirin, S. M. (1987). *Cocaine.* Washington, DC: American Psychiatric Press.

Weissman, A. N., & Beck, A. T. (1978, November). *Development and validation of the Dysfunctional Attitudes Scale: A preliminary investigation.* Paper presented at the meeting of the American Educational Research Association, Toronto, Canada.

Weissman, M. M. (1999). Depressed adolescents grown up. *Journal of the American Medical Association, 281,* 1707–1713.

Weissman, M. M., et al. (1991). Affective disorders. In L. N. Robins & D. A. Regier (Eds.), *Psychiatric disorders in America: The Epidemiologic Catchment Area Study* (pp. 53–80). New York: Free Press.

Weissman, M. M., & Markowtiz, J. C. (1994). Interpersonal psychotherapy: Current status. *Archives of General Psychiatry, 51,* 599–606.

Weisz, J. R., Pilkonis, P. A., Woody, S. R., & Follette, W. C. (2000). Stressing the (other) three Rs in the search for empirically supported treatments: Review procedures, research quality, relevance to practice and the public interest. *Clinical Psychology: Science and Practice, 7,* 243–258.

Weisz, J. R., Suwanlert, S., Chaiyasit, W., Weiss, B., Walter, B. R., & Anderson, W. W. (1988). Thai and American perspectives on over- and undercontrolled child behavior problems: Exploring the threshold model among parents, teachers, and psychologists. *Journal of Consulting and Clinical Psychology, 56,* 601–609.

Welch, M. R., & Kartub, P. (1978). Socio-cultural correlates of incidence of impotence: A cross-cultural study. *Journal of Sex Research, 14,* 218–230.

Welkowitz, L. A., Papp, L., Martinez, J., Browne, S., & Gorman, J. M. (1999). Instructional set and physiological response to CO_2 inhalation. *American Journal of Psychiatry, 156,* 745–748.

Wells, K. B., Sherbourne, C., Schoenbaum, M., Duan, N., Meredith, L., Unutzer, J., et al. (2000). Impact of disseminating quality improvement programs for depression in managed primary care: A randomized controlled trial. *Journal of the American Medical Association, 283,* 212–220.

Welsh, R. S. (2003). Prescription privileges: Pro or con. *Clinical Psychology: Science and Practice, 10,* 371–372. [Letter]

Weltzin, T. E., Cameron, J., Berga, S., & Kaye, W. H. (1994). Prediction of reproductive status in women with bulimia nervosa by past high weight. *American Journal of Psychiatry, 151,* 136–138.

Wender, P. H., Rosenthal, D., Kety, S. S., Schulsinger, F., & Welner, J. (1974). Cross-fostering: A research strategy

for clarifying the role of genetic and experiential factors in the etiology of schizophrenia. *Archives of General Psychiatry, 30,* 121–128.

Westen, D., & Gabbard, G. O. (2002). Developments in cognitive neuroscience: 1. Conflict, compromise, and connectionism. *Journal of the American Psychoanalytic Association, 50,* 53–98.

Westen, D., & Shedler, J. (1999). Revising and assessing axis II, Part II: Toward an empirically based and clinically useful classification of personality disorders. *The American Journal of Psychiatry, 156,* 273–285.

Wetzler, S., & Marlowe, D. B. (1993). The diagnosis and assessment of depression, mania, and psychosis by self-report. *Journal of Personality Assessment, 60,* 1–31.

Wexler, B. E., Gottschalk, C. H., Fulbright, R. K., Prohovnik, L., Lacadie, C. M., Rounsaville, B. J., et al. (2001). Functional magnetic resonance imaging of cocaine craving. *American Journal of Psychiatry, 158,* 86–95.

Whalen, C. K., Jamner, L. D., Henker, B., & Delfino, R. J. (2001). Smoking and moods in adolescents with depressive and aggressive dispositions: Evidence from surveys and electronic diaries. *Health Psychology, 20,* 99–111.

What causes migraine headaches? (2001) *Nidus Information Services, Inc.* Retrieved January 5, 2004, from http://www.ucdmc.ucdavis.edu/ucdhs/health/a-z/97migraine/doc97causes.html

Whiffen, V. E., & Gotlib, I. H. (1993). Comparison of postpartum and nonpostpartum depression: Clinical presentation, psychiatric history, and psychosocial functioning. *Journal of Consulting and Clinical Psychology, 61,* 485–493.

WHO World Mental Health Survey Consortium. (2004). Prevalence, severity, and unmet need for treatment of mental disorders in the World Health Organization World Mental Health Surveys. *Journal of the American Medical Association, 291,* 2581–2590.

Whooley, M. A., Kiefe, C. I., Chesney, M. A., Markovitz, J. H., Matthews, K., Hulley, S. B., et al. (2002). Depressive symptoms, unemployment, and loss of income. The CARDIA Study. *Archives of Internal Medicine, 162,* 2614–2620.

Wickenhaver, J. (1992, September 8). After the "Wild Man": Can an insane system be cured? *Manhattan Spirit,* pp. 13, 28.

Wickizer, T. M., Lessler, D., & Travis, K. M. (1996). Controlling inpatient psychiatric utilization through managed care. *American Journal of Psychiatry, 153,* 339–345.

Widiger, T. A. (1991). *DSM-IV* reviews of the personality disorders: Introduction to special series. *Journal of Personality Disorder, 5,* 122–134.

Widiger, T. A. (1992). Generalized social phobia versus avoidant personality disorder: A commentary on three studies. *Journal of Abnormal Psychology, 101,* 340–343.

Widiger, T. A., & Clark, L. A. (2000). Toward *DSM-V* and the classification of psychopathology. *Psychological Bulletin, 126,* 946–963.

Widiger, T. A., & Costa, P. T., Jr. (1994). Personality and personality disorders. *Journal of Abnormal Psychology, 103,* 78–91.

Wiers, R. W., & Kummeling, R. H. C. (2004). An experimental test of an alcohol expectancy challenge in mixed gender groups of young heavy drinkers. *Addictive Behaviors, 29,* 215–220.

Wiersma, D., et al. (2001). Cognitive behaviour therapy with coping training for persistent auditory hallucinations in schizophrenia: A naturalistic follow-up study of the durability of effects. *Acta Psychiatrica Scandinavica, 103,* 393–399.

Wilbur, C. B. (1986). Psychoanalysis and multiple personality disorder. In B. G. Braun (Ed.), *Treatment of multiple personality disorder.* Washington, DC: American Psychiatric Press.

Wilcox, M. A., Faraone, S. V., Su, J., Van Eerdewegh, P., & Tsuang, M. T. (2002). Genome scan of three quantitative traits in schizophrenia pedigrees. *Biological Psychiatry, 52,* 847–54.

Wilens, T. E., Biederman, J., Wozniak, J., Gunawardene, S., Wong, J., & Monuteaux, M. (2003). Can adults with attention-deficit/hyperactivity disorder be distinguished from those with comorbid bipolar disorder? Findings from a sample of clinically referred adults. *Biological Psychiatry, 54*, 8.

Wilkie, F. L., et al. (1998). Mild cognitive impairment and risk of mortality in HIV-1 infection. *Journal of Neuropsychiatry and Clinical Neuroscience, 10*, 125–132.

Wilkinson, D., et al. (2003). Donepezil in vascular dementia: A randomized, placebo-controlled study. *Neurology, 61*, 479–486.

Wilkinson-Ryan, T., & Westen, D. (2000). Identity disturbance in borderline personality disorders: An empirical investigation. *American Journal of Psychiatry, 157*, 528–541.

Williams, D. (1992). *Nobody nowhere: The extraordinary autobiography of an autistic.* New York: Times Books.

Williams, J. B., et al. (1992). The Structured Clinical Interview for DSM-III—(SCID). II: Multisite test-retest reliability. *Archives of General Psychiatry, 49*, 630–636.

Williams, J. E., Paton, C. C., Siegler, I. C., Eigenbrodt, M. L., Nieto, F. J., & Tyroler, H. A. (2000). Anger proneness predicts coronary heart disease risk: Prospective analysis from the Atherosclerosis Risk in Communities (ARIC) Study. *Circulation, 101*, 2034–2039.

Williams, N. M., Preece, A., Morris, D. W., Spurlock, G., Bray, N. J., Stephens, D. M., Norton, N., et al. (2004). Identification in 2 independent samples of a novel schizophrenia risk haplotype of the Dystrobrevin Binding Protein Gene (DTNBP1). *Archives of General Psychiatry, 61*, 336–344.

Williams, P. G., Wiebe, D. J., & Smith, T. W. (1992). Coping processes as mediators of the relationship between hardiness and health. *Journal of Behavioral Medicine, 15*, 237–255.

Williams, R. B., Marchuk, D. A., Gadde, K. M., Barefoot, J. C., Grichnik, K., Helms, M. J., et al. (2003) Serotonin-related gene polymorphisms and central nervous system serotonin function. *Neuropsychopharmacology, 28*, 533–541.

Willis, D. J. (2003, Fall). The case for prescription privileges. *The Clinical Psychologist, 56*, 1–4.

Wills, T. A., & Filer Fegan, M. (2001). Social networks and social support. In A. Baum, T. A. Revenson, & J. E. Singer (Eds.), *Handbook of health psychology* (pp. 3–18). Mahwah, NJ: Lawrence Erlbaum Associates.

Wilson, G. T. (1991). Chemical aversion conditioning in the treatment of alcoholism: Further comments: *Behaviour Research & Therapy, 29*, 415–419.

Wilson, G. T. (1994). Behavioral treatment of childhood obesity: Theoretical and practical implications. *Health Psychology, 13*, 371–372.

Wilson, G. T. (1997). Behavior therapy at century close. *Behavior Therapy, 28*, 449–457.

Wilson, G. T., & Fairburn, C. G. (1998). Treatment for eating disorders. In P. E. Nathan & J. M. Gorman (Eds.), *A guide to treatments that work* (pp. 501–530). New York: Oxford University Press.

Wilson, R. S., Barnes, L. L., Mendes de Leon, C. F., Aggarwal, N. T., Schneider, J. S., Bach, J., et al. (2002). Depressive symptoms, cognitive decline, and risk of AD in older persons. *Neurology, 59*, 364–370.

Wilson, R. S., &. Bennett, D. A. (2003). Cognitive activity and risk of Alzheimer's disease. *Current Directions in Psychological Science, 12*, 87–90.

Wilson, S. A., Becker, L. A., & Tinker, R. H. (1997). Fifteen-month follow-up of eye movement desensitization and reprocessing (EMDR) treatment for posttraumatic stress disorder and psychological trauma. *Journal of Consulting and Clinical Psychology, 65*, 1047–1056.

Winefield, H. R., & Harvey, E. J. (1994). Needs of family caregivers in chronic schizophrenia. *Schizophrenia Bulletin, 20*, 557–566.

Winerip, M. (1991, December 18). Soldier in battle for the retarded. *The New York Times*, pp. B1, B6.

Winerip, M. (1998, January 4). Binge nights. *The New York Times*, Education Section 4A, pp. 28–31, 42.

Winerip, M. (1999, May 23). Bedlam on the streets. *The New York Times*, pp. 42–49.

Winerman, L. (2004, May). Panel stresses youth suicide prevention. *Monitor on Psychology, 35*, p. 18.

Wing, R. R., & Polley, B. A. (2001). Obesity. In A. Baum, T. A. Revenson, & J. E. Singer (Eds), *Handbook of health psychology* (pp. 263–279). Mahwah, NJ: Erlbaum.

Wingert, P. (2000, December 4). No more "afternoon nasties." *Newsweek*, p. 59.

Winston, A., Laikin, M., Pollack, J., Samstag, L. W., McCullough, L., & Muran, J. C. (1994). Short-term psychotherapy of personality disorders. *American Journal of Psychiatry, 51*, 190–194.

Winston, A., Pollack, J., McCullough, L., Flegenheimer, W., Kestenbaum, R., & Trujillo, M. (1991). Brief psychotherapy of personality disorders. *Journal of Nervous & Mental Disease, 179*, 188–193.

Winterer, G., Coppola, R., Goldberg, T. E., Egan, M. F., Jones, D. W., et al. (2004). Prefrontal broadband noise, working memory, and genetic risk for schizophrenia. *American Journal of Psychiatry, 161*, 490–500.

Wisner, K. L, Parry, B. L., & Piontek, C. M. (2002). Postpartum depression. *New England Journal of Medicine, 347*, 194–199.

Woerner, M. G., Robinson, D. G., Alvir, J. M., Sheitman, B. B., Lieberman, J. A., & Kane, J. M. (2003). *American Journal of Psychiatry, 160*, 1514–1516.

Wolfe, D. A., et al. (2001). Child maltreatment: Risk of adjustment problems and dating violence in adolescence. *Journal of American Academy of Child & Adolescent Psychiatry, 40*, 282–289.

Wolpe, J. (1958). *Psychotherapy by reciprocal inhibition.* Stanford, CA: Stanford University Press.

Wolpe, J., & Lazarus, A. A. (1966). *Behavior therapy techniques.* New York: Pergamon Press.

Wonderlich, S. A., Brewerton, T. D., Jocic, Z., Dansky, B. S., & Abbott, D. W. (1997). Relationship of childhood sexual abuse and eating disorders. *Journal of the American Academy of Child and Adolescent Psychiatry, 36*, 1107–1115.

Wong, E. C., Kim, B. S. K., Zane, N. W. S., Kim, I. J., & Huang, J. S. (2003). Examining culturally based variables associated with ethnicity: Influences on credibility perceptions of empirically supported interventions. *Cultural Diversity and Ethnic Minority Psychology, 9*, 88–96.

Wong, J. L., & Whitaker, D. J. (1993). Depressive mood states and their cognitive and personality correlates in college students: They improve over time. *Journal of Clinical Psychology, 49*, 615–621.

Wong, M. M., Klingle, R. S., & Price, R. K. (2004). Alcohol, tobacco, and other drug use among Asian American and Pacific Islander Adolescents in California and Hawaii. *Addictive Behaviors, 29*, 127–141.

Wood, J. M., Bootzin, R. R., Rosenhan, D., Nolen-Hoeksema, S., & Jourden, R. (1992). Effects of 1989 San Francisco earthquake on frequency and content of nightmares. *Journal of Abnormal Psychology, 101*, 219–234.

Wood, M. D., Vinson, D. C., & Sher, K. J. (2001). Alcohol use and misuse. In A. Baum, T. A. Revenson, & J. E. Singer (Eds.), *Handbook of health psychology* (pp. 280–320). Mahwah, NJ: Erlbaum.

Woods, C. M., Vevea, J. L., Chambless, D. L., & Bayen, U. J. (2002). Are compulsive checkers impaired in memory? A meta-analytic review. *Clinical Psychology: Science and Practice, 9*, 353–366.

Woods, S. C., Schwartz, M. W., Baskin, D. G., & Seeley, R. J. (2000). Food intake and the regulation of body weight. *Annual Review of Psychology, 51*, 255–277.

Woodward, A. M., Dwinell, A. D., & Arons, B. S. (1992). Barriers to mental health care for Hispanic Americans: A literature review and discussion. *Journal of Mental Health Administration, 19*, 224–236.

Woodworth, M., & Porter, S. (2002). In cold blood: Characteristics of criminal homicides as a function of psychopathy. *Journal of Abnormal Psychology, 111*, 436–445.

Wootton, J. M., et al. (1997). Ineffective parenting and childhood conduct problems: The moderating role of callous-unemotional traits. *Journal of Consulting and Clinical Psychology, 65*, 301–308.

Wright, P., & Kantrowitz, B. (2002, October 7). Young and depressed. *Newsweek*, pp. 53–60.

Writing Group of the PREMIER Collaborative Research Group. (2003). Effects of comprehensive lifestyle modification on blood pressure control: Main results of the PREMIER Clinical Trial. *Journal of the American Medical Association, 289*, 2083–2093.

Wu, P., Hoven, C. W., Cohen, P., Liu, X., Moore, R. E., Tiet, Q., et al. (2001). Factors associated with use of mental health services for depression by children and adolescents. *Psychiatric Services, 52*(2), 189–195.

Wyatt v. Stickney, 334 F. Supp. 1341 (1972).

Y

Yager, J. (2003, December 23). Is there something fishy about bipolar disorder? *Journal Watch Psychiatry*. Retrieved December 24, 2003, from http://psychiatry.jwatch.org/cgi/content/full/2003/1223/5?q=etoc

Yancey, K. B. (2000, August 18). Treatment virtually cures fear of flying. *USA Today Online*. Retrieved November 23, 2003, from http://www.usatoday.com/life/cyber/tech/review/crh424.htm

Yang, Q., Rasmussen, S. A., & Friedman, J. M. (2002). Mortality associated with Down's syndrome in the USA from 1983 to 1997: A population-based study. *The Lancet, 359*, 1019–1025.

Yates, W. R. (2000). Testosterone in psychiatry: Risks and benefits. *Journal of the American Medical Association, 57*, 155–156.

Yatham, L. M., Liddle, P. F., Shiah, I. S., Scarrow, G., Lam, R. W., Adam, M. J., Zis, A. P., et al. (2000). Brain serotonin2 receptors in major depression: A positron emission tomography study. *Archives of General Psychiatry, 57*, 850–858.

Yeargin-Allsopp, M., Rice, C., Karapurkan, T., Doernberg, N., Boyle, C., & Murphy, C. (2003). Prevalence of autism in a US metropolitan area. *Journal of the American Medical Association, 289*, 49–55.

Yeh, C. J. (2003). Age, acculturation, cultural adjustment, and mental health symptoms of Chinese, Korean, and Japanese immigrant youths. *Cultural Diversity and Ethnic Minority Psychology, 9*, 34–48.

Yeni, P. G., Hammer, S. M., Carpenter, C. C., Cooper, D. A., Fischl, M. A., Gatell, J. M., et al. (2002). Antiretroviral treatment for adult HIV Infection in 2002: Updated Recommendations of the International AIDS Society-USA Panel. *Journal of the American Medical Association, 288*, 222–235.

Yeung, A., Howarth, S., Chan, R., Sonawalla, S., Nierenberg, A. A., & Fava, M. (2002). Use of the Chinese version of the Beck Depression Inventory for screening depression in primary care. *Journal of Nervous & Mental Disease, 190*, 94–99.

Yeung, P. P., & Greenwald, S. (1992). Jewish Americans and mental health: Results of the NIMH Epidemiologic Catchment Area Study. *Social Psychiatry and Psychiatric Epidemiology, 27*, 292–297.

Young, E. A., McFatter, R., & Clopton, J. R. (2001). Family functioning, peer influence, and media influence as predictors of bulimic behavior. *Eating Behaviors, 2*, 323–337.

Young, M. A., Fogg, L. F., Scheftner, W. A., & Fawcett, J. A. (1994). Interactions of risk factors in predicting suicide. *American Journal of Psychiatry, 51*, 434–435.

Young, T. J., & French, L. A. (1996). Suicide and homicide rates among U.S. Indian health service areas: The income inequality hypothesis. *Social Behavior and Personality, 24*, 365–366.

Young, T. K., & Sevenhuyser, G. (1989). Obesity in northern Canadian Indians: Patterns, determinants, and consequences. *American Journal of Clinical Nutrition, 49,* 786–793.

Youngberg v. Romeo, 102 S. Ct. 2452, 2463 (1982).

Yu, C. E., Dawson, G., Munson, J., D'Souza, I., Osterling, J., Estes, A., et al. (2002). Presence of large deletions in kindreds with autism. *American Journal of Human Genetics, 71,* 100–115.

Z

Zamanian, K., et al. (1992). Acculturation and depression in Mexican-American elderly. *Gerontologist, 11,* 109–121.

Zammit, S., Allebeck, P., Adreasson, S., Lundberg, I., & Lewis, G. (2002). Self reported cannabis use as a risk factor for schizophrenia in Swedish conscripts of 1969: Historical cohort study. *British Medical Journal, 325,* 1199.

Zanardi, R., Franchini, L., Gasperini, M., Perez, J., & Smeraldi, E. (1996). Double-blind controlled trial of sertraline versus paroxetine in the treatment of delusional depression. *American Journal of Psychiatry, 153,* 1631–1633.

Zanarini, M. C., Frankenburg, F. R., Hennen, J., & Silk, K. R. (2003). The longitudinal course of borderline psychopathology: 6-year prospective follow-up of the phenomenology of borderline personality disorder. *American Journal of Psychiatry, 160,* 274–283.

Zane, N., & Sue, S. (1991). Culturally responsive mental health services for Asian Americans: Treatment and training issues. In H. F. Myers, et al. (Eds.), *Ethnic minority perspectives on clinical training and services in psychology* (pp. 49–58). Washington, DC: American Psychological Association.

Zernike, K., & Petersen, M. (2001, August 19). Schools' backing of behavior drugs comes under fire. *The New York Times Online.*

Zhang, C. H., Hernan, M. A., Schwarzschild, M. A., Willett, W. C., Colditz, G. A., Speizer, F. E., et al. (2003). Nonsteroidal anti-inflammatory drugs and the risk of Parkinson disease. *Archives of Neurology, 60,* 1059–64.

Zickler, P. (2000). Brain imaging studies show long-term damage from methamphetamine abuse. *NIDA Notes, 15*(3), 11, 13.

Zickler, P. (2004, April). Smoking decreases key enzyme throughout body research findings. National Institute on Drug Abuse. *NIDA Notes, 19.* Retrieved May 10, 2004, from http://www.drugabuse.gov/NIDA_notes/NNvol19N1/Smoking.html

Zimand, E., Anderson, P., Gershon, G., Graap, K., Hodges, L., & Rothbaum, B. (2003). Virtual reality therapy: Innovative treatment for anxiety disorders. *Primary Psychiatry, 9,* 51–54.

Zinbarg, R. E., Brown, T. A., Barlow, D. H., & Rapee, R. M. (2001). Anxiety sensitivity, panic, and depressed mood: a reanalysis teasing apart the contributions of the two levels in the hierarchical structure of the Anxiety Sensitivity Index. *Journal of Abnormal Psychology, 110,* 372–377.

Zito, J. M., Safer, D. J., dosReis, S., Gardner, J. F., Boles, M., & Lynch, F. (2000). Trends in the prescribing of psychotropic medications to preschoolers. *Journal of the American Medical Association, 283,* 1025–1030.

Zlotnick, C., Bruce, S. E., Shea, M. T., & Keller, M. B. (2001). Delayed posttraumatic stress disorder (PTSD) and predictors of first onset of PTSD in patients with anxiety disorders. *Journal of Nervous & Mental Disease, 189,* 404–406.

Zoellner, L. A., Foa, E. B., Brigidi, B. D., & Przeworski, A. (2000). Are trauma victims susceptible to "false memories"? *Journal of Abnormal Psychology, 109,* 517–524.

Zola, S. M. (1999). Memory, amnesia, and the issue of recovered memory: Neurobiological aspects. *Clinical Psychology Review, 19,* 915–932.

Zorumski, C. F., & Isenberg, K. E. (1991). Insights into the structure and function of GABA-benzodiazepine receptors: Ion channels and psychiatry. *American Journal of Psychiatry, 148,* 162–172.

Zubenko, G. S., Mulsant, B. H., Sweet, R. A., Pasternak, R. E., & Tu, X. M. (1997). Mortality of elderly patients with psychiatric disorders. *American Journal of Psychiatry, 154,* 1360–1368.

Zubin, J., & Spring, B. (1977). Vulnerability—New view of schizophrenia. *Journal of Abnormal Psychology, 86,* 103–126.

Zuckerman, M. (1980). Sensation seeking. In H. London & J. Exner (Eds.), *Dimensions of personality.* New York: Wiley.

Zvolensky, M. J., Arrindell, W. A., Taylor, S., Bouvard, M., Cox, B. J., Stewart, S. H., et al. (2003). Cross-cultural assessment and abnormal psychology. *Behaviour Research and Therapy, 41,* 841–859.

Zvolensky, M. J., & Eifert, G. H. (2001). A review of psychological factors/processes affecting anxious responding during voluntary hyperventilation and inhalations of carbon dioxide-enriched air. *Clinical Psychology Review, 21,* 375–400.

Zvolensky, M. J., McNeil, D. W., Porter, C. A., & Stewart, S. H. (2001). Assessment of anxiety sensitivity in young American Indians and Alaska Natives. *Behaviour Research and Therapy, 39,* 477–493.

Zweig-Frank, H., & Paris, J. (1991). Parents' emotional neglect and overprotection according to the recollections of patients with borderline personality disorder. *American Journal of Psychiatry, 148,* 648–651.

Zwillich, C. W. (2000). Is untreated sleep apnea a contributing factor for chronic hypertension? *Journal of the American Medical Association, 283,* 1880–1881. [Editorial]

Chapter 1 Page 2: Tomek Sikora/ Getty Images Inc.—Image Bank; page 7: Kathleen Finlay/Masterfile Corporation; page 7: Pierre Perrin/ Corbis/Sygma; page 7: Catherine Karnow/Woodfin Camp and Associates; page 10: Arne Hodalic/Corbis/Bettmann; page 11: Bierwert/American Museum of Natural History; page 12: The Granger Collection; page 13: The Granger Collection; page 14: The Granger Collection; page 14: Corbis/Bettmann; page 17: © Bettmann/CORBIS; page 18: David Young-Wolff/PhotoEdit; page 19: The Granger Collection; page 19: The Granger Collection; page 23: Richard Hutchings/PhotoEdit; page 26: Corbis RF; page 29: Jose Luis Pelaez, Inc./Corbis/Bettmann.

Chapter 2 Page 36: Erwin Redl; page 43: Mario Tama/Getty Images, Inc.; page 45: Ron Chapple/ Getty Images, Inc.—Taxi; page 47: AP Wide World Photos; page 43: David Muir/Masterfile Corporation; page 48: Frank Siteman/Stock Boston; page 49: © New Line/Everett Collection, Inc.; page 50: Culver Pictures, Inc.; page 50: Scott Camazine/ Corbis/ Bettmann; page 50: PhotoEdit; page 52: The Granger Collection; page 52: Nina Leen/Getty Images/Time Life Pictures; page 56: Nancy Sheehan/ Index Stock Imagery, Inc.; page 56: Corbis/Rogers Ressmeyer/ Corbis/Bettmann; page 56: Ann Kaplan/Corbis/Bettmann; page 57: AP Wide World Photos; page 58: Gabor Demjen/Stock Boston; page 59: Albert Ellis Institute; page 60: Aaron T. Beck, M.D.; page 63: Frank Siteman/PictureQuest.

Chapter 3 Page 68: Diana Ong/SuperStock, Inc.; page 72: Stephanie Maze/ Corbis/Bettmann; page 73: Charles Gupton/Getty Images Inc.—Stone Allstock; page 78: The Image Works; page 79: Spencer Grant/ PhotoEdit; page 81: Pictor/ImageState/International Stock Photography Ltd.; page 86: Pearson Education/PH College; page 87: Reprinted by permission of the publishers from Henry A. Murray, *Thematic Apperception Test*, Cambridge, Massachusetts: Harvard University Press, © 1943 by the President and Fellows of Harvard College, © 1971 by Henry A. Murray; page 93: Michael Newman/ PhotoEdit; page 95: Richard T. Nowitz/Corbis/ Bettmann; page 96: Scott Camazine/Photo Researchers, Inc.; page 96: Brookhaven National Laboratory; page 97: Visuals Unlimited; page 97: Alexander Tsiaras/Science Source/Photo Researchers, Inc.; page 97: Magnetic Resonance Imaging of the Brain in Schizophrenia, pg. 35-44, 1990; 47:35/Archive of General Psychiatry/American Medical Association.

Chapter 4 Page 100: Images.com/Corbis/Bettmann; page 102: © Columbia/ Everett Collection, Inc.; page 105: Zigy Kaluzny/Getty Images Inc.—Stone Allstock; page 106: Kactus Foto/ SuperStock, Inc.; page 107: Grantpix/Photo Researchers, Inc.; page 109: Geri Engberg/ The Image Works; page 116: Will Hart; page 117: D. Young- Wolff/ PhotoEdit; page 120: From the *Wall Street Journal*—permission, Cartoon Features Syndicate; page 122: Rhoda Sidney; page 125: Will McIntyre/Photo Researchers, Inc.; page 129: Bill Aron/PhotoEdit; page 130: Michael Newman/PhotoEdit; page 133: Robert Ginn/PhotoEdit.

Chapter 5 Page 136: SuperStock, Inc.; page 138: Phyllis Picardi/Stock Boston; page 141: Biology Media/Science Source/Photo Researchers, Inc.; page 142: Richard Radstone/Getty Images, Inc.; page 145: Nejiah Feanny/Corbis/Sygma; page 146: Esbin/Anderson/Omni-Photo Communications, Inc.; page 146: Bob Daemmrich/Stock Boston; page 148: Photomondo/Getty Images, Inc.; page 148: Lawrence Migdale/ Stock Boston; page 151: Jose Luis Pelaez, Inc./Corbis/Bettmann; page 153: Jeff Greenberg/David R. Frazier Photolibrary, Inc.; page 156: Joel Gordon Photography; page 158: William Johnson/Stock Boston; page 158: Zigy Kaluzny/Getty Images Inc.—Stone Allstock; page 161: Michael Banks/ Getty Images Inc.—Stone Allstock; page 164: Alon Reininger/ Woodfin Camp & Associates.

Chapter 6 Page 168: Sandy Skoglund; page 172: Walter Smith/Corbis/Bettmann; page 179: Geri Engberg/Geri Engberg Photography; page 179: SuperStock, Inc.; page 179: David E. Dempster/Pearson Education/PH College; page 183: Corbis/Stephanie Maze/Corbis/Bettmann; page 185: M.H. Sharp/ Photo Researchers, Inc.; page 186: Jeff Maloney/Getty Images, Inc.- Photodisc; page 188: Laima E. Druskis/Pearson Education/PH College; page 190: Bob Mahoney/The Image Works; page 193: Getty Images Inc.—Stone Allstock; page 194: Sony Pictures/Photofest; page 198: Charles Piatiau/Corbis/Bettmann; page 194: Allan Tannenbaum/The Image Works; page 202: Lori Grinker/Contact Press Images Inc.

Chapter 7 Page 208: SuperStock, Inc.; page 211 (all three images): Film Still Archive/ The Museum of Modern Art/Film Stills Archive; page 215: Susan Greenwood/Getty Images, Inc.—Liaison; page 217: Werner H. Muller/Peter Arnold, Inc.; page 221: Spencer Grant/PhotoEdit; page 224: Siner Jeff/Corbis/Sygma; page 226: Matthew Borkoski/Stock Boston; page 230: Bald Headed Pictures/Taxi/Getty Images; page 231: Margot Granitsas/The Image Works; page 233: Peter Turnley/ Corbis/Bettmann; page 234: Stock Montage/Hulton Archive/Getty Images.

Chapter 8 Page 240: Sam Taylor-Wood, "Soliloquy VI". 1999. C-print. 87 3/4″ × 101 1/4″. TAYS.PH.8948. Courtesy of Sam Taylor-Wood and Matthew Marks Gallery, New York; page 242: Sean Gallup/Getty Images, Inc.; page 243: Joel Gordon Photography; page 247: Jon Gray/Getty Images Inc.—Stone Allstock; page 247: Dan McCoy/ Rainbow; page 251: AP Wide World Photos; page 253: Gemeente Museum, The Hague, Netherlands/SuperStock, Inc.; page 255: Lisa Quinones/Black Star; page 256: Tom & Dee Ann McCarthy/Corbis/Bettmann; page 257: Bebeto Matthews/Getty Images, Inc.; page 260: SuperStock, Inc.; page 264: Color Day Production/Getty Images Inc.—Image Bank; page 269: Michal Heron/Michal Heron Photography; page 276: Sarah Hollingsworth Lisanby, MD; page 279: William F. Campbell/Getty Images/Time Life Pictures; page 282: Mary Kate Denny/PhotoEdit.

Chapter 9 Page 286: Sandy Skoglund; page 289: Walter Bibikow/Getty Images Inc.—Image Bank; page 289: Lawrence Migdale/Pix; page 292: Mario Beauregard/Corbis/Bettmann; page 295: Ken Fisher/Getty Images Inc.—Stone Allstock; page 296: D. Wells/The Image Works; page 296: Paul Chesley/ Getty Images Inc.—Stone Allstock; page 298: Karen Moskowitz/Getty Images, Inc.; page 300: Corbis Digital Stock; page 302: Don Farrall/Getty Images, Inc.—Photodisc. Page 303: Peter Matthews/Black Star; page 312: Catherine Ursillo/Photo Researchers, Inc.; page 317: Tom & DeeAnn McCarthy/Corbis/Stock Market; page 318: Joel Gordon Photography; page 320: Jeff Greenberg/Lonely Planet Images/Photo 20-20; page 325 (both images): Mark and Linda Sobell.

Chapter 10 Page 330: Sandy Skoglund; page 333: Sisse Brimberg/ Woodfin Camp & Associates; page 334: Tony Freeman/PhotoEdit; page 336: Michael Weisbrot/The Image Works; page 339: Jill Greenberg/Jill Greenberg Studio, Inc.; page 339: Azzara Steve/Corbis/Sygma; page 346: Tom Raymond/Getty Images Inc.—Stone Allstock; page 346: Joel Gordon Photography; page 351: Alex Wong/Getty Images, Inc.—Liaison; page 353: Russell D. Curtis/Photo Researchers, Inc.; page 356: Pictor/ ImageState/International Stock Photography Ltd.; page 360: Ogust/The Image Works.

Chapter 11 Page 364: Eric Fischel, "The Bed, The Chair, The Sitter". 78″ × 93″. Oil on Linen. 1999-2000. Courtesy: Mary Boone Gallery, New York; page 366: Dr. Jayne Thomas, Deceased/Peg Greene; page 367: George Holton/Photo Researchers, Inc.; page 367: Ty Allison/Getty Images, Inc.; page 370: Corbis/Sygma; page 376: Roy Morsch/Corbis/Stock Market; page 378: Ira Wyman/Corbis/Sygma; page 381: Bob Daemmrich/The

Image Works; page 384: Randy Matusow; page 390: Fredrik D. Bodin; page 391: Michael Newman/PhotoEdit; page 395: Dazzo/Masterfile Corporation

Chapter 12   Page 400: Elia Alba Doll heads (multiplicities) copyright 2001. Courtesy of the artist and Henrique Faria Fine Art.; page 402: Photofest; page 407: Jonathan Nourok/PhotoEdit; page 410: "Soulful Feelings", 1991. 22″ × 30″. © Artwork by Danny Gayder, a participating artist of VSA arts, website http://www.vsarts.org; page 412: Bob Benyas Photography; page 414: Grunnitus/Photo Researchers, Inc.; page 415: Frieman Photography/Photo Researchers, Inc.; page 416: Corbis/Bettmann; page 416: Monte S. Buchsbaum, M.D., Mount Sinai School of Medicine, New York, N.Y.; 419: Courtesy of Thompson, et al., in PNAS; page 419: Nancy C. Andreasen, M.D./University of Iowa Hospitals & Clinics; page 419: Nancy C. Andreasen, M.D./University of Iowa Hospitals & Clinics; page 420: Monte S. Buchsbaum, M.D., Mount Sinai School of Medicine, New York, N.Y.; page 422: David Lees/ Corbis/Bettmann; page 427: Amy Etra/PhotoEdit; page 432: Patrick Molnar/ Getty Images Inc.—Stone Allstock

Chapter 13   Page 438: Barbara Kruger, "Power Pleasure Desire Disgust". Installation: November 1997. Courtesy: Mary Boone Gallery, New York; page 441: Savino/The Image Works; page 443: AP Wide World Photos; page 444: Greg Smith/ Corbis/SABA Press Photos, Inc.; page 446: Picture Desk, Inc./Kobal Collection; page 447: Globe Photos, Inc.; page 448: Douglas Kirkland/Corbis/Bettmann; page 450: Greg Ceo/Image Bank/Getty Images; page 452: Penny Tweedie/Getty Images Inc.—Stone Allstock; page 455: Laima E. Druskis/ Pearson Education/PH College; page 457: Bob Daemmrich/Stock Boston; page 458: Bob Daemmrich/Stock Boston; page 460: Richard Renaldi; page 463: AP Wide World Photos.

Chapter 14   Page 470: SuperStock, Inc.; page 473: Tony Freeman/PhotoEdit; page 473: M. Siluk/The Image Works; page 476: Erika Stone; page 480: Robin Nelson/PhotoEdit; page 482: Richard Hutchings/Photo Researchers, Inc. page 483: Tony Freeman/PhotoEdit; page 485: Paul, Conklin/PotoEdit; page 486: AP Wide World Photos; page 489: David Young-Wolff/PhotoEdit; page 493: Pascal Quittemelle/Stock Boston; Jeff Greenberg/PhotoEdit; page 496: David Young-Wolff/PhotoEdit; page 497: Jean Claude LeJeune/Stock Boston; page 500: Michael Newman/PhotoEdit; page 503: Palco Labs, Inc.

Chapter 15   Page 508: Gilles Barbier, "L'Hospice (or Nursing Home)". 2002. Six wax figures, television, various elements; variable dimensions. Collection Martin Z. Margulies, Miami, USA; Courtesy Galerie GP&N Vallois/Paris France; page 510: Frank Siteman/Stock Boston; page 514: Jeff Persons/Stock Boston; page 516: Paul Berton/Corbis/Bettmann; page 517: Arthur Tilley/Getty Images, Inc.—Taxi; page 517: Robert Ginn/PhotoEdit; page 519: AP/Wide World Photos; page 520 (both images): Robert P. Friedland, MD, Case Western Reserve University; page 521: AP Wide World Photos; page 523: Spike Walker/Getty Images Inc.—Stone Allstock; page 524: Karen Kasmauski/ Woodfin Camp & Associates; page 526: AP Wide World Photos; page 528: Catherine Bauknight/Corbis/Bettmann; page 530: AP Wide World Photos.

Chapter 16   Page 532: Sammlung Cleomir Jussiant, Antwerp, Belgium/SuperStock, Inc.; page 534: AP Wide World Photos; page 536: AP Wide World Photos; page 537: AP/Wide World Photos; page 538: Potter/CMSP/Custom Medical Stock Photo, Inc.; page 539: Republic Pictures/Stringer/Getty Images, Inc.; page 541 (both images): AP Wide World Photos; page 542: AP Wide World Photos; page 544: Brendan Smialowski/Stringer/Reuters NewsMedia/Corbis/Bettmann; page 546: AP Wide World Photos.

SINGLE PC LICENSE AGREEMENT AND LIMITED WARRANTY

READ THIS LICENSE CAREFULLY BEFORE OPENING THIS PACKAGE. BY OPENING THIS PACKAGE, YOU ARE AGREEING TO THE TERMS AND CONDITIONS OF THIS LICENSE. IF YOU DO NOT AGREE, DO NOT OPEN THE PACKAGE. PROMPTLY RETURN THE UNOPENED PACKAGE AND ALL ACCOMPANYING ITEMS TO THE PLACE YOU OBTAINED THEM.

1. GRANT OF LICENSE and OWNERSHIP: The enclosed computer programs ("Software") are licensed, not sold, to you by Prentice-Hall, Inc. ("We" or the "Company") and in consideration of your purchase or adoption of the accompanying Company textbooks and/or other materials, and your agreement to these terms. We reserve any rights not granted to you. You own only the disk(s) but we and/or our licensors own the Software itself. This license allows you to use and display your copy of the Software on a single computer (i.e., with a single CPU) at a single location for <u>academic</u> use only, so long as you comply with the terms of this Agreement. You may make one copy for back up, or transfer your copy to another CPU, provided that the Software is usable on only one computer.

2. RESTRICTIONS: You may <u>not</u> transfer or distribute the Software or documentation to anyone else. Except for backup, you may <u>not</u> copy the documentation or the Software. You may <u>not</u> network the Software or otherwise use it on more than one computer or computer terminal at the same time. You may <u>not</u> reverse engineer, disassemble, decompile, modify, adapt, translate, or create derivative works based on the Software or the Documentation. You may be held legally responsible for any copying or copyright infringement which is caused by your failure to abide by the terms of these restrictions.

3. TERMINATION: This license is effective until terminated. This license will terminate automatically without notice from the Company if you fail to comply with any provisions or limitations of this license. Upon termination, you shall destroy the Documentation and all copies of the Software. All provisions of this Agreement as to limitation and disclaimer of warranties, limitation of liability, remedies or damages, and our ownership rights shall survive termination.

4. LIMITED WARRANTY AND DISCLAIMER OF WARRANTY: Company warrants that for a period of 60 days from the date you purchase this SOFTWARE (or purchase or adopt the accompanying textbook), the Software, when properly installed and used in accordance with the Documentation, will operate in substantial conformity with the description of the Software set forth in the Documentation, and that for a period of 30 days the disk(s) on which the Software is delivered shall be free from defects in materials and workmanship under normal use. The Company does <u>not</u> warrant that the Software will meet your requirements or that the operation of the Software will be uninterrupted or error-free. Your only remedy and the Company's only obligation under these limited warranties is, at the Company's option, return of the disk for a refund of any amounts paid for it by you or replacement of the disk. THIS LIMITED WARRANTY IS THE ONLY WARRANTY PROVIDED BY THE COMPANY AND ITS LICENSORS, AND THE COMPANY AND ITS LICENSORS DISCLAIM ALL OTHER WARRANTIES, EXPRESS OR IMPLIED, INCLUDING WITHOUT LIMITATION, THE IMPLIED WARRANTIES OF MERCHANTABILITY AND FITNESS FOR A PARTICULAR PURPOSE. THE COMPANY DOES NOT WARRANT, GUARANTEE OR MAKE ANY REPRESENTATION REGARDING THE ACCURACY, RELIABILITY, CURRENTNESS, USE, OR RESULTS OF USE, OF THE SOFTWARE.

5. LIMITATION OF REMEDIES AND DAMAGES: IN NO EVENT, SHALL THE COMPANY OR ITS EMPLOYEES, AGENTS, LICENSORS, OR CONTRACTORS BE LIABLE FOR ANY INCIDENTAL, INDIRECT, SPECIAL, OR CONSEQUENTIAL DAMAGES ARISING OUT OF OR IN CONNECTION WITH THIS LICENSE OR THE SOFTWARE, INCLUDING FOR LOSS OF USE, LOSS OF DATA, LOSS OF INCOME OR PROFIT, OR OTHER LOSSES, SUSTAINED AS A RESULT OF INJURY TO ANY PERSON, OR LOSS OF OR DAMAGE TO PROPERTY, OR CLAIMS OF THIRD PARTIES, EVEN IF THE COMPANY OR AN AUTHORIZED REPRESENTATIVE OF THE COMPANY HAS BEEN ADVISED OF THE POSSIBILITY OF SUCH DAMAGES. IN NO EVENT SHALL THE LIABILITY OF THE COMPANY FOR DAMAGES WITH RESPECT TO THE SOFTWARE EXCEED THE AMOUNTS ACTUALLY PAID BY YOU, IF ANY, FOR THE SOFTWARE OR THE ACCOMPANYING TEXTBOOK. BECAUSE SOME JURISDICTIONS DO NOT ALLOW THE LIMITATION OF LIABILITY IN CERTAIN CIRCUMSTANCES, THE ABOVE LIMITATIONS MAY NOT ALWAYS APPLY TO YOU.

6. GENERAL: THIS AGREEMENT SHALL BE CONSTRUED IN ACCORDANCE WITH THE LAWS OF THE UNITED STATES OF AMERICA AND THE STATE OF NEW YORK, APPLICABLE TO CONTRACTS MADE IN NEW YORK, AND SHALL BENEFIT THE COMPANY, ITS AFFILIATES AND ASSIGNEES. HIS AGREEMENT IS THE COMPLETE AND EXCLUSIVE STATEMENT OF THE AGREEMENT BETWEEN YOU AND THE COMPANY AND SUPERSEDES ALL PROPOSALS OR PRIOR AGREEMENTS, ORAL, OR WRITTEN, AND ANY OTHER COMMUNICATIONS BETWEEN YOU AND THE COMPANY OR ANY REPRESENTATIVE OF THE COMPANY RELATING TO THE SUBJECT MATTER OF THIS AGREEMENT. If you are a U.S. Government user, this Software is licensed with "restricted rights" as set forth in subparagraphs (a)-(d) of the Commercial Computer-Restricted Rights clause at FAR 52.227-19 or in subparagraphs (c)(1)(ii) of the Rights in Technical Data and Computer Software clause at DFARS 252.227-7013, and similar clauses, as applicable.

Should you have any questions concerning this agreement please contact in writing: Legal Department, Prentice Hall, One Lake Street, Upper Saddle River, NJ 07458. If you need technical assistance with this product, call the Company Technical Support group at 1-800-677-6337. If you wish to contact the Company for any other reason, please contact in writing: Psychology Media Editor, Prentice Hall, One Lake Street, Upper Saddle River, NJ 07458.

DSM-IV-TR CLASSIFICATION (American Psychiatric Association 2000)

AXIS I

Clinical Syndromes

DISORDERS USUALLY FIRST DIAGNOSED IN INFANCY, CHILDHOOD, OR ADOLESCENCE

- **Learning Disorders**
  Reading Disorder
  Mathematics Disorder
  Disorder of Written Expression
  Learning Disorder Not Otherwise Specified

- **Motor Skills Disorder**
  Developmental Coordination Disorder

- **Communication Disorders**
  Expressive Language Disorder
  Mixed Receptive/Expressive Language Disorder
  Phonological Disorder
  Stuttering
  Communication Disorder Not Otherwise Specified

- **Pervasive Developmental Disorders**
  Autistic Disorder
  Rett's Disorder
  Childhood Disintegrative Disorder
  Asperger's Disorder
  Pervasive Developmental Disorder Not Otherwise Specified

- **Attention-Deficit and Disruptive Behavior Disorders**
  Attention-Deficit/Hyperactivity Disorder
  Predominantly Inattentive Type
  Predominantly Hyperactive-Impulsive Type
  Combined Type
  Oppositional Defiant Disorder
  Conduct Disorder
  Attention-Deficit/Hyperactivity Disorder Not Otherwise Specified
  Disruptive Behavior Disorder Not Otherwise Specified

- **Feeding and Eating Disorders of Infancy or Early Childhood**
  Pica
  Rumination Disorder
  Feeding Disorder of Infancy or Early Childhood Not Otherwise Specified

- **Tic Disorders**
  Tourette's Disorder
  Chronic Motor or Vocal Tic Disorder
  Transient Tic Disorder
  Tic Disorder Not Otherwise Specified

- **Elimination Disorders**
  Encopresis
  Enuresis

- **Other Disorders of Infancy, Childhood, or Adolescence**
  Separation Anxiety Disorder
  Selective Mutism
  Reactive Attachment Disorder of Infancy or Early Childhood
  Stereotypic Movement Disorder
  Disorder of Infancy, Childhood, or Adolescence Not Otherwise Specified

DELIRIUM, DEMENTIA, AND AMNESTIC AND OTHER COGNITIVE DISORDERS

- **Delirium**
  Delirium Due to a General Medical Condition
  Substance Intoxication Delirium
  Substance Withdrawal Delirium
  Delirium Due to Multiple Etiologies
  Delirium Not Otherwise Specified

- **Dementia**
  Dementia of the Alzheimer's Type
  Vascular Dementia
  Dementias Due to Other General Medical Conditions
  Dementia Due to HIV Disease
  Dementia Due to Head Trauma
  Dementia Due to Parkinson's Disease
  Dementia Due to Huntington's Disease
  Dementia Due to Pick's Disease
  Dementia Due to Creutzfeldt-Jakob Disease
  Substance-Induced Persisting Dementia
  Dementia Due to Multiple Etiologies
  Dementia Not Otherwise Specified

- **Amnestic Disorders**
  Amnestic Disorder Due to a General Medical Condition
  Substance-Induced Persisting Amnestic Disorder
  Amnestic Disorder Not Otherwise Specified

SUBSTANCE-RELATED DISORDERS

- **Alcohol Use Disorders**
  Alcohol Dependence
  Alcohol Abuse

- **Alcohol-Induced Disorders**
  Alcohol Intoxication
  Alcohol Withdrawal
  Alcohol Intoxication Delirium
  Alcohol Withdrawal Delirium
  Alcohol-Induced Persisting Dementia
  Alcohol-Induced Persisting Amnestic Disorder
  Alcohol-Induced Psychotic Disorder
  Alcohol-Induced Mood Disorder
  Alcohol-Induced Anxiety Disorder
  Alcohol-Induced Sexual Dysfunction
  Alcohol-Induced Sleep Disorder
  Alcohol-Related Disorder Not Otherwise Specified

- **Amphetamine Use Disorders**

- **Amphetamine-Induced Disorders**

- **Caffeine-Induced Disorders**

- **Cannabis Use Disorders**

- **Cannabis-Induced Disorders**

- **Cocaine Use Disorders**

- **Cocaine-Induced Disorders**

- **Hallucinogen Use Disorders**

- **Hallucinogen-Induced Disorders**

- **Inhalant Use Disorders**

- **Inhalant-Induced Disorders**

- **Nicotine Use Disorder**

- **Nicotine-Induced Disorder**

- **Opioid Use Disorders**

- **Opioid-Induced Disorders**

- **Phencyclidine Use Disorders**

- **Phencyclidine-Induced Disorders**

- **Sedative, Hypnotic, or Anxiolytic Use Disorders**

- **Sedative, Hypnotic, or Anxiolytic-Induced Disorders**

- **Polysubstance-Related Disorder**

- **Other (or Unknown) Substance Use Disorders**

- **Other (or Unknown) Substance-Induced Disorders**

SCHIZOPHRENIA AND OTHER PSYCHOTIC DISORDERS

- **Schizophrenia**
  Paranoid Type
  Disorganized Type
  Catatonic Type
  Undifferentiated Type
  Residual Type

- **Schizophreniform Disorder**

- **Schizoaffective Disorder**

- **Delusional Disorder**

- **Brief Psychotic Disorder**

- **Shared Psychotic Disorder (Folie à Deux)**

- **Psychotic Disorder Due to a General Medical Condition**

- **Substance-Induced Psychotic Disorder**

- **Psychotic Disorder Not Otherwise Specified**

MOOD DISORDERS

- **Depressive Disorders**
  Major Depressive Disorder
  Dysthymic Disorder
  Depressive Disorder Not Otherwise Specified

- **Bipolar Disorders**
  Bipolar I Disorder
  Single Manic Episode
  Most Recent Episode Hypomanic
  Most Recent Episode Manic
  Most Recent Episode Mixed
  Most Recent Episode Depressed
  Most Recent Episode Unspecified
  Bipolar II Disorder
  Cyclothymic Disorder
  Bipolar Disorder Not Otherwise Specified

- **Other Mood Disorders**
  Mood Disorder Due to a General Medical Condition
  Substance-Induced Mood Disorder
  Mood Disorder Not Otherwise Specified